UIKit

for Masterminds

How to take advantage of Swift and UIKit to create insanely great apps for iPhones, iPads, and Macs

J.D Gauchat

www.jdgauchat.com

The source code for this book is available at **www.formasterminds.com**

Copyright Registration Number: 1185933

ISBN: 978-1-7779782-0-4

1st Edition 2021

Table of Contents

Chapter 4—Introduction to Frameworks

Chapter 5—UIKit Framework

Chapter 6—Adaptivity

Chapter 7—Scroll Views

Chapter 8—Gesture Recognizers

Chapter 9—Navigation

Chapter 10—Table Views

Chapter 11—Collection Views

Chapter 12—Split View Controllers

Chapter 13—Alert Views

Chapter 14—Concurrency

Chapter 15—Storage

Chapter 16—Notifications

Chapter 17—iCloud

Chapter 18—Media

Chapter 19—Web

Chapter 20—Map Kit

Chapter 21—Drag and Drop

Chapter 22—Mac Catalyst

Chapter 23—App Store

Conventions

This book explores basic and advanced topics required to develop professional applications. Depending on your current level of knowledge, you may find some of these topics easy or difficult to learn. To help you navigate the book, we have identified each section with a label. The following is a description of what these labels represent.

Basic — The Basic label represents topics you can ignore if you already know the basics of Swift and app development. If you are learning how to develop applications for Apple devices for the first time, these sections are required.

Medium — The Medium label represents topics that are not required for every app. You can ignore the information presented in these sections until they are applied in practical situations later or when you need them in your own applications.

Advanced — The Advanced label represents topics that are only required in advanced applications or API development. The information presented in these sections is not required for the development of most applications, but it can be helpful if you want to improve your understanding of how Apple technologies work.

If you are new to app development, read all the Basic sections first and only read the Medium sections when you need it later to understand how the examples work.

Examples

Every single topic presented in this book is explained through examples that you can try yourself. We recommend that you open Xcode and try the examples as you learn, but you can download the codes and projects from our website to save time (**www.formasterminds.com**).

The examples in this book only apply the technologies you already know, so they not always represent best practices. There are several programming patterns and best practices you can follow. What applies to you depends on the characteristics of your application and what you want to achieve with it. We recommend you explore all the possibilities presented in this book but also experiment and try your own.

IMPORTANT: Apple technologies are extensive, and a book cannot teach you everything. After each topic is introduced, you should read the official specifications provided by Apple and look for additional examples on the Web. The links to the specifications, additional information, tutorials, and videos are available on our website **www.formasterminds.com**. Apple's official documentation is available at **developer.apple.com**. Frameworks and APIs references are available at **developer.apple.com/reference**.

Chapter 1
App Development

Basic 1.1 Overview

After the introduction of the iPhone in 2007 and its massive success, Apple decided to provide the tools for developers to create applications for it. The tools were already available for Mac computers, but the iPhone's small screen and unique characteristics called for a different approach. So, along with those already available, Apple introduced a specific set of tools to develop apps for these devices called UIKit.

UIKit (User Interface Kit) includes everything a developer needs to manage a device and create the elements of the graphic interface. It was designed to develop apps for iPhones and iPads, but thanks to a new system called Mac Catalyst, we can write applications for Mac computers, as well.

Basic Requirements

Apple requires developers to use the software provided by the company to create apps for its devices, and this software only works on Apple computers. For this reason, the options are limited, but the good news is that the tools and accounts we need are provided by the company for free.

Mac Computer—This in theory could be any Mac computer, but the development software always requires the latest operative system (currently macOS Monterey), so in practice we need a relatively new computer with a recommended 16GB of memory.

Xcode—This is the software provided by Apple for development. The latest version is number 13. It's free and the package comes with everything we need to create our apps, including an editor, the SDK (Software Development Kit), and a simulator to test the applications.

Apple Developer Account—This is a basic account we can get for free. From this account, we can manage our membership, create certificates, app identifiers and other information we need to test and publish our apps.

Apple Membership—This is the membership required to publish our apps in the App Store. As of this writing, the cost of this membership is $99 US dollars per year.

Mobile Device— This could be any of the devices available in the market that support the current versions of Apple's mobile operative systems (currently iOS 15, tvOS 15, watchOS 8, iPadOS 15, and macOS Monterey). Testing our applications on a real device is highly recommended and necessary before publishing.

In short, to develop applications for Apple devices we need a Mac Computer capable of running the operative system required by the latest version of Xcode (currently macOS Monterey), make sure that we have an Apple ID to access our Developer Account (**developer.apple.com**), and install the latest version of Xcode (currently 13).

Basic 1.2 Xcode

Xcode is a general-purpose IDE (Integrated Development Environment). It includes a very powerful editor with graphic tools to help us write our code, the SDKs (Software Development

Kits) for the creation of software for the iOS, iPadOS, macOS, watchOS, and tvOS operative systems, and compilers for the C, C++, Objective-C and Swift languages. From Xcode, we can program software for every Apple platform using any of these tools and programming languages.

Xcode is available as an app in the Mac App Store. To download this application, we must open the App Store from Launchpad (the application organizer that comes with macOS) or double click the App Store icon inside the Applications folder in Finder (macOS's file explorer).

If we search for the term "Xcode" in the App Store, the window shows Xcode's icon at the top and a button to download it (Figure 1-1, number 1).

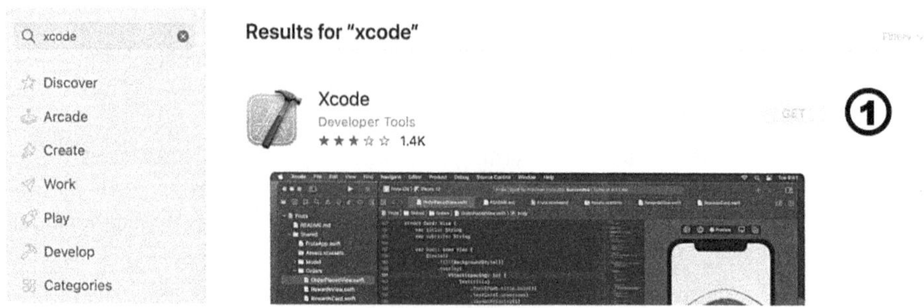

Figure 1-1: Xcode in the Mac App Store

Once the application is downloaded, the software is automatically installed. To start Xcode, we open Launchpad and click on the icon or double-click the program from the Applications folder in Finder. Figure 1-2 shows Xcode's welcome screen.

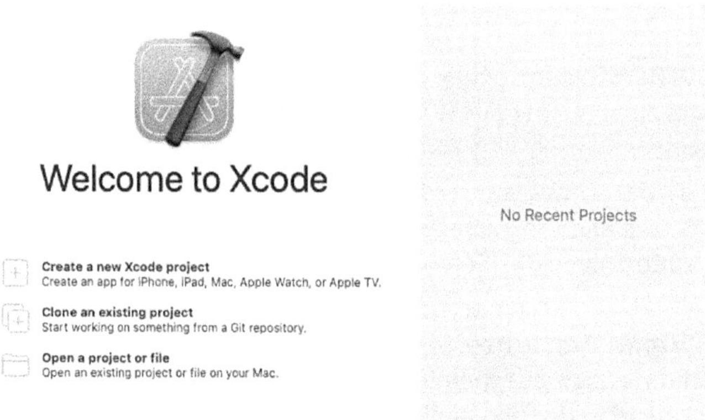

Figure 1-2: *Xcode's welcome screen*

The welcome screen offers a list of the recent projects on the right and buttons on the left to create a new project, open a project on our computer, or clone one stored in a repository.

Basic 1.3 Development

Even though some simple projects could be developed without programming a single line of code, we always need to write our own code if we want to create a useful application, and for that, we need programming languages, frameworks, and APIs.

Basic Programming Languages

Several years ago, Apple adopted and implemented a language called Objective-C to allow developers to create applications for its devices. Due to the technical level required to work with this language, the spectacular success of Apple's mobile devices did not impress developers the same way as consumers. The demand for more and better applications was growing fast, but the complicated nature of the system did not appeal to most developers who were used to working with more traditional tools. To solve this problem, in 2014 the company introduced a new programming language called *Swift*. Swift presents a simpler syntax that developers find familiar, while at the same time preserves that low-level nature necessary to take advantage of every aspect of Apple's devices. Swift was designed to replace Objective-C and, therefore, it is the language recommended to new developers.

Basic Frameworks and APIs

Programming languages by themselves cannot do much. They provide all the elements to interact with the system but are basic tools for data management. Because of the complexity of the information required to control sophisticated technologies and access every part of a system, it could take years to develop an application from scratch working with just the instructions of a programming language. Doing simple things like printing graphics on the screen or storing data in files would become a nightmare if programmers had to depend on the tools provided by programming languages alone. For this reason, languages are always accompanied by pre-programmed routines grouped in libraries and frameworks that through a simple interface called *API* (Application programming interface) allow programmers to incorporate to their apps amazing functionality with just a few lines of code. Apple provides all this functionality, including frameworks and their APIs, in a set of tools called SDK (Software Development Kit) that comes with Xcode.

Frameworks and APIs are critical for app development. As developers, we must learn and apply these tools if we want to create useful applications and, therefore, they will become the main subject of study in following chapters.

Basic Compiler

Computers do not understand Swift or any other programming language. These languages were created for us to give machines instructions we can understand. Our code must be converted to elemental orders that work at an electronic level, turning multiple switches on and off to represent the abstraction humans work with. The translation from the language humans understand to the language computers understand is done by a program called *compiler*.

Compilers have specific routines to translate instructions from programming languages to machine code. They are language and platform specific, which means that we need a specific compiler to program in one language and platform. There are a few compilers available for Apple systems, but the one currently implemented by Xcode is called *LLVM*. LLVM is capable of compiling code written in Swift, C, C++, and Objective-C.

With the compiler, the machinery to build an app is complete. Figure 1-3 shows all the elements involved. There are three main sources of code the compiler uses to build the application: our code in Swift, the frameworks our program requires, and a set of basic routines necessary for the app to run (called Application Loop in Figure 1-3). The process starts from Xcode. In this program we write our code, access frameworks through their APIs, and configure the app to be compiled (built). Combining our code, the codes from the frameworks our app requires and the basic routines (Application Loop), the compiler creates an executable program that may be run in a simulator, a device, or submitted to the App Store for distribution.

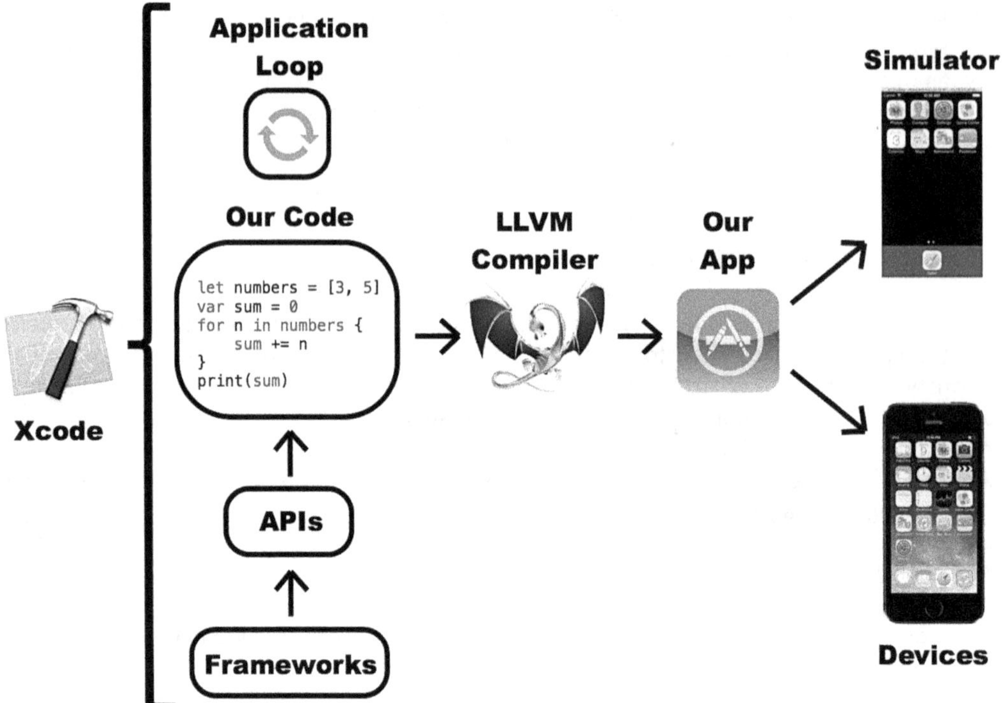

Figure 1-3: *Building an App*

IMPORTANT: The Application Loop is a group of elemental routines, common to every program, that connects your app to the operative system and provides a loop (a code that executes itself over and over again) to constantly check for events produced by the user or coming from the system. Although you never work directly with these routines, they are connected to your code to inform the state of the program, as we will see in further chapters.

Chapter 2
Introduction to Swift

Basic 2.1 Computer Programming

Computers can't do anything unless we write a program. A program is a succession of instructions that the computer must follow. We write the program using the instructions provided by a specific programming language, then a compiler translates these instructions into orders the computer can understand, and when we tell the computer to run the program, the orders are executed sequentially one by one.

The instructions are always listed in sequential order, but programming languages offer different ways to group them together and organize the code and the data that is going to be processed. Developing an app demands a deep understanding of these instructions and the combinations required to achieve the results we want. Since this may be daunting for beginners, Xcode includes a tool called *Playground* to learn how to program and test our code.

Basic Playground

As the name suggests, Playground offers a place to experiment and play around with our code before including it in our applications. Although we could start an Xcode project to create an application right away, it is better to work with Playground first to learn how to program and how to take advantage of some of the fundamental frameworks included in the SDK. Playground files are created from the Playground... option in the File menu at the top of the screen.

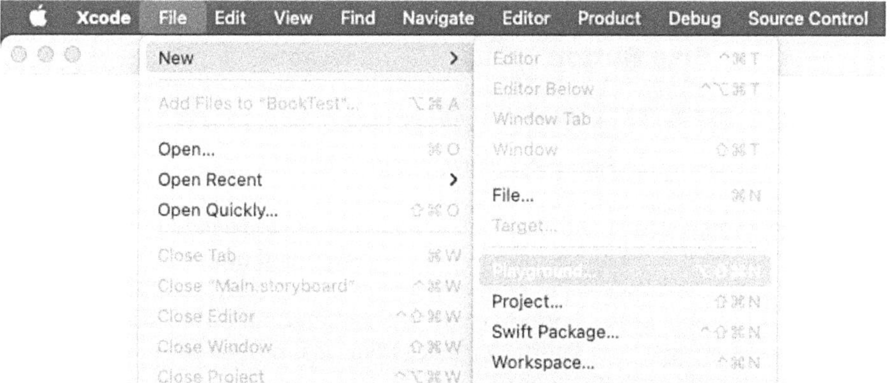

Figure 2-1: *Playground option*

This opens a window with a list of icons to select the template we want to use. Templates are files with pre-programmed code to help us get started with our project. The ones available at this time are called Blank (with just a few lines of code to start from scratch), Game (with basic code to program a video game), Map (with the code to display a map), and Single View (with the same code required to create a view for an application).

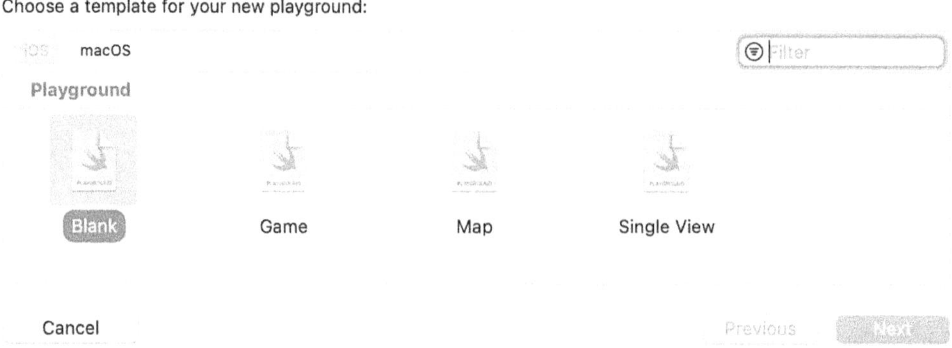

Figure 2-2: *Playground templates*

After we select the template, Xcode asks for the name of the Playground file and the place on our hard drive where we want to store it. Once the file is created, Xcode shows the Playground's interface on the screen. Figure 2-3 illustrates what we see when we create a Blank template.

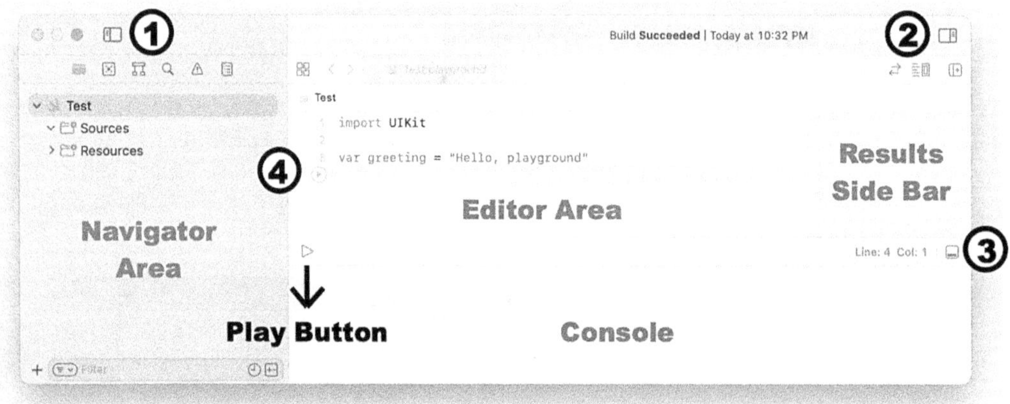

Figure 2-3: *Playground's interface*

Playground presents a simple interface with a toolbar at the top and four areas. The Navigator Area where we can see the resources included in our Playground project, the Editor Area where we write our code, the *Results Side Bar* on the right where the results produced by our code are displayed, and the Console at the bottom where we can read the errors produced by the code and print our own messages. The interface includes buttons to open or remove some of these panels. The button on the top-left corner removes the Navigator Area (number 1), the one on the top-right corner removes a panel called Utilities Area with information about the selected resource, and the button at the top-left corner of the Console area removes the console.

As illustrated in Figure 2-3, the Editor Area includes a button at the bottom of the panel to run and stop the code (Play Button). There is also a play button on the left side of the Editor Area that we can press if we want to execute parts of the code instead (number 4). When this button is pressed, the code is executed up to the line in which the button is located.

Playground can run the code automatically or wait until we press the Play button. By default, the mode is set to Automatically Run, but we can press and hold the Play button to access the menu to modify this behavior.

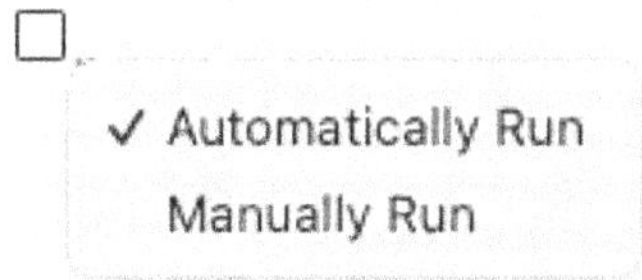

Figure 2-4: *Playground's running mode*

In the Editor Area, we can see the code we have programmed so far. When a new Playground file is created, Xcode offers a template that includes a few basic lines of code to start with. Listing 2-1, below, is the code currently generated for the Blank template.

```
import UIKit

var greeting = "Hello, playground"
```

Listing 2-1: *Playground template*

A computer program is just text written in a specific format. Each line of text represents an instruction. Sometimes a single line includes several instructions, and therefore each line is usually called *statement*. Every statement is an order, or a group of orders, required for the computer to perform a task. In the code of Listing 2-1, the first statement uses the instruction **import** to include in our code the pre-programmed codes from the UIKit framework, and the second statement uses the instruction **var** to store the text "Hello, playground" in memory.

If we press the Play Button to execute the code, we see what the code does inside the Results Side Bar (in this case, it shows the text stored in memory by the **var** instruction). When we move the mouse over this indication, two small buttons show up, as illustrated below.

Figure 2-5: *Quick Look and Show Result buttons*

The button on the left is called *Quick Look*, and it shows a popup window with a visual representation of the result of the execution of the code, such as the formatted text or an image. In this case, no visual effect is generated by the code, so we only see the plain text.

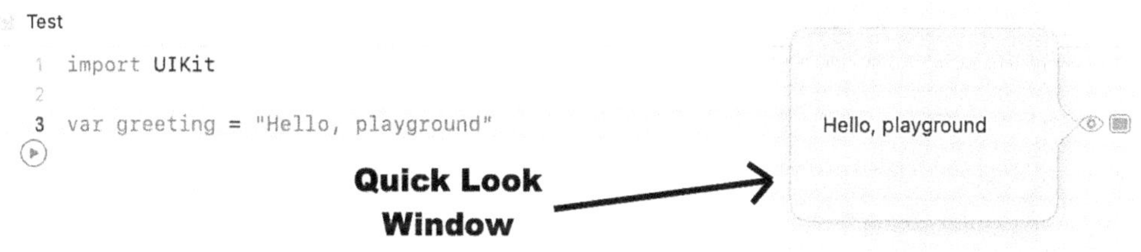

Figure 2-6: *Quick Look window*

The button on the right is called *Show Result*, and what it does is to open a window within our code with a visual representation of the results of the execution of the code over time. In this case, nothing changes, so only the "Hello, playground" text is shown.

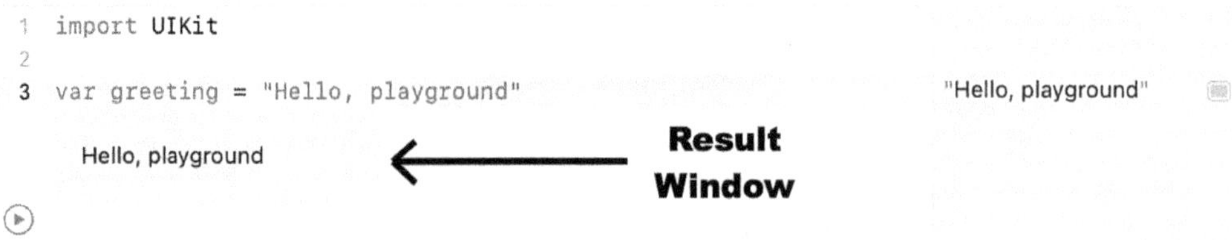

Figure 2-7: *Result window*

The code provided by Xcode for the Blank template is useless, but it shows the basic syntax of the Swift language and how to do elemental things in a program such as importing frameworks to add functionality and storing data in memory. The reason why one of the statements is storing data in memory is because this is the most important task of a program. A program's main functions are storing, retrieving, and processing data. Working with data in the computer's memory is a delicate process that demands meticulous organization. If we are not careful, data may be accidentally deleted, corrupted, or completely overwritten. To make sure this does not happen, programming languages introduce the concept of variables.

Basic 2.2 Variables

Variables are names representing values stored in memory. Once a variable is defined, its name remains the same but the value in memory they represent may change. This allows us to store and retrieve a value from memory without the need of remembering where in the memory the value was stored. With just mentioning the name of the variable we used to store the value, we can get it back or replace it with a new one. With variables, the system takes care of managing the memory for us, but we still need to know how memory works to find out what kind of values we can store.

Basic Memory

The computer's memory is like a huge honeycomb, with consecutive cells that can be in two possible states: activated or deactivated. They are electronic switches with on and off positions established by low and high energy levels.

Figure 2-8: *Memory cells*

Because of their two possible states, each cell is a small unit of information. One cell may represent two possible states (switch on or off), but by combining a sequence of cells we can represent more states. For example, if we combine two cells, we have four possible states.

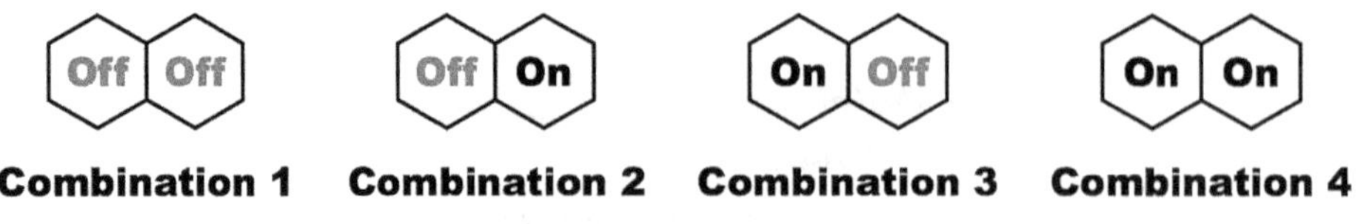

Figure 2-9: *Combining two cells*

With these two cells, we can now represent up to four states (4 possible combinations). If we had used three cells instead, then the possible combinations would have been 8 (eight states). The number of combinations doubles every time we add another cell to the group. This can be extended to represent any number of states we want.

Because of its characteristics, this system of switches is used to represent binary numbers, which are numbers expressed by only two digits: 0 and 1. An on switch represents the value 1 and an off switch represents the value 0. Basic units were determined with the purpose of identifying parts of this endless series of digits. One cell was called a *bit* and a group of 8 bits was called a *byte*. Figure 2-10 shows how a byte looks like in memory, with some of its switches on representing the binary number 00011101.

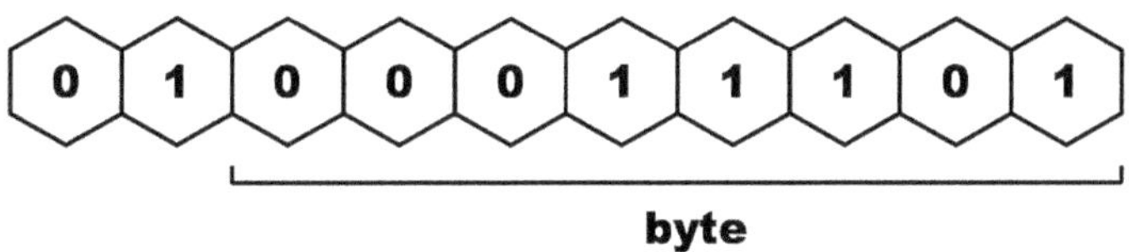

Figure 2-10: *Representation of one byte in memory*

The possible combinations of 8 bits are 256, therefore, a byte can represent binary numbers of 8 digits, which in turn can be converted to numbers that humans can understand, such as decimal numbers. With its 256 possible combinations, a byte can represent decimal numbers from 0 to 255. For instance, when the value of the byte in the example of Figure 2-10 is converted to the decimal system, we get the number 29 (00011101 = 29).

IMPORTANT: Numbers of one numeral system, like binary, can be converted to any other numeral system, like decimal. The binary system is the one a computer can understand because it translates directly to the electronic switches they are built with, but humans find this difficult to read, so we use other systems to express numbers, like the decimal system.

To represent larger numbers, bytes are grouped together. For example, if we take two bytes from memory, we get a binary number composed of a total of 16 bits (16 zeros and ones). A binary number of 16 bits can represent decimal numbers from 0 to 65535 (a total of 65536 possible combinations). To establish clearly defined data structures, each programming language declares its own units of data of a predetermined size. These units are usually called *primitive types*.

Basic Primitive Data Types

Primitive data types are units of data defined by the language. They are always the same size, so when we store a value of one of these data types, the computer knows exactly how much memory to use. The following is probably the most useful primitive data type provided by Swift.

Int—This data type defines integer numbers, which are numbers with no fractional component. In 64 bits systems, the size of this data type is 8 bytes and therefore it can store values from -9,223,372,036,854,775,808 to 9,223,372,036,854,775,807.

Although it is recommended to use the `Int` data type to store integers, some frameworks require a very specific type of integer. For this reason, Swift also defines the following data types.

Int8—This data type defines integer numbers of a size of 1 byte (8 bits). Because of its size, it can store values from -128 to 127.

Int16—This data type defines integer numbers of a size of 2 bytes (16 bits). Because of its size, it can store values from -32,768 to 32,767.

Int32—This data type defines integer numbers of a size of 4 bytes (32 bits). Because of its size, it can store values from -2,147,483,648 to 2,147,483,647.

Int64—This data type defines integer numbers of a size of 8 bytes (64 bits). Because of its size, it can store values from -9,223,372,036,854,775,808 to 9,223,372,036,854,775,807.

If we check the size of each type presented so far and calculate the possible combinations of bits, we will discover that the maximum values don't match. For example, an **Int8** uses 1 byte, which means it is composed of 8 bits, and for this reason it should be able to store numbers from 0 to 255 (256 possible combinations). The reason why an **Int8** has a positive limit of 127 is because it only uses 7 bits to store the value, the first bit on the left is reserved to indicate the sign (positive or negative). Although these limits are not restrictive, the language also provides the unsigned versions of these types in case we need to store larger positive values.

UInt—This is the same as **Int** but for unsigned values. Because it does not reserve a bit for the sign, in 64-bit systems it can store values from 0 to 18,446,744,073,709,551,615.

The specific data types for **UInt** are **UInt8**, **UInt16**, **UInt32**, and **UInt64**. These data types work exactly like the equivalents for **Int**, but they are intended to store only positive numbers.

Although all these data types are very useful, they are only good for storing binary values that can be used to represent integer numbers. Arithmetic operations also require the use of real numbers (e.g., 3.14 or 10.543). Computers cannot reproduce these types of values, but they can work with an approximation called floating-point numbers. The following are the most frequently used floating-point data types defined in the Swift language.

Float—This data type defines 32 bits floating-point numbers with a precision of 6 digits.

Double—This data type defines 64 bits floating-point numbers with a precision of at least 15 digits.

Floating-point types can handle large numbers using scientific notation, but because of their precision, it is recommended to declare a variable of type **Double** when performing calculations and use **Float** for minor tasks such as storing coordinates to position graphics on the screen.

Basic Declaration and Initialization

If we want to store data in memory, the first thing we need to do is to select the right type from the data types provided by the language and then create a variable of that type. This action is called *Declaration*, and it is done using the **var** instruction and the syntax **var name: type**.

```
var mynumber: Int
```

Listing 2-2: *Declaring variables*

This example creates a variable called **mynumber** of type **Int**. When the system reads this statement, it reserves a space in memory of 8 bytes long (64 bits) and assigns the name **mynumber** to that space. After the execution of this statement, we can use the variable **mynumber** to store in memory any integer value from -9,223,372,036,854,775,808 to 9,223,372,036,854,775,807.

IMPORTANT: You can use any character to declare the name of a variable, except for spaces, mathematical symbols, and some Unicode characters. Also, the name cannot start with a number, and Swift distinguishes between lowercase and uppercase characters (**MyInt** is considered a different variable than **myint**). You must also make sure that the name doesn't match any reserve word. If you declare a variable with an illegal name, Xcode will show you an error.

The memory is a reusable resource. The space reserved for a variable may have been used before by another variable or a piece of code may have been stored in the same location. For this reason, after the declaration of a variable we must always store a value in it to clear the space. This action is called *Initialization*.

```
var mynumber: Int
mynumber = 5
```

Listing 2-3: *Initializing variables*

In the new example of Listing 2-3, we first declare the variable as we did before, and then initialize it with the value 5 (we store the number 5 in the space of memory reserved for this variable). To store the value, we use the **=** (equal) symbol and the syntax **name = value**, where **name** is the name of the variable and **value** is the value we want to store (once the variable was declared, we do not have to use the **var** instruction or specify its type anymore).

Most of the time, we know what the variable's initial value will be right away. In cases like this, Swift allows us to declare and initialize the variable in just one line of code.

```
var mynumber: Int = 5
```

Listing 2-4: *Declaring and initializing variables in the same statement*

Do It Yourself: If you haven't done it yet, create a new Playground file with the Blank template. Replace all the statements of the Xcode's template by the code in Listing 2-4 and press the Play button. You should see the value 5 on the Results Side Bar. Repeat this process for the following examples.

Variables are called variables because their values are not constant. We can change them any time we want. To store a new value in the space of memory reserved for a variable, we must implement the same syntax used for initialization.

```
var mynumber: Int = 5
mynumber = 87
```

Listing 2-5: *Assigning a new value to a variable*

The process of storing a new value is called *assignment*. In these terms, we can say that in the example of Listing 2-5 we "initialize the variable **mynumber** with the number 5 and then assign the value 87 to it". The value 87 replaces the value 5 in memory. After that second statement is executed, every time we read the **mynumber** variable from other statements in the code it will return the value 87 (unless another value is assigned to the variable later).

IMPORTANT: Once a variable is declared, the values stored in that variable must be of the same type. If we declare a variable of type **Int**, we cannot store floating-point values in it later (e.g., 14.129).

Of course, we can create all the variables we want and of any type we need.

```
var mynumber: Int = 5
var myfavorite: Float = 14.129
```

Listing 2-6: *Declaring variables of different types*

The first statement of Listing 2-6 declares an integer variable and initializes it with the value 5. The second statement does the same but for a floating-point variable. When the values are of a clear data type, Swift can infer them and the syntax may be simplified, as shown next.

```
var mynumber = 5
var myfavorite = 14.129
```

Listing 2-7: *Declaring variables without specifying the type*

Swift infers the variable's data type from the value we are trying to assign to it. In this last example, the value 5 is clearly an integer and the value 14.129 is clearly a floating-point value, so Swift creates the variable **mynumber** of type **Int** and the variable **myfavorite** of type **Double** (it selects the most comprehensive type).

IMPORTANT: Xcode offers a simple tool we can use to see the data type assigned to a variable and get additional information. All you need to do is click on the name of the variable while holding down the Option key. This opens a popup window with the full declaration of the variable, including its data type, and any information we may need to identify the code's functionality. As we will see later, this not only applies to variables but also to instructions, including methods and properties.

An important feature of variables is that the value of one may be assigned to another.

```
var mynumber = 5
var myfavorite = mynumber
```

Listing 2-8: *Assigning variables to variables*

The second statement in Listing 2-8 reads the value of the **mynumber** variable and assigns it to the **myfavorite** variable. The type of **myfavorite** is inferred to be **Int** (the same of **mynumber**). After this code is executed, we have two integer variables, each with its own space in memory and the value 5 stored in them.

Basic Arithmetic Operators

Storing values in memory is what variables allow us to do, but those values do not have to be declared explicitly, they can also be the result of arithmetic operations. Swift supports the operations: **+** (addition), **-** (subtraction), ***** (multiplication), **/** (division) and **%** (remainder).

```
var mynumber = 5 + 10  // 15
```

Listing 2-9: *Assigning the result of an operation to a variable*

IMPORTANT: The text added at the end of the statement of Listing 2-9 is a comment that we used to show the value produced by the statement. Comments are ignored by the compiler but useful for programmers to remember vital information. They are introduced after the characters **//** (e.g., **// comment**) or in between the characters **/* */** (e.g., **/* comment */**). You can write the characters yourself or use Xcode's shortcut by selecting the lines of code you want to turn into a comment and press the keys Command and /.

When the system reads the statement in Listing 2-9, it adds 10 to 5 and assigns the result to **mynumber** (15). Of course, we can perform not only addition but any operation we want.

```
var mynumber = 2 * 25  // 50
var anothernumber = 8 - 40 * 2  // -72
var myfraction = 5.0 / 2.0  // 2.5
```

Listing 2-10: *Performing operations in variables of different type*

The first two statements in Listing 2-10 are easy to read. They perform arithmetic operations over integer numbers that produce an integer value as a result, so the variables **mynumber** and

anothernumber will be of type **Int**. A problem arises when we work with operations that may produce floating-point numbers. That is why in the third statement we specifically declared the values as floating-point numbers (adding the fractional part .0). This forces Swift to infer the variable's type as **Double** and produce a result of that type.

When the compiler finds an operation with two or more numbers and has to infer the type of the result, it converts the number of the less comprehensive type to the most comprehensive. For example, when we declare an **Int** and a **Double** in the same operation (e.g., 5 + 2.0), the **Int** value is converted and processed as **Double**, and therefore the result will also be **Double**.

```
var myfraction1 = 5.0 / 2.0  // 2.5
var myfraction2 = 5 / 2.0  // 2.5
var myfraction3 = 5 / 2  // 2
```

Listing 2-11: *Inferring the type from an operation*

This example declares and initializes three variables. In the first statement both numbers were declared as floating-point values, so the compiler infers a **Double** and creates the **myfraction1** variable of that type. In the second statement, we have an integer value and a floating-point value. Because of the floating-point value, the compiler interprets the integer (5) as a **Double** (5.0) and creates the **myfraction2** variable of type **Double**. But in the last statement there is no clear floating-point value. Both numbers were declared as integers (with no decimals). In this case, the compiler does not know what we want to do, so it interprets both numbers as integers and creates the **myfraction3** variable of type **Int**. When an operation produces a result that is expected to be an integer, any fractional part is discarded. In this example, the system gets rid of the decimal 5 from the result and only assigns the integer 2 to the variable. If we don't want to lose the fractional part, we must avoid inference and declare the data type ourselves as **Float** or **Double**.

Dividing integer numbers may be pointless most of the time, except in some circumstances when we need to know the remainder. The remainder is the amount left over by a division between two numbers and it is calculated using the **%** symbol.

```
var remainder1 = 11 % 3  // 2
var remainder2 = 20 % 8  // 4
var remainder3 = 5 % 2  // 1
```

Listing 2-12: *Calculating the remainder*

Listing 2-12 shows three examples of how to calculate the remainder of a division. Each statement calculates the remainder of dividing the first number by the second number and assigns the result to the variable. For instance, the first statement produces the remainder 2. The system divides 11 by 3 and finds a quotient of 3. Then, to get the remainder, it calculates 11 minus the multiplication of 3 times the quotient (**11 – (3 * 3) = 2**). The second statement produces a remainder of 4 and the third statement produces a remainder of 1. This last statement is particularly useful because it allows us to determine whether a value is odd or even. When we calculate the reminder of an integer divided by 2, we get a result according to its parity. If the number is even, the remainder is 0, and if the number is odd, the remainder is 1 (or -1).

Performing arithmetic operations becomes useful when instead of numbers we use variables.

```
var mynumber = 5
var total = mynumber + 10  // 15
```

Listing 2-13: *Adding numbers to variables*

This example declares the **mynumber** variable and initializes it with the value 5. In the next statement, the **total** variable is declared and initialized with the result of the addition of the current value of **mynumber** plus 10 (5 + 10).

In Listing 2-13, we used a new variable to store the result of the operation, but when the old value is not important anymore, we can store the result back into the same variable.

```
var mynumber = 5
mynumber = mynumber + 10  // 15
```

***Listing 2-14:** Performing operations on the variable's current value*

In this example, the current value of **mynumber** is added to 10 and the result is assigned to the same variable. After the execution of the second statement, the value of **mynumber** is 15.

Working with values previously stored in a variable allows our program to evolve and adapt to new circumstances. For instance, we could add 1 to the current value of a variable and store the result in the same variable to create a counter. Every time the statement is executed, the value of the variable is incremented by one unit. Recurrent increments and decrements of the values of variables are very important in computer programming. Because of this, Swift supports two operators that were specifically designed for this purpose.

- **+=** is a shorthand for **variable = variable + number**, where **number** is the value we want to add to the variable's current value.
- **-=** is a shorthand for **variable = variable - number**, where **number** is the value we want to subtract from the variable's current value.

With these operators, we can easily add or subtract a value to the current value of the variable and assign the result back to the same variable.

```
var mynumber = 5
mynumber += 4  // 9
```

***Listing 2-15:** Modifying the variable's value using incremental operators*

The process generated by the code in Listing 2-15 is straightforward. After the value 5 is assigned to the **mynumber** variable, the system reads the second statement, gets the current value of the variable, adds 4 to that value, and stores the result back to **mynumber** (9).

IMPORTANT: Swift also offers Overflow operators (**&+**, **&-**, **&***, **&/** and **&%**). These operators are useful when we think that an operation could produce a result that goes over the limit the data type can handle. For more information, visit our website and follow the links for this chapter.

Basic Constants

As mentioned before, the memory of a computer is a sequence of switches. There are millions and millions of switches, one after another, with no clear delimitations. To be able to know where the space occupied by a variable starts and ends, the system uses addresses. These addresses are just consecutive numbers that correspond to each byte of memory (8 bits). For example, if one byte is at the address 000000, the next byte will be at the address 000001, the next one at 000002, and so on. If we declare a variable of 4 bytes, the system reserves the four consecutive bytes and remember where they are so as not to overwrite them with the value of another variable. The task is easy when working with primitive types because their sizes are always the same, but the size of variables of more complex or custom data types depends on the values we assign to them. For example, the space in memory required to store the text "Hello" is smaller than the space required for the text "Hello World". Managing the memory for data of inconsistent sizes takes time and consumes more resources than working with fixed sizes. This is one of the reasons why Swift includes the concept of constants.

Constants are the same as variables, but their values cannot change. Once a constant is declared and initialized, we cannot change its value. Therefore, constants provide a secure way to store a value and help the system manage the memory. To declare them, we must apply the same syntax used for a variable but replace the **var** keyword by the **let** keyword.

```
let mynumber = 5
```

Listing 2-16: *Declaring and initializing a constant*

All the rules for variables also apply to constants; with the exception that we cannot assign a new value after the constant was already initialized. The **mynumber** constant declared in Listing 2-16 will always have the value 5.

IMPORTANT: When to use constants or variables depends on your application. As guidance, you can follow what Apple recommends: if a stored value in your code is not going to change, always declare it as a constant with the **let** keyword. Use variables only for storing values that need to be able to change.

Basic 2.3 Data Types

Besides primitive data types, Swift defines additional data types to allow us to work not only with numbers but also more complex values such as logical values (true or false), characters, or text.

Basic Characters

Because of their nature, computers cannot store decimal numbers, characters, or text. As we have seen in the previous section, the computer memory is only capable of storing 1s and 0s (switches on and off), but they can work with more complex values using tables that contain the information necessary to represent those values (numbers, letters, symbols, etc.). What the system stores in memory is not the character but the value corresponding to the index of the character on the table. For example, if we use the letter A, the value stored in memory will be the decimal number 65 (in its binary representation) because that's the position of the letter A on the table used by Swift to define these characters.

There are several standard tables of characters available. Swift is compliant with a table called *Unicode*. This is a comprehensive table that includes every character from almost any language in the world, and special characters, such as emojis. Due to its broad range, the space in memory required to store a single character varies from one character to another. For this reason, Swift provides the **Character** type to store these values.

```
var myletter: Character = "A"
```

Listing 2-17: *Declaring and initializing a* `Character` *variable*

A character is declared using the **Character** data type and initialized with the value between double quotes. In Listing 2-17, we declare a variable called **myletter** with the value A.

Besides the characters we can type from the keyboard, Unicode allows us to store emojis and symbols as characters, and Xcode offers a handy tool to select the graphics we want. By pressing the combination of keys Control + Command + Space, we can open a popup window and select a graphic with a click of the mouse.

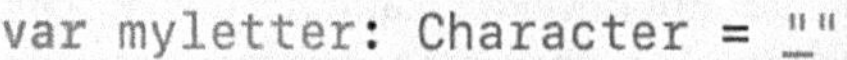

Figure 2-11: *Emojis and symbols*

Basic Strings

Individual characters are barely used in computer programming. Instead, we usually store strings of characters. The **String** type was created for this purpose.

```
let mytext: String = "My name is John"
```

Listing 2-18: *Declaring and initializing a* `String` *variable*

A string is a sequence of **Character** values. It is declared with the **String** type and the value between double quotes. These types of variables are very flexible; we may replace the string by another one of different length, concatenate two or more, or even modify parts of them. Concatenation is a common operation, and it is done with the **+** and **+=** operators.

```
var mytext = "My name is "
mytext = mytext + "John"  // "My name is John"
```

Listing 2-19: *Concatenating strings*

In Listing 2-19, the **mytext** variable is created with the value "My name is " and then the string "John" is added at the end of the current value to get the string "My name is John". The **+=** operator works in a similar way, and we can also combine them to get the string we want.

```
let name = "John"
var mytext = "My name is "
mytext += name  // "My name is John"
```

Listing 2-20: *Concatenating strings with the + and += operators*

With the **+** and **+=** operators we can concatenate strings with strings. To concatenate strings with characters and numbers we must implement a procedure called *String Interpolation*. The variables must be included inside the string between parentheses and prefixed by a backslash.

```
let age = 44
let mytext = "I am \(age) years old"  // "I am 44 years old"
```

Listing 2-21: *Including variables in strings*

In this code, the **age** variable is read and its current value is added to the string. The string "I am 44 years old" is then assigned to **mytext**. Using this tool, we can insert any value we want inside a string, including **Character** values, **String** variables, and arithmetic operations. In the following example, the value of **age** is multiplied by 12 and the result is included in the string.

```
let age = 44
let mytext = "I am \(age * 12) months old"   // "I am 528 months old"
```

Listing 2-22: *Performing operations inside strings*

Sometimes we need to include special characters in the string, like backslashes or quotes. Swift offers two ways to achieve this purpose. We can prefix the special character with another backslash, or we can enclose the entire string in hash characters, as shown next.

```
let text1 = "This is \"my\" age"   // "This is "my" age"
let text2 = #"This is "my" age"#   // "This is "my" age"
```

Listing 2-23: *Including special characters in a string*

Another important feature of strings is the possibility to create multiple lines of text. Again, Swift offers two alternatives. We can include the special characters **\n** where we want to generate a new line or we can use triple quotes (`"""`) and the compiler will consider the original format of the text and automatically insert the **\n** characters when required, as shown next.

```
let twolines = "This is the first line\nThis is the second line"
let multiline = """
This is the first line
This is the second line
"""
```

Listing 2-24: *Generating multiple lines of text*

The **`twolines`** constant defined in this example includes the **`\n`** characters in the text, which tells the compiler to generate two lines of text. If we press the Show Result button on the Results Side Bar, Xcode introduces a box below the code showing the two lines of text, one on top of the other. Something similar happens with the value of the **`multiline`** constant, although in this case the `"""` characters tell the compiler to add the **`\n`** characters at the end of each line for us.

Basic Booleans

Boolean variables are a type of variables that can only store two values: **`true`** or **`false`**. These variables are particularly useful when we want to execute an instruction or a set of instructions only if a condition is met. To declare a Boolean variable, we can specify the data type as **`Bool`** or let Swift infer it from the value, as in the following example.

```
var valid = true
```

Listing 2-25: *Declaring a Boolean variable*

The purpose of these variables is to simplify the process of identifying a condition. By using a Boolean variable instead of an integer, for example, we just need to check whether the value is equal to **`true`** or **`false`** to verify the condition. We will see some practical examples later.

Basic Optionals

As mentioned at the beginning of this chapter, after a variable is declared, we must provide its initial value. We cannot use a variable if it was not initialized. This means that a variable has a valid value all the time. But this is not always possible. Sometimes we do not have an initial value to assign to the variable during development or we need to indicate the absence of a value because the current one becomes invalid. For these situations, Swift defines a modifier that turns every data type into an optional type. This means that the variable marked as optional may have a value or be empty. To declare an optional, we add a question mark after the type's name.

```
var mynumber: Int?
```

***Listing 2-26:** Declaring an optional variable of type* `Int`

New values are assigned to optionals as we do with normal variables.

```
var mynumber: Int?
mynumber = 5
```

***Listing 2-27:** Assigning new values to optional variables*

The empty state is represented by the keyword **`nil`**. Therefore, when an optional variable is declared but not initialized, Swift assigns the **`nil`** keyword to the variable to indicate the absence of a value. Thus, if later we need to empty the variable, we can assign the keyword **`nil`** to it.

```
var mynumber: Int?
mynumber = 5
mynumber = nil
```

***Listing 2-28:** Using* `nil` *to empty an optional variable*

This example declares an optional integer, assigns the value 5 to it, and then declares the variable as empty with the keyword **`nil`**. Although optionals seem to work like regular variables, they do not expose their values. To read the value of an optional, we must unwrap it by adding an exclamation mark at the end of the name.

```
var mynumber: Int?
mynumber = 5
var total = mynumber! * 10  // 50
```

***Listing 2-29:** Unwrapping an optional variable*

The last statement of Listing 2-29 unwraps **`mynumber`** to get its value, multiplies this value by 10, and assigns the result to the **`total`** variable. This is only necessary when we need to use the value. If we just want to assign an optional to another optional, the process is as always.

```
var mynumber: Int?
mynumber = 5
var total = mynumber
```

***Listing 2-30:** Assigning an optional to another optional*

In this example, the system infers the type of the **`total`** variable to be an optional of type **`Int`** and assigns the value of **`mynumber`** to it. If we want to read the value of **`total`** later, we must unwrap it as we did with **`mynumber`** before.

IMPORTANT: Before unwrapping an optional, we need to make sure it contains a value (it is not equal to **`nil`**). If we try to unwrap an empty optional, the app will return an error and crash. Later in this chapter we will learn how to use conditional statements to check this condition.

There are times when we know that an optional will always have a value, but we do not know what the initial value is. For example, we could have a variable that receives a value from the system as soon as the application is executed. When the variable is declared in our code, we do not have a value to assign to it, but we know that the variable will have a value as soon as the user launches the app. For these situations, Swift includes *implicitly unwrapped optionals*. These are optional variables declared with the exclamation mark instead of the question mark. The system treats these variables as optionals until we use them in a statement, as shown next.

```
var mynumber: Int!
mynumber = 5
var total = mynumber * 10  // 50
```

Listing 2-31: *Declaring implicitly unwrapped optionals*

In this code, the **mynumber** variable was declared as an implicitly unwrapped optional and it was later initialized with the value 5. Notice that it was not necessary to write the exclamation mark when reading its value anymore. The system unwraps the **mynumber** variable automatically to use its value in the multiplication (this is only available for implicitly unwrapped optionals).

Basic Tuples

A tuple is a type of variable that contains a group of one or more values of equal or different type. It is useful when we need to store values that are somehow related to each other. Tuples are declared with their values and types separated by a comma and enclosed between parentheses.

```
var myname: (String, String) = ("John", "Doe")
```

Listing 2-32: *Declaring a tuple with two values*

In this example, the **myname** variable is declared to be a tuple that contains two **String** values. The values of this tuple are of the same type, but we can use any combination of values we want.

```
var myname = ("John", "Doe", 44)
```

Listing 2-33: *Declaring a tuple with values of different type*

To be able to read the values later, an index is automatically assigned to each of the values of the tuple. The first value will be at index 0, the second at index 1, and so on. Using the corresponding index and dot notation we can access the value we want.

```
var myname = ("John", "Doe", 44)
var mytext = "\(myname.0) is \(myname.2) years old" // "John is 44 years
old"
```

Listing 2-34: *Reading a tuple*

In Listing 2-34, we read the values of the **myname** tuple at index 0 and 2 to include them in a new string and assign the string to **mytext**. The same syntax may be used to modify a value.

```
var myname = ("John", "Doe", 44)
myname.0 = "George"
var mytext = "\(myname.0) is \(myname.2) years old"
```

Listing 2-35: *Changing the value of a tuple*

The second statement in Listing 2-35 assigns a new string to the first value of the tuple. The new value must be of the same data type as the old one or we will get an error. After the code is executed, the value of **mytext** is "George is 44 years old".

Indexes are a quick way to access the values of a tuple, but they do not help us remember what the values represent. To identify the values in a tuple, we can assign a name to each one of them. The name must be declared before the value and separated with a colon, as shown next.

```
var myname = (name: "John", surname: "Doe", age: 44)
var mytext = "\(myname.name) is \(myname.age) years old"
```

Listing 2-36: *Declaring names for the values of a tuple*

Swift also provides a way to copy the values of the tuple into independent variables.

```
var myname = ("John", "Doe", 44)
var (name, surname, age) = myname
var mytext = "\(name) \(surname) is \(age) years old"
```

Listing 2-37: *Creating multiple variables from the values of a tuple*

The names of the variables are declared between parentheses and the tuple is assigned to this construction. The values are assigned to the variables in the same order they are in the tuple. If only some of the values are required, the rest may be ignored with an underscore.

```
var myname = ("John", "Doe", 44)
var (name, _, age) = myname
var mytext = "\(name) is \(age) years old"
```

Listing 2-38: *Ignoring some of the values of a tuple*

Only the variables **name** and **age** are created in this last example (notice the underscore in the place of the second variable). The string assigned to **mytext** is "John is 44 years old".

Basic 2.4 Conditionals and Loops

Up to this point, we have been writing instructions in a sequence, one after another. In this programming pattern, the system executes each statement once. It starts with the one at the top and goes on until it reaches the end of the list. The purpose of Conditionals and Loops is to break this sequential flow. Conditionals allow us to execute one or more instructions only when a condition is met, and Loops let us execute a group of instructions repeatedly.

Basic If and Else

A simple but handful conditional statement available in Swift is **if**. With **if** we can check a condition and execute a group of instructions only when the condition is true. The instructions that are going to be executed must be declared between braces after the condition.

```
var age = 19
var message = "John is old"

if age < 21 {
   message = "John is young"
}
```

Listing 2-39: *Comparing two values with* `if`

Two variables are declared in this code. The **age** variable contains the value we want to check, and the **message** variable is the one we are going to modify depending on the state of the condition. The **if** statement compares the value of **age** with the number 21 using the character **<** (less than). This comparison returns the state of the condition (true or false). If the condition is true (the value of **age** is less than 21), the instruction between braces is executed, assigning a new value to the **message** variable, otherwise the instruction is ignored, and the execution continues with the instructions after the braces. In this case, the value of **age** is less than 21 and therefore the string "John is young" is assigned to the **message** variable.

IMPORTANT: The instruction between braces in the example of Listing 2-39 is displaced to the right. The whitespace on the left is used to help us differentiate the statements between braces from the rest of the statements. This whitespace is automatically generated for you by Xcode, but you can add it yourself, when necessary, by pressing the Tab key on your keyboard.

The **<** symbol we used in the last example to compare values is part of a group of operators called *comparison operators*. The following is the list of comparison operators available in Swift.

- **==** checks whether the value on the left is equal to the value on the right.
- **!=** checks whether the value on the left is different from the value on the right.
- **>** checks whether the value on the left is greater than the value on the right.
- **<** checks whether the value on the left is less than the value on the right.
- **>=** checks whether the value on the left is greater or equal than the value on the right.
- **<=** checks whether the value on the left is less or equal than the value on the right.

All these operators are applied the same way we did in the previous example. For instance, the following code modifies the value of **message** when the value of **age** is less or equal than 21.

```
var age = 21
var message = "John is old"
if age <= 21 {
   message = "John is young"
}
```

***Listing 2-40:** Comparing two values with the <= operator*

When only two results are required, we may define the condition using a Boolean. These values do not need to be compared with the expected value; they already return a state (true or false).

```
var underage = true
var message = "John is allowed"
if underage {
   message = "John is underage"
}
```

***Listing 2-41:** Conditions with Boolean values*

This code checks whether the value of the **underage** variable is **true** or **false**. If it is **true** (which means the condition is true), a new string is assigned to the **message** variable. If what we want is to execute the statements when the value is **false**, Swift offers a logical operator to toggle the condition. All we need to do is to precede the condition with an exclamation mark.

```
var underage = true
var message = "John is underage"
```

```
if !underage {
   message = "John is allowed"
}
```

Listing 2-42: *Using logical operators*

The original value of the **underage** variable in the code of Listing 2-42 is **true**, so when the **if** statement toggles the condition, the resulting condition is false and therefore the value of the **message** variable is not modified.

The exclamation mark is part of a group of logical operators provided by Swift.

- **!** (logical NOT) toggles the state of the condition. If the condition is true, it returns false, and vice versa.
- **&&** (logical AND) checks two conditions and returns true if both are true.
- **||** (logical OR) checks two conditions and returns true if one or both are true.

Logical operators work with any kind of conditions, not only Booleans. To work with complex conditions, it is recommended to enclose the condition between parentheses.

```
var smart = true
var age = 19
var message = "John is underage or dumb"

if (age < 21) && smart {
   message = "John is allowed"
}
```

Listing 2-43: *Using logical operators to check several conditions*

The **if** statement in Listing 2-43 compares the value of the **age** variable with 21 and checks the value of the **smart** variable. If **age** is less than 21 and **smart** is **true**, then the overall condition is true, and a new string is assigned to **message**. If any of the individual conditions is false, then the overall condition is false, and the block of instructions is not executed. In this case, both conditions are true and therefore the "John is allowed" string is assigned to **message**.

IMPORTANT: Using **&&** (AND) and **||** (OR) you can create a logical sequence of multiple conditions. The system evaluates one condition at a time from left to right and compares the results. If you want to make sure that the expressions are evaluated in the correct order, you can declare them within parentheses, as in **(true && false) || true**. The expression within the parentheses is evaluated first, and the result is then evaluated against the rest of the expression.

Although we can use comparison operators and logical operators in most of the data types available, optionals are slightly different. Their values are wrapped, so we cannot compare them with other values or check their state as we do with Booleans. Optionals must be compared against the keyword **nil** first and then unwrapped before working with their values.

```
var count = 0
var myoptional: Int? = 5

if myoptional != nil {
   let uvalue = myoptional!
   count = count + uvalue   // 5
}
```

Listing 2-44: *Checking whether an optional contains a value or not*

This example introduces the process we must follow to read the value of an optional variable. The optional is checked first against **nil**. If it is different from **nil** (which means it contains a value), we unwrap the optional inside the block of statements using an exclamation mark, assign its value to a constant, and use the constant to perform any operation necessary.

We always need to make sure that an optional has a value before unwrapping it. Because of this, Swift introduces a convenient syntax that checks the optional and unwraps its value at the same time. It is called *Optional Binding*.

```
var count = 0
var myoptional: Int? = 5
if let uvalue = myoptional {
   count = count + uvalue   // 5
}
```

Listing 2-45: *Using optional binding to unwrap an optional variable*

This code is cleaner and easy to read. The optional is unwrapped as part of the condition. If it is different from **nil**, its value is assigned to the **uvalue** constant and the statements in the block are executed, otherwise, the statements inside the block are ignored.

IMPORTANT: The constant created to unwrap the optional in this way is only available inside the block assigned to the **if** statement. If we try to read the value of this constant from outside the block, we will get an error. We will learn more about the scope of variables in Chapter 3.

If we want to unwrap several optionals at the same time using Optional Binding, we must declare the expressions separated by a comma. This also applies when we want to check other conditions in the same statement. For instance, the following example unwraps an optional and only executes the code between braces if its value is equal to 5.

```
var count = 0
var myoptional: Int? = 5
if let uvalue = myoptional, uvalue == 5 {
   count = count + uvalue   // 5
}
```

Listing 2-46: *Checking multiple conditions with Optional Binding*

The **if** statement in Listing 2-46 unwraps the optional first and, if there is a value, compares it with the number 5. The statements in the block are executed only if both conditions are true (the **myoptional** variable contains a value and the value is equal to 5).

Sometimes, a group of instructions must be executed for each state of the condition. For this purpose, Swift includes the **if else** statement. The instructions are declared in two blocks. The first block is executed when the condition is true, and the second block when the condition is false.

```
var mynumber = 6
if mynumber % 2 == 0 {
   mynumber = mynumber + 2   // 8
} else {
   mynumber = mynumber + 1
}
```

Listing 2-47: *Using* `if else` *to respond to both states of the condition*

This is a simple example that checks whether a value is odd or even using the remainder operator. The condition gets the remainder of the division between the value of the **mynumber** variable and 2 and compares the result against 0. If true, it means that the value of **mynumber** is even, so the first block is executed. If the result is different from 0, it means that the value is odd and the condition is false, so the block corresponding to the **else** instruction is executed instead.

The statements **if** and **else** may be concatenated to check for as many conditions as we need. In the following example, the first condition checks whether **age** is less than 21. If not true, the second condition checks whether **age** is over 21. And if not true, the final **else** block is executed.

```
var age = 19
var message = "The customer is "
if age < 21 {
   message += "underage"   // "The customer is underage"
} else if age > 21 {
   message += "allowed"
} else {
   message += "21 years old"
}
```

Listing 2-48: *Concatenating* `if else` *instructions*

If all we need from an **if** statement is to assign a value to a variable depending on a condition, we can use a shortcut provided by Swift called *ternary operator*. The ternary operator is a construction composed by the condition and the two values we want to return for each state, separated with the characters **?** and **:**, as in the following example.

```
var age = 19
var message = age < 21 ? "Underage" : "Allowed"   // "Underage"
```

Listing 2-49: *Implementing the ternary operator*

The first value is returned if the condition is true, and the second value is returned if the condition is false. The advantage of using the ternary operator is that it reduces the code significantly, but the result is the same as using an **if else** statement. In this case, the string "Underage" is assigned to the variable **message** because the value of **age** is less than 21.

Ternary operators can also be implemented to unwrap optionals. For instance, we can check whether an optional variable contains a value and assign it to another variable or give the variable a default value if the optional is empty.

```
var age: Int? = 19
var realage = age != nil ? age! : 0   // 19
```

Listing 2-50: *Unwrapping an optional with a ternary operator*

This code defines an optional variable called **age** with the value 19. Next, we use a ternary operator to unwrap it and assign its value to a new variable called **realage**. If the optional contains a value, its value is assigned to the variable, otherwise, the value 0 is assigned instead.

Assigning values by default when the optional is empty is very common. To simplify our work, Swift offers the nil-coalescing operator, which is represented by the characters **??**. This operator works like the ternary operator implemented before; it unwraps the optional and returns its value or returns another value if the optional is empty. In the following example, we create an empty optional called **age** and use the nil-coalescing operator to assign its value to the **maxage** variable or the value 100 if the optional is empty.

```
var age: Int?
var maxage = age ?? 100   // 100
```

Listing 2-51: *Unwrapping an optional with the nil-coalescing operator*

Basic Switch

We can repeat the **if** and **else** statements to check as many conditions as we need, but this pattern can make the code impossible to read and maintain. When several conditions must be verified, it is better to use the **switch** instruction instead. This instruction compares a value with a list of values and executes the statements corresponding to the value that matches. The possible matches are listed between braces using the **case** keyword, as in the following example.

```
var age = 19
var message = ""
switch age {
   case 13:
      message = "Happy Bar Mitzvah!"
   case 16:
      message = "Sweet Sixteen!"
   case 21:
      message = "Welcome to Adulthood!"
   default:
      message = "Happy Birthday!"   // "Happy Birthday!"
}
```

Listing 2-52: *Checking conditions with* switch

The cases must be exhaustive; every possible value of the variable being checked must be contemplated. If we do not include a **case** statement for every possible value, we must add a **default** statement at the end that is executed when no match is found.

In Listing 2-52, we compare the value of the **age** variable with a small set of values corresponding to special dates. If no **case** matches the value of the variable, the **default** statement is executed and the string "Happy Birthday!" is assigned to **message**.

When we need to execute the same set of instructions for more than one value, we can declare the values separated by comma.

```
var age = 6
var message = "You go to "
switch age {
   case 2, 3, 4:
      message += "Day Care"
   case 5, 6, 7, 8, 9, 10, 11:
      message += "Elementary School"   // "You go to Elementary School"
   case 12, 13, 14, 15, 16, 17:
      message += "High School"
   case 18, 19, 20, 21:
      message += "College"
   default:
      message += "Work"
}
```

Listing 2-53: *Checking multiple conditions per case*

The **switch** statement can also work with more complex data types, such as strings and tuples. In the case of tuples, **switch** provides additional options to build complex matching patterns. For example, the following code checks the second value of a tuple to determine the difference in age.

```
var message = ""
var ages = (10, 30)
```

```
switch ages {
   case (10, 20):
      message = "Too close"
   case (10, 30):
      message = "The right age"   // "The right age"
   case (10, 40):
      message = "Too far"
   default:
      message = "Way too far"
}
```

Listing 2-54: *Matching a tuple in a* `switch` *statement*

This example always compares the first value of the tuple against 10 but checks different matches for the second value. If a value does not matter, we can use an underscore to ignore it.

```
var message = ""
var ages = (10, 30)

switch ages {
   case (_, 20):
      message = "Too close"
   case (_, 30):
      message = "The right age"   // "The right age"
   case (_, 40):
      message = "Too far"
   default:
      message = "Way too far"
}
```

Listing 2-55: *Matching only the second value of a tuple*

An alternative offered by the **switch** statement to create complex matching patterns is to capture a value in a constant to be able to access it from the instructions of the **case**.

```
var message = ""
var ages = (10, 20)
switch ages {
   case (let x, 20):
      message = "Too close to \(x)"   // "Too close to 10"
   case (_, 30):
      message = "The right age"
   case (let x, 40):
      message = "Too far to \(x)"
   default:
      message = "Way too far"
}
```

Listing 2-56: *Capturing values with constants*

In this example, when the **switch** statement checks the first and third cases, it creates a constant called **x** and assigns the first value to it, so we can access and use the value from the statements inside the **case** (in this example, we just add the value to a string).

There is an even more complex matching pattern that involves the use of a clause called **where**. This clause allows us to check additional conditions. In the following example, we capture the values of the tuple with another tuple and compare them against each other.

```
var message = ""
var ages = (10, 20)
```

```
switch ages {
   case let (x, y) where x > y:
      message = "Too young"
   case let (x, y) where x == y:
      message = "The same age"
   case let (x, y) where x < y:
      message = "Too old"   // "Too old"
   default:
      message = "Not found"
}
```

Listing 2-57: *Comparing values with* `where`

Every time the **switch** statement tries to match a **case** in this example, it creates a tuple and assigns the values of **ages** to it. The **where** clause compares the values and when the condition returns true it executes the statements inside the **case**.

Basic While and Repeat While

The conditionals studied so far execute the statements only once. Sometimes the program requires executing a block of instructions several times until a condition is satisfied. An alternative offered by Swift to create these loops is the **while** statement (and its sibling **repeat while**).

The **while** statement checks a condition and executes the statements in its block while the condition is true. The following example initializes a variable with the value 0 and then checks its value in a **while** statement. If the value of the variable is less than 5, the statements inside the block are executed. After this, the condition is checked again. The loop keeps running until the condition becomes false (the value of the **counter** variable is equal or greater than 5).

```
var counter = 0
while counter < 5 {
   counter += 1
}
```

Listing 2-58: *Using* `while` *to create a loop*

If the first time the condition is checked returns false, the statements in the block are never executed. If we want to execute the statements at least once, we must use **repeat while**.

```
var counter = 10
repeat {
   counter += 1
} while counter < 5
```

Listing 2-59: *Using* `repeat while` *to create a loop*

In this case, the initial value of the **counter** variable is declared as 10. This is greater than 5, but since we are using the **repeat while** instruction, the statements in the block are executed before the condition is checked, so the final value of **counter** will be 11 (its value is incremented once and then the condition returns false, ending the loop).

Basic For In

The purpose of the **for in** loop is to iterate over collections of elements, like the strings of characters studied before. During the execution of a **for in** loop, the system reads the elements of the collection one by one in sequential order and assigns their values to a constant that can be used by the statements inside the block. In this case, the condition that must be satisfied for the loop to be over is reaching the end of the collection.

The syntax of a **for in** loop is **for constant in collection {}**, where **constant** is the name of the constant that we are going to use to capture the value of each element, and **collection** is the name of the collection of values that we want to iterate over.

```
var mytext = "Hello"
var message = ""

for letter in mytext {
   message += message != "" ? "-" : ""
   message += "\(letter)"
}
```

Listing 2-60: *Using* `for in` *to iterate over the characters of a string*

The code in Listing 2-60 defines two **String** variables: **mytext** with the text "Hello" and **message** with an empty string. Next, we use a **for in** loop to iterate over the characters of the string in **mytext** and add each character to the current value of **message**. In each cycle of the loop, the instruction takes one character from the value of **mytext**, assigns it to the **letter** constant, and executes the statements in the block. The first statement uses a ternary operator to check whether the value of **message** is an empty string. If not, it adds the **-** character at the end of it, otherwise, it adds an empty string. Finally, the second statement adds the current value of **letter** to the end of the **message** string.

In this example, the code works as follows: in the loop's first cycle, the character "H" is assigned to the **letter** constant. Because at this moment the **message** string is empty, nothing is added by the first statement. Then, the second statement adds the value of **letter** to the current value of **message** and the next cycle is executed. In this new cycle, the character "e" is assigned to the **letter** constant. This time, the **message** string already contains the letter "H", so the character "-" is added at the end by the first statement ("H-"), and then the second statement adds the letter "e" at the end of this new string ("H-e"). This process continues until all the characters in the **mytext** variable are processed. The final value of **message** is "H-e-l-l-o".

When the constant is not required inside the block, we can replace it with an underscore.

```
var mytext = "Hello"
var counter = 0

for _ in mytext {
   counter += 1
}
var message = "The string contains \(counter) letters"  // 5
```

Listing 2-61: *Iterating over a string without reading the characters*

In this example, we iterate over the value of **mytext** to count the number of characters in the string. The value of the **counter** variable is incremented by 1 each cycle, giving a total of 5.

A **for in** instruction may include the **where** clause to perform the next cycle only when a condition is met. For instance, the following code checks the value of the letter and only performs the cycle when the letter is not an L. In consequence, only the letters H, e, and o are counted.

```
var mytext = "Hello"
var counter = 0

for letter in mytext where letter != "l" {
   counter += 1
}
var message = "The string contains \(counter) letters"  // 3
```

Listing 2-62: *Adding a condition to a loop*

Basic Control Transfer Statements

Sometimes loops must be interrupted, independently of the condition. Swift offers instructions to break the execution of loops and conditionals. The following are the most frequently used.

continue—This instruction interrupts the current cycle and moves to the next. The system ignores the rest of the statements in the block after the instruction is executed.

break—This instruction interrupts the loop. The rest of the statements in the block and any pending cycles are ignored after the instruction is executed.

The **continue** instruction is applied when we do not want to execute the rest of the statements in the block, but we want to keep the loop running. For instance, the following code counts the letters in a string but ignores the letters "l".

```
var mytext = "Hello"
var counter = 0

for letter in mytext {
   if letter == "l" {
      continue
   }
   counter += 1
}
var message = "The string contains \(counter) letters"  // 3
```

Listing 2-63: *Jumping to the next cycle of the loop*

The **if** statement inside the **for in** loop of Listing 2-63 compares the value of **letter** with the letter "l". If the characters match, the **continue** instruction is executed, the last statement inside the loop is ignored, and the loop moves on to the next character in **mytext**. In consequence, the code counts all the characters that are different from "l" (H, e, and o).

Unlike the **continue** instruction, the **break** instruction interrupts the loop completely, moving the execution of the program to the statements after the loop. The following example only counts the characters in the string that are placed before the first letter "l".

```
var mytext = "Hello"
var counter = 0

for letter in mytext {
   if letter == "l" {
      break
   }
   counter += 1
}
var message = "The string contains \(counter) letters"  // 2
```

Listing 2-64: *Interrupting the loop*

Again, the **if** statement of Listing 2-64 compares the value of **letter** with the character "l", but this time it executes the **break** instruction when a match is found. If the character currently processed by the loop is "l", the **break** instruction is executed, and the loop is over, no matter how many characters are left in the string. In consequence, only the characters located before the first letter "l" are considered (H and e).

The **break** instruction is also useful to cancel the execution of a **switch** statement. The problem with the **switch** statement in Swift is that the cases must be exhaustive, which means that every possible value must be contemplated. When this is not possible or necessary, we can use the **break** instruction to ignore the values that are not applicable. For example, we can declare the cases for the values we need and then break the execution in the **default** case for the rest of the values that we do not care about.

```
var age = 19
var message = ""

switch age {
   case 13:
      message = "Happy Bar Mitzvah!"
   case 16:
      message = "Sweet Sixteen!"
   case 21:
      message = "Welcome to Adulthood!"
   default:
      break
}
```

Listing 2-65: *Ignoring values in a* `switch` *statement*

After the execution of this code, the **message** variable is empty because there is no **case** that matches the value of the **age** variable and therefore the code in **default** is executed and the **break** instruction returns the control to the statements after the **switch**.

Basic Guard

The **guard** instruction is intended to prevent the execution of the code that follows the statement. For example, we can break the execution of a loop when a condition is satisfied, as we do with an **if else** statement.

```
var mytext = "Hello"
var counter = 0

for letter in mytext {
   guard letter != "l" else {
      break
   }
   counter += 1
}
var message = "The string contains \(counter) letters"  // 2
```

Listing 2-66: *Interrupting a loop with* `guard`

The **guard** instruction works along with the **else** instruction and therefore it is very similar to the **if else** statement, but the code is only executed when the condition is false. In the example of Listing 2-66, the **for in** loop reads the characters of the string in **mytext** one by one, as we did before. If the characters are different from the letter "l", we increase the value of **counter** by 1, but when the value of **letter** is equal to "l", the condition of the **guard** instruction is false and therefore the **break** instruction is executed, interrupting the loop.

IMPORTANT: The advantage of **guard** over the **if else** statement is that the variable or constant defined in the condition outlives the statement, and therefore we can read its value outside the block. Although you can implement the **guard** instruction to break or continue a loop, the instruction was introduced to work along with the **return** instruction to interrupt the execution of a function. We will study the **return** instruction and functions later.

Chapter 3
Swift Paradigm

Basic 3.1 Programming Paradigms

Programs wouldn't be very useful if we were only able to write them as a consecutive set of instructions. At first, this was the only way to write a program, but soon programming languages incorporated tools to allow programmers to group instructions together and execute them every time necessary. The way instructions are organized is called *paradigm*. Different paradigms are now available, with the most common being the Object-Oriented Programming paradigm, or OOP. This paradigm emerges from the construction and integration of processing units called *objects*. Swift adopts OOP, but it is not focused as much on objects as other languages do. Instead, it implements other types of processing units called *structures* and *enumerations* along with blueprints called *protocols* to conform a new paradigm called *Protocol-Oriented Programing*. The Swift paradigm unifies objects, structures, and enumerations through protocols that define how these units behave and the type of functionality they have.

Do It Yourself: The examples in this chapter were designed to be tested in Playground. You just need to create a Playground file with a Blank template and then replace the code with the example you want to try.

Basic 3.2 Functions

The processing units that define the Swift paradigm (objects, structures, and enumerations) are capable of encapsulating data along with functionality. The data is stored in the same variables we studied before, but the functionality is provided by functions. Functions are blocks of code delimited by curly braces and identified by a name. The difference between functions and the block of codes used in loops and conditional statements is that there is no condition to satisfy; the statements inside a function are executed every time the function is called (executed). Functions are called by writing their names followed by parentheses. This call may be performed from anywhere in the code and every time necessary, which completely breaks the sequential processing of a program. Once a function is called, the execution of the program continues with the statements inside the function and only returns to the section of the code that called the function once the execution of the function is over.

Basic Declaration of Functions

Functions are declared with the **func** keyword followed by a name, parentheses, and the code between braces.

```
var mynumber = 5
func myfunction() {
   mynumber = mynumber * 2  // 10
}
myfunction()
```

Listing 3-1: *Declaring and calling functions*

The code in Listing 3-1 declares the **mynumber** variable, initializes it with the value 5, and then declares a function called **myfunction()**. The statements in a function are only processed when the function is called, so after the **myfunction()** function is declared, we call it with the instruction **myfunction()**. When our function is called, it multiplies the current value of **mynumber** times 2 and assigns the result back to the variable. Once all the statements inside the function are processed, the execution continues from the statement after the call.

As we already mentioned, once the function is declared, we can call it any time necessary and from anywhere in the program. For example, the following code runs a **while** loop that calls **myfunction()** a total of 5 times (the loop runs while **counter** is less than 5). Every time the function is executed, **mynumber**'s current value is multiplied by 2, getting a result of 160.

```
var mynumber = 5
var counter = 0
func myfunction() {
   mynumber = mynumber * 2  // 160
}
while counter < 5 {
   myfunction()
   counter += 1
}
```

Listing 3-2: *Calling functions from a loop*

The functions in these examples are modifying the value of an external variable (a variable that was not declared inside the function). Creating a function that works with values and variables that do not belong to the function itself could be dangerous; some variables may be modified by accident from other functions, the function may be called before the variables were even declared or initialized, or the variables that the function tries to modify may not be accessible by the function (functions have limited scope, as we will see later). To make sure that a function processes the right values, they must be sent to the function when it is called. The type of values the function can receive and the names they are going to take are specified within the function's parentheses separated by a comma. When the function is executed, these parameters are turned into constants that we can read inside the function to get their values.

```
func doubleValue(number: Int) {
   let total = number * 2
   let message = "Result: \(total)"  // "Result: 10"
}
doubleValue(number: 5)
```

Listing 3-3: *Sending values to a function*

In this example, we don't use external variables anymore. The value to be processed is sent to the function when it is called and received by the function through its parameter. The parameters are declared within the function's parentheses with the same syntax used for constants and variables. We must write the name and the data type separated by a colon. In this example, the function is declared with one parameter of type **Int** called **number**.

The call must include the name of the parameter and the value we want to send to the function. When the function of Listing 3-3 is called, the value between the parentheses of the call (5) is assigned to the **number** constant, the value of the constant is multiplied by 2, and finally the result is included in a string with string interpolation.

Of course, we can include as many parameters as we need. The following example multiplies two values and creates a string with the result.

```
func multiply(number1: Int, number2: Int) {
   let result = number1 * number2
   let message = "The result is \(result)"  // "The result is 80"
}
multiply(number1: 20, number2: 4)
```

Listing 3-4: *Sending different values to a function*

Functions may not only be called every time we need them, but also the values we provide to the function in the call may be different each time. This makes functions reusable.

```
func doubleValue(number: Int) {
   let total = number * 2
   let message = "Result: \(total)"
}
doubleValue(number: 5)  // "Result: 10"
doubleValue(number: 25)  // "Result: 50"
```

Listing 3-5: *Sending different values to a function*

The constants and variables declared inside a function, like **`total`** and **`message`**, are not accessible from other parts of the code. This means that a function can receive values, but the result produced by processing those values is trapped inside the function. To communicate this result to the rest of the code, functions can return a value using a special instruction called **`return`**. The **`return`** instruction finishes the processing of the function, so we must declare it after all the statements required have been processed, as in the following example.

```
func doubleValue(number: Int) -> Int {
   let total = number * 2
   return total
}
let result = doubleValue(number: 25)
let message = "The result is \(result)"  // "The result is 50"
```

Listing 3-6: *Returning a value from a function*

When we create a function that returns a value, the type of the value returned is specified in the declaration after the parentheses with the syntax **`-> Type`**, where **`Type`** is just the data type of the value that is going to be returned by the function. A function can only return values of the type indicated in its definition. For instance, the function in Listing 3-6 can only return integer values because we declared the returned type as **`-> Int`**.

When a function returns a value, the system calls the function first and then the value returned is processed inside the statement that made the call. For instance, in the code of Listing 3-6, we create the **`result`** variable and assign to this variable a call to the **`doubleValue()`** function. When the system processes this statement, the function is executed first and then the value returned (50) is assigned to the variable.

The values received and returned by a function may be of any available data type. The following example takes a string and returns a tuple with a string and an integer.

```
func sumCharacters(word: String) -> (String, Int) {
   var characters = ""
   var counter = 0
   for letter in word {
      characters += "\(letter) "
      counter += 1
   }
   return (characters, counter)
}
var (list, total) = sumCharacters(word: "Hello")
var message = "There are \(total) characters (\(list))"
```

Listing 3-7: *Returning a tuple*

The **`sumCharacters()`** function of Listing 3-7 receives a string (**`word: String`**) and returns a tuple composed of a string and an integer (**`-> (String, Int)`**). The function adds the characters to the **`characters`** variable and counts them with the **`counter`** variable, as we did before (see Listing 2-60). At the end, the tuple is returned, its values are assigned to the **`list`** and **`total`** variables, and then incorporated into a string ("There are 5 characters (H e l l o)").

Besides returning the result of an operation, the **return** instruction can also be used to interrupt the execution of a function. The **guard** instruction introduced in Chapter 2 is perfect for cases like this, as illustrated by the following example.

```
func doubleValue(number: Int) -> Int {
   guard number < 10 else {
      return number
   }
   return number * 2
}
let result = doubleValue(number: 25)
let message = "The result is \(result)"  // "The result is 25"
```

Listing 3-8: *Interrupting the execution of a function with* `guard`

The **doubleValue()** function of Listing 3-8 is similar to previous examples. It receives a number, multiplies it by 2, and returns the result, but this time we first check that the value received by the function is less than 10. If the value is equal or higher than 10, the **guard** instruction calls the **return** instruction with the received value, otherwise, the statements of the function are executed as normal. In this case, the value sent to the function is 25, therefore the condition is false, and the same value is returned.

Notice that in the example of Listing 3-8 we simplified our code including the multiplication in the **return** instruction. The **return** instruction can take single values or expressions like this. The instruction takes care of solving the expression (or operation, as in this case) and returning the result. For this reason, sometimes we may find functions with only one statement in charge of returning a value. If this is the case, we can remove the **return** keyword. In the following example, the call sends the number 25 to the function, the value is multiplied by 2, and returned, as in previous examples, but this time we didn't have to declare the **return** keyword because there is only one statement inside the function and therefore the compiler knows what to return.

```
func doubleValue(number: Int) -> Int {
   number * 2
}
let result = doubleValue(number: 25)
let message = "The result is \(result)"  // "The result is 50"
```

Listing 3-9: *Removing the* `return` *keyword*

Besides the **return** keyword, Swift offers the **inout** keyword to preserve a value after the function finishes processing. When a parameter is marked with **inout**, any changes performed on the value are stored in the original variable. This is useful when we call a function from another function (or block), and we want the modifications introduced by the second function to persist.

```
func first() {
   var number = 25
   second(value: &number)
   print("The result is \(number)")  // "The result is 50"
}
func second(value: inout Int) {
   value = value * 2
}
first()
```

Listing 3-10: *Modifying external variables from a function*

This code defines two functions: **first()** and **second()**. The **second()** function receives an **inout** parameter called **value**, which means that any modification on its value is stored in the original variable. The **first()** function defines a variable called **number** and then executes the **second()** function with it, so when the **second()** function multiplies this value times 2, the result (50) is stored in **number**. At the end, we execute the **first()** function to start the process. Notice that in the call to the **second()** function we include an ampersand before the variable's name (&). This tells the system that the variable is going to be modified by the function.

An important aspect of the definition of a function are the parameter's names. When we call a function, we must declare the names of the parameters. For example, the function **doubleValue()** of previous examples includes a parameter called **number**. Every time we call this function, we must include the name of the parameter (e.g., **doubleValue(number: 50)**). These names are called *argument labels*. Swift automatically generates argument labels for every parameter using their names. Sometimes the names assigned to the parameters of a function may be descriptive enough for the statements of the function but may be confusing when we perform the call. For cases like these, Swift allows us to define our own argument labels in the function's definition; we just need to declare them before the name of the parameter separated by a space.

```
func doubleValue(years number: Int) -> Int {
   number * 2
}
let result = doubleValue(years: 8)
let message = "The result is \(result)"  // "The results is 16"
```

***Listing 3-11:** Declaring argument labels*

The **doubleValue()** function in Listing 3-11 declares an argument label called **years** for the **number** parameter. From now on, the name of the parameter (**number**) is the one used by the statements of the function to access the value received from the call, while the argument label (**years**) is used when calling the function to identify the value.

If what we want instead is to remove an argument label, we can define it with an underscore.

```
func multiply(number1: Int, _ number2: Int) -> Int {
   number1 * number2
}
let result = multiply(number1: 25, 3)
let message = "The result is \(result)"  // "The result is 75"
```

***Listing 3-12:** Removing argument labels*

In this example, we preserved the behavior by default for the first parameter and removed the argument label for the second parameter. Now the call only has to include the argument label of the first parameter (**multiply(number1: 25, 3)**).

Every function we have defined so far requires the values to be specified in the call. We cannot omit any of the values that the function expects to receive, but Swift allows us to declare a default value for any of the function's parameters and avoid this requirement.

```
func sayhello(name: String = "Undefined") -> String {
   return "Your name is " + name
}
let message = sayhello()  // "Your name is Undefined"
```

***Listing 3-13:** Declaring default values for parameters*

The code in Listing 3-13 declares the function **sayhello()** with one parameter of type **String** called **name** and with the string "Undefined" as its default value. When the function is called without a value, the string "Undefined" is assigned to **name**.

Medium Generic Functions

Although creating two or more functions with the same name is not allowed, we can do it if their parameters are not the same. This is called *overloading* and allows us to define multiple functions with the same name to process different types of values.

```
func getDescription(value: Int) -> String {
   let message = "The value is \(value)"
   return message
}
func getDescription(value: String) -> String {
   let message = "The value is \(value)"
   return message
}
let result1 = getDescription(value: 3)  // "The value is 3"
let result2 = getDescription(value: "John")  // "The value is John"
```

Listing 3-14: *Declaring different functions with the same name*

These functions have the same name, but one receives an integer and the other a string. We can say that the function that receives the string overloads the function that receives the integer. When we call the **getDescription()** function, the system selects which function is going to be executed depending on the value of the argument (when we call the function with an integer, the first function is executed, and when we call it with a string, the second function is executed).

The advantage of creating functions with the same name is that there is only one name to remember. We call the function and Swift takes care of executing the right one depending on the values assigned to the arguments. But when the functions perform the same task and only differ in the type of value received, we end up with two or more pieces of code to maintain, which can introduce errors. In cases like this, we can declare only one function with a generic data type.

Generic data types are placeholders for real data types. When the function is called, the generic data type is turned into the data type of the value received. If we send an integer, the generic data type turns into an **Int** data type; if we send a string, it turns into a **String**. To define a generic function, we must declare the generic data type using a custom name between angle brackets after the function's name, as in the following example.

```
func getDescription<T>(value: T) -> String {
   let message = "The value is \(value)"
   return message
}
let result1 = getDescription(value: 3.5)  // "The value is 3.5"
let result2 = getDescription(value: "George")  // "The value is George"
```

Listing 3-15: *Defining generic functions*

This function is a generic function. The generic data type was called **T** (this is a standard name for a generic data type, but we can use any name we want). The function performs the same task, and it has the same name than the two functions from the previous example, but now we have reduced the amount of code in our program. When the function is called, the **T** generic data type is converted into the data type received and the value is processed (The first time the function is called in our example, **T** is turned into a **Double** and the second time into a **String**).

In our example, we only use one parameter and therefore the function can only work with one data type, but we can declare two or more generic data types separated by commas (e.g., **<T, U>**).

IMPORTANT: Although we can send any value of any type we want to a generic function, the operations we can perform on them are very limited due to the impossibility of the compiler to know the nature of the values received. For example, we can add two integers, but we can't add two Boolean values. To solve these issues, we can constraint the generic data types with protocols. We will study how to define protocols and how to use them later in this chapter.

Basic Standard Functions

The main advantage of functions is that we can call them from any part of the program that has access to them, and they will always perform the same operations. We don't even need to know how the function does it, we just send to the function the values we want to process and read the result. Because of these features, functions can be shared, and programmers can implement in their code pre-programmed functions provided by libraries and frameworks to incorporate additional functionality that would take them too long to develop themselves.

All the features of the Swift language we have implemented so far are included in a library called *Standard Library*. The Standard Library includes everything, from operators to primitive data types, as well as predefined functions. The following are some of the most frequently used.

print(String**)**—This function prints a string on the Xcode's console.

abs(Value**)**—This function returns the absolute value of an integer.

max(Values**)**—This function compares two or more values and returns the largest.

min(Values**)**—This function compares two or more values and returns the smallest.

There are also functions available to stop the execution of the application in case of an unrecoverable error.

fatalError(String**)**—This function stops the execution of the application and prints on the console the message provided by the argument.

precondition(Bool, String**)**—This function stops the execution of the application and prints a message on the console if a condition is false. The first argument is the condition to be checked and the second argument is the message we want to print on the console.

Of all the functions in the Swift Standard Library, **print()** is probably the most useful. Its purpose is to print messages on the Xcode's console that may help us to fix bugs in our code. In the following example, we use it to print the result of two operations.

```
let absolutenumber = abs(-25)
let minnumber = min(absolutenumber, 100)
print("The number is: \(minnumber)")  // "The number is: 25"
```

Listing 3-16: *Printing values on the console with* `print()`

The code in Listing 3-16 implements the **abs()** function to calculate the absolute value of -25, then gets the minimum value between **absolutenumber** and the number 100 with the **min()** function, and finally prints a message on the console with the result.

Sequences or collections of values are very important in computer programming. The strings studied in Chapter 2 are a clear example. A string is a sequence of values of type **Character**. As we will see later in this chapter, the Swift Standard Library includes several types of collections to store sequences of values that are important to the application or the user, but it also offers a few functions to create sequences of values our application may need temporarily to process information. The following are some of the most frequently used.

stride(from: Value, **through:** Value, **by:** Value**)**—This function returns a collection of values from the value specified by the **from** argument to the value specified by the **through** argument in intervals specified by the **by** argument.

stride(from: Value, **to:** Value, **by:** Value**)**—This function returns a collection of values from the value specified by the **from** argument to the value specified by the **through** argument in intervals specified by the **by** argument. The last value is not included.

repeatElement(Value, **count:** Int**)**—This function returns a collection with the number of elements specified by the **count** argument and with the value specified by the first argument.

zip(Collection, Collection**)**—This function returns a collection of tuples containing the values of the collections provided by the arguments in sequential order.

The following example applies some of these functions to create a list of tuples that contain a string and an integer.

```
let sequencetext = repeatElement("Hello", count: 5)
let sequencenumbers = stride(from: 0, to: 10, by: 2)
let finalsequence = zip(sequencetext, sequencenumbers)

for (text, number) in finalsequence {
   print("\(text) - \(number)")
}
```

Listing 3-17: *Creating collections of values*

The code in Listing 3-17 calls the **repeatElement()** function to create a collection of 5 elements, all of them with the string "Hello" ("Hello", "Hello", "Hello", "Hello", "Hello"). Next, the **stride()** function creates another collection with integers from 0 to 10, increased by 2, and without including the last one (0, 2, 4, 6, 8). Next, the **zip()** function merges these two collections in one collection of tuples, where each tuple has the corresponding values of each collection; the first tuple contains the first value of the **sequencetext** collection along with the first value of the **sequencenumbers** collection, and so on. Finally, we use a **for in** loop to iterate over the values of the **finalsequence** collection and print them on the console ("Hello - 0", "Hello - 2", "Hello - 4", "Hello - 6", "Hello - 8").

Basic Scopes

The conditionals and loops studied in Chapter 2 and the functions studied in this chapter have a thing in common; they all use blocks of code (statements between braces) to enclose their functionality. Blocks are independent processing units; they contain their own statements and variables. To preserve their independence and avoid conflicts between these units and the rest of the code, their variables and constants are isolated. Variables and constants declared inside a block are not accessible from other parts of the code; they can only be used inside the block in which they were created.

The space in the code where a variable is accessible is called *scope*. Swift defines two types of scopes: the global scope and the local scope (also referred as global space or local space). The variables and constants outside a block have global scope, while those declared inside a block have local scope. The variables and constants with global scope are accessible from any part of the code, while those with local scope are only accessible from the statements inside the block in which they were created (and the statements from blocks created inside their block). For better understanding, here is a practical example.

```
var multiplier = 1.2
var total = 0.0

func first() {
   let base = 10.0
   total += base * multiplier
}
```

```
func second() {
   let multiplier = 5.0
   let base = 3.5
   total += base * multiplier
}
first()
second()
print("Total: \(total)")  // "Total: 29.5"
```

Listing 3-18: *Using variables and constants of different scopes*

This example declares two variables in the global space, **multiplier** and **total**, and two functions with local constants. The **multiplier** and **total** variables are global and therefore they are accessible from anywhere in the code, but the constants defined inside the functions are available only to the statements inside the function in which they were created. Therefore, the **base** constant declared inside the **first()** function is only accessible from this function (neither the statements in the global space nor other functions or blocks outside **first()** have access to it), but we can modified the value of **total** from this function because it is a global variable.

The next function, **second()**, declares a new constant called **multiplier**. This constant has the same name as the **multiplier** variable declared before in the global space, but they have different scopes and therefore they are different variables. When we read the value of **multiplier** in the **second()** function to add a new value to the **total** variable, the **multiplier** that the system reads is the one declared inside the function because in that space this constant has precedence over the global variable with the same name (we can declare variables and constants with the same name as long as they have different scopes).

Medium Closures

Blocks of code, such as those used to create functions, conditionals, and loops, have their own scope, and know the variables that are available to them. Because of this, we can generate independent processing units that do not interfere with the operations of other units. This feature is so important in computer programming that Swift offers the possibility to create independent blocks called *Closures* to take advantage of it.

Closures are simple blocks of code with the syntax **{ (parameters) -> Type in statements }**. They are like functions (functions are closures with a name), but everything goes between braces and the **in** keyword is included to separate the data types from the statements.

Closures can be assigned to variables and executed using the name of the variable, as we do with functions. The name of the variable becomes the name of the closure, as shown next.

```
let multiplier = { (number: Int, times: Int) -> Int in
   let total = number * times
   return total
}
print("The result is \(multiplier(10, 5))")  // "The result is 50"
```

Listing 3-19: *Assigning closures to variables*

This example defines a closure and assigns it to the **multiplier** constant. After this, the name of the constant may be used to execute the closure. Notice that the parameters of the closure and the return type are declared with the same syntax as functions (**(number: Int, times: Int) -> Int**), but the parameters' names are not turned into argument labels and therefore they are ignored in the call.

An advantage of being able to assign closures to variables is the possibility to initialize them with the result of complex operations. The closure is assigned to the variable and executed right away adding parentheses at the end of the declaration. When the system reads the statement, it executes the closure and then assigns the value returned by the closure to the constant or variable.

```
let myaddition = { () -> Int in
   var total = 0
   let list = stride(from: 1, through: 9, by: 1)

   for number in list {
      total += number
   }
   return total
}()
print("The total is \(myaddition)")  // "The total is 45"
```

Listing 3-20: *Initializing a variable with the value returned by a closure*

The closure declared in Listing 3-20 doesn't receive any value and returns an integer (**() -> Int**). The code in the closure adds the values of a collection (1 to 9) and returns the result, but because we included the parentheses at the end of the definition, the value assigned to the **myaddition** constant is the one returned by the closure (45), not the closure itself. The task performed in this example is simple but executing a closure as soon as it is declared is a technique usually implemented for more complex processes such as loading a file or opening a database.

If the closure does not receive any parameter, we can simplify its syntax declaring the type of the constant or variable and letting Swift infer the type of the value returned by the closure. Notice that when the closure doesn't receive a value, we can also remove the **in** keyword.

```
let myaddition: Int = {
   var total = 0
   let list = stride(from: 1, through: 9, by: 1)

   for number in list {
      total += number
   }
   return total
}()
print("The total is \(myaddition)")  // "The total is 45"
```

Listing 3-21: *Simplifying a closure*

Closures cannot only be assigned to variables but also sent and returned from functions, as any other value. When a function receives a closure, the parameter's data type only has to include the data types the closure receives and returns, as in the following example.

```
let multiplier = { (number: Int, times: Int) -> Int in
   let total = number * times
   return total
}
func processclosure(myclosure: (Int, Int) -> Int) {
   let total = myclosure(10, 2)
   print("The total is: \(total)")  // "The total is: 20"
}
processclosure(myclosure: multiplier)
```

Listing 3-22: *Sending a closure to a function*

The first statement in Listing 3-22 defines a closure that multiplies two integers and returns the result. A function that receives a closure of this type is defined next. Notice that the data type of the value received by the function was declared as **(Int, Int) -> Int**. This indicates to the compiler that the **processclosure()** function can receive a closure that in turn receives two integer values and returns another integer. When the **processclosure()** function is called in the last statement, the value of the **multiplier** variable is sent to the function. The function assigns the closure to the **myclosure** constant, and the closure is executed inside the function using this name and the values 10 and 2, producing the result 20.

The closure was defined in the global space and was executed inside the **processclosure()** function, but we don't need to assign the closure to a variable, we can just define it in the call.

```
func processclosure(myclosure: (Int, Int) -> Int) {
   print("The total is: \(myclosure(10, 2))")  // "The total is: 20"
}
processclosure(myclosure: { (number: Int, times: Int) -> Int in
   return number * times
})
```

Listing 3-23: *Assigning the closure to the function's argument*

The code in Listing 3-23 works the same way as the previous example, but it was simplified by assigning the closure directly to the function's argument. This can be simplified even further by using a pattern called *Trailing Closures*. When the final argument of a function is a closure, we can declare the closure at the end of the call, as in the following example.

```
func processclosure(myclosure: (Int, Int) -> Int) {
   print("The total is: \(myclosure(10, 2))")  // "The total is: 20"
}
processclosure() { (number: Int, times: Int) -> Int in
   number * times
}
```

Listing 3-24: *Using Trailing Closures*

When we pass the closure this way, the call does not include the **myclosure** argument anymore. The closure declared after the parentheses is considered as the last argument of the function and therefore the argument label is not necessary.

The code in Listing 3-24 works the same way as previous examples, the only advantage is the reduction in the amount of code we had to write. And that can be simplified even further. In the last example we already removed the **return** keyword. As explained before, when the content of a function (or in this case a closure) includes only one statement, the compiler implies that the value produced by that statement is the one to return and therefore the **return** keyword is not required anymore. But when we are passing the closure to a function, Swift can also infer the data types of the values received by the closure and therefore we don't have to declare that either. Instead, we can represent these values using shorthand argument names. These are special placeholders composed by the $ symbol and an index starting from 0. The first value received by the closure is represented by $0, the second value by $1, and so on.

```
func processclosure(myclosure: (Int, Int) -> Int) {
   print("The total is: \(myclosure(10, 2))")  // "The total is: 20"
}
processclosure() { $0 * $1 }
```

Listing 3-25: *Inferring the closure's data types*

Again, the code is the same, but now the closure is extremely simple. When it is executed from the **processclosure()** function, it receives the values 10 and 2 and assigns them to the placeholders $0 and $1, respectively. Then, it multiplies their values and returns the result.

In the previous examples, we have executed the closure received by the function inside the same function, but there are situations in which a closure must be executed outside the function. This usually applies to asynchronous operations, as we will see later. If we want to execute a closure received by the function from outside the function, we must declare it as an *escape* closure. Escape closures are closures that remain in memory after the execution of the function is over. They are declared by preceding them with the **@escaping** keyword, as in the following example.

```
var myclosure: () -> Void = {}
func passclosure(closure: @escaping () -> Void) {
   myclosure = closure
}
passclosure() { () -> Void in
   print("Closure Executed")
}
myclosure()
```

Listing 3-26: *Declaring escaping closures*

In the code of Listing 3-26, we declare a variable called **myclosure** that stores a closure that doesn't receive or return any values (**() -> Void**) and then we assign an empty closure to it. After that, we define a function called **passclosure()** that receives an escaping closure and all it does is assign that closure to the **myclosure** variable. Next, we call the **passclosure()** function with a trailing closure that prints a message on the console. Up to this point, all we are doing is passing the closure to the function and the function is assigning that closure to the **myclosure** variable, so at the end we execute the closure in **myclosure** and the message is printed on the console.

IMPORTANT: When we define the data type of a closure, we must declare the data types of the values it receives and the data type of the values it returns. Therefore, if the closure doesn't return any value, we must declare the return type as **Void**, as we did in the example of Listing 3-26.

Basic 3.3 Structures

Structures are an essential part of the organizational paradigm proposed by Swift. They are custom data types that include not only the data but also the code in charge of processing that data. When we define a structure, what we are doing is declaring a data type that may contain variables and constants (called *properties*) and functions (called *methods*). Later we can declare variables and constants of this type to store information with the characteristics defined by the structure. These values (called *instances*) will be unique, each one with its own properties and methods.

Basic Definition of Structures

To define a new structure, we must use the **struct** keyword and enclose the data and functionality between braces.

```
struct Item {
   var name: String = "Not defined"
   var price: Double = 0
}
```

Listing 3-27: *Defining a structure*

This example defines a structure called **Item** with two properties (variables): **name** and **price**. The definition by itself does not create anything; it is just delineating the elements of the type (also called *members*), like a blueprint used to create the real structures. What we need to do to store values of this new data type in memory, as we would do with any other data type, is to declare a variable or constant of this type. The declaration is done as before, but the data type is the name of the structure and the initialization value is a special initializer with the syntax **Name()** (where **Name** is, again, the name of the structure).

```
struct Item {
   var name: String = "Not defined"
   var price: Double = 0
}
var purchase: Item = Item()
```

Listing 3-28: *Declaring a variable of type* `Item`

The code in Listing 3-28 creates a variable of type **Item** that stores an instance of the **Item** structure containing the properties **name** and **price**. The instance is created by the **Item()** initializer and then assigned to the **purchase** variable.

In the previous example, the properties of a new instance always take the values declared in the structure's definition (**"Not Defined"** and **0**), but we can change them as we do with any other variable. The only difference is that the properties are inside a structure, so every time we want to access them, we must mention the structure they belong to. The syntax implements dot notation, as in **variable.property**, where **variable** is the name of the variable that contains the instance of the structure and **property** is the name of the property we want to access.

```
struct Item {
   var name = "Not defined"
   var price = 0.0
}
var purchase = Item()
purchase.name = "Lamps"
purchase.price = 10.50

print("Product: \(purchase.name) $ \(purchase.price)")
```

Listing 3-29: *Assigning new values to the properties of a structure*

In this example, the properties of the **Item** structure and the **purchase** variable are declared as before, but this time we let Swift infer their data types. After the instance is created, new values are assigned to its properties using dot notation. Dot notation is not only used to assign new values but also to read the current ones. At the end, we read and print the values of the **name** and **price** properties on the console ("Product: Lamps $ 10.5").

IMPORTANT: Notice that we stored the structure in a variable (**var**). This is to be able to assign new values to its properties later. When the values of the properties in a structure are modified, instead of modifying the properties of the instance, the system creates a new structure and assigns the values to the properties of that instance. For this to be possible, the structure must be stored in a variable so it can be replaced by the new structure later.

Structures may be instantiated inside other structures, as many times as necessary. The dot notation is extended in these cases to reach every element in the hierarchy.

```
struct Price {
   var USD = 0.0
   var CAD = 0.0
}
struct Item {
   var name: String = "Not defined"
   var price: Price = Price()
}
```

```
var purchase = Item()
purchase.name = "Lamps"
purchase.price.USD = 10.50
```

Listing 3-30: *Structures inside structures*

Listing 3-30 defines two structures: **Price** and **Item**. The **price** property of the **Item** structure was defined as a property of type **Price**. Instead of storing a single value, now it can store a structure with two properties, **USD** and **CAD**, for American and Canadian dollars. When the **Item** structure is created and assigned to the **purchase** variable, the **Price** structure for the **price** property is also created with its values by default (**var price: Price = Price()**). By concatenating the names of the variables and properties containing these structures we can read and modify any value we want. For instance, the last statement in the code in Listing 3-30 accesses the **USD** property of the **price** structure inside the **purchase** structure to assign a price to the item in American Dollars (**purchase.price.USD = 10.50**).

In this example, the **price** object is created during instantiation, but this is not usually the case. Sometimes the values of the properties containing objects are defined after the instance is created and therefore those properties must be declared as optionals. The problem with optionals is that we always need to check whether the variable or property has a value before we use it. To simplify this task, Swift introduces Optional Chaining.

Optional Chaining is a simple tool to access objects, properties and methods in a hierarchical chain that contains optional components. As always, the access to these components is done through dot notation, but a question mark is added to the names of the properties that have optional values. When the system finds an optional, it checks whether it contains a value and continues processing the expression only in case of success. Here is the same example, but with the **price** property turned into an optional.

```
struct Price {
   var USD = 0.0
   var CAD = 0.0
}
struct Item {
   var name: String = "Not defined"
   var price: Price?
}
var purchase = Item()
purchase.name = "Lamps"
purchase.price?.USD = 10.50   // nil
```

Listing 3-31: *Accessing optional properties*

The **price** property in this code is declared as an optional (its initial value is not defined). Every time we read this property, we must unwrap its value, but if we use Optional Chaining, we can just concatenate the values with dot notation and add a question mark after the name of the optional (**purchase.price?.USD**). The system reads every component in the instruction and checks their values. If any of the optionals have no value, it returns **nil**, but when all the optionals have values, the instruction performs the task (in this case, assigning the number 10.50 to the **USD** property).

Medium Key Paths

Besides using dot notation to read and write a property, we can use key paths. A key path is a reference to a property that we can use to read and modify its value. The advantage of using key paths instead of dot notation is that they are stored in structures and therefore we can pass them to other parts of the code and then use them to access the values of the properties they are referencing without even knowing what those properties are. This can be useful when we need to interact with frameworks, or when we are extending code to include our own functionality.

Swift defines several structures to store key paths. For instance, a read-only key path is stored in an instance of a structure of type **KeyPath** and read-and-write key paths are stored in a structure of type **WritableKeyPath**. The syntax to define a key path includes a backward slash and the name of the data type followed by the name of the property we want to reference. To access the value of a property using a key path, Swift offers a syntax that includes square brackets after the instance's name and the keyword **keypath**, as illustrated in the following example.

```
struct Item {
   let name: String
   let price: Double
}
var purchase: Item = Item(name: "Lamps", price: 27.50)

let keyPrice = \Item.price
print(purchase[keyPath: keyPrice])  // "27.5"
```

Listing 3-32: *Creating key paths*

The code defines a structure with two properties: **name** and **price**. Next, we create a key path to reference the **price** property. Because the properties are defined as constants, the key path is created of type **KeyPath** (a read-only key path). In the last statement, we use this key path to access the value of the **price** property of the **purchase** instance and print it on the console.

We can easily create a read-and-write key path by defining the structure's properties as variables. In the following example, we turn the **name** and **price** properties into variables and modify the value of **price** using our **keyPrice** key path.

```
struct Item {
   var name: String
   var price: Double
}
var purchase: Item = Item(name: "Lamps", price: 27.50)

let keyPrice = \Item.price
purchase[keyPath: keyPrice] = 30.00
print(purchase.price)
```

Listing 3-33: *Using read and write key paths*

Basic Methods

If we could only store properties, structures would be just complex data types, like tuples, but structures may also include code. This is done through functions. Functions inside structures are called *methods*, but their definition and functionality are the same.

The syntax to execute a method is **variable.method()**, where **variable** is the name of the variable that contains the instance of the structure and **method** is the name of the method we want to call inside that structure, as shown in the following example.

```
struct Item {
   var name = "Not defined"
   var price = 0.0

   func total(quantity: Double) -> Double {
      return quantity * price
   }
}
var purchase = Item()
```

```
purchase.name = "Lamp"
purchase.price = 10.50

print("Total: \(purchase.total(quantity: 2))")  // "Total: 21.0"
```

Listing 3-34: Defining methods

In Listing 3-34, a method is declared as part of the definition of the **Item** structure. The method receives a value representing the number of items sold and calculates the total money spent in the transaction. We could have performed this operation outside the structure by reading the value of the **price** property but having a method in the structure itself presents some advantages. First, we don't have to worry about how the method calculates the value; we just call the method with the right value and let its statements perform the task, no matter how complex it is. And second, we do not have to write the operation over and over again, because it is always part of the instance of the structure we are working with.

A method can read the values of the instance's properties but cannot assign new values to them. If we want a method to be able to modify the values of the properties of its own instance, we must declare the **mutating** keyword before the **func** keyword in the structure's definition.

```
struct Item {
   var name = "Not defined"
   var price = 0.0

   mutating func changename(newname: String) {
      name = newname
   }
}
var purchase = Item()
purchase.changename(newname: "Lamps")

print("Product: \(purchase.name)")  // "Product: Lamps"
```

Listing 3-35: Assigning new values to properties from inside the structure

The **changename()** method of the **Item** structure in Listing 3-35 is declared as a mutating method so it can assign a new value to the **name** property. Therefore, we do not need to modify the **name** property directly, we can call this method with the value we want to store, and the method takes care of assigning the value to the property.

Basic Initialization

Every instance created from the structure's definition has the purpose to store and process specific data. For example, we can create multiple instances of the **Item** structure defined before to store information about different products. Each product will have its own name and price, so the properties of each instance must be initialized with the proper values. The initialization of an instance is a very common process, and it would be far too cumbersome if we had to assign the values one by one after the instances are created. For this reason, Swift provides different alternatives to initialize the values of a structure. One of them is called *memberwise initializer.*

Memberwise initializers detect the properties of the structure and declare their names as argument labels. Using these argument labels, we can provide the values for initialization between the parentheses of the initializer. The following code implements a memberwise initializer to initialize an instance of the **Item** structure declared in previous examples.

```
struct Item {
   var name = "Not defined"
   var price = 0.0
}
```

```
var purchase = Item(name: "Lamp", price: 10.50)
print("Purchase: \(purchase.name) $ \(purchase.price)")
```

Listing 3-36: Initializing properties

Memberwise initializers reduce the amount of code and simplify initialization. Also, if we use the memberwise initializer, we can ignore the values by default declared in the definition.

```
struct Item {
   var name: String
   var price: Double
}
var purchase = Item(name: "Lamp", price: 10.50)
print("Purchase: \(purchase.name) $ \(purchase.price)")
```

Listing 3-37: Using memberwise initializers to provide the initial values of a structure

The two types of initialization we have seen so far are not customizable enough. Some structures may have multiple properties to initialize or even methods that must be executed right away to get the proper values for the instance to be ready. To add more alternatives, Swift provides a method called **init()**. The **init()** method is called as soon as the instance is created, so we can use it to initialize properties or perform operations and initialize them with the results.

```
struct Price {
   var USD: Double
   var CAD: Double

   init() {
      USD = 5
      CAD = USD * 1.29
   }
}
var myprice = Price()
```

Listing 3-38: Initializing properties from the `init()` *method*

When the instance is generated by the initializer, the properties are created first and then the **init()** method is executed. Inside this method we can perform any operation we need to get the properties' initial values. In the example of Listing 3-38, we assign an initial value of 5 to the **USD** property and then multiply this value by the corresponding exchange rate to get the value of the **CAD** property (the same price in Canadian dollars).

As well as with any other method or function, the **init()** method may include parameters. These parameters are used to specify initial values from the initializer.

```
struct Price {
   var USD: Double
   var CAD: Double

   init(americans: Double) {
      USD = americans
      CAD = USD * 1.29
   }
}
var myprice = Price(americans: 5)
```

Listing 3-39: Declaring the parameters of the `init()` *method*

This is similar to what Swift creates for us in the background when we use memberwise initializers, but the advantage of declaring the **init()** method ourselves is that we can specify only the parameters we need (as in the last example) or even declare multiple **init()** methods to present several alternatives for initialization, as shown next.

```
struct Price {
   var USD: Double
   var CAD: Double

   init(americans: Double) {
      USD = americans
      CAD = USD * 1.29
   }
   init(canadians: Double) {
      CAD = canadians
      USD = CAD * 0.7752
   }
}
var myprice = Price(canadians: 5)
```

Listing 3-40: *Declaring multiple* `init()` *methods*

Swift identifies each function by its name and parameters, so we can declare several functions with the same name as long as they have different parameters. In the example of Listing 3-40, two **init()** methods were declared to initialize the instance of the structure. The first method receives a **Double** value with the name **americans** and the second method also receives a **Double** value but with the name **canadians**. The right method will be executed according to the argument included in the initializer. In this example, we use the argument **canadians** with the value 5, so the instance is initialized by the second method.

Medium Computed Properties

The properties we have declared up to this point are called *Stored Properties*. Their function is to store a value in memory. But there are other types of properties called *Computed Properties*. These properties do not store a value of their own, instead they have access to the rest of the properties of the structure and can perform operations to set and retrieve their values.

Two methods were included for computed properties to be able to set and retrieve a value: **get** and **set**. These methods are also called *getters* and *setters* and are declared between braces after the property's name. Although both methods are useful, only the **get** method is required.

```
struct Price {
   var USD: Double
   var ratetoCAD: Double

   var canadians: Double {
      get {
         return USD * ratetoCAD
      }
   }
}
var purchase = Price(USD: 11, ratetoCAD: 1.29)
print("Price in CAD: \(purchase.canadians)")  // "Price in CAD: 14.19"
```

Listing 3-41: *Declaring computed properties*

The structure defined in Listing 3-41 contains a stored property called **USD** to store the price in American dollars, a stored property called **ratetoCAD** to store the exchange rate for Canadian dollars, and a computed property called **canadians** that converts the US dollars into Canadian dollars and returns the result. Computed properties are like methods, they calculate the value every time the property is read. No matter if the value of the **ratetoCAD** property changes, the **canadians** property will always return the right price in Canadian dollars.

Computed properties with only a getter are called read-only properties because we can only read their values. When we declare a read-only property, we can omit the **get** method. And as we have seen before, when a block contains only one statement, it knows what to return, so we can also omit the **return** keyword. The previous example can therefore be simplified as follows.

```
struct Price {
   var USD: Double
   var ratetoCAD: Double

   var canadians: Double {
      USD * ratetoCAD
   }
}
var purchase = Price(USD: 11, ratetoCAD: 1.29)
print(purchase.canadians)  // "14.190000000000001"
```

Listing 3-42: *Defining read-only properties*

Including the **set** method for the **canadians** property we can, for example, set a new price using the same currency.

```
struct Price {
   var USD: Double
   var ratetoCAD: Double
   var ratetoUSD: Double

   var canadians: Double {
      get {
         USD * ratetoCAD
      }
      set {
         USD = newValue * ratetoUSD
      }
   }
}
var purchase = Price(USD: 11, ratetoCAD: 1.29, ratetoUSD: 0.7752)

purchase.canadians = 500
print("Price: \(purchase.USD)")  // "Price: 387.6"
```

Listing 3-43: *Adding the* set *method to set a new value*

The new structure defined in Listing 3-43 can retrieve and set a price in Canadian dollars. When we set a new value for the **canadians** property, the value is stored in a constant called **newValue** (the constant is created automatically for us). Using this constant, we can process the new value and perform the operations we need. In this example, the value of **newValue** is multiplied by the exchange rate to get the price in American dollars. The price is always stored in American dollars but using the **canadians** property we can set it and retrieve it in Canadian dollars.

If we want to use a different name for the new value, we can set the parameter's name between parentheses. In the following example, the parameter was called **CAD** and used instead of **newValue** to calculate the value for the **USD** property.

```
struct Price {
   var USD: Double
   var ratetoCAD: Double
   var ratetoUSD: Double
```

```
    var canadians: Double {
        get {
            USD * ratetoCAD
        }
        set(CAD) {
            USD = CAD * ratetoUSD
        }
    }
}
var purchase = Price(USD: 11, ratetoCAD: 1.29, ratetoUSD: 0.7752)
```

Listing 3-44: *Using a different name for the parameter of the* `set` *method*

Medium Property Observers

The properties of an instance of a structure may be modified at any moment by different processes, such as in response to user interaction or events produced by the system. To inform an instance that one of its properties was modified, Swift introduces Property Observers.

Property Observers are special methods, similar to **`get()`** and **`set()`**, that can be added to a property to execute code before and after a value is assigned to it. The methods are called **`willSet()`** and **`didSet()`**, and are declared between braces after the properties declaration.

```
struct Price {
    var increment: Double = 0
    var oldprice: Double = 0

    var price: Double {
        willSet {
            increment = newValue - price
        }
        didSet {
            oldprice = oldValue
        }
    }
}
var product = Price(price: 15.95)
product.price = 20.75
print("New price: \(product.price)")  // "New price: 20.75"
print("Old price: \(product.oldprice)")  // "Old price: 15.95"
```

Listing 3-45: *Adding observers to a property*

The **`Price`** structure in Listing 3-45 includes three properties: **`increment`**, **`oldprice`**, and **`price`**. We use the **`price`** property to store the value of an item, the **`oldprice`** property to store the previous price, and the **`increment`** property to store the difference between the old price and the new one. To set this last value, we declare property observers for the **`price`** property. Every time a new value is assigned to the property, the **`willSet()`** and **`didSet()`** methods are executed. Swift automatically creates a parameter called **`newValue`** for the **`willSet()`** method to provide access to the value that is going to be assigned to the property, and a parameter called **`oldValue`** for the **`didSet()`** method to provide access to the property's old value after the new value was assigned (we can change the names of these parameters as we did for the **`set()`** method in Listing 3-44). In our example, when the **`willSet()`** method is executed, the current value of **`price`** is subtracted from **`newValue`** to get the difference, and the result is assigned to the **`increment`** property. And in the **`didSet()`** method, we assign the old price provided by **`oldValue`** to the **`oldprice`** property to have access to the item's previous price later.

Basic Type Properties and Methods

The properties and methods declared above are accessible on the instances created from the definition of the structure. This means that we must create an instance of the structure to be able to access those properties and methods. But there are times when being able to execute properties and methods from the definition itself makes sense. We might need, for example, to get some information that affects all the instances, or call methods to create instances with standard values. In Swift, this is possible by declaring type properties and methods. These are properties and methods accessible from the data type, not the instance created from that type.

Type properties and methods for structures are declared adding the **static** keyword to their definition. Once a property or method is declared with this keyword, they are only accessible from the definition itself. In the following example, we include a type property called **currencies** to inform how many currencies the structure can handle.

```
struct Price {
   var USD: Double
   var CAD: Double

   static var currencies = 2
}
print(Price.currencies)  // 2
```

Listing 3-46: *Defining type properties*

As illustrated by the code in Listing 3-46, there is no need to create an instance to access a type property or method. After the definition, the **currencies** property is read using the name of the structure and dot notation (**Price.currencies**). If we create an instance from this definition, the only properties accessible from the instance will be **USD** and **CAD**. The **currencies** property is a type property, only accessible from the type itself. The same happens with methods.

```
struct Price {
   var USD: Double
   var CAD: Double

   static func reserve() -> Price {
      return Price(USD: 10.0, CAD: 11.0)
   }
}
var reserveprice = Price.reserve()
print("Price in USD: \(reserveprice.USD) CAD: \(reserveprice.CAD)")
```

Listing 3-47: *Defining type methods*

The structure in this example includes a type method called **reserve()**. The method creates and returns an instance of the **Price** structure with standard values. This is a common procedure and another way to create our own initializer. If we use the initializer by default, the values must be provided every time the instance is created, but with a type method all we need to do is to call the method on the type and we get in return an instance configured with specific values. In our example, the values correspond to a reserved price. We call the **reserve()** method on the **Price** type, the method creates an instance of the **Price** structure with the values 10.0 and 11.0, and then this instance is assigned to the **reserveprice** variable. At the end, the values of both properties are printed on the console to confirm that their values were defined by the **reserve()** method (again, the method is not accessible from the instance, only from the data type).

Advanced Generic Structures

At the beginning of this chapter, we explained how to create generic functions. These are functions that can process values of different data types. The function defines a placeholder for the data type and then adopts the data type of the received value. But generics data types are not exclusive to functions, we can also turn data types themselves, such as structures, into generic types. The advantage is that we can create independent processing units that can handle different types of values. To create a generic structure, we must declare the generic data type after the name of the structure and between angle brackets, as we did for functions.

```
struct MyStructure<T> {
   var myvalue:T

   func description() {
      print("The value is: \(myvalue)")  // "The value is: 5"
   }
}
let instance = MyStructure<Int>(myvalue: 5)
instance.description()
```

***Listing 3-48:** Defining generic structures*

This example defines a generic structure called **MyStructure** with one generic type called **T**. The structure contains a generic property called **myvalue** and a method that prints a message with its value. After the definition, we create an instance of this structure with an integer. The system replaces the **T** with the **Int** type, creates the instance, and assigns the value 5 to the **myvalue** property. In the last statement, we call the **description()** method to print the value.

When we create an instance of a generic structure, the data type we want the structure to work with is included after the name and between angle brackets, but this is only required when the initialization doesn't include any value. For example, the following code creates an instance of the same structure but with a string and lets Swift infer the generic data type from the value.

```
struct MyStructure<T> {
   var myvalue:T

   func description() {
      print("The value is: \(myvalue)")  // "The value is: Hello"
   }
}
let instance = MyStructure(myvalue: "Hello")
instance.description()
```

***Listing 3-49:** Using generic structures*

IMPORTANT: These are basic examples of how to create generic data types. As with functions, generics only become useful when we constrain the data using protocols. We will learn more about generics in the following sections and study protocols at the end of this chapter.

Basic Primitive Type Structures

Including properties and methods inside a structure and then assigning an instance of that structure to a variable is a simple way to wrap data and functionality in a single portable unit of code. Structures are usually used this way, as practical wrappers of code, and Swift takes advantage of this feature extensively. In fact, all the primitive data types defined in Swift are structures. The syntax **variable: Int = value**, for example, is a shortcut provided by Swift for the initializer **variable = Int(value)**. Every time we assign a new value to a variable of a primitive data type, we are assigning a structure that contains that value. The following are the initializers of some of the primitive data types studied in Chapter 2.

Int(Value)—This is the initializer of the **Int** data type. The argument is the value we want to assign to the instance. If no value is provided, the value 0 is assigned by default. Initializers for similar types are also available (**Int8()**, **Int16()**, **Int32()**, and **Int64()**).

UInt(Value)—This is the initializer of the **UInt** data type. The argument is the value we want to assign to the instance. If no value is provided, the value assigned is 0. Initializers for similar types are also available (**UInt8()**, **UInt16()**, **UInt32()**, and **UInt64()**).

Float(Value)—This is the initializer of the **Float** data type. The argument is the value we want to assign to the instance. If no value is provided, the value 0.0 is assigned by default.

Double(Value)—This is the initializer of the **Double** data type. The argument is the value we want to assign to the instance. If no value is provided, the value assigned is 0.0.

The structures for these data types were already defined for us in the Swift Standard Library. All we need to do to get an instance is to call its initializer with the value we want to store.

```
var mynumber = Int(25)
var myprice = Double(4.99)
```

Listing 3-50: *Initializing variables with standard initializers*

These initializers create a structure for each value and assign the instances to the variables. This is the same as assigning the values directly to the variable (e.g., **var myprice = 4.99**). There is no advantage in using initializers for primitive data types except when the value provided is of a different type. The definitions of these structures include several initializers that convert the value to the right type. This is usually called *casting*, and we can use it to turn a variable of one data type into another. For example, when we divide numbers, the system converts those numbers to the right type and performs the operation, but variables are already of a specific type and therefore they must be explicitly converted before the operation is performed or we get an error (The process does not really convert the variable; it just creates a new value of the right type).

```
var number1: Int = 10
var number2: Double = 2.5
var total = Double(number1) / number2  // 4.0
```

Listing 3-51: *Casting a variable*

The variables **number1** and **number2** defined in Listing 3-51 are of type **Int** and **Double**. To perform a division between them we must cast one of them to the data type of the other (arithmetic operations cannot be performed on values of different data type). Using the **Double()** initializer, we create a new value of type **Double** from the value of **number1** and perform the operation (the value 10.0 created by the initializer is divided by the value 2.5 of **number2** to get the result 4.0). The process is described as "casting the **number1** variable to a **Double**".

These initializers are also useful when working with **String** values. Sometimes the characters of a string represent numbers that we need to process. The problem is that strings cannot be processed as numbers. We cannot include a string in an arithmetic operation without first converting the string into a value of a numeric data type. Fortunately, the initializers for numeric types such as **Int** and **Double** can convert a value of type **String** into a number. If the operation cannot be performed, the initializer returns **nil**, so we can treat it as an optional value. In the following example, we convert the string "45" into the integer 45 and add the value 15 to it.

```
var units = "45"

if let number = Int(units) {
   let total = number + 15
   print("The total is \(total)")   // "The total is 60"
}
```

Listing 3-52: Extracting numbers from strings

The structures defined for primitive data types also have their own properties and methods. This includes type properties and methods. For instance, the following are the most frequently used properties and methods provided by the structures that process integer values (e.g., **Int**).

min—This type property returns the minimum value the data type can handle.

max—This type property returns the maximum value the data type can handle.

random(in: Range**)**—This type method returns a random number. The value is calculated from a range of integers provided by the **in** argument.

negate()—This method inverts the sign of the value.

isMultiple(of: Int**)**—This method returns **true** if the value is a multiple of the value provided by the **of** argument (this is similar to what we can achieve with the % operation).

The **min** and **max** properties are especially useful because they allow us to determine whether an operation could overflow a variable (produce a result that is greater or lesser than the minimum and maximum allowed).

```
var mynumber: Int8 = 120
let increment: Int8 = 10

if (Int8.max - mynumber) >= increment {   // (127 - 120) >= 10
   mynumber += increment
}
print(mynumber)   // "120"
```

Listing 3-53: Checking the maximum possible value for the `Int8` *type*

This example takes advantage of the **max** property to make sure that incrementing the value of a variable will not overflow the variable (the result will not be greater than the maximum the variable can handle). The code starts by defining a variable of type **Int8** to store the result of the operation and another to store the number we want to add. Then, we calculate how far the current value of **mynumber** is from the maximum value admitted by an **Int8** variable (**Int8.max – mynumber**) and compare this result with the value of **increment**. If the number of units we have left is greater or equal than the value of **increment**, we know that the operation can be performed without going over the limit (in this example, the operation is not performed because the addition of 120 + 10 produces a result greater than the limit of 127 admitted by **Int8**).

The type **Double** also includes its own selection of properties and methods. The following are the most frequently used.

pi—This type property returns the value of the constant pi.

infinity—This type property returns an infinite value.

minimum(Double, Double**)**—This type method compares the values provided by the arguments and returns the minimum.

maximum(Double, Double**)**—This type method compares the values provided by the arguments and returns the maximum.

random(in: Range)—This type method returns a random number. The value is calculated from a range of values of type **`Double`** provided by the **`in`** argument.

negate()—This method inverts the sign of the value.

squareRoot()—This method returns the square root of the value.

remainder(dividingBy: Double)—This method returns the remainder produced by dividing the value by the value specified by the **dividingBy** argument.

rounded(FloatingPointRoundingRule**)**—This method returns the value rounded according to the rule specified by the argument. The argument is an enumeration with the values **`awayFromZero`**, **`down`**, **`toNearestOrAwayFromZero`**, **`toNearestOrEven`**, **`towardZero`** and **`up`**.

In this case, the most useful method is probably **`rounded()`**. With this method, we can round a floating-point value to the nearest integer.

```
var mynumber: Double = 2.890
mynumber = mynumber.rounded(.toNearestOrAwayFromZero)
print("The round number is \(mynumber)")  // "The round number is 3.0"
```

Listing 3-54: *Rounding floating-point values*

Of course, Boolean values are also structures. Among others, the **`Bool`** data type offers the following methods.

toggle()—This method toggles the value. If the value is **`true`**, it becomes **`false`** and vice versa.

random()—This type method returns a random **`Bool`** value.

The following example checks the current value of a variable and changes the value to **`false`** if it is **`true`**.

```
var valid: Bool = true
if valid {
   print("It is Valid")
   valid.toggle()
}
print(valid)  // false
```

Listing 3-55: *Changing the value of a* `Bool` *variable*

Basic Range Structures

The **`random()`** method provided by some of the structures introduced above work with ranges of values (collections of values in sequential order). These are structures included in the Swift Standard Library that can manage open and close ranges of values. For instance, we can create a range between 1 and 5. If the range is open, it will include the values 1, 2, 3, and 4, but if the range is closed, it will include the values 1, 2, 3, 4, and 5. Swift includes two operators to generate ranges.

- **...** (three dots) creates a range from the value on the left to the value on the right, including both values in the range (e.g., 1...5 creates a range that includes the values 1, 2, 3, 4 and 5). The value on the right can be ignored to create a one-sided range. A one-sided range goes from the value on the left to the maximum value allowed for the type.

- **..<** (two dots and the less than character) creates a range from the value on the left to the value before the value on the right (e.g., 1..<5 creates a range that includes the values 1, 2, 3 and 4).

When we declare a range using these operators, Swift creates the proper structure according to the operator involved. A structure of type **`Range`** is created for an open range and a structure of type **`ClosedRange`** is created for a closed range. These structures provide common properties and methods to work with the range. The following are the most frequently used.

lowerBound—This property returns the range's lower value (the value on the left).

upperBound—This property returns the range's upper value (the value on the right).

contains(Element**)**—This method returns a Boolean value that determines if the value specified by the argument is inside the range.

clamped(to: Range**)**—This method compares the original range with the range specified by the **to** argument and returns a new range with the part of the ranges that overlap.

reversed()—This method returns a collection with the values in reversed order.

Ranges are useful in a variety of situations. For instance, if we need a loop with a fixed number of cycles, we can implement a **`for in`** loop with a range. The following example iterates over a closed range of integers from 0 to 10, generating a total of 11 cycles.

```
var total = 0
for value in 0...10 {
   total += value
}
print("The total is \(total)")  // "The total is 55"
```

Listing 3-56: *Using* `for in` *to iterate over a range*

Of course, we can also invert that loop.

```
var message = ""
var range = 0..<10

for item in range.reversed() {
   message += "\(item) "
}
print(message)  // "9 8 7 6 5 4 3 2 1 0 "
```

Listing 3-57: *Inverting a range*

This example creates a range from 0 to 9 with the **`..<`** operator and then calls the **`reversed()`** method to invert it. This method creates a collection with the values in reverse order, so we can read it with a **`for in`** loop. The statement inside the loop adds the values to the **`message`** string, and this string is printed at the end to confirm that the values were effectively reversed.

Ranges can also simplify **`switch`** statements that have to consider multiple values per case.

```
var age = 6
var message = "You have to go to "

switch age {
   case 2...4:
      message += "Day Care"
```

```
    case 5...11:
       message += "Elementary School"
    case 12...17:
       message += "High School"
    case 18..<22:
       message += "College"
    case 22...:
       message += "Work"
    default:
       message += "Breastfeeding"
}
print(message)  // "You have to go to Elementary School"
```

Listing 3-58: Using range operators in a `switch` *statement*

In this example, we compare an age with several ranges of ages. If the value of **age** is within one of the ranges, the instructions for that **case** are executed. As illustrated by this example, we can also declare only one side of a range and let the system determine the other. The last case creates a one-sided close range from the value 22 to the maximum value allowed for the type.

As mentioned before, ranges are used by the **random()** method of primitive data types to get a random value. The following example generates a loop that calculates multiple random values from 1 to 10. The condition stops the loop when the number returned by the method is equal to 5. Inside the loop, we also increment the value of the **attempts** variable to calculate the number of cycles required for the **random()** method to return our number.

```
var mynumber: Int = 0
var attempts = 0

while mynumber != 5 {
   mynumber = Int.random(in: 1...10)
   attempts += 1
}
print("It took \(attempts) attempts to get the number 5")
```

Listing 3-59: Calculating random numbers

Basic String Structures

Not only primitive data types and ranges are structures, but also the rest of the data types defined in the Swift Standard Library, including the **String** data type. As we have seen in Chapter 2, we can initialize a **String** structure by simply assigning a string (a text between double quotes) to a constant or a variable. This is another shortcut. In the background, instances of the **String** structure are created from the initializer included in the structure's definition.

String(Value**)**—This initializer creates a string from the value provided by the argument. The **String** structure defines multiple versions of this initializer to create strings from different types of values, including other strings, characters, and numbers.

Once the string is created, we can manipulate it with the properties and methods provided by the **String** structure. The following are the most frequently used.

isEmpty—This property returns a Boolean that indicates whether the value is an empty string. This is the same as comparing the string with an empty string (**string == ""**).

count—This property returns the total number of characters in the string.

first—This property returns the first character in the string.

last—This property returns the last character in the string.

lowercased()—This method returns a copy of the string in lowercase letters.

uppercased()—This method returns a copy of the string in uppercase letters.

hasPrefix(String**)**—This method returns a Boolean value that indicates whether the string begins with the text specified by the argument or not.

hasSuffix(String**)**—This method returns a Boolean value that indicates whether the string ends with the text specified by the argument or not.

contains(Character**)**—This method returns a Boolean value that indicates whether the character specified by the argument exists in the string or not.

Most of the time, we will assign a string directly to a variable as we have done so far, but the **String()** initializer may be useful when we need to convert values into strings. For instance, the following example converts the number 44 into a string and counts the number of characters.

```
var age = String(44)
var mytext = "Total digits \(age.count)"  // "Total digits 2"
```

Listing 3-60: *Converting a number into a string*

Swift strings are composed of Unicode characters, which occupy different amounts of memory, even when the characters look the same. Because of this, it is not possible to establish the position of a character using integer values. The index of the first character is always 0, but the index of the consecutive characters depends on the size of their predecessors. Swift solves this problem by defining a data type called **Index**. This is another structure defined inside the **String** structure designed to manage string indexes. The **String** structure includes properties and methods to work with these indexes and access the characters. The following are the most frequently used.

startIndex—This property returns the index value of the first character of the string.

endIndex—This property returns the index value of one position after the last character of the string. It is useful to manipulate range of characters, as we will see later.

firstIndex(of: Character**)**—This method returns the index where the character specified by the **of** argument appears for the first time in the string.

lastIndex(of: Character**)**—This method returns the last index where the character specified by the **of** argument appears in the string.

insert(Character, **at:** Index**)**—This method inserts into the string the character provided by the first argument at the position determined by the **at** argument.

insert(contentsOf: String, **at:** Index**)**—This method inserts into the string the value of the **contentsOf** argument at the position determined by the **at** argument.

remove(at: Index**)**—This method removes and returns the character at the position determined by the **at** argument.

prefix(through: Index**)**—This method returns a string created from the first character of the original string to the character at the index indicated by the **through** argument.

prefix(upTo: Index**)**—This method returns a string created from the first character of the original string to the character at the index indicated by the **upTo** argument, but without including this last character.

replaceSubrange(Range, **with:** String**)**—This method replaces the characters in the position determined by the range provided as the first argument with the string provided by the **with** argument.

removeSubrange(Range**)**—This method removes the characters in the positions determined by the range specified by the argument.

Strings are collection of values. To access a specific character in a string, we must declare the **Index** structure with the index of the character we want to read after the name of the variable that contains the string, enclosed in square brackets, as in the following example.

```
var text = "Hello World"
if !text.isEmpty {
   let start = text.startIndex
   let firstChar = text[start]

   print("First character is \(firstChar)")  // "First character is H"
}
```

Listing 3-61: *Processing the string's characters*

The first thing we do in this example is to check the value of the **isEmpty** property to make sure the string is not empty and there are characters to read (notice the **!** operator to invert the condition). Once we know we can proceed, we get the index of the string's first character from the **startIndex** property and read the character in that position using square brackets.

If we want to access a character in a different position, we must increment the value returned by **startIndex**. The trick is that, since **Index** values are not integers, we cannot just add a number to them. Instead, we must use the methods provided by the **String** structure.

index(after: Index**)**—This method increments the index specified by the **after** argument one unit and returns a new **Index** value with the result.

index(before: Index**)**—This method decrements the index specified by the **before** argument one unit and returns a new **Index** value with the result.

index(Index, **offsetBy:** Int**)**—This method increments the index specified by the first argument the amount of units specified by the **offsetBy** argument and returns a new **Index** value with the result.

The following example advances the initial index 6 positions to get a different character.

```
var text = "Hello World"
if text != "" {
   let start = text.startIndex
   let newIndex = text.index(start, offsetBy: 6)

   print("The character is \(text[newIndex])")  // "The character is W"
}
```

Listing 3-62: *Calculating a specific index*

The **index()** method applied in Listing 3-62 takes an integer to calculate the new index. The original index is increased the number of units indicated by the integer and the resulting **Index** value is returned. With this index, we get the character at the position 6 (indexes start from 0).

If we wanted to get the previous index, we could have specified a negative number of units for the offset value, but another way to move forward and backward is to implement the other versions of the **index()** method. The following example gets the next index after the initial index and prints the corresponding character on the screen.

```
var text = "John"
let start = text.startIndex
var next = text.index(after: start)
print("Second letter is \(text[next])")  // "Second letter is o"
```

Listing 3-63: *Getting the next index*

Once the right index is calculated, we can call some of the **String** methods to insert or remove characters. The **insert()** method, for instance, inserts a single character at the position indicated by its second argument. In the following example, we call it with the value of **endIndex** to add a character at the end of the string (**endindex** points to the position after the last character).

```
var text = "Hello World"
text.insert("!", at: text.endIndex)
print("New string is \(text)")  // "New string is Hello World!"
```

Listing 3-64: *Inserting a character in a string*

If we do not know where the character is located, we can find the index with the **index()** method. The value returned by this method is an optional containing the **Index** value of the first character that matches the argument or **nil** if no character is found. In the following example, we implement it to find the first space character and remove it with the **remove()** method.

```
var text = "Hello World"
var findIndex = text.firstIndex(of: " ")
if let index = findIndex {
   text.remove(at: index)
   print("New string is \(text)")  // "New string is HelloWorld"
}
```

Listing 3-65: *Removing a character*

If we want to work with groups of characters, we must implement ranges of **Index** values.

```
var text = "Hello World"
var start = text.startIndex
var findIndex = text.firstIndex(of: " ")
if let end = findIndex {
   print("First word is \(text[start..<end])") //"First word is Hello"
}
```

Listing 3-66: *Getting a range of characters*

The **firstIndex()** method in Listing 3-66 looks for a space character and returns its index. With this value, we can create a range from the first character to the space character and get the first word. But we must be careful because the **end** index is pointing to the space character, not to the last character of the word. To get the word without the space, we create an open range with the **..<** operator, so the character on the right is not included.

We can also use ranges to replace or remove parts of the text. The **String** structure offers the **replaceSubrange()** and **removeSubrange()** methods for this purpose.

```
var text = "Hello World"
var start = text.startIndex
var findIndex = text.firstIndex(of: " ")
if let end = findIndex {
   text.replaceSubrange(start..<end, with: "Goodbye")  // "Goodbye World"
}
findIndex = text.firstIndex(of: " ")
if let start = findIndex {
   text.removeSubrange(start...)  // "Goodbye"
}
```

Listing 3-67: *Working with ranges of characters*

The **replaceSubrange()** method in Listing 3-67 replaces the characters from the beginning of the string up to the character before the space character ("Hello") with the string "Goodbye", and the **removeSubrange()** method uses an open range to remove the characters of this sentence from the space character to the end of the string (" World"), getting the final string "Goodbye". Notice that after applying the methods over the same string, the indexes are lost and therefore they must be recalculated. That is why before calling the **removeSubrange()** method we search for the position of the space character once more and update the **findIndex** variable.

The rest of the methods provided by the **String** structure are straightforward. For instance, the following example implements two of them to check if a string contains the word "World" at the end and converts all the letters into uppercase letters.

```
let text = "Hello World"

if text.hasSuffix("World") {
   print(text.uppercased())   // "HELLO WORLD"
}
```

Listing 3-68: *Implementing* `String` *methods*

Basic Array Structures

The strings studied before and the values we have created in previous examples with functions such as **stride()** or **repeatElement()** are collections of values. Collections do not represent a value; they are containers for other values. A value of type **String** does not contain the string "Hello", it contains a collection of variables of type **Character**, with the values H, e, l, l, and o. Swift includes several collections like this, some were defined to contain specific values, like **String**, and others are generic (they are defined with a generic data type that can be turn into any other data type we need). One of those generic data types collections is **Array**.

Arrays are collections that contain an ordered list of values. They are generic structures that have the capacity to store all the values we need of any data type we want, but with the condition that once a data type is selected, all the values must be of that same type. For example, if we create an array of type **Int**, we will only be able to store values of type **Int** in it. Swift offers multiple syntaxes to create an array, including the following initializers.

Array<Type>()—This initializer returns an empty **Array** structure of the data type indicated by the value of **Type**.

Array(repeating: Value, **count:** Int**)**—This initializer returns an **Array** structure with copies of the same value. The **repeating** argument determines the value to copy, and the **count** argument determines how many copies the array will contain.

A shortcut to create an array is to declare the data type between square brackets followed by parentheses (e.g., **var list = [Int]()**), but the most frequently used is declaring the array with initial values enclosed in square brackets and separated by comma.

```
var list: [Int] = [15, 25, 35]
```

Listing 3-69: *Declaring arrays*

As with any other variable, Swift may infer the type from the values.

```
var list = [15, 25, 35]
```

Listing 3-70: *Declaring arrays with type inference*

The **list** array declared in these examples was initialized with three integer values, 15, 25 and 35. The values of an array are usually called *elements* or *items*. On these terms, we can say that the code of Listing 3-70 declares an array of three elements of type **Int**.

An index is assigned to each value automatically, starting from 0, and as with strings, we must specify the index of the value we want to read surrounded by square brackets.

```
var list = [15, 25, 35]
print(list[1])  // 25
```

***Listing 3-71:** Reading the array's elements*

The last statement of Listing 3-71 prints the value of the second element of the **list** array (the element at index 1) on the console. We can also use indexes to modify the values of an array.

```
var list = [15, 25, 35]
list[0] = 400
print(list)  // [400, 25, 35]
```

***Listing 3-72:** Assigning a new value to an element*

Assigning new values is only possible for elements that already exist in the array. To add a new element, or several, we can use the **+=** operator.

```
var list = [15, 25, 35]
list += [45, 55]
print(list)  // [15, 25, 35, 45, 55]
```

***Listing 3-73:** Adding new elements to an array*

The **+=** operator adds an array at the end of another array. In Listing 3-73, we use it to add two more elements to the array declared in the first statement. What the **+=** operator does is to concatenate two arrays and assign the result back to the same variable. If we want to use two or more arrays to create a new one, we can apply the **+** operator.

```
var list1 = [15, 25, 35]
var list2 = [45, 55, 65]
var final = list1 + list2  // [15, 25, 35, 45, 55, 65]
```

***Listing 3-74:** Concatenating two arrays*

It is possible to declare arrays of arrays. These types of arrays are called *multidimensional arrays*. Arrays inside arrays are listed separated by comma.

```
var list: [[Int]] = [[2, 45, 31], [5, 10], [81, 12]]
```

***Listing 3-75:** Creating multidimensional arrays*

This example creates an array of arrays of integers (notice the declaration of the array inside another array **[[Int]]**). To access the values, we must declare the indexes of each level in square brackets, one after another. The following example returns the first value (index 0) of the second array (index 1). The instruction looks for the array at index 1 and then gets the number at index 0.

```
var list: [[Int]] = [[2, 45, 31], [5, 10], [81, 12]]
print(list[1][0])  // 5
```

Listing 3-76: *Reading values from a multidimensional array*

To remove all the elements from an array, we can assign to the variable one of the initializers introduced before or just square brackets with no values.

```
var list = [15, 25, 35]
list = []
```

Listing 3-77: *Removing the elements of an array*

Arrays are collections of values and therefore we can iterate over their values with a **for in** loop, as we did with strings before.

```
var total = 0
let list = [15, 25, 35]

for value in list {
   total += value
}
print("The total is \(total)")  // "The total is 75"
```

Listing 3-78: *Reading an array with a* `for in` *loop*

The code in Listing 3-78 uses a **for in** loop to add the numbers of the **list** array to the **total** variable. At the end, we print the result. Although this is a legit way to do it, arrays offer multiple properties and methods to read and process their values.

count—This property returns the total number of elements in the array.

isEmpty—This property returns a Boolean value that indicates if the array is empty.

first—This property returns the first element of the array or **nil** if the array is empty.

last—This property returns the last element of the array or **nil** if the array is empty.

append(Element**)**—This method adds the value specified by the argument at the end of the array.

insert(Element, **at:** Int**)**—This method adds a new element in a specific position of the array. The first argument is the value we want to assign to the new element, and the **at** argument represents the position of the array where we want to insert the element.

remove(at: Int**)**—This method removes an element from the array at the index specified by the **at** argument.

removeFirst()—This method removes the first element of the array. It returns the value of the element deleted.

removeLast()—This method removes the last element of the array. It returns the value of the element deleted.

removeAll(where: Closure**)**—This method removes the elements in the array that meet the condition established by the closure assigned to the **where** argument.

removeSubrange(Range**)**—This method removes a range of elements from the array. The argument is a range of integers representing the indexes of the elements to remove.

replaceSubrange(Range, **with:** Array**)**—This method replaces a range of elements with the elements of the array provided by the **with** argument. The first argument is a range of integers corresponding to the indexes of the elements we want to replace.

dropFirst(Int**)**—This method removes the number of elements specified by the argument from the beginning of the array. If no amount is declared, only the first element is removed.

dropLast(Int**)**—This method removes the number of elements specified by the argument from the end of the array. If no amount is declared, only the last element is removed.

enumerated()—This method is used to iterate over the elements of the array. It returns a tuple containing the index and the value of the current element.

min()—This method compares the values of the elements and returns the smallest.

max()—This method compares the values of the elements and returns the largest.

sorted()—This method returns an array with the elements of the array in ascending order.

sorted(by: Closure**)**—This method returns an array with the elements of the array in the order determined by the closure provided to the **by** argument.

randomElement()—This method randomly selects an element from the array and returns it. If the array is empty, the value returned is `nil`.

shuffled()—This method returns an array with the elements of the array in random order.

reversed()—This method returns an array with the elements of the array in reverse order.

swapAt(Int, Int**)**—This method exchanges the values of the elements at the indexes specified by the arguments.

joined(separator: String**)**—This method returns a string that includes all the values in an array of strings joined by the string specified by the **separator** argument.

filter(Closure**)**—This method filters an array and returns another array with the values that passed the filter. The argument is a closure that processes the elements and returns a Boolean indicating whether the value passed the test or not.

map(Closure**)**—This method returns a new array containing the results of processing each of the values of the array.

compactMap(Closure**)**—This method returns a new array containing the results of processing each of the values of the array, but ignores the values that produce a `nil` result.

reduce(Value, Closure**)**—This method sends the values of the array to the closure one by one and returns the result of the operation. The first argument is the value that is going to be processed with the first value of the array.

contains(where: Closure**)**—This method returns a Boolean that determines if the array contains an element that meets the condition in the closure.

allSatisfy(Closure**)**—This method returns a Boolean value that determines if all the elements of the array comply with the requisites of a closure.

difference(from: Array**)**—This method returns a `CollectionDifference` structure containing all the changes that has to be performed to synchronize the array with the array provided by the **from** method. This method can work in conjunction with the `applying()` method to apply all the changes in the array at once.

In the previous example, we have seen how to iterate over the elements of an array with the `for in` loop, but that iteration only returns the value of the element, not its index. An alternative is provided by the `enumerated()` method, designed to work with these types of loops. Each cycle returns a tuple with the index and the value of the current element.

```
let fruits = ["Banana", "Orange", "Apple"]
var message = "My fruits:"

for (myindex, myfruit) in fruits.enumerated() {
   message += " \(myindex + 1)-\(myfruit)"
}
print(message)  // "My fruits: 1-Banana 2-Orange 3-Apple"
```

***Listing 3-79:** Reading indexes and values of an array*

This example uses the constants **myindex** and **myfruit** to capture the values produced by the **enumerated()** method and generates a string. Notice that since the array's indexes start from 0, we added 1 to **myindex** to start counting from 1.

Another useful property is **count**. As mentioned before, we can access each element of the array with the index between square brackets. But trying to read a value in an index that has not yet been defined will return an error. To make sure that the index exists, we can check whether it is greater than 0 and less than the total amount of elements in the array using this property.

```
let ages = [32, 540, 12, 27, 54]
let index = 3
if index > 0 && index < ages.count {
   print("The value is: \(ages[index])")  // "The value is: 27"
}
```

***Listing 3-80:** Checking whether an array contains a value in a specific index*

The methods to add and remove elements from an array are straightforward. The following example illustrates how to implement them.

```
var fruits = ["Banana", "Orange"]
if !fruits.isEmpty {
   fruits.append("Apple")  // ["Banana", "Orange", "Apple"]
   fruits.removeFirst()  // "Banana"
   fruits.insert("Pear", at: 1)  // ["Orange", "Pear", "Apple"]
   fruits.insert(contentsOf: ["Cherry", "Peach"], at: 2)
   // ["Orange", "Pear", "Cherry", "Peach", "Apple"]
}
```

***Listing 3-81:** Adding and removing elements*

IMPORTANT: Every time an array is modified, its indexes are reassigned. For instance, if you remove the first element of an array of three elements, the index 0 is reassigned to the second element and the index 1 to the third element. The system makes sure that the indexes are always consecutive and start from 0.

A more complex method is **removeAll(where:)**. This method removes several elements at once, but only those that meet a condition. The condition is established by a closure that processes each of the values in the array and returns **true** or **false** depending on whether the value meets the condition or not. In the following example, we compare each value with the string "Orange" and therefore all the values "Orange" are removed from the array.

```
var fruits = ["Banana", "Orange", "Apple", "Orange"]
fruits.removeAll(where: { (value) in
   value == "Orange"
})
print(fruits)  // ["Banana", "Apple"]
```

***Listing 3-82:** Removing all the elements that meet a condition*

Another method that work with a closure is **contains(where:)**. In the following example, we use this method to determine whether an array contains a value greater than 60 or not.

```
var list = [55, 12, 32, 5, 9]
let found = list.contains(where: { (value) in
   value > 60
})
print(found)  // false
```

Listing 3-83: *Finding if an element meets a condition*

We can also select a random value with the **randomElement()** method. This method selects a value from the array and returns an optional, so we must compare it against **nil** or use optional binding before processing it, as in the following example.

```
let fruits = ["Banana", "Orange", "Apple"]
if let randomValue = fruits.randomElement() {
   print("The selected value is: \(randomValue)")
}
```

Listing 3-84: *Selecting a random value from an array*

Another random operation is performed by the **shuffled()** method. With this method we can randomly sort the elements of an array.

```
var fruits = ["Banana", "Orange", "Apple"]
fruits = fruits.shuffled()
print(fruits)  // e.g.: ["Orange", "Apple", "Banana"]
```

Listing 3-85: *Changing the order of the elements of an array*

Besides working with all the elements of an array, we can do it with a range of elements.

```
var fruits = ["Banana", "Orange", "Apple", "Cherry"]
var someFruits = fruits[0..<2]  // ["Banana", "Orange"]

print("The new selection has \(someFruits.count) fruits")
```

Listing 3-86: *Reading a range of elements*

This example gets the elements at the indexes 0 and 1 from the **fruits** array and assigns them to the new **someFruits** array. Now we have two arrays: **fruits** with 4 elements and **someFruits** with 2.

Arrays created from a range of indexes are of type **ArraySlice**. This is another collection type provided by Swift to store temporary arrays that are composed of elements taken from other arrays. We can iterate over these types of arrays with a loop or read its elements as we do with normal arrays, but if we want to assign them to other array variables or use them for persistent storage, we must cast them as **Array** types using the **Array()** initializer. The initializer takes the values of the **ArraySlice** variable and returns a normal array, as shown next.

```
var fruits = ["Banana", "Orange", "Apple", "Cherry"]
var someFruits = fruits[0..<2]  // ["Banana", "Orange"]
var newArray = Array(someFruits)
```

Listing 3-87: *Casting arrays of type* ArraySlice

The **Array** structure also offers the **removeSubrange()** and **replaceSubrange()** methods to remove and replace a range of elements.

```
var fruits = ["Banana", "Orange", "Apple", "Banana", "Banana"]
fruits.removeSubrange(1...2)
fruits.replaceSubrange(0..<2, with: ["Cherry", "Cherry"])
print(fruits)  // "["Cherry", "Cherry", "Banana"]"
```

***Listing 3-88:** Removing and replacing elements*

In Listing 3-88, we call the **removeSubrange()** method to remove the range of elements from index 1 to 2, getting an array filled with the value "Banana", and then we call the **replaceSubrange()** method to replace the elements from index 0 to 1 with another array filled with "Cherries". This is just to illustrate how the methods work, but it shows a recurrent situation in app development where sometimes we need to fill a collection with elements of the same value. When working with arrays, this is easy to achieve. The **Array** structure includes an initializer that takes two arguments, **repeating** and **count**, and generates an array with the number of elements indicated by **count** and the value indicated by **repeating**.

```
var fruits = ["Banana", "Orange", "Apple"]
let total = fruits.count
let newArray = Array(repeating: "Cherry", count: total)
fruits.replaceSubrange(0..<total, with: newArray)
print(fruits)  // "["Cherry", "Cherry", "Cherry"]"
```

***Listing 3-89:** Initializing an array with elements of the same value*

In this example, we create an array with the same amount of elements as the **fruits** array and then use the **replaceSubrange()** method to replace every element with a new one.

The methods to remove and replace elements of an array are not selective enough; they affect the elements in a specific index or a range of indexes without considering their values. If we want to perform a more specific job, we must use the **filter()** method. This method takes a closure and sends each element to the closure for processing. If the closure returns **true**, the element is included in the new array, otherwise it is ignored, as shown next.

```
var fruits = ["Apple", "Grape", "Banana", "Grape"]
var filteredArray = fruits.filter({ $0 != "Grape" })
print(filteredArray)  // "["Apple", "Banana"]"
```

***Listing 3-90:** Filtering the values of an array*

The **filter()** method sends the values one by one to the closure, the closure replaces the placeholder (**$0**) with the current value, compares it with the value "Grape", and returns a Boolean with the result. If the value is **true**, the element is included in **filteredArray**.

If what we need is to modify the elements of an array all at once, we can use the **map()** method. This method sends to a closure the values of the array one by one and returns another array with the results produced by the closure.

```
let list = [2, 4, 8, 16]
let half = list.map({ $0 / 2 })
print(half)  // "[1, 2, 4, 8]"
```

***Listing 3-91:** Mapping an array*

The example in Listing 3-91 defines a list of integers and then calls the **map()** method on the array to divide each value by 2. The **map()** method sends the values of the array to the closure one by one, the closure replaces the placeholder (**$0**) with the current value, divides the number by 2, and returns the result. All the results are stored in a new array and that array is returned by the **map()** method when the process is over.

Of course, we can perform any kind of operations on the values in the closure. For instance, the following code converts the values into strings with the **String()** initializer.

```
let list = [1, 2, 3, 4, 5]
let listtext = list.map({ String($0) })
print(listtext)  // "["1", "2", "3", "4", "5"]"
```

Listing 3-92: *Converting the elements of an array into strings*

When all we want to do is to initialize a new structure with the value received by the closure, instead of a closure, Swift allows us to provide the structure's initializer. The value received by the closure is sent to the initializer and a new structure of that type is returned.

```
let list = [1, 2, 3, 4, 5]
let listtext = list.map(String.init)
print(listtext)  // "["1", "2", "3", "4", "5"]"
```

Listing 3-93: *Using a structure initializer with the* `map()` *method*

This example produces the same result as before, but instead of using a closure, we use a reference to the **String** initializer. The **map()** method sends the values to the initializer, the initializer returns a new **String** structure with that value, and the process continues as always.

Another way to process all the values of an array at once is with the **reduce()** method. This method works in a similar way than **map()**, but instead of storing the results in an array, it sends the result back to the closure to get only one value in return. For instance, the following code uses the **reduce()** method to get the result of the addition of all the numbers in an array.

```
let list = [2, 4, 8, 16]
let total = list.reduce(0, { $0 + $1 })
print(total)  // "30"
```

Listing 3-94: *Reducing an array*

The code in Listing 3-94 defines an array of integers and then calls the **reduce()** method on it. This method sends two values at a time to the closure. In the first cycle, the values sent to the closure are the ones provided by the first argument (**0**) and the first value of the array (**2**). In the second cycle, the values sent to the closure are the value returned by the closure in the first cycle (0 + 2 = **2**), and the second value of the array (**4**). The loop goes on until all the values of the array are processed.

When it comes to sorting the elements of an array, there are several options available. The most frequently used are **reversed()** and **sorted()** (and its variant **sorted(by:)**). The **reversed()** method takes the elements of an array and returns a new array with the same elements in reversed order. The value returned by the method is stored in a structure of type **ReversedCollection**. As we did before with the **ArraySlice** type, we can cast these values as **Array** structures with the **Array()** initializer.

```
var fruits = ["Apple", "Blueberry", "Banana"]
var array = Array(fruits.reversed())  // ["Banana", "Blueberry", "Apple"]
```

Listing 3-95: *Reversing the elements of an array*

The **sorted()** method sorts the array in ascending order and returns a new array.

```
var fruits = ["Blueberry", "Apple", "Banana"]
let basket = fruits.sorted()
print(basket)  // ["Apple", "Banana", "Blueberry"]
```

Listing 3-96: *Sorting the elements of an array*

If we want to sort the elements in a custom order, we can use the **sorted(by:)** method. This method works in a similar fashion to the **filter()** method studied before. It takes a function or a closure that receives the value of two elements and returns **true** if the first element should appear before the second element, or **false** otherwise.

```
var fruits = ["Apple", "Raspberry", "Banana", "Grape"]
var newArray = fruits.sorted(by: { $0 > $1 })
print(newArray[0])  // "Raspberry"
```

Listing 3-97: *Sorting the elements of an array in a custom order*

When the **sorted()** method is executed, it performs a loop. On each cycle, two values of the **fruits** array are sent to the closure. The closure compares the values and returns **true** or **false** accordingly. This indicates to the **sorted()** method which value should appear before the other in the new array, effectively sorting the elements. Unlike the example we programmed for the **filter()** method, this one does not compare the argument against a specific value. This allows us to order arrays of any data type. For example, we can use the closure to sort an array of integers.

```
var numbers = [55, 12, 32, 5, 9]
var newArray = numbers.sorted(by: { $0 < $1 })
print(newArray[0])  // 5
```

Listing 3-98: *Sorting an array of integers*

If we decide to work with specific data types, we can perform custom tasks. For example, we can count the characters in the strings and sort them according to their length.

```
var fruits = ["Apple", "Blueberry", "Banana", "Grape"]
var newArray = fruits.sorted(by: { $0.count < $1.count })
print(newArray)  // ["Apple", "Grape", "Banana", "Blueberry"]
```

Listing 3-99: *Sorting strings according to the number of characters*

Arrays also include two powerful methods to compare elements: **min()** and **max()**. These methods compare the values and return the smallest or largest, respectively.

```
let ages = [32, 540, 12, 27]

if let older = ages.max() {
   let digits = String(older)
   print("The maximum age is \(digits.count) digits long")
}
```

Listing 3-100: *Getting the largest element*

The code in Listing 3-100 takes the largest value from an array of integers and counts the number of digits in the returned value. Because the **max()** method returns an optional, we use optional binding to get its value. The rest of the code turns this value into a string and counts its characters to print the number of digits on the console.

Besides selecting the largest or smallest value with the **max()** and **min()** methods, we can also fetch values from the array using the **first** and **last** properties.

```
let ages = [32, 540, 12, 27]

if let firstAge = ages.first {
   print("The first person is \(firstAge) years old")   // 32
}
```

Listing 3-101: *Getting the first value of an array*

The value returned by the **first** property is also an optional, so we use optional binding again to get its value and store it in the **firstAge** constant. The **first** and **last** properties only get the first and last value, respectively. To search for any value in the array or its index, the **Array** structure offers the following methods.

firstIndex(of: Element**)**—This method performs a search from the beginning of the array and returns the index of the first element that matches the value of the **of** argument.

lastIndex(of: Element**)**—This method performs a search from the end of the array and returns the index of the first element that matches the value of the **of** argument.

firstIndex(where: Closure**)**—This method returns the index of the first value that meets the condition in the closure assigned to the **where** argument.

lastIndex(where: Closure**)**—This method returns the index of the last value that meets the condition in the closure assigned to the **where** argument.

first(where: Closure**)**—This method returns the first value that meets the condition in the closure assigned to the **where** argument.

last(where: Closure**)**—This method returns the last value that meets the condition in the closure assigned to the **where** argument.

If we only need the index of a particular element, we can use the **firstIndex(of:)** method. For instance, we can look for the first appearance of a number in an array and get the index.

```
let ages = [32, 540, 12, 27, 54]

if let index = ages.firstIndex(of: 540) {
   print("The value is at the position \(index)")   // 1
}
```

Listing 3-102: *Getting the index of a specific value,*

If what we need instead is to get the index of a value that meets certain condition, we can use methods like **firstIndex(where:)** or **lastIndex(where:)** depending on whether we want to search from the beginning or the end of the array.

```
let ages = [32, 540, 12, 27, 54]
let first = ages.firstIndex(where: { $0 < 30 })
if first != nil {
   print("The first value is at index \(first!)")   // 2
}
```

Listing 3-103: *Getting the index of a value that meets a condition*

In this example, we look for the index of a value smaller than 30. The **`firstIndex(where:)`** method reads every value of the array from the beginning and sends them to the closure assigned to the **`where`** argument. This closure assigns the current value to the placeholder and compares it against the number 30, if the value is greater than 30, the closure returns **`false`**, otherwise it returns **`true`** and the index of that value is assigned to the **`first`** variable. In this case, the first number in the array smaller than 30 is 12, and therefore the index assigned to the variable is 2.

Basic Set Structures

If we store two elements in an array, one element will automatically receive the index 0 and the other the index 1. This correlation between indexes and values never changes, allowing elements to be listed always in the right order and have elements with the same value at different indexes. Sets are like arrays, but they do not assign an index to their values and therefore there is no order or duplicated values. Sets are created from the **`Set`** structure.

Set<Type>()—This initializer returns an empty **`Set`** structure of the data type indicated by the value of **Type**.

This initializer can be used to create an empty set (e.g., **`let myset = Set<Int>()`**), but we can also use square brackets, as we do with arrays. The difference with arrays is that we must declare that we are creating a set with the **`Set`** keyword, as shown next.

```
var ages: Set<Int> = []
```

Listing 3-104: *Creating an empty set of integers*

If we initialize the set with some values, Swift can infer its type from the values' data type, simplifying the declaration.

```
var ages: Set = [15, 25, 35, 45]
```

Listing 3-105: *Creating a set of integers*

To process the elements of a set, we can use a **`for in`** loop, as we did before with strings and arrays, but sets also provide their own properties and methods for this purpose.

count—This property returns the number of elements in the set.

isEmpty—This property returns a Boolean that indicates whether the set is empty or not.

contains(Element**)**—This method returns a Boolean that indicates whether there is an element in the set with the value specified by the argument.

contains(where: Closure**)**—This method returns a Boolean that determines if the set contains an element that meets the condition in the closure.

min()—This method compares the elements in the set and returns the smallest.

max()—This method compares the elements in the set and returns the largest.

sorted()—This method returns an array with the elements of the set in ascending order.

sorted(by: Closure**)**—This method returns an array with the elements of the set in the order determined by the closure specified by the **by** argument.

randomElement()—This method randomly selects an element from the set and returns it. If the set is empty, the value returned is **`nil`**.

shuffled()—This method returns an array with the elements of the set in random order.

insert(Element**)**—This method inserts a new element in the set with the value provided by the argument.

union(Collection**)**—This method returns a new set created with the values of the original set plus the values provided by the argument (an array or another set).

subtract(Collection**)**—This method returns a new set created by subtracting the elements provided by the argument to the original set.

intersection(Collection**)**—This method returns a new set created with the values of the original set that match the values provided by the argument (an array or another set).

remove(Element**)**—This method removes from the set the element with the value provided by the argument.

isSubset(of: Set**)**—This method returns a Boolean that indicates whether or not the set is a subset of the set specified by the **of** argument.

isSuperset(of: Set**)**—This method returns a Boolean that indicates whether or not the set is a superset of the set specified by the **of** argument.

isDisjoint(with: Set**)**—This method returns a Boolean that indicates whether or not the original set and the set specified by the **with** argument have elements in common.

Using these methods, we can easily access and modify the values of a set. For instance, we can implement the **contains()** method to search for a value.

```
var fruits: Set = ["Apple", "Orange", "Banana"]

if fruits.contains("Apple") {
   print("Apple exists!")
}
```

Listing 3-106: *Using* `contains()` *to find an element in a set*

To insert a new element, we just have to execute the **insert()** method.

```
var fruits: Set = ["Apple", "Orange", "Banana"]

if !fruits.contains("Grape") {
   fruits.insert("Grape")
}
print("The set has \(fruits.count) elements")  // 4
```

Listing 3-107: *Inserting a new element*

In listing 3-107, we use the **contains()** method again to check if an element with the value "Grape" already exists in the set, but this is not really necessary. If the value is already part of the set, the **insert()** method does not perform any action.

To remove an element we must call the **remove()** method.

```
var fruits: Set = ["Apple", "Orange", "Banana"]

if let removed = fruits.remove("Banana") {
   print("\(removed) was removed")  // "Banana was removed"
}
```

Listing 3-108: *Removing an element from a set*

The **remove()** method removes the element which value matches the value of its argument and returns an optional with the value removed or **nil** in case of failure. In the code of Listing 3-108, we get the value returned by the method and print a message if it was removed successfully.

Sets are collections without order. Every time we read a set, the order in which its values are returned is not guaranteed, but we can use the **sorted()** method to create an array with the values of the set in order. The following example sorts the elements of the **fruits** set in alphabetical order, creating a new array we call **orderFruits**.

```
var fruits: Set = ["Apple", "Orange", "Banana"]
var orderFruits = fruits.sorted()
if let lastItem = orderFruits.last {
   print(lastItem)  // "Orange"
}
```

Listing 3-109: *Sorting the elements of a set*

The rest of the methods available are straightforward. The following example joins two sets with the **union()** method and then subtracts elements from the result with **subtract()**.

```
var fruits: Set = ["Apple", "Banana"]
var newSet = fruits.union(["Grapes"])  // "Banana", "Grapes", "Apple"
newSet.subtract(["Apple", "Banana"])  // "Grapes"
```

Listing 3-110: *Combining sets*

The **Set** structure also offer methods to compare sets. We can determine if a set is a subset or a superset of another set with the **isSubset()** and **isSuperset()** methods or check if two sets have elements in common with the **isDisjoint()** method. The following example implements the **isSubset()** method to check if the fruits in a basket come from the store. The code checks if the elements in the **basket** set are found in the **store** set and returns **true** in case of success.

```
var store: Set = ["Banana", "Apple", "Orange", "Pear"]
var basket: Set = ["Apple", "Orange"]

if basket.isSubset(of: store) {
   print("The fruits in the basket are from the store")
}
```

Listing 3-111: *Comparing sets*

Basic Dictionary Structures

There is only one way to access the elements of an array and that is through their numeric indexes. Dictionaries offer a better alternative. With dictionaries, we can define the indexes ourselves using any custom value we want. Each index, also known as *key*, must be explicitly declared along with its value. Swift offers multiple syntaxes to create a dictionary, including the following initializers.

Dictionary<Type1: Type2**>()**—This initializer returns an empty **Dictionary** structure with the keys and values of the data type indicated by the value of **Type1** and **Type2**.

Dictionary(grouping: Collection, **by:** Closure**)**—This initializer returns a **Dictionary** structure with the values provided by the **grouping** argument grouped in arrays according to the keys returned by the closure provided by the **by** argument.

If the data types are explicitly defined, we can also declare an empty dictionary with a simplified syntax, as in **var list: [String: String] = Dictionary()**, or use square brackets with a colon, as in **var list: [String: String] = [:]**. This shortcut is also used to define a dictionary with initial values. In this case, the keys and values are separated by a colon and the items are separated by comma, as in the following example.

```
var list: [String: String] = ["First": "Apple", "Second": "Orange"]
```

***Listing 3-112:** Declaring a dictionary with initial values*

The first value of each item is the key and the second is the value. Of course, if the keys and the values are of a clear data type, Swift can infer them.

```
var list = ["First": "Apple", "Second": "Orange"]
```

***Listing 3-113:** Declaring a dictionary with type inference*

As with arrays, if we want to read or replace a value, we must declare the key (index) in square brackets after the name of the dictionary.

```
var list = ["First": "Apple", "Second": "Orange"]
list["Second"] = "Banana"
```

***Listing 3-114:** Assigning a new value to an element of a dictionary*

The second statement in Listing 3-114 assigns a new value to the element identified with the keyword "Second". Now, the dictionary contains two elements with the values "Apple" and "Banana". If the keyword used to assign the new value exists, the system updates the value, but if the keyword does not exist, a new element is created, as shown next.

```
var list = ["First": "Apple", "Second": "Orange"]
list["Third"] = "Banana"
print(list)  // "["Second": "Orange", "First": "Apple", "Third": 
"Banana"]"
```

***Listing 3-115:** Adding a new element to a dictionary*

In this last example, the second statement assigns the value "Banana" to a keyword that does not exist. The system creates the new element with the specified keyword and value.

Dictionaries return optional values. If we try to read an element with a keyword that does not exist, the value returned is **nil**.

```
var list = ["First": "Apple", "Second": "Orange"]
print(list["Third"])  // nil
```

***Listing 3-116:** Reading an element that does not exist*

The code in Listing 3-116 tries to read a value with the keyword "Third" that does not exist in the **list** dictionary. As a result, the value **nil** is printed on the console. If the element exists and we want to read its value, we must unwrap it.

```
var list = ["First": "Apple", "Second": "Orange"]
if let first = list["First"], let second = list["Second"] {
   print("We have \(first) and \(second)")  // "We have Apple and Orange"
}
```

***Listing 3-117:** Reading the values*

Since dictionary elements are optionals, we can assign the value **nil** to remove them. The following example removes the element with the keyword "First".

```
var list = ["First": "Apple", "Second": "Orange"]
list["First"] = nil
```

Listing 3-118: *Removing an element from a dictionary*

As with arrays and sets, we can also iterate over the values of a dictionary with a **for in** loop. The value produced by each cycle of the loop is a tuple containing the key and the element's value.

```
var fruits = ["First": "Apple", "Second": "Orange"]
var message = "My fruits:"

for (myindex, myfruit) in fruits {
   message += " \(myindex)-\(myfruit)"
}
print(message)  // "My fruits: First-Apple Second-Orange"
```

Listing 3-119: *Using* `for in` *to iterate over a dictionary*

The **for in** loop in Listing 3-119 reads the elements of the **fruits** dictionary one by one, assigns the index and the value to the **myindex** and **myfruit** constants, and adds their values to the **message** variable, so at the end we get a string with all the keys and values in the dictionary.

Of course, dictionaries may also contain arrays as values. The declaration is simple, the key is declared as always, and the single value is replaced by an array.

```
var fruits: [String: [String]] = ["A": ["Apple", "Apricot"], "B":
["Banana", "Blueberries"]]
```

Listing 3-120: *Combining dictionaries with arrays*

Reading the values of a dictionary like this is a bit more complicated. Because dictionaries return optionals, we cannot just specify the indexes as we do for multidimensional arrays (see Listing 3-76). The value returned by the dictionary must be unwrapped before accessing its values.

```
var fruits: [String: [String]] = ["A": ["Apple", "Apricot"], "B":
["Banana", "Blueberries"]]
if let list = fruits["A"] {
   print(list[0])  // "Apple"
}
```

Listing 3-121: *Reading arrays inside dictionaries*

In this example, we create a dictionary with two values. The values are arrays of strings with a string as key. The code gets the array corresponding to the "A" key, unwraps it, and stores it in a constant. The **list** constant now contains the array assigned to the "A" key, and therefore when we read the element at index 0 of that array, we get the value "Apple".

This is actually how the **Dictionary(grouping:, by:)** initializer works. It takes the values of a collection and groups them together in arrays according to the value of a key returned by the closure, as in the following example.

```
let list = [15, 25, 38, 55, 42]
let group5 = Dictionary(grouping: list, by: {$0 % 5 == 0 ? "Yes" : "No"})
print(group5)  // "["No": [38, 42], "Yes": [15, 25, 55]]"
```

Listing 3-122: Grouping values by a key

The **Dictionary** initializer implemented in Listing 3-122 takes the values of the **list** array, sends them to the closure one by one, and creates a new dictionary with the keys returned by the closure. The closure receives the value and returns the strings "Yes" or "No" depending on whether the current value is multiple of 5. If the value is multiple of 5, it is included in an array with the key "Yes", otherwise it is included in an array with the key "No".

Dictionaries incorporate plenty of functionality by themselves, but they also include properties and methods to manage their values. The following are the most frequently used.

count—This property returns the total number of elements in the dictionary.

isEmpty—This property returns a Boolean value that indicates if the dictionary is empty.

keys—This property returns a collection with the keys in the dictionary.

values—This property returns a collection with the values in the dictionary.

sorted(by: Closure**)**—This method returns an array of tuples with each element of the dictionary (key and value) in the order determined by the closure.

randomElement()—This method randomly selects an element from the dictionary and returns a tuple with its key and value. If the dictionary is empty, the value returned is **nil**.

shuffled()—This method returns an array of tuples containing the keys and values of each element of the dictionary in random order.

updateValue(Value, **forKey:** Key**)**—This method updates the value of an element with the value and key specified by its arguments. If the key does not exist, the method creates a new element. It returns the previous value if the key exists or **nil** otherwise.

removeValue(forKey: Key**)**—This method removes the element with the key equal to the value of the **forKey** argument. It returns an optional containing the value of the deleted element or **nil** if no element with the specified key was found.

contains(where: Closure**)**—This method returns a Boolean value that determines if the dictionary contains an element that meets the condition in the closure.

Some of the methods provided by the **Dictionary** structure are like those included in the **Array** and **Set** structures, but others are more specific. For example, the **updateValue()** and **removeValue()** methods require the element's key to process the values.

```
var fruits = ["one": "Banana", "two": "Apple", "three": "Pear"]
fruits.updateValue("Banana", forKey: "three")  // "Pear"
fruits.removeValue(forKey: "one")  // "Banana"
print(fruits)  // "["three": "Banana", "two": "Apple"]"
```

Listing 3-123: Adding and removing elements from a dictionary

The **updateValue()** method updates the value of an element when there is already an element with that key or creates a new one if the key does not exist. This is the same as assigning a value directly to an element (see Listings 3-114 and 3-115), but the method returns the previous value, which may be useful sometimes.

Like sets, dictionaries are an unordered collection of values, but we can create an array with their elements in a specific order using the **sorted()** method. The method returns the values as tuples, with the element's key first and the value second.

```
var fruits = ["one": "Banana", "two": "Apple", "three": "Pear"]
var list = fruits.sorted(by: { $0.1 < $1.1 })
print(list)
```

Listing 3-124: *Sorting the values of a dictionary*

As with arrays, the **sorted()** method sends to the closure two values at a time, but the values in a dictionary are sent as tuples containing the key and value of each element. For instance, the first values sent to the closure in Listing 3-124 are ("one", "Banana") and ("two", "Apple"). These values take the place of the placeholders **$0** and **$1**, so if we want to order the elements according to their values (the names of the fruits), we must compare the values of the tuples at the index 1 (**$0.1 < $1.1**). The array returned is a collection of tuples in alphabetical order, with every element containing the keys and values of the dictionary (**[(key: "two", value: "Apple"), (key: "one", value: "Banana"), (key: "three", value: "Pear")]**).

Earlier, we saw how to iterate over the elements of a dictionary with a **for in** loop (see Listing 3-119). The loop gets each element and generates a tuple with the key and value. But there are times when we only need the element's key or the element's value. The **Dictionary** structure provides two properties for this purpose: **keys** and **values**. The properties return a collection containing only the keys or the values of the elements, respectively.

```
var fruits = ["one": "Banana", "two": "Apple", "three": "Pear"]

for key in fruits.keys {
   if key == "two" {
      print("We have an element with the key 'two'")
   }
}
```

Listing 3-125: *Iterating over the dictionary's keys*

The collections returned by the **keys** and **values** properties are structures of type **Keys** and **Values** defined inside the **Dictionary** structure. As we did before with other collection types, to work with their values we can turn them into arrays with the **Array()** initializer.

```
var fruits = ["one": "Banana", "two": "Apple", "three": "Pear"]
let keys = Array(fruits.keys)
print(keys)
```

Listing 3-126: *Reading the keys of a dictionary*

Basic 3.4 Enumerations

Enumerations are a way to create data types with a limited set of values. An enumeration type is like the Boolean type but with the possible values defined by the programmer. They are declared with the **enum** keyword, and the values are defined with the **case** keyword between braces.

```
enum Number {
   case one
   case two
   case three
}
```

Listing 3-127: *Defining an enumeration type*

This example defines an enumeration call **Number** with three possible values: **one**, **two,** and **three**. We can assign any names we want for the enumeration and its values. The values may also be declared just in one **case** statement separated by comma.

```
enum Number {
   case one, two, three
}
```

Listing 3-128: *Declaring the enumeration values in one statement*

An enumeration is a custom data type. As we did with structures, we must create a variable of this type and assign to that variable one of the possible values using dot notation.

```
enum Number {
   case one, two, three
}
var mynumber: Number = Number.one
```

Listing 3-129: *Declaring a variable of type* `Number`

Variables declared of this type may only have the values allowed by the type (**one**, **two,** or **three**). To assign a value, we must use the name of the enumeration and dot notation. The **mynumber** variable declared in Listing 3-129 is of type **Number** and has the value **one**.

Once the type of the variable was already defined, only the dot and the value are necessary to modify its value.

```
enum Number {
   case one, two, three
}
var mynumber = Number.one
mynumber = .two
```

Listing 3-130: *Assigning a new value to a variable of type* `Number`

In the last statement of Listing 3-130, we assign a new value to **mynumber**. The value **.two** may have been written as **Number.two**. Both syntaxes are valid, but Swift infers that the value provided is of the same type as the variable's type, so it is not necessary to declare the name anymore.

Like Booleans, enumeration types may be used as signals to indicate a state that can be checked later to decide whether to perform a certain task. Therefore, they are frequently used with conditionals and loops. The following example checks the value of an enumeration variable with a **switch** statement. This statement is particularly useful when working with enumerations because these data types have a limited set of values, making it easy to define a **case** for each one of them.

```
enum Number {
   case one
   case two
   case three
}
var mynumber = Number.two

switch mynumber {
   case .one:
      print("The number is 1")
   case .two:
      print("The number is 2")   // "The number is 2"
```

```
    case .three:
        print("The number is 3")
}
```

Listing 3-131: Using `switch` *with an enumeration type*

In this example, the **Number** enumeration is defined and then the **mynumber** variable is declared of this type and the value **two** is assigned to it. Next, a **switch** statement compares the value of this variable with the three possible values of its type and prints a message on the console.

Medium Raw Values

The cases of an enumeration can have values by default. These values are called *raw values*. Swift assigns values by default to every case, starting from 0, but we can assign our own to each case.

```
enum Number: String {
    case one = "Number One"
    case two = "Number Two"
    case three = "Number Three"
}
var mynumber = Number.one
```

Listing 3-132: *Assigning raw values to enumeration values*

Enumerations behave like structures. We can define our own properties and methods inside an enumeration, and they also include initializers, properties, and methods by default. The most useful property is called **rawValue**, which lets us read the raw value of each **case**.

```
enum Number: String {
    case one = "Number One"
    case two = "Number Two"
    case three = "Number Three"
}
var mynumber = Number.one
print("The value is \(mynumber.rawValue)")  // "The value is Number One"
```

Listing 3-133: *Reading raw values*

Additionally, enumerations include an initializer to create an instance from a raw value. Instead of declaring the variable using the value's name (**one**), we can use the initializer and the raw value. The initializer includes the **rawValue** argument to specify the value used to create the instance.

```
enum Number: String {
    case one = "Number One"
    case two = "Number Two"
    case three = "Number Three"
}
var mynumber = Number(rawValue: "Number Two")

if mynumber == .two {
    print("Correct Value")  // "Correct Value"
}
```

Listing 3-134: *Creating an enumeration from a raw value*

We can read the **case** value or the raw value to identify an instance of an enumeration type. In Listing 3-134, we create an instance of **Number** with the raw value "Number Two" and then check that the variable contains the proper **case** value with an **if** statement.

What makes enumerations part of the programming paradigm proposed by Swift is not their capacity to store different types of values but the possibility to include custom methods and computed properties. The following example adds a method to our **Number** enumeration that prints a message depending on the current value of the instance.

```
enum Number: Int {
   case one
   case two
   case three

   func printMessage() -> String {
      switch self {
         case .one:
            return "We are the best"
         case .two:
            return "We have to study more"
         case .three:
            return "This is just the beginning"
      }
   }
}
var mynumber = Number.two
print(mynumber.printMessage())   // "We have to study more"
```

***Listing 3-135:** Adding methods to an enumeration*

When we need to check the current value of the instance from inside a method, we must use the **self** keyword. This keyword refers to the instance where the method is being executed (in our case, **mynumber**), and this is how we can check for the instance's current value and return the right message. (We will learn more about the **self** keyword later.)

Medium Associated Values

Enumerations include the possibility to associate values to a case. These are values we can attach to a case when variables of that type are initialized. For instance, in the following example we create an enumeration that can store information about a character, but it provides the possibility to differentiate between letters and numbers.

```
enum MyCharacters {
   case number(Int, String)
   case letter(Character, String)
}
var character = MyCharacters.number(1, "Number One")

switch character {
   case .number(let value, let description):
      print("\(description) - \(value)")   // "Number One - 1"
   case .letter(let letter, let description):
      print("\(description) - \(letter)")
}
```

***Listing 3-136:** Associating values*

This example defines an enumeration called **MyCharacters** that includes two cases. The first case is called **number** and it takes two associated values: an integer and a string. The second case is called **letter** and it also takes two associated values: a character and a string. When we create a value of this type, we must select the case value, as always, but we must also specify the associated values. If the value of the enumeration is **number**, we must provide an integer and a string, and if the value is **letter**, we must provide a character and a string. In this example, we create an instance with the value **number** and the associated values 1 and "Number One".

In each case of the **switch** statement, we test whether the value is **number** or **letter** and extract their associated values with constants between parenthesis, as we did with tuples before (see Listing 2-37). If we need to test a single case, we can use an **if** or a **guard** statement and assign the value to the case we want to test.

```
enum MyCharacters {
   case number(Int, String)
   case letter(Character, String)
}
var character = MyCharacters.number(1, "Number One")

if case .number(let number, let text) = character {
   print("Number: \(number)")  // "Number: 1"
   print("Text: \(text)")  // "Text: Number One"
}
```

Listing 3-137: *Reading associated values from an* `if` *statement*

The syntax includes the **case** keyword and the necessary constants to receive the values. The statement is saying something like "Assign the value to this case, if not possible, return false". In our example, if the **character** variable doesn't contain a **MyCharacters** enumeration with the value **number**, the statement returns **false** and nothing is done, otherwise, the associated values in the **character** variable are assigned to the constants and printed on the console.

Advanced Collection Difference

Associated values are commonly implemented by libraries and frameworks to share data with our code. For instance, the **Array** structure defined in the Swift Standard Library includes the **difference()** method. We have introduced this method before. Its purpose is to compare two arrays and return a structure of type **CollectionDifference** that contains a collection of values that represent the difference between the arrays. These values are of type **Change**, an enumeration defined by the **CollectionDifference** structure that includes the following values and their associated values to represent single changes.

insert(offset: Int, **element:** Element, **associatedWith:** Int?**)**—This enumeration value represents the insertion of an element. It includes three associated values. The **offset** value indicates the index in which the element is inserted, the **element** value is the element, and the **associatedWith** value is the index of the element associated with this change.

remove(offset: Int, **element:** Element, **associatedWith:** Int?**)**—This enumeration value represents the removal of an element. It includes three associated values. The **offset** value indicates the index from which the element was removed, the **element** value is the removed element, and the **associatedWith** value is the index of the element associated with this change.

As we will see later, the code that comprises an application is usually divided into separate units that take care of very specific tasks, like storing the user's data or showing that data on the screen. This means that sometimes we may have two sets of data that represent the same information and therefore we must keep them synchronized. For instance, we may have data stored in an array that represents the information saved by the user on a file, and another array with a copy of that data that we are using to show the information on the screen. If the data from the file changes, we must update the data that is shown to the user. If that data is stored in ordered collections, such as arrays, we can synchronize them with the **difference()** method.

```
var list1 = [1, 2, 3, 4, 5]
var list2 = [2, 4, 8, 16, 32]

let diff = list1.difference(from: list2)
for change in diff {
   switch change {
   case .insert(let offset, let element, _):
      list2.insert(element, at: offset)
   case .remove(let offset, _, _):
      list2.remove(at: offset)
   }
}
print(list2)  // "[1, 2, 3, 4, 5]"
```

Listing 3-138: *Synchronizing arrays*

The code in Listing 3-138 defines two arrays: **list1** and **list2**. In this example, we are assuming that **list2** is the array that has to be synchronized with the changes in **list1**, so we determine the current differences by calling the **difference()** method on **list1**. This gives us a collection of **Change** values that tell us which elements of the **list2** array we must remove or add. Next, we create a **for in** loop to iterate over the collection. Because these values are enumeration values with associated values, we must use a **switch** statement to process them. In the case the value is **insert()**, we insert a new element in the **list2** array with the **insert()** method (see Listing 3-81), but if the value is **remove()**, we remove the element with the **remove()** method.

At the end of this process, the array stored in the **list2** variable will be the same as the one stored in the **list1** variable. Of course, we could have simplified this process by assigning **list1** to **list2** but knowing exactly which elements change in one array with respect to the other is useful when we need to perform tasks after a change is applied.

If we don't need to process the changes one by one but still want to modify the array with the values returned by the **difference()** method, we can call the **applying()** method offered by the **Array** structure to perform all the changes at once.

```
var list1 = [1, 2, 3, 4, 5]
var list2 = [2, 4, 8, 16, 32]

let diff = list1.difference(from: list2)
if let newlist = list2.applying(diff) {
   list2 = newlist
}
print(list2)  // "[1, 2, 3, 4, 5]"
```

Listing 3-139: *Applying all the changes at once*

The **applying()** method returns the array with all the changes applied, or **nil** if it can't apply the difference to the array, so we have to check this value and then assign the result back to **list2**. The result is the same as before, the array in **list2** contains the same values as **list1**, but with the difference that all the changes were performed at once.

Basic 3.5 Objects

Objects are data types that encapsulate data and functionality in the form of properties and methods, but unlike the structures and enumerations introduced before they are stored by reference, which means that more than one variable can refer to the same object in memory.

Basic Definition of Objects

Like structures and enumerations, objects are defined first and then instances are created from their definition. The definitions of objects are called *classes*, and what we called objects are the instances created from those classes. Classes are declared the same way as structures or enumerations, but instead of the **struct** or **enum** keywords we must use the **class** keyword.

```
class Employee {
   var name = "Undefined"
   var age = 0
}
```

Listing 3-140: *Defining a class*

This example defines a simple class called **Employee** with two properties: **name** and **age**. As always, this does not create anything, it is just defining a new custom data type. To store data in memory in this format, we must declare a constant or a variable of this type and assign to it an instance of the class created with an initializer.

```
class Employee {
   var name = "Undefined"
   var age = 0
}
let employee1 = Employee()
employee1.name = "John"
employee1.age = 32
```

Listing 3-141: *Creating an object from a class*

In Listing 3-141, the **Employee()** initializer creates a new instance of the class **Employee**. Since in this case the words instance and object are synonyms, we can say that we have created a new object called **employee1** containing two properties, **name** and **age**.

Of course, we can also modify the values of the properties of an object from its methods, but unlike structures, the object's methods can modify the properties of their own object without adding anything to the definition (they do not need to be declared as **mutating**).

```
class Employee {
   var name = "Undefined"
   var age = 0

   func changename(newname: String, newage: Int) {
      name = newname
      age = newage
   }
}
let employee1 = Employee()
employee1.changename(newname: "Martin", newage: 32)
print("Name: \(employee1.name)")  // "Name: Martin"
```

Listing 3-142: *Modifying properties from the object's methods*

In Listing 3-142, the **changename()** method is added to the **Employee** class to modify the values of its properties. After the instance is created, we call this method to assign the values "Martin" and 32 to the **name** and **age** properties, respectively.

Basic Type Properties and Methods

We have studied type properties and methods before with structures. These are properties and methods that are accessible from the data type and not from the instances created from that type. They work in classes the same way as in structures, but instead of the **static** keyword we must use the **class** keyword to define them.

```
class Employee {
   var name = "Undefined"
   var age = 0

   class func description() {
      print("This class stores the name and age of an employee")
   }
}
Employee.description()
```

Listing 3-143: *Declaring a type method for a class*

This example defines an **Employee** class with two properties: **name** and **age**. The type method declared next is just describing the purpose of the class. Every time the **description()** method is executed on the class, a description is printed on the console. Again, we don't have to create an instance because the method is executed on the class itself.

IMPORTANT: Classes can also use the **static** keyword to define type properties and methods. The difference between the **static** and **class** keywords is that properties and methods defined with the **static** keyword are immutable and those defined with the **class** keyword can be modified by subclasses. (We will learn about subclasses and inheritance later in this chapter.)

Basic Reference Types

Structures and enumerations are value types. This means that every time we assign a variable of any of these data types to another variable, the value is copied. For example, if we create an instance of a structure and then assign that instance to another variable, the instance is copied, and we end up with two instances of the same structure in memory.

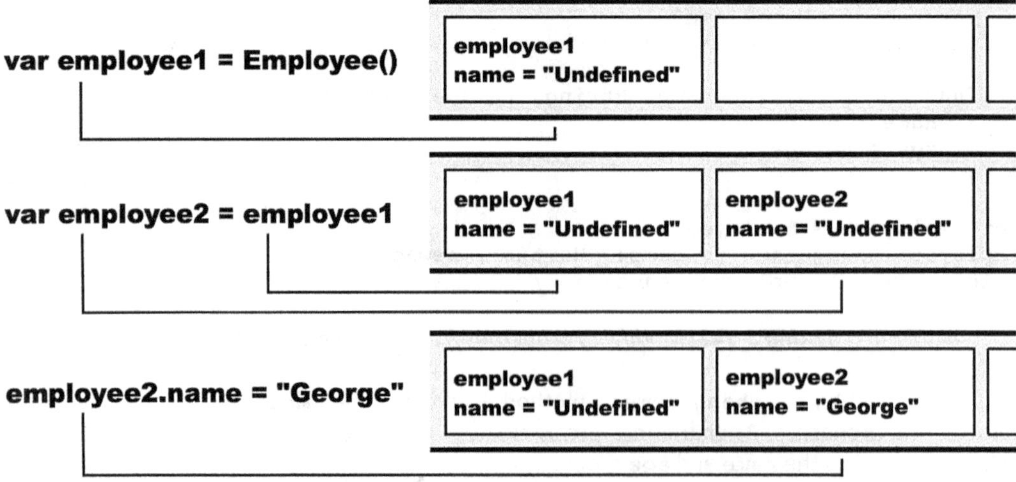

Figure 3-1: *Value types stored in memory*

Figure 3-1 shows how two different copies of the **Employee** structure, one referenced by the **employee1** variable and the other referenced by the **employee2** variable, are stored in memory. Any modification to the values of one of the instances will not affect the other, because they occupy different spaces in memory.

Objects, on the other hand, are passed by reference. This means that when we assign an object to a constant or a variable, a reference to the object is assigned to it, not a copy of the object. In the following example, the object in **employee2** is the same as the object in **employee1**. Any change in the **name** property is reflected in the other because both constants point to the same object in memory (they refer to the same instance).

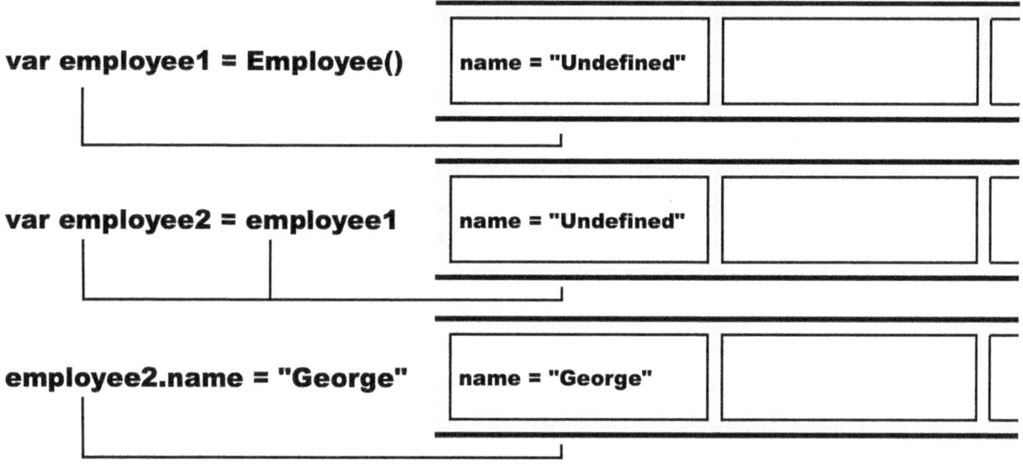

Figure 3-2: *Objects stored in memory*

Constants or variables that were assigned an object do not store the object; they store the value of the memory address where the object is located. When a constant or a variable containing this address is assigned to another constant or variable, only the address is copied, and therefore the object is not duplicated. This is the most important characteristic of objects, and what makes them suitable for situations in which data in memory must be accessed and shared by different parts of the code.

IMPORTANT: Because constants and variables store a reference to an object (a memory address), two or more variables in your code may reference the same object. If you need to know whether this is the case, you can compare the variables with the operators **===** (identical to) and **!==** (not identical to) provided by Swift. If what you need is to know whether two objects contain different information, you can use the basic operators **==** and **!=**, but you can only do this when the objects conform to the **Equatable** protocol; a protocol that determines how the objects will be compared. We will study protocols and the **Equatable** protocol later in this chapter.

Basic Self

Because the same object may be referenced by multiple constants or variables, every language that works with objects offers a way for the object to reference itself. In Swift this is done automatically, but there are situations in which this reference must be declared explicitly. For this purpose, Swift defines a special keyword called **self**. We have introduced this keyword earlier in this chapter to be able to read the current value of an enumeration from inside the instance (see Listing 3-135). In structures and objects, the **self** keyword works the same way; it references the instance the code belongs to.

The most common situation in which the use of this keyword is required is when we need to declare the names of the parameters of a method equal to the names of the object's properties.

If the names are the same, the system doesn't know whether we are referring to the property or the parameter. The **self** keyword clarifies the situation.

```
class Employee {
   var name = "Undefined"

   func changename(name: String) {
      self.name = name
   }
}
let employee1 = Employee()
employee1.changename(name: "Martin")
print("Name: \(employee1.name)")  // "Name: Martin"
```

***Listing 3-144:** Referring to the object with* `self`

The **self** keyword in the **changename()** method of Listing 3-144 represents the object created from the **Employee** class and helps the system understand what we are referring to when we use the word **name**. When we call the **changename()** method in the **employee1** object, the value of the **name** parameter is assigned to the object's **name** property (**self.name**). The **self** keyword in this example is a reference to the object stored in the **employee1** variable. This would be the same as declaring **employee1.name**, but since we do not know the name of the variable that is going to store the instance when the class is defined, we must use **self** instead.

Another useful application of the **self** keyword is to reference the data type itself. The value generated by reading the **self** keyword on a data type is called *metatype*. A metatype refers to the type itself, not an instance of it. For example, the value **Int.self** refers to the definition of the **Int** data type, not an integer number created from that type, as shown in the following example.

```
let reference = Int.self
let newnumber = reference.init(20)
print(newnumber)  // "20"
```

***Listing 3-145:** Referring to the data type with* `self`

The code in Listing 3-145 stores a reference to the **Int** data type in a constant and then uses that constant to create an instance of **Int** with the value 20. Notice that when working with metatypes we must declare the **init()** method implicitly to create an instance. Metatypes are widely used to pass references of data types to methods and initializers of other types, as we will see in further chapters.

Medium Memory Management

Because objects are stored by reference, they can be referenced by several variables at the same time. If a variable is erased, the object it references cannot be erased from memory because another variable could still be using it. This creates a situation in which the device's memory is filled with objects that are no longer necessary. The solution provided by Apple is an automatic system that counts the number of variables referencing an object and only removes the object from memory when all the references are erased (all the variables were erased, set to **nil**, or they were assigned a reference to another object). The system is called *ARC* (Automatic Reference Counting). ARC automatically erases the objects when there is no longer a constant or a variable containing a reference to that space in memory.

In an ideal scenario, this system works like magic, counting how many references we create to the same object and erasing that object when none of those references exist anymore. But there are situations in which we can create something called *Strong Reference Cycle*. This happens when two objects have a property that references the other object.

```
class Employee {
   var name: String?
   var location: Department?
}
class Department {
   var area: String?
   var person: Employee?
}
var employee: Employee? = Employee()
var department: Department? = Department()

employee?.name = "John"
employee?.location = department

department?.area = "Mail"
department?.person = employee
```

Listing 3-146: *Referencing one object from another*

This example defines two classes: **Employee** and **Department**. Both classes contain a property that references an object of the other class (**location** and **person**). After the definition, objects of each class are created and stored in the **employee** and **department** variables. The reference in the **department** variable is assigned to the **location** property of the **employee** object, and the reference in the **employee** variable is assigned to the **person** property of the **department** object. After this, each object contains a reference to the other, as shown below.

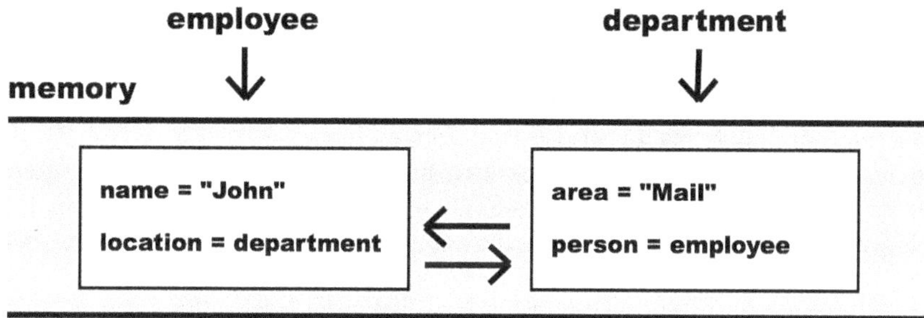

Figure 3-3: *Objects referencing each other*

At this point, each object is referenced by a variable and a property. The object of the **Employee** class is referenced by the **employee** variable and the **person** property, and the object of the **Department** class is referenced by the **department** variable and the **location** property. If, for some reason, we do not need to access these objects from our code anymore and erase or modify the values of the **employee** and **department** variables, ARC will not erase the objects from memory because their properties still have a reference that keeps them alive.

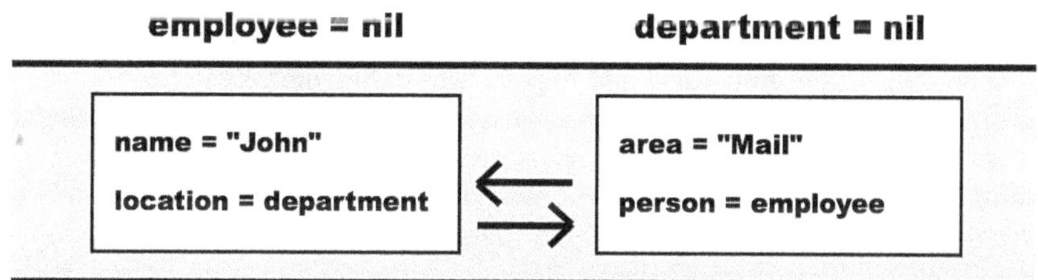

Figure 3-4: *Objects preserved in memory*

In this example, we assume that the value **nil** was assigned to the **employee** and **department** variables, and in consequence the objects are not accessible anymore, but they are preserved in memory because ARC has no way to know that they are no longer required.

Swift has solved this problem classifying the references into three categories: strong, weak, and unowned. Normal references are strong; they are always valid and the objects they point to are preserved in memory for as long as they exist. These are the kind of references we have been using so far, and that is why the cycle created by our example is called Strong Reference Cycle. The solution to break this cycle is to define one of the references as **weak** or **unowned**. When ARC encounters one of these types of references to be the last reference to an object, the object is erased from memory as if the reference had never existed.

```
class Employee {
   var name: String?
   var location: Department?
}
class Department {
   var area: String?
   weak var person: Employee?
}
var employee: Employee? = Employee()
var department: Department? = Department()

employee?.name = "John"
employee?.location = department

department?.area = "Mail"
department?.person = employee
```

Listing 3-147: *Assigning weak references*

In the code of Listing 3-147, the **person** property was declared as **weak**. Now, when the references from the variables are erased, the object created from the **Employee** class is erased from memory because the only reference left is the weak reference from the **person** property. After this object disappears, the object created from the **Department** class does not have any other strong reference either, so it is also erased from memory.

The unowned reference works the same way, but it differs with the weak reference on the type of values it applies to. Weak references apply to variables with optional values (they can be empty at some point) and unowned references apply to non-optional values (they always have a value).

IMPORTANT: Closures can create strong reference cycles if we try to access properties or methods defined outside the closure. If we need to reference properties or methods with **self** inside a closure, we can declare the reference to **self** as weak with the syntax **[weak self]** or **[unowned self]**. The expression must be declared before the closure's parameters (see Chapter 5, Listing 5-30). For more information on ARC and how to avoid strong reference cycles, visit our website and follow the links for this chapter.

Medium Inheritance

One of the main purposes of structures and objects is to define pieces of code that can be copied and shared. The code is defined once and then instances (copies) of that code are created every time they are required. This programming pattern works well when we define our own code but presents some limitations when working with code programmed by other developers and shared through libraries and frameworks. The programmers creating the code for us cannot anticipate how we are going to use it and all the possible variations required for every application. To provide a solution to this problem, classes incorporate inheritance. A class can inherit properties and methods from another class and then improve it adding some properties and methods of its own. This way, programmers can share classes and developers can adapt them to their needs.

To illustrate how inheritance works, the following examples present a situation in which a class must be expanded to contain additional information that was not initially contemplated.

```
class Employee {
   var name = "Undefined"
   var age = 0

   func createbadge() -> String {
      return "Employee \(name) \(age)"
   }
}
```

Listing 3-148: *Defining a basic class*

The **Employee** class declared in Listing 3-148 is a normal class, like those we have defined before. It has two properties and a method called **createbadge()** that returns a string with the values of the properties. This class would be enough to create objects that generate the string of text necessary to print a badge for every employee showing its name and age. But for the sake of argument, let's say that some of the employees require a badge that also displays the department they work in. One option is to define another class with the same properties and methods and add what we need, but this produces redundant code, and it is difficult to do when the class was taken from a library (they are usually too complex to modify or duplicate). The solution is to create a new class that inherits the characteristics of the basic class and adds its own properties and methods to satisfy the new requirements. To indicate that a class inherits from another class, we must write the name of the basic class after the name of the new class separated by a colon.

```
class Employee {
   var name = "Undefined"
   var age = 0

   func createbadge() -> String {
      return "Employee \(name) \(age)"
   }
}
class OfficeEmployee: Employee {
   var department = "Undefined"
}
```

Listing 3-149: *Inheriting properties and methods from another class*

The **OfficeEmployee** class added to our code in Listing 3-149 only has one property called **department**, but it inherits the **name** and **age** properties, and also the **createbadge()** method from the **Employee** class. All these properties and methods are available in any of the objects created from the **OfficeEmployee** class, as shown next.

```
class Employee {
   var name = "Undefined"
   var age = 0

   func createbadge() -> String {
      return "Employee \(name) \(age)"
   }
}
class OfficeEmployee: Employee {
   var department = "Undefined"
}
let employee = OfficeEmployee()
employee.name = "George"
employee.age = 25
employee.department = "Mail"
```

```
var badge = employee.createbadge()
print("Badge: \(badge)")  // "Badge: Employee George 25"
```

Listing 3-150: *Creating objects from a subclass*

A class like **Employee** is called *superclass*, and a class that inherits from another class like **OfficeEmployee** is called *subclass*. In these terms, we can say that the **OfficeEmployee** class is a subclass that inherits the properties and methods of its superclass **Employee**. A class can inherit from a superclass that already inherited from another superclass in an infinite chain. When a property is accessed, or a method is called, the system looks for it on the object's class and, if it is not there, it keeps looking in the superclasses up the hierarchical chain until it finds it.

IMPORTANT: Inheritance does not work the other way around. For example, considering the code in Listing 3-150, objects created from the class **OfficeEmployee** have access to the **department** property of this class and the properties and methods of the **Employee** class, but objects created from the **Employee** class do not have access to the **department** property.

Because of this hierarchical chain, sometimes a method does not have access to all the properties available for the object. For example, the **createbadge()** method called on the **employee** object created in Listing 3-150 have access to the properties declared on the **Employee** class but not those declared in the **OfficeEmployee** class. If we want the method to also print the value of the **department** property, we must implement it again in the **OfficeEmployee** class with the appropriate modifications. This is called *overriding*. To override a method of a superclass, we prefix it with the **override** keyword.

```
class Employee {
   var name = "Undefined"
   var age = 0

   func createbadge() -> String {
      return "Employee \(name) \(age)"
   }
}
class OfficeEmployee: Employee {
   var department = "Undefined"

   override func createbadge() -> String {
      return "Employee \(department) \(name) \(age)"
   }
}
let employee = OfficeEmployee()
employee.name = "George"
employee.age = 25
employee.department = "Mail"

var badge = employee.createbadge()
print("Badge: \(badge)")  // "Badge: Employee Mail George 25"
```

Listing 3-151: *Overriding an inherited method*

The new **OfficeEmployee** subclass of Listing 3-151 overrides the **createbadge()** method of its superclass to generate a string that includes the value of the **department** property. Now, when the method is executed from an object of this class, the method called is the one declared in **OfficeEmployee** (the old method from the superclass is ignored), and the badge generated includes the values of the three properties.

Using inheritance, we have created a new class without modifying previous classes or duplicating any code. The **Employee** class can create objects to store the name and age of an employee and generate a badge with this information, and the **OfficeEmployee** class can create objects to store the name, age, and the department of the employee and generate a more complete badge with the values of all these properties.

When we call the **createbadge()** method on the **employee** object created from the **OfficeEmployee** class in Listing 3-151, the method executed is the one defined in the **OfficeEmployee** class. If we want to execute the method on the superclass instead, we must use a special keyword called **super**. The **super** keyword is like the **self** keyword, but instead of referencing the object, **super** represents the superclass. It is often used when we have overridden a method, but we still need to execute the method on the superclass.

```
class Employee {
   var name = "Undefined"
   var age = 0

   func createbadge() -> String {
      return "Employee \(name) \(age)"
   }
}
class OfficeEmployee: Employee {
   var department = "Undefined"

   override func createbadge() -> String {
      let oldbadge = super.createbadge()
      return "\(oldbadge) \(department)"
   }
}
let employee = OfficeEmployee()
employee.name = "George"
employee.age = 25
employee.department = "Mail"

var badge = employee.createbadge()
print("Badge: \(badge)")  // "Badge: Employee George 25 Mail"
```

Listing 3-152: *Calling a method on the superclass*

This is the same as the previous example, but now, when the **createbadge()** method of an object created from the **OfficeEmployee** class is called, the method calls the **createbadge()** method of the superclass first and assigns the result to the **oldbadge** constant. The value of this constant is later added to the value of the **department** property to generate the final string.

Medium Type Casting

Inheritance not only transfers functionality from one class to another but also connects the classes together. The superclasses and their subclasses are linked together in a hierarchical chain. Because of this, whenever we declare a variable of the type of the superclass, objects of the subclasses can be assigned to that variable too. This is a very important feature that allows us to do things like creating arrays of objects that are of different classes but belong to the same hierarchy.

```
class Employee {
   var name = "Undefined"
   var age = 0
}
class OfficeEmployee: Employee {
   var deskNumber = 0
}
class WarehouseEmployee: Employee {
   var area = "Undefined"
}
var list: [Employee] = [OfficeEmployee(), WarehouseEmployee(),
OfficeEmployee()]
```

Listing 3-153: *Creating an array of objects from different subclasses*

This example defines a superclass called **Employee** and then two subclasses of **Employee** called **OfficeEmployee** and **WarehouseEmployee**. The purpose is to have the information for every employee in one class and then have classes for specific types of employee. Following this organization, we can create objects that only contain the **name**, **age**, and **deskNumber** properties to represent employees working at the office and objects that only contain the **name**, **age**, and **area** properties to represent employees working at the warehouse.

No matter the differences between one object and another, they all represent employees of the same company, so sooner or later we will have to include them on the same list. The class hierarchy allows us to do that. We can declare a collection of the data type of the superclass and then store objects of the subclasses in it, as we did in Listing 3-153 with the **list** array.

This is all good until we try to read the array. The elements of the array are all considered to be of type **Employee**, so we can only access the properties defined in the **Employee** class. Also, there is no way to know what type of object each element is. We could have an **OfficeEmployee** object at index 0 and later replace it by a **WarehouseEmployee** object. The indexes do not provide any information to identify the objects. Swift solve these problems with the **is** and **as** operators.

is—This operator returns a Boolean indicating whether the value is of a certain data type.

as—This operator converts a value of one class to another class when possible.

Identifying an object is easy with the **is** operator. This operator returns a Boolean value that we can use in an **if** statement to check the object's class.

```
var countOffice = 0
var countWarehouse = 0

for obj in list {
   if obj is OfficeEmployee {
      countOffice += 1
   } else if obj is WarehouseEmployee {
      countWarehouse += 1
   }
}
print("We have \(countOffice) employees working at the office")  //2
print("We have \(countWarehouse) employees working at the warehouse") //1
```

***Listing 3-154:** Identifying the object's data type*

In Listing 3-154, we create the **list** array again with objects from the same classes defined in the previous example, but this time we add a **for in** loop to iterate over the array and count how many objects of each class we have found. The **if** statement inside the loop uses the **is** operator to check if the current object stored in the **obj** constant is of type **OfficeEmployee** or **WarehouseEmployee** and increments the counter respectively (**countOffice** or **countWarehouse**).

Counting objects is not really what these operators are all about. The idea is to figure out the type with the **is** operator and then convert the object with the **as** operator to be able to access their properties and methods. The **as** operator converts a value of one type to another. The conversions are not always guaranteed, and that is why this operator comes in two more forms: **as!** and **as?**. These versions of the **as** operator work like optionals. The **as!** operator forces the conversion and returns an error if the conversion is not possible, and the **as?** operator tries to convert the object and returns an optional with the new object or **nil** in case of failure.

```
for obj in list {
   if obj is OfficeEmployee {
      let temp = obj as! OfficeEmployee
      temp.deskNumber = 100
```

```
   } else if obj is WarehouseEmployee {
      let temp = obj as! WarehouseEmployee
      temp.area = "New Area"
   }
}
```

Listing 3-155: *Casting an object*

When we use the **as!** operator we are forcing the conversion, so we need to make sure that the conversion is possible or otherwise the app will crash (this is the same that happens when we unwrap optionals with the exclamation mark). In the code of Listing 3-155, we only use this operator after we have already checked with the **is** operator that the object is of the right class. Once the object is casted (converted) into its original data type, we can access its properties and methods. In this example, the objects returned by the **as!** operator are stored in the **temp** constant and then new values are assigned to the **deskNumber** and **area** properties.

Checking for the type before casting is redundant. To simplify the code, we can use the **as?** operator. Instead of forcing the conversion and crashing the app, this version of the **as** operator tries to perform the conversion and returns an optional with the result of the operation.

```
for obj in list {
   if let temp = obj as? OfficeEmployee {
      temp.deskNumber = 100
   } else if let temp = obj as? WarehouseEmployee {
      temp.area = "New Area"
   }
}
```

Listing 3-156: *Casting an object with the* `as?` *operator*

In this example, we use optional binding to cast the object and assign the result to the **temp** constant. First, we try to cast **obj** as an **OfficeEmployee** object. If we are successful, we assign the value 100 to the **deskNumber** property, but if the value returned is **nil**, then we try to cast the object to the **WarehouseEmployee** class to modify its **area** property.

Casting can also be performed on the fly if we are sure that the conversion is possible. The statement to cast the object is the same but it must be declared between parentheses.

```
let myarea = (list[1] as! WarehouseEmployee).area
print("The area of employee 1 is \(myarea)")  // "Undefined"
```

Listing 3-157: *Casting an object on the fly*

In this example, we do not assign the object to any variable; we just cast the element of the **list** array at index 1 as a **WarehouseEmployee** object inside the parentheses and then access its **area** property. The value of this property is stored in the **myarea** constant and then printed on the console. Remember that conversions performed with the **as!** operator are only possible when we are sure it is going to be successful.

IMPORTANT: The **as!** operator is applied when the conversion is guaranteed to be successful, and the **as?** operator is used when we are not sure about the result. But we can also use the basic **as** operator when the Swift compiler can verify that the conversion will be successful, as when we are casting some primitive data types (e.g., **String** values into **NSString** objects).

The **as** operator works on objects that belong to the same class hierarchy. Because sometimes the objects that require casting are not in the same hierarchy, Swift defines several generic data types to represent values of any kind. The most frequently used are **Any**, **AnyObject**, and **AnyClass**. Taking advantage of these generic types, we can create collections with values that are not associated with each other.

```
class Employee {
   var name = "Undefined"
}
class Department {
   var area = "Undefined"
}
var list: [AnyObject] = [Employee(), Department(), Department()]

for obj in list {
   if let temp = obj as? Employee {
      temp.name = ""
   } else if let temp = obj as? Department {
      temp.area = ""
   }
}
```

Listing 3-158: *Working with objects of* `AnyObject` *type*

The **`list`** array declared in Listing 3-158 is of type **`AnyObject`** and therefore it can contain objects of any data type. To populate the array, we created two simple and independent classes: **`Employee`** and **`Department`**. A few objects are created from these classes and included in the array. The objects are later casted by the **`as?`** operator inside a **`for in`** loop and their corresponding properties are modified following the same procedure used in previous examples.

Basic Initialization

We have been initializing the properties during definition in every class declared so far. This is because classes do not provide memberwise initializers as structures do. The properties of a class have to be initialized explicitly in the definition or during instantiation by the **`init()`** method. This is the same method previously introduced for structures and we can use it in our classes as well.

```
class Employee {
   var name: String
   var age: Int

   init(name: String, age: Int) {
      self.name = name
      self.age = age
   }
}
let employee1 = Employee(name: "George", age: 28)
```

Listing 3-159: *Declaring a Designated Initializer*

The **`init()`** method declared for the **`Employee`** class in Listing 3-159 initializes every property of the class with the values specified in the **`Employee()`** initializer. This type of initializer is called *Designated Initializer*. When we declare a Designated Initializer, we need to make sure that all the properties are initialized.

If we know that in some circumstances our code will not be able to provide all the values during initialization, we can also declare a Convenience Initializer. A Convenience Initializer is an initializer that offers a convenient way to initialize an object with default values for some or all its properties. It is declared as an **`init()`** method but preceded with the **`convenience`** keyword. A Convenience Initializer must call the Designated initializer of the same class with the corresponding values.

```
class Employee {
   var name: String
   var age: Int

   init(name: String, age: Int) {
      self.name = name
      self.age = age
   }
   convenience init() {
      self.init(name: "Undefined", age: 0)
   }
}
let employee1 = Employee()
```

***Listing 3-160:** Declaring a Convenience Initializer*

When we create an instance of **Employee**, the system detects the number and type of arguments provided and executes the corresponding initializer. For example, if we provide the values for the **name** and the **age** parameters, the system executes the Designated Initializer because this is the initializer that contains the necessary parameters to receive those values, but if the initialization does not include any argument, the Convenience Initializer is executed instead and then the Designated Initializer is called with values by default ("Undefined" and 0).

Unlike structures, classes can inherit properties and methods from other classes, and this includes the **init()** method. When a subclass does not provide its own Designated Initializer, the initializer of its superclass is used instead.

```
class Employee {
   var name: String
   var age: Int

   init(name: String, age: Int) {
      self.name = name
      self.age = age
   }
}
class OfficeEmployee: Employee {
   var department: String = "Undefined"
}
let employee1 = OfficeEmployee(name: "George", age: 29)
```

***Listing 3-161:** Inheriting the Designated Initializer*

The code in Listing 3-161 defines the subclass **OfficeEmployee** that inherits from the **Employee** class. The **OfficeEmployee** class does not provide any initializer, so the only initializer available is the one provided by its superclass. This initializer only initializes the properties **name** and **age**. The **department** property of **OfficeEmployee** is explicitly initialized with the value "Undefined". To provide an initializer that also includes this property, we must declare a new Designated Initializer in the **OfficeEmployee** class.

```
class Employee {
   var name: String
   var age: Int

   init(name: String, age: Int) {
      self.name = name
      self.age = age
   }
}
```

```
class OfficeEmployee: Employee {
   var department: String

   init(name: String, age: Int, department: String) {
      self.department = department

      super.init(name: name, age: age)
   }
}
let employee1 = OfficeEmployee(name: "John", age: 24, department: "Mail")
```

Listing 3-162: *Declaring a Designated Initializer for the subclass*

The Designated Initializer of a subclass must initialize the properties of its own class first and then call the initializer of its superclass. This is done by calling the **init()** method on **super**. The **super** keyword refers to the superclass, so when the system executes the **super.init()** statement in the code of Listing 3-162, the **init()** method of the superclass is executed and the **name** and **age** properties of this class are initialized.

IMPORTANT: There are different ways to combine Designated and Convenience initializers. The possibility of classes to inherit from other classes in an unlimited chain can turn initialization into a very complex process. This book does not explore all the possibilities provided by Swift for initialization. For more information, visit our website and follow the links for this chapter.

Advanced Deinitialization

There is a counterpart of the initialization process called *Deinitialization*. Despite its name, this process is not directly related to the initialization process but rather to the ARC system. ARC, as we studied previously in this chapter, is an automatic system adopted by Swift to manage memory. Letting the system manage the memory and take care of removing the objects our program does no longer need presents a huge advantage, but it also means that we do not always know when an object is going to be removed. There are times when an object is using resources that must be closed or information that needs to be stored. Whatever the task, Swift offers the **deinit** method to execute any last-minute instructions we need before the object is erased from memory.

```
class Item {
   var quantity = 0.0
   var name = "Not defined"
   var price = 0.0

   deinit {
      print("This instance was erased")
   }
}
var purchase: Item? = Item()
purchase = nil
```

Listing 3-163: *Declaring a deinitializer*

This example defines a simple class with a deinitializer. The object is created and assigned to an optional variable. Right after that, the **nil** value is assigned to the same variable to erase the reference and test the **deinit** method, which prints a message on the console.

Advanced Access Control and Modifiers

Swift defines keywords (also called *modifiers*) that can be applied to entities (classes, structures, properties, methods, etc.) to confer them special attributes. We have already seen the **mutating** and **override** keyword, but there are more available, like the following.

lazy—This keyword defines a property whose initial value is not assigned until the property is used for the first time.

final—This keyword is used on a class when we don't want to allow the code to create subclasses of it. It must be declared before the **class** keyword.

The **lazy** keyword is frequently used when the property's value may take time to be determined and we do not want the initialization of the structure or the class to be delayed. For example, we may have a property that stores a name retrieved from a server, which is a resource intensive task that we should perform only when the value is required.

```
class Employee {
   lazy var name: String = {
      // Loading name from a server
      print("Loading...")

      return "Undefined"
   }()
   var age = 0
}
let employee = Employee()
```

***Listing 3-164:** Defining `lazy` properties*

The **Employee** class in Listing 3-164 defines two properties, **name** and **age**, but this time a closure is assigned to the **name** property to get the employee's name from a server (we will see how to retrieve information from the Web in Chapter 19). Because we declared this property as **lazy**, the closure will only be executed when we try to read the property's value. If we execute the example as it is, we get nothing in return, but if we read the **name** property with a statement at the end, we will see the text "Loading..." printed on the console.

The Swift language also includes keywords in charge of defining the level of access for each entity in our code. Access control in Swift is based on modules and source files, but it also applies to single properties and methods. Source files are the files we create for our application, the properties and methods are the ones we have created for our structures and classes in previous examples, and modules are units of code that are related. For instance, a single application and each of the frameworks included in it are considered modules (we will introduce frameworks in Chapter 4). Considering this classification, Swift defines five keywords to determine accessibility.

open—This keyword determines that an entity is accessible from the module it belongs to and other modules.

public—This keyword determines that an entity is accessible from the module it belongs to and other modules. The difference between **public** and **open** is that we can't create subclasses of **public** classes outside the module in which they were defined. This also applies to methods and properties (e.g., **public** methods can't be overridden outside the module in which they were declared).

internal—This keyword determines that an entity is accessible only inside the module in which it was created. This is the default access mode for applications. By default, every entity defined in our application is only accessible from inside the application.

private—This keyword determines that an entity is accessible only from the context in which it was created (e.g., a **private** property in a class will only be accessible from methods of the same class).

fileprivate—This keyword determines that an entity is accessible only from the file in which it was declared (e.g., a **fileprivate** property in a class will only be accessible by other entities defined inside the file in which it was declared).

As we will see later, most of these keywords apply to frameworks and are rarely used in single applications. By default, the properties and methods we include in our classes and structures are declared **internal**, which means that our classes and structures are only available from inside our application (module). Unless we are creating our own frameworks, this is all we need for our applications, and is the reason why we didn't have to specify any keyword when we defined our structures and classes before. All our classes and structures are accessible by the rest of the code inside our application, but if we want to have a level of control in our data types or avoid modifying values by mistake, we can declare some of them as **private**, as in the following example.

```
class Employee {
   private var name = "Undefined"
   private var age = 0

   func showValues() {
      print("Name: \(name)")
      print("Age: \(age)")
   }
}
let employee = Employee()
employee.showValues()
```

Listing 3-165: *Declaring* `private` *properties*

The code in Listing 3-165 defines the **name** and **age** properties of our **Employee** class as **private** and adds a method called **showValues()** to access their values. Due to access control, these properties are only accessible by the method in the class. If we try to read their values from outside the object using dot notation, Xcode will return an error (**employee.name**).

If what we want is to be able to read the property from outside the object but not allow assigning new values to it, we can declare it with a public getter but a private setter.

```
class Employee {
   private var name = "Undefined"
   public private(set) var age = 0

   func setAge(newAge: Int) {
      age = newAge
   }
}
let employee = Employee()
employee.setAge(newAge: 25)
print(employee.age)
```

Listing 3-166: *Declaring a public getter and private setter*

The **age** property in the **Employee** class of Listing 3-166 was declared as public, so everyone can read its value, but with a private setter (**private(set)**), so only the methods inside the class can modify it. To change the value, we defined the **setAge()** method. The code creates an instance of the class and calls the method, but this time we can read the value of the **age** property and print it on the console because it was declared with a public getter.

Basic 3.6 Protocols

The main characteristics of classes, and therefore objects, are the capacity to encapsulate data and functionality and the possibility to share and improve code through inheritance. This introduced an advantage over previous paradigms and turned Object-Oriented Programming into the industry standard for a while. But that changed with the introduction of protocols in Swift. Protocols define properties and methods that structures can have in common. This means that Swift's structures not only can encapsulate data and functionality, just like objects, but by conforming to protocols they can also share code. Figure 3-5 illustrates the differences between these two paradigms.

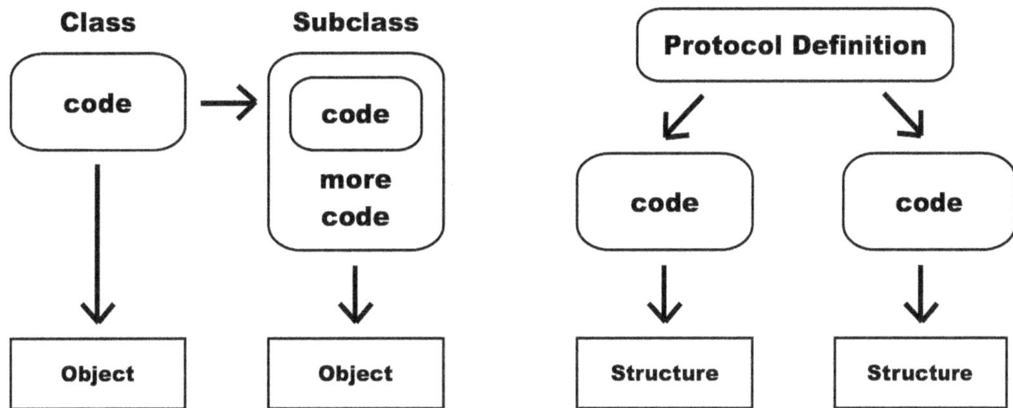

Figure 3-5: *Object-Oriented Programming versus Protocol-Oriented Programming*

In OOP, the code is implemented inside a class and then objects are created from that class. If we need to create objects with additional functionality, we must define a subclass that inherits the code from the superclass and adds some of its own. Protocols offer a slightly different approach. The properties and methods we want the structures to have in common are defined in the protocol and then implemented by the structures' definitions. This lets us associate different structures together through a common pattern. The code implemented by each structure is unique, but they follow a blueprint set by the protocol. If we know that a structure uses a protocol, we can always be sure that besides its own definitions, it will also include the properties and methods defined by the protocol. In addition, protocols can be extended to provide their own implementations of the properties and methods we want the structures to have in common, allowing the paradigm to completely replace classes and objects.

IMPORTANT: The Swift paradigm is built from the combination of structures and protocols, but protocols may also be adopted by enumerations and classes. For instance, Objective-C and the frameworks programmed in this language use protocols to offer a programming pattern called *Delegation*. We will study how classes conform to protocols and how to implement delegation later.

Basic Definition of Protocols

Protocols are defined with the **`protocol`** keyword followed by the name and the list of properties and methods between braces. No values or statements are assigned or declared inside a protocol, only the names and the corresponding types. Because of this, methods are defined as always, but they omit the braces and the statements, and properties must include the **`get`** and **`set`** keywords between braces to indicate whether they are read-only properties, or we can read and assign values to them (see Listing 3-43 for an example of getters and setters). To indicate that the structure conforms to the protocol, we must include the protocol's name after the structure's name separated by a colon, as shown in the following example.

```
protocol Printer {
   var name: String { get set }
   func printdescription()
}
struct Employees: Printer {
   var name: String
   var age: Int

   func printdescription() {
      print("Description: \(name) \(age)")  // "Description: John 32"
   }
}
let employee1 = Employees(name: "John", age: 32)
employee1.printdescription()
```

Listing 3-167: *Defining protocols*

A protocol tells the structure what properties and methods are required, but the structure must implement them. In the example of Listing 3-167, we define a protocol called **Printer** that includes the **name** property and the **printdescription()** method. The **Employees** structure defined next conforms to this protocol, and along with the protocol's property and method it also implements its own property called **age**. Although this property was not defined in the protocol, we can read it inside the **printdescription()** method and print its value.

The advantage of this practice is evident when structures of different types conform to the same protocol, as shown in the following example.

```
protocol Printer {
   var name: String { get set }
   func printdescription()
}
struct Employees: Printer {
   var name: String
   var age: Int

   func printdescription() {
      print("Description: \(name) \(age)")
   }
}
struct Offices: Printer {
   var name: String
   var employees: Int

   func printdescription() {
      print("Description: \(name) \(employees)") // "Description: Mail 2"
   }
}
let employee1 = Employees(name: "John", age: 32)
let office1 = Offices(name: "Mail", employees: 2)
office1.printdescription()
```

Listing 3-168: *Defining multiple structures that conform to the same protocol*

Although the structures created in Listing 3-168 from the **Employees** and **Offices** definitions are different (they have different properties), they both conform to the **Printer** protocol and provide their own implementation of the **printdescription()** method. The common functionality defined by the protocol ensures that no matter what type of structure we are working with, it will always have an implementation of **printdescription()**.

Protocols are also data types. We can treat a structure as if it is of the data type of the protocol it conforms to. This allows us to associate structures by their common functionality.

```
let employee1 = Employees(name: "John", age: 32)
let office1 = Offices(name: "Mail", employees: 2)

var list: [Printer] = [employee1, office1]
for element in list {
   element.printdescription()
}
```

Listing 3-169: *Using protocols as data types*

Listing 3-169 uses the same protocol and structures defined in the previous example, but this time it stores the instances in an array. The type of the array was defined as **Printer**, which means the array may contain structures of any type as long as they conform to the **Printer** protocol. Because of this, no matter the element's data type (**Employees** or **Offices**) we know that they always have an implementation of the **name** property and the **printdescription()** method.

When we process a structure or an object as a protocol type, we can only access the properties and methods defined by the protocol. If we need to access the instance's own properties and methods, we must cast it using the **as** operator as we did with classes before. The following example prints the value of the **age** property if the element of the array is of type **Employees**.

```
let employee1 = Employees(name: "John", age: 32)
let office1 = Offices(name: "Mail", employees: 2)

var list: [Printer] = [employee1, office1]
for element in list {
   if let employee = element as? Employees {
      print(employee.age)  // "32"
   }
   element.printdescription()
}
```

Listing 3-170: *Accessing the instance's own properties*

Because protocols are data types, we can use them to define variables, or return them from functions. The following example declares a function that returns a value of type **Printer**.

```
func getFile(type: Int) -> Printer {
   var data: Printer!
   if type == 1 {
      data = Employees(name: "John", age: 32)
   } else if type == 2 {
      data = Offices(name: "Mail", employees: 2)
   }
   return data
}
let file = getFile(type: 1)
file.printdescription()  // "Description: John 32"
```

Listing 3-171: *Returning values of a protocol data type*

The **getFile()** function in Listing 3-171 creates an instance of a structure depending on the value received. If the **type** parameter is equal to 1, it returns an instance of **Employees**, but if the value is equal to 2, it returns an instance of **Offices**. But because the value returned by the function is of type **Printer** we know it will always include the **printdescription()** method.

Advanced Generic Protocols

Protocols can also define generic properties and methods, but they work slightly different than the generic types studied before. When we want to define a protocol with a generic property or method, we first must define the name of the generic type with the **associatedtype** keyword.

```
protocol Printer {
   associatedtype protype
   var name: protype { get set }
}
struct Employees: Printer {
   var name: String
}
let employee = Employees(name: "John")
print(employee.name)  // "John"
```

Listing 3-172: *Defining generic protocols*

The code in Listing 3-172 defines a generic protocol called **Printer** and a structure that conforms to that protocol called **Employees**. The protocol defines a generic type with the name **protype** and then a property of that type. The property's real data type is defined by the structure or the class that conforms to the protocol. In this case, the **Employees** structure defines the **name** property to be of type **String**, and that's the type of values we can use in the instances of this structure, but we could have declared the property as an integer or any other data type we needed.

Medium Swift Protocols

The Swift language makes use of protocols extensively. Almost every API includes protocols that define common features and behavior for their data types, including enumerations, structures, and classes. But there are also important protocols defined in the Swift Standard Library that we can use to improve our custom data types. The following are some of the protocols available.

Equatable—This protocol defines a data type which values can be compared with other values of the same type using the operators == and !=.

Comparable—This protocol defines a data type which values can be compared with other values of the same type using the operators >, <, >=, and <=.

Numeric—This protocol defines a data type that only works with values that can participate in arithmetic operations.

Hashable—This protocol defines a data type that provides the hash value (unique identifier) required for the value to be included in collections, such as sets and dictionaries.

CaseIterable—This protocol defines a data type, usually an enumeration without associated values, that includes a property called **allCases** that contains the collection of all the cases included in the data type.

These protocols are responsible of elemental processes performed by the system and the Swift language. For example, when we compare two values with the == or != operators, the system checks whether the values conform to the **Equatable** protocol and then calls a type method in the values' data types to compare them and solve the condition (true or false, depending on whether the values are equal or not). Swift primitive data types conform to the **Equatable** protocol and implement its methods, but we can also implement them in our own data types to compare their values. For this purpose, we must declare that the data type conforms to the protocol and implement the methods required by it. The **Equatable** protocol requires only one method called **==** to check for equality (the system infers that if two values are not equal, they are different, and therefore the method for the != operator is optional). This method must have a name equal to the operator (**==**), receive the two values to compare, and return a Boolean value to communicate the result of the comparison. For instance, we can make our **Employees** structure conform to the **Equatable** protocol and implement a method with the name **==** to be able to compare two different instances of the same structure.

```
struct Employees: Equatable {
   var name: String
   var age: Int

   static func == (value1: Employees, value2: Employees) -> Bool {
      return value1.age == value2.age
   }
}
let employee1 = Employees(name: "John", age: 32)
let employee2 = Employees(name: "George", age: 32)

let message = employee1 == employee2 ? "Equal" : "Different"
print(message)  // "Equal"
```

***Listing 3-173:** Conforming to the* `Equatable` *protocol*

In this example, we use the **==** method to compare the values of the **age** properties and therefore the structures are going to be equal when the employees are the same age. In this case, both instances are created with the value 32 and therefore the value "Equal" is assigned to the **message** constant when we compare the objects with the ternary operator.

If what we want is to compare each of the properties in the structure, then we can omit the method. When we conform to the **Equatable** protocol, the compiler automatically generates the method for us to compare all the values of the structure (in this case, **name** and **age**).

```
struct Employees: Equatable {
   var name: String
   var age: Int
}
let employee1 = Employees(name: "John", age: 32)
let employee2 = Employees(name: "George", age: 32)

let message = employee1 == employee2 ? "Equal" : "Different"
print(message)  // "Different"
```

***Listing 3-174:** Letting the compiler create the protocol methods for us*

Because we did not declare the **==** method in the example of Listing 3-174, the system creates the method for us and compares the values of both properties. As a result, the objects are considered different (the ages are the same, but the names are different)

Of course, we could have compared the properties directly (**employee1.name == employee2.name**) but being able to compare the objects instead simplifies the code and allows us to use our structures (or objects) in APIs that require the values to be comparable. For example, when we created a generic function earlier in this chapter, we could not perform any operations on the values (see Listing 3-15). Because the data type we used in those functions is generic, Swift is incapable of knowing the capabilities of the data type and therefore Xcode returns an error if we try to perform operations on the values, but we can easily change the situation by making the generic type conform to a protocol. This feature is called *type constraint* because it constrains the generic type to a data type with certain capabilities. For instance, the function in the following example receives two generic values, but only of a data type that conforms to the **Equatable** protocol, and therefore we can compare the values inside the function.

```swift
struct Employees: Equatable {
   var name: String
   var age: Int
}
func compareValues<T: Equatable>(value1: T, value2: T) -> String {
   let message = value1 == value2 ? "equal" : "different"
   return message
}
let employee1 = Employees(name: "George", age: 55)
let employee2 = Employees(name: "Robert", age: 55)

let result = compareValues(value1: employee1, value2: employee2)
print("The values are \(result)")  // "The values are different"
```

***Listing 3-175:** Adding a type constraint to a generic function*

The conformance to the protocol is specified inside the angle brackets after the name of the generic type. The **compareValues()** function in Listing 3-175 declares the **T** type to conform to **Equatable** and then compares the values with a ternary operator and returns the result. In this case, the ages of the employees are the same (55), but the names are different ("George" and "Robert"), and therefore the system considers the structures to be different.

Another protocol used as a type constraint is **Numeric**. This protocol determines that the data types of the values received by the function must support arithmetic operations.

```swift
func calculateResult<T: Numeric>(value1: T, value2: T) {
   print(value1 + value2)  // 7.5
}
calculateResult(value1: 3.5, value2: 4)
```

***Listing 3-176:** Using the* `Numeric` *protocol to set a type constraint*

The **calculateResult()** function in Listing 3-176 is a generic function and therefore it can receive any value of any type, but because we set a type constraint with the **Numeric** protocol, the function can only receive values of data types that can participate in arithmetic operations.

Besides comparing for equality with the **Equatable** protocol, we can also compare magnitudes with the **Comparable** protocol. This protocol is like **Equatable**, but the system does not offer a default implementation of the type methods, we must implement them ourselves. The protocol requires four methods to represent the operations >, <, >= and <=. In the following example, we compare the ages of the employees.

```swift
struct Employees: Comparable {
   var name: String
   var age: Int

   static func > (value1: Employees, value2: Employees) -> Bool {
      return value1.age > value2.age
   }
   static func < (value1: Employees, value2: Employees) -> Bool {
      return value1.age < value2.age
   }
   static func >= (value1: Employees, value2: Employees) -> Bool {
      return value1.age >= value2.age
   }
   static func <= (value1: Employees, value2: Employees) -> Bool {
      return value1.age <= value2.age
   }
}
let employee1 = Employees(name: "George", age: 32)
let employee2 = Employees(name: "Robert", age: 55)
```

```
if employee1 > employee2 {
   print("\(employee1.name) is older")
} else {
   print("\(employee2.name) is older")  // "Robert is older"
}
```

Listing 3-177: *Conforming to the* `Comparable` *protocol*

When we compare two instances of the **`Employees`** structure, the system calls the corresponding type method and the method returns **`true`** or **`false`** according to the values of the **`age`** properties. Because in this example the value of **`age`** in the **`employee1`** structure is not greater than the value of **`age`** in the **`employee2`** structure, we get the message "Robert is older".

Another useful protocol is **`Hashable`**. Every time we include a structure or an object in a set or use them as the index of a dictionary, the system requires the data type to provide a hash value that can be used to uniquely identify each item. This is a random integer that is created based on the values of the properties. The function of the **`Hashable`** protocol is to define properties and methods to handle this value. Most of the data types defined by Swift conform to this protocol and that is why we do not have any problems when including these values in a set or as the index of dictionaries, but for custom structures and objects we must provide the hash value ourselves. Fortunately, if the values in our data type are already Hashable, we do not need a specific property to be used to create the hash value, all we need to do is to conform to the protocol and the system creates the value for us. The following example makes the **`Employees`** structure conform to the **`Hashable`** protocol, so we can include the instances in a set.

```
struct Employees: Hashable {
   var name: String
   var age: Int
}
let employee1 = Employees(name: "John", age: 32)
let employee2 = Employees(name: "Robert", age: 55)

let list: Set<Employees> = [employee1, employee2]
for item in list {
   print(item.name)
}
```

Listing 3-178: *Conforming to the* `Hashable` *protocol*

Hash values are random integers created based on the values of the properties. If we just conform to the protocol, the system uses the values of all the properties in the instance to create it (all the properties must be hashable), but we can specify which properties should be included by implementing the properties and methods defined by the protocol.

hashValue—This property returns the instance's hash value. It is of type **`Int`**.

hash(into: inout Hasher)—This method defines the properties that are going to be included in the hasher to create the hash value.

To calculate the hash value, the Swift Standard Library includes a structure called **`Hasher`**. This is the structure received by the **`hash(into:)`** method and it contains a method called **`combine()`** to tell the hasher which properties should be used to create the value. The following example illustrates how to implement the **`hash(into:)`** method and call the **`combine()`** method on the hasher to create a hash value from the value of the **`name`** property.

```
struct Employees: Hashable {
   var name: String
   var age: Int
```

```
    func hash(into hasher: inout Hasher) {
        hasher.combine(name)
    }
}
let employee = Employees(name: "George", age: 32)
print(employee.hashValue)  // e.g., 7722685913545470055
```

Listing 3-179: Defining our own hash value

At the end of Listing 3-179, we print the value of the **hashValue** property. Because the resulting value is always an integer calculated randomly every time the app is executed, we won't notice any difference, but this procedure may be useful when we manage sensitive information.

IMPORTANT: The Foundation framework includes a global function called **UUID()** that creates and returns a UUID value. This is a unique value that can be used to identify instances of custom data types. We will study Foundation in the next chapter and implement UUID values in Chapter 10.

The last protocol from our list is called **CaseIterable**. This is a simple protocol that defines a property called **allCases** to store a collection with all the cases in an enumeration. Again, the system automatically initializes this property, so all we need to do is to declare that the enumeration conforms to the protocol. In the following example, we define an enumeration with three cases and then iterate through the collection in the **allCases** property to print the names.

```
enum Departments: CaseIterable {
    case mail
    case marketing
    case managing
}
var message = ""
for department in Departments.allCases {
    message += "\(department) "
}
print(message)  // "mail marketing managing "
```

Listing 3-180: Conforming to the `CaseIterable` *protocol*

Medium Extensions

Protocols only define the properties and methods that the data types will have in common, but they do not include any implementation. However, we can implement properties and methods that will be common to all the data types that conform to the protocol by taking advantage of a feature of the Swift language called *extensions*. Extensions are special declarations that add functionality to an existent data type. We can use them with structures, enumerations, and classes, but they are particularly useful with protocols because this is the way protocols can provide their own functionality. The syntax includes the **extension** keyword followed by the name of the data type we want to extend. The following example recreates the **Printer** protocol introduced in previous examples and extends it with a method called **printdescription()**.

```
protocol Printer {
    var name: String { get set }
}
extension Printer {
    func printdescription() {
        print("The name is \(name)")
    }
}
```

```
struct Employees: Printer {
   var name: String
   var age: Int
}
struct Offices: Printer {
   var name: String
   var employees: Int
}
let employee = Employees(name: "John", age: 45)
let office = Offices(name: "Mail", employees: 2)

employee.printdescription()  // "The name is John"
office.printdescription()  // "The name is Mail"
```

Listing 3-181: *Extending a protocol*

In this example, we define a **Printer** protocol with just the **name** property and then extend it to include a common implementation of the **printdescription()** method. Now, the **Employees** and **Offices** structures in our example share the same implementation and produce the same result when their **printdescription()** methods are executed.

As we already mentioned, extensions are not only available for protocols but also for any other data type. We can use them to extend structures, enumerations, or classes. This is particularly useful when we do not have access to the definitions of the data types and need to add some functionality (like when they are part of a library or framework). In the following example, we extend the **Int** structure to provide a method that prints a description of its value.

```
extension Int {
   func printdescription() {
      print("The number is \(self)")
   }
}
let number = 25
number.printdescription()  // "The number is 25"
```

Listing 3-182: *Extending data types*

The **Int** data type is a structure defined in the Swift Standard Library. We cannot modify its definition, but we can extend it to add more functionality. In this example, we add a method called **printdescription()** to print a message with the current value (notice the use of the **self** keyword to refer to the instance). This method is not included in the original definition, but it is now available in our code.

Of course, we can also extend our own data types if we consider that appropriate. The following example extends our **Employees** structure to add a new method.

```
struct Employees {
   var name: String
   var age: Int
}
extension Employees {
   func printbadge() {
      print("Name: \(name) Age: \(age)")
   }
}
let employee = Employees(name: "John", age: 50)
employee.printbadge()  // "Name: John Age: 50"
```

Listing 3-183: *Extending custom data types*

Extensions can also be conditional. For instance, if we have a generic structure, we can add an extension only for specific types of values. The condition is determined by the **where** clause. The clause works like an **if** statement, so the extension is only applied if the condition is met.

```
struct Employees<T> {
   var value: T
}
extension Employees where T == Int {
   func doubleValue() {
      print("\(value) times 2 = \(value * 2)")
   }
}
let employee = Employees(value: 25)
employee.doubleValue()  // "25 times 2 = 50"
```

***Listing 3-184:** Defining a conditional extension*

In this example, we define a generic structure called **Employees** with a generic property called **value** and then define an extension for this structure with a method called **doubleValue()**, but this method will only be added to the instance if the data type used to create the instance is **Int**. At the end, we create an instance with the value 25 and call the method, which multiplies the value by 2 and prints a string with the result. This works because we created the instance with an integer, but if we try to use another type of value, Xcode will show an error.

Another useful implementation of extensions is the customization of string interpolation. We have introduced string interpolation in Chapter 2 and have been using it in almost every example to insert values into strings (e.g., **print("My name is \(name)")**). What we haven't mentioned is that these values are managed by a structure called **String.StringInterpolation** (a typealias of **DefaultStringInterpolation**) and that by extending this structure we can customize how the system processes the values. The **StringInterpolation** structure includes the following methods for this purpose.

appendInterpolation(Value**)**—This method interpolates the value provided by the argument into the final string.

appendLiteral(String**)**—This method adds the string provided by the argument to the interpolation.

To customize the interpolation, we extend the **StringInterpolation** structure with an overload of the **appendInterpolation()** method, process the value inside this method, and finally append the result to the interpolation with the **appendLiteral()** method.

```
extension String.StringInterpolation {
   mutating func appendInterpolation(celsius value: Double) {
      let fahrenheit = ((value * 9)/5) + 32
      appendLiteral(String(fahrenheit))
   }
}
print("Temperature in Fahrenheit \(celsius: 25)")
```

***Listing 3-185:** Customizing string interpolation*

The **appendInterpolation()** method can take as many parameters as we need. In this example, we define only one parameter with the name **value** and the label **celsius**. When we create a string with this label and a number, the method is executed. Inside, we use the formula to turn Celsius degrees into Fahrenheit and then add the result to the interpolation with the **appendLiteral()** method to get the string "Temperature in Fahrenheit 77.0".

Medium Delegates

As we have already seen, an instance of a structure or an object can be assigned to the property of another instance. For example, we could have an instance of a structure called **Employees** with a property that contains an instance of a structure called **Offices** to store information about the office where the employee works. This opens the door to new programming patterns where the instances adopt different roles. The most useful pattern is called *delegation*. A structure or object delegates responsibility for the execution of certain tasks to another structure or object.

```
struct Salary {
   func showMoney(name: String, money: Double) {
      print("The salary of \(name) is \(money)")
   }
}
struct Employees {
   var name: String
   var money: Double

   var delegate: Salary

   func generatereport() {
      delegate.showMoney(name: name, money: money)
   }
}
let salary = Salary()
var employee1 = Employees(name: "John", money: 45000, delegate: salary)

employee1.generatereport()  // "The salary of John is 45000.0"
```

Listing 3-186: *Delegating tasks*

The **Employees** structure in Listing 3-186 contains three properties. The properties **name** and **money** store the employee's data, while the **delegate** property stores the instance of the **Salary** structure in charge of printing that data. The code creates the **Salary** instance first and then uses this value to create the **Employees** instance. When we call the **generatereport()** method on the **employee1** structure at the end, the method calls the **showmoney()** method on **delegate**, effectively delegating the task of printing the data to this structure.

This pattern presents two problems. First, the structure that is delegating needs to know the data type of the structure that is going to become the delegate (in our example, the **delegate** property had to be declared of type **Salary**). Following this approach, not every structure can be a delegate, only the ones specified in the definition (only structures of type **Salary** can be delegates of structures of type **Employee**). The second problem is related to how we know which are the properties and methods that the delegate must implement. If the structure is too complex or is taken from a library, we could forget to implement some methods or properties and get an error when the structure tries to access them. Both problems are solved by protocols. Instead of declaring a specific structure as the delegate, we define a protocol and declare the **delegate** property to be of that type, as shown in the following example.

```
protocol SalaryProtocol {
   func showMoney(name: String, money: Double)
}
struct Salary: SalaryProtocol {
   func showMoney(name: String, money: Double) {
      print("The salary of \(name) is \(money)")
   }
}
```

```
struct Employees {
   var name: String
   var money: Double

   var delegate: SalaryProtocol

   func generatereport() {
      delegate.showMoney(name: name, money: money)
   }
}
let salary = Salary()
let employee1 = Employees(name: "John", money: 45000, delegate: salary)
employee1.generatereport()  // "The salary of John is 45000.0"
```

Listing 3-187: *Delegating with protocols*

The **delegate** property of the **Employees** structure is now of type **SalaryProtocol**, which means that it can store any instance of any type providing that it conforms to the **SalaryProtocol** protocol. As shown by this example, the advantage of protocols is that we can use structures of different types to perform the task. It doesn't matter what type they are as long as they conform to the delegate's protocol and implement its properties and methods. For example, we could create two different structures to print the data of our last example and assign to the delegate one instance or another depending on what we want to achieve.

```
protocol SalaryProtocol {
   func showMoney(name: String, money: Double)
}
struct Salary: SalaryProtocol {
   func showMoney(name: String, money: Double) {
      print("The salary of \(name) is \(money)")
   }
}
struct BasicSalary: SalaryProtocol {
   func showMoney(name: String, money: Double) {
      if money > 40000 {
         print("Salary is over the minimum")
      } else {
         print("The salary of \(name) is \(money)")
      }
   }
}
struct Employees {
   var name: String
   var money: Double
   var delegate: SalaryProtocol

   func generatereport() {
      delegate.showMoney(name: name, money: money)
   }
}
let salary = Salary()
var employee1 = Employees(name: "John", money: 45000, delegate: salary)

employee1.delegate = BasicSalary()
employee1.generatereport()  // "Salary is over the minimum"
```

Listing 3-188: *Using different delegates*

The **BasicSalary** structure added in Listing 3-188 conforms to the **SalaryProtocol** protocol and implements its **showMoney()** method, but unlike the **Salary** structure, it produces two different results depending on the employee's salary. The output produced by the execution of the **generatereport()** method on the **Employees** structure now depends on the type of structure we previously assigned to the **delegate** property.

Medium 3.7 Errors

Errors are common in computer programming. Either our code or the code provided by libraries and frameworks may return errors. No matter how many precautions we take, we can't never guarantee success and many problems may be found as our code tries to serve its purpose. For this reason, Swift introduces a systematic process to handle errors called *Error Handling*.

Medium Throwing Errors

When a method reports an error, it is said that it *throws* an error. Several frameworks provided by Apple are already programmed to throw errors, as we will see in further chapters, but we can also do it from our own structures and classes. To throw an error, we must use the **throw** and **throws** keywords. The **throw** keyword is used to throw the error and the **throws** keyword is specified in the method's declaration to indicate that the method can throw errors.

Because a method can throw multiple errors, we also must indicate the type of error found with values of an enumeration type. This is a custom enumeration that conforms to the **Error** protocol. For instance, let's consider the following example.

```
struct Stock {
   var totalLamps = 5
   mutating func sold(amount: Int) {
      totalLamps = totalLamps - amount
   }
}
var mystock = Stock()

mystock.sold(amount: 8)
print("Lamps in stock: \(mystock.totalLamps)")  // "Lamps in stock: -3"
```

Listing 3-189: *Producing an error inside a method*

The code in Listing 3-189 defines a structure called **Stock** that manages the stock of lamps available in the store. The class includes the **totalLamps** property to store the number of lamps we still have available and the **sold()** method to process the lamps sold. The method updates the stock by subtracting the number of lamps we have sold from the value of the **totalLamps** property. If the number of lamps sold is less than the number of lamps in stock, everything is fine, but when we sell more lamps than we have, as in this example, there is clearly a problem.

To throw an error, we must define the types of errors available for the method, declare the method as a throwing method adding the **throws** keyword in the declaration (between the arguments and the returning data types), detect the error, and throw it with the **throw** keyword.

```
enum Errors: Error {
   case OutOfStock
}
struct Stock {
   var totalLamps = 5
   mutating func sold(amount: Int) throws {
      if amount > totalLamps {
         throw Errors.OutOfStock
      } else {
         totalLamps = totalLamps - amount
      }
   }
}
var mystock = Stock()
```

Listing 3-190: *Throwing errors*

In this example, we declare an enumeration called **Errors** that conforms to the **Error** protocol and includes a case called **OutOfStock**. By declaring **sold()** as a throwing method with the **throws** keyword, we can now throw the **OutOfStock** error every time we try to sell more lamps than we have. If the lamps sold are more than the number of lamps in stock, the method throws the error, otherwise the stock is updated.

Medium Handling Errors

Now that we have a method that can throw errors, we must handle the errors when the method is executed. Swift includes the **try** keyword and the **do catch** statements for this purpose. The **do catch** statements create two blocks of code. If the statements inside the **do** block return an error, the statements in the **catch** block are executed. To execute a method that throws errors, we must call the method inside the **do** statement with the **try** keyword in front of it.

```
enum Errors: Error {
   case OutOfStock
}
struct Stock {
   var totalLamps = 5
   mutating func sold(amount: Int) throws {
      if amount > totalLamps {
         throw Errors.OutOfStock
      } else {
         totalLamps = totalLamps - amount
      }
   }
}
var mystock = Stock()

do {
   try mystock.sold(amount: 8)
} catch Errors.OutOfStock {
   print("We do not have enough lamps")
}
```

***Listing 3-191:** Handling errors*

The code in Listing 3-191 expands the previous example to handle the error thrown by the **sold()** method. Because of the addition of the **try** keyword, the system tries to execute the **sold()** method in the **mystock** structure and check for errors. If the method returns the **OutOfStock** error, the statements inside the **catch** block are executed. This pattern allows us to respond every time there is an error and report it to the user or correct the situation without having to crash the app or produce unexpected results.

Do It Yourself: Create a new Playground file. Copy the code in Listing 3-191 inside the file. You should see the message "We do not have enough lamps" printed on the console. Replace the number 8 with the number 3. Now the message should not be printed because there are enough lamps in stock.

IMPORTANT: You can add as many errors as you need to the **Errors** enumeration. The errors can be checked later with multiple **catch** statements in sequence. Also, you may add all the statements you need to the **do** block. The statements before **try** are always executed, while the statements after **try** are only executed if no error is found.

If the error is not one of the types we are expecting, we can print information about it. The information is stored in a constant called **error** that we can read inside the **catch** block.

```
enum Errors: String, Error {
   case OutOfStock = "Hello"
}
struct Stock {
   var totalLamps = 5
   mutating func sold(amount: Int) throws {
      if amount > totalLamps {
         throw Errors.OutOfStock
      } else {
         totalLamps = totalLamps - amount
      }
   }
}
var mystock = Stock()

do {
   try mystock.sold(amount: 8)
} catch {
   print(error)  // OutOfStock
}
```

Listing 3-192: *Getting information about the error*

On the other hand, if we do not care about the error, we can force the **`try`** keyword to return an optional with the syntax **`try?`**. If the method throws an error, the instruction returns **`nil`**, and therefore we can avoid the use of the **`do catch`** statements.

```
enum Errors: Error {
   case OutOfStock
}
struct Stock {
   var totalLamps = 5
   mutating func sold(amount: Int) throws {
      if amount > totalLamps {
         throw Errors.OutOfStock
      } else {
         totalLamps = totalLamps - amount
      }
   }
}
var mystock = Stock()
try? mystock.sold(amount: 8)  // nil
```

Listing 3-193: *Catching errors with* `try?`

The instruction at the end of Listing 3-193 returns the value **`nil`** if the method throws an error, or an optional with the value returned by the method if everything goes right.

Sometimes, we know beforehand that a throwing method is not going to throw an error and therefore we want to avoid writing unnecessary code. In cases like this, we can use the syntax **`try!`**. For instance, the following code checks if there are enough lamps before calling the **`sold()`** method, so we know that the instruction will never throw the **`OutOfStock`** error.

```
enum Errors: Error {
   case OutOfStock
}
struct Stock {
   var totalLamps = 5
   mutating func sold(amount: Int) throws {
```

```
      if amount > totalLamps {
         throw Errors.OutOfStock
      } else {
         totalLamps = totalLamps - amount
      }
   }
}
var mystock = Stock()

if mystock.totalLamps > 3 {
   try! mystock.sold(amount: 3)
}
print("Lamps in stock: \(mystock.totalLamps)")
```

***Listing 3-194:** Ignoring the errors*

Medium Results

Sometimes we need to return more than just an error. For this purpose, the Swift Standard Library defines the **Result** enumeration. The enumeration defines two cases with associated values to use in case of success or failure, called **success()** and **failure()**. The Result enumeration is generic, which means that the data types of the associated values can be anything we want. For instance, in the following examples we define a **Result** enumeration of type **<Int, Errors>** to return an integer and the **OutOfStock** error defined in the previous example.

```
enum Errors: Error {
   case OutOfStock
}
struct Stock {
   var totalLamps = 5

   mutating func sold(amount: Int) -> Result<Int, Errors> {
      if amount > totalLamps {
         return .failure(.OutOfStock)
      } else {
         totalLamps = totalLamps - amount
         return .success(totalLamps)
      }
   }
}
var mystock = Stock()

let result = mystock.sold(amount: 3)
switch result {
   case .success(let stock):
      print("Lamps in stock: \(stock)")
   case .failure(let error):
      if error == .OutOfStock {
         print("Error: Out of Stock")
      } else {
         print("Error")
      }
}
```

***Listing 3-195:** Returning an error with a* `Result` *enumeration*

The **sold()** method in Listing 3-195 now returns a **Result** value of type **<Int, Errors>**, so if an error occurs, the method can return a **failure()** value with the associated value **OutOfStock**, but if we have enough lamps to fulfill the order, we can return a **success()** value with the remaining number of lamps. The result can be read by a **switch** statement. We check whether the value returned by the method is **failure()** or **success()**, get the associated value with a **let** statement, and proceed accordingly. In this case, there are enough lamps available, so a message is printed on the console with the remaining stock.

Instead of using a **switch** statement, we can use the following method defined by the **Result** enumeration.

get()—This method returns the associated value of the **success()** case or throws an error with the associated value of the **failure()** case.

The only purpose of the **get()** method is to simplify the code. Now, instead of a **switch** statement, we can use a **do catch**.

```
enum Errors: Error {
   case OutOfStock
}
struct Stock {
   var totalLamps = 5

   mutating func sold(amount: Int) -> Result<Int, Errors> {
      if amount > totalLamps {
         return .failure(.OutOfStock)
      } else {
         totalLamps = totalLamps - amount
         return .success(totalLamps)
      }
   }
}
var mystock = Stock()

let result = mystock.sold(amount: 2)
do {
   let stock = try result.get()
   print("Lamps in stock: \(stock)")
} catch Errors.OutOfStock {
   print("Error: Out of Stock")
}
```

Listing 3-196: *Processing an error with the* `get()` *method*

The result is the same, but now all we need to do is to call the **get()** method. If the method doesn't return an error, the remaining stock is printed on the console, otherwise, the **catch** block is performed, and an error is printed instead.

Chapter 4

Introduction to Frameworks

Basic 4.1 Frameworks

The programming tools introduced in previous chapters are not enough to build professional applications. Creating an app requires accessing complex technologies and performing repetitive tasks that involve hundreds or even thousands of lines of code. Faced with this situation, developers always implemented pre-programmed codes that perform common tasks. These pieces of code are organized according to their purpose in what we know as frameworks.

Frameworks are libraries (pre-programmed code) and APIs (Application Programming Interfaces) that we can use to add functionality to our applications. This includes managing databases, creating graphics on the screen, storing files, accessing resources on the Web, sharing data online, and more. These frameworks are essential for creating professional applications for Apple devices and are therefore part of the SDK (Software Development Kit) included with Xcode.

Do It Yourself: The examples in this chapter were designed to be tested in Playground. You just need to create a Playground file with a Blank template and then replace the code with the example you want to try.

Basic Importing Frameworks

The Swift Standard Library we have been using in previous chapters is automatically loaded for us and available everywhere in our code, but when we require the use of other frameworks, we must indicate it to the system. This is done by adding the **`import`** instruction at the beginning of each file followed by the name of the framework we want to include (e.g., **`import Foundation`**). Once the framework is imported, it is included in our file, giving us access to all the structures, classes, functions, and any of the values defined in its code.

Basic 4.2 Foundation

Foundation is one of the oldest frameworks provided by Apple. It was written in Objective-C and developed by Steve Jobs's second company NeXT. It was created to manage basic tasks and store data. The framework provides its own data types (structures and classes) to store any value we want, including numbers and strings of characters, arrays and dictionaries, and a primary class called **`NSObject`** with basic behavior that every other class inherits from. Most of these definitions are now obsolete, replaced by Swift's data types, but others remain useful, as we will see next.

Basic More Standard Functions

As we have seen in Chapter 3, the Swift Standard Library includes a few standard functions, such as **`print()`** or **`abs()`**, but others are provided by frameworks like Foundation. The following are some of the basic functions and structures available when we import the Foundation framework.

pow(Float, Float**)**—This function returns the result of raising the first value to the power of the second value. The arguments may be numbers of type **`Float`** or **`Double`**.

sqrt(Float**)**—This function returns the square root of the value of its argument. The argument may be of type **`Float`** or **`Double`**.

log(Float**)**—This function returns the natural logarithm of a value. Similar functions are **`log2()`**, **`log10()`**, **`log1p()`**, and **`logb()`**. It can take a value of type **`Float`** or **`Double`**.

sin(Float)—This function returns the sine of a value. Similar functions are **asin()**, **sinh()**, and **asinh()**. The argument may be of type **Float** or **Double**.

cos(Float)—This function returns the cosine of a value. Similar functions are **acos()**, **cosh()**, and **acosh()**. The argument may be of type **Float** or **Double**.

tan(Float)—This function returns the tangent of a value. Similar functions are **atan()**, **atan2()**, **tanh()**, and **atanh()**. The argument may be of type **Float** or **Double**.

UUID()—This is an initializer that returns a structure of type **UUID** with a unique value that can be used to identify instances of custom structures, classes and more.

The application of these functions is straightforward, as shown in the following example.

```
import Foundation

let square = sqrt(4.0)
let power = pow(2.0, 2.0)
let maximum = max(square, power)

print("The maximum value is \(maximum)")  // "The maximum value is 4.0"
```

Listing 4-1: *Applying math functions*

The first thing we do in the code of Listing 4-1 is to import the Foundation framework. After this, we can implement any of the tools defined inside the framework, including the basic functions introduced above. This example gets the square root of 4.0, calculates 2.0 to the power of 2.0, and compares the results using the **max()** function from the Swift Standard Library.

Basic Strings

Foundation defines a class called **NSString** to store and manage strings of characters. The **String** structure offered by the Swift Standard Library for this same purpose adopts most of its functionality, turning the class obsolete, but because Swift coexists with old frameworks and data types, **NSString** objects are still required in some circumstances. The **NSString** class includes several Initializers to create these objects. The one usually implemented in Swift takes an argument called **string** with the string of characters we want to assign to the object.

```
import Foundation

var text: NSString = NSString(string: "Hello")
print(text)  // "Hello"
```

Listing 4-2: *Creating an* `NSString` *object*

If we already have a **String** value in our code, we can cast it into an **NSString** object with the **as** operator.

```
import Foundation

var text = "Hello World"
var newText = text as NSString
print(newText)  // "Hello World"
```

Listing 4-3: *Casting a* `String` *value into an* `NSString` *object*

A **String** structure can be turned into an **NSString** object with the **as** operator because they are interconnected. It is said that the **String** structure bridges with the **NSString** class. This means that we can access the functionality offered by the **NSString** class from the **String** structure, including the following properties and methods.

capitalized—This property returns a string with the first letter of every word in uppercase.

length—This property returns the number of characters in the string of an **NSString** object. (For **String** values, we should use the **count** property instead.)

localizedStringWithFormat(String, Values**)**—This type method creates a string from the string provided by the first argument and the values provided by the second argument. The first argument is a template used to create the string, and the second argument is the list of values we want to include in the string separated by comma.

contains(String**)**—This method returns a Boolean value that indicates whether or not the string specified by the argument was found inside the original string.

trimmingCharacters(in: CharacterSet**)**—This method erases the characters indicated by the **in** argument at the beginning and the end of the string and returns a new string with the result. The argument is a **CharacterSet** structure with type properties to select the type of characters we want to remove. The most frequently used properties are **whitespaces** (spaces) and **whitespacesAndNewlines** (spaces and new line characters).

compare(String, **options:** CompareOptions, **range:** Range?, **locale:** Locale?**)**—This method compares the original string with the string provided by the first argument and returns an enumeration of type **ComparisonResult** with a value corresponding to the lexical order of the strings. The **orderedSame** value is returned when the strings are equal, the **orderedAscending** value is returned when the original string precedes the value of the first argument, and the **orderedDescending** value is returned when the original string follows the value of the first argument. The **options** argument is a property of the **CompareOptions** structure. The properties available are **caseInsensitive** (it considers lowercase and uppercase letters to be the same), **literal** (performs a byte-to-byte comparison), **diacriticInsensitive** (ignores diacritic marks such as the visual stress on vowels), **widthInsensitive** (ignores the width difference in characters that occurs in some languages), and **forcedOrdering** (the comparison is forced to return **orderedAscending** or **orderedDescending** values when the strings are equivalent but not strictly equal). The **range** argument defines a range that determines the portion of the original string we want to compare. Finally, the **locale** argument is a **Locale** structure that defines localization. Except for the first argument, the rest of the arguments are optional.

caseInsensitiveCompare(String**)**—This method compares the original string with the string provided by the argument. It works exactly like the **compare()** method but with the option **caseInsensitiveSearch** set by default.

range(of: String, **options:** CompareOptions, **range:** Range?, **locale:** Locale?**)**—This method searches for the string specified by the first argument and returns a range to indicate where the string was found or **nil** in case of failure. The **options** argument is a property of the **CompareOptions** structure. The properties available for this method are the same we have for the **compare()** method, with the difference that we can specify three more: **backwards** (searches from the end of the string), **anchored** (matches characters only at the beginning or the end, not in the middle), and **regularExpression** (searches with a regular expression). The **range** argument defines a range that determines the portion of the original string where we want to search. Except for the first argument, the rest of the argument s are optional.

As we already mentioned, the **String** structure is bridged to the **NSString** class and therefore we can call these methods from **String** values, but because they are defined in the **NSString** class, we still must import the Foundation framework to be able to use them. Some of them are like those offered by the **String** structure but allow us to perform additional operations on the values. For instance, we can incorporate values into strings with string interpolation, but the **localizedStringWithFormat()** method offers a different approach.

This method takes a string with placeholders and replaces them with a list of values. The placeholders are declared with the % symbol followed by a character that represents the type of value we want to include. For example, if we want to replace the placeholder by an integer, we must use the characters %d.

```
import Foundation

var age = 44
var mytext = String.localizedStringWithFormat("My age is %d", age)
print(mytext)  // "My age is 44"
```

***Listing 4-4:** Creating a formatted string*

There are different placeholders available. The most frequently used are %d for integers, %f for floating-point numbers, %g to remove redundant 0 (zeros), and %@ for objects and structures. We can use any of these characters and as many times as necessary. This is like what we would get with string interpolation, but with this method we can also format the values. For instance, we can determine the number of digits a value will have by adding the amount before the letter.

```
import Foundation

let length = 12.3472
let total = 54
let decimals = String.localizedStringWithFormat("Decimals: %.2f", length)
let digits = String.localizedStringWithFormat("Digits: %.5d", total)
print(decimals)  // "Decimals: 12.35"
print(digits)  // "Digits: 00054"
```

***Listing 4-5:** Formatting numbers*

The code in Listing 4-5 formats two numbers, a double and an integer. The double is processed with the %.2f placeholder, which means that the value is going to be rounded to two decimals after the point, and the integer is processed with the %.5d placeholder, which means that the number in the string is going to contain a total of five digits.

Other methods provided by the **NSString** class perform operations that are already available for **String** values, but they produce a more comprehensive result. For example, the **compare()** method compares strings like the **==** operator, but the value returned is not just **true** or **false**.

```
import Foundation

var fruit = "Orange"
var search = "Apple"

var result = fruit.compare(search)
switch result {
   case .orderedSame:
      print("Fruit and Search are equal")
   case .orderedDescending:
      print("Fruit follows Search")  // "Fruit follows Search"
   case .orderedAscending:
      print("Fruit precedes Search")
}
```

***Listing 4-6:** Comparing `String` values*

The **compare()** method takes a string, compares it to the original string, and returns a **ComparisonResult** value to indicate the order. The **ComparisonResult** enumeration contains three values: **orderedSame**, **orderedDescending**, and **orderedAscending**. After comparing the values of the **fruit** and **search** variables in our example, the **result** variable contains one of these values according to the lexical order of the strings. In this case, the value "Orange" assigned to **fruit** is bigger (follows alphabetically) the value "Apple" assigned to **search**, so the value returned is **orderedDescending** (the order is descending from **fruit** to **search**).

The **compare()** method implemented in Listing 4-6 and the **==** operator studied in Chapter 2 consider a lowercase string different from an uppercase string. Adding an option to the **compare()** method we can compare two strings without considering lowercase or uppercase letters.

```
import Foundation

var fruit = "Orange"
var search = "ORANGE"

var result = fruit.compare(search, options: .caseInsensitive)
switch result {
   case .orderedSame:
      print("The values are equal")  // "The values are equal"
   case .orderedDescending:
      print("Fruit follows Search")
   case .orderedAscending:
      print("Fruit precedes Search")
}
```

Listing 4-7: *Comparing* String *values with options*

The strings stored in the **fruit** and **search** variables in Listing 4-7 are different, but because of the **caseInsensitive** option, they are considered equal. This type of comparison is very common, which is why the class includes the **caseInsensitiveCompare()** method that all it does is calling the **compare()** method with the **caseInsensitive** option already set.

Despite this being the most common scenario, we can perform more precise comparison by providing the range of characters we want to compare.

```
import Foundation

var phone = "905-525-6666"
var search = "905"

var start = phone.startIndex
var end = phone.firstIndex(of: "-")

if let endIndex = end {
   let result = phone.compare(search, options: .caseInsensitive, range:
start..<endIndex)
   if result == .orderedSame {
      print("The area code is the same")  // "The area code is the same"
   } else {
      print("The area code is different")
   }
}
```

Listing 4-8: *Comparing only a range of characters*

This example compares only the initial characters of a string to check the area code of a phone number. The code defines a range that goes from the first character of the **phone** variable to the position before the **-** character. This range is provided to the **compare()** method and in consequence the value of the **search** variable is compared only against the first three characters.

We can also use ranges to search for strings using the **range()** method. This method searches for a string inside another string and returns a range that determines where the string was found.

```
import Foundation

var text = "The Suitcase is Black"
var search = "black  "
search = search.trimmingCharacters(in: .whitespacesAndNewlines)

var range = text.range(of: search, options: .caseInsensitive)
if let rangeToReplace = range {
   text.replaceSubrange(rangeToReplace, with: "Red")
}
print(text)  // "The Suitcase is Red"
```

Listing 4-9: *Searching and replacing characters in a string*

The **range()** method returns an optional value that contains the range where the string was found or **nil** in case of failure. In Listing 4-9, we search for the value of the **search** variable inside the **text** variable and check the optional value returned. When we have a range to work with (which means that the value was found) we use it to call the **replaceSubrange()** method of the **String** structure to replace the characters in the range with the string "Red" (see Listing 3-67). Notice that because search values are usually provided by the user, we trim the value of the **search** variable with the **trimmingCharacters()** method to make sure that there are no space characters at the beginning or the end of the string (the two spaces after the word "black" are removed).

Basic Ranges

Although Swift includes range structures to store ranges of values, some frameworks programmed in Objective-C still implement an old Foundation class called **NSRange**. The **NSRange** class is slightly different from the Swift's **Range** structure. Instead of storing the initial and final values of the range, **NSRange** objects store the initial value and the length of the range.

NSRange(Range**)**—This initializer creates an **NSRange** object from a **Range** value.

NSRange(Range, **in:** String**)**—This initializer creates an **NSRange** object to represent a **Range** structure with string indexes.

Range(NSRange**)**—This initializer creates a **Range** structure from an **NSRange** value.

Range(NSRange, **in:** String**)**—This initializer creates a **Range** structure to represent an **NSRange** object with string indexes.

The **NSRange** class also includes two properties to retrieve its values: **location** and **length**. The following example initializes an **NSRange** object from a Swift range and prints its values.

```
import Foundation

let range = NSRange(4..<10)
print("Initial: \(range.location)")  // "Initial: 4"
print("Length: \(range.length)")  // "Length: 6"
```

Listing 4-10: *Creating and reading an* NSRange *value*

The initializer implemented in this example is for countable ranges. If we work with string indexes, we must use the initializer defined for strings. This is because the **String** structure works with Unicode characters while **NSString** objects work with a less comprehensive character encoding called *UTF-16*. Working with different character encodings means that the space the characters occupy in memory varies. A range that represents a series of characters in a **String** value may differ from a range that represents the same series of characters in an **NSString** value. The following example illustrates how to work with this initializer.

```swift
import Foundation

let text = "Hello World"
if let start = text.firstIndex(of: "W") {
   let newRange = NSRange(start..., in: text)
   print("Initial: \(newRange.location)")  // "Initial: 6"
   print("Length: \(newRange.length)")  // "Length: 5"
}
```

Listing 4-11: *Converting a range of string indexes*

Basic Numbers

Foundation offers a class called **NSNumber** to represent and store numbers. With the introduction of the Swift's primitive data types, the use of this class is no longer necessary, but there are a few old frameworks that still require these types of values. The class includes the following initializer.

NSNumber(value: Value**)**—This initializer creates an **NSNumber** object with the value specified by the **value** argument. The argument may be a value of any of the data types available in Swift for numbers.

The class also provides properties to perform the opposite operation, getting Swift data types from **NSNumber** objects. The following are the most frequently used.

intValue—This property returns an **Int** value with the object's number.

floatValue—This property returns a **Float** value with the object's number.

doubleValue—This property returns a **Double** value with the object's number.

The following example shows how to create **NSNumber** objects and how to get them back as Swift data types to perform operations.

```swift
import Foundation

var mynumber = NSNumber(value: 35)
var mydouble = mynumber.doubleValue * 2  // 70
```

Listing 4-12: *Working with* NSNumber *objects*

Besides its own data type, Foundation also provides the means to format numbers. Every time we print a number, all the digits are shown on the screen, including all the decimal digits. In Listing 4-4, we explained how to specify how many digits of a number we want to include in a string using placeholders (e.g., **%.2f**), but this is not customizable enough. To provide a better alternative, the framework includes the following formatting method.

formatted(FormatStyle**)**—This method formats the number according to the styles provided by the argument.

To format a number, we must call this method from the instance with the styles we want to apply to it. The styles are defined by a structure that conforms to the **FormatStyle** protocol. For numbers, the framework defines the **IntegerFormatStyle** and the **FloatingPointFormat-Style** structures. These structures include the following methods to style a number.

precision(Precision**)**—This method defines the number of digits included in the integer and decimal parts of the number. The argument is a **Precision** structure, which includes the **integerLength(Int)** and **fractionLength(Int)** methods to determine the number of digits in the integer and decimal parts, and the **integerAndFraction-Length(integer: Int, fraction: Int)** method to determine both.

rounded(rule: FloatingPointRoundingRule**)**—This method rounds the number to the nearest value. The **rule** argument is an enumeration with the values **up**, **down**, **awayFromZero**, **toNearestOrAwayFromZero**, **toNearestOrEven**, and **towardZero**.

grouping(Grouping**)**—This method determines if the digits of a number are going to be separated in groups (e.g., 9,000,000). The argument is a structure with the properties **automatic** (default) and **never**.

notation(Notation**)**—This method determines the number's notation. The argument is a structure with the properties **automatic** (default), **compactName**, and **scientific**.

sign(strategy: SignDisplayStrategy**)**—This method determines if the sign will be included (+ and -). The **strategy** argument is a **SignDisplayStrategy** structure, which includes the **automatic** (default) and **never** properties, and also the **always(includingZero: Bool)** method to determine if the sign is displayed or not.

decimalSeparator(strategy: DecimalSeparatorDisplayStrategy**)**—This method determines if a separator is going to be included after the number. The **strategy** argument is a structure with the properties **automatic** (default) and **always**.

The **FormatStyle** protocol defines the **number** property, which contains an instance of the **IntegerFormatStyle** or the **FloatingPointFormatStyle** structures, depending on the number's data type. From this instance, we can apply all the styles we want to a number.

```
import Foundation

let mynumber: Double = 32.56789
let text = mynumber.formatted(.number.precision(.fractionLength(2)))
print(text)  // "32.57"
```

Listing 4-13: *Formatting a number*

The styles are provided one by one with dot notation. We first get the styling structure from the **number** property (in this case, the number is a **Double** so the value of the property is an instance of the **FloatingPointFormatStyle** structure). Next, we call the **precision()** method, and send to this method the value returned by the **fractionLength()** method, which formats the number with 2 decimal digits. As a result, we get a string with the value "32.57" (the value is rounded up).

Styles can be concatenated, one after another, with dot notation. For instance, in the previous example, the number was rounded up by default, but we can change this behavior by applying the **rounded(rule:)** method, as shown next.

```
import Foundation

let mynumber: Double = 32.56789
let text =
mynumber.formatted(.number.precision(.fractionLength(2)).rounded(rule: .d
own))
print(text)  // "32.56"
```

Listing 4-14: *Rounding a number*

In this example, the **rounded(rule:)** method is called after the number is formatted with 2 decimal digits, so the rest of the digits are rounded down. The result is a string with the value "32.56".

The grouping, notation, and decimal separator styles usually apply to large numbers. For instance, by default, the digits of large numbers are separated in groups, as in 32,000,000, but we can change this behavior with the **grouping()** method.

```
import Foundation

let mynumber: Int = 32000000
let text = mynumber.formatted(.number.grouping(.never))
print(text)  // "32000000"
```

Listing 4-15: *Disabling grouping*

We can also show the sign in front of the number (+ or -). In the following example, we always show the sign except when the number is equal to 0.

```
import Foundation

let mynumber: Int = 32000000
let text =
mynumber.formatted(.number.sign(strategy: .always(includingZero: false)))
print(text)  // "+32,000,000"
```

Listing 4-16: *Adding the sign*

In addition to **number**, the **FormatStyle** protocol defines the **percent** property to style the number as a percentage, and the **currency(code:)** method to format monetary values. The **percent** property is a **Percent** structure that all it does is to add the % sign to the number.

```
import Foundation

let mynumber: Double = 32.55
let text = mynumber.formatted(.percent)
print(text)  // "32.55%"
```

Listing 4-17: *Formatting the number as a percentage value*

On the other hand, the **currency(code:)** method can produce a number with any format and currency symbol we want. The currency is defined by the string assigned to the argument. There are values for any currency available. For instance, the USD string is for American Dollars, the CAD string is for Canadian Dollars, EUR for Euros, and so on. The following example gets the number expressed in Canadian dollars (for more values, visit our website and follow the links for this chapter).

```
import Foundation

let mynumber: Double = 32.55
let text = mynumber.formatted(.currency(code: "CAD"))
print(text)  // "CA$32.55"
```

Listing 4-18: *Formatting currency values*

Basic Dates

Foundation defines multiple classes and structures to create and process dates, including **Date**, **Calendar**, **DateComponents**, **DateInterval**, **Locale**, and **TimeZone**. The data type in charge of creating the structure to store the actual date is **Date**. The following are some of its initializers.

Date()—This initializer creates a **Date** structure with the system's current date.

Date(timeIntervalSinceNow: TimeInterval**)**—This initializer creates a **`Date`** structure with a date calculated from the addition of the current date plus the time specified by the **timeIntervalSinceNow** argument. The argument is a value of type **`TimeInterval`** that indicates how many seconds the date is from the initial date.

Date(timeInterval: TimeInterval, **since:** Date**)**—This initializer creates a **`Date`** structure with a date calculated from the addition of the date specified by the **since** argument plus the time specified by the **timeInterval** argument. The argument is a value of type **`TimeInterval`** that indicates how many seconds the date is from the initial date.

The following example shows different ways to initialize a date.

```
import Foundation

var currentdate = Date()
var nextday = Date(timeIntervalSinceNow: 24 * 60 * 60)
var tendays = Date(timeInterval: -10 * 24 * 3600, since: nextday)
```

Listing 4-19: *Storing dates with* `Date` *structures*

If the initializer requires an interval, as those in the code of Listing 4-19, the value is specified in seconds. An easy way to calculate the seconds is multiplying every component. For example, the date for the **`nextday`** object created in our example is calculated adding 1 day to the current date. The number of seconds in 1 day are calculated by multiplying the 24 hours of the day by the 60 minutes in an hour by the 60 seconds in a minute (24 * 60 * 60). For the **`tendays`** object, we apply the same technique. This initializer adds the interval to a specific date (**`nextday`**). The seconds are calculated by multiplying the components, albeit this time it multiplies the previous result by -10 to get a date 10 days before **`nextday`** (we will see better ways to add components to a date later).

IMPORTANT: These methods require a value of type **`Double`** to declare the interval in seconds, but instead of **`Double`** the framework calls it **`TimeInterval`**. This is a typealias (an alternative name for an existing type). Once defined, aliases are used exactly like regular data types. To create your own type aliases, you can use the instruction **`typealias`** (e.g., **`typealias myinteger = Int`**).

Besides the initializers, the class also includes type properties that return special dates. Some of these properties produce values that are useful to set limits and sort lists.

distantFuture—This type property returns a **`Date`** structure with a value that represents a date in a distant future.

distantPast—This type property returns a **`Date`** structure with a value that represents a date in a distant past.

The **`Date`** structure also includes properties and methods to calculate and compare dates. The following are the most frequently used.

timeIntervalSinceNow—This property returns a **`TimeInterval`** value representing the difference in seconds between the date in the **`Date`** structure and the current date.

compare(Date**)**—This method compares the date in the **`Date`** structure with the date specified by the argument and returns an enumeration of type **`ComparisonResult`** with a value corresponding to the temporal order of the dates. The possible values are **`orderedSame`** (the dates are equal), **`orderedAscending`** (the date is earlier than the value), and **`orderedDescending`** (the date is later than the value).

timeIntervalSince(Date**)**—This method compares the date in the **Date** structure with the date specified by the argument and returns the interval between both dates in seconds.

addingTimeInterval(TimeInterval**)**—This method adds the seconds specified by the argument to the date in the **Date** structure and returns a new **Date** structure with the result.

addTimeInterval(TimeInterval**)**—This method adds the seconds specified by the argument to the date in the **Date** structure and stores the result in the same structure.

Comparing dates and calculating the intervals between dates is a constant requirement in app development. The following example compares the current date with a date calculated from a specific number of days. If the resulting date is later than the current date, the code prints a message on the console to show the time remaining in seconds.

```
import Foundation

var days = 7

var today = Date()
var event = Date(timeIntervalSinceNow: Double(days) * 24 * 3600)

if today.compare(event) == .orderedAscending {
   let interval = event.timeIntervalSince(today)
   print("We have to wait \(interval) seconds")
}
```

Listing 4-20: *Comparing two dates*

The dates in **Date** structures are not associated to any calendar. This means that to get the components in a date (year, month, day, etc.) we must decide first in the context of which calendar the date is going to be interpreted. The calendar for a date is defined by the **Calendar** structure. This structure provides properties and methods to process a date according to a specific calendar (Gregorian, Buddhist, Chinese, etc.). To initialize a **Calendar** structure, we have the following initializer and type property.

Calendar(identifier: Identifier**)**—This initializer creates a **Calendar** structure with the calendar specified by the argument. The **identifier** argument is a property of a structure called **Identifier** defined inside the **Calendar** structure. The properties available are **gregorian**, **buddhist**, **chinese**, **coptic**, **ethiopicAmeteMihret**, **ethiopicAmeteAlem**, **hebrew**, **ISO8601**, **indian**, **islamic**, **islamicCivil**, **japanese**, **persian**, **republicOfChina**, **islamicTabular** and **islamicUmmAlQura**.

current—This type property returns a structure with the current calendar set in the system.

A **Calendar** structure includes the following properties and methods to manage the calendar and to get and set new dates.

identifier—This property returns the value that identifies the calendar.

locale—This property sets or returns the **Locale** structure used by the **Calendar** structure to process dates. The value by default is the **Locale** structure defined by the system.

timeZone—This property sets or returns the **TimeZone** structure used by the **Calendar** structure to process dates. The value by default is the **TimeZone** structure set by the system.

dateComponents(Set, **from:** Date**)**—This method returns a **DateComponents** structure with the components indicated by the first argument from the date indicated by the **from** argument. The first argument is a set with properties of a structure called **Unit** that represent each component (**year**, **month**, **day**, **hour**, **minute**, **second**, etc.).

dateComponents(Set, **from:** Date, **to:** Date**)**—This method returns a **DateComponents** structure with the components indicated by the first argument, which values represent the difference between the dates specified by the **from** and **to** arguments. The first argument is a set with properties of a structure called **Unit** that represent each component. The most frequently used are **year**, **month**, **day**, **hour**, **minute**, and **second**.

date(byAdding: DateComponents, **to:** Date**)**—This method returns a **Date** structure with the value obtained by adding the components indicated by the **byAdding** argument to the date indicated by the **to** argument.

date(from: DateComponents**)**—This method returns a date created from the components provided by the **from** argument. The value returned is a **Date** structure.

The **Calendar** structure works along with the **DateComponents** structure to read and return components from a date. The instances created from the **DateComponents** structure include the properties **year**, **month**, **day**, **hour**, **minute**, **second**, and **weekday** to read and set the values of the components. The following example combines these tools to get the year of the current date.

```
import Foundation

var today = Date()
let calendar = Calendar.current
var components = calendar.dateComponents([.year], from: today)
print("The year is \(components.year!)")
```

Listing 4-21: *Extracting components from a date*

In Listing 4-21, we get a reference to the calendar set in the system from the **current** property and then use the **dateComponents()** method to get the year component of the current date.

Several components may be retrieved at once by adding the corresponding properties to the set. The following example gets the year, month, and day of the current date.

```
import Foundation

var today = Date()
let calendar = Calendar.current
var comp = calendar.dateComponents([.year, .month, .day], from: today)
print("Today \(comp.day!)-\(comp.month!)-\(comp.year!)")
```

Listing 4-22: *Extracting multiple components from a date*

DateComponents structures are used to retrieve the components of existing dates and to set the values for new dates. In the following example, a new **Date** structure is created from the values of a **DateComponents** structure.

```
import Foundation

let calendar = Calendar.current
var comp = DateComponents()
```

```
comp.year = 1970
comp.month = 8
comp.day = 21

var birthday = calendar.date(from: comp)  // "Aug 21, 1970, 12:00 AM"
```

***Listing 4-23:** Creating a new date from single components*

The **date(from:)** method of the **Calendar** structure returns a new date with the values provided by the **DateComponents** structure. The components which values are not explicitly defined take values by default (e.g., 12:00 AM).

Generating a new date requires a specific calendar. For example, in the code of Listing 4-23, the values of the components are declared with the format established by the Gregorian calendar. In this case, we rely on the calendar returned by the system, but if we want to use the same calendar no matter where the app is executed, we must set it ourselves from the **Calendar** initializer.

```
import Foundation

let id = Calendar.Identifier.gregorian
let calendar = Calendar(identifier: id)

var comp = DateComponents()
comp.year = 1970
comp.month = 8
comp.day = 13
var birthday = calendar.date(from: comp)  // "Aug 13, 1970 at 12:00 AM"
```

***Listing 4-24:** Using a Gregorian calendar*

Declaring a specific calendar is not only recommended when creating new dates but also when calculating dates by adding components, as in the following example.

```
import Foundation

let id = Calendar.Identifier.gregorian
let calendar = Calendar(identifier: id)
var comp = DateComponents()
comp.day = 120

var today = Date()
var appointment = calendar.date(byAdding: comp, to: today)
```

***Listing 4-25:** Adding components to a date*

The **date()** method implemented in Listing 4-25 adds components to a date and returns a new **Date** structure with the result. The component **day** was set to 120. The **date()** method takes this value and adds it to the date in the **today** structure (the current date), and returns the result.

A common task when working with multiple dates is getting the time between dates, such as the hours remaining for a process to complete or the days remaining for an event to begin. The **Calendar** structure includes a version of the **dateComponents()** method that allows us to compare two dates and get the difference expressed in a specific component.

```
import Foundation

let calendar = Calendar.current
var comp = DateComponents()
comp.year = 1970
comp.month = 8
comp.day = 21
```

```
var today = Date()
var birthdate = calendar.date(from: comp)

if let olddate = birthdate {
   let components = calendar.dateComponents([.day], from: olddate, to:
today)
   print("Days between dates: \(components.day!)")
}
```

***Listing 4-26:** Comparing dates*

This example calculates the days between a birthdate and the current date. The value returned by the **date()** method used to generate the birthdate returns an optional, so we unwrap it before calculating the difference. We assign this value to the **olddate** constant and then compare it with the current date. The number of days between the dates is returned and printed on the console.

Another way to specify intervals between dates is with the **DateInterval** structure. This structure allows us to create an interval with **Date** values. The following are its initializers.

DateInterval(start: Date, **end:** Date**)**—This initializer creates a **DateInterval** structure with the interval between the values provided by the **start** and **end** arguments.

DateInterval(start: Date, **duration:** TimeInterval**)**—This initializer creates a **DateInterval** structure with an interval that starts at the date specified by the **start** argument and last as long as the time specified by the **duration** argument.

The **DateInterval** structure also offers the following properties and methods.

start—This property sets or returns the initial **Date** of the interval.

end—This property sets or returns the final **Date** of the interval.

duration—This property sets or returns the duration of the interval in seconds.

contains(Date**)**—This method returns a Boolean value that indicates whether the date specified by the argument is inside the interval or not.

intersects(DateInterval**)**—This method returns a Boolean value that indicates if the interval intersects with the interval specified by the argument.

intersection(with: DateInterval**)**—This method returns a **DateInterval** value with the interval in which the original interval and the one provided by the **with** argument overlap.

A typical use of the **DateInterval** structure is to create an interval from two dates and check if a specific date falls within the interval, as in the following example.

```
import Foundation

let calendar = Calendar.current

var components = DateComponents()
components.year = 1970
components.month = 8
components.day = 21
var birthday = calendar.date(from: components)

components.year = 2020
components.month = 8
components.day = 21
var future = calendar.date(from: components)
```

```
if birthday != nil && future != nil {
   let today = Date()
   let interval = DateInterval(start: birthday!, end: future!)
   if interval.contains(today) {
      print("You still have time")  // "You still have time"
   }
}
```

Listing 4-27: Finding a date in an interval

The code in Listing 4-27 creates two dates, **birthday** and **future**, and then generates an interval from one date to another. The **contains()** method is used next to check whether the current date is within the interval or not.

As with numbers, Foundation also provides the tools to format dates. The **Date** structure defines two versions of the **formatted()** method for this purpose.

formatted(date: DateStyle, **time:** TimeStyle**)**—This methods formats the date with the styles specified by the arguments. The **date** argument defines the style for the date. It is a structure with the type properties **abbreviated**, **complete**, **long**, **numeric**, and **omitted**. And the **time** argument defines the style for the time. It is a structure with the type properties **complete**, **omitted**, **shortened**, and **standard**.

formatted(Date.FormatStyle**)**—This method formats the date with the styles specified by the argument. The argument is a **FormatStyle** structure defined by the **Date** structure.

If all we need is a standard format, we can call the **formatted(date:, time:)** method with the styles we want for the date and time. The method takes these values and returns a string with a date in the format defined by the current locale (the user's language and location).

```
import Foundation

let mydate = Date.now
let text = mydate.formatted(date: .abbreviated, time: .omitted)
print(text)  // "Jun 18, 2021"
```

Listing 4-28: Formatting dates

The code in Listing 4-28 gets the current date from the **now** property and then calls the method with the **abbreviated** and **omitted** values. This creates a string that contains a date with abbreviated text and no time ("Jun 18, 2021").

Standard styles include all the components of the date, but the **Date** structure includes an additional version of the **formatted()** method that takes a **FormatStyle** structure to format the date any way we want. The following are some of the methods included for customization.

day(Day**)**—This method includes the day. The argument defines the style for the day. It is a structure with the properties **defaultDigits**, **ordinalOfDayInMonth**, and **twoDigits**.

month(Month**)**—This method includes the month. The argument defines the style for the month. It is a structure with the properties **abbreviated**, **defaultDigits**, **narrow**, **twoDigits**, and **wide**.

year(Year**)**—This method includes the year. The argument defines the style for the year. It is a structure with the properties **defaultDigits** and **twoDigits**.

hour(Hour**)**—This method includes the hour. The argument defines the style for the hour. It is a structure with the properties **defaultDigitsNoAMPM** and **twoDigitsNoAMPM**.

minute(Minute)—This method includes the minutes. The argument defines the style for the minutes. It is a structure with the properties **defaultDigits** and **twoDigits**.

second(Second)—This method includes the seconds. The argument defines the style for the seconds. It is a structure with the properties **defaultDigits** and **twoDigits**.

weekday(Weekday)—This method includes the weekday. The argument defines the style for the day. It is a structure with the properties **abbreviated**, **narrow**, **oneDigit**, **short**, **twoDigits**, and **wide**.

The **FormatStyle** structure includes the following properties to configure the parameters used to format the date.

calendar—This property sets or returns the calendar used to format the date. It is of type **Calendar**.

locale—This property sets or returns the locale used to format the date. It is of type **Locale**.

timeZone—This property sets or return the time zone used to format the date. It is of type **TimeZone**.

Although we can create our own **FormatStyle** structure, the structure includes a type property called **dateTime** to return an instance with the calendar and standard values set by the device. If the configuration by default is enough, we can use this property to format the date, as shown next.

```
import Foundation

let mydate = Date.now
let text = mydate.formatted(.dateTime.weekday(.wide))
print(text)  // "Friday"
```

Listing 4-29: *Specifying a custom format*

The code in Listing 4-29 calls the **weekday()** method from the **FormatStyle** structure returned by the **dateTime** property to get the day of the week. In this case, we call the method with the value **wide**, which returns the day's full name ("Friday"). Only one component is included in this example, but we can add more by concatenating the methods with dot notation, as we did before for numbers.

```
import Foundation

let mydate = Date.now
let text = mydate.formatted(.dateTime.day().hour().month(.wide))
print(text)  // "June 18, 6 PM"
```

Listing 4-30: *Including multiple date components*

In this code, we implement the **day()**, **month()**, and **hour()** methods. The result is a string with a date that includes the month (full name), the day, and the hour ("June 18, 6 PM").

Notice that the order in which the methods are called doesn't matter. The date and time are always formatted with a standard format that depends on the user's locale (language and country). This is because the **formatted()** method processes dates according to local conventions, including the language, symbols, etc. This means that the components of a date are going to be interpreted according to the conventions currently set on the device. For example, the same date will look like this "Tuesday, August 6, 2021" for a user in the United States and like this "2021年8月6日 星期二" for a user in China. How dates are processed is determined by an object of the **Locale** structure. Every device has a **Locale** structure assigned by default, and our code will work with it unless we determine otherwise. To get a reference to the current structure or create a new one, the **Locale** structure includes the following initializer and type property.

Locale(identifier: String**)**—This initializer creates a **Locale** structure configured for the region determined by the value of the argument. The argument is a string that represents a language and a region (e.g., en_US for the United States, zh_CN for China).

current—This type property returns the **Locale** structure assigned by default to the device or defined by the user in the Settings app.

The **FormatStyle** structure includes the following method to format a date for a locale.

locale(Locale**)**—This method specifies the locale to use by the formatter.

Although it is recommended to use the **Locale** structure set by the system and keep the values by default, there are times when our application must present the information with a specific configuration. For example, we may need to create an application that always shows dates in Chinese, no matter where the user is located. We can do this by defining a **Locale** structure and then include the **locale()** method in the formatter with this value.

```
import Foundation

let mydate = Date.now
let chinaLocale = Locale(identifier: "zh_CN")
let text =
mydate.formatted(.dateTime.locale(chinaLocale).day().month().year())
print(text)  // "2021年6月18日"
```

Listing 4-31: *Specifying a different locale*

This example creates a new **Locale** structure with the zh_CN identifier, which corresponds to China and the Chinese language, and then formats the date with this locale and the **day()**, **month()**, and **year()** methods. The result is a string with the date in Chinese ("2021年6月18日").

IMPORTANT: The list of identifiers you can use to create a **Locale** structure is extensive, but you can print the type property **availableIdentifiers** from the **Locale** structure to get an array with all the values available.

The date stored in a **Date** structure is not a date but the number of seconds between the date represented by the object and an arbitrary date in the past (January 1st, 2001). To process these values and get the actual date, the **Calendar** structure needs to know the user's time zone. Foundation includes the **TimeZone** structure to manage time zones. An object is assigned by default to the system containing the time zone where the device is located (that is why when we display a date it coincides with the date in our device), but we can define a different one as we did with the **Locale** structure. To get a reference to the current structure or create a new one, the **TimeZone** structure includes the following initializer and type property.

TimeZone(identifier: String**)**—This initializer creates a **TimeZone** structure configured for the time zone determined by the value of the **identifier** argument. The argument is a string that represents the name of the time zone (e.g., "Europe/Paris", "Asia/Bangkok").

current—This type property returns the **TimeZone** structure assigned by default to the device or defined by the user in the Settings app.

The **FormatStyle** structure does not include a method to provide a specific time zone to format the date. For this purpose, we must create a custom instance and then assign the time zone to the structure's **timeZone** property, as in the following example.

```
import Foundation

if let tokyoTimeZone = TimeZone(identifier: "Asia/Tokyo"), let
madridTimeZone = TimeZone(identifier: "Europe/Madrid") {
   let mydate = Date.now
   let mytime = mydate.formatted(.dateTime.hour().minute().second())

   var dateTimeStyle = Date.FormatStyle()
   dateTimeStyle.timeZone = tokyoTimeZone
   let tokyoTime =
mydate.formatted(dateTimeStyle.hour().minute().second())

   dateTimeStyle.timeZone = madridTimeZone
   let madridTime =
mydate.formatted(dateTimeStyle.hour().minute().second())

   print("My Time: \(mytime)")  // "My Time: 9:25:19 PM"
   print("Tokyo Time: \(tokyoTime)")  // "Tokyo Time: 10:25:19 AM"
   print("Madrid Time: \(madridTime)")  // "Madrid Time: 3:25:19 AM"
}
```

***Listing 4-32:** Working with different time zones*

The code in Listing 4-32 creates two **TimeZone** structures, one for Tokyo's time zone and another for Madrid's. If successful, we initialize a **FormatStyle** structure and format the date twice, first for Tokyo and then for Madrid. Notice that the **TimeZone** structures are assigned to the **timeZone** property of the **FormatStyle** structure before using the structure to format each date.

IMPORTANT: The list of names for the time zones is stored in a database. The **TimeZone** structure offers the **knownTimeZoneIdentifiers** type property that you can print to see all the values available.

Medium Measurements

Some applications require the use of units of measurement, such as pounds, miles, liters, etc. Defining our own units present some challenges, but Foundation includes the **Measurement** structure to simplify our work. This structure includes two properties, one for the value and another for the unit. The initializer requires these two values to create the structure.

Measurement(value: Double, **unit:** Unit**)**—This initializer creates a **Measurement** structure with the values specified by the **value** and **unit** arguments. The **unit** argument is a property of a subclass of the **Dimension** class.

The value declared for the **Measurement** structure is the number that determines the magnitude, like 55 in 55 km, and the unit is a property of a subclass of the **Dimension** class that represents the unit of measurement, like km in 55 km. The **Dimension** class contains all the basic functionally required for measurement but is through its subclasses that the units of measurement are determined. Foundation offers multiple subclasses to define units for different types of dimensions. The following are the most frequently used.

UnitDuration—This subclass of the **Dimension** class defines the units of measurement for duration (time). The subclass includes the following properties to represent the units: **seconds**, **minutes**, and **hours**, with **seconds** defined as the basic unit.

UnitLength—This subclass of the **Dimension** class defines the units of measurement for length. The subclass includes the following properties to represent the units: **megameters**, **kilometers**, **hectometers**, **decameters**, **meters**, **decimeters**, **centimeters**, **millimeters**, **micrometers**, **nanometers**, **picometers**, **inches**, **feet**, **yards**, **miles**, **scandinavianMiles**, **lightyears**, **nauticalMiles**, **fathoms**, **furlongs**, **astronomicalUnits**, and **parsecs**, with **meters** defined as the basic unit.

UnitMass—This subclass of the **Dimension** class defines the units of measurement for mass. The subclass includes the following properties to represent the units: **kilograms**, **grams**, **decigrams**, **centigrams**, **milligrams**, **micrograms**, **nanograms**, **picograms**, **ounces**, **pounds**, **stones**, **metricTons**, **shortTons**, **carats**, **ouncesTroy**, and **slugs**, with **kilograms** defined as the basic unit.

UnitVolume—This subclass of the **Dimension** class defines the units of measurement for volume. The subclass includes the following properties to represent the units: **megaliters**, **kiloliters**, **liters**, **deciliters**, **centiliters**, **milliliters**, **cubicKilometers**, **cubicMeters**, **cubicDecimeters**, **cubicMillimeters**, **cubicInches**, **cubicFeet**, **cubicYards**, **cubicMiles**, **acreFeet**, **bushels**, **teaspoons**, **tablespoons**, **fluidOunces**, **cups**, **pints**, **quarts**, **gallons**, **imperialTeaspoons**, **imperialTablespoons**, **imperialFluidOunces**, **imperialPints**, **imperialQuarts**, **imperialGallons**, and **metricCups**, with **liters** defined as the basic unit.

The **Measurement** structure includes the following properties and methods to access the values and convert them to different units.

value—This property sets or returns the structure's value. It is of type **Double**.

unit—This property sets or returns the structure's unit of measurement. It is represented by a property of a subclass of the **Dimension** class.

convert(to: Unit)—This method converts the values of the **Measurement** structure to the unit specified by the **to** argument. The argument is a property of a subclass of **Dimension**.

converted(to: Unit)—This method converts the values of the **Measurement** structure to the unit specified by the **to** argument and returns a new **Measurement** structure with the result. The argument is a property of a subclass of the **Dimension** class.

The initialization of a **Measurement** structure is simple, we just need to provide the value for the magnitude and the property that represents the unit of measurement we want to use. The following example creates two structures to store a measurement of 30 centimeters and another of 5 pounds.

```
import Foundation

var length = Measurement(value: 30, unit: UnitLength.centimeters) //30 cm
var weight = Measurement(value: 5, unit: UnitMass.pounds)  // 5.0 lb
```

Listing 4-33: *Initializing* Measurement *structures*

If the measurements are of the same dimension (e.g., length), we can perform operations with their values. The **Measurement** structure allows the operations **+**, **-**, *****, **/**, and also the use of the comparison operators **==**, **!=**, **<**, **>**, **<=**, and **>=** to compare values. The following example adds two measurements in centimeters.

```
import Foundation

var length = Measurement(value: 200, unit: UnitLength.centimeters)
var width = Measurement(value: 800, unit: UnitLength.centimeters)

var total = length + width   // 1000.0 cm
```

Listing 4-34: *Adding the values of two* `Measurement` *structures*

If the units are different, the **`Measurement`** structure returned by the operation is defined with the dimension's basic unit. For example, if we are working with lengths, the basic unit is **`meters`**.

```
import Foundation

var length = Measurement(value: 300, unit: UnitLength.meters)
var width = Measurement(value: 2, unit: UnitLength.kilometers)

var total = length + width   // 2300.0 m
```

Listing 4-35: *Adding two values of different units*

The code in Listing 4-35 adds two lengths of different units (meters and kilometers). The system converts kilometers to meters and then performs the addition, returning a **`Measurement`** structure with a value in meters (the default unit).

If we want everything to be performed in the same unit, we can convert a value to a different unit using the **`convert()`** or **`converted()`** methods. In the following example, we convert the unit of the **`length`** variable to kilometers and perform the addition again in kilometers.

```
import Foundation

var length = Measurement(value: 300, unit: UnitLength.meters)
var width = Measurement(value: 2, unit: UnitLength.kilometers)
length.convert(to: UnitLength.kilometers)

var total = length + width   // 2.3 km
```

Listing 4-36: *Converting units*

The values of a **`Measurement`** structure are printed as they are stored and with the units they represent, but this is usually not what we need to show to our users. Fortunately, the **`Measurement`** structure defines the **formatted()** method to format these values.

formatted(Measurement.FormatStyle**)**—This method formats the measurement with the styles specified by the argument. The argument is a **`FormatStyle`** structure defined in the **`Measurement`** structure.

The **`formatted()`** method requires a **`FormatStyle`** structure to format the value. The structure includes the following initializer and type method to create an instance for every type of unit.

FormatStyle(width: UnitWidth, **locale:** Locale, **usage:** Measurement-FormatUnitUsage, **numberFormatStyle:** FloatingPointFormatStyle**)**—This initializer creates a **`FormatStyle`** structure with the format set by the arguments. The

width argument specifies how the unit is going to be displayed. It is a structure with the properties **abbreviated**, **narrow**, and **wide**. The **locale** argument specifies the locale. The **usage** argument specifies the purpose of the formatted measurement. The structure to declare this value includes properties for any type of measurement, including **asProvided** (UnitType), **food** (UnitEnergy), **general** (UnitType), **person**: (UnitLength), **personHeight** (UnitLength), **personWeight** (UnitMass), **road** (UnitLength), **weather** (UnitTemperature), and **workout** (UnitEnergy). Finally, the **numberFormatStyle** argument specifies the format of the value.

measurement(width: UnitWidth, **usage:** MeasurementFormatUnitUsage, **numberFormatStyle:** FloatingPointFormatStyle**)**—This method returns a **FormatStyle** structure with the format set by the arguments (the same required by the initializer).

The **FormatStyle** structure also includes an additional initializer and method specific to format temperatures.

FormatStyle(width: UnitWidth, **locale:** Locale, **usage:** MeasurementFormatUnitUsage, **hidesScaleName:** Bool, **numberFormatStyle:** FloatingPointFormatStyle**)**—This initializer creates a **FormatStyle** structure with the format set by the arguments. The **width** argument specifies how the unit is going to be displayed. It is a structure with the properties **abbreviated**, **narrow**, and **wide**. The **locale** argument specifies the locale. The **usage** argument specifies the purpose of the formatted measurement. The structure to declare this value includes properties for any type of measurement. The ones available are **asProvided** (UnitType), **food** (UnitEnergy), **general** (UnitType), **person** (UnitTemperature), **personHeight** (UnitLength), **personWeight** (UnitMass), **road** (UnitLength), **weather** (UnitTemperature), and **workout** (UnitEnergy). The **hidesScaleName** argument determines if the name of the unit is going to be displayed, and the **numberFormatStyle** argument specifies the format of the value.

measurement(width: UnitWidth, **locale:** Locale, **usage:** MeasurementFormatUnitUsage, **hidesScaleName:** Bool, **numberFormatStyle:** FloatingPointFormatStyle**)**—This method returns a **FormatStyle** structure with the format set by the arguments. The arguments are the same required by the initializer.

Most of the arguments in these initializers and methods are optional. If an argument is not declared, the formatter uses values by default. For instance, if we just want to show the full name of the unit, we can call the **measurement()** method with the **width** argument and the value **wide**.

```
import Foundation

let length = Measurement(value: 40, unit: UnitLength.kilometers)
let text = length.formatted(.measurement(width: .wide,
usage: .asProvided))
print(text)  // "40 kilometers"
```

Listing 4-37: *Formatting a measurement*

In this example, we have also included the **usage** argument with the **asProvided** value to tell the formatter to use the original units (kilometers). If this argument is not declared, the formatter uses the value by default, which formats the measurement for the configuration and locale set in the device. For instance, if we specify the **road** value instead, the formatter will format the value to represent a distance using the device's locale, which for a device running in the United States means that the original value will be converted to miles.

```
import Foundation

let length = Measurement(value: 40, unit: UnitLength.kilometers)
let text = length.formatted(.measurement(width: .wide, usage: .road))
print(text)  // "25 miles"
```

Listing 4-38: *Formatting a measurement for a specific purpose*

By default, the formatter rounds the number. That's why in this example the result of converting 40 kilometers to miles is 25, when it should've been 24.8548. If we want to specify a different format, we can add the **numberFormatStyle** argument and implement the methods provided by the **IntegerFormatStyle** and **FloatingPointFormatStyle** structures introduced before. For instance, we can specify a precision of 2 digits for the decimal part with the **fractionLength()** method, as shown next.

```
import Foundation

let length = Measurement(value: 40, unit: UnitLength.kilometers)
let text = length.formatted(.measurement(width: .wide, usage: .road,
numberFormatStyle: .number.precision(.fractionLength(2))))
print(text)  // "24.85 miles"
```

Listing 4-39: *Formatting the measurement's value*

The **formatted()** method in this example includes the **width argument** to get the unit's full name, the **usage argument** to format the value to represent distance, and the **numberFormat-Style argument** to format the value. The value is expressed in miles again, but it is more accurate.

If our application must display a value always with the same unit of measurement independently of the device's location, we can set a specific locale. The **formatted()** method doesn't include an **argument** to designate a locale, but the initializers included in the **FormatStyle** structure do. The following example formats the measurements in Chinese, no matter where the device is located.

```
import Foundation

let length = Measurement(value: 40, unit: UnitLength.kilometers)
let chinaLocale = Locale(identifier: "zh_CN")
var format = Measurement<UnitLength>.FormatStyle(width: .wide, locale:
chinaLocale, usage: .asProvided)
let text = length.formatted(format)
print(text)  // "40.00公里"
```

Listing 4-40: *Formatting a measurement for a specific locale*

The code in Listing 4-40 initializes a **FormatStyle** structure with the locale configured for China and then calls the **formatted()** method with this structure to format the value. Notice that the **FormatStyle** structure is defined inside the **Measurement** structure, which is a generic structure and therefore we must specify the type of values the structure is going to process. In this case, we are working with units of length so we must specify the **UnitLength** data type.

Medium Timer

Timers are objects created from the **Timer** class that perform an action after a specific period of time. There are two types of timers: repeating and non-repeating. Repeating timers perform the action and then reschedule themselves to do it again in an infinite loop. Non-repeating timers, on the other hand, perform the action once and then invalidate themselves. The **Timer** class includes the following properties and methods to create and manage timers.

isValid—This property returns a Boolean value that indicates if the timer can still be fired, or it was invalidated.

timeInterval—This property returns the time interval in seconds for repeating timers.

tolerance—This property sets or returns a period of tolerance in seconds to provide the system with more flexibility. It is a value of type **TimeInterval**. The value by default is 0.

scheduledTimer(withTimeInterval: TimeInterval, **repeats:** Bool, **block:** Closure**)**—This type method returns repeating and non-repeating timers depending on the values of its arguments. The **withTimeInterval** argument represents the seconds the timer must wait before performing the action, the **repeats** argument is a Boolean value that determines if the timer is repeating (**true**) or non-repeating (**false**), and the **block** argument is the closure to be execute when the time is up.

fire()—This method fires the timer without considering the time remaining.

invalidate()—This method invalidates the timer (stops the timer).

The **scheduledTimer()** method creates a timer according to the value of its arguments and automatically adds it to an internal loop that will process it when the time is up. The time is set in seconds with a **TimeInterval** value (a typealias of **Double**), and we can declare the closure as a trailing closure to simplify the code, as in the following example.

```
import Foundation

print("Wait 5 seconds...")
Timer.scheduledTimer(withTimeInterval: 5.0, repeats: false) { (timer) in
   print("The time is up")
}
```

Listing 4-41: *Creating a non-repeating timer*

The code in Listing 4-41 creates a non-repeating timer. It prints a message and then initializes a timer with the **scheduleTimer()** method. The timer is set to 5 seconds, non-repeating, and the closure just prints another message on the console. When we execute the code, the first message appears on the console and after 5 seconds the message "The time is up" is printed below.

The closure receives a reference to the **Timer** object that we can use to access the timer's properties or invalidate it. It was not required in the last example, but it may be useful when working with repeating timers, as in the following example.

```
import Foundation

var counter = 0

func startTimer() {
   Timer.scheduledTimer(withTimeInterval: 1.0, repeats: true)
{ (timerref) in
      report(timer: timerref)
   }
}
```

```
func report(timer: Timer) {
   print("\(counter) times")
   counter += 1
   if counter > 10 {
      print("Finished")
      timer.invalidate()
   }
}
startTimer()
```

Listing 4-42: *Creating a repeating timer*

In this code, we define two functions. The **startTimer()** function schedules the timer, and the **report()** function is executed when the time is up. In this last function, we count how many times the code is executed with the **counter** variable and print a message on the console with the number. If the value is greater than 10, we print the text "Finished" and invalidate the timer, so the function is not executed anymore (repeating timers keep running indefinitely until they are invalidated).

Basic 4.3 Core Graphics

Core Graphics is an old framework programmed in the C language. It was developed to provide a platform-independent two-dimensional drawing engine for Apple systems. The framework is composed of basic drawing tools and its own data types. Due to its characteristics, instead of being replaced, the framework was integrated with newer frameworks and, therefore, it remains in use.

Basic Data Types

What modern applications require the most from this old framework are its data types. In Swift, Core Graphics' data types are implemented as structures, with their own initializers, properties, and methods. They can store values that represent attributes of elements on the screen, such as position or size. The following is a structure included in the framework to specify floating-point values.

CGFloat—This structure is used to store values of type **Double** for drawing purposes.

A more complex structure is **CGSize**, designed to store values that represent dimensions. This data type includes the following initializer and properties.

CGSize(width: CGFloat, **height:** CGFloat**)**—This initializer creates a **CGSize** structure with the values specified by the **width** and **height** arguments. The structure defines initializers to create instances from values of type **Int**, **CGFloat**, and **Double**.

zero—This type property returns a **CGSize** structure with its values set to zero.

width—This property sets or returns the structure's width.

height—This property sets or returns the structure's height.

Another structure defined by the framework is **CGPoint**, which is used to define points in a two-dimensional coordinate system. It includes the following initializer and properties.

CGPoint(x: CGFloat, **y:** CGFloat**)**—This initializer creates a **CGPoint** structure with the coordinates specified by the **x** and **y** arguments. The structure defines initializers to create instances from values of type **Int**, **CGFloat**, and **Double**.

zero—This type property returns a **CGPoint** structure with its values set to zero.

x—This property sets or returns the structure's x coordinate.

y—This property sets or returns the structure's y coordinate.

There is also a more complex structure called **CGRect** that we can use to define and work with rectangles. This data type includes the following initializers and properties.

CGRect(origin: CGPoint, **size:** CGSize**)**—This initializer creates a **CGRect** structure to store the origin and size of a rectangle. The **origin** argument is a **CGPoint** structure with the coordinates of the rectangle's origin, and the **size** argument is a **CGSize** structure with the rectangle's width and height.

CGRect(x: CGFloat, **y:** CGFloat, **width:** CGFloat, **height:** CGFloat**)**—This initializer creates a **CGRect** structure to store the origin and size of a rectangle. The **x** and **y** arguments define the coordinates of the rectangle's origin, and the **width** and **height** arguments its size. The structure defines initializers to create instances from **Int**, **CGFloat**, and **Double** values.

zero—This type property returns a **CGRect** structure with its values set to zero.

origin—This property sets or returns a **CGPoint** structure with the coordinates of the rectangle's origin.

size—This property sets or returns a **CGSize** structure with the rectangle's width and height.

midX—This property returns the value of the rectangle's **x** coordinate located at the horizontal center of the rectangle.

midY—This property returns the value of the rectangle's **y** coordinate located at the vertical center of the rectangle.

The structures provided by Core Graphics are declared and initialized as any other structures in Swift, but we must import the Core Graphics framework first for the types to be recognized.

```
import CoreGraphics

var myfloat: CGFloat = 35
var mysize: CGSize = CGSize(width: 250, height: 250)
var mypoint: CGPoint = CGPoint(x: 20, y: 50)
var myrect: CGRect = CGRect(origin: mypoint, size: mysize)
```

Listing 4-43: *Initializing Core Graphics' structures*

The **CGSize** and **CGPoint** structures may be initialized with their member initializers, but the **CGRect** structure provides an additional initializer to create the instance from the values of its internal structures.

```
import CoreGraphics

var myrect = CGRect(x: 30, y: 20, width: 100, height: 200)

print("The origin is at \(myrect.origin.x) and \(myrect.origin.y)")
print("The size is \(myrect.size.width) by \(myrect.size.height)")
```

Listing 4-44: *Using the* CGRect *convenience initializer*

The **origin** and **size** properties of a **CGRect** value are **CGPoint** and **CGSize** structures, respectively, so they can be copied into other variables or properties as any other values.

```
import CoreGraphics

var myrect = CGRect(x: 30, y: 20, width: 100, height: 200)

var mypoint = myrect.origin
var mysize = myrect.size
print("The origin is at \(mypoint.x) and \(mypoint.y)")
print("The size is \(mysize.width) by \(mysize.height)")
```

***Listing 4-45:** Accessing the structures inside a* `CGRect` *structure*

When we don't have initial values for the coordinates or the size, we can use the **zero** type property to create a structure with all the values initialized to 0.

```
import CoreGraphics

var myrect = CGRect.zero

print("The origin is at \(myrect.origin.x) and \(myrect.origin.y)")
print("The size is \(myrect.size.width) by \(myrect.size.height)")
```

***Listing 4-46:** Assigning empty structures to a* `CGRect` *variable*

The **myrect** variable of Listing 4-46 is a **CGRect** structure with all its properties initialized with the value 0. Assigning the value of the **zero** property to a variable is the same as using the initializer **CGRect(x: 0, y: 0, width: 0, height: 0)**.

The **CGRect** structure also includes properties to calculate values from its coordinates and size. For example, the **midX** and **midY** properties return the coordinates at the center of each side.

```
import CoreGraphics

var rect = CGRect(x: 0, y: 0, width: 100, height: 100)

print("The horizontal center is \(rect.midX)")  // 50.0
```

***Listing 4-47:** Calculating the coordinate at the center of the rectangle*

IMPORTANT: In this chapter, we have explored the part of Core Graphics used by modern frameworks to build user interfaces, but the framework is extensive and includes tools for the creation of custom graphics. For more information, visit our website and follow the links for this chapter.

Chapter 5
UIKit Framework

Basic 5.1 UIKit

UIKit (User Interface Kit) is the framework provided by Apple to define the elements of the graphic interface. From text to buttons, all the standard elements that users interact with on the screen to insert, select and process information are defined by the classes in this framework. Although its primary function is to create the user interface, the framework also includes several classes to create the objects the application needs to work and to connect with the rest of the system.

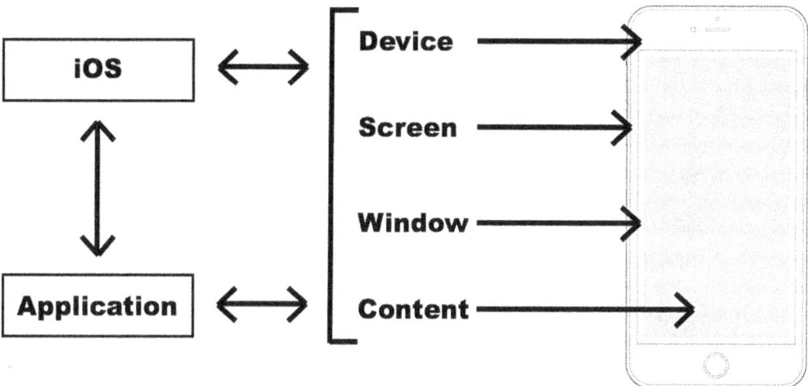

Figure 5-1: *App's ecosystem*

Basic Application

When the user taps on the icon to run the application, the first step performed by the system is to create an object of a class called **`UIApplication`** (the prefix UI stands for UIKit). This object starts a loop to keep the application running, it checks for events generated by the user or the system, reports changes in the state of the app, and provides access to the windows and the user interface.

The **`UIApplication`** object is automatically created as soon as our app is launched and works along with the system to keep the application responsive. There is nothing we need to do to set up this object, but there are times when we must access the object to configure the app or respond to changes reported by the system. For this purpose, the class includes the following type property.

shared—This type property returns a reference to the instance of the **`UIApplication`** class created for our application.

The **`UIApplication`** object designates a delegate and calls some methods on it that we can modify to perform custom tasks. The class includes the following property to access this delegate.

delegate—This property returns a reference to the object assigned as the delegate of the **`UIApplication`** object.

Devices like Mac computers and iPads can work with multiple instances of an app (multiple windows). In UIKit, these instances are called *Scenes*. Each copy of the app is a Scene, and the Scenes are associated to Scene sessions for configuration. The **`UIApplication`** class includes the following properties to manage the windows, the Scenes, and the Scene sessions of our application.

supportsMultipleScenes—This property returns a Boolean to indicate if the application supports multiple Scenes (multiple windows).

connectedScenes—This property returns a set with references to the Scenes that are currently connected to the application.

openSessions—This property returns a set with references to the Scene sessions currently active or archived by the system.

windows—This property returns an array of **UIWindow** objects representing the visible and hidden windows managed by the app.

The following example illustrates how to access the **UIApplication** object and how to read its properties.

```
import UIKit

let app = UIApplication.shared
if app.supportsMultipleScenes {
   print("Multiple Windows App")
} else {
   print("Single Window App")  // "Single Window App"
}
```

***Listing 5-1:** Accessing the* `UIApplication` *object*

In the code of Listing 5-1, we first import UIKit to have access to all the tools defined in this framework and then read the **shared** property to get a reference to the **UIApplication** object created for our app. With this reference, we check whether the application allows the user to open multiple windows or not by reading the **supportsMultipleScenes** property.

Do It Yourself: The examples in this section of the chapter were designed for testing on Playground. Playground was developed to learn, practice, and test code, but cannot simulate a system such as a mobile device, and therefore, UIKit classes only return values by default. Later in this chapter, we will learn how to create real applications with the Xcode main interface.

Basic Device

The UIKit framework also includes classes to manage the device in which the app is running and its screen. For the device, UIKit defines the **UIDevice** class. The following is the type property that returns the **UIDevice** object representing the current device.

current—This type property returns the instance of the **UIDevice** class that represents the device in which the app is currently running.

The following are some of the properties and methods provided by the **UIDevice** class to read the device's configuration and activate or deactivate some of its features.

systemName—This property returns a string with the name of the operative system.

systemVersion—This property returns a string with the version of the operative system.

orientation—This property returns a value that determines the current orientation of the device. It is an enumeration of type **UIDeviceOrientation** with the values **unknown**, **portrait**, **portraitUpsideDown**, **landscapeLeft**, **landscapeRight**, **faceUp**, and **faceDown**. For accuracy, the property requires the accelerometer to be enabled.

beginGeneratingDeviceOrientationNotifications()—This method enables the accelerometer and begins delivering notifications to communicate changes in the orientation.

endGeneratingDeviceOrientationNotifications()—This method tells the system that the accelerometer is no longer required and stops the delivery of notifications.

The implementation of this class is simple. We get an instance of the object that represents the current device and then read its properties, as shown next.

```
import UIKit

let current = UIDevice.current
let deviceName = current.systemName
let deviceVersion = current.systemVersion

print("\(deviceName) \(deviceVersion)")  // "iPadOS 15.0"
```

***Listing 5-2:** Getting information from the device*

The device's screen is represented by an object of the **UIScreen** class. This class provides information about the main screen and external screens connected to the device. The following are some of its properties.

main—This type property returns the **UIScreen** object that manages the main screen.

bounds—This property returns a **CGRect** value with the dimensions of the screen expressed in points. The values vary according to the device's orientation.

nativeBounds—This property returns a **CGRect** value with the dimensions of the screen expressed in pixels. The values are always returned considering the portrait orientation.

scale—This property returns a **CGFloat** value representing the scale of the screen. This is a value that translates between points and real pixels on the screen, as we will see next.

brightness—This property sets or returns a **CGFloat** value that determines the brightness of the screen. It takes values from 0.0 to 1.0.

The screen of a device is composed of a grid of hundreds of dots called *pixels*, ordered in rows and columns. The number of pixels varies from one device to another. To compensate for the disparities between devices, Apple adopted the concept of points (sometimes called *logical pixels*). The goal was to have a unit of measurement that is independent of the device and the density of the pixels on the screen. A point occupies a square of one or more pixels, depending on the device, but the developer does not need to know how many, it is all managed by the system.

At the time of writing, points in Apple mobile devices may represent a square of up to three pixels, depending on the device and the technology. The following is the list of devices available in the market that can run the latest operative system, along with the screen resolutions they support.

- iPhone 6S/7/8/SE2 375 x 667 points 750 x 1334 pixels 2x scale
- iPhone 6S/7/8 Plus 414 x 736 points 1080 x 1920 pixels 3x scale
- iPhone X/XS/11 Pro 375 x 812 points 1125 x 2436 pixels 3x scale
- iPhone XR/11 414 x 896 points 828 x 1792 pixels 3x scale
- iPhone XS Max/11 Pro Max 414 x 896 points 1242 x 2688 pixels 3x scale
- iPhone 12/13 Mini 375 x 812 points 1080 x 2340 pixels 3x scale
- iPhone 12/13 12/13 Pro 390 x 844 points 1170 x 2532 pixels 3x scale
- iPhone 12/13 Pro Max 428 x 926 points 1284 x 2778 pixels 3x scale

- iPad Pro 12.9in 1024 x 1366 points 2048 x 2732 pixels 2x scale
- iPad Pro 11in 834 x 1194 points 1668 x 2388 pixels 2x scale
- iPad Pro 10.5/ Air 3rd 834 x 1112 points 1668 x 2224 pixels 2x scale
- iPad Air 4th 820 x 1180 points 1640 x 2360 pixels 2x scale
- iPad 7th 810 x 1080 points 1620 x 2160 pixels 2x scale
- iPad 5th/6th/7th/8th 768 x 1024 points 1536 x 2048 pixels 2x scale
- iPad Pro 9.7in/Mini 4th/5th 768 x 1024 points 1536 x 2048 pixels 2x scale

The difference between points and pixels represents the scale. iPhones 3 and older had a scale of 1 (1 point represents 1 pixel), but modern iPhones have a scale up to 3 (1 point represents a square of 3 pixels), while iPads have a scale of 2 (1 point represents a square of 2 pixels). Working with points instead of pixels makes it easy for developers to create graphic interfaces that adapt to every device.

To determine the location of each point, Apple uses a coordinate system. The system counts the columns and rows from the top-left corner to the bottom-right corner, as illustrated next.

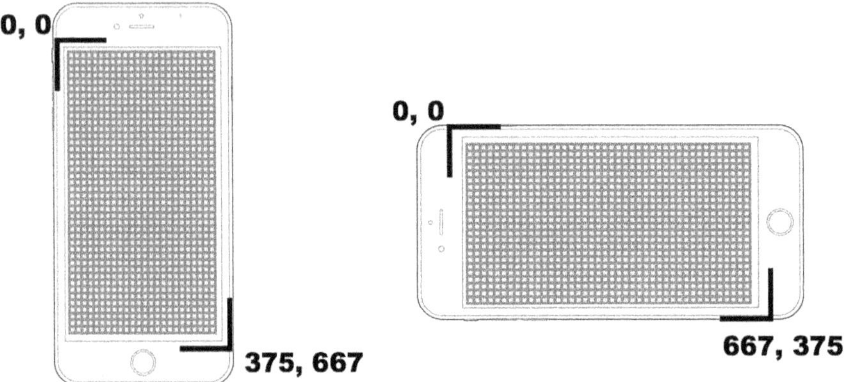

Figure 5-2: *Coordinate system*

The properties **`bound`**, **`nativeBounds`**, and **`scale`** included in the **`UIScreen`** class return the values corresponding to the screen of the device where the app is running. The **`bound`** and **`nativeBounds`** properties contain **`CGRect`** structures, while **`scale`** is just a **`CGFloat`** value.

```
import UIKit

let screen = UIScreen.main

let pointsWidth = screen.bounds.size.width
let pointsHeight = screen.bounds.size.height
print("Width: \(pointsWidth) x Height: \(pointsHeight)")

let pixelsWidth = screen.nativeBounds.size.width
let pixelsHeight = screen.nativeBounds.size.height
print("Width: \(pixelsWidth) x Height: \(pixelsHeight)")

print("Scale: \(screen.scale)")
```

Listing 5-3: *Getting information from the screen*

The native resolution in pixels is always returned considering a portrait orientation, but the size in points is returned according to the current orientation. For example, the iPhone X's screen is 375 points wide and 812 points tall in portrait, but 812 points wide and 375 points tall in landscape.

Basic Windows

The window is a space on the screen where the elements of the user interface are laid out. UIKit includes the **`UIWindow`** class to create the object that manages the windows in our app. When the system creates a new instance of our app (Scene), either because the app was just launched or because the user requested a new window, a **`UIWindow`** object is created and assigned to the Scene.

A **`UIWindow`** object defines the space occupied by the user interface, but the interface is created with objects called *Views*, as we will see next. Therefore, once the **`UIWindow`** object is initialized, we must tell the system which views are going to be shown first. The following is the property included by the class for this purpose.

rootViewController—This property sets or returns a reference to the object that controls the app's initial view.

There could be multiple windows available (one per Scene), and some may be hidden. The following are some of the properties and methods provided by the class to manage these situations.

isKeyWindow—This property returns a Boolean value that determines whether the window is the key window (the window currently in charge of receiving input from the user).

windowScene—This property sets or returns a reference of the Scene that contains the window. It is of type **`UIWindowScene`**.

makeKeyAndVisible()—This method positions the window in front of any other windows that may exist for the app and makes it visible.

Basic Views

The window is the space where the graphics are displayed, but it does not generate any visible content. The user's interface is built inside the window from similar containers called *Views*. These views are rectangular areas of custom size, designed to display graphics on the screen. Some views are used just as containers while others are improved to present graphic tools, such as buttons and switches, and graphic content, such as images and text. The views are organized in a hierarchy, one inside another, with a view of the size of the window as the root (usually called *main view* or *container view*), as illustrated next.

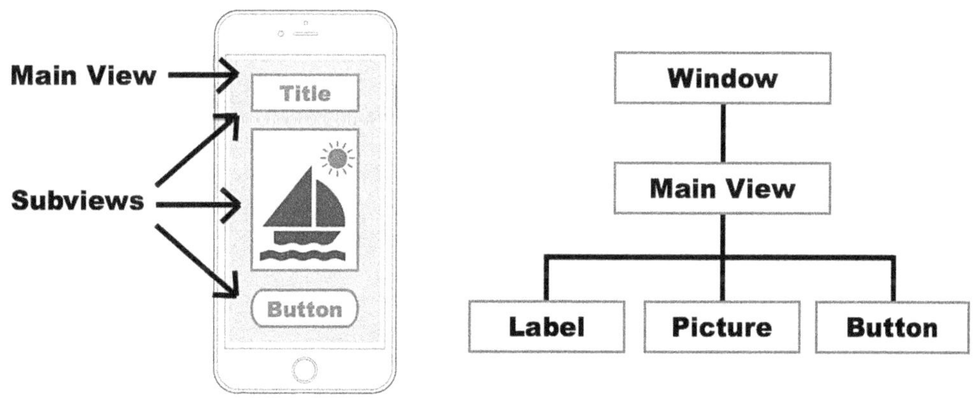

Figure 5-3: *Views hierarchy*

No matter the purpose of the view (to be a container or to present content), they are all created from objects of the **UIView** class. This is a basic class that is only capable of creating and managing the rectangular area occupied by the view, but subclasses of this class are defined to add functionality and present any type of content we want. Although the objects created directly from the **UIView** class are very limited, they have an extensive list of properties and methods to configure and draw their views. The following are the most useful initializer, properties, and methods available.

UIView(frame: CGRect**)**—This initializer creates a **UIView** object in the position and size determined by the **frame** argument.

frame—This property sets or returns a **CGRect** value that determines the position and size of the rectangular area occupied by the view.

bounds—This property sets or returns a **CGRect** value that determines the position and size of the rectangular area occupied by the view inside its own frame.

backgroundColor—This property sets or returns an object that determines the color of the view's background. The value is an object of the **UIColor** class.

alpha—This property sets or returns a **CGFloat** value that determines the view's alpha level (the level of transparency). The property takes values from 0.0 (transparent) to 1.0 (opaque).

isHidden—This property sets or returns a Boolean value that determines whether the view is visible (**false**) or hidden (**true**).

isOpaque—This property sets or returns a Boolean value that determines whether the view is opaque or not.

contentMode—This property sets or returns a value that determines the mode used by the view to lay out its content when its size changes (frequently used with images). It is an enumeration called **ContentMode** included in the **UIView** class. The values available are **scaleToFill**, **scaleAspectFit**, **scaleAspectFill**, **redraw**, **center**, **top**, **bottom**, **left**, **right**, **topLeft**, **topRight**, **bottomLeft**, and **bottomRight**.

clipsToBounds—This property sets or returns a Boolean value that determines whether the content of the view is confined to the view's bounds or not.

isUserInteractionEnabled—This property sets or returns a Boolean value that determines whether the view responds to the user's interaction (e.g., a tap of the finger).

isMultipleTouchEnabled—This property sets or returns a Boolean value that determines if the view can handle multiple touch events.

superview—This property returns a reference to the **UIVIew** object that is the container of the view. If the view is not inside another view, the value returned is **nil**.

subviews—This property returns an array containing references to the **UIView** objects that are inside the view (subviews).

tag—This property sets or returns an integer value that identifies the view.

viewWithTag(Int)—This method searches for a subview of the view with the tag specified by the argument. The value returned is an optional containing a **UIView** object or **nil** in case no view with that tag was found.

The window is positioned inside the screen, while the views are positioned inside the window and inside one another, generating a hierarchical structure (see Figure 5-3). As we already mentioned, the position of these elements is determined by a coordinate system. For instance, the next example creates a view of 375 points by 667 points, akin to the main view of a small iPhone.

```
import UIKit

var mainframe = CGRect(x: 0, y: 0, width: 375, height: 667)
let container = UIView(frame: mainframe)
```

Listing 5-4: Creating a view

The initializer of the **UIView** class takes a parameter called **frame** of type **CGRect** to establish the position and size of the view. The view created by the code in Listing 5-4 is positioned at the window's coordinates 0, 0 and has a size of 375 by 667 points.

Do It Yourself: Replace the code in your Playground file with the code in Listing 5-4. In the Results Side Bar, click on the Quick Look button corresponding to the line that creates the **container** object to see a representation of the view. At this moment, you will only be able to see a gray rectangle.

The background color of the **UIView** object is set as transparent by default. If we want to change the color, we must assign a new value to the **backgroundColor** property of the view. This value must be provided as an object of the **UIColor** class. This class includes some initializers and properties to create the objects. The following are the most frequently used.

UIColor(red: CGFloat, **green:** CGFloat, **blue:** CGFloat, **alpha:** CGFloat**)**—This initializer creates a **UIColor** object with a color set by the values of its arguments. It takes values from 0.0 to 1.0. The **red** argument defines the level of red, **green** the level of green, **blue** the level of blue, and **alpha** defines the alpha level (transparency).

UIColor(patternImage: UIImage**)**—This initializer creates a **UIColor** object with a color defined as the image provided by the **patternImage** argument. The image will be replicated as many times as necessary to fill the area to which the color is assigned.

The **UIColor** class also offers an extensive list of type properties that return a **UIColor** object with a predefined color. The following are the properties Apple recommends using to define standard colors because they adapt the color to the appearance (light or dark): **systemBlue**, **systemBrown**, **systemGreen**, **systemIndigo**, **systemOrange**, **systemPink**, **systemPurple**, **systemRed**, **systemTeal**, **systemYellow**, **systemCyan**, **systemMint**, **systemGray**, **systemGray2**, **systemGray3**, **systemGray4**, **systemGray5**, and **systemGray6**. There are also properties that return predefined colors for labels: **label**, **secondaryLabel**, **tertiaryLabel**, and **quaternaryLabel**. And properties with predefined fill colors: **systemFill**, **secondarySystemFill**, **tertiarySystemFill** and **quaternarySystemFill**. A few properties with predefined colors for backgrounds: **systemBackground**, **secondarySystemBackground**, and **tertiarySystemBackground**. Other properties that return colors for a variety of interface elements, such as **placeholderText**, **separator**, and **link**. A property called **clear** to assign a transparent color. Another called **tintColor** that represents the app's global tint color. And finally, some properties with fixed colors that do not adapt to the appearance: **black**, **blue**, **brown**, **cyan**, **darkGray**, **gray**, **green**, **lightGray**, **magenta**, **orange**, **purple**, **red**, **white**, and **yellow**.

UIColor objects are assigned to the views and most of the elements in the user interface to define their colors. They are created from the initializers or type properties listed above and then assigned to the corresponding properties, as in the following example.

```
import UIKit

let container = UIView(frame: CGRect(x: 0, y: 0, width: 375, height:
667))

var color = UIColor(red: 1.0, green: 0.0, blue: 0.0, alpha: 1.0)
container.backgroundColor = color
```

Listing 5-5: Assigning a background color to a view

The color for the **UIColor** object created in Listing 5-5 is defined by the initializer's arguments. The system used in this case is called RGB. The color is constructed by adding the values of every component: Red, Green, and Blue. In this example, the **red** argument was set to 1.0 while the rest of the colors were set to 0.0, defining a pure red. A similar color is returned by the type property **systemRed**, although with the difference that this color adapts to the appearance (light or dark).

```
import UIKit

let container = UIView(frame: CGRect(x: 0, y: 0, width: 375, height:
667))
let color = UIColor.systemRed
container.backgroundColor = color
```

Listing 5-6: Assigning an adaptable color to the view

Do It Yourself: Replace the code in your Playground file with the code in Listing 5-6. In the Result Side Bar, click on the Show Result button corresponding to the line that assigns the new color to the **backgroundColor** property of the view. You should see a rectangular red view within the Editor Area.

IMPORTANT: The **UIColor** initializer uses values from 0.0 to 1.0 to determine the levels of red, green, and blue that define the composition of the color, but RGB colors are usually determined with integer values from 0 to 255. If you prefer to work with these values, you can convert them dividing the values by 255.0. For example, if the level of red is 190, you can get the value for the initializer with the formula 190.0 / 255.0.

The user's interface is built by adding views to parent views that work as containers, creating the hierarchical structure introduced in Figure 5-3. The container view is called the *superview* and the views inside are called *subviews*. When a view is added to a superview, the object is stored in the **subviews** property of the superview. This is a property containing an array of views. To add and manage the views inside this array, the **UIView** class offers the following methods.

addSubview(UIView**)**—This method adds a view at the end of the **subviews** array.

insertSubview(UIView, **at:** Int**)**—This method inserts a view in the **subviews** array at the index indicated by the **at** argument.

insertSubview(UIView, **aboveSubview:** UIView**)**—This method inserts a view in the **subviews** array above the subview indicated by the **aboveSubview** argument.

insertSubview(UIView, **belowSubview:** UIView**)**—This method inserts a view in the **subviews** array below the subview indicated by the **belowSubview** argument.

bringSubviewToFront(UIView**)**—This method moves the subview specified by the argument to the end of the **subviews** array (to the front).

sendSubviewToBack(UIView**)**—This method moves the subview specified by the argument to the beginning of the **subviews** array (to the back).

removeFromSuperview()—This method removes a subview from its superview.

The subviews are shown on the screen according to their position on the **subviews** array. The subviews with a lower index are drawn first, so the views with a higher index are shown at the top. This is why the method most frequently used to add a view to another view is **addSubview()**. This method adds the view to the end of the **subviews** array, effectively drawing the view at the front.

```
import UIKit

let container = UIView(frame: CGRect(x: 0, y: 0, width: 375, height:
667))
container.backgroundColor = UIColor.systemRed

let subview1 = UIView(frame: CGRect(x: 20, y: 20, width: 335, height:
300))
subview1.backgroundColor = UIColor.systemGray4

let subview2 = UIView(frame: CGRect(x: 20, y: 347, width: 335, height:
300))
subview2.backgroundColor = UIColor.systemGray4

container.addSubview(subview1)
container.addSubview(subview2)
```

***Listing 5-7:** Adding subviews to a container view*

After creating the **container** view, the code in Listing 5-7 creates two more views and adds them as subviews with the **addSubview()** method. The **subviews** property of **container** now has two elements: the **subview1** and **subview2** views. These subviews are of different color, creating two smaller rectangles of 335 by 300 points inside the main view, as shown in Figure 5-4.

***Figure 5-4:** Views on Playground*

Every subview is attached to its superview and positioned on the screen according to its coordinate system. When we set the values of the **x** and **y** parameters in the **UIView** initializer for every view, we must consider the coordinates of their superviews, not the screen or other container views up the chain. For example, the position of the **subview1** view inside the **container** view is 20, 20, but its own coordinate system starts again from 0, 0 at its top-left corner. The same happens with **subview2**. Any views added to these subviews will have a position according to the coordinates of their superviews, not the coordinates of the **container** view or the window. Figure 5-5 illustrates these views and their coordinate systems.

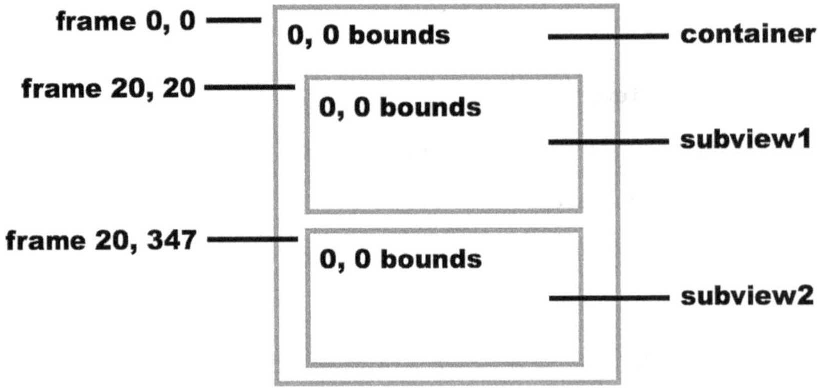

Figure 5-5: *Subviews and their coordinates*

These values are provided by the **frame** and **bounds** properties of the **UIView** objects that represent each view. For example, the **x** and **y** values of the **frame** property of **subview1** are 20, 20, but the **x** and **y** values of the **bounds** property of **subview1** are 0, 0, because the **bounds** property refers to the view's internal frame and its own coordinate system.

Basic UIView Subclasses

The views created from the **UIView** class are good as containers and organizers but do not present any content. The content is generated by subclasses of **UIView**. These subclasses overwrite some **UIView** methods and provide their own properties and methods to draw graphics inside the view or respond to user interaction. Considering how difficult and time consuming it is to create every single element of the interface from scratch, UIKit provides ready to use subclasses of **UIView** for the creation of standard elements. From labels and buttons to images and tables, there is a **UIView** subclass to present on the screen everything our app needs. Figure 5-6 shows a scheme with the **UIView** class and some of its most important subclasses.

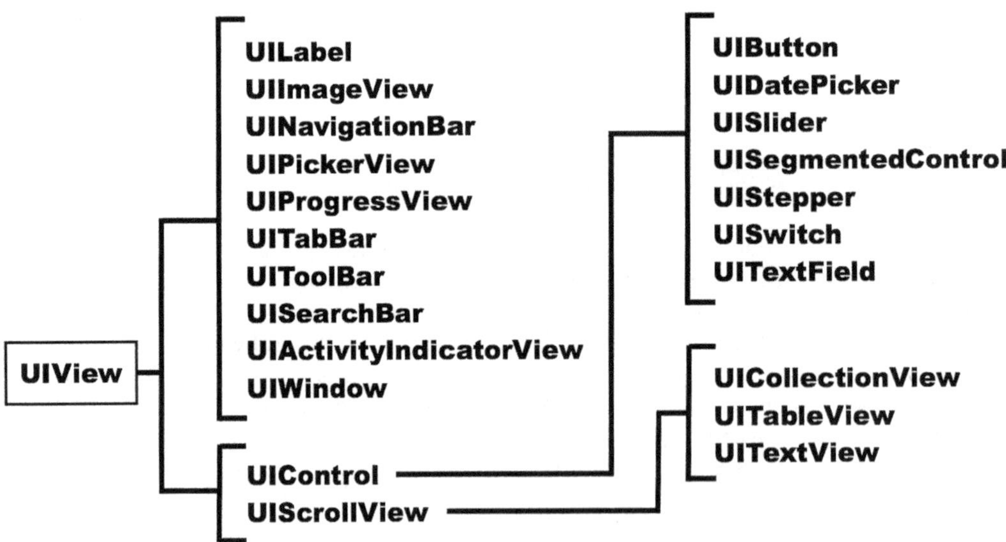

Figure 5-6: `UIView` *subclasses*

Some classes that add graphic content, such as **UILabel** or **UIImageView**, inherit directly from **UIView**, while classes that provide more complex functionality, such as **UIButton** or **UITableView**, inherit from intermediate subclasses. The two intermediate subclasses depicted in Figure 5-6, **UIControl** and **UIScrollView**, provide common functionality for their own subclasses. **UIControl** adds to **UIView** the capacity to respond to user interaction and report events, and **UIScrollView** adds the possibility to create views with scrollable content.

Basic Scenes

A **UIApplication** object runs the application, a **UIDevice** object provides information about the device, a **UIScreen** object describes and configures the screen, and **UIWindow** and **UIView** objects define the interface, but this is not enough to control the application. In some devices, multiple instances of the same application can run at the same time. For example, we may have two instances of the Text Editor on the screen processing two different documents, or two instances of a browser loading two different websites. To control these instances, the UIKit framework defines Scenes.

Scenes are what users call windows. Some devices, such as iPhones and iPods Touch, can only work with one Scene at a time (one window), but iPads and Mac computers can work with multiple Scenes (multiple windows). UIKit defines the **UIWindowScene** class to control each Scene. The following are some useful properties defined by this class.

windows—This property returns an array of **UIWindow** objects that represent the windows managed by the Scene.

screen—This property returns a reference to the **UIScreen** object that displays the content of the Scene.

interfaceOrientation—This property returns the interface orientation. It is an enumeration of type **UIInterfaceOrientation** with the values **unknown**, **portrait**, **portraitUpsideDown**, **landscapeLeft**, and **landscapeRight**. The enumeration also includes the Boolean properties **isLandscape** and **isPortrait** to quickly get the current orientation.

statusBarManager—This property returns a **UIStatusBarManager** object with the configuration of the status bar. This object includes properties like **isStatusBarHidden** (a Boolean value that determines whether the status bar is hidden or not) and **statusBarFrame** (a **CGRect** value with the position and size of the bar), among others.

A **UIWindowScene** object is automatically created per Scene and then **UIWindow** objects are created and assigned to the Scenes to display the user interface, as shown below.

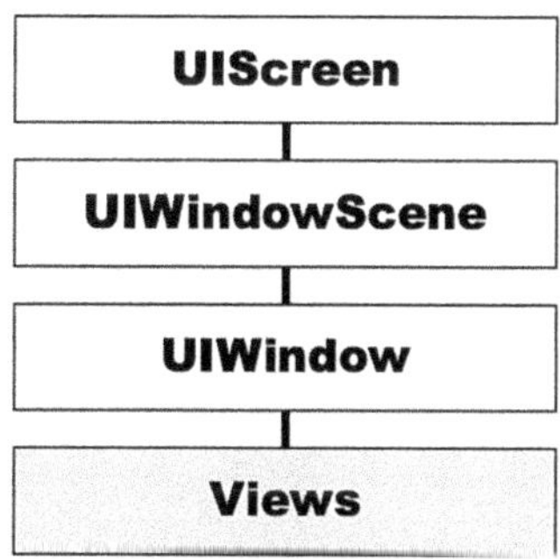

Figure 5-7: *Single Scene*

iPads and Mac computers allow multiple instances of our app to run at the same time. When the user opens multiple windows with our app, the system generates one Scene per window.

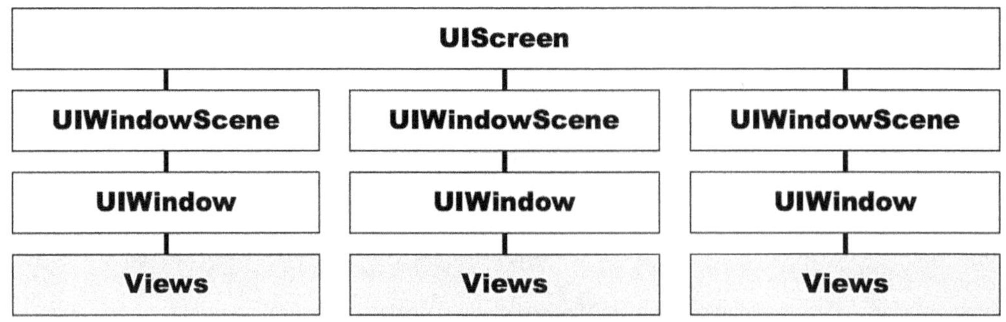

Figure 5-8: *Multiple Scenes*

No matter if the app is showing one Scene or several, the process to define the content of each one of them is the same. Once the window is created for the Scene, we must add all the views inside with the content we want to show to the user. We will study this process next.

Basic 5.2 Xcode

Creating the app's interface by adding subviews to the main view from our code, as we did in previous examples, may be appropriate for very small applications, but as the interface grows and new elements and functionality are introduced, the code becomes difficult to develop and maintain. This is especially true with mobile applications, where we not only have to define the initial interface but also adapt it to new conditions produced by the rotation of the screen or the app running on different devices. Xcode expedites our work by providing a set of graphic tools that allow us to create and modify the views and the application. This toolset includes an editor, a visual interface, resource managers, configuration panels, and debugging tools, all integrated into a single working space.

Basic Projects

Applications are built from several files and resources, including our own codes, frameworks, images, databases, and more. Xcode organizes these elements into projects. An Xcode project comprises all the information and resources necessary to create one application. The welcome window, illustrated in Figure 1-2, presents a button called *Create a new Xcode project* to initiate a project. When we click on this button, a new window presents the templates we can choose from to create our project.

Choose a template for your new project:

Multiplatform iOS macOS watchOS tvOS DriverKit Other Filter

Application

App Document App Game Augmented Reality App Sticker Pack App

Figure 5-9: *Selecting the type of project we want to create*

The options are organized in several categories—Multiplatform, iOS, macOS, watchOS, tvOS, DriverKit, and Other—representing each operative system Apple has to offer. In this book, we are going to learn how to develop applications for iPhones and iPads with UIKit, so we must select the App template under the iOS category, as shown in Figure 5-9.

Once we select the type of project we want to build, the next step is to provide information about the project. Figure 5-10, below, shows the values required for the App template and the iOS system.

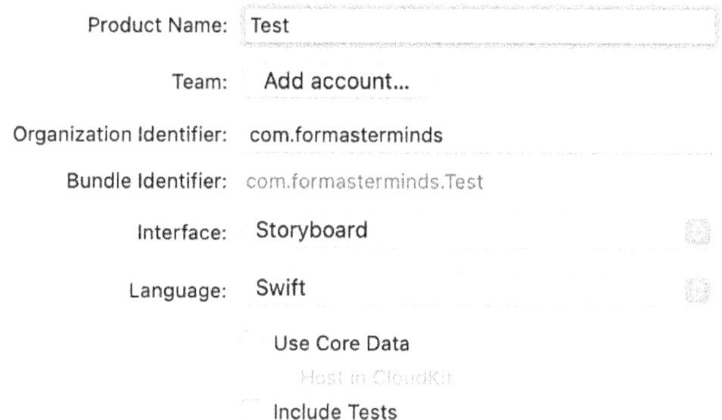

Figure 5-10: *Project configuration window*

The Product Name is the name of the project. By default, this is the name of our app and the folder where the project is stored, so we should write a name that is appropriate for our application. Next is the Team's account. This is the developer account created with our Apple ID at developer.apple.com, or our company's account. If we haven't yet registered our account with Xcode, we will see the Add Account button to add it (we explain how to add an account to Xcode below). The next value is the Organization Identifier. Xcode uses this value and the project's name to create a unique identifier for our app and therefore it is recommended to declare it with an inverted domain, as we did in our example (com.formasterminds). Using the inverted domain ensures that only our app will have that identifier (com.formasterminds.Test). Next, we must select the technology we are going to use to design the user interface. There are two options available: SwiftUI and Storyboard. SwiftUI is a system that allows us to declare the interface from code, while Storyboard is a graphic tool that produces a visual representation of the user interface and allows us to modify it by just dragging and dropping elements on the screen. To develop applications with the UIKit framework, we must select the Storyboard option. Finally, we must select the Swift language.

IMPORTANT: There are additional options at the bottom that we can check to prepare our template to work with complementary systems like Unit Testing and Core Data. For most projects, these options are not required, but we will explore some of them in following chapters (see Core Data in Chapter 15 and CloudKit in Chapter 17).

As mentioned above, the Team's field shows a list of developer accounts registered with Xcode. If we haven't yet inserted our developer account, we will see the Add Account button instead. Pressing this button opens a window to insert our Apple ID or create a new one.

Figure 5-11: *Registering Apple account in Xcode*

Once the Apple ID is inserted, the account is configured to work with our copy of Xcode. With the account selected and all the information inserted in the form, we can now press the Next button to designate the folder where our project is going to be stored. Xcode creates a folder for each project, so we only need to specify the destination folder where we are going to store all our projects and everything else is generated for us.

Do It Yourself: Open Xcode. In the welcome screen, click on the option Create a new Xcode project (Figure 1-2). You can also go to the File menu at the top of the screen and select the options New/Project. After this, you should see the templates window (Figure 5-9). Select the iOS tab, click on the App icon, and press Next. Now you should see the form of Figure 5-10. In Product Name, Insert the name of your project. In the Team option, select your developer account or press the Add Account button to register your account with Xcode. In Organization Identifier insert the inverted domain of your website or blog. Next, select the Storyboard interface and the Swift language. Make sure that the rest of the options are disabled. Finally, press Next and select a folder where to store your project.

IMPORTANT: Although it's not mandatory, you should get your own domain and website. Apple not only recommends the use of an inverted domain to generate the Bundle Identifier, but at the time of submitting your app to the App Store you will be asked to provide the web page used for promotion and where the users should go for support.

Basic Tools

After the project is created, Xcode generates the files required by the template and presents the main interface on the screen. Figure 5-12, next, shows what this interface looks like.

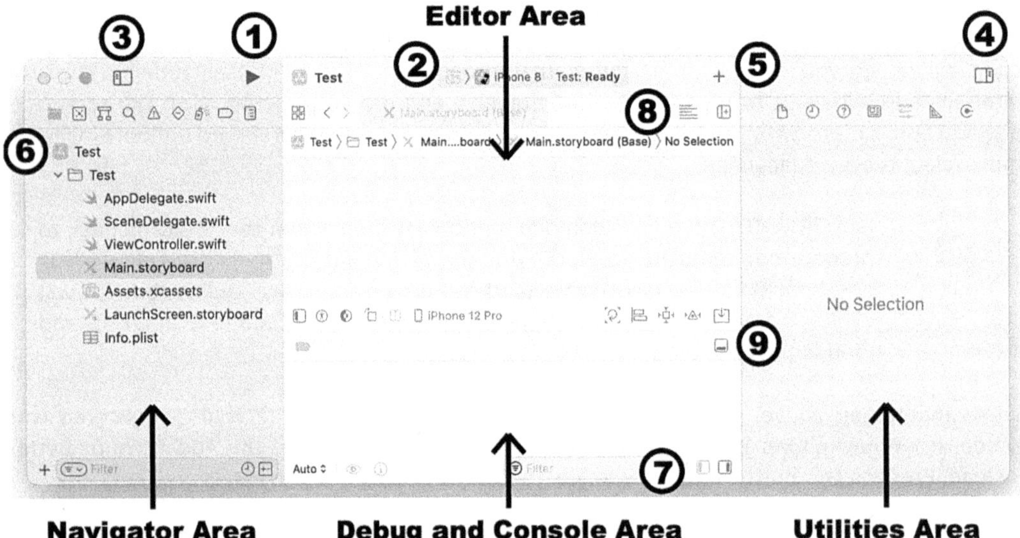

Figure 5-12: Xcode's interface

Like the Playground interface, the Xcode's main window is organized in several areas. There is a toolbar at the top, an area to edit the files at the center called *Editor Area*, and three removable panels on the sides and bottom called *Navigator Area*, *Debug and Console Area*, and *Utilities Area*.

Toolbar—This is the area at the top with buttons to control the appearance of the interface, and a display to show warnings, errors, and the app's status. It provides buttons to run and stop the app (Figure 5-12, number 1), a drop-down list to select the device or the simulator where we want to run the app (Figure 5-12, number 2), a button that opens a popup window with tools to create the user interface (Figure 5-12, number 5), and two buttons to show or remove the Navigator Area and the Utilities Area (Figure 5-12, number 3 and 4).

Navigator Area—This is a removable area that provides information about the files that comprise the application and tools for debugging (identify and remove errors in the code). From here, we can select the files to edit, create groups to organize those files, add resources, check for errors, and more. In addition to the files, this area shows an option at the top to configure the app (Figure 5-12, number 6).

Editor Area—This is the only non-removable area and is the one where we will do much of the work. The content of files and configuration panels are displayed here. Although the Editor Area cannot be removed, it includes buttons at the top to split the area into multiple editors or panels, as we will see later (Figure 5-12, number 8).

Debug and Console Area—This is a removable area that splits into two sections that can be shown or hidden by the buttons at the bottom (Figure 5-12, number 7). The section on the left provides information for debugging, while the section on the right is a console to display the results of the execution of our code, including warnings and errors.

Utilities Area—This is a removable area that provides additional information about the app and allows us to edit the configuration of the interface and its elements.

Basic Running the App

Xcode offers two ways to run our application: the simulator or a real device. The buttons to select these options, execute, and stop the app are on the toolbar.

Figure 5-13: *Buttons to run the app*

Applications are run on a specific destination. This destination could be different things, from real devices to windows or simulators, and have different configurations, including settings like the region where the device is located, and the human language used by the app to display the information on the screen. Xcode allows us to define and configure the possible destinations for our app using an arrangement called *Scheme*. When a project is created, a Scheme is automatically generated for us with options that are according to the type of project and our local settings (region and language set on the computer). For example, the default Scheme of a project for a mobile application includes several iOS simulators and offers access to the devices currently connected to the computer. The Scheme is selected from the button on the left of the Scheme section and the destination is selected from the button on the right. When the destination button is clicked, we can see a list of the devices and simulators available.

Figure 5-14: *Options available to run the app*

During development, the most common destination is the simulator. The simulator is a program included in the Xcode's package that can recreate a specific device in a separate window. It is a practical tool because it is fast, and it can simulate almost every feature of a device.

To test the app, all we need to do is to select the simulator from the Scheme and then click the Play button. Figure 5-15, below, shows the simulator configured as an iPhone, running the app created by the App template (an empty screen).

Figure 5-15: *iPhone simulator running the app created by the App template*

IMPORTANT: Pressing the Play button on the toolbar runs the application on the simulator or a device, but we can also build the app without running it. This is useful for checking your code for errors. You can build the app by pressing the Command + B keys on your keyboard or by selecting the Build option in the Product menu at the top of the screen.

Basic 5.3 Templates

Templates include files with resources and sample code that we can use to start building our application, but to take advantage of these files we need to understand first how Xcode suggests applications should be built and the tools it provides for this purpose.

Basic MVC

Xcode proposes an architectural paradigm that divides the application in three interconnected parts, the Model, the View, and the Controller (called MVC for short). Every part of the code performs a specific task and communicates to the other parts only the information strictly necessary. Figure 5-16 illustrates the elements involved.

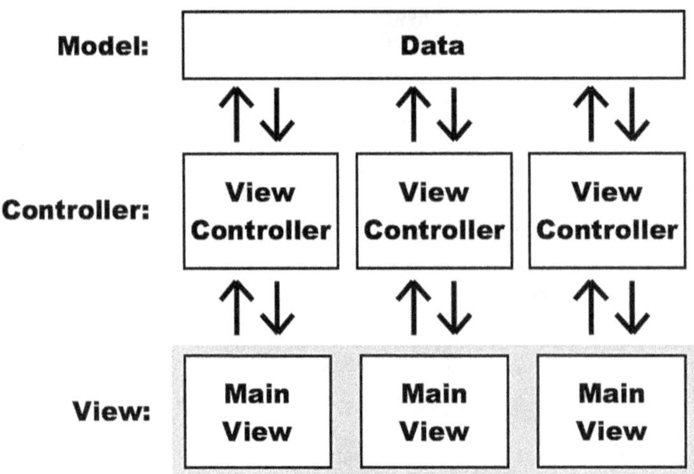

Figure 5-16: *MVC architecture*

The Model is the data the app is going to process, the View is the user interface (window and views), and the Controller is the object in charge of receiving input from the views, processing the data, and updating the interface. The objects managing the data and the views are not connected with each other, they send the information to the controller and this code decides what to do with it. This allows reusability. We can use the same code to control different views or replace the user's interface entirely without having to change a line of code in the rest of the program.

This structure is created from several objects. The interface is created from the **UIView** objects introduced before, which are connected to controller objects called *View Controllers*, and these objects are connected to the objects that manage the data. Although we can define all the objects from scratch, the files created by the App template provide the definition of some of the classes we need to create these objects and other resources.

AppDelegate.swift—This file defines a class called **AppDelegate** to create an object that is going to work as the delegate of the **UIApplication** object. Every time the state of the application changes, methods of this delegate are called to report the change.

SceneDelegate.swift—This file defines a class called **SceneDelegate** to create an object that is going to work as delegate of the Scenes (windows). When a Scene is created, an object of this class is assigned to it. Every time the state of the Scene changes, methods of this delegate are called to report the change to our code.

ViewController.swift—This file defines a class called **ViewController** to control the only view added to the Storyboard by the App template.

Main.storyboard—This file defines our app's Storyboard; a visual editor to create the user interface. The Storyboard provided by the App template includes only one view, but we can add more as we will see later.

Assets.xcassets—This is a folder called Assets Catalog used to organize the app's resources.

LaunchScreen.storyboard—This is a Storyboard with a single view used to define the app's launch screen (the screen shown by the system while the app is starting up).

Info.plist—This is a file with structured text to define the app's basic configuration.

Do It Yourself: Open the Navigator Area (the panel on the left). You should see the list of files created by the App template. If the files are not visible, click on the Project Navigator button at the top-left corner of the Navigator Area.

Medium Application Delegate

The first file on the list is called AppDelegate.swift and contains a class called **AppDelegate**. As we already mentioned, when the app is launched, the system creates an object of the **UIApplication** class to provide the basic functionality necessary for the app to process information and respond to user interaction. The object created from the **AppDelegate** class is assigned as the delegate of the **UIApplication** object. Every time the system needs to report a change in the state of the application to our code, it calls methods on this delegate. For this purpose, the **AppDelegate** class conforms to the **UIApplicationDelegate** protocol. The following are the methods defined by the protocol to initialize the app and configure the Scenes.

application(UIApplication, **didFinishLaunchingWithOptions:** Dictionary**)**—This is the first method called by the **UIApplication** object. It is called to let us know that all the necessary objects were already instantiated, and the app is ready to work.

application(UIApplication, **configurationForConnecting:** UISceneSession, **options:** UIScene.ConnectionOptions**)**—This method is called when a new Scene (window) is requested by the system or the user. The method must return a **UISceneConfiguration** object with the Scene's configuration.

application(UIApplication, **didDiscardSceneSessions:** Set)—This method is called when the user discards a Scene (closes a window). The **didDiscardSceneSessions** argument is a set with references to the **UISceneSession** objects representing the Scenes' sessions.

As soon as the app is launched, the **UIApplication** object calls the **application(UIApplication, didFinishLaunchingWithOptions:)** method. In this method, we can write all the code we need to prepare our application, such as declaring initial values, opening a database, checking the current settings, and more, as shown next.

```
import UIKit

@main
class AppDelegate: UIResponder, UIApplicationDelegate {
   var basicSalary: Double!

   func application(_ application: UIApplication,
didFinishLaunchingWithOptions launchOptions:
[UIApplication.LaunchOptionsKey: Any]?) -> Bool {

      basicSalary = 30000.0

      return true
   }
   func application(_ application: UIApplication,
configurationForConnecting connectingSceneSession: UISceneSession,
options: UIScene.ConnectionOptions) -> UISceneConfiguration {
      return UISceneConfiguration(name: "Default Configuration",
sessionRole: connectingSceneSession.role)
   }
}
```

Listing 5-8: *Defining a property in the app's delegate object*

This example adds a property called **basicSalary** to the **AppDelegate** class. When the **application(UIApplication, didFinishLaunchingWithOptions:)** method is called, we initialize this property with the value 30000.0. This is a simple but practical example that illustrates how we can add properties to the application delegate and initialize them when the app is launched. After the property is implemented in the delegate, we can access it from any part of our code through the **delegate** property of the **UIApplication** object, as we will see later.

The other two methods defined in the **UIApplicationDelegate** protocol are called when a Scene is created or discarded. When the system or the user generates a new window, the **application(UIApplication, configurationForConnecting:, options:)** method is called in the delegate. From this method, we must return the Scene's configuration, which is defined with an object of the **UISceneConfiguration** class. The class includes the following initializer.

UISceneConfiguration(name: String?, **sessionRole:** UISceneSession.Role)—This initializer returns a **UISceneConfiguration** object configured with the values provided by the arguments. The **name** argument is a string with the name that identifies the configuration. The **sessionRole** argument is a constant from a structure called **Role** that specifies the role of the Scene. The constant available to create Scenes for iPhones, iPads and Mac computers is called **windowApplication** (windows on the main screen).

This initializer provides the name of the configuration and the role of the Scene, but we also must declare the name of the class that is going to be assigned as the Scene's delegate. For this purpose, the **UISceneConfiguration** class includes the following property.

delegateClass—This property sets or returns the class that is going to be used to create the Scene's delegate (the object the system is going to use to report the state of the Scene).

There are two ways to define the delegate class. We can use the initializer to declare the name of the configuration and the role, and then assign the name of the class used to create the Scene's delegate to the **`delegateClass`** property, or we can define this value in a file called *Info.plist*. The App template implements this last approach. It defines the name of the configuration and the delegate class in the Info.plist file, as shown below, and then calls the initializer with that name.

Figure 5-17: *Scene definition in the info.plist file*

After a Scene is requested by the system or the user, the **`application(UIApplication, configurationForConnecting: UISceneSession, options: UIScene.Connection-Options)`** method is called and a **`UISceneConfiguration`** object is created using the configuration defined in the Info.plist file with the name "Default Configuration" and the role received by the method (**`connectingSceneSession.role`**).

IMPORTANT: The configuration defined by the App template is enough for most applications, so all we need to do is to leave the method as it is declared by the template and the Scenes will be properly configured. We will learn more about the info.plist file later, and how to work with multiple Scenes in Chapter 22.

Medium Scene Delegate

Another file generated by the App template is called SceneDelegate.swift and it defines the delegate for the Scenes (windows). The **`UIWindowScene`** object calls methods on this delegate to report changes in the Scene. From these methods, we can perform custom tasks every time a new Scene is created or the state of a Scene changes. The methods are defined by the **`UIWindowSceneDelegate`** protocol, which inherits from the **`UISceneDelegate`** protocol. The following are the most useful.

scene(UIScene, **willConnectTo:** UISceneSession, **options:** UIScene.ConnectionOptions**)**—This method is called when a new Scene is created.

sceneDidDisconnect(UIScene**)**—This method is called when a Scene was removed.

sceneDidBecomeActive(UIScene**)**—This method is called when a Scene becomes active and therefore it is responding to user events.

sceneWillResignActive(UIScene**)**—This method is called when a Scene is about to be moved to the background and stop responding to user events.

sceneWillEnterForeground(UIScene**)**—This method is called when a Scene is about to become visible and respond to user events.

sceneDidEnterBackground(UIScene**)**—This method is called when a Scene is no longer visible and does not respond to user events anymore.

In addition to these methods, the **`UIWindowSceneDelegate`** protocol also defines a property we must implement to store a reference to the window assigned to the Scene.

window—This property sets or returns a reference to the **`UIWindow`** object assigned to the Scene.

When a Scene is created, the system calls the **`scene(UIScene, willConnectTo:, options:)`** method on the Scene's delegate, creates a **`UIWindow`** object to represent the Scene's window, and assigns it to the **`window`** property. Because this method may be called not only when a new Scene is created but also in other circumstances, the code generated by the App template includes a **`guard`** statement to make sure that the **`UIScene`** object received by the method is an object of the **`UIWindowScene`** class. If the casting performs correctly, then we can proceed to execute any custom task we need to initialize the Scene, as shown next.

```
import UIKit

class SceneDelegate: UIResponder, UIWindowSceneDelegate {
   var window: UIWindow?

   func scene(_ scene: UIScene, willConnectTo session: UISceneSession,
options connectionOptions: UIScene.ConnectionOptions) {
      guard let _ = (scene as? UIWindowScene) else { return }

      print("The Scene is ready")
   }
}
```

Listing 5-9: *Initializing a Scene*

Basic Storyboard

The user interface is built with views inside a window. One view, usually called *main view* or *container view*, is responsible for organizing all the graphic elements on the screen. Several main views put together simulate virtual screens. This is how the app manages multiple screens and expands the interface in mobile devices. The main views replace one another inside the same window to give the impression of having more space than the window can offer.

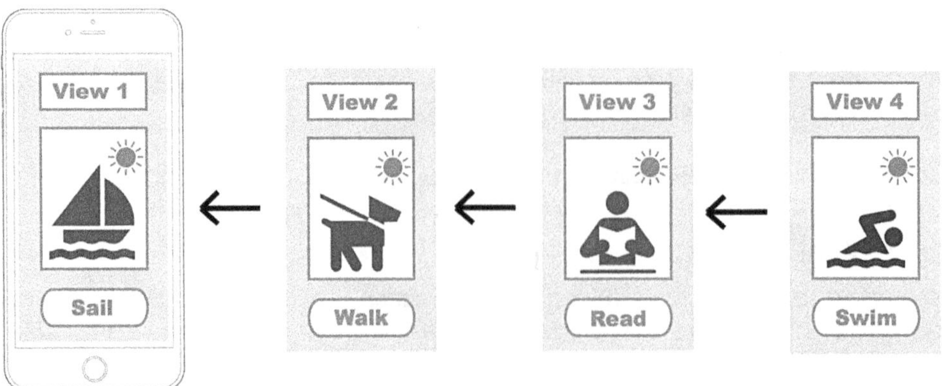

Figure 5-18: *Multiple views to expand the interface*

Creating and organizing these views and their content from code could demand hours of work. This is the reason why Xcode introduces a graphic tool called *Storyboard*. The Storyboard produces a result like Figure 5-18. It allows us to visually organize the main views and their content. Every component of the interface is displayed in the Editor Area, and we can drag and connect everything without writing a single line of code. All the information for the views created in the Storyboard is stored in an XML file. When the app is executed, this XML code is interpreted, the real objects are instantiated, and the views are drawn on the screen.

The files that store the information for the Storyboard have the **storyboard** extension. As we already mentioned, the App template includes the Main.storyboard file with a Storyboard for our app. Figure 5-19 shows what we see on the Editor Area when we click on that file (the shape and size of the view vary depending on the selected device, as we will see later).

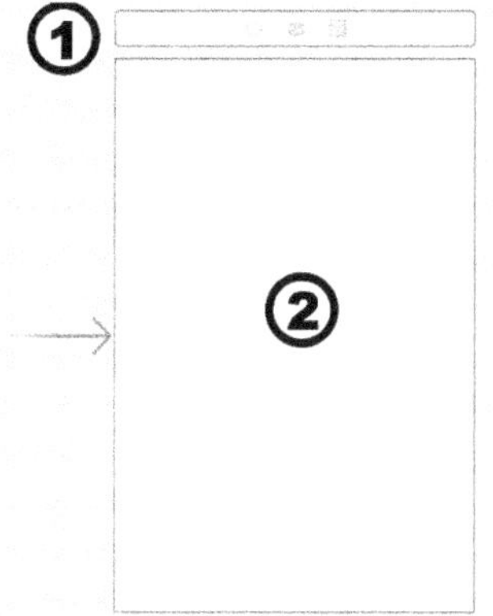

Figure 5-19: *Scene in the Storyboard*

The box shown in Figure 5-19 is called *scene* (not to be confused with the instances of our app which are also called *Scenes*, as we have seen in the previous section). The Storyboard uses these boxes to represent main views. Each scene contains a view where the interface is created (Figure 5-19, number 2) and a small bar at the top with options to configure the scene and the view controller (Figure 5-19, number 1). Clicking on the main area selects the main view and clicking on the bar selects the scene. The view controller may also be selected from the buttons shown on the bar when we click on it (see Figure 5-20, below). The button on the left represents the controller object responsible for the view, the button in the middle provides options to configure the element designated as first responder (introduced later), and the button on the right allows us to connect scenes together (studied in Chapter 9).

Figure 5-20: *Buttons to configure the scene*

The initial shape of the scenes resembles an iPhone, but we can change it anytime we want from the toolbar at the bottom of the Editor Area.

Figure 5-21: *Editor Area's toolbar*

All the buttons on this bar help us configure the Storyboard and its content, as described next.

Document Outline (1)—This button opens a panel on the left side of the Editor Area with a list of the scenes available in the Storyboard, the main views, content, and other components. From this list, we can select the elements of the interface, edit their names, remove them, or change their order.

Appearance (2)—These four buttons configure the Storyboard appearance. The first button opens a window to modify accessibility parameters, the second button toggles the appearance between Light and Dark, the third button rotates the scenes (portrait or landscape), and the fourth button simulates a split view (available on iPads).

Device Configuration (3)—This button opens a window with the list of devices we can select to change the appearance of the scenes.

Zoom (4)—These buttons allow us to zoom the Storyboard in and out.

Auto Layout (5)—These buttons open popup windows to create, configure, and resolve issues with constraints (we will study constraints and Auto Layout in Chapter 6).

When we select an option from these buttons, all the scenes in the Storyboard change to represent the new configuration, allowing us to design the interface for every device available.

Every time an element in the Storyboard is selected, the Utilities Area (the removable panel on the right) shows a series of panels for configuration. The panels are selected from the buttons at the top of the area. The most useful are the Attributes Inspector panel and the Size Inspector panel. From the Attributes Inspector panel, we can modify properties related to the attributes of the selected element, and from the Size Inspector panel we can change its size and position. Figure 5-22 shows how to open these panels and some of the properties they include when the main view is selected.

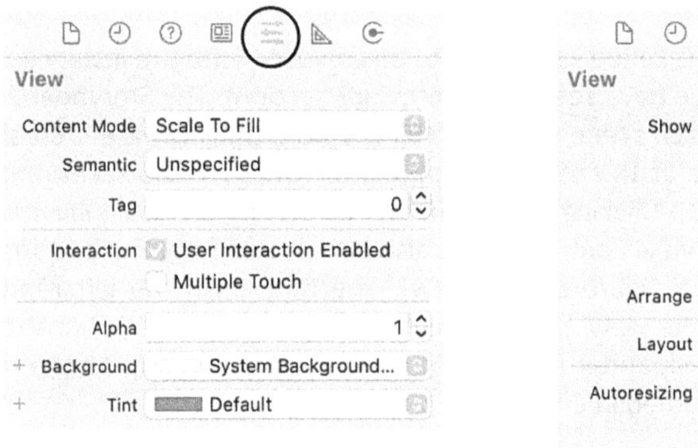

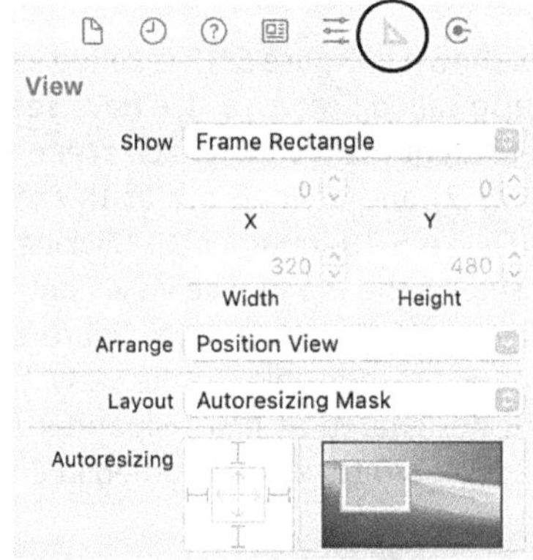

***Figure 5-22:** Attributes Inspector panel and Size Inspector panel*

The values in the panels of Figure 5-22 correspond to the same properties introduced before for `UIView` objects. For example, if we change the value of the Background field in the Attributes inspector panel (Figure 5-22, left), the selected value will be assigned to the `backgroundColor` property of the `UIView` object created to represent the main view. The same happens with the rest of the properties displayed on the panels. All the values defined in these panels will be assigned to the corresponding properties of the object created later to represent the element.

Do It Yourself: Click on the Main.storyboard file in the Navigator Area to see its content in the Editor Area. You should see something like Figure 5-19. Click on the main view to see the configuration options in the Utilities Area. Select a new color in the Background option to change the color of the view (Figure 5-22, left).

Basic View Controllers

Each scene in the Storyboard is responsible for showing a view and its content on the screen. To control the scenes and perform any standard function they require, the UIKit framework defines the **`UIViewController`** class. This is a basic class with properties and methods to manage a single scene and its views. Although the class provides all we need to control a scene, we do not work directly with objects created from it. Instead, we define a subclass of **`UIViewController`** for each scene in the Storyboard and add our own properties and methods to perform the tasks that are specific to the scene and our app.

As we will see in further chapters, applications with only one scene are rare. Usually, more scenes are added to the Storyboard to represent all the screens our users can navigate through to find the information they need. To know which object controls each scene, the scenes are associated to a view controller from the Identity Inspector panel. This is one of the configuration panels available in the Utilities Area when the scene is selected. To open the panel, we must select the scene and click on the third button at the top of the Utilities Area (circled in Figure 5-23).

Figure 5-23: *Identity Inspector panel*

The subclass that controls the scene is specified by the first option (Figure 5-23, number 1). We can write the name of the class or select it from the list. For instance, the App template includes the ViewController.swift file with a class called **`ViewController`** that inherits from the **`UIViewController`** class and is in charge of controlling the only scene in the Storyboard. If we select this scene, we will see that the **`ViewController`** class was already assign to this scene.

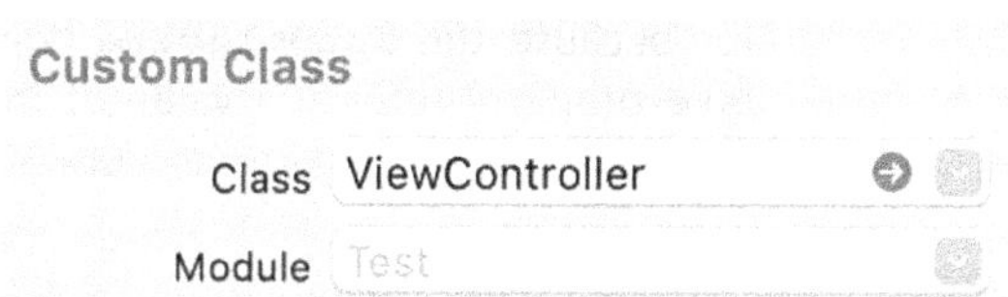

Figure 5-24: *ViewController class assigned to the initial scene*

The **`ViewController`** class provided by the App template is almost empty, except for the **`viewDidLoad()`** method. This is a method defined in the **`UIViewController`** class that is executed when the scene's main view and its content are created and loaded into memory. We must override this method in our subclass if we want to program our own response. Along with this method, the class includes a few more to report other states.

viewDidLoad()—This method is called after the main view is loaded into memory. It is the first method called on the object to indicate that the view is ready to be shown on the screen.

viewWillAppear()—This method is called after the **`viewDidLoad()`** method and before the main view is shown on the screen.

viewDidAppear()—This method is called after the main view is shown on the screen.

viewWillDisappear()—This method is called before the view is removed from the screen.

viewDidDisappear()—This method is called after the main view has been removed from the screen.

Usually we do not need other method than **viewDidLoad()** to set up the scene. This is the reason why it is the only one declared by the template. The following example modifies the **ViewController** class provided by the App template to read the property we added to the **UIApplication** delegate in Listing 5-8 and print its value on the console as soon as the scene's main view is loaded.

```
import UIKit

class ViewController: UIViewController {
   override func viewDidLoad() {
      super.viewDidLoad()

      let app = UIApplication.shared
      let mydelegate = app.delegate as! AppDelegate

      if let salary = mydelegate.basicSalary {
         print("Basic Salary is \(salary)")  // "Basic Salary is 30000.0"
      }
   }
}
```

***Listing 5-10:** Adding our own code to the ViewController.swift file*

The first thing we do inside the **viewDidLoad()** method of Listing 5-10 is to call the same method on the superclass (see **super** in Chapter 3). When a method is overridden, the original method is not executed anymore, but the original methods of some classes, like the **UIViewController** class, perform essential tasks necessary for the app to work properly, and that's why we must always call them before executing our own code.

In this example, our code gets a reference to the **UIApplication** object to read the properties defined in its delegate. First, we obtain this reference by reading the class' **shared** property. Next, we get a reference to the delegate object from the **delegate** property of the **UIApplication** object and assign it to the **mydelegate** constant (this is the object created from the class declared in the AppDelegate.swift file). Notice that we must cast this object as **AppDelegate** with the **as!** operator because the **AppDelegate** object is a subclass of the **UIResponder** class and the **delegate** property returns a value of that type. Finally, we use Optional Binding to read the **basicSalary** property in the delegate and print its value on the console.

The process carried out by this application is as follows. When the app is executed, the system creates all the basic objects, including the **UIApplication** object and its delegate, and then calls the **application(UIApplication, didFinishLaunchingWithOptions:)** method of the **AppDelegate** object to let us know that the app is ready. In this method, we initialize the **basicSalary** property (see Listing 5-8). When the execution of this method is over, the system looks in the Storyboard for the scene that has to show first and calls the **viewDidLoad()** method of its view controller. In this method, we get the value of the **basicSalary** property defined in the delegate object and print it on the console.

Do It Yourself: The last example assumes that you have already declared and initialized the **basicSalary** property in the app's delegate, as shown in Listing 5-8. Replace the code in your ViewController.swift file by the code in Listing 5-9. Select an iPhone simulator from the Scheme and press the Play button to execute the app (Figure 5-13). You should see the message "Basic Salary is 30000.0" printed on the console (Figure 5-12, Debug and Console Area).

IMPORTANT: The scenes defined in the Storyboard conform a path the user must follow to achieve a goal (e.g., access information, find a picture, etc.). The starting point of the path is determined by assigning the view controller object that controls the initial scene to a property of the **UIWindow** object called

rootViewController (see the **UIWindow** class introduced before). This may be done programmatically, but you can also do it from the Storyboard. All you need to do is to point the arrow on the screen to the scene you want to show first (Figure 5-19). If the arrow is not visible, you can specify the scene you want to show first from the Utilities Area. Select the scene in the Storyboard (clicking on the bar at the top), go to the Utilities Area, open the Attributes Inspector panel (Figure 5-22), and activate the option *Is Initial View Controller*.

The purpose of a view controller is to manage the scene's main view and its content. For this purpose, the **UIViewController** class defines the following property.

view—This property sets or returns the **UIView** object that represents the scene's main view.

When the app is launched, a **UIView** object is created to represent the scene's main view and this object is assigned to the **view** property. From this property, we can modify the attributes of the view, as we did in previous examples (see Listing 5-6). For instance, the following view controller change the view's background to blue as soon as the view is loaded.

```
import UIKit

class ViewController: UIViewController {
   override func viewDidLoad() {
      super.viewDidLoad()
      view.backgroundColor = .systemBlue
   }
}
```

Listing 5-11: *Modifying the main view from the view controller*

This code produces the same effect we achieve by changing the view's background color from the Attributes Inspector panel, but now we did it from code, after the view is loaded. This is required to have a functional application. From the Attribute Inspector panel, we set the interface's initial configuration, but then we must adapt that configuration and replace the content from code according to what the user requires or the state of the app, as we will learn in the next section.

Do It Yourself: Update the **ViewController** class in your project with the code in Listing 5-11. Run the application. You should see a blue screen. Replace the **systemBlue** value by any other color and run the application again.

Basic 5.4 Views

Templates include everything we need to start building our application. We get a Storyboard with the initial scene, a view controller to manage the scene's main view and its content, and all the necessary configuration files. After the template is created, we are ready to work on our application, and the first step is to add views to the scene to define the user interface. For this purpose, Xcode offers a tool called *Library*.

Basic Library

The Library is a popup window that opens when we press the Library button on the right side of the toolbar (Figure 5-12, number 5). This window presents a list with all the elements we can add to the Storyboard and the interface, including views, controls, and scenes.

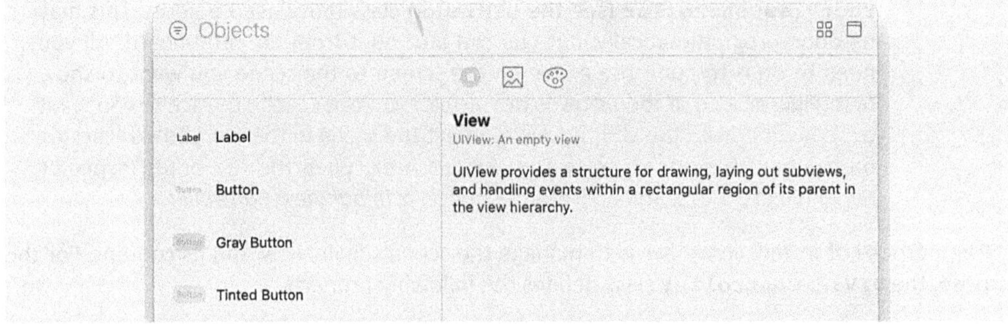

Figure 5-25: *Library*

The elements in the Library are incorporated into the view by dragging and dropping, as illustrated in Figure 5-26, below. If we want to drag more than one element, we can press and hold down the Option key to keep the window open.

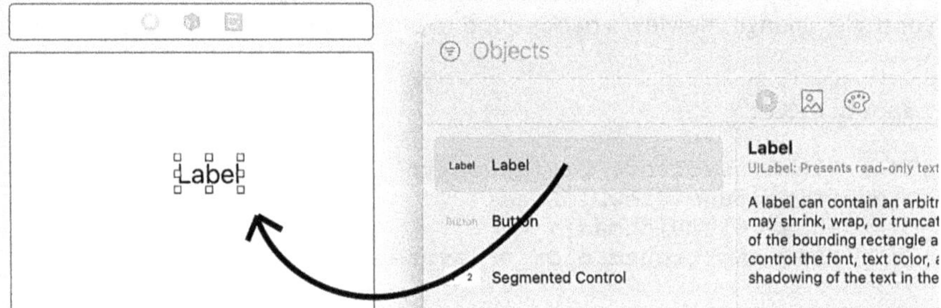

Figure 5-26: *Adding elements to the scene*

Once the element is dropped inside the view it becomes the selected element. Selected elements are surrounded by little squares that we can drag to change the size of their views. We can also drag the element to a new position and select another element by clicking on it.

Several elements may be selected at the same time by pressing and holding down the Shift key on the keyboard. Some elements, such as labels and buttons, allow us to double click on them to edit their content. For instance, we can double-click on the label added to the scene in Figure 5-26 and change the text to "My Title".

Figure 5-27: *New text for a label*

A label is a view that can display text on the screen. The view is the rectangular area that determines the space occupied by the label, and the text is the view's content. Therefore, the size of the text is independent of the size of the view. If the view is not big enough to fit the text inside, the text will be truncated, as in "My Ti...". In Chapter 6, we will learn how to adapt the views in the interface to the space available and their content, but for testing purposes, we can expand the view by dragging the square indicators around the label or define a specific size in points from the Size Inspector panel (see Figure 5-22, right).

IMPORTANT: An element dropped inside a view becomes one of its subviews. This is the same process performed by the `addSubview()` method of the `UIView` object (see Listing 5-7), with the difference that this time everything is done visually. All the views and subviews generated by this tool are stored as XML code and then the real objects are created when the application is launched.

Basic Guide Lines

While the element is being dragged over a view, Xcode shows lines to help us find the right place to drop it. There are lines that determine the horizontal and vertical center of the view, the superior, inferior, and lateral margins, and the position of one element relative to another. Figure 5-28 shows what we see when we drag a new label to the corner of the main view.

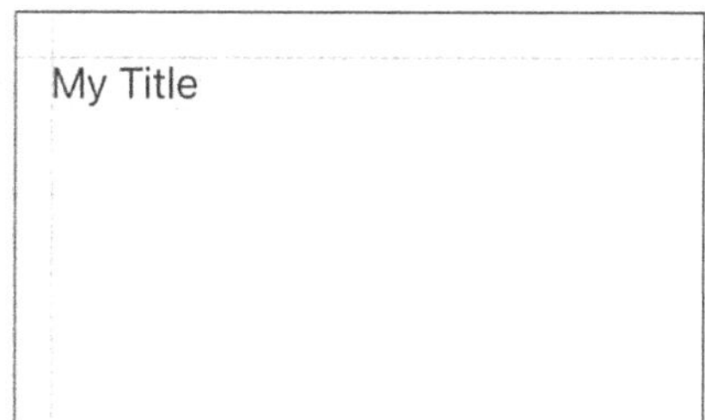

Figure 5-28: *Guide lines*

These lines become visible again when we drag the elements inside the view to find the right location and when we expand the area of the view by dragging the little squares around it.

Basic Outlets

As we already mentioned, the elements generated in the Storyboard, including views, subviews, and their properties, are stored as XML code in the storyboard file. Right after the app is launched, the objects for the main views and their content are created from this code. The **`UIView`** objects that represent the main views are connected to their view controllers through the **`view`** property (see Listing 5-11), but the objects that represent the subviews inside these main views (labels, buttons, etc.) are not connected to our code. They did not exist when we were programming our app (they were just XML code in the storyboard file), and therefore we cannot reference these objects from our code. To solve this problem, Xcode introduces the concepts of Outlets.

An Outlet is a property referencing an object in the user interface. These are normal properties but prefixed by the **`@IBOutlet`** attribute to indicate to Xcode that they are related to an element in the Storyboard. When the app is launched, the objects are created from the Storyboard and then assigned to their Outlets in our code. It is through these Outlets that we can access the objects from code and read and set the values of their properties.

There are different ways to create an Outlet and generate the connection. The simplest is to drag a line from the element in the scene to our view controller and let Xcode generate the codes on both ends. For this, we need to divide the Editor Area in two parts by selecting the Assistant option from the menu opened by the button at the editor's top-right corner, as illustrated below.

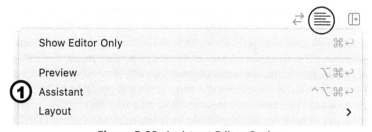

Figure 5-29: *Assistant Editor Option*

Once the Assistant option is selected (Figure 5-29, number 1), the Editor Area is split in two sections, with the main file on the left and an additional file opened on the right. If the element selected on the left is a scene in the Storyboard, the right area automatically shows its view controller. Figure 5-30, below, shows what we see when we open the Assistant Editor and select the scene with the label from Figure 5-26.

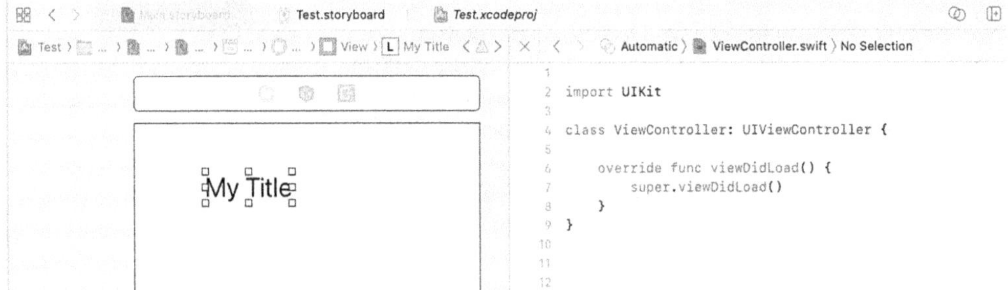

Figure 5-30: *Assistant Editor*

The connection between the elements in the view on the left and our code on the right is established by dragging a line from the element to the class while pressing and holding down the Control key on the keyboard. Xcode generates a blue line on the screen to show the connection that is being created and to indicate where the property is going to be placed in our code.

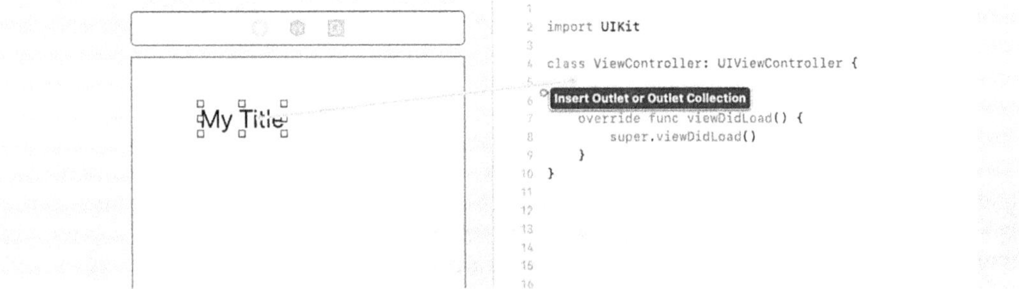

Figure 5-31: *Connection between a label and its view controller*

Outlets, as well as properties, should always be created at the beginning of the class. When we reach this place and release the mouse button, Xcode opens a popup window to configure the connection.

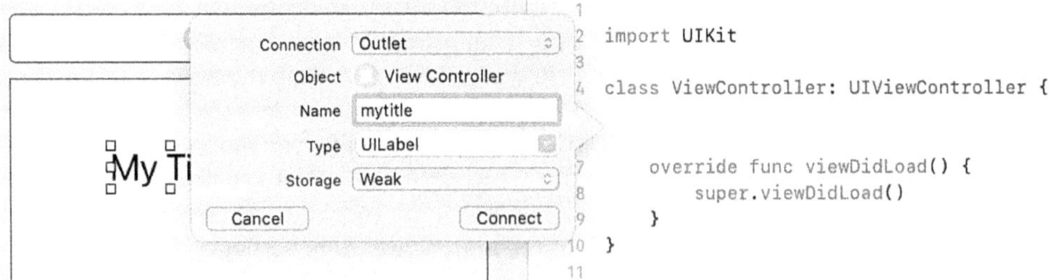

Figure 5-32: *Setting up a connection*

The window asks for the type of connection (Outlet or Outlet Collection) and additional information to generate the code. To create an Outlet, we must select the option Outlet in the Connection field, insert the name we want to assign to the property, its data type (for labels is **UILabel**), and the value that determines how the memory is going to be managed. The latter is usually specified as **weak**, because its container (the **UIView** object that represents the main view) already has a strong reference to the object (see Memory Management in Chapter 3).

In the example depicted in Figures 5-31 and 5-32, a label with the text My Title was added to the main view and then connected to the view controller with an Outlet called **mytitle**. When we click the Connect button in the popup window, Xcode generates the code for the Outlet.

```
import UIKit

class ViewController: UIViewController {
   @IBOutlet weak var mytitle: UILabel!

   override func viewDidLoad() {
      super.viewDidLoad()
   }
}
```

Listing 5-12: *Adding an Outlet for a label to the view controller*

Do It Yourself: If you haven't already, drag and drop a label from the Library into the scene in the Storyboard. Double-click the label to change its text to "My Title". Open the Assistant Editor (Figure 5-29). Position the mouse over the label and press and hold down the Control key on your keyboard. Press the mouse button and drag a line from the label to the beginning of the **ViewController** class. Release the mouse button when you see something like Figure 5-31. A popup window like the one in Figure 5-32 will open. Define the Connection as Outlet, the name as **mytitle**, the type as **UILabel**, and the Storage as **weak**. Click the Connect button to generate the code. Your view controller should look like Listing 5-12.

IMPORTANT: There are some names that are already in use by the UIKit classes or are reserved by the Swift language and we cannot use in our own properties or methods. For example, you cannot give a property the name **title** because the **UIViewController** class already defines a stored property with that name. To avoid conflicts, always use descriptive names such as **homeTitle** or **titleLabel**.

When an Outlet is created, Xcode generates code in our view controller and in the storyboard file. Something to keep in mind is that deleting the code for an Outlet in the view controller is not enough to break the connection. This only deletes the connection in our code, but it does nothing to the XML code in the storyboard file. To also erase the connection in the Storyboard, we must click the mouse's right button (Secondary click) when the pointer is over the element to open a popup window where we can edit the element's configuration, as shown below.

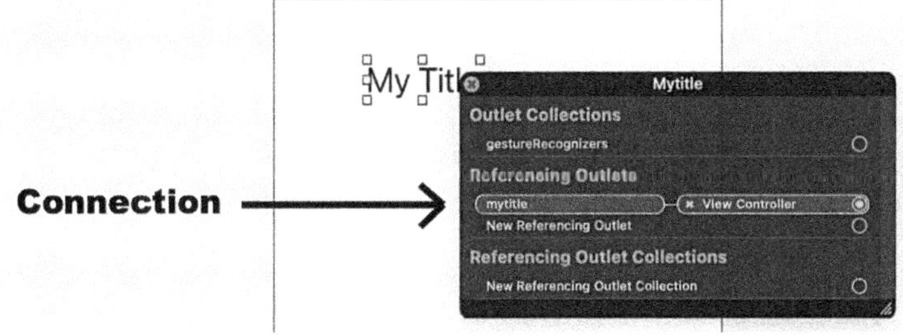

Figure 5-33: *Popup window to manage connections in the Storyboard*

The popup window shows all the connections created for the selected element. The name of the property is on the left and the name of the object is on the right. The name of the object includes a small x on the left that is highlighted by a circle when we move the mouse over. Clicking on this x erases the corresponding XML code in the storyboard file and completely breaks the connection (we can also erase the element if we do not need it anymore, and the connections are erased with it).

Basic Document Outline Panel

The Document Outline panel is an additional panel that opens on the left side of the Editor Area when we click on the button at the editor's bottom-left corner (see Figure 5-21, number 1). It offers a quick access to all the elements in the Storyboard and allows us to select them, connect them to Outlets and Actions in our code, change their names to make them easy to find, move them up or down in the hierarchy, delete them, and create constraints between them (we will study Actions later and constraints in Chapter 6).

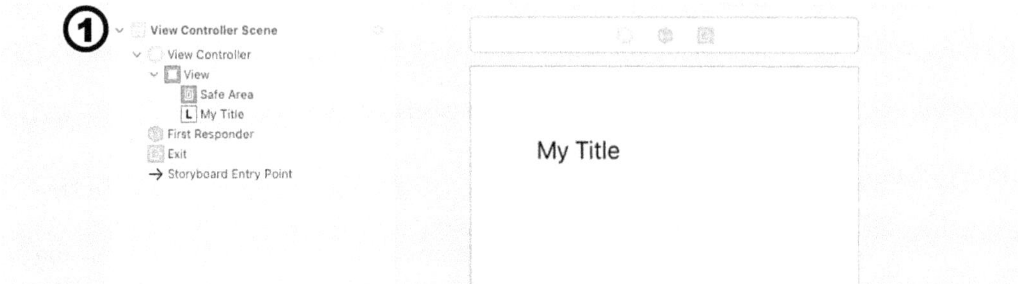

Figure 5-34: *Managing the elements of the scene*

The items are displayed in a hierarchical list. There are items at the top of the hierarchy to represent each scene in the Storyboard (Figure 5-34, number 1), and then items inside to represent the components of each scene. The items at the top are called View Controller, First Responder, and Exit (the three buttons in the scene's top bar). As we will see later, the First Responder represents the element that first responds to user interaction and the Exit control is used for navigation, but the View Controller represents the scene's view controller and therefore it contains the elements of the interface. The first element on the list is the main view (View). Inside this item we find an item with the title Safe Area that represents the area of the main view that is not superposed by toolbars or navigation bars. And finally, is the item that represents our label. By selecting any of these items in the Document Outline panel we are selecting the element they represent. For instance, if we select the item that represents the label, the label is selected on the scene.

The items take the name of the element they represent, and in the cases of labels and buttons, they are named after the text assigned to the elements. For example, the item that represents our label is called My Title, because that's the text assigned to the label. But we can change the name by selecting the item and pressing the Return key on the keyboard.

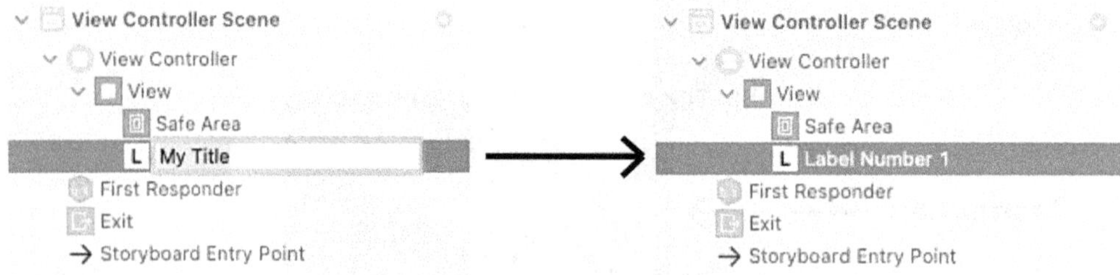

Figure 5-35: *Changing the item's name*

The items in the Document Outline panel represent the elements in the Storyboard and therefore edit their properties, move them up or down the hierarchy, change their positions and sizes, and connect them with our code. For instance, we can create an Outlet for our label by control-dragging a line from the item in the panel to the view controller.

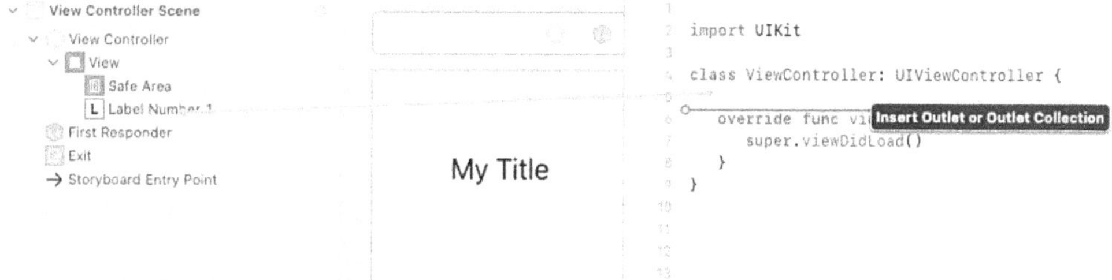

Figure 5-36: Creating Outlets

This is the same process introduced in Figure 5-32, but instead of dragging the line from the element in the scene, we do it form the item in the panel. This is useful when elements on the interface overlap each other and are hard to reach.

Basic Labels

The label we have added to the scene in the previous section is probably the most common element we can add to the user interface. Labels are views that draw one or multiple lines of text on the screen. They can be used to present information or to identify other elements on the interface. Labels are created from the **UILabel** class, a subclass of **UIView** that adds the additional functionality necessary to draw the text. The **UILabel** class doesn't define its own initializer but we can create objects of this class from code using the initializer inherited from the **UIView** class.

UILabel(frame: CGRect**)**—This initializer creates a **UILabel** object. The **frame** argument defines the position and size of the view that contains the text.

As seen in the previous section, labels can be added to the interface from the Library. All we need to do is to drag and drop the option and the label is included in the scene (see Figure 5-26).

Figure 5-37: *Label option in the Library*

After the label is created, we must assign a text to it and configure the view. The following are some of the properties included by the **UILabel** class for this purpose.

text—This property sets or returns the text displayed by the label.

attributedText—This property sets or returns the formatted text displayed by the label.

font—This property sets or returns the font used to display the label. Its value is an object of the **UIFont** class (we will introduce this class next).

textColor—This property sets or returns the color of the text. It is of type **UIColor**.

textAlignment—This property sets or returns the alignment of the text. It is an enumeration of type **NSTextAlignment** with the values **left** (to the left side of the view), **center** (to the center of the view), **right** (to the right side of the view), **justified** (the last line of the paragraph is aligned), and **natural** (uses the alignment associated with the text).

lineBreakMode—This property sets or returns the mode used to display lines of text that go beyond the view's boundaries. It is an enumeration of type **NSLineBreakMode** with the values **byWordWrapping** (the word that does not fit is moved to the next line),

byCharWrapping (the character that does not fit is moved to the next line), **byClipping** (characters that does not fit are not drawn), **byTruncatingHead** (the beginning of the text is replaced by ellipsis), **byTruncatingTail** (the end of the text is replaced by ellipsis), **byTruncatingMiddle** (the middle of the text is replaced by ellipsis).

numberOfLines—This property sets or returns the number of lines allowed for the text. If the text requires more lines than those set by this property, it is truncated according to the mode selected by the **lineBreakMode** property. The value 0 declares unlimited lines.

adjustFontSizeToFitWidth—This property sets or returns a Boolean value that determines whether the font size needs to be decreased for the text to fit inside the view. It only works when the **numberOfLines** property is set to a value different from 0.

shadowColor—This property sets or returns the color of the shadow. It is an optional property of type **UIColor**. When its value is **nil**, the text is drawn with no shadow.

shadowOffset—This property sets or returns the offset of the shadow. Its value is a **CGSize** structure that establishes the horizontal and vertical displacement.

When the label is added to the scene from the Library, we can modify the values of most of these properties from the Attributes Inspector panel.

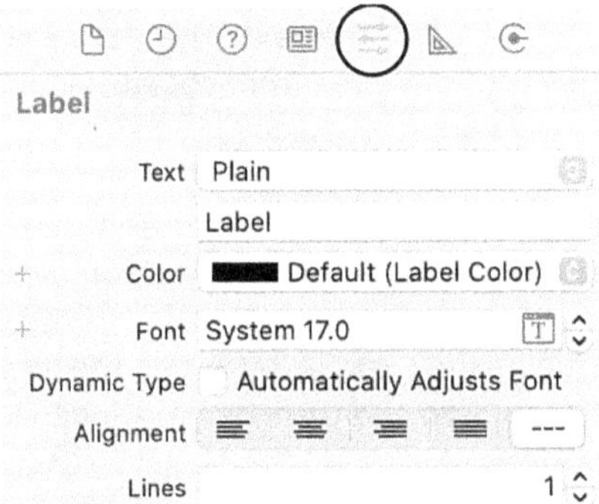

Figure 5-38: *Editing the properties of a label from the Utilities Area*

This is the same we have done for the main view before (see Figure 5-22), but of course the options available are specific for labels. For example, we can modify the text, color, and font of the label, and some aspects of the label's view as well, such as the background color.

Do It Yourself: Select the label on the scene. Insert a different text for the label and select a new color from the Color option. Click on the T button in the Font option to see the values available (we will learn more about these options next).

IMPORTANT: Classes like **UILabel** are subclasses of the **UIView** class. Other similar classes like **UIButton**, for example, are subclasses of **UIControl**, which is a subclass of **UIView**. Therefore, they not only have access to their own properties, but also to the properties they inherit from their superclasses. All these properties are available on the Attributes Inspector panel under the sections Control and View.

From the Attributes Inspector panel, we can set the label's initial conditions, but if our app needs to change these attributes later, we must do it from code by modifying the values of the **UILabel** properties. For instance, we can assign a new text to the label as soon as the view is loaded.

```
import UIKit

class ViewController: UIViewController {
   @IBOutlet weak var mytitle: UILabel!

   override func viewDidLoad() {
      super.viewDidLoad()
      mytitle.text = "Hello World"
   }
}
```

Listing 5-13: *Defining the label's text from code*

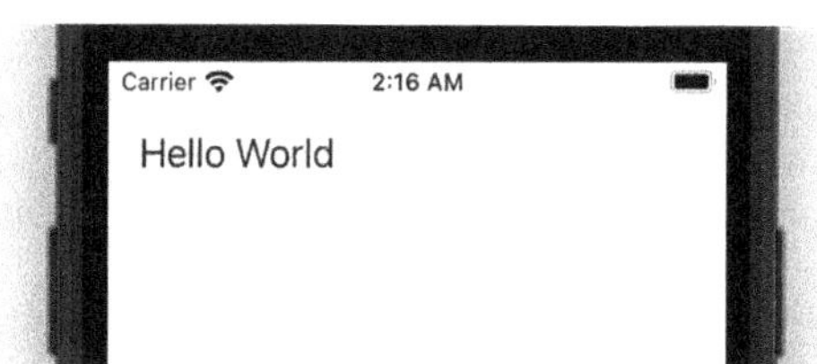

Figure 5-39: *Label with text defined from code*

Do It Yourself: Update the **ViewController** class with the code in Listing 5-13 and run the application. Something you may notice right away, is that the size of the label's view remains the same, no matter the text we assign to it. If the new text is longer than the original, it won't fit inside the view and it would be truncated, as explained before. To see the full text on the screen, expand the label's view by dragging the square indicators on the sides or define the size in points from the Size Inspector panel (see Figure 5-22, right). We will learn how to adapt the views to the space available in Chapter 6.

The size of the text is determined by the font set by the system. If we want to set a different size or font type, we must assign a new **UIFont** object to the **font** property of the **UILabel** object. **UIFont** objects are not only assigned to labels but also to other elements that display text on the screen. They contain properties and methods to store and manage fonts. The following are the most frequently used initializer and type methods included in the **UIFont** class to create these objects.

UIFont(name: String, **size:** CGFloat**)**—This initializer creates a **UIFont** object with the font referenced by the **name** argument and a size determined by the **size** argument. The **name** argument is a string with the font's PostScript name.

labelFontSize—This type property returns a **CGFloat** value with the size of the font used by the system to create **UILabel** objects.

buttonFontSize—This type property returns a **CGFloat** value with the size of the font used by the system to create **UIButton** objects (buttons).

systemFontSize—This type property returns a **CGFloat** value with the size of the font used by the system.

preferredFont(forTextStyle: TextStyle**)**—This type method returns a **UIFont** object with the font associated to the style specified by the **forTextStyle** argument and a size specified by the user in Settings. The argument is a property of a structure called **TextStyle** included in the **UIFont** class. The properties available are **body**, **callout**, **caption1**, **caption2**, **footnote**, **headline**, **subheadline**, **largeTitle**, **title1**, **title2**, **title3**.

systemFont(ofSize: CGFloat)—This type method returns a **UIFont** object with the font set by default on the system and a size determined by the **ofSize** argument.

boldSystemFont(ofSize: CGFloat)—This type method returns a **UIFont** object with the font of type bold set by default on the system and a size determined by the **ofSize** argument.

italicSystemFont(ofSize: CGFloat)—This type method returns a **UIFont** object with the font of type italic set by default on the system and a size determined by the **ofSize** argument.

Although we can create a font object with the initializer or any of the methods above, Apple recommends working with the **preferredFont()** method. The fonts returned by this method are called *Dynamic Types* because they are selected by the system according to the style specified by the argument and the size set by the user. The Settings app offers an option to change the font size for all the applications installed on the device. If our application implements Dynamic Types, it can respond to these changes and show the text on the screen with the size preferred by the user.

To assign a new font to a label, we must create the **UIFont** object with the styles we want and then assign it to the label's **font** property, as shown next.

```
import UIKit

class ViewController: UIViewController {
   @IBOutlet weak var mytitle: UILabel!

   override func viewDidLoad() {
      super.viewDidLoad()
      let myfont = UIFont.preferredFont(forTextStyle: .headline)
      mytitle.text = "Hello World"
      mytitle.font = myfont
   }
}
```

Listing 5-14: *Creating dynamic font types*

The code in Listing 5-14 creates a font with the **headline** style. This is the style used for titles and headers, but we can specify any style we want depending on the purpose of the text. For example, for long texts and content the preferred style is **body**. Every style uses different font types and they may look different, but the size is always determined by the system or the user from the Settings app.

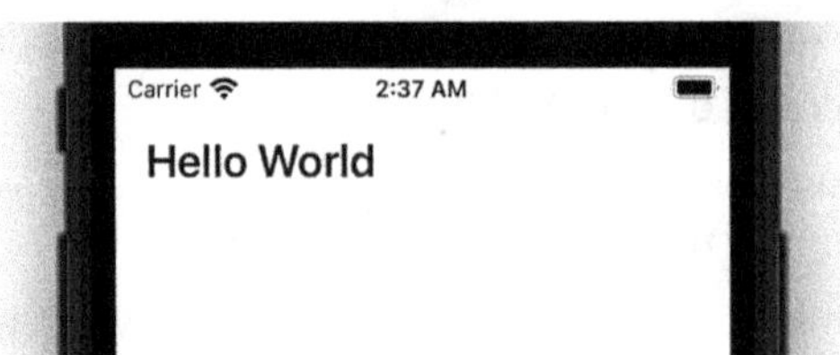

Figure 5-40: *Label with* `headline` *style*

IMPORTANT: Fonts with dynamic types automatically adapt their size to the size determined by the user from Settings (the option is available in General / Accessibility / Large Text), but if changes are performed after the app was installed and launched, we must listen to notifications from the system to force the app to adapt the fonts to the new size. We will learn how to listen to system notifications in Chapter 16.

If we do not want to use Dynamic Types, we can define the font with a specific family type and size using the **UIFont** initializer. The following example creates the **UIFont** object with a font called *Georgia-Italic* and a size of 30 points.

```
import UIKit

class ViewController: UIViewController {
   @IBOutlet weak var mytitle: UILabel!

   override func viewDidLoad() {
      super.viewDidLoad()
      let myfont = UIFont(name: "Georgia-Italic", size: 30)
      mytitle.text = "Hello World"
      mytitle.font = myfont
   }
}
```

***Listing 5-15:** Defining a specific font and size*

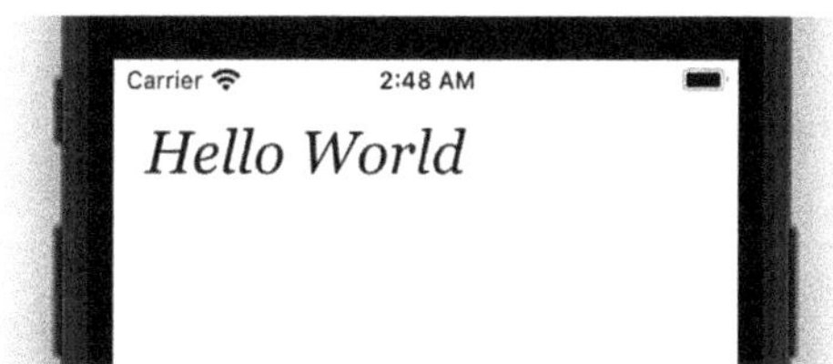

***Figure 5-41:** Label with custom font and size*

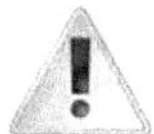

IMPORTANT: The font names for the **UIFont** initializer are the PostScript names. To find these names, open the Font Book application from your Applications folder, go to the View menu, and select the option Show Font Info. On the right column of the window, you will see the information for the selected font, starting by its PostScript name. Select the font you would like to include in your app to get its name. Most of the fonts in your computer are available in iOS, but you can also add your own fonts. For more information, visit our website and follow the links for this chapter.

The system also provides fonts that were carefully selected to optimize the design and produce a pleasant experience for the user. The **UIFont** class includes several type methods to get an object with these settings, as shown next.

```
import UIKit

class ViewController: UIViewController {
   @IBOutlet weak var mytitle: UILabel!

   override func viewDidLoad() {
      super.viewDidLoad()
      let myfont = UIFont.systemFont(ofSize: 30)
      mytitle.text = "Hello World"
      mytitle.font = myfont
   }
}
```

***Listing 5-16:** Using the system's standard font*

The **systemFont()** method applied in Listing 5-16 returns a **UIFont** object with the standard system font but with the size specified by the argument.

Figure 5-42: *Label with system font*

This time we declared a fix value of 30, but we can take advantage of some of the type methods of the **UIFont** class to set the size to some of the values defined by the system.

```
import UIKit

class ViewController: UIViewController {
   @IBOutlet weak var mytitle: UILabel!

   override func viewDidLoad() {
      super.viewDidLoad()
      let size = UIFont.buttonFontSize
      let myfont = UIFont.systemFont(ofSize: size)
      mytitle.text = "Hello World"
      mytitle.font = myfont
   }
}
```

Listing 5-17: *Getting the font size used by default for buttons*

This example reads the **buttonFontSize** property to get the size of the font used by the system to write the text inside buttons and assign it as the size of the **myfont** object. This is helpful when we want to present text along with some buttons and we need to keep everything proportional.

As explained before, we always have to make sure that the size of the label's view is big enough to display the text on the screen. But this is not always possible. Sometimes the size of the label's view cannot change or there is not enough room on the interface to expand it. The **UILabel** class provides the **lineBreakMode** property to determine how the text is going to be processed when it is longer than the width of its view. The value by default is **byTruncatingTail**, which means that the characters at the end of the text are going to be replaced by ellipsis. Other frequent values are **byTruncatingMiddle** to truncate the middle of the text, or **byClipping** to hide the characters that go beyond the view's boundaries. The following example assigns a longer text to the **text** property to see the effects of the line break modes applied to the label.

```
import UIKit

class ViewController: UIViewController {
   @IBOutlet weak var mytitle: UILabel!

   override func viewDidLoad() {
      super.viewDidLoad()
      mytitle.text = "This is a Beautiful Life"
      mytitle.lineBreakMode = .byClipping
   }
}
```

Listing 5-18: *Clipping the label's text*

For this example, we have given the view a width of 173 points from the Size Inspector panel and set the size of the font to 20 from the Attributes Inspector panel, so the view is not big enough to show the full text and therefore the text is clipped, as shown in Figure 5-43.

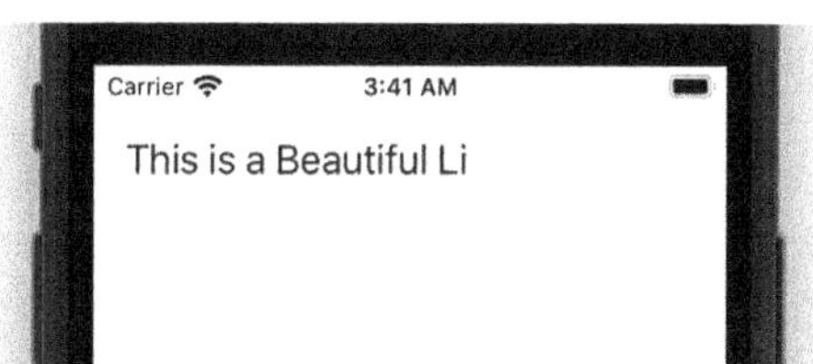

Figure 5-43: Label clipped

Do It Yourself: Update the **ViewController** class with the code in Listing 5-18. Select the label and change the size of the font to 20 from the Attributes Inspector panel (Figure 5-38). With the label selected, open the Size Inspector panel and assign a width of 173 points (Figure 5-22, right). Run the application. You should see the text clipped, as illustrated in Figure 5-43. Try every possible value for the **lineBreakMode** property to see how they work.

The **UILabel** class includes more properties to customize the text, including changing its color by assigning a **UIColor** object to the **textColor** property, or adding a shadow with the **shadowColor** and **shadowOffset** properties, as shown next.

```
import UIKit

class ViewController: UIViewController {
   @IBOutlet weak var mytitle: UILabel!

   override func viewDidLoad() {
      super.viewDidLoad()
      mytitle.text = "Hello World"
      mytitle.font = UIFont.systemFont(ofSize: 30)
      mytitle.textColor = UIColor.systemYellow
      mytitle.shadowColor = UIColor.systemGray
      mytitle.shadowOffset = CGSize(width: 2, height: 2)
   }
}
```

Listing 5-19: Customizing the text

Figure 5-44: Label with a shadow

These properties assign the styles to the whole text. Every time a new font, size or color is assigned to the **UILabel** object, all the characters in the text are affected. If we want some parts of the text to have a different style, we must create a separate label or assign the text to the **attributedText** property instead. This property takes a value of type **AttributedString**; a structure that contains the text and all the attributes that must be applied to it. The following are some of the structure's initializers.

AttributedString(String**)**—This initializer creates an **AttributedString** structure with the text specified by the argument.

AttributedString(String, **attributes:** AttributeContainer**)**—This initializer creates an **AttributedString** structure with the text specified by the first argument. The **attributes** argument is a container for all the attributes we want to apply to the text.

The attributes are determined by attribute keys defined in what is called an Attribute Scope. There is an enumeration called **AttributeScopes** with properties that contain an attribute scope for each platform (UIKit, appKit, SwiftUI, and Foundation). The attribute scope for UIKit is stored in the **uiKit** property. This is a structure of type **UIKitAttributes** with properties that represent all the attribute keys available for UIKit. The following are the most frequently used.

font—This property defines the text's font attribute. It is a value of type **UIFont**.

backgroundColor—This property defines the text's background color attribute. It is a value of type **UIColor**.

foregroundColor—This property defines the text's foreground color attribute. It is a value of type **UIColor**.

strokeColor—This property defines the text's stroke color attribute. It is a value of type **UIColor**.

strokeWidth—This property defines the text's stroke width attribute. It is a value of type **CGFloat**.

shadow—This property defines the text's shadow attribute. It is a value of type **NSShadow**.

To show a label with an attributed string, we must instantiate an **AttributedString** structure with the text we want to display, modify the structure's properties to define the attributes, and then assign the structure to the label's **attributedText** property.

```
import UIKit

class ViewController: UIViewController {
   @IBOutlet weak var mytitle: UILabel!

   override func viewDidLoad() {
      super.viewDidLoad()
      var mytext = AttributedString("Hello World!")
      mytext.font = UIFont.systemFont(ofSize: 24)
      mytext.foregroundColor = .systemRed
      mytitle.attributedText = NSAttributedString(mytext)
   }
}
```

Listing 5-20: *Assigning attributes to a label*

The code in Listing 5-20 creates an **AttributedString** structure with the text "Hello World!" and then assigns a system font of 24 points and the **systemRed** color to the text. Notice that the **attributedText** property of the **UILabel** object takes an **NSAttributedString** object. This is an old Foundation class not compatible with **AttributedString** values, but the class includes an initializer we can use to convert an **AttributedString** structure into an **NSAttributedString** object, as illustrated in this example. The result is shown in Figure 5-45.

Figure 5-45: *Label with attributes*

The previous example assigns the attributes to the entire text, but the purpose of the **AttributedString** structure is to assign different attributes to ranges of characters in the text. Like the **String** structure, the **AttributedString** structure identifies the positions of the characters with index values. To modify a specific portion of the text, all we need to do is to define a range of indexes that determine the positions of the first and last characters of the string we want to modify. The **AttributedString** structure includes a handy method for this purpose.

range(of: String**)**—This method returns a **Range** structure defined with the indexes of the first and last characters of the string specified by the **of** argument.

```
import UIKit

class ViewController: UIViewController {
   @IBOutlet weak var mytitle: UILabel!

   override func viewDidLoad() {
      super.viewDidLoad()
      var mytext = AttributedString("Hello World!")

      if let range = mytext.range(of: "World") {
         mytext[range].font = UIFont.systemFont(ofSize: 24)
         mytext[range].foregroundColor = .systemRed
         mytitle.attributedText = NSAttributedString(mytext)
      }
   }
}
```

***Listing 5-21:** Assigning attributes to a range of characters*

This example creates the **AttributedString** structure as before, and then gets the range of indexes that determines the position of the string "World". With this value, we assign a system font and a color to the text, but only to the characters inside the range.

***Figure 5-46:** Attributes assigned to a range of characters*

Attributes may be added to the label programmatically, as we have done so far, or from the Attributes Inspector panel (see Figure 5-38). If the label already contains some attributes and a new **AttributedString** structure is assigned to it, the old attributes will be removed. To preserver the current attributes, we must get the current attributed string from the label's **attributedText** property, add the new attributes, and assign the string back to the label. The problem is that the value returned by this property is an **NSAttributedString** object. To convert this object into an **AttributedString** structure, the structure includes the following initializer.

AttributedString(NSAttributedString, **including:** AttributeScope.Type**)**—This initializer creates an **AttributedString** structure from the **NSAttributedString** object specified by the first argument. The **including** argument is the scope's data type that defines the attribute keys used to generate the attributes for the string. Only the attributes in the **NSAttributedString** object that match the attributes in the scope are applied to the **AttributedString** structure.

The following example gets the attributed string from the label, converts it into an **AttributedString** structure, change its foreground color to blue, and assign it back to the label.

```
import UIKit

class ViewController: UIViewController {
   @IBOutlet weak var mytitle: UILabel!

   override func viewDidLoad() {
      super.viewDidLoad()
      if let oldtext = mytitle.attributedText {
         if let attrText = try? AttributedString(oldtext, including:
\.uiKit) {
            var mytext = attrText
            mytext.foregroundColor = .systemBlue
            mytitle.attributedText = NSAttributedString(mytext)
         }
      }
   }
}
```

Listing 5-22: *Assigning additional attributes to the label*

The **AttributedString** initializer takes an **NSAttributedString** object and the scope that defines the attribute keys we want to use to convert the text's attributes. In this case, we are using UIKit types, so we specify the keypath to the **uiKit** property of the **AttributeScopes** enumeration. This tells the initializer to use the attribute keys defined in the **UIKitAttributes** structure. After the **AttributedString** structure is ready, we assign it to a variable to be able to modify its attributes, change the foreground color to **systemBlue**, turn the value into an **NSAttributedString** object, and assign it back to the label. As a result, all the previous attributes are preserved, but the text is now shown in blue.

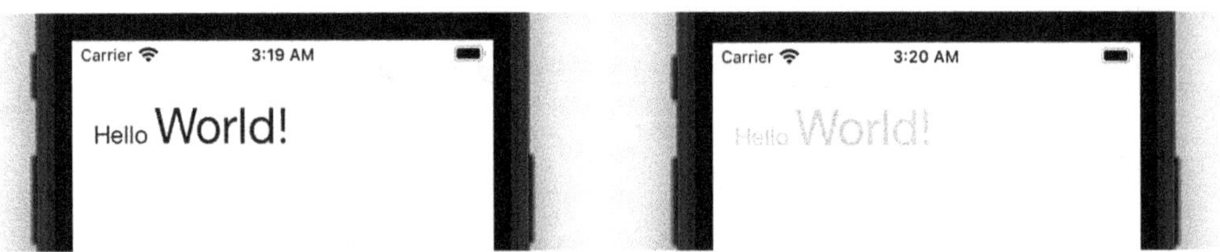

Figure 5-47: *Label with old and new attributes*

Do It Yourself: Select the label and go to the Attributes Inspector panel (Figure 5-38). Change the Text option from Plain to Attributed, select the word "World" and change the font size to 36. You should see something like Figure 5-47, left. Update the **ViewController** class with the code in Listing 5-22 and run the application. The label's color should now be blue, but the size of the text should remain the same, as illustrated in Figure 5-47, right.

As we do with **String** values, we can work directly with string indexes to modify any character we want. For this purpose, the **AttributedString** structure includes two properties, **characters** and **runs**. These properties return structures with sets of values that reference the characters in the string and the runs, which contains the attributes and the text to which they are applied. The **characters** property returns a structure of type **CharacterView**. The following are some of the properties and methods provided by this structure to manage the indexes.

indices—This property returns a collection with the characters' indexes.

count—This property returns an **`Int`** value with the number of characters in the string.

startIndex—This property returns the index of the first character. It is a value of type **`Index`**.

endIndex—This property returns the index of the last character. It is a value of type **`Index`**.

first—This property returns the string's first character. It is a value of type **`Character`**.

last—This property returns the string's last character. It is a value of type **`Character`**.

firstIndex(of: Character**)**—This method returns an **`Index`** value with the index of the first character that matches the character specified by the **of** argument.

index(Index, **offsetBy:** Int**)**—This method increments the index specified by the first argument the amount of units specified by the **offsetBy** argument and returns a new **`Index`** value with the result.

index(after: Index**)**—This method increments the index specified by the **after** argument one unit and returns a new **`Index`** value with the result.

index(before: Index**)**—This method decrements the index specified by the **before** argument one unit and returns a new **`Index`** value with the result.

The process to assign attributes to a range of characters is the same as before, but this time we must defined the range ourselves with the indexes obtained from the **`CharacterView`** structure.

```
import UIKit

class ViewController: UIViewController {
   @IBOutlet weak var mytitle: UILabel!

   override func viewDidLoad() {
      super.viewDidLoad()
      var mytext = AttributedString("Hello World!")

      let startIndex = mytext.characters.startIndex
      let endIndex = mytext.characters.index(startIndex, offsetBy: 5)

      mytext[startIndex...endIndex].font = UIFont.systemFont(ofSize: 24)
      mytext[startIndex...endIndex].foregroundColor = .systemRed
      mytitle.attributedText = NSAttributedString(mytext)
   }
}
```

Listing 5-23: *Assigning attributes to a customized range of characters*

In this example, we get the index of the string's first character from the **`startIndex`** property, then calculate the index of the string's fifth character with the **`index(offsetBy:)`** method, and finally assign the attributes to the characters in the range determined by these two indexes. In this case, this corresponds to the word "Hello".

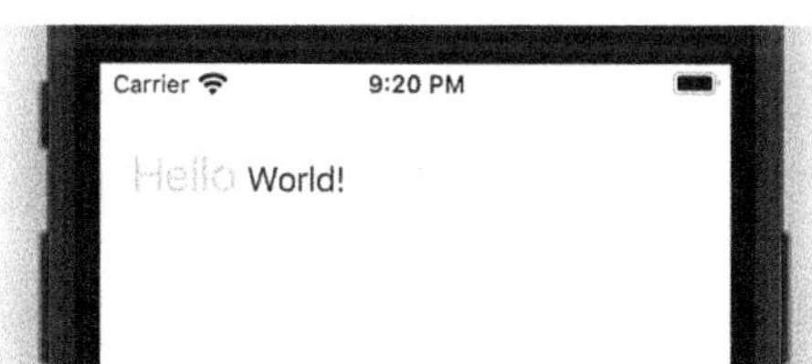

Figure 5-48: *Attributes assigned to a custom range of characters*

Most of the **AttributedString** properties require values of types we are familiar with, such as **UIFont** or **UIColor**, but some are of a more specific type. For example, the **shadow** property requires an object of the **NSShadow** class. This is a simple class with a few properties to configure the characteristics of a shadow.

shadowColor—This property defines the color of the shadow. It is a value of type **UIColor**.

shadowOffset—This property defines the offset of the shadow. It is a value of type **CGSize**, which determines the horizontal and vertical displacement.

shadowBlurRadius—This property defines the shadow's blur effect. It is a value of type **CGFloat**.

Effects like shadows are noticeable when they are applied to big fonts. In the following example, we assign the dynamic type **largeTitle** to the text's font and then apply a gray shadow with a horizontal and vertical offset of 2 and a blur radius of 5.

```
import UIKit

class ViewController: UIViewController {
   @IBOutlet weak var mytitle: UILabel!

   override func viewDidLoad() {
      super.viewDidLoad()
      var mytext = AttributedString("Hello World!")
      mytext.font = UIFont.preferredFont(forTextStyle: .largeTitle)

      let shadow = NSShadow()
      shadow.shadowColor = UIColor.systemGray
      shadow.shadowOffset = CGSize(width: 2, height: 2)
      shadow.shadowBlurRadius = 5
      mytext.shadow = shadow
      mytitle.attributedText = NSAttributedString(mytext)
   }
}
```

Listing 5-24: *Applying a shadow to the text*

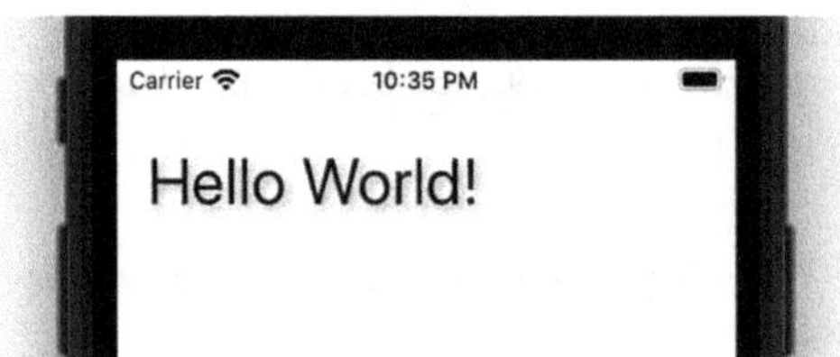

Figure 5-49: *Label with a shadow*

If our interface contains multiple labels that require the same attributes, instead of applying the attributes one by one to each label, we can create a container with the **AttributeContainer** structure and apply all the attributes at once. The following are some of the methods included in the **AttributedString** structure to work with an attributes container.

setAttributes(AttributeContainer**)**—This method assigns the attributes in a container to the text. All the previous attributes are removed.

mergeAttributes(AttributeContainer**)**—This method assigns the attributes in a container to the text. The new attributes are merged with the previous attributes.

replaceAttributes(AttributeContainer, **with:** AttributeContainer**)**—This method replaces the attributes specified by the container in the first argument with the attributes in the container specified by the **with** argument.

Instead of assigning the attributes to the text, they are first defined in the container and later applied to the text with one of the methods listed above, as in the following example.

```
import UIKit

class ViewController: UIViewController {
   @IBOutlet weak var mytitle: UILabel!

   override func viewDidLoad() {
      super.viewDidLoad()
      var mytext = AttributedString("Hello World!")

      var container = AttributeContainer()
      container.font = UIFont.preferredFont(forTextStyle: .body)
      container.backgroundColor = .systemGray4
      mytext.setAttributes(container)

      mytitle.attributedText = NSAttributedString(mytext)
   }
}
```

Listing 5-25: *Applying multiple attributes at once*

The properties of a container are the same we used before to assign the attributes directly to the text. The **AttributeContainer** structure is created first, and then all the attributes are assigned to it as always. In this example, we change the font style to **body** and the background color to gray.

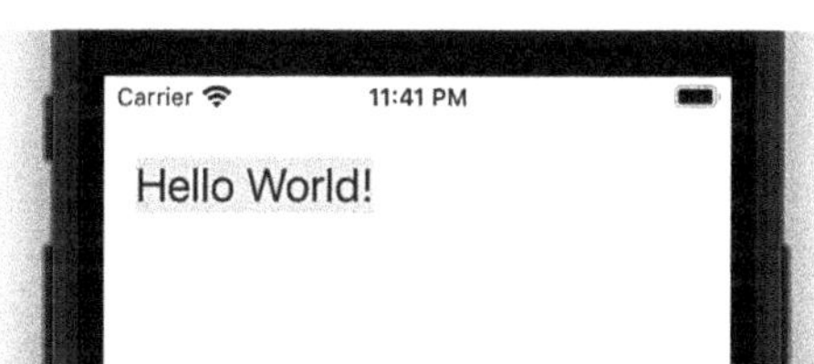

Figure 5-50: *Attributes applied to a label from a container*

So far, we have worked with the string's characters, accessible from the **characters** property, but there is also the **runs** property which returns a collection of runs that we can use to edit the attributes and the text. Runs are the sections in the text with a unique combination of attributes. For instance, if we assign a red color to the string "World!" and keep the rest with the color by default, we will have two runs, one with the string "World!" and the foreground color red, and another with the rest of the text and the foreground color by default.

Runs are defined by the **Run** structure, which includes the following properties.

attributes—This property returns an **AttributeContainer** structure with all the attributes assigned to the run's text.

range—This property returns a **Range** structure that determines the location of the run in the string.

By iterating over the **runs** property, we can read the attributes currently assigned to the text and modify the sections one by one.

```
import UIKit

class ViewController: UIViewController {
   @IBOutlet weak var mytitle: UILabel!

   override func viewDidLoad() {
      super.viewDidLoad()
      var mytext = AttributedString("Hello World!")

      if let range = mytext.range(of: "World") {
         mytext[range].backgroundColor = .systemRed
      }
      for run in mytext.runs {
         if run.attributes.backgroundColor == .systemRed {
            let range = run.range
            mytext[range].backgroundColor = .systemGray4
         }
      }
      mytitle.attributedText = NSAttributedString(mytext)
   }
}
```

Listing 5-26: *Modifying the attributes of a run*

The code in Listing 5-26 assigns the **systemRed** color to the word "World" and then looks for the run with that attribute to change the value to **systemGray4**. The run we are looking for can be found by checking the **backgroundColor** property of the run's **AttributeContainer** structure. If the value is **systemRed**, it means that the run corresponds to the word "World" so we get the run's range and assign a new background color to that section of the string. As a result, the background of the word "World" is initially red, but it is changed to gray before assigning the text to the label.

IMPORTANT: The **AttributedString** structure also includes initializers to assign attributes to the text with a markup language. These are special characters that can be inserted directly into the string to define the attributes. For more information, visit our website and follow the links for this chapter.

Basic Actions

Some elements of the interface are not limited to show text or graphics on the screen; they can also process user interaction. Buttons, Switches, Segmented Controls, and others are designed to respond to the user and fire an event to report the situation to the application. For instance, a button performs an action when pressed, such as saving values in a database, or replacing the current scene by another one. To perform these actions, we need to connect the button in the interface with a method in our code. For this purpose, Xcode implements Actions.

Adding an Action to an element is like adding an Outlet. We must drag a line from the control to the view controller class while pressing and holding down the Control key, and then provide the information for the connection. For instance, in the following example, we have changed the label's text to "Pressed: 0" and added a button below with the title "Press Here". Figure 5-51 shows what we see when we try to add an Action to the button.

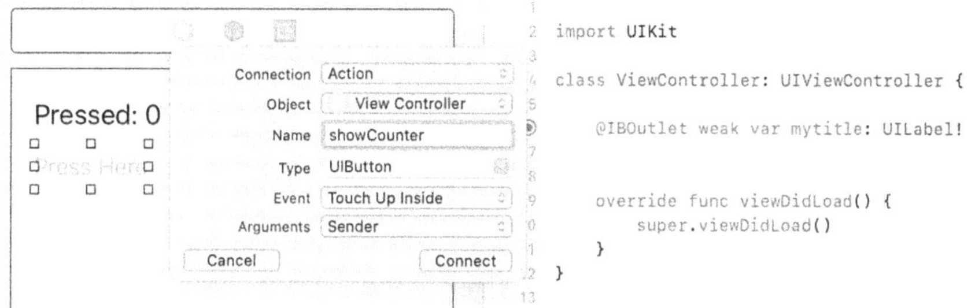

Figure 5-51: *Adding an Action for a button*

The first thing we need to do in the popup window is to select the type of the connection as Action. In the options, we must insert the name of the method that will be executed when the action is performed, the type of the object that performed the action, and the type of event that will trigger the action (Buttons respond to the Touch Up Inside event, but there are others, as we will see later). The last option, Arguments, determines the values we want to send to the method. The option includes three possible values: None (no value is sent to the method), Sender (a reference to the object that represents the control is sent to the method), and Sender and Event (a reference to the object that represents the control and information about the event that triggered the action are sent to the method). By default, this value is set to Sender, which will add to the method a parameter called **sender** to receive a reference to the object (buttons are created by objects of type **UIButton**, as we will see later).

After all the information is declared, Xcode generates the codes in both ends (the Storyboard and the view controller). The declaration of the method in our view controller is like any other, but it is prefixed by the **@IBAction** attribute to establish its relationship with the element in the Storyboard.

```
import UIKit

class ViewController: UIViewController {
   @IBOutlet weak var mytitle: UILabel!
   var counter: Int = 0

   @IBAction func showCounter(_ sender: UIButton) {
      counter += 1
      mytitle.text = "Pressed: \(counter)"
   }
}
```

Listing 5-27: *Defining an Action for the button*

Along with the Outlet for the label, the view controller in Listing 5-27 includes a property called **counter** to count the number of times the user pressed the button. When the button is pressed, the **UIButton** object that represents the button added to the scene in the Storyboard calls the **showCounter()** method in our view controller, the value of the **counter** property is incremented by 1, and the text in the **mytitle** label is updated with the result.

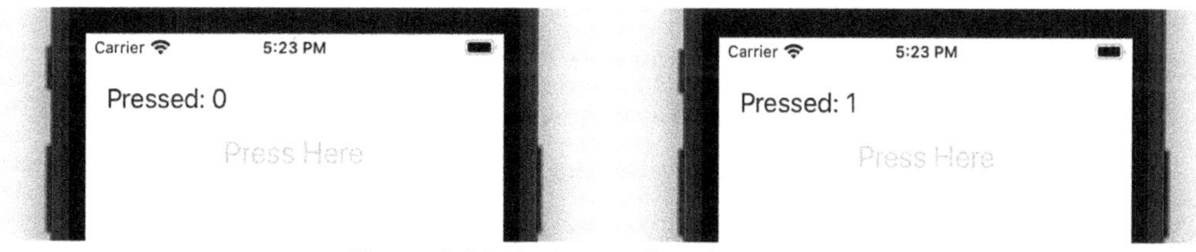

Figure 5-52: *Button performing an action*

Do It Yourself: Change the label's title in the Storyboard to "Pressed: 0". Open the Library and drag the option called Button to the scene. You should see something like the interface in Figure 5-51. Create an Action for the button with the name **`showCounter`**, the Type **`UIButton`**, the Event Touch Up Inside, and the rest of the values by default. Update the **`ViewController`** class with the code in Listing 5-27. Run the application and press the button. You should see the value on the label change, as illustrated in Figure 5-52.

Basic Buttons

The button implemented in the previous section is a control created from the **`UIButton`** class. There are multiple types of buttons available, with different styles and functionalities. The following is the initializer provided by the class to create a button from code.

UIButton(configuration: Configuration, **primaryAction:** UIAction?**)**—This initializer creates a **`UIButton`** object with the configuration specified by the **configuration** argument, and the action specified by the **primaryAction** argument.

The configuration is determined by a structure defined in the **`UIButton`** class called **`Configuration`**. The structure includes the following type methods to get a predefined configuration for every type of button available.

plain()—This type method creates a configuration for a button with a transparent background.

filled()—This type method creates a configuration for a button filled with a background color.

gray()—This type method creates a configuration for a button with a gray background.

tinted()—This type method creates a configuration for a button with a tinted background color.

Of course, these buttons can be added to the scene in the Storyboard from the Library.

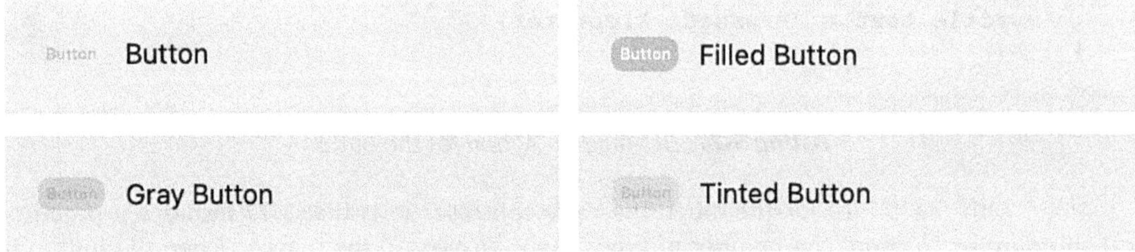

Figure 5-53: *Button options in the Library*

The following are some of the properties included in the **`Configuration`** structure to modify the characteristics of these buttons.

title—This property sets or returns a string with the button's title.

subtitle—This property sets or returns a string with the button's subtitle.

attributedTitle—This property sets or returns the button's attributed title. It is a value of type **`AttributedString`**.

attributedSubtitle—This property sets or returns the button's attributed subtitle. It is a value of type **`AttributedString`**.

titlePadding—This property sets or returns a **CGFloat** value that determines the distance between the button's title and subtitle.

titleAlignment—This property sets or returns a value that determines the title's alignment. It is an enumeration of type **TitleAlignment** with the values **automatic**, **center**, **leading**, and **trailing**.

Buttons can also include an image on the sides. The **Configuration** structure includes the following properties to set up this image.

image—This property sets or returns the buttons image. It is a **UIImage** object.

imagePadding—This property sets or returns a **CGFloat** value that determines the distance between the image and the text.

imagePlacement—This property sets or returns a value that determines the position of the image in relation to the text. It is an **NSDirectionalRectEdge** structure with the properties **all**, **bottom**, **leading**, **top**, and **trailing**.

showsActivityIndicator—This property sets or returns a Boolean value that determines if the button will include an activity indicator (a wheel that spins to indicate that an operation is in progress).

The **Configuration** structure also includes properties to configure the button.

baseBackgroundColor—This property sets or returns the button's background color. It is a value of type **UIColor**. The color automatically adapts to the state of the button (normal, pressed, and disabled).

baseForegroundColor—This property sets or returns the color of the button's content. It is a value of type **UIColor**. The color automatically adapts to the state of the button (normal, pressed, and disabled).

cornerStyle—This property sets or returns a value that determines the style of the corners. It is an enumeration of type **CornerStyle** with the values **dynamic**, **fixed**, **capsule**, **large**, **medium**, and **small**.

buttonSize—This property sets or returns a value that determines the size of the button. It is an enumeration of type **Size** with values that define predefined sizes. The values available are **large**, **medium**, **mini**, and **small**.

contentInsets—This property sets or returns a value that determines the padding around the button's content. It is a structure of type **NSDirectionalEdgeInsets**. The structure includes the following initializer to set the padding for each side: **NSDirectionalEdgeInsets(top: CGFloat, leading: CGFloat, bottom: CGFloat, trailing: CGFloat)**.

IMPORTANT: Some of these properties work with **leading** and **trailing** values. Instead of using names like left and right, UIKit implements these values because the side they reference depends on the human language set on the device. In English, for example, leading represents the left side of the element and trailing the right, but this may change for other languages. We will learn more about leading and trailing in Chapter 6.

In UIKit, the most common way to incorporate a button into the user interface is by dragging the option from the Library to the scene in the Storyboard, as we have done for the label and the button in previous examples. For instance, we can implement the previous interface, but now with two buttons, one to increment the value on the label and another to decrement it.

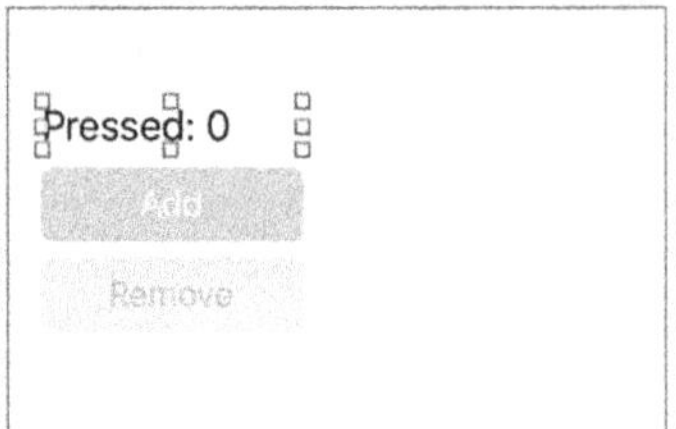

Figure 5-54: *Interface to test buttons*

For this application to work, we need to define two Actions in the view controller, one for the Add button and another for the Remove button, as shown next.

```
import UIKit

class ViewController: UIViewController {
   @IBOutlet weak var mytitle: UILabel!
   var counter: Int = 0

   @IBAction func addToCounter(_ sender: UIButton) {
      counter += 1
      mytitle.text = "Pressed: \(counter)"
   }
   @IBAction func removeFromCounter(_ sender: UIButton) {
      counter -= 1
      mytitle.text = "Pressed: \(counter)"
   }
}
```

Listing 5-28: *Responding to multiple buttons*

When the Add button is pressed, the **addToCounter()** method is executed, the value of the **counter** property is incremented, and the label is updated with the result. If the Remove button is pressed instead, the **removeFromCounter()** method is executed, the value of the property is decremented, and the label is updated again with the new value.

Do It Yourself: Keep the label but remove the button from the interface of the previous example. Add a Filled button and a Tilted button below the label. Double-click the buttons to change their titles to Add and Remove. Drag the squares around the elements to expand their views and get an interface like the one in Figure 5-54. Remove the Action added to the view controller in the previous example and create an Action called **addToCounter()** for the Add button and another called **removeFromCounter()** for the Remove button. Complete the **ViewController** class with the code in Listing 5-28. Run the application and press the buttons. You should see the value on the label change.

By default, the buttons are configured with only a title, but they can contain a title, a subtitle, and an image.

Figure 5-55: *Button's configurations*

When we are designing the interface in the Storyboard, the button's configuration can be modified from the Attributes Inspector panel. Most of the properties provided by the **Configuration** structure are available in this panel, as shown below.

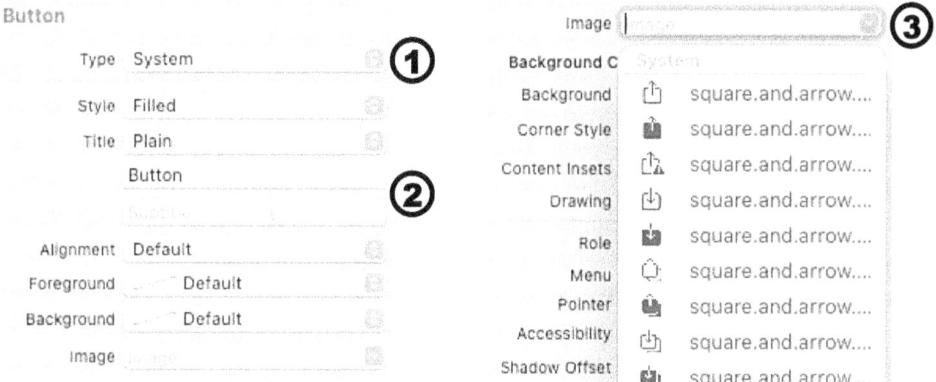

***Figure 5-56:** Configuration properties in the Attributes Inspector panel*

The first option sets the type of button we want to create. It includes some standard designs and provides compatibility with older systems. To customize our button, we need to set the type as System (Figure 5-56, number 1). Next, we can determine the style (Plain, Gray, Tinted, or Filled) and the type of text we want to use for the title (Plain or Attributed). Next, there are two fields to insert the button's title and subtitle (Figure 5-56, number 2). To include an image, there is an Image option below. The field can take custom images or images defined by the system. The images provided by the system are called SF Symbols. These symbols are identified by a name and are scalable, which means that the image adapts to the size of the text. For instance, the image added to the button in Figure 5-55 is called trash.fill. Once we select the image, it is added to the button in the position determined by the Placement option (we will learn more about SF Symbols and how to include our own images into the project later in this chapter).

Of course, all this customization can be made from code. The **`UIButton`** class includes the following properties and methods to update the configuration of a button.

configuration—This property sets or returns a **`Configuration`** structure with the button's configuration.

configurationUpdateHandler—This property sets or returns a closure used to update the button's configuration. The closure receives a value with a reference to the button.

setNeedsUpdateConfiguration()—This method asks the system to update the button's configuration.

All we need to do to change the button's configuration is to get the current configuration from the **`configuration`** property, modify the properties we want to change, and assign the configuration back to the button. If the button is added to the scene in the Storyboard, as in this example, we need an Outlet to access it. The following example includes an Outlet connected to the Add button of the interface in Figure 5-54 and change its title when the button is pressed.

```
import UIKit

class ViewController: UIViewController {
   @IBOutlet weak var addButton: UIButton!
   @IBOutlet weak var mytitle: UILabel!
   var counter: Int = 0

   @IBAction func addToCounter(_ sender: UIButton) {
      counter += 1
      mytitle.text = "Pressed: \(counter)"

      var configuration = addButton.configuration
      configuration?.title = "Adding \(counter)"
      addButton.configuration = configuration
   }
```

```
    @IBAction func removeFromCounter(_ sender: UIButton) {
        counter -= 1
        mytitle.text = "Pressed: \(counter)"
    }
}
```

Listing 5-29: *Modifying the button's configuration*

In this example, we get the button's current configuration, modify the value of the **title** property with a string that includes the current value of the **counter** property, and then assign the configuration back to the button. As a result, every time the button is pressed, the title is updated to display the state of the counter.

Notice that when the Remove button is pressed, the Add button is not updated. When changes in the configuration depend on actions unrelated to the button, we can define the configuration from the **configurationUpdateHandler** property and then call the **setNeedsUpdateConfiguration()** method to force an update. The closure assigned to the **configurationUpdateHandler** property is executed every time the button is pressed and when the **setNeedsUpdateConfiguration()** method is called, as shown in the following example.

```
import UIKit

class ViewController: UIViewController {
    @IBOutlet weak var addButton: UIButton!
    @IBOutlet weak var mytitle: UILabel!
    var counter: Int = 0

    override func viewDidLoad() {
        super.viewDidLoad()
        addButton.configurationUpdateHandler = { [unowned self] button in
            var current = button.configuration
            current?.title = "Add Me"
            current?.showsActivityIndicator = counter > 0 ? true : false
            current?.imagePlacement = .trailing
            current?.imagePadding = 15
            button.configuration = current
        }
    }
    @IBAction func addToCounter(_ sender: UIButton) {
        counter += 1
        mytitle.text = "Pressed: \(counter)"
    }
    @IBAction func removeFromCounter(_ sender: UIButton) {
        counter -= 1
        mytitle.text = "Pressed: \(counter)"
        addButton.setNeedsUpdateConfiguration()
    }
}
```

Listing 5-30: *Updating the button's configuration*

The closure assigned to the **configurationUpdateHandler** property receives a reference to the button that we can use to get the current configuration, perform the changes, and assign the configuration back to the button, as done before. In this example, we change the button's title to "Add Me" and add an activity indicator to the button depending on the value of the **counter** property. If the value of **counter** is greater than 0, the indicator is added to the button, otherwise it is removed.

The Activity Indicator is an animated image that looks like a rotating wheel, so we can configure it the same way we do with images. In this example, we assign the value **trailing** to the **imagePlacement** property, which positions the indicator on the button's right-hand side and assign a padding of 15 points between the indicator and the title.

The closure assigned to the **configurationUpdateHandler** property is executed every time the Add button is pressed, so there is nothing we need to do from the **addToCounter()** method to update the button, but to update the Add button when the Remove button is pressed, we must call the **setNeedsUpdateConfiguration()** method on the Add button, as we did in the **removeFromCounter()** method of Listing 5-30. The result is shown below.

Figure 5-57: *New button configuration*

Do It Yourself: Connect the Add button to the view controller with an Outlet called **addButton**. Update the **ViewController** class with the code in Listing 5-30. Run the application and press the Add Me button. You should see the number on the label change and the activity indicator appearing on the button's right-hand side (see Figure 5-57, right). Press the Remove button to reduce the value to 0 or less. The indicator should be removed.

IMPORTANT: The closure in Listing 5-30 accesses the **counter** property defined in the **ViewController** class. To access this property, the closure must reference the **ViewController** object with **self**. Using **self** inside a closure can create a strong reference cycle. To avoid it, you can mark **self** with the **unowned** keyword between square brackets, as we did in this example. If **self** is not required inside the closure, this declaration can be removed.

Although most of the time the buttons will be added to the scenes in the Storyboard, there are times when an application needs to define a button and its action from code. The buttons are created from the **UIButton** initializer introduced before, and the actions are created from the **UIAction** class. When a button on a scene is connected to the view controller with the **@IBAction** attribute, Xcode and the compiler take care of creating the **UIAction** object for us, but when the button is defined from code, we must provide this object ourselves. For this purpose, the class includes the following initializer.

UIAction(title: String, **image:** UIImage?, **identifier:** Identifier?, **state:** State, **handler:** Closure**)**—This initializer creates an action for a control. The **title** and **image** argument are the text and the image we want to use to represent the control. The **identifier** argument is a structure defined in the **UIAction** class that can be initialized with a string to identify the action. The **state** argument is an enumeration that specifies the action's initial state. The possible values are **on**, **off**, and **mixed**. And the **handler** argument is the closure or the function to execute when the action is performed. The closure or function receives one value with a reference to the **UIAction** object.

Most of the arguments are optional. For instance, if we already have a configuration for the button, we only need to provide the closure that defines the action to perform when the button is pressed, as in the following example.

```
import UIKit

class ViewController: UIViewController {
   var counter: Int = 0
```

```
    override func viewDidLoad() {
        super.viewDidLoad()
        var buttonConfig = UIButton.Configuration.filled()
        buttonConfig.title = "Press Me"
        buttonConfig.subtitle = "Do it now!"
        buttonConfig.baseBackgroundColor = .systemBrown

        let mybutton = UIButton(configuration: buttonConfig, primaryAction:
UIAction(handler: { [unowned self] action in
            print("Value of counter is: \(counter)")
            counter += 1
        }))
        mybutton.frame = CGRect(x: 20, y: 50, width: 150, height: 50)
        view.addSubview(mybutton)
    }
}
```

Listing 5-31: *Creating a button from code*

The button in this example is configured with the title "Press Me", the subtitle "Do It Now!", and a brown background. After the **Configuration** structure is ready, we create the **UIButton** object with this value and a **UIAction** object with a closure that prints a message and increments the value of the **counter** property when the button is pressed. Finally, the button is added to the main view with the **addSubview()** method and presented on the screen (see Listing 5-7).

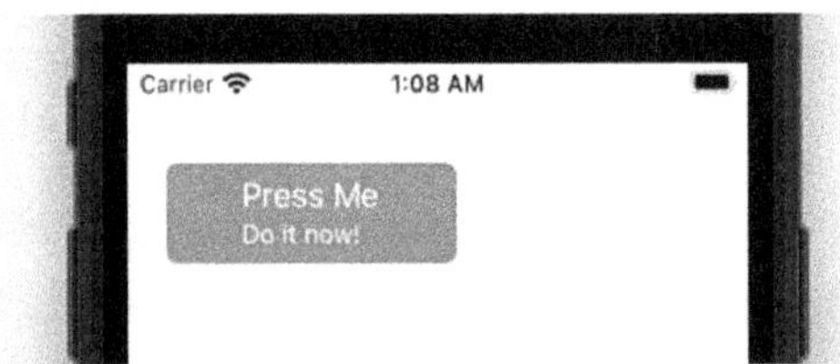

Figure 5-58: *Button added to the interface from code*

Do It Yourself: Remove all the elements from the previous interface. Update the **ViewController** class with the code in Listing 5-31. Run the application. You should see the button in Figure 5-58.

IMPORTANT: In our example, before adding the button, we had to specify the position and size by assigning a **CGRect** value to the **frame** property (the **UIButton** class inherits this property from the **UIView** class). This is necessary for the system to know where to position the button, but it is not the recommended practice. We use it here for didactic purposes, but the elements on the interface should be positioned and sized with constraints or added as the content of Stack Views, as we will see in Chapter 6.

If all we want is to create a simple button with a title and an image, we can provide the button's configuration from the **UIAction** object, as in the following example.

```
import UIKit

class ViewController: UIViewController {
    var counter: Int = 0

    override func viewDidLoad() {
        super.viewDidLoad()
```

```
        let mybutton = UIButton(configuration: .filled(), primaryAction: 
UIAction(title: "Press Here", handler: { [unowned self] action in
            print("Value of counter is: \(counter)")
            counter += 1
        }))
        mybutton.frame = CGRect(x: 20, y: 50, width: 150, height: 50)
        view.addSubview(mybutton)
    }
}
```

Listing 5-32: Configuring a button with an Action

In this example, we create the button with the configuration by default returned by the **`filled()`** method and then define the button's title and action from the **`UIAction`** object.

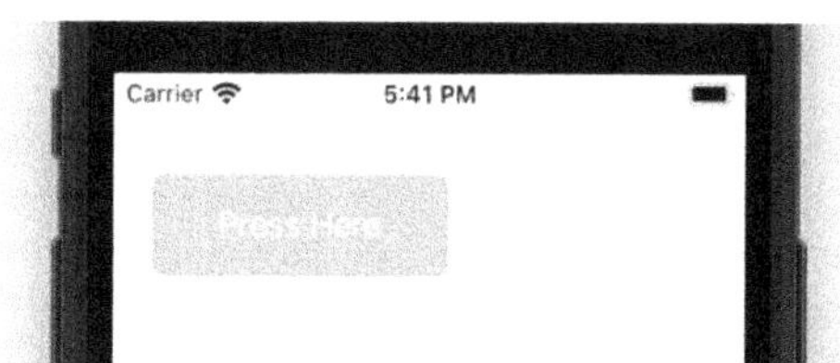

Figure 5-59: Button configured from an Action

The **`UIButton`** class is not a subclass of **`UIView`** but an intermediate class called **`UIControl`** (see Figure 5-6). The **`UIControl`** class provides all the functionality required by controls like buttons, switches, sliders, and more. By implementing the properties and methods defined by this class, we have more options to manage the controls. The following are the most frequently used.

isEnabled—This property sets or returns a Boolean value that indicates whether the element is enabled or not.

isSelected—This property sets or returns a Boolean value that indicates whether the element is selected or not.

addAction(UIAction, **for:** UIControl.Event**)**—This method adds an action to a control. The first argument defines the action, and the **for** argument is a property of a structure called **`Event`** that specifies the event that triggers the action. The properties available are **`touchDown`**, **`touchDownRepeat`**, **`touchDragInside`**, **`touchDragOutside`**, **`touchDragEnter`**, **`touchDragExit`**, **`touchUpInside`**, **`touchUpOutside`**, **`touchCancel`**, **`valueChanged`**, **`menuActionTriggered`**, **`primaryActionTriggered`**, **`editingDidBegin`**, **`editingChanged`**, **`editingDidEnd`**, and **`editingDidEndOnExit`**.

removeAction(UIAction, **for:** UIControl.Event**)**—This method removes from the control the action specified by the first argument and for the event specified by the **for** argument.

Because **`UIButton`** is a subclass of **`UIControl`**, all these properties and methods are available from the objects that represent the buttons. For instance, we can call the **`addAction()`** method on a button in a scene in the Storyboard to define the button's action from code.

The following example assumes that we have included a button to the scene from the Library and connected that button to the view controller with an Outlet called **`myButton`**. Using this Outlet, we can add an action to the button, as shown next.

```
import UIKit

class ViewController: UIViewController {
   @IBOutlet weak var myButton: UIButton!
   var counter: Int = 0

   override func viewDidLoad() {
      super.viewDidLoad()
      myButton.addAction(UIAction(handler: { [unowned self] action in
         print("Value of counter is: \(counter)")
      }), for: .touchUpInside)
   }
}
```

Listing 5-33: *Adding an action to a button from code*

This is a hybrid alternative from previous procedures. Instead of adding the button to the interface and connect it to the view controller with a **@IBAction** or programming the button and the action from code, we add the button to the interface and add the action from code with the **addAction()** method provided by the **UIControl** class. The method is called with a **UIAction** object that performs the same action as before (print a message on the console), and the event **touchUpInside**, which is fired after the button is pressed and released, so the closure is going to be executed only when these actions occur.

Do It Yourself: Remove any element in the scene and add a Filled button, as in the interface of Figure 5-54. Connect the button to the **ViewController** class with an Outlet called **myButton**. Update the class with the code in Listing 5-33 and run the application. Press the button. You should see a message printed on the console.

IMPORTANT: The **touchUpInside** event is the most common for buttons, but other controls usually implement the **valueChanged** event that is fired every time the value managed by the control changes, as we will see later.

The **UIControl** class also includes the **isEnabled** property to enable or disable the button. By default, all buttons are enabled, but we can assign the value **false** to this property to disable them.

```
import UIKit

class ViewController: UIViewController {
   @IBOutlet weak var myButton: UIButton!

   override func viewDidLoad() {
      super.viewDidLoad()
      myButton.addAction(UIAction(handler: { [unowned self] action in
         print("Button Pressed")
         self.myButton.isEnabled = false
      }), for: .touchUpInside)
   }
}
```

Listing 5-34: *Disabling a button*

In this view controller, we modify the action defined in the previous example to disable the button after it is pressed, but we can enable or disable the button from anywhere in the code, no matter how the action is implemented.

Another useful property included in the **UIControl** class is **isSelected**. This property can be used to turn a standard button into a toggle button (a button that represents two states, on or off). The **UIButton** class offers the following property for this purpose.

changesSelectionAsPrimaryAction—This property sets or returns a Boolean value that indicates whether the button is going to track a selection (**true**) or perform the action (**false**).

If we assign the value **true** to this property, the button toggles the value of its **isSelected** property every time it is pressed, but it doesn't perform any other action (the action assigned to the button is ignored), so we can use it to allow the user to select between two states. The following example defines a toggle button and displays the current state on the screen.

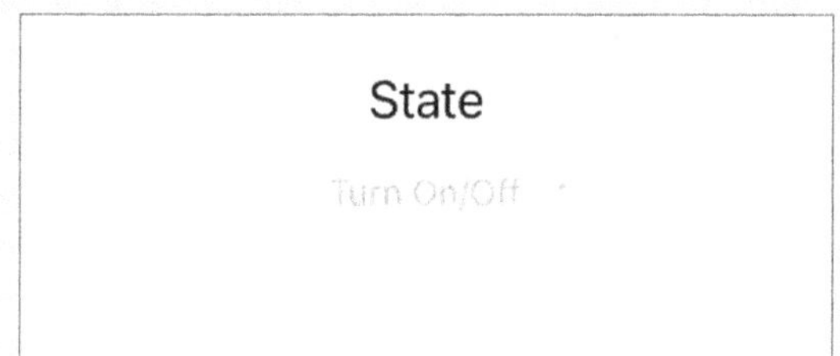

Figure 5-60: *Interface to test toggle buttons*

We need to set the **changesSelectionAsPrimaryAction** to **true**, but we can also set the initial state with the **isSelected** property, as shown next.

```
import UIKit

class ViewController: UIViewController {
   @IBOutlet weak var myLabel: UILabel!
   @IBOutlet weak var myButton: UIButton!

   override func viewDidLoad() {
      super.viewDidLoad()
      myButton.changesSelectionAsPrimaryAction = true
      myButton.isSelected = false
   }
   @IBAction func turnOption(_ sender: UIButton) {
      if sender.isSelected {
         myLabel.text = "Is On"
      } else {
         myLabel.text = "Is Off"
      }
   }
}
```

Listing 5-35: *Turning a button into a toggle button*

We can use any style we want to create a toggle button, but if we use a Plain button, as we did in the interface of Figure 5-60, it will reflect the current state.

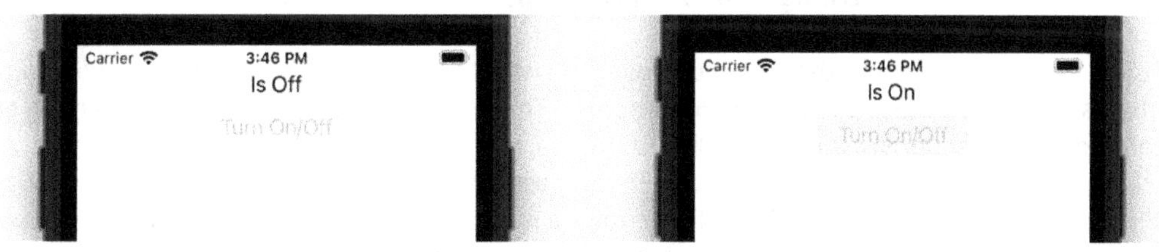

Figure 5-61: *Toggle button*

Do It Yourself: Remove the elements in the scene and add a label and a Plain button, as in the interface of Figure 5-60. Connect the label to the view controller with an Outlet called **myLabel** and the button with an Outlet called **myButton**. Update the **ViewController** class with the code in Listing 5-35. Run the application and press the button to toggle the state.

Buttons can also open a contextual menu when pressed. The **UIControl** class includes the following property to assign this functionality to a button.

showsMenuAsPrimaryAction—This property sets or returns a Boolean value that indicates whether the button is going to show a menu (**true**) or perform the action (**false**).

The menu is created from the **UIMenu** class. The following is the initializer with the arguments required to define contextual menus.

UIMenu(title: String, **children:** [UIAction]**)**—This initializer creates a menu with the options specified by the arguments. The **title** argument defines the title displayed at the top of the menu (an empty string removes the title), and the **children** argument is an array of objects that represent the options available.

The **UIButton** class includes the following property to associate a menu with the button.

menu—This property sets or returns the **UIMenu** object associated to the button.

The menu is created from a **UIMenu** object, and the options are created from **UIAction** objects. The **UIAction** objects require a title or an image, and the closure or the function that is going to be executed when the option is selected. In the following example, all the options execute the same function, but we can assign different functionality to each option if necessary.

```
import UIKit

class ViewController: UIViewController {
   @IBOutlet weak var myButton: UIButton!

   override func viewDidLoad() {
      super.viewDidLoad()
      myButton.showsMenuAsPrimaryAction = true

      myButton.menu = UIMenu(children: [
         UIAction(title: "Option 1", handler: selectOption),
         UIAction(title: "Option 2", handler: selectOption),
         UIAction(title: "Option 3", handler: selectOption)
      ])
   }
   func selectOption(action: UIAction) {
      print(action.title)
   }
}
```

Listing 5-36: *Displaying a menu with a button*

The first thing we do in the view controller in Listing 5-36 is to assign the value **true** to the button's **showsMenuAsPrimaryAction** property. This turns the menu as the primary action and therefore other actions assigned to the button are ignored. The menu is created next and assigned to the **menu** property. Notice that in this case we didn't need a title for the menu, so the **title** parameter is ignored. Now the button shows a menu when pressed and a message is printed on the console when the user selects an option.

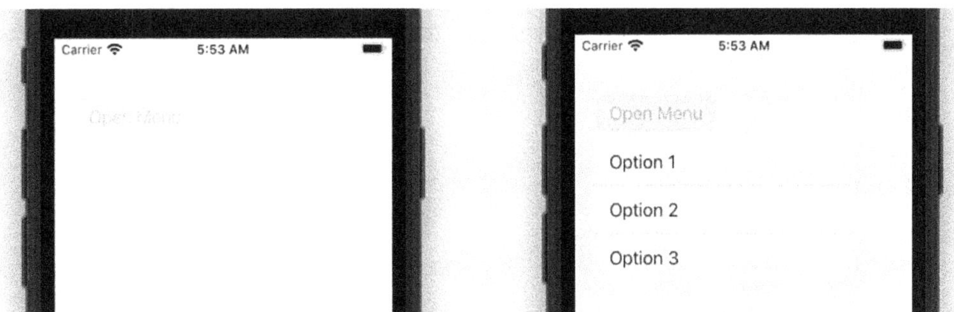

Figure 5-62: *Contextual menu*

Do It Yourself: Remove the elements in the scene and add a Tinted button from the Library. Connect the button to the view controller with an Outlet called **myButton**. Update the **ViewController** class with the code in Listing 5-36. Run the application, press the button, and select an option. You should see the option's title printed on the console.

In the last example, we have printed on the console the text we get from the action's **title** property. This property returns the title assigned to the action when it was created. Along with the title, the **UIAction** class defines properties to access every value assigned to the action, including **title**, **image**, **identifier**, and **state**. From the values of these properties, we can identify the action and optimize the response. For instance, we can assign an identifier to each action and then read the value of this identifier to know which option was selected by the user.

```
import UIKit

class ViewController: UIViewController {
   @IBOutlet weak var myButton: UIButton!

   override func viewDidLoad() {
      super.viewDidLoad()
      myButton.showsMenuAsPrimaryAction = true

      myButton.menu = UIMenu(children: [
         UIAction(title: "Option 1", identifier:
UIAction.Identifier("1"), handler: selectOption),
         UIAction(title: "Option 2", identifier:
UIAction.Identifier("2"), handler: selectOption),
         UIAction(title: "Option 3", identifier:
UIAction.Identifier("3"), handler: selectOption)
      ])
   }
   func selectOption(action: UIAction) {
      let id = action.identifier.rawValue
      if id == "1" {
         print("Option 1")
      }
   }
}
```

Listing 5-37: *Identifying the option selected by the user*

The **Identifier** structure includes an initializer that takes a string, which we can read later from the **rawValue** property. In this example, we identify the actions with the values 1, 2, and 3, and then check the identifier from the **selectOption()** method to print a message if the first option is selected.

The button generated by the previous examples is called Pull Down button because it displays a menu below, but there is another version called Pop Up that displays a popup menu and updates the button's title to reflect the option selected by the user. To turn a Pull Down button into a Pop Up button, all we have to do is to assign the value **true** to the **changesSelection-AsPrimaryAction** property (this is the same property used to define a toggle button, as we have seen in the example of Listing 5-35).

```
import UIKit

class ViewController: UIViewController {
   @IBOutlet weak var myButton: UIButton!

   override func viewDidLoad() {
      super.viewDidLoad()
      myButton.showsMenuAsPrimaryAction = true
      myButton.changesSelectionAsPrimaryAction = true

      myButton.menu = UIMenu(children: [
         UIAction(title: "Option 1", handler: selectOption),
         UIAction(title: "Option 2", state: .on, handler: selectOption),
         UIAction(title: "Option 3", handler: selectOption)
      ])
   }
   func selectOption(action: UIAction) {
      print(action.title)
   }
}
```

Listing 5-38: *Defining a Pop Up button*

The only requirement to create a Pop Up button is to define the **changesSelection-AsPrimaryAction** property, but we can also set the selected option by including the **state** parameter, as we did for the Option 2 in this example. If no option is selected, the first option is selected by default.

The Pop Up button works the same way as the Pull Down button, but the selected option is shown as the button's title.

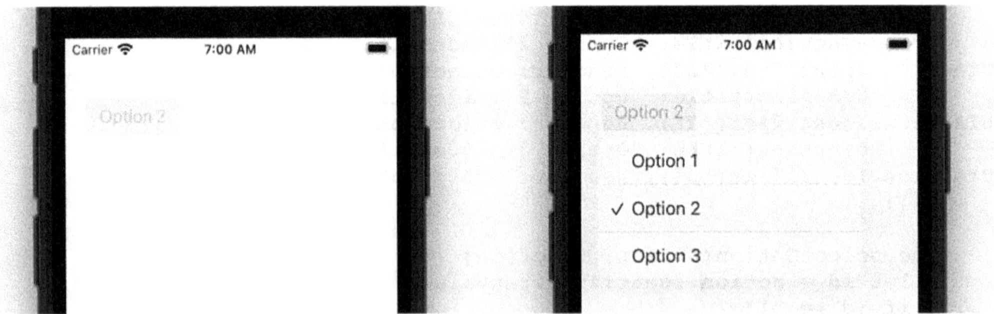

Figure 5-63: *Pop Up button*

The **UIMenu** class includes properties to manage the menu and the options. The most useful are the **children** property to access the options and the **selectedElements** property to return an array with objects that represent the selected options. The following is an action for an additional button that will print the title of the selected option when the button is pressed.

```
@IBAction func processOptions(_ sender: UIButton) {
   if let selected = myButton.menu?.selectedElements.first as? UIAction {
      print("Selected: \(selected.title)")
   }
}
```

Listing 5-39: *Getting the selected option*

The **selectedElements** property returns an array of **UIMenuElement** objects that we must cast to **UIAction** objects to access the option's values. In this example, we get the first element of the array (only one option is selected), get the **UIAction** object, and print the title on the console.

Do It Yourself: Add another button to the scene. Connect the button to the view controller with an Action called **processOptions()** and complete the method with the code in Listing 5-39. Run the application, select an option from the menu, and press the new button. You should see the name of the selected option printed on the console.

We can also select an option from code. All we need to do is to get the **UIAction** object that represents the option from the **children** property and modify the action's **state** property. For example, the following method gets the object that represents the second option (the option at index 1), casts the object to a **UIAction** object, and assigns the value **on** to the action's **state** property to select that option. Now, every time the button is pressed, the second option in the Pop Up button is selected.

```
@IBAction func processOptions(_ sender: UIButton) {
   let action = myButton.menu?.children[1] as? UIAction
   action?.state = .on
}
```

***Listing 5-40:** Selecting an option from code*

Basic Outlet Collections

An Outlet Collection is a type of Outlet that can reference one or more elements. It is useful when several elements of the interface must be modified at the same time. The property created for the Outlet is an array containing references to each element. By iterating over the array, we can reach every element connected to the Outlet and access their properties.

The following example presents an interface with three buttons. The Say Hello and Say Goodbye buttons print messages on the console and the Disable button is used to disable the first two.

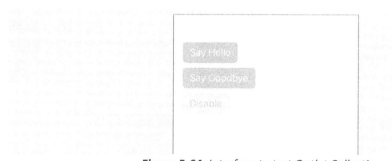

***Figure 5-64:** Interface to test Outlet Collections*

To create the functionality for this interface, we need an Action for every button and an Outlet Collection for the first two. The Outlet Collection is created by dragging a line from the first element to the view controller, as we did before, but this time the Connection is set as Outlet Collection. The subsequent connections can be created by dragging a line from the indicator on the left of the **@IBOutlet** property to the next element on the list, as shown below.

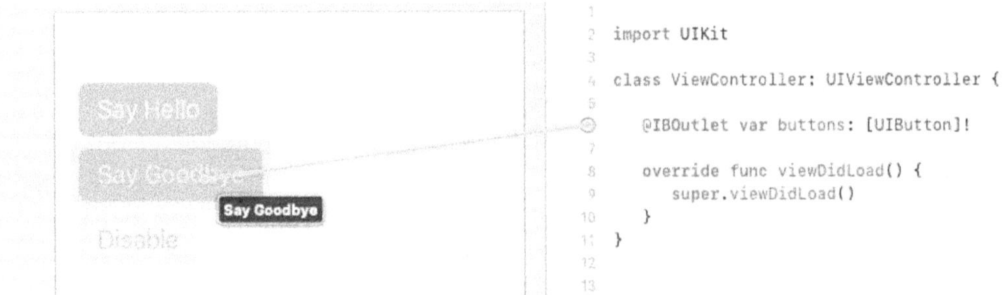

Figure 5-65: *Connecting multiple elements to the same Outlet*

After the Outlet Collection is defined and the first two buttons are connected, we must create the Actions. Listing 5-41, next, shows the view controller with the connections and all the Actions required for this example.

```
import UIKit

class ViewController: UIViewController {
   @IBOutlet var buttons: [UIButton]!

   @IBAction func sayHello(_ sender: UIButton) {
      print("Hello!")
   }
   @IBAction func sayGoodbye(_ sender: UIButton) {
      print("Goodbye!")
   }
   @IBAction func disableButtons(_ sender: UIButton) {
      for button in buttons {
         button.isEnabled = false
      }
   }
}
```

Listing 5-41: *Implementing an Outlet Collection*

The methods for the Say Hello and Say Goodbye buttons (**sayHello()** and **sayGoodbye()**) print messages on the console, but the method for the Disable button (**disableButtons()**) deactivates the other two buttons by modifying their **isEnabled** property. To access the property of every button, we iterate over the **buttons** array created to store the references for the Outlet Collection. When the Disable button is pressed, the **disableButtons()** method assigns the value **false** to the **isEnabled** property of each button in the Outlet Collection and therefore the first two buttons are disabled (they are shown in color gray and do not respond to the user anymore).

Do It Yourself: Clean the interface and code in your project. Drag and drop three buttons to the view to create the interface in Figure 5-64. Control-drag a line from the first button to the code and create an Outlet Collection called **buttons** (remember to set the type of connection as Outlet Collection). Control-drag a line from the indicator on the left side of the **@IBOutlet** property to the second button to add that button to the collection (Figure 5-65). Create the Actions for every button and complete the methods with the code in Listing 5-41. Every time you press any of the first two buttons, a message is printed on the console, but when you press the third button, the other buttons are disabled.

Progress View

UIKit includes the **UIProgressView** class to create a progress bar. This control was designed to show the progress of a task over time. The class includes its own initializer, a property, and a method to set and read the progress.

UIProgressView(progressViewStyle: Style**)**—This initializer creates a **UIProgressView** object with values by default and the style set by the argument. The argument is an enumeration called **Style** included in the **UIProgressView** class. The values available are **default** (standard progress bar) and **bar** (progress bar for toolbars).

progress—This property sets or returns the current progress. The possible values are between 0.0 and 1.0. The value by default is 0.0.

setProgress(Float, **animated:** Bool**)**—This method sets the value of the **progress** property. The first argument is a value between 0.0 and 1.0, and the **animated** argument indicates if the transition will be animated.

As always, the control can be added to a scene in the Storyboard from the Library.

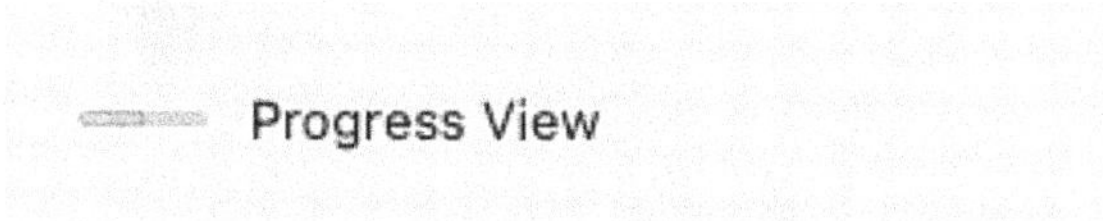

Figure 5-66: *Progress View in the Library*

In the interface, the bar looks like a line with two colors, one to indicate the progress and another to provide a reference to how much is left to process.

Figure 5-67: *Progress bar in the scene*

The class also includes the following properties to configure the appearance of the bar.

progressTintColor—This property sets or returns the color of the part of the progress bar that is filled. It is an optional of type **UIColor**.

trackTintColor—This property sets or returns the color of the part of the progress bar that is not filled. It is an optional of type **UIColor**.

progressImage—This property sets or returns the image used to illustrate the part of the progress bar that is filled. It is an optional of type **UIImage**.

trackImage—This property sets or returns the image used to illustrate the part of the progress bar that is not filled. It is an optional of type **UIImage**.

The progress is set with values from 0.0 to 1.0. By default, the value is 0.5, which sets the progress to 50%. This value can be changed from the Attributes Inspector panel or in code, as shown next.

```
import UIKit

class ViewController: UIViewController {
   @IBOutlet weak var progressbar: UIProgressView!

   override func viewDidLoad() {
      super.viewDidLoad()
      progressbar.progress = 0.2
      progressbar.tintColor = UIColor.systemRed
      progressbar.trackTintColor = UIColor.systemYellow
   }
}
```

Listing 5-42: *Customizing the progress bar*

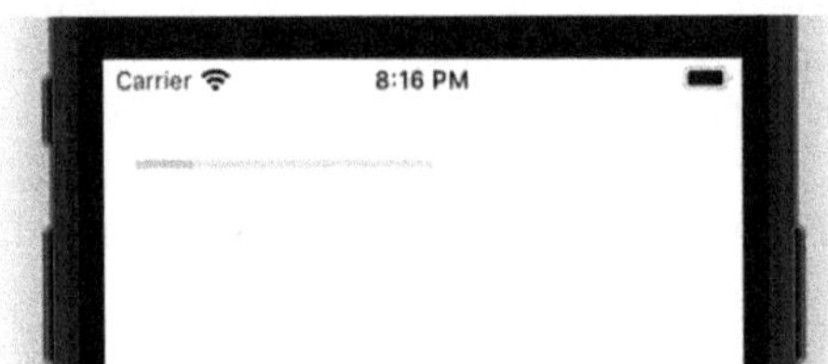

Figure 5-68: *Custom progress bar*

Do It Yourself: Delete the elements in the scene. Drag a Progress View from the Library to the scene. Connect it to the **ViewController** class with an Outlet called **progressbar**. Update the view controller with the code in Listing 5-42 and run the application. You should see the interface in Figure 5-68.

Basic Activity Indicator

The Activity Indicator creates a spinning wheel that indicates that a task is in progress, but unlike progress bars, this type of indicator has no implicit limitations. We have introduced it before when working with buttons (see Listing 5-30). In that case, the indicator was automatically created by the **UIButton** class, but we can initialize the object ourselves from the **UIActivityIndicatorView** class. The following are the initializer and some of the properties and methods provided by the class.

UIActivityIndicatorView(style: UIActivityIndicatorView.Style**)**—This initializer creates a **UIActivityIndicatorView** object with the style set by the argument. The argument is an enumeration called **Style** included in the **UIActivityIndicatorView** class. The values available are **large** (large indicator) and **medium** (standard indicator).

color—This property sets or returns the color of the indicator.

hidesWhenStopped—This property sets or returns a Boolean value that determines if the indicator is going to be hidden when the animation stops.

isAnimating—This property returns a Boolean value that determines whether the indicator is animating or not.

startAnimating()—This method starts the animation.

stopAnimating()—This method stops the animation.

The following is the option in the Library to add the indicator to a scene in the Storyboard.

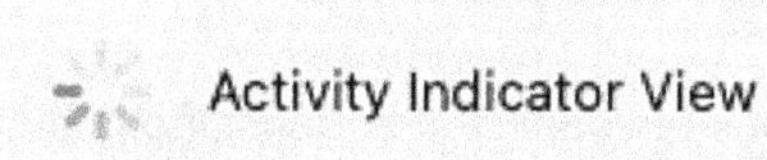

Figure 5-69: Activity Indicator in the Library

The activity indicator is usually implemented to show that a process has started. In the following example, we activate and deactivate the indicator every time a toggle button is pressed.

Figure 5-70: Interface to test the Activity Indicator

The view controller must include Outlets for the indicator and the button, and an action for the button to activate and deactivate the indicator when pressed.

```
import UIKit

class ViewController: UIViewController {
   @IBOutlet weak var myButton: UIButton!
   @IBOutlet weak var activity: UIActivityIndicatorView!

   override func viewDidLoad() {
      super.viewDidLoad()
      myButton.changesSelectionAsPrimaryAction = true
      activity.color = UIColor.systemRed
   }
   @IBAction func turnOnOff(_ sender: UIButton) {
      if activity.isAnimating {
         activity.stopAnimating()
         myButton.setTitle("Turn On", for: .normal)
      } else {
         activity.startAnimating()
         myButton.setTitle("Turn Off", for: .selected)
      }
   }
}
```

Listing 5-43: Working with an Activity Indicator

The code in Listing 5-43 configures the button as a toggle button with the **changesSelectionAsPrimaryAction** property and then assigns a red color to the indicator. When the app is launched, the indicator is not active, but if the button is pressed, the **turnOnOff()** method is called and the Activity Indicator is activated. In this method, we check the current condition by reading the **isAnimating** property, and then start or stop the indicator accordingly.

Do It Yourself: Delete previous elements in the scene. Drag an Activity Indicator and a Plain button from the Library to the scene and connect them to the **ViewController** class with Outlets called **myButton** and **activity**. Connect the button with an action called **turnOnOff()**. Complete the view controller with the code in Listing 5-43 and run the application. Press the button. You should see the indicator spinning.

Basic Segmented Control

A Segmented Control creates a bar of interconnected buttons (if one button is pressed, the other buttons are deactivated). The control is defined by the `UISegmentedControl` class, which includes the following initializer.

UISegmentedControl(frame: CGRect, **actions:** [UIAction]**)**—This initializer creates a `UISegmentedControl` object that performs a specific action for each button. The **frame** argument determines the position and size of the view, and the **actions** argument is an array of objects that define the buttons and the actions.

Each button of the segment is identified by an index starting from 0. The properties and methods in the class use this index to access and modify the buttons.

numberOfSegments—This property returns the number of buttons in the control.

selectedSegmentIndex—This property sets or returns the selected button in the control.

setAction(UIAction, **forSegmentAt:** Int**)**—This method sets a new action for a button. The first argument represents the action we want to assign to the button, and the **forSegmentAt** argument determines the index of the button to be modified.

insertSegment(action: UIAction, **at:** Int, **animated:** Bool**)**—This method inserts a new button with the action and in the position specified by the arguments. The **action** argument determines the action for the button, the **at** argument specifies the index in which the button will be inserted, and the **animated** argument determines whether the process will be animated or not.

removeSegment(at: Int, **animated:** Bool**)**—This method removes the button at the index specified by the **at** argument. The **animated** argument indicates if the process will be animated.

setEnabled(Bool, **forSegmentAt:** Int**)**—This method sets the condition of the button at the index specified by the **forSegmentAt** argument. The first argument determines whether the button is enabled (`true`) or disabled (`false`).

As with any other control, the Library offers an option to add a Segmented Control to a scene in the Storyboard.

Figure 5-71: *Segmented Control in the Library*

By default, the control is added to the scene with two buttons, but we can define more from the Attribute Inspector panel and change their titles with a double-click. For instance, the following interface includes a Segmented Control with the two buttons by default but new titles, and a label we are going to modify according to the button selected by the user.

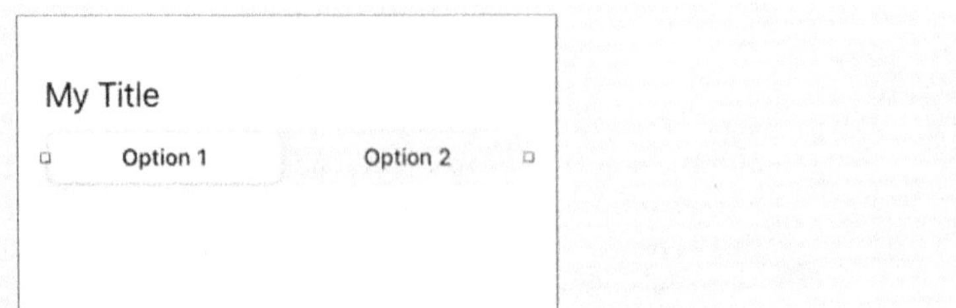

Figure 5-72: *Segmented Control with two buttons*

The way a Segmented Control works is by keeping track of the selected segment. An index value is assigned to each segment, from left to right, starting from 0. When a new segment is selected, the value of its index is assigned to the **selectedSegmentIndex** property of the **UISegmentedControl** object that represents the element and the Value Changed event is fired. By creating an Action that responds to this event, we can check the **selectedSegmentIndex** property and execute the corresponding code according to its value.

```
import UIKit

class ViewController: UIViewController {
   @IBOutlet weak var mytitle: UILabel!

   @IBAction func changeOption(_ sender: UISegmentedControl) {
      if sender.selectedSegmentIndex == 0 {
         mytitle.textColor = .label
      } else if sender.selectedSegmentIndex == 1 {
         mytitle.textColor = .systemRed
      }
   }
}
```

Listing 5-44: *Responding to the Value Changed event of a Segmented Control*

The **ViewController** class in Listing 5-44 includes an Action called **changeOption()** for the Segmented Control. When the user selects a segment by pressing a button, the Value Changed event is fired and the **changeOption()** method is executed. Inside this method, we check the value of the **selectedSegmentIndex** property of the **sender** object (the Segmented Control) and change the color of the label accordingly (black for the segment at index 0 and red for the segment at index 1).

Do It Yourself: Delete the elements in the scene. Drag and drop a label and a Segmented Control from the Library into the scene (Figure 5-72). Double-click on the label and each segment to change the text. Create an Outlet for the label called **mytitle** and an Action for the control with the name **changeOption()** (Remember to set the Type **UISegmentedControl** and the Event Value Changed). Update the view controller with the code in Listing 5-44. Run the application. You should be able to change the color of the label by pressing the buttons.

The buttons included in a Segmented Control added from the Library are not associated to any action. If we want the buttons to perform a task when pressed, we must add the actions from code with the **setAction(forSegmentAt:)** method, as shown in the following example.

```
import UIKit

class ViewController: UIViewController {
   @IBOutlet weak var mytitle: UILabel!
   @IBOutlet weak var options: UISegmentedControl!

   override func viewDidLoad() {
      super.viewDidLoad()
      options.setAction(UIAction(title: "Black", image: nil, handler:
{ action in
         print("Black Pressed")
      }), forSegmentAt: 0)
      options.setAction(UIAction(title: "Red", image: nil, handler:
{ action in
         print("Red Pressed")
      }), forSegmentAt: 1)
   }
```

```
    @IBAction func changeOption(_ sender: UISegmentedControl) {
        if sender.selectedSegmentIndex == 0 {
            mytitle.textColor = .label
        } else if sender.selectedSegmentIndex == 1 {
            mytitle.textColor = .systemRed
        }
    }
}
```

Listing 5-45: *Adding actions to a Segmented Control*

In this example, we connected the Segmented Control on the interface with an Outlet and then call the **setAction(forSegmentAt:)** method twice to add an action to each button. The **UIAction** initializer includes a title, image, and a closure to execute when the button is pressed, so the title of the segment is modified every time a new action is assigned to it. In this case, we define the titles "Black" and "Red" and then print a message on the console when the buttons are pressed.

Segmented Controls also include tools to add, remove, and edit segments. For example, we can insert a new segment with the **insertSegment()** method.

```
import UIKit

class ViewController: UIViewController {
    @IBOutlet weak var mytitle: UILabel!
    @IBOutlet weak var options: UISegmentedControl!

    override func viewDidLoad() {
        super.viewDidLoad()
        options.setAction(UIAction(title: "Black", image: nil, handler:
{ action in
            print("Black Pressed")
        }), forSegmentAt: 0)
        options.setAction(UIAction(title: "Red", image: nil, handler:
{ action in
            print("Red Pressed")
        }), forSegmentAt: 1)

        let total = options.numberOfSegments
        options.insertSegment(action: UIAction(title: "Blue", image: nil,
handler: { action in
            print("Blue Pressed")
        }), at: total, animated: false)

        options.setEnabled(false, forSegmentAt: 0)
    }
    @IBAction func changeOption(_ sender: UISegmentedControl) {
        switch sender.selectedSegmentIndex {
        case 0:
            mytitle.textColor = .label
        case 1:
            mytitle.textColor = .systemRed
        case 2:
            mytitle.textColor = .systemBlue
        default:
            mytitle.textColor = .label
        }
    }
}
```

Listing 5-46: *Modifying a Segmented Control*

The view controller in Listing 5-46 defines the actions for the segments as we did before, but then inserts a new segment at the end of the list. To know the index, we read the **numberOfSegments** property. This property returns the number of segments in the control, so we can use it as index to add another one at the end.

To respond to the selection, we replace the **if else** statement from previous examples with a **switch** statement and three cases, one per button. Notice that the first segment is disabled with the **setEnabled()** method, so only the Red and Blue buttons are available.

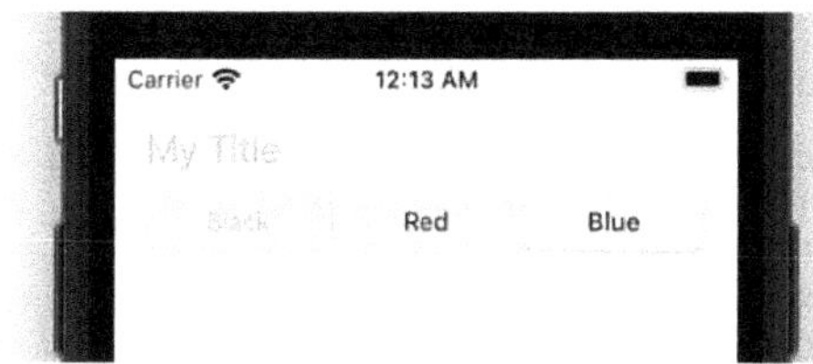

Figure 5-73: Segments added and modified from code

Switch

As its name indicates, the Switch control is a switch on the screen that the user can turn on and off. UIKit includes the **UISwitch** class to create these controls. The class doesn't implement any initializer, but we can use the **UIView** initializer to create a Switch from code or drag the option from the Library.

UISwitch(frame: CGRect**)**—This initializer creates a **UISwitch** object with the position and size specified by the argument.

Figure 5-74: Switch in the Library

Switches are turned on and off by the user, but the class includes some tools to modify the state from code.

isOn—This property sets or returns the state of the switch. It is a Boolean value that determines the state of the switch; on (**true**) or off (**false**).

setOn(Bool, **animated:** Bool**)**—This method sets the state of the switch. The first argument sets the switch on (**true**) or off (**false**), and the **animated** argument determines if the transition will be animated.

Switches can have only two states, on or off (**true** or **false**), and therefore they are appropriate when only two conditions are possible. For instance, we can replace the Segmented Control from the previous interface with a Switch to change the label's color between two values.

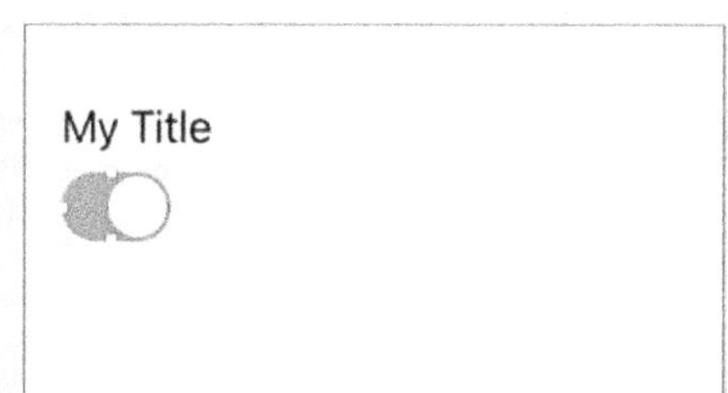

Figure 5-75: Interface to test a Switch

When the Switch is turned on or off, it fires a Value Changed event, so we can define an Action to listen to this event and read the **isOn** property to check the state and perform a task accordingly.

```
import UIKit

class ViewController: UIViewController {
   @IBOutlet weak var mytitle: UILabel!

   @IBAction func turnSwitch(_ sender: UISwitch) {
      if sender.isOn {
         mytitle.textColor = .label
      } else {
         mytitle.textColor = .systemRed
      }
   }
}
```

Listing 5-47: *Changing the color of a label with a Switch*

When the switch is turned on, its background color changes. We can modify this color and the color of the button using the following properties.

onTintColor—This property sets or returns the color of the switch's background when it is turned on. It is an optional of type **UIColor**.

thumbTintColor—This property sets or returns the color of the switch's button. It is an optional of type **UIColor**.

In the following example, we connect the Switch with an Outlet to modify the appearance from code, and then apply custom colors to the knob and the background.

```
import UIKit

class ViewController: UIViewController {
   @IBOutlet weak var mytitle: UILabel!
   @IBOutlet weak var mySwitch: UISwitch!

   override func viewDidLoad() {
      super.viewDidLoad()
      let colorBackground = UIColor(red: 0.9, green: 0.9, blue: 1.0, 
alpha:1.0)
      let colorButton = UIColor(red: 0.5, green: 0.5, blue: 1.0, alpha: 
1.0)
      mySwitch.onTintColor = colorBackground
      mySwitch.thumbTintColor = colorButton
   }
   @IBAction func turnSwitch(_ sender: UISwitch) {
      if sender.isOn {
         mytitle.textColor = .label
      } else {
         mytitle.textColor = .systemRed
      }
   }
}
```

Listing 5-48: *Changing the colors of the switch*

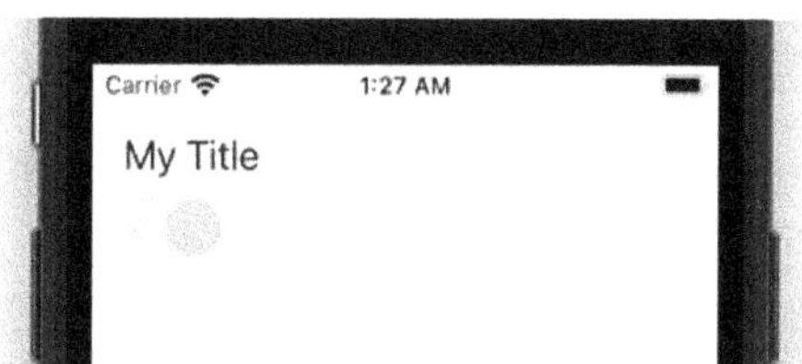

Figure 5-76: Switch with custom colors

Do It Yourself: Recreate the interface from Figure 5-75. Create an Outlet for the label called **`mytitle`** and an Action for the Switch with the name **`mySwitch()`**, the Type **`UISwitch`**, the Event Value Changed, and the rest of the values by default. Complete the **`ViewController`** class with the code in Listing 5-48. Run the application. Every time you turn the switch on or off, the color of the label should change between black and red.

Basic Slider

Sliders allow the user to select a value from a range of values. The control is presented as a horizontal bar with a round indicator that points to the selected value. It is defined by the **`UISlider`** class. We can create it from code with the **`UIView`** initializer or add it to a scene from the option in the Library.

UISlider(frame: CGRect**)**—This initializer creates a **`UISlider`** object with the position and size specified by the argument.

Figure 5-77: Slider in the Library

By default, Sliders are created with a range of values between 0.0 and 1.0 and the indicator pointing at the value 0.5, but we can adapt the control to our needs from the Attributes Inspector panel or the properties and methods provided by the **`UISlider`** class.

value—This property sets or returns the selected value. When the value is set, the indicator is moved to the corresponding position. It takes a value of type **`Float`**.

minimumValue—This property sets or returns the minimum value. It is of type **`Float`**.

maximumValue—This property sets or returns the maximum value. It is of type **`Float`**.

setValue(Float, **animated:** Bool**)**—This method sets the selected value as the value specified by the first argument and moves the indicator to the corresponding position. The **animated** argument is a Boolean value that determines if the change will be animated.

The Slider is usually applied to analog systems where a specific value is not required (e.g., volume control, brightness, etc.). For the following example, we implement a Progress View along with a Slider with values by default.

Figure 5-78: Progress View and Slider working together

```
import UIKit

class ViewController: UIViewController {
   @IBOutlet weak var progress: UIProgressView!

   @IBAction func updateProgress(_ sender: UISlider) {
      progress.progress = sender.value
   }
}
```

Listing 5-49: *Incrementing or decrementing a value with a Slider*

When the user moves the pointer, the value in the **value** property changes, the Value Changed event is fired, and the Action assigned to the Slider is performed. In this example, we defined the action with a method called **updateProgress()**. In this method, we take the current value of the Slider from the **value** property and assign it to the **progress** property of the **UIProgressView** object to update the progress bar.

Do It Yourself: Delete the elements in the scene. Add a Progress View and a Slider from the Library (as illustrated in Figure 5-78). Create an Outlet for the progress bar called **progress** and an Action for the Slider called **updateProgress()**. Update the view controller with the code in Listing 5-49. The progress bar should change according to the position of the Slider.

As we have seen above, we can specify different values for the Slider from the Attributes Inspector panel and from code, but the class also provides properties to customize the Slider, change colors, and add images on the sides to represent minimum and maximum values.

minimumTrackTintColor—This property sets or returns the color of the bar on the left side of the indicator. It is an optional of type **UIColor**.

maximumTrackTintColor—This property sets or returns the color of the bar on the right side of the indicator. It is an optional of type **UIColor**.

minimumValueImage—This property sets or returns the image that represents the minimum value. It is an optional of type **UIImage**.

maximumValueImage—This property sets or returns the image that represents the maximum value. It is an optional of type **UIImage**.

```
import UIKit

class ViewController: UIViewController {
   @IBOutlet weak var progress: UIProgressView!
   @IBOutlet weak var slider: UISlider!

   override func viewDidLoad() {
      super.viewDidLoad()
      slider.minimumValue = 0.0
      slider.maximumValue = 10.0
      slider.value = 0.0

      slider.minimumTrackTintColor = UIColor.systemRed
      slider.maximumTrackTintColor = UIColor.systemYellow
   }
   @IBAction func updateProgress(_ sender: UISlider) {
      let currentValue = sender.value / 10
      progress.progress = currentValue
   }
}
```

Listing 5-50: *Working with custom values*

In this example, we connect the Slider to the view controller with an Outlet called slider to modify its values and appearance. Now the Slider is presented with different colors and runs from 0.0 to 10.0. The rest of the application works the same but notice that we couldn't assign the value of the Slider directly to the Progress View, as we did before. By default, the Progress View and the Slider work with the same range of values (0.0 to 1.0). If we change the range for the Slider, we must adapt the number returned by this element to the Progress View range to be able to display the correct level of progress. In our example, the value of the Slider goes from 0 to 10, so we divide the value of the **`value`** property by 10 to get a number between 0.0 and 1.0 that we can assign to the progress bar.

Basic Stepper

A Stepper includes two buttons with the minus and plus symbols that users can press to increment or decrement a value. It is defined by the **`UIStepper`** class. We can create a Stepper from code with the **`UIView`** initializer or add it to a scene from the option in the Library.

UIStepper(frame: CGRect**)**—This initializer creates a **`UIStepper`** object with the position and size specified by the argument.

Figure 5-79: Stepper in the Library

A Stepper is set with values by default. The minimum is set to 0.0, the maximum to 100.0, the initial value to 0.0, and the incremental value to 1.0, but we can adapt the control to our needs from the Attributes Inspector panel or the class properties.

value—This property sets or returns the current value of the Stepper.

minimumValue—This property sets or returns the minimum value. It is of type **`Double`**.

maximumValue—This property sets or returns the maximum value. It is of type **`Double`**.

stepValue—This property sets or returns the number by which the current value of the Stepper will be incremented or decremented. It is of type **`Double`**.

The class also includes properties to configure the control's behavior and appearance.

autorepeat—This property sets or returns a Boolean value that indicates if the value is incremented automatically. If it is set to **`true`**, the value of the Stepper is incremented repeatedly while the user holds the button down.

isContinuous—This property sets or returns a Boolean value that indicates if the updated values are reported during the user interaction or only when the user interaction ends.

wraps—This property sets or returns a Boolean value that determines how the value is processed when it reaches the minimum or maximum values allowed. If **`true`**, when the value goes beyond the limit the opposite limit is assigned to it and the value keeps decrementing or incrementing in a loop. On the other hand, when the property is **`false`**, the value stops decrementing or incrementing when a limit is reached.

tintColor—This property sets or returns the color of the control.

A Stepper works the same way as other controls we have already introduced. When the user presses a button, the control fires a Value Changed event, so we can define an Action to respond to this event and process the new value or perform a task. For instance, we can show the current value with a label, as in the following example.

Figure 5-80: *Interface to test the Stepper*

The values of the Stepper's properties may be modified from the Attribute inspector panel or from code. This example illustrates how to set the values from the view controller.

```
import UIKit

class ViewController: UIViewController {
   @IBOutlet weak var stepper: UIStepper!
   @IBOutlet weak var counterLabel: UILabel!

   override func viewDidLoad() {
      super.viewDidLoad()
      stepper.value = 0.0
      stepper.minimumValue = 0.0
      stepper.maximumValue = 10.0
      stepper.stepValue = 1.0
   }
   @IBAction func increment(_ sender: UIStepper) {
      counterLabel.text = String(sender.value)
   }
}
```

Listing 5-51: *Customizing the values of a Stepper*

The view controller defines an Outlet for the Stepper and change its values when the view is loaded. We set an initial value of 0, a minimum value of 0, a maximum value of 10, and declare the step with a value of 1.0, so the user can select a value from 0 to 10 in steps of 1. The Stepper was also connected to the view controller with an Action called **increment()**, so every time the user presses a button, the new value is assigned to the label and displayed on the screen.

Do It Yourself: Delete the elements in the scene. Add a label and a Stepper to the scene. Double-click the label to change its text to "0.0", as illustrated in Figure 5-80. Create an Outlet for the label called **counterLabel** and an Action for the Stepper called **increment()**. Update the **ViewController** class with the code in Listing 5-51. Run the application. The value in the label should be incremented or decremented every time you press the buttons of the Stepper.

Basic Text Field

A Text Field is a rectangular box on the screen that activates the keyboard to let the user insert characters or paste text in it. It is defined by the **UITextField** class. We can create a Text Field from code with the **UIView** initializer or add it to a scene from the option in the Library.

UITextField(frame: CGRect)—This initializer creates an object of the **UITextField** class with a position and size determined by the **frame** argument.

Text Text Field

Figure 5-81: Text Field option in the Library

The following are the most frequently used properties included in the class.

text—This property sets or returns the text inside the field. It is an optional of type **String**.

placeholder—This property sets or returns the message that is displayed while the field is empty. It is an optional of type **String**.

font—This property sets or returns the font used by the Text Field to show the text. It is an optional of type **UIFont**.

textColor—This property sets or returns the color of the text. It is an optional of type **UIColor**.

textAlignment—This property sets or returns the text's alignment. It is an enumeration of type **NSTextAlignment** with the values **left**, **center**, **right**, **justified**, and **natural**.

clearsOnBeginEditing—This property sets or returns a Boolean value that determines whether the text inside the field should be erased when the user begins editing.

borderStyle—This property sets or returns the value of the style for the border. It is an enumeration called **BorderStyle** included in the **UITextField** class. The values available are **none** (no border), **line** (single line around the field), **bezel** (single line with shadows), and **roundedRect** (lines with round corners).

background—This property sets or returns the background image. It is an optional value of type **UIImage**. The image replaces the border defined by the **borderStyle** property.

The **UITextField** class also conforms to a protocol called **UITextInputTraits** that defines a set of properties to configure the input produced by the keyboard and the keyboard itself.

autocapitalizationType—This property sets or returns a value that determines when the Shift key will be automatically pressed to insert uppercase letters. It is an enumeration of type **UITextAutocapitalizationType** with the values **none** (Shift is never activated), **words** (Shift is activated to capitalize each word), **sentences** (Shift is activated to capitalize sentences), and **allCharacters** (Shift is always activated).

autocorrectionType—This property sets or returns a value that determines whether auto-correction is enabled while typing. It is an enumeration of type **UITextAutocorrectionType** with the values **default**, **no**, and **yes**.

spellCheckingType—This property sets or returns a value that determines whether spell checking is enabled while typing. It is an enumeration of type **UITextSpellCheckingType** with the values **default**, **no**, and **yes**.

keyboardType—This property sets or returns a value that determines what type of keyboard to open. It is an enumeration of type **UIKeyboardType** with the values **default**, **asciiCapable**, **numbersAndPunctuation**, **URL**, **numberPad**, **phonePad**, **namePhonePad**, **emailAddress**, **decimalPad**, **twitter**, and **webSearch**.

returnKeyType—This property sets or returns a value that determines the title of the Return key. It is an enumeration of type **UIReturnKeyType** with the values **default**, **go**, **google**, **join**, **next**, **route**, **search**, **send**, **yahoo**, **done**, and **emergencyCall**.

isSecureTextEntry—This property sets or returns a Boolean value that determines whether the text should be hidden (used to hide passwords). The value by default is **false**.

As with any other element, we can set up the Text Field from the Attributes Inspector panel and later change some aspects and read its values from code. To illustrate this process, we are going to implement the following interface, which includes a label, a Text Field with the placeholder "Insert title here", and a button to process the text inserted by the user.

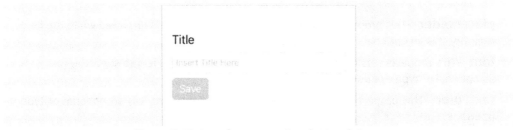

Figure 5-82: *Interface to receive the user's input*

As we do with any other element in the interface, to access the text inserted by the user and modify the characteristics of the Text Field from code, we must create an Outlet. The interface in Figure 5-82 requires two Outlets, one for the label and another for the Text Field, and an Action for the Save button to process the text.

```
import UIKit

class ViewController: UIViewController {
   @IBOutlet weak var titleLabel: UILabel!
   @IBOutlet weak var titleInput: UITextField!

   @IBAction func changeTitle(_ sender: UIButton) {
      if titleInput.text != "" {
         titleLabel.text = titleInput.text
         titleInput.text = ""
      }
   }
}
```

Listing 5-52: *Processing the user's input*

The code in Listing 5-52 does not introduce anything new, but thanks to the Text Field we are now able to process input from the user. When the user taps on the Save button, the **changeTitle()** method is executed and the label's text is replaced with the text inserted by the user. The first thing we do is to confirm that the Text Field is not empty comparing its **text** property with an empty string (**titleInput.text != ""**). When there is text to process, the value of this property is assigned to the label's **text** property (**titleLabel.text = titleInput.text**), effectively replacing the text on the screen with the text inserted by the user. Finally, the Text Field is cleared to receive new input.

Do It Yourself: Delete the elements in the scene. Add a label with the word "Title", a Text Field with the placeholder "Insert title here", and a button called "Save" (Figure 5-82). Create Outlets for the label and the Text Field called **titleLabel** and **titleInput**. Create an Action for the Save button called **changeTitle()**. Update the view controller with the code in Listing 5-52. Run the application, insert a text, and press the Save button. You should see the text replacing the title.

In the example of Listing 5-52, we compare the value inserted by the user with an empty string. If the string is not empty, we process it. But sometimes users unintentionally add space characters at the beginning or the end of the string. The **String** structure includes a convenient method defined specifically to remove these unwanted characters.

trimmingCharacters(in: CharacterSet**)**—This method erases the characters indicated by the **in** argument at the beginning and end of the string and returns a string with the result. The argument is a **CharacterSet** structure with the set of characters we want to erase.

The **trimmingCharacters()** method takes a structure of type **CharacterSet** to know what to remove. This structure creates sets of characters for searching operations. The definition includes a few type properties to create structures with standard sets. The most useful are **whitespaces** and **whitespacesAndNewlines**, which return sets that contain invisible characters, like spaces, tabulations, or characters that represent new lines. The following example implements the **whitespaces** property to remove the space characters at the beginning and the end of the string inserted by the user. Notice that this time we take advantage of the **isEmpty** property defined by the **String** structure to check if the string is empty or not. This produces the same result as before but can simplify our code in some circumstances.

```
import UIKit

class ViewController: UIViewController {
   @IBOutlet weak var titleLabel: UILabel!
   @IBOutlet weak var titleInput: UITextField!

   @IBAction func changeTitle(_ sender: UIButton) {
      var text = titleInput.text!
      text = text.trimmingCharacters(in: .whitespaces)

      if !text.isEmpty {
         titleLabel.text = text
         titleInput.text = ""
      }
   }
}
```

Listing 5-53: *Trimming text*

The **UITextField** class, as well as other classes that create visual controls on the screen, is a subclass of the **UIControl** class and the **UIControl** class is a subclass of the **UIView** class, therefore, **UITextField** objects have access to all their properties and methods, such as the **backgroundColor** property to change the background color or the **isEnabled** property to enable or disable the field. The following example modifies the **isEnabled** property to disable the Text Field after the first input.

```
import UIKit

class ViewController: UIViewController {
   @IBOutlet weak var titleLabel: UILabel!
   @IBOutlet weak var titleInput: UITextField!

   @IBAction func changeTitle(_ sender: UIButton) {
      var text = titleInput.text!
      text = text.trimmingCharacters(in: .whitespaces)
      if !text.isEmpty {
         titleLabel.text = text
```

```
            titleInput.text = ""
            titleInput.placeholder = "Text Field Disabled"
            titleInput.isEnabled = false
        }
    }
}
```

Listing 5-54: Disabling the Text Field

The **changeTitle()** method in Listing 5-54 assigns the new text to the label as before, but now it also modifies the **isEnabled** property to disable the field and shows a new placeholder to report the situation to the user. Once the Text Field is disabled, the user cannot type anymore.

These properties provide some level of customization, but they are not enough to control the user's input. Sometimes we need to determine what the user is allowed to insert or how the Text Field should respond. For this purpose, the **UITextField** class includes the **delegate** property to designate a delegate to the Text Field. The **UITextField** object calls methods on this delegate object to report the state of the process. The object assigned as the Text Field's delegate must conform to the **UITextFieldDelegate** protocol, which includes the following methods.

textFieldShouldBeginEditing(UITextField**)**—This method is called by the Text Field on the delegate object to know if edition should be allowed. The method must return a Boolean value that indicates if edition is allowed or not.

textFieldDidBeginEditing(UITextField**)**—This method is called by the Text Field on the delegate object when the user begins editing its content.

textFieldShouldEndEditing(UITextField**)**—This method is called by the Text Field on the delegate object when the user tries to switch focus to another element. The method must return a Boolean value that indicates if edition should stop or not.

textFieldDidEndEditing(UITextField**)**—This method is called by the Text Field on the delegate object after the element loses focus.

textField(UITextField, **shouldChangeCharactersIn:** NSRange, **replacementString:** String**)**—This method is called by the Text Field on the delegate object every time the user inserts or deletes a character or a string of characters. The **shouldChangeCharactersIn** argument determines the range of characters on the field affected by the operation, and the **replacementString** argument is the new character or string of characters inserted by the user. The method must return a Boolean value that indicates whether the text should be replaced or not.

textFieldShouldClear(UITextField**)**—This method is called by the Text Field on the delegate object to know if the Text Field should be cleared when the Clear button is pressed. The method must return a Boolean value that indicates whether the Text Field should be cleared or not.

textFieldShouldReturn(UITextField**)**—This method is called by the Text Field on the delegate object when the user taps the Return key on the keyboard. The method must return a Boolean value that indicates if the action should be considered or not.

Usually, the object assigned as the Text Field's delegate is the same view controller that controls the scene to which the Text Field belongs. In the following example, the **ViewController** object is assigned to the **delegate** property of the Text Field and then the **textFieldShouldBeginEditing()** method is implemented. This method is another way to enable or disable a Text Field. The **UITextField** object calls it as soon as the user taps on the Text Field. If the value returned by the method is **false**, the user is not allowed to insert text.

```
import UIKit

class ViewController: UIViewController, UITextFieldDelegate {
   @IBOutlet weak var titleLabel: UILabel!
   @IBOutlet weak var titleInput: UITextField!

   override func viewDidLoad() {
      super.viewDidLoad()
      titleInput.delegate = self
   }
   @IBAction func changeTitle(_ sender: UIButton) {
      titleLabel.text = titleInput.text
   }
   func textFieldShouldBeginEditing(_ textField: UITextField) -> Bool {
      return false
   }
}
```

Listing 5-55: *Assigning a delegate to the Text Field and declaring its methods*

The first thing we need to do in our view controller is to declare that the class conforms to the **UITextFieldDelegate** protocol, so the **UITextField** object knows that this object implements the protocol methods. This is done by adding the name of the protocol after the name of the class, separated by a comma (see Protocols and Delegates in Chapter 3). Next, we must declare the view controller object as the delegate of the Text Field, so the **UITextField** object knows what object implements the protocol methods. This is part of the Text Field's configuration, so it has to be done before anything else, and that is why we assign the **self** keyword to the **delegate** property inside the **viewDidLoad()** method (**self** is a reference to the object that the code belongs to, in this case, the **ViewController** object). Now the **UITextField** object can use the **delegate** property to access our view controller object and report changes in the state of the Text Field by calling the corresponding methods. For example, when the user taps on the Text Field to start writing on it, the **UITextField** object calls the **textFieldShouldBeginEditing()** method to know if the user is allowed to type on it (in our example, we return **false**, indicating that the user is not allowed).

The methods of the **UITextFieldDelegate** protocol are optional, which means we can implement only the ones we need. If the method does not exist inside the delegate, the Text Field uses the values by default. For example, if we do not declare the **textFieldShouldBegin-Editing()** method, as we did in Listing 5-55, the Text Field considers the value to be **true** and allows the user to edit the field.

The **textFieldShouldBeginEditing()** method is a very simple method, but we can declare others to control more aspects of the interaction between the user and the Text Field. For example, if we want to control what the user is allowed to type in the field, we can implement the **textField(shouldChangeCharactersIn:, replacementString:)** method. Every time the user types a character, the **UITextField** object calls this method to know whether it should include the entry or not. Implementing this method, we can process the input while it is entered.

```
import UIKit

class ViewController: UIViewController, UITextFieldDelegate {
   @IBOutlet weak var titleLabel: UILabel!
   @IBOutlet weak var titleInput: UITextField!

   override func viewDidLoad() {
      super.viewDidLoad()
      titleInput.delegate = self
   }
```

```
    @IBAction func changeTitle(_ sender: UIButton) {
        titleLabel.text = titleInput.text
    }
    func textField(_ textField: UITextField, shouldChangeCharactersIn
range: NSRange, replacementString string: String) -> Bool {
        if let text = textField.text {
            let total = text.count + string.count - range.length
            if total > 10 {
                return false
            }
        }
        return true
    }
}
```

Listing 5-56: *Determining the number of characters allowed*

The **textField(shouldChangeCharactersIn:, replacementString:)** method receives three values from the Text Field: a reference to the **UITextField** object, an **NSRange** value that represents the range of characters in the Text Field that are going to be replaced by the new entry, and a **String** value with the new entry. Based on these values, we must determine if the entry should be included in the field or not and return a Boolean value to communicate our decision. For example, a common task is to limit the number of characters allowed in the field. We add the number of characters currently stored in the **text** property to the number of characters the user wants to introduce minus the length of the range and return **false** if the value exceeds the maximum allowed. This procedure is followed in the example of Listing 5-56. We count the characters in the **text** property and the **string** parameter, add both values, subtract the length of the array, which represents the number of characters currently selected by the user, and finally store the total in the **total** constant. The value of **total** is then compared to 10 (the maximum number of characters we want to allow in the Text Field for this example) and the value **false** is returned if **total** is greater than this number, rejecting the new entry.

The possibilities of control are limitless. We can filter the input in any way we want. For instance, we could let the user insert only numbers.

```
func textField(_ textField: UITextField, shouldChangeCharactersIn range:
NSRange, replacementString string: String) -> Bool {
    if (Int(string) != nil && textField.text != "0") || string == "" {
        return true
    }
    return false
}
```

Listing 5-57: *Allowing only numbers*

To determine if the user inserted a number we use the **Int()** initializer. If the value returned by **Int()** is not **nil**, it means that the **string** parameter contains a number. But there are a few other things we must contemplate to create this filter. The first is that, although the number 0 is a valid integer number, an integer number of two digits or more cannot begin with 0. Therefore, we ought to validate the entry only if the current value in the Text Field is not equal to 0. These two values, the value created by the initializer and the current value of the **text** property, determine two of the conditions we need to check to validate the entry, but there is one more. When the user presses a key that does not produce any character, such as the Delete key, the value assigned to the **string** parameter is an empty string and therefore we also need to check this value to determine if the entry is valid or not. Inside the method of Listing 5-57, we create a logical sequence to check all these conditions. If **string** contains a number and the current value of the **text** property is not 0, or the value of **string** is an empty string, the logical sequence evaluates to true, and the entry is validated.

Do It Yourself: Replace the **`textField(shouldChangeCharactersIn:, replacementString:)`** method of Listing 5-56 by the method of Listing 5-57. Run the application. You should only be allowed to type numbers. If you type the number 0 first, the system will not let you insert any additional number.

Another useful method of the **`UITextFieldDelegate`** protocol is **`textFieldShouldReturn()`**. This method is called every time the user presses the Return key on the keyboard. As an example, we can use it to perform the same action as the Save button.

```
import UIKit

class ViewController: UIViewController, UITextFieldDelegate {
   @IBOutlet weak var titleLabel: UILabel!
   @IBOutlet weak var titleInput: UITextField!

   override func viewDidLoad() {
      super.viewDidLoad()
      titleInput.delegate = self
   }
   @IBAction func changeTitle(_ sender: UIButton) {
      assignTitle()
   }
   func textFieldShouldReturn(_ textField: UITextField) -> Bool {
      assignTitle()
      return true
   }
   func assignTitle() {
      titleLabel.text = titleInput.text
   }
}
```

Listing 5-58: *Responding to the keyboard*

Because we are performing the same action for both, the Save button and the Return key, we process the text in a new method called **`assignTitle()`** and then call this method every time the button or the key are pressed. When the user presses the Return key, the **`textFieldShouldReturn()`** method is called. This method executes the **`assignTitle()`** method to replace the label's text and then returns the value **`true`** to tell the system to implement the default behavior for the Return key.

Other methods of the **`UITextFieldDelegate`** protocol are called when the editing begins or ends. For example, we can implement the **`textFieldDidBeginEditing()`** method to highlight the active Text Field. The following example changes the Text Field's background color to a light gray when the user taps on it to start typing.

```
func textFieldDidBeginEditing(_ textField: UITextField) {
   textField.backgroundColor = UIColor.systemGray4
}
```

Listing 5-59: *Highlighting the Text Field*

If our interface includes two or more Text Fields, we can take advantage of other methods like **`textFieldDidEndEditing()`**. Instead of performing a task when the Text Field is tapped, with this method we can do it when the Text Field loses focus (the user taps somewhere else). For example, if we expand our interface to include another Text Field, we can highlight only the one currently selected. Figure 5-83 shows what an interface like this looks like.

Figure 5-83: *Interface with two Text Fields*

In this example, the original Text Field is used to introduce the title and the new Text Field is used for the subtitle, so now the Save button must assign both values to the label.

```
import UIKit

class ViewController: UIViewController, UITextFieldDelegate {
   @IBOutlet weak var titleLabel: UILabel!
   @IBOutlet weak var titleInput: UITextField!
   @IBOutlet weak var subtitleInput: UITextField!

   override func viewDidLoad() {
      super.viewDidLoad()
      titleInput.delegate = self
      subtitleInput.delegate = self
   }
   @IBAction func changeTitle(_ sender: UIButton) {
      if titleInput.text != "" && subtitleInput.text != "" {
         titleLabel.text = titleInput.text! + " - " + subtitleInput.text!
         titleInput.text = ""
         subtitleInput.text = ""
      }
   }
   func textFieldDidBeginEditing(_ textField: UITextField) {
      textField.backgroundColor = UIColor.systemGray4
   }
   func textFieldDidEndEditing(_ textField: UITextField) {
      textField.backgroundColor = UIColor.white
   }
}
```

Listing 5-60: *Highlighting two Text Fields*

This view controller includes an Outlet called **`subtitleInput`** for the new Text Field and assigns itself as the delegate for both Text Fields. Every time the user types on any of the Text Fields, the protocol methods are called in our view controller. In this example, we have implemented the **`textFieldDidBeginEditing()`** and the **`textFieldDidEndEditing()`** methods to change the background colors. When the user taps on one of the Text Fields to start typing, its background becomes gray, as it did in the previous example, but now when the user taps on the other Text Field, the first one loses focus and it calls the **`textFieldDidEndEdition()`** method. From this method, we change the Text Field's background color back to white to reflect the new state.

Do It Yourself: Add a new Text Field to the interface, as shown in Figure 5-83. Connect this element to the view controller with an Outlet called **`subtitleInput`**. Update the **`ViewController`** class with the code in Listing 5-60. Run the application and tap on one Text Field and then the other to see how their background colors change.

Working with two or more Text Fields in the same view and connected to the same delegate presents a challenge. The methods called on the delegate are always the same, no matter which Text Field performed the call. This is the reason why all the methods defined in the **UITextFieldDelegate** protocol include a parameter with a reference to the **UITextField** object that performed the call. We can use this reference to modify the object, as we did before, but also to identify the Text Field we are working with. One simple way to do this is to assign a value to the object's **tag** property. A different value is assigned to the **tag** property of every Text Field from the Attributes Inspector panel and then the property is read from code to know which Text Field called the method. For example, the following view controller implements the **textField(shouldChangeCharactersIn:, replacementString:)** method to establish different limits to the number of characters the user can type on each field.

```
import UIKit

class ViewController: UIViewController, UITextFieldDelegate {
   @IBOutlet weak var titleLabel: UILabel!
   @IBOutlet weak var titleInput: UITextField!
   @IBOutlet weak var subtitleInput: UITextField!

   override func viewDidLoad() {
      super.viewDidLoad()
      titleInput.delegate = self
      subtitleInput.delegate = self
   }
   @IBAction func changeTitle(_ sender: UIButton) {
      if titleInput.text != "" && subtitleInput.text != "" {
         titleLabel.text = titleInput.text! + " - " + subtitleInput.text!
         titleInput.text = ""
         subtitleInput.text = ""
      }
   }
   func textField(_ textField: UITextField, shouldChangeCharactersIn
range: NSRange, replacementString string: String) -> Bool {
      var maximum = 0
      if textField.tag == 1 {
         maximum = 10
      } else {
         maximum = 15
      }
      if let text = textField.text {
         let total = text.count + string.count - range.length
         if total > maximum {
            return false
         }
      }
      return true
   }
}
```

***Listing 5-61:** Identifying Text Fields*

This example assumes that the values of the Text Fields' **tag** properties were defined as 1 and 2, respectively. The **textField(shouldChangeCharactersIn:, replacementString:)** method checks this value to know which Text Field is making the call (**textField.tag == 1**), sets the value of the **maximum** variable, and then compares the result with the total amount of characters allowed to validate the entry (**total > maximum**).

Do It Yourself: Select each Text Field in the Storyboard and assign the corresponding values to their **tag** properties from the Attributes Inspector panel (1 for the title and 2 for the subtitle). Update the **ViewController** class with the code in Listing 5-61. Run the application. The title should be limited to 10 characters and the subtitle to 15.

Basic Text View

A Text View is a scrollable view that can be used to display and insert long texts. If the size of the text surpasses the size of the view, the view allows the user to scroll it. It is defined by the **UITextView** class. We can create a Text Field from code with the **UIView** initializer or add it to a scene from the option in the Library.

UITextView(frame: CGRect**)**—This initializer creates an object of the **UITextView** class with a position and size determined by the **frame** argument.

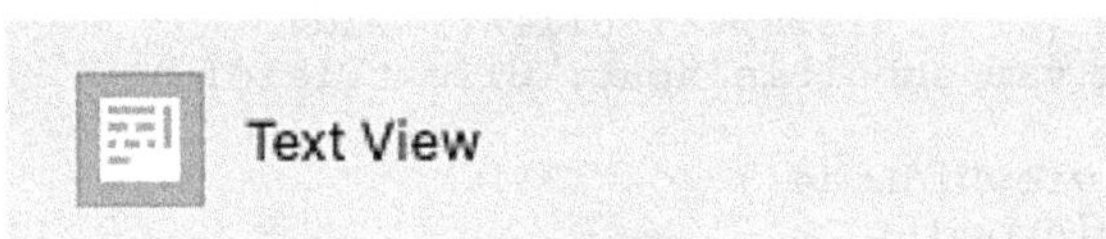

Figure 5-84: *Text View option in the Library*

The following are the most frequently used properties included in the **UITextView** class.

text—This property sets or returns the text in the view. It is an optional of type **String**.

attributedText—This property sets or returns an **NSAttributedString** object with the Text View's attributed text.

font—This property sets or returns the font used by the Text View to display the text. It is an optional of type **UIFont**.

textColor—This property sets or returns the color of the text. It is an optional of type **UIColor**.

textAlignment—This property sets or returns the text's alignment. It is an enumeration of type **NSTextAlignment** with the values **left**, **center**, **right**, **justified**, and **natural**.

isEditable—This property sets or returns a Boolean value that determines whether the user is allowed to edit the text inside the Text View or not.

isSelectable—This property sets or returns a Boolean value that determines whether the user is allowed to select text inside the Text View or not.

selectedRange—This property sets or returns the range of the text selected inside the Text View. It is of type **NSRange**.

scrollRangeToVisible(NSRange**)**—This method scrolls the view to show on the screen the text that corresponds to the range specified by the argument.

The **UITextView** class can also designate a delegate to report the state of the process. The object assigned as the Text View's delegate must conform to the **UITextViewDelegate** protocol, which includes the following methods.

textViewShouldBeginEditing(UITextView**)**—This method is called by the Text View on the delegate object to know if edition should be allowed. The method returns a Boolean value that indicates if edition is allowed or not.

textViewDidBeginEditing(UITextView**)**—This method is called by the Text View on the delegate object when the user begins editing its content.

textViewShouldEndEditing(UITextView**)**—This method is called by the Text View on the delegate object when the user tries to switch focus to another element. The method returns a Boolean value that indicates if edition should stop or not.

textViewDidEndEditing(UITextView**)**—This method is called by the Text View on the delegate object when the element loses focus.

textView(UITextView, **shouldChangeTextIn:** NSRange, **replacementText:** String**)**—This method is called by the Text View on the delegate object every time the user inserts or deletes a character or a string of characters. The **shouldChangeTextIn** argument determines the range of characters on the view affected by the operation, and the **replacementText** argument is the new character or string inserted by the user. The method returns a Boolean value that indicates whether the text should be replaced or not.

textViewDidChange(UITextView**)**—This method is called by the Text View on the delegate object when the user changes the text or any of its attributes.

textViewDidChangeSelection(UITextView**)**—This method is called by the Text View on the delegate object when the user selects text.

As always, we can provide the values for all the properties from the Attributes Inspector panel, including the text to show inside the view. When a Text View is selected, the panel includes an option at the top to indicate the type of text we want to assign to the view: Plain or Attributed. If the Attributed option is selected, additional buttons appear to assign the attributes.

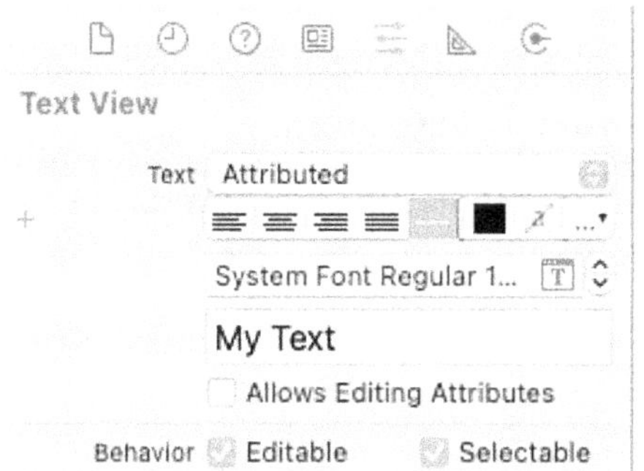

Figure 5-85: *Attributed text for the Text View*

From the Attributes Inspector panel, we can change every aspect of the text or parts of it, but this only sets the Text View's initial value. If we want to modify the view's content or replace it when the app is running, we must do it from code. The **`UITextView`** class offers two properties to access the object's content: **`text`** and **`attributedText`**. With the **`text`** property, we can set plain text with common attributes, and with the **`attributeText`** property we can assign attributed text to the view.

The following example introduces a new interface with a button and a Text View. The purpose of the button is to assign new attributes to the characters selected by the user.

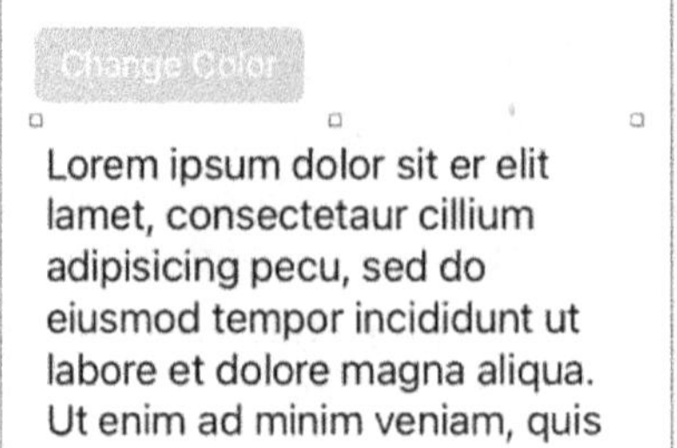
Change Color
Lorem ipsum dolor sit er elit lamet, consectetaur cillium adipisicing pecu, sed do eiusmod tempor incididunt ut labore et dolore magna aliqua. Ut enim ad minim veniam, quis

Figure 5-86: *Interface to test Text Views*

The view controller for this interface is simple, we just need an Outlet to reference the Text View and an Action for the button. Because we want to modify the attributes of the text (change the color of the characters selected by the user) we must convert the **`NSAttributedString`** object returned by the **`attributedText`** property of the **`UITextView`** object into an **`AttributedString`** structure with the structure's initializer defined for this purpose, as explained before (see Listing 5-22).

```
import UIKit

class ViewController: UIViewController {
   @IBOutlet weak var message: UITextView!

   @IBAction func selection(_ sender: UIButton) {
      if let text = message.attributedText {
         if let attrText = try? AttributedString(text, including:
\.uiKit) {
            if let newRange = Range(message.selectedRange, in: attrText)
{
               var newText = attrText
               newText[newRange].foregroundColor = .systemRed
               message.attributedText = NSAttributedString(newText)
            }
         }
      }
   }
}
```

Listing 5-62: *Adding attributes to the attributed text of a Text View*

After we convert the **`NSAttributedString`** object into an **`AttributedString`** structure, we get the range of indexes that determines the characters selected by the user and process the string. The range is provided by the Text View's **`selectedRange`** property, but this is an **`NSRange`** object and we need a **`Range`** structure with **`Index`** values, so we use the **`Range(in:)`** initializer to convert it to the right type (see Ranges in Chapter 4). Once the attributed string and the range are ready, the procedure is the same implemented in previous examples. We add the attribute to the range of characters and then assign the resulting string back to the Text View.

Do It Yourself: Delete the elements in the scene. Add a button called Change Color and a Text View to get an interface like Figure 5-86. Connect the Text View to the view controller with an Outlet called **`message`** and the button with an Action called **`selection()`**. Update the **`ViewController`** class with the code in Listing 5-62. Run the application, double click a word to select it, and press the Change Color button to change its color to red.

Of course, the characters selected by the user are not the only one we can modify. Any range of characters can be changed at any moment. For example, we could search for specific words in the text and change the attributes for only those characters. In the following example, we search for the string "John" and change the color of these characters to blue as the user types in the Text View.

```
import UIKit

class ViewController: UIViewController, UITextViewDelegate {
   @IBOutlet weak var message: UITextView!
   override func viewDidLoad() {
      super.viewDidLoad()
      message.delegate = self
   }
   func textViewDidChange(_ textView: UITextView) {
      if let text = message.attributedText {
         if let attrText = try? AttributedString(text, including:
\.uiKit) {
            let currentPos = message.selectedRange
            var newText = attrText
            let chars = newText.characters

            for pos in chars.indices {
               let distance = chars.distance(from: pos, to:
chars.endIndex)
               let endPos = chars.index(pos, offsetBy: min(distance, 4))
               let word = String(chars[pos..<endPos])
               if word == "John" {
                  newText[pos..<endPos].foregroundColor = .systemBlue
               }
            }
            message.attributedText = NSAttributedString(newText)
            message.selectedRange = currentPos
         }
      }
   }
}
```

Listing 5-63: *Adding attributes to a range of characters*

The code in Listing 5-63 works with the same interface used before, but this time we assign the view controller as the Text View's delegate and implement the **textViewDidChange()** method. This method is called by the **UITextView** object every time the content of the Text View changes. This way, when the user types or erases a character, our code is aware of it and can process the new value.

There are several steps we must take to find the words we want to modify. After turning the **NSAttributedString** object returned by the Text View into an **AttributedString** structure, we store the value of the **selectedRange** property. This is to capture to cursor's current position and set it back in the same position after the new attributed string is assigned to the Text View. Next, we assign the structure to a variable to be able to modify its attributes, get the collection of characters from the **characters** property, and finally iterate through the indexes of this collection to get the index of each character in the string and process it. Each cycle of the loop gets the index of a character in the string. To find a word, we must create a range between this index and the one that indicates the end of the word. In this case, the word we are looking for is "John" and therefore the last index is 4 positions after the initial index. First, we get the distance between the initial position and the end of the string to make sure the indexes are not out of range. Then, we get the index of the last character with the **index(offsetBy:)** method. And finally, we use these values to get the range of characters in that position and compare it to the word "John". If the strings match, we assign the **foregroundColor** attribute to that portion of the string, changing the characters color to blue.

Do It Yourself: Update the **`ViewController`** class with the code in Listing 5-63 and run the application. Tap on the text to activate the cursor and write the text "John". You should see the color of the word change to blue.

Medium Keyboard

iOS has a particular way to control the keyboard. It does not consider the keyboard as a tool, but rather a way to detect events produced by the user, and therefore it keeps it on screen for as long as the element that made it appear is still capable of processing the input. To dismiss the keyboard, we must tell the system that the element is no longer able to process the events, and this is done by altering the chain of response.

When an event occurs, such as a tap on the screen, the system determines which element is going to process it. The position of the elements on the screen does not always reflects this responsibility. To figure out which element is responsible to process an event, the system considers the elements hierarchy and creates a virtual chain in which some elements in certain positions, called *Responders*, receive the event, and then decide whether to process it or deliver it to the next element in the chain. Some events, like key events from the keyboard, are sent to specific elements called *First Responders*.

First Responders are designated by the system or our code. This is what the system does when the user taps on a Text Field or a Text View; it declares the element as the First Responder, so all the events are first sent to it. And this is also how the system manages the keyboard. The keyboard opens when an element that is capable of handling key events becomes the First Responder, and it is closed when the element ceases to be the First Responder (it resigns as First Responder).

The UIKit framework defines the **`UIResponder`** class to manage Responders and respond to events. The following are its most frequently used properties and methods.

isFirstResponder—This property returns a Boolean value that indicates whether the element is the current designated First Responder or not.

becomeFirstResponder()—This method designates the element as the First Responder.

resignFirstResponder()—This method notifies the element that it has to resign its condition of First Responder.

touchesBegan([UITouch], **with:** UIEvent?**)**—This method is called by the system in responder objects (views and view controllers) when the user starts touching the screen.

touchesMoved([UITouch], **with:** UIEvent?**)**—This method is called by the system in responder objects (views and view controllers) when the finger touching the screen moves.

touchesEnded([UITouch], **with:** UIEvent?**)**—This method is called by the system in responder objects (views and view controllers) when the user stops touching the screen.

touchesCancelled([UITouch], **with:** UIEvent?**)**—This method is called by the system in responder objects (views and view controllers) when a touch event is cancelled by the system.

The **`UIResponder`** class is a basic class that most of the UIKit classes inherit from. Because of this, all the elements created from UIKit classes have access to its properties and methods and are capable of handling events. If we want to open the keyboard, we can call the **`becomeFirstResponder()`** method on an element capable of handling key events (which produces the same effect as the user tapping on the element). Closing the keyboard is as simple as calling the **`resignFirstResponder()`** on the element currently assigned as First Responder.

The following example shows how to implement these two methods. This view controller assumes that we have an interface with a Text Field, a label, and a button, as the one presented in Figure 5-82.

```
import UIKit

class ViewController: UIViewController {
   @IBOutlet weak var titleLabel: UILabel!
   @IBOutlet weak var titleInput: UITextField!

   @IBAction func changeTitle(_ sender: UIButton) {
      if titleInput.text != "" {
         titleLabel.text = titleInput.text
         titleInput.text = ""
         titleInput.resignFirstResponder()
      } else {
         titleInput.becomeFirstResponder()
      }
   }
}
```

Listing 5-64: *Opening and closing the keyboard from code*

The view controller in Listing 5-64 includes Outlets for the label and the Text Field, and an Action for the button. When the user taps the Save button, the **changeTitle()** method checks the content of the Text Field as before. If something was inserted into the field, the method assigns that value to the label and then executes the **resignFirstResponder()** method to force the Text Field to resign its condition as First Responder. When the system detects that there is no First Responder that can process key events, it closes the keyboard. On the other hand, if the **changeTitle()** method cannot find any text inside the Text Field, it executes the **becomeFirstResponder()** method, turning the Text Field into the First Responder and compelling the system to open the keyboard.

Do It Yourself: Create an interface like the one presented in Figure 5-82. Connect the label, the Text Field and the button with the corresponding Outlets and Action. Update the **ViewController** class with the code in Listing 5-64. Run the application and click the Save button. The keyboard will pop up and the Text Field will show the cursor. Write something in the Text Field and press the Save button again. The keyboard should be dismissed.

IMPORTANT: The simulator includes the same keyboard of a real device, but it can also work with the computer's keyboard. To select one keyboard or another, open the I/O menu at the top of the screen, go to Keyboard and select the option of your preference.

The **becomeFirstResponder()** method is not always necessary. Usually, the user taps on the element when it needs to type something on it and this action automatically makes the element the First Responder, compelling the system to open the keyboard. But the execution of the **resignFirstResponder()** method is required every time we want to dismiss the keyboard because there is no automatic action to do it. In our previous example, we called this method when the Save button was pressed, but a more intuitive interface will also close the keyboard when the user taps somewhere else on the screen. These types of events are detected by the event-handling methods included in the **UIResponder** class, as shown next.

```
import UIKit

class ViewController: UIViewController {
   @IBOutlet weak var titleLabel: UILabel!
   @IBOutlet weak var titleInput: UITextField!

   @IBAction func changeTitle(_ sender: UIButton) {
      if titleInput.text != "" {
         titleLabel.text = titleInput.text
         titleInput.text = ""
      }
   }
   override func touchesBegan(_ touches: Set<UITouch>, with event:
UIEvent?) {
      super.touchesBegan(touches, with: event)
      titleInput.resignFirstResponder()
   }
}
```

Listing 5-65: *Dismissing the keyboard when the user touches the screen*

The **touchesBegan()** method implemented in Listing 5-65 is called on the view controller when the user touches the screen. We override this method in our view controller to perform custom tasks. In this case, we use it to call the **resignFirstResponder()** method on the Text Field to dismiss the keyboard. As a result, the keyboard is opened when the user taps on the Text Field and closed when the user taps somewhere else (except on the Save button, because the button provides its own response to the event).

Calling the **resignFirstResponder()** method on an element only removes the status of First Responder for that element. If we have several elements that can become First Responders, such as the multiple Text Fields we had in the example of Figure 5-83, we must call the method on each one of them. To simplify our work, the **UIView** class includes a special method that looks at the view and its subviews to find the current First Responder and ask the element to resign.

endEditing(Bool**)**—This method looks for the First Responder in a view and its subviews and asks it to resign its condition. The argument indicates whether the element should be forced to resign or not.

The following example implements the same view controller of Listing 5-65 but instead of calling the **resignFirstResponder()** method on each Text Field it calls the **endEditing()** method on the main view (the **view** property). This method finds the current First Responder inside the view and forces it to resign its condition. It is the same process, but now we do not have to call the **resignFirstResponder()** method for every Text Field in the view.

```
import UIKit

class ViewController: UIViewController {
   @IBOutlet weak var titleLabel: UILabel!
   @IBOutlet weak var titleInput: UITextField!

   @IBAction func changeTitle(_ sender: UIButton) {
      if titleInput.text != "" {
         titleLabel.text = titleInput.text
         titleInput.text = ""
      }
   }
```

```
    override func touchesBegan(_ touches: Set<UITouch>, with event:
UIEvent?) {
        super.touchesBegan(touches, with: event)
        view.endEditing(true)
    }
}
```

Listing 5-66: Finding the First Responder

Basic Picker View

A Picker View is a view that allows the user to select a value from a list. The values are organized in rows and components (columns). Each component represents a list of values, and each row represents an individual value. The components scroll independently.

Pickers are defined by the **UIPickerView** class. We can create a Picker View from code with the **UIView** initializer or add it to a scene from the option in the Library.

UIPickerView(frame: CGRect**)**—This initializer creates an object of the **UIPickerView** class with a position and size determined by the **frame** argument.

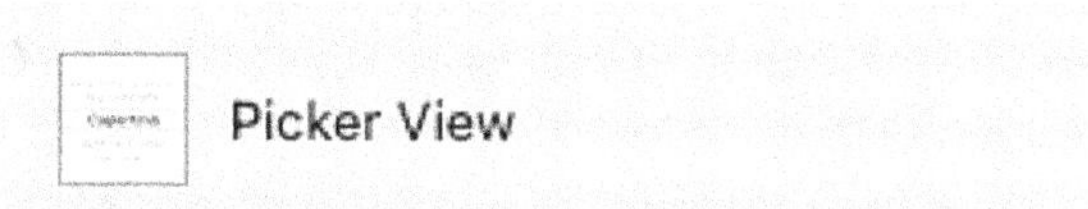

Figure 5-87: *Picker View option in the Library*

To identify each row and component, the picker creates indexes starting from 0. The first value of a row will be at index 0, the second at index 1, and so on. The items in a picker are organized this way so we can associate it with arrays in our code and easily present and retrieve values. The class defines the following properties and methods to interact with the picker.

numberOfComponents—This property returns a value of type **Int** that represents the number of components in the picker.

numberOfRows(inComponent: Int**)**—This method returns a value of type **Int** that represents the number of rows in a component. The argument indicates the index of the component we want to access.

selectedRow(inComponent: Int**)**—This method returns a value of type **Int** that represents the index of the selected row in the component specified by the **inComponent** argument.

reloadAllComponents()—This method forces the picker to update the values of its components.

reloadComponent(Int**)**—This method forces the picker to update the values of a component. The argument indicates the index of the component we want to update.

selectRow(Int, **inComponent:** Int, **animated:** Bool**)**—This method selects the row with the index specified by the first argument in the component specified by the **inComponent** argument. The **animated** argument determines whether the selection should be animated or not. The method rotates the wheel until the selected row is positioned at the center.

The **UIPickerView** class also defines two properties, **delegate** and **dataSource**, to assign delegate objects that will configure the picker and provide the values for the rows. The object assigned to the **delegate** property must conform to the **UIPickerViewDelegate** protocol, which includes the following methods.

pickerView(UIPickerView, **titleForRow:** Int, **forComponent:** Int**)**—This method is called by the **UIPickerView** object on the delegate when it needs a value for the row indicated by the **titleForRow** argument in the component indicated by the **forComponent** argument. The method must return a string with the value for the row.

pickerView(UIPickerView, **attributedTitleForRow:** Int, **forComponent:** Int**)**—This method is called by the **UIPickerView** object on the delegate when it needs a value for the row indicated by the **attributedTitleForRow** argument in the component indicated by the **forComponent** argument. The method must return an **NSAttributedString** object.

pickerView(UIPickerView, **didSelectRow:** Int, **inComponent:** Int**)**—This method is called by the **UIPickerView** object on the delegate when the user selects a row (moves the wheel to get a new value at the center). The **didSelectRow** and **inComponent** arguments contain the indexes of the selected row and component.

On the other hand, the object assigned to the **dataSource** property must conform to the **UIPickerViewDataSource** protocol, which includes the following methods.

numberOfComponents(in: UIPickerView**)**—This method is called by the **UIPickerView** object on the data source delegate to know the number of components to display. The method must return an **Int** value with the number of components we want.

pickerView(UIPickerView, **numberOfRowsInComponent:** Int**)**—This method is called by the **UIPickerView** object on the data source delegate to know how many rows to display in a component. The **numberOfRowsInComponent** argument specifies the index of the component (the method is called for every component in the picker).

Picker Views are usually combined with other controllers to process the values selected by the user. The interface in Figure 5-88, below, includes a picker that we are going to use to show a list of years and a label that is going to display the year selected by the user.

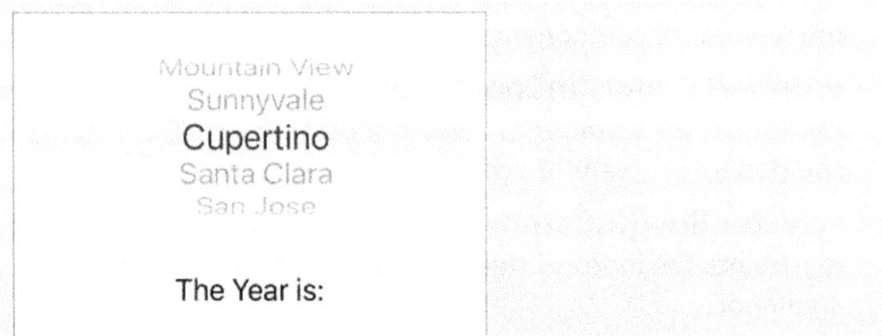

Figure 5-88: *Interface to test a Picker View*

When the picker is added to a scene from the Library, Xcode shows it with some values by default, as illustrated in Figure 5-88, but the real values are provided by the delegate object assigned to the **dataSource** property. This is a normal delegate, but because its purpose is to provide data it is usually called *data source* (hence the name of the property). As always, the delegates could be any objects we want, but it is common practice to declare the view controller in charge of the picker to be the delegate as well as the data source, as in the following example.

```
import UIKit

class ViewController: UIViewController, UIPickerViewDelegate,
UIPickerViewDataSource {
   @IBOutlet weak var showYear: UILabel!
   @IBOutlet weak var pickerYears: UIPickerView!
   var years: [String]!
```

```
    override func viewDidLoad() {
        super.viewDidLoad()
        pickerYears.delegate = self
        pickerYears.dataSource = self
        years = ["1944", "1945", "1946", "1947", "1948", "1949", "1950"]
    }
    func numberOfComponents(in pickerView: UIPickerView) -> Int {
        return 1
    }
    func pickerView(_ pickerView: UIPickerView, numberOfRowsInComponent
component: Int) -> Int {
        return years.count
    }
    func pickerView(_ pickerView: UIPickerView, titleForRow row: Int,
forComponent component: Int) -> String? {
        return years[row]
    }
    func pickerView(_ pickerView: UIPickerView, didSelectRow row: Int,
inComponent component: Int) {
        let year = years[row]
        showYear.text = "The Year is: \(year)"
    }
}
```

Listing 5-67: *Providing values for the picker*

This view controller defines Outlets for the label and the Picker View, and an array called **years** to store the values we want to assign to the picker. In the **viewDidLoad()** method, we use the Outlet to declare the view controller as the picker's delegate and data source, and also initialize the **years** array with a list of values.

After the properties are initialized, we must configure the picker and load the data from the delegate and data source methods. We first implement the **numberOfComponents()** method to tell the picker that we want one component to show the list of years (one column). The next method, **pickerView(numberOfRowsInComponent:)**, performs a similar function, but this time for the rows. Inside this method, we count how many values are in the **years** array and return that number to indicate how many rows we need to show them all. Next is the **pickerView(titleForRow:, forComponent:)** method, called by the picker to get the value for each row. The first call will be for the row at index 0, then for the row at index 1, and so on. Using these indexes, we get the corresponding value from the **years** array and return it. Notice that this method returns a **String** value. If we have an array of integers, as in this case, before returning each value we must convert it to a **String** using string interpolation or the **String()** initializer (e.g., **String(number)**).

The last method, **pickerView(didSelectRow:, inComponent:)**, is called by the picker when the user rotates the wheel and selects a new value. The index of the selected row is reported by the method through its **didSelectRow** argument. Using this index, we can retrieve the value from the array and assign it to the label.

Do It Yourself: Delete the elements in the scene. Add a Picker View and a label to the scene, as shown in Figure 5-88. Connect the label and the picker to the view controller with Outlets called **showYear** and **pickerYears,** respectively. Update the **ViewController** class with the code in Listing 5-67 and run the application. Every time you rotate the wheel, the selected year should be shown on the label.

The **pickerView(didSelectRow:, inComponent:)** method allows us to get the value as soon as it is selected, but we can also read the selected value any time we want with the **selectedRow()** method. To test it, we can add a button to the interface and an Action to the view controller to change the value of the label every time the button is pressed.

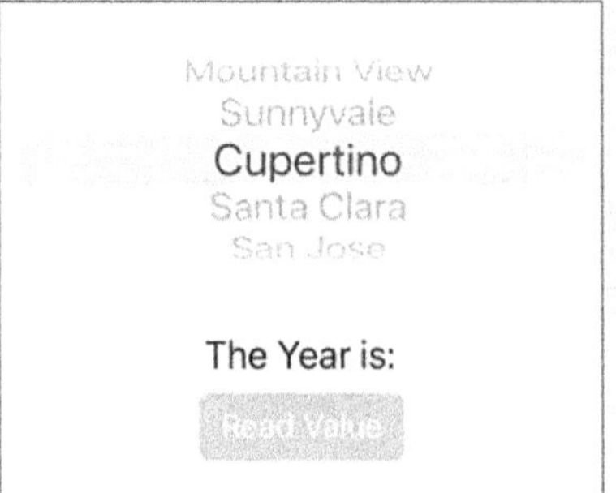

Figure 5-89: *Interface to get the value currently selected*

In this example, the method for the action replaces the **pickerView(didSelectRow:, inComponent:)** method, but they could work together if necessary.

```
import UIKit

class ViewController: UIViewController, UIPickerViewDelegate,
UIPickerViewDataSource {
   @IBOutlet weak var showYear: UILabel!
   @IBOutlet weak var pickerYears: UIPickerView!
   var years: [String]!

   override func viewDidLoad() {
      super.viewDidLoad()
      pickerYears.delegate = self
      pickerYears.dataSource = self
      years = ["1944", "1945", "1946", "1947", "1948", "1949", "1950"]
   }
   func numberOfComponents(in pickerView: UIPickerView) -> Int {
      return 1
   }
   func pickerView(_ pickerView: UIPickerView, numberOfRowsInComponent
component: Int) -> Int {
      return years.count
   }
   func pickerView(_ pickerView: UIPickerView, titleForRow row: Int,
forComponent component: Int) -> String? {
      return years[row]
   }
   @IBAction func getYear(_ sender: UIButton) {
      let row = pickerYears.selectedRow(inComponent: 0)
      showYear.text = "The Year is: \(years[row])"
   }
}
```

Listing 5-68: *Reading the selected value*

In the **getYear()** method of Listing 5-68, we call the **selectedRow()** method to get the index of the selected row for the component at index 0 (we only have one component in our picker) and then use the value of the **row** constant to retrieve the year from the array and assign it to the label.

Besides the user rotating the wheel, there is also a method that allows us to select a value from code. This is particularly useful when we want the picker to suggest a value to the user. The following example initializes the picker with the year 1945.

```
override func viewDidLoad() {
   super.viewDidLoad()
   pickerYears.delegate = self
   pickerYears.dataSource = self
   years = ["1944", "1945", "1946", "1947", "1948", "1949", "1950"]

   if let index = years.firstIndex(of: "1945") {
      pickerYears.selectRow(index, inComponent: 0, animated: false)
   }
}
```

Listing 5-69: *Selecting the initial value*

Because we want to initialize the picker with this value, we call the method from the **viewDidLoad()** method. First, we search for the value "1945" in the array with the **firstIndex(of:)** method, and then we select the row using the index returned by this method. The value of the **animated** argument was set to **false** because we want the picker to show the right value as soon as it is displayed, but we can take advantage of this argument to create a smooth transition when the selection is done after the picker was already shown to the user.

Do It Yourself: Replace the **viewDidLoad()** method in the previous example by the one in Listing 5-69 and run the app. The selected value in the picker should be "1945".

With a few modifications, we can easily create a picker with more than one component. The following example includes two components to let the user select a year and a city.

```
import UIKit

class ViewController: UIViewController, UIPickerViewDelegate,
UIPickerViewDataSource {
   @IBOutlet weak var showYear: UILabel!
   @IBOutlet weak var pickerYears: UIPickerView!
   var cities: [String]!
   var years: [String]!

   override func viewDidLoad() {
      super.viewDidLoad()
      pickerYears.delegate = self
      pickerYears.dataSource = self
      cities = ["Mountain View", "Sunnyvale", "Cupertino", "Santa Clara"]
      years = ["1944", "1945", "1946", "1947", "1948", "1949", "1950"]
   }
   func numberOfComponents(in pickerView: UIPickerView) -> Int {
      return 2
   }
   func pickerView(_ pickerView: UIPickerView, numberOfRowsInComponent
component: Int) -> Int {
      if component == 0 {
         return cities.count
      } else {
         return years.count
      }
   }
   func pickerView(_ pickerView: UIPickerView, titleForRow row: Int,
forComponent component: Int) -> String? {
      if component == 0 {
         return cities[row]
      } else {
         return years[row]
```

```
      }
   }
   @IBAction func getYear(_ sender: UIButton) {
      let rowCity = pickerYears.selectedRow(inComponent: 0)
      let rowYear = pickerYears.selectedRow(inComponent: 1)
      showYear.text = "The Year is: \(years[rowYear]) in \
(cities[rowCity])"
   }
}
```

Listing 5-70: *Creating a picker with multiple components*

This view controller provides values for two components. The **years** array for the years and the **cities** array for the cities. To tell the picker that we want two components, the value 2 was returned from the **numberOfComponents()** method. From this point on, we must consider the component every time we interact with the picker. If the index of the component is 0, we are working with the **cities** array, and when the index is 1, we are working with the **years** array. The **getYear()** method was also expanded to read the selected value from each component and assign them to the label. The result is shown below.

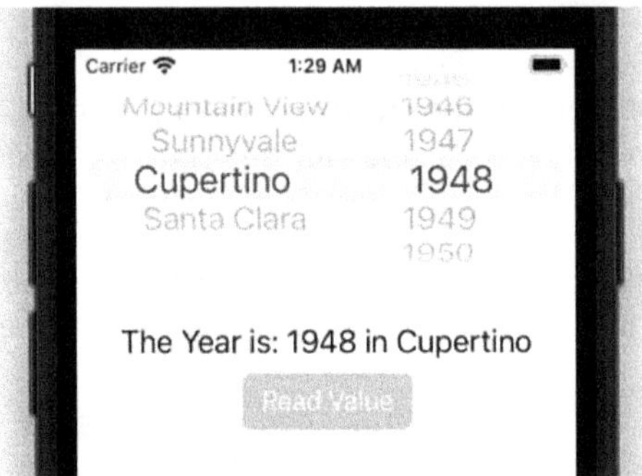

Figure 5-90: *Picker with two components*

Basic Date Picker

The Date Picker was designed to simplify the creation of pickers for dates and times. It is defined by the **UIDatePicker** class (a subclass of **UIPickerView**). With this class, we can create objects that show dates, dates and times, and a countdown timer. This picker can be created from code, using the **UIView** initializer or by dragging the option from the Library.

UIDatePicker(frame: CGRect)—This initializer creates an object of the **UIDatePicker** class with a position and size determined by the **frame** argument.

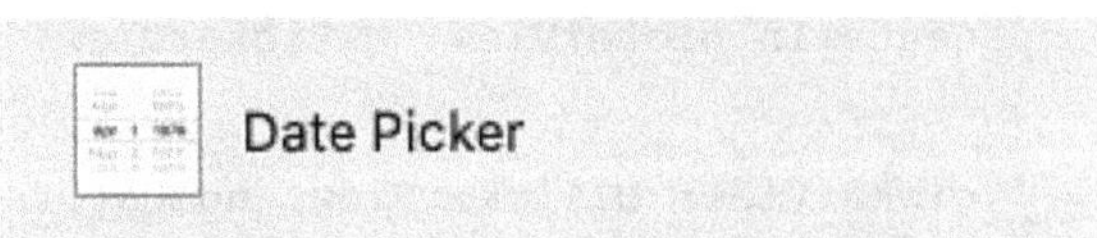

Figure 5-91: *Date Picker option in the Library*

The class provides the following properties to configure the picker.

datePickerMode—This property sets or returns the picker's mode. It is an enumeration called **Mode** with the values **time**, **date**, **dateAndTime**, and **countDownTimer**.

preferredDatePickerStyle—This property sets or returns the style of the picker. It is an enumeration called **UIDatePickerStyle** with the values **automatic** (selected according to the platform), **compact** (label that expands into a calendar), **inline** (editable field or calendar, depending on the platform), and **wheels** (standard wheel picker).

maximumDate—This property sets or returns the maximum date the picker can show. It is a conditional of type **`Date`**.

minimumDate—This property sets or returns the minimum date the picker can show. It is a conditional of type **`Date`**.

date—This property sets or returns the selected date. It is of type **`Date`**.

minuteInterval—This property sets or returns an integer value that determines the interval at which the minutes should be shown (1 by default).

countDownDuration—This property sets or returns a value of type **`TimeInterval`** that indicates the seconds from which the timer starts counting down.

setDate(Date, **animated:** Bool**)**—This method selects a new date. The first argument is a **`Date`** value that specifies the date we want to select, and the **animated** argument is a Boolean value that determines whether we want the selection to be animated or not.

The class also includes three properties to determine the type of data to show. If the properties are not defined, they take the default values set on the device.

calendar—This property sets or returns the calendar to use by the picker. It is an optional of type **`Calendar`**.

locale—This property sets or returns the locale (regional information) to use by the picker. It is an optional of type **`Locale`**.

timeZone—This property sets or returns the time zone of the date shown by the picker. It is an optional of type **`TimeZone`**.

There are three types of Date Pickers: Compact, Wheels, and Inline, as shown below.

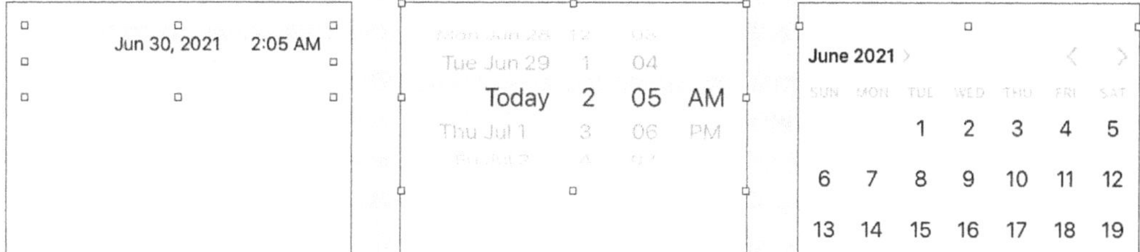

Figure 5-92: *Date Picker styles*

By default, the Style is set to Automatic, which means that the system is going to select the appropriate style according to the space available on the interface. If we want the keep a consistent style, we can set a specific value from code or from the Attributes Inspector panel. For instance, in the following example we have selected the Wheel style, to show the picker as a wheel, the Date mode to show only dates, and set a minimum and a maximum date.

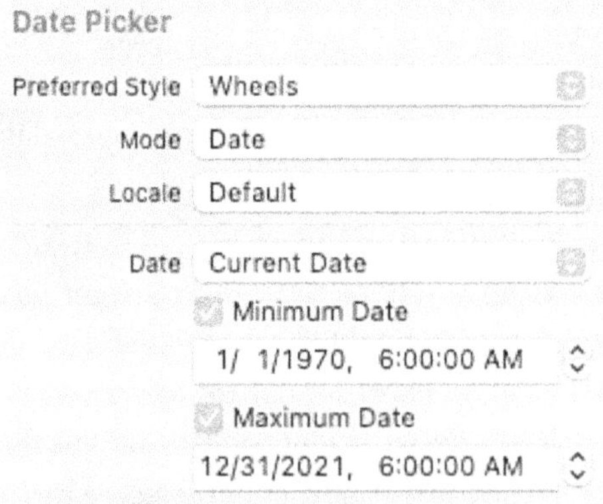

Figure 5-93: *Date Picker properties*

A Date Picker does not work with delegates, we interact with the picker directly through its properties and methods. To illustrate how this works, we are going to create an interface like the one used for Picker Views, as shown below.

Figure 5-94: *Interface to test Date Pickers*

The view controller for this interface only needs to include two Outlets for the picker and the label, and an Action for the button.

```
import UIKit

class ViewController: UIViewController {
   @IBOutlet weak var picker: UIDatePicker!
   @IBOutlet weak var showDate: UILabel!

   @IBAction func getDate(_ sender: UIButton) {
      let selectedDate = picker.date
      let format = selectedDate.formatted(date: .abbreviated,
time: .omitted)
      showDate.text = "Date: \(format)"
   }
}
```

Listing 5-71: *Displaying the selected date*

Getting the date selected on the picker is as simple as reading the **date** property. This property is of type **Date**, which means we can format the date and show it to the user (see Dates in Chapter 4). In this example, we call the **formatted()** method with the **abbreviated** and **omitted** values to generate a string with a date and no time.

Of course, we also declare an initial value for Date Pickers. The value may be assigned directly to the **date** property or by calling the **setDate()** method. The only difference is that with the method we have the chance to animate the selection. The **viewDidLoad()** method below initializes the picker with the date 08-13-2010.

```
override func viewDidLoad() {
   super.viewDidLoad()
   let calendar = Calendar.current
   var components = DateComponents()
   components.year = 2010
   components.month = 8
   components.day = 13

   if let newDate = calendar.date(from: components) {
      picker.date = newDate
   }
}
```

***Listing 5-72:** Setting the initial date*

The code in Listing 5-72 implements a **DateComponents** structure and the **date()** method of the **Calendar** structure to create a date. Because the **date()** method returns an optional, we unwrap it before assigning it to the **date** property. Once we add the **viewDidLoad()** method to the previous example, the initial values of the picker will be August 13, 2010.

Do It Yourself: Delete the elements in the scene. Add a Date Picker, a label, and a button to the scene (Figure 5-94). Select the Date Picker and change the Style to Wheel and the mode to Date from the Attributes Inspector panel. Connect the label and the picker to Outlets called **showDate** and **picker**, respectively. Connect the button to an Action called **getDate()**. Update the **ViewController** class with the code in Listing 5-71. You can also add the **viewDidLoad()** method of Listing 5-72 to define an initial value. Run the application, select a date, and press the button to assign it to the label. Stop the app. Select the picker on the scene and try different styles from the Attributes Inspector panel to see how they look and work.

Basic 5.7 Images

The screens of Apple devices have different resolutions and scales. In some devices, one point represents one pixel and in others more. At this moment, three scales have been defined: 1x, 2x, and 3x. The 1x scale defines one point as one pixel, the 2x scale defines 1 point as a square of 2 pixels, and the 3x scale defines one point as a square of three pixels. For this reason, every time we want to show images in our interface, we must consider the conversion between pixels and points. For example, if we have an image of 300 pixels wide and 400 pixels tall, in a device with a scale of 1x the image will almost fill the screen, but in a device with a scale of 2x the image will look half its size. The image is occupying the same space, 300 by 400 pixels, but because of the higher resolution these pixels represents a smaller area on the screen in devices with scales of 2x or 3x, as shown below.

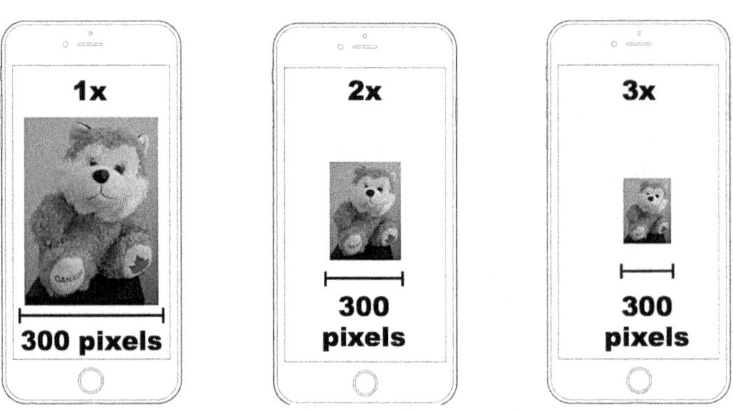

Figure 5-95: *Same image in devices with different scale*

One solution to this problem is to scale up a small image in devices with higher resolution or scale down a big image in devices with lower resolution. For example, we can expand an image of 300 x 400 pixels to 600 x 800 pixels and make it look like the same size in a screen with a scale of 2x (a space of 300 x 400 points represents 600 x 800 pixels at this scale), or we could start with an image of 600 x 800 pixels and reduce it to 300 x 400 pixels for devices with half the scale. One way or another, we have a problem. If we expand a small image to fill the screen, it loses quality, and if we reduce it, it occupies unnecessary space in memory because the image is never shown in its original resolution. Fortunately, there is a more efficient solution. It requires us to include in our project three versions of the same image, one for every scale. Considering the image of our example, we will need one picture of the husky in a size of 300 x 400 pixels for devices with a scale of 1x, another of 600 x 800 pixels for devices with a scale of 2x, and a third one of 900 x 1200 for devices with a scale of 3x. Now, the images can be shown in the same size and with the same quality no matter the device or the scale.

Figure 5-96: *Different images for specific scales*

Providing the same image in different resolutions solves the problem but introduces some complications. We must create three versions of the same image and then select which one is going to be shown depending on the scale of the device. To help us select the right image, Apple systems detect the scale that corresponds to the image by reading a suffix on the file's name. What we need to do is to provide three files with the same name but with suffixes that determine the scale for which they were designed. The file containing the image for the 1x scale (300 x 400 pixels in our example) only requires the name and the extension (e.g., **husky.png**), the name of the file with the image for the 2x scale (600 x 800) must include the suffix @2x (e.g., **husky@2x.png**), and the name of the file with the image for the 3x scale (900 x 1200) must include the suffix @3x (e.g., **husky@3x.png**). Every time the interface requires an image, the system reads the suffixes and loads the one corresponding to the scale of the screen.

IMPORTANT: There is a useful app in the App Store for Mac computers called *Prepo* that can take an image of a scale of 3x and reduce it to create the versions for the rest of the scales. It can also help you generate the icons for your app.

There are two ways to incorporate images into our project. One is to drag the files to the Navigator Area and the second alternative is to use a tool called *Assets Catalog*. The first option is simple. We must create the images for the resolutions we want to provide and then drag them from Finder to the Navigator Area, as shown in Figure 5-97.

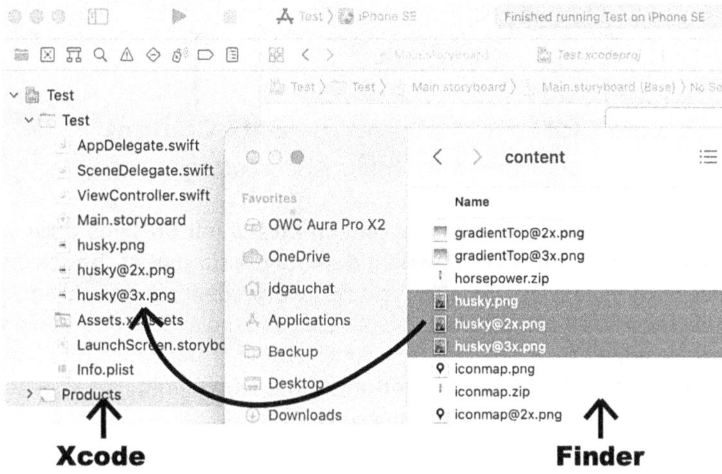

Figure 5-97: *Dragging files from Finder to our Xcode's project*

When we drop the files into our Xcode project, a window asks for information about the destination and the target. If we want the files to be copied to the project's folder (recommended), we must activate the option *Copy items if needed*, as shown in Figure 5-98 below. We also must indicate that the files are going to be added to the target created for our project selecting the target in the *Add to targets* option (the project used in this example was called *Test*).

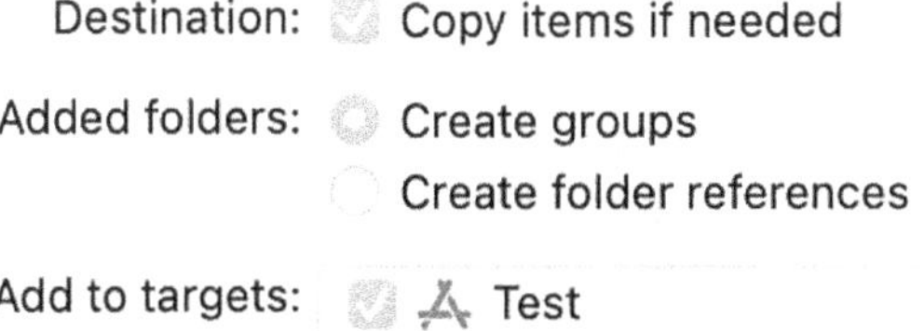

Figure 5-98: *Options to add files to the project*

After these options are selected and the Finish button is pressed, Xcode includes the files with the rest of the files in our project.

Basic Assets Catalog

Although we could include all the images for our application by adding the files to the project, as we did in Figure 5-97, this is not practical. Sometimes dozens, if not hundreds, of images are necessary to create an app. No matter how we name or classify these files, it will still be very difficult to keep them organized. For this purpose, the UIKit framework defines a class called **`UIImageAsset`** that creates a container called *Assets Catalog* to organize the project's resources, including images, icons, colors, and more. Templates include an Assets Catalog for our app and Xcode offers a simple interface to edit its content. To open the interface, we must click on the file in the Navigator Area called Assets.xcassets. Figure 5-99 shows what we see in the Editor Area.

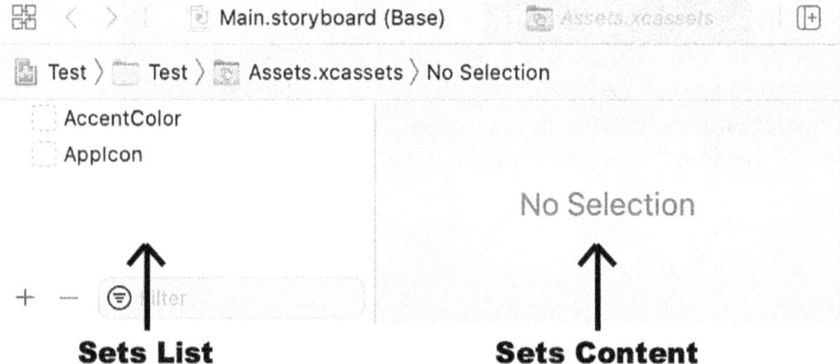

Figure 5-99: *Empty Assets Catalog*

The interface includes two columns: the column on the left presents a list with the sets of resources available and the column on the right displays the content of the selected set (e.g., the three images for each scale). The list also includes two predefined sets called AccentColor and AppIcon to define the default tint color for the controls and the app's icons, as we will see later.

New sets can be added from the Add New Asset option in the Editor menu at the top of the screen or by pressing the + button at the bottom of the left column. For instance, Figure 5-100 shows what we see when we create a new Image set.

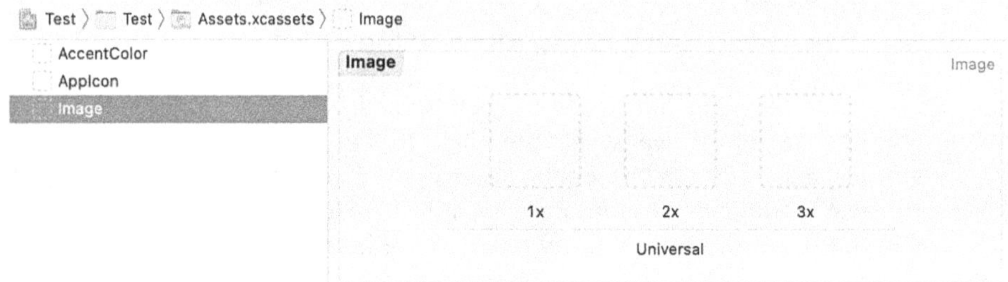

Figure 5-100: *New set of images*

The name of the set is the name we must use to get the image from code. Xcode calls the new set *Image* but we can click on it and press Enter to change it any time we want. By default, a set for an image includes the three versions of the image, one for each scale. Once the set is created, we can drag the files to the corresponding squares. For example, the file husky.png from our previous example goes inside the 1x square, the file husky@2x.png goes inside the 2x square, and the file husky@3x.png goes inside the 3x square. Figure 5-101, below, shows the Editor Area after the images are dragged from Finder to the Assets Catalog and the name of the set is changed to "husky".

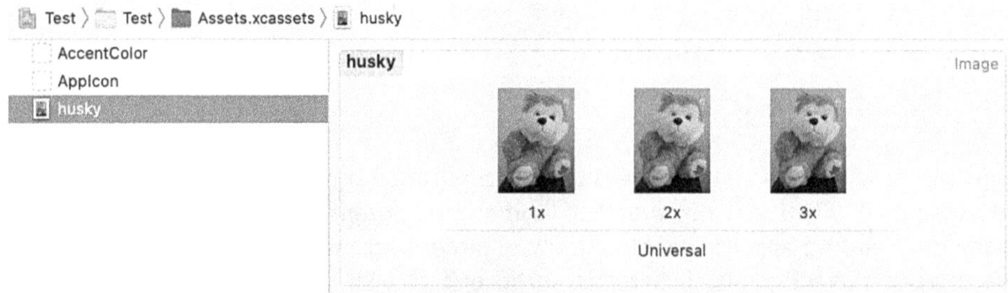

Figure 5-101: *Husky set is ready*

Once the images are loaded to the catalog, the set is ready to use. We do not need to copy the files to the project's folder anymore or anything like it. All we need to do is to load the image from our app using the name defined for the set ("husky" in our example). But this process is still a little bit tedious. An easy way to create a new set is to drag the three images for the set to the Assets Catalog and let Xcode define everything for us. For instance, we can drag and drop the files door.png, door@2x.png, and door@3x.png and Xcode takes care of creating the set, assigning each image to the corresponding scale, and give it the name "door".

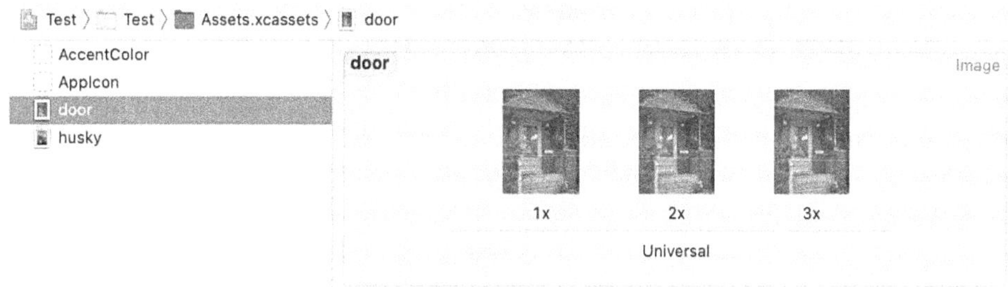

Figure 5-102: *New door set*

Besides the possibility of including a version of the image for every scale, we can also add versions for different devices and parameters. When a set is selected, the Attributes Inspector panel on the right shows a list of properties, including Devices, Appearances, and more. By default, the set is shown in any device (Universal) and for any type of interface, but we can change it by modifying the values of these attributes. For example, if we select the iPad option from the list of devices (Figure 5-103, number 1), new placeholders are added to the interface (Figure 5-103, number 2).

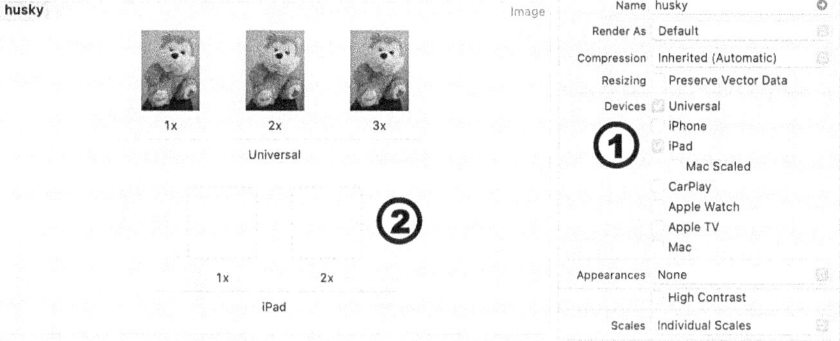

Figure 5-103: *Set for specific devices*

After the images are added to the set, the system selects the appropriate version according to the scale, the device, and the characteristics of the interface.

Basic Image

Because the purpose of images is not only to be presented on the screen but also to be used in the construction of patterns and customized controls, the UIKit framework provides a class called **UIImage** to load images. The **UIImage** class can load one image at a time but includes multiple initializers to load the image from a variety of sources. The following are the most frequently used.

UIImage(named: String)—This initializer creates an object that contains the image from the file specified by the **named** argument. The argument is a string with the name of the file, or the image set in the Assets Catalog.

UIImage(data: Data, **scale:** CGFloat**)**—This initializer creates an object that contains an image generated from the data provided by the **data** argument and with an associated scale specified by the **scale** argument. If the scale is 1, the last argument can be ignored.

UIImage(cgImage: CGImage, **scale:** CGFloat, **orientation:** Orientation**)**—This initializer creates an object that contains an image generated from a **CGImage** object and with a scale and orientation defined by the arguments. The **CGImage** class is defined by the Core Graphics framework to store a low-level representation of an image, and the **orientation** argument is an enumeration with the values **up**, **down**, **left**, **right**, **upMirrored**, **downMirrored**, **leftMirrored**, and **rightMirrored**.

The **UIImage** class includes a few type properties to return objects with standard images. The properties available are **add**, **remove**, **actions**, **checkmark**, and **strokedCheckmark**. There are also properties and methods to get information about the image and process it. The following are the most frequently used.

size—This property returns a **CGSize** value with the size of the image.

scale—This property returns a **CGFloat** value with the scale of the image.

imageOrientation—This property returns a value that identifies the orientation of the image. It is an enumeration called **Orientation** included in the **UIImage** class. The values available are **up**, **down**, **left**, **right**, **upMirrored**, **downMirrored**, **leftMirrored**, and **rightMirrored**.

cgImage—This property returns the image in the Core Graphic format. It is of type **CGImage**, a Core Graphic data type.

pngData()—This method converts the image into raw data in the PNG format and returns a **Data** structure with it.

jpegData(compressionQuality: CGFloat**)**—This method converts the image into raw data in the JPEG format and returns a **Data** structure with it. The **compressionQuality** argument is a value between 0.0 and 1.0 that determines the level of compression.

Working with images from code is very simple. We must create the **UIImage** object with the source we want and then apply it to the elements on the interface or show it on the screen. Many elements include properties that take a **UIImage** object. For instance, the **UIColor** class can take a **UIImage** object to create a pattern that later can be applied to the background of a view. In the following example, we load an image called oranges.png and apply it to the background of the scene's main view. The example assumes that we have created a set in the Assets Catalog called *oranges* with the files oranges.png, oranges@2x.png, and oranges@3x.png (the files are available on our website).

```
import UIKit

class ViewController: UIViewController {
   override func viewDidLoad() {
      super.viewDidLoad()
      if let mypattern = UIImage(named: "oranges") {
         view.backgroundColor = UIColor(patternImage: mypattern)
      }
   }
}
```

Listing 5-73: *Adding a background pattern to the main view*

The **UIImage()** initializer implemented in Listing 5-73 looks for an image in the Assets Catalog with the name "oranges" and returns a **UIImage** object if the image is found and successfully loaded, or the value **nil** otherwise. In this example, we use the image to create a background pattern with a **UIColor** object. When a **UIColor** object is initialized with an image, the object takes that image and fills the area with it, as shown below.

Figure 5-104: *Main view with a background pattern*

Do It Yourself: Create a new project. Download the three oranges.png files from our website or provide your own. Drag the files to the Assets Catalog to create a set called *oranges*. Update the **ViewController** class with the code in Listing 5-73. Run the application. You should see something like Figure 5-104.

Some elements, such as buttons, use **UIImage** objects to customize their appearance. Once the images are added to the project, we can assign them to the element from the Attributes Inspector panel. The following example shows how to create a custom button using an image.

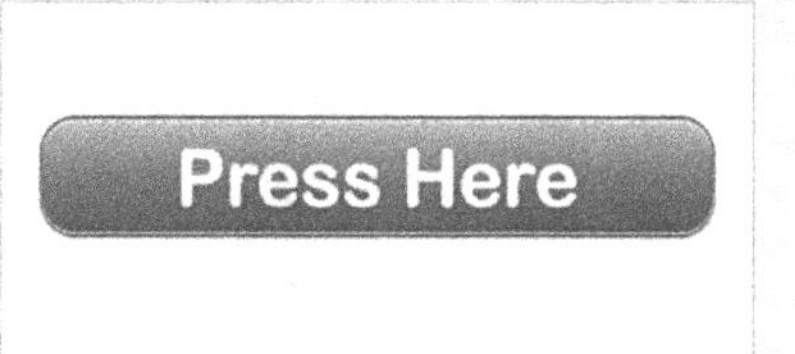

Figure 5-105: *Button with a custom image*

The button is added to the scene from the Library as always, but with a Custom Type, a Default Style, no title, and the image we want to show, as illustrated in Figure 5-106 below. (This example uses the images buttonnormal.png, buttonnormal@2x.png, and buttonnormal@3x.png, available on our website.)

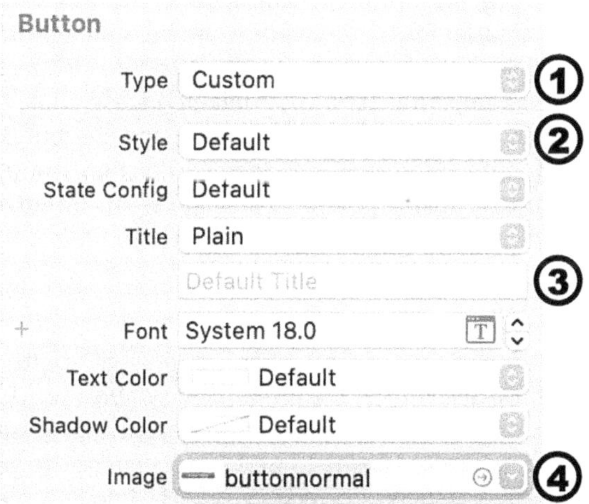

Figure 5-106: *Configuring the button from the Attributes Inspector panel*

Custom buttons can present more images depending on their state. If, for example, we want the button to show a different image when it is pressed, we must add it for the Highlighted state, as shown in Figure 5-107 below (number 1). Once this option is selected, the Image field is emptied to let us pick the new image for that state. This example uses the images buttondown.png, buttondown@2x.png, and buttondown@3x.png, available on our website.

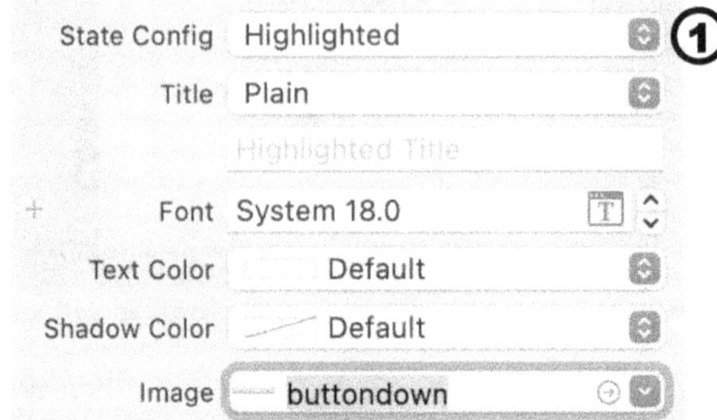

Figure 5-107: *Adding an image for the Highlighted state*

When the app is executed, the **`UIImage`** objects that represent the images we have added for the button are created and shown on the screen. The interface displays the button with the image defined for the Default state and replaces it by the second image when the button is pressed.

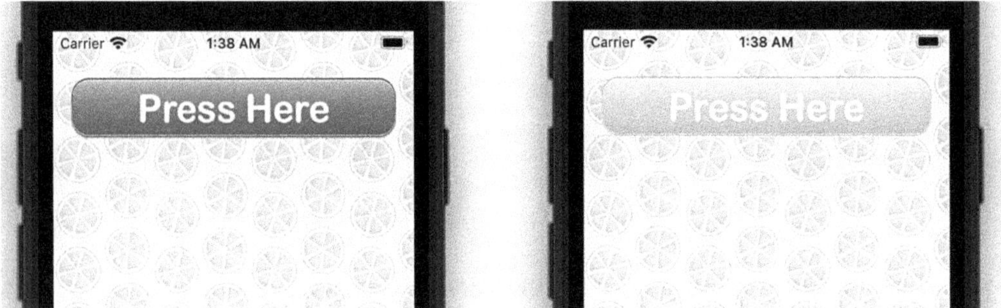

Figure 5-108: *Custom button with a different image when pressed (right)*

Do It Yourself: Download the three buttonnormal.png files and the three buttondown.png files from our website and add them to the Assets Catalog of the project created for the previous example. Add a button from the Library to the scene. Select the button, go to the Attributes Inspector panel, and set the Type as Custom, the style as Default, erase the title, and select the buttonnormal image for the Default state and the buttondown image for the Highlighted state (Figures 5-106 and 5-107). Run the application. When you press the button, the image should change, as illustrated in Figure 5-108 (right).

Basic SF Symbols

Although we can implement our own images, when working with buttons, markers, or indicators, it is better to use SF Symbols. SF Symbols are predefined symbols provided by Apple to represent functionality, such as the image of an envelope to represent the possibility to send emails or a magnifying glass representing the possibility to perform a search. The graphics are identified with a string, are scalable, and come in different versions, which simplifies the integration with the rest of the interface.

There are plenty of symbols available to cover every need our application may have. To help us find the symbols we want, Apple provides a free application called SF Symbols that we can download from developer.apple.com (Develop/Downloads/Release/Applications). The app includes options to search for symbols by name or category.

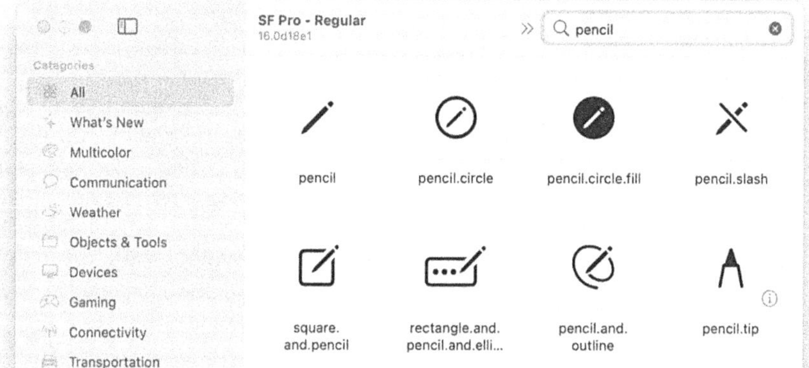

Figure 5-109: *SF Symbols app*

We have introduced SF Symbols before in this chapter. They are implemented by buttons to show images along with the title, but we can create them ourselves with the **`UIImage`** initializer.

UIImage(systemName: String, **withConfiguration:** Configuration**)**—This initializer creates an object that contains an SF symbol. The **systemName** argument is the name of the symbol, and the **withConfiguration** argument is the symbol's configuration, including font, size, weight, and more.

The **withConfiguration** argument is optional. For instance, if we only provide the symbol's name, the system creates an SF Symbol with values by default. In the following example, we change the configuration of a Filled button on the interface to include an image with an SF Symbol.

```
import UIKit

class ViewController: UIViewController {
   @IBOutlet weak var myButton: UIButton!

   override func viewDidLoad() {
      super.viewDidLoad()
      myButton.configurationUpdateHandler = { button in
         var current = button.configuration
         current?.title = "Add Comment"
         current?.image = UIImage(systemName: "trash")
         current?.imagePadding = 15
         button.configuration = current
      }
   }
}
```

Listing 5-74: *Implementing SF Symbols*

This view controller changes the button’s configuration as we did before, but this time we include an image with the symbol of a trash can.

Figure 5-110: *Button with an SF Symbol*

Do It Yourself: Delete the elements in the scene. Add a Filled button from the Library. Connect the button to the **ViewController** class with an Outlet called **mybutton**. Update the class with the code in Listing 5-74 and run the application. You should see a button like the one in Figure 5-110.

SF Symbols come in different versions. For instance, the symbol with the name "trash" implemented in our example has a version with a circle around the can, another with a line across, and more. These are called *variants*. Symbol's names follow a pattern we can use to identify a variant. First, we write the base name, and then specify the variants with dot notation.

```
import UIKit

class ViewController: UIViewController {
   @IBOutlet weak var myButton: UIButton!

   override func viewDidLoad() {
      super.viewDidLoad()
      myButton.configurationUpdateHandler = { button in
         var current = button.configuration
         current?.title = "Add Comment"
         current?.image = UIImage(systemName: "trash.circle")
         current?.imagePadding = 15
         button.configuration = current
      }
   }
}
```

Listing 5-75: *Selecting a variant of an SF Symbols*

This example loads a symbol with the name "trash.circle", which represents the image of a trash can surrounded by a circle.

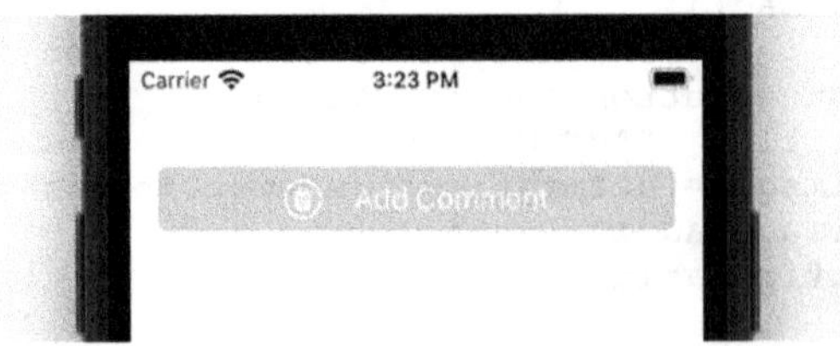

Figure 5-111: *Button with a variant of an SF Symbol*

SF Symbols adopt the size of the text or the elements they are applied to, but when the symbol is used independently, there is no reference for the system to set the size or the appearance. In cases like this, or when we want to specify a different configuration than the one set by the system, we can provide a configuration object. These objects are created from the **SymbolConfiguration** class. The class includes multiple initializers. The following are the most frequently used.

SymbolConfiguration(pointSize: CGFloat, **weight:** SymbolWeight**)**—This initializer creates an object with the configuration defined by the arguments. The **pointSize** argument determines the font size the symbol uses as reference, and the **weight** argument determines the font's weight. This last argument is a **SymbolWeight** enumeration with the values **unspecified**, **ultraLight**, **thin**, **light**, **regular**, **medium**, **semibold**, **bold**, **heavy**, and **black**. The enumeration also includes the **fontWeight()** method to declare a weight.

SymbolConfiguration(textStyle: TextStyle, **scale:** SymbolScale**)**—This initializer creates an object with the configuration defined by the arguments. The **textStyle** argument is a Dynamic Font (e.g., **body**, **headline**, etc.), and the **scale** argument specifies the symbol's scale. This is an enumeration with the values **unspecified**, **small**, **medium**, and **large**.

SymbolConfiguration(font: UIFont, **scale:** SymbolScale**)**—This initializer creates an object with the configuration defined by the arguments. The **font** argument is the font the symbol uses as reference, and the **scale** argument specifies the symbol's scale. This is an enumeration with the values **unspecified**, **small**, **medium**, and **large**.

The purpose of the configuration object is to define the characteristics of the font the system will use as reference to draw the symbol. For instance, we can specify a size of 30 points.

```
import UIKit

class ViewController: UIViewController {
   @IBOutlet weak var myButton: UIButton!

   override func viewDidLoad() {
      super.viewDidLoad()
      let config = UIImage.SymbolConfiguration(pointSize: 30,
weight: .regular)

      myButton.configurationUpdateHandler = { button in
         var current = button.configuration
         current?.title = "Add Comment"
         current?.image = UIImage(systemName: "trash", withConfiguration:
config)
         current?.imagePadding = 15
         button.configuration = current
      }
   }
}
```

Listing 5-76: *Configuring an SF Symbols*

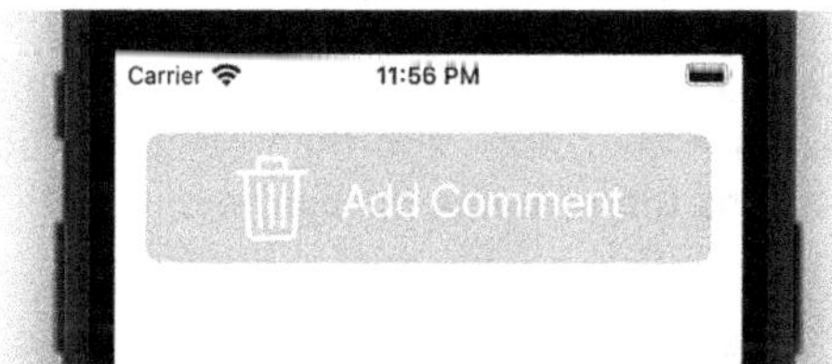

Figure 5-112: *SF Symbol with a custom size*

In additions to the base color, some symbols can include up to three more colors. And these colors can also be defined with a configuration object. The **SymbolConfiguration** class includes the following initializers for this purpose.

SymbolConfiguration(paletteColors: [UIColor]**)**—This initializer creates a configuration object to set the colors to the colors specified by the **paletteColors** argument.

SymbolConfiguration(hierarchicalColor: UIColor**)**—This initializer creates a configuration object that defines all the symbol's colors from a base color specified by the **hierarchicalColor** argument.

These initializers return a configuration object that defines the symbol's colors, but they do not provide an alternative to define other attributes, such as the size or weight. To combine the configuration object created by any of the previous initializers with an object created by the color initializers, the **`SymbolConfiguration`** class includes the following method.

applying(SymbolConfiguration**)**—This method combines the configuration object with the object specified by the argument.

Not all symbols are multicolor. In fact, most symbols are monochrome. To know which symbols can handle multiple colors, we can use the SF Symbols app. Once we find the symbol we want, the configuration is done as before. The following example illustrate how to configure the bell.circle symbol with two colors and a custom size.

```
import UIKit

class ViewController: UIViewController {
   @IBOutlet weak var myButton: UIButton!

   override func viewDidLoad() {
      super.viewDidLoad()
      let configSize = UIImage.SymbolConfiguration(pointSize: 35, weight:
.regular)
      let configColors = UIImage.SymbolConfiguration(paletteColors:
[.systemRed, .white])
      let config = configSize.applying(configColors)

      myButton.configurationUpdateHandler = { button in
         var current = button.configuration
         current?.title = "Add Comment"
         current?.image = UIImage(systemName: "bell.circle.fill",
withConfiguration: config)
         current?.imagePadding = 15
         button.configuration = current
      }
   }
}
```

Listing 5-77: *Defining the colors of an SF Symbols*

This view controller defines a configuration object to determine the symbol's size, a second configuration object to determine the colors, and then combines both configurations with the **`applying()`** method and assigns the resulting configuration to the **`UIImage`** object as we did before.

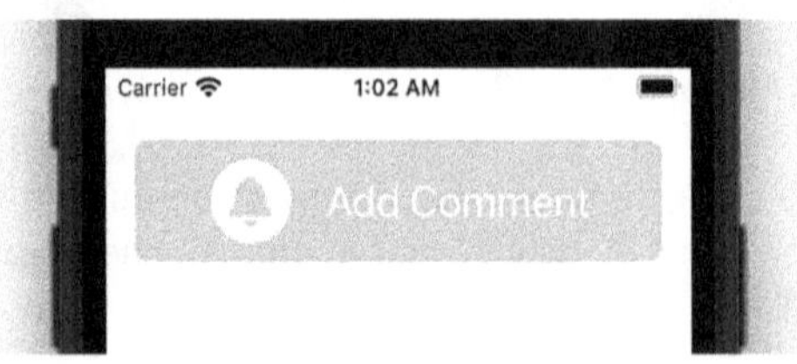

Figure 5-113: *SF Symbol with custom colors*

Basic Image View

UIImage objects may be added to views, buttons, or other elements to create customized controls, but if we just want to show the image on the screen, we must create an Image View. This view is defined by the **UIImageView** class, which includes the following initializer.

UIImageView(image: UIImage?)—This initializer creates a **UIImageView** object with the image provided by the **image** argument.

UIImageView objects can also be incorporated to the Storyboard from the option in the Library.

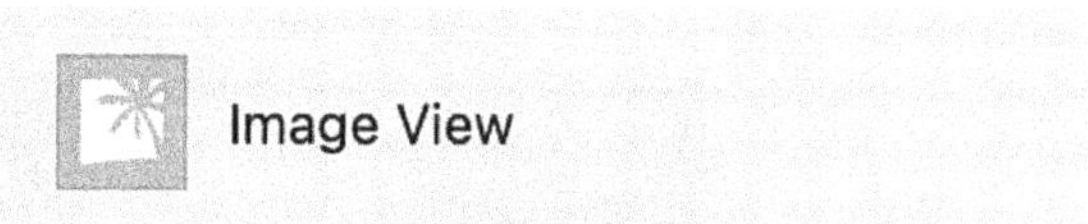

Figure 5-114: *Image View option in the Library*

The class includes properties to retrieve the image and configure the view.

image—This property sets or returns the image. It is an optional of type **UIImage**.

isUserInteractionEnabled—This property sets or returns a Boolean value that determines if the Image View responds to user events. By default, it is set to **false**.

Image Views are views that contain images and therefore they are added to the interface as any other view. The following interface includes a button at the top and an Image View at the bottom to display the selected image.

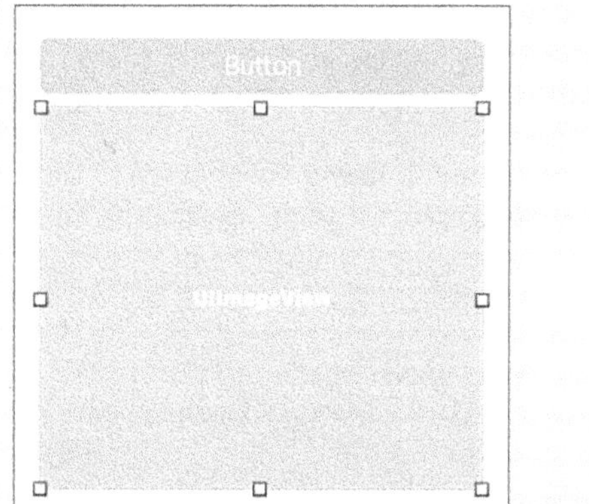

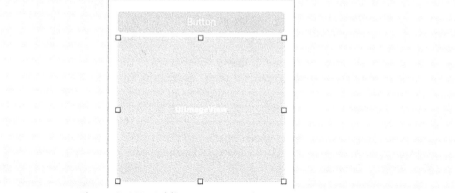

Figure 5-115: *Adding an Image View to a scene*

To assign an image to the view, we can modify its **image** property from code or select it from the Attributes Inspector panel, as shown below.

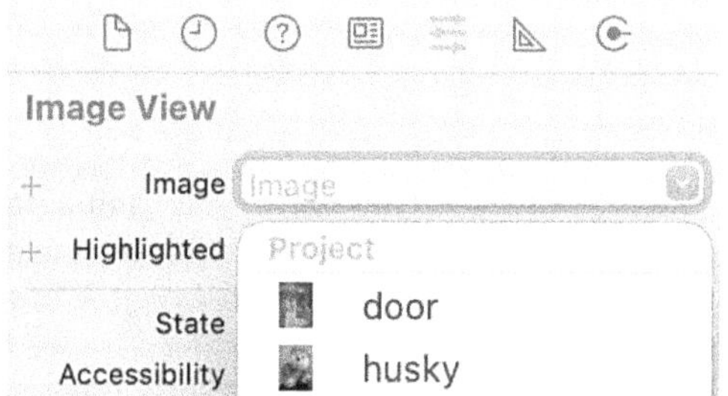

Figure 5-116: *Assigning an image to the Image View*

Image Views have their own size, independent of the size of the image they contain. When we load an image, we must tell the system how to accommodate the image inside the view. This is done by modifying the value of the **contentMode** property provided by the **UIView** class. This property can take several values, with the most useful being Scale to Fill, Aspect Fit, and Aspect Fill. Scale to Fill expands or contracts the image to fit the size of the view, Aspect Fit scales the image to fit the size of the view, maintaining its aspect ratio, and Aspect Fill scales the image to always fill the view but also keeping its aspect ratio, which means some parts of the image may lay outside the boundaries of the view and, depending on the configuration, they may be hidden. Figure 5-117 shows what the image of the husky looks like when the view is set to different modes.

***Figure 5-117:** Different modes applied to the same Image View*

Do It Yourself: Delete the elements in the scene. Add a Filled button and an Image View from the Library. Expand the views to resemble the interface in Figure 5-115. Download the husky.png, husky@2x.png and husky@3x.png files from our website and add them to the Assets Catalog. Select the Image View and assign the husky.png image to it from the Attributes Inspector panel (Figure 5-116). Try different Content Mode settings to see how the image is affected.

Image Views, as any other element, may be connected to the view controller with Outlets and then modified from code. For example, we could replace the image when the button is pressed.

```
import UIKit

class ViewController: UIViewController {
   @IBOutlet weak var pictureView: UIImageView!
   var door: UIImage!

   override func viewDidLoad() {
      super.viewDidLoad()
      door = UIImage(named: "door")
   }
   @IBAction func changePicture(_ sender: UIButton) {
      pictureView.image = door
   }
}
```

***Listing 5-78:** Replacing the picture when the button is pressed*

The view controller includes an Outlet to the Image View and a property to store the image. When the view is loaded, we create the **UIImage** object with the image of the door and assign it to the **door** property. Once we have this object, we can assign it to the **image** property of the Image View any time we want to show the image on the screen. In fact, the image can be replaced at any time. For instance, we can store two **UIImage** objects with different images and show one or the other depending on a condition, as in the following example.

```swift
import UIKit

class ViewController: UIViewController {
   @IBOutlet weak var pictureView: UIImageView!
   var currentActive: Bool = false
   var husky: UIImage!
   var door: UIImage!

   override func viewDidLoad() {
      super.viewDidLoad()
      husky = UIImage(named: "husky")
      door = UIImage(named: "door")
   }
   @IBAction func changePicture(_ sender: UIButton) {
      if currentActive {
         pictureView.image = husky
      } else {
         pictureView.image = door
      }
      currentActive.toggle()
   }
}
```

Listing 5-79: *Switching pictures*

The Image View is the same as before, but now we have two **UIImage** objects, one with the image of the husky and another with the image of the door. When the button is pressed, we check the value of the **currentActive** property and assign one of the images to the view. At the end, we toggled the value of this property so next time the other image is assigned instead. The result is shown next. Every time the button is pressed, the image on the screen changes.

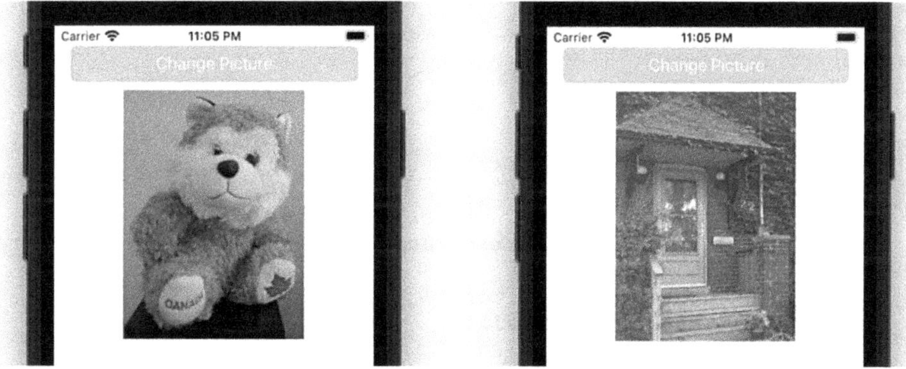

Figure 5-118: *Different images for the same Image View*

Do It Yourself: Add the images of the husky and the door to the Assets Catalog (the images are available on our website). Connect the Image View to the **ViewController** class with an Outlet called **pictureView** and the button with an Action called **changePicture()**. Update the class with the code in Listing 5-79 and run the application. Press the button to change the picture on the screen.

Basic Processing Images

To save storage space and bandwidth, images are compressed in formats such as Jpeg and PNG. When it is time to display the image on the screen, the system decompresses the data and resizes the image to fit inside the view according to the content mode set for the Image View. Letting the system take care of these tasks for us is fine when we are working with just a few images or displaying one image at a time, but it can affect performance when multiple images are shown on the screen at the same time, as it happens when working with Table Views and Collection Views (see Chapter 10 and Chapter 11). To ensure that performance is not affected by these processes, we should always provide images of a size that matches their screen size and decompress them beforehand. For this purpose, the `UIImage` class includes the following methods.

preparingThumbnail(of: CGSize**)**—This method returns a new image created from the original and with a size determined by the **of** argument.

prepareThumbnail(of: CGSize, **completionHandler:** Closure**)**—This method creates a new image from the original and calls a closure with the result. The **of** argument determines the size of the image. The closure receives a `UIImage` object with the result.

preparingForDisplay()—This method decompresses the original image and returns a new one ready to be shown on the screen.

prepareForDisplay(completionHandler: Closure**)**—This method decompress the original image and calls a closure when the process is over. The closure receives a `UIImage` object with the result.

The process of preparing an image to be shown on the screen is often only necessary in high performance applications but reducing the size of an image is a very common requirement. For instance, the resolution of photographs taken by the camera is too high for database storage. In cases like this, we can use the `preparingThumbnail(of:)` method to reduce the size of the image or create thumbnails. As an example, we can use it to get a thumbnail of our husky image.

```
import UIKit

class ViewController: UIViewController {
   @IBOutlet weak var pictureView: UIImageView!
   var husky: UIImage!

   override func viewDidLoad() {
      super.viewDidLoad()
      husky = UIImage(named: "husky")
   }
   @IBAction func changePicture(_ sender: UIButton) {
      let thumbnail = husky.preparingThumbnail(of: CGSize(width: 100,
height: 100))
      pictureView.contentMode = .top
      pictureView.image = thumbnail
   }
}
```

Listing 5-80: *Reducing the size of an image*

This example works with the same interface introduced in Figure 5-115. The image is connected to the `pictureView` outlet, and the button to the `changePicture()` action. When the button is pressed, we call the `preparingThumbnail(of:)` method to create an image of a maximum of 100 points. Notice that we change the view's content mode to `top`. This is to make sure that the image is shown on the screen in its original size. (By default, the content mode of an Image View is set to Aspect Fit, which causes the image to stretch to take up the available space.)

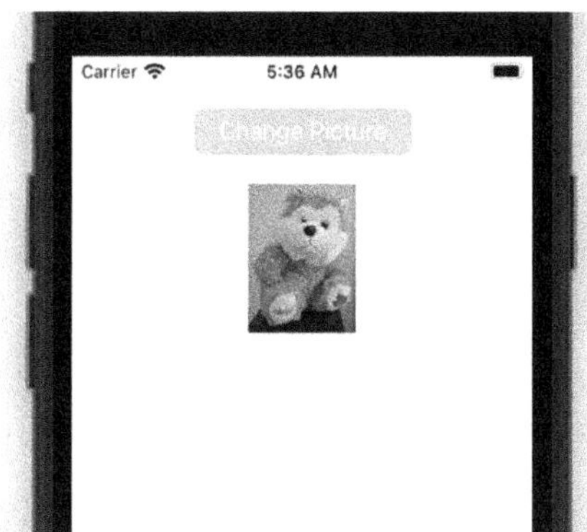

Figure 5-119: *Thumbnail*

IMPORTANT: The **`UIImage`** class also defines two asynchronous methods to perform these tasks: **`byPreparingForDisplay()`** and **`byPreparing-Thumbnail(ofSize: CGSize)`**. The advantage of asynchronous methods is that the system can perform other tasks while the methods finish processing. We will study concurrency in Chapter 14. For an example on how to implement these methods, see Chapter 16, Listing 16-13.

Basic Visual Effects

Modern versions of iOS make extensive use of transparency and Apple encourages developers to adopt these types of design in their own apps. The purpose is to create the illusion of depth so that the user feels that the content extends beyond the screen. One of the tricks used to achieve this effect is to make images appear blurry. The UIKit framework includes the **`UIVisualEffectView`** class to achieve this effect. The class includes an initializer with an argument to define the effect.

UIVisualEffectView(effect: UIVisualEffect?**)**—This initializer creates a **`UIVisual-EffectView`** object with the effect set by the **effect** argument.

The framework currently offers two subclasses of the **`UIVisualEffect`** class to define the effect: **`UIBlurEffect`** and **`UIVibrancyEffect`**. The following are the initializers.

UIBlurEffect(style: Style**)**—This initializer creates a **`UIBlurEffect`** object with the style defined by the **style** argument. The argument is an enumeration with multiple values, including the following to create an effect for light and dark appearances: **`systemUltraThinMaterial`**, **`systemThinMaterial`**, **`systemMaterial`**, **`system-ThickMaterial`**, and **`systemChromeMaterial`**.

UIVibrancyEffect(blurEffect: UIBlurEffect**)**—This initializer creates a **`UIVibrancy-Effect`** object to add vibrancy to a blur effect. The vibrancy is used to highlight a view inside a blur view.

The Library includes two options to add an effect view with a blur effect to a scene.

Figure 5-120: *Visual Effect View options in the Library*

These options create a view that we must place over the views we want to affect. For instance, we can add a Visual Effect View with Blur over a background image. We add the Image View for the background first, then the effect view, and finally the rest of the interface, as shown below.

Figure 5-121: Interface with a Visual Effect View

The Attributes Inspector panel includes the option to select the style. The value defines different levels of opacity. In our example, we used the Ultra Thin Material effect.

Do It Yourself: Download the background.jpg image from our website and add it to the Assets Catalog. Add an Image View to the scene and assign the background image to it. Expand the Image View to fill the main view (Figure 5-121, left). Add a Visual Effect View with Blur on top of the Image View (Figure 5-121, center). Select the Blur Style for this view from the Attributes Inspector panel. Add a button and another Image View on top of the Visual Effect View to get the interface in Figure 5-121, right.

Basic Dark Appearance

The interface of Apple devices can be presented with two appearances: Light and Dark. The user sets the preferred appearance from the Settings app and the applications must adapt their interfaces to it. The appearance by default is Light, but users can change it from the Display & Brightness option, as illustrated below.

Figure 5-122: *Different appearances for the interface*

There are two types of resources we need to adapt to these appearances: colors and images. Although we could perform these changes from code, the Assets Catalog allows us to set different resources for each appearance. For instance, we can specify different images for Any, Light, or Dark. The option is called Appearance (Figure 5-123, number 1).

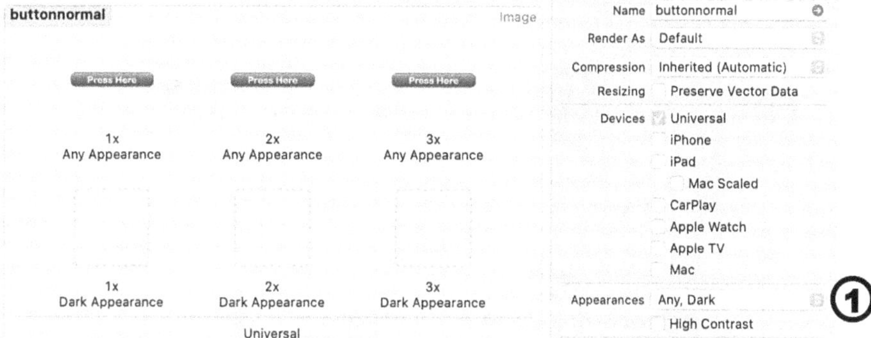

Figure 5-123: *Set of images for the Any and Dark appearances*

The images for the Dark appearance are added as before, by dragging the file for each resolution to the squares on the screen. For instance, we can complete this example to define a button for the Light appearance and another for Dark.

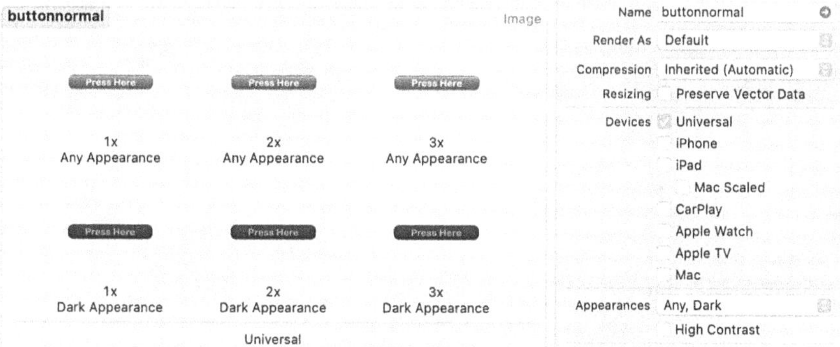

Figure 5-124: *Set of buttons for the Dark appearance*

Once we have images for both appearances, we can test them from the Storyboard or the simulator. The option in the Storyboard is available from the **Device Configuration panel** (see Figure 5-21), and in the simulator the option is available in the Features menu at the top of the screen (Toggle Appearance). For instance, this is how the buttons look like on the Storyboard when we change the appearance from Light to Dark.

Figure 5-125: *Button in Light and Dark appearances*

Most colors provided by the system are automatically adapted to the appearance. This is the reason why the background changes from white to black in our example (The color assigned to the main view by default is called System Background Color and is white in Light appearance and black in Dark appearance). But we can define our own sets of colors from the Assets Catalog. The set is added from the Editor menu (**Add New Set / Color Set**) and the appearance is selected from the Attributes Inspector panel. Xcode adds placeholders to the interface for each of the selected options (Figure 5-126, number 1). Clicking on a placeholder adds options at the bottom of the Attributes Inspector panel to select the color we want for the appearance (Figure 5-126, number 2).

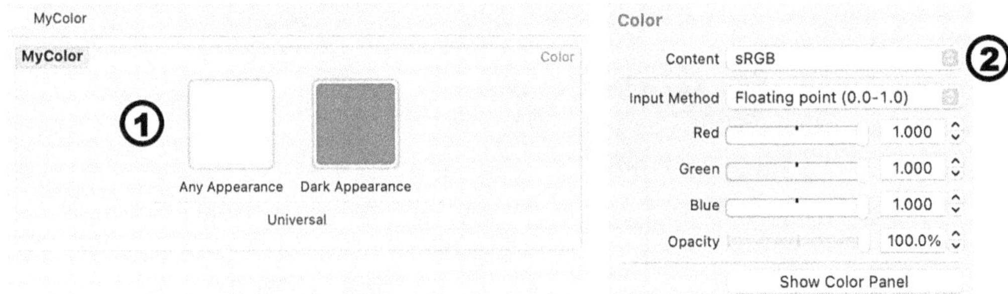

Figure 5-126: *Colors for Light and Dark appearances*

In this example, we have created a color set called MyColor with the color white for the Light appearance and orange for the Dark appearance. This color set can be later assigned to any view as we do with a normal color. For instance, if we assign the MyColor set to the main view in the interface of Figure 5-125, the background turns orange in Dark appearance.

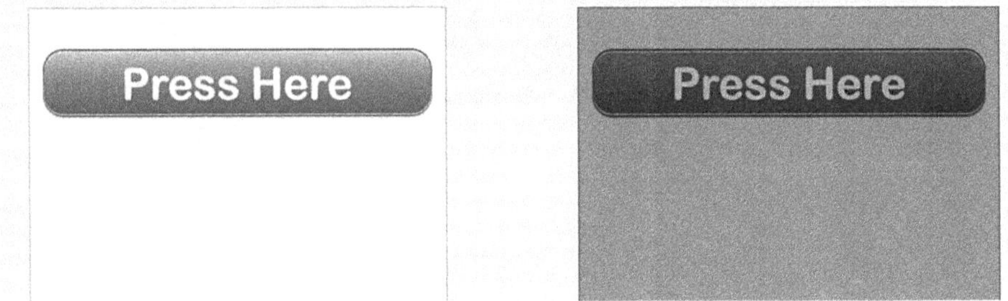

Figure 5-127: *Background with custom colors for Light and Dark appearances*

Basic Icons

Icons are the little images that the user taps or clicks to launch the app. By default, the Assets Catalog includes a set called *AppIcon* to manage the icons we must provide for the application. The set includes placeholders for every icon we need and for every scale and device available.

Icons may be created with any image edition software available in the market. A file must be created for every size required. For example, the first two placeholders require images of 20 points, which means that we need to create an image of a size of 40x40 pixels for the 2x scale and an image of a size of 60x60 pixels for the 3x scale. After all the images are created, we must drag them to corresponding squares, as we do with any other image. Figure 5-128 shows what the AppIcon set may look like once all the images are added (sample files are available on our website).

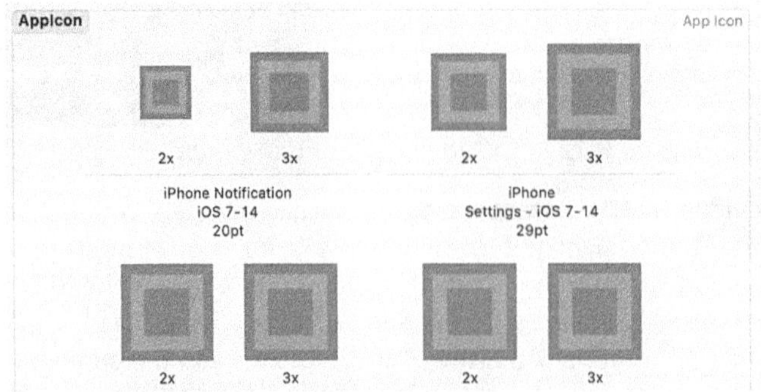

Figure 5-128: *AppIcon set with the icons for iPhones and iPads*

Basic Accent Color

Along with the *AppIcon* set, the Assets Catalog also includes a set called AccentColor to define the interface's accent color (also known as tint color). This is the color used by some controls, such as buttons and sliders. The color by default is blue, but we can modify the AccentColor set to define a new one. For instance, below, we assign an orange color to the Universal Accent Color. From that moment on, all the controls in every device will be orange, unless we specify something else later.

Figure 5-129: *Accent Color*

Basic Launching Image

The launching image is the image that is shown when the app is launched. No matter how small the app, it always takes a few seconds to load. These images are required to give the user the impression that the app is responsive. Xcode provides an additional file with a single scene to create a launching image. This file is called LaunchScreen.storyboard, and it is included in the Navigator Area along with the rest of the files created by the template.

Apple's guidelines recommend creating a launching image that gives the user the impression that the app is already running. For example, we can add an Image View with an image that simulates the app's interface. Figure 5-130, below, shows a possible launching screen for the app created in our last example. We added an Image View to the main view with the background.jpg image set in the Aspect Fill mode. Because the background is the same as the app's background, the transition between this image and the app's interface will look smooth to the user.

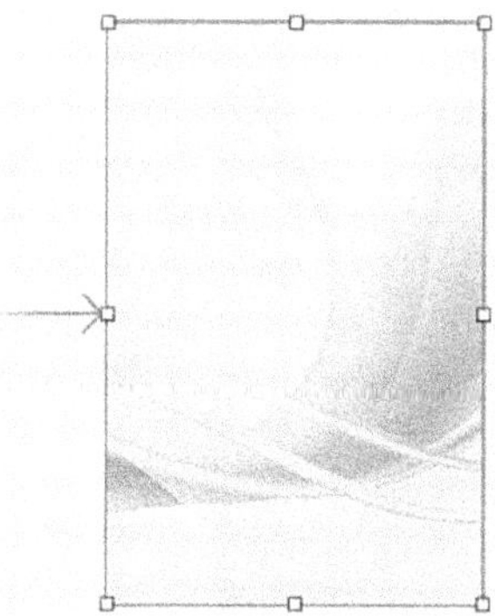

Figure 5-130: *Launching Image for our app*

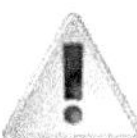

IMPORTANT: Although we could add any element from the Library to this scene, only some of them are appropriate. The content of this view is shown before the app is launched, so there is no code we can process at that moment.

Chapter 6
Adaptivity

Basic 6.1 Adaptivity

Adaptivity is a term that describes the capacity of the interface to adapt to changes in the size of the screen, either because the app is running on devices with different screens, the space available is not the same as before, or the device is rotated. Adaptivity is just an idea, accomplished by the combination of two technologies called *Auto Layout* and *Size Classes*. Combining these tools, we can develop different versions of the interface for every device and orientation.

Basic 6.1 Auto Layout

The position and size of the views added to the interface in the examples in Chapter 5 were determined by their current position and size on the scene. If we wanted to move the view to a different position or change its size, we could have dragged the view or the little squares around it. When we organize the interface this way, the final position and size on the scene determines the position and size of the view. When the app is launched, the objects that represent the views are created and the values that determine their positions and sizes on the scene are assigned to their **`frame`** properties. Using the values in this property, the system draws the views on the screen. This is an intuitive way to organize the interface, but the initial values do not adapt to changes in the space available, orientation, or the device.

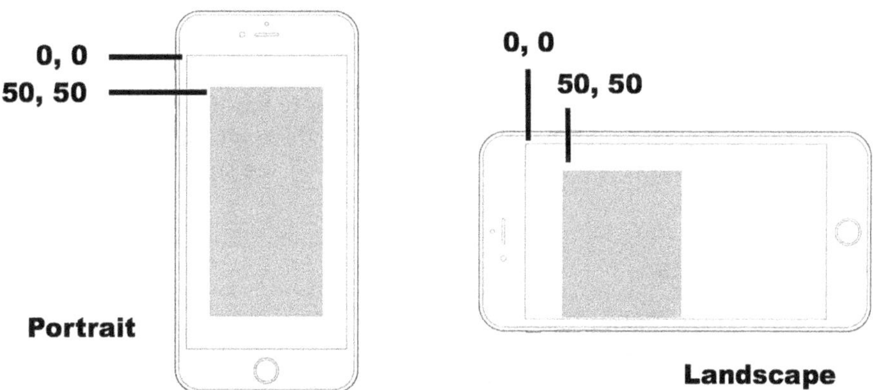

Figure 6-1: *View positioned with absolute values*

This example shows what happens when we determine the position and size of a view in portrait mode and then rotate the device. In landscape mode, half of the gray box generated by the view disappears at the bottom of the screen because there is not enough vertical space available to show it all. Although we could solve this problem by assigning new values to the view's **`frame`** property every time the space changes, this approach presents a difficult challenge. All the values for every view in the interface must be modified, not only when the screen is rotated but also for every type of screen available. And the list of possible scenarios grows every time a new device enters the market or new features are introduced, like the split-screen mode in iPads that allow users to run two apps simultaneously. The solution is provided by Auto Layout.

Auto Layout is a system that implements a set of rules to organize the elements on the interface. The rules establish the relationship between elements and between the elements and their containers. These rules are simple statements that determine things like how far a view should be from another view, or how a group of views should be aligned. As an example, Figure 6-2, next, presents a container with a button, the position and size of which are determined by four rules. These specific rules tell the system how far the button should be from the sides of its container. The example on the left is what we would see during implementation, when all the rules are assigned to the element. The illustration on the right represents the element during execution, when the position and size of the button have already been modified to abide to the rules.

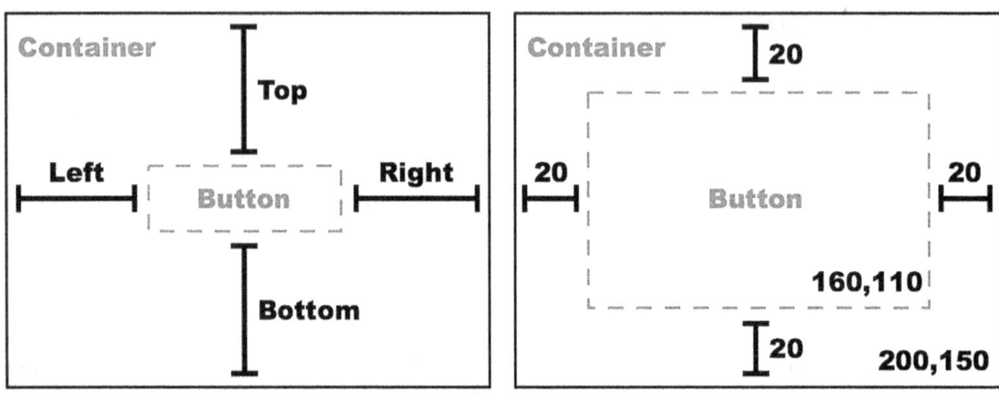

***Figure 6-2:** Rules applied to a button*

The rules applied to the button in Figure 6-2 are saying things like "this button always has to be 20 points from the top of its container" and "this button always has to be 20 points from the left edge of its container". Every rule determines one aspect of the relationship between the button and its container to help the system determine the position and size of the button every time the space available changes. Because of this, we no longer need to declare explicit values to lay out the elements; they are calculated by the system after all the rules have been considered.

IMPORTANT: When we use Auto Layout, the values assigned to the `frame` property of every view in the Storyboard are not considered by the system anymore. Assigning new values to this property has no effect on the position and size of the element on the screen, but there are situations in which the values of this property are still useful. We will see some examples in further chapters.

Basic Constraints

Computers cannot understand human expressions like "position the view 50 points from the edge of the container". For this reason, Auto Layout defines a set of specific rules that we can configure and combine to organize the interface. Auto Layout's rules are called *Constraints*, and they are comprehensive enough to allow us to create any design we want.

There are two main groups of constraints: Pin constraints and Align constraints. Pin constraints define space, such as the space between a view and the edge of its container, while Align constraints define how the views should be aligned with respect to other views or their containers. The following list describes the Pin constraints available.

Top Space—This constraint defines the space between the top of the element and its nearest neighbor or the top edge of the container (superview).

Bottom Space—This constraint defines the space between the bottom of the element and its nearest neighbor or the bottom edge of the container (superview).

Leading Space—This constraint defines the space between the left side of the element and its nearest neighbor or the left edge of the container (superview).

Trailing Space—This constraint defines the space between the right side of the element and its nearest neighbor or the right edge of the container (superview).

Width—This constraint defines the width of the element.

Height—This constraint defines the height of the element.

Aspect Ratio—This constraint defines the aspect ratio of the element.

Equal Widths—This constraint declares that two elements will have the same width. If the width of one of the elements changes, the same value is assigned to the other element affected by the constraint.

Equal Heights—This constraint declares that two elements will have the same height. If the height of one of the elements changes, the same value is assigned to the other element affected by the constraint.

The following are the constraints for alignment:

Horizontal in Container—This constraint aligns the center of the element with the center of its container in the horizontal axis.

Vertical in Container—This constraint aligns the center of the element with the center of its container in the vertical axis.

Leading Edges—This constraint aligns two elements to their left side.

Trailing Edges—This constraint aligns two elements to their right side.

Top Edges—This constraint aligns two elements to their top edge.

Bottom Edges—This constraint aligns two elements to their bottom edge.

Horizontal Centers—This constraint aligns two elements to their horizontal center.

Vertical Centers—This constraint aligns two elements to their vertical centers.

Baselines—This constraint aligns two elements to their baselines.

Most of these constraints are straightforward, but some of them adapt to the circumstances. For example, the constraints that affect the left or right side of the elements are called *Leading* and *Trailing* because they are applied to a side according to the human language set in the system. In English, for example, the leading space is on the left side of the element and the trailing space is on the right, but in Arabic languages is the opposite.

Basic Assigning Constraints

Every element on the interface requires constraints to define its position and size. Xcode offers a series of buttons at the bottom of the Storyboard to add and manage constraints.

Figure 6-3: *Buttons to work with constraints*

These buttons have different functions, from adding constraints to helping us solve the issues that arise along the way. The button on the left (1) updates the values of the view's frame if they do not match the values of the constraints, the next button (2) opens a menu with options to add constraints for alignment (Align menu), the following button (3) opens a menu to add constraints for space (Pin menu), the next one (4) opens a menu with options to help us solve issues with constraints or let the system place the constraints for us, and the last button on the right (5) embeds the view or the scene in containers like Stack Views or Navigation Controllers, as we will see later.

To add a constraint to an element, we select the element in the scene and then click the button to open the Align or Pin menus. Figure 6-4 shows the menus displayed by these buttons.

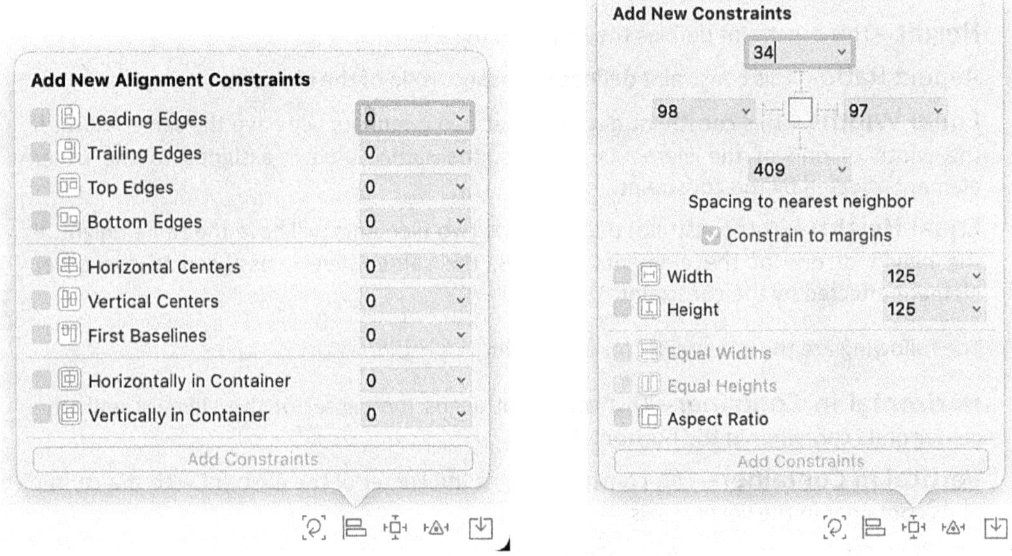

Figure 6-4: *Align and Pin menus*

These menus list all the types of constraints described before, but they adapt the options to the types and number of elements selected. For example, the constraints that require two elements are disabled when only one element is selected. After we activate the constraint that we want to add to the element, the Add Constraints button is highlighted. Clicking this button, adds the constraint to the view. Figure 6-5 shows the process of adding a Top Space constraint to a view.

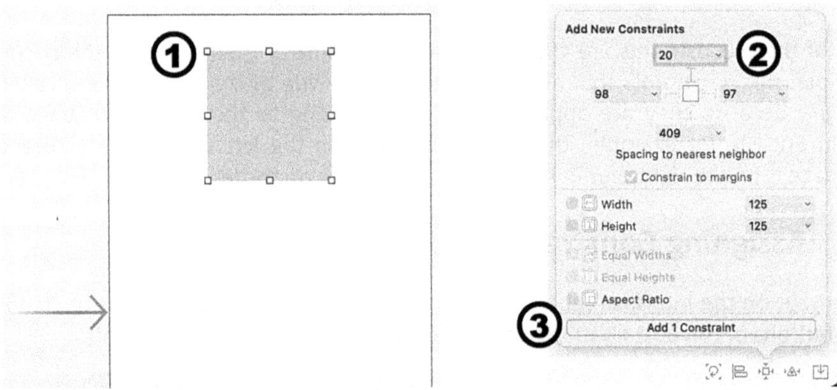

Figure 6-5: *Adding a Top Space constraint to a single view*

Space constraints are added from the Pin menu. We must select the view (Figure 6-5, number 1), click the Pin button at the bottom of the Editor Area to open the Pin menu (Figure 6-3, number 3), activate the constraint we want to add (Figure 6-5, number 2), and press the Add Constraint button to add it to the view (Figure 6-5, number 3). Space constraints are selected by clicking the red line between their value and the square in the middle that represents the view, as shown below.

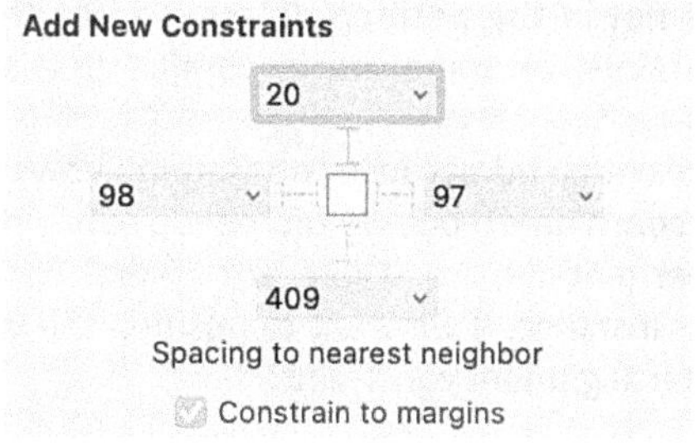

Figure 6-6: *Tool to add Space constraints*

The constraint's value is set by default to the value defined in the scene, but we can change it to any value we want. In our example, we have activated the Top Space constraint with a value of 20. This means that when the system reads this constraint it will position the top of the view 20 points from its nearest neighbor. If there are no other elements at the top, the distance is determined from the top of the element to the top edge of its container. And if multiple destinations are available, like another view or the container, we can click on the arrow to select which one we want to use to connect the constraint.

IMPORTANT: The Pin menu includes an option called *Constraint to margins*. If the option is activated, the Space constraint is set between the view and the margin of the main view. This margin is a standard value defined by Apple that varies from one device to another. Most views do not consider this option and therefore the Space constraints are pinned to the edge of the main view, but if you find that a view was pinned to the margin instead, you can remove the constraint and create it again with this option deactivated or select the constraint and remove the margin from the Attributes Inspector panel.

After the constraints have been selected and configured, we can press the Add Constraints button at the bottom of the menu to effectively add the constraints to the view. The menu is closed and Xcode shows lines in the Storyboard representing the constraints. Every time an element is selected, the lines that represent its constraints are shown on the screen (Figure 6-7, number 1).

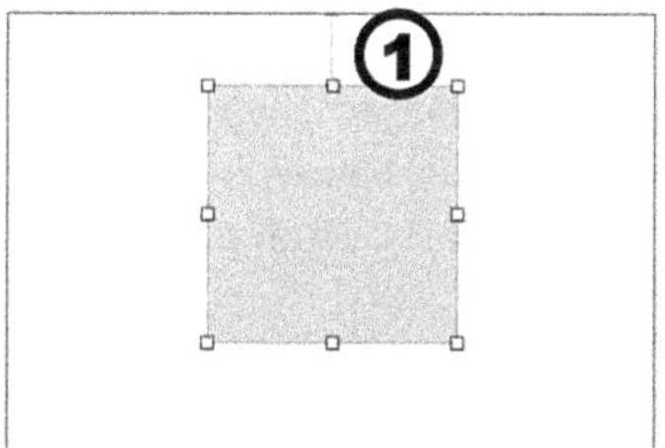

Figure 6-7: *View with a Top Space constraint*

Do It Yourself: Create a new project. Drag an empty view from the Library to the main view (the option in the Library is called *View*). Assign a background color, a size, and a position like the view depicted in Figure 6-5. With the view selected, open the Pin menu, and add a Top Space constraint (Figure 6-5). Keep the value of the constraint as suggested by Xcode. You should see the line representing the constraint as shown in Figure 6-7, number 1.

Although a constraint determines a specific rule, one constraint alone cannot provide enough information for the system to determine the element's position and size. When this happens, Xcode shows the constraint in the Storyboard in red. The color indicates that the constraints assigned to the element are insufficient. There is a total of three colors: blue, orange and red. The constraints are shown in blue when the system has enough information to display the element, orange when the element is not in the position determined by the constraints, and red when there are not enough constraints, or some are in conflict (the system cannot satisfy all the constraints at the same time).

In our example, the constraint is red because the system knows about the vertical position of the view (the value of the **y** coordinate), but we did not specify yet how it should be positioned horizontally and how to determine its size. There are several options available, depending on what we want to achieve. For instance, if we want to position the view at the center of the main view, we must add a Horizontal alignment constraint.

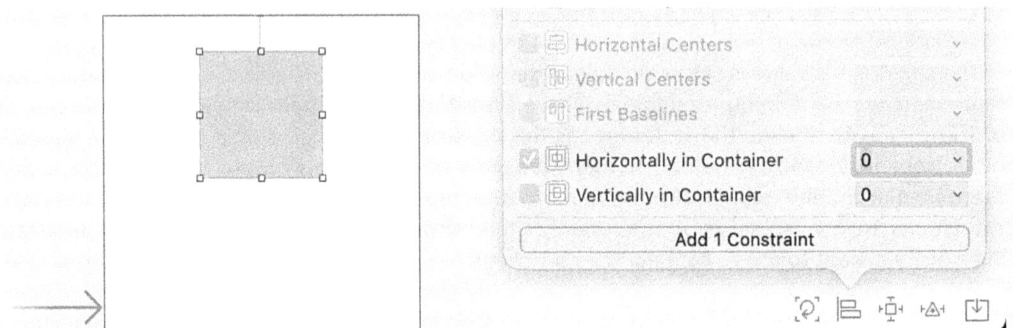

Figure 6-8: *Adding an alignment constraint*

These types of constraints are added from the Align menu, as illustrated in Figure 6-8. The constraints available for single elements are the Horizontal in Container (to center the element horizontally) and the Vertical in Container (to center the element vertically). The rest of the options are only available when multiple elements are selected. All the options in this menu also have a value that determines the constraint's offset. By default, the value is 0, which positions the view at the center of its container, but we can change it to displace the view to the left (negative values) or the right (positive values). In this example, we have selected the Horizontal in Container constraint with an offset value of 0 to center the view horizontally in its container (the main view).

Now, the view is centered on the screen, but the constraints are still red. The two constraints we have added so far (the Top Space constraint and the Horizontal in Container constraint) tell the system that the top of the view must be 20 points from the top of the container and aligned at the center. This is enough to establish the position, but we haven't provided the information for the size. The box could expand or contract to always be at a certain distance from the sides of the container, as we did with the button in Figure 6-2, or it could have a specific size. For this example, we have decided to go with the last option and give our view a size of 125 by 125 points with Width and Height constraints.

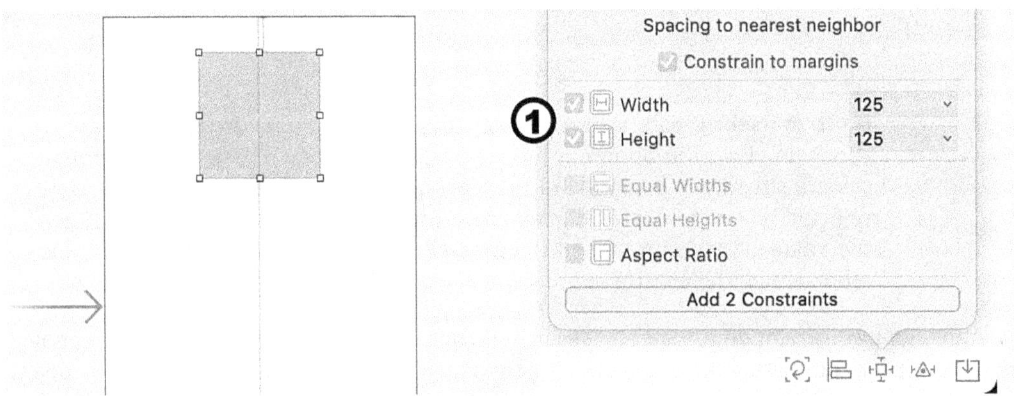

Figure 6-9: *Adding the Width and Height constraints*

The Width and Height constraints tell the system that the view will always have a specific width and height. The size is determined by the values declared for each constraint in the Pin menu, as shown in Figure 6-9, number 1. By default, the menu shows the current values defined in the Storyboard, but we can change them to declare the size we want. Figure 6-10, below, shows our view with all of its constraints.

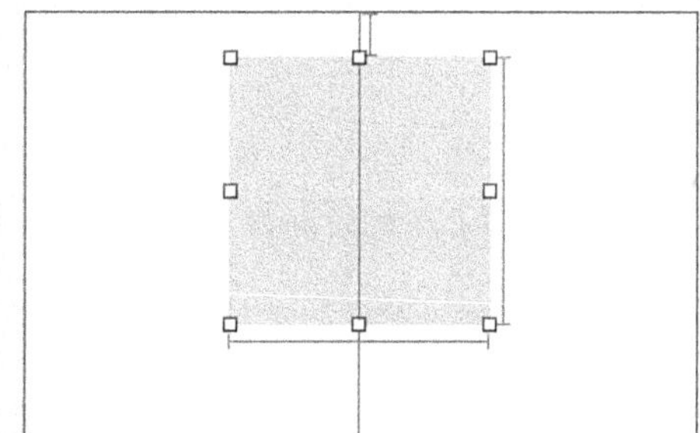

Figure 6-10: *View with all the necessary constraints*

All the constraints are now blue because the system has enough information to draw the view. The Top Space and Horizontal in Container constraints set the position, while the Width and Height constraints determine the size. No matter what the orientation or the size of the screen, our view will be drawn at 20 points from the top, at the center of the screen, and with a size of 125 by 125 points.

Do It Yourself: Add the Horizontal in Container constraint to the view, as shown in Figure 6-8, and the Width and Height constraints, as shown in Figure 6-9. Click on the Orientation button to change the orientation of the scene to landscape (Figure 5-21, number 2). You should see the view at the center and 20 points from the top, no matter the orientation.

Unless we have a good reason to set a specific size, we should always let the size of the elements be determined by the relationship between the element and its siblings or the container. For instance, if we want the view of our example to always be at the center of the screen, it is better to set Leading and Trailing constraints to define the space on the sides and let the system determine the width, as illustrated below.

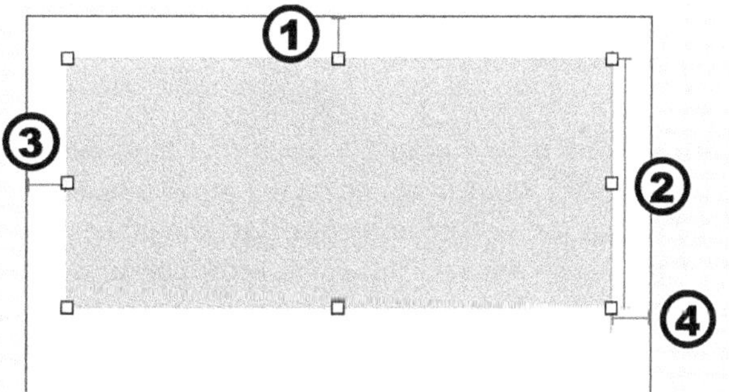

Figure 6-11: *Space constraints to define the width of the element*

In this example, the position and size of the view are determined by the Top Space (1), Height (2), Leading Space (3), and Trailing Space (4) constraints. The Leading Space and Trailing Space constraints tell the system that the view must be at a certain distance from the edge of the container, and it should shrink or expand to always be at that distance.

The view in Figure 6-11 has an absolute height determined by the Height constraint, but we could also change that assigning a Bottom space constraint or an Aspect Ratio constraint, as in the following example.

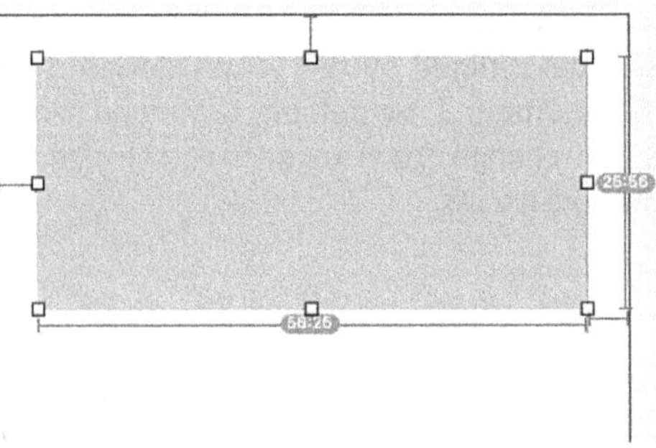

Figure 6-12: *Aspect Ratio constraint*

The example in Figure 6-12 implements an Aspect Ratio constraint to determine the view's height. The width is determined by the Leading Space and Trailing Space constraints, but the height is defined to be proportional to the current width by the Aspect Ratio constraint. When the view expands because of the Space constraints on the sides, it also gets proportionally taller. Because of these constraints, the view always has the same rectangular shape.

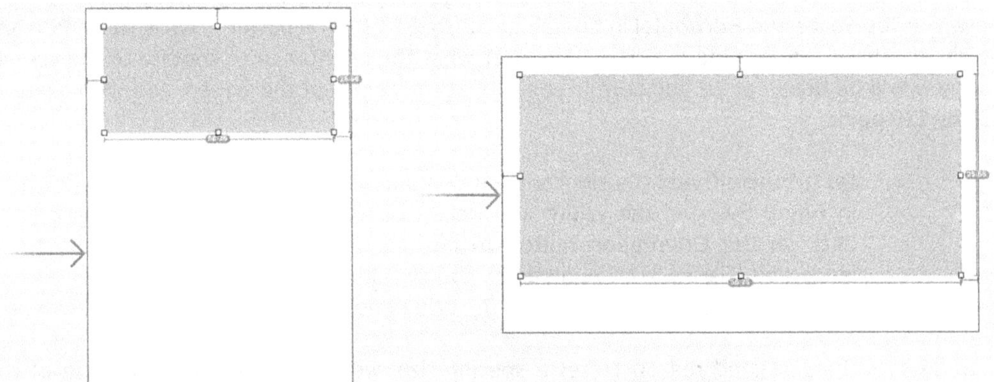

Figure 6-13: *Same aspect ratio in portrait and landscape*

Do It Yourself: To reproduce the interface in Figure 6-13, you can select and erase the Height constraint from the previous example and add an Aspect Ratio constraint instead (see Figure 6-12). Click on the Orientation button to change the orientation of the scene to landscape. You should see something like Figure 6-13 (right).

IMPORTANT: The aspect ratio is a value that determines how many points on one side correspond to the points on the other side. For example, a ratio of 1:2 determines that for each point on one side, the other side should have two. The Aspect Ratio constraint sets this value according to the current aspect ratio of the view. Next, we will see how to modify this value and specify a custom ratio.

Basic Editing Constraints

Every constraint has associated values to determine its properties, such as the distance, the width of the element, etc. Assigning new values to the constraints changes how they affect the elements and how the interface is built. The Align and Pin menus only allow us to add new constraints, not to edit the ones already created. Xcode offers different alternatives to access and edit the constraints. The simplest is to select the element and open the Size Inspector panel in the Utilities Area (Figure 5-22, right). The constraints associated with the element are listed at the bottom.

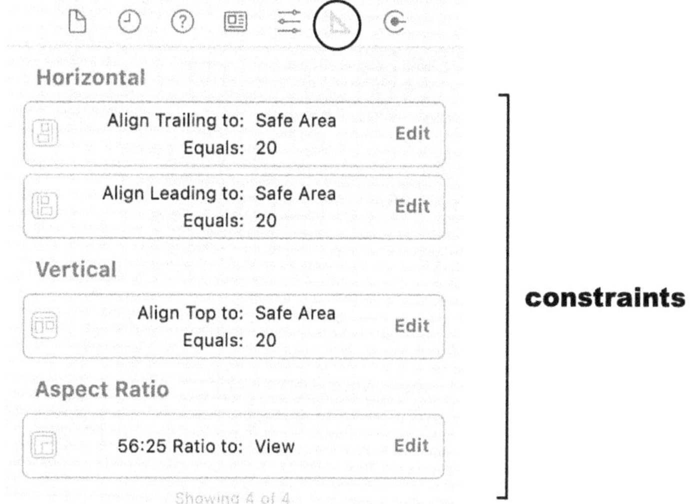

Figure 6-14: *List of constraints on the Size Inspector panel*

The constraints are listed at the bottom of the panel. Figure 6-14 shows the four constraints added to the view of our last example (Trailing Space, Leading Space, Top Space, and Aspect Ratio). Each constraint on the list includes an Edit button to edit the values. Figure 6-15, below, shows the window that opens when we click on this button. Changing the values in this window automatically modifies the constraint (this menu also opens if we double-click the constraint in the Storyboard).

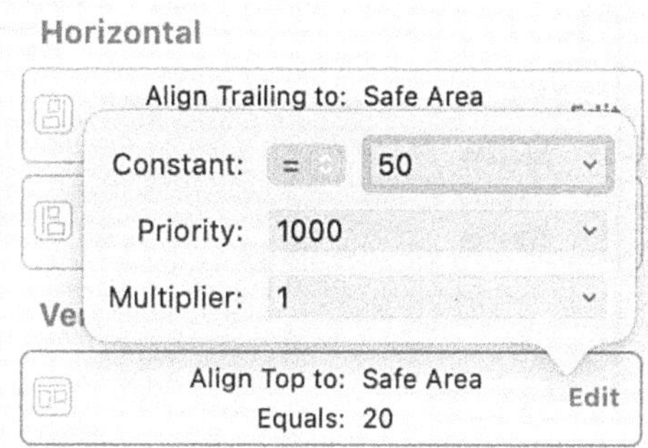

Figure 6-15: *Popup window to edit the values of a constraint*

There are different options available to configure a constraint. The option that determines the value of the constraint, such as the distance or the width, is called *Constant*.

Do It Yourself: Select the scene in the Storyboard. Click on the button to show the Size Inspector panel (circled in Figure 6-14). Click on the Edit button of any of the constraints to change their values. Try, for example, to assign a value of 50 to the Top Space constraint, as we did in Figure 6-15. The changes will be immediately reflected in the Storyboard when possible.

Constraints have their own panel with more configuration options. To open this panel, we can double click the constraint on the Size Inspector panel (Figure 6-14), select the constraint from the Storyboard, or click on the item that represents the constraint inside the Document Outline panel. When a constraint is selected, its values are shown in the Utilities Area. Figure 6-16, below, shows this panel after the Top Space constraint from our example is selected. From this panel, we can change all the constraint's values and some aspects of the elements the constraint is connected to.

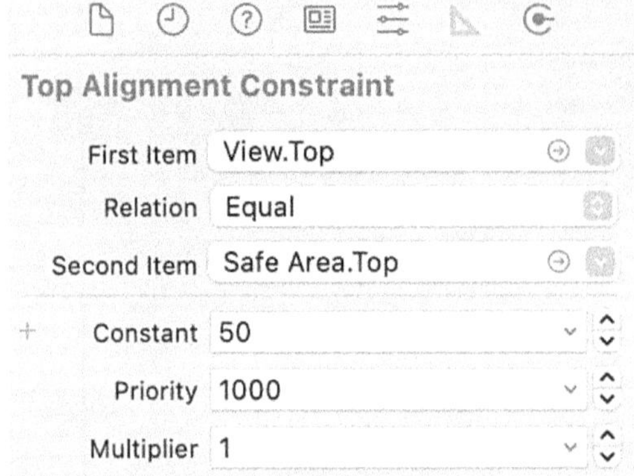

Figure 6-16: *Constraint editor in the Utilities Area*

Basic Safe Area

The system defines a layout guide called *Safe Area* where we can place the content of our interface. This is the area determined by the space remaining inside the scene's view after all the toolbars and special views are displayed by the system. For example, if we don't specify otherwise, the system displays a status bar at the top of the screen. This bar can adapt to different devices and orientations, and it might be completely removed at any time. To make sure that our content never overlaps the bar, we can pin it to the edges of the Safe Area.

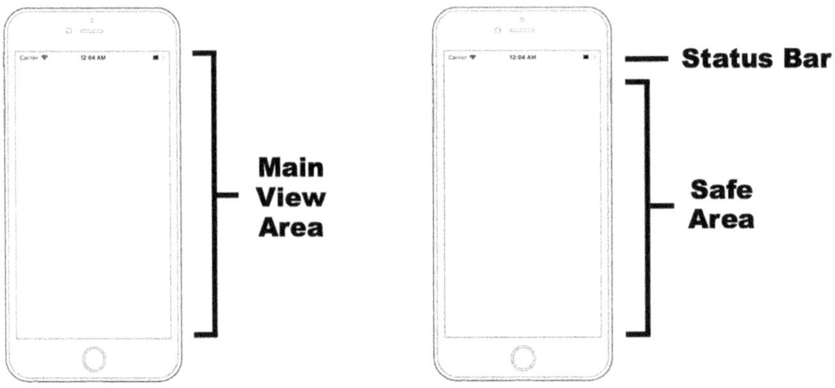

Figure 6-17: *Safe Area*

For example, the following interface includes a view that is positioned and sized with pin constraints with a value of 0. This expands the view to the edges of the scene.

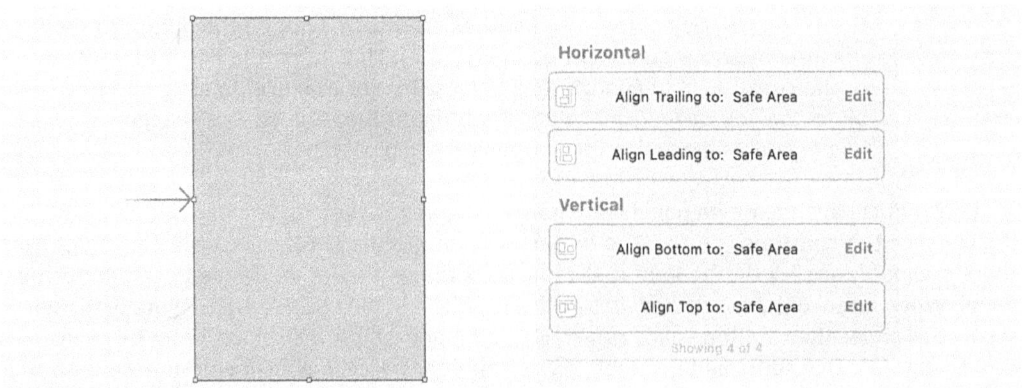

Figure 6-18: *Pinning a view to the Safe Area*

By default, the pin constraints assigned to the view are attached to the Safe Area, so the view will be drawn below the status bar. If instead we want our view to be pinned to the top edge of the main view, we must change the constraint's configuration from the Size Inspector panel.

When we select a constraint, the Size Inspector panel shows the two elements the constraint is attached to. To connect the top of our view to the top of the main view, we must change the second item of the relationship to Superview, as shown below.

Figure 6-19: *Pinning a view to its superview*

Figure 6-20, below, shows what we see in the simulator with the Top constraint attached to the Safe Area (left), and what happens when we attach it to the superview (right).

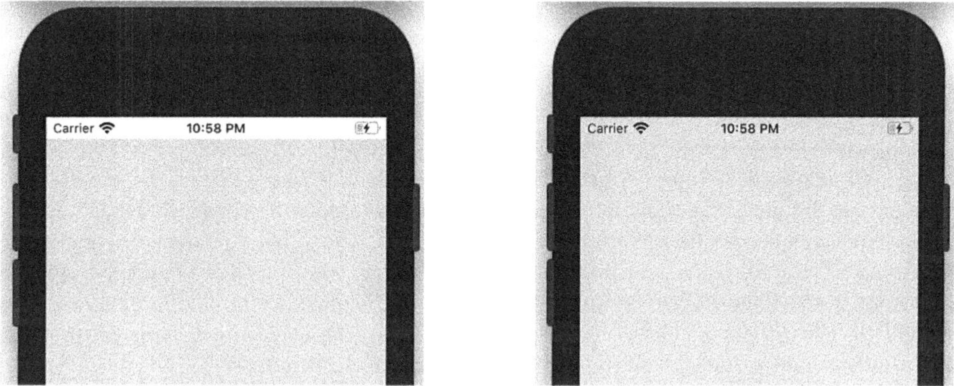

Figure 6-20: *View pinned to the Safe Area or the superview*

The option to select the element attached to the constraint is also available in the Pin menu. When we select a Space constraint to add it to a view, we can click the arrow on the right-hand side of the value and select the destination view, as shown below.

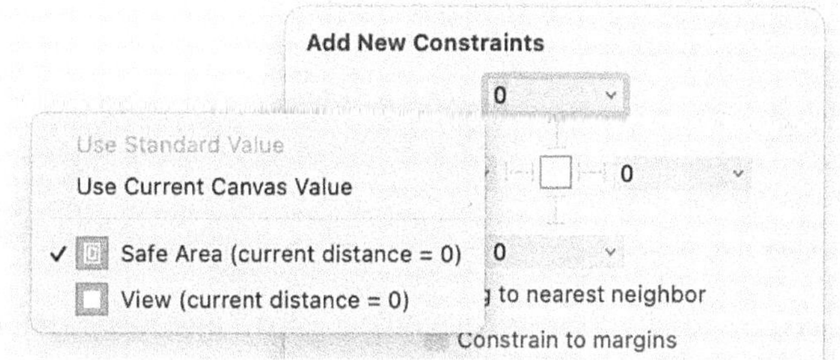

Figure 6-21: *Selecting the destination view*

The menu displays a list of all the elements available to attach to the constraint. In this example, only the Safe Area and the main view are available, but there may be others, as we will see later.

Basic Resolving Auto Layout Issues

As mentioned before, Xcode shows the constraints in different colors depending on the information they provide. We have seen the lines in red when there were not enough constraints to position or size the element and blue when the system had all the information required to place the element on the screen. But there is another situation. Sometimes the constraints are enough, but Xcode cannot determine the position and size of the views in the Storyboard and therefore there is a mismatch between what we see in the Storyboard and what the user will see after the constraints are applied. This situation may occur because Xcode decides that it is better to show the view in the current position and with the current size to make easy for us to edit the interface, or it just cannot determine the new position and size under the present conditions. To help us identify the problem, Xcode shows the constraints in orange with dashed lines that delimit the area where the view should be.

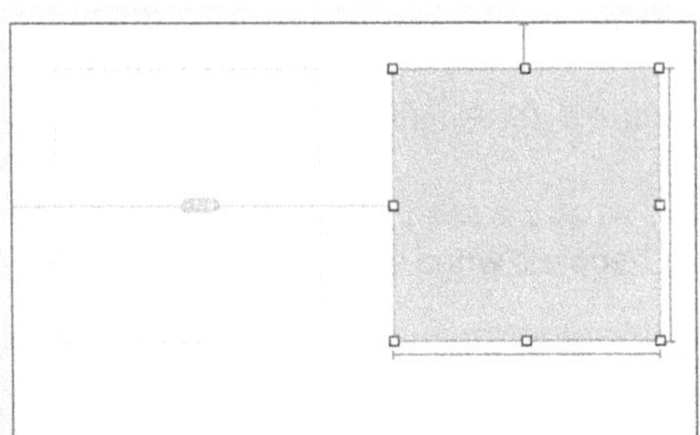

Figure 6-22: *Element in the wrong position*

The interface in Figure 6-22 presents a simple view with a Top Space constraint and Width and Height constraints to determine its size. The horizontal position was specified by a Leading Space constraint, but the view was moved to the right and therefore Xcode shows dashed lines around the area in which it should be according to the constraints. This is just an indication, and we could keep adding or modifying the constraints until the design is over, but if we need the Storyboard to represent the final interface, we must solve the issue. One option is to update the view's frame to match the constraints' values. This is done by selecting the view and clicking on the Update Frames button at the bottom of the Editor Area (Figure 6-3, number 1). Once we press this button, the values of the view's frame are updated, and the view is moved to the place determined by the constraints.

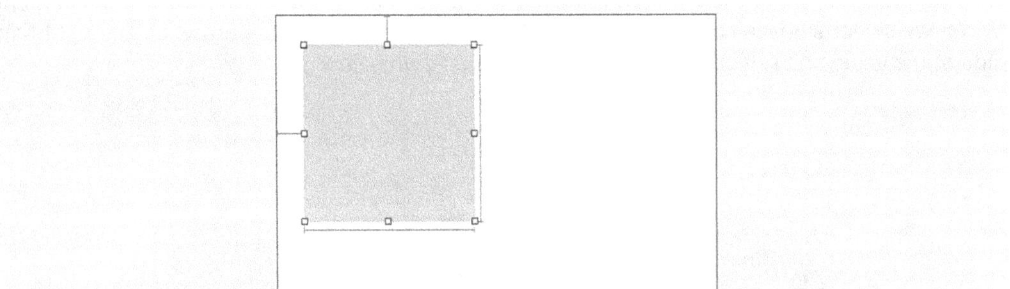

Figure 6-23: *Element in the position determined by the constraints*

For complex issues, Xcode offers the Resolve Auto Layout Issues menu (Figure 6-3, number 4). The Resolve Auto Layout Issues menu not only allows us to solve problems with the constraints, but it can also help us determine what the right constraints are for our interface. The following are the options available (the options are available twice, one for the selected views and another for all of them).

Update Constraints Constants—This option updates the values of the constraints to match the current position and size of the view.

Add Missing Constraints—This option adds the constraints for us. Xcode estimates what the constraints should be according to the current position and size of the views in the Storyboard and automatically adds those constraints. It is useful as a starting point.

Reset to Suggested Constraints—This option modifies the current constraints to take them back to the state established by Xcode when the suggested constraints were generated.

Clear Constraints—This option erases the constraints. We can select it when the constraints are not working and we have decided to start from scratch, but it is also useful when working with different Size Classes, as we will see later.

Xcode offers tools with more specific information to help us identify and solve complex problems with constraints. An easy way to get this information is from the Error button at the top of the Editor Area (Figure 6-24, number 1).

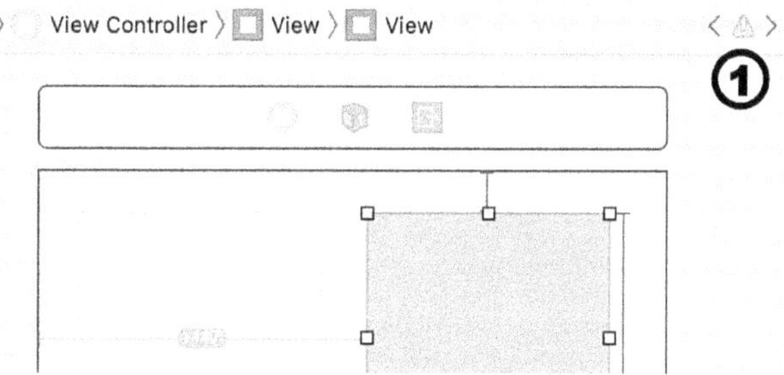

Figure 6-24: *Errors and Warnings*

This button displays a list of the errors and warnings that are affecting our application. Figure 6-25, below, shows the warning displayed when a view is not in the position determined by the constraints.

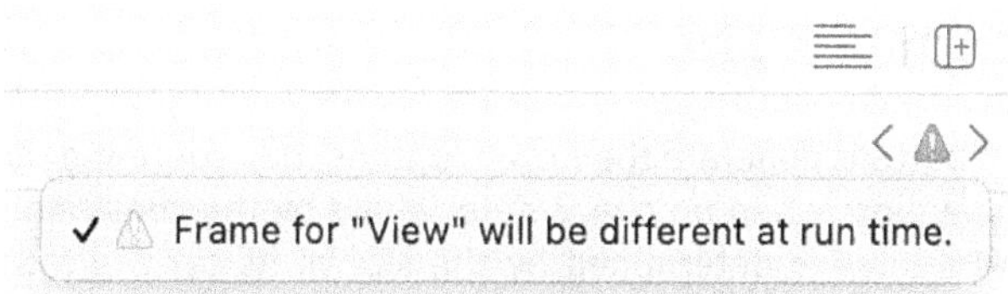

Figure 6-25: *Current issues with constraints*

Another way to get a detailed explanation of the issues regarding our constraints is from the Document Outline panel (Figure 5-21, number 1). The panel displays a list of the elements and constraints in the interface, and it provides a small button at the top right corner whenever there is an issue with the constraints (Figure 6-26, number 1).

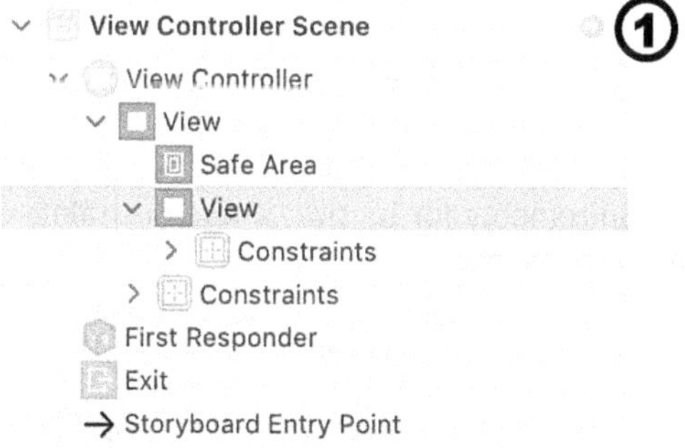

Figure 6-26: *Getting the list of issues from the Document Outline panel*

When we click this button, the list of views and constraints is replaced by the list of issues our interface currently has.

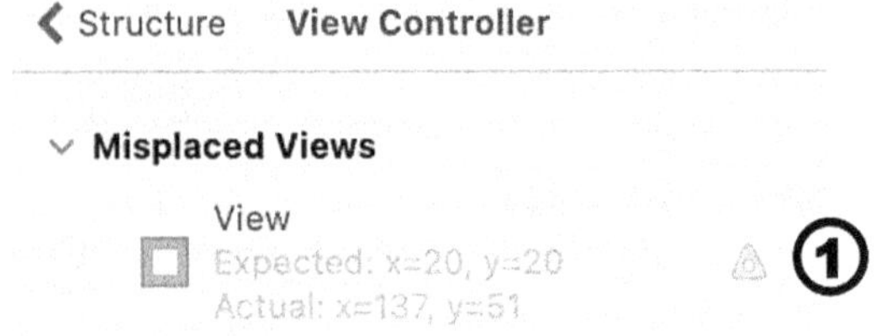

Figure 6-27: List of issues in the Document Outline panel

All the issues are listed with detailed information, such as the current and expected values, the constraints needed, etc. Every item of the list also includes another button (Figure 6-27, number 1) to open a popup menu with suggestions and solutions.

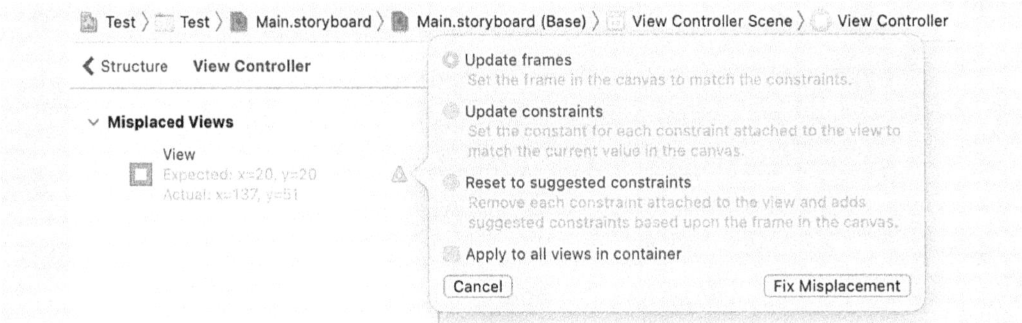

Figure 6-28: Automatic solutions for constraint issues

Some of the options in this menu are available in the Resolve Auto Layout Issues menu, but they are adapted to the issue we are dealing with.

Basic Intrinsic Content Size

Elements like labels and buttons generate their own content. This content defines a minimum size that the element's view adopts when no size is determined by the constraints. For example, the intrinsic content size of a label is determined by the size of its text. Because of this property, sometimes all we need for an element is to declare enough constraints to determine its position.

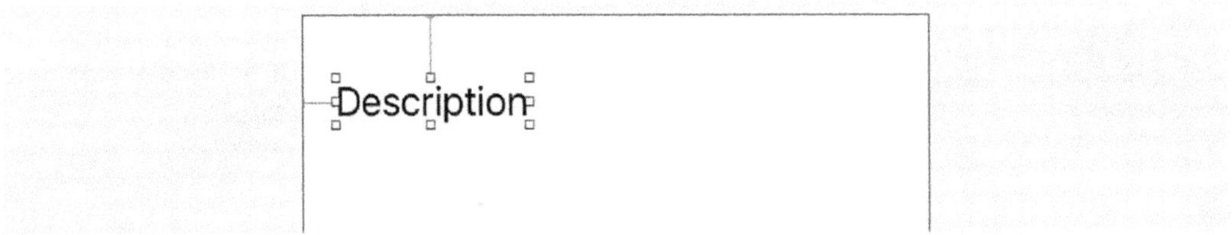

Figure 6-29: Label defined with intrinsic content size

The label in Figure 6-29 has only two constraints, Top Space of 30 points and Leading Space of 16 points. There are no requirements for its size. If no constraints are defined, the label's view automatically adopts the size of its text.

If we need to know what the current intrinsic content size of a view is, the **`UIView`** class includes the following property to return this value.

intrinsicContentSize—This property returns a **`CGSize`** value with the view's intrinsic content size.

The following example connects a label with an Outlet called **`mytitle`**, assigns a new text to the label, and prints the new values of its intrinsic content size on the console.

```
import UIKit

class ViewController: UIViewController {
   @IBOutlet weak var mytitle: UILabel!

   override func viewDidLoad() {
      super.viewDidLoad()
      mytitle.text = "Description: My New Label"

      let labelSize = mytitle.intrinsicContentSize
      print("New Width: \(labelSize.width)")
      print("New Height: \(labelSize.height)")
   }
}
```

Listing 6-1: *Reading the intrinsic content size*

Do It Yourself: Delete the elements in the scene. Add a label with a Top Space and a Leading Space constraint to define its position (see Figure 6-29). Create an Outlet for the label called **mytitle**. Update the **ViewController** class with the code in Listing 6-1 and run the application. The label's text is modified as soon as the app is executed, and the new values of its intrinsic content size are printed on the console.

Basic Multiple Views Constraints

Xcode provides an additional tool to add constraints that makes it easy to connect elements with each other. It requires the same procedure we use to create Outlets and Actions, but instead of control-dragging a line to the view controller we do it to another view, as shown below.

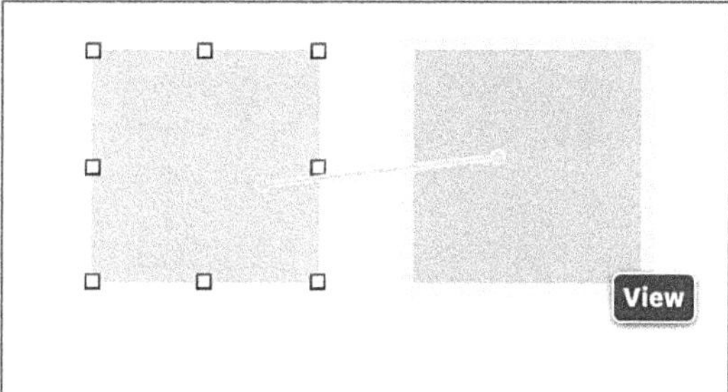

Figure 6-30: *Control-drag to add a constraint*

When the mouse button is released, Xcode shows a popup menu over the target to select the constraint we want to add.

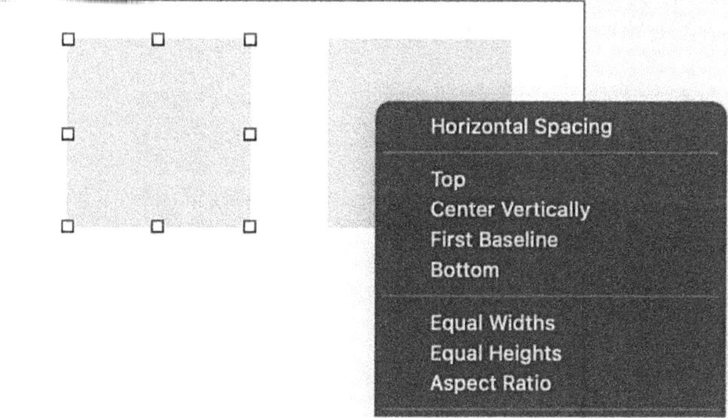

Figure 6-31: *Quick menu to add constraints*

The menu shows multiple options depending on what Xcode thinks we are trying to do. For example, when we control-drag a horizontal line from one view to another, the menu shows the Horizontal Spacing option at the top to let us add a Space constraint between the views.

Although this technique is useful to connect views together, we can also use it to add all the same constraints applied before. For example, by control-dragging a line from a view to its superview we can add a Top Space constraint.

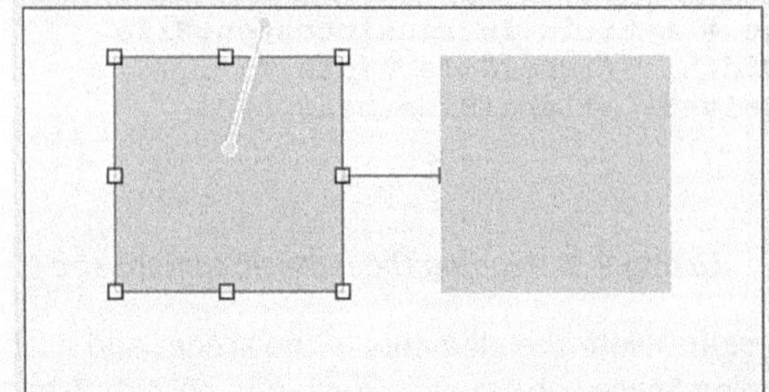

Figure 6-32: *Adding a Top Space constraint to the superview*

IMPORTANT: If you hold down the Command key or the Shift key when the menu is open, you can select multiple constraints. After all the constraints are selected, press the Return key to add them to the views.

When we drag and drop a line inside the same view, the menu displayed by Xcode includes options like Width, Height, and Aspect Ratio. Figure 6-33 shows the options available after a horizontal line is dragged from and into the view on the left.

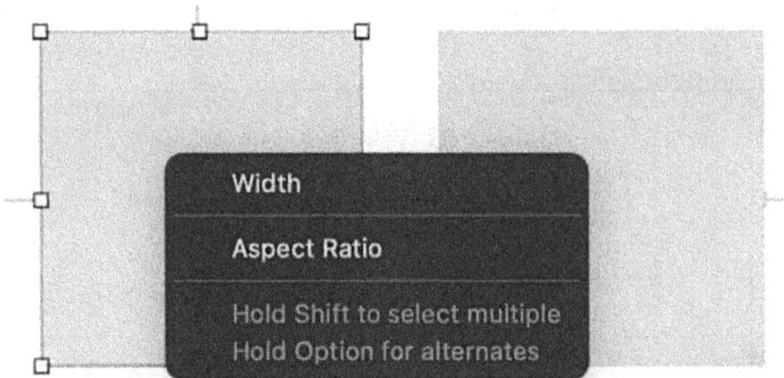

Figure 6-33: *Popup menu to add a Width constraint*

When working with two views connected with each other, we need to make sure that the constraints provide enough information for the system to position and size both views, but there are different options available, depending on what we want to achieve. For instance, we can define the width for only one view and let the system determine the width of the other. In the example of Figure 6-34, below, we pinned the views to the sides and with each other, but only added a Width constraint for the view on the left.

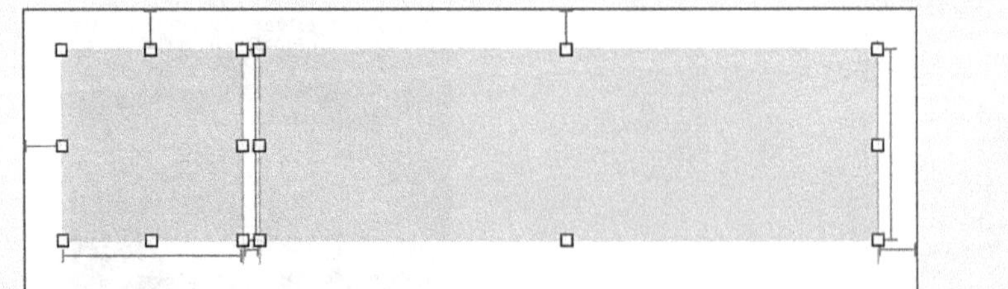

Figure 6-34: *Adapting multiple views to the space available*

Because we defined a fixed width for the left view only, that view is always of the same size while the view on the right expands or contracts to fill the space available. If we had defined both views with a fixed size, the system would not have been able to adapt the interface to the size of the screen and it would have returned an error message.

Do It Yourself: Delete the elements in the scene. Add two square views as in Figure 6-30. Control-drag from the left view to the right view to add a Space constraint (the option is called Horizontal Spacing). Control-drag from the left view to the top of the main view to add a Top Space constraint (the option is called Top Space to Safe Area). Repeat the process for the right view. Control-drag from the left view to the left side of the main view to create a Leading Space constraint (called Leading Space to Safe Area). Repeat the process with the view on the right to create a Trailing Space constraint (called Trailing Space to Safe Area). Control-drag a horizontal line inside the view on the left to create a Width constraint (Figure 6-29). Finally, control-drag a vertical line inside each view to create Height constraints.

Another problem that arises when working with multiple views is how to align them to a single point. A common solution involves the use of invisible views in between. The following example centers two labels in the main view using a third view as a separator.

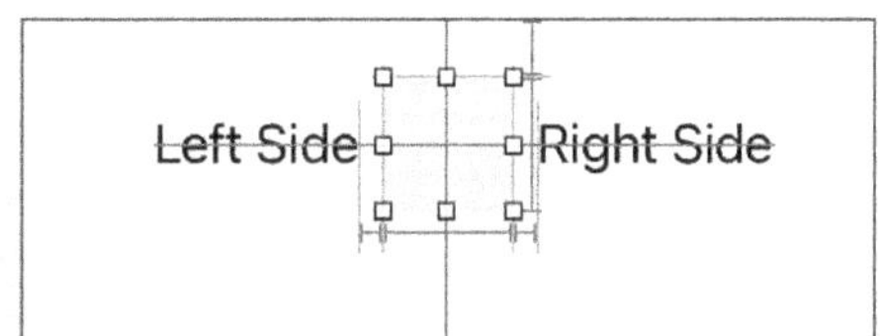

Figure 6-35: *Labels centered with an invisible view*

The supplementary view is centered in the main view, and it has a fixed width and height, and the labels are pinned to the sides of this view and centered with Vertical Center constraints. The result is that the labels are always oriented towards the center of the main view.

To hide the view, we can select the option Hidden from the Attributes Inspector panel or assign the value **`true`** to the view's **`isHidden`** property from code. This property makes the view visible during development, but it hides it when the app is executed.

Do It Yourself: Delete the elements in the scene. Add a square view at the center of the main view with a Top Space constraint, a Horizontal in Container constraint, and Width and Height constraints, as shown in Figure 6-35. Add two labels on each side of the view. Control-drag lines from each label to the view to add a Space constraint (Horizontal Spacing) and a Vertical Center constraint (Center Vertically). Select the view and mark the option Hidden from the Attributes Inspector panel. Change the orientation of the scene to see how the labels adapt to the space available.

Besides the Vertical Center constraint applied in the last example to center the labels vertically with the view, there are other alignment constraints available. These constraints are added from the Align menu and their application is straightforward, as shown below.

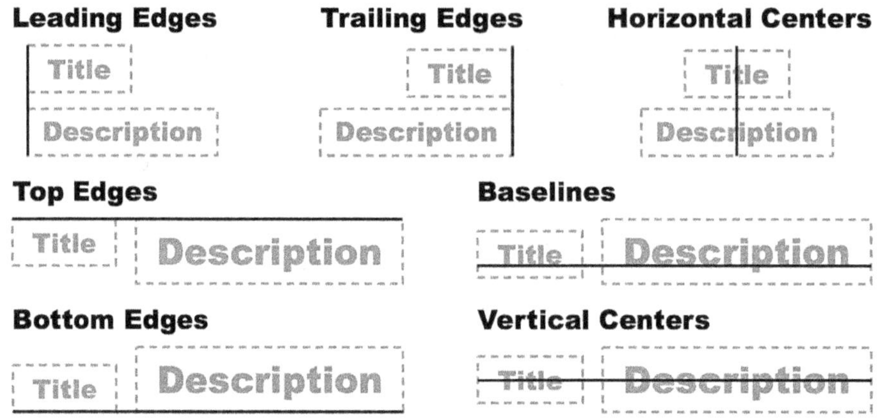

Figure 6-36: *Alignment constraints for multiple views*

These types of constraints provide the alternative to build more complex layouts. For example, they can help us determine the size of an element according to the space occupied by two or more elements. Figure 6-37, below, illustrates this situation.

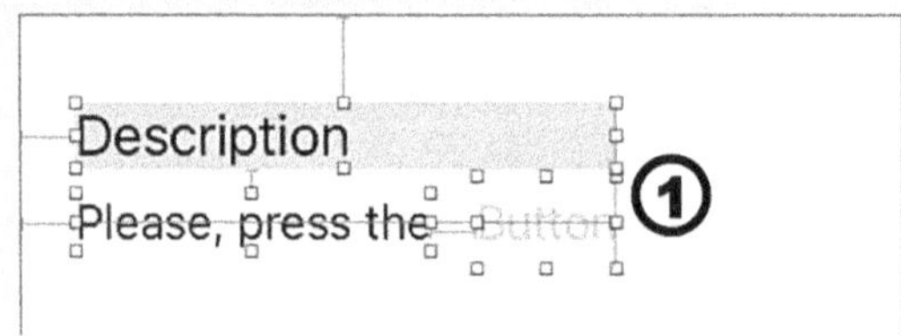

Figure 6-37: *Label's width determined by a Trailing Edge constraint*

This example includes two labels, "Description" and "Please, press the", and a Plain button with the title "Button". All the elements have Space constraints to the sides of the container and between them to establish their positions. Their sizes are determined by their intrinsic content size, except for the label at the top. The width of this label is determined by a Trailing Edge constraint connected to the button (called *Trailing* on the quick menu). Because of this, the label at the top always expands to reach the right side of the button (Figure 6-37, number 1).

Basic Relations and Priorities

The constraints we have defined so far are constant. This means that their values do not change, and the system must satisfy every one of them or return an error in case of failure. But some interfaces require more flexibility. Sometimes constraints need only an approximate value or they are not required all the time. For these situations, constraints include two more configuration values called *Relation* and *Priority*. The Relation determines the relationship between the constraint and its constant value, while the priority determines which constraint is more important. Important constraints are satisfied first and then the system tries to satisfy the rest as close as possible. The possible relations are the following:

- **Equal** determines that the constraint's value must be equal to the constant value. This is the relation by default.
- **Less Than or Equal** determines that the constraint's value can be equal or less than the constant value.
- **Greater Than or Equal** determines that the constraint's value can be equal or greater than the constant value.

On the other hand, the priorities are defined by an integer value between 1 and 1000. For common situations, Xcode declares three predefined states:

- **Low (250)** determines a low priority.
- **High (750)** determines a high priority.
- **Required (1000)** determines that the constraint is required.

There are multiple situations in which these values become useful. For example, we may have a label that we want to be of a specific size, but to change if new text is assigned to it. The following interface includes a label and a view. The label was defined with a Width constraint of 100, a Leading Space constraint that pins it to the left side of the main view, and a Vertical Center constraint that keeps it vertically centered with the view. The view has a Height constraint to define its height and Space constraints to define its position and the distance between its left side and the label, but its width is determined by the space available. The result is that the view expands or contracts, but the label has always the same width (100 points).

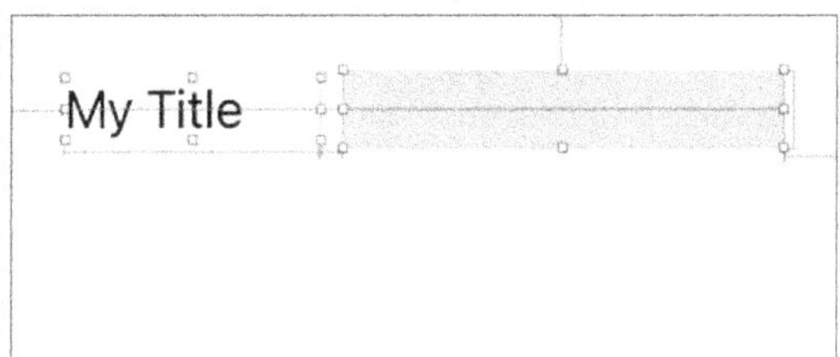

Figure 6-38: *Label with a fixed width of 100 points*

A problem arises when a text longer than 100 points is assigned to the label. Because the Width constraint determines a fixed size of 100 points, the new text is truncated, as shown below.

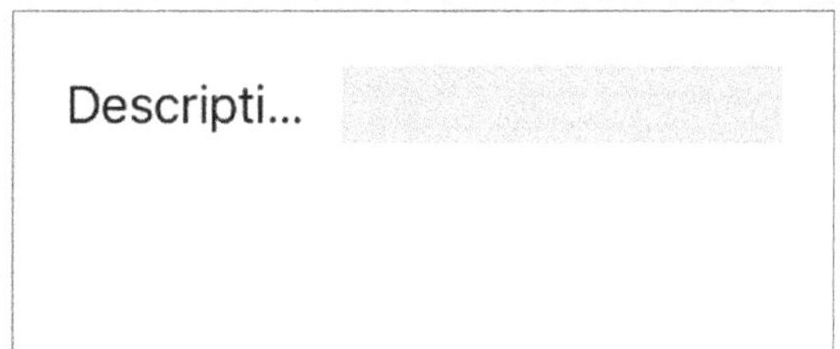

Figure 6-39: *The longer text is clipped*

What we want is for the label to stay at a size of 100 points but to grow when the space is not enough to show the full text. We need the value of the Width constraint to be Greater Than or Equal to 100 points. To change the relation, we must select the constraint, click the button on the right side of the Relation value, and select the option from the quick menu, as shown next.

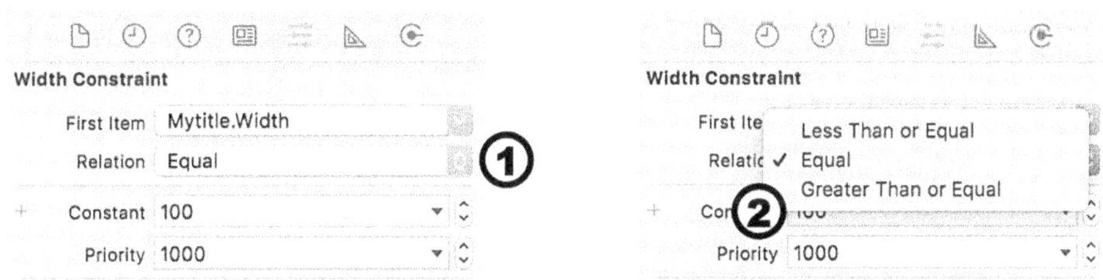

Figure 6-40: *New Relation for the constraint*

After the Greater Than or Equal relation is selected, the system tries to keep the label's width at 100 points whenever possible, but it lets the label expand if necessary. Now the text is not truncated when it is longer than 100 points and the view fills the remaining space.

Figure 6-41: The label expands to display the full text

Do It Yourself: Delete the elements in the scene. Add a label on the left side of the main view with the text "My Title" and a size of 24 points. Insert a view on the right with a gray background (Figure 6-38). Add a Leading Space constraint and a Trailing Space constraint to the label. Add a Width constraint to the label with a value of 100. Add a Top Space constraint and a Trailing Space constraint to the view. Add a Height constraint to the view to define its height. And lastly, add a Vertical Center constraint between the label and the view (Figure 6-38). Assign the text "Description Label" to the label from the Attributes Inspector panel (Figure 6-39). Select the label's Width constraint and change its relationship to Greater Than or Equal, as shown in Figure 6-40. You should see something like Figure 6-41.

There are times when two or more constraints must be constant, but they cannot be always satisfied. In cases like this, the system needs to know which one is more important. In the interface of Figure 6-42, below, two views are on the sides of a label. The views expand to occupy the space around the label, but they cannot reduce their sizes further than 50 points.

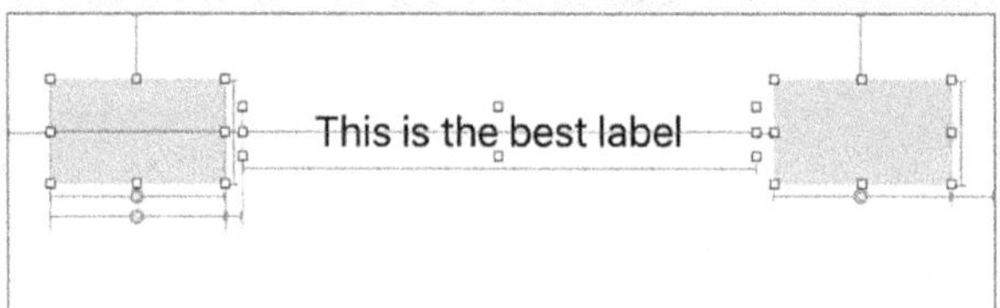

Figure 6-42: *Testing conflicting constraints*

In our example, the label was defined with a Width constraint equal to 250 points. The views are pinned to the main view and to the label with Space constraints and they also have a Width constraint but this time Greater Than or Equal to 50. The views are also connected to each other by an Equal Width constraint to make their widths equal. This means that the label will always have the same size, but the views will expand or contract to fill the space available. When there is plenty of space, the constraints work as expected. The views expand to fill the space between the label and the edge of the main view (Figure 6-42). A problem arises when there is not enough space to simultaneously satisfy all the Width constraints. The label must always be 250 points wide, and the views' width cannot be less than 50 points. The constraints are fine when there is enough space, but when there is no room for all the elements, they are displayed in red, as shown below.

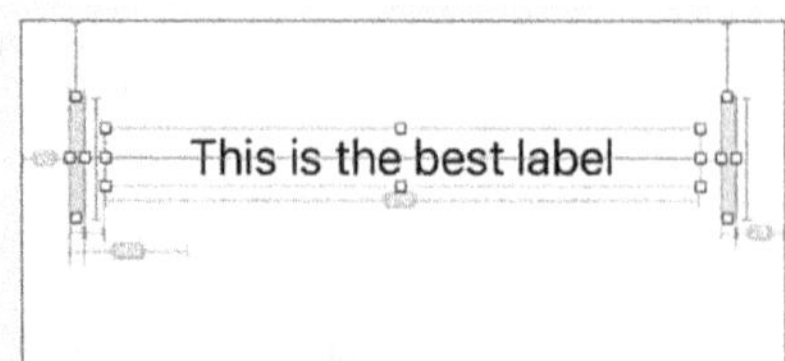

Figure 6-43: *Unable to satisfy constraints*

IMPORTANT: In these situations, the app will not crash but the system will print an error on the console with the message "Unable to simultaneously satisfy constraints" followed by a list of all the constraints that couldn't be satisfied.

By default, the Width constraint of the label is equally important than the Width constraints of the views and the system does not know what to do when there is not enough space to satisfy them all. The solution is simple. We must tell the system that it is important for us that the width of the views is never less than 50 points, but we do not care as much about the width of the label. This is achieved by reducing the priority of the label's width.

The constraints with a higher-priority value are satisfied first, and then the system tries to satisfy the rest as close as possible. Figure 6-44, below, shows what we see if we assign a priority of, for example, 750 to the label's Width constraint. Now the label's width is reduced to make room for the views and the constraint that is not satisfied is shown with a dashed line.

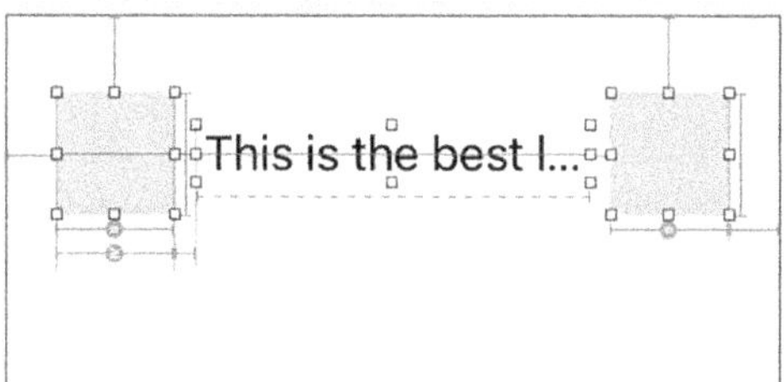

Figure 6-44: *Label's Width constraint with a lower priority*

IMPORTANT: Besides Constant, Relation, and Priority, there is an additional value available to configure constraints called *Multiplier*. The multiplier is multiplied by the value of the constant to get a proportional value. For example, when the Multiplier value of an Equal Width constraint is set to 2, the element will be twice as wide as the original. The system also uses the Multiplier to set the value for the Aspect Ratio constraint.

There are two more types of priorities that are useful for elements with intrinsic content size, such as labels, buttons, and images. They are called *Content Hugging* priority and *Content Compression Resistance* priority. Figure 6-45 shows the controls available on the Size Inspector panel to modify their values.

Content Hugging Priority
Horizontal 251
Vertical 251
Content Compression Resistance Priority
Horizontal 750
Vertical 750

Figure 6-45: *Options to modify content priorities*

The Content Hugging priority determines how much the element wants to stay of the size of its content and avoid expanding (it hugs its content). On the other hand, the Content Compression Resistance priority determines how much the element wants to stay of the size of its content and avoid contracting (resist compression). Figure 6-46, below, presents an example of two labels with a visible background to demonstrate how this works.

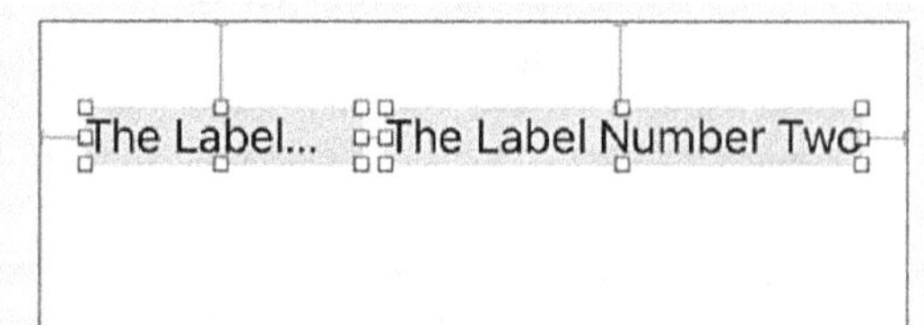

Figure 6-46: *Interface to test content priorities*

The labels are pinned to the main view and to each other with Space constraints. Their widths were not defined, so they will expand or contract according to the space available. Which label expands, and which one contracts is decided by the system considering their priorities. For this example, we have decided to assign to the label on the right higher values for its priorities. Its horizontal Content Hugging priority was declared as 750 and its Content Compression Resistance priority was declared as 1000. This will not let the label on the right expand or contract, so it is always the label on the left that adapts to the space available.

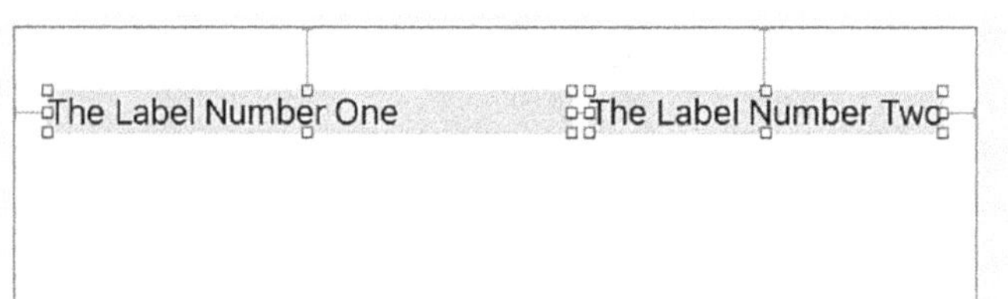

Figure 6-47: *Labels with different content priorities*

If, for example, we want the label on the right to contract when there is not enough space, we can change its Content Compression Resistance priority to a value smaller than the value of the label on the left. Figure 6-48 shows the result of assigning a value of 250 to the Content Compression Resistance priority to the label on the right and a value of 750 to the label on the left. The label on the left continues to expand when more space is available, but now it is the label on the right that contracts to make room when there is not enough space for both.

Figure 6-48: *Labels with different compression values*

IMPORTANT: The priorities can be set for both the horizontal and vertical axis. The horizontal values usually apply to elements like labels and buttons, while the vertical values are frequently used with Text Fields and images.

Basic Stack Views

Constraints were developed to affect single properties, such as a specific dimension of an element or the distance from one element to another. Because of this, designing an interface, even a simple one, requires an intricate network of constraints interconnecting the elements together. Fortunately, this elaborated system can be simplified by including our views inside other views that act as containers, which distributes the constraints in hierarchy levels.

In the following example, we have positioned a view at the top of the main view and added a label inside. The constraints for the view are connected to the main view (left), but the constraints for the label are connected to its container (right).

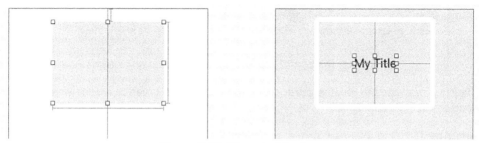

Figure 6-49: *Views inside views*

Figure 6-49 shows the constraints for the view and the label. The view has a Width and a Height constraint to define its size and a Top and a Horizontally alignment constraint to determine its position. The label, on the other hand, has Horizontal and Vertical alignment constraints to determine its position inside the view. Because of this distribution, the view may move on the screen according to the space available, but the label is always at the center of its container.

The width and the height of the container view were determined by a Width and Height constraints, but we can also let the content define the size of the container. The trick is to assign Space constraints to the sides and at the top and bottom of the content. The system calculates the width and height of the content from these constraints and expands or contracts the container to match the size of its content. In the following example, we assigned Leading, Trailing, Top and Bottom space constraints to the label. From these constraints and the label's intrinsic size, the system can calculate the size of the container view and therefore we no longer need the Width and Height constraint for the view (the size of the content determines the size of its container).

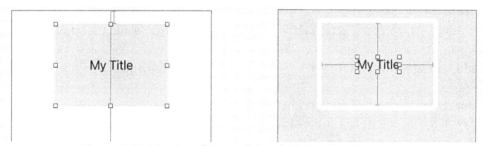

Figure 6-50: *The size of the container is defined by the content*

Using views as containers is a common practice. They create a hierarchy of constraints that simplify our work, but they still present a challenge. Every time we need to modify the interface, adding or removing elements from these containers, we still have to deal with their constraints. Considering that containers usually display their content in columns or rows, UIKit defines the **UIStackView** class to simplify this work. This class creates a special view that manages a horizontal or vertical stack of views and all their constraints. This means that using a Stack View to contain our views, we do not have to worry about their constraints anymore; all we need to do is to add or remove the views we want to include in the stack and the Stack View takes care of assigning all the necessary constraints to place them horizontally or vertically. The following is one of the initializers provided by the class to create these container views.

UIStackView(arrangedSubviews: [UIView]**)**—This initializer creates a Stack View that contains the views specified by the argument. The **arrangedSubviews** argument is an array with references to all the views we want to include in the stack.

As always, the Library offers the options to add them to our interface.

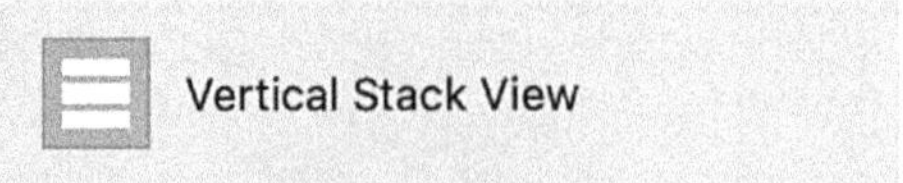

Figure 6-51: *Horizontal and Vertical Stack Views in the Library*

The class provides the following properties and methods to organize the views and the space available inside the Stack View.

arrangedSubviews—This property returns an array with references to the views managed by the Stack View.

axis—This property sets or returns a value that defines the Stack View's axis (the orientation in which the views are going to be laid out). It is an enumeration called **`Axis`** included in the **`UILayoutConstraint`** class. The values available are **`horizontal`** and **`vertical`**.

alignment—This property sets or returns a value that determines how the views inside the Stack View are going to be aligned. It is an enumeration called **`Alignment`** included in the **`UIStackView`** class. The values available are **`fill`**, **`leading`**, **`center`**, and **`trailing`**.

distribution—This property sets or returns a value that determines how the views are going to be distributed along the Stack View's axis. It is an enumeration called **`Distribution`** included in the **`UIStackView`** class. The values available are **`fill`** (the views are resized according to their index), **`fillEqually`** (the views are equally resized), **`fillProportionally`** (the views are resized proportionally according to their intrinsic content size), **`equalSpacing`** (the space between the views is distributed equally), and **`equalCentering`** (the space between the center of the views is equal).

spacing—This property sets or returns a **`CGFloat`** value that defines the space between views.

addArrangedSubview(UIView**)**—This method adds a view to the end of the Stack View.

insertArrangedSubview(UIView, **at:** Int**)**—This method adds a view to the Stack View at the index specified by the **at** argument.

removeArrangedSubview(UIView**)**—This method removes a view from the Stack View.

To include a Stack View in our interface, we just need to drag the option from the Library to the scene. The Stack View is represented by a white rectangle that we can pin to the main view, the Safe Area, or other views. Once the Stack View is in place, we can add all the subviews we want.

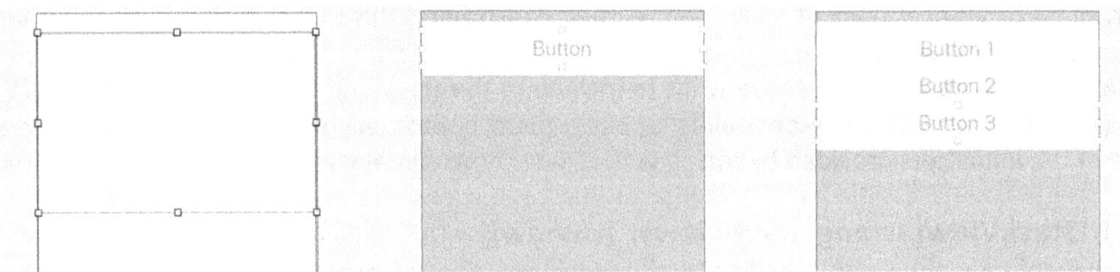

Figure 6-52: *Buttons inside a Stack View*

In this example, we pinned the Stack View with Space constraints to the top and the sides of the Safe Area and then dragged three buttons inside. Notice that we did not define the view's height because the system can determine the size from the size of the content. Every time we add or remove a view from the stack, the Stack View's height is updated (see Figure 6-52).

Once the content of the Stack View is defined, we can determine how the views are going to be aligned. By default, the **alignment** property is set to **fill**, which means that the views will expand to occupy all the space available, but we can also align them to the center, left or right by changing the Stack View's configuration, as shown below (we assigned a gray background to the buttons to be able to see the space occupied by their views).

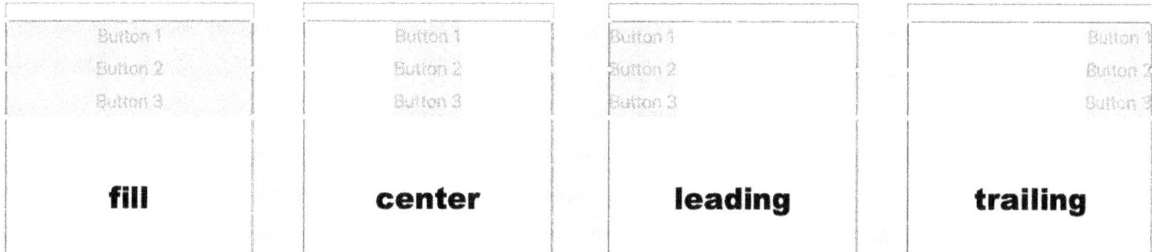

Figure 6-53: *Views inside a Stack View with different alignments*

The value of the property may be defined from code through an Outlet connected to the Stack View, or from the Attributes Inspector panel. To see the values, we must select the Stack View from the Document Outline panel or by holding down the Shift key and clicking the mouse's right button over the Stack View's content. The options include the values for alignment, distribution, and spacing. The latter generates a space between the views.

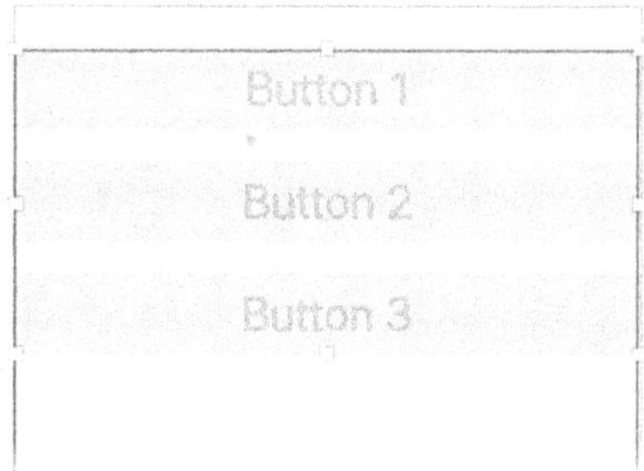

Figure 6-54: *Space between views*

In this example, we assigned a value of 15 to the **spacing** property. We can also change the distribution to define how the space between views is distributed. In the following example, we pinned the Stack View to the bottom of the Safe Area and apply some of the values of the **distribution** property to it (Fill, Fill Equally, and Equal Spacing, in that order).

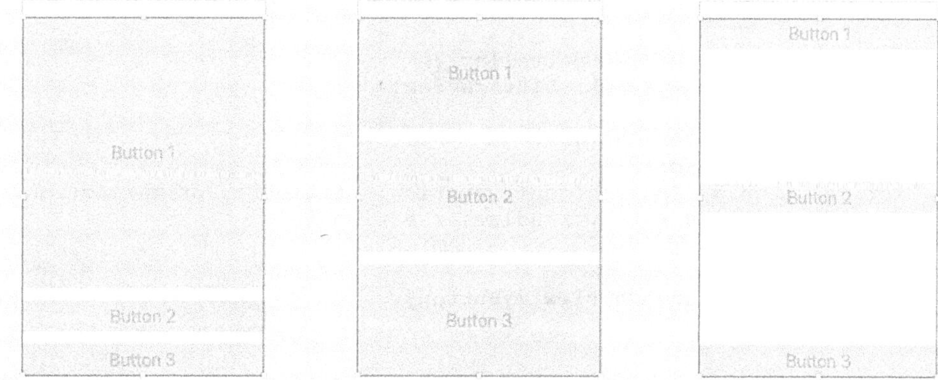

Figure 6-55: *Different distributions*

Stack Views can only manage one row or one column of views (horizontal or vertical), but they can be nested, providing an alternative for the creation of more complex arrangements. For example, we can add a horizontal Stack View at the top of our vertical Stack View to show two images side by side.

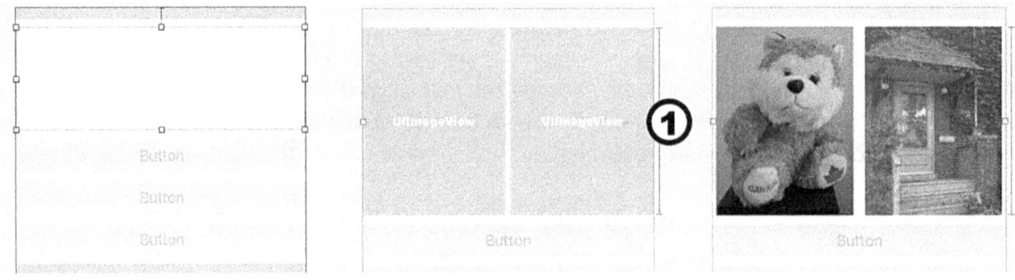

***Figure 6-56:** Nested Stack Views*

In Figure 6-56, we added a horizontal Stack View on top of the buttons with a **fillEqually** distribution and a spacing of 10, and then put two Image Views inside (Figure 6-56, center). The horizontal Stack View positions the Image Views side by side, with a width determined by the space available and a height determined by the height of the images. Therefore, to give the horizontal Stack View a specific height, we had to assign a Height constraint (Figure 6-56, number 1).

The advantage of using Stack Views to organize the interface is clear; we define the constraints to place the Stack View and the view takes care of assigning the constraints to its content. Depending on our design, we may use Stack Views to organize most of our interface or work with constraints, as we did so far. But Stack Views are also useful when we need to add to the interface a view from code, as in the following example.

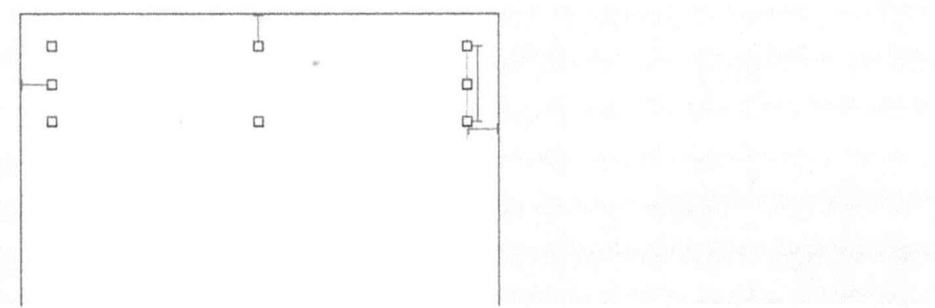

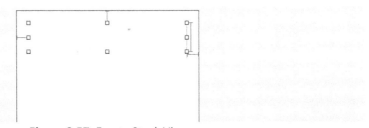

***Figure 6-57:** Empty Stack View*

The interface in Figure 6-57 contains an empty vertical Stack View with Top, Leading and Trailing constraints to define its position and width, and a Height constraint to define its height. Now we can incorporate any view we want to the interface by adding it as the content of this Stack View.

```
import UIKit

class ViewController: UIViewController {
   @IBOutlet weak var myStack: UIStackView!

   override func viewDidLoad() {
      super.viewDidLoad()
      let myButton = UIButton(configuration: .filled(), primaryAction:
UIAction(title: "Press Here", handler: { action in
         print("Hello")
      }))
      myStack.addArrangedSubview(myButton)
   }
}
```

***Listing 6-2:** Adding a view to the Stack View programmatically*

This view controller defines an Outlet called **myStack** to access the Stack View and then adds a **UIButton** to the stack with the **addArrangedSubview()** method. Because the button is the only view contained by the Stack View, it takes its position and size.

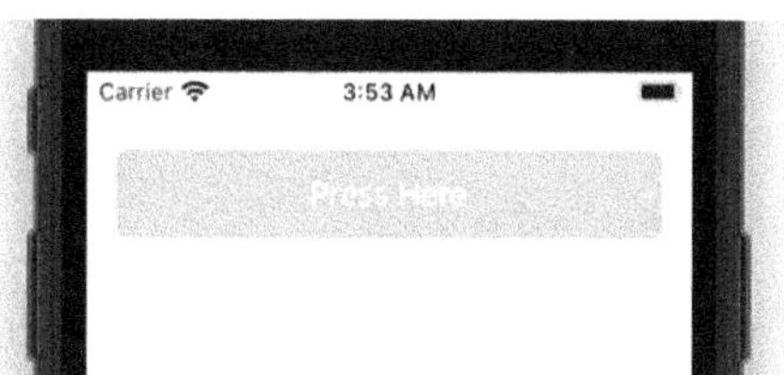

Figure 6-58: Button added to a Stack View from code

Medium Constraint Objects

The information for the constraints is stored as XML code in the Storyboard's file along with the rest of the information for the interface. Once the application is executed, the objects that represent the constraints are created. These objects are instances of the **NSLayoutConstraint** class. The objects defined in the Storyboard are automatically created from this class, but we can also use it to create our own constraints from code. The class includes the following initializer.

NSLayoutConstraint(item: Any, **attribute:** Attribute, **relatedBy:** Relation, **toItem:** Any?, **attribute:** Attribute, **multiplier:** CGFloat, **constant:** CGFloat**)**—This initializer creates a **NSLayoutConstraint** object from the information provided by the arguments. The **item** and **toItem** arguments are references to the elements affected by the constraint, the **attribute** argument specifies the type of constraint on each side of the connection, and the **relatedBy**, **multiplier**, and **constant** arguments provide the values.

This initializer takes all the necessary values to configure the constraint, including the views involved, the value of the Relation, Multiplier and Constant, and the attributes of the views that are going to be controlled by the constraint, such as the side, dimension, etc. The **NSLayoutConstraint** class includes the following enumerations to set these attributes and their relation.

Attribute—This enumeration defines the part of the object that should be used to set the constraint. The possible values are **left**, **right**, **top**, **bottom**, **leading**, **trailing**, **width**, **height**, **centerX**, **centerY**, **baseline**, and **notAnAttribute**.

Relation—This enumeration defines the relation between the first and the second attributes. The possible values are **lessThanOrEqual**, **equal**, and **greaterThanOrEqual**.

The **NSLayoutConstraint()** initializer returns **NSLayoutConstraint** objects but do not add the constraints to the view. The constraints are managed by methods of the **UIVIew** class.

constraints—This property returns an array with the **NSLayoutConstraint** objects that represent the constraints managed by the view.

addConstraint(NSLayoutConstraint**)**—This method adds a constraint to the view.

addConstraints([NSLayoutConstraint]**)**—This method adds an array of constraints to the view.

removeConstraint(NSLayoutConstraint**)**—This method removes from the view the constraint referenced by the argument.

removeConstraints([NSLayoutConstraint]**)**—This method removes from the view the constraints referenced by the argument.

The **NSLayoutConstraint** initializer takes one or two views, depending on the type of constraint, the attributes we want to associate to the constraint, and its values. The following example applies a Top Space, a Width, and a Horizontal in Container constraints to a label.

```
import UIKit

class ViewController: UIViewController {
   override func viewDidLoad() {
      super.viewDidLoad()

      let mylabel = UILabel(frame: CGRect.zero)
      mylabel.text = "Hello World"
      mylabel.textAlignment = .center
      mylabel.translatesAutoresizingMaskIntoConstraints = false
      view.addSubview(mylabel)

      let constraint1 = NSLayoutConstraint(item: mylabel,
attribute: .top, relatedBy: .equal, toItem: view, attribute: .top,
multiplier: 1, constant: 50)
      let constraint2 = NSLayoutConstraint(item: mylabel,
attribute: .width, relatedBy: .equal, toItem: nil,
attribute: .notAnAttribute, multiplier: 1, constant: 200)
      let constraint3 = NSLayoutConstraint(item: mylabel,
attribute: .centerX, relatedBy: .equal, toItem: view,
attribute: .centerX, multiplier: 1, constant: 0)
      view.addConstraints([constraint1, constraint2, constraint3])
   }
}
```

***Listing 6-3:** Laying out elements with constraints defined in code*

This example adds the label to the main view and then defines its constraints. The Top Space constraint is added by establishing a relation between the label's **top** attribute and the main view's **top** attribute. The Width constraint, on the other hand, only affects one element. In this case, the values for the second element and its attribute are not necessary, so they are declared as null with the values **nil** and **notAnAttribute**, respectively.

IMPORTANT: When elements are introduced to the interface without constraints, Xcode uses an old system called *Autoresizing* to position and size them. The information generated by this system is later applied to create constraints for the elements and present the interface on the screen. If the constraints are added from code though, the system doesn't know that there are constraints available and tries to create its own. To tell the system that the Autoresizing constraints are not necessary, you must set the view's **translatesAutoresizingMaskIntoConstraints** property to **false**. Assigning the value **false** to this property avoids the creation of automatic constraints and ensures that those you define in code will not conflict with those defined by the system. The property must be defined for every view added to the interface.

Constraints created from code may be added or removed. The following example takes advantage of the **removeConstraint()** method of the **UIVIew** class to change the position of a label when a button is pressed.

```
import UIKit

class ViewController: UIViewController {
   var mylabel: UILabel!
   var constraintLeft: NSLayoutConstraint!
   var constraintRight: NSLayoutConstraint!
   var constraintCenter: NSLayoutConstraint!
```

```
    override func viewDidLoad() {
        super.viewDidLoad()
        mylabel = UILabel(frame: CGRect.zero)
        mylabel.text = "Center"
        mylabel.translatesAutoresizingMaskIntoConstraints = false
        view.addSubview(mylabel)

        let constraintLabel = NSLayoutConstraint(item: mylabel!, attribute:
.top, relatedBy: .equal, toItem: view, attribute: .top, multiplier: 1,
constant: 50)
        view.addConstraint(constraintLabel)

        constraintLeft = NSLayoutConstraint(item: mylabel!,
attribute: .left, relatedBy: .equal, toItem: view, attribute: .left,
multiplier: 1, constant: 20)
        constraintRight = NSLayoutConstraint(item: mylabel!,
attribute: .right, relatedBy: .equal, toItem: view, attribute: .right,
multiplier: 1, constant: -20)
        constraintCenter = NSLayoutConstraint(item: mylabel!,
attribute: .centerX, relatedBy: .equal, toItem: view,
attribute: .centerX, multiplier: 1, constant: 0)
        view.addConstraint(constraintCenter)

        let button = UIButton(configuration: .filled(), primaryAction:
UIAction(title: "Move Label", handler: { [unowned self] action in
            self.moveLabel()
        }))
        button.translatesAutoresizingMaskIntoConstraints = false
        view.addSubview(button)

        let constraintButton1 = NSLayoutConstraint(item: button, attribute:
.top, relatedBy: .equal, toItem: mylabel, attribute: .bottom, multiplier:
1, constant: 30)
        let constraintButton2 = NSLayoutConstraint(item: button, attribute:
.centerX, relatedBy: .equal, toItem: view, attribute: .centerX,
multiplier: 1, constant: 0)
        view.addConstraints([constraintButton1, constraintButton2])
    }
    func moveLabel() {
        let text = mylabel.text!
        switch text {
            case "Right":
            view.removeConstraint(constraintRight)
            view.addConstraint(constraintLeft)
            mylabel.text = "Left"
        case "Left":
            view.removeConstraint(constraintLeft)
            view.addConstraint(constraintCenter)
            mylabel.text = "Center"
        case "Center":
            view.removeConstraint(constraintCenter)
            view.addConstraint(constraintRight)
            mylabel.text = "Right"
        default:
            break
        }
    }
}
```

Listing 6-4: *Removing constraints*

The code in Listing 6-4 creates a label and a button. The button must always be at the center of the screen, so we added a permanent Horizontal in Container constraint setting the **centerX** attributes of the button and the main view as **equal**, but the label moves every time the button is pressed. To achieve this, we have defined three properties with the necessary constraints: **constraintLeft**, **constraintRight**, and **constraintCenter**. After the constraints for the button are defined, these three constraints are also defined and the **constraintCenter** constraint is added to the label to establish its initial position at the center. Because of this, the initial interface positions both elements at the center of the screen. But this changes when the user presses the button and the **moveLabel()** method is executed. This method checks the current text assigned to the label and compares it to the strings "Right", "Left", and "Center" to establish the current position. Then, it removes and adds the constraints to move the label to the next place. For example, if the current value is "Right", it means that the label is at the right side of the main view, so we must move it to the left. The code removes the **constraintRight** constraint, adds the **constraintLeft** constraint, and changes the label's text to "Left". Figure 6-59 shows the three different configurations we see on the screen after the button is pressed.

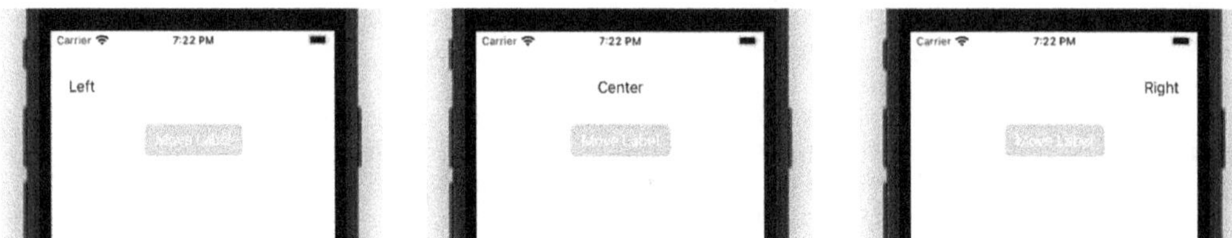

Figure 6-59: *Different constraints for a label*

Besides adding and deleting constraints, we can also edit their values. For this purpose, the **NSLayoutConstraint** class offers the following properties.

firstItem—This property sets or returns a reference to the first element associated with the constraint. It is an optional of type **AnyObject**.

secondItem—This property sets or returns a reference to the second element associated with the constraint. It is an optional of type **AnyObject**.

firstAttribute—This property sets or returns the value of the first element's attribute. It is an **NSLayoutConstraint.Attribute** enumeration value.

secondAttribute—This property sets or returns the value of the second element's attribute. It is an **NSLayoutConstraint.Attribute** enumeration value.

priority—This property sets or returns the constraint's priority value. It is a structure of type **UILayoutPriority** with the properties **required**, **defaultHigh**, **defaultLow**, and **fittingSizeLevel**.

relation—This property sets or returns the constraint's relation value. It is an **NSLayoutConstraint.Relation** enumeration value.

multiplier—This property sets or returns the multiplier value. It is a **CGFloat** value.

constant—This property sets or returns the constant value. It is a **CGFloat** value.

The following example creates a button at the center of the screen that expands or contracts when it is pressed. The first group of constraints determine its vertical position (50), horizontal position (**centerX**), and height (50), while the last constraint determines its width. The value of the Width constraint is changed by the **expandButton()** method every time the button is pressed.

```
import UIKit

class ViewController: UIViewController {
   var button: UIButton!
   var buttonTitle = "Expand"
   var constraintWidth: NSLayoutConstraint!
```

```
    override func viewDidLoad() {
        super.viewDidLoad()
        button = UIButton(configuration: .filled(), primaryAction:
UIAction(handler: { [unowned self] action in
            self.expandButton()
        }))
        button.configurationUpdateHandler = { [unowned self] button in
            var config = button.configuration
            config?.title = buttonTitle
            button.configuration = config
        }
        button.translatesAutoresizingMaskIntoConstraints = false
        view.addSubview(button)

        let constraintButton1 = NSLayoutConstraint(item: button!,
attribute: .top, relatedBy: .equal, toItem: view, attribute: .top,
multiplier: 1, constant: 50)
        let constraintButton2 = NSLayoutConstraint(item: button!,
attribute: .height, relatedBy: .equal, toItem: nil,
attribute: .notAnAttribute, multiplier: 1, constant: 50)
        let constraintButton3 = NSLayoutConstraint(item: button!,
attribute: .centerX, relatedBy: .equal, toItem: view,
attribute: .centerX, multiplier: 1, constant: 0)
        view.addConstraints([constraintButton1, constraintButton2,
constraintButton3])

        constraintWidth = NSLayoutConstraint(item: button!,
attribute: .width, relatedBy: .equal, toItem: nil,
attribute: .notAnAttribute, multiplier: 1, constant: 150)
        view.addConstraint(constraintWidth)
    }
    func expandButton() {
        if constraintWidth.constant < 280 {
            buttonTitle = "Contract"
            constraintWidth.constant = 280
        } else {
            buttonTitle = "Expand"
            constraintWidth.constant = 150
        }
    }
}
```

***Listing 6-5:** Updating constraints*

IMPORTANT: We cannot only modify the constraints added from code but also those created in the Storyboard. All we need to do is to control-drag a line from the constraint to the view controller to create an Outlet. This Outlet is like any other we have created so far, but instead of referencing a view it references the **`NSLayoutConstraint`** object that represents the constraint.

Creating one constraint at a time with **`NSLayoutConstraint`** objects takes time and requires several lines of code. Apple provides two solutions to this problem: a visual format and layout anchors. The latter is the most popular nowadays because it declares the constraints using properties. The following are the properties defined in the **`UIView`** class for this purpose.

topAnchor—This property returns an object that represents the view's top edge.

bottomAnchor—This property returns an object that represents the view's bottom edge.

leadingAnchor—This property returns an object that represents the view's leading edge.

trailingAnchor—This property returns an object that represents the view's trailing edge.

widthAnchor—This property returns an object that represents the view's width.

heightAnchor—This property returns an object that represents the view's height.

centerXAnchor—This property returns an object that represents the view's horizontal center.

centerYAnchor—This property returns an object that represents the view's vertical center.

leftAnchor—This property returns an object that represents the view's left edge.

rightAnchor—This property returns an object that represents the view's right edge.

firstBaselineAnchor—This property returns an object that represents the baseline of the top line of text in the view.

lastBaselineAnchor—This property returns an object that represents the baseline of the last line of text in the view.

These properties contain objects defined by subclasses of the **NSLayoutAnchor** class called **NSLayoutXAxisAnchor**, **NSLayoutYAxisAnchor**, and **NSLayoutDimension**. The following are the most frequently used methods included in these classes to add the constraints.

constraint(equalTo: NSLayoutAnchor, **constant:** CGFloat**)**—This method returns an **NSLayoutConstraint** object with a constraint that defines one anchor as equal to the other anchor, and with an offset determined by the **constant** argument.

constraint(greaterThanOrEqualTo: NSLayoutAnchor, **constant:** CGFloat**)**—This method returns an **NSLayoutConstraint** object with a constraint that defines one anchor as greater than or equal to the other anchor, and with an offset determined by the **constant** argument.

constraint(lessThanOrEqualTo: NSLayoutAnchor, **constant:** CGFloat**)**—This method returns an **NSLayoutConstraint** object with a constraint that defines one anchor as less than or equal to the other anchor, and with an offset determined by the **constant** argument.

constraint(equalTo: NSLayoutDimension, **multiplier:** CGFloat**)**—This method returns an **NSLayoutConstraint** object with a constraint that defines the size attribute of the view equal to the specified anchor multiplied by the value of the **multiplier** argument (used to defined equal widths and heights or to create Aspect Ratio constraints).

constraint(equalToConstant: CGFloat**)**—This method returns an **NSLayout-Constraint** object with a constraint that defines the size attribute of the view equal to the value of the **equalToConstant** argument.

constraint(greaterThanOrEqualToConstant: CGFloat**)**—This method returns an **NSLayoutConstraint** object with a constraint that defines the size attribute of the view greater than or equal to the value of the **greaterThanOrEqualToConstant** argument.

constraint(lessThanOrEqualToConstant: CGFloat**)**—This method returns an **NSLayoutConstraint** object with a constraint that defines the size attribute of the view less than or equal to the value of the **lessThanOrEqualToConstant** argument.

Depending on the types of constraints we need, we may use one method or another. For example, the following view controller creates an empty view and implements the **constraint(equalTo:, constant:)** method to add Space constraints to every side.

```swift
import UIKit

class ViewController: UIViewController {
   override func viewDidLoad() {
      super.viewDidLoad()
      let grayView = UIView(frame: CGRect.zero)
      grayView.backgroundColor = UIColor.systemGray4
      grayView.translatesAutoresizingMaskIntoConstraints = false
      view.addSubview(grayView)

      let constraint1 = grayView.leadingAnchor.constraint(equalTo:
view.leadingAnchor, constant: 0)
      let constraint2 = grayView.trailingAnchor.constraint(equalTo:
view.trailingAnchor, constant: 0)
      let constraint3 = grayView.topAnchor.constraint(equalTo:
view.topAnchor, constant: 0)
      let constraint4 = grayView.bottomAnchor.constraint(equalTo:
view.bottomAnchor, constant: 0)
      view.addConstraints([constraint1, constraint2, constraint3,
constraint4])
   }
}
```

Listing 6-6: *Attaching constraints to the view's anchors*

The constraints in this example are created from the Leading anchor of our view to the Leading anchor of the main view. The same for the Trailing anchor, the Top anchor and the Bottom anchor. Finally, the constraints are added to the view with the **addConstraints()** method, as we did before. Because we use a constant of value 0, the view expands to fill the main view's area.

Figure 6-60: *View pinned from its anchors*

The **NSLayoutConstraint** class offers a Boolean property called **isActive** to activate or the deactivate a constraint. Using this property, we can tell the system which constraints are going to affect the layout, and because the process of activating or deactivating a constraint automatically calls the **addConstraint()** and **removeConstraint()** methods, we don't have to call these methods anymore, as shown in the following example.

```swift
import UIKit

class ViewController: UIViewController {
   override func viewDidLoad() {
      super.viewDidLoad()

      let grayView = UIView(frame: CGRect.zero)
      grayView.backgroundColor = UIColor.systemGray4
      grayView.translatesAutoresizingMaskIntoConstraints = false
      view.addSubview(grayView)
```

```
        grayView.centerXAnchor.constraint(equalTo: view.centerXAnchor,
constant: 0).isActive = true
        grayView.centerYAnchor.constraint(equalTo: view.centerYAnchor,
constant: 0).isActive = true
        grayView.widthAnchor.constraint(equalToConstant: 125).isActive =
true
        grayView.heightAnchor.constraint(equalToConstant: 125).isActive =
true
    }
}
```

Listing 6-7: Adding constraints with the `isActive` *property*

In this example, we assign the value **`true`** to the **`isActive`** property of each constraint using dot notation. The **`NSLayoutConstraint`** object is created first with the **`constraint()`** method and then the value **`true`** is assigned to the constraint's property, activating the constraint. The code creates two Alignment constraints to position a view at the center of the main view and Width and Height constraints to determine its size. The result is shown below.

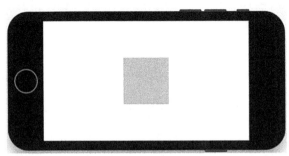

Figure 6-61: Constraints activated with the `isActive` *property*

The constraints not only can be attached to the anchors of the views but also to the anchors of layout guides like the Safe Area. The following are some of the properties provided by the **`UIView`** class to access these layout guides.

safeAreaLayoutGuide—This property returns a **`UILayoutGuide`** object with anchor properties we can use to define constraints between the views and the Safe Area.

readableContentGuide—This property returns a **`UILayoutGuide`** object with anchor properties we can use to define constraints between the views and the readable area of their superviews (the area in which the lines of text are short enough to be readable).

keyboardLayoutGuide—This property returns a **`UIKeyboardLayoutGuide`** object (a subclass of **`UILayoutGuide`**) with anchor properties we can use to define constraints between the views and the area occupied by the keyboard.

Layout guide objects include the same properties as **`UIView`** objects to define the anchors and therefore we can use them to create the constraints. The following example creates constraints between a view and the Safe Area.

```
import UIKit

class ViewController: UIViewController {
    override func viewDidLoad() {
        super.viewDidLoad()
        let grayView = UIView(frame: CGRect.zero)
        grayView.backgroundColor = UIColor.systemGray4
        grayView.translatesAutoresizingMaskIntoConstraints = false
        view.addSubview(grayView)
```

```
        let safeGuide = view.safeAreaLayoutGuide
        grayView.leadingAnchor.constraint(equalTo: safeGuide.leadingAnchor,
constant: 0).isActive = true
        grayView.trailingAnchor.constraint(equalTo:
safeGuide.trailingAnchor, constant: 0).isActive = true
        grayView.topAnchor.constraint(equalTo: safeGuide.topAnchor,
constant: 0).isActive = true
        grayView.bottomAnchor.constraint(equalTo: safeGuide.bottomAnchor,
constant: 0).isActive = true
    }
}
```

Listing 6-8: *Attaching constraints to the Safe Area's Layout Guide*

The code in Listing 6-8 defines a constant called **safeGuide** to store a reference to the Safe Area's Layout Guide, and then defines the constraints between the view's anchors and the anchors of the guide. Because of this, the view does not overlap the status bar.

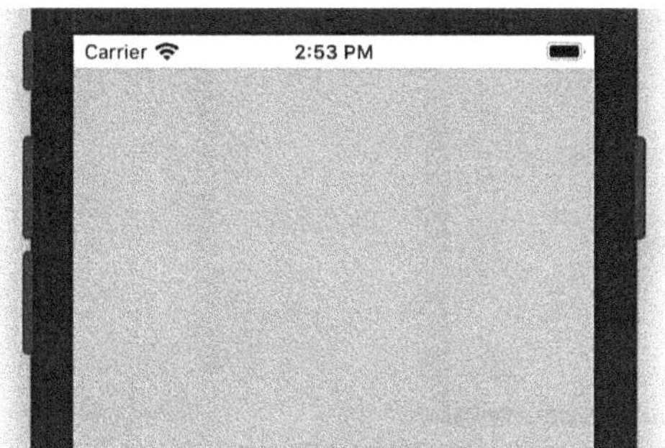

Figure 6-62: *Constraints between a view and the Safe Area's Layout Guide*

A very useful layout guide is the one provided for the keyboard. The **UIKeyboardLayoutGuide** class provides information about the space occupied by the keyboard. With this guide, we can prevent the interface from being covered or hidden behind the keyboard. For instance, if we have a Text View, we want to modify the view's height to make sure the user can always see what is typing.

```
import UIKit

class ViewController: UIViewController {
    override func viewDidLoad() {
        super.viewDidLoad()
        let commentsView = UITextView(frame: CGRect.zero)
        commentsView.backgroundColor = UIColor.systemGray5
        commentsView.font = UIFont.preferredFont(forTextStyle: .body)
        commentsView.translatesAutoresizingMaskIntoConstraints = false
        view.addSubview(commentsView)

        let keyboardGuide = view.keyboardLayoutGuide
        commentsView.leadingAnchor.constraint(equalTo: view.leadingAnchor,
constant: 16).isActive = true
        commentsView.trailingAnchor.constraint(equalTo:
view.trailingAnchor, constant: -16).isActive = true
        commentsView.topAnchor.constraint(equalTo: view.topAnchor,
constant: 20).isActive = true
        commentsView.bottomAnchor.constraint(equalTo:
keyboardGuide.topAnchor, constant: -20).isActive = true
    }
```

```
    override func touchesBegan(_ touches: Set<UITouch>, with event: UIEvent?) {
        view.endEditing(true)
    }
}
```

Listing 6-9: Adapting the interface to make room for the keyboard

This view controller creates a **UITextView** object and adds it to the main view. The Leading, Trailing, and Top constraints are attached to the main view, but the view's bottom is connected to the keyboard's Top anchor with a space of 20 points. This means that the bottom of the Text View is always going to be 20 points from the top of the keyboard, no matter if the keyboard is open or not.

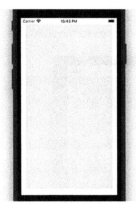

Figure 6-63: *Interface adapted to the keyboard*

IMPORTANT: Notice that some constants were defined with negative values. This is because of the order of the views associated with the constraints. For instance, if we assign a Trailing constraint from the Text View to the main view, the value must be negative for the space to be on the left side of the view's trailing side, but that changes if instead we assign the constraint from the main view to the Text View.

Medium Updating Frames

Usually, the views are updated automatically in every drawing cycle (an automatic cycle that updates the screen several times per second), but sometimes we may need to get the current position or size of an element before this process takes place (e.g., read the **frame** property of a view modified by a constraint). To make sure that we get the right values, we can ask the system to update the interface. The **UIView** class includes the following methods for this purpose.

setNeedsLayout()—This method informs the system that the current layout is invalid and it should be updated in the next drawing cycle.

layoutIfNeeded()—This method asks the system to update the layout.

These methods must be called on the **view** property of the view controller one after another to update the main view and its content. First we call the **setNeedsLayout()** method to tell the system that the current layout is invalid and then the **layoutIfNeeded()** method to force it to refresh the interface. After the methods are executed, we can read any of the element's properties, such as **frame**, and we will get values that reflect what the user sees on the screen. The **UIView** class also includes the following methods to update the constraints.

setNeedsUpdateConstraints()—This method informs the system that the current constraints need an update.

updateConstraintsIfNeeded()—This method asks the system to update the constraints.

These methods work the same way than the ones for the layout. We must call the **`setNeedsUpdateConstraints()`** method first to tell the system that the constraints need update, and then the **`updateConstraintsIfNeeded()`** method to ask the system to perform the update.

Basic 6.3 Size Classes

The way Auto Layout organizes the interface is by telling the system how every element should be laid out. In practice, this is only useful when the space available preserves its original proportions. Things change when we compare devices with very different screens, such as an iPhone and an iPad, or the same device in different orientations. In these disparate conditions, the interface must adapt in a way Auto Layout cannot handle. To get the design we want in every possible configuration, the values of the elements and constraints must be drastically modified, and some of them even removed or added. To know when to perform these changes, the system classifies the space available based on the magnitude of the horizontal and vertical dimensions. The size is called *Regular* if it is big enough to fit a regular interface or *Compact* otherwise. This classification is, of course, arbitrary. Apple's developers decided what should be considered Compact and what Regular based on the screen's sizes of the devices currently available in the market.

The Compact and Regular values conform a unit of measurement called *Size Classes* (this has nothing to do with the classes defined to create objects). Because of the rectangular shape of the screen, the interface is defined by two Size Classes, one for the horizontal space and another for the vertical space. For example, the Size Classes defining the space available for iPhones in portrait mode are Compact for their horizontal space and Regular for their vertical space because in this orientation the screen's width is constrained but its height has enough space to display a normal user interface. Every device is assigned different Size Classes, depending on the size of their screens and orientations.

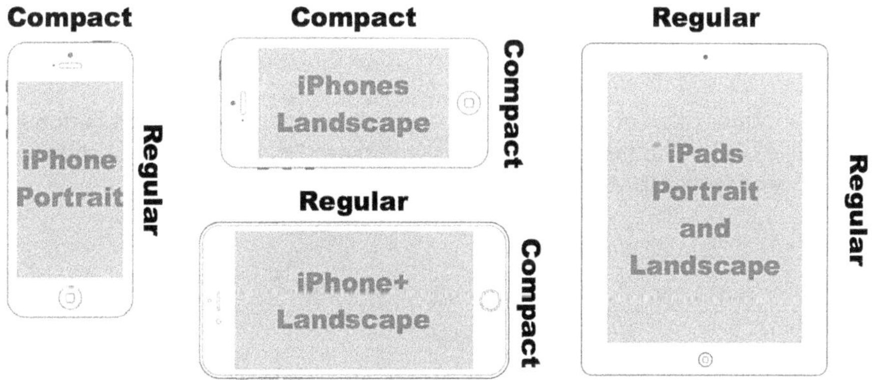

Figure 6-64: *Size Classes assigned to mobile devices*

The combinations presented in Figure 6-64 are the only four possible combinations of Size Classes: Compact width and Regular height, Compact width and Compact height, Regular width and Compact height, and Regular width and Regular height. By selecting the appropriate Size Classes for the width and height, it is possible to adapt our interface to any space available.

Basic Adapting Properties

Xcode offers tools to introduce modifications for specific Size Classes. For example, we can add a label to an interface for the Size Classes Compact width and Regular height and the label will be shown only on iPhones in portrait mode or on a narrow split view in iPads. With these tools, we cannot only add or remove elements but also modify some properties and add, remove, or modify constraints for any combination of Size Classes we want.

The simplest change we can perform for a Size Class is to modify the value of a property. Some attributes like the background color or the font size can be changed from the Attributes Inspector panel. When an element on the interface is selected, this panel shows the values of its properties. The properties that can be adapted to a specific Size Class include a + button on the side. Figure 6-65, below, shows the button available for the Font when a label is selected.

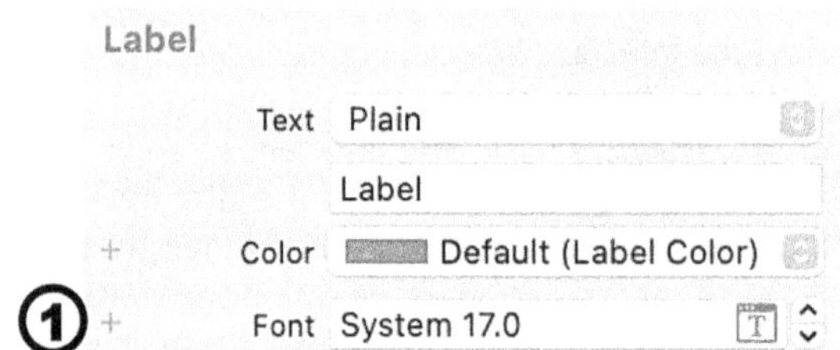

Figure 6-65: *Adapting a font from the Attributes Inspector panel*

When we click on the + button to add a font for a Size Class, Xcode shows a popup menu to select the combination of Size Classes we want to associate with the font, along with other values we will introduce later.

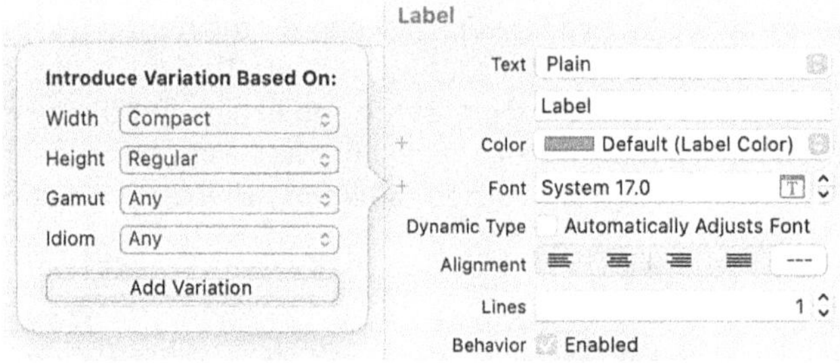

Figure 6-66: *Menu to select a combination of Size Classes*

After the combination of Size Classes is selected and the Add Variation button is pressed, a new Font field is added to the Attributes Inspector panel. Figure 6-67, below, shows what we see when a font is added for the Size Classes Compact width and Regular height.

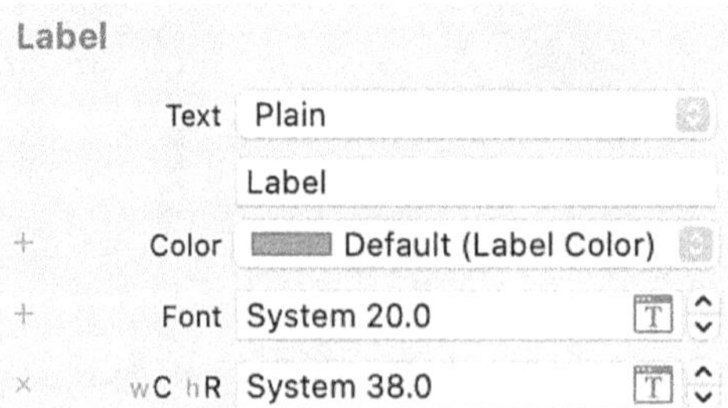

Figure 6-67: *New font size for a label in Compact width and Regular height*

In this example, we have defined the font size for the label as 38 points when the interface is presented on iPhones in portrait mode (Compact width and Regular height). The label is displayed with a size of 38 points in this configuration and with a size of 20 points anywhere else.

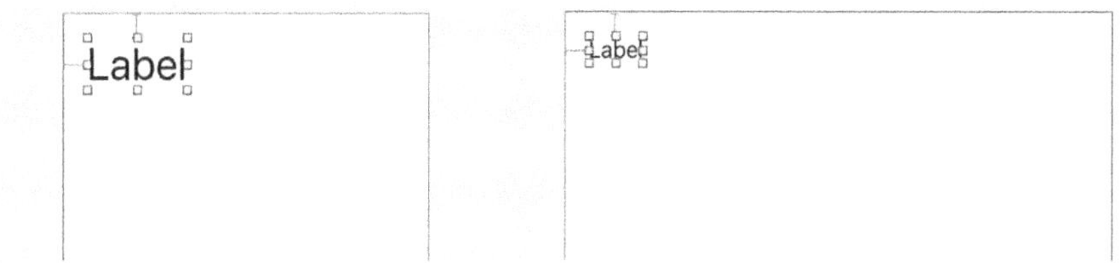

Figure 6-68: *Different font size in portrait and landscape*

In this example, we have selected a combination of Size Classes to affect a very specific configuration, but the system also contemplates the possibility of adapting the interface for the Size Class corresponding to only one dimension (horizontal or vertical) without considering the other. The option is called *Any* and it is available from the Size Classes menu. For example, we can select the Size Classes Regular width and Any height to affect only iPads and large iPhones in landscape orientation.

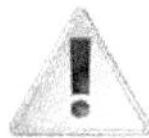

IMPORTANT: The configuration by default is for the Size Classes Any width and Any height, which means it will be applied to any configuration of Size Classes unless another value has been provided for a specific Size Class.

Basic Adapting Constraints

There are three things we can do with constraints: modify their values, deactivate them, and add new ones. The values are not modified; instead, new values are added for a specific configuration. For example, if we want our label to be 50 points from the top when the interface is presented in iPhones in portrait orientation, we can select the label's Top Space constraint and add a new value for Compact width and Regular height from the Attributes Inspector panel (Figure 6-69, number 1).

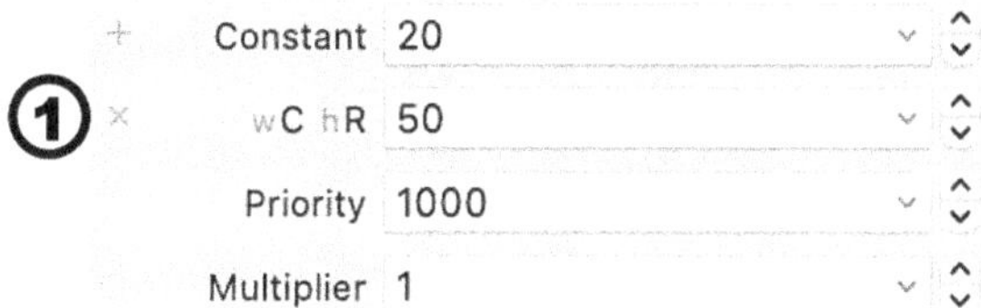

Figure 6-69: *Different value for the constraint in Compact width and Regular height*

IMPORTANT: The Attributes Inspector panel shows an **x** button on the left side of every additional value to remove it. When a value is removed, the constraint takes back the value defined for the Size Classes Any width and Any height.

Modifying values of constraints for specific Size Classes is the same we have done so far with Auto Layout. To perform more drastic changes, we must remove and add constraints. The constraints are not really removed but rather uninstalled. We install a constraint for specific Size Classes and uninstall it for others. For example, if we want our label to be pinned to the left side of the main view in iPhones in portrait mode but to appear at the center of the screen when the device is in landscape mode, we must uninstall the Leading Space constraint for Compact width and Compact height and install a Horizontally in Container constraint.

Constraints are uninstalled from the Attributes Inspector panel. The following figure shows this panel after the Leading Space constraint assigned to the label in our example is selected.

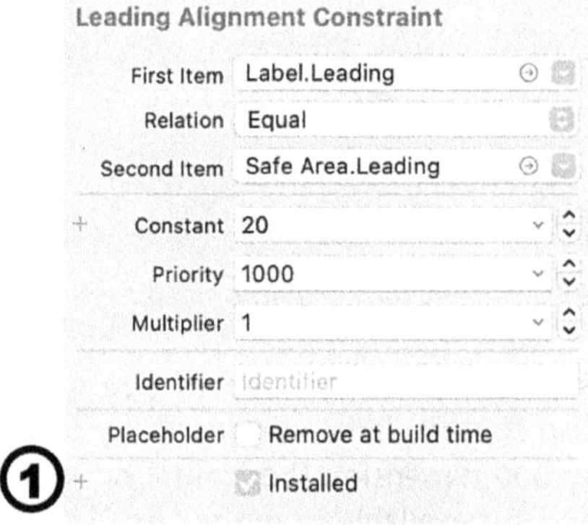

Figure 6-70: Installed option

The option to uninstall the selected constraint is shown at the bottom of the panel (Figure 6-70, number 1). The option available by default corresponds to Any width and Any height, which means that the constraint is applied in any combination of Size Classes. To uninstall this constraint, we first add the option for a specific configuration clicking the + button on the left. The following example adds a configuration for Compact width and Compact height.

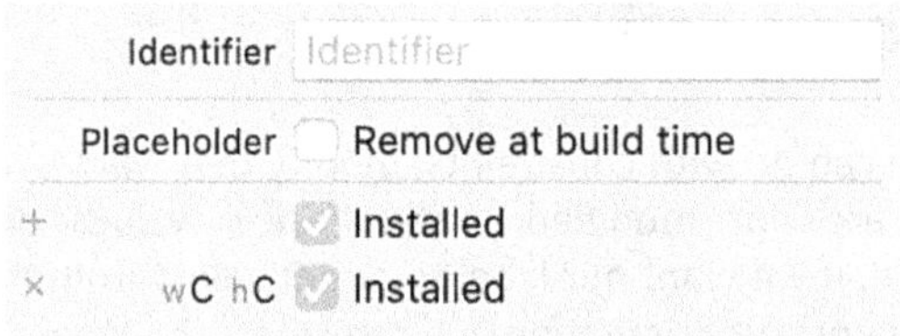

Figure 6-71: *Adding the Installed option for a specific configuration*

Once the new option is added, we must uninstall the constraint by clicking the checked button.

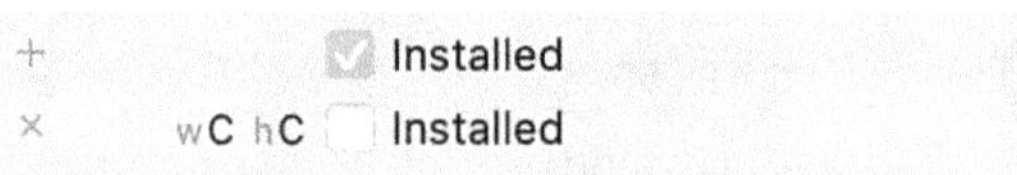

Figure 6-72: *Uninstalling a constraint for Compact width and Compact height*

The constraint still exists, but it is not functional in Compact width and Compact height. This means that in that configuration (small iPhones in landscape mode), the label now needs new constraints. The new constraints are added as we did before from the Auto Layout buttons, but we must install them only for Compact width and Compact height to affect the label only on that configuration. After adding a Horizontally in Container constraint to center the label, we add the Installed option for Compact width and Compact height and uninstall the constraint for all the rest of the configurations, as shown in Figure 6-73.

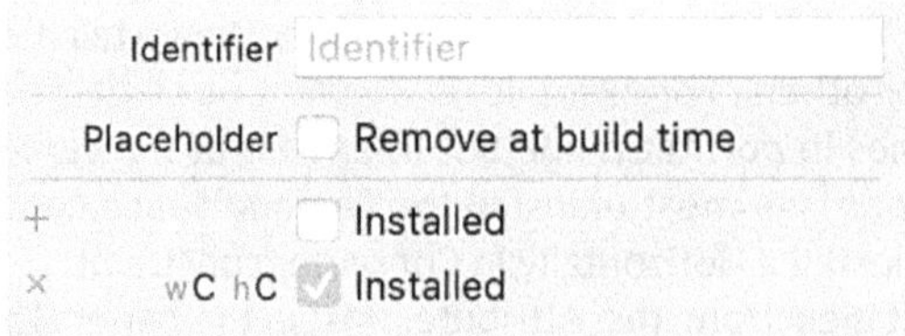

Figure 6-73: *Horizontal alignment constraint installed only for Compact width and height*

Now, there is a Leading Space constraint that is installed for the label in any configuration except Compact width and Compact height, and a Horizontally in Container constraint (Center X) that is installed only in Compact width and Compact height. The result is shown below; the label is always pinned to the left side except in small iPhones in landscape mode.

Figure 6-74: Different constraints applied to the same label

Do It Yourself: This example assumes that you have created the previous example with a single label and added the Top and Leading Space constraints shown in Figure 6-68. Select a small iPhone and change the orientation to landscape (Figure 5-21, number 2). Select the label's Leading Space constraint. In the Attributes Inspector panel, click the **+** button of the Installed option and add a new option for the Compact width and Compact height (Figure 6-71). Click on that option to deactivate it (Figure 6-72). Select the label and add a Horizontally in Container constraint (Figure 6-74, right). Install this constraint for the Size Classes Compact width and Compact height and uninstall it for the rest (Figure 6-73). The label should be displayed on the left anywhere except for small iPhones in landscape mode.

Basic Adapting Elements

The process to add or remove an element is the same we used for constraints, we select the element and install it or uninstall it for the configuration of Size Classes we want to affect.

Figure 6-75: Installed option for views

Medium Trait Collection

Every time the interface is displayed, each element receives a Trait Collection object with information about its own space on the screen, including the horizontal and vertical Size Classes. And this is how we can recognize the current Size Classes from code. The objects are created from the **`UITraitCollection`** class. The instantiation of these objects is automatic, but we can also create our own using the initializers provided by the class.

UITraitCollection(horizontalSizeClass: UIUserInterfaceSizeClass**)**—This initializer creates a **`UITraitCollection`** object with the value specified by the argument. The argument is an enumeration with the values **`unspecified`**, **`compact`**, and **`regular`**.

UITraitCollection(verticalSizeClass: UIUserInterfaceSizeClass**)**—This initializer creates a **`UITraitCollection`** object with the value specified by the argument. The argument is an enumeration with the values **`unspecified`**, **`compact`**, and **`regular`**.

These initializers are useful when we need to set a configuration for a specific Trait Collection from code, but more useful are the properties provided by the class to read the object's values.

horizontalSizeClass—This property returns the value of the horizontal Size Class represented by the **UITraitCollection** object. It is an enumeration of type **UIUserInterfaceSizeClass** with the values **unspecified**, **compact**, and **regular**.

verticalSizeClass—This property returns the value of the vertical Size Class represented by the **UITraitCollection** object. It is an enumeration of type **UIUserInterface-SizeClass** with the values **unspecified**, **compact**, and **regular**.

userInterfaceIdiom—This property returns a **UIUserInterfaceIdiom** enumeration value to indicate the platform the app is running on. The values available are **phone**, **pad**, **tv**, **carPlay**, **mac**, and **unspecified**.

displayScale—This property returns a **CGFloat** value that represents the screen's scale.

Views and view controllers conform to a protocol called **UITraitEnvironment** that defines a property to store the **UITraitCollection** object and a method to report changes.

traitCollection—This property returns a **UITraitCollection** object with the current Trait Collection associated to the view or the view controller.

traitCollectionDidChange(UITraitCollection?**)**—This method is called by views and view controllers that conform to the **UITraitEnvironment** protocol every time their Trait Collection changes. The argument represents the previous trait collection.

We can access this property and method from every view controller and our views. The following example overrides the **traitCollectionDidChange()** method to print on the console the values of the current Trait Collection.

```
import UIKit

class ViewController: UIViewController {
   override func traitCollectionDidChange(_ previousTraitCollection: 
UITraitCollection?) {
      super.traitCollectionDidChange(previousTraitCollection)

      var horizontal: String?
      var vertical: String?

      switch traitCollection.horizontalSizeClass {
         case .regular:
            horizontal = "Regular"
         case .compact:
            horizontal = "Compact"
         default:
            break
      }
      switch traitCollection.verticalSizeClass {
         case .regular:
            vertical = "Regular"
         case .compact:
            vertical = "Compact"
         default:
            break
      }
      if horizontal != nil && vertical != nil {
         print("The configuration is \(horizontal!) width and \
(vertical!) height")
      }
   }
}
```

Listing 6-10: *Detecting changes in the Trait Collection*

Every time the Size Classes assigned to the main view change, the system calls the **traitCollectionDidChange()** method on its view controller. From this method, we can read the information of the current trait collection from the **traitCollection** property, as we did in Listing 6-10, or get information about the previous Trait Collection from the **previousTraitCollection** parameter (to know about the previous conditions of the space occupied by the view).

The code in Listing 6-10 reads the **horizontalSizeClass** and **verticalSizeClass** properties of the **UITraitCollection** object and according to their values assigns the strings "Regular" or "Compact" to the corresponding variables (**horizontal** or **vertical**). At the end, we use the values of these variables to print a message with the current configuration on the console.

Do It Yourself: Create a new project. Complete the **ViewController** class with the code in Listing 6-10 and run the application. Every time the simulator is rotated, the code prints a message on the console to report the current Size Classes. You can rotate the simulator from the menu or by pressing the keys Command + arrows.

View controllers also adhere to the **UIContentContainer** protocol that among other methods defines two to report when the trait collection is going to change.

viewWillTransition(to: CGSize, **with:** UIViewControllerTransition-Coordinator**)**—This method is called to inform the view controller that its view is going to change size. The **to** argument specifies the new dimensions of the view, and the **with** argument is an object that adheres to the **UIViewControllerTransition-Coordinator** protocol, which defines a few methods to allow us to customize the transition process.

willTransition(to: UITraitCollection, **with:** UIViewControllerTransition-Coordinator**)**—This method is called to inform the view controller that the Trait Collection is going to change. The **to** argument defines the new Trait Collection, and the **with** argument is an object that adheres to the **UIViewControllerTransition-Coordinator** protocol, which defines a few methods to allow us to modify the transition process.

The **viewWillTransition()** method is called every time the main view is going to change to a different size, but the **willTransition()** method is only called when the Trait Collection is going to change. For example, when an iPhone rotates from portrait to landscape, both methods are called because the size of the view and the Size Classes change from one orientation to another. But iPads present a different situation. The size of the main view differs from portrait to landscape, but the Size Classes are always Regular (Regular width and Regular height), so the **willTransition()** method is never called. For this reason, it is better to implement the **viewWillTransition()** method every time we need to detect the change in the space available and only use the **willTransition()** method when we have to perform a task related to Trait Collections. The following example implements the **viewWillTransition()** method to detect rotation in any device.

```
import UIKit

class ViewController: UIViewController {
   override func viewWillTransition(to size: CGSize, with coordinator:
UIViewControllerTransitionCoordinator) {
      super.viewWillTransition(to: size, with: coordinator)
```

```
      let width = size.width
      let height = size.height
      if width > height {
         print("We are going Landscape")
      } else {
         print("We are going Portrait")
      }
   }
}
```

Listing 6-11: *Detecting rotation*

The **`viewWillTransition()`** method includes the **`size`** parameter with the dimensions the main view is going to take after the transition is over. In the example of Listing 6-11, we get the view's width and height from this parameter and compare their values to determine the new orientation. We are going to landscape if the width is greater than the height or to portrait otherwise. In this example, we use the **`viewWillTransition()`** method to report the new orientation, but these methods may be used to perform changes on elements and constraints that are not possible to anticipate in the Storyboard.

The value received by the **`with`** parameter in both methods is an object that conforms to the **`UIViewControllerTransitionCoordinator`** protocol. This protocol defines a few methods to allow us to customize the transition process. The following is the most relevant:

animate(alongsideTransition: Block?, **completion:** Block?**)**—This method executes a closure during the transition process and another after the transition is complete. The **alongsideTransition** and **completion** arguments are the closures we want to execute while the transition occurs or when it is over, respectively.

The **`animate()`** method must be called on the coordinator object inside the transition methods introduced before every time we want to participate in the transition process.

```
import UIKit

class ViewController: UIViewController {
   override func viewWillTransition(to size: CGSize, with coordinator: UIViewControllerTransitionCoordinator) {
      super.viewWillTransition(to: size, with: coordinator)

      coordinator.animate(alongsideTransition: nil, completion: {(context: UIViewControllerTransitionCoordinatorContext!) in
         let mainView = context.containerView
         print("\(mainView.frame.width) / \(mainView.frame.height)")
      })
   }
}
```

Listing 6-12: *Performing a task after the transition is over*

In this example, we call the **`animate()`** method with a closure for the **completion** argument. The closure receives a value that conforms to the **`UIViewControllerTransition-CoordinatorContext`** protocol, which among other properties, it provides the **`containerView`** property with a reference to the view that is causing the transition. In this case, we use this reference to read the view's **`width`** and **`height`** properties and print their values on the console.

Basic Orientation

Auto Layout and Trait Collections tell the application how to present the interface on the screen according to the space available and its characteristics (Compact or Regular), but the app is the one that determines the orientations available.

The first level of control is provided by the app's settings. Xcode includes an entry at the top of the Navigator Area to access an editor where we can configure our app (Figure 5-12, number 6). When we click this entry, a project editor is shown in the Editor Area. The editor is divided in panels, with each panel allowing the configuration of different aspects of the application, including basic things like setting the possible orientations to instructions on how the code should be compiled. Figure 6-76 shows some of the panels available.

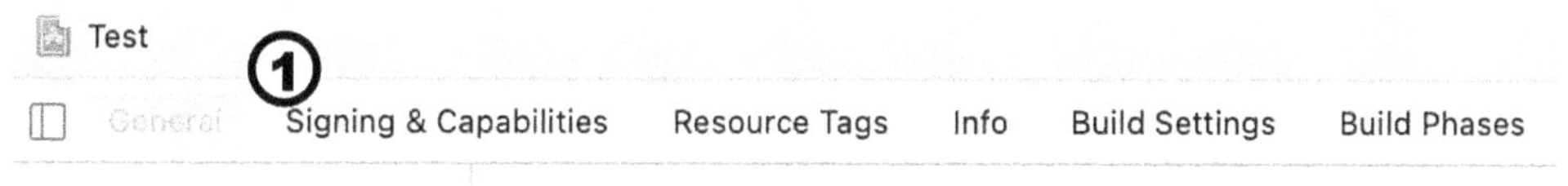

Figure 6-76: *Configuration panes*

The panel we will probably use the most is General (Figure 6-76, number 1). Here, we can set the app's version, declare the oldest iOS version our app supports, and control the orientations available, among other things. Figure 6-77, below, illustrates the section of this panel where we can activate and deactivate the orientations.

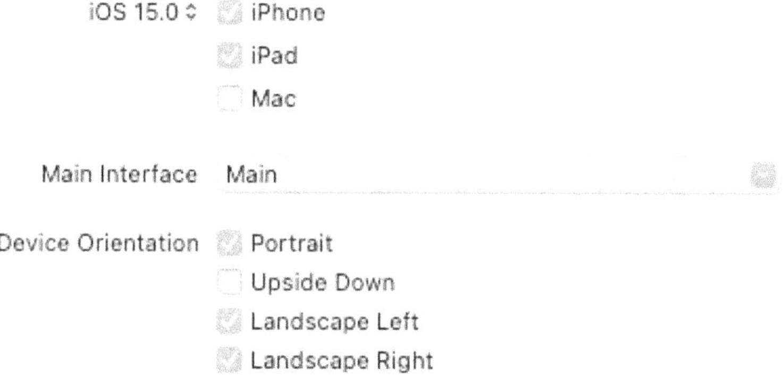

Figure 6-77: *Orientations*

The panel shows the four options available (Portrait, Upside Down, Landscape Left, and Landscape Right). If any of these options is deactivated, the interface of our app does not change when the device rotates to that orientation. The options are pre-set by Xcode according to the selected device (iPhone or iPad). All the orientations are automatically activated for iPad and Universal, but the Upside Down orientation is deactivated if we are creating a project for iPhones. This is to avoid the user making the mistake of answering a call with the phone upside down.

IMPORTANT: If you want to configure different orientations for each device, select only the device you want to modify and perform the changes. Once you finish, select again all the devices you want your application to run in. The setup is preserved in a plist file you can read and modify from the Info panel.

These options affect the entire app. The rotation of the initial view controller and every view controller we add later to the Storyboard will be limited to the options activated in this panel. If we want to define the orientation for each view controller, we must specify it in the definition of our subclass. The **`UIViewController`** class includes the following properties for this purpose.

shouldAutorotate—This computed property returns a Boolean value that indicates whether we want the main view to autorotate or not.

supportedInterfaceOrientations—This computed property returns a value that determines the orientations supported by the view controller. It returns a property of the **UIInterfaceOrientationMask** structure. The properties available are **portrait**, **landscapeLeft**, **landscapeRight**, **portraitUpsideDown**, **landscape**, **all**, and **allButUpsideDown**.

These are computed properties that only return a value, but we can override them in our view controller and make them return a different value to specify the behavior we want.

```
import UIKit

class ViewController: UIViewController {
   override var shouldAutorotate: Bool {
      return false
   }
}
```

Listing 6-13: *Deactivating rotation for a view controller*

The **shouldAutorotate** property indicates whether the main view should respond to the device's rotation. When we return the value **true** from this property, the main view is rotated in any of the orientations available (those activated in the app's settings), but when we return **false**, the main view is presented in the current orientation and then never rotated.

Another way to tell the system if the main view should rotate or not is by overriding the **supportedInterfaceOrientations** property. With this property, we can select exactly the orientations available for each view controller by returning a value or a set of values of type **UIInterfaceOrientationMask**.

```
import UIKit

class ViewController: UIViewController {
   override var supportedInterfaceOrientations:
UIInterfaceOrientationMask {
      return .landscape
   }
}
```

Listing 6-14: *Allowing only landscape orientation*

In this example, we return the value **landscape** to let the interface adapt to any of the landscape orientations (left or right). The main view of this view controller will only adapt when the device is in landscape mode. If we want to specify two or more possible orientations, we must declare them in a set (e.g., **[.portrait, .landscapeLeft]**).

IMPORTANT: The settings defined on the General panel have precedence over the view controllers. If we deactivate the landscape modes from the panel, for example, those orientations will not be available in any view controller, no matter the values returned by their methods.

Chapter 7
Scroll Views

Basic 7.1 Scroll Views

Scroll Views are views that display content larger than the area they cover. They allow the user to scroll the content or zoom in and out any part of it. The UIKit framework provides the **UIScrollView** class to create these types of views. A few classes inherit from **UIScrollView** to take advantage of its capabilities, like the **UITextView** class studied in Chapter 5, but Scroll Views can manage any type of content we need. Figure 7-1 illustrates what the user sees when scrolling a picture that is larger than the area occupied by the view.

Figure 7-1: *User scrolling through the Scroll View's content area*

A Scroll View can be created from code with the **UIView** initializer or added to the Storyboard from the option in the Library.

UIScrollView(frame: CGRect**)**—This initializer creates a Scroll View with the position and size determined by the **frame** argument.

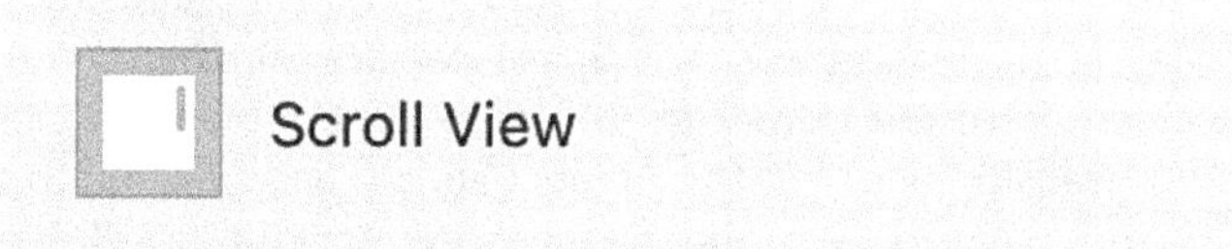

Figure 7-2: *Scroll View option in the Library*

Basic Implementing Scroll Views

The content of a Scroll View is inside a delimited area called *content area*. This area is like a canvas and the Scroll View like a window that allows the user to see one part of the canvas at a time (see Figure 7-1). Therefore, there are two areas to define: the area of the Scroll View and the area of its content. This demands the creation of two sets of constraints, the ones we need to position and size the view in the interface and those necessary to declare the size of the scrollable content. The constraints for the Scroll View are applied as always, but the constraints for the content must determine the content's size. For instance, if the content is composed of an empty view, we must declare constraints that determine the size of the view (width and height), including all the space around it (left, right, top and bottom). From these constraints, the Scroll View can calculate the size of its content and show it on the screen. But not all constraints are always necessary. If the content of the Scroll View is an Image View, for example, only the space constraints around it are necessary, because its size is determined by the intrinsic content size of the Image View (the size of the content will be the same as the size of the image), as shown in the following example.

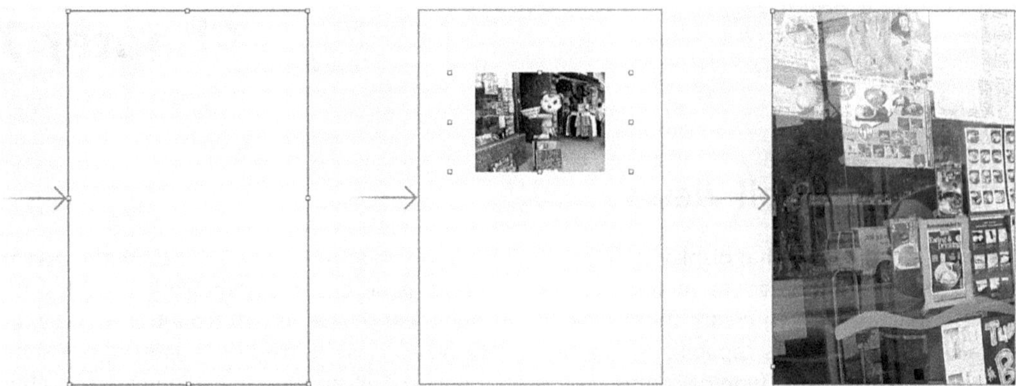

Figure 7-3: Scroll View with an image

To create the interface in Figure 7-3, we must add the Scroll View first and pin it to the main view with Leading, Trailing, Top and Bottom constraints. After that, we add the Image View to the Scroll View with the image we want to display (in this case, we use the file doll.jpg, available on our website). Finally, we pin the Image View to the Scroll View with Leading, Trailing, Top and Bottom constraints. Because of these constraints, the Scroll View's content adopts the size of the image (its intrinsic content size), and users can scroll the image to see the part they want.

Figure 7-4: Scrollable Image

Do It Yourself: Create a new project. Add a Scroll View to the scene and pin it to the sides of the main view with Space constraints (Figure 7-3, left). Drag an Image View from the Library to the Scroll View. Download the doll.jpg image from our website, add it to the Assets Catalog, and assign it to the Image View (Figure 7-3, center). Pin the image view to the Scroll View with Space constraints. Remember to click on the arrows to make sure that the destination of these constraints is the Scroll View (see Chapter 6, Figure 6-21). You should see the image expand to its original size (Figure 7-3, right). Run the application and scroll the image.

Basic Customizing Scroll Views

Although we could define the whole interface inside a Scroll View, as we will see at the end of this chapter, working with constraints inside a Scroll View introduces some complications. For that reason, the Scroll View and its content are usually defined from code. The following are some of the properties and methods included in the **UIScrollView** class to manage the view and its content.

contentSize—This property sets or returns the size of the content area. It is a structure of type **CGSize**.

contentOffset—This property sets or returns the **x** and **y** coordinates that determine the positions of the piece of content the Scroll View is currently showing on the screen. It is a structure of type **`CGPoint`**, with a value by default of 0, 0.

contentInset—This property sets or returns the content's padding. This is the space between the edges of the Scroll View and its content. It is a structure of type **`UIEdgeInsets`** with the properties **`top`**, **`left`**, **`bottom`**, and **`right`**, and a value by default of 0, 0, 0, 0.

isScrollEnabled—This property is a Boolean value that determines if scrolling is enabled.

isPagingEnabled—This property is a Boolean value that determines whether the Scroll View considers its content as pages or not.

showHorizontalScrollIndicator—This property is a Boolean value that determines whether the horizontal scroll indicator is visible or not.

showVerticalScrollIndicator—This property is a Boolean value that determines whether the vertical scroll indicator is visible or not.

zoomScale—This property sets or returns the current scale of the content. It is of type **`CGFloat`** with a default value of 1.0.

maximumZoomScale—This property sets or returns the maximum possible scale for the content. It is of type **`CGFloat`** with a default value of 1.0.

minimumZoomScale—This property sets or returns the minimum possible scale for the content. It is of type **`CGFloat`** with a default value of 1.0.

zoom(to: CGRect, **animated:** Bool**)**—This method zooms the content to make visible the area specified by the **to** argument. The **`animated`** argument indicates whether the process will be animated or not.

scrollRectToVisible(CGRect, **animated:** Bool**)**—This method scrolls the content to make visible the area specified by the first argument. The **`animated`** argument indicates whether the process will be animated or not.

Scroll Views can also designate a delegate for configuration and to report changes on their state. The delegate must conform to the **`UIScrollViewDelegate`** protocol and implement its methods. The following are the most frequently used.

viewForZooming(in: UIScrollView**)**—This method is called by the Scroll View on its delegate to know which view is going to be zoomed in or out.

scrollViewDidScroll(UIScrollView**)**—This method is called by the Scroll View on its delegate when the user scrolls the content.

scrollViewDidZoom(UIScrollView**)**—This method is called by the Scroll View on its delegate when the user zooms the content in or out.

There are two ways to add the Scroll View to the interface from code. We can create the **`UIScrollView`** object, add it to the main view or a container view, and then define the constraints from code, as explained in Chapter 6. But a better alternative is to add a Stack View to the main view and then add the Scroll View as the content of the Stack View, as in the following example.

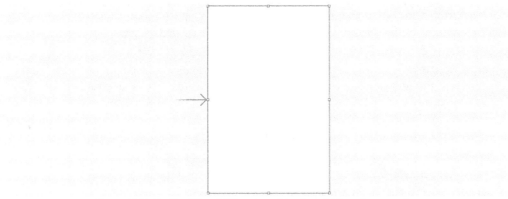

Figure 7-5: *Vertical Stack View to add a Scroll View from code*

Once the Stack View is added to the interface, we must connect it to an Outlet in the view controller and then create and add the Scroll View and its content from code, as shown next.

```
import UIKit

class ViewController: UIViewController {
   @IBOutlet weak var stackContainer: UIStackView!

   override func viewDidLoad() {
      super.viewDidLoad()
      let imgView = UIImageView(image: UIImage(named: "doll"))
      let imgWidth = imgView.frame.size.width
      let imgHeight = imgView.frame.size.height

      let mainScroll = UIScrollView(frame: .zero)
      mainScroll.contentSize = CGSize(width: imgWidth, height: imgHeight)
      mainScroll.addSubview(imgView)
      stackContainer.addArrangedSubview(mainScroll)
   }
}
```

Listing 7-1: *Adding a Scroll View from code*

The same way we did with constraints, every time we add a Scroll View from code, we must define the size of the Scroll View and the size of its content area. Because we are embedding the Scroll View in a Stack View, its size will be determined by the size of the Stack View in the Storyboard, but the size of the content area must be defined in code from the **contentSize** property. In the example of Listing 7-1, we create an Image View to add to the content area and then declare the size of the area as the size of the image (we did not have to declare the frame of the Image View because the initializer takes the values from the image). After the content area is ready, we create the **UIScrollView** object and add the Image View as its content with the **addSubview()** method. Finally, the Scroll View is added to the Stack View with the **addArrangedSubview()** method. The result is the same shown in Figure 7-4.

Do It Yourself: Create a new project. Add a Stack View to the main view and pin it to the sides (Figure 7-5). Create an Outlet for the Stack View called **stackContainer** and complete the view controller with the code in Listing 7-1. Download the image doll.jpg from our website and add it to the Assets Catalog. Run the application and scroll the image.

The result of the previous example is the same achieved when the Scroll View was added to the Storyboard (see Figure 7-4), but there is an issue that requires our attention. Despite connecting the Stack View to the top of the main view, the image appears below the status bar. This is because by default the Scroll View positions its content inside the Safe Area. To modify this behavior, the **UIScrollVIew** class includes the following property.

contentInsetAdjustmentBehavior—This property determines how the Scroll View is going to adjust the content's offsets. It is an enumeration of type **ContentInset-AdjustmentBehavior** with the values **automatic**, **scrollableAxes**, **never**, and **always**.

If we want to make sure that the scrollable content is shown full screen, we can define this property with the value **never**, as shown next.

```
import UIKit

class ViewController: UIViewController {
   @IBOutlet weak var stackContainer: UIStackView!

   override func viewDidLoad() {
      super.viewDidLoad()
      let imgView = UIImageView(image: UIImage(named: "doll"))
      let imgWidth = imgView.frame.size.width
      let imgHeight = imgView.frame.size.height

      let mainScroll = UIScrollView(frame: .zero)
      mainScroll.contentSize = CGSize(width: imgWidth, height: imgHeight)
      mainScroll.contentInsetAdjustmentBehavior = .never
      mainScroll.addSubview(imgView)

      stackContainer.addArrangedSubview(mainScroll)
   }
}
```

Listing 7-2: *Showing the content full screen*

The content area of a Scroll View may contain as many views as we want. The following example includes a second image with a logo at the top-left corner of the area (the image is called logo.png and is available on our website).

```
import UIKit

class ViewController: UIViewController {
   @IBOutlet weak var stackContainer: UIStackView!

   override func viewDidLoad() {
      super.viewDidLoad()

      let imgView = UIImageView(image: UIImage(named: "doll"))
      let imgWidth = imgView.frame.size.width
      let imgHeight = imgView.frame.size.height

      let mainScroll = UIScrollView(frame: .zero)
      mainScroll.contentSize = CGSize(width: imgWidth, height: imgHeight)
      mainScroll.addSubview(imgView)

      let logoView = UIImageView(frame: CGRect(x: 25, y: 25, width: 249,
height: 249))
      logoView.image = UIImage(named: "logo")
      mainScroll.addSubview(logoView)

      stackContainer.addArrangedSubview(mainScroll)
   }
}
```

Listing 7-3: *Adding more views to the content area*

The example in Listing 7-3 creates the Image View for the logo with a frame in the position 25, 25, and then adds it to the Scroll View. Because the image with the logo is added after the image with the doll, it is shown at the top, but it is fixed at the position 25, 25 in the content area and therefore it scrolls along with the rest of the content, as shown below.

Figure 7-6: *Two images in the content area*

As we already mentioned, the area occupied by the Scroll View on the interface may be different from the area occupied by its content. If we know the size of the content area, we can position and size content using coordinates, as we did in the previous example, but this is something difficult to do when the content has to be positioned and sized relative to the sides of the content area or to the sides of the Scroll View. For these situations, the **`UIScrollView`** class offers two layout guides that allow us to set constraints between the views and the content area or between the views and the Scroll View. The following are the properties included in the class to access these guides.

frameLayoutGuide—This property returns a layout guide that represents the frame of the Scroll View.

contentLayoutGuide—This property returns a layout guide that represents the frame of the content area.

Using these guides, we can integrate the content of the Scroll View with the rest of the interface. For instance, we can position the logo of our previous example relative to the sides of the Scroll View, which will keep it fixed in place.

```
import UIKit

class ViewController: UIViewController {
   @IBOutlet weak var stackContainer: UIStackView!

   override func viewDidLoad() {
      super.viewDidLoad()
      let imgView = UIImageView(image: UIImage(named: "doll"))
      let imgWidth = imgView.frame.size.width
      let imgHeight = imgView.frame.size.height

      let mainScroll = UIScrollView(frame: .zero)
      mainScroll.contentSize = CGSize(width: imgWidth, height: imgHeight)
      mainScroll.contentInsetAdjustmentBehavior = .never
      mainScroll.addSubview(imgView)

      let logoView = UIImageView(image: UIImage(named: "logo"))
      logoView.translatesAutoresizingMaskIntoConstraints = false
      mainScroll.addSubview(logoView)

      logoView.topAnchor.constraint(equalTo:
mainScroll.frameLayoutGuide.topAnchor, constant: 25).isActive = true
      logoView.leadingAnchor.constraint(equalTo:
mainScroll.frameLayoutGuide.leadingAnchor, constant: 25).isActive = true
```

```
        stackContainer.addArrangedSubview(mainScroll)
    }
}
```

Listing 7-4: Pinning content to the frame of the Scroll View

This example adds the images of the doll and the logo to the Scroll View, as we did before, but instead of declaring the position and size of the logo with a **CGRect** value, we do it with constraints. We define two constraints to pin the view to the top-left corner of the Scroll View, one from the Top anchor of the view to the Top anchor of the Frame layout guide, and another from the Leading anchor of the view to the Leading anchor of the Frame layout guide.

Because the logo is now pinned to the sides of the Scroll View, it always keeps its initial position and does not scroll with the rest of the content anymore, as illustrated below.

Figure 7-7: Content pinned to the Scroll View

Basic Zooming

Setting the size of the content area gives enough information to the Scroll View to allow the user to scroll the content, but to zoom in and out we must define the maximum and minimum scales allowed with the **minimumZoomScale** and **maximumZoomScale** properties, and also conform to the **UIScrollViewDelegate** protocol and implement its **viewForZooming()** method to declare which view is going to participate in the process.

```
import UIKit

class ViewController: UIViewController, UIScrollViewDelegate {
    @IBOutlet weak var stackContainer: UIStackView!
    var imgView: UIImageView!

    override func viewDidLoad() {
        super.viewDidLoad()
        imgView = UIImageView(image: UIImage(named: "doll"))
        let imageWidth = imgView.frame.size.width
        let imageHeight = imgView.frame.size.height

        let mainScroll = UIScrollView(frame: .zero)
        mainScroll.contentSize = CGSize(width: imageWidth, height:
imageHeight)
        mainScroll.contentInsetAdjustmentBehavior = .never
        mainScroll.delegate = self
        mainScroll.addSubview(imgView)

        mainScroll.minimumZoomScale = 1.0
        mainScroll.maximumZoomScale = 4.0
        stackContainer.addArrangedSubview(mainScroll)
    }
    func viewForZooming(in scrollView: UIScrollView) -> UIView? {
        return imgView
    }
}
```

Listing 7-5: Allowing zooming

The view controller in Listing 7-5 conforms to the **UIScrollViewDelegate** protocol and declares itself as the delegate of the **mainScroll** view. It also declares a minimum scale of 1.0 and a maximum scale of 4.0, and stores a reference to the Image View in the **imgView** property to be able to return it from the **viewForZooming()** method. When the Scroll View detects that the user is trying to zoom in or out, it calls this method on its delegate to know which view in the content area is going to be affected by the action and begins to zoom until a limit is reached.

The zoom scale is considered to be 1.0 at the initial state. If we set absolute values for the **minimumScale** and **maximumScale** properties when the initial image is larger than the area of the Scroll View, as in the previous example, the user will not be able to zoom out enough to see the whole image on the screen. There are different ways to accommodate these values, depending on the effects we want to achieve in our application. For instance, the following example calculates the minimum scale from the initial size of the image.

```
import UIKit

class ViewController: UIViewController, UIScrollViewDelegate {
   @IBOutlet weak var stackContainer: UIStackView!
   var imgView: UIImageView!

   override func viewDidLoad() {
      super.viewDidLoad()

      view.setNeedsLayout()
      view.layoutIfNeeded()

      imgView = UIImageView(image: UIImage(named: "doll"))
      let imageWidth = imgView.frame.size.width
      let imageHeight = imgView.frame.size.height

      let mainScroll = UIScrollView(frame: .zero)
      mainScroll.contentSize = CGSize(width: imageWidth, height:
imageHeight)
      mainScroll.contentInsetAdjustmentBehavior = .never
      mainScroll.delegate = self
      mainScroll.addSubview(imgView)

      let scrollWidth = stackContainer.frame.size.width
      let scrollHeight = stackContainer.frame.size.height
      let minScale = min(scrollWidth / imageWidth, scrollHeight /
imageHeight)
      let maxScale = max(minScale * 4.0, 1.0)

      mainScroll.minimumZoomScale = minScale
      mainScroll.maximumZoomScale = maxScale

      stackContainer.addArrangedSubview(mainScroll)
   }
   func viewForZooming(in scrollView: UIScrollView) -> UIView? {
      return imgView
   }
}
```

Listing 7-6: *Calculating the minimum and maximum scales*

To calculate what should be the minimum scale so the user can zoom out to see the whole image on the screen, we need to obtain the current values of the Scroll View's **width** and **height** properties. Because the Scroll View is going to have the same size of the Stack View, we can read the values from this view, but the problem is that those values are not updated when the main view is loaded but during the system's updating cycles. To force the system to update the values at the time we need them, we have to call the main view's **setNeedsLayout()** and **layoutIfNeeded()** methods (see Chapter 6). If we do not execute these methods before reading the view's **frame** property, the values returned might be those defined in the Storyboard (this is not always required, it depends on when in the process we try to read the frames).

The minimum scale is calculated in Listing 7-6 by dividing one of the Scroll View's dimensions by the same dimension of the Image View. For example, if we divide the width of the Scroll View by the width of the Image View, we get the scale necessary to let the user zoom out until the image fits the width of the view. But because we want the user to be able to see the whole image, we have to calculate the scale for both dimensions and get the smaller value. We do this by comparing the result of both formulas with the **`min`** function (**`min(scrollWidth / imageWidth, scrollHeight / imageHeight)`**). This will be our minimum scale. From this value we get the maximum scale multiplying it by 4.

IMPORTANT: If you want the image to be presented from the beginning at the minimum scale, you can set the initial zoom scale with the **`zoomScale`** property. Add the statement **`mainScroll.zoomScale = minScale`** to the Scroll View configuration.

Basic Pages

The **`UIScrollView`** class includes functionality to split the content area into pages. The size of the pages is determined by the size of the Scroll View, so when the user swipes a finger on the screen, the current visible portion of the content area is completely replaced by the section that represents the next page. To activate this mode, we assign the value **`true`** to the **`isPagingEnabled`** property and configure the content to represent the virtual pages. The following is a simple example that presents three images, spot1.png, spot2.png, and spot3.png, one per page.

```
import UIKit

class ViewController: UIViewController {
   @IBOutlet weak var stackContainer: UIStackView!

   override func viewDidLoad() {
      super.viewDidLoad()
      let images = ["spot1", "spot2", "spot3"]

      view.setNeedsLayout()
      view.layoutIfNeeded()
      let scrollWidth = stackContainer.frame.size.width
      let scrollHeight = stackContainer.frame.size.height

      let mainScroll = UIScrollView(frame: .zero)
      mainScroll.contentSize = CGSize(width: scrollWidth * 
CGFloat(images.count), height: scrollHeight)
      mainScroll.contentInsetAdjustmentBehavior = .never
      mainScroll.isPagingEnabled = true

      var posX: CGFloat = 0
      for img in images {
         let imgView = UIImageView(frame: CGRect(x: posX, y: 0, width: 
scrollWidth, height: scrollHeight))
         imgView.image = UIImage(named: img)
         imgView.contentMode = .scaleAspectFill
         imgView.clipsToBounds = true

         mainScroll.addSubview(imgView)
         posX = posX + scrollWidth
      }
      stackContainer.addArrangedSubview(mainScroll)
   }
}
```

Listing 7-7: *Organizing the content area in pages*

The Image Views need to be of the size of the Scroll View and positioned side by side to represent the pages. This is the reason why in Listing 7-7 we declare the frame of every Image View. The values for the frame's **width** and **height** properties are determined by the size of the Scroll View (**scrollWidth** and **scrollHeight**), and the coordinates for the position are calculated according to the page the view represents. The first Image View is added at the coordinate 0, 0, but the second Image View is displaced to the right a distance determined by the width of the Scroll View. To calculate this value, we use the **posX** variable. In every cycle of the loop, the variable is incremented with the value of the **scrollWidth** property to establish the horizontal position of the next view. As a result, the images are positioned on the content area one after another, from left to right.

Notice that we also set the **contentMode** of each Image View to **scaleAspectFill** to fill the entire Image View with the picture and the **clipsToBounds** property to **true** to make sure that the image will never be drawn outside the view's boundaries.

Do It Yourself: This example assumes that you are still working with the interface in Figure 7-5. Update the view controller with the code in Listing 7-7. Download the images spot1.png, spot2.png, and spot3.png from our website and add them to the Assets Catalog. Run the application. When you scroll the content, the interface should transition from right to left or left to right, from one image to another.

The UIKit framework includes a special type of control called Page Control that is particularly useful in these kinds of applications. The control displays dots on the screen that represent each page available and changes their colors according to the visible page. There is an option available in the Library to add a Page Control to the Storyboard.

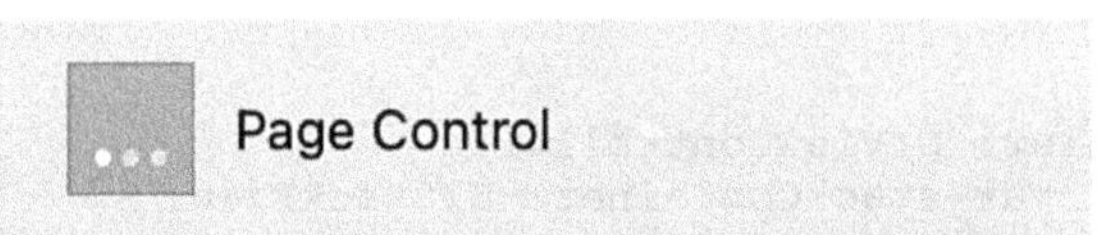

Figure 7-8: *Page Control option in the Library*

The control is created from the **UIPageControl** class. The class provides the following properties for configuration.

currentPage—This property sets or returns the number of the current page.

numberOfPages—This property sets or returns the number of pages represented by the control (the number of dots shown on the screen). It is of type **Int**.

hidesForSinglePage—This property is a Boolean value that determines whether the control should be hidden when there is only one page.

pageIndicatorTintColor—This property sets or returns the color of the dots when the pages they represent are not visible. It is an optional of type **UIColor**.

currentPageIndicatorTintColor—This property sets or returns the color of the dot that represents the visible page. It is an optional of type **UIColor**.

backgroundStyle—This property sets or returns the style of the control. It is an enumeration defined in the **UIPageControl** class called **BackgroundStyle**. The possible values are **automatic** (selects the style according to the state), **prominent** (shows a full background), and **minimal** (shows a minimal background).

preferredIndicatorImage—This property sets or returns a **UIImage** object with the image we want to assign to the indicators.

setIndicatorImage(UIImage?, **forPage:** Int**)**—This method sets the image for the indicator of a specific page. The first argument is the image we want to assign to the indicator, and the **forPage** argument is the page for which the indicator is going to be shown.

To add a Page Control to the interface, we could reduce the height of the Stack View to make room for it or put the control over the Stack View. For the following example, we have decided to go with the last option and add the Page Control on top of the Stack View. The control has a gray background with an opacity of 0.4 to make it translucent.

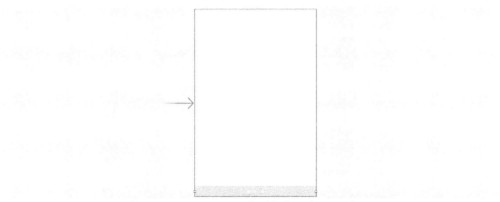

Figure 7-9: *Page Control added to the interface*

Do It Yourself: Views that are dragged over a Stack View become its subviews. This is not the desirable behavior for the interface in Figure 7-9. What you want is to put the Page Control over the Stack View, not inside. To achieve this, you can momentarily reduce the height of the Stack View, drag the Page Control inside the main view, set its constraints, and then update the frames to move the Stack View back to its original size, or just uninstall the Stack View until the Page Control is added and pinned to the sides. Alternatively, you can drag the Page Control inside the Stack View and then change its position in the hierarchy from the Document Outline panel. Once the Page Control is ready, go to the Attributes Inspector panel and change its background color to gray with an opacity of 40% (Custom color).

The Page Control is configured by default for three pages, but we can change the initial values from the Attributes Inspector panel. This is usually not necessary since the content to display with this type of control is loaded dynamically and its properties are configured from the view controller, as shown in the following example.

```
import UIKit

class ViewController: UIViewController, UIScrollViewDelegate {
   @IBOutlet weak var stackContainer: UIStackView!
   @IBOutlet weak var pageCounter: UIPageControl!

   var mainScroll: UIScrollView!
   var page: Int = 0

   override func viewDidLoad() {
      super.viewDidLoad()
      let images = ["spot1", "spot2", "spot3"]
      pageCounter.numberOfPages = images.count
      pageCounter.pageIndicatorTintColor = UIColor.black
      pageCounter.currentPageIndicatorTintColor = UIColor.white

      view.setNeedsLayout()
      view.layoutIfNeeded()
      let scrollWidth = stackContainer.frame.size.width
      let scrollHeight = stackContainer.frame.size.height
```

```
        mainScroll = UIScrollView(frame: .zero)
        mainScroll.contentSize = CGSize(width: scrollWidth *
CGFloat(images.count), height: scrollHeight)
        mainScroll.contentInsetAdjustmentBehavior = .never
        mainScroll.isPagingEnabled = true
        mainScroll.delegate = self

        var posX: CGFloat = 0
        for img in images {
            let imgView = UIImageView(frame: CGRect(x: posX, y: 0, width:
scrollWidth, height: scrollHeight))
            imgView.image = UIImage(named: img)
            imgView.contentMode = .scaleAspectFill
            imgView.clipsToBounds = true

            mainScroll.addSubview(imgView)
            posX = posX + scrollWidth
        }
        stackContainer.addArrangedSubview(mainScroll)
    }
    func scrollViewDidScroll(_ scrollView: UIScrollView) {
        let pageWidth = stackContainer.frame.size.width
        let getPage = round(mainScroll.contentOffset.x / pageWidth)
        let currentPage = Int(getPage)

        page = currentPage
        pageCounter.currentPage = page
    }
}
```

Listing 7-8: Calculating the page

To represent the pages on the screen with the Page Control, we not only have to configure the control but also get the number of the current visible page. The **UIScrollView** class does not offer any property or method to return this value; we must calculate it ourselves. Fortunately, the delegate protocol offers a method called **scrollViewDidScroll()** that is executed every time the user scrolls the content. Also, the system automatically updates the Scroll View's **contentOffset** property with the current displacement of the content area every time the content is scrolled. By implementing these tools, we can calculate the current page. The value is obtained dividing the value of the **x** property of the **contentOffset** structure by the size of the page (the width of the Scroll View). Because the result is a floating-point number, we round it, turn it into an integer, and assign it to the Page Control's **currentPage** property to show the current page on the screen.

Do It Yourself: Connect the Page Control to an Outlet called **pageCounter**. Complete your view controller with the code in Listing 7-8 and run the application. The Page Control should indicate the current visible page.

Letting the user zoom in or out the entire content area when the Scroll View is configured to work with pages would defeat the purpose of pages, but it is possible to let the user zoom each page individually. Scroll Views may be created inside other Scroll Views, and we can use this feature to build complex interfaces where a view may have parts of its content presented with vertical scrolling and other parts with horizontal scrolling. We can also use this feature to allow zooming a page in or out. All we have to do is to embed the content of each page inside additional Scroll Views, set their maximum and minimum scales, and implement the **viewForZooming()** method of the **UIScrollViewDelegate** protocol to tell the Scroll Views that zooming is allowed (see Listing 7-6).

```
import UIKit

class ViewController: UIViewController, UIScrollViewDelegate {
   @IBOutlet weak var stackContainer: UIStackView!
   @IBOutlet weak var pageCounter: UIPageControl!

   var mainScroll: UIScrollView!
   var imageViews: [UIImageView] = []
   var page: Int = 0

   override func viewDidLoad() {
      super.viewDidLoad()
      let images = ["spot1", "spot2", "spot3"]
      pageCounter.numberOfPages = images.count
      pageCounter.pageIndicatorTintColor = UIColor.black
      pageCounter.currentPageIndicatorTintColor = UIColor.white

      view.setNeedsLayout()
      view.layoutIfNeeded()
      let scrollWidth = stackContainer.frame.size.width
      let scrollHeight = stackContainer.frame.size.height

      mainScroll = UIScrollView(frame: .zero)
      mainScroll.contentSize = CGSize(width: scrollWidth *
CGFloat(images.count), height: scrollHeight)
      mainScroll.contentInsetAdjustmentBehavior = .never
      mainScroll.isPagingEnabled = true
      mainScroll.delegate = self

      var posX: CGFloat = 0
      for img in images {
         let childScroll = UIScrollView(frame: CGRect(x: posX, y: 0,
width: scrollWidth, height: scrollHeight))
         childScroll.contentSize = CGSize(width: scrollWidth, height:
scrollHeight)
         childScroll.contentInsetAdjustmentBehavior = .never
         childScroll.minimumZoomScale = 1.0
         childScroll.maximumZoomScale = 4.0
         childScroll.delegate = self

         let imgView = UIImageView(frame: CGRect(x: 0, y: 0, width:
scrollWidth, height: scrollHeight))
         imgView.image = UIImage(named: img)
         imgView.contentMode = .scaleAspectFill
         imgView.clipsToBounds = true
         imageViews.append(imgView)

         childScroll.addSubview(imgView)
         mainScroll.addSubview(childScroll)
         posX = posX + scrollWidth
      }
      stackContainer.addArrangedSubview(mainScroll)
   }
   func scrollViewDidScroll(_ scrollView: UIScrollView) {
      let pageWidth = stackContainer.frame.size.width
      let getPage = round(mainScroll.contentOffset.x / pageWidth)

      let currentPage = Int(getPage)
      if currentPage != page {
         let scroll = imageViews[page].superview as! UIScrollView
         scroll.setZoomScale(1.0, animated: true)
         page = Int(currentPage)
         pageCounter.currentPage = page
      }
   }
```

```
    func viewForZooming(in scrollView: UIScrollView) -> UIView? {
        return imageViews[page]
    }
}
```

Listing 7-9: *Zooming the pages in and out*

The code in Listing 7-9 creates Scroll Views to embed every Image View and then adds them as subviews of the **mainScroll** view. Notice that the minimum and maximum scales are set only for the nested Scroll Views, not for the **mainScroll** view, because we only want to make the zoom available for the Scroll Views assigned to each page.

There is also an aesthetic change inside the **scrollViewDidScroll()** method. This method is executed every time the user scrolls the pages, but the scroll does not always causes the current page to be replaced. We check this condition comparing the current page with the previous one and set the zoom scale back to 1.0 if the new page is different. This returns the images to the initial state every time the user moves to another page.

The examples we have studied so far create applications that let the user transition from one image to another with the move of a finger. But this presents a problem. Because the size of the pages is determined from the size of the Scroll View, the application does not work anymore if the device is rotated, or the size of the Scroll View changes for some reason. To solve this issue, we must implement the methods defined for Trait Collections to detect and report changes in size (see Chapter 6, Listing 6-10). The following example implements the **viewWillTransition()** method to update the frames of the Image Views and their Scroll Views when the device is rotated.

```
import UIKit

class ViewController: UIViewController, UIScrollViewDelegate {
    @IBOutlet weak var stackContainer: UIStackView!
    @IBOutlet weak var pageCounter: UIPageControl!

    var mainScroll: UIScrollView!
    var imageViews: [UIImageView] = []
    var page: Int = 0
    var rotating = false

    override func viewDidLoad() {
        super.viewDidLoad()
        let images = ["spot1", "spot2", "spot3"]
        pageCounter.numberOfPages = images.count
        pageCounter.pageIndicatorTintColor = UIColor.black
        pageCounter.currentPageIndicatorTintColor = UIColor.white

        view.setNeedsLayout()
        view.layoutIfNeeded()

        mainScroll = UIScrollView(frame: .zero)
        mainScroll.contentInsetAdjustmentBehavior = .never
        mainScroll.isPagingEnabled = true
        mainScroll.delegate = self

        for img in images {
            let childScroll = UIScrollView(frame: .zero)
            childScroll.contentInsetAdjustmentBehavior = .never
            childScroll.minimumZoomScale = 1.0
            childScroll.maximumZoomScale = 4.0
            childScroll.delegate = self

            let imgView = UIImageView(frame: .zero)
            imgView.image = UIImage(named: img)
            imgView.contentMode = .scaleAspectFit
            imgView.clipsToBounds = true
            imageViews.append(imgView)
```

```
         childScroll.addSubview(imgView)
         mainScroll.addSubview(childScroll)
      }
      stackContainer.addArrangedSubview(mainScroll)

      updateSize()
   }
   func updateSize() {
      let scrollWidth = stackContainer.frame.size.width
      let scrollHeight = stackContainer.frame.size.height

      var posX: CGFloat = 0
      for imgView in imageViews {
         let scroll = imgView.superview as! UIScrollView
         scroll.frame = CGRect(x: posX, y: 0, width: scrollWidth, height:
scrollHeight)
         scroll.contentSize = CGSize(width: scrollWidth, height:
scrollHeight)
         imgView.frame = CGRect(x: 0, y: 0, width: scrollWidth, height:
scrollHeight)
         posX = posX + scrollWidth
      }
      mainScroll.contentSize = CGSize(width: scrollWidth *
CGFloat(imageViews.count), height: scrollHeight)

      let scrollView = imageViews[page].superview as! UIScrollView
      mainScroll.contentOffset = CGPoint(x: scrollView.frame.origin.x, y:
0)
   }
   func scrollViewDidScroll(_ scrollView: UIScrollView) {
      if !rotating {
         let pageWidth = stackContainer.frame.size.width
         let getPage = round(mainScroll.contentOffset.x / pageWidth)
         let currentPage = Int(getPage)

         if currentPage != page {
            let scroll = imageViews[page].superview as! UIScrollView
            scroll.setZoomScale(1.0, animated: true)
            page = Int(currentPage)
            pageCounter.currentPage = page
         }
      }
   }
   func viewForZooming(in scrollView: UIScrollView) -> UIView? {
      return imageViews[page]
   }
   override func viewWillTransition(to size: CGSize, with coordinator:
UIViewControllerTransitionCoordinator) {
      super.viewWillTransition(to: size, with: coordinator)

      rotating = true
      coordinator.animate(alongsideTransition: nil, completion:
{(context: UIViewControllerTransitionCoordinatorContext!) in
         let scroll = self.imageViews[self.page].superview as!
UIScrollView
         scroll.setZoomScale(1.0, animated: true)

         self.updateSize()
         self.rotating = false
      })
   }
}
```

Listing 7-10: *Adapting the content area to a new orientation*

An important change introduced in this example is that now the definition of the frames for the Scroll Views and their Image Views are in a separate method. This is because every time the size of the **mainScroll** view changes, the code must update the values of the frames. We still define the pages inside the **viewDidLoad()** method, but we call our **updateSize()** method at the end to define their frames. This method is called again when the user rotates the device.

Every time the system detects a rotation or changes on the interface, it calls the **viewWillTransition()** method. In this method, we call the **animate()** method of the transition coordinator to update the values of the frames as soon as the transition is over (the statements were declared inside the closure for the completion handler). There are two more important things we do inside this method: we restore the zoom level of the current page back to its initial scale and modify the value of a Boolean property called **rotating** to inform the rest of the code that the interface is rotating. This is because we do not want to calculate the number of the current page inside the **scrollViewDidScroll()** method until all the values for the frames are updated. The **updateSize()** method also updates the value of the **contentOffset** property of the **mainScroll** view at the end to scroll the content to the right position after the rotation (when the device is rotated, the value of this property is not updated by the system).

Do It Yourself: Copy the code you want to try inside your view controller and run the application. In the example of Listing 7-10, we defined the value of the **contentMode** property as **scaleAspectFit** so the user can see the entire images on the screen. Try other values to find out which one is better for your application.

Medium Scrolling the Interface

Scroll Views allow us to display any content that does not fit entirely on the screen, including the interface itself. There are times when our interface contains so many elements and controls that there is not enough space to show them all, some get hidden when the device is rotated, or are overlapped by the keyboard. There are different ways to define the interface inside a Scroll View, but the simplest is to add a single view inside the Scroll View and then use this view as the container for the rest of the interface. Figure 7-10 illustrates this process. The Scroll View is added to the main view (left), then a single view is added to the Scroll View (center), and finally the view is expanded to fill the Scroll View.

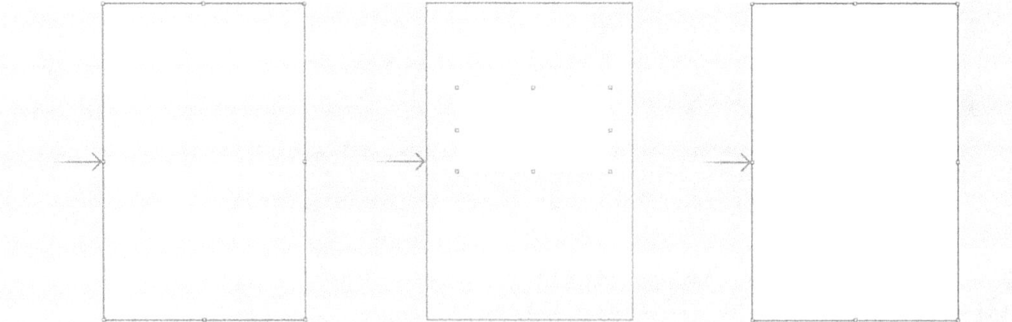

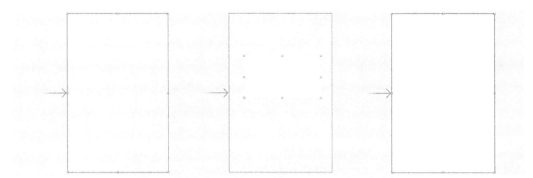

Figure 7-10: *Scroll View with an empty view inside*

Both views must be pinned to the edges of their respective containers with Top, Bottom, Leading and Trailing Space constraints. The Scroll View can be pinned to the Safe Area and the view inside the Scroll View must be pinned to the edges of the Scroll View, as we did for the Image View in the example of Figure 7-3. Figure 7-11, below, shows all the constraints required.

Scroll View **Container View**

Figure 7-11: *Initial constraints for the views*

Do It Yourself: Create a new project. Add a Scroll View to the scene and expand it to the edges of the main view (Figure 7-10, left). Select the Scroll View, open the Pin menu and create Leading, Trailing, Top, and Bottom constraints to pin it to the Safe Area. Add an empty view inside the Scroll View, expand it to occupy the Scroll View's area (Figure 7-10, right), and create Leading, Trailing, Top, and Bottom constraints to pin it to the sides of the Scroll View (make sure that the destination is the Scroll View). The constraints are shown in red because the system does not have enough information to determine the size of the content area yet.

Now that the Scroll View and the container are ready, we must create the constraints necessary to determine the size of the scrollable content. The vertical size is determined by the elements inside the view and their constraints, but the horizontal size is determined by the space available. This requires the creation of two more constraints that pin the container view to the left and right sides of the main view. Figure 7-12 illustrates the process. We have to control-drag a line from the view inside the Scroll View to the main view in the Document Outline panel and create Leading and Trailing constraints with a value of 0.

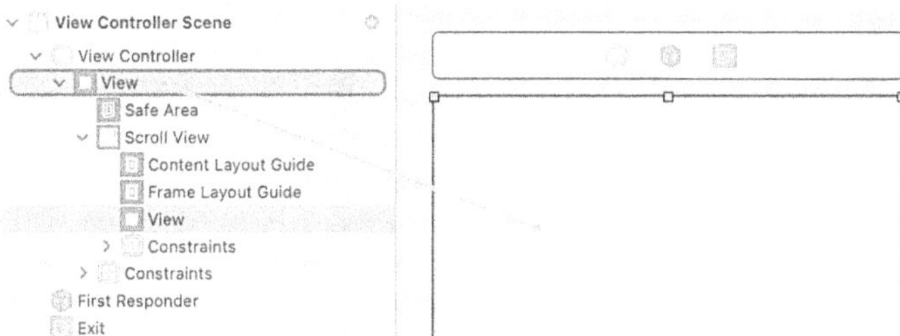

Figure 7-12: *Additional constraints for the container view*

Every time the device is rotated or the space available changes, these constraints change the width of the view inside the Scroll View and this new size is communicated to the Scroll View by the Space constraints added before.

Do It Yourself: Control-drag a line from the view inside the Scroll View to the item that represents the main view in the Document Outline panel (Figure 7-12). Create a Leading and a Trailing constraint with a value of 0.

So far, we have determined the width of the content area. To determine the height, we must add the elements of the interface inside the container view and set constraints that connect them to each side of the view (including top and bottom). In the following example, we have added a Text Field, an Image View, a Text View, and a button. Figure 7-13 shows this interface, including all the required constraints. Notice that we have added constraints from the elements to every side of their container view, including the bottom, to help the system determine the height of the interface by adding the values of all the constraints and the heights of the elements.

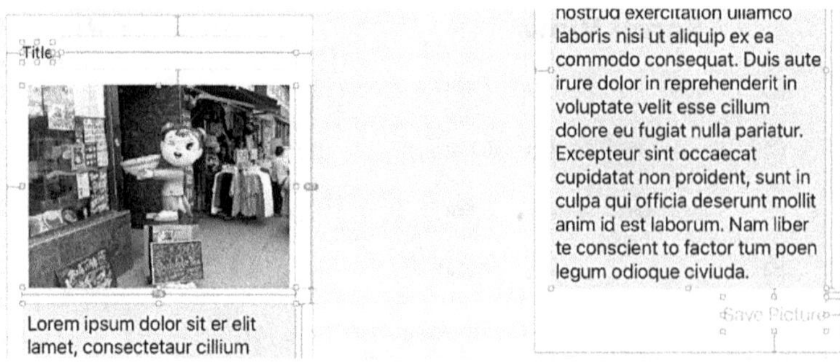

Figure 7-13: *Scrollable interface*

These interfaces are usually bigger than the standard size of the scenes. Xcode offers the alternative to set a specific size for the scene, so we can design longer interfaces in the Storyboard. The tool is called *Simulated Size* and it is available in the Size Inspector panel when the scene is selected. It includes two options: Fixed and Freeform. When we select Freeform, the panel allows us to change the values of the main view's width and height, as shown next.

Figure 7-14: *Simulated Size tool*

Once all the elements of our interface are added to the container view and all the constraints for these elements are defined, the Scroll View is ready to determine the size of its content area and allow us to scroll to see the parts that are not visible, as shown below.

Figure 7-15: *Scrolling the interface*

Do It Yourself: Select the scene in the Storyboard. Open the Size Inspector panel and select the Freeform option from the Simulated Size tool. Set the size of the main view to 320 x 800 or any value you want. Expand the Scroll View and the container view to fit the new size. Add the elements shown in Figure 7-13 to the container view, including the Text View with a gray background. Set the proper constraints to pin the elements to each other and to the sides of the view (Figure 7-13). Remember to assign Height or Aspect Ratio constraints to the elements that do not have intrinsic content size or need a specific size, such as the image View and the Text View. Run the application. You should be able to scroll the interface vertically, as shown in Figure 7-15.

Chapter 8
Gesture Recognizers

Basic 8.1 Gestures

Gestures are actions performed by the user on the screen, such as tapping, swiping, or pinching. These gestures are difficult to detect because all that the screen returns are the position of the fingers, not information on how the fingers were moved. This is the reason why Apple introduced gesture recognizers. A gesture recognizer is an object that performs all the necessary calculations to detect a gesture. The UIKit framework defines a base class called **UIGestureRecognizer** to provide the basic functionality for gesture recognizers and multiple subclasses with additional properties and methods to create recognizers for specific gestures.

UITapGestureRecognizer—This class creates a gesture recognizer that recognizes single or multiple taps. The class includes the integer properties **numberOfTapsRequired** and **numberOfTouchesRequired** to determine the number of taps that need to occur and the number of fingers that have to participate for the gesture to be recognized.

UIPinchGestureRecognizer—This class creates a gesture recognizer that recognizes a pinching gesture (zoom in or out). The class includes the properties **scale** and **velocity** to set a scaling factor and return the velocity of the pinch. The properties are of type **CGFloat**.

UIRotationGestureRecognizer—This class creates a gesture recognizer that recognizes a rotating gesture. The class includes the properties **rotation** and **velocity** to set the rotation in radians and return the velocity in radians per second. They are of type **CGFloat**.

UISwipeGestureRecognizer—This class creates a gesture recognizer that recognizes a swiping gesture. The class includes the properties **direction** and **numberOfTouchesRequired** to set the direction allowed and the number of fingers that must touch the screen for the gesture to be recognized. The **direction** property is a structure (or a set of structures) of type **UISwipeGestureRecognizerDirection** with the properties **right**, **left**, **up**, and **down**.

UIPanGestureRecognizer—This class creates a gesture recognizer that recognizes a panning gesture. The class includes the method **translation(in: UIView?)** to return the current position of the gesture relative to the starting position, the method **velocity(in: UIView?)** to return the velocity of the gesture expressed in points per second, and the properties **maximumNumberOfTouches** and **minimumNumberOfTouches** to set the number of fingers that must touch the view for the gesture to be recognized.

UIScreenEdgePanGestureRecognizer—This class creates a gesture recognizer that recognizes a panning gesture that starts near the edge of the screen. The class includes the **edges** property to determine the edges that recognize the gesture. The property is a structure of type **UIRectEdge** with the properties **top**, **left**, **bottom**, **right**, and **all**.

UILongPressGestureRecognizer—This class creates a gesture recognizer that recognizes a long-press gesture (the user presses one or more fingers on the screen for a certain period of time). The class includes the properties **minimumPressDuration** (a **Double** value to indicate the minimum time the fingers must press the screen), **numberOfTouchesRequired** (the number of fingers that must touch the screen), **numberOfTapsRequired** (the number of taps), and **allowableMovement** (a **CGFloat** value that indicates the movement allowed).

The **UIGestureRecognizer** class provides an initializer to create objects from every subclass and also general properties and methods. The following are the most frequently used.

init(target: Any?, **action:** Selector?**)**—This initializer creates a gesture recognizer configured with the target and the action specified by the arguments. The **target** argument is the object where the action will be executed, and the **action** argument is the method to be executed when the gesture is detected.

state—This property returns the current state of the gesture recognizer. It is an enumeration called **State** included in the **UIGestureRecognizer** class. The values available are **possible**, **began**, **changed**, **ended**, **cancelled**, **failed**, and **recognized**.

view—This property returns a reference to the view the gesture recognizer is attached to.

isEnabled—This property sets or returns a Boolean value that determines whether or not the gesture recognizer is enabled.

numberOfTouches—This property returns the number of touches involved in the gesture.

location(in: UIView?**)**—This method returns a **CGPoint** value that indicates the coordinates where the gesture occurred in the view specified by the **in** argument.

location(ofTouch: Int, **in:** UIView?**)**—This method returns a **CGPoint** value that indicates the coordinates where a touch occurred in the view specified by the **in** argument. The **ofTouch** argument is the index of the touch we want to check.

Gesture recognizers may be added to an element from code or in the Storyboard from the Library.

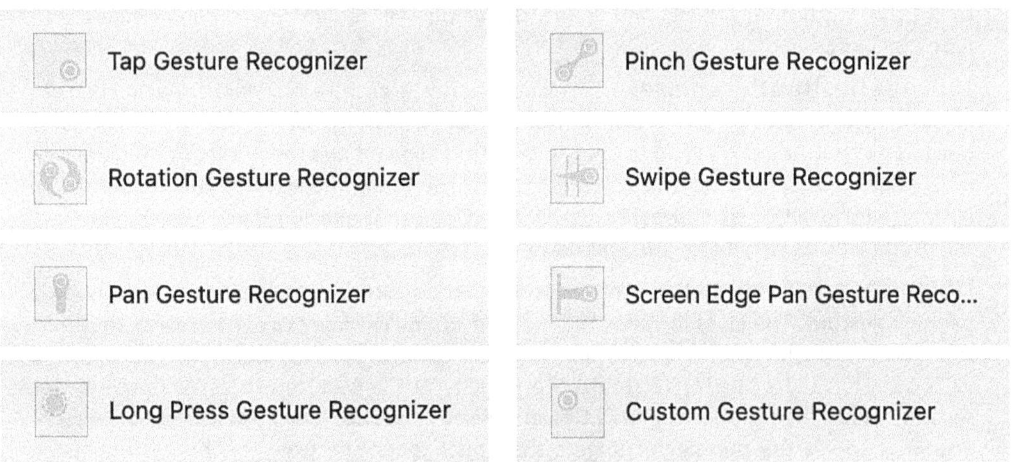

Figure 8-1: *Gesture Recognizer options in the Library*

Although gesture recognizers may be added to any of the views provided by the UIKit framework, not all of them are ready to recognize gestures. The **UIView** class offers two Boolean properties we can modify called **isUserInteractionEnabled** and **isMultipleTouch-Enabled** to activate detection of gestures and multiple touch. If we want to use gestures in a view that disables these options by default, like an Image View for example, we have to change their values from code or from the Attributes Inspector panel, as shown next.

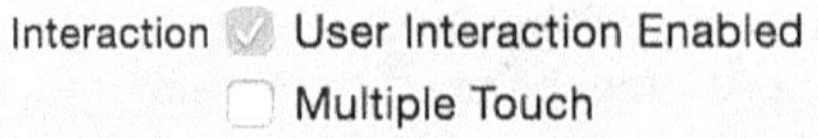

Interaction ☑ User Interaction Enabled
☐ Multiple Touch

Figure 8-2: *Options to enable interaction*

Gesture recognizers are added to the Storyboard as any other element. All we need to do is to drag the gesture recognizer from the Library and drop it on the view we want to recognize the gesture. Xcode adds an icon to the top of the scene to represent it. Figure 8-3 shows what the icon looks like after we add a Pan Gesture to an Image View on the interface.

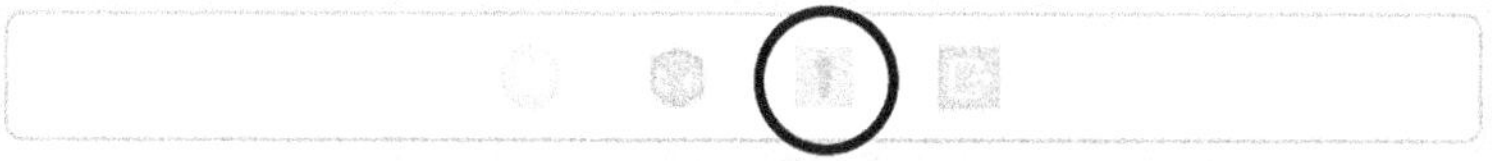

Figure 8-3: *Gesture Recognizer's icon*

For this example, we included an Image View with the picture of the husky (husky.png) that we are going to fade in and out responding to the Pan Gesture.

Figure 8-4: *Image View with a Pan Gesture*

The view controller needs an Outlet for the Image View and an Action for the gesture. To create the Action, we must control-drag a line from the gesture's icon (Figure 8-3) or from the item that represents the gesture in the Document Outline panel.

```
import UIKit

class ViewController: UIViewController {
   @IBOutlet weak var picture: UIImageView!
   var previous: CGFloat = 0

   @IBAction func fadingOut(_ sender: UIPanGestureRecognizer) {
      let translation = sender.translation(in: picture)
      let delta = translation.x - previous
      let width = picture.frame.size.width
      let alpha = picture.alpha + (delta / width)

      if alpha > 0.1 && alpha < 1 {
         picture.alpha = alpha
      }
      if sender.state == .ended {
         previous = 0
      } else {
         previous = translation.x
      }
   }
}
```

Listing 8-1: *Responding to a gesture*

Each gesture returns different kind of information. In the case of the pan gesture, the object includes a few methods that calculate and return the current position and velocity of the gesture. Every time a gesture begins, or a change occurs on its state, the object calls the Action method with a reference to itself (**sender: UIPanGestureRecognizer**). From this reference, we can read and process the information provided by the gesture object and perform custom tasks. In Listing 8-1, we call the **translation()** method to get the value of the current position and calculate the difference between the old horizontal position and the new one. From this difference and the width of the image, we can get a proportional value that added to the alpha value allows us to associate the movement of the finger with changes in the translucency of the picture.

Because the limits of the gesture's position may vary, we check that the alpha value obtained from those numbers does not go over 1.0 or below 0.1 (at 0.0 the Image View does not recognize the gesture anymore), and then assign it to the **alpha** property of the Image View to reflect the changes. To keep track of the old position and be able to compare it with the new one, we store it in the **previous** property. Every time the action is called to report changes in the gesture, the new value is stored in this property. But because the position of a pan gesture is considered to be 0 at the point when the gesture begins, we cannot keep using the values of a previous gesture and therefore the value of the **previous** property must return to 0 when the gesture is over. This is detected at the end by reading the value of the gesture's **state** property.

Do It Yourself: Create a new project. Download the husky.png image from our website and add it to the Assets Catalog. Add an Image View to the main view and assign the image of the husky to it. In the same panel, activate the option called *User Interaction Enabled* for the Image View (Figure 8-2). Drag the option Pan Gesture from the Library and drop it over the Image View. You should see the icon pictured in Figure 8-3. Create an Outlet for the image called **picture**. Control-drag a line from the gesture's icon to the view controller to create an Action called **fadingOut()**. Complete the view controller with the code in Listing 8-1 and run the application. The picture should fade in and out when you move your finger from side to side.

IMPORTANT: Gesture recognizers cannot be added to different views. If we want to use the same recognizer for different views, we must create new objects, but several gesture recognizers of the same type may be connected to the same Action.

Gesture recognizers may be added to any view from code. The object is created first with the **UIGestureRecognizer** initializer and then configured and added to the view. The **UIView** class offers the following methods to manage gesture recognizers.

addGestureRecognizer(UIGestureRecognizer**)**—This method adds a gesture recognizer to the view. The argument is an object of a **UIGestureRecognizer** subclass.

removeGestureRecognizer(UIGestureRecognizer**)**—This method removes a gesture recognizer from the view. The argument is a reference to the gesture added before with the **addGestureRecognizer()** method.

Gesture recognizers implement an old protocol from Objective-C to define the action to perform when the gesture is recognized. This protocol is called *target/action* because it requires the specification of the object that is going to respond to the event (the target) and a method that will be executed when the gesture occurs (the action). The target is a reference to the object, usually specified as **self** (the object in charge of the response is the same object that initialized the gesture recognizer) and the method is specified with a selector. Selectors are declared with the instruction **#selector(method)** and the syntax for the method must include the names of its parameters followed by a semicolon, as in **#selector(showCounter(sender:))**. Because this is an old Objective-C feature, it also requires the methods to be prefixed by the **@objc** keyword.

The following example adds a Tap gesture to a Scroll View to zoom in and out to specific points of the image. This code assumes that we have added a Stack View to the initial scene and pin it to the Safe Area, as we did for some of the examples in the previous chapter.

```
import UIKit

class ViewController: UIViewController, UIScrollViewDelegate {
   @IBOutlet weak var stackContainer: UIStackView!

   var mainScroll: UIScrollView!
   var image: UIImageView!
   var zooming = false

   override func viewDidLoad() {
      super.viewDidLoad()
      image = UIImageView(image: UIImage(named: "doll"))

      mainScroll = UIScrollView(frame: .zero)
      mainScroll.contentSize = CGSize(width: image.frame.size.width,
height: image.frame.size.height)
      mainScroll.minimumZoomScale = 1.0
      mainScroll.maximumZoomScale = 4.0
      mainScroll.delegate = self
      mainScroll.addSubview(image)

      let gesture = UITapGestureRecognizer(target: self, action:
#selector(zoomPicture))
      mainScroll.addGestureRecognizer(gesture)

      stackContainer.addArrangedSubview(mainScroll)
   }
   func viewForZooming(in scrollView: UIScrollView) -> UIView? {
      return image
   }
   @objc func zoomPicture(sender: UITapGestureRecognizer) {
      if !zooming {
         let position = sender.location(in: mainScroll)
         mainScroll.zoom(to: CGRect(x: position.x, y: position.y, width:
1, height: 1), animated: true)
         zooming = true
      } else {
         mainScroll.setZoomScale(1.0, animated: true)
         zooming = false
      }
   }
}
```

Listing 8-2: *Adding gestures from code*

The **UIGestureRecognizer** initializer requires two values: a reference to the object where the action will be performed and the method that is going to be executed when the gesture is detected. Because we are going to perform all the tasks on the view controller, we declare the target as **self** and create a method called **zoomPicture()** to perform the action (Notice that the method was prefixed with the **@objc** keyword to be able to call it from a selector).

This example follows the procedure studied in Chapter 7 to configure the Scroll View and allow the user to scroll and zoom the picture. When the Scroll View is ready, the code creates a **UITapGestureRecognizer** object and adds it to the view with the **addGesture-Recognizer()** method. In consequence, every time the user taps on the Scroll View, the **zoomPicture()** method is executed. In this method, we zoom in or out, depending on the value of the **zooming** property. To zoom in, the code gets the position of the tap in the view from the **location()** method and then zooms in to a rectangle in that position. To zoom out, we just set the scale back to 1.0.

Do It Yourself: Create a new project. Add a Stack View to the main view and pin it to the Safe Area. Connect the Stack View with an Outlet called **`stackContainer`**. Download the doll.jpg image from our website and add it to the Assets Catalog. Complete the view controller with the code in Listing 8-2. Run the application and tap on the image. The image should zoom in the area around your finger.

Chapter 9
Navigation

Basic 9.1 Multiple View Controllers

Apps that only require one scene and a simple interface are rare these days. Because of the limited space, developing apps for mobile devices demands the creation of multiple scenes to represent virtual screens that replace one another in response to the user (see Figure 5-18). Practical applications contain multiple scenes connected with each other following a predetermined path that users can take to navigate and get the information they need.

Xcode templates, like the App template we have been using so far to create our projects, provide initial scenes to start from. The rest of the scenes are added later to the Storyboard as needed from options included in the Library. The option to add single scenes that are controlled by **`UIViewController`** objects is called *View Controller*.

Figure 9-1: *View Controller option in the Library*

Dragging this option to the Storyboard creates a new scene with its own main view. After the scenes are added, they can be dragged from the top bar to different positions to represent what users will see when they navigate the interface. Figure 9-2 shows what the Storyboard looks like after we add a new scene and move it to the right side of the initial scene.

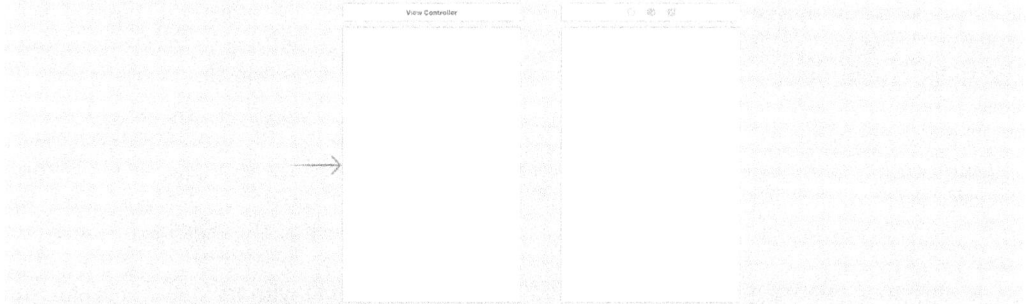

Figure 9-2: *Second scene added to the Storyboard*

We can add all the scenes we need to build our interface. Every scene represents a new screen, and their main views will be shown on the device's screen one at a time.

Do It Yourself: Create a new project. Drag the View Controller option from the Library to the Storyboard. Arrange the scenes to look like Figure 9-2.

The option to add a new scene to the Storyboard is called View Controller because it adds a scene that is controlled by an object created from a subclass of the **`UIViewController`** class, but the view controller is not included along with the scene, we ought to create the file ourselves.

Files are created from the File menu. If we click on the File menu and go over the New option, a submenu shows the option File. Once we click on this option, a window is opened to select the type of file we want to create (we can also use a shortcut pressing the Command + N keys).

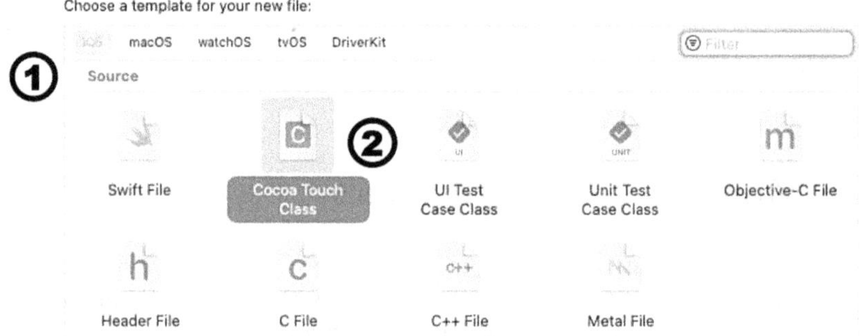

Figure 9-3: *Templates for new files*

There are several options available. The **`UIViewController`** class is part of the Cocoa Touch API, therefore, to create a file with a **`UIViewController`** subclass for the new scene, we must click on the Cocoa Touch Class option in the Source panel (Figure 9-3, number 1 and 2). Another window opens to insert the name and select the class we want to create our subclass from.

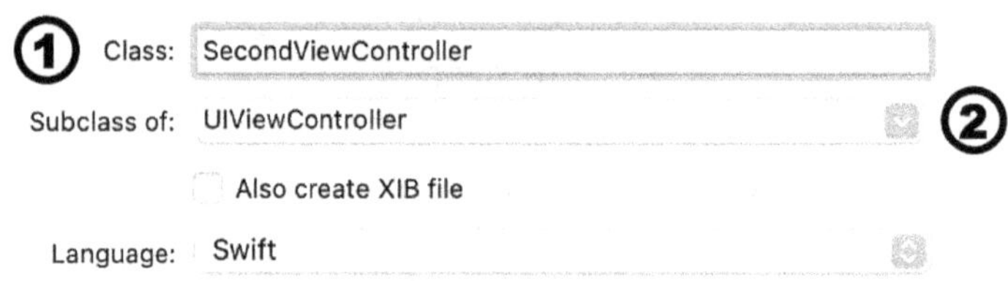

Figure 9-4: *Creating the subclass*

The first value is the name of the class (Figure 9-4, number 1). This value is going to be used as the name of the subclass and the file. It is good practice to start with a word that describes the purpose of the scene and end with the words "ViewController" to reflect the type of class declared inside the file (for this example, we called it *SecondViewController*). The next option is the superclass of our subclass. For scenes with a single view this is the **`UIViewController`** class.

The last two options determine if the process will create a new scene (this is not necessary because we have already created the scene in the Storyboard), and the language Xcode is going to use to create the file (the last language we use is always shown by default). After the information is ready, the file is created and included with the rest of the files in the Navigator Area.

At this point, we have the scene in the Storyboard and the file with its view controller, but they are not connected. Xcode does not assign the new file to the scene automatically; we must do it ourselves from the Identity Inspector panel. This is one of the configuration panels available in the Utilities Area when the scene is selected. To open the panel, select the scene and click on the fourth button at the top of the Utilities Area (circled in Figure 9-5).

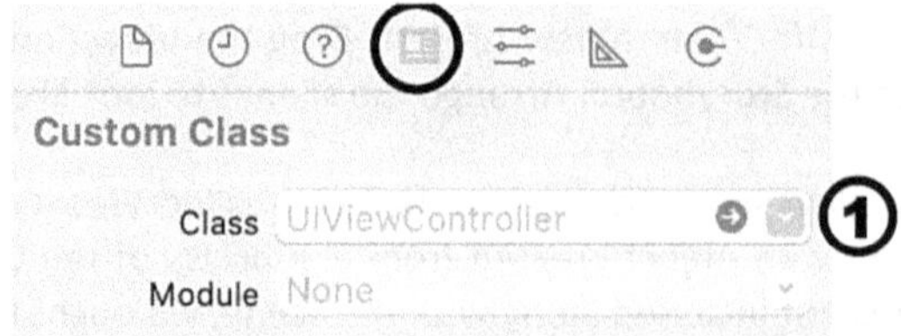

Figure 9-5: *Identity Inspector panel*

The subclass that controls the scene is specified by the first option (Figure 9-5, number 1). We can write the name of the class or select it from the list. Figure 9-6, below, illustrates what the panel looks like after we select the **`SecondViewController`** class.

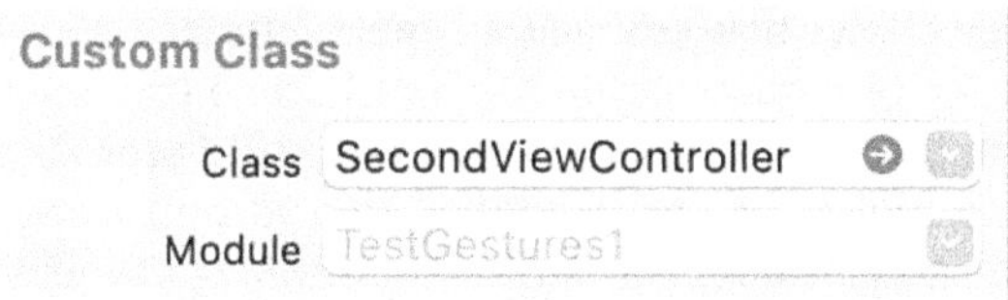

Figure 9-6: *Class assigned to the scene*

Now, the second scene has its own view controller, and we are ready to go. The procedure to create the interface for this scene and connect it to our code is the same as before. We must drag the elements we want to add to the main view and then connect them to the code in their respective view controllers (**`ViewController`** for the scene on the left and **`SecondViewController`** for the scene on the right).

Do It Yourself: Create the subclass for the second scene named **`SecondViewController`**. Select the second scene by clicking on the bar at the top or on the view controller icon (Figure 5-20). Open the Identity Inspector panel in the Utilities Area (Figure 9-5) and assign the subclass you have just created to the scene (Figure 9-5, number 1). Open the Assistant Editor (Figure 5-29) and click on the scenes in the Storyboard to select them. You should see the selected scene on the left and the corresponding view controller on the right of the Editor area.

Basic Segues

The scenes must be connected to each other to allow the user to navigate from one scene to another. For this purpose, the UIKit framework introduces the **`UIStoryboardSegue`** class. From this class, we can create objects called *Segues* that connect the scenes and perform the transition. There are different types of segues available, as shown next.

Show—This segue is used with scenes embedded in a Navigation Controller. It produces a transition from right to left.

Show Detail—This segue is used with scenes embedded in a Split View Controller. It shows a Detail View (a second scene on the same screen) when there is enough space available (iPads), or replaces the current scene by the new one when the space is limited (iPhones).

Present Modally—This segue presents the next scene over the current scene. The type of transition is set by the **`modalTransitionStyle`** property of the view controller that triggers the transition. The possible values are **`coverVertical`** (the scene appears from the bottom), **`flipHorizontal`** (the scenes are turned around), **`crossDissolve`** (the scenes are dissolved), and **`partialCurl`** (the old scene is curled up to reveal the new one).

Present As Popover—This segue presents a scene as a popover.

Custom—This segue allows developers to provide a custom transition.

Segues are fully integrated into the Storyboard and are created by control-dragging lines between scenes. They can be created from one scene to another or from a specific element, such as a button, depending on how we want the user to be able to navigate. The type of segue we use also depends on the type of interface we are building. For instance, the Present Modally and Present As Popover segues are used for small interfaces with only a few scenes, or when we need to provide additional information, such as a screen to let the user modify the app's settings. On the other hand, the Show segue is required when we embed the scenes in a Navigation Controller, as we will see later.

The following example shows how to build a simple interface with Present Modally segues. The interface includes a list of buttons inside the initial scene (the scene pointed by the arrow) and an Image View inside the second scene. The purpose is to provide buttons in one scene the user can tap to select a picture, and then transition to a second scene that shows the selected picture. The second scene also includes a Slider to rate the image, as illustrated below.

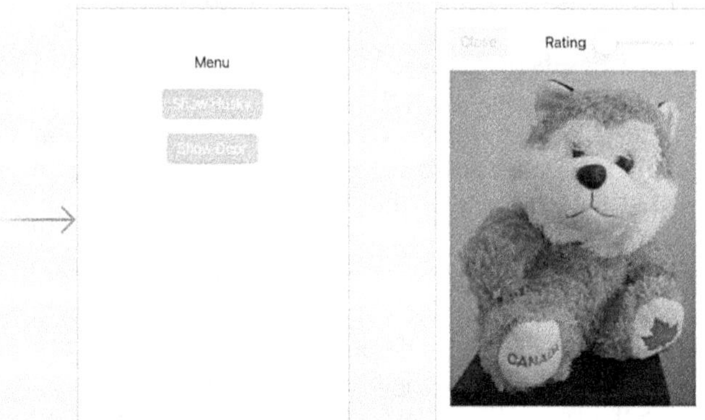

Figure 9-7: *Interface with two scenes*

If we run the app at this point, only the initial scene is shown on the screen and the buttons do not perform any action. To let the user transition from one scene to another, we must create a segue from the button Show Husky to the second scene. The process is illustrated below.

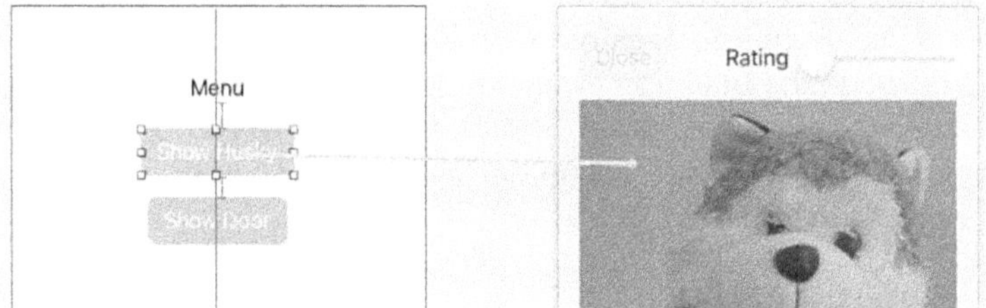

Figure 9-8: *Segue from a button to the second scene*

The line is control-dragged from the button to the second scene. When the mouse button is released, Xcode opens a menu to select the type of segue we want to create.

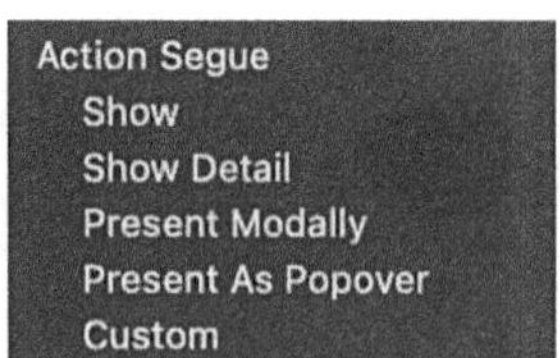

Figure 9-9: *Popup menu listing the type of segues available*

Independent scenes like those implemented in this example can only be connected using a Modal Segue (Present Modally) or a Popover Segue (Present As Popover). What segue to implement depends on the requirements of our application and the type of information contained in the scene. In this example, we have decided to use a Modal Segue (also known as Present Modally).

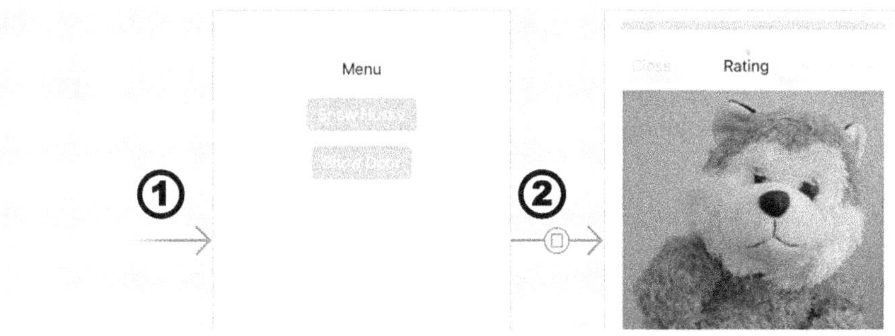

Figure 9-10: *Segue in the Storyboard*

IMPORTANT: Modal and Popover Segues are implemented in small applications or to open scenes that present additional information. Later in this chapter, we will learn how to create more complex and professional interfaces with Navigation Controllers and Show segues.

After adding the segue, the Storyboard shows two arrows, one pointing to the scene on the left (Figure 9-10, number 1) and another connecting the scenes (Figure 9-10, number 2). The single arrow on the left indicates what scene is going to be shown first when the app is executed, and the arrow in between is pointing to the scene that is going to be shown when the segue is triggered (the button is pressed). The arrows illustrate the path or possible paths the user can follow while interacting with our application, which is the main function of the Storyboard; to help us create a story.

Do It Yourself: Add a label and two buttons called Show Husky and Show Door to the initial scene. Add a Tinted button called Close, the label "Rating", a Slider, and an Image View to the second scene. From the Utilities Area, set the value of the Slider to 0, the minimum to 0, and the maximum to 5. Add the image husky.png to the Assets Catalog and assign it to the Image View. Apply all the necessary constraints to get an interface like Figure 9-7 (remember to assign higher Content Hugging and Content Compression priorities to the button or the Image View if necessary). Control-drag a line from the button Show Husky to the second scene (Figure 9-8). Select the Present Modally segue. Run your app and press the Show Husky button. You should see the second scene sliding from the bottom of the screen to the top.

Modal Segues were introduced for the purpose of connecting single views and presenting additional information, but still offer a few options for configuration. Among those options is a list of transitions we can choose from. The transition by default is called *Cover Vertical* and it slides the destination view from bottom to top, but we can change it from the Utilities Area. When we click on a segue in the Storyboard, the Utilities Area presents a configuration panel to edit the segue.

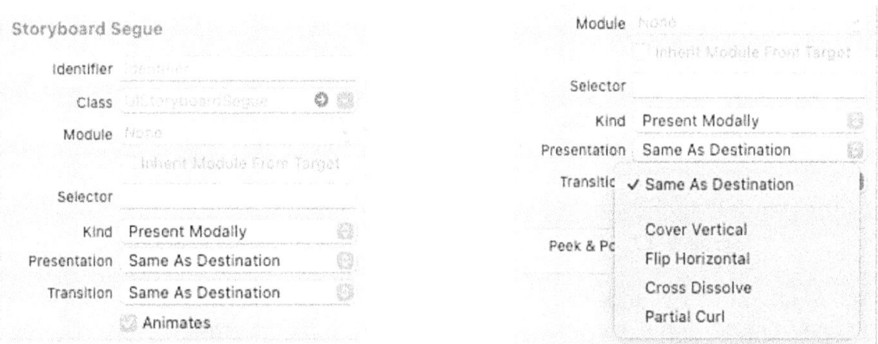

Figure 9-11: *Configuring the segue*

From this panel, we can specify a name to reference the segue from code (Identifier), set our own custom segue (Class), or select the type of segue, presentation, and transition we want. The picture on the right shows the Transition menu with the types available. Selecting any of these options changes the way the destination scene is presented.

Basic Unwind Segues

Modal Segues allow us to move forward in the Storyboard, but we can also move backward with a special kind of segue called *Unwind Segue*. To set up these segues we must follow a few unconventional steps. First, we must write an Action on the view controller that presents the next scene, and then connect to that Action the element in the second scene that triggers the Unwind Segue. This is because the view controller responsible for transitioning back to the previous scene is the one that presented the destination scene. In our example, this is the **ViewController** class.

So far, we have let Xcode generate the code for the **@IBAction**, but we can also write it ourselves and then create the connection, as shown next.

```
import UIKit

class ViewController: UIViewController {
   @IBAction func goBack(_ segue: UIStoryboardSegue) {
   }
}
```

Listing 9-1: *Adding the Action for the Unwind Segue*

The code in Listing 9-1 is an example of how to write the Action in the view controller that presents the destination scene. The method can have any name we want but it must include a parameter of type **UIStoryboardSegue** to provide access to the view controller that is been removed. Once this code is ready, we can connect the element in the destination scene to the Action. This is done by control-dragging a line from the element to the icon at the top of the scene called *Exit*.

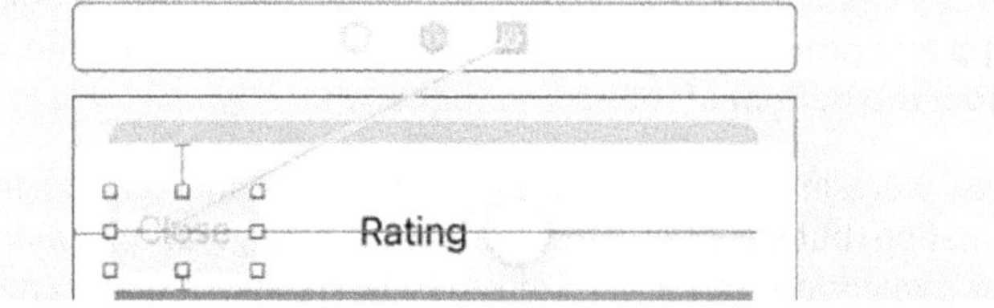

Figure 9-12: *Exit icon*

In Figure 9-12, the Close button inside the second scene is connected to the Exit icon. When the mouse is released, a menu shows the Actions available in the **ViewController** class.

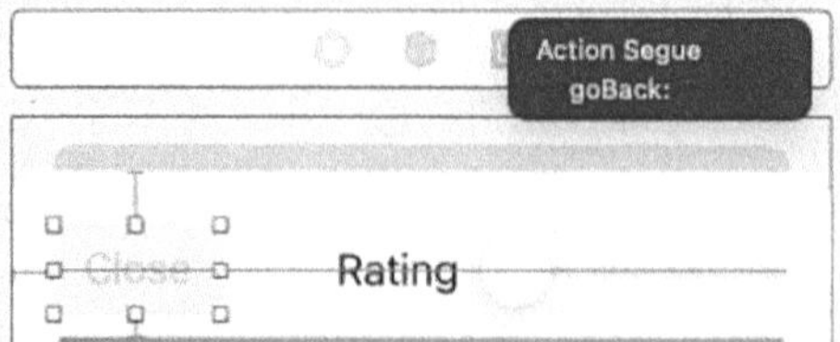

Figure 9-13: *Menu to select the Action for the Unwind Segue*

Once the **goBack()** Action is selected from this menu, the Close button is connected to the Action defined before in the **ViewController** class and the process is over. The system will remove the scene every time the button is pressed.

Do It Yourself: Write the Action in your **`ViewController`** class as shown in Listing 9-1. Control-drag a line from the Close button in the second scene to the Exit button, as shown in Figure 9-12. Select the **`goBack()`** action from the menu (Figure 9-13). Run the application and press the Show Husky button to present the second scene. Press the Close button to go back to the initial scene.

IMPORTANT: An Unwind Segue can transition back to any scene in the Navigation Controller that is part of the path the user is following. All we need to do is to define the Action for the view controller we want to go back to and then select that Action from the menu. The system transitions back to the view controller with the Action, no matter how many scenes are in between.

The Action in our **`ViewController`** class was declared with no statements. This is enough to perform the Unwind Segue, but we can take advantage of this method and its parameter to get information about the view controllers that participate in the transition. The **`UIStoryboardSegue`** class includes the following properties for this purpose.

source—This property returns a reference to the view controller that is displayed at the beginning of the transition. The value returned is a generic **`UIViewController`** object that we must cast to the corresponding type.

destination—This property returns a reference to the view controller that is displayed at the end of the transition. The value returned is a generic **`UIViewController`** object that we must cast to the corresponding type.

identifier—This property returns the string we used in Interface Builder to identify the segue (see Figure 9-11). Using this property, we know what segue was triggered and can get information about the scene that is going to be shown on the screen.

The **`source`** and **`destination`** properties are required depending on the process. If we want to access the view controller that is going to be removed, we read the **`source`** property (the origin of the transition), but if we want to access the view controller which scene is going to be presented on the screen, we access the **`destination`** (the destination of the transition). To illustrate this process, we can add some code to the **`SecondViewController`** class. This code processes the input from the Slider and adds a property we can read when the Unwind Segue is triggered.

```
import UIKit

class SecondViewController: UIViewController {
   @IBOutlet weak var sliderRating: UISlider!
   var rating: Int = 0

   override func viewDidLoad() {
      super.viewDidLoad()
      sliderRating.value = Float(rating)
   }
   @IBAction func changeRating(_ sender: UISlider) {
      let value = round(sender.value)
      sliderRating.value = value
      rating = Int(value)
   }
}
```

Listing 9-2: *Processing changes in the Slider*

The code in Listing 9-2 adds an integer property called **`rating`** to the **`SecondViewController`** class to keep track of the rating set by the user. The code also includes an Outlet for the Slider to set its initial value equal to the value of **`rating`** and an Action to update the value of this property every time the Slider is moved (see **`UISlider`** in Chapter 5).

Because the Slider works with consecutive floating-point values and our rating is established by integers between 0 and 5, before assigning the selected value to the **rating** property we must round the number to the nearest integer with the **round()** function and assign it back to the Slider to reflect the right rating on the screen. This makes the indicator jump from one integer to another, helping the user identify the rating that wants to assign to the picture.

Now that we have the **rating** property, we can read it from the Unwind Segue's Action in the **ViewController** class.

```
import UIKit

class ViewController: UIViewController {
   var ratingHusky: Int = 0

   @IBAction func goBack(_ segue: UIStoryboardSegue) {
      let controller = segue.source as! SecondViewController
      ratingHusky = controller.rating
   }
}
```

Listing 9-3: *Reading properties from the source*

From the **source** property of the **UIStoryboardSegue** object received by the Action, we get a reference to the view controller that is being removed and access its properties. In our example, this is the **SecondViewController** class. We get the value, cast it as **SecondViewController**, and store it in the **controller** constant. Now that we have access to the view controller of the second scene, we read its **rating** property and store its value in the **ratingHusky** property of the **ViewController** class. Copying the value to a property in the **ViewController** object is necessary because the **SecondViewController** object and all its properties are destroyed as soon as the scene is removed.

This is the first part of the process; we let the user select a rating and when it moves back to the menu screen, we preserve the selected value in the **ratingHusky** property. If we run the application at this moment and move the Slider to specify a rating, once we go back to the initial scene and tap the Show Husky button a second time, the Slider is again in its initial position. This is because the value of the Slider is always set as the value of the **rating** property when the main view is loaded. To get the Slider to show the value previously selected by the user, we must send the value of the **ratingHusky** property in the **ViewController** object back to the **SecondViewController** object every time the Show Husky button is pressed. The **UIViewController** class provides the following methods for this purpose.

prepare(for: UIStoryboardSegue, **sender:** Any?**)**—This method is called by the system in the view controller object when a segue is triggered and before the transition is initiated. We can override this method in our view controller to access the destination view controller and modify its properties.

performSegue(withIdentifier: String, **sender:** Any?**)**—This method triggers the segue identified with the string specified by the **withIdentifier** argument. The **sender** argument is the object that triggers the segue (usually declared as **self**).

The method we need to implement to send the information to the second view controller is **prepare()**. This is one of those methods that are called by the system in the view controller and can be overridden to perform custom tasks. In this case, we can override it to access the view controller that is going to be opened and modify its properties before its main view is shown on the screen. The following example expands the code in our **ViewController** class to update the value of the **rating** property in the **SecondViewController** class before the transition is performed.

```
import UIKit

class ViewController: UIViewController {
   var ratingHusky: Int = 0

   @IBAction func goBack(_ segue: UIStoryboardSegue) {
      let controller = segue.source as! SecondViewController
      ratingHusky = controller.rating
   }
   override func prepare(for segue: UIStoryboardSegue, sender: Any?) {
      let controller = segue.destination as! SecondViewController
      controller.rating = ratingHusky
   }
}
```

Listing 9-4: *Sending values to the second view controller before its main view is loaded*

Now the process is complete. The **prepare()** method updates the value of the **rating** property with the value of the **ratingHusky** property before the second scene is shown on the screen, and this value is used by the **SecondViewController** object to update the Slider as soon as the main view is loaded. When the user taps the Close button, the **goBack()** Action is executed in the **ViewController** class and the process is reversed (the **ratingHusky** property is updated with the current value of the **rating** property). In consequence, the rating set by the user is always preserved in the **ratingHusky** property inside the view controller of the initial scene and it is used to update the Slider every time the second scene is opened.

Do It Yourself: Copy the code in Listing 9-4 in your **ViewController** class. Create an Outlet called **sliderRating** and an Action called **changeRating()** for the Slider in the second scene. Complete the **SecondViewController** class with the code in Listing 9-2. Run the application. The Slider should always reflect the rating set by the user.

IMPORTANT: Never try to access Outlets of one view controller from another. Always transfer data through normal properties because there is no guarantee that the Outlets will be connected to the objects in the Storyboard until the main view is fully loaded.

The same procedure can be applied to the second button of the menu to let the user select another image. All we need to do is to add a new scene to the Storyboard and connect it to the Show Door button using another Modal Segue, as shown below.

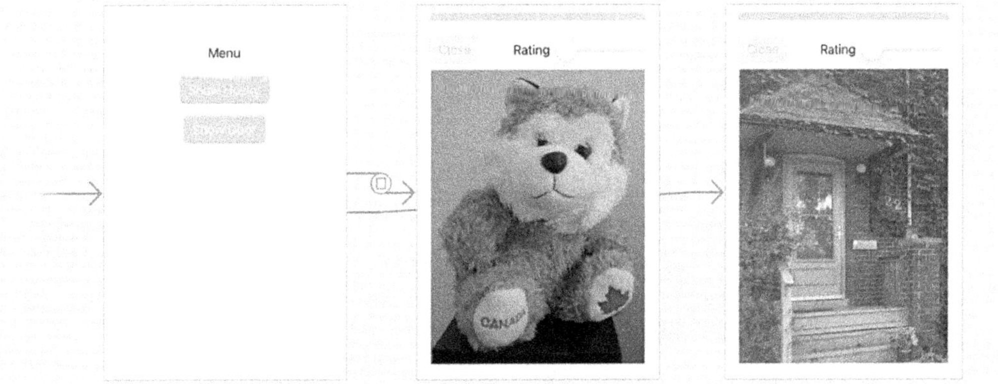

Figure 9-14: *Interface with three scenes*

The process to add the third scene is the same as before; we drag the View Controller option to the Storyboard and build the interface. Like the second scene, this one also needs its own view controller. For this example, we call it **ThirdViewController**. Because we use the same type of elements and process the same information, the code for this view controller is the same defined for the **SecondViewController** class in Listing 9-2, including the Outlet and Action for the Slider. What changes is how the **ViewController** class manages the information that is coming from and going to these view controllers. Now we have two segues, one that opens the scene with the husky and another that opens the scene with the door, and therefore the code in the **ViewController** class must recognize the segue that is being triggered to know how to proceed. This is why the segue's configuration panel includes an option called *Identifier* (Figure 9-11). The string provided to this option is assigned to the **identifier** property of the **UIStoryboardSegue** object and that is how we know which segue was triggered.

As explained before, to change the segue's configuration we must select it and open the Utilities Area (Figure 9-11). For normal segues it is easy, we select them on the Storyboard and modify their values from the Attributes Inspector panel, but the only way to select an Unwind Segue is from the Document Outline panel. The items in this panel that represent Unwind Segues are preceded by a round icon, as illustrated below (number 1).

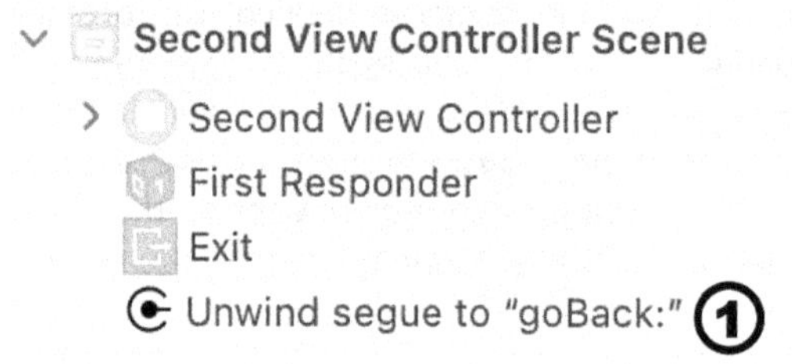

Figure 9-15: *Unwind Segue in the Document Outline panel*

For our example, we identified the segues that point to the scenes with the strings "showHusky" and "showDoor", and the Unwind Segues with the strings "removeHusky" and "removeDoor", respectively. Once all the segues have been identified, our **ViewController** class can check these values and modify the right properties.

```
import UIKit

class ViewController: UIViewController {
   var ratingHusky: Int = 0
   var ratingDoor: Int = 0

   @IBAction func goBack(_ segue: UIStoryboardSegue) {
      if segue.identifier == "removeHusky" {
         let controller = segue.source as! SecondViewController
         ratingHusky = controller.rating
      } else if segue.identifier == "removeDoor" {
         let controller = segue.source as! ThirdViewController
         ratingDoor = controller.rating
      }
   }
   override func prepare(for segue: UIStoryboardSegue, sender: Any?) {
      if segue.identifier == "showHusky" {
         let controller = segue.destination as! SecondViewController
         controller.rating = ratingHusky
      } else if segue.identifier == "showDoor" {
         let controller = segue.destination as! ThirdViewController
         controller.rating = ratingDoor
      }
   }
}
```

Listing 9-5: *Processing values according to the segue*

The **prepare()** method is executed every time a segue is triggered. The method in our example compares the value of the **identifier** property of the **segue** object with the strings "showHusky" and "showDoor". If the value is equal to "showHusky", it gets the reference to the **SecondViewController** object and updates the value of its **rating** property with the value of the **ratingHusky** property. If, on the other hand, the value of **identifier** is equal to "showDoor", it gets the reference to the **ThirdViewController** object and updates its **rating** property with the value of the **ratingDoor** property. A similar control is performed for the **goBack()** action, although this time we had to check the identifiers for the Unwind Segues ("removeHusky" and "removeDoor").

Do It Yourself: Add a new scene to the Storyboard and recreate the same interface of the second scene but with the image of the door (you can copy and paste the elements from one scene to another). Add a segue of type Present Modally from the Show Door button to the new scene. Control-drag a line from the Close button to the Exit icon to create the Unwind Segue for the third scene. Create a file with a subclass of **UIViewController** called **ThirdViewController** and assign it to the third scene. Create an Outlet called **sliderRating** and an Action called **changeRating** for the Slider and complete the code of the **ThirdViewController** class with the code in Listing 9-2. Select the segues in the Storyboard and assign the identifiers "showHusky" and "showDoor" (Figure 9-11). Select the Unwind Segues from the Document Outline panel and assign the identifiers "removeHusky" and "removeDoor" (Figure 9-15). Update the **ViewController** class with the code in Listing 9-5. Run the application. The Sliders should always reflect the rating selected by the user for each image.

IMPORTANT: Unwind Segues are not the only way to transition back to the previous scene. We can also dismiss a modal scene, or navigate back with the tools provided by Navigation Controllers. We will learn how to dismiss a modal scene in Chapter 12 and how to work with Navigation Controllers later in this chapter.

Basic Segues in Code

Creating a scene for every image available, as we did in the previous example, may be enough for small applications but real applications demand some sort of process in which the content of a scene is generated dynamically according to the information available. In this scenario, a scene provides an updated list of options and a segue connects it to another scene in charge of presenting the information selected by the user. The segue is therefore not triggered by a specific element on the interface but from code by the **performSegue()** method introduced before.

Depending on the number of values available, the list may be presented with a Table View, as we will see in Chapter 10, or with controls like pickers. The following example implements a Picker View to present a predefined list of pictures the user can choose from.

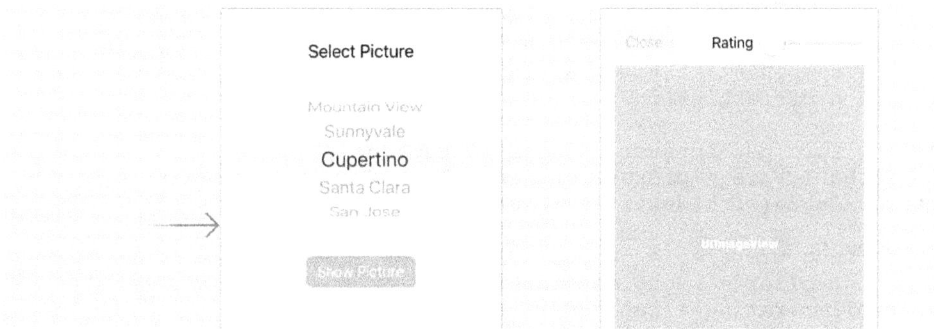

Figure 9-16: Interface to process every option available

The initial scene for this new application contains a Picker View and a button. When the button is pressed, the code for this view controller executes the **performSegue()** method to trigger a segue that transitions to the second scene. There are different ways to create this segue. The simplest is to control-drag a line from the view controller's icon to the second scene, as shown below.

Figure 9-17: *Creating a segue from one scene to another*

IMPORTANT: Segues that are not associated with an element must always have an identifier, so they can be referenced from code (see Figure 9-11). For this example, we are going to call it "showPicture".

No matter how the segue is triggered, the system always calls the **prepare()** method before performing the transition. In the following view controller, we use this method to report to the second scene which was the item selected on the picker. With this information, the second scene loads the corresponding image and sets the Slider to display the rating.

```
import UIKit

class ViewController: UIViewController, UIPickerViewDelegate,
UIPickerViewDataSource {
   @IBOutlet weak var pickerPictures: UIPickerView!
   var picturesList: [String]!
   var ratings: [Int]!
   var selectedPicture: Int!

   override func viewDidLoad() {
      super.viewDidLoad()
      pickerPictures.delegate = self
      pickerPictures.dataSource = self

      picturesList = ["Husky", "Door"]
      ratings = [0, 0]
      selectedPicture = 0
   }
   func numberOfComponents(in pickerView: UIPickerView) -> Int {
      return 1
   }
   func pickerView(_ pickerView: UIPickerView, numberOfRowsInComponent
component: Int) -> Int {
      return picturesList.count
   }
   func pickerView(_ pickerView: UIPickerView, titleForRow row: Int,
forComponent component: Int) -> String? {
      return picturesList[row]
   }
   @IBAction func getPicture(_ sender: UIButton) {
      selectedPicture = pickerPictures.selectedRow(inComponent: 0)
      performSegue(withIdentifier: "showPicture", sender: self)
   }
   override func prepare(for segue: UIStoryboardSegue, sender: Any?) {
      let controller = segue.destination as! SecondViewController
      controller.rating = ratings[selectedPicture]
      controller.picture = picturesList[selectedPicture]
   }
```

```
    @IBAction func goBack(_ segue: UIStoryboardSegue) {
        let controller = segue.source as! SecondViewController
        ratings[selectedPicture] = controller.rating
    }
}
```

Listing 9-6: *Storing the data*

Most of the code in Listing 9-6 is composed of the delegate methods that configure the picker (see **UIPickerView** in Chapter 5), but we also have the **goBack()** action implemented before for the Unwind Segue and the **prepare()** method to send the information to the second scene when the segue created in Figure 9-17 is triggered. To store the data, we have created three properties: **picturesList**, **ratings**, and **selectedPicture**. The **picturesList** property is an array of strings to store the names of the available pictures, the **ratings** property is an array of integers to store the rating of each picture, and the **selectedPicture** property is a single integer that stores the index of the selected picture. This last property is used to keep track of the picture we are currently working with. When the **prepare()** method sends the information to the second scene, it takes the values from the **picturesList** and **ratings** arrays corresponding to the index determined by the **selectedPicture** property. Likewise, when the **goBack()** method processes the rating set by the user, it stores its value in the position of the **ratings** array corresponding to the **selectedPicture** property.

The interface includes the Show Picture button to select the picture. This button has been connected with an Action called **getPicture()** that gets the value selected in the picker, assigns it to the **selectedPicture** property, and then executes the **performSegue()** method to trigger the segue and load the second scene (the segue was identified with the name "showPicture").

Unwind Segues can also be created from the view controller to the Exit button and then triggered by code. To create an Unwind Segue that is not connected to an element, we must control-drag a line from the view controller's icon at the top of the scene to the Exit button.

Figure 9-18: *Creating an Unwind Segue for a view controller*

The view controller for the second scene now has to execute the **performSegue()** method to trigger the Unwind Segue when the user wants to go back to the previous scene. To this end, we have included an Action connected to the Close button in the **SecondViewController** class (the Unwind Segue was identified with the string "goBack").

```
import UIKit

class SecondViewController: UIViewController {
    @IBOutlet weak var sliderRating: UISlider!
    @IBOutlet weak var pictureView: UIImageView!
    var rating: Int = 0
    var picture: String!

    override func viewDidLoad() {
        super.viewDidLoad()
        sliderRating.value = Float(rating)
        pictureView.image = UIImage(named: picture.lowercased())
    }
    @IBAction func changeRating(_ sender: UISlider) {
        let value = round(sender.value)
        sliderRating.value = value
        rating = Int(value)
    }
```

```
    @IBAction func goBack(_ sender: UIButton) {
        performSegue(withIdentifier: "goBack", sender: self)
    }
}
```

***Listing 9-7:** Showing the data*

Besides triggering the Unwind Segue, the code in Listing 9-7 introduces additional changes necessary to process the image selected in the initial scene. The view controller includes a new property to store the name of the image selected by the user and load its file (**`picture`**). This property is used to load the file, create the **`UIImage`** object, and assign it to the Image View. Notice that the value of the **`picture`** property was lowercased to match the names of the images.

Do It Yourself: Create a new project. Add a second scene with a class called **`SecondViewController`**. Design the interface according to Figure 9-16. The initial scene includes a Picker View and a button, and the second scene is the same implemented for previous examples. Create a Present Modally segue from the initial scene to the second scene (Figure 9-17). Assign the identifier "showPicture" to this segue. Copy the code in Listing 9-6 into the ViewController.swift file and the code in Listing 9-7 into the SecondViewController.swift file. Create an Unwind Segue for the second scene as shown in Figure 9-18. Open the Document Outline panel, select this segue, and give it the identifier "goBack". Connect the Slider and the Image View to their respective Outlets, and the Slider and the Close button to their respective Actions. Run the application. You should be able to select the pictures from the picker and change their ratings.

Basic 9.2 Navigation Controllers

The view controllers used so far are called *Content View Controllers* because they manage their own content. They are created from custom subclasses of the **`UIViewController`** class and can present and control a single scene. For this reason, these view controllers have limitations when it comes to replacing their own scene by another or providing the means to organize the interface. This is the reason why the UIKit framework includes several subclasses of **`UIViewController`** that introduce better alternatives to work with multiple scenes. The view controllers created from these classes are called *Container View Controllers* because they contain other view controllers. The most widely used is the Navigation Controller, created from the **`UINavigationController`** class. This class creates a container view controller that organizes the scenes in sequential order, as shown below.

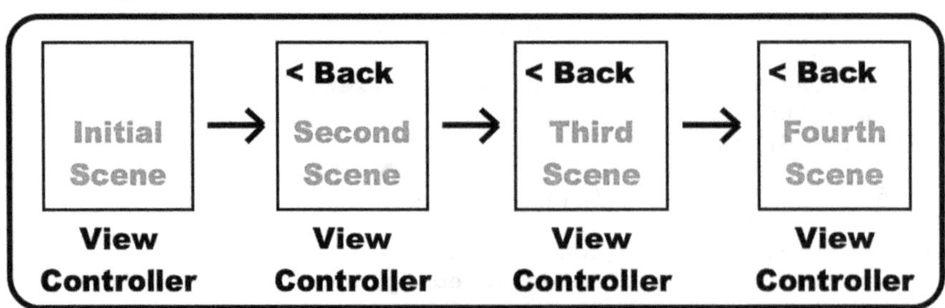

***Figure 9-19:** View controllers managed by a Navigation Controller*

As shown in Figure 9-19, the scenes managed by a Navigation Controller are presented in sequence. The first scene opens the second scene, the second scene opens the third scene, and so on. When the user decides to go back, the sequence is reversed, the current scene is removed, and the previous one is shown on the screen. To keep track of the view controllers in the sequence, the Navigation Controller stores a reference to each one of them in an array called *stack* and then puts or pulls view controllers from the stack every time their scenes must be presented or removed.

The possible sequences are defined in the Storyboard, but the stack is generated in real time. If we define different paths, as illustrated in Figure 9-20 below, the Navigation Controller only stores in the stack the view controllers on the path the user decides to follow.

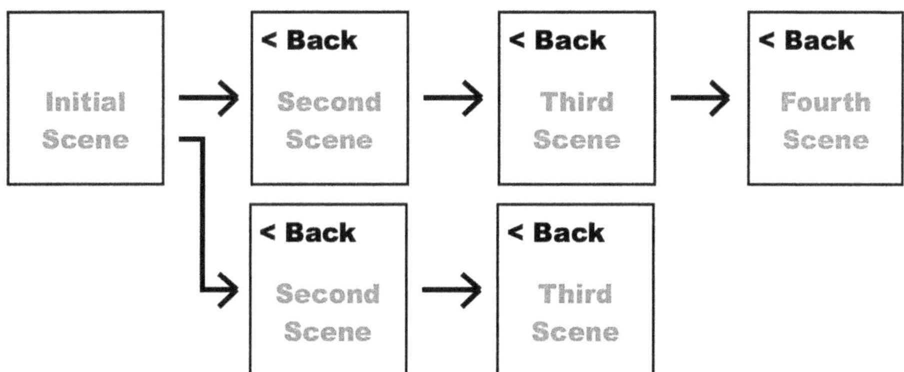

Figure 9-20: *Navigation Controller with multiple paths*

The difference between building a structure like this with a Navigation Controller rather than the single view controllers and Modal segues implemented before is that Navigation Controllers incorporate additional functionality that makes it easy for us to create a path for the user to navigate through. They use a segue of type Show that transitions from right to left (or left to right when the scene is being removed) reflecting on the screen the sequential order of the scenes in the stack. They also incorporate bars to identify each scene and their predecessors, and properties and methods to control the navigation. The following are the most frequently used.

viewControllers—This property is an array that contains references to the view controllers currently managed by the `UINavigationController` object.

topViewController—This property returns the view controller at the top of the stack (usually the view controller displayed on the screen).

visibleViewController—This property returns the view controller currently shown on the screen. The view controller may belong to the Navigation Controller or to a scene opened modally.

popViewController(animated: Bool**)**—This method removes the top view controller from the stack and makes the previous one active. The **animated** argument indicates whether the transition will be animated or not.

pushViewController(UIViewController, **animated:** Bool**)**—This method adds the view controller referenced by the first argument to the stack. The **animated** argument indicates whether the transition will be animated or not.

popToRootViewController(animated: Bool**)**—This method removes all the view controllers from the stack except the initial view controller. The **animated** argument indicates whether the transition will be animated or not.

Basic Navigation Controllers in the Storyboard

There are two ways to add a Navigation Controller to the Storyboard. If we have already designed the interface, Xcode offers an option to embed the scenes inside a Navigation Controller. We must select the scene that we want to be the initial scene for the Navigation Controller and then go to the Editor menu at the top of the screen, open the option Embed In, and select Navigation Controller (Editor/Embed In/Navigation Controller). The other alternative is to drag the Navigation Controller option from the Library. This option creates the Navigation Controller along with its initial scene. Figure 9-21 illustrates what a single scene looks like after it is embedded in a Navigation Controller.

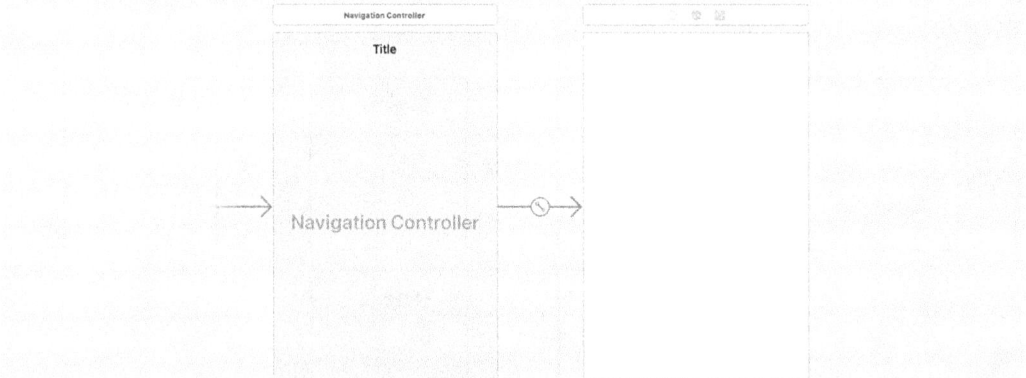

Figure 9-21: *Initial scene embedded in a Navigation Controller*

The scene on the left represents the Navigation Controller and the scene on the right is our initial scene. The arrow is now pointing to the Navigation Controller and a segue connects this controller to the initial scene. This segue is called *Root View Controller* because it indicates which is the first scene displayed by the Navigation Controller. When the app is executed, the system loads the Navigation Controller first and then looks for its root view controller to show the initial scene on the screen.

IMPORTANT: If you opt for the option to add the Navigation Controller from the Library, there is an additional step you must follow. When the initial scene is deleted and a new one is added to the Storyboard, the arrow pointing to the initial scene disappears. To get back the arrow, you must select the scene you want to be the initial scene (in this case, the Navigation Controller), go to the Attributes Inspector panel, and activate the option *Is Initial View Controller*.

More scenes may be added to the interface as before, but instead of using the Present Modally segue to connect the scenes, we must create segues of type Show. Figure 9-22, next, illustrates what we see when we add a second scene and connect it using this segue. The initial scene includes a label with the text "Root View" and a button with the title "Open Second View". The button was connected to the second scene with a Show segue (the first option of the popup menu). When the user presses the button, the second scene is shown on the screen transitioning from right to left.

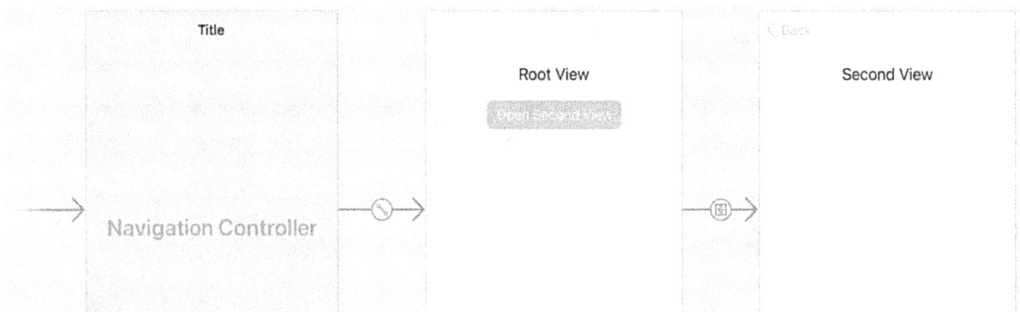

Figure 9-22: *Navigation stack in the Storyboard*

The Show segue performs the transition to move from one scene to another, but the Navigation Controller takes care of the rest. It adds a Navigation Bar at the top that we can use to identify the scenes and a Back button to each scene to allow the user to return to the previous one. All the functionality for this button is already implemented by the controller, so unless we want to customize the process, there is nothing else we need to do to allow the user to navigate back and forward.

Do It Yourself: Create a new project. Select the scene, open the Editor menu at the top of the screen, go to Embed In, and select the option Navigation Controller. The Storyboard should look like Figure 9-21. Drag the View Controller option from the Library to add another scene to the Storyboard. Add a label and a button to the initial scene and a label to the second scene, as illustrated in Figure 9-22 (Make sure that the elements are positioned below the Navigation Bar at the top). Control-drag a line from the button in the initial scene to the second scene to create a Show segue. Create a file with the view controller for the second scene called `SecondViewController`, as we did before. Run the application and press the button. Press the Back button to go back to the initial scene.

Basic Navigation Bar

As we just mentioned, the Navigation Controller introduces a Navigation Bar at the top of every scene to help the user navigate. Navigation Bars are just empty views. Their content is not generated by the bar itself but by objects of the `UINavigationItem` class. In turn, these objects are containers for other views that represent things like the title of the scene and buttons, as shown below.

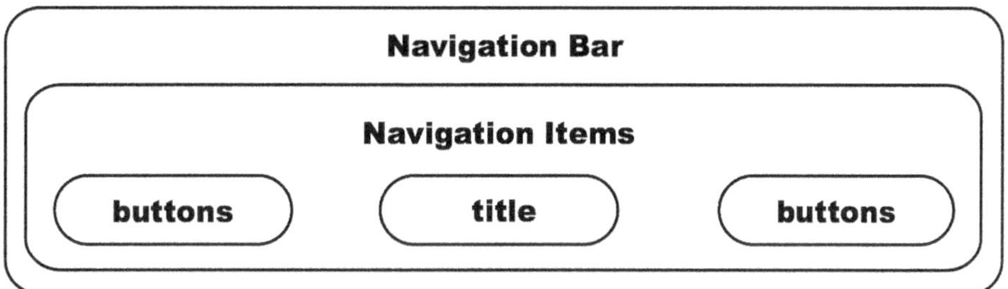

Figure 9-23: *Elements of the Navigation Bar*

Navigation Items are created automatically by the system along with the Navigation Bar, but we can remove them and add them again from the Library if necessary.

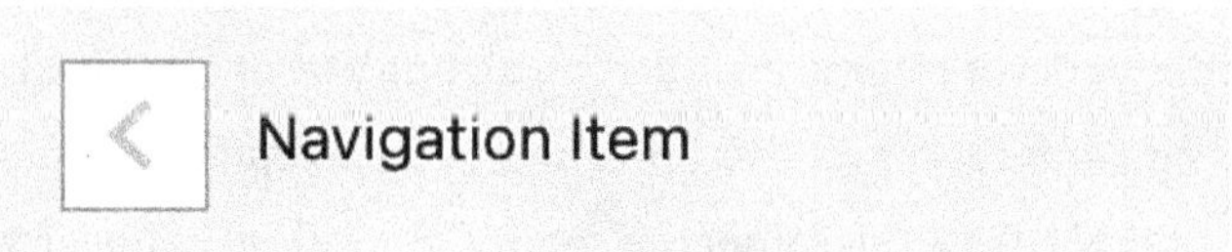

Figure 9-24: *Navigation Item option in the Library*

Navigation items may include a title, a prompt, and buttons on the sides. As we have seen in the previous section of this chapter, one button is automatically generated by the Navigation Controller to help the user navigate back to the previous scene. By default, this button has the same title as the previous scene or the title Back if the scene has no title, but we can define our own, along with the scene's title and prompt, from the Attributes Inspector panel.

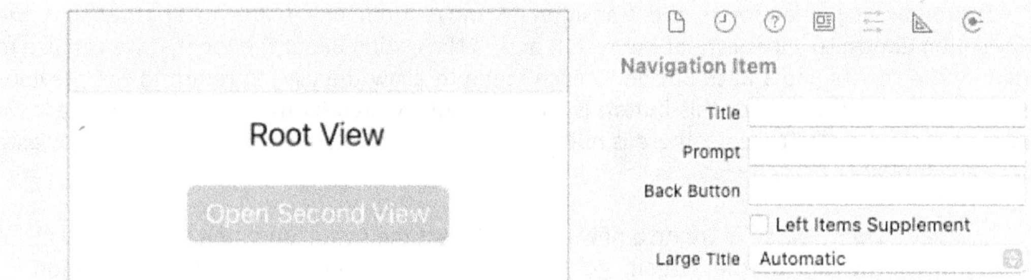

Figure 9-25: *Configuring the Navigation Item*

The values inserted in the first two fields (Title and Prompt) are shown in the current scene, but the value of the third field corresponds to the title of the Back button the system is going to show in the next scene to go back to this one. For example, if we select the Navigation Item of the initial scene in our interface and insert the title "Menu" for the bar and the title "Go Back" for the button, we will see something like Figure 9-26, below. The scene's title is shown at the center of the Navigation Bar and the Back button in the second scene now reads "Go Back".

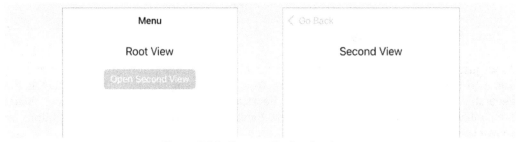

Figure 9-26: *Custom Navigation Items*

Do It Yourself: Click on the Navigation Bar of the initial scene, open the Attributes Inspector panel, and assign the value "Menu" to the Title option and the value "Go Back" to the Back Button option (Figure 9-25). You should see something like Figure 9-26. You can also double-click the bar to change the title from the Storyboard.

IMPORTANT: If a title is provided but no value is defined for the Back button, the button adopts the title of the scene (the Back button in our example would have the title "Menu").

Of course, the items of a **`UINavigationItem`** object may be modified from code. The **`UIViewController`** class offers a property called **`navigationItem`** to access the Navigation Item and its properties. The following are the most frequently used.

title—This property sets or returns the title. It is an optional of type **`String`**.

prompt—This property sets or returns the prompt. It is an optional of type **`String`**.

largeTitleDisplayMode—This property sets or returns a value of an enumeration called **`LargeTitleDisplayMode`** included in the **`UINavigationItem`** class that determines whether the Navigation Bar will show large titles or not. The values available are **`automatic`** (it is determined by the system depending on the previous scene), **`always`**, and **`never`**.

backBarButtonItem—This property sets the Back button for the scene. It is an optional of type **`UIBarButtonItem`**.

hidesBackButton—This property is a Boolean value that determines whether the Back button is visible. The property must be defined in the scene that shows the button.

The following is the view controller assigned to the second scene of our example. When the view is loaded, we modify the value of the **title** property of the Navigation Item to change the scene's title to "Second".

```
import UIKit

class SecondViewController: UIViewController {
   override func viewDidLoad() {
      super.viewDidLoad()
      navigationItem.title = "Second"
   }
}
```

Listing 9-8: *Assigning the scene's title from code*

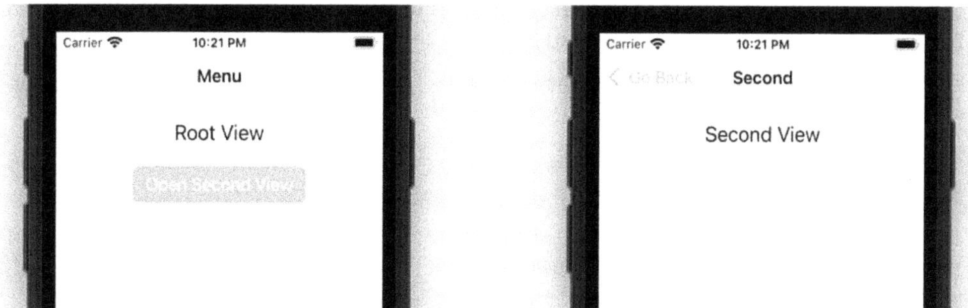

Figure 9-27: *Scene's title defined from code*

The Navigation Bar was designed to work with scrollable content and therefore it adapts to the content's offset. If the content is not scrolled (the top of the content is visible to the user), the bar presents a scroll edge appearance, but if the content has been scrolled, the bar presents a standard appearance. By default, the scroll edge appearance is transparent, and that's why we don't see any bar at the top of our scenes in the Storyboard, but in the standard appearance the bar is displayed in a translucent gray, so we can see it when the content is scrolled. Figure 9-28 shows what we see when the scene contains a table, and the table is scrolled (We will study Table Views in Chapter 10).

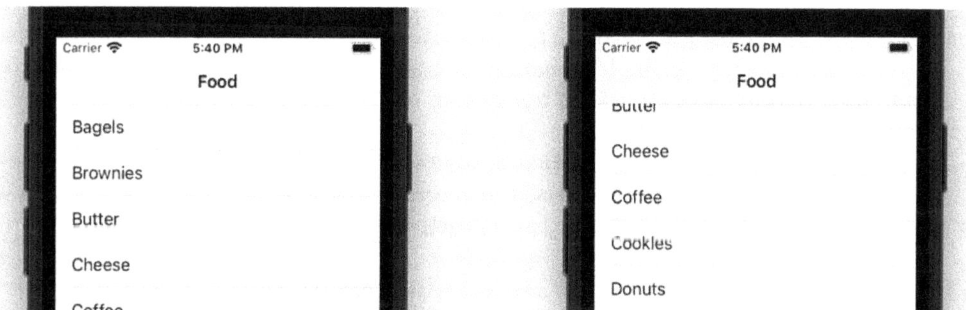

Figure 9-28: *Navigation Bar with scrollable content*

When the bar is presented in a Compact vertical Size Class, the height of the bar is reduced to make room for the content. In this case, the bar can present a different appearance.

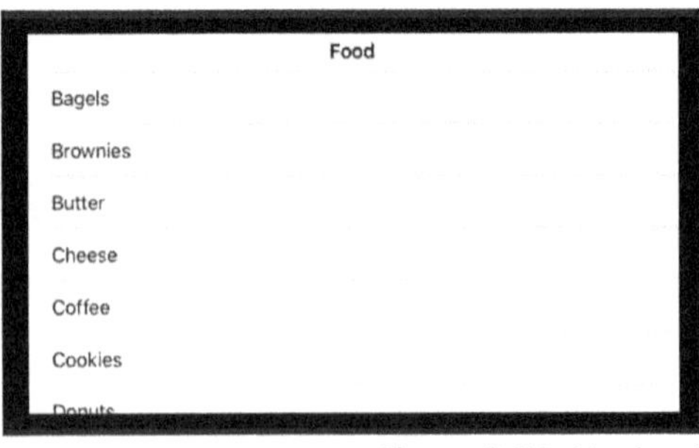

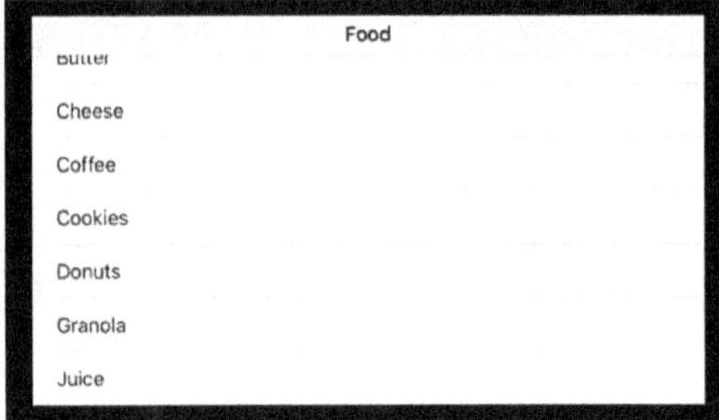

Figure 9-29: Navigation Bar in landscape mode

The Navigation Bar is created from an object of the **`UINavigationBar`** class, which includes properties to modify the appearance of the bar in all these conditions.

standardAppearance—This property sets or returns the appearance of the Navigation Bar when it is displayed with a standard height.

compactAppearance—This property sets or returns the appearance of the Navigation Bar when it is displayed with a compact height.

scrollEdgeAppearance—This property sets or returns the appearance of the Navigation Bar when it is displayed in a standard height and the content is not scrolled.

compactScrollEdgeAppearance—This property sets or returns the appearance of the Navigation Bar when it is displayed in a compact height and the content is not scrolled.

The appearance is defined by a **`UINavigationBarAppearance`** object. The class includes properties for configuration. The following are the most frequently used.

titleTextAttributes—This property sets or returns the attributes of the text for the title. The value is a dictionary with **`NSAttributedString`** keys.

largeTitleTextAttributes—This property sets or returns the attributes of the text for large titles. The value is a dictionary with **`NSAttributedString`** keys.

titlePositionAdjustment—This property sets or returns the position of the title. It is an object of type **`UIOffset`**, which includes the **`horizontal`** and **`vertical`** properties to set the title's horizontal and vertical offsets.

setBackIndicatorImage(UIImage?, **transitionMaskImage:** UIImage?**)**—This method sets the image for the back button. The arguments are the images we want to assign to the button in the normal and transition mode.

The **`titleTextAttributes`** and **`largeTitleTextAttributes`** properties works with a dictionary of **`NSAttributedString`** keys. The **`Dictionary`** structure includes the following initializer to convert an **`AttributeContainer`** structure into this type of dictionary.

Dictionary(AttributeContainer, **including:** AttributeScope.Type**)**—This initializer creates a dictionary with the attributes defined by the **`AttributeContainer`** structure according to the scope specified by the **including** argument.

The **`UINavigationBarAppearance`** class inherits from the **`UIBarAppearance`** class, which includes additional properties for configuration. The following are the most frequently used.

backgroundColor—This property sets or returns the bar's background color.

backgroundImage—This property sets or returns the bar's background image.

backgroundImageContentMode—This property sets the background image content mode. The possible values are **scaleToFill**, **scaleAspectFit**, **scaleAspectFill**, **redraw**, **center**, **top**, **bottom**, **left**, **right**, **topLeft**, **topRight**, **bottomLeft**, and **bottomRight**.

backgroundEffect—This property sets or returns the bar's blur effect. It is an optional of type **UIBlurEffect**. The value **nil** defines no effect.

The **UIViewController** class offers a property called **navigationController** to get a reference to the Navigation Controller the view controller belongs to. In turn, the **UINavigationController** class includes the **navigationBar** property with a reference to the **UINavigationBar** object that manages the Navigation Bar. From these properties, we can access the bar from our view controllers and define the appearance, as in the following example.

```
import UIKit

class ViewController: UIViewController {
   override func viewDidLoad() {
      super.viewDidLoad()
      var container = AttributeContainer()
      container.font = UIFont.preferredFont(forTextStyle: .title1)
      container.foregroundColor = UIColor.white

      let standard = UINavigationBarAppearance()
      standard.backgroundColor = UIColor.systemRed
      if let keys = try? Dictionary(container, including: \.uiKit) {
         standard.titleTextAttributes = keys
      }
      let compact = UINavigationBarAppearance()
      compact.backgroundColor = UIColor.yellow

      let bar = navigationController?.navigationBar
      bar?.scrollEdgeAppearance = standard
      bar?.compactScrollEdgeAppearance = compact
   }
}
```

Listing 9-9: *Configuring the Navigation Bar for standard and compact heights*

The standard and compact appearances are only applied when the content is scrolled. If we don't have scrollable content, as in this case, only the scroll edge appearance is applied and that's all we need to configure the bar. The view controller in Listing 9-9 creates two **UINavigationBarAppearance** objects, one for the standard and another for the compact appearance. The configuration for the standard appearance includes a red background while the background for the compact appearance is defined yellow. Once the **UINavigationBar-Appearance** objects are ready, we assign them to the bar's **scrollEdgeAppearance** and **compactScrollEdgeAppearance** properties to change the configuration for each mode.

Notice that the attributes for the title are defined with an **AttributeContainer** structure, but the **titleTextAttributes** property takes a dictionary of attribute keys, so we had to use the **Dictionary** initializer to convert the **AttributeContainer** structure to this format.

Because we assigned different configurations for the standard and compact heights, the Navigation Bar changes appearance every time the Size Classes change, as it happens when an iPhone rotates from portrait to landscape.

Figure 9-30: Different appearances for standard and compact bars

Do It Yourself: Update the **ViewController** class with the code in Listing 9-9. Run the application. You should see a red bar (Figure 9-30, left). Rotate the device to landscape. Now the bar should be compact and yellow (Figure 9-30, right).

The **UINavigationController** class also includes properties and methods to assign some functionality to the Navigation Bar.

hidesBarsOnTap—This property takes a Boolean value that indicates whether the bars should be hidden when the user taps on the screen.

hidesBarsOnSwipe—This property takes a Boolean value that indicates whether the bars should be hidden when the user swipes the finger on the screen.

hidesBarsWhenKeyboardAppears—This property takes a Boolean value that indicates whether the bars should be hidden when the keyboard is visible.

hidesBarsWhenVerticallyCompact—This property takes a Boolean value that indicates whether the bars should be hidden when the vertical Size Class is Compact.

isNavigationBarHidden—This property returns a Boolean value that indicates if the Navigation Bar is currently hidden.

setNavigationBarHidden(Bool, **animated:** Bool**)**—This method hides or shows the Navigation Bar. The first argument indicates whether the bar will be hidden, and the **animated** argument determines if the process is going to be animated.

These are Boolean properties used to activate or deactivate Navigation Bar features. For instance, we can assign the value **true** to the **hidesBarsOnTap** property to allow the user to hide or show the bar by tapping on the screen.

```
import UIKit

class ViewController: UIViewController {
   override func viewDidLoad() {
      super.viewDidLoad()
      var container = AttributeContainer()
      container.font = UIFont.preferredFont(forTextStyle: .title1)
      container.foregroundColor = UIColor.white

      let standard = UINavigationBarAppearance()
      standard.backgroundColor = UIColor.systemRed
      if let keys = try? Dictionary(container, including: \.uiKit) {
         standard.titleTextAttributes = keys
      }
      let compact = UINavigationBarAppearance()
      compact.backgroundColor = UIColor.yellow
```

```
        let bar = navigationController?.navigationBar
        bar?.scrollEdgeAppearance = standard
        bar?.compactScrollEdgeAppearance = compact

        navigationController?.hidesBarsOnTap = true
    }
}
```

Listing 9-10: *Setting up Navigation Bar features*

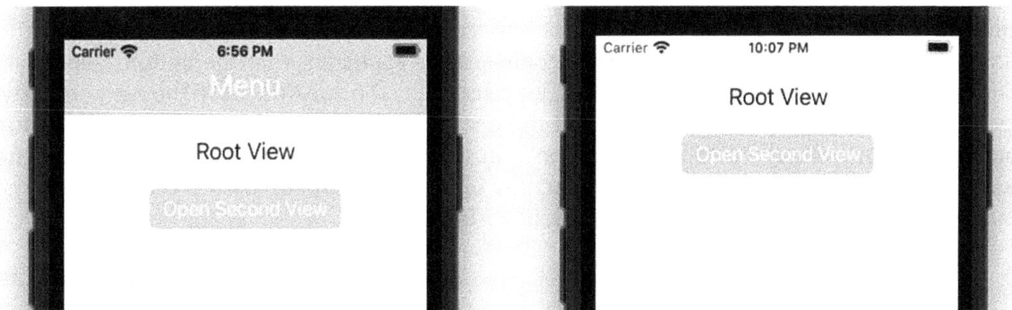

Figure 9-31: *Navigation Bar removed when the user taps the screen*

In addition to the bar, we can also modify the appearance of the buttons. The **UINavigationBarAppearance** class defines the following properties for this purpose.

buttonAppearance—This property sets or returns the appearance of the buttons. It is an appearance object of type **UIBarButtonItemAppearance**.

backButtonAppearance—This property sets or returns the appearance of the back button. It is an appearance object of type **UIBarButtonItemAppearance**.

The **UIBarButtonItemAppearance** class defines the properties **normal**, **disabled**, **highlighted**, and **focused** to set the appearance for the buttons on every state. To change the appearance of the Navigation Bar buttons, we must create the **UIBarButtonItemAppearance** object, then modify the properties for the state we want to change, and finally assign the object to one of the appearance properties (**buttonAppearance** or **backButtonAppearance**). The following example illustrates how to change the font of the back button in the normal state.

```
import UIKit

class ViewController: UIViewController {
    override func viewDidLoad() {
        super.viewDidLoad()
        var container = AttributeContainer()
        container.font = UIFont.preferredFont(forTextStyle: .title1)

        let buttonAppearance = UIBarButtonItemAppearance()
        if let textAttributes = try? Dictionary(container, including:
\.uiKit) {
            buttonAppearance.normal.titleTextAttributes = textAttributes
        }
        let standard = UINavigationBarAppearance()
        standard.backgroundColor = UIColor.systemGray4
        standard.backButtonAppearance = buttonAppearance
        standard.setBackIndicatorImage(UIImage(systemName:
"arrow.backward.circle"), transitionMaskImage: UIImage(systemName:
"arrow.backward.circle"))

        let compact = UINavigationBarAppearance()
        compact.backgroundColor = UIColor.yellow
```

```
        let bar = navigationController?.navigationBar
        bar?.scrollEdgeAppearance = standard
        bar?.compactScrollEdgeAppearance = compact
    }
}
```

Listing 9-11: *Configuring the back button*

The first thing we do in the view controller of Listing 9-11 is to create the **AttributeContainer** structure with the attributes we want to assign to the button's text. In this case, we define a dynamic font of type **title1**. Then, we initialize the **UIBarButtonItemAppearance** object to configure the appearance for the button. Depending on the state of the button we want to affect, we must apply the appearance to the right property. In our example, we modify the attributes of the text for the **normal** property, which affects the button's normal state. When the button's appearance is ready, we assign it to the **backButtonAppearance** property of the **UINavigationBarAppearance** object and give the button a new image. Now the Back button is shown in big letters.

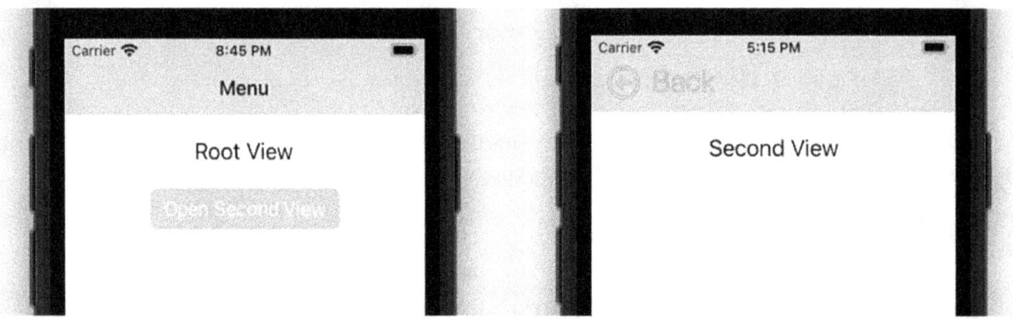

Figure 9-32: *Custom appearance for the back button*

Basic Large Titles

Navigation Bars offer two formats to display the titles: small and large. Small titles are shown by default, as illustrated by the previous examples, but we can specify our preference using the **prefersLargeTitles** property provided by the **UINavigationBar** class. The option is also available from the Attributes Inspector panel when we select the Navigation Bar.

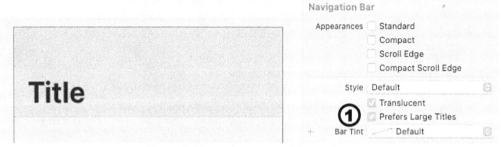

Figure 9-33: *Prefers Large Titles option*

After the property is set to **true** or the option is selected from the Attributes Inspector panel, the Navigation Bars show large titles, as illustrated bellow.

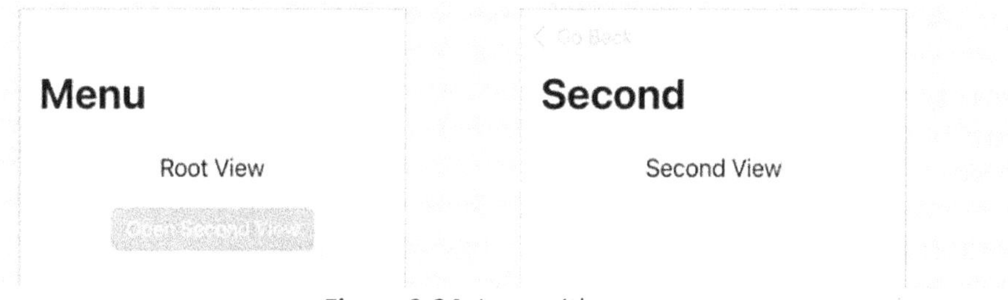

Figure 9-34: *Large titles*

The **prefersLargeTitles** property activates large titles for every scene in the navigation stack, but the **UINavigationItem** class offers the **largeTitleDisplayMode** property to change this behavior. The option is also available for each scene from the Attributes Inspector panel.

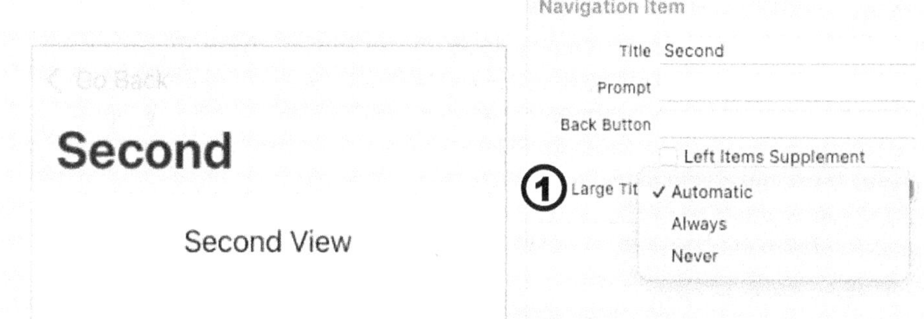

Figure 9-35: *Large Titles option for each scene*

Of course, we can also modify the **largeTitleDisplayMode** property from code. The values available are **automatic**, **always**, and **never**. For example, we can deactivate large titles in the second scene of our example by assigning the value **never** to this property.

```
import UIKit

class SecondViewController: UIViewController {
   override func viewDidLoad() {
      super.viewDidLoad()
      navigationItem.title = "Second"
      navigationItem.largeTitleDisplayMode = .never
   }
}
```

Listing 9-12: *Deactivating large titles*

Now, the initial scene shows large titles, but the second scene displays the standard title with a small font.

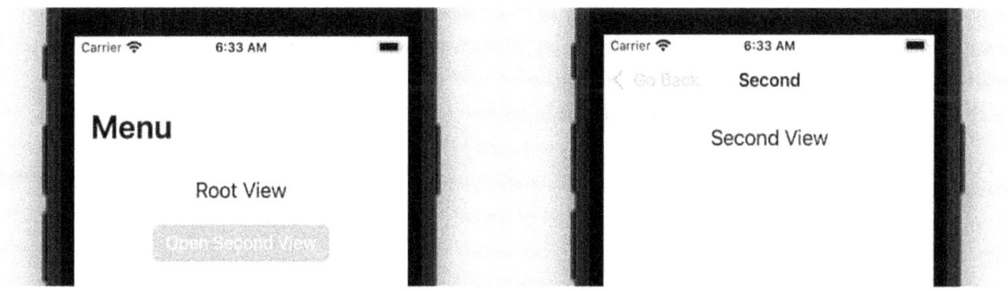

Figure 9-36: *Large and small titles*

Basic Bar Buttons

Besides the Back button, we can also add custom buttons to the Navigation Bar. These are not regular buttons; they are created from the **`UIBarButtonItem`** class with the following initializers.

UIBarButtonItem(title: String?, **image:** UIImage?, **primaryAction:** UIAction?, **menu:** UIMenu?**)**—This initializer creates a bar button with the configuration specified by the arguments. The **title** and **image** arguments are the button's title and image, respectively. The **primaryAction** argument specifies the action the button performs when pressed. And the **menu** argument specifies the contextual menu to be presented by the button.

UIBarButtonItem(systemItem: SystemItem, **primaryAction:** UIAction?, **menu:** UIMenu?**)**—This initializer creates a predefined bar button. The **systemItem** argument determines the type of button we want to create. It is an enumeration called **`SystemItem`** included in the **`UIBarButtonItem`** class with the values **`done`**, **`cancel`**, **`edit`**, **`save`**, **`add`**, **`flexibleSpace`**, **`fixedSpace`**, **`compose`**, **`reply`**, **`action`**, **`organize`**, **`bookmarks`**, **`search`**, **`refresh`**, **`stop`**, **`camera`**, **`trash`**, **`play`**, **`pause`**, **`rewind`**, **`fastForward`**, **`undo`**, **`redo`**, and **`close`**. The **primaryAction** argument defines the action, and the **menu** argument defines the contextual menu to be presented by the button.

As always, there is also an option in the Library to add a bar button to a scene.

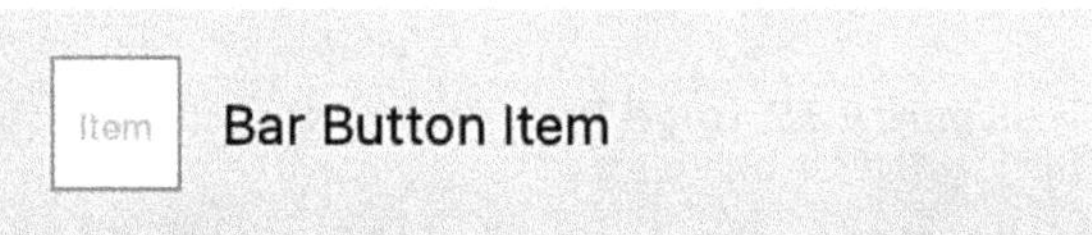

Figure 9-37: *Bar Button Item option in the Library*

The bar buttons may be added to the left or the right side of the bar, but if we add them to the left in a scene that is not the initial scene, the buttons replace the Back button. Figure 9-37 shows the interface of our example after a Bar Button Item was dragged from the Library to the right side of the Navigation Bar in the initial scene.

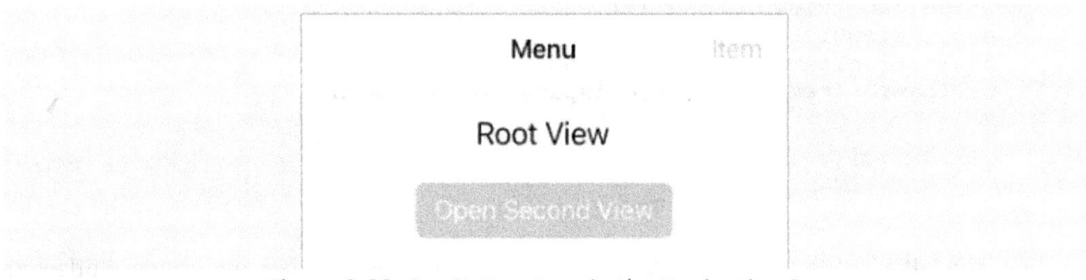

Figure 9-38: *Bar Button Item in the Navigation Bar*

The title of the button by default is "Item", but we can change it from the Attributes Inspector panel, as well as specify the button's design, add custom images for portrait and landscape modes, and define a tint color (the original colors of the images are ignored). Figure 9-39 shows what we see when the Camera value of the System Item option is selected.

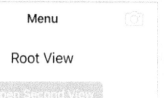

Figure 9-39: *Predefined Bar Button Item*

The **UINavigationItem** class includes the following properties to add the buttons from code.

leftBarButtonItems—This property is an array of **UIBarButtonItem** objects that defines the bar buttons for the left side of the bar.

rightBarButtonItems—This property is an array of **UIBarButtonItem** objects that defines the bar buttons for the right side of the bar.

leftItemsSupplementBackButton—This property is a Boolean value that determines whether the Back button is shown along with the items on the left side of the bar or not. By default, the Back button is not shown when there are custom buttons in its place. We can change this behavior by setting this property to **true**.

Bar buttons are created from the **UIBarButtonItem** class, which is a subclass of the **UIBarItem** class. Together, these classes define properties and methods to configure the buttons.

title—This property sets or returns the button's title. It is an optional of type **String**.

image—This property sets or returns the button's image. It is an optional of type **UIImage**.

landscapeImagePhone—This property sets or returns the image for the button that is going to be shown when the device is in landscape mode. It is an optional of type **UIImage**.

tintColor—This property sets or returns the button's tint color.

primaryAction—This property sets or returns the **UIAction** object with the action to be performed when the button is pressed.

menu—This property sets or returns a **UIMenu** object with the contextual menu to be presented when the button is pressed.

The arguments included in the **UIBarButtonItem** initializers are optional. For instance, we can define a button with a title or an image. If the button contains an image, then the **title** argument may be ignored. The same happens with the **menu** argument, which only applies when we want the button to open a contextual menu. For instance, the following example illustrates how to add a simple button with an image to the initial scene in our project.

```
import UIKit

class ViewController: UIViewController {
   override func viewDidLoad() {
      super.viewDidLoad()
      let button = UIBarButtonItem(image: UIImage(systemName: "trash"),
primaryAction: UIAction(handler: { action in
         print("Button pressed")
      }))
      button.tintColor = UIColor.systemRed
```

```
        navigationItem.rightBarButtonItems = [button]
    }
}
```

Listing 9-13: *Adding buttons to the Navigation Bar*

The view controller in Listing 9-13 creates a bar button with an SF Symbol of a trash can and an action that prints a message on the console. After the button is created, we change its color to red and assign it to the **rightBarButtonItems** property to add it to the Navigation Bar.

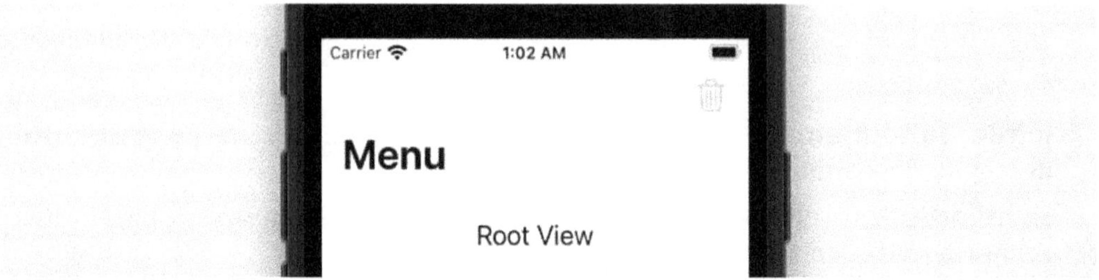

Figure 9-40: *Custom bar button*

Do It Yourself: Erase the button with the camera added before to the initial scene if necessary. Update the **ViewController** class with the code in Listing 9-13. Run the application. You should see a red trash can at the top (Figure 9-40).

We can also use a **UIBarButtonItem** object to define the back button for the destination scene. In this case, we only need to specify the button's title, because the action is already determined by the Navigation Controller.

```
import UIKit

class ViewController: UIViewController {
    override func viewDidLoad() {
        super.viewDidLoad()
        let button = UIBarButtonItem(title: "Close")
        button.tintColor = UIColor.systemGreen

        navigationItem.backBarButtonItem = button
    }
}
```

Listing 9-14: *Replacing the back button*

The button is created first, as before, but then it is assigned to the **backBarButtonItem** property of the Navigation Item, effectively replacing the original back button. Now, every time we open the second scene, the button reads "Close".

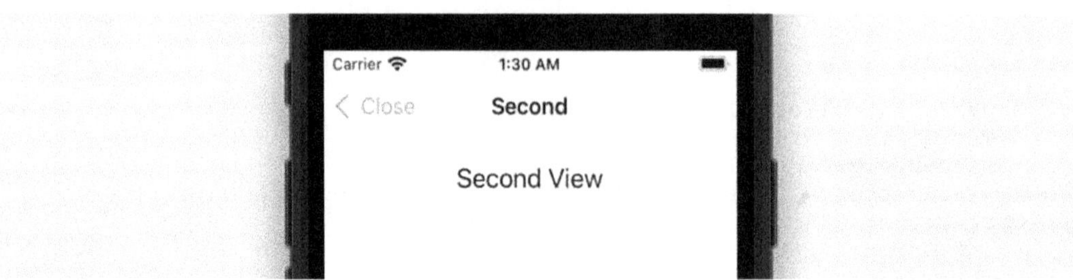

Figure 9-41: *Custom back button*

Like buttons, bar buttons can also display contextual menus. The **UIBarButtonItem** class includes the **menu** property to associate a menu with the button. All we need to do is to set the primary action as **nil** and define the menu as we did for the **UIButton** class in Chapter 5.

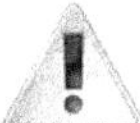

IMPORTANT: Bar buttons are created from the **UIBarButtonItem** class instead of the **UIButton** class because they were specifically designed to fit in the narrow space of a Navigation Bar, but you can implement normal buttons if the Navigation Bar is configured with large titles. All you need to do is to set the Prefers Large Titles option and drag the buttons from the Library to the Navigation Bar.

Basic Toolbar

In addition to the Navigation Bar, UIKit includes a class called **UIToolbar** to add an additional bar to the scene. A Navigation Controller includes a Toolbar by default, but it is hidden. If we want to see how the Toolbar is going to affect our interface, we can select the Navigation Controller and set the option from the Attributes Inspector panel to show it in the Storyboard.

Navigation Controller
Bar Visibility Shows Navigation Bar
Shows Toolbar ①
Hide Bars On Swipe
On Tap
When Keyboard Appears
When Vertically Compact

Figure 9-42: *Option to show the Toolbar in the Storyboard*

The Toolbar is not visible in the scenes, but elements pinned to the bottom of the Safe Area will move up and bar buttons added to the view will be included in the Toolbar. The buttons are defined by the **UIBarButtonItem** class. This is the same class used before to add buttons to the Navigation Bar. The **UIViewController** class offers the following property and method to manage these buttons from code.

toolbarItems—This property is an array of **UIBarButtonItem** objects with the buttons.

setToolbarItems([UIBarButtonItem]?, **animated:** Bool**)**—This method assigns the bar buttons provided by the first argument to the toolbar. The **animated** argument determines if the process will be animated.

For configuration, the **UIToolbar** class includes the same properties available for Navigation Bars (**standardAppearance**, **compactAppearance**, **scrollEdgeAppearance**, and **compactScrollEdgeAppearance**). These properties take a **UIToolbarAppearance** object. The **UIToolbarAppearance** class inherits from the **UIBarAppearance** class and therefore it provides all the same properties for configuration, but it also includes the following property to change the appearance of the buttons.

buttonAppearance—This property sets or returns the appearance of the buttons. It is an appearance object of type **UIBarButtonItemAppearance**.

The Toolbar is not shown on the screen unless it includes at least one button. The buttons can be added by dragging the Bar Button Item option in the Library to the main view, as we did for Navigation Bars, or from code implementing the methods described above. The following example shows how to define a Toolbar with a custom appearance and one button.

```swift
import UIKit

class ViewController: UIViewController {
   override func viewDidLoad() {
      super.viewDidLoad()
      let standard = UIToolbarAppearance()
      standard.backgroundColor = UIColor.yellow
      navigationController?.toolbar.scrollEdgeAppearance = standard

      let button = UIBarButtonItem(image: UIImage(systemName: "trash"),
primaryAction: UIAction(handler: { action in
         print("Button pressed")
      }))
      button.tintColor = UIColor.systemRed
      self.setToolbarItems([button], animated: false)
   }
}
```

Listing 9-15: *Configuring the appearance of the Toolbar*

The code defines a **UIToolbarAppearance** object with a yellow background and assigns it to the **scrollEdgeAppearance** property of the Navigation Controller's **toolbar** property to modify the Toolbar's appearance. After this, we create a bar button, as we did before for the Navigation Bar, and add it to the Toolbar with the **setToolbarItems()** method provided by the view controller. The result is shown below.

Figure 9-43: *Custom Toolbar in portrait and landscape mode*

Do It Yourself: Update the **ViewController** class with the code in Listing 9-15 and run the application. Rotate the screen. You should see something like Figure 9-43. You can also select the Navigation Controller, set the Shows toolbar option from the Attributes Inspector panel, and drag bar buttons to the Toolbar from the Library to see how the buttons are created in the Storyboard.

Basic Custom Navigation

It is possible to hide the Navigation Bar and provide our own navigation tools. The option is available in the Attributes Inspector panel when the Navigation Controller is selected (see Figure 9-44). Clicking on the Shows Navigation Bar option deactivates the bar and removes it from the scenes. Once the Navigation Bar is deactivated, it is our responsibility to provide the tools the user needs to navigate.

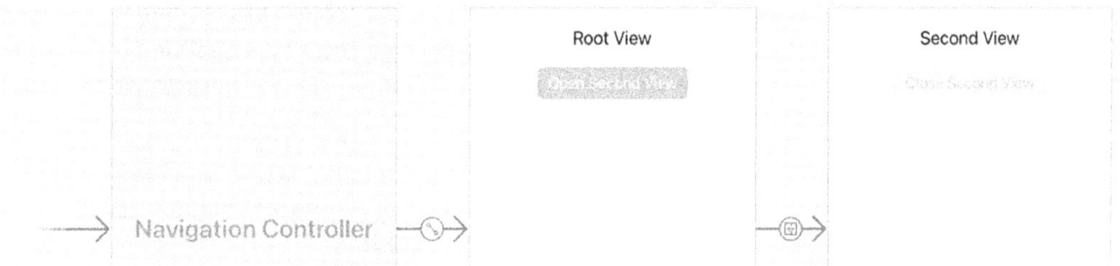

Figure 9-44: *Interface without the Navigation Bar*

Figure 9-44 introduces a simple interface. With the Navigation Bar removed, we do not have a Back button anymore, so we added a button in the second view called Close Second View to remove it. The view controller for this scene has to include an Action for the button that calls the **`popViewController()`** method of its Navigation Controller. This method removes the current view and asks the Navigation Controller to show the previous view in the stack.

```
import UIKit

class SecondViewController: UIViewController {
   @IBAction func closeView(_ sender: UIButton) {
      navigationController?.popViewController(animated: true)
   }
}
```

Listing 9-16: *Defining our own method to navigate back*

Basic Data Model

View controllers managed by a Navigation Controller serve a common purpose and therefore often share common data. When working with Navigation Controllers, we should not send information from one view controller to another, as we did before with single view controllers, but instead create a unique source of data. One of the objects frequently used to store this data is the **`AppDelegate`** object. The advantage presented by this object is that it is the delegate of the **`UIApplication`** object created to run the application and therefore it is accessible from anywhere in the code.

As an example, we are going to recreate the application developed at the beginning of this chapter using a Navigation Controller. The interface includes two scenes embedded in a Navigation Controller, one with the buttons to select the picture and another with an Image View and a Slider to show the picture and rate it.

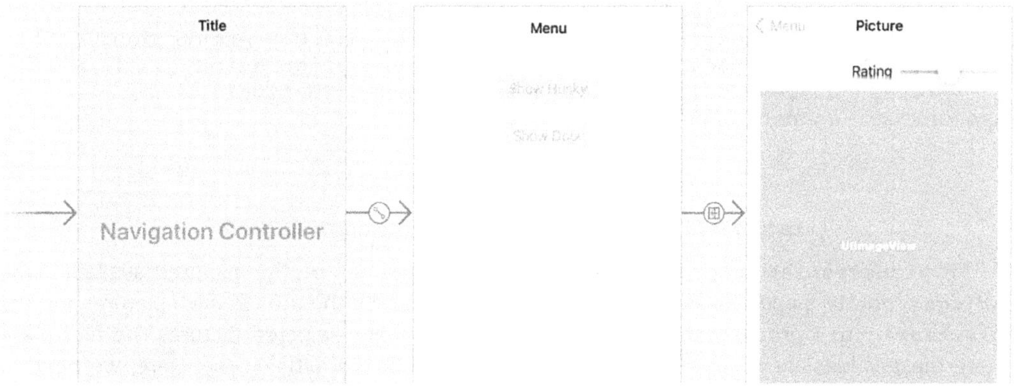

Figure 9-45: *Picture application created with a Navigation Controller*

The application works as before, the system shows the initial scene with the menu first and then when the user clicks on any of the buttons it transitions to the second scene to show the selected picture, but because this time we use a Navigation Bar, we do not have to worry about the button required to go back to the previous scene.

Do It Yourself: Create a new project. Embed the initial scene in a Navigation Controller. Add a second scene to the Storyboard. Connect the initial scene to the second scene with a Show segue (Figure 9-17). Assign the string "showPicture" to the segue's identifier (Figure 9-11). Create a new file with a view controller called **SecondViewController** and assign it to the second scene (Figures 9-5 and 9-6). Click on the Navigation Bars and assign the title "Menu" to the initial scene and "Picture" to the second scene (Figure 9-25). Add buttons called Show Husky and Show Door to the initial scene and assign the values 0 and 1 to their **tag** properties from the Attributes Inspector panel (this is to identify which button was pressed). Add an Image View, a label with the text "Rating", and a Slider to the second scene. Set a value of 0, a minimum of 0, and a maximum of 5 for the Slider. Assign a higher vertical Content Hugging Priority and Content Compression Resistance Priority to the Slider if necessary. Add the pictures husky.png and door.png to the Assets Catalog. The interface should look like Figure 9-45.

The code is also like previous examples, but the **picturesList**, **ratings**, and **selectedPicture** properties we used before to store the information are going to be defined in the application's delegate, so every time the rating is modified in the second scene, we do not need to send the data back to the initial view controller; all we need to do is access the app's delegate and change the values of its properties. The following code illustrates how the properties should be declared and initialized in the delegate.

```
import UIKit

@main
class AppDelegate: UIResponder, UIApplicationDelegate {
   var picturesList: [String]!
   var ratings: [Int]!
   var selectedPicture: Int!

   func application(_ application: UIApplication,
didFinishLaunchingWithOptions launchOptions:
[UIApplication.LaunchOptionsKey: Any]?) -> Bool {
      picturesList = ["Husky", "Door"]
      ratings = [0, 0]
      selectedPicture = 0
      return true
   }
   func application(_ application: UIApplication,
configurationForConnecting connectingSceneSession: UISceneSession,
options: UIScene.ConnectionOptions) -> UISceneConfiguration {
      return UISceneConfiguration(name: "Default Configuration",
sessionRole: connectingSceneSession.role)
   }
}
```

Listing 9-17: *Storing common data in the app's delegate*

The **picturesList** property is an array with the names of the pictures available, the **ratings** property is another array with the ratings assigned by the user to each picture, and the **selectedPicture** property stores the index of the currently selected picture. The first place where these values are required is in the view controller of the initial scene. Here, we need to update the **selectedPicture** property every time a button is pressed so that the rest of the application knows which picture was selected by the user.

```
import UIKit

class ViewController: UIViewController {
   var mydelegate: AppDelegate!

   override func viewDidLoad() {
      super.viewDidLoad()
      let app = UIApplication.shared
      mydelegate = app.delegate as? AppDelegate
   }
   @IBAction func goToPicture(_ sender: UIButton) {
      mydelegate.selectedPicture = sender.tag
      performSegue(withIdentifier: "showPicture", sender: self)
   }
}
```

Listing 9-18: *Storing the index of the selected picture*

The first thing we do in the **ViewController** class is to get a reference to the application's delegate. We first get a reference to the **UIApplication** object created for the application and then read its **delegate** property. The property we need to modify in the delegate is the **selectedPicture** property that stores the index of the selected picture. For this purpose, we have connected both buttons, Show Husky and Show Door, to one Action called **goToPicture()**. When any of the buttons is pressed, we take the value of their **tag** property and assign it to the **selectedPicture** property (the value 0 represents the husky and the value 1 the door).

At the end, we call the **performSegue()** method to transition to the second scene. Notice that this time we do not need to send any value to **SecondViewController** because this view controller also takes the values from the app's delegate, as shown next.

```
import UIKit

class SecondViewController: UIViewController {
   @IBOutlet weak var sliderRating: UISlider!
   @IBOutlet weak var pictureView: UIImageView!
   var mydelegate: AppDelegate!

   override func viewDidLoad() {
      super.viewDidLoad()
      let app = UIApplication.shared
      mydelegate = app.delegate as? AppDelegate

      let selected = mydelegate.selectedPicture ?? 0
      let picture = mydelegate.picturesList[selected]
      let rating = mydelegate.ratings[selected]
      sliderRating.value = Float(rating)
      pictureView.image = UIImage(named: picture.lowercased())
   }
   @IBAction func changeRating(_ sender: UISlider) {
      let value = round(sender.value)
      sliderRating.value = value
      let selected = mydelegate.selectedPicture ?? 0
      mydelegate.ratings[selected] = Int(value)
   }
}
```

Listing 9-19: *Showing the selected picture and storing the rating in the app's delegate*

In this view controller, we read the three properties of the app's delegate to configure the view. First, we get the index of the selected picture and use it to read the picture's name and rating from the **picturesList** and **ratings** arrays. This information is used next to update the Slider and the Image View before the interface is shown on the screen. The **selectedPicture** and **ratings** properties are also used in the Action connected to the Slider to update the value of the rating with the one selected by the user.

Do It Yourself: Update the **AppDelegate** class in the AppDelegate.swift file with the code in Listing 9-17. Connect the Show Husky and Show Door buttons in the initial scene to an Action called **goToPicture()**. Complete the **ViewController** class with the code in Listing 9-18. Connect the Slider and the Image View of the second scene to Outlets called **sliderRating** and **pictureView**, respectively. Create an Action for the Slider called **changeRating()**. Complete the **SecondViewController** class with the code in Listing 9-19. Run the application and modify the rating of the pictures to verify that the values are preserved.

The use of the app's delegate to store data is only recommended when the amount of data is not significant. For large amounts of data, it is better to create global objects or structures that the application can access every time necessary and where we can safely manage the information available. To do this in Swift is very easy. All the files are in the global space and are processed as soon as the application is launched. If we want to create a global object or structure that we can access from anywhere in our code, all we need to do is define it and initialize it in a new Swift file.

As any other files, Swift files are created from the File menu or pressing Command + N on the keyboard, but instead of selecting the Cocoa Touch Class option we click on the Swift File option (Figure 9-3). The name of the file in this case is just for reference, because except for a few comments and **import** statements, no code is created for the template. Once the file is added to the list of files in our application, we can define our custom classes or structures inside. For our example, we have created a file called ApplicationData.swift and define a structure inside with the same name and all the properties necessary for our application.

```
import Foundation

struct ApplicationData {
   var picturesList: [String]
   var ratings: [Int]
   var selectedPicture: Int

   init() {
      picturesList = ["Husky", "Door"]
      ratings = [0, 0]
      selectedPicture = 0
   }
}
var AppData = ApplicationData()
```

Listing 9-20: *Defining a global structure to store common data*

IMPORTANT: The **ApplicationData** structure represents the model in our MVC, or Model-View-Controller (see Chapter 5). In our example, the Views (scenes) are created from the Storyboard, the Controllers are the view controllers we associate with those views (scenes), and the Model is now the **ApplicationData** structure defined in Listing 9-20. This model and the one created with the app's delegate before are suitable for small to medium applications, but there are multiple models and programming patterns available for professional applications. For instance, some applications implement singletons. Singletons are defined by classes that make sure that one and only one object can be instantiated from the class. For more information, visit our website and follow the links for this chapter.

The structure declared in Listing 9-20 contains the same information as before, but it provides a unique place to store and manage all the information for our app. Now we can access this data from anywhere in the code by just reading and writing the content of the **AppData** variable. The following example shows how the **ViewController** of our application gets the data from **AppData**.

```
import UIKit

class ViewController: UIViewController {
   @IBAction func goToPicture(_ sender: UIButton) {
      AppData.selectedPicture = sender.tag
      performSegue(withIdentifier: "showPicture", sender: self)
   }
}
```

***Listing 9-21:** Accessing the data model from the* `ViewController` *class*

Since we do not have to get a reference to the app's delegate anymore, all we need in the **ViewController** class is the Action for the buttons. When a button is pressed, the **goToPicture()** method is executed as always, but this time instead of accessing the **selectedPicture** property from the app's delegate we do it from the **AppData** structure.

The code for the **SecondViewController** can also be simplified. Getting the data from a global structure makes everything easier.

```
import UIKit

class SecondViewController: UIViewController {
   @IBOutlet weak var sliderRating: UISlider!
   @IBOutlet weak var pictureView: UIImageView!

   override func viewDidLoad() {
      super.viewDidLoad()
      let selected = AppData.selectedPicture
      let picture = AppData.picturesList[selected]
      let rating = AppData.ratings[selected]
      sliderRating.value = Float(rating)
      pictureView.image = UIImage(named: picture.lowercased())
   }
   @IBAction func changeRating(_ sender: UISlider) {
      let value = round(sender.value)
      sliderRating.value = value
      let selected = AppData.selectedPicture
      AppData.ratings[selected] = Int(value)
   }
}
```

***Listing 9-22:** Accessing the data model from the* `SecondViewController` *class*

Do It Yourself: Erase the properties in the **AppDelegate** class. Open the File menu, click on New, and select the option File to create a new Swift file. In the next window, click on the Swift File icon and insert the name ApplicationData.swift. Open the new file and update the code with the model in Listing 9-20. Replace the **ViewController** class with the class in Listing 9-21 and the **SecondViewController** class with the class in Listing 9-22. Run the application. It should work as before but now the data is taken from the **AppData** structure.

Basic

9.3 Tab Bar Controllers

A Tab Bar Controller is a simple container view controller that designates two areas on the screen: one for the scenes and a smaller one at the bottom for a bar with tabs that users can tap to select the scene they want to see. Each tab is associated with only one scene and therefore we can use them to move from one scene to another.

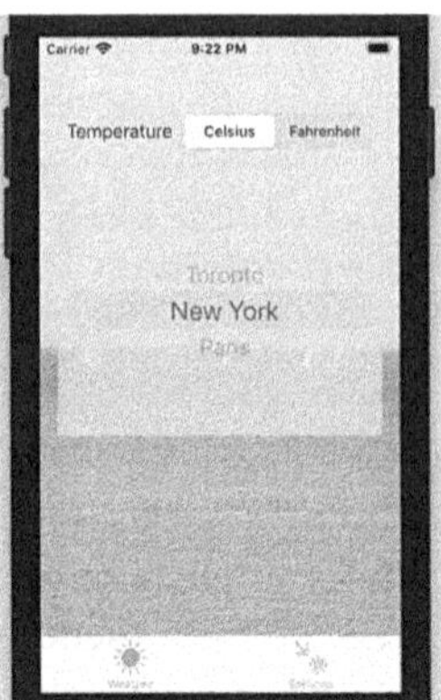

Figure 9-46: *Application based on a Tab Bar Controller*

As with Navigation Controllers, there are two ways to add a Tab Bar Controller to the Storyboard. We can embed a scene inside a Tab Bar Controller from the Editor menu (Editor/ Embed In/Tab Bar Controller) or drag the Tab Bar Controller option from the Library. Figure 9-47, below, shows what we see when we embed a single scene in a Tab Bar Controller.

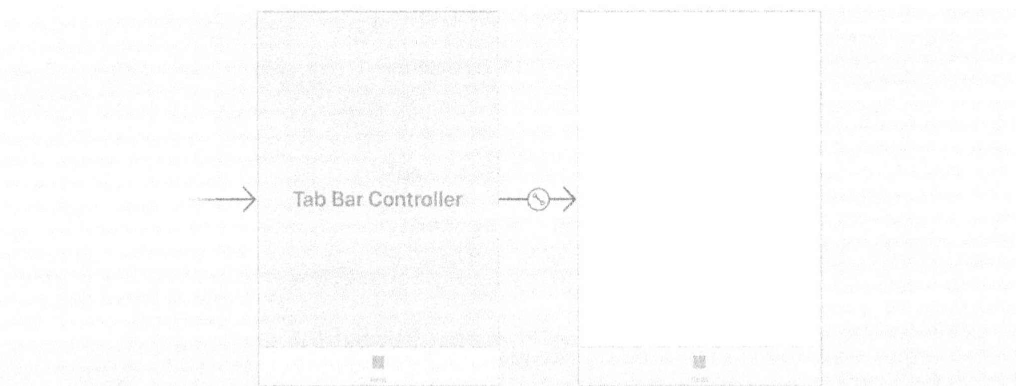

Figure 9-47: *Initial scene embedded in a Tab Bar Controller*

The scenes managed by the Tab Bar Controller are connected with a segue called *View Controllers*. If we want to incorporate another scene to the Tab Bar Controller, we must add it to the Storyboard and create a View Controllers segue from the Tab Bar Controller to the new scene.

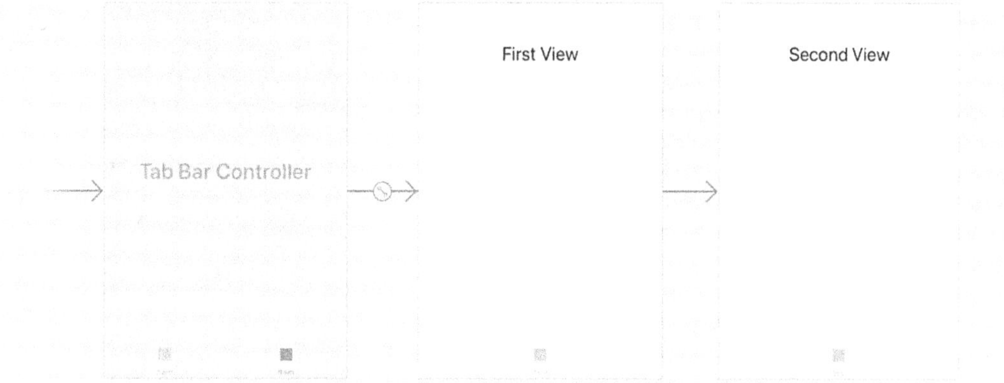

Figure 9-48: *Multiple scenes managed by the Tab Bar Controller*

We can add all the scenes we want. When a scene is added to the Tab Bar Controller, the system automatically includes the corresponding tab at the bottom of the scene. The Tab Bar Controller gets the tabs from the scenes and generates the bar (Figure 9-48, left). If there is not enough space on the bar to place all the tabs available, the controller adds a tab called *More* that the user can tap to select the tabs that are not visible.

Basic Tabs

The bar is managed by the Tab Bar Controller, but the tabs are provided by the view controllers to which they belong. To change the values and appearance of the tabs, we can click on them and edit their values from the Attributes Inspector panel.

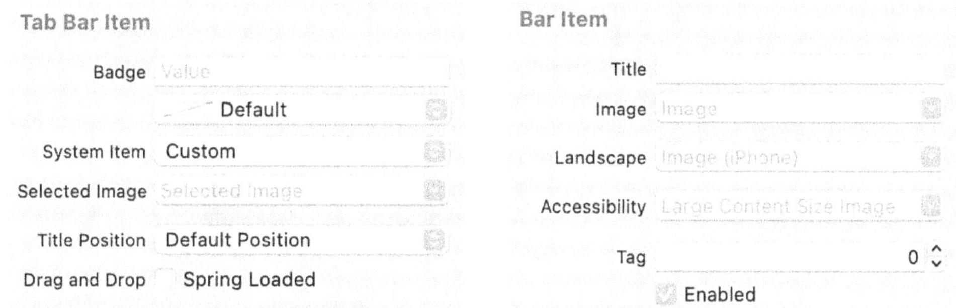

Figure 9-49: *Options to configure the tab*

Each tab has a title, image, selected image, and a landscape image to identify the scenes they represent. There are two alternatives to configure the tab: we can provide a custom name and images, or we can select a tab predefined by the system from the option called *System Item*. If we click on this field, a popup window shows a list of all the tabs available. Figure 9-50 shows what the bottom of the scenes look like after the style Favorites and Search were selected for the tabs.

Figure 9-50: *Tabs defined by the system*

These options define the image and the name. If we want to provide our own values, we must set the System Item option to Custom and specify the information below. We can provide our own images or specify an SF Symbol. Custom images must be provided with a size of 30 pixels by

30 pixels (60x60 for the 2x scale and 90x90 for the 3x scale) and a transparent background. For our example, we have created the images iconweather.png for the initial scene and iconsettings.png for the second scene. Figure 9-51, below, shows what the bar looks like when we select these images and insert the titles "Weather" and "Settings".

Figure 9-51: *Custom tabs*

Do It Yourself: Create a project and embed the initial scene in a Tab Bar Controller (Editor/Embed In/Tab Bar Controller). Add a second scene and create a segue of type View Controllers from the Tab Bar Controller to the new scene. Add labels to identify each scene, as shown in Figure 9-48. Create a view controller called **`SecondViewController`** and assign it to the second scene. Download from our website the images iconweather.png and iconsettings.png and add them to the Assets Catalog. Click on the initial scene's tab, go to the Bar Item section in the Attributes Inspector panel, and insert the name "Weather" and the image iconweather.png. Repeat the same with the name "Settings" and the image iconsettings.png for the second scene. The bars should look like Figure 9-51. Run the application and tap on the items to select a scene.

Tabs are created from the **`UITabBarItem`** class. This is a subclass of the **`UIBarItem`** class, which is also used to create the buttons for Navigation Controllers. In addition to the properties defined by the **`UIBarItem`** class to configure the items, like **`title`**, **`image`**, and **`landscape-ImagePhone`**, the **`UITabBarItem`** class includes the following.

badgeValue—This property sets or returns the value of the tab's badge (shown inside a circle at the top-right corner of the tab's icon). It is an optional of type **`String`**.

The tabs are configured from the view controllers to which they belong. The **`UIViewController`** class includes the **`tabBarItem`** property to access the view controller's tab. The next example adds an Action for a button to update the badge when the button is pressed.

```
import UIKit

class ViewController: UIViewController {
   var counter = 1

   @IBAction func updateBadge(_ sender: UIButton) {
      if let item = self.tabBarItem {
         item.title = "New Weather"
         item.badgeValue = String(counter)
         counter += 1
      }
   }
}
```

Listing 9-23: *Updating the badge from the view controller*

This code gets a reference to the view's tab from the **`tabBarItem`** property, updates the tab's title with the string "New Weather" and the **`badgeValue`** property with the value of the **`counter`** property. The counter is incremented every time the button is pressed to illustrate how the badge is modified by the system. Figure 9-52 shows what we see when we run the app for the first time and after the button is pressed 12 times.

Figure 9-52: Tab with a badge and a new title

Do It Yourself: Add a button to the initial scene of the interface in Figure 9-48. Connect the button to an Action called **updateBadge()**. Complete the **ViewController** class with the code in Listing 9-23. Run the application and press the button. You should see something like Figure 9-52.

Basic Tab Bar Controller

View controllers manage their own tabs, but the bar and the list of view controllers available is managed by the Tab Bar Controller. The **UITabBarController** class includes the following properties to store the view controllers, keep a reference to the selected one, and access the bar.

tabBar—This property returns a reference to the **UITabBar** object that represents the bar.

viewControllers—This property sets or returns the view controllers managed by the Tab Bar Controller. It is an array of **UIViewController** objects.

selectedViewController—This property returns a reference to the view controller of the scene currently shown to the user.

selectedIndex—This property returns the index of the view controller that is currently being shown to the user. It is a value of type **Int**.

The bar is created from the **UITabBar** class, which includes the **standardAppearance** and **scrollEdgeAppearance** properties to modify the bar's appearance. These properties take an object of type **UITabBarAppearance**. This is a subclass of **UIBarAppearance**, which is also available for Navigation Bars and Toolbars. Therefore, a **UITabBarAppearance** object includes properties we used before like **backgroundEffect**, **backgroundColor**, and **backgroundImage**, but also its own properties. The following are the most frequently used.

stackedLayoutAppearance—This property sets or returns a **UITabBarItemAppearance** object that provides the appearance of the items in the standard configuration.

compactInlineLayoutAppearance—This property sets or returns a **UITabBarItemAppearance** object that provides the appearance of the items in the compact configuration.

inlineLayoutAppearance—This property sets or returns a **UITabBarItemAppearance** object that provides the appearance of the items in the inline configuration.

stackedItemPositioning—This property sets or returns a value that determines the position of the buttons. It is an enumeration of type **ItemPositioning** with the values **fill**, **centered**, and **automatic**.

stackedItemSpacing—This property sets or returns a **CGFloat** value that determines the space between items.

stackedItemWidth—This property sets or returns a **CGFloat** value that determines the width of the items.

The **UITabBarAppearance** class defines the appearance of the bar. If we want to modify the appearance of the items, we must assign an appearance object to the **stackedLayout-Appearance**, **compactInlineLayoutAppearance**, or **inlineLayoutAppearance** properties. These properties take an object of type **UITabBarItemAppearance**, which in turn includes the **normal**, **selected**, **disabled**, and **focused** properties to configure the appearance of the items in every state. The values are defined by the **UITabBarItemState-Appearance** class, which includes the following properties for configuration.

titleTextAttributes—This property sets or returns the attributes of the item's title. The value is a dictionary with **NSAttributedString** keys.

titlePositionAdjustment—This property sets or returns the position of the item's title. It is an object of type **UIOffset**, which includes the **horizontal** and **vertical** properties to set the horizontal and vertical offsets.

iconColor—This property sets or returns the color of the item's image.

badgeTextAttributes—This property sets or returns the attributes of the text displayed by the badge. The value is a dictionary with **NSAttributedString** keys.

badgeBackgroundColor—This property sets or returns the badge's background color.

The **UIViewController** class includes the **tabBarController** property to access the Tab Bar Controller to which the scene belongs, but because there is usually only one Tab Bar Controller per application it is better to create a subclass of **UITabBarController** and manage the view controllers and the bar from it. For our example, we have created a file called MyTabViewController.swift with a subclass of the **UITabBarController** called **MyTabViewController** and assign it to the Tab Bar Controller of the interface in Figure 9-48.

```
import UIKit

class MyTabViewController: UITabBarController {
    override func viewDidLoad() {
        super.viewDidLoad()
        var attributesNormal = AttributeContainer()
        attributesNormal.foregroundColor = .systemGray

        var attributesSelected = AttributeContainer()
        attributesSelected.foregroundColor = .systemGreen

        let standard = UITabBarAppearance()
        standard.backgroundColor = .systemGray5
        standard.stackedLayoutAppearance.normal.iconColor = .systemGray
        standard.compactInlineLayoutAppearance.normal.iconColor
= .systemGray
        standard.inlineLayoutAppearance.normal.iconColor = .systemGray
        if let attr = try? Dictionary(attributesNormal, including:
\.uiKit) {
            standard.stackedLayoutAppearance.normal.titleTextAttributes =
attr

standard.compactInlineLayoutAppearance.normal.titleTextAttributes = attr
            standard.inlineLayoutAppearance.normal.titleTextAttributes =
attr
        }
        standard.stackedLayoutAppearance.selected.iconColor = .systemGreen
        standard.compactInlineLayoutAppearance.selected.iconColor
= .systemGreen
        standard.inlineLayoutAppearance.selected.iconColor = .systemGreen
        if let attr = try? Dictionary(attributesSelected, including:
\.uiKit) {
```

```
            standard.stackedLayoutAppearance.selected.titleTextAttributes =
attr
            standard.compactInlineLayoutAppearance.selected.titleText-
Attributes = attr
            standard.inlineLayoutAppearance.selected.titleTextAttributes =
attr
        }
        self.tabBar.standardAppearance = standard
    }
}
```

Listing 9-24: Modifying the appearance of the bar

A Tab Bar can adopt three different configurations. The standard configuration is when the bar is shown with a standard height and the text below the image. The appearance for this configuration is defined by the **stackedLayoutAppearance** property (the elements of the tab are stacked). Another possible configuration is compact. In this configuration, the height of the Tab Bar is reduced to make room for the content. This appearance is defined by the **compactInlineLayoutAppearance** property. Finally, there is a configuration in which the elements of the tab are shown side by side (the image on the left and the text on the right). This appearance is defined by the **inlineLayoutAppearance** property. The configuration is determined by the system according to the space available, but we can assign the same appearance to all the three properties to make sure that the Tab Bar always looks the same, as we did in this example.

The process to configure the bar is like those implemented before to configure the Navigation Bar and the Toolbar. In this case, we start by creating two **AttributeContainer** structures to define the attributes for the text, then we create the **UITabBarAppearance** object and proceed to define the appearances for every configuration (standard, compact, and inline). Finally, we access the Tab Bar with the **tabBar** property provided by the **UITabBarController** object and assign the appearance object to the **standardAppearance** property of the bar to modify its appearance.

Do It Yourself: Create a new file with a subclass of the **UITabBarController** class called **MyTabViewController** and assign it to the Tab Bar Controller introduced in Figure 9-48. Complete the subclass with the code in Listing 9-24. The application now shows the items in gray, but they change to green when selected.

By default, the items on the bar are expanded to fill the space available, but we can center the items and then assign a custom width and space in between with the rest of the properties provided by the **UITabBarAppearance** class.

```
import UIKit

class MyTabViewController: UITabBarController {
   override func viewDidLoad() {
      super.viewDidLoad()
      let standard = UITabBarAppearance()
      standard.stackedItemPositioning = .centered
      standard.stackedItemWidth = 50
      standard.stackedItemSpacing = 50
      self.tabBar.standardAppearance = standard
   }
}
```

Listing 9-25: Configuring the items

The **stackedItemPositioning** property can take two values, **fill** and **centered**. The value by default is **fill**, which causes the items to expand proportionally to fill the available space. This means that the size and space in between items is determined by the system. But if the value **centered** is assigned to this property, as we did in Listing 9-25, we can assign a custom size and space in between. In our example, we give the items a width and a space of 50 points.

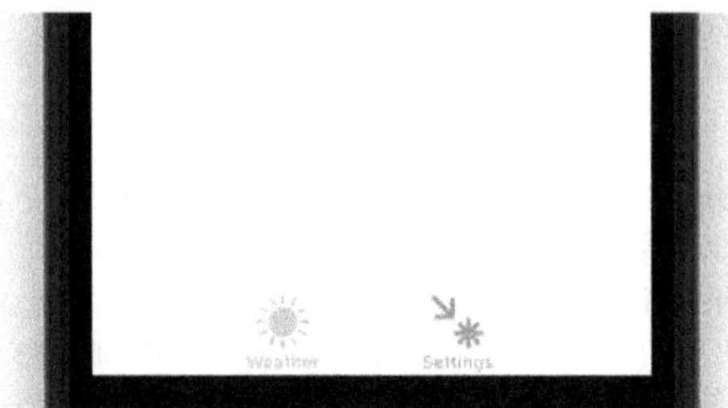

Figure 9-53: *Items with custom size*

There are more tasks we can perform from the **UITabBarController** subclass other than configuring the bar. Important things like establishing which scene will be shown first or setting the badges for each tab can be done from this subclass. The following example modifies the **selectedIndex** property to declare the second scene as the initial scene.

```
import UIKit

class MyTabViewController: UITabBarController {
   override func viewDidLoad() {
      super.viewDidLoad()
      let list = viewControllers!
      let controller = list[0] as! ViewController
      controller.tabBarItem?.badgeValue = String(20)

      self.selectedIndex = 1
   }
}
```

Listing 9-26: *Initializing the Tab Bar Controller*

The view controllers managed by the Tab Bar Controller are stored in an array called **viewControllers** in the order they were connected in the Storyboard. In our example, the view controller for the Weather scene was stored at index 0 and the view controller for the Settings scene was stored at index 1. Therefore, to add a badge to the first scene, we get the first element of the **viewControllers** array, cast it as **ViewController** (the array contains elements of type **UIViewController**), and access its properties. On the other hand, the Settings view controller is at index 1, so we assign the value 1 to the **selectedIndex** property to declare this as the initial scene.

Basic Tab Bar Controller Delegate

Tab Bar Controllers can use a delegate object to report when something happened or is about to happen with the tabs. The UIKit framework includes the **UITabBarControllerDelegate** protocol for this purpose. The following are some of the methods defined by the protocol.

tabBarController(UITabBarController, **didSelect:** UIViewController**)**—This method is called by the **UITabBarController** object when a tab is selected. The **didSelect** argument is a reference to the view controller of the selected tab.

tabBarController(UITabBarController, **shouldSelect:** UIViewController**)**—This method is called by the **UITabBarController** object to know whether it should let the user select a tab. The method returns a Boolean value that communicates the decision made by the app. The **shouldSelect** argument is a reference to the view controller of the selected tab.

The delegate object may be an external object or the **UITabBarController** subclass that is controlling our Tab Bar Controller. The following example defines our **MyTabViewController** class as its own delegate to perform a task when a tab is selected.

```
import UIKit

class MyTabViewController: UITabBarController, UITabBarControllerDelegate
{
   override func viewDidLoad() {
      super.viewDidLoad()
      delegate = self
   }
   func tabBarController(_ tabBarController: UITabBarController,
didSelect viewController: UIViewController) {
      let list = viewControllers!
      let controller = list[1]
      if viewController === controller {
         print("It's Settings")
      }
   }
}
```

Listing 9-27: *Defining the Tab Bar Controller's delegate*

To turn the **MyTabViewController** class of our example into its own delegate, we must declare that the class conforms to the **UITabBarControllerDelegate** protocol first, and then assign **self** to its **delegate** property. From that moment on, the **MyTabViewController** object will call the delegate's methods on itself. In Listing 9-27, we declare the method that is called when the user selects a tab. To check which tab was selected, we implement the identity operator (===) to compare the value on the **viewController** argument with the reference stored at index 1 in the **viewControllers** array. This reference corresponds to the **SecondViewController** object and therefore the task is performed when the Settings view is show on the screen (the === operator compares objects' references).

There are other ways to detect the type of the selected view controller. For example, we could try to convert it to one of our **UIViewController** subclasses with the **as?** operator and compare the value returned by the conversion to **nil**. If the view controller received by the method is of type **SecondViewController**, the condition will be true, and we can perform the task as we did in Listing 9-27. Following this procedure, we could also read the properties of this object, as shown next.

```
import UIKit

class MyTabViewController: UITabBarController, UITabBarControllerDelegate
{
   override func viewDidLoad() {
      super.viewDidLoad()
      delegate = self
   }
   func tabBarController(_ tabBarController: UITabBarController,
shouldSelect viewController: UIViewController) -> Bool {
      if let controller = viewController as? SecondViewController {
         let control = controller.myproperty
```

```
            if control != 0 {
               return false
            }
         }
         return true
      }
   }
```

Listing 9-28: Allowing the selection of a tab

The protocol method implemented in this example is called when a tab is selected but before the scene is shown on the screen. From this method, we must return a Boolean value to indicate whether the action is valid or not. To know what value to return, the code in Listing 9-28 detects the scene the user is trying to open by casting the value in the **viewController** argument to the class corresponding to the view controller of the Settings scene (**SecondViewController**). In case of success, we store the result in the **controller** constant and use this reference to access a property called **myproperty**. If the value of this property is different from 0, the code returns **false** and does not let the user select the tab.

Do It Yourself: Copy the example you want to try in the MyTabViewController.swift file created before and run the application. The code in Listing 9-28 assumes that you have declared a property called **myproperty** in the **SecondViewController** class assigned to the second scene and initialize it with an integer. If the value is different from 0, the delegate method returns **false** and therefore you will not be able to select the Settings tab.

Chapter 10
Table Views

Basic 10.1 Tables

Computers are experts at organizing information in lists of values, and therefore it didn't take long for computer systems to adopt the concepts of tables to present this type of information. A table is an organizational system that proposes an arrangement of data in rows and columns. Apple has always provided the tools to create tables on its systems, but the small screens of mobile devices forced the company to introduce a customized version of tables composed of only one column.

Despite their simplicity, tables in iOS are very powerful. They provide tools to manage the data, organize it in single lists or sections, and are built inside a Scroll View, allowing the content to be shown with no limitations whatsoever. Figure 10-1 shows the three possible configurations (Plain, Grouped, and Inset Grouped).

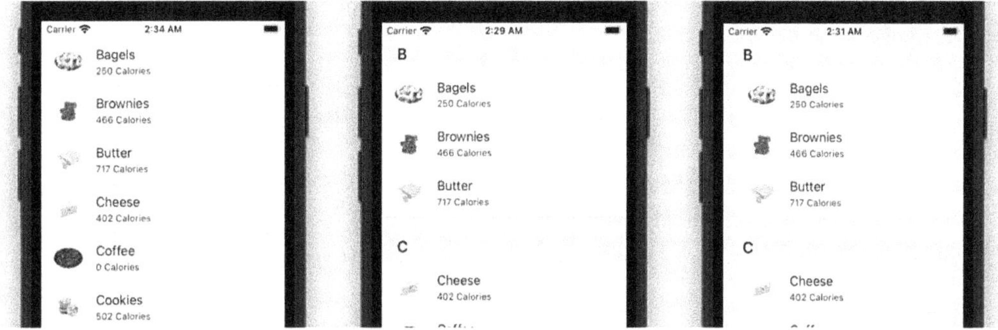

Figure 10-1: *Table Views styles*

iOS tables can present the information on a list, like the table on the left of Figure 10-1, or organized in groups, like the ones at the center and right of Figure 10-1, and they can also display images and text, as in this example, only text, or be completely customized, as we will see later.

IMPORTANT: There are at least two ways to create and configure Table Views. Traditionally, Table Views work with delegate objects that provide the configuration and the data, but since iOS 14, the data is provided by Diffable Data Sources and the cells are defined by configuration objects. This is how Table Views work in iOS 15 and therefore it is the approach we take in this book. To learn more about the old Table View delegates, visit our website and follow the links for this chapter.

Basic Table Views

Tables are created from the **`UITableView`** class. The following are the initializer provided by the class to create a table from code and the option in the Library to add a table to a scene.

UITableView(frame: CGRect, **style:** Style**)**—This initializer creates a **`UITableView`** object with the frame specified by the **frame** argument. The **style** argument is an enumeration called **`Style`** with the values **`plain`**, **`grouped`**, and **`insetGrouped`**.

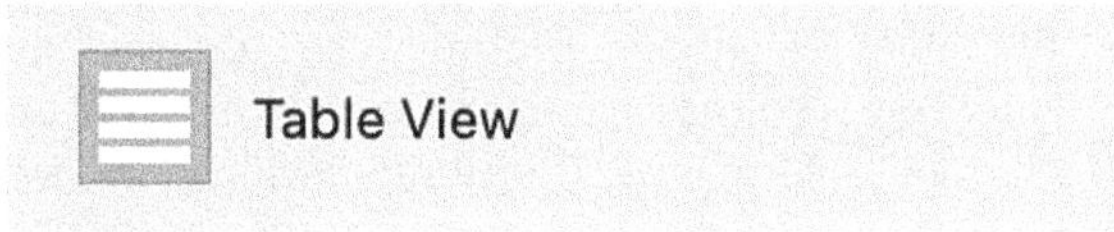

Figure 10-2: *Table View option in the Library*

The **UITableView** class includes multiple properties and methods to configure the table. The following are the most frequently used.

allowsSelection—This property sets or returns a Boolean value that determines if the user is allowed to select a cell or not.

allowsMultipleSelection—This property sets or returns a Boolean value that determines if the user is allowed to select multiple cells or not.

isEditing—This property sets or returns a Boolean value that indicates whether the table is in edition mode or not. The edition mode is used to delete or move rows.

rowHeight—This property sets or returns a **CGFloat** value that determines the cells' height.

estimatedRowHeight—This property sets or returns a **CGFloat** value that determines the approximate size of the cell. It is intended to improve performance.

separatorStyle—This property sets or returns the style for the cells' separators. It is an enumeration called **SeparatorStyle** with the values **none** and **singleLine**.

separatorColor—This property sets or returns the color for the cells' separators. It is an optional of type **UIColor**.

separatorInset—This property sets or returns the padding for the cells' separators. It is a structure of type **UIEdgeInsets** with the properties **top**, **left**, **bottom**, and **right** (only the left and right values are considered).

indexPathForSelectedRow—This property returns an **IndexPath** structure with the location of the currently selected cell.

selectRow(at: IndexPath?, **animated:** Bool, **scrollPosition:** ScrollPosition**)**—This method selects the cell at the location specified by the **at** argument. The **animated** argument indicates whether the process is going to be animated or not, and the **scrollPosition** argument indicates if the table will scroll to the position of the cell and how. It is an enumeration called **ScrollPosition** with the values **none**, **top**, **middle**, and **bottom**.

deselectRow(at: IndexPath, **animated:** Bool**)**—This method deselects the cell at the location specified by the **at** argument. The **animated** argument indicates whether the process is going to be animated or not.

scrollToRow(at: IndexPath, **at:** ScrollPosition, **animated:** Bool**)**—This method scrolls the Table View to show on the screen the cell at the position indicated by the **at** argument. The **position** argument indicates if the table scrolls to the position of the cell and how. It is an enumeration called **ScrollPosition** with the values **none**, **top**, **middle**, and **bottom**. The **animated** argument indicates whether the process is going to be animated.

setEditing(Bool, **animated:** Bool**)**—This method sets the value of the **isEditing** property. The first argument is the value we want to assign to the property, and the **animated** argument determines if the change will be animated.

Basic Table View Cells

Tables present the information in cells, one per row, with each cell in charge of displaying a unique piece of data. Cells are created from the **UITableViewCell** class, but we do not instantiate each cell for the table, we define a prototype cell and then ask the system to create the cells from this prototype. This is so the system can keep in memory only the cells required at any given moment and improve performance. The Library includes the following option to add a prototype cell to the table.

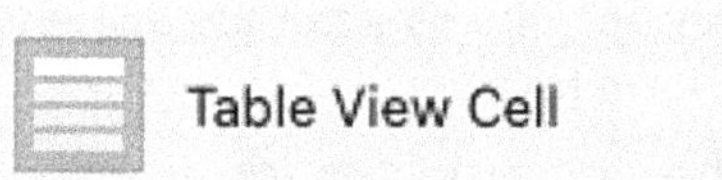

Figure 10-3: *Table View Cell option in the Library*

If we want to include a prototype cell from code (a process called registration), we can use the following method.

register(AnyClass?, **forCellReuseIdentifier:** String**)**—This method registers a prototype cell. The fist argument is the class that is going to be used to create the cells (the **`UITableViewCell`** class or a subclass of it), and the **forCellReuseIdentifier** argument specifies the string the table is going to use to identify this prototype cell.

Once we have a prototype cell, we can use it to display the information on the table. The following is the method we need to implement to get a reference to the cell for a row.

dequeueReusableCell(withIdentifier: String, **for:** IndexPath**)**—This method returns a reusable cell with the identifier specified by the **withIdentifier** argument. The **for** argument is an **`IndexPath`** structure that determines the cell's location.

This method gets the cell for a row, but the content of that cell is defined by a configuration object. This is an object created from the **`UIListContentConfiguration`** structure. The **`UITableViewCell`** class includes the following method to create a **`UIListContentConfiguration`** structure with a configuration by default.

defaultContentConfiguration()—This method returns a **`UIListContentConfiguration`** structure with a default configuration.

The **`UIListContentConfiguration`** structure also includes type methods that return standard configurations for cells, including **`cell()`**, **`subtitleCell()`**, **`valueCell()`**, **`sidebarCell()`**, **`sidebarSubtitleCell()`**, **`accompaniedSidebarCell()`**, and **`accompaniedSidebarSubtitleCell()`**.

After we get the configuration, we must assign the values we want to display inside the cell. A standard cell can display three values by default: a text, a secondary text, and an image. The **`UIListContentConfiguration`** structure includes the following properties to specify these values.

text—This property sets or returns the cell's main text. It is an optional of type **`String`**.

attributedText—This property sets or returns the cell's attributed text. It is an optional of type **`NSAttributedString`**.

secondaryText—This property sets or returns the cell's secondary text. It is an optional of type **`String`**.

secondaryAttributedText—This property sets or returns the cell's attributed secondary text. It is an optional of type **`NSAttributedString`**.

image—This property sets or returns the cell's image. It is an optional of type **`UIImage`**.

The **`attributedText`** and **`secondaryAttributedText`** properties allow us to declare the cell's main and secondary texts with attributed strings, but we can also specify the text and secondary text with a string and assign common attributes. The **`UIListContentConfiguration`** structure includes the following properties to assign attributes to the texts and the image.

textProperties—This property sets or returns a **TextProperties** structure with the attributes we want to assign to the main text.

secondaryTextProperties—This property sets or returns a **TextProperties** structure with the attributes we want to assign to the secondary text.

imageProperties—This property sets or returns an **ImageProperties** structure with the attributes we want to assign to the image.

The attributes for the text are defined by a **TextProperties** structure. For this purpose, the structure includes the following properties.

font—This property sets or returns the font. It is a value of type **UIFont**.

color—This property sets or returns the color. It is a value of type **UIColor**.

alignment—This property sets or returns the alignment. It is a **TextAlignment** enumeration with the values **center**, **justified**, and **natural**.

lineBreakMode—This property sets or returns the mode used to truncate the text. It is an **NSLineBreakMode** enumeration with the values **byWordWrapping**, **byCharWrapping**, **byClipping**, **byTruncatingHead**, **byTruncatingTail**, and **byTruncatingMiddle**.

numberOfLines—This property sets or returns the maximum lines of text allowed. It is a value of type **Int**. The value 0 indicates unlimited lines.

On the other hand, the attributes for the image are defined by an **ImageProperties** structure. For this purpose, the structure includes the following properties.

cornerRadius—This property sets or returns a **CGFloat** value that determines the image's corner radius.

maximumSize—This property sets or returns a **CGSize** value with the image's width and height. The image is resized to meet these values.

reservedLayoutSize—This property sets or returns a **CGSize** value that determines the space reserved for the images (used to align the images with the rest of the content).

After the configuration object is defined, we must assign it to the cell. The **UITableViewCell** class includes the following properties for this purpose.

contentConfiguration—This property sets or returns the **UIListContent-Configuration** structure that determines the cell's configuration.

automaticallyUpdatesContentConfiguration—This property sets or returns a Boolean value that indicates whether the configuration is going to be updated when the state of the cell changes. The value by default is **true**.

In addition to the text, the secondary text, and the image, a cell can also include a view on the side. These views, called accessories, are used to reflect or propose user interaction. For instance, there is an accessory called Disclosure Indicator used to indicate to the user that there is more information available for the item. Accessories are defined by the cell. The **UITableViewCell** includes the following property for this purpose.

accessoryType—This property sets or returns the type of the accessory view. It is an enumeration called **AccessoryType** with the values **none**, **disclosureIndicator**, **detailDisclosureButton**, **checkmark**, and **detailButton**.

Basic Data Source

The data is provided to the Table View by two objects: an object of the **UITableViewDiffableDataSource** class, which takes care of defining the cells, and an object of the **NSDiffableDataSourceSnapshot** class, responsible for keeping the Table View up to date. The **UITableViewDiffableDataSource** class provides the following initializer and methods to generate the cells and apply the changes.

UITableViewDiffableDataSource(tableView: UITableView, **cellProvider:** Closure**)**—This initializer creates a data source for the Table View specified by the **tableView** argument. The **cellProvider** argument is a closure that is called every time a cell is required. The closure receives three values: a reference to the Table View, the cell's index path, and a reference to the data that must be shown by the cell.

snapshot()—This method returns a reference to the current snapshot used by the data source to get the data.

apply(NSDiffableDataSourceSnapshot, **animatingDifferences:** Bool, **completion:** Closure**)**—This method applies the snapshot provided by the first argument to the data source object. It is used to update the Table View with new values. The **animatingDifferences** argument determines if the changes on the table will be animated, and the **completion** argument is a closure to be executed when the process is over. These last two arguments may be ignored.

defaultRowAnimation—This property sets or returns a value that determines how the insertion or deletion of cells will be animated. It is an enumeration of type **RowAnimation** with the values **fade**, **right**, **left**, **top**, **bottom**, **middle**, **automatic**, and **none**.

The **UITableViewDiffableDataSource** object generates the cells from a snapshot of the data created by a **NSDiffableDataSourceSnapshot** object. The following are some of the properties and methods defined by the **NSDiffableDataSourceSnapshot** class to process the values.

numberOfItems—This property returns the number of values managed by the snapshot. There is also the **numberOfSections** property to return the number of sections.

itemIdentifiers—This property returns an array with the identifiers of the values managed by the snapshot. There is also the **sectionIdentifiers** property for the sections.

numberOfItems(inSection: SectionIdentifierType**)**—This method returns the number of items in the section specified by the **inSection** argument.

appendItems([ItemIdentifierType], **toSection:** SectionIdentifierType?**)**—This method adds to the snapshot the items specified by the first argument in the section specified by the **toSection** argument. If there is only one section, the second argument may be ignored.

appendSections([SectionIdentifierType]**)**—This method adds to the snapshot the sections specified by the argument.

insertItems([ItemIdentifierType], **afterItem:** ItemIdentifierType**)**—This method inserts the items specified by the first argument after the item specified by the **afterItem** argument.

insertItems([ItemIdentifierType], **beforeItem:** ItemIdentifierType**)**—This method inserts the items specified by the first argument before the item specified by the **beforeItem** argument.

insertSections([SectionIdentifierType], **afterSection:** SectionIdentifierType**)**—This method inserts the sections specified by the first argument after the section specified by the **afterSection** argument.

insertSections([SectionIdentifierType], **beforeSection:** SectionIdentifier-Type**)**—This method inserts the sections specified by the first argument before the section specified by the **beforeSection** argument.

deleteItems([ItemIdentifierType]**)**—This method removes from the snapshot the items specified by the argument.

deleteSections([SectionIdentifierType]**)**—This method removes from the snapshot the sections specified by the argument.

reconfigureItems([ItemIdentifierType]**)**—This method updates the values for the items specified by the argument.

deleteAllItems()—This method removes all the items from the snapshot.

moveItem(ItemIdentifierType, **afterItem:** ItemIdentifierType**)**—This method moves the item specified by the first argument to the position after the item specified by the **afterItem** argument.

moveItem(ItemIdentifierType, **beforeItem:** ItemIdentifierType**)**—This method moves the item specified by the first argument to the position before the item specified by the **beforeItem** argument.

moveSection(SectionIdentifierType, **afterSection:** SectionIdentifierType**)**—This method moves the section specified by the first argument to the position after the section specified by the **afterSection** argument.

moveSection(SectionIdentifierType, **beforeSection:** SectionIdentifierType**)**—This method moves the section specified by the first argument to the position before the section specified by the **beforeSection** argument.

reloadItems([ItemIdentifierType]**)**—This method reloads the items specified by the argument. It updates the items with the current values from the model.

reloadSections([SectionIdentifierType]**)**—This method reloads the sections specified by the argument. It updates the sections with the current values from the model.

Basic Index Paths and Identifiers

Cells and sections are identified by their position in the Table View. Sections are assigned a consecutive index starting from 0, and then the cells inside each section are also identified with a consecutive index starting from 0. Therefore, to identify a cell, we need the index of the cell and the index of the section the cell belongs to. Table Views store this information in a structure of type **`IndexPath`**. The values are returned by the following properties.

section—This property returns the index of the section where the cell is located.

row—This property returns the index of the cell.

item—This property returns the index of the item in a Collection View.

`IndexPath` structures are automatically defined by the Table View, but there are situations in which we must create them ourselves. The structure includes the following initializer.

IndexPath(item: Int, **section:** Int**)**—This initializer creates an **`IndexPath`** structure with the values provided by the arguments.

As we already mentioned, Table Views get the data to display from a diffable data source. Diffable data sources work with their own identifiers; they use the identification values provided by the data. Because Table Views still need to call their delegate methods to perform most of the configuration tasks, there are times when we need to convert **IndexPath** values into identifiers and vice versa. The **UITableViewDiffableDataSource** class includes the following methods for this purpose.

indexPath(for: ItemIdentifierType**)**—This method returns an **IndexPath** structure with the location of the cell identified by the value provided by the argument.

itemIdentifier(for: IndexPath**)**—This method returns the identifier of the cell at the index path specified by the argument.

Basic Implementing Table Views

Table Views are normal views and therefore they are positioned and sized inside the main view with constraints. Although we can give them any size we want, due to the type of information they manage, they are usually defined of the size of the screen.

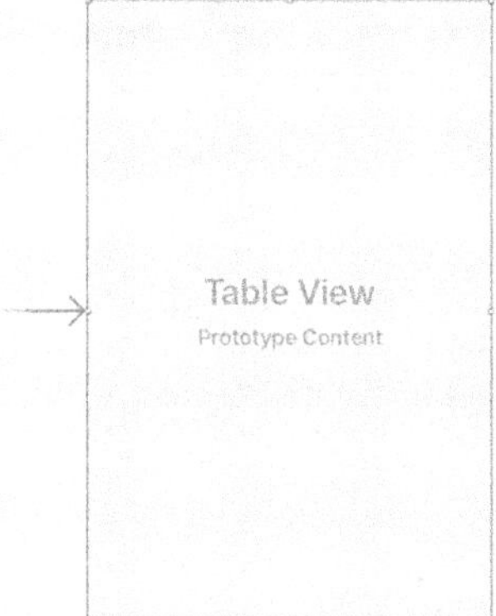

Figure 10-4: *Table View pinned to the Safe Area*

To provide the data for the table, we need three elements: the model where the data is stored, a snapshot to keep the table up to date with the changes in the model, and a diffable data source to configure the cells. We have seen how to create a model in Chapter 9 (see Listing 9-20), but diffable data sources and snapshots have a few requirements. Diffable data sources do not work with the data itself, they store the data identifiers. These identifiers must conform to the **Hashable** protocol, so the values can be differentiated. Swift standard data types, such as strings, integers, and enumerations, conform to this protocol by default, but if we want to use custom data types to store the data, they must conform to the **Identifiable** protocol and define the **id** property required by the protocol with a **Hashable** value.

Table Views require at least one section to show the data, so we also need identifiers for the sections. In the following model, we provide an enumeration with a single value to represent the only section we need for now, and a class with a **Hashable** identifier to store the data.

```
import UIKit

enum Sections {
   case main
}
class ItemsData: Identifiable {
   var id: UUID = UUID()
   var name: String
   var image: String
   var calories: Int
   var selected: Bool
```

```
    init(_ name: String, _ image: String, _ calories: Int, _ selected: 
Bool) {
        self.name = name
        self.image = image
        self.calories = calories
        self.selected = selected
    }
}
struct ApplicationData {
    var dataSource: UITableViewDiffableDataSource<Sections, ItemsData.ID>!

    var items: [ItemsData] = [] {
        didSet {
            items.sort(by: { $0.name < $1.name })
        }
    }
    init() {
        items.append(ItemsData("Bagels", "bagels", 250, false))
        items.append(ItemsData("Brownies", "brownies", 466, false))
        items.append(ItemsData("Butter", "butter", 717, false))
        items.append(ItemsData("Cheese", "cheese", 402, false))
        items.append(ItemsData("Coffee", "coffee", 0, false))
        items.append(ItemsData("Cookies", "cookies", 502, false))
        items.append(ItemsData("Donuts", "donuts", 452, false))
        items.append(ItemsData("Granola", "granola", 471, false))
        items.append(ItemsData("Juice", "juice", 23, false))
        items.append(ItemsData("Lemonade", "lemonade", 40, false))
        items.append(ItemsData("Lettuce", "lettuce", 15, false))
        items.append(ItemsData("Milk", "milk", 42, false))
        items.append(ItemsData("Oatmeal", "oatmeal", 68, false))
        items.append(ItemsData("Potatoes", "potato", 77, false))
        items.append(ItemsData("Tomatoes", "tomato", 18, false))
        items.append(ItemsData("Yogurt", "yogurt", 59, false))
    }
}
var AppData = ApplicationData()
```

Listing 10-1: *Defining a model for a diffable data source*

The **ItemsData** class includes four properties for the values (**name**, **image**, **calories**, and **selected**), and the **id** property defined with a **UUID** value. This is a structure that always produces a unique value and that's what we are going to use to identify each item on the table.

Next is the definition of the structure to contain the model. This is the same **ApplicationData** structure we used before for the examples in Chapter 9. The structure includes a property called **dataSource** to store the diffable data source, a property called **items** to store the values for each cell, and an initializer to provide initial values to work with.

Notice that the **UITableViewDiffableDataSource** class is generic, and therefore it must be declared with the data types of the values is going to store (the data types used to identify the sections and the items). For the sections it is easy, the identifier is a value of type **Sections**, but the data type of the items' identifiers depends on the data type of the **id** property. In this case, we could have specified the **UUID** data type, but the **Identifier** protocol defines a typealias for the property's data type called **ID** (a typealias is an alternative name for a data type). By using this typealias we make sure that the data type assigned to the diffable data source is the same assigned to the **id** property. This makes the code more readable and easy to update.

The **items** property includes the **didSet** method to sort the values alphabetically every time changes are introduced by the user (the values are modified, deleted, or new values are added).

With the model ready, now the view controller has all the information it needs to configure the table and present the data on the screen.

```
import UIKit

class ViewController: UIViewController {
   @IBOutlet weak var myTable: UITableView!

   override func viewDidLoad() {
      super.viewDidLoad()
      myTable.register(UITableViewCell.self, forCellReuseIdentifier:
"myCell")

      AppData.dataSource = UITableViewDiffableDataSource<Sections,
ItemsData.ID>(tableView: myTable) { tableView, indexPath, itemID in
         let cell = tableView.dequeueReusableCell(withIdentifier:
"myCell", for: indexPath)

         if let item = AppData.items.first(where: { $0.id == itemID }) {
            var config = cell.defaultContentConfiguration()
            config.text = item.name
            cell.contentConfiguration = config
         }
         return cell
      }
      var snapshot = NSDiffableDataSourceSnapshot<Sections,
ItemsData.ID>()
      snapshot.appendSections([.main])
      snapshot.appendItems(AppData.items.map({ $0.id }))
      AppData.dataSource.apply(snapshot)
   }
}
```

Listing 10-2: *Defining the diffable data source and the snapshot*

A Table View needs a prototype cell. This is like a template the table uses to create all the cells it needs to display the data. Although prototype cells can be added to the Table View in the Storyboard, Apple's technologies are leaning towards the optimizations of elements created from code, so in this example we have decided to follow that approach. Using the **register()** method, we define a prototype cell with the myCell identifier and then to create the diffable data source with this cell.

The **UITableViewDiffableDataSource** initializer takes a reference to the Table View and a closure that is called every time the table needs a cell (defined as a trailing closure in this example). The closure receives three values we must use to create and configure the cell: a reference to the Table View, the index path with the location of the cell, and the **UUID** value that identifies the item to be shown in that row. The cell is created by the **dequeueReusableCell()** method. This method creates a new **UITableViewCell** object from a prototype cell or returns an existent object from a cell that is not currently in use. Whatever the origin, we always must update the configuration with the values of the current item, and the first step is to get the item. For this purpose, we call the **first(where:)** method on the **items** array. This method compares the value of the **id** property of each item with the ID received by the closure and returns the item which ID matches. With this value, we can finally configure the cell.

The configuration is defined by a **UIListContentConfiguration** structure. In this example, we use the instance returned by the **defaultContentConfiguration()** method. This is a standard configuration that includes the image on the left, the text on top, and a secondary text with a smaller font at the bottom. Although the configuration structure provides styles for every element in the cell, we can define only those we need. In this case, we only want the cell to show the name of the item, so we assign that value to the **text** property. After the configuration structure is ready, we assign it to the **contentConfiguration** property to apply it to the cell.

The Table View shows the cells on the screen, the diffable data source configures the cells with the data, but the data is managed by a snapshot created from a **NSDiffableDataSourceSnapshot** object. This class is also generic and requires us to specify the data types of the identifiers we are going to work with. In this case, **Sections** for the sections and **ItemsData.ID** for the data. After the object is created, we must add the sections with the **appendSections()** method and all the items IDs we want to show to the user with the **appendItems()** method. Notice that because the **items** array contains a list of items, we map the array with the **map()** method to get an array of identifiers instead. Finally, the snapshot is applied to the diffable data source with the **apply()** method and the values appear on the screen.

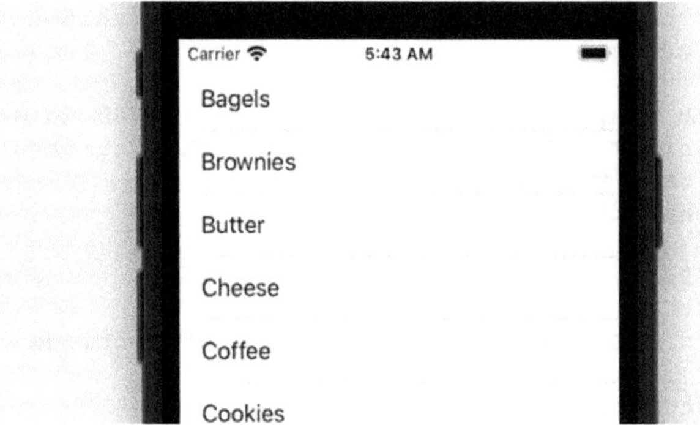

Figure 10-5: *Table View with standard configuration*

Do It Yourself: Create a new project. Add a Table View to the scene and pin it to the Safe Area. Connect the table to an Outlet in the view controller called **myTable**. Create a Swift file called ApplicationData.swift to store the code in Listing 10-1. Complete the **ViewController** class with the code in Listing 10-2. Run the application. You should see a Table View like in Figure 10-5.

IMPORTANT: By default, the **apply()** method tells the data source to animate the changes, but you can modify that behavior by specifying the **animatingDifferences** argument with the value **false**.

We can take advantage of the rest of the elements in a standard cell to present more information. The following example configures the cell with a text, a secondary text, and an image. Notice that because the code for the diffable data source has grown, we have moved it along with the snapshot to two custom methods (**prepareDataSource()** and **prepareSnapshot()**).

```
import UIKit

class ViewController: UIViewController {
   @IBOutlet weak var myTable: UITableView!

   override func viewDidLoad() {
      super.viewDidLoad()
      myTable.register(UITableViewCell.self, forCellReuseIdentifier:
"myCell")
      prepareDataSource()
      prepareSnapshot()
   }
   func prepareDataSource() {
      AppData.dataSource = UITableViewDiffableDataSource<Sections,
ItemsData.ID>(tableView: myTable) { tableView, indexPath, itemID in
         let cell = tableView.dequeueReusableCell(withIdentifier:
"myCell", for: indexPath)
```

```
        if let item = AppData.items.first(where: { $0.id == itemID }) {
           var config = cell.defaultContentConfiguration()
           config.text = item.name
           config.secondaryText = "\(item.calories) Calories"
           config.image = UIImage(named: item.image)
           config.imageProperties.maximumSize = CGSize(width: 40,
height: 40)
           cell.contentConfiguration = config
        }
        return cell
     }
  }
  func prepareSnapshot() {
     var snapshot = NSDiffableDataSourceSnapshot<Sections,
ItemsData.ID>()
     snapshot.appendSections([.main])
     snapshot.appendItems(AppData.items.map({ $0.id }))
     AppData.dataSource.apply(snapshot)
  }
}
```

Listing 10-3: *Including more information in the cell*

This diffable data source includes the text, as before, but also the secondary text and the image. Notice that the images we used are too big for the table, so we specify the maximum size with a **CGSize** value. The images are reduced, and the cell's layout adapts to the elements available.

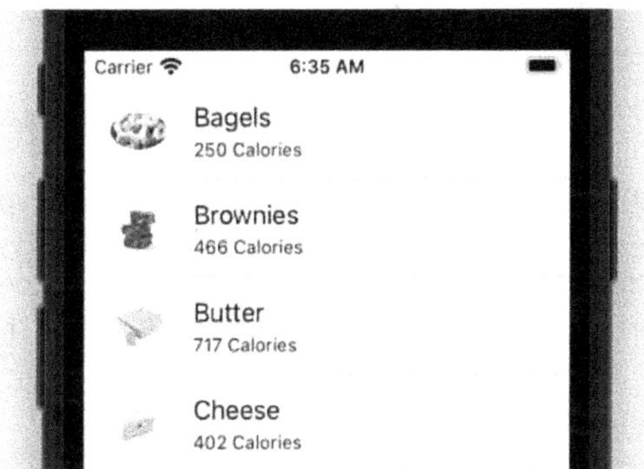

Figure 10-6: *Cells with all the standard elements*

Do It Yourself: Download the thumbnails.zip file from our website and add the images to the Assets Catalog. Update the **ViewController** class with the code in Listing 10-3. Run the application. You should see something like Figure 10-6.

The same way we assign attributes to the image, we can assign attributes to the text. There are two ways to do it. We can assign attributed strings to the text and secondary text with the **attributedText** and **secondaryAttributedText** properties or define the attributes independently from the **textProperties** and **secondaryTextProperties** properties. For instance, if all we want to do is to assign different colors to the texts, we can modify the **color** property of the **TextProperties** structure returned by the **textProperties** and **secondaryTextProperties** properties, as shown next.

```
func prepareDataSource() {
   AppData.dataSource = UITableViewDiffableDataSource<Sections,
ItemsData.ID>(tableView: myTable) { tableView, indexPath, itemID in
      let cell = tableView.dequeueReusableCell(withIdentifier: "myCell",
for: indexPath)
```

```
        if let item = AppData.items.first(where: { $0.id == itemID }) {
           var config = cell.defaultContentConfiguration()
           config.text = item.name
           config.textProperties.color = .systemBlue
           config.secondaryText = "\(item.calories) Calories"
           config.secondaryTextProperties.color = .systemGray

           config.image = UIImage(named: item.image)
           config.imageProperties.maximumSize = CGSize(width: 40, height:
40)
           cell.contentConfiguration = config
        }
        return cell
    }
}
```

Listing 10-4: *Configuring the texts*

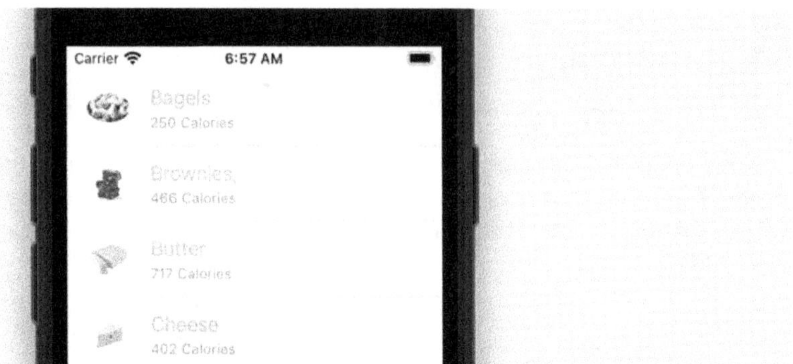

Figure 10-7: *Elements with custom attributes*

The **UIListContentConfiguration** structure also includes type methods that return a configuration structure with some predefined colors and styles. For instance, the **sidebarCell()** method returns a configuration that shows the secondary text in gray. Another useful method is **valueCell()**, which returns a configuration that shows the main text on the left and the secondary text on the right, as show next.

```
func prepareDataSource() {
   AppData.dataSource = UITableViewDiffableDataSource<Sections,
ItemsData.ID>(tableView: myTable) { tableView, indexPath, itemID in
      let cell = tableView.dequeueReusableCell(withIdentifier: "myCell",
for: indexPath)
      if let item = AppData.items.first(where: { $0.id == itemID }) {
         var config = UIListContentConfiguration.valueCell()
         config.text = item.name
         config.secondaryText = "\(item.calories) Calories"
         cell.contentConfiguration = config
      }
      return cell
   }
}
```

Listing 10-5: *Implementing standard configurations*

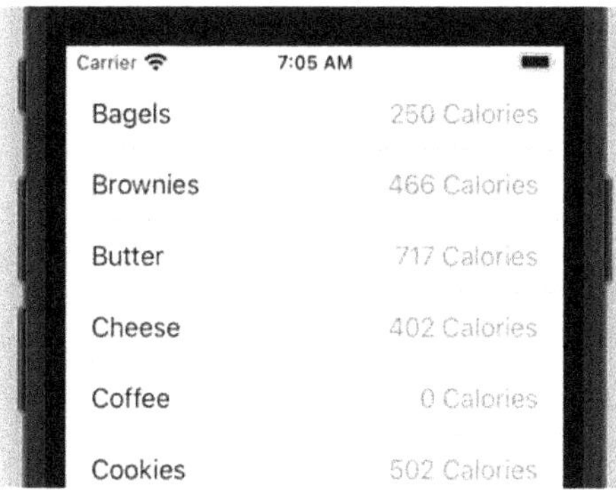

Figure 10-8: *Standard configuration*

Basic Background

In addition to the cell's content, we can also configure the cell's background. The background's configuration is defined by a **`UIBackgroundConfiguration`** structure. Like the **`UIListContentConfiguration`** structure, the **`UIBackgroundConfiguration`** structure includes type methods that return standard configurations for a cell, including **`listPlainCell()`**, **`listGroupedCell()`**, **`listSidebarCell()`**, and **`listAccompanied-SidebarCell()`**. The class also includes properties for customization. The following are the most frequently used.

backgroundColor—This property sets or returns the background color. It's an optional of type **`UIColor`**.

backgroundInsets—This property returns the index of the cell.

strokeWidth—This property sets or returns the padding between the content and the background views. It is a value of type **`NSDirectionalEdgeInsets`**.

strokeColor—This property sets or returns the color of the border around the background view. It is an optional of type **`UIColor`**.

cornerRadius—This property sets or returns a **`CGFloat`** value that determines the radius of the corners.

image—This property sets or returns the background's image. It is an optional of type **`UIImage`**.

imageContentMode—This property sets or returns the mode to use to layout the image inside the background view. It is the same **`ContentMode`** enumeration provided by the **`UIView`** class that we use to layout the content of a **`UIImageView`**. The most useful values are **`scaleToFill`**, **`scaleAspectFit`**, and **`scaleAspectFill`**.

After the configuration object is defined, we must assign it to the cell. The **`UITableViewCell`** class includes the following properties for this purpose.

backgroundConfiguration—This property sets or returns the **`UIBackground-Configuration`** structure that determines the cell's background configuration.

automaticallyUpdatesBackgroundConfiguration—This property sets or returns a Boolean value that indicates whether the background configuration is going to be updated when the state of the cell changes. The value by default is **`true`**.

The process to define and apply a background configuration to the cell is the same we used to configure the content. We must get a standard configuration from the type methods, customize it, and then assign it to the cell.

```
import UIKit

class ViewController: UIViewController {
   @IBOutlet weak var myTable: UITableView!

   override func viewDidLoad() {
      super.viewDidLoad()
      myTable.register(UITableViewCell.self, forCellReuseIdentifier:
"myCell")
      myTable.rowHeight = 80
      myTable.separatorStyle = .none

      prepareDataSource()
      prepareSnapshot()
   }
   func prepareDataSource() {
      AppData.dataSource = UITableViewDiffableDataSource<Sections,
ItemsData.ID>(tableView: myTable) { tableView, indexPath, itemID in
         let cell = tableView.dequeueReusableCell(withIdentifier:
"myCell", for: indexPath)
         if let item = AppData.items.first(where: { $0.id == itemID }) {
            var config = cell.defaultContentConfiguration()
            config.text = item.name
            config.image = UIImage(named: item.image)
            config.imageProperties.maximumSize = CGSize(width: 60,
height: 60)
            cell.contentConfiguration = config

            var backgroundConfig =
UIBackgroundConfiguration.listPlainCell()
            backgroundConfig.backgroundColor = .systemGray6
            backgroundConfig.backgroundInsets =
NSDirectionalEdgeInsets(top: 5, leading: 5, bottom: 5, trailing: 5)
            backgroundConfig.cornerRadius = 10
            cell.backgroundConfiguration = backgroundConfig
         }
         return cell
      }
   }
   func prepareSnapshot() {
      var snapshot = NSDiffableDataSourceSnapshot<Sections,
ItemsData.ID>()
      snapshot.appendSections([.main])
      snapshot.appendItems(AppData.items.map({ $0.id }))
      AppData.dataSource.apply(snapshot)
   }
}
```

Listing 10-6: *Assigning a background configuration to the cell*

The diffable data source in Listing 10-6 configures the cell with the main title, the image, and a gray background. Notice that we also took advantage of the Table View's **rowHeight** and **separatorStyle** to assign a height of 80 points to the cell and remove the separator. We have also enlarged the images, which are now 60x60 points in size. The result is shown below.

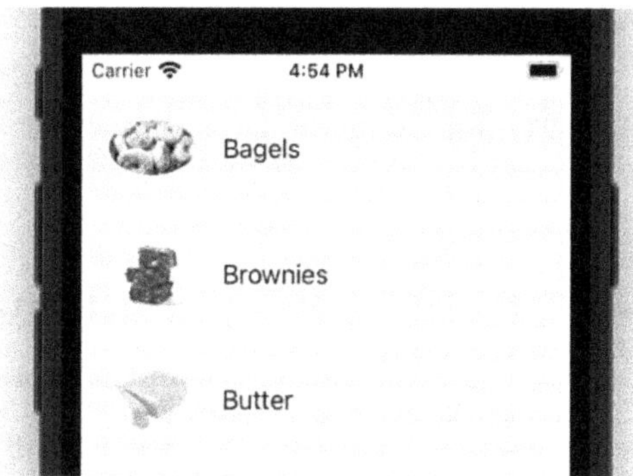

Figure 10-9: Custom background

Do It Yourself: Update the **ViewController** class with the code in Listing 10-6. Run the application. You should see something like Figure 10-9. Try to use an image for the background instead of a color by modifying the background's **image** and **imageContentMode** properties.

Basic States

Cells can be in a variety of different states. For instance, if the user taps on a cell, the cell becomes selected (the cell is in the selected state). If the user swipes a cell to the side (a gesture used to delete a cell), it is said that the cell is in the swipe state. The states are reported by Boolean properties of the **UICellConfigurationState** structure. Some of the properties available are **isSelected**, **isHighlighted**, **isFocused**, **isDisabled**, **isEditing**, **isSwiped**, and **isExpanded**. To process these states, the **UITableViewCell** class includes the following properties.

configurationState—This property returns the cell's current state. It is a **UICellConfigurationState** value.

configurationUpdateHandler—This property sets or returns a closure that is executed every time the state of the cell changes. The closure receives two values: a reference to the cell and a **UICellConfigurationState** value to report the cell's current state.

With the **UICellConfigurationState** value, we can define configurations for every state. For this purpose, the **UIListContentConfiguration** and **UIBackgroundConfiguration** structures define a method that returns a configuration object for any state we want.

updated(for: State**)**—This method returns a configuration for the state specified by the **for** argument.

The closure assigned to the cell's **configurationUpdateHandler** property is executed every time the state of the cell changes and also after it is created, so we can define the configurations for all the states from it. For instance, we can update the diffable data source from the previous example to assign a background to the cell and modify it every time the cell is selected.

```
func prepareDataSource() {
   AppData.dataSource = UITableViewDiffableDataSource<Sections,
ItemsData.ID>(tableView: myTable) { tableView, indexPath, itemID in
      let cell = tableView.dequeueReusableCell(withIdentifier: "myCell",
for: indexPath)
```

```
        if let item = AppData.items.first(where: { $0.id == itemID }) {
           var config = cell.defaultContentConfiguration()
           config.text = item.name
           config.image = UIImage(named: item.image)
           config.imageProperties.maximumSize = CGSize(width: 60, height:
60)
           cell.contentConfiguration = config

           cell.configurationUpdateHandler = { cell, state in
              var backgroundConfig =
UIBackgroundConfiguration.listPlainCell().updated(for: state)
              backgroundConfig.backgroundInsets =
NSDirectionalEdgeInsets(top: 5, leading: 5, bottom: 5, trailing: 5)
              backgroundConfig.cornerRadius = 10

              if state.isSelected {
                 backgroundConfig.backgroundColor = .systemBlue
              } else {
                 backgroundConfig.backgroundColor = .systemGray6
              }
              cell.backgroundConfiguration = backgroundConfig
           }
        }
        return cell
     }
  }
```

***Listing 10-7:** Defining a background configuration for multiple states*

The code in Listing 10-7 defines the content configuration as before, but the background configuration is defined by the closure. The first step is to get a reference to the configuration for the current state. For this purpose, we get a standard configuration with the **`listPlainCell()`** method and then call the **`updated()`** method on it to get the configuration for the state determined by the argument received by the closure. Next, we proceed to define the configuration. The padding around the background view and the round corners are the same for every state, so we always specify the same values, but we want the background color to be different when the cell is selected, so we check if the cell is in the selected state with the **`isSelected`** property and modify this attribute accordingly. Now the cells are gray but become blue when they are selected by the user.

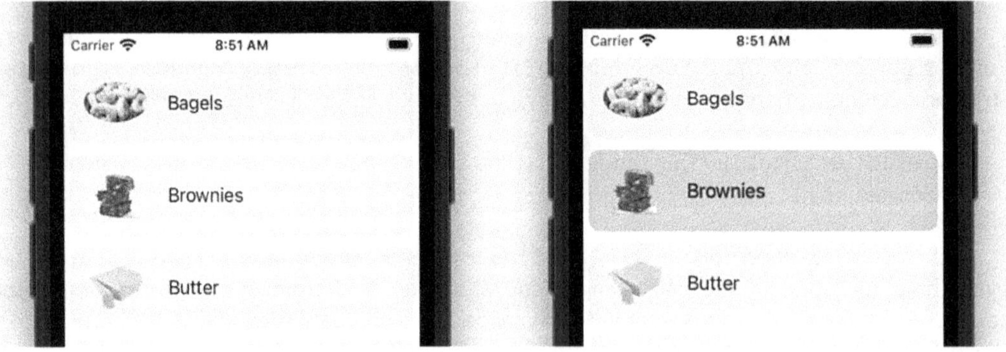

***Figure 10-10:** Different background for each state*

Do It Yourself: Update the **`ViewController`** class introduced in Listing 10-6 with the code in Listing 10-7. Run the application and select a cell. You should see something like Figure 10-10.

Basic Cell Subclass

The **dequeueReusableCell()** method creates a **UITableViewCell** object from the prototype cell. This object generates a standard cell that we must configure to show the values we want. But this code can get long and difficult to maintain. An alternative is to create a **UITableViewCell** subclass and move all the cell configuration from the view controller to this class. To specify the cell's configuration, the **UITableViewCell** class defines the following method.

updateConfiguration(using: State)—This method is called every time the cell needs to update the configuration for a specific state.

The file for the subclass is created as we did before for view controllers, only this time we must select the **UITableViewCell** class as the superclass. As always, there are no requirements for the name, but it is better to give it a name related to the cell (for our example, we call it **FoodCell**). Inside the subclass, we must implement the **updateConfiguration()** method, and also a property to store a copy of the data to be displayed, as shown in the following example.

```
import UIKit

class FoodCell: UITableViewCell {
   var item: ItemsData!

   override func updateConfiguration(using state:
UICellConfigurationState) {
      var config = self.defaultContentConfiguration()
      config.text = item.name
      self.contentConfiguration = config
   }
}
```

Listing 10-8: *Configuring the cells from a* UITableViewCell *subclass*

The code in Listing 10-8 defines a subclass of **UITableViewCell** called **FoodCell**. The class includes a property called **item** to store a value of type **ItemsData**, and overrides the **updateConfiguration()** method to define the cell's configuration. In this case, we define a simple configuration with just the item's name, but this method can also include a background configuration and all the values we need.

Now that the configuration of the cell is defined in the cell's subclass, all the diffable data source needs to do is to create the cell from this class and assign the item to the cell's property.

```
import UIKit

class ViewController: UIViewController {
   @IBOutlet weak var myTable: UITableView!

   override func viewDidLoad() {
      super.viewDidLoad()
      myTable.register(FoodCell.self, forCellReuseIdentifier: "myCell")
      prepareDataSource()
      prepareSnapshot()
   }
   func prepareDataSource() {
      AppData.dataSource = UITableViewDiffableDataSource<Sections,
ItemsData.ID>(tableView: myTable) { tableView, indexPath, itemID in
         let cell = tableView.dequeueReusableCell(withIdentifier:
"myCell", for: indexPath) as! FoodCell
```

```
         if let item = AppData.items.first(where: { $0.id == itemID }) {
            cell.item = item
         }
         return cell
      }
   }
   func prepareSnapshot() {
      var snapshot = NSDiffableDataSourceSnapshot<Sections,
ItemsData.ID>()
      snapshot.appendSections([.main])
      snapshot.appendItems(AppData.items.map({ $0.id }))
      AppData.dataSource.apply(snapshot)
   }
}
```

Listing 10-9: *Creating a cell from a custom subclass*

Because we are now creating the cells from our subclass, we must register the prototype cell with this data type, and cast the value returned by the **dequeueReusableCell()** method to **FoodCell**. Once we have the **FoodCell** object, all we need to do in the diffable data source is to assign the current item to the **item** property, so the cell knows which values to display. All the work has been moved from the diffable data source to the cell, but the result is the same as before.

Do It Yourself: Create a new file with a **UITableViewCell** subclass called **FoodCell**. Complete the class with the code in Listing 10-8. Update the **ViewController** class with the code in Listing 10-9. Run the application. You should see an interface like the one in Figure 10-5.

IMPORTANT: The current template generated by Xcode for subclasses of **UITableViewCell** includes the methods **awakeFromNib()** and **setSelected()**. The **awakeFromNib()** method is like the **viewDidLoad()** method. It is called as soon as the cell is loaded, and it is used to initialize it. The **setSelected()** method, on the other hand, is called when the cell is selected.

Basic Custom Cell

Sometimes the configuration and elements provided by a standard cell may not be enough to satisfy the requirements of our application. There are different options available to customize the cells. One alternative is provided by the **UIListContentConfiguration** structure. In addition to all the properties defined by this structure to assign attributes to the texts and the image, the structure also includes the following to define the padding between the elements and their container.

imageToTextPadding—This property sets or returns a **CGFloat** value that determines the padding between the image and the main text.

textToSecondaryTextHorizontalPadding—This property sets or returns a **CGFloat** value that determines the padding between the text and the secondary text when they are displayed side by side.

textToSecondaryTextVerticalPadding—This property sets or returns a **CGFloat** value that determines the padding between the text and the secondary text when they are displayed on top of each other.

directionalLayoutMargins—This property sets or returns a value that determines the padding between the elements and the container view (also known as Content View). It is a value of type **NSDirectionalEdgeInsets**.

prefersSideBySideTextAndSecondaryText—This property sets or returns a Boolean value that determines if the main and secondary texts are going to be shown side by side.

For example, the following cell is configured with a padding of 50 points on the left, which displaces the content to the right.

```
import UIKit
class FoodCell: UITableViewCell {
   var item: ItemsData!

   override func updateConfiguration(using state:
UICellConfigurationState) {
      var config = self.defaultContentConfiguration()
      config.text = item.name
      config.secondaryText = "\(item.calories) Calories"
      config.image = UIImage(named: item.image)
      config.imageProperties.maximumSize = CGSize(width: 60, height: 60)
      config.directionalLayoutMargins = NSDirectionalEdgeInsets(top: 0,
leading: 50, bottom: 0, trailing: 0)
      self.contentConfiguration = config
   }
}
```

Listing 10-10: *Defining the cell's padding*

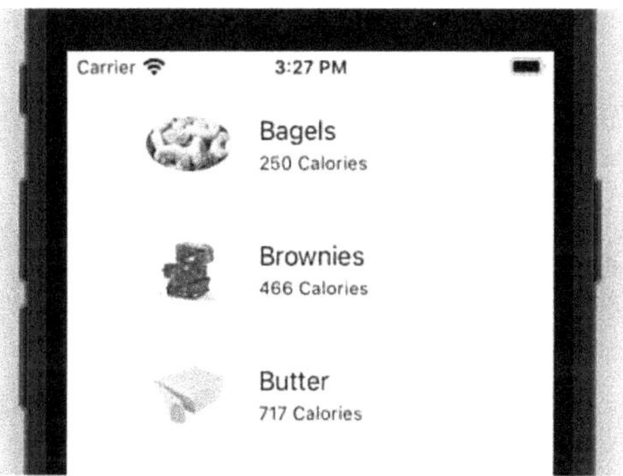

Figure 10-11: *Cell with custom padding*

Table View cells include a view, called *Content View*, where all the cell's content is placed. When working with configuration structures, the object that represents this view is created from a subclass of **UIView** that conforms to the **UIContentView** protocol. Although we can define our own subclasses, as we will see later, UIKit includes a subclass called **UIListContentView** that comes with all the elements necessary to present standard values on the screen. This includes the two labels for the text and secondary text, and the Image View for the image. This view is automatically pinned to the sides of the cell, so the text can use all the space available. There are different ways to add custom elements along with those included by a List Content View. An alternative is to create our own **UIListContentView** object and define the constraints to make room for additional views. For instance, below is a cell with a List Content View on the left and a custom button on the right.

Figure 10-12: *Cell with custom views*

The List Content View is pinned to the top, leading, and bottom of the cell's Content View with Space constraints, and our custom button is occupying the space on the right with Space constraints to the List Content View and the cell's Content View. Now the area available for the text, secondary text, and image is not the entire cell but the space left by the button.

To produce this layout, we must work with a few new elements. First, we need to access the cell's Content View. The **UITableViewCell** class includes the following property for this purpose.

contentView—This property returns a reference to the cell's Content View. It is a value of type **UIView**.

Instead of working with the **UIListContentView** object created by the configuration structure, we must create our own. The **UIListContentView** class includes the following initializer.

UIListContentView(configuration: UIListContentConfiguration**)**—This initializer creates a List Content View with the configuration defined by the argument.

The configuration of the cell doesn't change, but now the configuration structure is provided by our custom **UIListContentView** object. The following example shows the process we follow to create the cell of Figure 10-12.

```
import UIKit

class FoodCell: UITableViewCell {
   private var customView: UIListContentView!
   private var customButton: UIButton!
   var item: ItemsData!

   override func updateConfiguration(using state:
UICellConfigurationState) {
      createViews()

      if let configuration = self.customView.configuration as?
UIListContentConfiguration {
         var config = configuration.updated(for: state)
         config.text = item.name
         config.secondaryText = "Calories: \(item.calories)"
         config.image = UIImage(named: item.image)
         config.imageProperties.maximumSize = CGSize(width: 60, height:
60)
         self.customView.configuration = config
      }
   }
}
```

Listing 10-11: *Configuring a cell with a custom List Content View*

Two properties were added to the **FoodCell** class to store our List Content View and the button, but the configuration is defined inside the **updateConfiguration()** method, as before. The **UIListContentView** class includes the **configuration** property to set and return the configuration structure assigned to the view. The property returns a value of type **UIContentConfiguration** that we must cast to the data type of the configuration structure we used to create the view (in this case, **UIListContentConfiguration**). If the casting is successful, we get a copy for the current state, then assign the item's values to the configuration properties, and finally assign the configuration back to the view.

Every time the cell calls the **updateConfiguration()** method to get the configuration for the cell, we call our **createViews()** method to create the views. This method must create the List Content View and the **UIButton** to delete the cell, along with all the constraints necessary to achieve the layout in Figure 10-12.

```
func createViews() {
   guard contentView.viewWithTag(999) == nil else { return }

   customView = UIListContentView(configuration: .subtitleCell())
   customView.translatesAutoresizingMaskIntoConstraints = false
   self.contentView.addSubview(customView)

   customView.topAnchor.constraint(equalTo: self.contentView.topAnchor,
constant: 8).isActive = true
   customView.leadingAnchor.constraint(equalTo:
self.contentView.leadingAnchor, constant: 16).isActive = true
   customView.bottomAnchor.constraint(equalTo:
self.contentView.bottomAnchor, constant: -8).isActive = true

   customButton = UIButton(configuration: .plain(), primaryAction:
UIAction(image: UIImage(systemName: "trash"), handler: { [unowned self]
action in
      self.eraseItem()
   }))
   customButton.translatesAutoresizingMaskIntoConstraints = false
   customButton.tag = 999
   self.contentView.addSubview(customButton)

   customButton.leadingAnchor.constraint(equalTo:
customView.trailingAnchor, constant: 8).isActive = true
   customButton.trailingAnchor.constraint(equalTo:
self.contentView.trailingAnchor, constant: -16).isActive = true
   customButton.centerYAnchor.constraint(equalTo:
customView.centerYAnchor).isActive = true
   customButton.widthAnchor.constraint(equalToConstant: 30).isActive =
true
   customButton.heightAnchor.constraint(equalToConstant: 30).isActive =
true
}
```

***Listing 10-12:** Defining the views for a custom cell*

The **createViews()** method is called every time the state of the cell changes, so we need to make sure that the views are created only once. For this purpose, we assign the number 999 to the button's **tag** property and check whether a view with that tag already exists inside the cell's Content View. If no view is found, we proceed to create them.

The views and the constraints are created as before. We create the object, set the **translatesAutoresizingMaskIntoConstraints** property to false to stop the system from defining the constraints for us, add the view to the container (in this case the cell's Content View), and then assign the constraints.

The action for the button executes a method called **eraseItem()** which purpose is to erase the item and update the snapshot to show the change on the screen, as shown below.

```
func eraseItem() {
   AppData.items.removeAll(where: { $0.id == item.id })

   var currentSnapshot = AppData.dataSource.snapshot()
   currentSnapshot.deleteItems([item.id])
   AppData.dataSource.apply(currentSnapshot)
}
```

***Listing 10-13:** Deleting a custom cell*

With these changes, the cell now contains a List Content View with a standard configuration to present an image, a text, and a secondary text, along with a button on the right-hand side to delete the item. When the button is pressed, the item is deleted from the model and the cell is removed.

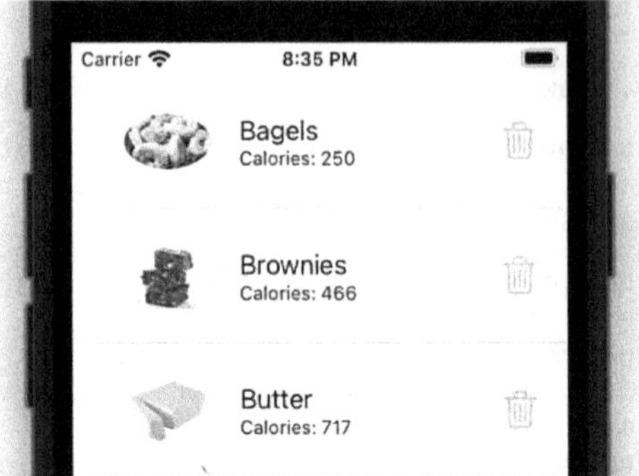

Figure 10-13: *Cells with custom views*

Do It Yourself: Update the **FoodCell** class with the code in Listing 10-11. Add to the class the methods in Listings 13-12 and 13-13. Run the application and press the trashcan button to erase a cell.

Custom views added to a standard cell are not part of the cell's configuration and therefore they are not optimized by the system. If we want our custom views to be part of the cell's configuration, or to define a configuration with custom elements, we must provide our own configuration structure and **UIView** subclass. To define the configuration, UIKit includes the **UIContentConfiguration** protocol, which requires the implementation of the following methods.

makeContentView()—This method is called by the cell when it needs a Content View. The method must return a **UIView** object that conforms to the **UIContentView** protocol.

updated(for: State)—This method is called by the cell to get the configuration structure for a state. The method must return the configuration structure we want to implement for the state specified by the **for** argument.

The definition of the configuration structure is simple. We must include properties to store the values that the cell is going to display and implement the two required methods.

```
struct CustomConfig: UIContentConfiguration {
   var name: String!
   var picture: UIImage!

   func makeContentView() -> UIView & UIContentView {
      let content = CustomContentView(configuration: self)
      return content
   }
   func updated(for state: UIConfigurationState) -> CustomConfig {
      return self
   }
}
```

Listing 10-14: *Defining a custom configuration structure*

In this example, the cell is going to show the item's name and image, so we include two properties called **name** and **picture** to store those values. The **makeContentView()** method creates and returns our custom Content View (called **CustomContentView** in this example), and because the configuration in this case is going to be the same for every state, the **updated()** method just returns the instance of the structure.

For the Content View, we need a subclass of **UIView** that conforms to the **UIContentView** protocol, which only requirement is a property called **configuration** to store a reference to our configuration structure. Along with this property, we must also create the elements the cell needs to display the values on the screen. For instance, the class in the following example creates a label and an Image View to show the item's name and image, and adds them to the view with the necessary constraints to place the name on the left and the image on the right.

```
class CustomContentView: UIView, UIContentView {
   let picture = UIImageView(frame: .zero)
   let name = UILabel(frame: .zero)

   var configuration: UIContentConfiguration {
      didSet {
         newConfiguration()
      }
   }
   init(configuration: UIContentConfiguration) {
      self.configuration = configuration
      super.init(frame: .zero)

      picture.translatesAutoresizingMaskIntoConstraints = false
      picture.contentMode = .scaleAspectFit
      self.addSubview(picture)

      let cp1 = picture.widthAnchor.constraint(equalToConstant: 100)
      let cp2 = picture.heightAnchor.constraint(equalToConstant: 100)
      let cp3 = picture.trailingAnchor.constraint(equalTo:
self.trailingAnchor, constant: -16)
      let cp4 = picture.topAnchor.constraint(equalTo: self.topAnchor,
constant: 10)
      let cp5 = picture.bottomAnchor.constraint(equalTo:
self.bottomAnchor, constant: -10)
      cp5.priority = .defaultLow
      self.addConstraints([cp1, cp2, cp3, cp4, cp5])

      name.translatesAutoresizingMaskIntoConstraints = false
      name.numberOfLines = 1
      name.font = UIFont.preferredFont(forTextStyle: .title1)
      self.addSubview(name)

      let cn1 = name.leadingAnchor.constraint(equalTo:
self.leadingAnchor, constant: 16)
      let cn2 = name.trailingAnchor.constraint(equalTo:
picture.leadingAnchor, constant: 0)
      let cn3 = name.centerYAnchor.constraint(equalTo:
picture.centerYAnchor)
      self.addConstraints([cn1, cn2, cn3])

      newConfiguration()
   }
   func newConfiguration() {
      if let config = self.configuration as? CustomConfig {
         name.text = config.name
         picture.image = config.picture
      }
   }
   required init?(coder: NSCoder) {
      fatalError("Error")
   }
}
```

Listing 10-15: *Defining a custom Content View*

The **CustomContentView** class defined in Listing 10-15 is initialized from the **makeContentView()** method in the configuration structure. When this method is executed, it sends the configuration structure to the **CustomContentView** initializer. In this initializer, we assign that value to the **configuration** property and proceed to create the views. We create the **UIImageView** object first, add it to the Content View, and define the constraints to place it on the right side of the cell. Then we do the same for the **UILabel** object, which is pinned to the left and centered with the image.

The values of these elements change after they are created and each time a new configuration is assigned to the view. To apply these changes, we included a method called **newConfiguration()** and call it whenever necessary. The method gets the configuration structure by casting the value of the **configuration** property to our custom data type (**CustomConfig**) and updates the elements with the current values.

IMPORTANT: Notice that the class in Listing 10-15 includes an additional initializer prefixed by the **required** keyword. The **UIView** class conforms to the **NSCoding** protocol, which requires this initializer to be able to encode and decode the view for archiving. We will learn more about archiving in Chapter 15.

With the configuration structure and the Content View ready, we can finally configure the cell. The process is the same as before, but instead of using a standard configuration, we implement our **CustomConfig** structure.

```
import UIKit

class FoodCell: UITableViewCell {
   var item: ItemsData!

   override func updateConfiguration(using state:
UICellConfigurationState) {
      var config = CustomConfig().updated(for: state)
      config.name = item.name
      config.picture = UIImage(named: item.image)
      self.contentConfiguration = config
   }
}
```

Listing 10-16: *Implementing a custom configuration*

When the **CustomConfig** structure is assigned to the cell's **contentConfiguration** property, the cell calls the **makeContentView()** method, this method returns the **CustomContentView** object, the view created by this object is assigned as the cell's Content View, and the values are shown on the screen.

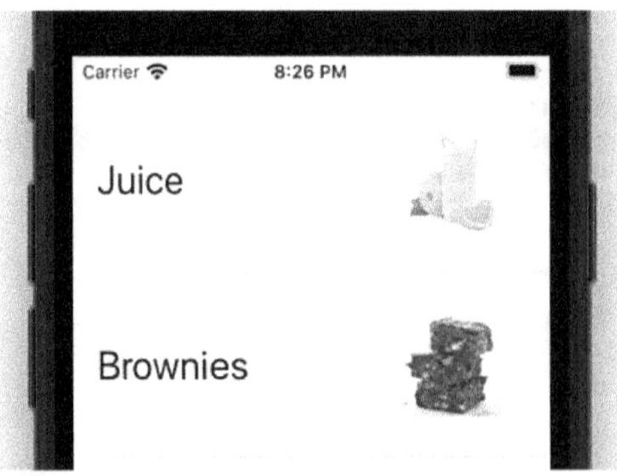

Figure 10-14: *Table with custom cells*

Do It Yourself: Add the `CustomConfig` structure introduced in Listing 10-14 to the FoodCell.swift file (below the `FoodCell` class). Do the same for the `CustomContentView` class of Listing 10-15. Update the `FoodCell` class with the code in Listing 10-16. Run the application. You should see the table of Figure 10-14.

Basic Table View Delegates

Traditionally, the content and configuration of a Table View was provided by delegate methods. These methods were defined by two protocols: `UITableViewDelegate` and `UITableViewDataSource`. Because now the data and the configuration are provided by diffable data sources and snapshots, some of the methods defined by these protocols have become obsolete, but a few remain useful. The following are some of the methods defined in the `UITableViewDelegate` protocol we still need to implement in our applications.

tableView(UITableView, **didSelectRowAt:** IndexPath**)**—This method is called by the table after the user selects a cell. The **didSelectRowAt** argument indicates the cell's location.

tableView(UITableView, **didDeselectRowAt:** IndexPath**)**—This method is called by the table when a cell is deselected. The **didDeselectRowAt** argument indicates the cell's location.

tableView(UITableView, **heightForHeaderInSection:** Int**)**—This method is called by the table to get the height of the header for the section at the index indicated by the **heightForHeaderInSection** argument. The method must return a `CGFloat` value with the header's height.

tableView(UITableView, **heightForFooterInSection:** Int**)**—This method is called by the table to get the height of the footer for the section at the index indicated by the **heightForFooterInSection** argument. The method must return a `CGFloat` value with the footer's height.

tableView(UITableView, **leadingSwipeActionsConfigurationForRowAt:** IndexPath**)**—This method is called by the table to get the actions to display on the left side of each row when they are in edition mode. It must return a `UISwipeActionsConfiguration` object containing the `UIContextualAction` objects that define the actions.

tableView(UITableView, **trailingSwipeActionsConfigurationForRowAt:** IndexPath**)**—This method is called by the table to get the actions to display on the right side of each row when they are in edition mode. It must return a `UISwipeActionsConfiguration` object containing the `UIContextualAction` objects that define each action.

Although the data is provided by a diffable data source, the table still relies on methods defined by the `UITableViewDataSource` protocol for advanced configuration. The following are the most frequently used.

tableView(UITableView, **titleForHeaderInSection:** Int**)**—This method is called by the table to get the title for the header of the section indicated by the **titleForHeaderInSection** argument. The method must return a `String` value with the header's title.

tableView(UITableView, **titleForFooterInSection:** Int**)**—This method is called by the table to get the title for the footer of the section indicated by the **titleForFooter-InSection** argument. The method must return a `String` value with the footer's title.

tableView(UITableView, **canEditRowAt:** IndexPath**)**—This method is called by the table to know if the user is allowed to edit a row. The method must return a Boolean value to indicate if the row at the path determined by the **canEditRowAt** argument can be edited.

tableView(UITableView, **commit:** EditingStyle, **forRowAt:** IndexPath**)**—This method is called by the table when the user inserts or deletes a row. It is implemented along with the edition tools provided by Table Views. The **commit** argument is an enumeration called **EditingStyle** included in the **UITableViewCell** class that indicates the type of operation performed. The possible values are **delete** and **insert**.

sectionIndexTitles(for: UITableView**)**—This method is called by the table to get the strings that represent the sections in the table's index. The method must return an array of strings with the values for the indexes.

tableView(UITableView, **sectionForSectionIndexTitle:** String, **at:** Int**)**—This method is called by the table to get the section corresponding to an index title. The method must return an integer value with the section's index. The **sectionForSection-IndexTitle** argument is a string with the index's title, and the **at** argument is the position where the title is located on the index.

tableView(UITableView, **moveRowAt:** IndexPath, **to:** IndexPath**)**—This method is called when the user moves a cell to a different position on the table. It is implemented along with the edition tools provided by Table Views. The **moveRowAt** argument is the index path in which the cell is currently located and the **to** argument is the index path where the cell is going to be placed.

tableView(UITableView, **canMoveRowAt:** IndexPath**)**—This method is called when the user tries to move a cell to a different position. The method must return a Boolean value to indicate if the action is allowed. The **canMoveRowAt** argument indicates the cell's location.

The methods defined by the **UITableViewDelegate** protocol are easy to implement. All we need to do is to define an object that conforms to the protocol (usually the view controller) and assign it as the table's delegate, so all the protocol methods are called on it, as shown next.

```
import UIKit

class ViewController: UIViewController, UITableViewDelegate {
   @IBOutlet weak var myTable: UITableView!

   override func viewDidLoad() {
      super.viewDidLoad()
      myTable.register(UITableViewCell.self, forCellReuseIdentifier:
"myCell")
      myTable.delegate = self
      prepareDataSource()
      prepareSnapshot()
   }
   func prepareDataSource() {
      AppData.dataSource = UITableViewDiffableDataSource<Sections,
ItemsData.ID>(tableView: myTable) { tableView, indexPath, itemID in
         let cell = tableView.dequeueReusableCell(withIdentifier:
"myCell", for: indexPath)
         if let item = AppData.items.first(where: { $0.id == itemID }) {
            cell.configurationUpdateHandler = { cell, state in
               var config =
cell.defaultContentConfiguration().updated(for: state)
               config.text = item.name
               config.secondaryText = "\(item.calories) Calories"
               config.image = UIImage(named: item.image)
```

```
                config.imageProperties.maximumSize = CGSize(width: 40,
height: 40)
                cell.contentConfiguration = config

                cell.accessoryType = item.selected ? .checkmark : .none
            }
        }
        return cell
    }
  }
  func prepareSnapshot() {
     var snapshot = NSDiffableDataSourceSnapshot<Sections,
ItemsData.ID>()
     snapshot.appendSections([.main])
     snapshot.appendItems(AppData.items.map({ $0.id }))
     AppData.dataSource.apply(snapshot)
  }
  func tableView(_ tableView: UITableView, didSelectRowAt indexPath:
IndexPath) {
     if let itemID = AppData.dataSource.itemIdentifier(for: indexPath) {
        if let item = AppData.items.first(where: { $0.id == itemID }) {
           item.selected.toggle()
        }
     }
     tableView.deselectRow(at: indexPath, animated: true)
  }
}
```

Listing 10-17: *Selecting multiple items*

In this example, we make the view controller conform to the **UITableViewDelegate** protocol and assign it as the Table View's delegate using the **delegate** property provided by the **UITableView** class. Assigning the value **self** to this property, the view controller becomes the table's delegate, and we can proceed to implement the protocol methods we need. In this case, we implement the **tableView(UITableView, didSelectRowAt:)** method to modify the value of the item's **selected** property every time the user selects a cell.

First, we get the item's identifier from the cell's index path with the **itemIdentifier()** method provided by the data source. The **itemIdentifier()** method takes the **IndexPath** value received by the protocol method, which contains the indexes of the section and the row where the selected cell is located, and returns the corresponding identifier for the item in the cell. With the identifier, we get the item from the model, as before, and modify its values. In this example, we toggle the value of the item's **selected** property with the **toggle()** method. If the value was **true**, it becomes **false**, and vice versa, indicating whether the item is selected or not.

Because we are modifying the value of the item's **selected** property every time a cell is selected, we don't need the table to show the selected cell anymore, so we deselect it with the Table View's **deselectRow()** method. To show the user which items are currently selected and which not, we add an accessory view to the cell. The **UITableViewCell** class includes the **accessoryType** property to define the type of accessory we want to show. When we want to display the accessory, we must assign one of the values available or the value **none** to hide it. In our example, we use the **checkmark** type. If the value of the **selected** property is **true**, we assign this value to the **accessoryType** property and a checkmark is shown on the screen for that item, otherwise, the value assigned to the property is **none** and the accessory is hidden. The result is shown below.

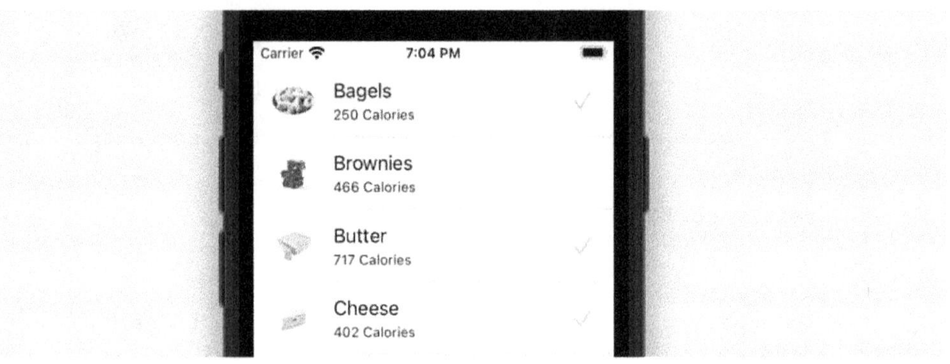

Figure 10-15: Selected cells highlighted with Checkmark accessories

Do It Yourself: Update the **`ViewController`** class with the code in Listing 10-17. In this example, we are using a standard cell, so the custom cell defined in the previous section is no longer required. Run the application and select multiple cells. You should see the checkmarks indicating the selected cells.

Basic 10.2 Table Views in Navigation Controllers

Tables in iOS are meant to work along with other scenes to provide more functionality. The addition of rows, for example, requires a separate scene to provide the fields and buttons the user needs to insert the information. This is the reason why we frequently see applications with tables embedded in Navigation Controllers. Navigation Controllers present scenes with a transition that feels more natural to the user and helps establish the relationship between the table and the rest of the scenes. Figure 10-16 shows what a scene with a table looks like after it is embedded in a Navigation Controller.

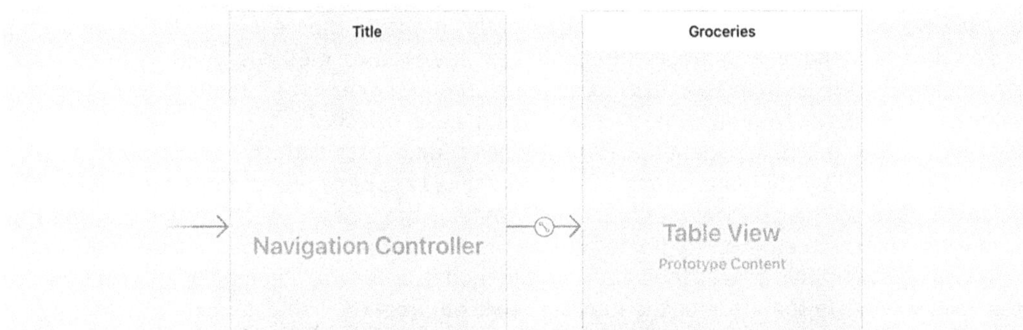

Figure 10-16: Table View embedded in a Navigation Controller

A common function provided by tables is the possibility to select a row to see more information related to the item. For instance, considering the previous examples, we may add a scene that presents the nutritional values associated with an item every time the user taps on a cell.

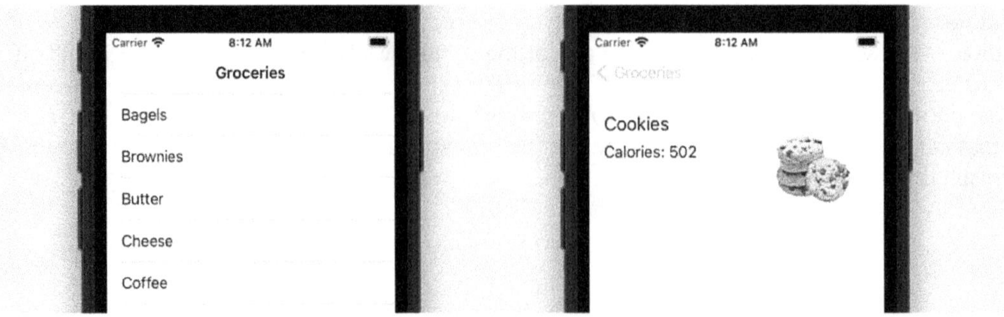

Figure 10-17: Table with a Detail View

The scene that presents the additional information is called *Detail View*, because it shows details about the selected item. To create a Detail View, we must add a new scene to the Storyboard and connect a Show segue from the table's view controller to the new scene (Figure 9-17). For our example, we have populated the Detail View with a label, an Image View, and a Text View to display the values (Figure 10-18, right).

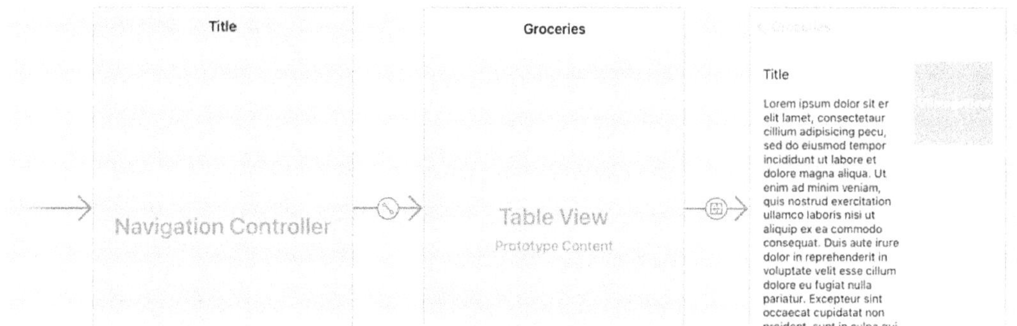

Figure 10-18: *Detail View in the Storyboard*

A Table View inside a Navigation Controller works the same way as before. To access the detail view when a cell is selected, we must implement the **`tableView(UITableView, didSelectRowAt:)`** method (see Listing 10-17), trigger the segue with the **`performSegue()`** method (see Listing 9-6), and send the data to the Detail View with the **`prepare()`** method (see Listing 9-4).

```
import UIKit

class ViewController: UIViewController, UITableViewDelegate {
   @IBOutlet weak var myTable: UITableView!
   var selected: ItemsData!

   override func viewDidLoad() {
      super.viewDidLoad()
      myTable.register(UITableViewCell.self, forCellReuseIdentifier:
"myCell")
      myTable.delegate = self
      prepareDataSource()
      prepareSnapshot()
   }
   func tableView(_ tableView: UITableView, didSelectRowAt indexPath:
IndexPath) {
      if let itemID = AppData.dataSource.itemIdentifier(for: indexPath) {
         if let item = AppData.items.first(where: { $0.id == itemID }) {
            selected = item
         }
      }
      performSegue(withIdentifier: "showDetails", sender: self)
   }
   override func prepare(for segue: UIStoryboardSegue, sender: Any?) {
      if segue.identifier == "showDetails" {
         let controller = segue.destination as! DetailViewController
         controller.selected = selected
      }
   }
   func prepareDataSource() {
      AppData.dataSource = UITableViewDiffableDataSource<Sections,
ItemsData.ID>(tableView: myTable) { tableView, indexPath, itemID in
         let cell = tableView.dequeueReusableCell(withIdentifier:
"myCell", for: indexPath)
```

```
            if let item = AppData.items.first(where: { $0.id == itemID }) {
               var config = cell.defaultContentConfiguration()
               config.text = item.name
               cell.contentConfiguration = config
            }
            return cell
         }
      }
      func prepareSnapshot() {
         var snapshot = NSDiffableDataSourceSnapshot<Sections,
ItemsData.ID>()
         snapshot.appendSections([.main])
         snapshot.appendItems(AppData.items.map({ $0.id }))
         AppData.dataSource.apply(snapshot)
      }
}
```

Listing 10-18: *Opening the Detail View when a cell is selected*

The **tableView(UITableView, didSelectRowAt:)** method in Listing 10-18 gets the selected item with the **itemIdentifier()** method, as we did before, and assigns it to a property called **selected**. After this reference is stored, we can call the **performSegue()** method to open the Detail View (the segue was identified with the name "showDetails").

When a segue is triggered, the system calls the **prepare()** method. In our example, we implement this method to get a reference to the view controller of the Detail View and pass the item stored in the **selected** property to the **selected** property of the destination controller.

Accordingly, the view controller for the Detail View must include the **selected** property along with Outlets for each of the elements on the interface to show the information on the screen. We call this view controller **DetailViewController**.

```
import UIKit

class DetailViewController: UIViewController {
   @IBOutlet weak var titleItem: UILabel!
   @IBOutlet weak var imageItem: UIImageView!
   @IBOutlet weak var nutritionItem: UITextView!
   var selected: ItemsData!

   override func viewWillAppear(_ animated: Bool) {
      super.viewWillAppear(animated)
      if selected != nil {
         titleItem.text = selected.name
         imageItem.image = UIImage(named: selected.image)
         nutritionItem.text = "Calories: \(selected.calories)"
      }
   }
}
```

Listing 10-19: *Showing the details of the selected row*

The **DetailViewController** class checks whether the **selected** property contains an item or not and then assigns the values to the Outlets to display the item on the screen.

Do It Yourself: Embed the initial scene in a Navigation Controller and assign the title Groceries to it. You should see something like Figure 10-16. Add another scene to the Storyboard. Create a Show segue from the scene with the table to the second scene (Figure 9-17) and identify the segue with the string "showDetails". Add a label, an Image View, and a Text View to the second scene to get an interface like the one in Figure 10-18. Create a subclass of **UIViewController** for the second scene called **DetailViewController**.

Create the Outlets for the elements in the scene with the names used in Listing 10-19. Update the **ViewController** class with the code in Listing 10-18 and complete the **DetailViewController** class with the code in Listing 10-19. Run the application and select a row. You should see something like Figure 10-17.

Once selected, the rows remain in that state until the user selects another row. This means that when the user comes back from the Detail View, the selected row is still visible. As we have seen before, to deselect a row we have to call the Table View's **deselectRow()** method (see Listing 10-19). Where we call this method depends on what we want to achieve with our app. The only thing we need to remember is that once the row is deselected, the **indexPathForSelectedRow** property returns **nil** (because no row is selected anymore), so we always must deselect the cell after the value of its row is no longer required. The following example implements the **viewWillAppear()** method to deselect the cells when the user comes back from the Detail View (the **viewDidLoad()** method is only called when the scene is loaded, but the **viewWillAppear()** method is called every time the scene is about to be shown on the screen).

```
override func viewWillAppear(_ animated: Bool) {
   super.viewWillAppear(animated)
   if let path = myTable.indexPathForSelectedRow {
      myTable.deselectRow(at: path, animated: true)
   }
}
```

Listing 10-20: *Deselecting the selected row*

Do It Yourself: Add the method in Listing 10-20 to the view controller of Listing 10-18. Run the application and select a row. Go back to the Table View. The selected row should be deselected.

Basic Adding Rows

Navigation controllers not only provide a natural transition between views but also a bar where we can put buttons to let the user manage the table and the information it contains (see Chapter 9). A very common feature added to the table from this bar is a button that opens a view with a form to add new items to the list. There is even a predefined style for Bar Button Items called *Add* that creates a button with a plus sign. Figure 10-19, below, shows the Add button inserted on the right side of the bar and a new scene with an input field to add items to the model. The new scene is connected to the Add button with a Show segue.

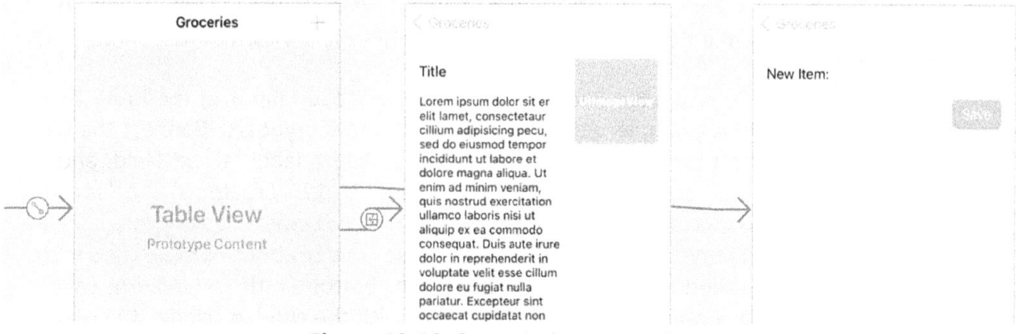

Figure 10-19: *Scene to insert new items*

The addition of new items is very simple, we provide the form for the user to insert the data and then store it in the model (In our case, this is the **items** array in the **AppData** structure). To keep it simple, we have included only a Text Field to let the user insert the name of the item (Figure 10-19, right). The rest of the information is filled with placeholders ("noimage" and "Not Defined"). The following is the code for the view controller of the new scene (we call it **AddItemViewController**).

```
import UIKit

class AddItemViewController: UIViewController {
   @IBOutlet weak var newItem: UITextField!

   @IBAction func saveItem(_ sender: UIButton) {
      var text = newItem.text!
      text = text.trimmingCharacters(in: .whitespaces)
      if text != "" {
         let lower = text.lowercased()
         let final = lower.capitalized

         let itemData = ItemsData(final, "noimage", 0, false)
         AppData.items.append(itemData)

         var snapshot = NSDiffableDataSourceSnapshot<Sections, 
ItemsData.ID>()
         snapshot.appendSections([.main])
         snapshot.appendItems(AppData.items.map({ $0.id }))
         AppData.dataSource.apply(snapshot, animatingDifferences: false)

         navigationController?.popViewController(animated: true)
      }
   }
}
```

***Listing 10-21:** Adding items to the model*

The view controller includes an Outlet for the Text Field called **newItem** and an Action for the button called **saveItem()**. When the button is pressed, the **saveItem()** method trims the text in the Text Field with the **trimmingCharacters()** method (see Listing 5-53), and then compares it with an empty string. If the user's input is not empty, the code capitalizes the string, creates the **ItemsData** structure to store the information for the new item, and adds it to the **items** array with the **append()** method.

This process modifies the model, but we still need to update the snapshot to provide the new information to the data source and update the table. In this case, we must consider that the model sorts the data in alphabetical order and therefore we can't just append the new item to the current snapshot. Items appended to an existent snapshot are added at the end of the list, but the position for the new item may be different, depending on the name inserted by the user. In consequence, we must create a new **NSDiffableDataSourceSnapshot** object and provide all the values again as we did in the **prepareSnapshot()** method before.

Do It Yourself: Add a Bar Button Item to the Navigation Bar over the Table View of our previous example. Add a new scene to the Storyboard. Connect the bar button to the new scene with a Show segue. Add a label, a Text Field, and a button to the scene, as shown in Figure 10-19. Create a subclass of **UIViewController** called **AddItemViewController** and assign it to the new scene. Connect the Text Field to the **AddItemViewController** class with an Outlet called **newItem** and the Save button with an Action called **saveItem()**. Complete this view controller with the code in Listing 10-21. Run the application, press the plus button, insert a text, and press the Save button. The new item should be added to the table.

Basic Deleting Rows

The same way we can add items we can also delete them. The process is as simple as deleting the item from the model and updating the snapshot, but there are several ways to allow the user to do it. An alternative is to include a button in the Detail View that the user can press to delete the item. In that scene, we know what item was selected by the user because we have a reference in the **selected** property, and the user also knows what item is going to be deleted because the item's information is on the screen. Figure 10-20 shows the Detail View of our example modified to include a Delete button below the thumbnail.

Title
Lorem ipsum dolor sit er
elit lamet, consectetaur
cillium adipisicing pecu,
sed do eiusmod tempor
incididunt ut labore et
dolore magna aliqua. Ut
enim ad minim veniam,
quis nostrud exercitation

Figure 10-20: *Delete button*

The Delete button must be connected to an Action in the **DetailViewController** class to delete the item from the model and close the scene. To delete the item from the **items** array, we can use the value of the **id** property and the **removeAll(where:)** method provided by the **Array** structure, as in the following example.

```
@IBAction func deleteItem(_ sender: UIButton) {
   if selected != nil {
      AppData.items.removeAll(where: { $0.id == selected.id })

      var currentSnapshot = AppData.dataSource.snapshot()
      currentSnapshot.deleteItems([selected.id])
      AppData.dataSource.apply(currentSnapshot)

      navigationController?.popViewController(animated: true)
   }
}
```

Listing 10-22: *Removing the selected item*

The **removeAll(where:)** method implemented in the code in Listing 10-22 reads the value of the **id** property of each item in the array and removes the item which value matches the value of the **id** property of the selected item. After the item is removed from the model, we also remove it from the current snapshot with the **deleteItems()** method, and the scene is closed.

Do It Yourself: Add a button called Delete to the Detail View of the previous example (Figure 10-20). Connect the button to an Action in the **DetailViewController** class called **deleteItem()**. Complete the method with the code in Listing 10-22. Run the application. Select a row and press the Delete button. The item should be removed from the table.

IMPORTANT: The user should be warned every time the code is going to delete data from the model. UIKit offers the **UIAlertController** class to create views for this purpose. We will study how to create Alert Views in Chapter 13.

In addition to any custom techniques, Table Views also provide built-in functionality to allow the user to remove items from the table. The table includes an editing mode that when activated shows a button on the left to delete the item and a button on the right to confirm the action.

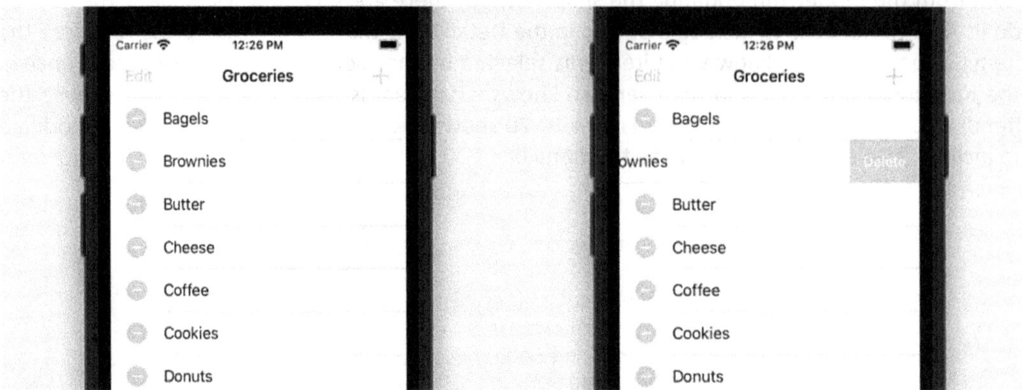

Figure 10-21: *Table in editing mode*

The process to activate and deactivate this mode involves the **isEditing** property, the **setEditing()** method (both from the **UITableView** class), and two methods defined in the **UITableViewDataSource** protocol: the **tableView(UITableView, canEditRowAt:)** method to tell the table whether a row can be edited or not, and the **tableView(UITable-View, commit:, forRowAt:)** method to process the deletion.

The first step is to provide a way for the user to decide when to activate or deactivate the mode. For our example, we have added a Bar Button Item to the Navigation Bar called Edit.

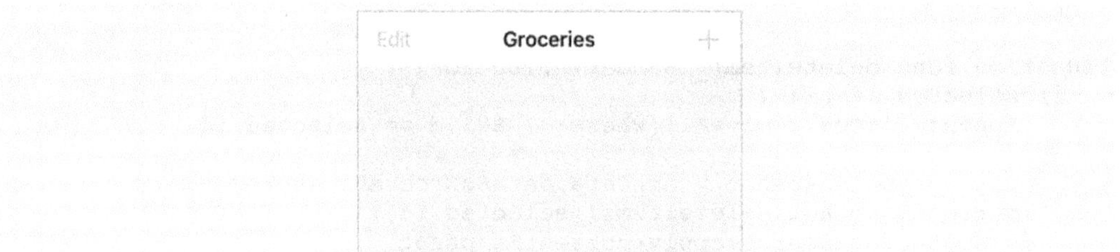

Figure 10-22: *Edit button*

The purpose of the Edit button is to activate or deactivate the edition mode depending on its current state. To determine the state, we can read the **isEditing** property, and to set the new state we must call the **setEditing()** method, as in the following example.

```
@IBAction func editItems(_ sender: UIBarButtonItem) {
   if myTable.isEditing {
      myTable.setEditing(false, animated: true)
   } else {
      myTable.setEditing(true, animated: true)
   }
}
```

Listing 10-23: *Activating and deactivating the editing mode*

The **editItems()** method in Listing 10-23 checks the value of the **isEditing** property and sets the mode to **false** if the property is **true**, or to **true** if the property is **false**. When the value is set to **true**, the Table View calls the **tableView(UITableView, canEditRowAt:)** method on the data source delegate and allows the user to edit the rows or not, based on the value returned by the method (**true** or **false**).

Data source delegate methods are implemented by the diffable data source, so if we want to provide our own implementation, we must define a subclass of the **UITableView-DiffableDataSource** class. For this example, we have created a Swift file called MyDataSource.swift to store our subclass called **MyDataSource**.

```
import UIKit

class MyDataSource: UITableViewDiffableDataSource<Sections, ItemsData.ID>
{
   override func tableView(_ tableView: UITableView, canEditRowAt
indexPath: IndexPath) -> Bool {
      return true
   }
   override func tableView(_ tableView: UITableView, commit editingStyle:
UITableViewCell.EditingStyle, forRowAt indexPath: IndexPath) {
      if editingStyle == UITableViewCell.EditingStyle.delete {
         if let itemID = self.itemIdentifier(for: indexPath) {
            AppData.items.removeAll(where: { $0.id == itemID })

            var currentSnapshot = self.snapshot()
            currentSnapshot.deleteItems([itemID])
            self.apply(currentSnapshot)
         }
      }
   }
}
```

Listing 10-24: *Implementing the data source delegate methods*

The **MyDataSource** subclass in Listing 10-24 implements the two methods we need to manage the editing mode. First, we override the **tableView(UITableView, canEditRowAt:)** method and return the value **true**. This tells the table that all the rows are editable. Next, we override the **tableView(UITableView, commit:, forRowAt:)** method. This method is called when the user presses the Delete button on the table (see Figure 10-21, right). The method receives an **EditingStyle** value with a value that corresponds to the action performed by the user. If the value is **delete**, which means the user wants to delete the row, we delete the item from the model and the snapshot following the same procedure used before in the **DetailViewController** class (see Listing 10-22). Notice that this time we reference the data source with **self** because we are inside a **UITableViewDiffableDataSource** subclass.

To implement this subclass in our code, we must define the **dataSource** property in our model with the **MyDataSource** data type and create the diffable data source from this subclass.

```
func prepareDataSource() {
   AppData.dataSource = MyDataSource(tableView: myTable) { tableView,
indexPath, itemID in
      let cell = tableView.dequeueReusableCell(withIdentifier: "myCell",
for: indexPath)
      if let item = AppData.items.first(where: { $0.id == itemID }) {
         var config = cell.defaultContentConfiguration()
         config.text = item.name
         cell.contentConfiguration = config
      }
      return cell
   }
}
```

Listing 10-25: *Implementing our data source subclass*

The **prepareDataSource()** method in Listing 10-25 replaces the same method in our **ViewController** class, but the only difference is that now instead of creating the diffable data source from the **UITableViewDiffableDataSource** class, we do it from our subclass (This example assumes that we have defined the **dataSource** property in our model with the data type **MyDataSource**, as in **var dataSource: MyDataSource!**).

Do It Yourself: Add a Bar Button Item with the title "Edit" to the Navigation Bar at the top of the Table View (Figure 10-22). Connect the button to an Action in the **ViewController** class called **editItems()** and complete the method with the code in Listing 10-23. Create a new Swift file called MyDataSource.swift for the code in Listing 10-24. Open the ApplicationData.swift file and change the data type of the **dataSource** property to **MyDataSource** (**var dataSource: MyDataSource!**). Replace the **prepareDataSource()** method in the **ViewController** class with the method in Listing 10-25. Run the application and press the Edit button. You should see the edition buttons appear on the table's left-hand side. Press one of these buttons. The row should displace to the left and reveal the Delete button on the right. Press this button to delete the row.

IMPORTANT: Tables include a hidden feature that simplifies the deletion of rows and the execution of custom tasks. If the delegate methods are implemented, as we did in the **MyDataSource** subclass, the feature is activated, which allows the user to uncover the Delete button by swiping the row to the left. If this feature is enough for your application, there is no need to add an Edit button to activate or deactivate the mode, all you need to do is implement the delegate methods.

We can also show our own buttons on the left and right side of the rows implementing the methods **tableView(UITableView, trailingSwipeActionsConfigurationForRowAt:)** and **tableView(UITableView, leadingSwipeActionsConfigurationForRowAt:)** defined by the **UITableViewDelegate** protocol. These methods are called when the user swipes a row to one side or the other and are in charge of defining the buttons displayed by the table and the actions they perform. For this purpose, UIKit includes two classes: the **UISwipeActionsConfiguration** class, to provide the actions and configuration values, and the **UIContextualAction** class to define each button and action. The following are the initializer and property provided by the **UISwipeActionsConfiguration** class.

UISwipeActionsConfiguration(actions: [UIContextualAction]**)**—This initializer returns an object with the actions provided by the argument and the configuration defined by its properties.

performsFirstActionWithFullSwipe—This is a Boolean property that determines if the first action included in the object is going to be executed when the user performs a full swipe.

To define the buttons and actions, we must create an object of the **UIContextualAction** class. The following are its initializer and properties.

UIContextualAction(style: Style, **title:** String?, **handler:** Closure**)**—This initializer returns a **UIContextualAction** object with the definition of a button. The **style** argument defines the style of the button. It is an enumeration called **Style** included in the **UIContextualAction** class. The values available are **normal** (color gray) and **destructive** (color red). The **title** argument is a string with the text to be shown on the button, and the **handler** argument is the closure that is going to be executed when the action is performed. The closure receives three values: a reference to the action, a reference to the button's view, and another closure that takes a Boolean to declare whether the action was successful or not.

title—This property sets or returns a string with the button's title.

backgroundColor—This property sets or returns a **UIColor** object with the button's background color.

image—This property sets or returns a **UIImage** object with the button's image.

If we implement these methods in our view controller instead of the **tableView(UITableView, commit:, forRowAt:)** method in the diffable data source, the Delete button is replaced by our own buttons. For instance, in the following example we create our own Delete button with a blue background and a different title.

```
func tableView(_ tableView: UITableView,
trailingSwipeActionsConfigurationForRowAt indexPath: IndexPath) ->
UISwipeActionsConfiguration? {
   let button = UIContextualAction(style: .normal, title: "Remove",
handler: { (action, view, completion) in
      if let itemID = AppData.dataSource.itemIdentifier(for: indexPath) {
         AppData.items.removeAll(where: { $0.id == itemID })

         var currentSnapshot = AppData.dataSource.snapshot()
         currentSnapshot.deleteItems([itemID])
         AppData.dataSource.apply(currentSnapshot)
      }
      completion(true)
   })
   button.backgroundColor = UIColor.systemBlue

   let config = UISwipeActionsConfiguration(actions: [button])
   config.performsFirstActionWithFullSwipe = false
   return config
}
```

Listing 10-26: *Creating our own actions*

When the user swipes a row to the left, the table calls the method in Listing 10-26 to know which buttons to display. In this example, we create an action called **button** with the style **normal**, the title "Remove", and a closure that performs the same action as before (it gets the item's identifier, it removes it from the model, and updates the snapshot). Notice that at the end of the closure we call the completion handler received by the third argument with the value **true** to indicate that the action was performed successfully, otherwise the button is not removed. Finally, we create a new **UISwipeActionsConfiguration** object with this action, set its **performsFirstActionWithFullSwipe** property to **false** so the user cannot perform the action with a full swipe, and return it.

This method is defined by the **UITableViewDelegate** protocol, so we must implement it in the **ViewController** class and make the class conform to the protocol, as done before (see Listing 10-18). The method replaces the **tableView(UITableView, commit:, forRowAt:)** method implemented in the **MyDataSource** subclass of Listing 10-24, but we still have to implement the **tableView(UITableView, canEditRowAt:)** method in the data source to tell the table that the user is allowed to edit the rows.

Do It Yourself: Add the method in Listing 10-26 to the **ViewController** class. Remove the **tableView(UITableView, commit:, forRowAt:)** from the **MyDataSource** class. Run the application and swipe a row to the left. You should see a blue button with the title "Remove". Press the button to remove the row.

Basic Moving Rows

The edition mode also allows users to move cells to a different position on the table. This option is presented as an icon on the right side of the cells. To activate it, we must implement two methods defined by the **UITableViewDataSource** protocol: the **tableView(UITableView, moveRowAt:, to:)** method to modify the data when a cell is moved to a different position, and the **tableView(UITableView, canMoveRowAt:)** method to tell the table that the user is allowed to move the row.

The cells are automatically placed in their new position every time the user performs the action, but we also need to make sure that the new order is reflected in the model and the snapshot, so the next time the table loads its content, it shows the cells in the order determined by the user. The following example presents a possible implementation of these delegate methods.

```
import UIKit

class MyDataSource: UITableViewDiffableDataSource<Sections, ItemsData.ID>
{
   override func tableView(_ tableView: UITableView, canEditRowAt
indexPath: IndexPath) -> Bool {
      return true
   }
   override func tableView(_ tableView: UITableView, canMoveRowAt
indexPath: IndexPath) -> Bool {
      return true
   }
   override func tableView(_ tableView: UITableView, moveRowAt
sourceIndexPath: IndexPath, to destinationIndexPath: IndexPath) {
      guard sourceIndexPath != destinationIndexPath else { return }

      let item = AppData.items[sourceIndexPath.row]
      AppData.items.remove(at: sourceIndexPath.row)
      AppData.items.insert(item, at: destinationIndexPath.row)

      if let itemOrigin = self.itemIdentifier(for: sourceIndexPath), let
itemDestination = self.itemIdentifier(for: destinationIndexPath) {
         var currentSnapshot = self.snapshot()
         if sourceIndexPath.row > destinationIndexPath.row {
            currentSnapshot.moveItem(itemOrigin, beforeItem:
itemDestination)
         } else {
            currentSnapshot.moveItem(itemOrigin, afterItem:
itemDestination)
         }
         self.apply(currentSnapshot, animatingDifferences: false)
      }
   }
}
```

Listing 10-27: *Reorganizing the model when a cell is moved*

In the subclass of Listing 10-27, we return **true** from the **tableView(UITableView, canEditRowAt:)** method to allow the user to edit the table, and from the **tableView(UITableView, canMoveRowAt:)** method to allow the user to move the rows. Then, we implement the **tableView(UITableView, moveRowAt:, to:)** method to sort the items in the model and the snapshot. This method receives two values indicating the original position of the cell and the position where the user is trying to move it. First, we check that these values are not equal. If they are equal, which means the cell was moved to the same position, we return nothing and finish the process, otherwise, we proceed to modify the model. We get a reference to the item being moved, remove it from the array with the **`remove(at:)`** method, and then add it again in the new position with the **`insert(at:)`** method. After that, we get the identifiers of the items in both positions and modify the snapshot. To move the item to the new position, we must call different methods depending on the order. If the new position is below the current position, we move the item with the **`moveItem(beforeItem:)`** method. Otherwise, we must use the **`moveItem(afterItem:)`** method. The snapshot is finally applied with no animation. This is to avoid conflicts with the table's natural animation.

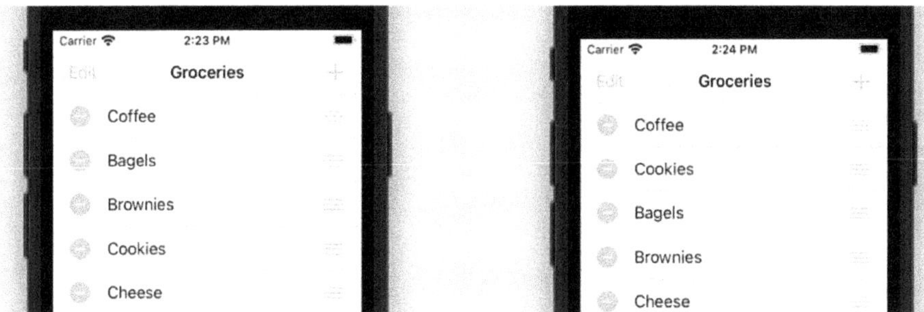

***Figure 10-23:** Editing mode to move cells*

To move a cell, the user must drag the cell from the icon to the new position. In the example of Figure 10-23, we moved the Cookies cell to the second row. When the change is performed, the Table View calls the delegate methods of Listing 10-27 and the item corresponding to the cell is moved to an index that reflects its new position on the table.

Do It Yourself: Update the **`MyDataSource`** class with the code in Listing 10-27. Run the application and press the Edit button. You should see the icons to move the cells. Drag a cell to a new position from one of these icons. The table should reorder the cells, as shown in Figure 10-23.

IMPORTANT: The model we have been using so far automatically organizes the items in alphabetical order (see Listing 10-1). If we want the user to decide the order of the items, we must use a model that allows it. To test the example of Listing 10-27, you must delete the **`didSet()`** method of the **`items`** property in the **`ApplicationData`** structure (**`var items: [ItemsData] = []`**). This makes sure that the model delivers the items in the order they are stored.

Basic Modifying Rows

To allow users to modify the items, we must provide a form where they can insert the new values. For our example, we have added a button called Edit Item to the Detail View (Figure 10-24, number 1) and a scene connected to this button with a Show segue. The scene presents the same interface used before to add items (Figure 10-24, number 2).

***Figure 10-24:** Button and interface to modify items*

The view controller for the new scene must receive a reference to the item to be modified, show the current value in the Text Field for reference, and then assign the new value inserted by the user to the **name** property of the **ItemsData** structure when the Save button is pressed. We called this view controller **EditItemViewController**.

```
import UIKit

class EditItemViewController: UIViewController {
   @IBOutlet weak var newName: UITextField!
   var selected: ItemsData!

   override func viewDidLoad() {
      super.viewDidLoad()
      if selected != nil {
         newName.text = selected.name
         newName.becomeFirstResponder()
      }
   }
   @IBAction func saveItem(_ sender: UIButton) {
      var text = newName.text!
      text = text.trimmingCharacters(in: .whitespaces)
      if text != "" {
         let lower = text.lowercased()
         let final = lower.capitalized
         selected.name = final

         var currentSnapshot = AppData.dataSource.snapshot()
         currentSnapshot.reloadItems([selected.id])
         AppData.dataSource.apply(currentSnapshot)

         navigationController?.popViewController(animated: true)
      }
   }
}
```

Listing 10-28: *Modifying an item*

In this view controller, we define the **selected** property again to receive the item from the Detail View. Then, in the **viewDidLoad()** method, we assign the item's name to the Text Field and make it the first responder with the **becomeFirstResponder()** method. This automatically activates the keyboard and shows the cursor on the Text Field for the user to start typing.

When the Save button is pressed, the **saveItem()** method trims the text, capitalizes it, and assigns it to the **name** property of the selected item. Finally, the snapshot is updated with the **reloadItems()** method and the view is closed.

To tell the view controller which item to edit, we must send it from the Detail View with the **prepare()** method, as shown next.

```
override func prepare(for segue: UIStoryboardSegue, sender: Any?) {
   if segue.identifier == "showEditItem" {
      let controller = segue.destination as! EditItemViewController
      controller.selected = selected
   }
}
```

Listing 10-29: *Sending the selected item*

Do It Yourself: Add a Bar Button Item to the Detail View with the title "Edit Item" (Figure 10-24, number 1). Add a new scene to the Storyboard with a label, a Text Field, and a Save button (Figure 10-24, number 2). Connect the Edit Item button to this new scene with a Show segue called "showEditItem". Create a new subclass of **UIViewController** called **EditItemViewController**

and assign it to the new scene. Connect the Text Field to this view controller with an Outlet called **newName** and the Save button with an Action called **saveItem()**. Complete the view controller with the code in Listing 10-28. Add the **prepare()** method in Listing 10-29 to the **DetailViewController** class. Run the application. Select an item on the table, press the Edit Item button, and change the name. You should see the changes in the Detail View and the table.

Basic 10.3 Table View Controller

Table Views that take up the entire screen are very common in mobile applications. To simplify the creation of these tables, the UIKit framework provides a subclass of the **UIViewController** class called **UITableViewController**, which includes a full-screen table. The class has several advantages over adding the Table View ourselves. It conforms to the Table View protocols by default, the controller is fully integrated with Navigation Controllers, search bars and controls to refresh the data, and it even offers another type of cells called *Static Cells* that allow us to present the cells as they are defined in the Storyboard. The Library includes the Table View Controller option to add this view controller to the interface.

Table View Controller

Figure 10-25: *Table View Controller option in the Library*

A Table View Controller looks like any other scene but with a full-screen table inside. The difference is that the Table View is integrated into the scene and its size cannot be changed.

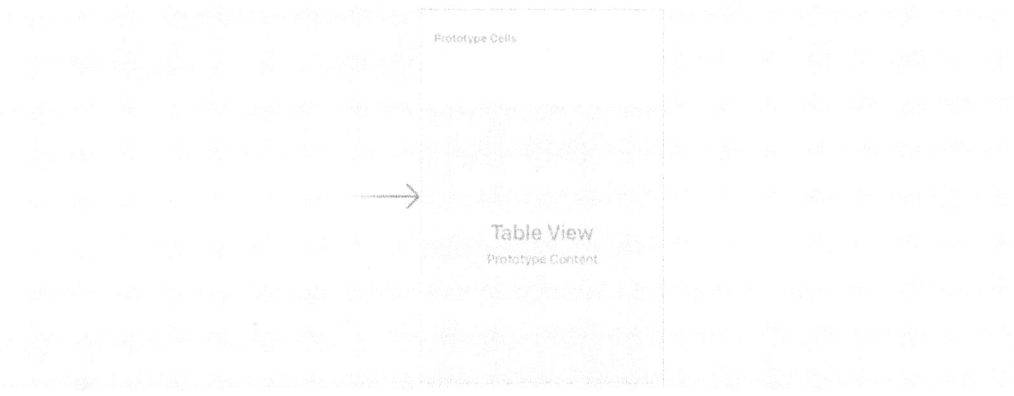

Figure 10-26: *Table View Controller in the Storyboard*

To manage the Table View, we must create a subclass of the **UITableViewController** class and assign it to the scene in the Storyboard. The file is created as any other file but with the **UITableViewController** class as the superclass. Also, the Table View includes a prototype cell. We can use this prototype cell or register the cell as we have done so far in our examples.

```
import UIKit

class MyTableViewController: UITableViewController {
   override func viewDidLoad() {
      super.viewDidLoad()
      tableView.register(UITableViewCell.self, forCellReuseIdentifier:
"myCell")
      prepareDataSource()
      prepareSnapshot()
   }
```

```
   func prepareDataSource() {
      AppData.dataSource = UITableViewDiffableDataSource<Sections,
ItemsData.ID>(tableView: tableView) { tableView, indexPath, itemID in
         let cell = tableView.dequeueReusableCell(withIdentifier:
"myCell", for: indexPath)
         if let item = AppData.items.first(where: { $0.id == itemID }) {
            var config = cell.defaultContentConfiguration()
            config.text = item.name
            cell.contentConfiguration = config
         }
         return cell
      }
   }
   func prepareSnapshot() {
      var snapshot = NSDiffableDataSourceSnapshot<Sections,
ItemsData.ID>()
      snapshot.appendSections([.main])
      snapshot.appendItems(AppData.items.map({ $0.id }))
      AppData.dataSource.apply(snapshot)
   }
}
```

Listing 10-30: *Managing the table from a subclass of* `UITableViewController`

The **`UITableViewController`** class includes a property called **`tableView`** with a reference to the Table View. This saves us from creating the Outlet for the table. The rest of the configuration and code work the same way as before.

Do It Yourself: Create a new project. Delete the initial scene and add a Table View Controller from the Library (Figure 10-25). Select the scene, open the Attributes Inspector panel, and activate the option Is Initial View Controller to designate it as the initial scene. Create a new file with a subclass of **`UITableViewController`** called **`MyTableViewController`** and assign it to the scene. Complete the class with the code in Listing 10-30. This example assumes that you have included into the project the model from Listing 10-1. Run the application. You should see a table with the items in the model listed by name.

IMPORTANT: A Table View Controller automatically deselects a cell when the table is shown on the screen. For this reason, we do not have to deselect the cell anymore, as we did in the example of Listing 10-20. The **`UITableViewController`** class offers a Boolean property called **`clearsSelectionOnViewWillAppear`** to activate or deactivate this feature.

Medium Refresh Control

Table View Controllers include a feature usually provided by modern applications that allow the user to refresh the data by scrolling down the table. When the user keeps scrolling down the table, a spinning wheel appears at the top to indicate that the system is refreshing the data.

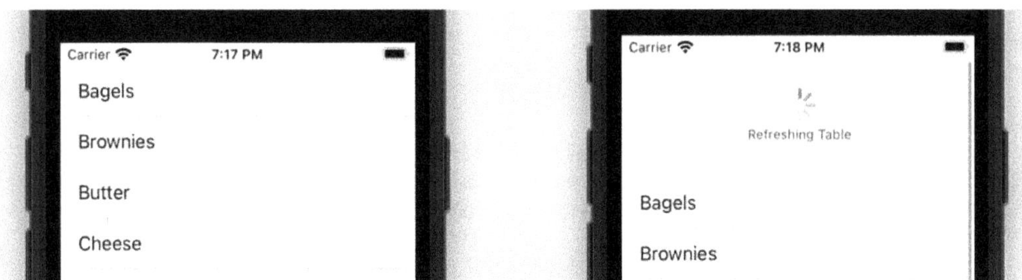

Figure 10-27: *Refresh Control*

The graphics are created by the Table View Controller, but UIKit defines the **`UIRefreshControl`** class to manage the control. The class includes the following properties and methods to configure the control and report the state of the process.

tintColor—This property sets or returns a **`UIColor`** value that defines the control's color.

attributedTitle—This property sets or returns the text shown in the control. It is a value of type **`NSAttributedString`**.

isRefreshing—This is a Boolean property that indicates if the control is in the process of refreshing the data.

beginRefreshing()—This method tells the control that the process of refreshing the data was initiated.

endRefreshing()—This method tells the control that the process is over.

The **`UITableView`** class inherits the following property from the **`UIScrollView`** class to assign the control to the table.

refreshControl—This property sets or returns a reference to the Refresh Control associated to the table.

When the user scrolls down the table, the Table View Controller shows the Refresh Control and fires a **`valueChanged`** event to indicate to the code that it should perform the corresponding tasks. Therefore, to respond to the control, we must add an action to the Refresh Control for this event with the **`addAction(for:)`** method, as shown in the following example.

```
import UIKit

class MyTableViewController: UITableViewController {
   var refresh: UIRefreshControl!

   override func viewDidLoad() {
      super.viewDidLoad()
      tableView.register(UITableViewCell.self, forCellReuseIdentifier:
"myCell")
      prepareDataSource()
      prepareSnapshot()

      refresh = UIRefreshControl()
      refresh.addAction(UIAction(handler: { [unowned self] action in
         self.refreshTable()
      }), for: .valueChanged)

      let text = AttributedString("Refreshing Table")
      refresh.attributedTitle = NSMutableAttributedString(text)
      tableView.refreshControl = refresh
   }
```

```
    func refreshTable() {
        prepareSnapshot()
        refresh.endRefreshing()
    }
    func prepareDataSource() {
        AppData.dataSource = UITableViewDiffableDataSource<Sections,
ItemsData.ID>(tableView: tableView) { tableView, indexPath, itemID in
            let cell = tableView.dequeueReusableCell(withIdentifier:
"myCell", for: indexPath)
            if let item = AppData.items.first(where: { $0.id == itemID }) {
                var config = cell.defaultContentConfiguration()
                config.text = item.name
                cell.contentConfiguration = config
            }
            return cell
        }
    }
    func prepareSnapshot() {
        var snapshot = NSDiffableDataSourceSnapshot<Sections,
ItemsData.ID>()
        snapshot.appendSections([.main])
        snapshot.appendItems(AppData.items.map({ $0.id }))
        AppData.dataSource.apply(snapshot)
    }
}
```

Listing 10-31: *Presenting a Refresh Control*

The view controller in Listing 10-31 initializes the control, adds an action to it, and then assigns it to the table. The closure calls the **`refreshTable()`** method to respond to the event. When the user uncovers the control, the **`valueChanged`** event is fired and the method is executed. In this example, we just reload the snapshot with the **`prepareSnapshot()`** method, but this is where we usually access a server to download information, or read a database. After the update, we call the **`endRefreshing()`** method to indicate to the control that the process is over.

Do It Yourself: Update the **`MyTableViewController`** class from the previous example with the code in Listing 10-31. Run the application and scroll down the table to activate the control. This example defines an attributed text for the control, so you will see something like the right picture of Figure 10-27.

Basic 10.4 Search

Table Views can manage thousands of rows, and therefore users can sometimes have a hard time finding what they are looking for. For this reason, the UIKit framework defines the **`UISearchController`** class. This class creates a controller that includes the functionality necessary to allow the user to search for values in the model and present them on the screen. The controller must be created with the following initializer.

UISearchController(searchResultsController: UIViewController?)—This initializer creates a search controller associated with the view controller indicated by the argument. The argument is a reference to the view controller we want to use to present the information or **`nil`** if we want to use the current view controller.

The **`UISearchController`** object creates a search bar with a text field and buttons to let the user perform the search. The following are the properties included in the object to access the bar and configure the controller.

searchBar—This property returns a reference to the **UISearchBar** object created by the controller to present the search bar.

obscuresBackgroundDuringPresentation—This property sets or returns a Boolean value that indicates if the background is obscured during the presentation of the search bar.

hidesNavigationBarDuringPresentation—This property sets or returns a Boolean value that determines whether the Navigation Bar should be hidden during the presentation of the search bar.

The controller also includes the **searchResultsUpdater** property to store a delegate object that receives the value introduced by the user, performs the search, and updates the interface. The object assigned to this property must conform to the **UISearchResultsUpdating** protocol and implement the following method.

updateSearchResults(for: UISearchController**)**—This method is called by the search controller to process the value inserted by the user.

To present the search bar, we must assign the controller to the Navigation Item of the Navigation Bar. The **UINavigationItem** class offers the following properties for this purpose.

searchController—This property sets or returns a reference to the search controller we want to present in the Navigation Bar.

hidesSearchBarWhenScrolling—This property sets or returns a Boolean value that indicates whether the search bar will be hidden when the table is scrolled.

The process is simple. We must embed a Table View Controller in a Navigation Controller, create the search controller with the **UISearchController** initializer, declare the Table View Controller as the delegate, and implement the method of the **UISearchResultsUpdating** protocol to process the input.

Search controllers provide tools for the user to perform the search, but it is up to us to take this input and select the items in our model that match the term. There are different ways to do it. When working with arrays, one alternative is to use the **filter()** method introduced in Chapter 3. The following is the code required by our model to filter the data and store the result.

```
var searchValue: String = ""
var filteredItems: [ItemsData] {
   get {
      if searchValue.isEmpty {
         return items
      } else {
         var list = items.filter( { (item) -> Bool in
            let value1 = item.name.lowercased()
            let value2 = searchValue.lowercased()
            return value1.hasPrefix(value2)
         })
         list.sort(by: { (value1, value2) in value1.name < value2.name })
         return list
      }
   }
}
```

Listing 10-32: *Filtering the data*

The code in Listing 10-32 defines the two properties we must add to our model. The **searchValue** property stores the value searched by the user, and **filteredItems** is a computed property that always returns an array with the items that match the search. Because the snapshot is going to be updated with the values from the **filterItems** property every time the user inserts or deletes a character, we cannot compare entire words, we must look for values in the **items** array the first letters of which match the characters inserted by the user. The **hasPrefix()** method introduced in Chapter 3 is perfect for this situation. The method compares two strings and returns **true** if the first string is found at the beginning of the second string (the method is case sensitive, so we lowercased both strings before comparing).

Because the model manages the search, the view controller is simple. We need to create the search controller and conform to the **UISearchResultsUpdating** protocol to process the input.

```
import UIKit

class MyTableViewController: UITableViewController,
UISearchResultsUpdating {
   override func viewDidLoad() {
      super.viewDidLoad()
      tableView.register(UITableViewCell.self, forCellReuseIdentifier:
"myCell")
      prepareDataSource()
      prepareSnapshot()

      let searchController = UISearchController(searchResultsController:
nil)
      searchController.searchResultsUpdater = self
      searchController.obscuresBackgroundDuringPresentation = false
      navigationItem.searchController = searchController
   }
   func prepareDataSource() {
      AppData.dataSource = UITableViewDiffableDataSource<Sections,
ItemsData.ID>(tableView: tableView) { tableView, indexPath, itemID in
         let cell = tableView.dequeueReusableCell(withIdentifier:
"myCell", for: indexPath)
         if let item = AppData.items.first(where: { $0.id == itemID }) {
            var config = cell.defaultContentConfiguration()
            config.text = item.name
            cell.contentConfiguration = config
         }
         return cell
      }
   }
   func prepareSnapshot() {
      var snapshot = NSDiffableDataSourceSnapshot<Sections,
ItemsData.ID>()
      snapshot.appendSections([.main])
      snapshot.appendItems(AppData.filteredItems.map({ $0.id }))
      AppData.dataSource.apply(snapshot)
   }
   func updateSearchResults(for searchController: UISearchController) {
      if let text = searchController.searchBar.text {
         AppData.searchValue = text.trimmingCharacters(in: .whitespaces)
         prepareSnapshot()
      }
   }
}
```

Listing 10-33: *Processing the input from the search controller*

The first thing we do in this view controller is to create a search controller. In the initializer, we specify the **nil** value to declare this view controller as the one responsible for showing the results. The view controller is also assigned as the delegate of the search controller through the **searchResultsUpdater** property, and the search controller is finally assigned to the **searchController** property of the Navigation Item to show the search bar on the screen.

When the user inserts a character in the search bar, the search controller calls the **updateSearchResults(for:)** method with a reference to the search controller. From this reference, we read the value inserted by the user, assign it to the **searchValue** property in the model, and then update the snapshot with the **prepareSnapshot()** method. (Notice that the snapshot is created with the values of the **filteredItems** property instead of the **items** property.) The result is shown below.

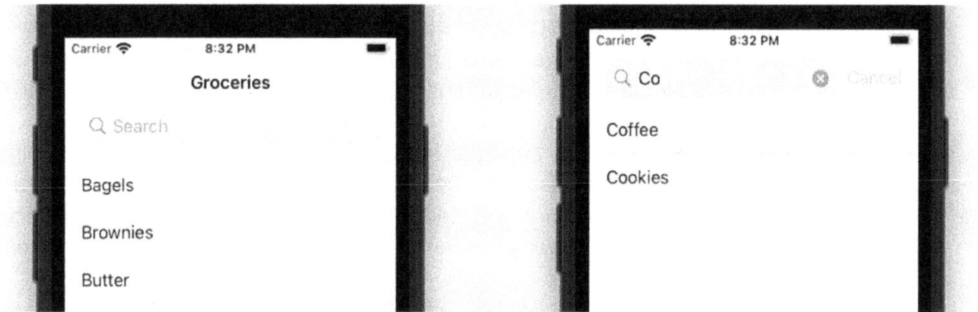

Figure 10-28: *Search controller in the Navigation Bar*

Do It Yourself: Embed the Table View Controller in a Navigation Controller. Insert the title Groceries for the scene. Add the code in Listing 10-32 to the **ApplicationData** structure (below the definition of the **items** property). Update the **MyTableViewController** class with the code in Listing 10-33. Run the application. You should see the search bar at the top. Insert a value. The table should be updated with the items that match the value, as shown in Figure 10-28.

IMPORTANT: In the example of Listing 10-33, we assigned the value **false** to the **obscuresBackgroundDuringPresentation** property to not let the controller obscure the interface when the bar is selected, but you can also assign the value **false** to the **hidesNavigationBarDuringPresentation** property to keep the Navigation Bar visible and take advantage of the **hidesSearchBarWhenScrolling** property of the Navigation Item to keep the search bar visible when the table is scrolled up.

Basic Search Bar

The bar created by the controller is an object of the **UISearchBar** class, which includes several methods and properties for configuration. In the example of Listing 10-33, we used the **text** property to get the value inserted by the user, but there are more available.

text—This property sets or returns the text in the field. It is an optional of type **String**.

placeholder—This property sets or returns the placeholder. It is an optional of type **String**.

tintColor—This property sets or returns the color of the bar's elements. It is an optional of type **UIColor**.

IMPORTANT: The **UISearchBar** class also conforms to the **UITextInput-Traits** protocol and implements its properties to configure the keyboard and some features for the Text Field. For more information, see **UITextField** in Chapter 5.

The **UISearchBar** class can also designate its own delegate object to report the state of the bar. The delegate must conform to the **UISearchBarDelegate** protocol and implement its methods.

searchBarTextDidBeginEditing(UISearchBar**)**—This method is called by the bar on its delegate when the edition begins (the user taps on the bar to perform a search).

searchBarTextDidEndEditing(UISearchBar**)**—This method is called by the bar on its delegate when the edition ends.

searchBarCancelButtonClicked(UISearchBar**)**—This method is called by the bar on its delegate when the Cancel button is pressed.

searchBar(UISearchBar, **selectedScopeButtonIndexDidChange:** Int**)**—This method is called by the bar on its delegate when a button in the scope bar is pressed. The button's index is provided by the second argument.

The last method works with a feature provided by search bars called *Scope Bar* (see Figure 10-29, below). This is an additional bar displayed below the search bar with selectable buttons (like Segmented Controls). When a button is selected, the others are automatically deselected. The **UISearchBar** class includes the following properties to create and configure these buttons.

showsScopeBar—This property is a Boolean value that determines whether the scope bar is displayed or not. When the value is set to **true**, an additional bar is shown at the bottom of the Search Bar with buttons to select the scope of the search.

scopeButtonTitles—This property sets or returns an array of strings with the title for the buttons.

selectedScopeButtonIndex—This property sets or returns the index of the selected button in the scope bar. It is of type **Int**.

The bar assigns an index to every button and every time a button is selected it calls the **searchBar(UISearchBar, selectedScopeButtonIndexDidChange:)** method on its delegate with the button's index, which we can use to refine the search. For example, we can search items by title or by the number of calories. The following is the update required in our model to filter the items depending on the button selected by the user.

```
var searchValue: String = ""
var selectedButton: Int = 0
var filteredItems: [ItemsData] {
   get {
      if searchValue.isEmpty {
         return items
      } else {
         var list = items.filter( { (item) -> Bool in
            if selectedButton == 0 {
               let value1 = item.name.lowercased()
               let value2 = searchValue.lowercased()
               return value1.hasPrefix(value2)
            } else if selectedButton == 1 {
              if let maximum = Int(searchValue),item.calories < maximum {
                  return true
               }
            }
            return false
         })
         list.sort(by: { (value1, value2) in value1.name < value2.name })
         return list
      }
   }
}
```

Listing 10-34: *Expanding the model to work with a scope bar*

The code in Listing 10-34 defines the properties we need to add to our model to manage the search and the scope bar. This includes a property called **selectedButton** to store the index of the active button, so we know what to search for. In the closure for the **filteredItems** property, we filter the items according to the value of this property. If the value is 0, which means the first button is active, we filter the items by title, but if the value is 1, the filter gets the number inserted by the user and only returns **true** if the item's calories are lower than that value.

The view controller must implement the **searchBar(UISearchBar, selectedScopeButtonIndexDidChange:)** method to store the index of the selected button in the model and adapt the interface accordingly.

```
import UIKit

class MyTableViewController: UITableViewController,
UISearchResultsUpdating, UISearchBarDelegate {
   override func viewDidLoad() {
      super.viewDidLoad()
      tableView.register(UITableViewCell.self, forCellReuseIdentifier:
"myCell")
      prepareDataSource()
      prepareSnapshot()

      let searchController = UISearchController(searchResultsController:
nil)
      searchController.searchResultsUpdater = self
      searchController.obscuresBackgroundDuringPresentation = false
      navigationItem.searchController = searchController
      navigationItem.hidesSearchBarWhenScrolling = false

      let searchBar = searchController.searchBar
      searchBar.delegate = self
      searchBar.placeholder = "Search Product"
      searchBar.showsScopeBar = true
      searchBar.scopeButtonTitles = ["Names", "Calories"]
      searchBar.selectedScopeButtonIndex = 0
   }
   func prepareDataSource() {
      AppData.dataSource = UITableViewDiffableDataSource<Sections,
ItemsData.ID>(tableView: tableView) { tableView, indexPath, itemID in
         let cell = tableView.dequeueReusableCell(withIdentifier:
"myCell", for: indexPath)
         if let item = AppData.items.first(where: { $0.id == itemID }) {
            var config = cell.defaultContentConfiguration()
            config.text = item.name
            cell.contentConfiguration = config
         }
         return cell
      }
   }
   func prepareSnapshot() {
      var snapshot = NSDiffableDataSourceSnapshot<Sections,
ItemsData.ID>()
      snapshot.appendSections([.main])
      snapshot.appendItems(AppData.filteredItems.map({ $0.id }))
      AppData.dataSource.apply(snapshot)
   }
   func updateSearchResults(for searchController: UISearchController) {
      if let text = searchController.searchBar.text {
         AppData.searchValue = text.trimmingCharacters(in: .whitespaces)
         prepareSnapshot()
      }
   }
```

```
    func searchBar(_ searchBar: UISearchBar,
selectedScopeButtonIndexDidChange selectedScope: Int) {
        AppData.selectedButton = selectedScope
        prepareSnapshot()
        searchBar.placeholder = selectedScope == 0 ? "Search Product" :
"Maximum Calories"
        searchBar.text = ""
    }
}
```

Listing 10-35: *Adding a scope bar*

After creating the search controller, the code in Listing 10-35 gets a reference to the search bar to modify its properties. We first declare the view controller as the bar's delegate, then assign the string "Search Product" as placeholder, and finally create two buttons for the scope bar.

To respond to the user, we have implemented the **searchBar(UISearchBar, selectedScopeButtonIndexDidChange:)** method. This method is called when a button is pressed in the scope bar. Here, we assign the index of the active button to the model's **selectedScope** property to notify the model the type of information it must look for and update the snapshot. After that, we change the bar's placeholder to help the user identify the value that the Text Field is expecting and clean the bar to show all the original values on the screen. Consequently, if the Names button is selected, the model tries to match the value with the names of the items, but when the Calories button is selected, we compare the value to the number of calories in each item.

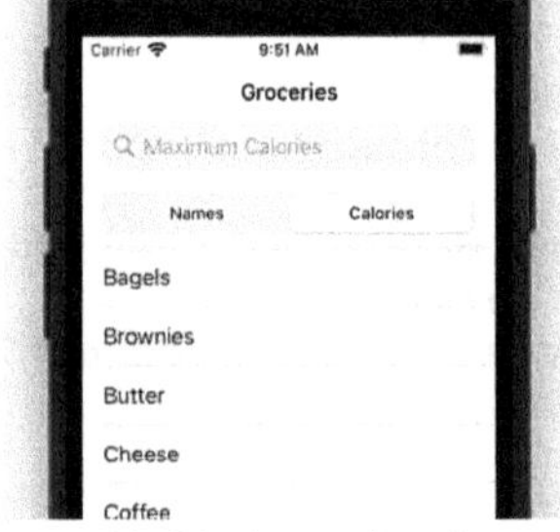

Figure 10-29: *Scope bar in action*

Basic 10.5 Sections

Tables organize the information in sections. The model used so far declares the sections with an enumeration called **Sections**. The enumeration only includes one value called **main** because our examples only required one section, but we can declare more. An alternative is to add more values to the **Sections** enumeration, but if the sections are dynamic (they are generated according to the information inserted by the user), we should define our own data type to identify them.

There are different ways to organize this information. For this example, we have decided to create and additional class for the sections and store the values in two arrays, one for the sections and another for the items.

```
import UIKit

class Sections: Identifiable {
    var id: UUID = UUID()
    var name: String

    init(name: String) {
        self.name = name
    }
}
```

```
class ItemsData: Identifiable {
   var id: UUID = UUID()
   var name: String
   var image: String
   var calories: Int
   var selected: Bool
   var section: String

   init(_ name: String, _ image: String, _ calories: Int, _ selected: Bool, _ section: String) {
      self.name = name
      self.image = image
      self.calories = calories
      self.selected = selected
      self.section = section
   }
}
struct ApplicationData {
   var dataSource: MyDataSource!
   var sections: [Sections] = []
   var items: [ItemsData] = []

   init() {
      sections.append(contentsOf: [Sections(name: "B"), Sections(name: "C"), Sections(name: "D"), Sections(name: "G"), Sections(name: "J"), Sections(name: "L"), Sections(name: "M"), Sections(name: "O"), Sections(name: "P"), Sections(name: "T"), Sections(name: "Y")])
      items.append(contentsOf: [ItemsData("Bagels", "bagels", 250, false, "B"), ItemsData("Brownies", "brownies", 466, false, "B"), ItemsData("Butter", "butter", 717, false, "B")])
      items.append(contentsOf: [ItemsData("Cheese", "cheese", 402, false, "C"), ItemsData("Coffee", "coffee", 0, false, "C"), ItemsData("Cookies", "cookies", 502, false, "C")])
      items.append(contentsOf: [ItemsData("Donuts", "donuts", 452, false, "D")])
      items.append(contentsOf: [ItemsData("Granola", "granola", 471, false, "G")])
      items.append(contentsOf: [ItemsData("Juice", "juice", 23, false, "J")])
      items.append(contentsOf: [ItemsData("Lemonade", "lemonade", 40, false, "L"), ItemsData("Lettuce", "lettuce", 15, false, "L")])
      items.append(contentsOf: [ItemsData("Milk", "milk", 42, false, "M")])
      items.append(contentsOf: [ItemsData("Oatmeal", "oatmeal", 68, false, "O")])
      items.append(contentsOf: [ItemsData("Potatoes", "potato", 77, false, "P")])
      items.append(contentsOf: [ItemsData("Tomatoes", "tomato", 18, false, "T")])
      items.append(contentsOf: [ItemsData("Yogurt", "yogurt", 59, false, "Y")])
   }
}
var AppData = ApplicationData()
```

Listing 10-36: *Storing the data in sections*

The **Sections** class includes the **id** property to identify each section and the **name** property to store the section's name. We have also incorporated an additional property to the **ItemsData** class to store the name of the section to which the item belongs. The property to store the sections is called **sections** and the property to store the items is called **items**. After the properties are defined, we initialize them with a few values to test the model.

The model classifies the data, but the sections are defined by the snapshot, as shown next.

```
import UIKit

class MyTableViewController: UITableViewController {
   override func viewDidLoad() {
      super.viewDidLoad()
      tableView.register(UITableViewCell.self, forCellReuseIdentifier:
"myCell")
      prepareDataSource()
      prepareSnapshot()
   }
   func prepareDataSource() {
      AppData.dataSource = MyDataSource(tableView: tableView)
{ tableView, indexPath, itemID in
         let cell = tableView.dequeueReusableCell(withIdentifier:
"myCell", for: indexPath)
         if let item = AppData.items.first(where: { $0.id == itemID }) {
            var config = cell.defaultContentConfiguration()
            config.text = item.name
            cell.contentConfiguration = config
         }
         return cell
      }
   }
   func prepareSnapshot() {
      var snapshot = NSDiffableDataSourceSnapshot<Sections.ID,
ItemsData.ID>()
      snapshot.appendSections(AppData.sections.map({ $0.id }))
      for section in AppData.sections {
         let itemIDs = AppData.items.compactMap({ value in
            return value.section == section.name ? value.id : nil
         })
         snapshot.appendItems(itemIDs, toSection: section.id)
      }
      AppData.dataSource.apply(snapshot)
   }
}
```

Listing 10-37: *Defining a snapshot with sections*

The sections are now identified by the value of the **id** property, so we must define the **NSDiffableDataSourceSnapshot** object with the **Sections.ID** data type, as we did before for the items. The section ids are added to the snapshot with the **appendSections()** method, as always, but this time the items are added to the sections they belong to with the **appendItems(toSection:)** method. To get the list of items per section, we iterate through the **sections** array and filter the items with the **compactMap()** method. This method is similar to **map()**, but only returns the values that are different from **nil**. This means that we can process the items and include in the result only the identifiers of those that belong to the current section (if the item doesn't belong to the section, we return **nil** to ignore it).

This organizes the items in sections, but we still need to provide the titles for the headers of each section. An alternative is to implement the **tableView(UITableView, titleForHeaderInSection:)** method of the **UITableViewDataSource** protocol in our **UITableViewDiffableDataSource** subclass, as in the following example.

```
import UIKit

class MyDataSource: UITableViewDiffableDataSource<Sections.ID,
ItemsData.ID> {
```

```
    override func tableView(_ tableView: UITableView,
titleForHeaderInSection section: Int) -> String? {
        return AppData.sections[section].name
    }
}
```

Listing 10-38: *Declaring the sections' titles*

The **tableView(UITableView, titleForHeaderInSection:)** method is called by the table every time it needs the title of a section. In this method, we read the value of the section's **name** property and return it. The table takes this value and turns it into the section's title.

When items are split in sections, we can take advantage of the multiple styles available for Table Views. Figure 10-30, below, shows what we see when we run our application with the Table View's Style option set to Plain, Grouped and Inset Grouped.

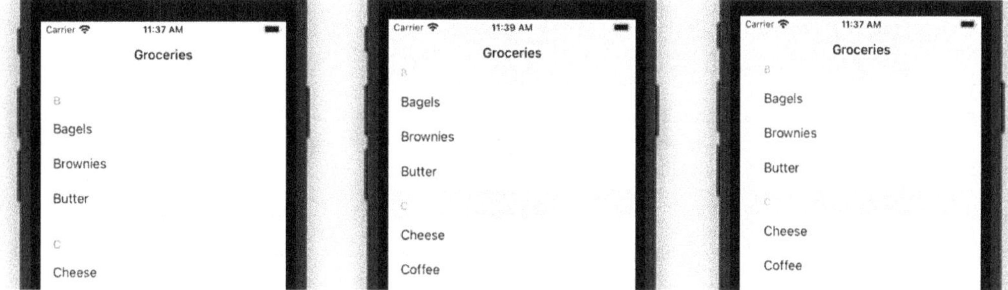

Figure 10-30: *Items in sections*

Do It Yourself: Update the model with the code in Listing 10-36 and the **MyTableViewController** class with the code in Listing 10-37. Create a Swift file called MyDataSource.swift for the code in Listing 10-38. Select the Table View and modify the Style option from the Attributes Inspector panel to configure the table with the style you want. Run the application. You should see the table of Figure 10-30. (As of this writing, the Style option applies different styles to the table. Select and deselect the options until you get the style you want.)

Like cells, section headers are created from prototypes. After the **tableView-(UITableView, titleForHeaderInSection:)** method returns the title for the header, the Table View creates a header view from a prototype view and shows it on the screen. Although this is enough for some applications, we can define and configure our own prototype. The **UITableView** class includes the following methods to register a prototype and create a view from it.

register(AnyClass?, **forHeaderFooterViewReuseIdentifier:** String**)**—This method registers a prototype header or footer view. The fist argument is the class that is going to be used to create the cells (the **UITableViewHeaderFooterView** class or a subclass of it), and the **forHeaderFooterViewReuseIdentifier** argument specifies the string the table is going to use to identify this prototype view.

dequeueReusableHeaderFooterView(withIdentifier: String**)**—This method returns a **UITableViewHeaderFooterView** object to represent a header or footer view. The object is created from the prototype with the identifier defined by the **withIdentifier** argument.

To further optimize performance, header and footer views are configured with configuration structures. The **UIListContentConfiguration** structure defines several type methods to return standard configurations for headers and footers, including **plainHeader()**, **groupedHeader()**, **sidebarHeader()**, **plainFooter()**, **groupedFooter()**, **prominent-InsetGroupedHeader()**, and **extraProminentInsetGroupedHeader()**.

There are two methods defined in the **UITableViewDelegate** protocol we need to implement to provide a custom header. The **tableView(UITableView, viewForHeaderInSection:)** method creates and returns the view for the header, and the **tableView(UITableView, heightForHeaderInSection:)** method specifies the header's height. The following view controller shows how to implement these methods in our example.

```
import UIKit

class MyTableViewController: UITableViewController {
   override func viewDidLoad() {
      super.viewDidLoad()
      tableView.register(UITableViewCell.self, forCellReuseIdentifier:
"myCell")
      tableView.register(UITableViewHeaderFooterView.self,
forHeaderFooterViewReuseIdentifier: "myHeader")
      prepareDataSource()
      prepareSnapshot()
   }
   func prepareDataSource() {
      AppData.dataSource = MyDataSource(tableView: tableView)
{ tableView, indexPath, itemID in
         let cell = tableView.dequeueReusableCell(withIdentifier:
"myCell", for: indexPath)
         if let item = AppData.items.first(where: { $0.id == itemID }) {
            var config = cell.defaultContentConfiguration()
            config.text = item.name
            cell.contentConfiguration = config
         }
         return cell
      }
   }
   func prepareSnapshot() {
      var snapshot = NSDiffableDataSourceSnapshot<Sections.ID,
ItemsData.ID>()
      snapshot.appendSections(AppData.sections.map({ $0.id }))
      for section in AppData.sections {
         let itemIDs = AppData.items.compactMap({ value in
            return value.section == section.name ? value.id : nil
         })
         snapshot.appendItems(itemIDs, toSection: section.id)
      }
      AppData.dataSource.apply(snapshot)
   }
   override func tableView(_ tableView: UITableView,
viewForHeaderInSection section: Int) -> UIView? {
      let header =
tableView.dequeueReusableHeaderFooterView(withIdentifier: "myHeader")!

      var config =
UIListContentConfiguration.prominentInsetGroupedHeader()
      config.text = AppData.sections[section].name
      config.directionalLayoutMargins = NSDirectionalEdgeInsets(top: 0,
leading: 15, bottom: 0, trailing: 0)
      header.contentConfiguration = config
      return header
   }
   override func tableView(_ tableView: UITableView,
heightForHeaderInSection section: Int) -> CGFloat {
      return 40
   }
}
```

Listing 10-39: *Configuring the headers*

The first thing we do in this view controller is to register the prototype view for the headers with the identifier "myHeader". Using this identifier, we create the header views with the configuration provided by the **prominentInsetGroupedHeader()** method and the appropriate margins and height for an Inset Grouped table. The result is show below.

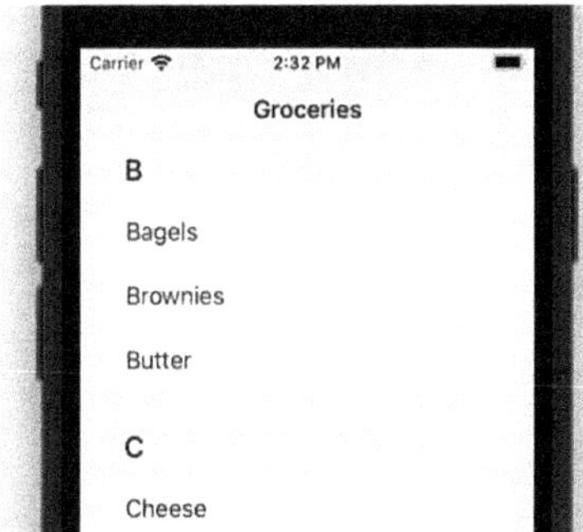

Figure 10-31: *Table with custom headers*

Do It Yourself: Update the **MyTableViewController** class with the code in Listing 10-39. The header's view and title are now provided by the **tableView(UITableView, viewForHeaderInSection:)** method, so you can remove the method added to the **MyDataSource** class in Listing 10-38. Run the application. You should see something like Figure 10-31.

When working with sections, we can also provide an index on the table's right-hand side to help the user navigate through the items. The **UITableViewDataSource** protocol includes the **sectionIndexTitles()** method to provide an array with the titles for the indexes, and the **tableView(UITableView, sectionForSectionIndexTitle:, at:)** method to specify the section to which the titles belong. The following example implements these methods in our **MyDataSource** subclass to create the indexes from the names of the sections.

```
import UIKit

class MyDataSource: UITableViewDiffableDataSource<Sections.ID, ItemsData.ID> {
   override func tableView(_ tableView: UITableView, titleForHeaderInSection section: Int) -> String? {
      return AppData.sections[section].name
   }
   override func sectionIndexTitles(for tableView: UITableView) -> [String]? {
      let titles = AppData.sections.map({ $0.name })
      return titles
   }
   override func tableView(_ tableView: UITableView, sectionForSectionIndexTitle title: String, at index: Int) -> Int {
      if let index = AppData.sections.firstIndex(where: { $0.name == title }) {
         return index
      }
      return 0
   }
}
```

Listing 10-40: *Showing the index*

The **sectionIndexTitles()** method in Listing 10-40 creates an array with the values of the items' **name** properties and returns it. This gives the table the list of titles for the sections, but because we could include titles for sections that do not yet exist on the table, we also implement the **tableView(UITableView, sectionForSectionIndexTitle:, at:)** method to provide the indexes of the sections corresponding to each title. This method is called every time the table needs to know which section a title belongs to, so we search for the title in the **sections** array with the **firstIndex(where:)** method and return it. The result is shown below (number 1).

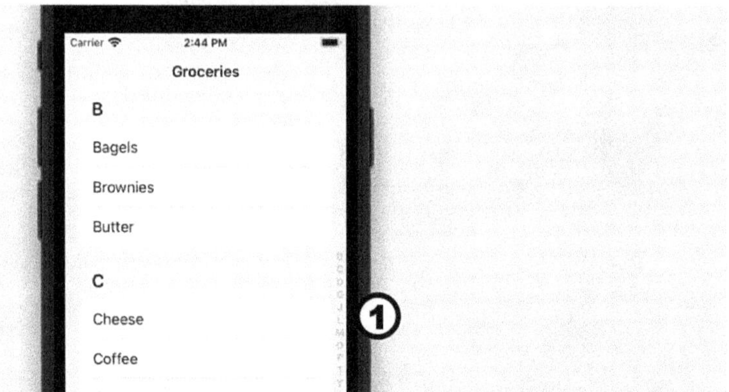

Figure 10-32: Table indexes

Do It Yourself: Update the **MyDataSource** class with the code in Listing 10-40. Run the application. You should see the index on the right, as illustrated in Figure 10-32. Tapping on these buttons scrolls the table to the corresponding section.

Basic Deleting Sections

When working with sections, we must take care of creating new sections and deleting those that are not required anymore. The process always depends on how our model is organized. For instance, the following example shows how to delete a section when all the section's items have been removed.

```
import UIKit

class MyDataSource: UITableViewDiffableDataSource<Sections.ID,
ItemsData.ID> {
   override func tableView(_ tableView: UITableView,
titleForHeaderInSection section: Int) -> String? {
      return AppData.sections[section].name
   }
   override func tableView(_ tableView: UITableView, canEditRowAt
indexPath: IndexPath) -> Bool {
      return true
   }
   override func tableView(_ tableView: UITableView, commit editingStyle:
UITableViewCell.EditingStyle, forRowAt indexPath: IndexPath) {
      if editingStyle == UITableViewCell.EditingStyle.delete {
         if let itemID = self.itemIdentifier(for: indexPath), let
sectionID = self.sectionIdentifier(for: indexPath.section) {
            AppData.items.removeAll(where: { $0.id == itemID })

            var currentSnapshot = self.snapshot()
            currentSnapshot.deleteItems([itemID])
            if currentSnapshot.numberOfItems(inSection: sectionID) <= 0 {
               AppData.sections.removeAll(where: { $0.id == sectionID })
               currentSnapshot.deleteSections([sectionID])
            }
```

```
                self.apply(currentSnapshot)
            }
        }
    }
}
```

Listing 10-41: *Deleting empty sections*

The **MyDataSource** method in Listing 10-41 includes the protocol method necessary to return the section's name, and the two we need to edit the rows (see Listing 10-24). When the Delete button is pressed, we get the item and section IDs, and then delete the item, as we did before, but now we get the number of items in the item's section and if there are no items left, we proceed to delete the section in the model and the snapshot.

Do It Yourself: Update the **MyDataSource** class with the code in Listing 10-41. Run the application, swipe a cell to the left to reveal the Delete button, and press the button to delete the cell. If there are no items left in the section, the section is deleted as well.

Basic 10.6 Static Tables

Table View Controllers offer the possibility to create static tables. Static tables present a fixed number of cells and therefore are particularly useful when we have a limited number of options or predefined data to display. To turn the table of a Table View Controller into a static table, we must select it and change the Content option in the Attributes Inspector panel to Static Cells.

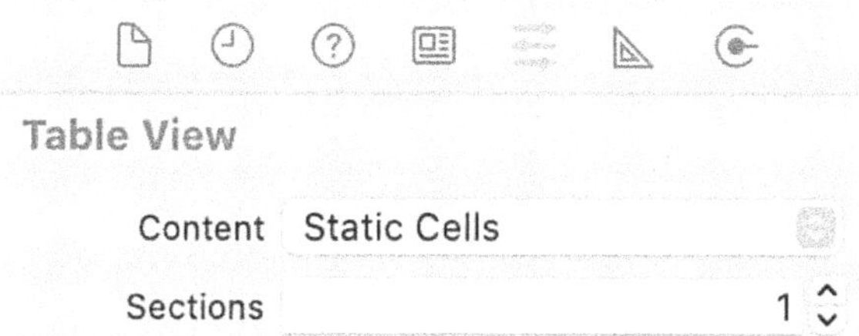

Figure 10-33: *Option to change the type of cells*

Once the option is selected, the table replaces the prototype cells with three custom cells.

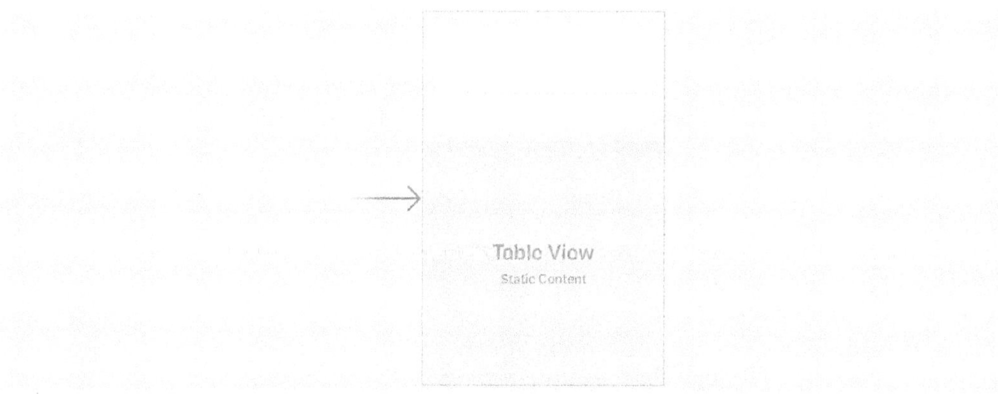

Figure 10-34: *Empty static cells in an Inset Grouped table*

From this point on, the cells and their content are designed in the Storyboard by dragging the elements from the Library to the cells, as we do with any other view. We can add new cells by dragging the Table View Cell option from the Library, and new sections may be added by modifying the value of the Section option from the Attributes Inspector panel. When a section is selected, the Attributes Inspector panel offers options to specify the titles for the section's header and footer.

If the scene in the Storyboard is not tall enough to fit all the cells we need, we can set a different size from the Simulated Size option in the Size Inspector panel, as we did for Scroll Views in Chapter 7. Figure 10-35, below, shows a possible design. For this example, we changed the table's style to Inset Grouped, use custom cells, and added labels and a section with a single cell to present an Image View.

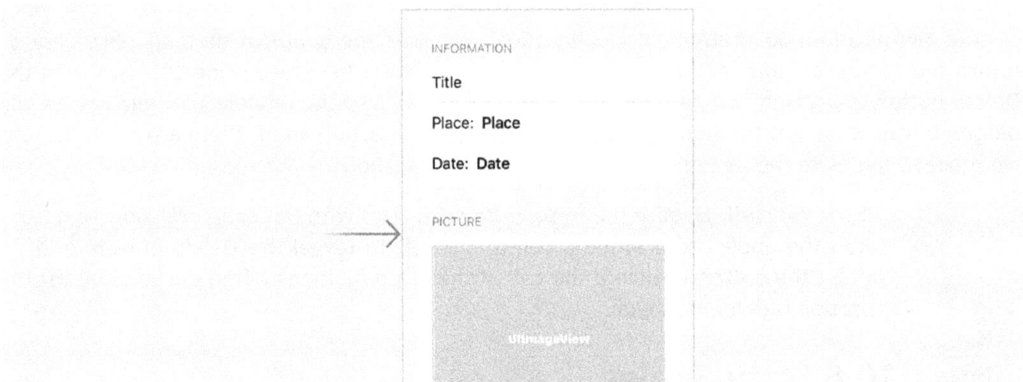

Figure 10-35: *Definition of static cells*

The custom cells for a static table do not need their own **UITableViewCell** subclass; all we need to do is to connect the elements directly to Outlets in the view controller. The following is the code for the **UITableViewController** subclass necessary to control the interface of Figure 10-35.

```
import UIKit

class MyTableViewController: UITableViewController {
   @IBOutlet weak var titleLabel: UILabel!
   @IBOutlet weak var placeLabel: UILabel!
   @IBOutlet weak var dateLabel: UILabel!
   @IBOutlet weak var picture: UIImageView!

   override func viewDidLoad() {
      super.viewDidLoad()
      titleLabel.text = "Toronto's Waterfront"
      placeLabel.text = "Toronto"

      let now = Date.now
      dateLabel.text = now.formatted(date: .abbreviated, time: .omitted)
      picture.image = UIImage(named: "Toronto")
   }
}
```

Listing 10-42: *Defining the content of static cells*

In the view controller for a static table, we do not have to declare a snapshot or a data source because everything has been defined in the Storyboard, but we can assign new values to the elements in the cells. In Listing 10-42, we assign strings to the labels, a date, and an image to the Image View. The result is shown below.

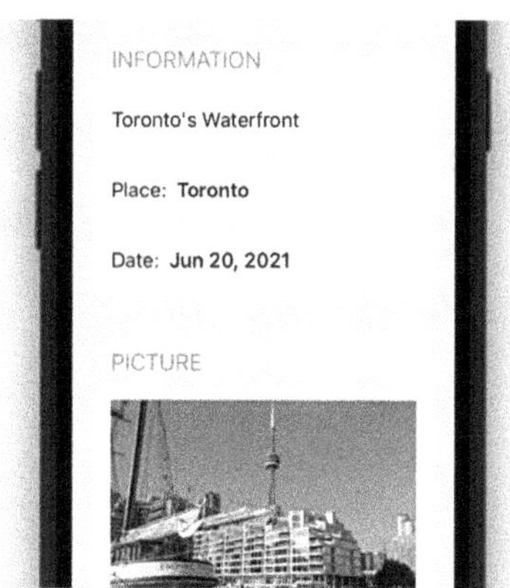

Figure 10-36: *Application with a static table*

Do It Yourself: Create a new project. Download the image Toronto.jpg from our website and add it to the Assets Catalog. Delete the scene and add a Table View Controller from the Library (Figure 10-25). Select the scene, open the Attributes Inspector panel, and activate the option Is Initial View Controller. Select the table and change the value of the Content option to Static Cells. Assign the value 2 to Sections to add another section to the table. Select the cells you don't need and press the Delete button to remove them. Modify the sizes of the cells from the Size Inspector panel to fit the elements and add labels to the cells of the first section and an Image View to the cell of the second section. Assign the necessary constraints to get the interface in Figure 10-35. Select the sections to change their titles. Create a subclass of **`UITableViewController`** called **`MyTableViewController`** and assign it to the scene. Complete the class with the code in Listing 10-42 and connect the elements on the cells to the Outlets in the code. Run the application. You should see something like Figure 10-36.

Chapter 11
Collection Views

Basic 11.1 Collection Views

Collection Views are like Table Views, with the difference that they can present the information with a customizable layout. They come with a grid-like layout by default, but we can modify it or replace it entirely to present the views any way we want.

Figure 11-1: *Collection Views*

Collection Views are defined by the **UICollectionView** class. As any other views, they may be created from code or added to a scene from the option in the Library.

UICollectionView(frame: CGRect, **collectionViewLayout:** UICollectionView-Layout**)**—This initializer creates a **UICollectionView** object with the frame specified by the **frame** argument and the layout object provided by the **collectionViewLayout** argument.

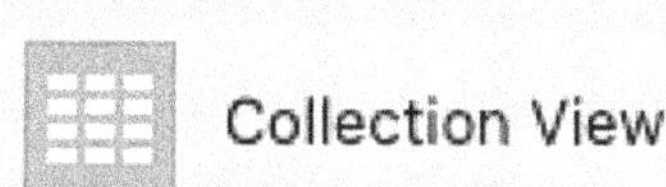

Figure 11-2: *Collection View option in the Library*

Although we can use this option to add a Collection View to a scene, the Library also includes an option to add a scene to the Storyboard that comes with a full-screen Collection View.

Figure 11-3: *Collection View Controller option in the Library*

The following are some of the properties and methods included in the **UICollectionView** class to configure the view.

allowsSelection—This property is a Boolean value that determines whether the selection of cells is allowed or not.

allowsMultipleSelection—This property is a Boolean value that determines whether multiple selection of cells is allowed or not.

collectionViewLayout—This property sets or returns the layout object in charge of setting the layout for the cells. It is an object of a subclass of **UICollectionView-Layout**.

indexPathsForSelectedItems—This property returns an array of **IndexPath** structures with the indexes of the selected cells.

deselectItem(at: IndexPath, **animated:** Bool**)**—This method deselects the cell at the position indicated by the **at** argument. The **animated** argument indicates if the process is going to be animated.

scrollToItem(at: IndexPath, **at:** ScrollPosition, **animated:** Bool**)**—This method scrolls the Collection View to show on the screen the cell at the position indicated by the first **at** argument. The second **at** argument is a property of a structure called **ScrollPosition** included in the **UICollectionView** class that indicates how the Collection View is going to scroll. The properties available are **top**, **bottom**, **left**, **right**, **centeredVertically**, and **centeredHorizontally**. And the **animated** argument is a Boolean value that indicates if the process is going to be animated

Basic Collection View Cells

The views displayed by a Collection View are also called cells. Cells in a Collection View are created from the **UICollectionViewCell** class, but they do not include any standard elements by default. Therefore, to create a cell, we must define a subclass of the **UICollectionViewCell** class and add our own views to the cell's Content View. The class includes the following property for this purpose.

contentView—This property returns the cell's Content View. All the elements added to customize the cell are incorporated as subviews of this view.

Just like the cells in a Table View, these cells are created from prototype cells. To register a prototype cell, the **UICollectionView** class defines the **CellRegistration** structure.

CellRegistration(handler: Closure**)**—This initializer registers and configures a prototype cell. The **handler** argument is a closure that is called every time a cell is required. The closure receives three values: a reference to the cell, the index path with the location of the cell, and a reference to the data that must be shown by the cell.

The following is the method provided by the **UICollectionView** class to create cells from a prototype cell.

dequeueConfiguredReusableCell(using: CellRegistration, **for:** IndexPath, **item:** Item?**)**—This method returns a cell with the configuration defined by the **CellRegistration** structure specified by the **using** argument. The **for** argument indicates the cell's location, and the **item** argument is the data to be shown by the cell.

Basic Collection View Delegate

Collection Views can designate a delegate to respond to user interaction. UIKit includes the **UICollectionViewDelegate** protocol to define this delegate object. The following are the methods we need to implement to respond to the selection of a cell.

collectionView(UICollectionView, **didSelectItemAt:** IndexPath**)**—This method is called by the Collection View on its delegate when a cell is selected.

collectionView(UICollectionView, **didDeselectItemAt:** IndexPath**)**—This method is called by the Collection View on its delegate when a cell is deselected.

Basic Data Source

As with tables, the snapshot is created from the **NSDiffableDataSourceSnapshot** class, but UIKit defines a specific class to create the diffable data source for Collection Views called **UICollectionViewDiffableDataSource**. The class provides the following initializer.

UICollectionViewDiffableDataSource(collectionView: UICollectionView, **cellProvider:** Closure)—This initializer creates a data source for the Collection View specified by the **collectionView** argument. The **cellProvider** argument is a closure that is called every time a cell is required. The closure receives three values: a reference to the Collection View, the index path with the location of the cell, and a reference to the data that must be shown by the cell.

Basic 11.2 Implementing Collection Views

As already mentioned, Collection Views can be initialized from code, added to a scene from the Library, or included with a Collection View Controller. Because Collection Views usually filled the screen, the latter is the recommended option. Figure 11-4 shows what a Collection View Controller looks like in the Storyboard.

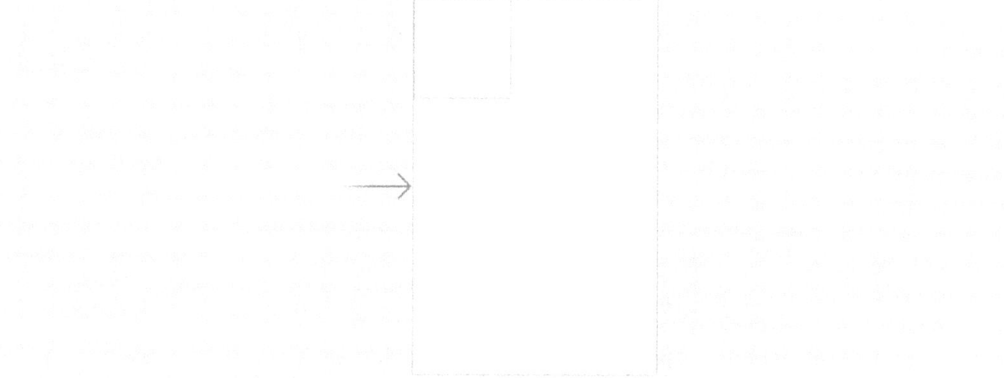

Figure 11-4: *Collection View Controller*

The Collection View included with the scene comes with a prototype cell (the square at the top of the scene in Figure 11-4). Before iOS 14, this was the recommended way to create our prototype cells, but modern cells are registered and configured from code. For this purpose, we must define our own subclass of **UICollectionViewCell**.

All the subclass needs to do is to create the views we want to use to show the values. In the following example, we define a subclass called **FoodCell** with an Image View to show the item's pictures.

```
import UIKit

class FoodCell: UICollectionViewCell {
   let picture = UIImageView()

   override init(frame: CGRect) {
      super.init(frame: frame)
      picture.translatesAutoresizingMaskIntoConstraints = false
      picture.contentMode = .scaleAspectFit
      self.contentView.addSubview(picture)
```

```
      picture.topAnchor.constraint(equalTo: self.contentView.topAnchor,
constant: 8).isActive = true
      picture.bottomAnchor.constraint(equalTo:
self.contentView.bottomAnchor, constant: -8).isActive = true
      picture.leadingAnchor.constraint(equalTo:
self.contentView.leadingAnchor, constant: 8).isActive = true
      picture.trailingAnchor.constraint(equalTo:
self.contentView.trailingAnchor, constant: -8).isActive = true
   }
   required init?(coder: NSCoder) {
      fatalError("Error")
   }
}
```

Listing 11-1: Creating a Collection View cell

The **FoodCell** class includes a property called **picture** to store the Image View. This is the property that we access later to configure the cell with the image of each item. When the cell is initialized, we set up the Image View with Space constraints to pin it to the sides of the Content View.

The steps to set up the Collection View are the same as for Table Views, but the process is different. The configuration of the cell is done by the closure assigned to the **CellRegistration** structure, so all that is left to do for the diffable data source is to create the cell with the **dequeueConfiguredReusableCell()** method and return it. (For this example, we are implementing the same model used for Table Views in Chapter 10, Listing 10-1. The only difference is that now the diffable data source must be defined with the **UICollectionViewDiffableDataSource** class.)

```
import UIKit

class MyCollectionViewController: UICollectionViewController {
   override func viewDidLoad() {
      super.viewDidLoad()
      let cellRegistration = UICollectionView.CellRegistration<FoodCell,
ItemsData.ID> { cell, indexPath, itemID in
         if let item = AppData.items.first(where: { $0.id == itemID }) {
            cell.picture.image = UIImage(named: item.image)
         }
      }
      AppData.dataSource = UICollectionViewDiffableDataSource<Sections,
ItemsData.ID>(collectionView: collectionView) { (collection, indexPath,
itemID) in
         return collection.dequeueConfiguredReusableCell(using:
cellRegistration, for: indexPath, item: itemID)
      }
      var snapshot = NSDiffableDataSourceSnapshot<Sections,
ItemsData.ID>()
      snapshot.appendSections([.main])
      snapshot.appendItems(AppData.items.map({ $0.id }))
      AppData.dataSource.apply(snapshot)
   }
}
```

Listing 11-2: Configuring a Collection View

The **CellRegistration** structure is generic. To create an instance, we specify the cell's data type (**FoodCell**) and the data type we use to identify the values in the model (**ItemsData.ID**). The initializer creates the prototype cell and provides the closure to configure it. This closure is called later every time a new cell is required by the Collection View. In our example, we get the item from the item's ID, and assign the item's image to the cell's **picture** property.

Next, we create the diffable data source. Because the cell is already configured by the **CellRegistration** structure, all we need to do here is to call the **dequeueConfiguredReusableCell()** method with a reference to the configuration structure to create the cell and return it.

The cells, the diffable data source, and the snapshot define the content of the Collection View, but how the cells are going to be laid out is defined by a layout object. Collection Views come with a default layout called *Flow* layout. This layout is configured to position the cells in a grid, which means the cells will be displayed in as many rows and columns as the available space allows.

Figure 11-5: *Flow layout*

Do It Yourself: Create a new project. Remove the initial scene and add a Collection View Controller from the Library. Select the scene and activate the option Is Initial View Controller from the Attributes Inspector panel. Create a file with a subclass of **UICollectionViewCell** called **FoodCell**. Update this class with the code in Listing 11-1. Create a Swift file called ApplicationData.swift with the model in Chapter 10, Listing 10-1. Define the **dataSource** property in the model with the **UICollectionViewDiffableDataSource** class (**var dataSource: UICollectionViewDiffableDataSource<Sections, ItemsData.ID>!**). Create a subclass of **UICollectionViewController** called **MyCollectionViewController**. Update this class with the code in Listing 11-2. Download the thumbnails from our website and add them to the Assets Catalog. Run the application. You should see something like Figure 11-5. Rotate the device to see how the layout adapts the cells to the space available.

Collection View cells can be selected, but they do not show any indication to the user (the background color doesn't change). If we want to change the background every time a cell is selected or deselected, we must apply a background configuration. Like Table View cells, Collection View cells include the **configurationUpdateHandler** property to take a closure that we can use to configure the cell every time the state changes, and the **backgroundConfiguration** property to assign the background configuration to the cell. The implementation is the same used for Table Views (see Background in Chapter 10).

```
import UIKit

class MyCollectionViewController: UICollectionViewController {
   override func viewDidLoad() {
      super.viewDidLoad()
      prepareDataSource()
      prepareSnapshot()
   }
```

```
    func prepareDataSource() {
        let cellRegistration = UICollectionView.CellRegistration<FoodCell,
ItemsData.ID> { cell, indexPath, itemID in
            if let item = AppData.items.first(where: { $0.id == itemID }) {
                cell.picture.image = UIImage(named: item.image)
            }
            cell.configurationUpdateHandler = { cell, state in
                var backgroundConfig =
UIBackgroundConfiguration.listPlainCell().updated(for: state)
                backgroundConfig.cornerRadius = 10

                if state.isSelected {
                    backgroundConfig.backgroundColor = .systemGray5
                } else {
                    backgroundConfig.backgroundColor = .systemBackground
                }
                cell.backgroundConfiguration = backgroundConfig
            }
        }
        AppData.dataSource = UICollectionViewDiffableDataSource<Sections,
ItemsData.ID>(collectionView: collectionView) { (collection, indexPath,
itemID) in
            return collection.dequeueConfiguredReusableCell(using:
cellRegistration, for: indexPath, item: itemID)
        }
    }
    func prepareSnapshot() {
        var snapshot = NSDiffableDataSourceSnapshot<Sections,
ItemsData.ID>()
        snapshot.appendSections([.main])
        snapshot.appendItems(AppData.items.map({ $0.id }))
        AppData.dataSource.apply(snapshot)
    }
}
```

Listing 11-3: *Configuring the background of a Collection View cell*

Figure 11-6: *Different background for selected cells*

Basic Flow Layout

How the cells are laid out in a collection view is determined by an object created from a subclass of the **UICollectionViewLayout** class. Although we can create our own subclass to define any layout we want, UIKit includes a subclass called **UICollectionViewFlowLayout** that provides a highly customizable grid-like layout called Flow layout. This is the layout assign to the Collection View by default and the one we have been using so far. In our examples, we implemented this layout with standard settings, but the class includes the following properties for configuration.

scrollDirection—This property sets or returns the direction of the scroll. It is an enumeration called **ScrollDirection** included in the **UICollectionView** class. The values available are **vertical** and **horizontal** (with **vertical** set by default).

minimumInteritemSpacing—This property sets or returns a `CGFloat` value that determines the space between cells. In vertical scrolling, the value determines the space between cells in the same row, but in horizontal scrolling it determines the space between items in the same column.

minimumLineSpacing—This property sets or returns a `CGFloat` value that determines the space between cells. In vertical scrolling, the value determines the space between rows, but in horizontal scrolling it determines the space between columns.

sectionInset—This property sets or returns the margins for the sections. It is a structure of type `UIEdgeInsets` with the properties `top`, `bottom`, `left`, and `right`.

itemSize—This property sets or returns the size of the cells. It is a value of type `CGSize`.

estimatedItemSize—This property sets or returns the approximate size of dynamic sized cells. Declaring an estimated size can help the Collection View calculate the size of the cells when it is determined by the size of their content. It is a value of type `CGSize`.

The Flow layout can also designate a delegate to specify a custom configuration for each cell. The methods are defined by the `UICollectionViewDelegateFlowLayout` protocol. The following are the most frequently used.

collectionView(UICollectionView, **layout:** UICollectionViewLayout, **sizeForItemAt:** IndexPath**)**—This method is called by the layout object to get the size of a cell. It must return a `CGSize` value with the size of the cell at the location indicated by the **sizeForItemAt** argument.

collectionView(UICollectionView, **layout:** UICollectionViewLayout, **insetForSectionAt:** Int**)**—This method is called by the layout object to get the `UIEdgeInsets` structure with the inset values for the section (the margins). The **insetForSectionAt** argument is an integer with the section's index.

collectionView(UICollectionView, **layout:** UICollectionViewLayout, **minimumLineSpacingForSectionAt:** Int**)**—This method is called by the layout object to get the `CGFloat` value that determines the minimum space between lines in a section. The **minimumLineSpacingForSectionAt** argument is an integer with the section's index.

collectionView(UICollectionView, **layout:** UICollectionViewLayout, **minimumInteritemSpacingForSectionAt:** Int**)**—This method is called by the layout object to get the `CGFloat` value that determines the minimum space between cells in a section. The **minimumInteritemSpacingForSectionAt** argument is an integer with the section's index.

There are different ways to determine the size of the cells. By default, the size is set by the Collection View. The Size Inspector panel includes options to set these values.

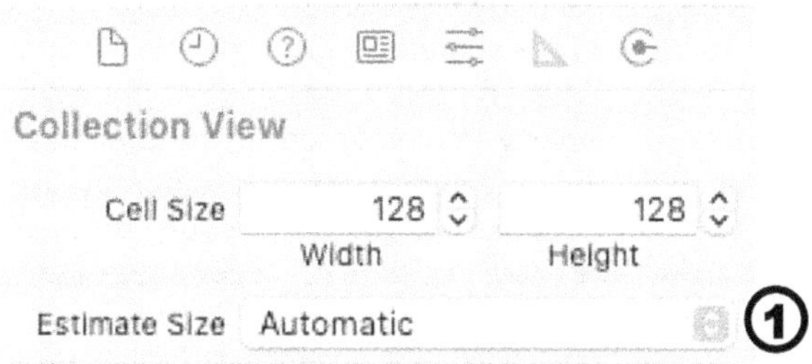

Figure 11-7: *Cell size*

Below the Cell Size option there is an option called Estimate Size (Figure 11-7, number 1). If the value of this option is Automatic or Custom, the cells are display with the size determined in this panel, but we can set the size from the layout by selecting the option None. When the size of the cells is not determined by the Collection View, we can set it from the layout object, as shown next.

```
override func viewDidLoad() {
   super.viewDidLoad()
   let layout = collectionView.collectionViewLayout as!
UICollectionViewFlowLayout
   layout.itemSize = CGSize(width: 100, height: 100)
   layout.sectionInset = UIEdgeInsets(top: 20, left: 20, bottom: 20,
right: 20)
   prepareDataSource()
   prepareSnapshot()
}
```

Listing 11-4: *Configuring Flow layout*

The layout object is stored in the **collectionViewLayout** property. This property returns a generic object of type **UICollectionViewLayout** that we need to cast to our subclass (in this case, **UICollectionViewFlowLayout**). The code in Listing 11-4 shows the changes we must introduce to the **viewDidLoad()** method of our example to get the layout object and modify its properties. In this case, we assign a **CGSize** value to the **itemSize** property to give the cells a size of 100x100 points and add a padding around them with the **sectionInset** property.

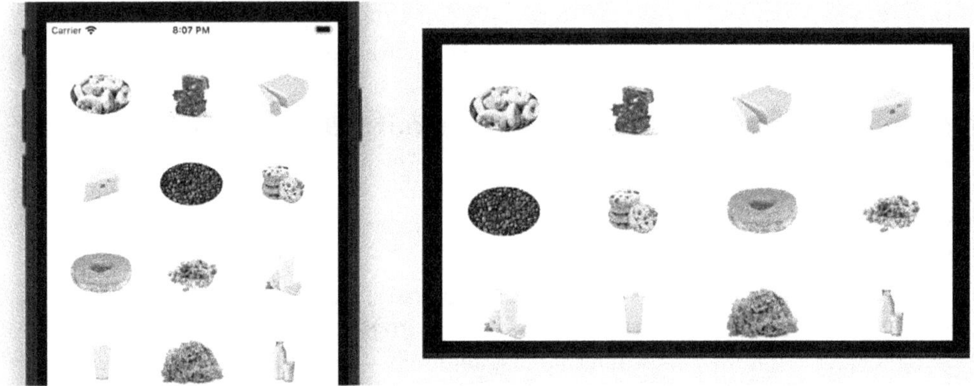

Figure 11-8: *Cells with custom size and margins*

Do It Yourself: Update the **viewDidLoad()** method in the **MyCollectionViewController** class with the code in Listing 11-4. Select the Collection View in the Storyboard, open the Size Inspector panel, and select the None option for the Estimate Size parameter (Figure 11-7, number 1). Run the application. You should see something like Figure 11-8.

The value of the **itemSize** property implemented in the previous example is assigned to every cell in the Collection View. If we want to assign a different size for each cell, we can conform to the **UICollectionViewDelegateFlowLayout** protocol and implement the **collectionView(UICollectionView, layout:, sizeForItemAt:)** method. From this method, we can return the size of each cell, as shown next.

```
import UIKit

class MyCollectionViewController: UICollectionViewController,
UICollectionViewDelegateFlowLayout {
   override func viewDidLoad() {
      super.viewDidLoad()
      collectionView.delegate = self
      prepareDataSource()
      prepareSnapshot()
   }
   func prepareDataSource() {
      let cellRegistration = UICollectionView.CellRegistration<FoodCell,
ItemsData.ID> { cell, indexPath, itemID in
         if let item = AppData.items.first(where: { $0.id == itemID }) {
            cell.picture.image = UIImage(named: item.image)
         }
      }
      AppData.dataSource = UICollectionViewDiffableDataSource<Sections,
ItemsData.ID>(collectionView: collectionView) { (collection, indexPath,
itemID) in
         return collection.dequeueConfiguredReusableCell(using:
cellRegistration, for: indexPath, item: itemID)
      }
   }
   func prepareSnapshot() {
      var snapshot = NSDiffableDataSourceSnapshot<Sections,
ItemsData.ID>()
      snapshot.appendSections([.main])
      snapshot.appendItems(AppData.items.map({ $0.id }))
      AppData.dataSource.apply(snapshot)
   }
   func collectionView(_ collectionView: UICollectionView, layout
collectionViewLayout: UICollectionViewLayout, sizeForItemAt indexPath:
IndexPath) -> CGSize {
      var width: CGFloat = 146
      var height: CGFloat = 100

      if indexPath.item % 3 == 0 {
         width = 292
         height = 200
      }
      return CGSize(width: width, height: height)
   }
}
```

Listing 11-5: *Declaring a specific size for each cell*

The layout object calls the protocol methods on the delegate assigned to the Collection View's **delegate** property, so we must designate our view controller as the delegate for these methods to be called. The Flow layout calls the **collectionView(UICollectionView, layout:, sizeForItemAt:)** method every time it needs to know the size of a cell to calculate the layout. In this example, we decided to assign a size of 146x100 points to every cell, except when the index of the cell is multiple of 3. When the remainder of the division of the index by 3 is equal to 0, we assign a size of 292x200 points. As a result, every three items, the cell is displayed in a larger size.

Figure 11-9: Cells of different size

Do It Yourself: Update the **`MyCollectionViewController`** class with the code in Listing 11-5 and run the application. You should see something like Figure 11-9.

Medium Custom Layout

With Flow layout, we can achieve many designs, but the number of cells displayed in a row or column is always determined by the layout according to the space available. Flow layout gets the dimensions of the Collection View, subtracts the margins and the space between cells, and then positions the cells that fit into the remaining space. If, for example, we set the **`minimumInteritemSpacing`** property to a value too big to fit two cells in the same row, Flow layout will show only one cell and move the second cell to a new row. The only way to make sure that the cells are organized the way we want, is to define a custom layout object.

Although we can create our own subclass of the **`UICollectionViewLayout`** class to define a custom layout, the framework includes a more flexible alternative called *Compositional Layouts*. Compositional layouts are defined by the **`UICollectionViewCompositionalLayout`** class and their main characteristic is that they can organize (compose) a layout from smaller parts. There are three main parts in a compositional layout: the item (a cell), the group (a group of cells), and the section (a subdivision of the layout that can include one or multiple groups). Figure 11-10, below, illustrates these parts in a simple layout.

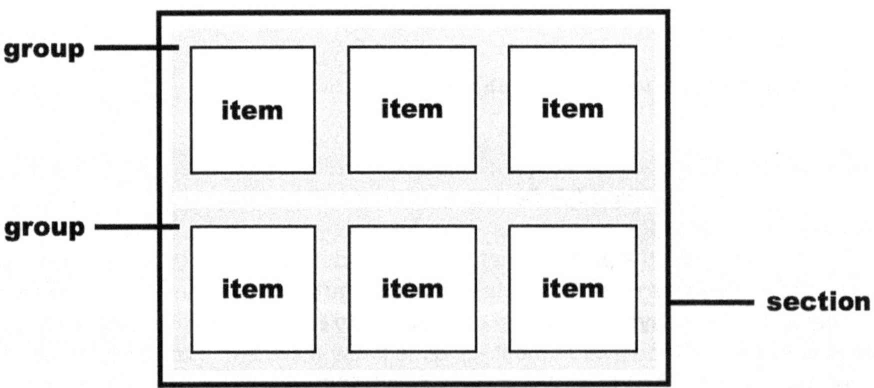

Figure 11-10: Compositional layout

The items are grouped horizontally or vertically, the groups repeat over and over again to show all the items available, and one or multiple sections can be used to present these groups. Each part is highly configurable and flexible, starting with the layout itself. The following are the initializers included in the **`UICollectionViewCompositionalLayout`** class to create the layout.

UICollectionViewCompositionalLayout(section: NSCollectionLayoutSection**)**—This initializer creates a compositional layout with the section specified by the argument.

UICollectionViewCompositionalLayout(section: NSCollectionLayoutSection, **configuration:** UICollectionViewCompositionalLayoutConfiguration**)**—This initializer creates a compositional layout with the section specified by the **section** argument and with the configuration specified by the **configuration** argument.

UICollectionViewCompositionalLayout(sectionProvider: Closure**)**—This initializer creates a compositional layout with the section returned by the closure specified by the **sectionProvider** argument.

UICollectionViewCompositionalLayout(sectionProvider: Closure, **configuration:** UICollectionViewCompositionalLayoutConfiguration**)**—This initializer creates a compositional layout with the section returned by the closure specified by the **sectionProvider** argument and with the configuration specified by the **configuration** argument.

The layout is configured with an object of the **`UICollectionViewCompositionalLayoutConfiguration`** class. The class includes the following properties to configure the layout.

interSectionSpacing—This property sets or returns a **`CGFloat`** value that determines the space between sections.

scrollDirection—This property sets or returns a value that determines the scrolling orientation. It is an enumeration of type **`ScrollDirection`** with the values **`vertical`** and **`horizontal`**.

Once we have the layout, we must define its parts. The items are defined by the **`NSCollectionLayoutItem`** class. The class includes the following initializers.

NSCollectionLayoutItem(layoutSize: NSCollectionLayoutSize**)**—This initializer creates an item of the size specified by the **layoutSize** argument.

NSCollectionLayoutItem(layoutSize: NSCollectionLayoutSize, **supplementaryItems:** [NSCollectionLayoutSupplementaryItem]**)**—This initializer creates an item of the size specified by the **layoutSize** argument for the supplementary views specified by the **supplementaryItems** argument.

The **`NSCollectionLayoutItem`** class also includes the following properties to configure the items.

contentInsets—This property sets or returns a structure of type **`NSDirectionalEdgeInsets`** with the insets for the content's left, right, top, and bottom sides. These values are defined from the structure's initializer (**`NSDirectionalEdgeInsets(top: CGFloat, leading: CGFloat, bottom: CGFloat, trailing: CGFloat)`**).

edgeSpacing—This property sets or returns an object of type **`NSCollectionLayoutEdgeSpacing`** that defines the space on the sides of the layout. The space is defined with an object of type **`NSCollectionLayoutSpacing`**, which includes the type methods **`fixed(CGFloat)`** for fixed values, and **`flexible(CGFloat)`** for flexible values. The values for each side are declared by the **`NSCollectionLayoutEdgeSpacing`** class' initializer (**`NSCollectionLayoutEdgeSpacing(leading: NSCollectionLayoutSpacing?, top: NSCollectionLayoutSpacing?, trailing: NSCollectionLayoutSpacing?, bottom: NSCollectionLayoutSpacing?)`**).

The items are organized in groups. The framework includes the **NSCollectionLayout-Group** class to create them. The class includes the following methods to define and configure a group.

horizontal(layoutSize: NSCollectionLayoutSize, **subitems:** [NSCollection-LayoutItem]**)**—This method returns a group with the items in horizontal order. The **layoutSize** argument determines the size of the group, and the **subitems** argument determines the type of items the group is going to contain. The number of items in the group is determined by the space available.

horizontal(layoutSize: NSCollectionLayoutSize, **subitem:** NSCollection-LayoutItem, **count:** Int**)**—This method returns a group with the items in horizontal order. The **layoutSize** argument determines the size of the group, the **subitem** argument determines the type of items the group is going to contain, and the **count** argument specifies how many.

vertical(layoutSize: NSCollectionLayoutSize, **subitems:** [NSCollection-LayoutItem]**)**—This method returns a group with the items in vertical order. The **layoutSize** argument determines the size of the group, and the **subitems** argument determines the type of items the group is going to contain. The number of items in the group is determined by the space available.

vertical(layoutSize: NSCollectionLayoutSize, **subitem:** NSCollection-LayoutItem, **count:** Int**)**—This method returns a group with the items in vertical order. The **layoutSize** argument determines the size of the group, the **subitem** argument determines the type of items the group is going to contain, and the **count** argument specifies how many.

custom(layoutSize: NSCollectionLayoutSize, **itemProvider:** Closure**)**—This method returns a group with the size determined by the **layoutSize** argument and the item returned by the closure assigned to the **itemProvider** argument.

The **NSCollectionLayoutGroup** class also includes a property to specify the space between items.

interItemSpacing—This property sets or returns an object of type **NSCollection-LayoutSpacing** to define the space between items. The class includes the methods **fixed(CGFloat)** for fixed values, and **flexible(CGFloat)** for flexible values.

Groups are the components of sections and sections are defined with the **NSCollectionLayoutSection** class. The class includes the following initializer.

NSCollectionLayoutSection(group: NSCollectionLayoutGroup**)**—This initializer creates a section with the type of groups specified by the **group** argument.

To configure the section, the **NSCollectionLayoutSection** class includes the following properties.

contentInsets—This property sets or returns a structure of type **NSDirectional-EdgeInsets** with the inset for the left, right, top and bottom sides of the section. These values are defined from the structure's initializer (**NSDirectionalEdgeInsets(top: CGFloat, leading: CGFloat, bottom: CGFloat, trailing: CGFloat)**).

interGroupSpacing—This property sets or returns a **CGFloat** value that determines the space between groups.

orthogonalScrollingBehavior—This property sets or returns a value that determines the section's scrolling behavior. When it is declared, the section scrolls perpendicular to the layout. It is an enumeration of type **UICollectionLayoutSectionOrthogonalScrollingBehavior** with the values **continuous**, **continuousGroupLeadingBoundary**, **groupPaging**, **groupPagingCentered**, **paging**, and **none**.

The size of items and groups is determined by objects of type **NSCollectionLayoutSize**. The class includes the following initializer.

NSCollectionLayoutSize(widthDimension: NSCollectionLayoutDimension, **heightDimension:** NSCollectionLayoutDimension**)**—This initializer creates an **NSCollectionLayoutSize** object with the dimensions determined by the arguments. The arguments are objects of type **NSCollectionLayoutDimension**. This class includes the type methods **absolute(CGFloat)** to provide absolute values, **estimated(CGFloat)** to provide a size estimate, **fractionalWidth(CGFloat)** to calculate the value from the width of the container, and **fractionalHeight(CGFloat)** to calculate the value from the height of the container. The fractional values are specified with numbers from 0.0 to 1.0.

It is time to see an example of how to compose a complex layout with all these tools. The process is simple, we must create a **UICollectionViewCompositionalLayout** object with a definition of the layout's items, groups, and sections, and assign it to the Collection View. In the following example, we create this object from a method and then call the method from **viewDidLoad()** to create the custom layout and assign it to the Collection View as soon as the scene is loaded.

```
import UIKit

class MyCollectionViewController: UICollectionViewController {
   override func viewDidLoad() {
      super.viewDidLoad()
      let customLayout = createLayout()
      collectionView.collectionViewLayout = customLayout
      prepareDataSource()
      prepareSnapshot()
   }
   func prepareDataSource() {
      let cellRegistration = UICollectionView.CellRegistration<FoodCell,
ItemsData.ID> { cell, indexPath, itemID in
         if let item = AppData.items.first(where: { $0.id == itemID }) {
            cell.picture.image = UIImage(named: item.image)
         }
      }
      AppData.dataSource = UICollectionViewDiffableDataSource<Sections,
ItemsData.ID>(collectionView: collectionView) { (collection, indexPath,
itemID) in
         return collection.dequeueConfiguredReusableCell(using:
cellRegistration, for: indexPath, item: itemID)
      }
   }
   func prepareSnapshot() {
      var snapshot = NSDiffableDataSourceSnapshot<Sections,
ItemsData.ID>()
      snapshot.appendSections([.main])
      snapshot.appendItems(AppData.items.map({ $0.id }))
      AppData.dataSource.apply(snapshot)
   }
```

```
    func createLayout() -> UICollectionViewCompositionalLayout {
        let itemSize =
NSCollectionLayoutSize(widthDimension: .fractionalWidth(0.5),
heightDimension: .fractionalWidth(0.5))
        let item = NSCollectionLayoutItem(layoutSize: itemSize)
        item.contentInsets = NSDirectionalEdgeInsets(top: 10, leading: 5,
bottom: 5, trailing: 10)

        let groupSize =
NSCollectionLayoutSize(widthDimension: .fractionalWidth(1),
heightDimension: .fractionalWidth(0.5))
        let group = NSCollectionLayoutGroup.horizontal(layoutSize:
groupSize, subitems: [item])

        let section = NSCollectionLayoutSection(group: group)

        let layout = UICollectionViewCompositionalLayout(section: section)
        return layout
    }
}
```

Listing 11-6: *Assigning a compositional layout to the Collection View*

The process to define a compositional layout is declarative. We define the object that configures the items, then the object that configures the groups, then the object that configures the sections, and finally the layout object that contains the sections. In the **createLayout()** method of Listing 11-6, we begin by defining the size of the items. To adapt the items to the space available, we use fractional values. The width dimension was declared as half the width of the container, and we do the same for the height. This means that the system is going to get the width of the group, divide it by half (width * 0.5), and assign the result to the item's width and height. For instance, if the screen has a width of 320 points and the group is declared of the same size, the items are going to have a size of 160 by 160 points (320 * 0.5). With this size, we instantiate the **NSCollectionLayoutItem** object and then assign a new value to the **contentInsets** property to separate the items from each other and the edges of the container.

With the items configured, we proceed to define the group that is going to contain those items. First, the size of the group is declared with fractional values. This time, we assign a width that is 100% the size of the group's container (**fractionalWidth(1)**) and a height that is half the width. Again, if the screen is 320 points wide, the group is going to have a width of 320 points and a height of 160. Next, we use the **horizontal()** type method to create the group using the size we just calculated and an array with the **NSCollectionLayoutItem** object defined before. This asks the layout to align the items in the group horizontally and fit as many as possible. Finally, the section is defined with this group and the layout is defined with that section.

This example creates a simple layout, like the one built with a Flow layout before, but with the difference that the size of the items is determined by the space available. The layout organizes the items in one section and one group, and because the size of each item was specified as half the width of the container, only two are included per group, no matter the space available.

Figure 11-11: *Compositional layout*

Do It Yourself: Update the `MyCollectionViewController` class with the code in Listing 11-6. Run the application and rotate the device. You should see the cells adapting to the space available, as illustrated in Figure 11-11.

Designing the perfect layout for our application is easy with a compositional layout. For instance, we can include five columns of items by assigning a fractional size of 0.2 to the items.

```
func createLayout() -> UICollectionViewLayout {
   let itemSize =
NSCollectionLayoutSize(widthDimension: .fractionalWidth(0.2),
heightDimension: .fractionalWidth(0.2))
   let item = NSCollectionLayoutItem(layoutSize: itemSize)
   item.contentInsets = NSDirectionalEdgeInsets(top: 10, leading: 5,
bottom: 5, trailing: 10)

   let groupSize =
NSCollectionLayoutSize(widthDimension: .fractionalWidth(1),
heightDimension: .fractionalWidth(0.2))
   let group = NSCollectionLayoutGroup.horizontal(layoutSize: groupSize,
subitems: [item])

   let section = NSCollectionLayoutSection(group: group)

   let layout = UICollectionViewCompositionalLayout(section: section)
   return layout
}
```

Listing 11-7: *Customizing a compositional layout*

In this example, the width and height of the items were declared as 20% the width of the container, which means that a total of five items will fit in a group. Notice that the height of the group was defined as 20% of the width of the container, so it matches the size of the items.

Figure 11-12: *Compositional layout with five columns*

Basic Supplementary Views

Besides cells, Collection Views use other views to include additional content such as headers and footers. These views are called *Supplementary Views* and are managed by the layout object. For instance, the Flow layout includes two supplementary views, one for the header and another for the footer of every section.

As well as cells, supplementary views are reusable; they are created from prototype views. The **UICollectionView** class defines the **SupplementaryRegistration** structure to register these views. The structure includes the following initializer.

SupplementaryRegistration(elementKind: String, **handler:** Closure**)**—This initializer registers and configures a prototype view. The **elementKind** argument is an identifier that determines the type of view to create (header, footer, etc.), and the **handler** argument is a closure that is called every time a supplementary view is required. The closure receives three values: a reference to the view, the view's identifier, and the index path with the location.

Although we can use whatever value we want to identify the view, the **`UICollectionView`** class includes the following type properties with predefined identifiers for headers and footers.

elementKindSectionHeader—This property returns a string to identify a header.

elementKindSectionFooter—This property returns a string to identify a footer.

Once the prototype view is created, we must create the supplementary views from it and provide them to the Collection View. The **`UICollectionViewDiffableDataSource`** includes the following property for this purpose.

supplementaryViewProvider—This property sets a closure that the Collection View executes to get the supplementary views (e.g., headers and footers). The closure receives three values: a reference to the Collection View, a string that describes the type of view required, and the index path with the location of the view.

The closure assigned to the **`supplementaryViewProvider`** property must create the supplementary view from a prototype and return it. The **`UICollectionView`** class includes the following method for this purpose.

dequeueConfiguredReusableSupplementary (using: Supplementary-Registration, **for:** IndexPath**)**—This method returns a supplementary view with the configuration defined by the **`SupplementaryRegistration`** structure specified by the **using** argument. The **for** argument indicates the view's location.

The **`SupplementaryRegistration`** structure is generic, which means it needs to know the data type of the view is going to use to create the prototype views. UIKit defines the **`UICollectionReusableView`** class to create these views. The process is the same we have used before for custom cells in Table Views. We must define the properties to reference the elements in the view and then create those elements when the view is initialized. The following example defines a reusable view with a background image and a label at the center.

```
import UIKit

class MyHeader: UICollectionReusableView {
   var pictureView = UIImageView()
   var textView = UILabel()

   override init(frame: CGRect) {
      super.init(frame: frame)
      pictureView.translatesAutoresizingMaskIntoConstraints = false
      pictureView.contentMode = .scaleToFill
      self.addSubview(pictureView)

      pictureView.topAnchor.constraint(equalTo: self.topAnchor).isActive
= true
      pictureView.bottomAnchor.constraint(equalTo:
self.bottomAnchor).isActive = true
      pictureView.leadingAnchor.constraint(equalTo:
self.leadingAnchor).isActive = true
      pictureView.trailingAnchor.constraint(equalTo:
self.trailingAnchor).isActive = true
```

```
      textView.translatesAutoresizingMaskIntoConstraints = false
      textView.font = UIFont.preferredFont(forTextStyle: .title1)
      self.addSubview(textView)

      textView.centerXAnchor.constraint(equalTo:
self.centerXAnchor).isActive = true
      textView.centerYAnchor.constraint(equalTo:
self.centerYAnchor).isActive = true
   }
   required init?(coder: NSCoder) {
      fatalError("Error")
   }
}
```

Listing 11-8: *Defining a reusable view*

Once we have our view class, we can register the prototype and create the supplementary views. The following are the changes we need to introduce to our **prepareDataSource()** method.

```
func prepareDataSource() {
   let cellRegistration = UICollectionView.CellRegistration<FoodCell,
ItemsData.ID> { cell, indexPath, itemID in
      if let item = AppData.items.first(where: { $0.id == itemID }) {
         cell.picture.image = UIImage(named: item.image)
      }
   }
   AppData.dataSource = UICollectionViewDiffableDataSource<Sections,
ItemsData.ID>(collectionView: collectionView) { (collection, indexPath,
itemID) in
      return collection.dequeueConfiguredReusableCell(using:
cellRegistration, for: indexPath, item: itemID)
   }
   let headerRegistration =
UICollectionView.SupplementaryRegistration<MyHeader>(elementKind:
UICollectionView.elementKindSectionHeader) { headerView, kind, indexPath
in
      headerView.pictureView.image = UIImage(named: "gradientTop")
      headerView.textView.text = "My Food"
   }
   AppData.dataSource.supplementaryViewProvider = { view, kind, indexPath
in
      return
self.collectionView.dequeueConfiguredReusableSupplementary(using:
headerRegistration, for: indexPath)
   }
}
```

Listing 11-9: *Defining the supplementary views*

After the cells are defined as always, we create a **SupplementaryRegistration** structure using our view's data type (**MyHeader**). In the closure, we initialize the properties of the view with a background image called gradientTop (available on our website) and the title "My Food".

Creating supplementary views from this prototype is simple. We just have to assign a closure to the **supplementaryViewProvider** property of the diffable data source, call the **dequeueConfiguredReusableSupplementary()** method with the registration structure, and return the view produced by it, as we did for cells before.

This creates the views, but they are not included in the Collection View. This is the responsibility of the layout object. For instance, Compositional layout works with **NSCollectionLayoutBoundarySupplementaryItem** objects to define headers and footers. The class includes the following initializer.

NSCollectionLayoutBoundarySupplementaryItem(layoutSize: NSCollectionLayoutSize, **elementKind:** String, **alignment:** NSRectAlignment**)**—This initializer creates a layout item called *boundary supplementary item* that is used to add headers and footers to a section. The **layoutSize** argument determines the size of the view, the **elementKind** argument is the identifier we used to create the view, and the **alignment** argument determines the position of the view in relation to the section. It is an enumeration with the values **top**, **topLeading**, **leading**, **bottomLeading**, **bottom**, **bottomTrailing**, **trailing**, **topTrailing**, and **none**.

Once the boundary supplementary item is created, we must assign it to the section. The **NSCollectionLayoutSection** class includes the following property for this purpose.

boundarySupplementaryItems—This property sets or returns an array of **NSCollectionLayoutBoundarySupplementaryItem** objects that represent the supplementary items associated with the section.

The following are the changes we need to introduce to the compositional layout of our example to add the header to the Collection View.

```
func createLayout() -> UICollectionViewLayout {
   let itemSize =
NSCollectionLayoutSize(widthDimension: .fractionalWidth(0.5),
heightDimension: .fractionalWidth(0.5))
   let item = NSCollectionLayoutItem(layoutSize: itemSize)
   item.contentInsets = NSDirectionalEdgeInsets(top: 10, leading: 5,
bottom: 5, trailing: 10)

   let groupSize =
NSCollectionLayoutSize(widthDimension: .fractionalWidth(1),
heightDimension: .fractionalWidth(0.5))
   let group = NSCollectionLayoutGroup.horizontal(layoutSize: groupSize,
subitems: [item])

   let section = NSCollectionLayoutSection(group: group)
   let headerSize =
NSCollectionLayoutSize(widthDimension: .fractionalWidth(1.0),
heightDimension: .absolute(60))
   let sectionHeader =
NSCollectionLayoutBoundarySupplementaryItem(layoutSize: headerSize,
elementKind: UICollectionView.elementKindSectionHeader, alignment: .top)
   section.boundarySupplementaryItems = [sectionHeader]

   let layout = UICollectionViewCompositionalLayout(section: section)
   return layout
}
```

Listing 11-10: *Adding supplementary views to a compositional layout*

In this example, we define a **NSCollectionLayoutSize** object with a flexible width and a height of 45 points. The boundary supplementary item is created next with this value and the "Header" identifier (this is the same identifier we used to create the view before). Notice that the layout doesn't know whether we are adding a header or a footer, so we specify the **top** value for the **alignment** argument to show the view at the top of the section. Finally, the item is assigned to the section and shown on the screen.

***Figure 11-13:** Collection View header*

Do It Yourself: Create a file with a subclass of **UICollectionReusableView** called **MyHeader**. Complete the class with the code in Listing 11-8. Update the **prepareDataSource()** method in the **MyCollectionViewController** class with the code in Listing 11-9 and the **createLayout()** method with the code in Listing 11-10. Download the image gradientTop from our website and add it to the Assets Catalog. Run the application. You should see the header of Figure 11-13.

Basic Sections

Collection Views may organize the information in sections. The sections must be defined in the model and then the snapshot must be created from these values, as we did with Table Views. There are just a few changes we must introduce in our example to work with more than one section. For the model, we can use the one defined in Chapter 10 for Table Views (see Listing 10-36). As always, we must define the **dataSource** property with the **UICollectionView-DiffableDataSource** class, but the rest of the code remains the same.

In the view controller, the changes are minor. The diffable data source now has to work with section IDs (Section.ID), and the supplementary view for the header must display the section's name instead of a predefined string, as shown next.

```
func prepareDataSource() {
   let cellRegistration = UICollectionView.CellRegistration<FoodCell,
ItemsData.ID> { cell, indexPath, itemID in
      if let item = AppData.items.first(where: { $0.id == itemID }) {
         cell.picture.image = UIImage(named: item.image)
      }
   }
   AppData.dataSource = UICollectionViewDiffableDataSource<Sections.ID,
ItemsData.ID>(collectionView: collectionView) { (collection, indexPath,
itemID) in
      return collection.dequeueConfiguredReusableCell(using:
cellRegistration, for: indexPath, item: itemID)
   }
   let headerRegistration =
UICollectionView.SupplementaryRegistration<MyHeader>(elementKind:
UICollectionView.elementKindSectionHeader) { headerView, kind, indexPath
in
      headerView.pictureView.image = UIImage(named: "gradientTop")
      headerView.textView.text = AppData.sections[indexPath.section].name
   }
   AppData.dataSource.supplementaryViewProvider = { view, kind, indexPath
in
```

```
        return self.collectionView.dequeueConfiguredReusable-
Supplementary(using: headerRegistration, for: indexPath)
    }
}
```

Listing 11-11: *Working with multiple sections*

The snapshot is the same we used for Table Views. The following is the **prepareSnapshot()** method for this example.

```
func prepareSnapshot() {
    var snapshot = NSDiffableDataSourceSnapshot<Sections.ID,
ItemsData.ID>()
    snapshot.appendSections(AppData.sections.map({ $0.id }))
    for section in AppData.sections {
        let itemIDs = AppData.items.compactMap({ value in
            return value.section == section.name ? value.id : nil
        })
        snapshot.appendItems(itemIDs, toSection: section.id)
    }
    AppData.dataSource.apply(snapshot)
}
```

Listing 11-12: *Snapshot for multiple sections*

Because the **SupplementaryRegistration** structure defines the content of the header views, no changes are required for the layout and therefore the rest of the code remains the same. The result is shown below.

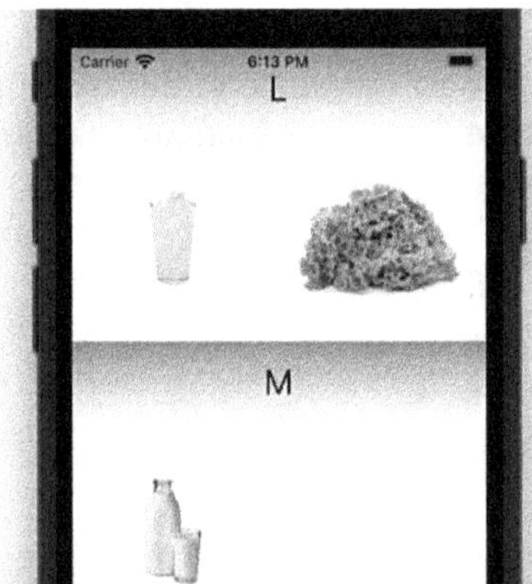

Figure 11-14: *Sections with headers*

Do It Yourself: Update the ApplicationData.swift file with the model in Chapter 10, Listing 10-36. Define the **dataSource** property in the model with the **UICollectionViewDiffableDataSource** class (**var dataSource: UICollectionViewDiffableDataSource<Sections.ID, Items-Data.ID>!**). Update the **prepareDataSource()** and **prepareSnapshot()** methods in your view controller with the codes in Listing 11-11 and 11-12. Run the application. You should see something like Figure 11-14.

The information included in the sections of our example belong to the same topic. In this case, all items represent food. But Collection Views can work with information provided by multiple sources or with different characteristics. For instance, a Collection View may include two sections, one to show the items available and another to display those selected by the user. In cases like this, it may be useful to create a snapshot for each section. The framework provides the **NSDiffableDataSourceSectionSnapshot** class for this purpose. As a normal snapshot, the class includes all the properties and methods required to add and remove items, but also some that are specific to section snapshots. The following are the most frequently used.

items—This property returns an array with the identifiers of the items in the section.

rootItems—This property returns an array with the identifiers of the items at the top of the snapshot's hierarchy.

append([ItemIdentifierType], **to:** ItemIdentifierType?**)**—This method adds the items specified by the first argument to the section specified by the **to** argument.

contains(ItemIdentifierType**)**—This method returns a Boolean value that determines whether the item specified by the argument is included in the section.

expand([ItemIdentifierType]**)**—This method expands the section to show the items specified by the argument.

collapse([ItemIdentifierType]**)**—This method collapses the section to hide the items specified by the argument.

isExpanded(ItemIdentifierType**)**—This method returns a Boolean value to indicate whether the item specified by the argument is in the expanded state.

As we will see in the next section of this chapter, section snapshots are frequently used to create hierarchical lists, but they are also useful when the information of each section is unique. For example, the following model defines two sections, one for the items selected by the user and another for the items that are still available to select.

```
import UIKit

enum Sections {
   case selected, available
}
class ItemsData: Identifiable {
   var id: UUID = UUID()
   var name: String
   var image: String
   var calories: Int
   var selected: Bool

   init(_ name: String, _ image: String, _ calories: Int, _ selected:
Bool) {
      self.name = name
      self.image = image
      self.calories = calories
      self.selected = selected
   }
}
struct ApplicationData {
   var dataSource: UICollectionViewDiffableDataSource<Sections,
ItemsData.ID>!
   var items: [ItemsData] = [] {
      didSet {
         items.sort(by: { $0.name < $1.name })
      }
   }
   init() {
      items.append(contentsOf: [ItemsData("Bagels", "bagels", 250,
false), ItemsData("Brownies", "brownies", 466, false),
ItemsData("Butter", "butter", 717, false), ItemsData("Cheese", "cheese",
402, false), ItemsData("Coffee", "coffee", 0, false),
ItemsData("Cookies", "cookies", 502, false), ItemsData("Donuts",
"donuts", 452, false), ItemsData("Granola", "granola", 471, false),
ItemsData("Juice", "juice", 23, false), ItemsData("Lemonade", "lemonade",
```

```
40, false), ItemsData("Lettuce", "lettuce", 15, false), ItemsData("Milk",
"milk", 42, false), ItemsData("Oatmeal", "oatmeal", 68, false),
ItemsData("Potatoes", "potato", 77, false), ItemsData("Tomatoes",
"tomato", 18, false), ItemsData("Yogurt", "yogurt", 59, false)])
   }
}
var AppData = ApplicationData()
```

Listing 11-13: *Defining a model to test section snapshots*

The sections are identified by the **Sections** enumeration. The enumeration includes two values: **selected**, for the selected items, and **available**, for the items available to select. The diffable data source is defined with this data type, but the rest of the code in the model is the same as before.

In the view controller, we need to create two section snapshots and then update their content when an item is selected by the user, as shown next.

```
import UIKit

class MyCollectionViewController: UICollectionViewController {
   override func viewDidLoad() {
      super.viewDidLoad()
      let customLayout = createLayout()
      collectionView.collectionViewLayout = customLayout
      prepareDataSource()
      prepareSnapshot()
   }
   func prepareDataSource() {
      let cellRegistration = UICollectionView.CellRegistration<FoodCell,
ItemsData.ID> { cell, indexPath, itemID in
         if let item = AppData.items.first(where: { $0.id == itemID }) {
            cell.picture.image = UIImage(named: item.image)
         }
      }
      AppData.dataSource = UICollectionViewDiffableDataSource<Sections,
ItemsData.ID>(collectionView: collectionView) { (collection, indexPath,
itemID) in
         return collection.dequeueConfiguredReusableCell(using:
cellRegistration, for: indexPath, item: itemID)
      }
      let headerRegistration =
UICollectionView.SupplementaryRegistration<MyHeader>(elementKind:
UICollectionView.elementKindSectionHeader) { headerView, kind, indexPath
in
         if let sectionID = AppData.dataSource.sectionIdentifier(for:
indexPath.section) {
            headerView.pictureView.image = UIImage(named: "gradientTop")
            headerView.textView.text = sectionID == .selected ?
"Selected" : "Available"
         }
      }
      AppData.dataSource.supplementaryViewProvider = { view, kind,
indexPath in
         return
self.collectionView.dequeueConfiguredReusableSupplementary(using:
headerRegistration, for: indexPath)
      }
   }
   func prepareSnapshot() {
      var snapshot = NSDiffableDataSourceSnapshot<Sections,
ItemsData.ID>()
      snapshot.appendSections([.selected, .available])
      AppData.dataSource.apply(snapshot, animatingDifferences: true)
```

```
      let selectedIDs = AppData.items.compactMap({ value in
         return value.selected ? value.id : nil
      })
      var selectedSnapshot =
NSDiffableDataSourceSectionSnapshot<ItemsData.ID>()
      selectedSnapshot.append(selectedIDs)
      AppData.dataSource.apply(selectedSnapshot, to: .selected,
animatingDifferences: false)

      let availableIDs = AppData.items.compactMap({ value in
         return value.selected ? nil : value.id
      })
      var availableSnapshot =
NSDiffableDataSourceSectionSnapshot<ItemsData.ID>()
      availableSnapshot.append(availableIDs)
      AppData.dataSource.apply(availableSnapshot, to: .available,
animatingDifferences: false)
   }
   func createLayout() -> UICollectionViewLayout {
      let itemSize =
NSCollectionLayoutSize(widthDimension: .fractionalWidth(0.33),
heightDimension: .fractionalWidth(0.33))
      let item = NSCollectionLayoutItem(layoutSize: itemSize)

      let groupSize =
NSCollectionLayoutSize(widthDimension: .fractionalWidth(1),
heightDimension: .fractionalWidth(0.33))
      let group = NSCollectionLayoutGroup.horizontal(layoutSize:
groupSize, subitems: [item])

      let section = NSCollectionLayoutSection(group: group)
      let headerSize =
NSCollectionLayoutSize(widthDimension: .fractionalWidth(1.0),
heightDimension: .absolute(60))
      let sectionHeader =
NSCollectionLayoutBoundarySupplementaryItem(layoutSize: headerSize,
elementKind: UICollectionView.elementKindSectionHeader, alignment: .top)
      section.boundarySupplementaryItems = [sectionHeader]

      let layout = UICollectionViewCompositionalLayout(section: section)
      return layout
   }
   override func collectionView(_ collectionView: UICollectionView,
didSelectItemAt indexPath: IndexPath) {
      if let itemID = AppData.dataSource.itemIdentifier(for: indexPath) {
         if let item = AppData.items.first(where: { $0.id == itemID }) {
            if item.selected {
               var selectedSnapshot =
AppData.dataSource.snapshot(for: .selected)
               selectedSnapshot.delete([itemID])
               AppData.dataSource.apply(selectedSnapshot, to: .selected,
animatingDifferences: true)
               item.selected = false

               let availableIDs = AppData.items.compactMap({ value in
                  return value.selected ? nil : value.id
               })
               var availableSnapshot =
NSDiffableDataSourceSectionSnapshot<ItemsData.ID>()
               availableSnapshot.append(availableIDs)
               AppData.dataSource.apply(availableSnapshot,
to: .available, animatingDifferences: false)
            } else {
               var availableSnapshot =
AppData.dataSource.snapshot(for: .available)
```

```
                availableSnapshot.delete([itemID])
                AppData.dataSource.apply(availableSnapshot,
to: .available, animatingDifferences: true)
                item.selected = true

                let selectedIDs = AppData.items.compactMap({ value in
                   return value.selected ? value.id : nil
                })
                var selectedSnapshot =
NSDiffableDataSourceSectionSnapshot<ItemsData.ID>()
                selectedSnapshot.append(selectedIDs)
                AppData.dataSource.apply(selectedSnapshot, to: .selected,
animatingDifferences: false)
            }
         }
      }
   }
}
```

Listing 11-14: *Moving items between section snapshots*

There are only a few changes in this view controller from the previous one. First, we modify the diffable data source to work with **Sections** values. Another small change is in the registration of the header view. Depending on the section identifier, we display the string "Selected" or "Available". The big changes are in the **prepareSnapshot()** method. A normal snapshot is defined first to manage the two sections. After this snapshot is applied, we filter the items and create two section snapshots, one with the list of selected items and another with the unselected items.

To let the user select or deselect an item, we implement the **collection-View(UICollectionView, didSelectItemAt:)** method defined by the **UICollection-ViewDelegate** protocol, which is called every time the user taps on a cell. In this method, we perform two operations, depending on whether the item was previously selected (the value of the item's **selected** property is **true**). First, we delete the item from the current section and then create a new snapshot to update the other section (If the item is selected, we remove it from the **selected** section and update the **available** section, or vice versa).

Now we have two sections that manage different information.

Figure 11-15: *Section snapshots*

Do It Yourself: Update the ApplicationData.swift file with the code in Listing 11-13 and the **MyCollectionViewController** class with the code in Listing 11-14. Run the application and select an item. You should see the item moving to the Selected section.

Basic 11.3 Lists

Collection Views can also display the items as a one-column list, in a format that emulates Table Views. The difference with Table Views is that Collection View Lists are more versatile and better optimized. In fact, Apple recommends implementing a Collection View List instead of a Table View when possible. The **UICollectionViewCompositionalLayout** class includes the following type method to produce a compositional layout that organizes the views in a list.

list(using: UICollectionLayoutListConfiguration**)**—This type method creates a compositional layout that displays the views on a list. The **using** argument is a structure that defines the style for the list.

Like Table Views, a Collection View List can have different styles or appearances. This configuration is determined by a **UICollectionLayoutListConfiguration** structure.

UICollectionLayoutListConfiguration(appearance: Appearance**)**—This initializer creates a configuration structure to define the appearance of the list. The **appearance** argument is an enumeration with the values **plain**, **grouped**, **insetGrouped**, **sidebar**, and **sidebarPlain**.

To create the cells, the framework includes the **UICollectionViewListCell** class. The class implements the **defaultContentConfiguration()** method to configure the content and the following properties for the accessories and layout.

accessories—This property sets or returns an array of **UICellAccessory** structures that represent the accessories to show in the cell.

indentationLevel—This property sets or returns an integer value that determines the level of indentation for the cell.

indentationWidth—This property sets or returns a **CGFloat** value with the width of an indentation level.

indentsAccessories—This property sets or returns a Boolean value that determines whether the cell indents accessories on the leading edge.

To turn a Collection View into a list, we must get the List Layout with the **list()** method, assign it to the Collection View, register a **UICollectionViewListCell**, and configure the cell as we did before for Table Views.

```
import UIKit

class MyCollectionViewController: UICollectionViewController {
   override func viewDidLoad() {
      super.viewDidLoad()
      let config =
UICollectionLayoutListConfiguration(appearance: .grouped)
      let layout = UICollectionViewCompositionalLayout.list(using:
config)
      collectionView.collectionViewLayout = layout

      prepareDataSource()
      prepareSnapshot()
   }
   func prepareDataSource() {
      let cellRegistration =
UICollectionView.CellRegistration<UICollectionViewListCell, ItemsData.ID>
{ cell, indexPath, itemID in
```

```
        if let item = AppData.items.first(where: { $0.id == itemID }) {
            var config = cell.defaultContentConfiguration()
            config.text = item.name
            config.secondaryText = "Calories: \(item.calories)"
            config.image = UIImage(named: item.image)
            config.imageProperties.maximumSize = CGSize(width: 60,
height: 60)
            cell.contentConfiguration = config
        }
    }
    AppData.dataSource =
UICollectionViewDiffableDataSource<Sections.ID,
ItemsData.ID>(collectionView: collectionView) { (collection, indexPath,
itemID) in
        return collection.dequeueConfiguredReusableCell(using:
cellRegistration, for: indexPath, item: itemID)
    }
  }
  func prepareSnapshot() {
    var snapshot = NSDiffableDataSourceSnapshot<Sections.ID,
ItemsData.ID>()
    snapshot.appendSections(AppData.sections.map({ $0.id }))
    for section in AppData.sections {
        let itemIDs = AppData.items.compactMap({ value in
            return value.section == section.name ? value.id : nil
        })
        snapshot.appendItems(itemIDs, toSection: section.id)
    }
    AppData.dataSource.apply(snapshot)
  }
}
```

Listing 11-15: *Creating a Collection View List*

This view controller creates a configuration structure with the **grouped** appearance, gets the layout with this value, and assigns it to the Collection View. The rest of the code is very similar to previous examples, especially those designed for Table Views. The result is shown below.

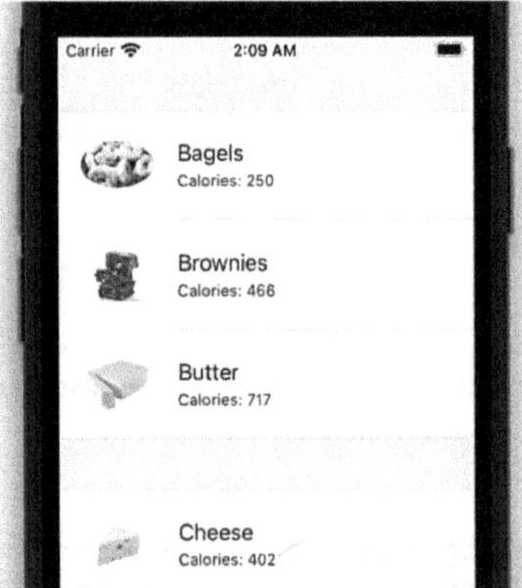

Figure 11-16: *Collection View List*

Do It Yourself: Create a new project. Replace the initial scene with a Collection View Controller. Create a subclass of **UICollectionViewController** called **MyCollectionViewController** and assign it to the scene. Update the class with the code in Listing 11-15. Create a Swift file called ApplicationData.swift for the model in Chapter 10, Listing 10-36. Remember to update the **dataSource** property to work with the diffable data source for Collection Views (**var dataSource: UICollectionViewDiffableDataSource<Sections.ID, ItemsData.ID>!**). Add the thumbnails to the Assets Catalog. Run the application. You should see the interface in Figure 11-16.

Headers and footers are still added to the Collection View by the diffable data source, but now the layout configuration must specify the type of header or footer we want to use. The **UICollectionLayoutListConfiguration** class includes the following properties for this purpose.

headerMode—This property sets or returns an enumeration value that determines the type of header to use for the list. The values available are **none**, **supplementary**, and **firstItemInSection**.

footerMode—This property sets or returns an enumeration value that determines the type of footer to use for the list. The values available are **none** and **supplementary**.

As always, we need a **UICollectionReusableView** subclass to design the header. The following example includes a label with a **headline** style at the center of the view.

```
import UIKit

class MyHeader: UICollectionReusableView {
   var textView = UILabel()

   override init(frame: CGRect) {
      super.init(frame: frame)
      textView.translatesAutoresizingMaskIntoConstraints = false
      textView.font = UIFont.preferredFont(forTextStyle: .headline)
      self.addSubview(textView)

      textView.centerXAnchor.constraint(equalTo:
self.centerXAnchor).isActive = true
      textView.topAnchor.constraint(equalTo: self.topAnchor, constant:
16).isActive = true
      textView.bottomAnchor.constraint(equalTo: self.bottomAnchor,
constant: -16).isActive = true
   }
   required init?(coder: NSCoder) {
      fatalError("Error")
   }
}
```

Listing 11-16: *Defining the header for a list*

Although we must explicitly declare in the layout configuration structure that we are working with supplementary views, the process for registering and creating these views remain the same.

```
import UIKit

class MyCollectionViewController: UICollectionViewController {
   override func viewDidLoad() {
      super.viewDidLoad()
      var config =
UICollectionLayoutListConfiguration(appearance: .grouped)
      config.headerMode = .supplementary
      let layout = UICollectionViewCompositionalLayout.list(using:
config)
      collectionView.collectionViewLayout = layout

      prepareDataSource()
      prepareSnapshot()
   }
```

```
    func prepareDataSource() {
        let cellRegistration =
UICollectionView.CellRegistration<UICollectionViewListCell, ItemsData.ID>
{ cell, indexPath, itemID in
            if let item = AppData.items.first(where: { $0.id == itemID }) {
                var config = cell.defaultContentConfiguration()
                config.text = item.name
                config.secondaryText = "Calories: \(item.calories)"
                config.image = UIImage(named: item.image)
                config.imageProperties.maximumSize = CGSize(width: 60,
height: 60)
                cell.contentConfiguration = config
            }
        }
        AppData.dataSource =
UICollectionViewDiffableDataSource<Sections.ID,
ItemsData.ID>(collectionView: collectionView) { (collection, indexPath,
itemID) in
            return collection.dequeueConfiguredReusableCell(using:
cellRegistration, for: indexPath, item: itemID)
        }
        let headerRegistration =
UICollectionView.SupplementaryRegistration<MyHeader>(elementKind:
UICollectionView.elementKindSectionHeader) { headerView, kind, indexPath
in
            headerView.textView.text =
AppData.sections[indexPath.section].name
        }
        AppData.dataSource.supplementaryViewProvider = { view, kind,
indexPath in
            return
self.collectionView.dequeueConfiguredReusableSupplementary(using:
headerRegistration, for: indexPath)
        }
    }
    func prepareSnapshot() {
        var snapshot = NSDiffableDataSourceSnapshot<Sections.ID,
ItemsData.ID>()
        snapshot.appendSections(AppData.sections.map({ $0.id }))
        for section in AppData.sections {
            let itemIDs = AppData.items.compactMap({ value in
                return value.section == section.name ? value.id : nil
            })
            snapshot.appendItems(itemIDs, toSection: section.id)
        }
        AppData.dataSource.apply(snapshot)
    }
}
```

***Listing 11-17:** Adding supplementary views to the list*

Do It Yourself: Create a file with a subclass of **UICollectionReusableView** called **MyHeader**. Complete the class with the code in Listing 11-16. Update the **MyCollectionViewController** class with the code in Listing 11-17. Run the application. You should see the headers with the title of each section.

Another aspect of the list we can configure are the separators (the lines between cells). The **UICollectionLayoutListConfiguration** structure includes the following properties for this purpose.

showsSeparators—This property sets or returns a Boolean value that determines whether the separators are displayed or not.

separatorConfiguration—This property sets or returns a value that defines the configuration for the separators. It is a structure of type **`UIListSeparatorConfiguration`**.

itemSeparatorHandler—This property sets or returns a closure that is executed to get the configuration for the separator of each item.

The configuration is defined by the **`UIListSeparatorConfiguration`** structure. The following are some of its properties.

color—This property sets or returns a **`UIColor`** value with the separator's color.

topSeparatorVisibility—This property sets or returns a value that determines whether the separator at the top of the cell is visible or not. It is a **`Visibility`** enumeration with the values **`automatic`**, **`hidden`**, and **`visible`**.

bottomSeparatorVisibility—This property sets or returns a value that determines whether the separator at the bottom of the cell is visible or not. It is a **`Visibility`** enumeration with the values **`automatic`**, **`hidden`**, and **`visible`**.

topSeparatorInsets—This property sets or returns an **`NSDirectionalEdgeInsets`** value that defines the padding around the separator at the top of the cell.

bottomSeparatorInsets—This property sets or returns an **`NSDirectionalEdgeInsets`** value that defines the padding around the separator at the bottom of the cell.

A list displays lines between the cells, but also at the top and bottom of each section. We can modify this behavior from the closure assigned to the **`itemSeparatorHandler`** property. In the following example, we change the color of the separators to red and then remove the separators at the top and bottom of each section.

```
override func viewDidLoad() {
   super.viewDidLoad()
   var config = UICollectionLayoutListConfiguration(appearance: .grouped)
   config.headerMode = .supplementary
   config.separatorConfiguration.color = .systemRed

   config.itemSeparatorHandler = { indexPath, config in
      let row = indexPath.item
      let section = indexPath.section

      var lastRow = 0
      if let sectionID = AppData.dataSource.sectionIdentifier(for:
section) {
         lastRow = AppData.dataSource.snapshot().numberOfItems(inSection:
sectionID)
         lastRow = lastRow > 0 ? lastRow - 1 : 0
      }
      var configuration = config
      configuration.topSeparatorVisibility = row ==
0 ? .hidden : .automatic
      configuration.bottomSeparatorVisibility = row ==
lastRow ? .hidden : .automatic
      return configuration
   }
   let layout = UICollectionViewCompositionalLayout.list(using: config)
   collectionView.collectionViewLayout = layout

   prepareDataSource()
   prepareSnapshot()
}
```

Listing 11-18: *Configuring cell's separators*

The code in Listing 11-18 assigns a closure to the **itemSeparatorHandler** property to configure the separators cell by cell. To know if the current cell is the first one in the section, we just read the index and hide the top separator when it is equal to 0 (The first row is always at the index 0), but to know whether the cell is the last one in the section, we get the number of items in the section minus 1 and compare that value with the index of the current cell. If they match, it means that the cell is the last one in the section, so we hide the bottom separator.

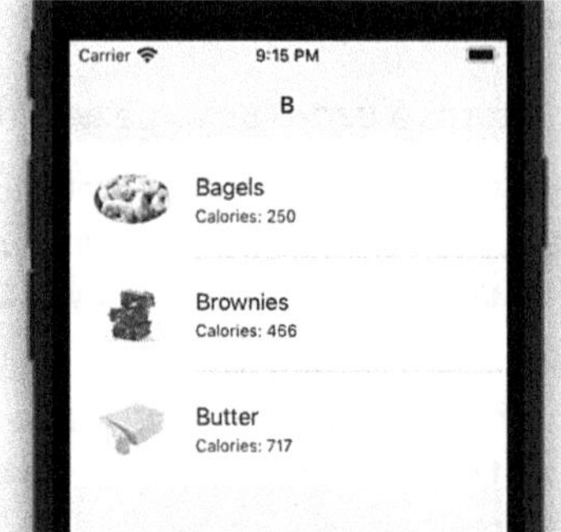

Figure 11-17: *Custom separators*

As Table Views, Collection View Lists can also include accessories. These are small icons on the left or right side of the cell that incorporate additional functionality. The accessories are defined by the **UICellAccessory** structure. The following are some of its methods.

disclosureIndicator(displayed: DisplayedState, **options:** Disclosure-IndicatorOptions**)**—This method returns an accessory that indicates that there is information to disclose. The **displayed** argument indicates when the accessory is displayed, and the **options** argument defines the accessory's configuration.

checkmark(displayed: DisplayedState, **options:** CheckmarkOptions**)**—This method returns an accessory that presents a checkmark. The **displayed** argument indicates when the accessory is displayed, and the **options** argument defines the accessory's configuration.

delete(displayed: DisplayedState, **options:** DeleteOptions, **actionHandler:** Closure**)**—This method returns an accessory that allows the user to delete a cell. The **displayed** argument indicates when the accessory is displayed, the **options** argument defines the accessory's configuration, and the **actionHandler** is the closure to be executed after the user performs the action.

reorder(displayed: DisplayedState, **options:** ReorderOptions**)**—This method returns an accessory that allows the user to reorder the cells. The **displayed** argument indicates when the accessory is displayed, and the **options** argument defines the accessory's configuration.

All these accessories use similar values for configuration. For instance, a value of the **DisplayedState** enumeration determines when the accessory is going to be displayed. The values available are **always**, **whenEditing**, and **whenNotEditing**. The options for each accessory are defined by specific structures, but they usually share the same properties, like **isHidden** to hide the accessory, or **tintColor** to change its color. Although we can modify any of these values, usually those assigned by default are more than enough. For instance, in the following example we add an accessory of type checkmark to the cells when they are selected or remove it when not.

```
let cellRegistration =
UICollectionView.CellRegistration<UICollectionViewListCell, ItemsData.ID>
{ cell, indexPath, itemID in
   if let item = AppData.items.first(where: { $0.id == itemID }) {
      var config = cell.defaultContentConfiguration()
      config.text = item.name
      config.secondaryText = "Calories: \(item.calories)"
      config.image = UIImage(named: item.image)
      config.imageProperties.maximumSize = CGSize(width: 60, height: 60)
      cell.contentConfiguration = config

      let selected = item.selected
      cell.accessories = selected ? [.checkmark()] : []
   }
}
```

Listing 11-19: *Adding accessories to the cells*

The code in Listing 11-19 defines a new registration for our cell. The cell is configured as before, but now we get the value of the item's **selected** property and assign to the cell a **checkmark** accessory or an empty array depending on the property's value.

To let the user select or deselect a cell, we can implement the **collectionView (UICollectionView, didSelectItemAt:)** method again.

```
override func collectionView(_ collectionView: UICollectionView,
didSelectItemAt indexPath: IndexPath) {
   if let itemID = AppData.dataSource.itemIdentifier(for: indexPath) {
      if let item = AppData.items.first(where: { $0.id == itemID }) {
         item.selected.toggle()

         var current = AppData.dataSource.snapshot()
         current.reconfigureItems([itemID])
         AppData.dataSource.apply(current)

         collectionView.deselectItem(at: indexPath, animated: true)
      }
   }
}
```

Listing 11-20: *Selecting and deselecting a cell in a list*

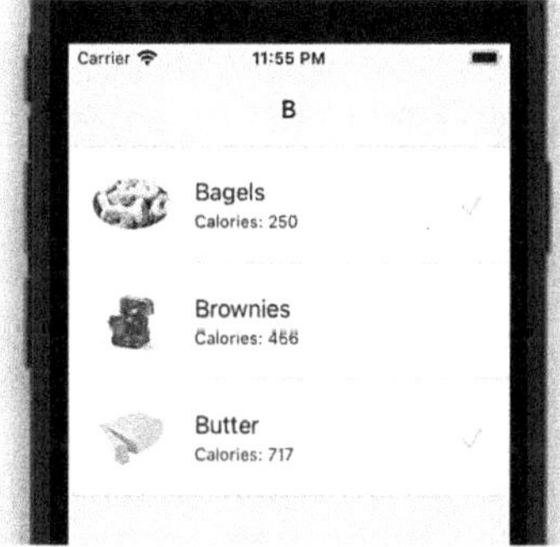

Figure 11-18: *Checkmark accessories*

Collection View Lists can also implement functionality to allow users to delete cells. The system works in the same way as with Table Views. The **UICollectionView** class includes the **isEditing** property to activate or deactivate the editing mode (**true** or **false**), and the **UICollectionLayoutListConfiguration** structure includes the following properties to provide the actions for the swipe gesture.

leadingSwipeActionsConfigurationProvider—This property takes a closure to configure swipe actions for the cell's leading edge. The closure receives an **IndexPath** value with the location of the cell and must return a **UISwipeActionsConfiguration** object with the buttons we want to show.

trailingSwipeActionsConfigurationProvider—This property takes a closure to configure swipe actions for the cell's trailing edge. The closure receives an **IndexPath** value with the location of the cell and must return a **UISwipeActionsConfiguration** object with the buttons we want to show.

The process to add these buttons to the cell is the same we used before for Table Views. The buttons are defined with the **UIContextualAction** class, and then the **UISwipeActionsConfiguration** object is initialized with these values and returned. The following example adds a trailing button to delete the cell.

```
override func viewDidLoad() {
   super.viewDidLoad()
   var config = UICollectionLayoutListConfiguration(appearance: .grouped)
   config.headerMode = .supplementary

   config.trailingSwipeActionsConfigurationProvider = { indexPath in
      let button = UIContextualAction(style: .normal, title: "Remove",
handler: { (action, view, completion) in
         if let itemID = AppData.dataSource.itemIdentifier(for:
indexPath), let sectionID = AppData.dataSource.sectionIdentifier(for:
indexPath.section) {
            AppData.items.removeAll(where: { $0.id == itemID })

            var currentSnapshot = AppData.dataSource.snapshot()
            currentSnapshot.deleteItems([itemID])
            if currentSnapshot.numberOfItems(inSection: sectionID) <= 0 {
               AppData.sections.removeAll(where: { $0.id == sectionID })
               currentSnapshot.deleteSections([sectionID])
            }
            AppData.dataSource.apply(currentSnapshot)
         }
         completion(true)
      })
      let config = UISwipeActionsConfiguration(actions: [button])
      return config
   }
   let layout = UICollectionViewCompositionalLayout.list(using: config)
   collectionView.collectionViewLayout = layout

   prepareDataSource()
   prepareSnapshot()
}
```

Listing 11-21: *Defining the buttons for swipe gestures*

The closure assigned to the **trailingSwipeActionsConfigurationProvider** property in Listing 11-21 creates a button with an action that removes the cell and the section if there are no cells left. The button is used to create the **UISwipeActionsConfiguration** object, and the object is returned to configure the list.

Figure 11-19: *Swipe button to delete the cells*

Do It Yourself: Replace the **`viewDidLoad()`** method in your **`MyCollectionViewController`** class with the method of Listing 11-21. Run the application and swipe a cell to the left. Press the Delete button. The cell should be deleted. If you want to activate the editing mode, as we did for Table Views in Chapter 10, assign the value **`true`** to the **`isEditing`** property of the **`UICollectionView`** object (**`collectionView.isEditing = true`**) and add the delete accessory to the cell (**`cell.accessories = [.delete()]`**).

Collection View Lists can also work along with section snapshots to create a hierarchical list. This is a list in which some items can expand or collapse to display or hide other items. The main items, also called *parents*, work as containers for other items, called *children*, that the user can see by tapping on the top item's accessory.

We don't need anything new to create these types of lists, all the functionality is provided by section snapshots, but the information in the model must be organized accordingly. For instance, the following model includes a structure to store all the items, but the structure includes a property with an array of instances of the same structure to store the items that are going to be shown when the parent item is expanded.

```
import UIKit

enum Sections {
   case main
}
struct MainItems: Identifiable {
   var id = UUID()
   var name: String!
   var options: [MainItems]!
}
struct ApplicationData {
   var dataSource: UICollectionViewDiffableDataSource<Sections,
MainItems.ID>!

  let items = [
      MainItems(name: "Food", options: [
         MainItems(name: "Oatmeal", options: nil),
         MainItems(name: "Bagels", options: nil),
         MainItems(name: "Brownies", options: nil),
         MainItems(name: "Cheese", options: nil),
         MainItems(name: "Cookies", options: nil),
         MainItems(name: "Donuts", options: nil)
      ]),
      MainItems(name: "Beverages", options: [
         MainItems(name: "Coffee", options: nil),
         MainItems(name: "Juice", options: nil),
         MainItems(name: "Lemonade", options: nil)
      ])
   ]
```

```
}
var AppData = ApplicationData()
```

Listing 11-22: Defining a model for a hierarchical list

The **MainItems** structure includes the **name** property to store the item's text, and the **options** property to store the children. In this example, we store two parent items called "Food" and "Beverages", and the children for each parent are stored in the item's **options** property. When the user taps on the "Food" or "Beverages" items, all the items stored in their **options** property are shown on the screen.

For this feature to work, we must mirror this organization in a section snapshot. The section snapshot is created first and then the items are added with the **append([ItemIdentifier-Type], to: ItemIdentifierType?)** method, where the **to** argument is the identifier of the parent to which the children belong or **nil** if the item to be added is a parent item, as shown next.

```
import UIKit

class MyCollectionViewController: UICollectionViewController {
   override func viewDidLoad() {
      super.viewDidLoad()
      let config =
UICollectionLayoutListConfiguration(appearance: .plain)
      let layout = UICollectionViewCompositionalLayout.list(using:
config)
      collectionView.collectionViewLayout = layout

      prepareDataSource()
      prepareSnapshot()
   }
   func prepareDataSource() {
      let cellRegistration =
UICollectionView.CellRegistration<UICollectionViewListCell, MainItems.ID>
{ cell, indexPath, itemID in
         if let item = self.getItem(id: itemID) {
            var config = cell.defaultContentConfiguration()
            config.text = item.name
            cell.contentConfiguration = config
            cell.accessories = item.options != nil ?
[.outlineDisclosure()] : []
         }
      }
      AppData.dataSource = UICollectionViewDiffableDataSource<Sections,
MainItems.ID>(collectionView: collectionView) { (collection, indexPath,
itemID) in
         return collection.dequeueConfiguredReusableCell(using:
cellRegistration, for: indexPath, item: itemID)
      }
   }
   func prepareSnapshot() {
      var snapshot = NSDiffableDataSourceSectionSnapshot<MainItems.ID>()
      for mainItem in AppData.items {
         snapshot.append([mainItem.id], to: nil)
         snapshot.append(mainItem.options.map({ $0.id }), to:
mainItem.id)
      }
      AppData.dataSource.apply(snapshot, to: .main, animatingDifferences:
false)
   }
   func getItem(id: MainItems.ID) -> MainItems? {
      var item = AppData.items.first(where: { $0.id == id })
```

```
        if item == nil {
           for main in AppData.items {
              if let found = main.options.first(where: { $0.id == id }) {
                 item = found
                 break
              }
           }
        }
        return item
     }
}
```

Listing 11-23: *Creating a hierarchical list*

The **prepareSnapshot()** method in Listing 11-23 creates the **NSDiffableDataSource-SectionSnapshot** structure and then adds all the items from the **items** array. First, we add the parent and then the children stored in the parent's **options** property. The rest of the code is similar to previous examples, but because we are working with nested items, we use a method called **getItem()** to get the item from the item's identifier. First, the method compares the identifier with the parent's identifier. If the item is not found (it is not a parent item), we iterate through the **items** array to look for the item inside the **options** array. The item is returned, and the cell is configured as before.

Notice that the cell includes an Outline Disclosure accessory. This is an accessory specifically designed to work with hierarchical lists (also known as expandable/collapsible outlines). The accessory shows an arrow that points down when the parent item is expanded, as shown below.

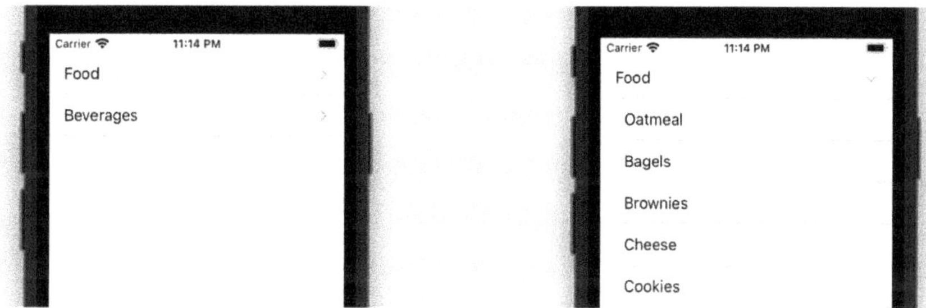

Figure 11-20: *Hierarchical list*

Do It Yourself: Replace the model in your project with the one in Listing 11-22. Update the **MyCollectionViewController** class with the code in Listing 11-23. Run the application and tap on a parent item to expand it.

Chapter 12
Split View Controllers

Basic 12.1 Universal Container

The container view controllers studied so far are good for devices with small screens, such as iPhones and iPods, but the space available in devices like the iPads and large iPhones in landscape mode demand a more elaborated design. UIKit includes a subclass of **`UIViewController`** called **`UISplitViewController`** that can present up to three scenes at a time: the primary scene, the supplementary scene, and the secondary scene.

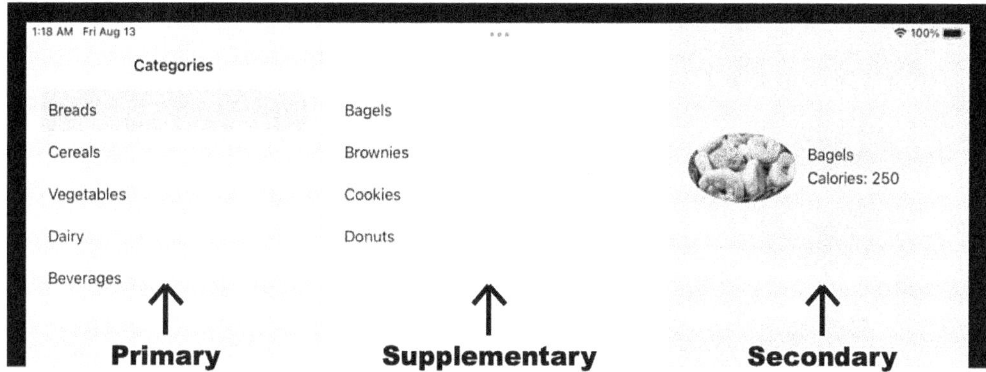

Figure 12-1: *Split View Controller with three columns*

The Primary and Supplementary columns are removable, and they are presented on the screen depending on the number of columns and the space available. By default, on iPads in landscape mode, only one of the removable columns is shown. In a two-column design, the Split View Controller displays the Primary column, while in a three-column design the Supplementary column is shown instead. But on iPads on portrait mode and large iPhones in landscape mode, only the Secondary column is displayed, and a button is provided in the navigation bar to open the removable columns.

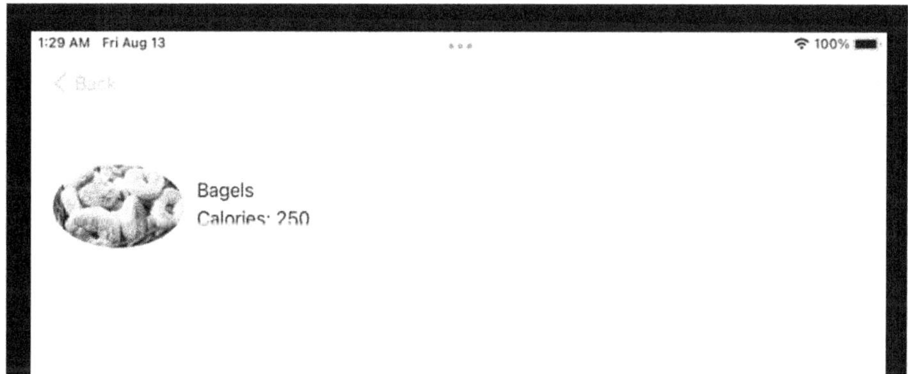

Figure 12-2: *Button on the navigation bar to open removable columns*

iPhones in portrait mode present a different configuration; the columns are displayed as in a Navigation Controller. They replace one another and buttons are included to navigate back.

Figure 12-3: *Split View Controller in iPhones in portrait mode*

Split View Controllers can be configured with two or three columns (Primary and Secondary, or Primary, Supplementary, and Secondary) and the removable columns may be shown on the left of the Secondary column or on top of it. This style is defined by the controller's display mode. There are a total of six display modes available.

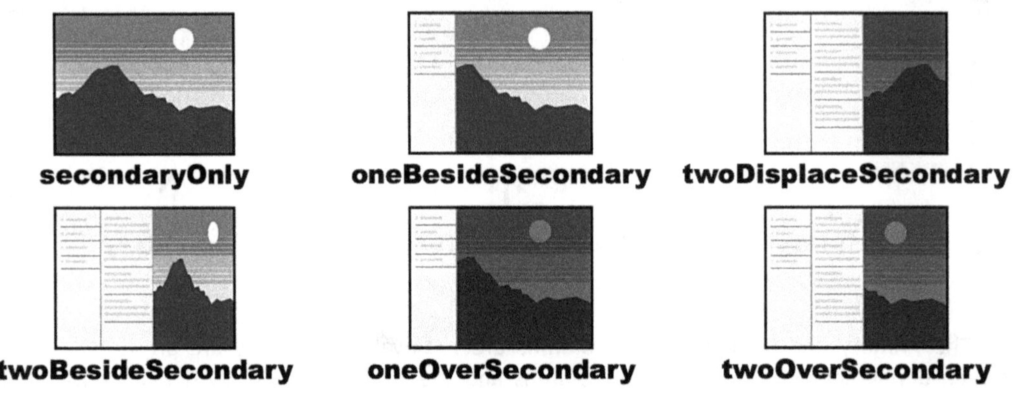

Figure 12-4: *Display modes for Split View Controllers*

Basic Split View Controller

Split View Controllers are created from the **`UISplitViewController`** class. As with any other view, they can be added to the interface from code or to the Storyboard from the Library.

UISplitViewController(style: Style)—This initializer creates a Split View Controller of the type specified by the **style** argument. The argument is an enumeration with the values **`unspecified`** (defines a classic Split View Controller), **`doubleColumn`** (defines a controller with two columns), and **`tripleColumn`** (defines a controller with three columns).

Figure 12-5: *Split View Controller option in the Library*

The option in the Library adds to the Storyboard a two-column Split View Controller, which includes the scenes for the Primary and Secondary columns. The Primary scene is embedded in a visible Navigation Controller, like those we have implemented before. On the other hand, the Secondary scene is a single view embedded in a Navigation Controller that is automatically assigned to the scene by the Split View Controller, as shown below.

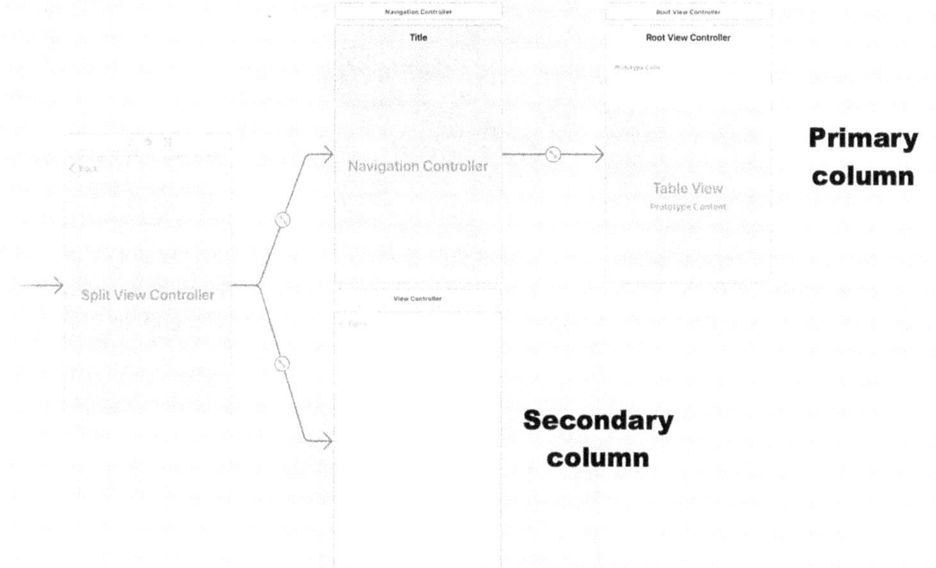

Figure 12-6: *Split View Controller in the Storyboard*

By default, this Split View Controller is configured with two columns (Primary and Secondary), but we can modify this configuration and other values from the Attributes Inspector panel.

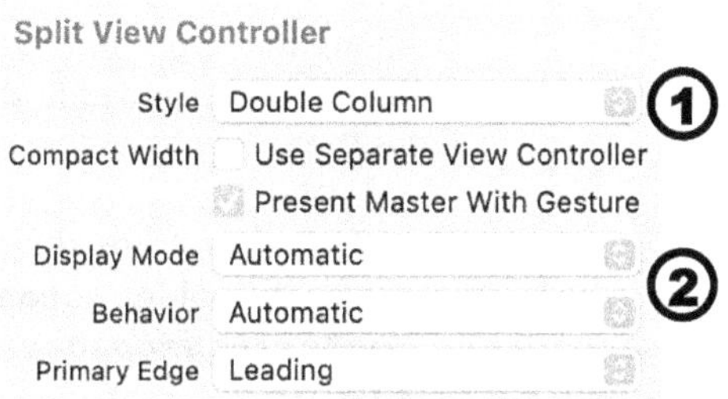

Figure 12-7: *Split View Controller configuration*

The panel includes the Style option to configure the Split View Controller with two or three columns (Figure 12-7, number 1), and the Display Mode and Behavior options to change the controller's display mode and behavior, respectively (Figure 12-7, number 2). The Display Mode determines how the columns are shown on the screen, and the split Behavior determines how the Secondary column is going to behave when the removable columns are visible. There are three values available: Tile, Overlay, and Displace.

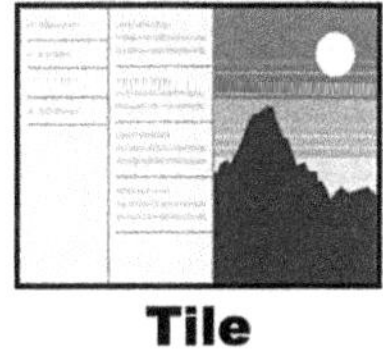

Figure 12-8: *Split behavior*

If we change the configuration of the Split View Controller to three columns, an additional scene is added to the Storyboard, but we can always remove or add these scenes manually. After adding the scenes, all we need to do is to control-drag a line from the Split View Controller to the scene and select the type of segue according to their role on the interface. For this purpose, the Storyboard defines four special segues called *Relationship Segues*, as shown next.

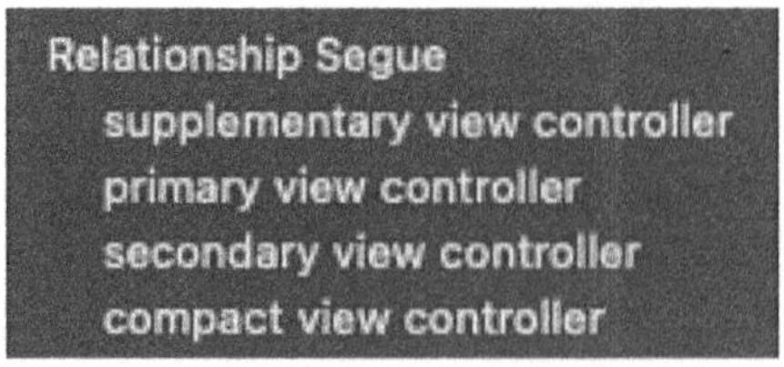

Relationship Segue
supplementary view controller
primary view controller
secondary view controller
compact view controller

Figure 12-9: *Relationship Segues for Split View Controllers*

Another useful segue when working with Split View Controllers is the Show Detail segue. This segue is used to connect the Primary or Supplementary scenes to the Secondary scene (the segue is triggered from the Primary or Supplementary scenes to open a scene in the Secondary column).

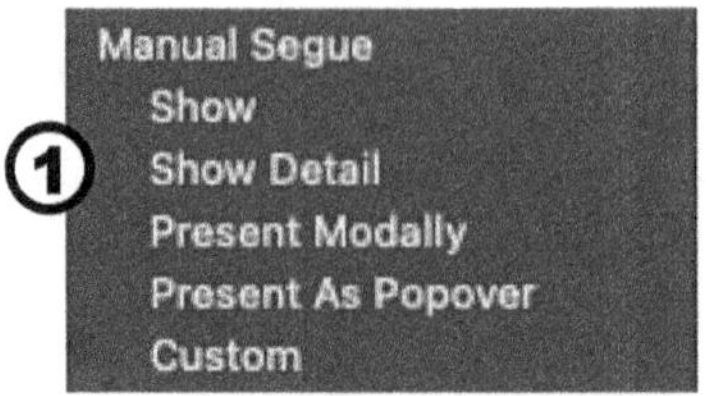

Figure 12-10: *Show Detail Segue*

Basic Split View Controller Configuration

Because Split View Controllers automatically expand and collapse to adapt to the space available, they are perfect to create universal applications that work on iPads and iPhones, but they still require some configuration. In addition to the options included in the Attributes Inspector panel, the **`UISplitViewController`** class includes the following properties.

preferredDisplayMode—This property sets or returns the preferred display mode. It is an enumeration called **`DisplayMode`** with the values **`secondaryOnly`**, **`oneBeside-Secondary`**, **`oneOverSecondary`**, **`twoBesideSecondary`**, **`twoOverSecondary`**, **`twoDisplaceSecondary`**, and **`automatic`**.

displayMode—This property returns the current display mode. It is an enumeration called **`DisplayMode`** with the values **`secondaryOnly`**, **`oneBesideSecondary`**, **`oneOverSecondary`**, **`twoBesideSecondary`**, **`twoOverSecondary`**, **`twoDisplace-Secondary`**, and **`automatic`**.

preferredSplitBehavior—This property sets of returns the preferred split behavior, which determines how the Secondary scene should appear in relation to the removable columns. It is an enumeration called **`SplitBehavior`** with the values **`tile`**, **`overlay`**, **`displace`**, and **`automatic`**.

isCollapsed—This property returns a Boolean value that determines the state of the interface. The value **`true`** means that the interface is collapsed (the controller is presenting only one column and it cannot be expanded), and the value **`false`** means the interface is expanded (the controller is presenting or can present two or more columns).

presentsWithGesture—This property sets or returns a Boolean value that determines whether a hidden view can be shown with a swipe gesture. Some configurations, like the iPad in portrait mode, present only one view and allow the user to make the other visible by swiping the finger or pressing a button. This property activates or deactivates these features.

showsSecondaryOnlyButton—This property sets or returns a Boolean value that determines whether the navigation bar of the Secondary column includes a button to show or hide the removable columns.

Besides the tools provided by the Split View Controller to show or hide the removable views, the **UISplitViewController** class includes the following methods to control the scenes.

viewController(for: Column**)**—This method returns a reference to the view controller presented in the column specified by the **for** argument. The argument is an enumeration with the values **primary**, **supplementary**, **secondary**, and **compact**.

setViewController(UIViewController?, **for:** Column**)**—This method assigns a new view controller to the column specified by the **for** argument. The first argument is a reference to the view controller (the scene) we want to show in the column, and the **for** argument is an enumeration with the values **primary**, **supplementary**, **secondary**, and **compact**.

show(Column**)**—This method makes a column visible. The argument is an enumeration with the values **primary**, **supplementary**, **secondary**, and **compact**.

hide(Column**)**—This method hides a column. The argument is an enumeration with the values **primary**, **supplementary**, **secondary**, and **compact**.

The **UISplitViewController** class also includes the following properties to suggest a size for the Primary and Supplementary columns.

preferredPrimaryColumnWidthFraction—This property sets or returns a **CGFloat** value that determines the width of the Primary column in relation to the Secondary column. The value must be specified with a number between 0.0 and 1.0. For example, a value of 0.5 gives the Primary column a size of 50% the width of the space available.

preferredPrimaryColumnWidth—This property sets or returns a **CGFloat** value with the preferred width of the Primary column.

primaryColumnWidth—This property returns a **CGFloat** value with the width of the Primary column.

minimumPrimaryColumnWidth—This property sets or returns a **CGFloat** value that determines the minimum width of the Primary column.

maximumPrimaryColumnWidth—This property sets or returns a **CGFloat** value that determines the maximum width of the Primary column.

preferredSupplementaryColumnWidthFraction—This property sets or returns a **CGFloat** value that determines the width of the Supplementary column in relation to the Secondary column. The value must be specified with a number between 0.0 and 1.0. For example, a value of 0.5 gives the Supplementary column a size of 50% the width of the space available.

preferredSupplementaryColumnWidth—This property sets or returns a **CGFloat** value with the preferred width of the Supplementary column.

supplementaryColumnWidth—This property returns a **CGFloat** value with the width of the Supplementary column.

minimumSupplementaryColumnWidth—This property sets or returns a **CGFloat** value that determines the minimum width of the Supplementary column.

maximumSupplementaryColumnWidth—This property sets or returns a **CGFloat** value that determines the maximum width of the Supplementary column.

IMPORTANT: The values set by these properties are suggestions to the Split View Controller, but the controller decides what size, mode, and behavior to apply depending on the device and space available.

Basic Split View Controller Delegate

Split View Controllers can also designate a delegate to report changes in the columns. The delegate must conform to the **UISplitViewControllerDelegate** protocol. The following are the methods defined in this protocol to manage a two or three-columns Split View Controller.

splitViewController(UISplitViewController, **topColumnForCollapsingToProposedTopColumn:** Column**)**—This method is called by the Split View Controller on its delegate before collapsing into one column. The method receives a **Column** value representing the column the controller is proposing to show and must return another **Column** value representing the column we really want to show.

splitViewController(UISplitViewController, **willHide:** Column**)**—This method is called by the Split View Controller on its delegate when a column is going to be hidden. The method receives a **Column** value representing the affected column.

splitViewController(UISplitViewController, **willShow:** Column**)**—This method is called by the Split View Controller on its delegate when a column is going to be shown. The method receives a **Column** value representing the affected column.

splitViewControllerDidCollapse(UISplitViewController**)**—This method is called by the Split View Controller on its delegate to report that the interface has collapsed.

splitViewControllerDidExpand(UISplitViewController**)**—This method is called by the Split View Controller on its delegate to report that the interface has expanded.

splitViewController(UISplitViewController, **displayModeForExpandingToProposedDisplayMode:** DisplayMode**)**—This method is called by the Split View Controller on its delegate when it needs to know which display mode to use when the interface is expanding. The method must return a **DisplayMode** value.

Basic 12.2 Implementing Split View Controllers

An application based on a Split View Controller works like any other we have built so far. The elements of the interface are added to the scenes and view controllers are assigned to the scenes to manage their content. For example, based on the scenes provided by a two-column Split View Controller, we can create an application to manage the same grocery list used in previous chapters. When an item is selected in the Primary column, the Secondary column shows the item's thumbnail, name, and calories. Figure 12-11, below, shows the modifications we need to introduce to the scenes for the Primary and Secondary columns to manage this information.

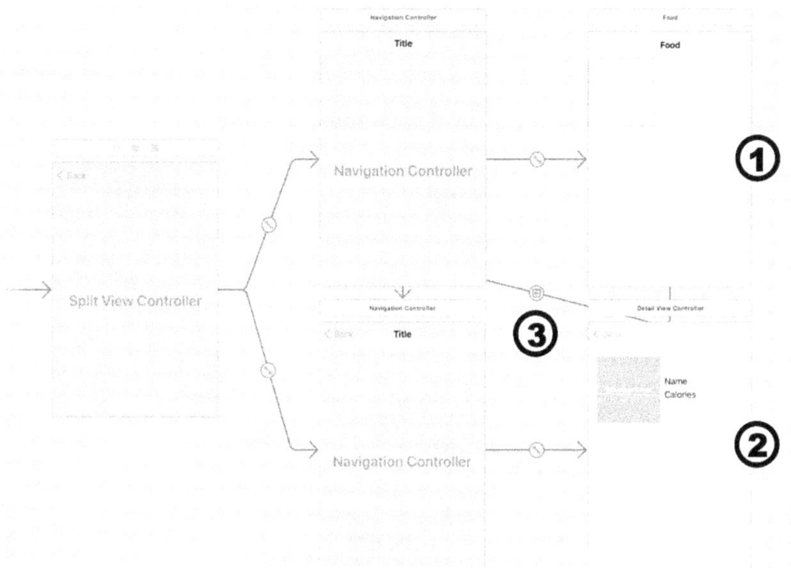

Figure 12-11: *Split View controller with custom Primary and Secondary scenes*

In this example, we have replaced the Table View Controller included in the standard Split View Controller with a Collection View Controller. The scene for the Secondary column was embedded in a Navigation Controller, and an Image View and two labels have been added to show the item's values on the screen. Notice that the Primary scene was connected to the Navigation Controller of the Secondary scene with a Show Detail segue, so every time an item is selected in the Primary column, its values are shown in the Secondary column.

Do It Yourself: Create a new project. Erase the initial scene and add a Split View Controller from the Library (Figures 12-5 and 12-6). Select the Split View Controller and activate the option Is Initial View Controller from the Attributes Inspector panel. Replace the Table View Controller with a Collection View Controller and connect it to the Navigation Controller with a Root View Controller segue (Figure 12-11, number 1). Double click on the Navigation Bar to change its title to "Food". Embed the Secondary scene in a Navigation Controller and add an Image View and two labels to the scene (Figure 12-11, number 2). Control-drag a line from the Collection View Controller to the Navigation Controller of the Secondary scene to create a Show Detail segue (Figure 12-11, number 3). Give the segue the identifier "showSecondary".

As always, the first step is to define the data model. For this example, we are going to use the same model implemented for Table Views in Chapter 10 (see Listing 10-1). All we need to remember is to define the diffable data source to work with a Collection View (**`var dataSource: UICollectionViewDiffableDataSource<Sections, ItemsData.ID>!`**).

The view controller for the Primary scene must define the diffable data source and the snapshot to provide the data to the Collection View (see Collection Views in Chapter 11), but it also must perform the Show Detail segue to open a new scene every time an item is selected.

```
import UIKit

class PrimaryViewController: UICollectionViewController {
   var selected: ItemsData.ID!

   override func viewDidLoad() {
      super.viewDidLoad()
```

```
        let config =
UICollectionLayoutListConfiguration(appearance: .sidebar)
        let layout = UICollectionViewCompositionalLayout.list(using:
config)
        collectionView.collectionViewLayout = layout

        prepareDataSource()
        prepareSnapshot()
    }
    func prepareDataSource() {
        let cellRegistration =
UICollectionView.CellRegistration<UICollectionViewListCell, ItemsData.ID>
{ cell, indexPath, itemID in
            if let item = AppData.items.first(where: { $0.id == itemID }) {
                var config = cell.defaultContentConfiguration()
                config.text = item.name
                cell.contentConfiguration = config
            }
        }
        AppData.dataSource = UICollectionViewDiffableDataSource<Sections,
ItemsData.ID>(collectionView: collectionView) { collection, indexPath,
itemID in
            return collection.dequeueConfiguredReusableCell(using:
cellRegistration, for: indexPath, item: itemID)
        }
    }
    func prepareSnapshot() {
        var snapshot = NSDiffableDataSourceSnapshot<Sections,
ItemsData.ID>()
        snapshot.appendSections([.main])
        snapshot.appendItems(AppData.items.map({ $0.id }))
        AppData.dataSource.apply(snapshot)
    }
    override func collectionView(_ collectionView: UICollectionView,
didSelectItemAt indexPath: IndexPath) {
        if let itemID = AppData.dataSource.itemIdentifier(for: indexPath) {
            selected = itemID
            performSegue(withIdentifier: "showSecondary", sender: nil)
        }
    }
    override func prepare(for segue: UIStoryboardSegue, sender: Any?) {
        if segue.identifier == "showSecondary" {
            if let navigator = segue.destination as? UINavigationController
{
                let controller = navigator.topViewController as!
SecondaryViewController
                controller.selected = selected
            }
        }
    }
}
```

Listing 12-1: *Controlling the Primary scene*

When possible, Apple recommends using a Collection View List with a side bar configuration to display the content of the Primary and Supplementary columns. In this example, we configure the layout with a **sidebar** appearance and the cells to display the item's name, so we get a list of items on the Primary column. When an item is selected, the Collection View Controller calls the **collectionView(UICollectionView, didSelectItemAt:)** method. In this method, we get the selected item with the **itemIdentifier()** method, store the identifier in a property, and perform the Show Detail segue (identified with the name "showSecondary").

In the **prepare()** method, the value of the **selected** property is sent to the view controller of the Secondary scene to show the values on the screen. Notice that the Show Detail segue is connected to the Navigation Controller, so we first get a reference to the Navigation Controller of the Secondary scene, then read the **topViewController** property of the Navigation Controller to get a reference to the view controller of the Secondary scene, and finally pass the value of the **selected** property to this view controller.

All the view controller of the Secondary scene needs to do is to get the item from the identifier and show its values on the screen.

```
import UIKit

class SecondaryViewController: UIViewController {
   @IBOutlet weak var itemThumbnail: UIImageView!
   @IBOutlet weak var itemName: UILabel!
   @IBOutlet weak var itemCalories: UILabel!
   var selected: ItemsData.ID!

   override func viewDidLoad() {
      super.viewDidLoad()
      if selected != nil {
        if let item = AppData.items.first(where: {$0.id == selected!}) {
             itemThumbnail?.image = UIImage(named: item.image)
             itemName?.text = item.name
             itemCalories?.text = "Calories: \(item.calories)"
        }
      }
   }
}
```

Listing 12-2: Displaying the item in the Secondary scene

By default, iPads display the Primary and Secondary columns side by side in landscape, and only the Secondary column in portrait mode. In landscape mode, the Split View Controller includes a button in the navigation bar to hide or show the Primary column (Figure 12-12, number 1), but in portrait mode the Primary column can be opened with a swipe gesture from the left or by pressing the back button included in the navigation bar (Figure 12-12, number 2).

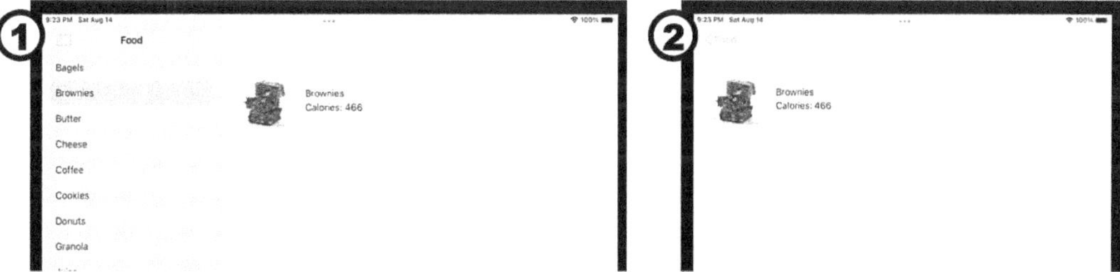

Figure 12-12: *Split View Controller in landscape and portrait modes*

Do It Yourself: Create a Swift file called ApplicationData.swift with the model in Listing 10-1 (Chapter 10). Update the definition of the **dataSource** property to work with Collection Views (var **dataSource: UICollectionView-DiffableDataSource<Sections, ItemsData.ID>!**). Create a file with a subclass of **UICollectionViewController** called **Primary-ViewController** and assign it to the Primary scene. Update the class with the code in Listing 12-1. Create a file with a subclass of **UIViewController** called **SecondaryViewController** and assign it to the Secondary scene. Update the class with the code in Listing 12-2. Connect the elements in the scene to their respective Outlets. Download the food thumbnails from our website and add them to the Assets Catalog. Run the application in the iPad and iPhone simulators. Rotate the simulator to see how the Split View Controller responds in every device.

Basic Swipe Gesture

As we already mentioned, Split View Controllers include a gesture and a button that allow the user to change the display mode (show or hide the Primary column), but if we want to provide our own tools to control the columns, we can remove these features by assigning the value **false** to the **presentsWithGesture** property.

The property can be modified from any view controller, but a good practice is to create a subclass of the **UISplitViewController** class to take care of the controller's configuration.

```
import UIKit

class MySplitViewController: UISplitViewController {
   override func viewDidLoad() {
      super.viewDidLoad()
      presentsWithGesture = false
   }
}
```

Listing 12-3: *Configuring the Split View Controller*

The **UISplitViewController** subclass in Listing 12-3 assigns the value **true** to the **presentsWithGesture** property as soon as the Split View Controller is loaded. Now the Split View Controller doesn't offer the built-in features to allow the user to manipulate the interface.

Do It Yourself: Create a subclass of the **UISplitViewController** class called **MySplitViewController** and assign it to the Split View Controller in the Storyboard. Complete the class with the code in Listing 12-3. Run the application. You shouldn't see the button to remove the Primary column anymore and shouldn't be able to open the column with a swipe gesture either.

Of course, if we still want the user to be able to show or hide the removable columns, we must provide our own tools. For this purpose, the **UIViewController** class defines the **splitViewController** property to access the Split View Controller, and the **UISplitViewController** class includes the **show()** and **hide()** methods to show or hide a column. For instance, we can add a button to the Navigation Bar of the Secondary scene and then call the **show()** or **hide()** methods depending on what we need to do.

```
import UIKit

class SecondaryViewController: UIViewController {
   @IBOutlet weak var itemThumbnail: UIImageView!
   @IBOutlet weak var itemName: UILabel!
   @IBOutlet weak var itemCalories: UILabel!
   var selected: ItemsData.ID!

   override func viewDidLoad() {
      super.viewDidLoad()
      let buttonMode = UIBarButtonItem(title: "Menu", image: nil,
primaryAction: UIAction(handler: { [unowned self] action in
         self.showColumn()
      }), menu: nil)
      navigationItem.leftBarButtonItem = buttonMode

      if selected != nil {
         if let item = AppData.items.first(where: {$0.id == selected!}) {
            itemThumbnail?.image = UIImage(named: item.image)
```

```
            itemName?.text = item.name
            itemCalories?.text = "Calories: \(item.calories)"
         }
      }
   }
   func showColumn() {
      if splitViewController?.isCollapsed == true {
         splitViewController?.hide(.secondary)
      } else {
         if splitViewController?.displayMode == .secondaryOnly {
            splitViewController?.show(.primary)
         } else {
            splitViewController?.hide(.primary)
         }
      }
   }
}
```

Listing 12-4: *Managing the columns from code*

In this example, we create a **UIBarButtonItem** object and add it to the bar as soon as the Secondary scene is loaded. When pressed, the button calls the **showColumn()** method where we check the current state of the interface and show or hide the scenes accordingly. If the interface is collapsed, it means that we are in an iPhone in portrait mode, so we hide the Secondary scene to force the system to transition back to the Primary scene. If not, we show or hide the Primary scene depending on the display mode.

Figure 12-13: *Custom button for the Split View Controller*

Do It Yourself: Update the **SecondaryViewController** class with the code in Listing 12-4 and run the application. You should see the Menu button in the Secondary scene. Press the button to hide or show the Primary column.

Basic Display Mode

Due to the reduced size of the screens in iPads in portrait mode and large iPhones in landscape mode, the Split View Controller presents the columns with a display mode of type **secondaryOnly**, which means that only the secondary column is visible. But we can recommend an alternative mode and split behavior by assigning a different value to the **preferredDisplayMode** and the **preferredSplitBehavior** properties.

```
import UIKit

class MySplitViewController: UISplitViewController {
   override func viewDidLoad() {
      super.viewDidLoad()
      presentsWithGesture = false
      preferredDisplayMode = .oneBesideSecondary
      preferredSplitBehavior = .tile
   }
}
```

Listing 12-5: *Changing the Split View Controller display mode*

The code in Listing 12-5 recommends the Split View Controller to use the mode **oneBesideSecondary** and the split behavior **tile** (the columns share the space available). In consequence, the Split View Controller displays the Primary column beside the Secondary column when possible.

Figure 12-14: *Custom display mode and split behavior in iPads*

Do It Yourself: Update the **MySplitViewController** class with the code in Listing 12-5 (if you haven't created this subclass yet, you can do it as explained for the example in Listing 12-3). Run the application. The Primary column should always be visible, regardless of the orientation, as illustrated in Figure 12-14.

Basic Default Item

When our application is launched, no item has been selected by the user yet, so the Secondary scene has nothing to show. Depending on the characteristics of our application, we may provide a placeholder or just select an item at random. For instance, we can modify our **SecondaryViewController** class to get the first item in the model when no item was selected.

```
override func viewDidLoad() {
   super.viewDidLoad()
   let buttonMode = UIBarButtonItem(title: "Menu", image: nil,
primaryAction: UIAction(handler: { [unowned self] action in
      self.showColumn()
   }), menu: nil)
   navigationItem.leftBarButtonItem = buttonMode

   if selected == nil {
      if let item = AppData.items.first {
         selected = item.id
      }
   }
   if let item = AppData.items.first(where: { $0.id == selected! }) {
      itemThumbnail?.image = UIImage(named: item.image)
      itemName?.text = item.name
      itemCalories?.text = "Calories: \(item.calories)"
   }
}
```

Listing 12-6: *Selecting the item by default*

Listing 12-6 are the changes we need to introduce to the **viewDidLoad()** method of the **SecondaryViewController** class to show an item by default. If the value of the **selected** property is **nil**, which means no item was selected by the user, we get the first item in the **items** array and assign it to the **selected** property, so that item is shown on the screen.

Do It Yourself: Update the **viewDidLoad()** method in your **SecondaryViewController** class with the code in Listing 12-6 and run the application. You should see the first item in the model on the screen.

Basic Default Column

When the app is launched, the Split View Controller decides how to display the columns. If there is only space available for one column, by default it will show the Secondary. This means that, for example, when we launch the app in an iPhone in portrait mode, we will always see the Secondary column until an action is performed. The **UISplitViewControllerDelegate** protocol defines the **splitViewController(UISplitViewController, topColumnForCollapsingToProposedTopColumn:)** method to change this predefined behavior. The method is called by the Split View Controller to know what column we want to show when the interface is collapsed. For instance, the view controller in the following example conforms to the **UISplitViewControllerDelegate** protocol and implements this method to ask the Split View Controller to show the Primary column first.

```
import UIKit

class MySplitViewController: UISplitViewController,
UISplitViewControllerDelegate {
   override func viewDidLoad() {
      super.viewDidLoad()
      presentsWithGesture = false
      preferredDisplayMode = .oneBesideSecondary
      preferredSplitBehavior = .tile
      delegate = self
   }
   func splitViewController(_ svc: UISplitViewController,
topColumnForCollapsingToProposedTopColumn proposedTopColumn:
UISplitViewController.Column) -> UISplitViewController.Column {
      return .primary
   }
}
```

Listing 12-7: *Declaring the initial column for a collapsed interface*

For this example, we have decided to designate our **UISplitViewController** subclass as the Split View Controller delegate, but any other view controller would work as well. In this case, we implement the protocol method and return the value **primary**, so the Split View Controller shows the Primary column first when the app is launched in a collapsed interface.

Do It Yourself: Update the **MySplitViewController** class with the code in Listing 12-7. Run the application on the iPhone simulator in portrait mode. You should see the Primary scene on the screen.

Basic Compact Scene

With the delegate method implemented in the previous section we can select the column we want to show first from those available, but Split View Controllers can also include an additional scene that is only shown in a collapse interface. The scene is added to the Split View Controller with a Compact View Controller segue or introduced to the Storyboard by selecting the option Use Separate View Controller from the Attributes Inspector panel (see Figure 12-7). Once we select this option, the Compact scene is added to the Storyboard (Figure 12-15, number 1).

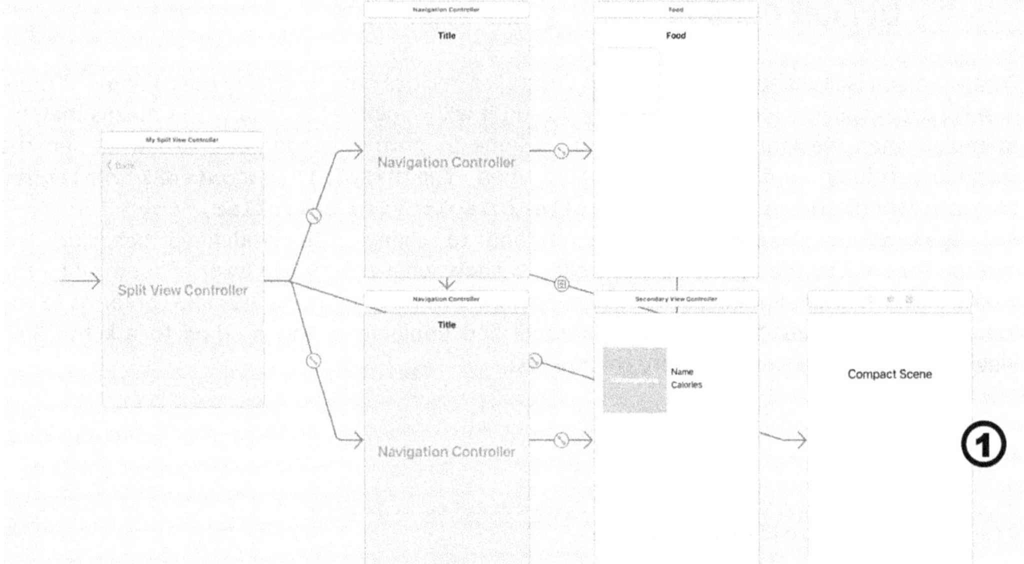

Figure 12-15: *Compact scene*

The Compact scene is used when the interface for a Compact Size Class is radically different from the rest. Once this scene is added to the Split View Controller, it is displayed every time the interface collapses, unless we specify otherwise from the delegate method.

Figure 12-16: *Compact scene in a collapsed interface*

Do It Yourself: Select the Split View Controller in the Storyboard and activate the Use Separate View Controller option in the Attributes Inspector panel. You should see a new scene in the Storyboard connected to the Split View Controller with a Compact View Controller segue. Remove the delegate method added to the **`UISplitViewController`** subclass in Listing 12-7 to let the Split View Controller select the initial scene. Add a label to identify the scene and run the application on the iPhone simulator in portrait mode. You should see the interface of Figure 12-16.

Basic Three-Column Design

Split View Controllers can be configured with two or three columns. So far, we have been using a two-column design, but we can easily add an additional column by changing the Style option in the Attributes Inspector panel to Triple Column (see Figure 12-7, number 1). Once we select this option, a Supplementary scene is added to the Storyboard and connected to the Split View Controller with a Supplementary View Controller segue.

Xcode adds a single view to the Storyboard, but we can replace it with any type of scene we want. For our example, we are going to use the Primary scene to show a list of categories, and the Supplementary scene to show the items belonging to each category, so we need a Collection View Controller. Figure 12-17, below, shows what the interface looks like after we replace the scene with a Collection View Controller (number 1).

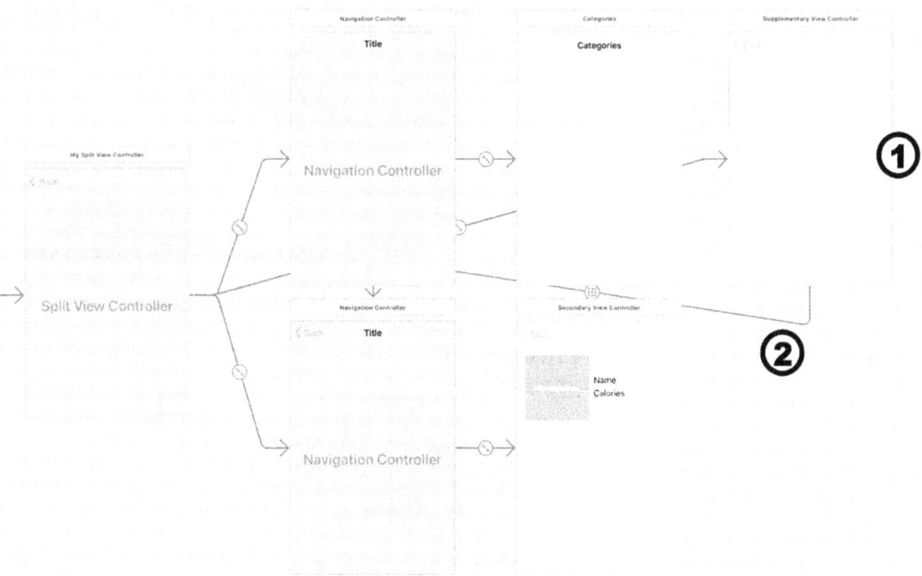

***Figure 12-17:** Scenes for a three-column Split View Controller*

Do It Yourself: Remove the Compact scene added in the previous example and add a Collection View Controller. Connect this scene to the Split View Controller with a Supplementary View Controller segue (Figure 12-17, number 1). Remove all the configuration changes added to the **`UISplitViewController`** subclass before to allow the Split View Controller to provide the standard buttons to manage the columns. Remove the Show Detail segue and add a new one from the Supplementary scene to the Navigation Controller of the Secondary scene (Figure 12-17, number 2). Assign the identifier "showSecondary" to this segue. The rest of the interface is the same as before, but because we are going to use the Primary scene to show the list of categories, you should change its title to Categories, as we did in the interface in Figure 12-17.

For this example, we need to organize the items in categories. The following model defines a class to store the categories called **`Categories`**, which includes an array of **`ItemsData`** objects to store the items for each category.

```
import UIKit

enum Sections {
   case main
}
class Categories: Identifiable {
   var id: UUID = UUID()
   var name: String
   var items: [ItemsData]

   init(_ name: String, _ items: [ItemsData]) {
      self.name = name
      self.items = items
   }
}
class ItemsData: Identifiable {
   var id: UUID = UUID()
   var name: String
   var image: String
   var calories: Int
   var selected: Bool
```

```
   init(_ name: String, _ image: String, _ calories: Int, _ selected: 
Bool) {
      self.name = name
      self.image = image
      self.calories = calories
      self.selected = selected
   }
}
struct ApplicationData {
   var dataSourceCategories: UICollectionViewDiffableDataSource<Sections, 
Categories.ID>!
   var dataSource: UICollectionViewDiffableDataSource<Sections, 
ItemsData.ID>!
   var categories: [Categories] = []
   var selectedCategory: Categories!

   init() {
      categories.append(Categories("Breads", [ ItemsData("Bagels", 
"bagels", 250, false), ItemsData("Brownies", "brownies", 466, false), 
ItemsData("Cookies", "cookies", 502, false), ItemsData("Donuts", 
"donuts", 452, false) ]))
      categories.append(Categories("Cereals", [ ItemsData("Granola", 
"granola", 471, false), ItemsData("Oatmeal", "oatmeal", 68, false) ]))
      categories.append(Categories("Vegetables", [ ItemsData("Lettuce", 
"lettuce", 15, false), ItemsData("Potatoes", "potato", 77, false), 
ItemsData("Tomatoes", "tomato", 18, false) ]))
      categories.append(Categories("Dairy", [ ItemsData("Butter", 
"butter", 717, false), ItemsData("Cheese", "cheese", 402, false), 
ItemsData("Milk", "milk", 42, false), ItemsData("Yogurt", "yogurt", 59, 
false) ]))
      categories.append(Categories("Beverages", [ ItemsData("Coffee", 
"coffee", 0, false), ItemsData("Juice", "juice", 23, false), 
ItemsData("Lemonade", "lemonade", 40, false) ]))

      selectedCategory = categories.first
   }
}
var AppData = ApplicationData()
```

Listing 12-8: *Defining a model to work with a three-column Split View Controller*

The model includes properties to store two diffable data sources, one for the categories (**dataSourceCategories**) and another for the items (**dataSource**). Using these data sources, we can define the view controllers to list the categories in the Primary scene and the items in the Supplementary scene. The following is the code for the Primary view controller.

```
import UIKit

class PrimaryViewController: UICollectionViewController {
   override func viewDidLoad() {
      super.viewDidLoad()
      let config = 
UICollectionLayoutListConfiguration(appearance: .sidebar)
      let layout = UICollectionViewCompositionalLayout.list(using: 
config)
      collectionView.collectionViewLayout = layout

      prepareDataSource()
      prepareSnapshot()
   }
  func prepareDataSource() {
      let cellRegistration = 
UICollectionView.CellRegistration<UICollectionViewListCell, 
Categories.ID> { cell, indexPath, itemID in
```

```
         if let item = AppData.categories.first(where: { $0.id ==
itemID }) {
            var config = cell.defaultContentConfiguration()
            config.text = item.name
            cell.contentConfiguration = config
         }
      }
      AppData.dataSourceCategories =
UICollectionViewDiffableDataSource<Sections,
Categories.ID>(collectionView: collectionView) { collection, indexPath,
itemID in
         return collection.dequeueConfiguredReusableCell(using:
cellRegistration, for: indexPath, item: itemID)
      }
   }
   func prepareSnapshot() {
      var snapshot = NSDiffableDataSourceSnapshot<Sections,
Categories.ID>()
      snapshot.appendSections([.main])
      snapshot.appendItems(AppData.categories.map({ $0.id }))
      AppData.dataSourceCategories.apply(snapshot)
   }
   override func collectionView(_ collectionView: UICollectionView,
didSelectItemAt indexPath: IndexPath) {
      if let categoryID =
AppData.dataSourceCategories.itemIdentifier(for: indexPath), let category
= AppData.categories.first(where: { $0.id == categoryID }) {
         if let controller =
splitViewController?.viewController(for: .supplementary) as?
SupplementaryViewController {
            AppData.selectedCategory = category
            controller.prepareSnapshot()

            if splitViewController?.isCollapsed == true {
               splitViewController?.show(.supplementary)
            }
         }
      }
   }
}
```

Listing 12-9: *Showing the categories*

The view controller in Listing 12-9 shows the list of categories, so the diffable data source and the snapshot are defined with the **Categories.ID** type and the **categories** array. Again, we implement the **collectionView(UICollectionView, didSelectItemAt:)** method to respond to the selection of a cell. In this method, we get the item's identifier and send it to the Supplementary scene.

The Supplementary scene displays the items that belong to the category selected by the user, so we get the **Categories** object that represents the selected category from the **categories** array and store it in a property in the model (We store it in a property in the model to make it available for the Supplementary and the Secondary scenes). After the selected category is assigned to the **selectedCategory** property, we call the **prepareSnapshot()** method in the Supplementary scene to update the Collection View, and then arrange the columns on the screen. By default, the Split View Controller can manage the columns in expanded interfaces without any help, but we still have to call the **show()** method to show the Supplementary scene in a collapsed interface.

When opened, the Supplementary scene reads the selected category from the model and shows the items on the screen.

```
import UIKit

class SupplementaryViewController: UICollectionViewController {
   var selected: ItemsData.ID!

   override func viewDidLoad() {
      super.viewDidLoad()
      let config =
UICollectionLayoutListConfiguration(appearance: .sidebarPlain)
      let layout = UICollectionViewCompositionalLayout.list(using:
config)
      collectionView.collectionViewLayout = layout

      navigationItem.title = "Food"

      prepareDataSource()
      prepareSnapshot()
   }
   func prepareDataSource() {
      let cellRegistration =
UICollectionView.CellRegistration<UICollectionViewListCell, ItemsData.ID>
{ cell, indexPath, itemID in
         if let item = AppData.selectedCategory?.items.first(where:
{ $0.id == itemID }) {
            var config = cell.defaultContentConfiguration()
            config.text = item.name
            cell.contentConfiguration = config
         }
      }
      AppData.dataSource = UICollectionViewDiffableDataSource<Sections,
ItemsData.ID>(collectionView: collectionView) { collection, indexPath,
itemID in
         return collection.dequeueConfiguredReusableCell(using:
cellRegistration, for: indexPath, item: itemID)
      }
   }
   func prepareSnapshot() {
      var snapshot = NSDiffableDataSourceSnapshot<Sections,
ItemsData.ID>()
      snapshot.appendSections([.main])
      let items = AppData.selectedCategory?.items.map({ $0.id })
      snapshot.appendItems(items ?? [])
      AppData.dataSource.apply(snapshot, animatingDifferences: false)
   }
   override func collectionView(_ collectionView: UICollectionView,
didSelectItemAt indexPath: IndexPath) {
      if let itemID = AppData.dataSource.itemIdentifier(for: indexPath) {
         selected = itemID
         performSegue(withIdentifier: "showSecondary", sender: nil)
      }
   }
   override func prepare(for segue: UIStoryboardSegue, sender: Any?) {
      if segue.identifier == "showSecondary" {
         if let navigator = segue.destination as? UINavigationController
{
            let controller = navigator.topViewController as!
SecondaryViewController
            controller.selected = selected
         }
      }
   }
}
```

Listing 12-10: *Showing the items in a category*

This view controller performs the same tasks as the view controller for the Primary scene, but now the snapshot is created from the **items** property of the selected category, so only the items that belong to that category are shown on the screen.

When an item is selected in the Supplementary scene, it must be sent to the Secondary scene to show the values on the screen. This is the same process used before for a two-column Split View Controller; we assign the item to the **selected** property and perform the Show Detail segue.

No changes are required for the view controller that controls the Secondary scene, except that this time we get the item by default from the selected category (this is why we assigned the selected category to a property in the model).

```
import UIKit

class SecondaryViewController: UIViewController {
   @IBOutlet weak var itemThumbnail: UIImageView!
   @IBOutlet weak var itemName: UILabel!
   @IBOutlet weak var itemCalories: UILabel!
   var selected: ItemsData.ID!

   override func viewDidLoad() {
      super.viewDidLoad()
      if selected == nil {
         if let item = AppData.selectedCategory.items.first {
            selected = item.id
         }
      }
      if let item = AppData.selectedCategory?.items.first(where: { $0.id
== selected! }) {
         itemThumbnail?.image = UIImage(named: item.image)
         itemName?.text = item.name
         itemCalories?.text = "Calories: \(item.calories)"
      }
   }
}
```

Listing 12-11: *Showing the item's values*

In iPads in landscape mode, the columns are shown by default, but in iPads in portrait mode and large iPhones in landscape mode, the removable columns are hidden and only the Secondary column is visible, and in iPhones in portrait mode (collapsed interfaces) the columns are shown one at a time, but buttons are always provided to access the rest of the columns.

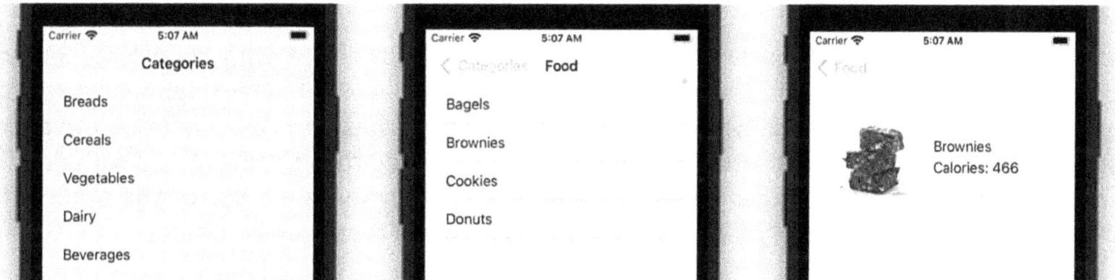

Figure 12-18: *Three-column Split View Controller on an iPhone*

Do It Yourself: Update the ApplicationData.swift file in your project with the model in Listing 12-8. Update the **PrimaryViewController** class and the **SecondaryViewController** class with the codes in Listings 12-9 and 12-11. Create a subclass of **UICollectionViewController** called **SupplementaryViewController** and assign it to the Supplementary scene. Complete this class with the code in Listing 12-10. Run the application and test it in different devices and orientations to see how the columns work.

Basic Secondary Only Button

Split View Controllers include buttons to open the removable columns and offer the possibility to tap anywhere on the Secondary column to hide them. But in a three-column design, we can also add a standard button for this purpose. All we need to do to activate this feature is to assign the value **true** to the **showsSecondaryOnlyButton** property, as in the following example.

```
import UIKit

class MySplitViewController: UISplitViewController {
   override func viewDidLoad() {
      super.viewDidLoad()
      showsSecondaryOnlyButton = true
   }
}
```

Listing 12-12: *Adding the Secondary Only button*

The button is automatically added to the navigation bar of the Secondary scene when a removable column is displayed on the side. The user can tap this button to show or hide the removable column.

Figure 12-19: *Secondary Only button*

Do It Yourself: Create or update the **UISplitViewController** subclass with the code in Listing 12-12. Run the application in the iPad simulator in landscape mode. You should see the Supplementary and Secondary columns on the screen. Press the Secondary Only button to hide or show the Supplementary column.

Basic 12.3 Modal Scenes

Besides showing and hiding columns, we can expand the interface with modal scenes and popovers. We have already introduced modal scenes in Chapter 9. They are normal scenes but connected with a *Present Modally* segue. In iPhones, these scenes open as a sheet on top of the current scene, but in iPads and large iPhones in landscape mode they are presented with designs that take advantage of the larger screens. These presentation styles are set by the segue. The options are available from the Attributes Inspector panel when the segue is selected.

- **Full Screen** presents a scene of the size of the screen over the current interface.
- **Current Context** presents a scene in the place and of the size of the designated area.
- **Page Sheet** presents a scene as a sheet that emerges from the bottom of the screen.
- **Form Sheet** presents a scene as a sheet over the current interface and in the center of the screen.
- **Over Full Screen** presents a scene over the interface and with the size of the screen (but without hiding the current scenes).

- **Over Current Context** presents a scene in the place and with the size of the designated area (but without hiding the current scene).

Because modal scenes are not part of the main interface and are not added to the navigation stack of a Navigation Controller, we must provide a way for the user to control them. In Chapter 9, we studied how to do this with an Unwind Segue, but the **`UIViewController`** class also offers some properties and methods to present and dismiss these scenes programmatically.

modalPresentationStyle—This property sets or returns the scene's presentation style. It is an enumeration of type **`UIModalPresentationStyle`** with the values **`automatic`**, **`fullScreen`**, **`pageSheet`**, **`formSheet`**, **`currentContext`**, **`custom`**, **`overFullScreen`**, **`overCurrentContext`**, **`popover`**, **`blurOverFullScreen`**, and none.

modalTransitionStyle—This property sets or returns the transition style. It is an enumeration of type **`UIModalTransitionStyle`** with the values **`coverVertical`**, **`flipHorizontal`**, **`crossDissolve`**, and **`partialCurl`**. Notice that some of these transitions are only available for the Full Screen presentation style.

present(UIViewController, **animated:** Bool, **completion:** Block**)**—This method presents a modal scene. The first argument is a reference to the view controller of the scene we want to present, the **`animated`** argument determines whether the process will be animated, and the **`completion`** argument is an optional closure that is executed after the scene is presented on the screen.

dismiss(animated: Bool, **completion:** Block?**)**—This method dismisses the scene. The **animated** argument is a Boolean value that determines whether the process will be animated, and the **completion** argument is a closure that is executed after the scene is closed.

Modal scenes are used to present additional information. For instance, we can connect a scene to the Secondary scene with an Image View to let the user see a larger image of the selected item.

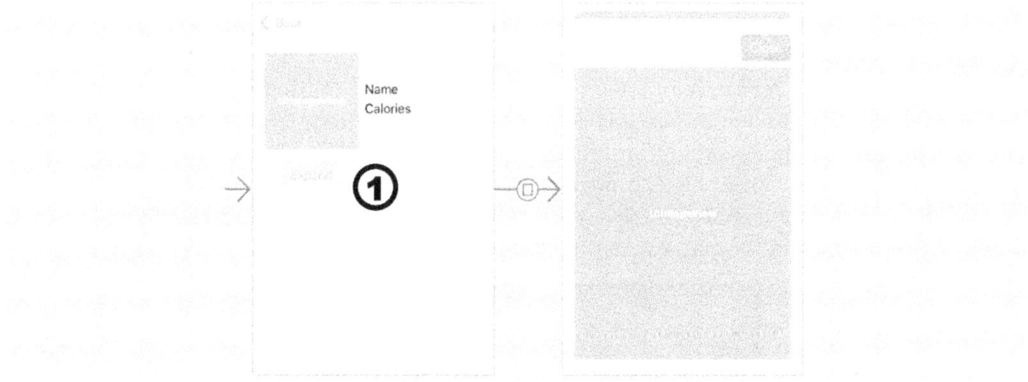

Figure 12-20: *Interface with a Modal Segue*

In Figure 12-20, we have modified the Secondary scene of our example to incorporate a button below the item's thumbnail with the title "Expand" (number 1) and have connected this button with a Present Modally segue to a scene that includes an Image View. Now we can pass the selected item from the Secondary scene to the new scene to show a larger picture on the screen. For this purpose, the **`SecondaryViewController`** class has to implement the **`prepare()`** method.

```
override func prepare(for segue: UIStoryboardSegue, sender: Any?) {
   if segue.identifier == "showPicture" {
      let controller = segue.destination as! PictureViewController
      controller.selected = selected
   }
}
```

Listing 12-13: *Sending the selected item to the new scene*

The view controller for the new scene must include a property called **`selected`** to receive the identifier of the selected item and then update the Image View using the item's values. We called this view controller **`PictureViewController`**.

```
import UIKit

class PictureViewController: UIViewController {
   @IBOutlet weak var bigThumbnail: UIImageView!
   var selected: ItemsData.ID!

   override func viewDidLoad() {
      super.viewDidLoad()

      if selected != nil {
         if let item = AppData.selectedCategory?.items.first(where:
{ $0.id == selected! }) {
            bigThumbnail.image = UIImage(named: item.image)
         }
      }
   }
   @IBAction func closeScene(_ sender: UIButton) {
      dismiss(animated: true, completion: nil)
   }
}
```

Listing 12-14: *Showing a large version of the item's thumbnail*

This view controller is very similar to the view controller used for the Secondary scene. It defines the **`selected`** property to receive the selected item and shows the values on the screen (only the image in this case), but it also includes an Action for the Close button to call the **`dismiss()`** method and close the scene.

Depending on the presentation style selected and the device running the application, the modal scene will adopt different designs. For example, on an iPhone in portrait mode, the scene is always shown as a sheet with a transition determined by the Transition option, but on an iPad the scene is shown with the selected presentation style (in large iPhones in landscape mode, a presentation other than Full Screen always defaults to Page Sheet). Figure 12-21, below, is what we see when we present the scene with the Page Sheet mode on an iPad.

Figure 12-21: *Page Sheet presentation style*

Do It Yourself: Add a button below the thumbnail in the Secondary scene with the title "Expand" (Figure 12-20, number 1). Add a scene to the Storyboard and connect the button to this scene with a Present Modally segue. Assign the segue the identifier "showPicture" and the Presentation style Page Sheet. Add a button with the title "Close" and an Image View to the new scene (Remember to assign a higher Vertical Content Hugging Priority to the button if necessary). Create a subclass of **UIViewController** called **PictureViewController** and assign it to the new scene. Connect the Image View and the button with an Outlet called **bigThumbnail** and an Action called **closeScene()**. Complete the **PictureViewController** class with the code in Listing 12-14 and add the method in Listing 12-13 to the **SecondaryViewController** class. Run the application on the iPad simulator, select an item, and press the Expand button. You should see something like Figure 12-21.

The modal scene in this example was presented as a Page Sheet. There are two modes available for Page Sheets: large and medium. A large Page Sheet is displayed at full height, and a medium Page Sheet is shown at approximately half the height of the screen. By default, the presentation is large, but we can set a different mode by modifying the controller before the scene is shown on the screen.

UIKit defines a class called **UIPresentationController** to manage the presentation of modal scenes. When a modal scene is created and presented, an object of the **UIPresentationController** class is automatically created to manage the presentation. Page Sheets are created from a subclass of the **UIPresentationController** class called **UISheetPresentationController**. This class includes a property called **detents** that we can use to define the presentation mode. The property takes an array of objects of a class called **Detent**, which includes the following type methods.

medium()—This type method returns a **Detent** object to create a medium Page Sheet.

large()—This type method returns a **Detent** object to create a large Page Sheet.

To provide access to the **UISheetPresentationController** object created for our modal scene, the **UIViewController** class includes the **sheetPresentationController** property. From this property, we can modify the **detents** property to set the Page Sheet's mode. These changes can be performed in the **prepare()** method, before the segue is triggered, as shown next.

```
override func prepare(for segue: UIStoryboardSegue, sender: Any?) {
   if segue.identifier == "showPicture" {
      let controller = segue.destination as! PictureViewController
      controller.selected = selected

      if let sheet = controller.sheetPresentationController {
         sheet.detents = [.medium()]
      }
   }
}
```

Listing 12-15: *Defining a medium Page Sheet*

The **sheetPresentationController** property only returns a value if the presentation style is Page Sheet, so we check whether there is a value in the property and then modify the object's **detents** property. This property takes an array of **Detent** objects. By assigning an array with the value returned by the **medium()** method, the Page Sheet is displayed at half the height of the screen.

Figure 12-22: *Medium Page Sheet*

When the scene is presented as a Form Sheet or a Popover, we can specify its size from the Attributes Inspector panel. The option is called *Use Preferred Explicit Size*, and it appears at the bottom of the panel when the scene is selected (Figure 12-22, number 1).

Figure 12-23: *Use Preferred Explicit Size option*

This is not the same option as the Simulated Size offered by the Size Inspector panel (Figure 7-14). The Simulated Size option determines the size of the scene in the Storyboard, while the Use Preferred Explicit Size option sets the size the scene is going to have when the application is running. We can set both options to the same values if we want to work on a scene that matches what the user is going to see on the screen. Figure 12-24, below, shows the modal scene from the previous example presented on an iPad as a Form Sheet and with an explicit size of 300 x 400.

Figure 12-24: *Form Sheet presentation with an explicit size*

Do It Yourself: Select the Modal segue and change the Presentation style to Form Sheet. Select the scene, open the Attributes Inspector panel, go to the bottom, activate the option Use Preferred Explicit Size, and assign a size of 300 x 400 points (Figure 12-23). Run the application, select an item, and press the Expand button. You should see something like Figure 12-24.

Adding scenes to the interface with Modal segues is easy, but there are times when our application requires the addition of the scenes dynamically from code. There are several alternatives, but the easiest way to do it is to add the scene to the Storyboard, as always, but disconnected from the rest of the interface. These scenes are not connected to other scenes with segues, but they can be managed from the object created to represent the Storyboard.

When the app is executed, the Storyboard is loaded and processed. The objects representing the scenes and their content are created and connected with each other, but the system also creates an object that represents the Storyboard itself. This object is instantiated from the **`UIStoryboard`** class and offers the following methods to access its content.

instantiateInitialViewController()—This method instantiates and returns the view controller of the initial scene in the Storyboard.

instantiateViewController(withIdentifier: String**)**—This method instantiates and returns the view controller of the scene in the Storyboard that was identified with the string specified by the **withIdentifier** argument.

Independent scenes are added to the Storyboard the same way we do with other scenes, the only difference is that they are not connected to the rest of the scenes. Once the scene is ready, the process to generate its content and view controller are the same. For our example, we will add to our project the scene down below with a view controller called **`SingleViewController`**.

Figure 12-25: *Single scene in the Storyboard*

The view controller for this scene only needs an Action for the Close button.

```
import UIKit

class SingleViewController: UIViewController {
   @IBAction func closeHelp(_ sender: UIButton) {
      dismiss(animated: true, completion: nil)
   }
}
```

Listing 12-16: *Dismissing a single scene*

To be able to present this scene from code, we must assign it an identifier from the Identity Inspector panel. The option is called *Storyboard ID*. For our example, we identified the scene with the string "helpView".

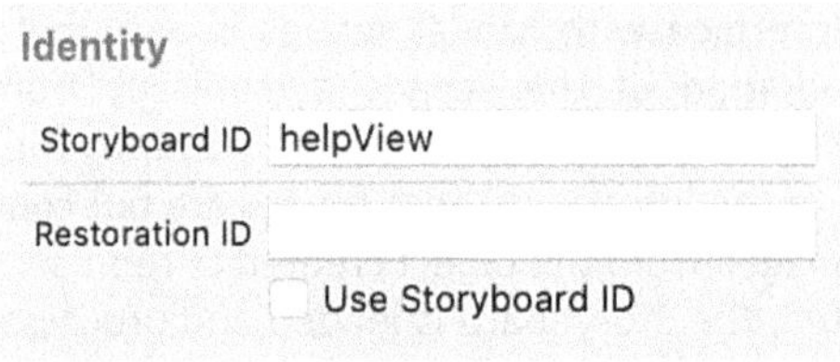

Identity

Storyboard ID helpView

Restoration ID

Use Storyboard ID

Figure 12-26: *Option to assign an identifier to a scene*

To demonstrate how to open these scenes, we have incorporated a Bar Button Item called "Help" to the Navigation Bar of the Primary scene. When the button is pressed, the **PrimaryViewController** class has to instantiate the view controller for this scene with the **instantiateViewController()** method and present it with the **present()** method.

```
@IBAction func showHelp(_ sender: UIBarButtonItem) {
   if let story = storyboard {
      let controller = story.instantiateViewController(withIdentifier:
"helpView") as! SingleViewController
      controller.modalPresentationStyle = .pageSheet
      present(controller, animated: true, completion: nil)
   }
}
```

Listing 12-17: *Instantiating the scene from code*

To provide access to the **UIStoryboard** object, the **UIViewController** class offers the **storyboard** property. In Listing 12-17, we read this property and execute the **instantiateViewController()** method to create an instance of the **SingleViewController** class. The instance is stored in the **controller** constant and its scene is presented on the screen with the **present()** method and the Presentation style **pageSheet**.

Do It Yourself: Add a new scene to the Storyboard with a label and a button (Figure 12-25). Create a **UIViewController** subclass called **SingleViewController**. Select the scene, open the Identity Inspector panel, and assign the subclass to the scene and the string "helpView" to the Storyboard ID option (Figure 12-26). Connect the Close button to the **SingleViewController** class with an Action called **closeHelp()** and complete the class with the code in Listing 12-16. Add a Bar Button Item called Help to the navigation bar of the Primary scene and connect it to the **PrimaryViewController** class with an Action called **showHelp()**. Complete the method with the code in Listing 12-17. Run the application, open the Primary column, and press the Help button to open the scene.

Medium Presentation Controller

As we already mentioned, when a modal scene is presented, an object of the **UIPresentationController** class is automatically created to manage the presentation. This object is assigned to a property of the view controller that is being presented called **presentationController**. From this property, we can access the object and read its current configuration. The following are its most frequently used properties.

presentingViewController—This property returns a reference to the view controller that initiated the presentation.

presentedViewController—This property returns a reference to the view controller that is being presented.

containerView—This property returns a reference to the scene in which the presentation occurs.

presentationStyle—This property returns the presentation style used to present the scene. It is an enumeration of type **UIModalPresentationStyle** with the values **automatic**, **fullScreen**, **pageSheet**, **formSheet**, **currentContext**, **custom**, **overFullScreen**, **overCurrentContext**, **popover**, **blurOverFullScreen**, and none.

adaptivePresentationStyle—This property returns the presentation style used when the horizontal Size Class becomes compact.

We can also designate a delegate for the **UIPresentationController** object to change its configuration according to the current state of the interface. The delegate must conform to the **UIAdaptivePresentationControllerDelegate** protocol and implement its methods.

adaptivePresentationStyle(for: UIPresentationController**)**—This method is called on the delegate to know the presentation style to use when the horizontal Size Class becomes compact.

presentationController(UIPresentationController, **viewControllerForAdaptivePresentationStyle:** UIModalPresentationStyle**)**—This method is called on the delegate to get the view controller to present for the style determined by the second argument.

The **UIPresentationController** object has two presentation styles, one for the normal state and another for the adaptive state. The adaptive state is the state in which the horizontal Size Class is compact. This is the state we will find in small iPhones or when the app is opened in an iPad in multitasking mode. When a modal scene is presented in these conditions, the presentation style is automatically changed to **pageSheet**, but we can specify the style we want implementing the protocol methods. The advantage of these methods is that they are called not only to know the presentation style to use in the adaptive state but also to get the view controller we want to present, and therefore we can designate a completely different view controller for each state. The following example adds another scene to our Storyboard to present when the interface is in an adaptive state.

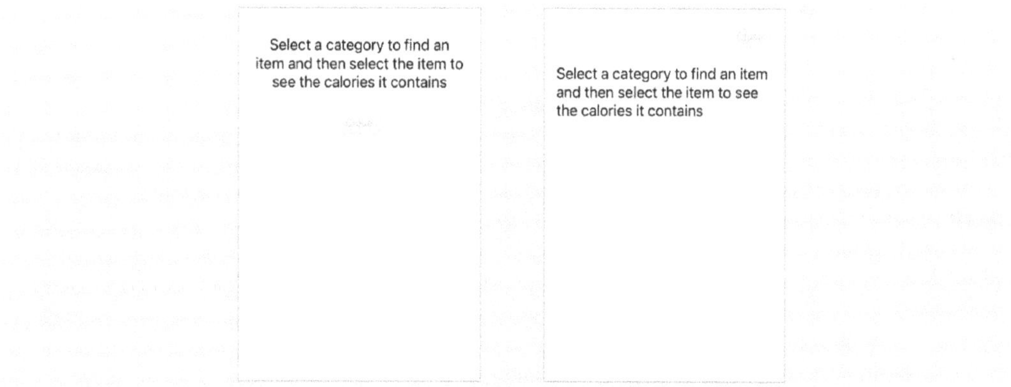

Figure 12-27: *Two interfaces for the same modal scene*

The scene on the left is the same introduced in Figure 12-25, and the one on the right is the new scene we will open in the adaptive state (when the horizontal Size Class is compact). In this example, we just change the position of the Close button, so on iPads the button will be shown at the bottom and on iPhones at the top, but other changes and elements may be introduced to adapt the scene to each device and situation. To control this new scene, we have created a class called **iPhoneViewController** with the Action for the button.

```
import UIKit

class iPhoneViewController: UIViewController {
   @IBAction func closeHelp(_ sender: UIButton) {
      dismiss(animated: true, completion: nil)
   }
}
```

Listing 12-18: *Dismissing the adaptive scene*

We now have the two scenes to present when the Help button is pressed, so all that is left to do is to implement the protocol methods in the **PrimaryViewController** class to load the scene on the right every time the horizontal Size Class is Compact.

```
import UIKit

class PrimaryViewController: UICollectionViewController,
UIAdaptivePresentationControllerDelegate {
   override func viewDidLoad() {
      super.viewDidLoad()
      let config =
UICollectionLayoutListConfiguration(appearance: .sidebar)
      let layout = UICollectionViewCompositionalLayout.list(using:
config)
      collectionView.collectionViewLayout = layout

      prepareDataSource()
      prepareSnapshot()
   }
   func prepareDataSource() {
      let cellRegistration =
UICollectionView.CellRegistration<UICollectionViewListCell,
Categories.ID> { cell, indexPath, itemID in
         if let item = AppData.categories.first(where: { $0.id ==
itemID }) {
            var config = cell.defaultContentConfiguration()
            config.text = item.name
            cell.contentConfiguration = config
         }
      }
      AppData.dataSourceCategories =
UICollectionViewDiffableDataSource<Sections,
Categories.ID>(collectionView: collectionView) { collection, indexPath,
itemID in
         return collection.dequeueConfiguredReusableCell(using:
cellRegistration, for: indexPath, item: itemID)
      }
   }
   func prepareSnapshot() {
      var snapshot = NSDiffableDataSourceSnapshot<Sections,
Categories.ID>()
      snapshot.appendSections([.main])
      snapshot.appendItems(AppData.categories.map({ $0.id }))
      AppData.dataSourceCategories.apply(snapshot)
   }
   override func collectionView(_ collectionView: UICollectionView,
didSelectItemAt indexPath: IndexPath) {
      if let categoryID =
AppData.dataSourceCategories.itemIdentifier(for: indexPath), let category
= AppData.categories.first(where: { $0.id == categoryID }) {
```

```
        if let controller =
splitViewController?.viewController(for: .supplementary) as?
SupplementaryViewController {
            AppData.selectedCategory = category
            controller.prepareSnapshot()

            if splitViewController?.isCollapsed == true {
               splitViewController?.show(.supplementary)
            }
         }
      }
   }
   @IBAction func showHelp(_ sender: UIBarButtonItem) {
      if let story = storyboard {
         let controller = story.instantiateViewController(withIdentifier:
"helpView") as! SingleViewController
         controller.modalPresentationStyle = .formSheet

         let presentation = controller.presentationController
         presentation?.delegate = self

         present(controller, animated: true, completion: nil)
      }
   }
   func adaptivePresentationStyle(for controller:
UIPresentationController) -> UIModalPresentationStyle {
      return .fullScreen
   }
   func presentationController(_ controller: UIPresentationController,
viewControllerForAdaptivePresentationStyle style:
UIModalPresentationStyle) -> UIViewController? {
      var controller: iPhoneViewController!
      if style == .fullScreen {
         if let story = storyboard {
            controller = story.instantiateViewController(withIdentifier:
"iPhoneView") as? iPhoneViewController
         }
      }
      return controller
   }
}
```

Listing 12-19: *Showing an alternative modal scene*

As always, the first thing we need to do is to conform to the protocol and declare the object as the delegate. Although we have done this dozens of times before, in this opportunity we want our class to be the delegate of the **UIPresentationController** object of the view controller that is being presented, so we must get a reference to this object from the **presentationController** property first and then modify its **delegate** property. In our example, we can access this property from the instance created by the **showHelp()** method. We get the reference first and then assign **self** to its **delegate** property. With the delegate set, we can now implement its methods.

In our example, we have set the presentation style as **formSheet**. This is the standard style for interfaces in the normal state (e.g., iPads in landscape mode), but it is automatically adapted to a **pageSheet** style for interfaces in the adaptive state (e.g., iPhones in portrait mode). If we want the modal scene to be shown full screen in the adaptive state, we need to change the style to **fullScreen**. When the scene is in the adaptive state, the **UIPresentationController** object calls the **adaptivePresentationStyle()** method to know what presentation style to use, so we return the **fullScreen** value and the presentation is set to the style we want.

At this point, the presentation style is different for an iPad than an iPhone, but the scene shown on the screen is always the same. To specify a different scene for the adaptive state we implement the **presentationController(UIPresentationController, viewControllerForAdaptivePresentationStyle:)** method. This method is called by the **UIPresentationController** object on its delegate to know the scene it must present for each style, so this is our chance to instantiate the scene's view controller we just added to the interface in Figure 12-27 and return it when the style is **fullScreen** (we have identified this scene in the Storyboard with the string "iPhoneView"). The result is shown in Figure 12-28, below. If we open the view on an iPad or on a large iPhone in landscape mode, the scene with the button at the bottom is presented on the screen, but if we do the same on an iPhone in portrait mode, the scene with the button at the top is open instead.

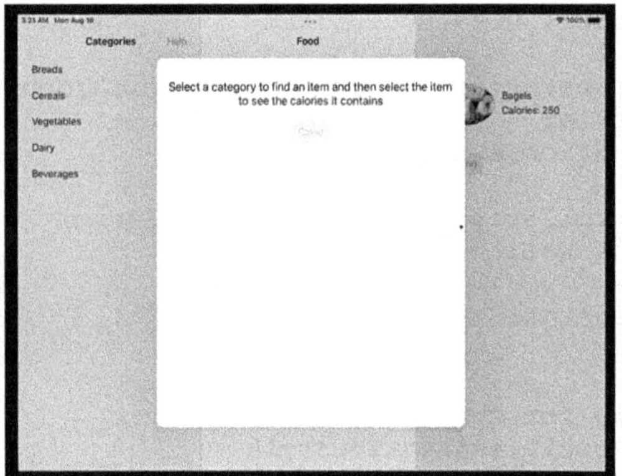

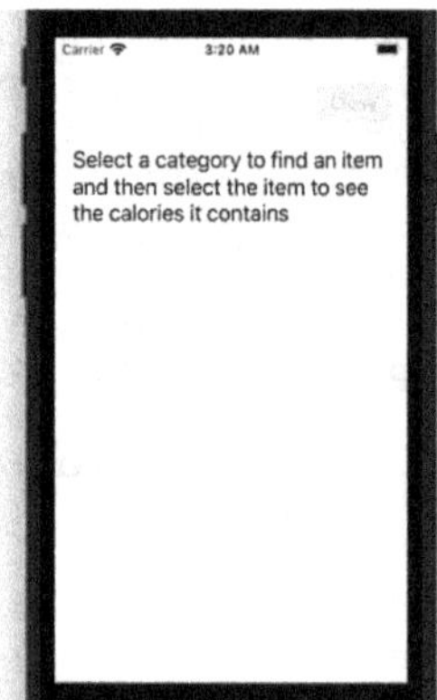

Figure 12-28: *Alternative scenes for different devices*

Do It Yourself: Add a new scene to the Storyboard. Add a button and a label to reproduce the interface in Figure 12-27 (right). Create a new subclass of **UIViewController** called **iPhoneViewController**. Select the scene, open the Identity Inspector panel, assign the subclass to the scene, and give it the Storyboard ID "iPhoneView". Connect the Close button to an Action called **closeHelp()** and complete the class with the code in Listing 12-18. Update the **PrimaryViewController** class with the code in Listing 12-19. Run the application on different devices to see how the modal scenes are displayed.

Medium Popover Presentation Controller

Page Sheets are created from a subclass of the **UIPresentationController** class. This is because the system needs more information to present the sheets, like the height mode. The same happens with popovers. Popovers are created from a subclass called **UIPopoverPresentationController**, which provides all the information necessary to present the popover, such as its margins or the anchor point that determines its position. The following are some of the properties added by the subclass to configure the popover.

popoverLayoutMargins—This property sets or returns the margins that define the maximum portion of the screen designated for the popover. It is a value of type **UIEdgeInsets**.

permittedArrowDirections—This property sets or returns a value that determines the position of the popover's arrow. Every popover contains a little arrow that points to the element that triggered the presentation. This property is used to set the position of that arrow. It is a structure of type **UIPopoverArrowDirection** with the properties **up**, **down**, **left**, **right**, **any**, and **unknown**.

arrowDirection—This property returns the arrow's direction. It is a structure of type **UIPopoverArrowDirection** with the properties **up**, **down**, **left**, **right**, **any**, and **unknown**.

sourceView—This property sets or returns the view to which the popover is anchored. It is an optional value of type **`UIView`**.

sourceRect—This property sets or returns a **`CGRect`** value with the rectangle of the view to which the popover is anchored.

barButtonItem—This property sets or returns the Bar Button Item to which the popover is anchored. It is an optional value of type **`UIBarButtonItem`**.

The **`UIPopoverPresentationController`** object can also work with a delegate to report the state of the popover. The delegate must conform to the **`UIPopoverPresentation-ControllerDelegate`** protocol, which defines the following methods.

prepareForPopoverPresentation(UIPopoverPresentationController**)**—This method is called to notify the delegate that the popover is about to be presented on the screen.

popoverPresentationControllerShouldDismissPopover(UIPopoverPresentationController**)**—This method is called to know if the popover should be dismissed or not.

popoverPresentationControllerDidDismissPopover(UIPopoverPresentationController**)**—This method is called to notify the delegate that the popover was dismissed.

popoverPresentationController(UIPopoverPresentationController, **willRepositionPopoverTo:** CGRect, **in:** UIView**)**—This method is called to notify the delegate that the popover is going to be repositioned to the rectangle and view determined by the arguments.

The steps to add a popover to the Storyboard are the same as for modal scenes, with the exception that we must use a specific segue called *Present As Popover*. Figure 12-29 shows a small scene connected to a button in our Secondary scene with this type of segue. The purpose of the button is to open a popover that shows how many calories are provided by 10 units of the item. The button has been connected to a scene with an explicit size of 300 x 100.

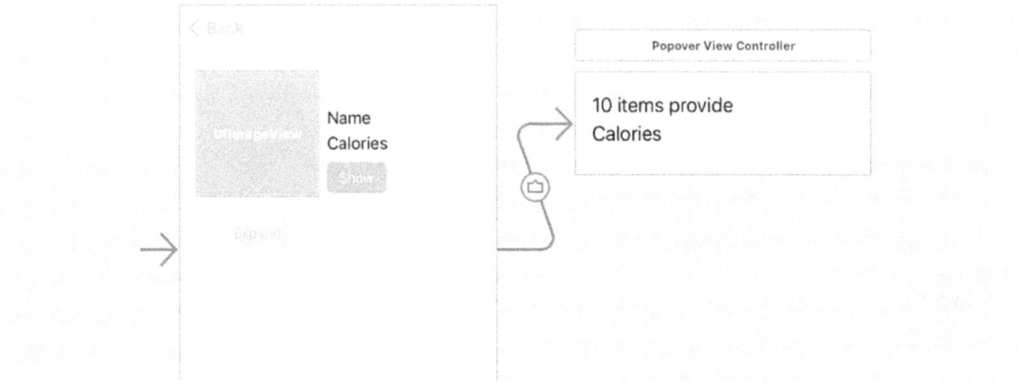

Figure 12-29: *Popover in the Storyboard*

A Present As Popover segue assigns values by default to the **`UIPopoverPresentation-Controller`** object, but we can modify some of them from the Attributes Inspector panel.

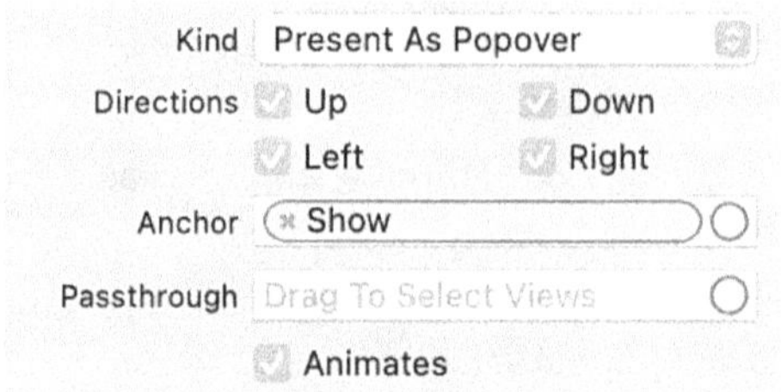

Figure 12-30: *Popover configuration*

The most important option is Directions. These values indicate where the arrow that points to the element that triggered the presentation is going to be located. For example, if we position the arrow at the top (Up), the scene is going to be positioned below the element. By default, the segue activates all the values to let the system decide the most appropriate, but we can suggest a specific position by activating only the ones we want.

The popover of our example shows a message with the calories provided by 10 items, so we must pass the selected item from the Secondary scene to the popover, calculate the calories, and show the result on the screen.

The first step is to modify the **prepare()** method of the **SecondaryViewController** class to send the item's identifier to the popover view controller when the popover's segue is triggered. The segue was identified with the "showPopover" string.

```
override func prepare(for segue: UIStoryboardSegue, sender: Any?) {
   if segue.identifier == "showPicture" {
      let controller = segue.destination as! PictureViewController
      controller.selected = selected
   } else if segue.identifier == "showPopover" {
      let controller = segue.destination as! PopoverViewController
      controller.selected = selected
   }
}
```

Listing 12-20: *Sending the item to the popover*

The view controller for the popover must calculate the total calories provided by 10 items and assign the result to the label. We called it **PopoverViewController**.

```
import UIKit

class PopoverViewController: UIViewController {
   @IBOutlet weak var messageLabel: UILabel!
   @IBOutlet weak var caloriesLabel: UILabel!
   var selected: ItemsData.ID!

   override func viewDidLoad() {
      super.viewDidLoad()
      if selected != nil {
         if let item = AppData.selectedCategory?.items.first(where:
{ $0.id == selected! }) {
            messageLabel.text = "10 \(item.name) provide"
            caloriesLabel.text = "\(item.calories * 10) Calories"
         }
      }
   }
}
```

Listing 12-21: *Displaying information in a popover*

The code in Listing 12-21 defines two Outlets to control the labels, one for the message and another for the calories. When the view is loaded, we prepare the strings with the item's name and calories and assign them to the labels to show them on the screen.

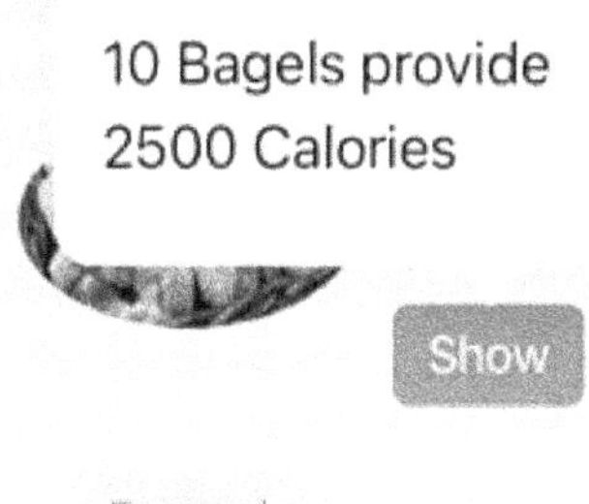

Figure 12-31: *Popover*

If we leave the segue with the configuration by default, the system decides where to position the arrow and the scene for us. In this case, it decided that it was better to present the scene at the top of the Show button, but we can select a different position by deactivating the directions we don't want. For instance, the following is what we see if only the Left arrow is activated.

Figure 12-32: *Popover with a Left arrow*

Do It Yourself: Add a button with the title "Show" below the labels in the Secondary scene. Add a new scene to the Storyboard and connect the button to this scene with a Present As Popover segue. Give the segue the identifier "showPopover". Add two labels to the popover, as shown in Figure 12-29. Select this scene and modify its explicit size from the Attributes Inspector panel (Figure 12-23). You can also modify the size in the Storyboard from the Size Inspector panel (Figure 7-14). Create a subclass of **`UIViewController`** called **`PopoverViewController`** and assign it to the new scene. Complete the subclass with the code in Listing 12-21. Connect the labels to the **`messageLabel`** and **`caloriesLabel`** Outlets. Update the **`prepare()`** method in the **`SecondaryViewController`** class with the code in Listing 12-20. Run the application in the iPad simulator, select an item, and press the Show button. You should see something like Figure 12-31. Select the popover segue, go to the Attributes Inspector panel, and deactivate the directions Up, Down, and Right. Run the application again. You should see something like Figure 12-32.

This works fine on iPads. The scene is presented as a popover, and it can be dismissed tapping anywhere else on the screen. But in a compact horizontal Size Class, the popover is shown as a Page Sheet and the only way for the user to close it is to drag it down. To solve this problem, we can implement the protocol methods we used before for modal scenes. One alternative is to return the **`none`** value from the **`adaptivePresentationStyle()`** method. This tells the **`UIPresentationController`** object that we want the scene to be presented with its original presentation style, so the scene always looks like a popover, no matter the Size Class.

UIKit defines a special protocol for popovers called **UIPopoverPresentationController-Delegate**. This protocol inherits from the **UIAdaptivePresentationControllerDelegate** protocol, so all the methods defined in that protocol are also available for popovers. The following are the modifications we need to introduce to the **SecondaryViewController** class to conform to this protocol and modify the popover's adaptive style.

```
import UIKit

class SecondaryViewController: UIViewController,
UIPopoverPresentationControllerDelegate {
   @IBOutlet weak var itemThumbnail: UIImageView!
   @IBOutlet weak var itemName: UILabel!
   @IBOutlet weak var itemCalories: UILabel!
   var selected: ItemsData.ID!

   override func viewDidLoad() {
      super.viewDidLoad()
      if selected == nil {
         if let item = AppData.selectedCategory.items.first {
            selected = item.id
         }
      }
      if let item = AppData.selectedCategory?.items.first(where: { $0.id
== selected! }) {
         itemThumbnail?.image = UIImage(named: item.image)
         itemName?.text = item.name
         itemCalories?.text = "Calories: \(item.calories)"
      }
   }
   override func prepare(for segue: UIStoryboardSegue, sender: Any?) {
      if segue.identifier == "showPicture" {
         let controller = segue.destination as! PictureViewController
         controller.selected = selected
      } else if segue.identifier == "showPopover" {
         let controller = segue.destination as! PopoverViewController
         controller.selected = selected
         controller.popoverPresentationController?.delegate = self
      }
   }
   func adaptivePresentationStyle(for controller:
UIPresentationController) -> UIModalPresentationStyle {
      return .none
   }
}
```

Listing 12-22: *Modifying the adaptive style*

The **UIViewController** class includes the **popoverPresentationController** property to access the **UIPopoverPresentationController** object in charge of presenting the popover. From this object, we assign the **SecondaryViewController** class as the popover's delegate and then implement the **adaptivePresentationStyle()** method to return the value **none**. From now on, every time the popover is about to be presented in a compact horizontal Size Class, the **UIPopoverPresentationController** object receives the **none** value and therefore does not adapt the presentation style (the popover is not shown as a Page Sheet). Figure 12-33 shows what the popover looks like on an iPhone in portrait mode.

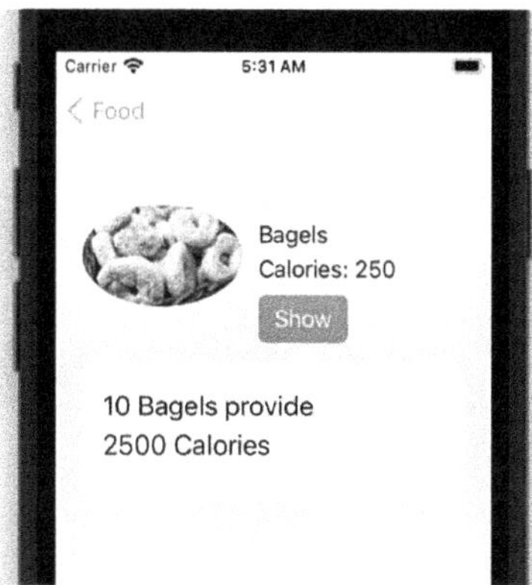

Figure 12-33: *Popover on an iPhone in portrait mode*

Do It Yourself: Update the `SecondaryViewController` class with the code in Listing 12-22. Run the application on the iPhone simulator, select an item and press the Show button to open the popover.

Chapter 13

Alert Views

Basic 13.1 Alert Views

Alert views are predefined modal scenes that can display messages and receive input from the user. Their purpose is to deliver important information that requires immediate attention. For example, an Alert View may be used to ask the user for confirmation before deleting a file or data from the model. They may include a title, a message, Text Fields, and buttons, and be presented full screen or as popovers on some devices. UIKit includes a subclass of the **`UIViewController`** class called **`UIAlertController`** to define these views, but there is no option to add them to the Storyboard, they ought to be created from code with the following initializer.

UIAlertController(title: String?, **message:** String?, **preferredStyle:** Style**)**—This initializer creates a **`UIAlertController`** object configured with the values assigned to the arguments. The **title** argument is the text displayed at the top, the **message** argument is the message displayed below the title, and the **preferredStyle** argument is an enumeration with the values **`alert`** and **`actionSheet`**, to indicate the scene's type (Alert or Action Sheet).

The class also includes properties and methods to add and configure the scene's elements.

title—This property sets or returns the title.

message—This property sets or returns the message

actions—This property returns an array with references to the actions (buttons) in the scene.

textFields—This property returns an array with references to the Text Fields in the scene.

addAction(UIAlertAction**)**—This method adds a new action to the scene. Actions are objects that create buttons for the scene with specific configurations and purposes.

addTextField(configurationHandler: Block**)**—This method adds a Text Field to the scene. The argument is a closure that provides the configuration for the Text Field.

Alert Views present buttons along with the text to receive input from the user. The buttons are created from the **`UIAlertAction`** class. The class includes the following initializer and properties.

UIAlertAction(title: String?, **style:** Style, **handler:** Block**)**—This initializer creates a **`UIAlertAction`** object configured with the values assigned to the arguments. The **title** argument is the title for the button. The **style** argument defines the purpose of the button. The possible values are **`default`** (for a generic type of button), **`cancel`** (for a button that cancels the request), and **`destructive`** (for a button that performs a destructive task, such as deleting a file). The **handler** argument is a closure that is executed when the button is pressed.

title—This property returns a string with the title of the button.

style—This property returns the button's type. It is an enumeration called **`Style`** with the values **`default`**, **`cancel`**, and **`destructive`**.

isEnabled—This property sets or returns a Boolean value that determines whether the button is enabled or not.

There are two types of Alert Views: Alerts and Action Sheets. Alert Views of type Alert are presented at the center of the screen, while those of type Action Sheet are anchored to the bottom of the screen in small devices or presented as popovers in devices with larger screens. They may include messages and buttons, but only the Alert types can include Text Fields.

Basic Alerts

Alert Views of type Alert are usually presented to inform the user that a specific task has been completed or that something went wrong. For example, we may show an Alert View of type Alert to report an error when the user tries to save the value of an empty Text Field. The following interface includes a Text Field and a button to allow the user to enter a name. If the user presses the button before inserting any text, the code displays an Alert View reminding the user that a name is required.

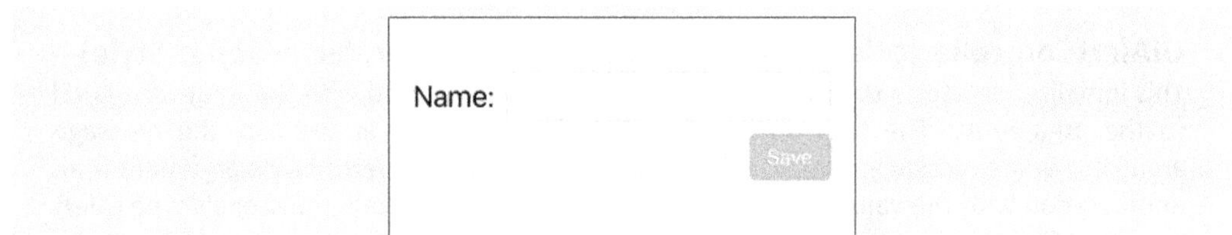

Figure 13-1: *Interface to test Alert Views*

The view controller for this scene must check whether the Text Field contains text or not and show the alert if it is empty.

```
import UIKit

class ViewController: UIViewController {
   @IBOutlet weak var nameText: UITextField!

   @IBAction func saveName(_ sender: UIButton) {
      var text = nameText.text!
      text = text.trimmingCharacters(in: .whitespaces)
      if text == "" {
         showAlert()
      } else {
         print("Value stored: \(text)")
         nameText.text = ""
      }
   }
   func showAlert() {
      let alert = UIAlertController(title: "Error", message: "Insert your
name in the field", preferredStyle: .alert)
      let action = UIAlertAction(title: "OK", style: .default, handler:
nil)
      alert.addAction(action)
      present(alert, animated: true, completion: nil)
   }
}
```

Listing 13-1: *Presenting an Alert View*

The view controller in Listing 13-1 includes an Outlet for the Text Field called **`nameText`** and an Action for the button called **`saveName()`**. When the user presses the button, the Action checks the value of the **`text`** property. If the value is empty, it calls the **`showAlert()`** method to present an Alert View, otherwise it prints a message on the console and clears the field.

The **showAlert()** method creates the view controller with the **UIAlertController()** initializer, which includes the title, the message, and the view's type (Alert in this case). Next, it creates and adds a **UIAlertAction** object for every button to be included. The initializer for this class also allows us to define the information required, like the title for the button, its purpose, and a closure that is going to be executed when the button is pressed. For this example, we need only one button of type Default with no action, so the handler is declared as **nil**. The action is added to the Alert View with the **addAction()** method and then the scene is presented on the screen with the **present()** method, as we did for modal scenes in Chapter 12. If we run the application and press the Save button before typing any text, an Alert View reminds us that we must enter our name.

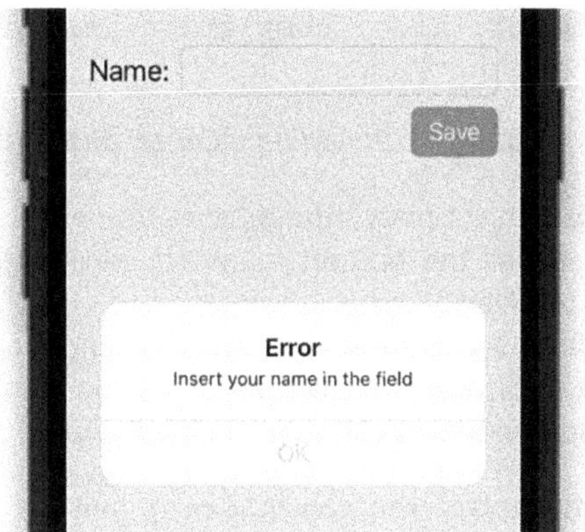

Figure 13-2: *Alert View of type Alert with a single button*

Do It Yourself: Create a new project. Add a label, a Text Field, and a button to the scene. Connect the Text Field to the view controller with an Outlet called **nameText** and the button to an Action called **saveName()**. Complete the **ViewController** class with the code in Listing 13-1. Run the application and press the button. You should see the alert shown in Figure 13-2.

The OK button in our example doesn't do anything other than dismissing the scene. If we want to perform a task, we must provide a closure for the **handler** argument of the **UIAlertAction** initializer. For instance, the following code changes the background color of the Text Field after the OK button is pressed.

```
func showAlert() {
   let alert = UIAlertController(title: "Error", message: "Insert the name in the field", preferredStyle: .alert)
   let action = UIAlertAction(title: "OK", style: .default, handler: { (action) in
      self.nameText.backgroundColor = UIColor(red: 255.0/255.0, green: 230.0/255.0, blue: 230.0/255.0, alpha: 1.0)
   })
   alert.addAction(action)
   present(alert, animated: true, completion: nil)
}
```

Listing 13-2: *Changing the background color of the Text Field when the button is pressed*

We can include more buttons in the Alert View by adding more actions. The following example asks the user if the application should store the value anyway and offers a Cancel button to cancel the operation.

```
func showAlert() {
   let alert = UIAlertController(title: "The field is empty", message:
"Are you sure do you want to store an empty string?",
preferredStyle: .alert)
   let action = UIAlertAction(title: "Yes", style: .default, handler:
{ (action) in
      print("Value stored")
   })
   alert.addAction(action)
   let cancel = UIAlertAction(title: "Cancel", style: .cancel, handler:
nil)
   alert.addAction(cancel)
   present(alert, animated: true, completion: nil)
}
```

Listing 13-3: *Adding a Cancel button*

The **UIAlertController** object places the buttons inside the scene in the order they were declared in code. We may add all the buttons we need, except for buttons of type Cancel, of which only one is permitted per Alert View.

Because we did not include a closure for the **handler** argument of the Cancel button, the function of the button is just to dismiss the view, but all buttons can perform additional tasks, we just need to provide the closure in the **UIAlertAction** initializer.

Do It Yourself: Replace the **showAlert()** method in your project with the methods in Listings 13-2 and 13-3 to test each example.

Alert Views of type Alert may also include Text Fields. Text Fields are usually added to an Alert View to get input from the user or to create sign-up or log-in forms. For instance, we can create an interface with an initial scene that allows the user to log in, and a second scene that opens if the values inserted by the user match the data in the model. The interface below includes a welcoming window with a button called Log In to open an Alert View to insert an email and a password.

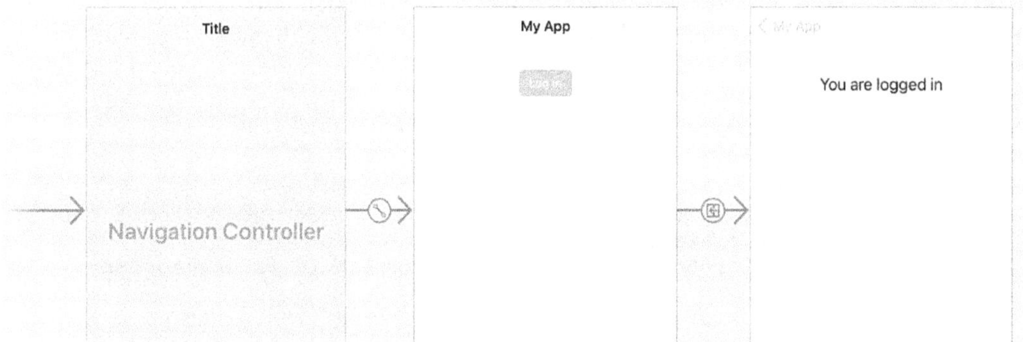

Figure 13-3: *Interface to log in*

Text Fields are added to the Alert View with the **addTextField()** method. In our example we need two: one for the email and another for the password. The view controller of the initial scene must include an Action for the Log In button to create the Alert View.

```
import UIKit

class ViewController: UIViewController {
   @IBAction func loginUser(_ sender: UIButton) {
      let alert = UIAlertController(title: "Insert Email and Password",
message: nil, preferredStyle: .alert)
```

```
      let cancel = UIAlertAction(title: "Cancel", style: .cancel,
handler: nil)
      alert.addAction(cancel)

      let action = UIAlertAction(title: "Login", style: .default,
handler: { (action) in
         if let fields = alert.textFields {
            let email = fields[0].text
            let password = fields[1].text

            if email == "test@yahoo.com" && password == "12345" {
               self.performSegue(withIdentifier: "showMainScreen",
sender: self)
            }
         }
      })
      alert.addAction(action)

      alert.addTextField(configurationHandler: { (textField) in
         textField.placeholder = "Email"
      })
      alert.addTextField(configurationHandler: { (textField) in
         textField.placeholder = "Password"
         textField.isSecureTextEntry = true
      })
      present(alert, animated: true, completion: nil)
   }
}
```

Listing 13-4: *Creating and processing a login form*

The **`addTextField()`** method includes an argument that takes a closure to configure the Text Field. For the email, we only need a placeholder, but the Text Field for the password should be declared as secure with the **`isSecureTextEntry`** property, so the password is not displayed on the screen.

The Alert View includes two buttons: Cancel and Login. When the user presses the Login button, we compare the values inserted in the fields with the data we have in our model (usually a database in the device or in a server). To access the Text Fields from inside the closure, we read the **`textFields`** property of the Alert View. This property contains an array with references to the Text Fields available. The indexes of the array follow the order of the Text Fields in the code (the first one is at index 0, the next one at index 1, and so on). For this example, we keep it simple and compare the values of each Text Field with hard-coded strings. If the values match, we perform the segue to open the second scene where the user can begin working with our app (the segue is a Show segue identified with the string "showMainScreen").

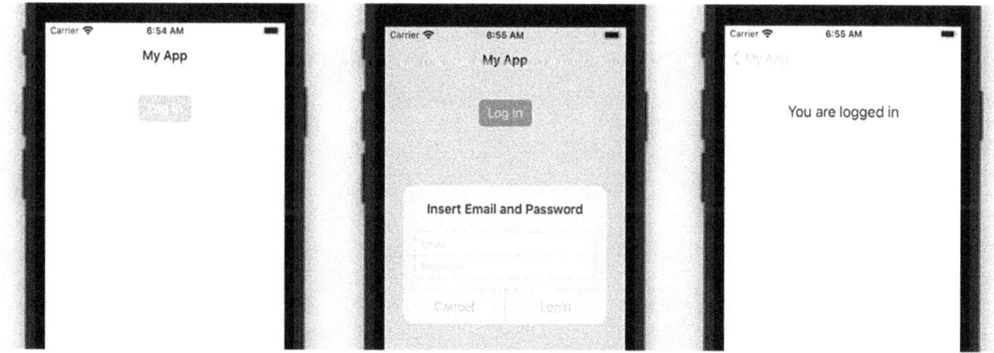

Figure 13-4: *Alert View with Text Fields*

Do It Yourself: Create a new project. Embed the scene in a Navigation Controller. Add a button with the title Log In to the scene. Add a second scene to the Storyboard. Add a label with the text "You are logged in" to the second scene. Connect the first scene to the second scene with a Show segue. Give the segue the identifier "showMainScreen". Connect the Log In button with an Action called **loginUser()**. Complete the Action with the code in Listing 13-4. Run the application and press the button. Insert the email "test@yahoo.com" and password "12345". Press Login. You should see something like Figure 13-4.

Basic Action Sheets

Action Sheets are generally presented when the user must decide between multiple available options. As shown in the following example, the creation of Action Sheets is like Alert Views, but the initializer must be defined with the style **actionSheet**. The example assumes that the interface contains a button connected to an Action called **openSheet()**.

```
import UIKit

class ViewController: UIViewController {
   @IBAction func openSheet(_ sender: UIButton) {
      let alert = UIAlertController(title: "Emails", message: "What do
you want to do with the message?", preferredStyle: .actionSheet)

      let action1 = UIAlertAction(title: "Move to Inbox",
style: .default, handler: nil)
      alert.addAction(action1)
      let action2 = UIAlertAction(title: "Delete", style: .destructive,
handler: nil)
      alert.addAction(action2)
      let cancel = UIAlertAction(title: "Cancel", style: .cancel,
handler: nil)
      alert.addAction(cancel)

      present(alert, animated: true, completion: nil)
   }
}
```

Listing 13-5: *Creating an Action Sheet*

The code in Listing 13-5 creates an Alert View of type Action Sheet when the user presses the button on the interface. This Action Sheet contains a total of three buttons: a **default** button called Move to Inbox, a **destructive** button called Delete, and a **cancel** button called Cancel. We didn't include any handler for the buttons, so their only purpose is to dismiss the scene, but the example illustrates how an Action Sheet is created and how the buttons are organized. No matter the position of the buttons in the code, the **cancel** button is always displayed at the bottom, in a separate box, and the **destructive** button is highlighted in red.

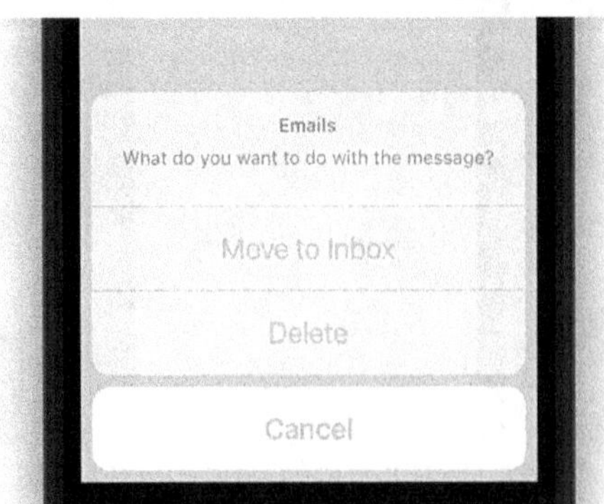

Figure 13-5: *Action Sheet*

Do It Yourself: Create a new project. Add a button called Open Sheet to the scene. Connect the button to the **ViewController** class with an Action called **openSheet()**. Complete the Action with the code in Listing 13-5. Run the application on an iPhone simulator and press the button. You should see something like Figure 13-5.

As we already mentioned, Action Sheets are presented as modal scenes at the bottom of the screen in small devices, but as popovers in iPads. The problem is that the system cannot display a popover without the necessary information. If we execute the previous application on an iPad, we get an error and the application crashes. To make sure that the code works on every device, we must configure the presentation controller. For this purpose, the **UIAlertController** object includes the **popoverPresentationController** property with a reference to the **UIPopoverPresentationController** object in charge of the presentation when the presentation style is **popover**. The values we need to provide are the view to which the Action Sheet is anchored, the rectangle inside the view the popover's arrow points to, and the direction of the arrow.

```
import UIKit

class ViewController: UIViewController {
   @IBAction func openSheet(_ sender: UIButton) {
      let alert = UIAlertController(title: "Emails", message: "What do
you want to do with the message?", preferredStyle: .actionSheet)

      if let popover = alert.popoverPresentationController {
         popover.sourceView = sender
         popover.sourceRect = sender.bounds
         popover.permittedArrowDirections = [.up]
      }
      let action1 = UIAlertAction(title: "Move to Inbox",
style: .default, handler: nil)
      alert.addAction(action1)
      let cancel = UIAlertAction(title: "Cancel", style: .cancel,
handler: nil)
      alert.addAction(cancel)
      let action2 = UIAlertAction(title: "Delete", style: .destructive,
handler: nil)
      alert.addAction(action2)
      present(alert, animated: true, completion: nil)
   }
}
```

Listing 13-6: *Presenting the Action Sheet as a popover in iPads*

The view controller in Listing 13-6 adds the configuration for the popover to the previous example. We decided to anchor the popover to the button that opens the Alert View, so we assign the reference received by the Action to the **sourceView** property of the **UIPopoverPresentationController** object. This anchors the popover to the button, but we still must determine to which part of the button's view the arrow is going to point to. By assigning the internal frame of the button's view to the **sourceRect** property we make sure that the arrow always points to one side of the button and the button is not covered by the view. Finally, we set the **permittedArrowDirections** property with the value **up**, so the scene is positioned below the button.

The Action Sheet adapts the presentation style to the space available and also the design. If we run the example in Listing 13-6 on an iPad, the Cancel button is automatically removed because the user can dismiss the popover by tapping anywhere else on the screen.

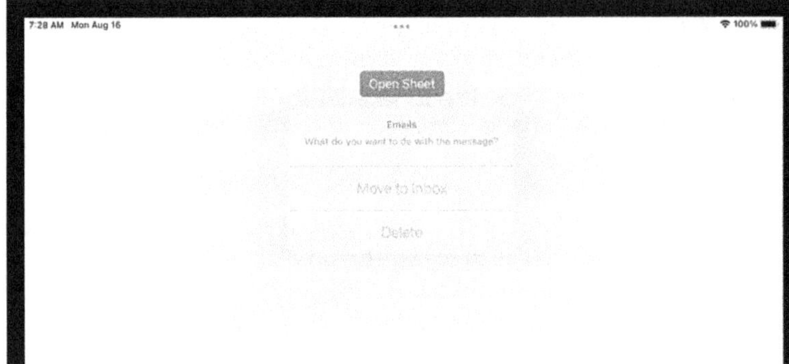

Figure 13-6: *Action Sheet on an iPad*

Do It Yourself: Update the **`ViewController`** class with the code in Listing 13-6. Run the application on an iPad simulator and press the button. You should see something like Figure 13-6.

Chapter 14
Concurrency

Basic 14.1 Asynchronous and Concurrent Tasks

Apple systems can take advantage of the multiple cores in modern processors to execute different pieces of code simultaneously, increasing the amount of work the application can perform at any given time. For example, we may have a code that downloads a file from the Internet and another code that shows the progress on the screen. In cases like this, we cannot wait for one code to finish to execute the other; we need the two pieces of code to run simultaneously.

Units of code that are prepared to run in parallel are called *Tasks*. In Swift, tasks can be implemented through asynchronous and concurrent programming. Asynchronous programming is a programming pattern in which the code waits for a process to finish before completing the task. This allows the system to share computing resources among many processes. While waiting, the system can use the resources to perform other tasks. On the other hand, concurrent programming implements code that can take advantage of multiple core processors to execute tasks simultaneously.

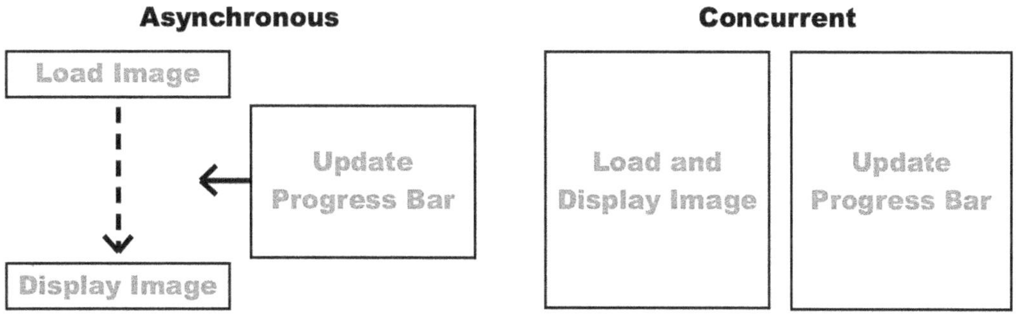

Figure 14-1: *Asynchronous and concurrent programming*

Because multiple applications can run at the same time, the system doesn't allocate certain number of cores per application. What it does is to create execution threads, assign the tasks to the threads, and then decide which threads are going to be executed by which core depending on the available resources. In the example of Figure 14-1, left, there is an asynchronous task that loads and image from the Web and then displays it on the screen. While waiting for the image to download, the thread is free to perform other tasks, so the system may use it to execute a different task that updates the progress bar. On the right, the tasks were created as concurrent tasks and therefore they are executed simultaneously in different threads.

Basic Tasks

Asynchronous and concurrent code is defined by tasks. The Swift Standard Library includes the **`Task`** structure to create and manage these tasks. The following is the structure's initializer.

> **Task(priority:** TaskPriority?, **operation:** Closure**)**—This initializer creates and runs a new task. The **priority** argument is a structure that helps the system decide when to execute the task. The structure includes type properties to defined standard priorities. The currently available are **`background`**, **`high`**, **`low`**, **`medium`**, **`userInitiated`**, and **`utility`**. The **operation** argument is a closure with the statements to be executed by the task.

The **Task** structure includes the following properties to cancel a task.

isCancelled—This property returns a Boolean value that indicates if the task was cancelled.

cancel()—This method cancels the task.

There are also a few type properties and methods available to get information from the current task or create tasks that perform specific processes. The following are the most frequently used.

currentPriority—This property returns the priority of the current task. It is a **TaskPriority** structure with the properties **background**, **high**, **low**, **medium**, **userInitiated**, and **utility**.

isCancelled—This property returns a Boolean value that indicates whether the current task was cancelled.

sleep(UInt64)—This method suspends the current task the time specified by the argument in nanoseconds.

Basic Async and Await

Asynchronous and concurrent tasks are defined in Swift with the **async** and **await** keywords. For instance, to create an asynchronous task, we mark a method with **async** and then wait for that method to complete with **await**. This means that an asynchronous method can only be called with the **await** keyword from inside another asynchronous method, which creates an indefinite cycle. To start the cycle, we can create an asynchronous task with the **Task** structure, as shown next.

```
import UIKit

class ViewController: UIViewController {
   override func viewDidLoad() {
      super.viewDidLoad()
      Task(priority: .background) {
         let imageName = await loadImage(name: "image1")
         print(imageName)
      }
   }
   func loadImage(name: String) async -> String {
      await Task.sleep(3 * 1000000000)
      return "Name: \(name)"
   }
}
```

Listing 14-1: *Creating an asynchronous task*

The **Task** structure in this example is created with a **background** priority, which means that the task is not going to have priority over other parallel tasks. In the closure, we called the **loadImage()** method and then print the value returned. This is a method we defined to simulate the process of downloading an image form the Web. We will learn how to download data and connect to the Web later, but for now we use the **sleep()** method to pause the task for 3 seconds and pretend that the image is downloading (the method takes a value in nanoseconds). Once this pause is over, the method returns a string with the name received from the task. To define the method as asynchronous, we add the **async** keyword after the parameters, and then call it with the **await** keyword to indicate that the task must wait for this process to be over.

The application creates the task and adds it to the thread. When the system is ready to run it, it executes the closure. In the closure, we call the **loadImage()** method and wait for its completion. The method pauses for 3 seconds and then returns a string. After this, the task continues executing the statements, and a message is printed on the console.

Do It Yourself: Create a new project. Update the **ViewController** class with the code in Listing 14-1. Run the application. You should see a message appear on the console after 3 seconds. Use this project to try the rest of the examples.

A task can perform multiple asynchronous processes. For instance, in the following example we call the **loadImage()** method three times to download three images.

```
import UIKit

class ViewController: UIViewController {
   override func viewDidLoad() {
      super.viewDidLoad()
      Task(priority: .background) {
         let imageName1 = await loadImage(name: "image1")
         let imageName2 = await loadImage(name: "image2")
         let imageName3 = await loadImage(name: "image3")
         print("\(imageName1), \(imageName2), and \(imageName3)")
      }
   }
   func loadImage(name: String) async -> String {
      await Task.sleep(3 * 1000000000)
      return "Name: \(name)"
   }
}
```

Listing 14-2: *Running multiple asynchronous tasks*

The processes are executed one by one, in sequential order. The task waits for a process to be over before executing the next. In this case, the whole task is going to take 9 seconds to finish (3 seconds per process). The more processes we add to an asynchronous task, the more is going to take to finish. For this reason, sometimes we might need to cancel a task before it is completed.

Cancelling a task is easy. We must assign the task to a variable and then call the **cancel()** method on it. But the processes are not automatically cancelled; we must detect whether the task has been cancelled with the **isCancelled** property and stop the process ourselves.

```
import UIKit

class ViewController: UIViewController {
   override func viewDidLoad() {
      super.viewDidLoad()
      let myTask = Task(priority: .background) {
         let imageName = await loadImage(name: "image1")
         print(imageName)
      }
      Timer.scheduledTimer(withTimeInterval: 2.0, repeats: false)
{ (timer) in
         print("The time is up")
         myTask.cancel()
      }
   }
   func loadImage(name: String) async -> String {
      await Task.sleep(3 * 1000000000)
      if !Task.isCancelled {
         return "Name: \(name)"
      } else {
```

```
            return "Task Cancelled"
         }
      }
}
```

Listing 14-3: *Cancelling a task*

This example assigns the previous task to a constant and then creates a timer to call the **cancel()** method on the task 2 seconds later. In the **loadImage()** method, we read the **isCancelled** property and respond accordingly. If the task was cancelled, we return the "Task Cancelled" message, otherwise, the name is returned as before. Notice that in this case we are working inside a process executed by the task, so we use the type property instead of the instance property (we read the **isCancelled** property from the data type, not the instance). This property returns **true** or **false** depending on the state of the current task. As a result, the task is cancelled before it is completed.

Tasks can receive and return values. The **Task** structure includes the **value** property to provide access to the value returned by the task. Of course, we also need to wait for the task to complete before reading this value, as shown next.

```
import UIKit

class ViewController: UIViewController {
   override func viewDidLoad() {
      super.viewDidLoad()
      Task(priority: .background) {
         let imageName = await loadImage(name: "image1")
         print(imageName)
      }
   }
   func loadImage(name: String) async -> String {
      let result = Task(priority: .background) { () -> String in
         let imageData = await getMetadata()
         return "Name: \(name) Size: \(imageData)"
      }
      let message = await result.value
      return message
   }
   func getMetadata() async -> Int {
      await Task.sleep(3 * 1000000000)
      return 50000
   }
}
```

Listing 14-4: *Reading a value returned by a task*

Because we need to wait for the task to finish before using the value, we have defined a second task. The process starts as always, with a task that calls the **loadImage()** method, but now we create a second task in this method that returns a string. This task executes another asynchronous method that waits for 3 seconds and returns the number 50000. After this process is over, the task creates a string with the name and the number and returns it. We then get the string from the **value** property, and return it to the original task, which prints it on the console.

So far, we have worked with asynchronous methods, but we can also define asynchronous properties. All we need to do is to define the getter with the **async** keyword, as shown next.

```
import UIKit

class ViewController: UIViewController {
   var thumbnail: String {
      get async {
         await Task.sleep(3 * 1000000000)
```

```
            return "mythumbnail"
         }
      }
      override func viewDidLoad() {
         super.viewDidLoad()
         Task(priority: .background) {
            let imageName = await thumbnail
            print(imageName)
         }
      }
}
```

Listing 14-5: *Defining and asynchronous properties*

This time, instead of calling a method, the task reads a property. The property suspends the tasks for 3 seconds and returns a string. Again, we are suspending the task for didactic purposes, but we can perform any demanding task we want in this property, such as downloading an image from the Web or processing data.

Basic Errors

Asynchronous tasks are not always successful, so we must be prepared to process the errors returned. If we are creating our own tasks, we can define the errors with an enumeration that conforms to the **Error** protocol, as explain in Chapter 3 (see Listing 3-190). The following example defines a structure with two errors, one to return when no metadata is found on the server (**noData**), and another for when the image is not available (**noImage**).

```
import UIKit

enum MyErrors: Error {
   case noData, noImage
}
class ViewController: UIViewController {
   override func viewDidLoad() {
      super.viewDidLoad()

      Task(priority: .background) {
         do {
            let imageName = try await loadImage(name: "image1")
            print(imageName)
         } catch MyErrors.noData {
            print("Error: No Data Available")
         } catch MyErrors.noImage {
            print("Error: No Image Available")
         }
      }
   }
   func loadImage(name: String) async throws -> String {
      await Task.sleep(3 * 1000000000)

      let error = true
      if error {
         throw MyErrors.noImage
      }
      return "Name: \(name)"
   }
}
```

Listing 14-6: *Responding to errors*

The **loadImage()** method in this example always throws a **noImage** error to test the code. The task checks for errors with a **do catch** statement and prints a message on the console to report the result. Notice that when an asynchronous function can throw errors, we must declare the **throws** keyword after **async**, as shown in Listing 14-6.

Basic Concurrency

Asynchronous tasks are useful when we want to free resources for the system to perform other tasks, like updating the interface, but when we want to run two tasks simultaneously, we need concurrency. For this purpose, the Swift Standard Library defines the **async let** statement. To turn an asynchronous task into multiple concurrent tasks, all we need to do is to declare the processes with the **async let** statement, as shown next.

```
import UIKit

class ViewController: UIViewController {
   override func viewDidLoad() {
      super.viewDidLoad()
      let currentTime = Date()

      Task(priority: .background) {
         async let imageName1 = loadImage(name: "image1")
         async let imageName2 = loadImage(name: "image2")
         async let imageName3 = loadImage(name: "image3")

         let listNames = await "\(imageName1), \(imageName2), and \
(imageName3)"
         print(listNames)
         print("Total Time: \(Date().timeIntervalSince(currentTime))")
      }
   }
   func loadImage(name: String) async -> String {
      await Task.sleep(3 * 1000000000)
      return "Name: \(name)"
   }
}
```

Listing 14-7: *Defining a concurrent task*

Every time a process is declared with the **async let** statement the system creates a new concurrent task that runs in parallel with the rest of the tasks. In the example of Listing 14-7, we create three concurrent tasks (imageName1, imageName2, and imageName3). The process is the same as before, they call the **loadImage()** method, the method pauses the task for 3 seconds, and returns a string. But because this time the processes run in parallel, the time they take to complete is around 3 seconds (not 9 seconds, as in the example of Listing 14-2). Notice that to make sure the tasks are running concurrently we calculate the seconds they take to complete with a **Date** structure and print the interval on the console.

Medium Actors

When working with concurrent tasks, we could run into a problem called *data race*. A data race happens when two or more tasks running in parallel try to access the same data. For instance, they try to modify the value of a property at the same time. This could lead to errors or serious bugs. To solve this issue, the Swift Standard Library includes actors.

Actors are data types that isolate parallel tasks from one another, so when a task is modifying the values of an actor, other tasks are forced to wait. Actors are reference types and are defined like classes, but instead of the **class** keyword, they are declared with the **actor** keyword. Another important difference with classes is that the properties and methods must be accessed asynchronously (we must wait with the **await** keyword). This ensures that the code can wait until the actor is free to respond (no other task is accessing the actor).

The following example illustrates how actors work. The code declares an actor with two properties and a method, creates an instance, and then calls the method from multiple tasks.

```
import UIKit

actor ItemData {
   var name: String
   var counter: Int

   init(name: String) {
      self.name = name
      self.counter = 0
   }
   func changeName(newName: String) {
      name = newName
      counter += 1
   }
}
class ViewController: UIViewController {
   var item: ItemData!

   override func viewDidLoad() {
      super.viewDidLoad()
      item = ItemData(name: "Undefined")

      Task(priority: .background) {
         async let imageName1 = loadImage(name: "potatos")
         async let imageName2 = loadImage(name: "milk")
         async let imageName3 = loadImage(name: "orange")

         let listNames = await "\(imageName1), \(imageName2), and \
(imageName3)"
         print(listNames)
      }
   }
   func loadImage(name: String) async -> String {
      await item.changeName(newName: name)

      let count = await item.counter
      return "\(name) \(count)"
   }
}
```

Listing 14-8: *Defining an actor*

The method in the **ItemData** actor updates the value of the **name** property and then increments the value of the **counter** property by 1 to keep a count on the number of times the name was modified. When the view is loaded, we create an instance of this actor with the name "Undefined" and then define a task with three concurrent tasks inside. The concurrent tasks call the **loadImage()** method. In this method we call the **changeName()** method to modify the name in the actor and then return this value along with the current value of the **counter** property. Notice that we wait for both, the method and the property, to make sure the tasks don't overlap.

Basic Main Actor

As we already mentioned, tasks are assigned to execution threads and then the system distributes these threads among the multiple cores of a processor to perform the tasks as fast and smoothly as possible. A thread can manage multiple tasks, and multiple threads may be created for our application. Besides the threads initialized to process asynchronous and concurrent tasks, the system always creates a thread, called *main thread*, to start the application and run non-asynchronous codes, including the code that creates and updates the interface. This means that if we try to modify the interface from an asynchronous or concurrent task, we may cause a data race or a serious bug. To avoid these conflicts, the Swift Standard Library defines the Main Actor. The Main Actor is an actor created by the system that makes sure that every task that wants to interact with the main code or modify the elements of the interface waits for other tasks to finish.

Swift provides two easy ways to make sure that our code runs on the Main Actor (the main thread): the **@MainActor** modifier and the **run()** method. With the **@MainActor** modifier we can mark an entire method to run on the main thread, while the **run()** method executes a closure in the main thread. For instance, in the following example we mark the **loadImage()** method with **@MainActor** to make sure that the code inside the method is executed in the main thread and we are able to modify the value of a label.

```
import UIKit

class ViewController: UIViewController {
   @IBOutlet weak var myLabel: UILabel!

   override func viewDidLoad() {
      super.viewDidLoad()
      Task(priority: .background) {
         await loadImage(name: "image1")
      }
   }
   @MainActor func loadImage(name: String) async {
      myLabel.text = name
      print(name)
   }
}
```

Listing 14-9: *Executing a method in the Main Actor*

This code creates an asynchronous task as before, but now the method is marked with **@MainActor**, so the code is executed in the main thread, and we can safely assign a text to the label.

Do It Yourself: Update the **ViewController** class with the code in Listing 14-9. Add a label to the scene and connect it with the **myLabel** Outlet. Run the application. You should see the text "image1" on the screen.

Most of the time, only part of our code deals with the interface, but the rest can be executed in the current thread. For cases like this, we can implement the **run()** method. This is a type method defined by the **MainActor** structure (the structure used to create the Main Actor). The method takes a closure with the statements we need to execute in the main thread.

```
import UIKit

class ViewController: UIViewController {
   @IBOutlet weak var myLabel: UILabel!

   override func viewDidLoad() {
      super.viewDidLoad()

      Task(priority: .background) {
         await loadImage(name: "image1")
      }
   }
```

```
    func loadImage(name: String) async {
       await MainActor.run {
          myLabel.text = name
       }
       print(name)
    }
}
```

Listing 14-10: *Executing code in the Main Actor*

This code is the same as before, but now only the statement that modifies the interface runs in the main thread, while the rest of the statements in the method keep running in the thread assigned to the task. Notice that the **`run()`** method is marked with **`await`**. The **`await`** keyword is necessary because the method may have to wait for the main thread to be free to execute the statements.

The **`run()`** method can also return a value. This is useful when we need to get information from the interface. In the following example, we get the label's current text and print it on the console.

```
import UIKit

class ViewController: UIViewController {
   @IBOutlet weak var myLabel: UILabel!

   override func viewDidLoad() {
      super.viewDidLoad()

      Task(priority: .background) {
         await loadImage(name: "image1")
      }
   }
   func loadImage(name: String) async {
      let labelText: String = await MainActor.run {
         let text = myLabel.text
         return text ?? ""
      }
      print(labelText)
   }
}
```

Listing 14-11: *Returning a value from the Main Actor*

Medium Asynchronous Sequences

Sometimes, information may be returned as a sequence of values, but the values may not be available all at once. In cases like this, we can create an asynchronous sequence. This sequence is like an array, but the values are returned asynchronously, so we must wait for each value to be ready.

The Swift Standard Library includes two protocols to create asynchronous sequences: the **`AsyncSequence`** protocol to define the sequence and the **`AsyncIteratorProtocol`** protocol to define the code that iterates through the sequence to return the values. The **`AsyncSequence`** protocol requires the data type to include a typealias with the name **`Element`** that represents the data type returned by the sequence, and the following method.

makeAsyncIterator()—This method returns the instance of the iterator in charge of producing the values. The value returned is an instance of a data type that conforms to the **`AsyncIteratorProtocol`** protocol.

On the other hand, the **AsyncIteratorProtocol** protocol only requires the data type to implement the following method.

next()—This method returns the next element on the list. The method is called over and over again until the value returned is **nil**, which indicates the end of the sequence.

To create an asynchronous sequence, we must define two data types, one that conforms to the **AsyncSequence** to describe the data type of the values returned by the sequence and initialize the iterator, and another that conforms to the **AsyncIteratorProtocol** protocol to produce the values. In the following example, we define an asynchronous sequence that processes an array of strings one by one and returns a sequence of **String** values.

```
import UIKit

struct ImageIterator : AsyncIteratorProtocol {
   let imageList: [String]
   var current = 0

   mutating func next() async -> String? {
      guard current < imageList.count else {
         return nil
      }
      await Task.sleep(3 * 1000000000)

      let image = imageList[current]
      current += 1
      return image
   }
}
struct ImageLoader : AsyncSequence {
   typealias Element = String
   let imageList: [String]

   func makeAsyncIterator() -> ImageIterator {
      return AsyncIterator(imageList: imageList)
   }
}
class ViewController: UIViewController {
   var imageList = ["image1", "image2", "image3"]

   override func viewDidLoad() {
      super.viewDidLoad()
      Task(priority: .background) {
         let loader = ImageLoader(imageList: imageList)
         for await image in loader {
            print(image)
         }
      }
   }
}
```

Listing 14-12: *Defining an asynchronous sequence*

The code in Listing 14-12 simulates the process of asynchronously downloading images from the Web. The iterator with the **next()** method is defined first. In this method, we read the strings from the **imageList** array and update a counter to know when we have reached the end (the value of the counter is equal or greater than the number of elements in the array). Notice that we also wait for 3 seconds to pretend that we are downloading the image from the Web.

The asynchronous sequence is defined next by the **ImageLoader** structure. The structure includes a typealias called **Element** to indicate that the sequence returns **String** values, and the **makeAsyncIterator()** method to initialize the iterator. Now everything is ready to read the values in the sequence, so we start a task, create an instance of the **ImageLoader** sequence, and then iterate through the elements with a **for in** loop. Notice that the **for in** loop requires the **await** keyword to wait for each element of the sequence. The loop runs until the value returned by the iterator is **nil**.

Do It Yourself: Update the **ViewController** class with the code in Listing 14-12. Remember to delete the label from the scene if you don't use it anymore. Run the application. You should see the values in the **imageList** array printed on the console every 3 seconds.

Medium Task Group

A task group is a container for dynamically generated tasks. Once the group is created, we can add and manage tasks from code as required by the application. The Swift Standard Library defines the following global methods to create a group.

withTaskGroup(of: Type, **returning:** Type, **body:** Closure**)**—This method creates a task group. The **of** argument defines the data type returned by the tasks, the **returning** argument defines the data type returned by the group, and the **body** argument is the closure where the tasks are defined. If no values are returned, the arguments may be ignored.

withThrowingTaskGroup(of: Type, **returning:** Type, **body:** Closure**)**—This method creates a task group that can throw errors. The **of** argument defines the data type returned by the tasks, the **returning** argument defines the data type returned by the group, and the **body** argument is the closure where the tasks are defined. If no values are returned, the arguments may be ignored.

The group is defined by an instance of the **TaskGroup** structure, which includes properties and methods to manage the tasks in the group. The following are the most frequently used.

isCancelled—This property returns a Boolean value that indicates whether the group was cancelled.

isEmpty—This property returns a Boolean value that indicates whether the group has any remaining tasks.

addTask(priority: TaskPriority?, **operation:** Closure**)**—This method adds a task to the group. The **priority** argument is a structure that helps the system decide when to execute the task. The structure includes type properties to defined standard priorities. The currently available are **background**, **high**, **low**, **medium**, **userInitiated**, and **utility**. And the **operation** argument is a closure with the statements to be executed by the task.

cancelAll()—This method cancels all the tasks in the group.

A task group is an asynchronous sequence of tasks. This sequence is generic, which means that the tasks, and the group, can return any types of values. This is the reason why the methods to create a task group have two arguments to specify the data types returned by the tasks and the group. These two methods are the same. The one we implement depends on whether we want to throw errors or not. These methods create a **TaskGroup** structure that works with the data types specified by the arguments and send the instance to the closure. Using this value inside the closure, we can add to the group all the tasks we want, as shown next.

```
import UIKit

class ViewController: UIViewController {
   override func viewDidLoad() {
      super.viewDidLoad()
      Task(priority: .background) {
         await withTaskGroup(of: String.self) { group in
            group.addTask(priority: .background) {
               let imageName = await self.loadImage(name: "image1")
               return imageName
            }
            group.addTask(priority: .background) {
               let imageName = await self.loadImage(name: "image2")
               return imageName
            }
            group.addTask(priority: .background) {
               let imageName = await self.loadImage(name: "image3")
               return imageName
            }
            for await result in group {
               print(result)
            }
         }
      }
   }
   func loadImage(name: String) async -> String {
      await Task.sleep(3 * 1000000000)
      return "Name: \(name)"
   }
}
```

Listing 14-13: *Defining a task group*

In this example, we create a task group that doesn't throw errors. The group doesn't return a value either, but the tasks return a string, so we declare the **of** argument of the **withTaskGroup()** method with a reference to the **String** data type (**String.self**). The tasks are added to the group one after another. Each task performs the same process as before. They call the **loadImage()** method asynchronously and get a string in return.

Because a task group is an asynchronous sequence of tasks, we can iterate though the values with a **for in** loop, as we did for the asynchronous sequence created in the previous section of this chapter. Every time a task is completed, the group returns the value produced by the task until no tasks remain, in which case the value **nil** is returned to finish the loop.

IMPORTANT: Task Groups store the tasks in sequence. You can remove, filter, or even check whether a group contains a specific task. The topic is beyond the scope of this book. For more information, visit our website and follow the links for this chapter.

Chapter 15
Storage

Basic 15.1 User Preferences

Up to this point, all the data was stored in arrays created in the model, and the values were hard-coded, meaning they are always the same every time the app is launched. If we added a new value to the model, it was only preserved for as long as the app was running, but as soon as the app was closed, the values were lost, and everything was back to the initial state. To preserve the values and all the changes introduced by the user, we need to store the data permanently on the device. Apple includes several systems for storing data. They all work with files but can take various forms, from simple text files to databases (indexed data).

Basic User Defaults

The simplest system available on Apple devices is called *Users Defaults*. This system was designed to store user preferences, which may include values set by the user to determine how the app should work and values set by the app to restore previous states. These values are stored in a system-managed database and therefore continue to exist after the application is closed and for as long as the user or the application decides to keep them.

The Foundation framework defines a class called **UserDefaults** to manage this system. Only one **UserDefaults** object is assigned per application, so we can reference this object anywhere in the code and always process the same values. The class offers the following type property to get a reference to the **UserDefaults** object created for the app.

standard—This type property returns a reference to the app's **UserDefaults** object.

The values are assigned to the **UserDefaults** object with an associated key that we can use to retrieve them later. The types of values we can work with are restricted to Property List values (**NSNumber**, **NSString**, **NSDate**, **NSArray**, **NSDictionary**, **NSData**, and the equivalents in Swift), but we can also work with other types of values, including custom objects, by converting them into **NSData** objects, as we will see in further chapters. The **UserDefaults** class includes the following methods to store, retrieve, and delete values of any of these types.

set(Any?, **forKey:** String**)**—This method stores the value specified by the first argument with the key specified by the **forKey** argument. If the value already exists, it is updated.

object(forKey: String**)**—This method retrieves the value associated with the key specified by the **forKey** argument. If the value does not exist, it returns **nil**.

removeObject(forKey: String**)**—This method removes the value associated with the key specified by the **forKey** argument.

Because the methods above process values of any type, they return them as objects of type **Any**. This means that we always need to cast the values to the right data type before using them. To simplify our work, the class includes methods to retrieve the values for specific types.

bool(forKey: String**)**—This method retrieves a value of type **Bool**. If there is no value set for the key, the method returns the value **false**.

float(forKey: String**)**—This method retrieves a value of type **Float**. If there is no value set for the key, the method returns the value 0.0.

integer(forKey: String**)**—This method retrieves a value of type **Int**. If there is no value set for the key, the method returns the value 0.

double(forKey: String**)**—This method retrieves a value of type **Double**. If there is no value set for the key, the method returns the value 0.0.

string(forKey: String**)**—This method retrieves a value of type **String**.

array(forKey: String**)**—This method retrieves an array.

dictionary(forKey: String**)**—This method retrieves a dictionary.

data(forKey: String**)**—This method retrieves a value of type **Data**.

url(forKey: String**)**—This method retrieves a value of type **URL**.

The User Defaults system can store any amount of data we want, but it is recommendable to use it to store short strings and small values. Its main purpose is to serve as a storage system for the app's settings. For instance, we can use the User Defaults system to allow the user to store a limit on the number of items managed by the application, and then set that limit back every time the app is executed. The interface below includes a Stepper and a label to illustrate how the process works.

− + 0

Figure 15-1: *Interface to store settings*

The view controller for this scene must update the value of the label when the interface is shown on the screen and store it in the User Defaults system every time the user sets a new one.

```
import UIKit

class ViewController: UIViewController {
   @IBOutlet weak var counter: UIStepper!
   @IBOutlet weak var counterLabel: UILabel!
   var defaultValues: UserDefaults!

   override func viewDidLoad() {
      super.viewDidLoad()
      defaultValues = UserDefaults.standard
      if let number = defaultValues.object(forKey: "counter") as? Double{
         counter.value = number
         counterLabel.text = String(number)
      }
   }
   @IBAction func incrementValue(_ sender: UIStepper) {
      let current = counter.value
      defaultValues.set(current, forKey: "counter")
      counterLabel.text = String(current)
   }
}
```

Listing 15-1: *Storing values in the User Defaults system*

The way we store the value is simple. We get a reference to the **UserDefaults** object of our application and then call any of the methods provided by the object to this effect. In Listing 15-1, we declare a property called **defaultValues** to store a reference to the object and use the **object()** and **set()** methods to read and store a value with the "counter" key. The **object()** method returns an optional of type **AnyObject**, so we unwrap the value and cast it to the original data type (in this case a **Double**). If there is already a value stored with the "counter" key, we assign it to the **value** property of the Stepper to start counting from that number and to the label to show it on the screen.

The Stepper is connected to an Action called **incrementValue().** When the user presses the buttons, this method gets the current value, stores it in the User Defaults system with the "counter" key, and updates the label. In consequence, the label always displays the current value, even after the app was closed.

Do It Yourself: Create a new project. Add a Stepper and a label to the scene. Connect the Stepper to the view controller with an Outlet called **counter** and the label with an Outlet called **counterLabel**. Connect the Stepper with an Action called **incrementValue()**. Complete the **ViewController** class with the code in Listing 15-1 and run the application. Press the buttons of the Stepper to change the value on the label. Wait a few second for the system to register the change. Stop the execution of the app from the Stop button in Xcode. Run the application again. The value on the label should be the last one stored by the app.

As we already mentioned, we can also store values generated by the app. For example, we may add a value to User Settings to keep track of the time the user has spent without using the app. The following example updates the last view controller to store this value. The code reads the value when the main view is loaded, compares it with the current date, and prints the difference on the console. At the end, we update the value with the current date for the next cycle.

```
import UIKit

class ViewController: UIViewController {
   @IBOutlet weak var counter: UIStepper!
   @IBOutlet weak var counterLabel: UILabel!
   var defaultValues: UserDefaults!

   override func viewDidLoad() {
      super.viewDidLoad()
      defaultValues = UserDefaults.standard
      if let number = defaultValues.object(forKey: "counter") as? Double{
         counter.value = number
         counterLabel.text = String(number)
      }
      if let lastDate = defaultValues.object(forKey:"lastDate") as? Date{
         let calendar = Calendar.current
         let components =
calendar.dateComponents([.year, .month, .day, .hour, .minute, .second],
from: lastDate, to: Date())
         print("You haven't use this app in \(components.year!) years, \
(components.month!) months, \(components.day!) days, \(components.hour!)
hours, \(components.minute!) minutes, \(components.second!) seconds")
      }
      defaultValues.set(Date(), forKey: "lastDate")
   }
   @IBAction func incrementValue(_ sender: UIStepper) {
      let current = counter.value
      defaultValues.set(current, forKey: "counter")
      counterLabel.text = String(current)
   }
}
```

Listing 15-2: *Storing app values*

Do It Yourself: Update the **ViewController** class with the code in Listing 15-2 and run the application. Wait a few seconds and stop the application from Xcode. Wait a few more seconds and run it again. You should see the time between runs printed on the console.

The interface introduced in Figure 15-1 was designed for didactic purposes, but scenes presenting the app's settings are usually set apart from the main interface. In Figure 15-2, below, we introduce a new interface with a dedicated scene to set the app's settings. The initial scene was embedded in a Navigation Controller. This scene contains a Text View and a bar button called Settings to navigate to the settings scene. On the other hand, the settings scene was created with a Table View Controller and a static table with two sections and three cells to present the controls users can manipulate to set their preferences. The cell in the first section contains a Segmented Control with three buttons to set the color of the text: Dark, Medium, and Light, and the cells in the second section contain Switches to set whether the Text View is going to be editable and have auto-correction activated or not.

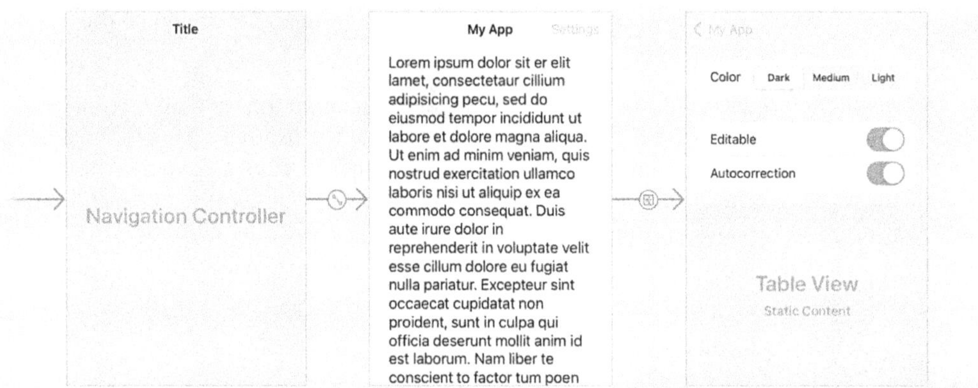

Figure 15-2: *Interface with an additional scene for the app's settings*

The view controller for the initial scene reads the values and updates the Text View.

```
import UIKit

class ViewController: UIViewController {
   @IBOutlet weak var textEditor: UITextView!

   override func viewWillAppear(_ animated: Bool) {
      super.viewWillAppear(animated)

      let defaultValues = UserDefaults.standard
      if let color = defaultValues.object(forKey: "color") as? Int {
         let colorList = [UIColor.black, UIColor.gray, UIColor.lightGray]
         textEditor.textColor = colorList[color]
      }
      if let editable = defaultValues.object(forKey:"editable") as? Bool{
         textEditor.isEditable = editable
      }
      if let correction = defaultValues.object(forKey: "correction") as?
Bool {
         if correction {
            textEditor.spellCheckingType = .yes
         } else {
            textEditor.spellCheckingType = .no
         }
      }
   }
}
```

Listing 15-3: *Configuring the Text View according to the values set by the user*

For this example, we use three values called "color", "editable", and "correction" to store the current settings. If the values were already set, which means that the user changed them from the settings screen at some point in the past, we configure the Text View with those values, otherwise the application uses the values assigned in the Storyboard. For example, the color for the text in the Text View is set as black by default in the Storyboard, but if there is a value stored with the key "color" we use it to get the current color from an array (black, gray, or light gray).

In the view controller for the settings scene, we must read the values as well to update the elements, but also get the user's input and store the new values for future reference. We call this view controller **SettingsViewController**.

```
import UIKit

class SettingsViewController: UITableViewController {
   @IBOutlet weak var controlColors: UISegmentedControl!
   @IBOutlet weak var controlEditable: UISwitch!
   @IBOutlet weak var controlCorrection: UISwitch!
   var defaultValues: UserDefaults!

   override func viewDidLoad() {
      super.viewDidLoad()

      defaultValues = UserDefaults.standard
      if let color = defaultValues.object(forKey: "color") as? Int {
         controlColors.selectedSegmentIndex = color
      }
      if let editable = defaultValues.object(forKey: "editable") as? Bool
{
         controlEditable.isOn = editable
      }
      if let correction = defaultValues.object(forKey: "correction") as?
Bool {
         controlCorrection.isOn = correction
      }
   }
   @IBAction func saveColor(_ sender: UISegmentedControl) {
      let current = controlColors.selectedSegmentIndex
      defaultValues.set(current, forKey: "color")
   }
   @IBAction func saveEditable(_ sender: UISwitch) {
      let current = controlEditable.isOn
      defaultValues.set(current, forKey: "editable")
   }
   @IBAction func saveCorrection(_ sender: UISwitch) {
      let current = controlCorrection.isOn
      defaultValues.set(current, forKey: "correction")
   }
}
```

Listing 15-4: *Saving the settings*

The settings scene contains a Segmented Control with the buttons Dark, Medium, and Light, and two Switches to set the edition and autocorrection features of the Text View. These elements were connected to Outlets that we use in the **viewDidLoad()** method to update their states according to the values selected by the user, and also to Actions that update the settings every time these values are changed (the Value Changed event is fired). In consequence, every time the user opens the settings scene, the states of the elements are modified according to the values stored in User Settings, and as soon as the user moves a Switch or taps a button in the Segmented Control, the new value is stored in the system.

Do It Yourself: Create a new project. Embed the scene in a Navigation Controller. Add a bar button called Settings and a Text View. Add a Table View Controller to the Storyboard. Connect the Settings button to the new scene with a Show Segue. Select the table, go to the Attributes Inspector panel, and change the Content option to Static Cells, and the value of Sections to 2. Select the header of each section and erase their titles. Leave only one cell for the first section and two for the second section. Add labels, a Segmented Control with the buttons Dark, Medium, and Light, and switches to the interface (Figure 15-2, right). Create a subclass of the **`UITableViewController`** class called **`SettingsViewController`** and assign it to the second scene. Complete the **`ViewController`** class and the **`SettingsViewController`** class with the codes in Listings 15-3 and 15-4. Connect the elements to their Outlets and Actions. Run the application and set new values. Wait a few seconds for the system to store the values in User Defaults. Stop the application and run it again. The Text View should be always configured according to the values stored in the system.

So far, we have used a generic method to retrieve the values, but the methods for specific types provided by the **`UserDefault`** class can simplify our code. The following example updates the **`ViewController`** class of Listing 15-3 to read the values with the methods according to their type.

```
import UIKit

class ViewController: UIViewController {
   @IBOutlet weak var textEditor: UITextView!

   override func viewWillAppear(_ animated: Bool) {
      super.viewWillAppear(animated)

      let defaultValues = UserDefaults.standard
      let color = defaultValues.integer(forKey: "color")
      let colorList = [UIColor.black, UIColor.gray, UIColor.lightGray]
      textEditor.textColor = colorList[color]
      textEditor.isEditable = defaultValues.bool(forKey: "editable")

      let correction = defaultValues.bool(forKey: "correction")
      if correction {
         textEditor.spellCheckingType = .yes
      } else {
         textEditor.spellCheckingType = .no
      }
   }
}
```

***Listing 15-5:** Reading values with specific methods*

The code is simplified because we no longer need to unwrap the values, but there is a problem. Some of these methods return values by default. For example, the **`integer()`** method will return the value 0 if no value was stored before for the "color" key. In the case of the color, we want the value by default to be 0, so the text is displayed in black the first time the user runs the application, but the value by default for Booleans is **`false`**, which means that the features we set for the Text View will be deactivated by default. If we want these features activated, we must provide our own default values. The **`UserDefaults`** class includes the **`register()`** method to set these values. The method receives a dictionary of type **`[String: Any]`** with the keys and values we want to set by default and stores them in the User Defaults system. Because the values may be modified from anywhere in our app, it is good practice to set them when the app is launched, as in the following example.

```
import UIKit

@main
class AppDelegate: UIResponder, UIApplicationDelegate {
   func application(_ application: UIApplication,
didFinishLaunchingWithOptions launchOptions:
[UIApplication.LaunchOptionsKey: Any]?) -> Bool {
      let list: [String : Any] = ["color": 0, "editable": true,
"correction": false]
      let defaultValues = UserDefaults.standard
      defaultValues.register(defaults: list)
      return true
   }
   func application(_ application: UIApplication,
configurationForConnecting connectingSceneSession: UISceneSession,
options: UIScene.ConnectionOptions) -> UISceneConfiguration {
      return UISceneConfiguration(name: "Default Configuration",
sessionRole: connectingSceneSession.role)
   }
}
```

Listing 15-6: *Setting values by default*

Do It Yourself: Replace the code in your **ViewController** class with the code in Listing 15-5. Update the **AppDelegate** class with the code in Listing 15-6. Open the simulator, press the Home button, and delete the application to clean the User Default system (the simulator works exactly like a real device, you have to keep pressing the mouse button on the icon of the app you want to delete and click the Remove App option). Run the application again. The settings should be set according to the values you specified in the **list** dictionary.

Basic 15.2 Files

iOS, like any other operative system, allows users to create and access files, but the iOS file system is like no other. The system restricts applications to their own space (called Sandbox) and a handful of directories to ensure that they do not interfere with each other. This means that we can only access the files and directories that belong to our app.

Foundation defines a class called **FileManager** to manage files and directories. One object of this class is assigned to the app and from it we can create, delete, copy, and move files and directories in our app's storage space. The class offers the following type property to get a reference to this object.

default—This type property returns a reference to the app's **FileManager** object.

The **FileManager** class offers multiple properties and methods to manage files and directories. The following are the most frequently used.

urls(for: SearchPathDirectory, **in:** SearchPathDomainMask**)**—This method returns an array with the location of a directory. The **for** argument is an enumeration with values that represent common system directories, such as Documents, and the **in** argument is an enumeration with values that determine the domain in which the files are located.

createDirectory(at: URL, **withIntermediateDirectories:** Bool, **attributes:** Dictionary?**)**—This method creates a new directory. The **at** argument specifies the location, including the name and the extension. The **withIntermediateDirectories** argument indicates whether intermediate directories will also be created. And the **attributes** argument is a dictionary with values that determine the directory's attributes (e.g., ownership). The value `nil` sets the attributes by default, which are usually enough for iOS applications.

createFile(atPath: String, **contents:** Data?, **attributes:** Dictionary?**)**—This method creates a file. The **atPath** argument specifies the location of the file, including its name and extension. The **contents** argument represents the content of the file. And the **attributes** argument is a dictionary with values that determine the file's attributes (e.g., ownership). The value `nil` sets the attributes by default.

contents(atPath: String**)**—This method returns the content of the file at the path specified by the **atPath** argument. The value returned is an optional of type `Data`.

contentsOfDirectory(atPath: String**)**—This method returns an array with the paths of the files and directories inside the directory indicated by the **atPath** argument.

copyItem(atPath: String, **toPath:** String**)**—This method copies the file or directory at the path specified by the **at** argument to the path specified by the **to** argument.

moveItem(atPath: String, **toPath:** String**)**—This method moves the file or directory at the path specified by the **at** argument to the path specified by the **to** argument.

removeItem(atPath: String**)**—This method removes the file or directory at the path indicated by the **atPath** argument.

fileExists(atPath: String**)**—This method returns a Boolean value that determines whether the file or the directory at the path specified by the **atPath** argument exists or not.

attributesOfItem(atPath: String**)**—This method returns a dictionary with the attributes of the file or directory at the location indicated by the **atPath** argument. The `FileManager` class provides constants to define the attributes, including `creationDate`, `modificationDate`, `size`, and `type`, among others.

Basic URLs and Paths

As in any other operative system, files in iOS are organized in directories. There is a basic directory called *root* that can contain files and other directories, which in turn can contain other files and directories, creating a tree-like structure. To reproduce this route in code, iOS adopts a common syntax that separates each part of the route with a forward slash (/), starting with a single slash to indicate the root directory, as in /Pictures/Travels/Hawaii.png. This is called *path*, and it is used to access any file on the system.

Paths are a simple way to access files but are not enough to identify the location of a file in the storage system. This is because in practice files are usually not stored in a single storage space, but in several units or even in remote servers. Following a long path to find a file also takes time and consumes resources. For these reasons, locations are always identified by URLs (Uniform Resource Locator). URLs are just strings, like paths, but provide more information to the system and follow a convention that systems can use to manage and access local or remote files. Foundation defines a structure to work with URLs called `URL`. The following are some of the initializers, properties and methods provided by this structure to work with files.

URL(fileURLWithPath: String**)**—This initializer returns a `URL` object referencing a local file or directory. The **fileURLWithPath** argument is a string with the file's path.

URL(fileURLWithPath: String, **relativeTo:** URL**)**—This initializer returns a `URL` object referencing a local file or directory. The **fileURLWithPath** argument is a string with the file's path, and the **relativeTo** argument is a `URL` object referencing the base URL.

path—This property returns the path of a URL. It is a conditional of type `String`.

pathComponents—This property returns an array of **`String`** values that represent the components of a path extracted from a URL (the strings between forward slashes).

lastPathComponent—This property returns a string with the last component of a path extracted from a URL. It is usually used to get the file's name and extension.

pathExtension—This property returns a string with the extension of the path extracted from a URL. It is usually used to get the file's extension.

appendingPathComponent(String**)**—This method returns a new **`URL`** structure with the URL of the original object plus the component specified by the argument.

IMPORTANT: The **`FileManager`** class includes methods to work with both paths and URLs. For example, there are two versions of the **`createDirectory()`** method, one to create the directory from a path and another from a URL. The methods that work with paths take care of converting the path into a URL and are usually easier to implement, but you can use any method you need. For a complete list, visit our website and follow the links for this chapter.

Basic Files and Directories

When the application is installed on the device, iOS creates a group of standard directories that we can use. The most useful are the Documents directory, where we can store the user's files, and the Application Support directory, for files that our app needs to create during runtime. The location of these directories is not guaranteed, so we must always ask iOS for the current URL that points to the directory or file we want to access.

To get the location of common directories like Documents, the **`FileManager`** class includes the **`urls()`** method. The method requires two arguments. The first argument is an enumeration with values that represent different directories. There are several values available for the iOS and OSX operative systems, including **`documentDirectory`** to reference the Documents directory and **`applicationSupportDirectory`** to reference the Application Support directory. The second argument is another enumeration with values that indicate the domain where the directory is located. The system organizes directories and files in separate domains depending on their intended usage. The domain where our app's files are stored is the User Domain, identified with the constant **`userDomainMask`**. In consequence, to get the URL of any of the directories generated for our app and start creating files to store the user's data, we must get a reference to the **`FileManager`** object and then call the **`urls()`** method with the values that represent the location we want to use. The following example shows how to get the Documents directory's URL.

```
import UIKit

class ViewController: UIViewController {
   override func viewDidLoad() {
      super.viewDidLoad()
      let manager = FileManager.default
      let documents = manager.urls(for: .documentDirectory,
in: .userDomainMask)
      let docURL = documents.first!
      print(docURL)
   }
}
```

Listing 15-7: *Getting the Documents directory's URL*

The **urls()** method returns an array of optional **URL** structures with all the possible locations of the directory. In the case of the Documents directory, the right value is the first item of the array, so in Listing 15-7 we get this value from the **first** property, unwrap it, assign it to the **docURL** constant, and print it on the console.

Do It Yourself: Create a new project. Update the **ViewController** class with the code in Listing 15-7. Run the application. You should see the URL of the Documents directory printed on the console.

Now that we have the URL, we can start adding other directories and files inside the Documents directory. The **FileManager** class includes the **createFile()** method to create new files. The method requires three values: the path where the file is going to be created (including the file's name and extension), a value with the file's content, and the file's attributes. The content and the attributes are optional. If we declare these values as **nil**, the file is created empty and with attributes by default, as in the following example.

```
import UIKit

class ViewController: UIViewController {
   override func viewDidLoad() {
      super.viewDidLoad()
      let manager = FileManager.default
      let documents = manager.urls(for: .documentDirectory,
in: .userDomainMask)
      let docURL = documents.first!

      let newFileURL = docURL.appendingPathComponent("mytext.txt")
      let path = newFileURL.path
      manager.createFile(atPath: path, contents: nil, attributes: nil)
   }
}
```

Listing 15-8: *Creating a file inside Documents*

The path must represent the route to the file, including its name and extension. The **URL** class includes the **appendingPathComponent()** method to extend a URL. The method adds a string to the end of the URL and takes care of including the necessary forward slashes to ensure its validity. In Listing 15-8, we use it to get the URL of the new file. After this, we obtain its path from the **path** property, and finally call the **createFile()** method to create the file (if the file already exists, the method does nothing). At the end, the Documents directory of this application contains an empty file called *mytext.txt*.

In the same way that we create a file, we can create a directory. The method to create a directory is called **createDirectory()**. Again, the method takes three values: the path of the new directory (including its name), a Boolean value that indicates if we want to create all the directories included in the path (in case the path includes directories we have not created yet), and the attributes. This method throws an error if it cannot complete the task, so we must handle it with **try**.

```
import UIKit

class ViewController: UIViewController {
   override func viewDidLoad() {
      super.viewDidLoad()
      let manager = FileManager.default
      let documents = manager.urls(for: .documentDirectory,
in: .userDomainMask)
      let docURL = documents.first!
```

```
      let newDirectoryURL = docURL.appendingPathComponent("myfiles")
      let path = newDirectoryURL.path
      do {
         try manager.createDirectory(atPath: path,
withIntermediateDirectories: false, attributes: nil)
      } catch {
         print("The directory already exists")
      }
   }
}
```

Listing 15-9: Creating a directory inside Documents

The **FileManager** class also offers methods to list the content of a directory. We can use the **contentsOfDirectory()** method to get an array of strings with the names of the files and directories in a specific path. In the following example, we create another method to list files and directories. The method receives the URL we want to search for and then creates a **for in** loop to print the items found.

```
import UIKit

class ViewController: UIViewController {
   override func viewDidLoad() {
      super.viewDidLoad()
      let manager = FileManager.default
      let documents = manager.urls(for: .documentDirectory,
in: .userDomainMask)
      let docURL = documents.first!
      listItems(directory: docURL)
   }
   func listItems(directory: URL) {
      let manager = FileManager.default
      if let list = try? manager.contentsOfDirectory(atPath:
directory.path) {
         if list.isEmpty {
            print("The directory is empty")
         } else {
            for item in list {
               print(item)
            }
         }
      }
   }
}
```

Listing 15-10: Listing the content of a directory

In this example, we get the Documents directory's URL and then call the **listItems()** method to list the files and directories inside it. The **listItems()** method gets its own reference of the **FileManager** object and then calls the **contentsOfDirectory()** method to get the list of items. Notice that this method throws errors, so we use **try?** to handle them. If the value returned is not **nil** and not empty, we print every item on the console (in our case, this would be the myfiles directory and the mytext.txt file created in previous examples).

In the example of Listing 15-8, we have created a file inside the Documents directory, but we can also create files inside our custom directories. For example, we can add a new file to the myfiles directory created in Listing 15-9.

```
import UIKit

class ViewController: UIViewController {
   override func viewDidLoad() {
      super.viewDidLoad()
      let manager = FileManager.default
      let documents = manager.urls(for: .documentDirectory,
in: .userDomainMask)
      let docURL = documents.first!

      let newFileURL = docURL.appendingPathComponent("myfiles/
anotherfile.txt")
      let path = newFileURL.path
      let created = manager.createFile(atPath: path, contents: nil,
attributes: nil)
      if !created {
         print("We couldn't create the file")
      }
   }
}
```

Listing 15-11: *Creating files in a custom directory*

The code in Listing 15-11 adds the necessary components to the Documents directory's URL and then creates the file as done before. In this example, we add the components all at once, separating each component with a forward slash, but we could have called the **appendingPathComponent()** method for every component and add them one by one.

We can also move a file or directory from one location to another. All we have to do is to provide the paths for the origin and destination and then call the **moveItem()** method. For example, we can move the mytext.txt file to the myfiles directory created before.

```
import UIKit

class ViewController: UIViewController {
   override func viewDidLoad() {
      super.viewDidLoad()
      let manager = FileManager.default
      let documents = manager.urls(for: .documentDirectory,
in: .userDomainMask)
      let docURL = documents.first!

      let originURL = docURL.appendingPathComponent("mytext.txt")
      let destinationURL = docURL.appendingPathComponent("myfiles/
mytext.txt")
      let originPath = originURL.path
      let destinationPath = destinationURL.path
      do {
         try manager.moveItem(atPath: originPath, toPath:
destinationPath)
      } catch {
         print("File was not moved")
      }
   }
}
```

Listing 15-12: *Moving files*

We can also copy files from one directory to another. The following example copies the anotherfile.txt file created inside the myfiles directory into the Documents directory.

```
import UIKit

class ViewController: UIViewController {
   override func viewDidLoad() {
      super.viewDidLoad()
      let manager = FileManager.default
      let documents = manager.urls(for: .documentDirectory,
in: .userDomainMask)
      let docURL = documents.first!

      let originURL = docURL.appendingPathComponent("myfiles/
anotherfile.txt")
      let destinationURL =
docURL.appendingPathComponent("anotherfile.txt")
      let originPath = originURL.path
      let destinationPath = destinationURL.path
      do {
         try manager.copyItem(atPath: originPath, toPath:
destinationPath)
      } catch {
         print("File was not copied")
      }
   }
}
```

Listing 15-13: *Copying files*

Removing files or directories is also an easy task. All we need to do is to get the path to the item and then call the **removeItem()** method.

```
import UIKit

class ViewController: UIViewController {
   override func viewDidLoad() {
      super.viewDidLoad()
      let manager = FileManager.default
      let documents = manager.urls(for: .documentDirectory,
in: .userDomainMask)
      let docURL = documents.first!

      let fileURL = docURL.appendingPathComponent("anotherfile.txt")
      let path = fileURL.path
      do {
         try manager.removeItem(atPath: path)
      } catch {
         print("File was not removed")
      }
   }
}
```

Listing 15-14: *Removing files*

Do It Yourself: Update the **ViewController** class with the codes in Listings 15-11, 15-12, 15-13, and 15-14, and run the application every time. Incorporate the **listItems()** method of Listing 15-10 to the class so you can see the files being created and moved.

Basic Files Attributes

Some applications need to know more than the name of the file. The **FileManager** class offers the **attributesOfItem()** method to get the file attributes, such as the date of creation or the size. The method returns a dictionary with predefined keys to identify each value. There are several constants available we can use as keys. The most useful are **creationDate** (the date the file was created), **modificationDate** (last time it was modified), **size**, and **type**. The following code gets the attributes of the mytext.txt file created in previous examples.

```
import UIKit

class ViewController: UIViewController {
   override func viewDidLoad() {
      super.viewDidLoad()
      let manager = FileManager.default
      let documents = manager.urls(for: .documentDirectory,
in: .userDomainMask)
      let docURL = documents.first!

      let fileURL = docURL.appendingPathComponent("myfiles/mytext.txt")
      let filePath = fileURL.path
      if let attributes = try? manager.attributesOfItem(atPath:filePath){
         let type = attributes[.type] as! FileAttributeType
         let size = attributes[.size] as! Int
         let date = attributes[.creationDate] as! Date
         if type != FileAttributeType.typeDirectory {
            print("Name: \(fileURL.lastPathComponent)")
            print("Size: \(size)")
            print("Created: \(date)")
         }
      }
   }
}
```

***Listing 15-15:** Reading the file's attributes*

The attributes are returned as **Any** values, so we cast them to their corresponding data types. Most of the values are of data types we already know, such as **Int** or **Date**, but the **type** key returns a property of a structure called **FileAttributeType** that represent the resource's type. There are properties available to represent different types of resources. The most frequently used are **typeRegular** to represent files and **typeDirectory** to represent directories. If we want to know if the resource is a file, we can compare the value returned by the **type** key with the **typeDirectory** property, as we did in the example of Listing 15-15. If they are different, it means that the resource is a file, and we can process its attributes.

Basic Files Content

Storage systems, like hard drives and solid-state drives, store information the only way a computer knows, as a series of ones and zeros. Therefore, the information that we want to store in files must be converted into a stream of bytes which can then be converted back to the original data. Foundation offers the **Data** structure for this purpose.

Although we can work directly with a **Data** structure, most frameworks include tools to convert our data into **Data** structures that we can process or store on files. For example, the **UIImage** class includes the **pngData()** and **jpegData()** methods to convert images into **Data** structures (see Chapter 5). Another common data type that provides tools to convert data is the **String** structure. This structure includes a method that turns a string into data an also an initializer that can get back the string from a **Data** structure.

String(data: Data, **encoding:** Encoding)—This initializer creates a **`String`** value with the text in the **`Data`** structure specified by the **data** argument. The **encoding** argument is a value provided by properties of a structure called **`Encoding`** that determine the type of encoding used to generate the string. The most frequently used are **`unicode`**, **`utf8`**, and **`ascii`**.

data(using: Encoding, **allowLossyConversion:** Bool)—This method returns a **`Data`** structure containing the string in the original **`String`** value. The **using** argument is a value provided by properties of the **`Encoding`** structure that determine the type of encoding used to generate the string. The most frequently used are **`unicode`**, **`utf8`**, and **`ascii`**. The **allowLossyConversion** argument determines the precision of the conversion.

The structures and classes capable of processing **`Data`** structures and files also provide specific methods to write and read a file. For example, the **`String`** structure includes the following method to turn a string into data and store it in a file, all at once.

write(to: URL, **atomically:** Bool, **encoding:** Encoding)—This method converts a string into a **`Data`** structure and stores it in the file located at the URL specified by the **to** argument. The **atomically** argument determines if we want the data to be stored in an auxiliary file first to ensure that the original file is not corrupted (the value **`true`** is recommended). The **encoding** argument is a value provided by properties of the **`Encoding`** structure that determine the type of encoding used to generate the string. The most frequently used are **`unicode`**, **`utf8`**, and **`ascii`**.

With these tools, we can store information generated by the user in a file and keep it updated. For example, we can get input from the user through a Text View and store the text in a file.

Figure 15-3: *Interface to generate file content*

The view controller for the scene in Figure 15-3 must perform two tasks: store the text from the Text View in a file every time the user introduces a change, and read the content back from the file every time the user loads the application and show it on the screen.

```
import UIKit

class ViewController: UIViewController, UITextViewDelegate {
   @IBOutlet weak var diaryText: UITextView!
   var fileURL: URL!

   override func viewDidLoad() {
      super.viewDidLoad()
```

```
        diaryText.delegate = self
        let manager = FileManager.default
        let documents = manager.urls(for: .documentDirectory,
in: .userDomainMask)
        let docURL = documents.first!
        fileURL = docURL.appendingPathComponent("userdata.txt")
        let filePath = fileURL.path
        if manager.fileExists(atPath: filePath) {
           if let content = manager.contents(atPath: filePath) {
              diaryText.text = String(data: content, encoding: .utf8)
           }
        } else {
           manager.createFile(atPath: filePath, contents: nil, attributes:
nil)
        }
    }
    func textViewDidChange(_ textView: UITextView) {
        let text = diaryText.text!
        do {
           try text.write(to: fileURL, atomically: true, encoding: .utf8)
        } catch {
           print("Error")
        }
    }
}
```

Listing 15-16: Managing the file's content

The first thing we do in this **ViewController** class is to call the **fileExists()** method to check if the file where we are going to store the data already exists. If the file exists, we read its content with the **contents()** method, convert the data into a string with the **String** initializer, and assign the string to the Text View. This way, the last text stored in the file is always displayed on the screen as soon as the app is launched. If the file does not exist, however, we create it with the **createFile()** method and no content (**nil**). To keep the file updated with the text inserted by the user in the Text View, we declare the **ViewController** class as the delegate of the Text View and implement the **textViewDidChange()** method. This method is called by the Text View every time its content changes (see Chapter 5). Inside the method we read the current text and call its **write()** method to store it in the file. Now, everything the user writes in the Text View is preserved and always available.

Do It Yourself: Create a new project. Add a label and a Text View to the initial scene to get the interface in Figure 15-3. Connect the Text View to the **ViewController** class with an Outlet called **diaryText**. Complete the **ViewController** class with the code in Listing 15-16. Run the application and insert a text in the Text View. Stop the application from Xcode and run it again. You should see the text on the screen.

Basic Bundle

A bundle is a container for all the app's files and directories. One bundle is created per app, so by accessing the bundle we get access to all the files included in the application. To create and manage bundles, Foundation defines the **Bundle** class. The class offers properties and methods to work with bundles, including the following to access the app's bundle.

main—This type property returns a reference to the app's bundle.

bundleURL—This property returns a **URL** structure with the bundle's URL.

bundlePath—This property returns a string with the bundle's path.

Because we are not able to determine the location of our app's files and resources during development, every time we want to access these files from code, we need to get their URLs from the **Bundle** object. The **Bundle** class provides the following methods for this purpose.

url(forResource: String?, **withExtension:** String?**)**—This method returns a **URL** structure with the URL of a file or directory inside the bundle. The first argument specifies the name of the file or directory we are looking for, and the **withExtension** argument specifies its extension (set as **nil** for resources that do not have an extension).

path(forResource: String?, **ofType:** String?**)**—This method returns the path of a file or directory inside the bundle. The first argument specifies the name of the file or directory we are looking for, and the **ofType** argument specifies its extension (set as **nil** for resources that do not have an extension).

The **Bundle** object is frequently used in professional applications to access files that are required for some services, like databases, for example, but we can also take advantage of this object to load files with initial data to populate the model when the app is launched for the first time or to restore the initial state.

The following example loads a text file called quote.txt from the bundle as soon as the application is launched. The file must be added to the project during development by dragging it from Finder to the Navigator Area, as we did for images before (see Figure 5-97).

```
import UIKit

@main
class AppDelegate: UIResponder, UIApplicationDelegate {
   func application(_ application: UIApplication,
didFinishLaunchingWithOptions launchOptions:
[UIApplication.LaunchOptionsKey: Any]?) -> Bool {
      let bundle = Bundle.main
      let filePath = bundle.path(forResource: "quote", ofType: "txt")

      let manager = FileManager.default
      if let data = manager.contents(atPath: filePath!) {
         let message = String(data: data, encoding: .utf8)
         print(message!)
      }
      return true
   }
   func application(_ application: UIApplication,
configurationForConnecting connectingSceneSession: UISceneSession,
options: UIScene.ConnectionOptions) -> UISceneConfiguration {
      return UISceneConfiguration(name: "Default Configuration",
sessionRole: connectingSceneSession.role)
   }
}
```

Listing 15-17: *Loading a file added to the project*

The code in Listing 15-17 gets a reference to the app's bundle and then finds the path for the quote.txt file with the **path()** method. After we get the path, we can read the file as we did before. In this example, we print the string on the console, but this information is usually stored in the model or assigned to the objects that requires it.

Do It Yourself: Create a new project and update its **AppDelegate** class with the code in Listing 15-17. Create a text file with a text editor, write some text in it, save it with the name quote.txt, and add it to your project. Run the application. You should see the text inside the file printed on the console.

Basic 15.3 Archiving

The methods we have just studied to store data in files are enough for simple models but present some limitations. We can only work with single values and with classes that already provide a way to turn their content into data. Professional applications rely on more elaborated models that include collection of values and custom objects. To give us more flexibility, Foundation offers the **NSCoder** class. This class can encode and decode values to **Data** structures for storage purposes in a process called *Archiving*.

An **NSCoder** object not only encodes an object but also the objects it is connected to, preserving the connections and the hierarchy. For example, we may have two objects with properties that reference the other object. Object 1 references Object 2 and Object 2 references Object 1. With archiving, both objects are encoded, stored, and then decoded and connected again when we need them.

Basic Encoding and Decoding

The **NSCoder** class provides all the methods necessary to encode and decode the values of an object, but all the work is done by instances of two **NSCoder** subclasses called **NSKeyedArchiver** and **NSKeyedUnarchiver**. The **NSKeyedArchiver** class calls the **encode()** method on the objects to encode their values and stores the data in a **Data** structure or a file. The **NSKeyedUnarchiver** class, on the other hand, initializes the objects with the protocol's initializer and returns the original values.

The **NSKeyedArchiver** class offers the following type method to encode an Object Graph and store it in a **Data** structure.

> **archivedData(withRootObject:** Any, **requiringSecureCoding:** Bool**)**—This type method encodes the Object Graph of the object specified by the **withRootObject** argument and stores it in a **Data** structure. The **requiringSecureCoding** argument is a Boolean value that determines whether the data will be secured or not.

The **NSKeyedUnarchiver** class offers the following type method to decode an Object Graph from a **Data** structure.

> **unarchivedObject(ofClass:** Class, **from:** Data**)**—This type method decodes the data specified by the **from** argument and returns the original Object Graph. The **ofClass** argument determines the data type of the decoded object.
>
> **unarchivedObject(ofClasses:** [AnyClass], **from:** Data**)**—This type method decodes the data specified by the **from** argument and returns the original Object Graph. The **ofClasses** argument determines the data types of the decoded object.

Implementing these methods, we can generate **Data** structures for processing, or we can just store and retrieve the data from a file. In the following example, we encode and decode a string to a **Data** structure and use **FileManager** methods to create and read the file.

```
import UIKit

class ViewController: UIViewController {
   override func viewDidLoad() {
      super.viewDidLoad()

      let manager = FileManager.default
      let documents = manager.urls(for: .documentDirectory,
in: .userDomainMask)
      let docURL = documents.first!
```

```
        let fileURL = docURL.appendingPathComponent("quotes.dat")
        let filePath = fileURL.path
        if manager.fileExists(atPath: filePath) {
           if let content = manager.contents(atPath: filePath) {
              if let result = try? 
NSKeyedUnarchiver.unarchivedObject(ofClass: NSString.self, from: content) 
as String? {
                 print(result)
              }
           }
        } else {
           let quote = "Fiction is the truth inside the lie"
           if let fileData = try? 
NSKeyedArchiver.archivedData(withRootObject: quote, 
requiringSecureCoding: false) {
              manager.createFile(atPath: filePath, contents: fileData, 
attributes: nil)
           }
        }
    }
}
```

Listing 15-18: *Encoding and decoding data*

Listing 15-18 presents a view controller with a simple example. A single string is encoded and stored in a file called quotes.dat. As we did in previous examples, we first check if the file exists with the **fileExists()** method and then proceed accordingly. If the file does not exist, we convert the string in the **quote** constant to a **Data** value with the **archivedData()** method and create a file with it, but if the file already exists, we read its content with the **contents()** method and decode the data with the **unarchivedObject()** method to get back the string.

The **unarchivedObject()** method can only work with data types that conform to a protocol called **NSSecureCoding**. That is the reason why we had to specify the **NSString** class as the value of the **ofClass** argument and convert it at the end to a **String** structure with the **as** operator (the **NSString** class conforms to the **NSSecureCoding** protocol but the **String** structure does not).

Do It Yourself: Create a new project. Update the **ViewController** class with the code in Listing 15-18. Run the application. The first time, the file is created, and no message is printed on the console. Stop and run the application again. Now you should see the quote on the console.

The methods of the **NSKeyedArchiver** and **NSKeyedUnarchiver** classes work with Property List values (**NSNumber**, **NSString**, **NSDate**, **NSArray**, **NSDictionary**, **NSData**, and the equivalents in Swift). In the previous example, we had to use an **NSString** value, but if we want to archive our own data types, we must convert them to Property List values. Foundation offers two classes for this purpose, **PropertyListEncoder** and **PropertyListDecoder**, which include the following methods to encode and decode values.

encode(Value**)**—This method of the **PropertyListEncoder** class encodes a value into a Property List value.

decode(Type, **from:** Data**)**—This method of the **PropertyListDecoder** class decodes a Property List value into a value of the data type specified by the first argument. The **from** argument is a **Data** structure with the data to be decoded.

Another requirement for custom structures is that they implement the initializers and methods defined in the **NSSecureCoding** protocol for the system to be able to encode and decode the data. Fortunately, the Swift Standard Library defines a protocol called **Codable** that turns a structure into an encodable and decodable data type. All we need to do, is to make our structure conform to the protocol and the compiler takes care of adding all the methods required to encode and decode its values. The following example creates a structure to store information about books.

```
import Foundation

struct Book: Codable {
   var title: String
   var author: String
   var edition: Int
}
```

Listing 15-19: *Encoding and decoding a custom data type*

Once our custom structure is defined, we can create instances of it and archive them. The next example follows the same procedure as before. When the main view is loaded, we check if the file already exists and read it or create a new one. To archive and unarchive the data, we use the same methods, but this time we encode or decode the values into a Property List.

```
import UIKit

class ViewController: UIViewController {
   override func viewDidLoad() {
      super.viewDidLoad()

      let manager = FileManager.default
      let documents = manager.urls(for: .documentDirectory,
in: .userDomainMask)
      let docURL = documents.first!

      let fileURL = docURL.appendingPathComponent("userdata.dat")
      let filePath = fileURL.path
      if manager.fileExists(atPath: filePath) {
         if let content = manager.contents(atPath: filePath) {
            if let result = try?
NSKeyedUnarchiver.unarchivedObject(ofClass: NSData.self, from: content)
as Data? {
               let decoder = PropertyListDecoder()
               if let books = try? decoder.decode([Book].self, from:
result) {
                  for book in books {
                     print("\(book.title) - \(book.author) - \
(book.edition)")
                  }
               }
            }
         }
      } else {
         let book1 = Book(title: "IT", author: "Stephen King", edition:
2)
         let book2 = Book(title: "Pet Sematary", author: "Stephen King",
edition: 1)
         let book3 = Book(title: "The Shining", author: "Stephen King",
edition: 1)
         let list = [book1, book2, book3]

         let encoder = PropertyListEncoder()
         if let data = try? encoder.encode(list) {
```

```
            if let fileData = try?
NSKeyedArchiver.archivedData(withRootObject: data, requiringSecureCoding:
false) {
                manager.createFile(atPath: filePath, contents: fileData,
attributes: nil)
            }
          }
       }
    }
}
```

Listing 15-20: *Encoding and decoding arrays of custom structures*

In this example, we store an array of three **Book** structures. First, we convert the array into a Property List value with the **encode()** method of the **PropertyListEncoder** class, then we archive the data, and finally we store it in a file called userdata.dat. To get the information back from the file, we decode the data with the **decode()** method of the **PropertyListDecoder** class and print the values on the console.

Do It Yourself: Create a new project. Create a new Swift file called Book.swift for the structure in Listing 15-19. Update the **ViewController** class with the code in Listing 15-20. As happened with the previous example, the first time you run the application, the file is created and nothing is printed on the console, but if you run the application again, the view controller decodes the content of the file created before and prints the values of every **Book** object on the console.

Basic 15.4 Core Data

With archiving, we can store not only objects but also their connections. This organization is called *Object Graph*. Archiving is a good tool to store an Object Graph on file but presents some limitations. The Object Graph stored this way is difficult to expand or modified. The entire graph must be stored in the file again after the smallest change, and it is not easy to control the connections between objects to determine exactly which objects will be stored. The solution is called *Core Data*. Core Data is an Object Graph manager that defines and manages its own objects and connections and stores them in a database. We can determine the composition of the objects and their relationships. The system takes care of encoding and decoding the objects, preserving consistency and maximizing efficiency.

Basic Data Model

The structure of the Core Data's Object Graph is defined with a data model. This has nothing to do with the data model of the MVC pattern implemented in previous chapters; a Core Data model is a definition of the type of objects the graph is going to contain (called *Entities*) and their connections (called *Relationships*).

A model can be created from code, but Xcode offers a practical editor to define the structure of the graph. The model is stored in a file and then the file is compiled and included in the Core Data system created for our app. Xcode offers a template to create this file.

Figure 15-4: *Option to create a Core Data model in the iOS panel*

The file may be created with any name we want but it must have the extension xcdatamodel. Once created, it is included in our project along with the rest of the files. Clicking on it reveals the Xcode editor in the Editor Area.

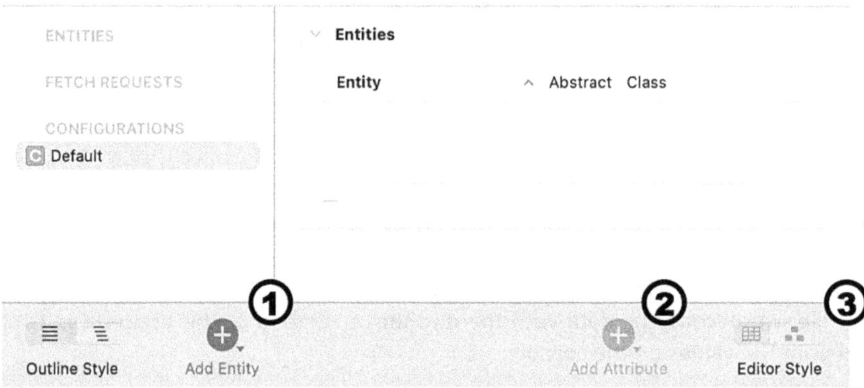

Figure 15-5: *Model editor*

The model contains three main components: Entities, Attributes, and Relationships. Entities are the descriptions of the objects, Attributes are the descriptions of the objects' properties, and Relationships are the connections allowed between the objects. The first step is to add Entities to the model. Entities are created from the Add Entity button at the bottom of the editor (Figure 15-5, number 1). When we press this button, Xcode creates an entity with the generic name "Entity".

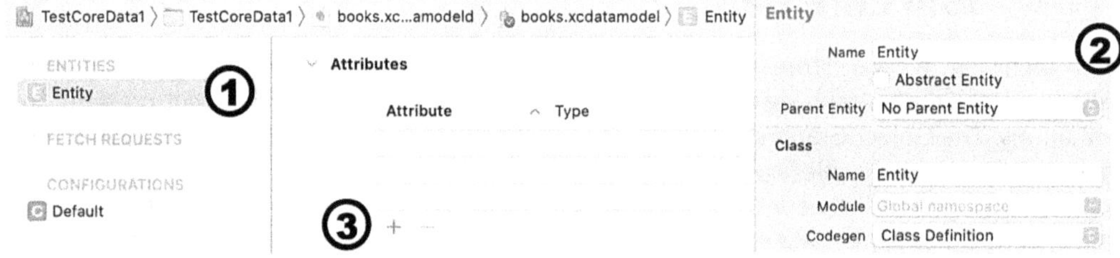

Figure 15-6: *New Entities*

We can change the name of the newly created entity by double-clicking the name (Figure 15-6, number 1) or by editing the Name field in the Data Model Inspector panel (Figure 15-6, number 2).

An entity defines the composition of the objects that are going to be part of the Object Graph, so the next step is to declare the type of values those objects are going to store. For this purpose, entities include Attributes (properties). To add an attribute, we select the entity and press the + button under the Attributes area (Figure 15-6, number 3) or press the Add Attribute button at the bottom of the editor (Figure 15-5, number 2). The attribute is added with the generic name "attribute" and the data type Undefined. Again, we can change the name of the attribute by double-clicking on it or editing the Name field in the Data Model Inspector panel. For our example, we called the entity *Books* and the first attribute *title* (Figure 15-7, number 1).

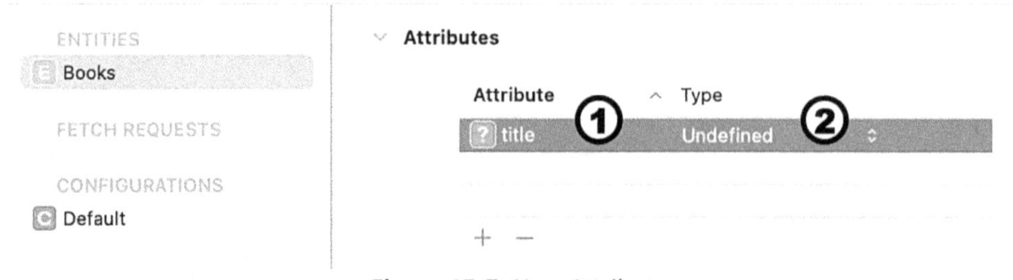

Figure 15-7: *New Attribute*

IMPORTANT: The name of entities must start with an uppercase letter and the names of attributes and relationships with a lowercase letter.

Every attribute must be associated with a data type for the objects to know what kind of values they can manage (Figure 15-7, number 2). Clicking on the attribute's type, we can open a menu to select the right data type. The most frequently used are Integer 16, Integer 32, Integer 64, Double, Float, String, Boolean, Date, and Binary Data. The Integer 16, 32, or 64 options are for **`Int16`**, **`Int32`**, and **`Int64`** values, Double and Float are for **`Double`** and **`Float`** values, String is for **`String`** values, Boolean is for **`Bool`** values, Date is for **`Date`** values, and Binary Data is for **`Data`** values.

An entity may contain as many attributes as our objects need. For example, we may add a few more attributes to complement the information required for books.

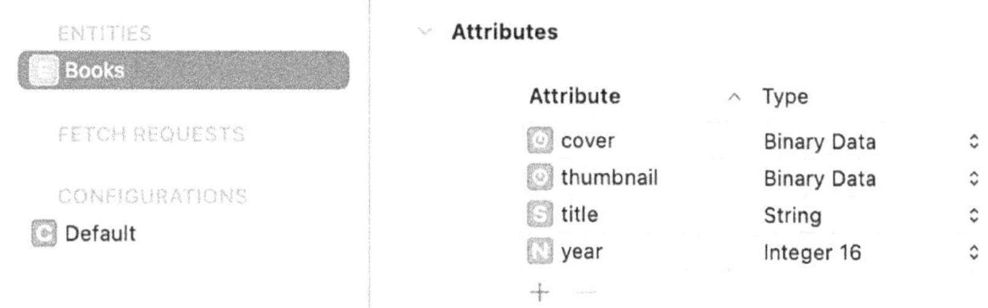

Figure 15-8: *Multiple Attributes*

In the example of Figure 15-8, we added an attribute called *year* to store the year in which the book was published, and two attributes of type Binary Data to store images (the book's cover and thumbnail). The data types used by these attributes are analog to the Swift data types we have being working so far. The title attribute takes a **`String`** value, the year attribute stores a value of type **`Int16`**, and the images are going to be stored as **`Data`** structures.

Most values don't require much consideration, but images are made of big chunks of data. Storing large amounts of data in a Persistent Store can affect the system's performance and slow down essential processes like searching for values or migrating the model. One alternative is to store the images in separate files, but it can get cumbersome to coordinate hundreds of files with the data in the database. Fortunately, Core Data can perform the process for us. All we need to do is to store the image as Binary Data and select the option Allows External Storage, available in the Data Model inspector panel inside the Utilities Area, as shown in Figure 15-9, below. After the option is selected, the images assigned to that attribute are going to be stored in separate files managed by the system.

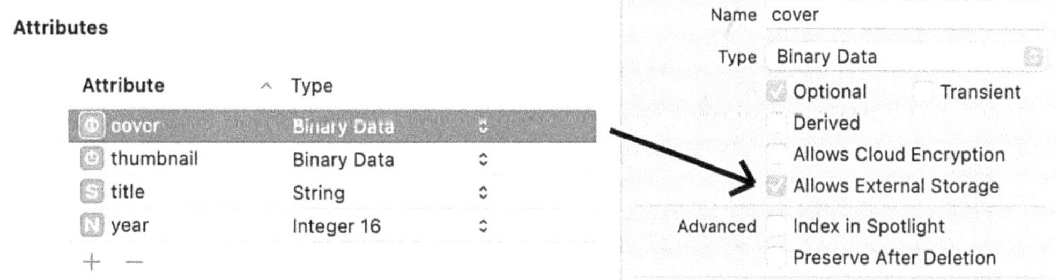

Figure 15-9: *Option to store images outside the Persistent Store*

We could have also included another attribute for the author's name in the Books entity, but here is when we need to think about the structure of the Object Graph and how the information will be stored. If we include a String type attribute for the author's name inside the Books entity, every time the user inserts a new book it will have to type the name of the author. This is error prone, time consuming, and when several books of the same author are available, it is impossible to make sure that all share the same exact name (one book could have the author's middle name and others just the first one, for example). Without the certainty of having the exact same name, we can never incorporate features in our app such as ordering the books by author or getting the list of books written by a particular author. Things get worse when, along with the name, we also decide to store other information about the author, like his or her date of birth. A proper organization of this information demands separate objects and therefore we must create new entities to represent them. Additional entities are added to the model in the same way as we did with the first one. Figure 15-10, next, shows our model with a new entity called *Authors* containing an attribute called *name*.

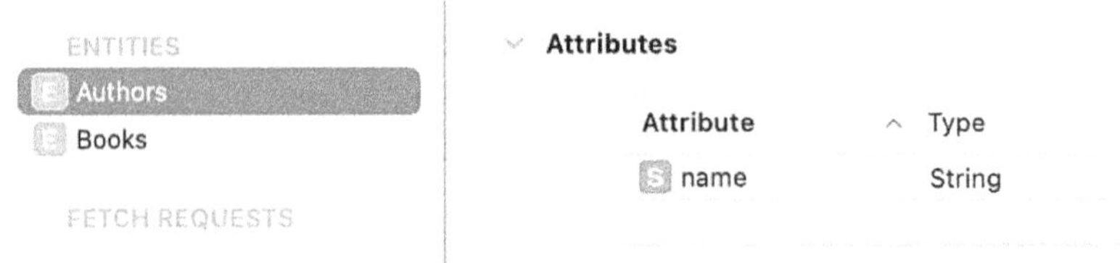

Figure 15-10: *Multiple Entities*

Entities are blueprints that we use to define the characteristics of the objects we want to store. For instance, when we want to store a new book in our example, we create a new object based on the Books entity. That object will have four properties corresponding to the values of its title, year, cover, and thumbnail. The same happens when we want to store information of an author. We create a new object based on the Authors entity and assign the name of the author to its name property. At the end, we will have two objects in the storage space, one for the book and another for the author. But if we want to retrieve these objects later, we need a way to know what Books object is related to what Authors object. To create this connection, the Core Data model includes Relationships.

Relationships are like properties in one object containing references to other objects. They could have a reference to only one object or a set of objects. For example, in the Books entity, we can create a relationship that contains a reference to only one object of the Authors entity, because there could only be one author per book (for this example we are assuming that our app is storing books written only by one author). On the contrary, in the Authors entity, we need to establish a relationship that contains references to multiple Books objects, because an author may have written several books, not just one. Core Data calls these relationships according to the number of objects they may reference. The names are To-One and To-Many and they are created pressing the **+** button in the Relationships area below the Attributes area. Figure 15-11, below, shows a relationship called *author* we have created for the Books entity of our example.

Figure 15-11: *Relationship for the Books entity*

A relationship only needs two values: its name (the name of the property) and the destination (the type of objects it is referencing), but it requires some parameters to be set. We must tell the model if the relationship is going to be optional, define its type (To-One or To-Many), and determine what should happen to the destination object if the source object is deleted (the Delete Rule). All these options are available in the Data Model Inspector panel when the relationship is selected.

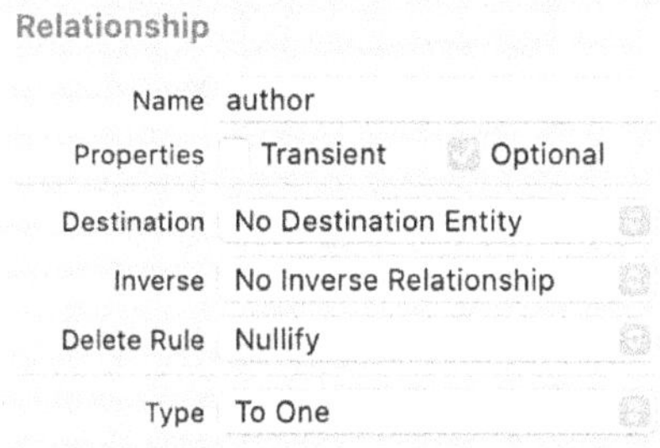

***Figure 15-12:** Relationship settings*

By default, the relationship is set to Optional, which means that the source may be connected to a destination object or not (a book can have an author or not), the Type of the relationship is set to To-One (a book can only have one author), and the Delete Rule is set to Nullify. The following are all the values available for this rule.

- **Deny:** If there is at least one object at the destination, the source is not deleted (if there is an Authors object assigned to the Books object, the book is not deleted).
- **Nullify:** The connections between objects are removed, but the objects at the destination are not deleted (if a Books object is deleted, the Authors object associated with that book loses the connection but it is not deleted).
- **Cascade:** The objects at the destination are deleted when the source is deleted (the Authors object is deleted if one of its books is deleted).
- **No Action:** The objects at the destination are not deleted or modified (the connections are preserved, even when the source object does not exist anymore).

To find the right rule for a relationship, we must think in terms of the information we are manipulating. Is it right to delete the author if one of its books is deleted? In our case, the answer is simple. An author can have more than one book, so we cannot delete the author when a book is deleted because there could be other books that are connected to that same author. Therefore, the Nullify rule set by default is the right one for this relationship. But this could change when we create the opposite relationship, connecting the Authors entity to the Books entity. We need this second relationship to search for books that belong to an author. Figure 15-13 shows a relationship called *books* that we have created for the Authors entity.

***Figure 15-13:** Relationship for the Authors entity*

IMPORTANT: Relationships must always be bidirectional. If we set a relationship from entity A to entity B, we must set the opposite relationship from entity B to A. Core Data offers another type of relationship called *Fetched Properties* to connect entities in only one direction. You can add a Fetched Property from the area below the Relationships area.

The new relationship added in Figure 15-13 is in the Authors entity, so every Authors object will have a property called **books** that we can use to retrieve the Books objects connected to the author. Because one author can have many books, the setting of this relationship is going to differ from the previous one. In this case, we must set the Type of the relationship as To-Many (to many books) and modify the Delete Rule according to how we want our application to respond when an author is deleted. If we don't want to keep books that do not have an author assigned, we should select the Cascade option, so when an author is deleted all his or her books are deleted too. But if we don't mind having books with no author around, then the option should be kept as Nullify.

IMPORTANT: The Delete Rules are a way to ensure that the objects remaining in the Object Graph are those that our application and the user need. But we can always set the rule to Nullify and take care of deleting all the objects ourselves.

There is a third value for the relationship called *Inverse*. Once we set the relationships on both sides, it is highly recommended to set this value. It just tells the model what the name of the opposite relationship is. Core Data needs this to ensure the consistency of the Object Graph. Figure 15-14 shows the final setup for both relationships.

Relationship for the Books entity

Relationship	Destination	Inverse
author	Authors	books

Relationship for the Authors entity

Relationship	Destination	Inverse
books	Books	author

Figure 15-14: *Inverse Relationships*

Two relationships are simple to follow, but multiple relationships connecting several entities together can turn the model into an indecipherable mess. To help us identify every component of the model, Xcode offers an additional visualization style that displays the entities as boxes and the relationships as arrows connecting the boxes. The option, called *Editor Style*, is at the bottom of the Editor Area (Figure 15-5, number 3). Figure 15-15, below, shows what our model looks like when we switch to this style (Notice that the To-Many relationship is represented by double arrows).

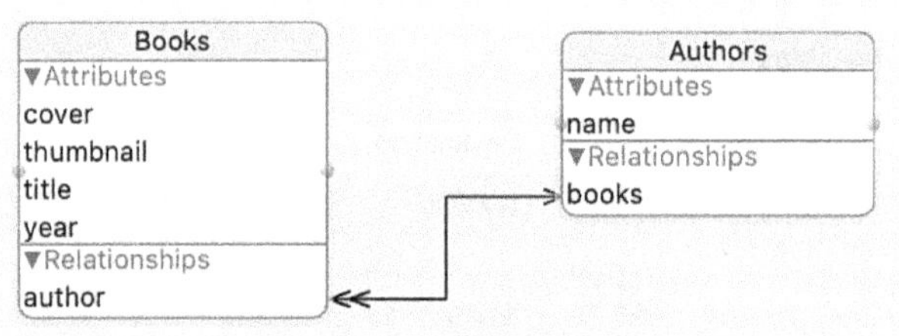

Figure 15-15: *Graphical representation of the model*

Do It Yourself: Create a new project. Open the File menu at the top of the screen, go to New and select the File option to create a new file. Move to the Core Data section in the iOS panel and select the Data Model option (Figure 15-4). Save the file with the name books.xcdatamodeld. Click on this file to open the editor (Figure 15-5). Press the Add Entity button to create two new entities with the names Authors and Books. Create the attributes for these entities as illustrated in Figures 15-8 and 15-10. Create the relationships for every entity as shown in Figure 15-14. Set the books relationship to To-Many and keep the rest of the values by default. Click on the Editor Style button to see a graphical representation of the model.

Basic Core Data Stack

The creation of the model is just the first step in the definition of the Core Data system. Once we have all the entities along with their attributes and relationships set up, we must initialize Core Data. Core Data is created from a group of objects that manage all the processes, from the organization of the Object Graph to the storage of the graph in a database. There is an object that manages the model, an object that stores the data on file, and an object that intermediates between this Persistent Store and our own code. The scheme is called *stack*. Figure 15-16 illustrates a common Core Data stack.

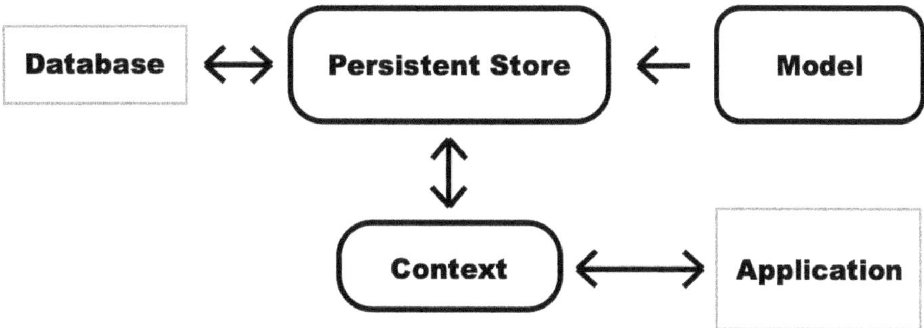

Figure 15-16: *Core Data stack*

The code in our application interacts with the Context to manage the objects and access their values, the Context asks the Persistent Store to read or add new objects to the graph, and the Persistent Store processes the Object Graph and saves it in the database.

The Core Data framework offers classes to create objects that represent every part of the stack. The **`NSManagedObjectModel`** class manages the model, the **`NSPersistentStore`** class manages a Persistent Store, the **`NSPersistentStoreCoordinator`** class is used to manage all the Persistent Stores available (a Core Data stack can have multiple Persistent Stores), and the **`NSManagedObjectContext`** creates and manages the context that intermediates between our app and the Persistent Store. Although we can instantiate these objects and create the stack ourselves, the framework offers the **`NSPersistentContainer`** class, which takes care of everything for us. The class includes the following initializer and also properties to access each object of the stack.

NSPersistentContainer(name: String**)**—This initializer creates an **`NSPersistentContainer`** object that defines a Core Data stack. The **name** argument is a string representing the name of the container. This value must match the name of the Core Data model (the file's name, without the extension).

managedObjectModel—This property sets or returns an **`NSManagedObjectModel`** object that represents the Core Data model.

persistentStoreCoordinator—This property sets or returns the **`NSPersistentStoreCoordinator`** object that manages the Persistent Stores available.

viewContext—This property sets or returns the **`NSManagedObjectContext`** object in charge of the stack's context that we use to access and modify the Object Graph.

To create the Core Data stack from our app, we must initialize a new **`NSPersistentContainer`** object and then load the Persistent Stores (one by default). Because the stores may take time to load, the class offers a specific method for this purpose.

loadPersistentStores(completionHandler: Closure**)**—This method loads the Persistent Stores and executes a closure when the process is over. The closure receives two arguments, an **`NSPersistentStoreDescription`** object with the configuration of the stack, and an optional **`NSError`** value to report errors.

All the communication between our app and the data in the Persistent Store is done through the context. The context is created by the container from the **NSManagedObjectContext** class. This class includes properties and methods to manage the context and the objects in the Persistent Store. The following are the most frequently used.

hasChanges—This property returns a Boolean value that indicates if the context has changes that have to be saved in the Persistent Store.

save()—This method saves the changes in the Persistent Store.

reset()—This method resets the context to a basic state. All the objects and modifications our app introduced to the context are ignored.

delete(NSManagedObject**)**—This method deletes an object in the Persistent Store.

count(for: NSFetchRequest**)**—This method returns the number of objects found in the Persistent Store for the request. The **for** argument specifies the request.

When working with Core Data, the Core Data's Persistent Store becomes our app's data model. Therefore, Apple recommends initializing the Core Data stack in the app's delegate. In fact, Xcode includes an option to create the Core Data stack that generates this code for us. All we need to do is to activate the Use Core Data option when the project is created (see Figure 5-10). The following example shows the code included by the Xcode template when this option is selected.

```
import UIKit
import CoreData

@main
class AppDelegate: UIResponder, UIApplicationDelegate {
   func application(_ application: UIApplication,
didFinishLaunchingWithOptions launchOptions:
[UIApplication.LaunchOptionsKey: Any]?) -> Bool {
      return true
   }
   func application(_ application: UIApplication,
configurationForConnecting connectingSceneSession: UISceneSession,
options: UIScene.ConnectionOptions) -> UISceneConfiguration {
      return UISceneConfiguration(name: "Default Configuration",
sessionRole: connectingSceneSession.role)
   }
   lazy var persistentContainer: NSPersistentContainer = {
      let container = NSPersistentContainer(name: "books")
      container.loadPersistentStores(completionHandler:
{ (storeDescription, error) in
         if let error = error as NSError? {
            fatalError("Unresolved error \(error), \(error.userInfo)")
         }
      })
      return container
   }()
}
```

Listing 15-21: *Initializing the Core Data stack in the app's delegate*

The **AppDelegate** class in Listing 15-21 defines a computed property called **persistentContainer** to create the Persistent Store. Apple recommends declaring this property as **lazy**, so the Core Data stack is only initialized when required. The property creates an instance of the **NSPersistentContainer** class with the name of the Core Data model (in our example, we called it "books"). This object creates the stack but does not load the Persistent

Stores; this is the job of the **loadPersistentStores()** method. After completion, this method executes a closure with two values: a reference to the Persistent Store just created, and an **Error** value to report errors. Errors are infrequent, but if an error occurs, we should warn the user. The code provided by Xcode just calls the **fatalError()** function to stop the execution of the app.

The **NSManagedObjectContext** object stored in the **viewContext** property of the Persistent Store is the one we use in our app's view controllers to add, fetch, and remove objects from the store. To read this property from the view controllers we must access the app's delegate, as explained in Chapter 5 (see Listing 5-10). The following code illustrates a possible implementation. We read the property in the app's delegate and assign its value to a local property that we can use later from other methods in the view controller to access the context.

```
import UIKit
import CoreData

class ViewController: UIViewController {
   var context: NSManagedObjectContext!

   override func viewDidLoad() {
      super.viewDidLoad()
      let app = UIApplication.shared
      let appDelegate = app.delegate as! AppDelegate
      context = appDelegate.persistentContainer.viewContext
   }
}
```

Listing 15-22: *Accessing the context from a view controller*

Do It Yourself: Update the **AppDelegate** class with the code in Listing 15-21. Replace the value of the **name** argument in the **NSPersistentContainer** initializer by the name of your model's file (books). At this moment, the app doesn't do anything other than creating the stack.

Basic Managed Objects

Core Data does not store our custom objects; it defines a class called **NSManagedObject** for this purpose. Every time we want to store information in the database, we must create an **NSManagedObject** object, associate that object to an Entity, and store the data the entity allows. For example, if we create an object associated to the Books entity, we are only allowed to store five values that corresponds to the Entity's attributes and relationship (title, year, cover, thumbnail, and author). The class includes the following initializer and methods to create and manage the objects.

NSManagedObject(context: NSManagedObjectContext**)**—This initializer creates an instance of the **NSManagedObject** class and adds it to the context specified by the argument.

fetchRequest()—This type method generates a fetch request for an entity. A fetch request is a request we use to fetch objects of a particular entity from the Persistent Store.

To simplify our work, the system allows us to define subclasses of the **NSManagedObject** class that correspond to the entities of our model (Instead of creating instances of the **NSManagedObject** class, we create instances of the **Books** and **Authors** classes). Because this is common practice for any developer, Xcode does it automatically for us. All we need to do is to associate each Entity with a subclass from the Data Model Inspector panel. The option is available in a section called *Class*.

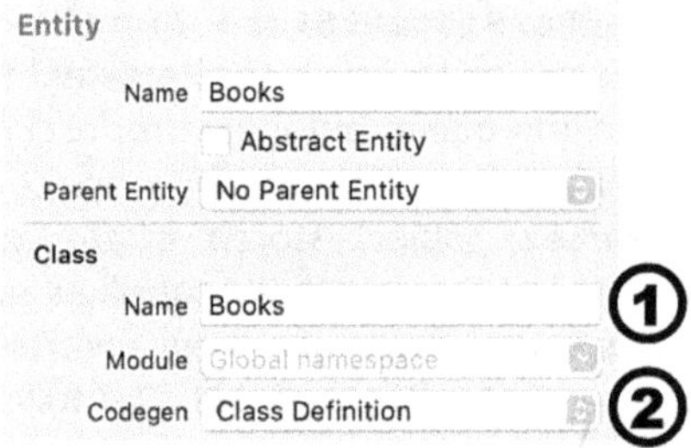

Figure 15-17: *Entity's subclass*

To ask Xcode to create the subclasses for us, we must select the entities one by one, click on the Class Definition value for the Codegen option (number 2), and make sure that the name of the subclass is specified in the Name field (number 1). Once the options are set, the classes are automatically created. For example, when we set these options for the entities in our model, Xcode creates a subclass of **NSManagedObject** called **Books** with the properties **title**, **year**, **cover**, **thumbnail**, and **author**, and a subclass called **Authors** with the properties **name** and **books**. From now on, all we need to do to store a book in the Persistent Store is to create an instance of the **Books** class using the **NSManagedObject** initializer.

Do It Yourself: Click on the Core Data model file to open the model. Select the Books entity, open the Data Model Inspector panel, and make sure that the value of the Codegen option is set to Class Definition and the name of the class is assigned to the Name field (Figure 15-17). Repeat the same process for the Authors entity.

IMPORTANT: The subclasses of the **NSManagedObject** class created to represent each entity in our model are not visible in Xcode. They are created internally and automatically modified every time entities or attributes are added or removed from the model. If you decide not to use these subclasses, you can select the value Manual/None from the Codegen option and work directly with **NSManagedObject** objects or define your own subclasses.

Basic Asynchronous Access

Reading and writing information on a database is a delicate process. The database may be accessed by different parts of the application and from different threads, which can cause errors or even data corruption. To make sure the data is accurate and safe, we must access the database from the same thread assigned to the Core Data context. For this purpose, the **NSManagedObjectContext** class includes the following asynchronous method.

perform(schedule: ScheduledTaskType, Closure**)**—This asynchronous method performs a closure in the thread assigned to the Core Data context. The **schedule** argument determines how the closure is going to be executed. It is an enumeration with the values **immediate** (the closure runs asynchronously), and **enqueued** (the closure runs concurrently). If the argument is ignored, the closure is executed asynchronously.

Basic Storing Objects

All the interaction between our code and the Persistent Store is done through the context. When we want to access the objects already stored, add new ones, remove them, or modify any of their values, we must do it in the context and then move those changes from the context to the Persistent Store. To illustrate how this process works, we are going to create a simple example that allows us to add, delete, and list books.

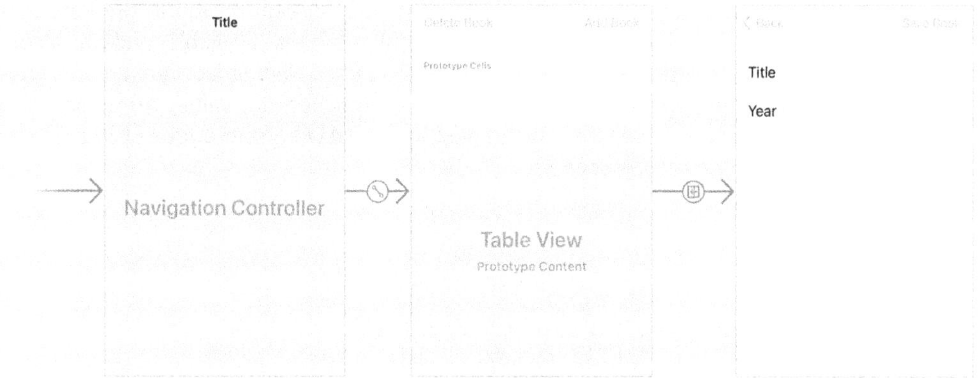

Figure 15-18: *Interface to list and add books*

The interface includes a Table View Controller embedded in a Navigation Controller and a second scene with a form to add values. The Navigation Bar of the Table View Controller includes two bar buttons: Delete Book to delete books and Add Book to add new ones. The Add Book button is connected to the second scene with a Show segue. This scene includes two Text Fields to let the user insert the title and year of a new book and a bar button called Save Book to save it.

Do It Yourself: Delete the initial scene. Add a Table View Controller to the Storyboard and embed it in a Navigation Controller (remember to designate the Navigation Controller as the initial view controller). Add two bar buttons to the Navigation Bar called Delete Book and Add Book. Add a new scene. Connect the Add Book button to this scene with a Show segue. Add a bar button to the second scene called Save Book. Add two labels and two Text Fields to the second scene.

The Persistent Store stores the app's data in a database, but we still need an MVC data model to temporarily store the data for the scenes. Core Data makes this work easy. Core Data objects conform to the **`Identifiable`** protocol and include the following property to provide a unique identifier.

objectID—This property returns the object's unique identifier. It is a value of type **`NSManagedObjectID`**.

The identifiers are defined by the **`NSManagedObjectID`** class, and the objects are returned as **`NSManagedObject`** objects (**`Books`** and **`Authors`**), so all our model needs to do is to create a diffable data source that works with **`NSManagedObjectID`** values and provide an array to store the objects retrieved from the database, as shown next.

```
import UIKit
import CoreData

enum Sections {
   case main
}
struct ApplicationData {
   var dataSourceBooks: UITableViewDiffableDataSource<Sections,
NSManagedObjectID>!
   var listOfBooks: [Books] = []
}
var AppData = ApplicationData()
```

Listing 15-23: *Defining the model to work with Core Data*

The purpose of our application is to show the list of objects already stored in the Persistent Store and create new ones. The initial scene is going to list all the books available, and the second scene will create new objects with the values provided by the user. New objects are created from the **NSManagedObject** initializer of our subclass (**Books**) and then the values are assigned to this object's properties. The process is introduced next in the **EditBookViewController** class we have created to control the second scene.

```
import UIKit
import CoreData

class EditBookViewController: UIViewController {
   @IBOutlet weak var bookTitle: UITextField!
   @IBOutlet weak var bookYear: UITextField!
   var context: NSManagedObjectContext!

   override func viewDidLoad() {
      super.viewDidLoad()
      let app = UIApplication.shared
      let appDelegate = app.delegate as! AppDelegate
      context = appDelegate.persistentContainer.viewContext

      bookTitle.becomeFirstResponder()
   }
   @IBAction func saveBook(_ sender: UIBarButtonItem) {
      let title = bookTitle.text!.trimmingCharacters(in: .whitespaces)
      let year = Int16(bookYear.text!)
      if title != "" && year != nil {
         Task(priority: .high) {
            await storeBook(title: title, year: year!)
         }
      }
   }
   func storeBook(title: String, year: Int16) async {
      await context.perform {
         let newBook = Books(context: self.context)
         newBook.title = title
         newBook.year = year
         newBook.thumbnail = UIImage(named: "nothumbnail")?.pngData()

         do {
            try self.context.save()
            self.closeScene()
         } catch {
            print("Error: \(error)")
         }
      }
   }
   func closeScene() {
      Task(priority: .high) {
         await MainActor.run {
            navigationController?.popViewController(animated: true)
         }
      }
   }
}
```

Listing 15-24: *Adding new objects to the Persistent Store*

As illustrated in this example, the first thing we need to do in any view controller that wants to access Core Data is to get a reference to the context from the app's delegate. In the view controller of Listing 15-24, we assigned the context to a property called **context** for easy access.

When the Save Book button is pressed, the **saveBook()** method checks if the values in the Text Fields are valid and executes an asynchronous method called **storeBook()** to create the **Books** object and store it in the Persistent Store. This method performs two asynchronous tasks: the **perform()** method of the Core Data context to safely access the Persistent Store, and the **run()** method of the Main Actor to remove the scene from the main thread when the process is over (see Concurrency in Chapter 14). To store the values in the Persistent Store, we create a new object with the **Books()** initializer. This not only creates a new object of type **Books** but it also adds it to the context. Next, we assign the values inserted by the user to the object's **title** and **year** properties and also a placeholder image called nothumbnail to the **thumbnail** property (the image is available on our website). The title and year values are assigned directly to the properties, but the image must be converted to a **Data** structure with the **pngData()** method of the **UIImage** object (see **UIImage** in Chapter 5). Notice that the system automatically assigns the value **nil** to the rest of the properties (**cover** and **author**).

The **Books()** initializer inserts the new object into the context, but this change is not permanent. If we close the app after the values are assigned to the properties, the object is lost. To persist the changes, we must save the context with the **save()** method. This method takes the information in the context and modifies the Persistent Store with it, so everything is stored on file.

Do It Yourself: Create a Swift file called ApplicationData.swift for the model in Listing 15-23. Create a subclass of the **UIViewController** class called **EditBookViewController** and assign it to the second scene. Connect the first Text Field with an Outlet called **bookTitle** and the second Text Field with an Outlet called **bookYear**. Connect the Save Book button with an Action called **saveBook()**. Complete the class with the code in Listing 15-24.

The process to get the objects back from the Persistent Store is the opposite. Instead of moving the changes in the context to the Persistent Store, we get the objects from the Persistent Store and move them into the context. Once the objects are in the context, we can read their properties, modify the values, or delete them. Core Data defines the **NSFetchRequest** class to request objects from the Persistent Store. The following are some of the properties included by the class for configuration.

predicate—This property sets or returns the predicate used to filter the objects. It is a value of type **NSPredicate**; a Foundation class used to establish logical conditions that describe objects in the Persistent Store.

sortDescriptors—This property sets or returns an array of sort descriptors that determine what the order of the objects obtained by the request should be. It is an array of values of type **NSSortDescriptor**, a Foundation class used to sort the objects according to the value of a property in ascending or descending order.

fetchLimit—This property sets or returns the maximum number of objects that the request should return. It takes a value of type **Int**.

resultType—This property sets or returns a value that determines the type of data returned by the request. The framework offers the **NSFetchRequestResultType** structure with properties to define the value. The properties available are **managedObjectResultType** (it returns values of type **NSManagedObject**), **managedObjectIDResultType** (it returns the identification values of the **NSManagedObject** objects instead of the objects themselves), **dictionaryResultType** (it returns a dictionary with the values of the properties), and **countResultType** (it returns an integer value with the total of objects found).

propertiesToFetch—This property sets or returns an array of values that determine the properties we want to get (by default, all the properties of the **NSManagedObject** objects are returned). The properties of an entity (attributes) are represented by objects of the **NSPropertyDescription** class, or subclasses of it.

Every time we want to read objects from the Persistent Store, we must create an **NSFetchRequest** object to determine what type of objects we want. Because the request has to be associated to an entity, the subclasses of the **NSManagedObject** class representing our entities include the **fetchRequest()** method. This method returns an **NSFetchRequest** object already associated to the entity. Once the request object is ready, we must fetch the objects with the **fetch()** method provided by the context. The following is the view controller for the Table View of our example. The code performs a request, stores the objects in the model, and shows their values on the screen.

```
import UIKit
import CoreData

class BooksViewController: UITableViewController {
   var context: NSManagedObjectContext!

   override func viewDidLoad() {
      super.viewDidLoad()
      let app = UIApplication.shared
      let appDelegate = app.delegate as! AppDelegate
      context = appDelegate.persistentContainer.viewContext

      tableView.register(UITableViewCell.self, forCellReuseIdentifier:
"booksCell")
      prepareDataSource()
   }
   override func viewWillAppear(_ animated: Bool) {
      super.viewWillAppear(animated)
      Task(priority: .high) {
         await loadRequest()

         await MainActor.run {
            prepareSnapshot()
         }
      }
   }
   func prepareDataSource() {
      AppData.dataSourceBooks = UITableViewDiffableDataSource<Sections,
NSManagedObjectID>(tableView: tableView) { tableView, indexPath, itemID
in
         let cell = tableView.dequeueReusableCell(withIdentifier:
"booksCell", for: indexPath)
         if let item = AppData.listOfBooks.first(where: { $0.objectID ==
itemID }) {
            var config = cell.defaultContentConfiguration()
            config.text = item.title
            config.secondaryText = item.author?.name ?? "Undefined"
            config.secondaryTextProperties.color = .systemGray

            if let data = item.thumbnail, let image = UIImage(data: data)
{
               config.image = image
            } else {
               config.image = UIImage(named: "nothumbnail")
            }
            config.imageProperties.maximumSize = CGSize(width: 60,
height: 60)
            cell.contentConfiguration = config
         }
         return cell
      }
   }
```

```
    func loadRequest() async {
        await context.perform {
            let request: NSFetchRequest<Books> = Books.fetchRequest()
            do {
                AppData.listOfBooks = try self.context.fetch(request)
            } catch {
                print("Error: \(error)")
            }
        }
    }
    func prepareSnapshot() {
        var snapshot = NSDiffableDataSourceSnapshot<Sections,
NSManagedObjectID>()
        snapshot.appendSections([.main])
        snapshot.appendItems(AppData.listOfBooks.map({ $0.objectID }))
        AppData.dataSourceBooks.apply(snapshot)
    }
}
```

Listing 15-25: *Fetching values from the Persistent Store*

There are different places from where we can perform a request, depending on the requirements of our application. In this example, we created an asynchronous method called **`loadRequest()`** and then execute it from the **`viewWillAppear()`** method, so the objects are retrieved and the table is updated every time the user opens the scene.

To make a request, we first get the **`NSFetchRequest`** object by calling the **`fetchRequest()`** method on the subclass of the objects we want to read (in this case we want to get books, so we call it on the **`Books`** class). Once the request is ready, we fetch the objects with the **`fetch()`** method and assign them to the **`listOfBooks`** property in our model.

The rest of the process is like any other example we have seen so far. The snapshot gets the identifiers of the **`Books`** objects in the **`listOfBooks`** property and provides them to the diffable data source, and the diffable data source reads the properties of each object and configures the cell to show the values on the screen. The only difference is in how we process the images. In this case, the images are stored in the Persistent Store as **`Data`** objects, so we must check whether there is data available or not and then initialize the **`UIImage`** object with that data (**`UIImage(data: data)`**). If no image was assigned to the object, we show the placeholder image. The result is illustrated below.

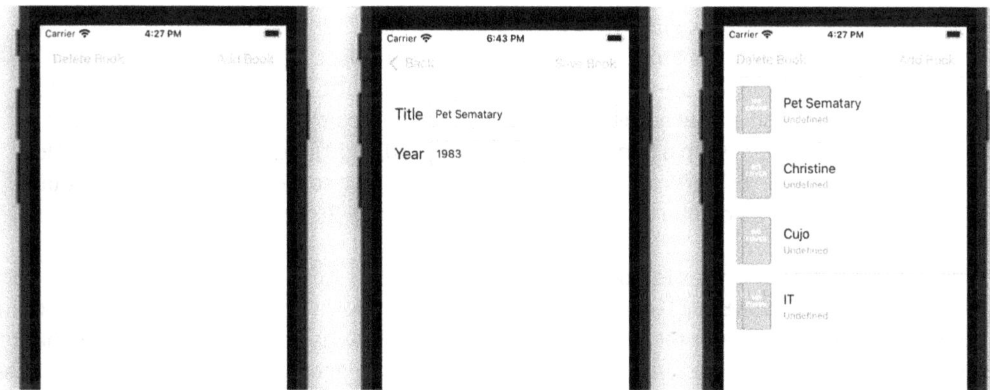

Figure 15-19: *Adding books to a Persistent Store*

Do It Yourself: Create a **`UITableViewController`** subclass called **`BooksViewController`** and assign it to the Table View Controller. Complete the class with the code in Listing 15-25. Download the nothumbnail.png image from our website and add it to the Assets Catalog. Run the application. The first screen shows an empty Table View (Figure 15-19, left). Press the Add Book button and insert the values of a book (Figure 15-19, center). At the end, the table should look like the right picture in Figure 15-19.

IMPORTANT: Snapshot updates must always be performed from the same thread. This could be the main thread or a background thread, but it must always be the same. This is the reason why in the view controller of Listing 15-25 we call the **`prepareSnapshot()`** method from the Main Actor.

The next step is to allow the user to insert the authors. This demands our application to provide additional scenes where the user can select and add new objects. For our example, we have decided to expand the interface with another Table View Controller to list the authors available and an additional scene to insert more. To provide access to these new scenes, we have added a button called Select to the **`EditBookViewController`**'s scene, along with a label to show the name of the selected author (Figure 15-20, left).

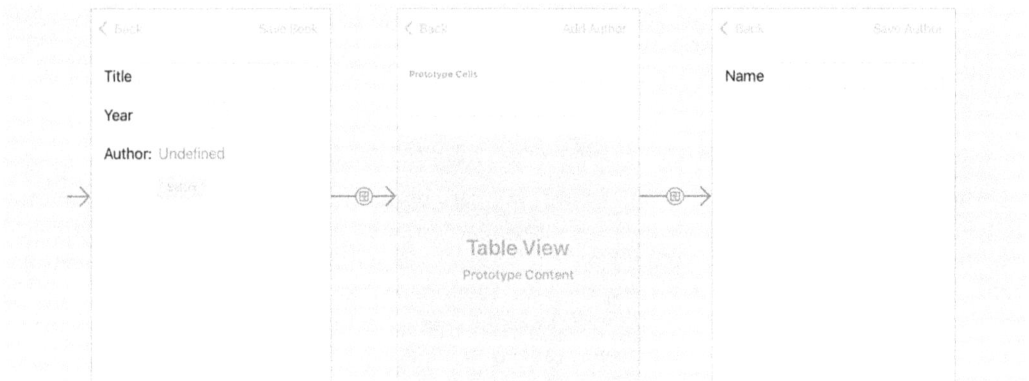

Figure 15-20: *Interface to list and add authors*

When the user presses the Add Book button in the initial scene (Figure 15-18, center), the next scene now shows three input options: a Text Field to insert the title of the book, a Text Field to insert the year, and the Select button to select the author (Figure 15-20, left). This button is connected to the Table View Controller for the authors with a Show segue (Figure 15-20, center). In addition, we have included a bar button called Add Author to open a scene that includes a Text Field to insert the name of a new author (Figure 15-20, right).

Do It Yourself: Add two labels and a button called Select to the **`EditBookViewController`**'s scene (Figure 15-20, left). Add a Table View Controller to the Storyboard and connect the Select button to this scene with a Show segue (Figure 15-20, center). Add a bar button called Add Author to this scene. Add a new scene to the Storyboard and connect the Add Author button to this scene with a Show segue (Figure 15-20, right). Add a label, an input field, and a bar button called Save Author to the last scene. Your interface should look like the combination of Figures 15-18 and 15-20.

Every time an author is selected or created, we must get its **`Authors`** object and send it back to the **`EditBookViewController`** class to assign it to the book. As we have already seen, there are different ways to do it, but for this example we are going to use Unwind Segues (see Chapter 9, Figure 9-12). We need two Unwind Segues, one that is triggered when the user selects an author from the Table View Controller, and another that is triggered when the user inserts a new author. When the Unwind Segues are triggered, we must get the **`Authors`** object that represents the author and update the scene with the value of its **`name`** property. To receive and process this information, we must modify the **`EditBookViewController`** class to include the Action for the Unwind Segues and properties to store and manage the **`Authors`** object.

```
import UIKit
import CoreData

class EditBookViewController: UIViewController {
   @IBOutlet weak var bookTitle: UITextField!
   @IBOutlet weak var bookYear: UITextField!
   @IBOutlet weak var authorName: UILabel!
   var context: NSManagedObjectContext!
   var selectedAuthor: Authors!

   override func viewDidLoad() {
      super.viewDidLoad()
      let app = UIApplication.shared
      let appDelegate = app.delegate as! AppDelegate
      context = appDelegate.persistentContainer.viewContext

      bookTitle.becomeFirstResponder()
   }
   @IBAction func saveBook(_ sender: UIBarButtonItem) {
      let title = bookTitle.text!.trimmingCharacters(in: .whitespaces)
      let year = Int16(bookYear.text!)
      if title != "" && year != nil {
         Task(priority: .high) {
            await storeBook(title: title, year: year!)
         }
      }
   }
   func storeBook(title: String, year: Int16) async {
      await context.perform {
         let newBook = Books(context: self.context)
         newBook.title = title
         newBook.year = year
         newBook.author = self.selectedAuthor

         do {
            try self.context.save()
            self.closeScene()
         } catch {
            print("Error: \(error)")
         }
      }
   }
   func closeScene() {
      Task(priority: .high) {
         await MainActor.run {
            navigationController?.popViewController(animated: true)
         }
      }
   }
   @IBAction func backAuthor(_ segue: UIStoryboardSegue) {
      if segue.identifier == "backFromList" {
         let controller = segue.source as! AuthorsViewController
         selectedAuthor = controller.selectedAuthor
         authorName.text = selectedAuthor.name
      } else if segue.identifier == "backFromNew" {
         let controller = segue.source as! EditAuthorViewController
         selectedAuthor = controller.selectedAuthor
         authorName.text = selectedAuthor.name
      }
   }
}
```

Listing 15-26: *Adding an author to the book*

This view controller manages the scene that allows the user to insert new books, but it also must process the author selected by the user and assign it to the book. When the user selects or inserts a new author from the scenes added to the interface in Figure 15-20, the **backAuthor()** method is executed (due to the Unwind Segues). In this method, the code gets the **Authors** object that represents the author, assigns it to the **selectedAuthor** property, and updates the label on the screen with the value of its **name** property. (This process is done for each Unwind Segue, so no matter if the author is selected from the table or inserted in the form, its name is always shown on the screen and the **Authors** object is assigned to the book when the user presses the Save Book button.)

The process to list and create new **Authors** objects is the same we used for books. We perform a request to get the **Authors** objects from the Persistent Store and store them in a property in the model. The following are the properties we must add to the model to manage this information.

```
import UIKit
import CoreData

enum Sections {
   case main
}
struct ApplicationData {
   var dataSourceBooks: UITableViewDiffableDataSource<Sections,
NSManagedObjectID>!
   var dataSourceAuthors: UITableViewDiffableDataSource<Sections,
NSManagedObjectID>!
   var listOfBooks: [Books] = []
   var listOfAuthors: [Authors] = []
}
var AppData = ApplicationData()
```

Listing 15-27: *Defining a model to manage books and authors*

With the model ready, we can now load and show the authors to the user. The following is the view controller to manage the Table View Controller added to the interface for this purpose (see Figure 15-20). We call it **AuthorsViewController**.

```
import UIKit
import CoreData

class AuthorsViewController: UITableViewController {
   var context: NSManagedObjectContext!
   var selectedAuthor: Authors!

   override func viewDidLoad() {
      super.viewDidLoad()
      let app = UIApplication.shared
      let appDelegate = app.delegate as! AppDelegate
      context = appDelegate.persistentContainer.viewContext

      tableView.register(UITableViewCell.self, forCellReuseIdentifier:
"authorsCell")
      prepareDataSource()
   }
   override func viewWillAppear(_ animated: Bool) {
      super.viewWillAppear(animated)
      Task(priority: .high) {
         await loadRequest()

         await MainActor.run {
            prepareSnapshot()
         }
      }
```

```
   }
   func prepareDataSource() {
      AppData.dataSourceAuthors = UITableViewDiffableDataSource<Sections, 
NSManagedObjectID>(tableView: tableView) { tableView, indexPath, itemID 
in
         let cell = tableView.dequeueReusableCell(withIdentifier: 
"authorsCell", for: indexPath)
         if let item = AppData.listOfAuthors.first(where: { $0.objectID 
== itemID }) {
            var config = cell.defaultContentConfiguration()
            config.text = item.name
            cell.contentConfiguration = config
         }
         return cell
      }
   }
   func loadRequest() async {
      await context.perform {
         let request: NSFetchRequest<Authors> = Authors.fetchRequest()
         do {
            AppData.listOfAuthors = try self.context.fetch(request)
         } catch {
            print("Error: \(error)")
         }
      }
   }
   func prepareSnapshot() {
      var snapshot = NSDiffableDataSourceSnapshot<Sections, 
NSManagedObjectID>()
      snapshot.appendSections([.main])
      snapshot.appendItems(AppData.listOfAuthors.map({ $0.objectID }))
      AppData.dataSourceAuthors.apply(snapshot, animatingDifferences: 
false)
   }
   override func tableView(_ tableView: UITableView, didSelectRowAt 
indexPath: IndexPath) {
      if let itemID = AppData.dataSourceAuthors.itemIdentifier(for: 
indexPath) {
         if let item = AppData.listOfAuthors.first(where: { $0.objectID 
== itemID }) {
            selectedAuthor = item
         }
         performSegue(withIdentifier: "backFromList", sender: self)
      }
   }
}
```

Listing 15-28: *Listing authors*

Other than changing the name of the array (**listOfAuthors**), the rest of the code, including the fetch request, is the same we used to list books. The code also implements the protocol method **tableView(UITableView, didSelectRowAt:)** to assign the author selected by the user to the **selectedAuthor** property and trigger the Unwind Segue (the example assumes that we have created an Unwind Segue from the Table View Controller to the **backAuthor()** Action and have identified the segue with the string "backFromList".

The view controller to add new authors is also very similar to the one we used to add new books. We have to take the text inserted by the user in the Text Field, create the new **Authors** object to represent the author, save the context, and finally trigger the Unwind Segue to move back to the **EditBookViewController**'s scene (again, the example assumes that we have created an Unwind Segue from this scene to the **backAuthor()** Action identified with the string "backFromNew"). We called this view controller **EditAuthorViewController**.

```swift
import UIKit
import CoreData

class EditAuthorViewController: UIViewController {
   @IBOutlet weak var authorName: UITextField!
   var context: NSManagedObjectContext!
   var selectedAuthor: Authors!

   override func viewDidLoad() {
      super.viewDidLoad()
      let app = UIApplication.shared
      let appDelegate = app.delegate as! AppDelegate
      context = appDelegate.persistentContainer.viewContext

      authorName.becomeFirstResponder()
   }
   @IBAction func saveAuthor(_ sender: UIBarButtonItem) {
      let name = authorName.text!.trimmingCharacters(in: .whitespaces)
      if name != "" {
         Task(priority: .high) {
            await storeAuthor(name: name)
         }
      }
   }
   func storeAuthor(name: String) async {
      await context.perform {
         self.selectedAuthor = Authors(context: self.context)
         self.selectedAuthor.name = name

         do {
            try self.context.save()
            self.closeScene()
         } catch {
            print("Error: \(error)")
         }
      }
   }
   func closeScene() {
      Task(priority: .high) {
         await MainActor.run {
            performSegue(withIdentifier: "backFromNew", sender: self)
         }
      }
   }
}
```

Listing 15-29: *Inserting new authors*

With these additions, our basic app is complete. When we pressed the Select button, the app opens a Table View with all the authors available (Figure 15-21, center). If there are no authors or the author we want is not on the list, we can press the Add Author button and insert a new one (Figure 15-21, right). Every time we select an author from the list or insert a new one, the app goes back to the scene with the book's information and shows the name of the author on the screen (Figure 15-21, left). When the book is saved, the **Authors** object that represents the author is assigned to the book's **author** property and therefore the name of the author is now shown on the list of books.

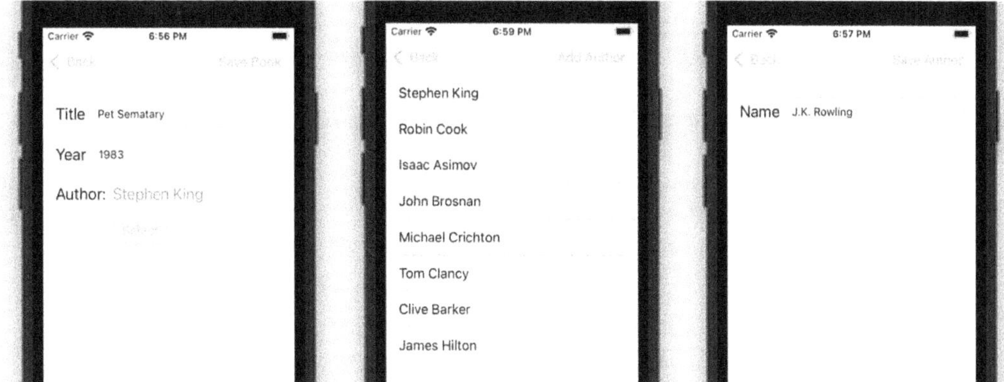

Figure 15-21: *Assigning an author to a book*

Do It Yourself: Update the model with the code in Listing 15-27. Update the **EditBookViewController** class with the code in Listing 15-26. Connect the label that is going to show the name of the author to the **authorName** Outlet. Create a **UITableViewController** subclass called **AuthorsView-Controller** and assign it to the new Table View Controller (Figure 15-20, center). Complete the class with the code in Listing 15-28. Create an Unwind Segue to the **backAuthor()** method for this scene with the identifier "backFromList". Create a **UIViewController** subclass called **EditAuthor-ViewController** and assign it to the last scene (Figure 15-20, right). Connect the Text Field in this scene with an Outlet called **authorName** and complete the **EditAuthorViewController** class with the code in Listing 15-29. Create an Unwind Segue to the **backAuthor()** method for this scene with the identifier "backFromNew". Run the application and press the Add New Book button. Press the Select button and select or insert a new author. Insert the rest of the information and save the book. You should see the list of books with their respective authors.

Basic Counting Objects

The **NSManagedObjectContext** class includes the **count()** method to count the number of objects in a request. The method returns an integer with the number of objects we would get if we call the **fetch()** method with the same request. For example, we can use it in the **EditBookViewController** class to get the number of authors already available. The request is always the same, but instead of fetching the objects we count them with the **count()** method.

```
override func viewDidLoad() {
   super.viewDidLoad()
   let app = UIApplication.shared
   let appDelegate = app.delegate as! AppDelegate
   context = appDelegate.persistentContainer.viewContext

   bookTitle.becomeFirstResponder()

   Task(priority: .background) {
      await context.perform {
         let request: NSFetchRequest<Authors> = Authors.fetchRequest()
         if let total = try? self.context.count(for: request) {
            print("Total Authors: \(total)")
         }
      }
   }
}
```

Listing 15-30: *Counting the authors available*

Do It Yourself: Replace the **`viewDidLoad()`** method in the **`EditBook-ViewController`** class with the method in Listing 15-30. Run the application and press the Add Book button. You should see the total number of authors available in the Persistent Store printed on the console.

If what we want is to get the number of objects associated to a To-Many relationship, we can count the number of items returned by the property that represents the relationship. For example, we can count the number of books of every author and show it next to the name.

```
func prepareDataSource() {
   AppData.dataSourceAuthors = UITableViewDiffableDataSource<Sections,
NSManagedObjectID>(tableView: tableView) { tableView, indexPath, itemID
in
      let cell = tableView.dequeueReusableCell(withIdentifier:
"authorsCell", for: indexPath)
      if let item = AppData.listOfAuthors.first(where: { $0.objectID ==
itemID }) {
         var config = cell.defaultContentConfiguration()

         let name = item.name ?? "Undefined"
         var total = 0
         if let totalBooks = item.books {
            total = totalBooks.count
         }
         config.text = "\(name) (\(total))"

         cell.contentConfiguration = config
      }
      return cell
   }
}
```

***Listing 15-31:** Counting the books of each author*

The **`prepareDataSource()`** method in Listing 15-31 replaces the same method in the **`AuthorsViewController`** class of Listing 15-28. Instead of assigning just the name of the author to the cell's label, we count the books associated to the author and create a string with this value and the author's name. Now the user can see how many books are available per author.

Basic Predicates

The requests performed in previous examples are getting all the objects associated to an entity. The Core Data framework defines the **`NSPredicate`** class to fetch only the objects that comply to certain conditions. For example, we could get only the books that were published in the year 1983. The class defines the following initializer to create a predicate with all the conditions we need.

NSPredicate(format: String, **argumentArray:** [Any]?**)**—This initializer creates a **`NSPredicate`** object with the conditions set by the **format** argument. The **argumentArray** argument is an optional array of values that replace placeholders in the string assigned to the **format** argument. The **argumentArray** argument may be ignored or replaced by a list of values separated by commas.

To filter values in a request, we must create the **`NSPredicate`** object and assign it to the request's **`predicate`** property, as shown next.

```
func loadRequest() async {
   await context.perform {
      let request: NSFetchRequest<Books> = Books.fetchRequest()
      request.predicate = NSPredicate(format: "year = 1983")
      do {
         AppData.listOfBooks = try self.context.fetch(request)
      } catch {
         print("Error: \(error)")
      }
   }
}
```

Listing 15-32: *Filtering books by year*

This example defines an **NSPredicate** object for the **BooksViewController** class to search for books published in 1983 (the **year** property is equal to 1983).

If we are trying to search for a value in a relationship, we can concatenate the properties with dot notation. For example, the following request looks for books written by the author Stephen King.

```
func loadRequest() async {
   await context.perform {
      let request: NSFetchRequest<Books> = Books.fetchRequest()
      request.predicate = NSPredicate(format: "author.name = 'Stephen
King'")
      do {
         AppData.listOfBooks = try self.context.fetch(request)
      } catch {
         print("Error: \(error)")
      }
   }
}
```

Listing 15-33: *Filtering books by author*

The name of the author was inserted inside the string using single quotes, but we do not always know beforehand what value we need to search for. To incorporate the value of a variable inside the formatted string, we can use placeholders. Placing the characters %@ inside the string, for example, indicates to the initializer that the value after the comma goes in that place.

```
func loadRequest() async {
   let search = "Stephen King"

   await context.perform {
      let request: NSFetchRequest<Books> = Books.fetchRequest()
      request.predicate = NSPredicate(format: "author.name = %@", search)
      do {
         AppData.listOfBooks = try self.context.fetch(request)
      } catch {
         print("Error: \(error)")
      }
   }
}
```

Listing 15-34: *Creating filters with placeholders*

We may include all the placeholders and arguments we need. The placeholders are replaced by the arguments one by one, in consecutive order, as with formatted strings (see **String** structures in Chapter 3). For example, we can search for books of a particular author and year. (Notice that since the value of the **year** property is an integer, we use the %d placeholder.)

```
func loadRequest() async {
   let search = "Stephen King"
   let year = 1983

   await context.perform {
      let request: NSFetchRequest<Books> = Books.fetchRequest()
      request.predicate = NSPredicate(format: "author.name = %@ && year =
%d", search, year)
      do {
         AppData.listOfBooks = try self.context.fetch(request)
      } catch {
         print("Error: \(error)")
      }
   }
}
```

Listing 15-35: Creating filters with multiple values

Do It Yourself: Replace the **viewWillAppear()** method in the **BooksViewController** class with any of the methods introduced above to see how predicates work. Add books with different authors and years to test them.

IMPORTANT: The placeholder %@ is replaced by the value specified in the arguments between quotes. If you need to add the value to the predicate without the quotes, you must use the placeholder %K instead (called *Dynamic Key*).

Predicates use comparison and logical operators like those offered by Swift. For example, we can compare values with the operators **=**, **!=**, **>**, **<**, **>=** and **<=**, and also concatenate conditions with the characters **&&** (or the word **AND**), **||** (or the word **OR**) and **!** (or the word **NOT**). Predicates also include keywords for a more precise search. The following are the most frequently used.

BEGINSWITH—The condition determined by this keyword is true when the expression on the left begins with the expression on the right.

CONTAINS—The condition determined by this keyword is true when the expression on the left contains the expression on the right.

ENDSWITH—The condition determined by this keyword is true when the expression on the left ends with the expression on the right.

LIKE—The condition determined by this keyword is true when the expression on the left is equal to the expression on the right.

IN—The condition determined by this keyword is true when the expression on the left is equal to any of the values included in the expression on the right. The values are provided as an array between parentheses.

These keywords may be accompanied by the characters **c** or **d** between square brackets to specify a case insensitive or diacritic insensitive search. For example, we may search for authors with a name beginning with the word "stephen", without considering uppercase or lowercase letters.

```
func loadRequest() async {
   let search = "stephen"

   await context.perform {
      let request: NSFetchRequest<Books> = Books.fetchRequest()
      request.predicate = NSPredicate(format: "author.name BEGINSWITH[c]
%@", search)
      do {
         AppData.listOfBooks = try self.context.fetch(request)
      } catch {
         print("Error: \(error)")
      }
   }
}
```

Listing 15-36: *Filtering values with predicate keywords*

IMPORTANT: Diacritics are the small marks used in some languages to change the pronunciation of a letter, like the visible stress over Spanish vowels. When we specify the character **d** between square brackets, the search ignores these marks and looks for the letter in its basic form. The **c** and **d** characters are usually implemented together, as in **[cd]**.

A practical application of predicates is to check for duplicates. Storing duplicated values is something that all applications should be prepared to avoid. For example, if we open our application and insert an author that already exists, two **Authors** objects with the same name will be stored in the Persistent Store. To avoid this situation, we can use a request with a predicate that searches for authors of the same name before creating a new object. The following example modifies the **storeAuthor()** method of the **EditAuthorViewController** class to avoid duplicates.

```
func storeAuthor(name: String) async {
   await context.perform {
      let request: NSFetchRequest<Authors> = Authors.fetchRequest()
      request.predicate = NSPredicate(format: "name = %@", name)

      if let total = try? self.context.count(for: request), total <= 0 {
         self.selectedAuthor = Authors(context: self.context)
         self.selectedAuthor.name = name

         do {
            try self.context.save()
            self.closeScene()
         } catch {
            print("Error: \(error)")
         }
      }
   }
}
```

Listing 15-37: *Checking for duplicates*

The method in Listing 15-37 creates a request for the Authors entity and uses the value inserted in the Text Field to create a predicate. The predicate looks for objects with the name equal to the value of the **name** constant. In the next statement, we call the **count()** method with this request to get the number of objects that match the condition. If the value returned is 0, we know that there are no authors in the Persistent Store with that name and can create and add a new one.

Do It Yourself: Replace the **storeAuthor()** method in the **EditAuthorViewController** class with the method in Listing 15-37. Run the application and try to insert an author that already exists. Use the same filter in the **EditBookViewController** class to avoid duplicates when inserting new books. You can create a predicate that checks for books with the same title and author (the placeholder characters %@ can take any type of values and objects, including **NSManagedObject** objects like **Books** and **Authors**).

Basic Sort Descriptors

Objects returned from a request are usually in the order they were created, but this is not guaranteed. To sort the objects in a specific order, we can associate the request with an object of type **NSSortDescriptor**. This class creates objects that specify an order according to the values of a property. The sorting criteria is determined by methods provided by the values themselves. For example, data types like **Date** implement only the **compare()** method to compare their values, but the **NSString** class implements other methods that allow us to do things like order strings without differentiating between lowercase and uppercase letters (see **NSString** in Chapter 4). By default, an **NSSortDescriptor** object uses the **compare()** method to compare any type of value, but we can specify others from the initializer.

NSSortDescriptor(key: String?, **ascending:** Bool, **selector:** Selector?**)**—This initializer creates an **NSSortDescriptor** object that orders the objects according to the value of the property specified by the **key** argument. This argument is a string with the name of the property, the **ascending** argument determines if the objects are sorted in ascending or descending order, and the **selector** argument is a method that determines the sorting criteria.

The **FetchRequest** class includes the **sortDescriptors** property to define the order of a request. All we need to do is to create at least one **NSSortDescriptor** object and assign it to this property. The following example sorts the **Books** objects by title in ascending order.

```
func loadRequest() async {
   await context.perform {
      let request: NSFetchRequest<Books> = Books.fetchRequest()
      let sort = NSSortDescriptor(key: "title", ascending: true)
      request.sortDescriptors = [sort]
      do {
         AppData.listOfBooks = try self.context.fetch(request)
      } catch {
         print("Error: \(error)")
      }
   }
}
```

Listing 15-38: *Sorting the books by title*

The **sortDescriptors** property takes an array of **NSSortDescriptor** objects, so we can specify different conditions to sort the list. The order is established according to the location of the objects in the array. For example, we can sort the books by author first and then by year.

```
func loadRequest() async {
   await context.perform {
      let request: NSFetchRequest<Books> = Books.fetchRequest()
      let sort1 = NSSortDescriptor(key: "author.name", ascending: true)
      let sort2 = NSSortDescriptor(key: "year", ascending: true)
      request.sortDescriptors = [sort1, sort2]
```

```
      do {
         AppData.listOfBooks = try self.context.fetch(request)
      } catch {
         print("Error: \(error)")
      }
   }
}
```

Listing 15-39: *Sorting books by author and year*

By default, **NSSortDescriptor** objects use the **compare()** method to sort the values, but we can implement others. These methods must be assigned to the **selector** argument of the **NSSortDescriptor** initializer. The most frequently used is **caseInsensitiveCompare()** because it compares values without differentiating between lowercase and uppercase letters. The following example implements this method to sort the books by title.

```
func loadRequest() async {
   await context.perform {
      let request: NSFetchRequest<Books> = Books.fetchRequest()
      let sort = NSSortDescriptor(key: "title", ascending: true,
selector: #selector(NSString.caseInsensitiveCompare(_:)))
      request.sortDescriptors = [sort]
      do {
         AppData.listOfBooks = try self.context.fetch(request)
      } catch {
         print("Error: \(error)")
      }
   }
}
```

Listing 15-40: *Sorting by title without differentiating between lowercase and uppercase letters*

Do It Yourself: Replace the **loadRequest()** method in the **BooksView-Controller** class with any of the methods introduced above to see how sort descriptors work. Change the value of the **ascending** argument to see how the order changes in each case.

Basic Modifying Objects

Modifying objects in the Persistent Store is easy. We just need to get the object from the Persistent Store, assign the new values to the object's properties, and save the context. In our application, this means letting the user select a book and provide a form to allow him to modify the title and year. For this purpose, we can use the same scene designed to insert new books. All we need is an additional Show segue, as shown next.

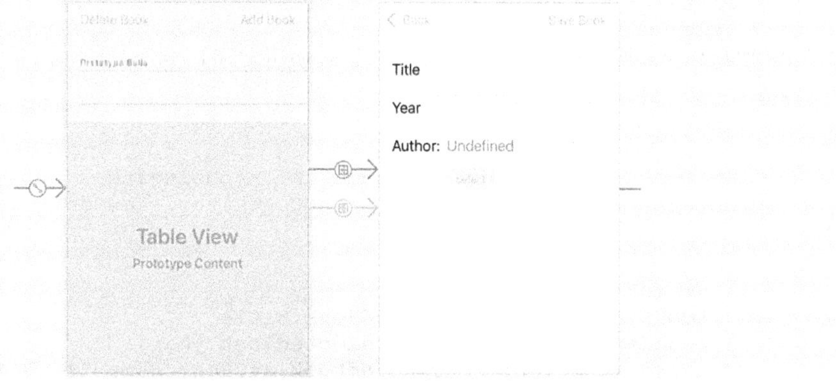

Figure 15-22: *Interface to modify books*

The interface in Figure 15-22 includes a Show segue from the Table View Controller to the second scene identified with the name "showEditBook". When the user selects a cell, we must perform this segue and send the **Books** object representing the book selected by the user from the **BooksViewController** view controller to the **EditBookViewController** view controller to allow the user to edit its values. The following are the methods we need in the **BooksViewController** class for this purpose.

```
override func tableView(_ tableView: UITableView, didSelectRowAt
indexPath: IndexPath) {
   performSegue(withIdentifier: "showEditBook", sender: self)
}
override func prepare(for segue: UIStoryboardSegue, sender: Any?) {
   if segue.identifier == "showEditBook" {
      if let path = tableView.indexPathForSelectedRow {
         if let itemID = AppData.dataSourceBooks.itemIdentifier(for:
path) {
            if let item = AppData.listOfBooks.first(where: { $0.objectID
== itemID }) {
               let controller = segue.destination as!
EditBookViewController
               controller.selectedBook = item
            }
         }
      }
   }
}
```

Listing 15-41: *Sending the book selected by the user*

The protocol method performs the segue when a cell is selected by the user, and the **prepare()** method gets the index path of the selected row, uses this value to get the **Books** object from the model, and assigns it to a property in the **EditBookViewController** class called **selectedBook**.

The **EditBookViewController** class must receive this object and show its values to the user. But we must also contemplate that the user might be trying to insert a new book instead. The following are all the changes we need to introduce to this class to respond to both situations.

```
import UIKit
import CoreData

class EditBookViewController: UIViewController {
   @IBOutlet weak var bookTitle: UITextField!
   @IBOutlet weak var bookYear: UITextField!
   @IBOutlet weak var authorName: UILabel!
   var context: NSManagedObjectContext!
   var selectedAuthor: Authors!
   var selectedBook: Books!

   override func viewDidLoad() {
      super.viewDidLoad()
      let app = UIApplication.shared
      let appDelegate = app.delegate as! AppDelegate
      context = appDelegate.persistentContainer.viewContext

      bookTitle.becomeFirstResponder()

      if selectedBook != nil {
         bookTitle.text = selectedBook.title
         bookYear.text = String(selectedBook.year)
         authorName.text = selectedBook.author?.name ?? "Undefined"
```

```
            selectedAuthor = selectedBook.author
         }
      }
      @IBAction func saveBook(_ sender: UIBarButtonItem) {
         let title = bookTitle.text!.trimmingCharacters(in: .whitespaces)
         let year = Int16(bookYear.text!)
         if title != "" && year != nil {
            Task(priority: .high) {
               await storeBook(title: title, year: year!)
            }
         }
      }
      func storeBook(title: String, year: Int16) async {
         await context.perform {
            if self.selectedBook != nil {
               self.selectedBook.title = title
               self.selectedBook.year = year
               self.selectedBook.author = self.selectedAuthor
            } else {
               let newBook = Books(context: self.context)
               newBook.title = title
               newBook.year = year
               newBook.author = self.selectedAuthor
            }
            do {
               try self.context.save()
            } catch {
               print("Error: \(error)")
            }
         }
         await MainActor.run {
            if let book = self.selectedBook {
               var currentSnapshot = AppData.dataSourceBooks.snapshot()
               currentSnapshot.reloadItems([book.objectID])
               AppData.dataSourceBooks.apply(currentSnapshot)
            }
            self.closeScene()
         }
      }
      func closeScene() {
         navigationController?.popViewController(animated: true)
      }
      @IBAction func backAuthor(_ segue: UIStoryboardSegue) {
         if segue.identifier == "backFromList" {
            let controller = segue.source as! AuthorsViewController
            selectedAuthor = controller.selectedAuthor
            authorName.text = selectedAuthor.name
         } else if segue.identifier == "backFromNew" {
            let controller = segue.source as! EditAuthorViewController
            selectedAuthor = controller.selectedAuthor
            authorName.text = selectedAuthor.name
         }
      }
   }
```

Listing 15-42: *Editing a book*

The scene for the view controller in Listing 15-42 opens when the user taps the Add Book button or when a cell is selected. What allows us to distinguish one situation from the other is the value of the **selectedBook** property. If this property is **nil**, it means that the user wants to insert a new book, but when the property contains a **Books** object, it means that the user selected a book and wants to edit its values. We first check the value of this property in the **viewDidLoad()** method. If it is different from **nil**, we show the book's values on the screen and assign the book's author to the **selectedAuthor** property, otherwise the fields are left empty for the user to insert a new book.

When the user taps the Save Book button to save the book, we check the value of the **selectedBook** property again. If it is different from **nil**, we modify the values of the **Books** object in the **selectedBook** property with those inserted by the user, otherwise, we create a new **Books** object. This way, the scene fulfills two purposes: it allows the user to edit the values of an existent book or add a new one.

Notice that the snapshot considers the items that are added or removed from the model, but it does not update their values. Therefore, after the user modifies the values of a book, we must call the **reloadItems()** method on the current snapshot to update the item. (We call this method in the Main Actor to avoid thread conflicts, as explained before.)

Do It Yourself: Create a Show segue from the Table View Controller to the second scene and identify it with the name "showEditBook" (Figure 15-22). Add the methods in Listing 15-41 to the **BooksViewController** class. Update the **EditBookViewController** class with the code in Listing 15-42. Run the application and select a book. You should see the values of the book on the screen. Modify the book's title and press the Save Book button. The changes should appear on the Table View.

Basic Deleting Objects

The interface introduced in Figure 15-18 includes a bar button called Delete Book to activate the table's edition mode. To delete an **NSManagedObject** object, the **NSManagedObjectContext** class offers the **delete()** method. The method takes a reference to the **NSManagedObject** object we want to delete and removes it from the context. As always, the change is only performed in the context, so we must save it, or the object will not be deleted from the Persistent Store.

As seen in Chapter 10, the edition mode is activated by the **setEditing()** method of the **UITableView** object (see Listings 10-23), but the values are processed by delegate methods defined in the **UITableViewDataSource** protocol, so we must create our own subclass of the **UITableViewDiffableDataSource** class (see Listing 10-24).

Because we are going to modify the request and the snapshot from different objects (the view controller and the diffable data source) we must rethink our programming pattern. In our example, this means moving the **loadRequest()** and **prepareSnapshot()** methods from the view controller to the model, as shown next.

```
import UIKit
import CoreData

enum Sections {
   case main
}
class ApplicationData {
   var dataSourceBooks: MyDataSource!
   var dataSourceAuthors: UITableViewDiffableDataSource<Sections,
NSManagedObjectID>!

   var listOfBooks: [Books] = []
   var listOfAuthors: [Authors] = []

   func loadRequestBooks(context: NSManagedObjectContext) async {
      await context.perform {
         let request: NSFetchRequest<Books> = Books.fetchRequest()
         let sort = NSSortDescriptor(key: "title", ascending: true,
selector: #selector(NSString.caseInsensitiveCompare(_:)))
         request.sortDescriptors = [sort]
```

```
            do {
               self.listOfBooks = try context.fetch(request)
            } catch {
               print("Error")
            }
         }
   }
   func prepareSnapshotBooks() {
      var snapshot = NSDiffableDataSourceSnapshot<Sections,
NSManagedObjectID>()
      snapshot.appendSections([.main])
      snapshot.appendItems(self.listOfBooks.map({ $0.objectID }))
      dataSourceBooks.apply(snapshot)
   }
}
var AppData = ApplicationData()
```

Listing 15-43: *Defining the request and the snapshot from the model*

To make sure that there is no confusion on what the purpose of the methods is, we renamed them to **loadRequestBooks()** and **prepareSnapshotBooks()**. The code is the same, but now the **loadRequestBooks()** method includes a parameter to receive a reference to the Core Data context to be able to perform the request.

The property to store the diffable data source for the books was defined of type **MyDataSource**. This is the subclass of the **UITableViewDiffableDataSource** class we need to implement the protocol methods.

```
import UIKit
import CoreData

class MyDataSource: UITableViewDiffableDataSource<Sections,
NSManagedObjectID> {
   override func tableView(_ tableView: UITableView, canEditRowAt
indexPath: IndexPath) -> Bool {
      return true
   }
   override func tableView(_ tableView: UITableView, commit editingStyle:
UITableViewCell.EditingStyle, forRowAt indexPath: IndexPath) {
      if editingStyle == .delete {
         if let itemID = AppData.dataSourceBooks.itemIdentifier(for:
indexPath) {
            let app = UIApplication.shared
            let appDelegate = app.delegate as! AppDelegate
            let context = appDelegate.persistentContainer.viewContext

            if let item = AppData.listOfBooks.first(where: { $0.objectID
== itemID }) {
               Task(priority: .high) {
                  await deleteBook(context: context, item: item)
               }
            }
         }
      }
   }
   func deleteBook(context: NSManagedObjectContext, item: Books) async {
      await context.perform {
         context.delete(item)
         do {
            try context.save()
         } catch {
            print("Error: \(error)")
         }
      }
```

```
        await AppData.loadRequestBooks(context: context)

        await MainActor.run {
           AppData.prepareSnapshotBooks()
        }
     }
}
```

Listing 15-44: *Implementing the protocol methods to delete a book*

The subclass in Listing 15-44 implements the two delegate methods we need; one to tell the Table View that the user is allowed to edit the rows, and the other to process the removal of the object (see Chapter 10). When the user taps on the Delete button on a row, the second method is called, we get a reference to the **Books** object from the model and call an asynchronous method to delete it. After the object is deleted, we proceed to save the context and update the request and the snapshot by calling the methods in the model.

The **BooksViewController** view controller must include an Action for the button to turn the table's edition mode on and off and use our **MyDataSource** class to create the diffable data source. The rest of the code remains the same.

```
import UIKit
import CoreData

class BooksViewController: UITableViewController {
   var context: NSManagedObjectContext!

   override func viewDidLoad() {
      super.viewDidLoad()
      let app = UIApplication.shared
      let appDelegate = app.delegate as! AppDelegate
      context = appDelegate.persistentContainer.viewContext

      tableView.register(UITableViewCell.self, forCellReuseIdentifier:
"booksCell")
      prepareDataSource()
   }
   override func viewWillAppear(_ animated: Bool) {
      super.viewWillAppear(animated)
      Task(priority: .high) {
         await AppData.loadRequestBooks(context: context)

         await MainActor.run {
            AppData.prepareSnapshotBooks()
         }
      }
   }
   func prepareDataSource() {
      AppData.dataSourceBooks = MyDataSource(tableView: tableView)
{ tableView, indexPath, itemID in
         let cell = tableView.dequeueReusableCell(withIdentifier:
"booksCell", for: indexPath)
         if let item = AppData.listOfBooks.first(where: { $0.objectID ==
itemID }) {
            var config = cell.defaultContentConfiguration()
            config.text = item.title
            config.secondaryText = item.author?.name ?? "Undefined"
            config.secondaryTextProperties.color = .systemGray

            if let data = item.thumbnail, let image = UIImage(data:data){
               config.image = image
            } else {
```

```
                config.image = UIImage(named: "nothumbnail")
            }
            config.imageProperties.maximumSize = CGSize(width: 60,
height: 60)
            cell.contentConfiguration = config
        }
        return cell
    }
  }
  override func tableView(_ tableView: UITableView, didSelectRowAt
indexPath: IndexPath) {
     performSegue(withIdentifier: "showEditBook", sender: self)
  }
  override func prepare(for segue: UIStoryboardSegue, sender: Any?) {
     if segue.identifier == "showEditBook" {
        if let path = tableView.indexPathForSelectedRow {
           if let itemID = AppData.dataSourceBooks.itemIdentifier(for:
path) {
              if let item = AppData.listOfBooks.first(where:
{ $0.objectID == itemID }) {
                 let controller = segue.destination as!
EditBookViewController
                 controller.selectedBook = item
              }
           }
        }
     }
  }
  @IBAction func editBooks(_ sender: UIBarButtonItem) {
     let editing = !tableView.isEditing
     tableView.setEditing(editing, animated: true)
  }
}
```

Listing 15-45: *Deleting a book*

Do It Yourself: Update the **ApplicationData** structure with the code in Listing 15-43. Create a new file called MyDataSource.swift for the class in Listing 15-44. Update the **BooksViewController** class with the code in Listing 15-45 and connect the Delete Book button on the interface with the **editBooks()** Action. Run the application, press the Delete Book button, and press the Delete button. The book should be removed from the list.

IMPORTANT: If you need to delete several objects in the same action, you should call the **save()** method at the end to improve performance. This also applies to other operations with the context. The context should be saved only after all the operations are performed.

Basic Fetched Results Controller

Storing the results of a request in an array is not recommended in most situations. Tables and Collection Views can handle thousands of items and putting all those items in an array might consume too many resources. The solution is to get only the objects the interface needs at a particular moment, but this is error prone and demands our code to keep track of the elements already loaded and request only those that we do not have. Programming an application to do this work efficiently is difficult. For this reason, Core Data offers the **NSFetchedResults-Controller** class. This class provides highly optimized code that intermediates between the app and the Persistent Store; taking care of fetching the objects the interface needs and updating the list of objects available when some are modified, added, or removed. To create the controller, the class provides the following initializer.

NSFetchedResultsController(fetchRequest: NSFetchRequest, **managedObjectContext:** NSManagedObjectContext, **sectionNameKeyPath:** String?, **cacheName:** String?**)**—This initializer creates an **NSFetchedResultsController** object that fetches **NSManagedObject** objects from the Persistent Store. The **fetchRequest** argument is an **NSFetchRequest** object with the request we want the controller to use to fetch the objects, the **managedObjectContext** argument is a reference to the Core Data context, the **sectionNameKeyPath** argument identifies the name of the property used to create the table's sections, and the **cacheName** argument defines the name of the file used to cache the objects returned by the request.

When working with an **NSFetchedResultsController** object, we must ask this object for any information we need about the request (the objects, their location, etc.). The class offers the following properties and methods to access these values.

fetchRequest—This property returns a reference to the **NSFetchRequest** object that defines the request used by the controller.

fetchedObjects—This property returns an array with the **NSManagedObjects** currently fetched by the controller.

sections—This property returns an array of objects with information about the sections. The objects implement the properties defined in the **NSFetchedResultsSectionInfo** protocol to provide this information.

sectionIndexTitles—This property returns an array of strings with the titles for the index of every section.

performFetch()—This method executes the controller's fetch request. The controller does not return any value until this method is called.

object(at: IndexPath**)**—This method returns the **NSManagedObject** object at the index path specified by the **at** argument.

indexPath(forObject: ResultType**)**—This method returns the index path of the **NSManagedObject** object specified by the **forObject** argument. The value returned is an **IndexPath** structure.

After the **NSFetchedResultsController** object is initialized, we must call the **performFetch()** method to perform the request. The results produced by the request are stored in a temporary container and automatically updated by the **NSFetchedResultsController** object every time a modification is introduced (an object is modified, deleted, moved, or new objects are added). Because of the close relationship between this controller and the views, it is important to make sure that all the changes are immediately reflected on the interface. Core Data simplifies this task with the addition of the **NSFetchedResultsControllerDelegate** protocol. This protocol defines the following method to update the snapshot and in consequence the values on the screen.

controller(NSFetchedResultsController, **didChangeContentWith:** NSDiffableDataSourceSnapshot**)**—This method is called on the delegate when the content managed by the **NSFetchedResultsController** object has changed. The method receives a snapshot that we must apply to the diffable data source to update the interface.

There are a few changes we must introduce to our previous example to implement a **NSFetchedResultsController** object. The first thing we need is a property in the model to store this object.

```
import UIKit
import CoreData

enum Sections {
   case main
}
struct ApplicationData {
   var dataSourceBooks: MyDataSource!
   var dataSourceAuthors: UITableViewDiffableDataSource<Sections,
NSManagedObjectID>!

   var fetchedController: NSFetchedResultsController<Books>!
   var listOfAuthors: [Authors] = []
}
var AppData = ApplicationData()
```

Listing 15-46: *Updating the model to work with a Fetched Results Controller*

The **fetchedController** property replaces the previous **listOfBooks** property (the **Books** objects are not going to be stored in an array but instead provided by the **NSFetchedResultsController** object). Notice that we have also removed the methods to create the request and the snapshot because now everything is managed by the Fetched Results Controller.

The Fetched Results Controller is created from **NSManagedObject** objects (**Books** and **Authors**), but the diffable data source and the snapshots are created with their **NSManagedObjectID** values. To get the **NSManagedObject** object from these identifiers, the **NSManagedObjectContext** class includes the following methods.

existingObject(with: NSManagedObjectID**)**—This method returns the object identified with the identifier specified by the **with** argument or **nil** if no object is found in the context.

object(with: NSManagedObjectID**)**—This method returns the object identified with the identifier specified by the **with** argument. If the object is not found in the context, it is fetched from the Persistent Store.

The following are the changes required in the **BooksViewController** class to get the **Books** objects from a Fetched Results Controller.

```
import UIKit
import CoreData

class BooksViewController: UITableViewController,
NSFetchedResultsControllerDelegate {
   var context: NSManagedObjectContext!

   override func viewDidLoad() {
      super.viewDidLoad()
      let app = UIApplication.shared
      let appDelegate = app.delegate as! AppDelegate
      context = appDelegate.persistentContainer.viewContext

      tableView.register(UITableViewCell.self, forCellReuseIdentifier:
"booksCell")
      prepareDataSource()
      prepareFetchedController()
   }
   override func viewWillAppear(_ animated: Bool) {
      super.viewWillAppear(animated)
      do {
         try AppData.fetchedController.performFetch()
```

```
      } catch {
         print("Error")
      }
   }
   func prepareDataSource() {
      AppData.dataSourceBooks = MyDataSource(tableView: tableView)
{ tableView, indexPath, itemID in
         let cell = tableView.dequeueReusableCell(withIdentifier:
"booksCell", for: indexPath)
         if let item = try? self.context.existingObject(with: itemID) as?
Books {
            var config = cell.defaultContentConfiguration()
            config.text = item.title
            config.secondaryText = item.author?.name ?? "Undefined"
            config.secondaryTextProperties.color = .systemGray

            if let data = item.thumbnail, let image = UIImage(data:data){
               config.image = image
            } else {
               config.image = UIImage(named: "nothumbnail")
            }
            config.imageProperties.maximumSize = CGSize(width: 60,
height: 60)
            cell.contentConfiguration = config
         }
         return cell
      }
   }
   func prepareFetchedController() {
      let request: NSFetchRequest<Books> = Books.fetchRequest()
      let sort = NSSortDescriptor(key: "title", ascending: true,
selector: #selector(NSString.caseInsensitiveCompare(_:)))
      request.sortDescriptors = [sort]
      AppData.fetchedController =
NSFetchedResultsController(fetchRequest: request, managedObjectContext:
context, sectionNameKeyPath: nil, cacheName: nil)
      AppData.fetchedController.delegate = self
   }
   func controller(_ controller:
NSFetchedResultsController<NSFetchRequestResult>, didChangeContentWith
snapshot: NSDiffableDataSourceSnapshotReference) {
      let newsnapshot = snapshot as
NSDiffableDataSourceSnapshot<Sections, NSManagedObjectID>
      AppData.dataSourceBooks.apply(newsnapshot, animatingDifferences:
true)
   }
   override func tableView(_ tableView: UITableView, didSelectRowAt
indexPath: IndexPath) {
      performSegue(withIdentifier: "showEditBook", sender: self)
   }
   override func prepare(for segue: UIStoryboardSegue, sender: Any?) {
      if segue.identifier == "showEditBook" {
         if let path = tableView.indexPathForSelectedRow {
            if let itemID = AppData.dataSourceBooks.itemIdentifier(for:
path) {
               if let item = try? context.existingObject(with: itemID)
as? Books {
                  let controller = segue.destination as!
EditBookViewController
                  controller.selectedBook = item
               }
            }
         }
      }
   }
```

```
    @IBAction func editBooks(_ sender: UIBarButtonItem) {
        let editing = !tableView.isEditing
        tableView.setEditing(editing, animated: true)
    }
}
```

Listing 15-47: Working with a Fetched Results Controller

To define the Fetched Results Controller, we created a method called **prepareFetchedController()** and execute it as soon as the view is loaded. The **NSFetchedResultsController** object requires a request with a sort descriptor to know the order in which the **Books** objects are going to be offered to the table. In this example, we create the **NSFetchRequest** object for the Books entity and assign to it a sort descriptor that sorts the books by title.

Besides the request, the **NSFetchedResultsController** initializer requires three more values: a reference to the context, the name of the property that is going to be used to create the sections for the table, and the name of the file used to cache the information for better performance. The last two parameters are not going to be used in this example, so we declared them as **nil**.

A Fetched Results Controller calls a protocol method to update the snapshot every time a change in the context is detected. The view controller in Listing 15-47 conforms to the **NSFetchedResultsControllerDelegate** protocol to be able to implement this method. In the method, all we need to do is to cast the generic snapshot to an object with the right data types and apply it to the diffable data source. This process updates the Table View and shows the new values on the screen.

Once we have the **NSFetchedResultsController** object, we must call the **performFetch()** method to fetch the objects from the Persistent Store. Because this process is required every time there are changes in the context, we call it in the **viewWillAppear()** method to make sure that every time the user opens this scene, the Fetched Results Controller is updated.

The diffable data source is the same as before, except this time instead of getting the object from an array in the model we call the **existingObject(with:)** method with the identifier received by the closure to get the object from the context. This returns the **Books** object associated to that identifier that we can use to configure the cell.

We do the same in the **prepare()** method. When the user selects a book to edit the values, we get the identifier as always, and then call the **existingObject(with:)** method again to get the **Books** object and send it to the **EditBookViewController** object.

The **existingObject(with:)** method must also be implemented in the **MyDataSource** class to get the object the user wants to delete, as shown next.

```
import UIKit
import CoreData

class MyDataSource: UITableViewDiffableDataSource<Sections,
NSManagedObjectID> {
    override func tableView(_ tableView: UITableView, canEditRowAt
indexPath: IndexPath) -> Bool {
        return true
    }
    override func tableView(_ tableView: UITableView, commit editingStyle:
UITableViewCell.EditingStyle, forRowAt indexPath: IndexPath) {
        if editingStyle == .delete {
            if let itemID = AppData.dataSourceBooks.itemIdentifier(for:
indexPath) {
                let app = UIApplication.shared
                let appDelegate = app.delegate as! AppDelegate
                let context = appDelegate.persistentContainer.viewContext
```

```
            if let item = try? context.existingObject(with: itemID) as?
Books {
               Task(priority: .high) {
                  await deleteBook(context: context, item: item)
               }
            }
         }
      }
   }
   func deleteBook(context: NSManagedObjectContext, item: Books) async {
      await context.perform {
         context.delete(item)
         do {
            try context.save()
         } catch {
            print("Error: \(error)")
         }
      }
   }
}
```

Listing 15-48: *Working with objects identifiers*

The process is the same as before, but now we call the **existingObject(with:)** method to get the **Books** object to be deleted. Notice that we also define the data type for the **UITableViewDiffableDataSource** object as **NSManagedObjectID**.

Do It Yourself: Update the **ApplicationData** structure with the code in Listing 15-46, the **BooksViewController** class with the code in Listing 15-47, and the **MyDataSource** class with the code in Listing 15-48. Run the application. Everything works as before but now the books are provided by the Fetched Results Controller.

Basic Search

The process to allow users to search for values in a Table View associated with an **NSFetchedResultsController** object does not differ from any other we have seen before. We must define a Search Controller, conform to the **UISearchResultsUpdating** and **UISearchBarDelegate** protocols, and implement their methods (see Chapter 10, Listing 10-35). In the **updateSearchResults(for:)** method, we must modify the predicate of the request assigned to the **NSFetchedResultsController** object to search for the value inserted by the user, and we also need to implement the **searchBarCancelButtonClicked()** method to assign an empty predicate to clear the controller and list all the books available again when the Cancel button is pressed. The following is the **BooksViewController** class we need to allow the user to search for books by title.

```
import UIKit
import CoreData

class BooksViewController: UITableViewController,
NSFetchedResultsControllerDelegate, UISearchResultsUpdating,
UISearchBarDelegate {
   var context: NSManagedObjectContext!
   var searchController: UISearchController!

   override func viewDidLoad() {
      super.viewDidLoad()
      let app = UIApplication.shared
      let appDelegate = app.delegate as! AppDelegate
      context = appDelegate.persistentContainer.viewContext
```

```
      searchController = UISearchController(searchResultsController: nil)
      searchController.searchResultsUpdater = self
      searchController.obscuresBackgroundDuringPresentation = false
      searchController.searchBar.delegate = self
      navigationItem.searchController = searchController

      tableView.register(UITableViewCell.self, forCellReuseIdentifier:
"booksCell")
      prepareDataSource()
      prepareFetchedController()
   }
   override func viewWillAppear(_ animated: Bool) {
      super.viewWillAppear(animated)
      do {
         try AppData.fetchedController.performFetch()
      } catch {
         print("Error")
      }
   }
   func prepareDataSource() {
      AppData.dataSourceBooks = MyDataSource(tableView: tableView)
{ tableView, indexPath, itemID in
         let cell = tableView.dequeueReusableCell(withIdentifier:
"booksCell", for: indexPath)
         if let item = try? self.context.existingObject(with: itemID) as?
Books {
            var config = cell.defaultContentConfiguration()
            config.text = item.title
            config.secondaryText = item.author?.name ?? "Undefined"
            config.secondaryTextProperties.color = .systemGray

            if let data = item.thumbnail, let image = UIImage(data:data){
               config.image = image
            } else {
               config.image = UIImage(named: "nothumbnail")
            }
            config.imageProperties.maximumSize = CGSize(width: 60,
height: 60)
            cell.contentConfiguration = config
         }
         return cell
      }
   }
   func prepareFetchedController() {
      let request: NSFetchRequest<Books> = Books.fetchRequest()
      let sort = NSSortDescriptor(key: "title", ascending: true,
selector: #selector(NSString.caseInsensitiveCompare(_:)))
      request.sortDescriptors = [sort]
      AppData.fetchedController =
NSFetchedResultsController(fetchRequest: request, managedObjectContext:
context, sectionNameKeyPath: nil, cacheName: nil)
      AppData.fetchedController.delegate = self
   }
   func controller(_ controller:
NSFetchedResultsController<NSFetchRequestResult>, didChangeContentWith
snapshot: NSDiffableDataSourceSnapshotReference) {
      let newsnapshot = snapshot as
NSDiffableDataSourceSnapshot<Sections, NSManagedObjectID>
      AppData.dataSourceBooks.apply(newsnapshot, animatingDifferences:
true)
   }
   override func tableView(_ tableView: UITableView, didSelectRowAt
indexPath: IndexPath) {
      performSegue(withIdentifier: "showEditBook", sender: self)
   }
```

```
    override func prepare(for segue: UIStoryboardSegue, sender: Any?) {
       if segue.identifier == "showEditBook" {
          if let path = tableView.indexPathForSelectedRow {
             if let itemID = AppData.dataSourceBooks.itemIdentifier(for:
path) {
                if let item = try? context.existingObject(with: itemID)
as? Books {
                   let controller = segue.destination as!
EditBookViewController
                   controller.selectedBook = item
                }
             }
          }
       }
    }
    func updateSearchResults(for searchController: UISearchController) {
       if let text = searchController.searchBar.text {
          let search = text.trimmingCharacters(in: .whitespaces)
          if !search.isEmpty {
             let request = AppData.fetchedController.fetchRequest
             request.predicate = NSPredicate(format: "title CONTAINS[cd]
%@", search)
             try? AppData.fetchedController.performFetch()
          }
       }
    }
    func searchBarCancelButtonClicked(_ searchBar: UISearchBar) {
       let request = AppData.fetchedController.fetchRequest
       request.predicate = nil
       try? AppData.fetchedController.performFetch()
    }
    @IBAction func editBooks(_ sender: UIBarButtonItem) {
       let editing = !tableView.isEditing
       tableView.setEditing(editing, animated: true)
    }
}
```

Listing 15-49: *Searching for books by title*

To perform a search, we do not have to replace the request or create a new **NSFetchedResultsController** object, all we need to do is to assign a new predicate to the current request and call the **performFetch()** method to execute the request again. In Listing 15-49, we modify the predicate every time the text in the search bar changes and assign the original predicate back when the search is cancelled (in this case, there was no original predicate, so we declare it as **nil**).

Do It Yourself: Update the **BooksViewController** class with the code in Listing 15-49. Run the application. The rows and sections should appear or disappear according to the term inserted in the bar.

Basic Sections

Of course, an **NSFetchedResultsController** object can work with sections. The object can take a property of an **NSManagedObject** object and generate sections with its values. For example, we can create one section for every author. The **NSFetchedResultsController** object splits the information in sections, with every section containing the books of a particular author, and automatically assigns the name of the author to the section's title. All we need to do is to declare the property we want to use as the value of the **sectionNameKeyPath** argument in the object's initializer, as shown in the following example.

```
func prepareFetchedController() {
   let request: NSFetchRequest<Books> = Books.fetchRequest()
   let sort1 = NSSortDescriptor(key: "author.name", ascending: true,
selector: #selector(NSString.caseInsensitiveCompare(_:)))
   let sort2 = NSSortDescriptor(key: "title", ascending: true, selector:
#selector(NSString.caseInsensitiveCompare(_:)))
   request.sortDescriptors = [sort1, sort2]

   AppData.fetchedController = NSFetchedResultsController(fetchRequest:
request, managedObjectContext: context, sectionNameKeyPath:
"author.name", cacheName: nil)
   AppData.fetchedController.delegate = self
}
```

Listing 15-50: *Organizing the* Books *objects in sections*

The value of the **sectionNameKeyPath** argument determines the property we want to use to separate the objects in sections (**author.name** in this case), but we also need to sort the objects to coincide with this configuration. When working with sections, the first sort descriptor must sort the objects by the value of the same property we used to generate the sections. In the example of Listing 15-50, we first sort the sections by the value of the **name** property of the **author** relationship, and then add another **NSSortDescriptor** object to sort the objects inside each section by the value of the **title** property.

To display the sections' titles, the data source must implement the **tableView(UITableView, titleForHeaderInSection:)** method, as we did in previous examples (see Listing 10-38). In this method, we must get the section's title (the author's name) and return it. This information is provided by **NSFetchedResultsController** objects through properties defined in a protocol called **NSFetchedResultsSectionInfo**. The following are the properties available.

numberOfObjects—This property returns the number of objects in the section.

objects—This property returns an array with references to the objects in the section.

name—This property returns the name of the section.

indexTitle—This property returns the index's title for the section (by default, the index's title is the capitalized first letter of the name of the section).

Using these properties, we can get the name of each section from the Fetched Results Controller and return it. The following is the method we need to add to the **MyDataSource** class.

```
override func tableView(_ tableView: UITableView, titleForHeaderInSection
section: Int) -> String? {
   if let sections = AppData.fetchedController.sections {
      let sectionInfo = sections[section]
      return sectionInfo.name
   }
   return nil
}
```

Listing 15-51: *Implementing the protocol method to get the sections' titles*

When the data source needs the title for a section, it calls the delegate method implemented in Listing 15-51. In this method, we get the list of sections from the **sections** property, read the information of the current section, and use the **name** property to return its name. Now the table presents sections of books organized by author and ordered by title.

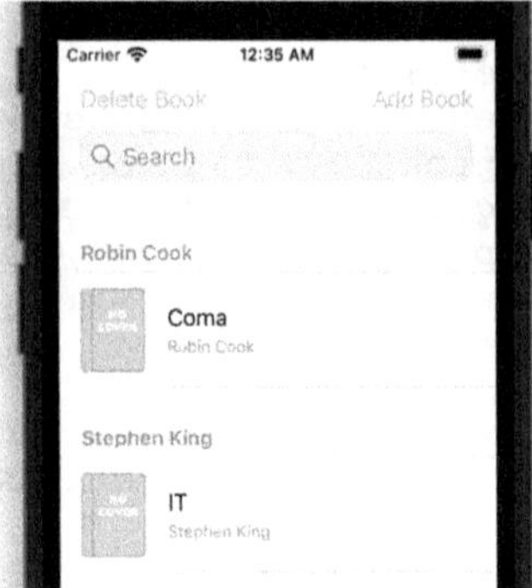

Figure 15-23: *Organizing the books in sections*

Do It Yourself: Update the **prepareFetchedController()** method in the **BooksViewController** class with the code in Listing 15-50. Add the method in Listing 15-51 to the **MyDataSource** class. Run the application. You should see the books ordered by author, as shown in Figure 15-23.

If we want to incorporate an index for the sections, as we did in the examples of Chapter 10, we must implement the **sectionIndexTitles()** method in the data source and return the array we get from the **sectionIndexTitles** property, as in the following example (the property returns an array with the initial letters of the sections' names capitalized).

```
override func sectionIndexTitles(for tableView: UITableView) -> [String]?
{
   return AppData.fetchedController.sectionIndexTitles
}
```

Listing 15-52: *Generating an index*

Do It Yourself: Add the method in Listing 15-52 to the **MyDataSource** class and run the application again. You should see the index on the right side of the table (see Chapter 10, Figure 10-32).

Medium To-Many Relationships

The previous examples assumed that there was only one author per book, but sometimes multiple authors collaborate to write a book. To assign multiple **Authors** objects to a book, we must turn the author relationship of the Books entity into a To-Many relationship, as shown below.

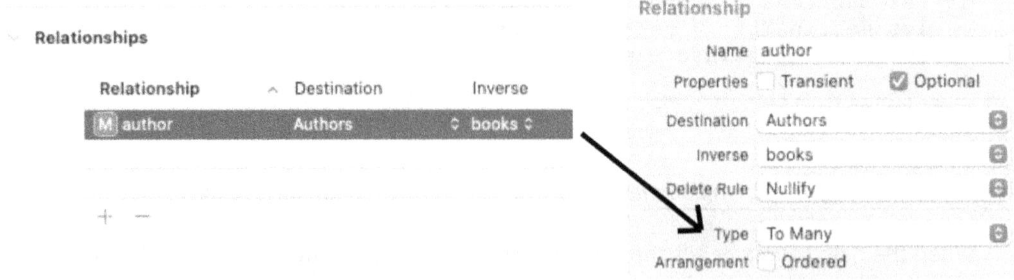

Figure 15-24: *Many-To-Many relationship*

Now, both relationships are of type To-Many, which means we can assign multiple books to an author and multiple authors to a book. This introduces a problem. Before, every time we wanted to assign an author to a book, we just had to create a new **Authors** object and assign it to the book's **author** property. Core Data was taking care of adding the book to the **books** property of the **Authors** object, along with the rest of the books associated to that author. But we can't do that when both relationships are To-Many. In that case, we must read and write the values ourselves.

The values of a To-Many relationship are stored in an **NSSet** object. This is a class defined by the Foundation framework to store sets of values. To read the values in an **NSSet**, we can cast it as a Swift set, but to turn a Swift set or array into an **NSSet** object, we must implement the following initializers.

NSSet(set: Set**)**—This initializer creates an **NSSet** object with the set provided by the attribute.

NSSet(array: Array**)**—This initializer creates an **NSSet** object with the array provided by the attribute.

In our application, the first place we need to read these values is in the **BooksViewController** class. Every time a cell is configured, we must cast the **NSSet** object returned by the book's **author** property to a Swift set and create a string with the names of all the authors assigned to the book to show them on the screen, as shown next.

```
import UIKit
import CoreData

class BooksViewController: UITableViewController,
NSFetchedResultsControllerDelegate {
   var context: NSManagedObjectContext!

   override func viewDidLoad() {
      super.viewDidLoad()
      let app = UIApplication.shared
      let appDelegate = app.delegate as! AppDelegate
      context = appDelegate.persistentContainer.viewContext

      tableView.register(UITableViewCell.self, forCellReuseIdentifier:
"booksCell")
      prepareDataSource()
      prepareFetchedController()
   }
   override func viewWillAppear(_ animated: Bool) {
      super.viewWillAppear(animated)
      do {
         try AppData.fetchedController.performFetch()
      } catch {
         print("Error")
      }
   }
   func prepareDataSource() {
      AppData.dataSourceBooks = MyDataSource(tableView: tableView)
{ tableView, indexPath, itemID in
         let cell = tableView.dequeueReusableCell(withIdentifier:
"booksCell", for: indexPath)
         if let item = try? self.context.existingObject(with: itemID) as?
Books {
            var config = cell.defaultContentConfiguration()
            config.text = item.title
            var authors: String!
```

```
            if let list = item.author as? Set<Authors> {
               let listNames = list.map({ $0.name ?? "Undefined" })
               if !listNames.isEmpty {
                  authors = listNames.joined(separator: ", ")
               }
            }
            config.secondaryText = authors ?? "Undefined"
            config.secondaryTextProperties.color = .systemGray
            if let data = item.thumbnail, let image = UIImage(data:data){
               config.image = image
            } else {
               config.image = UIImage(named: "nothumbnail")
            }
            config.imageProperties.maximumSize = CGSize(width: 60,
height: 60)
            cell.contentConfiguration = config
         }
         return cell
      }
   }
   func prepareFetchedController() {
      let request: NSFetchRequest<Books> = Books.fetchRequest()
      let sort = NSSortDescriptor(key: "title", ascending: true,
selector: #selector(NSString.caseInsensitiveCompare(_:)))
      request.sortDescriptors = [sort]
      AppData.fetchedController =
NSFetchedResultsController(fetchRequest: request, managedObjectContext:
context, sectionNameKeyPath: nil, cacheName: nil)
      AppData.fetchedController.delegate = self
   }
   func controller(_ controller:
NSFetchedResultsController<NSFetchRequestResult>, didChangeContentWith
snapshot: NSDiffableDataSourceSnapshotReference) {
      let newsnapshot = snapshot as
NSDiffableDataSourceSnapshot<Sections, NSManagedObjectID>
      AppData.dataSourceBooks.apply(newsnapshot, animatingDifferences:
true)
   }
   override func tableView(_ tableView: UITableView, didSelectRowAt
indexPath: IndexPath) {
      performSegue(withIdentifier: "showEditBook", sender: self)
   }
   override func prepare(for segue: UIStoryboardSegue, sender: Any?) {
      if segue.identifier == "showEditBook" {
         if let path = tableView.indexPathForSelectedRow {
            if let itemID = AppData.dataSourceBooks.itemIdentifier(for:
path) {
               if let item = try? context.existingObject(with: itemID)
as? Books {
                  let controller = segue.destination as!
EditBookViewController
                  controller.selectedBook = item
               }
            }
         }
      }
   }
   @IBAction func editBooks(_ sender: UIBarButtonItem) {
      let editing = !tableView.isEditing
      tableView.setEditing(editing, animated: true)
   }
}
```

Listing 15-53: *Reading the values of a To-Many relationship*

In this example, we cast the value of the **author** property to a **Set<Authors>** value. This creates a Swift set with **Authors** objects representing all the authors assigned to the book, so we map the values into an array of strings and call the **joined()** method to create a single string with the names separated by comma.

Now that the cells can show multiple authors per book, is time to allow the user to assign them. The following are the changes we must introduce to the **EditBookViewController** class to allow the user to select multiple authors per book.

```
import UIKit
import CoreData

class EditBookViewController: UIViewController {
   @IBOutlet weak var bookTitle: UITextField!
   @IBOutlet weak var bookYear: UITextField!
   @IBOutlet weak var authorName: UILabel!
   var context: NSManagedObjectContext!
   var selectedAuthors: [Authors] = []
   var selectedBook: Books!

   override func viewDidLoad() {
      super.viewDidLoad()
      let app = UIApplication.shared
      let appDelegate = app.delegate as! AppDelegate
      context = appDelegate.persistentContainer.viewContext

      bookTitle.becomeFirstResponder()

      if selectedBook != nil {
         bookTitle.text = selectedBook.title
         bookYear.text = String(selectedBook.year)

         var authors: String!
         if let list = selectedBook.author as? Set<Authors> {
            let listNames = list.map({ $0.name ?? "Undefined" })
            if !listNames.isEmpty {
               authors = listNames.joined(separator: ", ")
            }
            selectedAuthors = Array(list)
         }
         authorName.text = authors ?? "Undefined"
      }
   }
   @IBAction func saveBook(_ sender: UIBarButtonItem) {
      let title = bookTitle.text!.trimmingCharacters(in: .whitespaces)
      let year = Int16(bookYear.text!)
      if title != "" && year != nil {
         Task(priority: .high) {
            await storeBook(title: title, year: year!)
         }
      }
   }
   func storeBook(title: String, year: Int16) async {
      await context.perform {
         if self.selectedBook != nil {
            self.selectedBook.title = title
            self.selectedBook.year = year
            self.selectedBook.author = NSSet(array: self.selectedAuthors)
         } else {
            let newBook = Books(context: self.context)
            newBook.title = title
            newBook.year = year
            newBook.author = NSSet(array: self.selectedAuthors)
         }
```

```
            do {
               try self.context.save()
            } catch {
               print("Error: \(error)")
            }
         }
         await MainActor.run {
            if let book = self.selectedBook {
               var currentSnapshot = AppData.dataSourceBooks.snapshot()
               currentSnapshot.reloadItems([book.objectID])
               AppData.dataSourceBooks.apply(currentSnapshot)
            }
            self.closeScene()
         }
      }
   override func prepare(for segue: UIStoryboardSegue, sender: Any?) {
      if segue.identifier == "selectAuthor" {
         let controller = segue.destination as! AuthorsViewController
         controller.selectedAuthors = selectedAuthors
      }
   }
   func closeScene() {
      navigationController?.popViewController(animated: true)
   }
   @IBAction func backAuthor(_ segue: UIStoryboardSegue) {
      if segue.identifier == "backFromList" {
         let controller = segue.source as! AuthorsViewController
         selectedAuthors = controller.selectedAuthors
      } else if segue.identifier == "backFromNew" {
         let controller = segue.source as! EditAuthorViewController
         selectedAuthors.append(controller.selectedAuthor)
      }
      var authors: String!
      let listNames = selectedAuthors.map({ $0.name ?? "Undefined" })
      if !listNames.isEmpty {
         authors = listNames.joined(separator: ", ")
      }
      authorName.text = authors ?? "Undefined"
   }
}
```

Listing 15-54: *Assigning multiple authors per book*

The values are now stored in an array, so we always know which are the authors selected by the user. If the user is editing a book, we read the **author** property of the selected book and follow the same procedure as before to turn the value into a Swift set and show the names of the authors on the screen. Notice that at the end of the process, we assign the set of **Authors** objects to the **selectedAuthors** property to initialize the array (**selectedAuthors = Array(list)**). When the user decides to save the book, we perform the inverse procedure. The values in the **selectedAuthors** array are stored in an **NSSet** object and assigned to the **author** property.

To show the user the authors currently selected, we implement the **prepare()** method and send the value of the **selectedAuthors** property to the **AuthorsViewController** controller. The controller receives this value, and adds or removes authors from the array according to the selections performed by the user on the table, as shown below.

```
import UIKit
import CoreData

class AuthorsViewController: UITableViewController {
   var context: NSManagedObjectContext!
   var selectedAuthors: [Authors]!
```

```
   override func viewDidLoad() {
      super.viewDidLoad()
      let app = UIApplication.shared
      let appDelegate = app.delegate as! AppDelegate
      context = appDelegate.persistentContainer.viewContext

      tableView.register(UITableViewCell.self, forCellReuseIdentifier:
"authorsCell")
      prepareDataSource()
   }
   override func viewWillAppear(_ animated: Bool) {
      super.viewWillAppear(animated)
      Task(priority: .high) {
         await loadRequest()

         await MainActor.run {
            prepareSnapshot()
         }
      }
   }
   func prepareDataSource() {
      AppData.dataSourceAuthors = UITableViewDiffableDataSource<Sections,
NSManagedObjectID>(tableView: tableView) { tableView, indexPath, itemID
in
         let cell = tableView.dequeueReusableCell(withIdentifier:
"authorsCell", for: indexPath)
         if let item = AppData.listOfAuthors.first(where: { $0.objectID
== itemID }) {
            var config = cell.defaultContentConfiguration()
            config.text = item.name ?? "Undefined"
            cell.contentConfiguration = config

            let selected = self.selectedAuthors.contains(where: { $0.name
== item.name })
            cell.accessoryType = selected ? .checkmark : .none
         }
         return cell
      }
   }
   func loadRequest() async {
      await context.perform {
         let request: NSFetchRequest<Authors> = Authors.fetchRequest()
         do {
            AppData.listOfAuthors = try self.context.fetch(request)
         } catch {
            print("Error: \(error)")
         }
      }
   }
   func prepareSnapshot() {
      var snapshot = NSDiffableDataSourceSnapshot<Sections,
NSManagedObjectID>()
      snapshot.appendSections([.main])
      snapshot.appendItems(AppData.listOfAuthors.map({ $0.objectID }))
      AppData.dataSourceAuthors.apply(snapshot, animatingDifferences:
false)
   }
   override func tableView(_ tableView: UITableView, didSelectRowAt
indexPath: IndexPath) {
      if let itemID = AppData.dataSourceAuthors.itemIdentifier(for:
indexPath) {
         if let item = AppData.listOfAuthors.first(where: { $0.objectID
== itemID }) {
```

```
            if selectedAuthors.contains(where: { $0.name == item.name }){
               if let index = selectedAuthors.firstIndex(of: item) {
                  selectedAuthors.remove(at: index)
               }
            } else {
               selectedAuthors.append(item)
            }
         }
         performSegue(withIdentifier: "backFromList", sender: self)
      }
   }
}
```

Listing 15-55: Selecting and deselecting authors

This is the view controller that displays all available authors. To show which one has been previously selected, we add a checkmark to the cell when the author is already in the **selectedAuthors** array. Then, when a cell is selected by the user, we check whether the author was previously selected or not. If it was selected, we remove it from the **selectedAuthors** array, otherwise, we add it to the array. This makes sure that the array only contains the authors currently selected by the user.

After the user selects or deselects an author, we perform the Unwind Segue, get the array back from the **EditBookViewController** controller, and update the names on the screen (see the **backAuthor()** method in Listing 15-54). Now the user can select or deselect an author and add as many authors to a book as needed.

Do It Yourself: Open the Core Data model. Select the Books entity and change the Type of the author relationship to To-Many (Figure 15-24). Update the **BooksViewController** class with the code in Listing 15-53, the **EditBookViewController** class with the code in Listing 15-54, and the **AuthorsViewController** class with the code in Listing 15-55. Assign the "selectAuthor" identifier to the segue that connects the **EditBookViewController** scene to the **AuthorsViewController** scene. Run the application. Press the Add Book button. Press the Select button to add an author. You should be able to add as many authors as you want.

These types of relationships also change the way we search for values. For instance, we cannot search for a book by author as we did before because now a book may be associated to many authors. In this case, we must tell the predicate to search for the value inside the set of authors. For this purpose, predicates can include the following keywords.

ANY—This keyword returns true when the condition is true for some of the values in the set.

ALL—This keyword returns true when the condition is true for all the values in the set.

NONE—This keyword returns true when the condition is false for all the values in the set.

We have introduced predicate keywords earlier in this chapter. They are included in the format string to determine the way the predicate filters the data. For our example, we can add the ANY keyword in front of the comparison to get the books with an author relationship that contains at least one author with a specific name, as shown next.

```
override func viewWillAppear(_ animated: Bool) {
   super.viewWillAppear(animated)
   do {
      try AppData.fetchedController.performFetch()
```

```
   } catch {
      print("Error")
   }
   let request: NSFetchRequest<Books> = Books.fetchRequest()
   request.predicate = NSPredicate(format: "ANY author.name == %@",
"Stephen King")
   if let list = try? context.fetch(request) {
      for book in list {
         print(book.title!)
      }
   }
}
```

Listing 15-56: *Fetching books by author*

This example updates the **`viewWillAppear()`** method of the **`BooksViewController`** class to include a request that finds all the books associated with an author named "Stephen King". The predicate reads all the **`Authors`** objects in the relationship and returns the book when one of the names matches the string.

Do It Yourself: Update the **`viewWillAppear()`** method in the **`BooksViewController`** class with the code in Listing 15-56. Run the application and insert a few books with the author Stephen King. You should see the names of the books associated with that author printed on the console.

The example we have been working on so far turns the **`NSSet`** object returned by the author relationship into an array of **`Authors`** objects and then adds or removes authors from this array, but if we need to add or remove values directly from the **`NSSet`** object, we must turn it into an **`NSMutableSet`** object. This class creates a mutable set and therefore it allows us to add or remove values from the object. To create an **`NSMutableSet`** object from an **`NSSet`** object, the **`NSManagedObject`** class includes the following method.

mutableSetValue(forKey: String**)**—This method reads the **`NSSet`** object of the relationship indicated by the **forKey** attribute and returns an **`NSMutableSet`** with the values.

The **`NSMutableSet`** class includes the following methods to add and remove items in the set.

add(Any**)**—This method adds the object specified by the argument to the set.

remove(Any**)**—This method removes the object specified by the argument from the set.

The following example shows a possible implementation of these methods. We get the object representing the author with the name "Stephen King" and then remove that author from every book.

```
override func viewWillAppear(_ animated: Bool) {
   super.viewWillAppear(animated)
   do {
      try AppData.fetchedController.performFetch()
   } catch {
      print("Error")
   }
   let request: NSFetchRequest<Authors> = Authors.fetchRequest()
   request.predicate = NSPredicate(format: "name == %@", "Stephen King")
   if let list = try? context.fetch(request), list.count > 0 {
      let author = list[0]
```

```
        if let books = AppData.fetchedController.fetchedObjects {
           for book in books {
              let authorSet = book.mutableSetValue(forKey: "author")
              authorSet.remove(author)
              book.author = authorSet
           }
        }
        try? context.save()
     }
}
```

Listing 15-57: *Systematically removing authors from books*

This example updates the **viewWillAppear()** method of the **BooksViewController** class again to modify all the **Books** objects in the Persistent Store as soon as the app is launched. First, we perform a request to get the **Authors** object with the name "Stephen King". Then, we read the **fetchedObjects** property of the Fetched Results Controller to get the list of books fetched by the controller, and use a **for in** loop to modify them one by one. In the loop, we turn the **NSSet** object returned by the author relationship into an **NSMutableSet** object, remove from the set the **Authors** object fetched before with the **remove()** method, and assign the result back to the author relationship, effectively removing that author from every book.

Do It Yourself: Update the **viewWillAppear()** method in the **BooksViewController** class with the code in Listing 15-57. Run the application. The author Stephen King should be removed from every book.

Chapter 16
Notifications

Basic 16.1 Notification Center

Besides the techniques we have seen so far to transfer data between different parts of the application, such as sending values from one view controller to another or providing a common model from which every view controller can get the information it needs, we can also report changes across the application with notifications. Foundation includes the **NotificationCenter** class to create an object that serves as a Notification Center for the whole application. We can send notifications (messages) to this object and then listen to those notifications from anywhere in the code. The class includes the following property to get a reference to the app's Notification Center.

default—This type property returns the **NotificationCenter** object assigned to the application by default.

The Notification Center is like a bulletin board; we can post a notification from anywhere in the code and then read it from other objects. The **NotificationCenter** class defines the following methods to post and read notifications.

post(name: Name, **object:** Any?, **userInfo:** Dictionary**)**—This method posts a notification to the Notification Center. The **name** argument determines the name of the notification, the **object** argument is a reference to the object that sent the notification, and the **userInfo** argument is a dictionary with the information we want to pass to the observer.

notifications(named: Name, **object:** AnyObject?**)**—This method returns a **Notifications** object with an asynchronous sequence that contains all the notifications posted to the Notification Center. The **named** argument is the name of the notification we want to read, and the **object** argument is a reference to the object that sent the notification (set to **nil** if we want to read notifications posted by any object).

Notifications are created from the **Notification** class. The **post()** method automatically creates a **Notification** object to represent the notification we want to post, but we can also do it ourselves from the **Notification** class initializer.

Notification(name: Name, **object:** Any?, **userInfo:** Dictionary**)**—This initializer creates a **Notification** object with the information defined by the arguments. The **name** argument determines the name of the notification, the **object** argument is a reference to the object that is sending the notification, and the **userInfo** argument is a dictionary with the information we want to send with the notification.

The class includes the following properties to read the values of the notification.

name—This property returns the name of the notification.

object—This property returns a reference to the object that posted the notification.

userInfo—This property returns the dictionary attached to the notification.

The name of the notification is created from a structure included in the **Notification** class called **Name**. The structure provides the following initializer to define custom names.

Name(String)—This initializer creates a structure that represents the notification's name. The argument is a string with the name we want to assign to the notification.

Notifications are used for multiple purposes. We can post a notification after a long process is over to tell a view controller that it is time to update the interface, we can communicate view controllers with each other in a large interface, or keep a view controller up to date posting notifications from the model. The following example implements a model that posts a notification every time a new value is inserted by the user. For didactic purposes, we are going to use a simple interface that includes just enough scenes to show the number of values available and insert new ones.

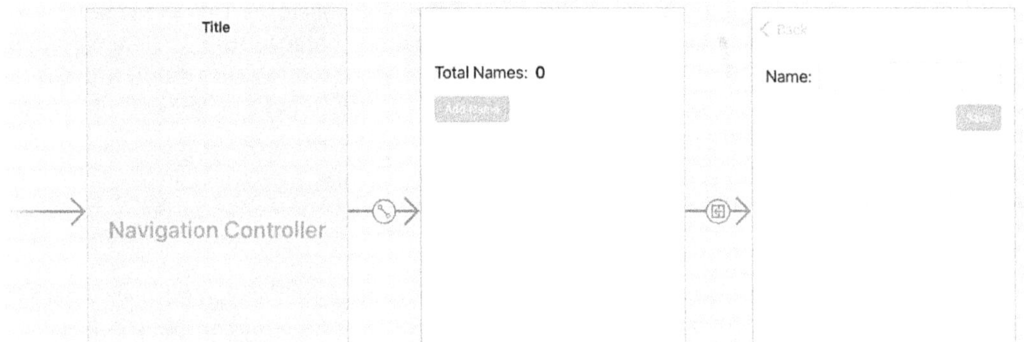

Figure 16-1: *Interface to test notifications*

The model must store the value inserted by the user in the Text Field and then post a notification, so the initial scene can update its interface.

```
import Foundation

struct ApplicationData {
   var names: [String] = []

   mutating func addNewName(newName: String) {
      names.append(newName)

      let center = NotificationCenter.default
      let name = Notification.Name("Update Data")
      center.post(name: name, object: nil, userInfo: nil)
   }
}
var AppData = ApplicationData()
```

Listing 16-1: *Sending notifications from the model*

The **`ApplicationData`** structure created for this example contains only one property called **`names`** with an array of strings, but we have also included a method called **`addNewName()`** to assign new values to it. After adding the new value to the **`names`** array, the method gets a reference to the **`NotificationCenter`** object assigned to our app and posts a notification we called "Update Data" to report the change.

The Notification Center creates an asynchronous sequence with all the notifications received (see Asynchronous Sequences in Chapter 14). The sequence is managed by a **`Notifications`** object that we can get from the **`notifications()`** method. To read this sequence, all we need to do is to create an asynchronous **`for in`** loop with this object.

```
import UIKit

class ViewController: UIViewController {
   @IBOutlet weak var counter: UILabel!

   override func viewDidLoad() {
      super.viewDidLoad()
      Task(priority: .background) {
         await readNotifications()
      }
   }
   func readNotifications() async {
      let center = NotificationCenter.default
      let name = Notification.Name("Update Data")

      for await _ in center.notifications(named: name, object: nil) {
         let current = AppData.names
         await MainActor.run {
            self.counter.text = String(current.count)
         }
      }
   }
}
```

***Listing 16-2:** Listening to notifications*

Because we must wait for the notifications to arrive, we mark the **for in** loop with the **await** keyword and put it inside an asynchronous method. Every time a notification is received, the loop performs a cycle, we get the total number of names stored in the **names** array and assign it to the label. Notice that we call the **run()** method on the Main Actor to make sure that the statement that interacts with the label runs in the main thread (see Main Actor in Chapter 14).

The values in the model are added from the second scene. The view controller for this scene has to take the value inserted by the user in the Text Field and call the **addNewName()** method to add it to the model.

```
import UIKit

class SecondViewController: UIViewController {
   @IBOutlet weak var name: UITextField!

   @IBAction func saveName(_ sender: UIButton) {
      if let value = name.text {
         AppData.addNewName(newName: value)
      }
      name.text = ""
   }
}
```

***Listing 16-3:** Adding new values to the model*

When a name is inserted into the Text Field and the Save button is pressed, the **saveName()** method adds the value to the model by calling the model's **addNewName()** method. The model receives the value, stores it in the **names** array, and posts an "Update Data" notification. The Notification Center stores the notification in the asynchronous sequence, the **for in** loop in the **ViewController** object detects that a new value is available in the sequence, performs a cycle, and the current number of values stored in the **names** array is shown on the screen.

Do It Yourself: Create a new project. Embed the initial scene in a Navigation Controller. Add a second scene to the Storyboard. Add two labels and a button to the initial scene, and a label, a Text Field, and a button to the second scene (Figure 16-1). Connect the button in the initial scene to the second scene with a Show segue. Create a Swift file called ApplicationData.swift for the model in Listing 16-1. Create a subclass of the **UIViewController** class called **SecondViewController** and assign it to the second scene. Complete the **ViewController** class with the code in Listing 16-2, and the **SecondViewController** class with the code in Listing 16-3. Connect the elements to their respective Outlets and Actions. Run the application, press the button to go to the second scene, and insert a few names. Move back to the initial scene. The interface should show the total number of names inserted in the form.

The **Notification** object that represents the notification includes the **userInfo** property, which allows us to send information from one object to another. The values that can be included in this dictionary are Property List values (**NSNumber**, **NSString**, **NSDate**, **NSArray**, **NSDictionary**, **NSData**, and the equivalents in Swift). There are multiple applications for this property. Considering our previous example, we could include the string inserted by the user and perform an additional task when the notifications are related to a specific name, as we do next.

```
import Foundation

struct ApplicationData {
   var names: [String] = []

   mutating func addNewName(newName: String) {
      names.append(newName)

      let center = NotificationCenter.default
      let name = Notification.Name("Update Data")
      let info = ["type": newName]
      center.post(name: name, object: nil, userInfo: info)
   }
}
var AppData = ApplicationData()
```

Listing 16-4: *Adding information to the notification*

The code in Listing 16-4 declares a dictionary with the key "type" and the value inserted by the user and assigns it to the **userInfo** argument of the **post()** method. Now, we can check this value from our **ViewController** class.

```
func readNotifications() async {
   let center = NotificationCenter.default
   let name = Notification.Name("Update Data")

   for await notification in center.notifications(named: name, object:
nil) {
      if let info = notification.userInfo {
         let type = info["type"] as? String
         if type == "John" {
            print("Our name was inserted")
         }
      }
      let current = AppData.names
      await MainActor.run {
```

```
            self.counter.text = String(current.count)
         }
      }
   }
```

Listing 16-5: Reading the value in the notification

The values from the dictionary are returned as values of type **Any**, so we must cast them to the right type. The example in Listing 16-5 reads the value of the "type" key, cast it as a **String**, and then compares it with the string "John". If the values match, we print a message on the console.

Do It Yourself: Update the **ApplicationData** structure with the code in Listing 16-4 and the **readNotifications()** method in the **ViewController** class with the code in Listing 16-5. Run the application. A message should be printed on the console every time you insert the name John.

If we do not want to post any more notifications, we can stop the process in the model (a simple **if else** statement will suffice), but if we want to stop processing the notifications from a receiver, we must cancel the task. For instance, if we have two or more view controllers that are processing the notifications but we want only one of them to stop doing it, we can store the task in a constant and called the **cancel()** method, as we did in Chapter 14 (see Listing 14-3).

The following example cancels the task in our **ViewController** class after 10 seconds, so the label is no longer updated with any of the values inserted by the user after the time expires.

```
override func viewDidLoad() {
   super.viewDidLoad()
   let myTask = Task(priority: .background) {
      await readNotifications()
   }
   Timer.scheduledTimer(withTimeInterval: 10.0, repeats: false){ timer in
      myTask.cancel()
   }
}
```

Listing 16-6: Cancelling the task

Basic System Notifications

Besides the notifications posted by our app, the system also posts notifications to the Notification Center all the time to report changes in the interface or in other objects running the application. There are hundreds of these notifications available, including many defined in some of the classes we already studied. For example, the **UITextView** class includes notifications like **textDidChangeNotification** to report that the content of the Text View changed. The following is a simple **ViewController** class we can use to test this notification (the example assumes that we have an interface with a Text View). Every time the user changes the text, the Text View posts the **textDidChangeNotification** notification and the view controller responds by printing a message on the console.

```
import UIKit

class ViewController: UIViewController {
   @IBOutlet weak var mainText: UITextView!

   override func viewDidLoad() {
      super.viewDidLoad()
      Task(priority: .background) {
         await receiveNotifications()
      }
```

```
   }
   func receiveNotifications() async {
      let center = NotificationCenter.default
      let name = UITextView.textDidChangeNotification

      for await notification in center.notifications(named: name, object:
nil) {
         if notification.name == name {
            print("The Text View was modified")
         }
      }
   }
}
```

Listing 16-7: Responding to the Text View notification

Do It Yourself: Create a new project. Add a Text View to the initial scene. Update the **ViewController** class with the code in Listing 16-7. Run the application and type some text inside the Text View. You should see a message on the console every time a character is added or removed.

Another useful notification is called **didChangeNotification**, defined in a structure called **UIContentSizeCategory**. This notification is posted every time the user changes the size of the Dynamic Font types from the Settings app.

We introduced Dynamic Font types in Chapter 5. They can be created from code with the **preferredFont()** method of the **UIFont** class (see Listing 5-14) or selected from the Attributes Inspector panel. There are different types available, such as Body, Headline, and more. When we select one of these types, the system sets the size of the font to match the size selected by the user from the Settings app (Accessibility/Display & Text Size/Large Text). The problem is that the views that were already loaded are not automatically updated. To make sure that all the important text in our interface is updated to the current size selected by the user, we must listen to the **didChangeNotification** notification and perform the update ourselves.

```
import UIKit

class ViewController: UIViewController {
   @IBOutlet weak var mainText: UITextView!

   override func viewDidLoad() {
      super.viewDidLoad()
      mainText.font = UIFont.preferredFont(forTextStyle: .body)

      Task(priority: .background) {
         await receiveNotifications()
      }
   }
   func receiveNotifications() async {
      let center = NotificationCenter.default
      let name = UIContentSizeCategory.didChangeNotification
      for await notification in center.notifications(named: name, object:
nil) {
         if notification.name == name {
            await MainActor.run {
               self.mainText.font =
UIFont.preferredFont(forTextStyle: .body)
            }
         }
      }
   }
}
```

Listing 16-8: Responding to font size changes in the Settings app

When the system detects a change in the size of the fonts performed from the Settings app, it posts the **didChangeNotification** notification to tell the applications that the content size is different. In the example of Listing 16-8, we initialize the Text View with a font of type **body** and then reassign this font type every time a notification is received. This forces the system to update the interface and show the text inside the Text View in the size selected by the user.

Do It Yourself: Update the **ViewController** class with the code in Listing 16-8. Run the application, click the Home button to go to the home screen, and change the size of the font from the Settings app (Accessibility/Display & Text Size/Large Text). Click the Home button again and open the app. You should see the text in the new size selected from Settings.

There is at least one more notification worth mentioning called **orientationDidChange-Notification**, defined in the **UIDevice** class. This notification is posted to the Notification Center by the system when the orientation of the device changes, but only if the accelerometer is enabled. As we mentioned in Chapter 5, the **UIDevice** class offers two methods to activate the accelerometer. Every time we want to know the orientation of the device, we must call the **beginGeneratingDeviceOrientationNotifications()** method first to make sure that we are getting accurate information, and when our app does not require updates anymore, we must call the **endGeneratingDeviceOrientationNotifications()** method to tell the system that it can turn off the accelerometer. In the following example, we apply these methods and print the current orientation on the console.

```
import UIKit

class ViewController: UIViewController {
   var device = UIDevice.current

   override func viewWillAppear(_ animated: Bool) {
      device.beginGeneratingDeviceOrientationNotifications()

      Task(priority: .background) {
         await receiveNotifications()
      }
   }
   override func viewDidDisappear(_ animated: Bool) {
      device.endGeneratingDeviceOrientationNotifications()
   }
   func receiveNotifications() async {
      let center = NotificationCenter.default
      let name = UIDevice.orientationDidChangeNotification
      for await notification in center.notifications(named: name, object:
nil) {
         if notification.name == name {
            let orientation = device.orientation
            switch orientation {
               case .portrait, .portraitUpsideDown:
                  print("Portrait")
               case .landscapeLeft, .landscapeRight:
                  print("Landscape")
               default:
                  print("Undefined")
            }
         }
      }
   }
}
```

***Listing 16-9:** Detecting the current orientation*

Because we want to detect every rotation while the view is visible, we enable the accelerometer in the **viewWillAppear()** method. Every time the system detects a rotation, it posts a notification. When a notification is received, we get the current orientation from the **orientation** property of the **UIDevice** object and print a message on the console.

Notice that we also called the **endGeneratingDeviceOrientationNotifications()** method in the **viewDidDisappear()** method. This is not necessary in our application because we only have one scene, but in a more complex interface it is good practice to tell the system that we no longer require updates on the state of the device. The system stops posting notifications and powers down the accelerometer if no other part of the application is using it.

Do It Yourself: To try this last example, remove the Text View from the scene and update the **ViewController** class with the code in Listing 16-9. Run the application and rotate the device. You should see the orientation printed on the console every time it changes.

Basic 16.2 User Notifications

A different type of notification is the User Notification. These are notifications that the system shows to the user when the app has an event to report, such as the completion of a task or real-life events that the user wants to be reminded of. There are three different types of User Notifications: alert, badge, and sound. A badge-type notification displays a badge with a number over the app's icon, a sound-type notification plays a sound, and an alert-type notification may be displayed as a banner, an Alert View, or a message on the lock screen, depending on the current state of the device and the configuration set by the user. They can be scheduled all at once or independently. For instance, we can schedule a notification that displays an alert and plays a sound, another that displays an alert and shows a badge, or another that just plays a sound.

IMPORTANT: User Notifications are divided into Local Notifications and Remote Notifications (also known as Push Notifications). Local Notifications are notifications generated by the application running on the device, while Remote Notifications are generated by remote servers and received by the system through the network. In this chapter, we are going to study Local Notifications. For more information on Remote Notifications, visit our website and follow the links for this chapter.

Basic User Notifications Framework

User Notifications are created and managed by classes of the User Notifications framework. The framework includes multiple classes to control every step of the process, of which the most important is the **UNUserNotificationCenter** class. This class creates a Notification Center to schedule and manage user notifications. This is like the Notification Center studied before but specific for User Notifications. The system creates a **UNUserNotificationCenter** object to serve as the Notification Center for the application that we can retrieve with the following type method.

current()—This type method returns a reference to the **UNUserNotificationCenter** object assigned to the app.

From the **UNUserNotificationCenter** object, we can manage the notifications. The first step is to request authorization from the user. The class includes the following methods for this purpose.

requestAuthorization(options: UNAuthorizationOptions**)**—This asynchronous method requests authorization from the user to show notifications and returns a Boolean value to report the result. The **options** argument is a set of properties that determine the type of notifications we want to show. The properties available are **badge**, **sound**, **alert**, **carPlay**, **criticalAlert**, **provisional**, and **announcement**.

notificationSettings()—This asynchronous method returns a **UNNotification-Settings** object with the current settings. The most useful property is **authorizationStatus**, which returns an enumeration value with the authorization status (the user may change the status of the authorization anytime from the Settings app). The possible values are **notDetermined**, **denied**, **authorized**, **provisional**, and **ephemeral**.

For the notifications to be sent, they must be added to the User Notification Center. The **UNUserNotificationCenter** class includes the following methods to add and remove them.

add(UNNotificationRequest**)**—This asynchronous method schedules a new notification in the User Notification Center. The argument is the request for the notification.

removePendingNotificationRequests(withIdentifiers: [String]**)**—This method removes the pending notifications with the identifiers specified by the argument.

The framework includes the **UNMutableNotificationContent** class to store the content of a notification. The following are the properties included in this class to set the notification's values.

title—This property sets or returns the notification's title.

subtitle—This property sets or returns the notification's subtitle.

body—This property sets or returns the notification's message.

badge—This property sets or returns a number to show over the app's icon.

sound—This property sets or returns the sound we want to play when the notification is delivered to the user. It is an object of type **UNNotificationSound**.

userInfo—This property sets or returns a dictionary with the information we want to send with the notification.

These properties define the information the notification is going to show to the user. Some of these properties store strings, except for the **badge** property which takes an **NSNumber** object, and the **sound** property which takes an object of the **UNNotificationSound** class. This class includes the following initializer and property to get the object.

UNNotificationSound(named: UNNotificationSoundName**)**—This initializer creates a **UNNotificationSound** object with the sound specified by the **named** argument.

default—This type property returns a **UNNotificationSound** object with the sound defined by the system.

The names of the sounds are defined by a structure of type **UNNotificationSoundName**. The structure includes the following initializer.

UNNotificationSoundName(rawValue: String**)**—This initializer creates a **UNNotificationSoundName** object with the name of the file that contains the sound we want to play with the notification.

The **UNMutableNotificationContent** class also allows us to set the level of interruption. By default, notifications are **active**, which means they are going to turn on the screen and play sound, but they can also be set to **`passive`** (they do not turn on the screen), **`timeSensitive`** (they are displayed immediately, but considering user settings), and **`critical`** (they bypass user settings). The class includes the following property to define the interruption level.

interruptionLevel—This property sets or returns a value that determines the importance and delivery timing of the notification. It is a **`UNNotification-InterruptionLevel`** enumeration with the values **`active`** (default), **`critical`**, **`passive`**, and **`timeSensitive`**.

User Notifications are posted to the User Notification Center and then presented by the system when a certain condition is met. These conditions are established by objects called *Triggers*. There are three types of triggers available for Local Notifications: Time Interval, (the notification is delivered after a certain period of time), Calendar (the notification is delivered on a specific date), and Location (the notification is delivered in a specific location). The framework defines three classes to create these triggers: **`UNTimeIntervalNotificationTrigger`**, **`UNCalendarNotificationTrigger`**, and **`UNLocationNotificationTrigger`**.

UNTimeIntervalNotificationTrigger(timeInterval: TimeInterval, **repeats:** Bool**)**—This initializer creates a Time Interval trigger that will deliver the notification after the period of time determined by the **timeInterval** argument (in seconds). The **repeats** argument determines if the notification will be delivered once or infinite times.

UNCalendarNotificationTrigger(dateMatching: DateComponents, **repeats:** Bool**)**—This initializer creates a Calendar trigger that delivers the notification at the date determined by the **dateMatching** argument. The **repeats** argument determines if the notification will be delivered once or infinite times.

UNLocationNotificationTrigger(region: CLCircularRegion, **repeats:** Bool**)**—This initializer creates a Location trigger that delivers the notification when the device is inside a region in the real world determined by the **region** argument. The **repeats** argument determines if the notification will be delivered once or infinite times.

To deliver a notification, we must create a request that contains the notification, an identifier, and a trigger. The framework defines the **`UNNotificationRequest`** class for this purpose.

UNNotificationRequest(identifier: String, **content:** UNNotificationContent, **trigger:** UNNotificationTrigger?**)**—This initializer creates a request to deliver the notification specified by the **content** argument and at the time or place specified by the **trigger** argument. The **identifier** argument is a string that we can use later to manage the request.

As we already mentioned, before sending user notifications we must ask the user for permission. Apple recommends doing it only when we really need it. For instance, if our application contains a scene with a switch for the user to activate notifications, we should ask permission in this scene and not right after the app is launched. The following example illustrates how to do it.

```
import UIKit
import UserNotifications

class ViewController: UIViewController {
   var center: UNUserNotificationCenter!
   @IBOutlet weak var sendButton: UIButton!

   override func viewDidLoad() {
      center = UNUserNotificationCenter.current()
      sendButton.isEnabled = false
```

```
      Task(priority: .high) {
         do {
            let authorized = try await
center.requestAuthorization(options: [.alert, .sound])
            await MainActor.run {
               self.sendButton.isEnabled = authorized
            }
         } catch {
            print("Error: \(error)")
         }
      }
   }
}
```

Listing 16-10: *Asking permission to send notifications*

This example assumes that we have a button on the interface to send notifications. We first get a reference to the **UNUserNotificationCenter** object assigned to the app, and then start a task to ask for authorization to show alert banners and sound. The **requestAuthorization()** method is asynchronous, so we wait for the user to respond and then enabled or disable the button according to the value returned by the method (**true** if the user authorizes the app or **false** otherwise).

When the **requestAuthorization()** method is called, it creates an Alert View with a message and two buttons to let the user decide, as shown below.

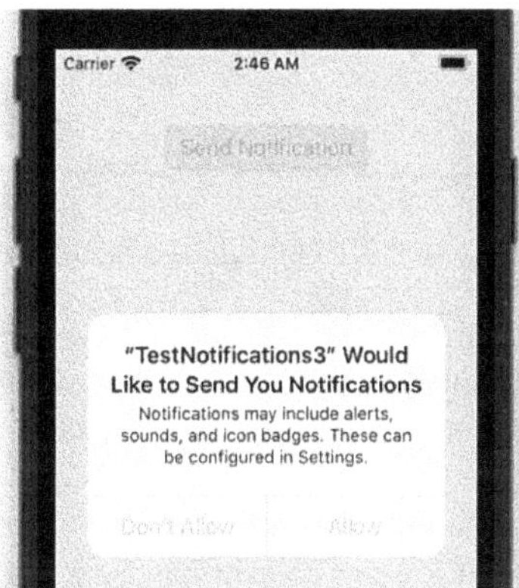

Figure 16-2: *Authorization to deliver notifications*

If the user doesn't allow the app to show notifications, it can be done later from the Settings app, so the app should always test whether authorization was granted or not and warn the user in case an action is required. For this purpose, the **UNUserNotificationCenter** class includes the **notificationSettings()** method. We should always consult this method before sending notifications to make sure that the app is still authorized to do it. For instance, we can add an Action for the button to call a method that checks the status and sends a notification every time it is pressed.

```
@IBAction func checkAuthorization(_ sender: UIButton) {
   Task(priority: .background) {
      let authorization = await center.notificationSettings()
      if authorization.authorizationStatus == .authorized {
         await self.sendNotification()
      }
   }
}
```

Listing 16-11: *Checking authorization status*

The **notificationSettings()** method is asynchronous, so we wait for the method to return a value and then check the authorization status. If the value of the **authorizationStatus** property is equal to **authorized**, it means that we are authorized to send notifications and can proceed. The **add()** method used to send a notification is also asynchronous, so after the authorization is confirmed, we call our own asynchronous method to send the notification.

```
func sendNotification() async {
   let content = UNMutableNotificationContent()
   content.title = "Reminder"
   content.body = "This is the body of the message"
   content.sound = UNNotificationSound(named:
UNNotificationSoundName(rawValue: "alarm.mp3"))

   let trigger = UNTimeIntervalNotificationTrigger(timeInterval: 30,
repeats: false)

   let id = "reminder-\(UUID())"
   let request = UNNotificationRequest(identifier: id, content: content,
trigger: trigger)

   do {
      try await center.add(request)
      await MainActor.run {
         self.sendButton.isEnabled = false
      }
   } catch {
      print("Error: \(error)")
   }
}
```

Listing 16-12: *Scheduling a notification*

The process to schedule a notification is simple. We must create an instance of the **UNMutableNotificationContent** class with the values we want the notification to show to the user, create a trigger (in this case we use a Time Interval trigger), create an instance of the **UNNotificationRequest** class with these values to request the delivery of the notification, and finally add the request to the User Notification Center with the **add()** method. Notice that the request identifier must be unique. In our example, we define this unique identifier with a string that includes the word "reminder" followed by a random value generated by the **UUID()** function.

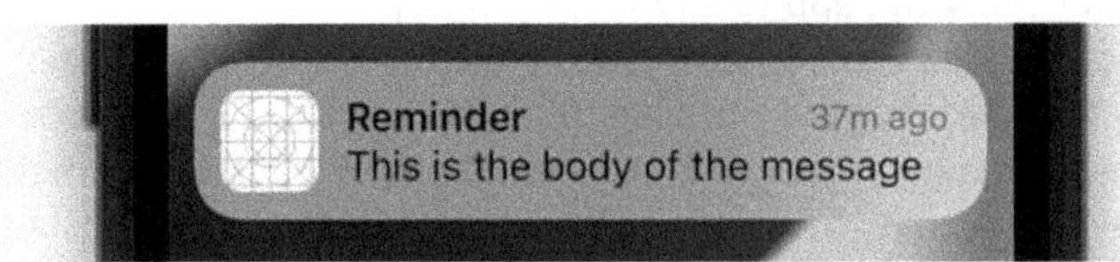

Figure 16-3: *Notification*

Do It Yourself: Create a new project. Add a button to the scene and connect it to the **ViewController** class with an Outlet called **sendButton** and an Action called **checkAuthorization()**. Complete the **ViewController** class with the code in Listing 16-10 and the methods in Listings 16-11 and 16-12. Download the alarm.mp3 file from our website and add it to your project (you can drag and drop the file from Finder). The first time you run the application the system will ask you to allow the app to deliver notifications. Press the Allow button. The button on the interface should be enabled. Press this button to send the notification. Press the Home button to close the app. You should see the notification popping up on the screen after 30 seconds, as shown in Figure 16-3

Basic Media Attachments

Besides text and sounds, notifications can also include other types of media, such as images and videos. The **UNMutableNotificationContent** class includes the following property to attach additional media to the notification.

attachments—This property sets or returns an array of **UNNotificationAttachment** objects with the media files we want to show with the notification.

The attachments are loaded by an object of the **UNNotificationAttachment** class. The class includes the following initializer.

UNNotificationAttachment(identifier: String, **url:** URL, **options:** Dictionary?**)**—This initializer creates an attachment with the media loaded from the URL specified by the **url** argument. The **identifier** argument is the attachment's unique identifier. And the **options** argument is a dictionary with predefined values to configure the media. The most useful are **UNNotificationAttachmentOptionsThumbnail-ClippingRectKey** to use only a portion of an image, and **UNNotification-AttachmentOptionsThumbnailTimeKey** to select a frame from a video.

To attach an image or a video to the notification, we must create the **UNNotification-Attachment** object and assign it to the content's **attachments** property. The object takes a unique identifier, that we can create as we always do, and the URL of the file that contains the media we want to add to the notification. This means that we need the media in a file or to create the file ourselves. The following example illustrates how to take an image from the Assets Catalog, store it in a file, and assign it to the notification.

```
func sendNotification() async {
   let content = UNMutableNotificationContent()
   content.title = "Reminder"
   content.body = "This is the body of the message"

   let idImage = "attach-\(UUID())"
   if let urlImage = await getThumbnail(id: idImage) {
      if let attachment = try? UNNotificationAttachment(identifier:
idImage, url: urlImage, options: nil) {
         content.attachments = [attachment]
      }
   }
   let trigger = UNTimeIntervalNotificationTrigger(timeInterval: 10,
repeats: false)

   let id = "reminder-\(UUID())"
   let request = UNNotificationRequest(identifier: id, content: content,
trigger: trigger)
   do {
      try await center.add(request)
      await MainActor.run {
         self.sendButton.isEnabled = false
      }
   } catch {
      print("Error: \(error)")
   }
}
func getThumbnail(id: String) async -> URL? {
   let manager = FileManager.default
   if let docURL = manager.urls(for: .documentDirectory,
in: .userDomainMask).first {
```

```
        let fileURL = docURL.appendingPathComponent("\(id).png")
        if let image = UIImage(named: "husky") {
           if let thumbnail = await image.byPreparingThumbnail(ofSize:
CGSize(width: 100, height: 100)) {
              if let imageData = thumbnail.pngData() {
                 if let _ = try? imageData.write(to: fileURL) {
                    return fileURL
                 }
              }
           }
        }
     }
     return nil
}
```

***Listing 16-13:** Attaching an image to a notification*

Because we need to load, process, and save the image in a file, we moved the code to a new method called **getThumbnail()**. In this method, we get the URL of the Documents directory, append the name of the file, and then load the image from the Assets Catalog, convert it to data, and store it. The file's URL is returned by the method and used by the code to attach the image to the notification. The result is shown below. The image is displayed inside the banner and expanded when the user drags the banner down.

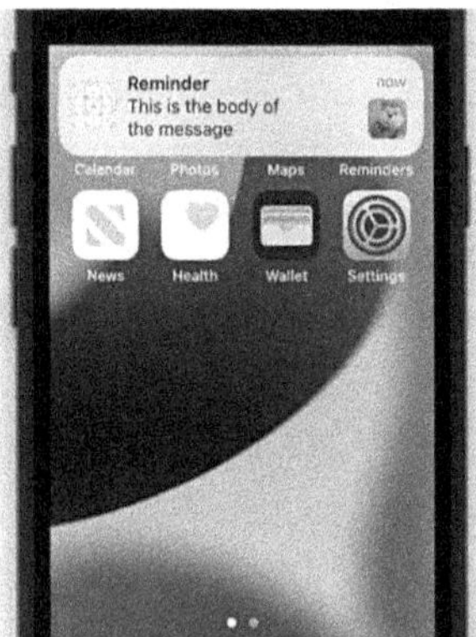

***Figure 16-4:** Attachment*

Do It Yourself: Update the **sendNotification()** method in the **ViewController** class with the code in Listing 16-13 and add the **getThumbnail(id:)** method below. Download the husky.png image from our website and add it to the Assets Catalog. Run the application. Press the button to post a notification, and press the Home button to close the app. You should see a notification with the picture of the husky, as in Figure 16-4.

Basic Provisional Notifications

Asking the user for permission can be a bit disruptive for some applications. If we consider that due to the characteristics of our app the user's acceptance to receive notifications may be implicit, we can post provisional notifications. These are quiet notifications that only show in the Notification Center (they are not displayed in the Locked or Home screens) and include buttons for the user to decide whether to keep them or turn them off. To get our app to post provisional notifications, all we need to do is to add the **provisional** option to the **requestAuthorization()** method, as shown next.

```
override func viewDidLoad() {
   center = UNUserNotificationCenter.current()
   sendButton.isEnabled = false

   Task(priority: .background) {
      do {
         let authorized = try await center.requestAuthorization(options:
[.alert, .sound, .provisional])
         await MainActor.run {
            self.sendButton.isEnabled = authorized
         }
      } catch {
         print("Error: \(error)")
      }
   }
}
```

Listing 16-14: *Scheduling provisional notifications*

If we use provisional notifications, the user is not prompted for authorization, the app is automatically authorized to post notifications, but the status is set as **`provisional`** instead of **`authorized`**, so we must consider this condition when we check the status.

```
@IBAction func checkAuthorization(_ sender: UIButton) {
   Task(priority: .background) {
      let authorization = await center.notificationSettings()
      let status = authorization.authorizationStatus
      if status == .authorized || status == .provisional {
         await self.sendNotification()
      }
   }
}
```

Listing 16-15: *Checking the status of a provisional authorization*

Because provisional notifications are only shown on the Notification Center, the user must open the Notification Center to see them, and then press the Manage button to decide whether to keep them or turn them off.

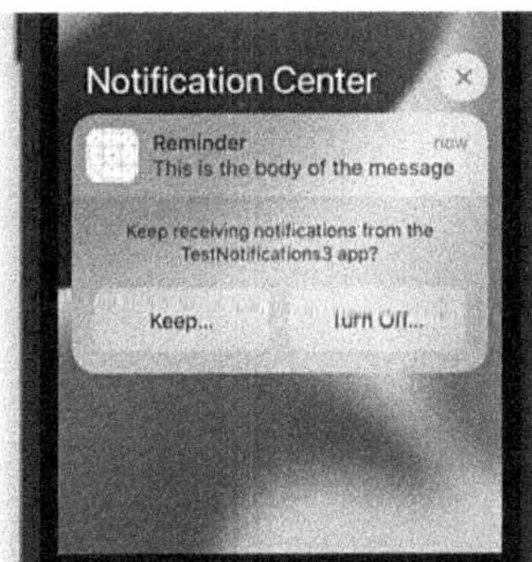

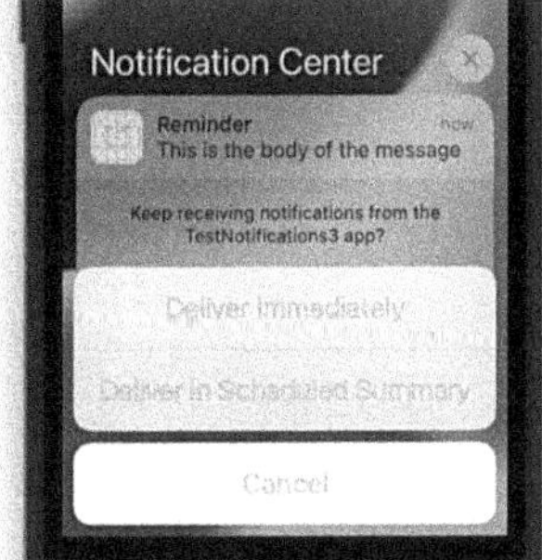

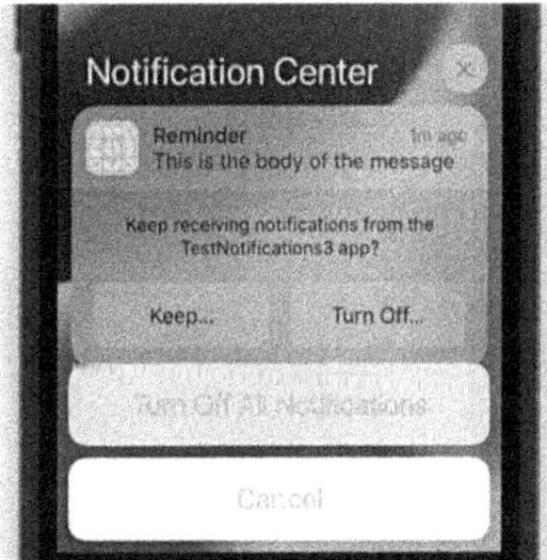

Figure 16-5: *Provisional notifications in the Notification Center*

Do It Yourself: Update the **`viewDidLoad()`** method with the code in Listing 16-14 and the **`checkAuthorization()`** method with the code in Listing 16-15. Uninstall the app and run it again from Xcode. Post a notification. Go to the Home screen and drag your finger from the top to open the Notification Center. You should see the provisional notification, as shown in Figure 16-5.

Basic Notifications Delegate

If the user is working with the app when a notification is delivered, the notification is not displayed on the screen, but we can assign a delegate to the User Notification Center to change this behavior. For this purpose, the framework defines the **UNUserNotificationCenter-Delegate** protocol, which allows us to do two things: we can decide whether to show the notification when the app is running and respond to actions performed by the user.

userNotificationCenter(UNUserNotificationCenter, **willPresent:** UNNotification, **withCompletionHandler:** Block**)**—This method is called by the User Notification Center on the delegate when the application is active and a notification has to be delivered. The **withCompletionHandler** argument is a closure that we must execute to tell the system what to do with the notification. The closure receives an argument of type **UNNotificationPresentationOptions** to define what type of notification to show. The possible values are **badge**, **banner**, **list**, and **sound**.

userNotificationCenter(UNUserNotificationCenter, **didReceive:** UNNotificationResponse, **withCompletionHandler:** Block**)**—This method is called by the User Notification Center when the user interacts with the notification (performs an action). The **didReceive** argument is an object with information about the notification and the action performed, and the **withCompletionHandler** argument is a closure we must execute after the response is processed.

When a notification is triggered and the app is being executed, the User Notification Center calls the **userNotificationCenter(UNUserNotificationCenter, willPresent:, withCompletionHandler:)** method on its delegate to ask the application what to do. In this method, we can perform any task we want and then execute the closure received by the method to specify what we want the system to do with the notification. If we do not want to show the notification, we must execute the closure with no parameters, otherwise we must provide a value that determines the type of notification we want to show.

As always, all we need to do is to declare our view controller as the delegate and implement the protocol methods. In the following example, we implement the **userNotification-Center(UNUserNotificationCenter, notification:, completionHandler:)** method to show the notification while the app is running.

```
import UIKit
import UserNotifications

class ViewController: UIViewController, UNUserNotificationCenterDelegate{
   var center: UNUserNotificationCenter!
   @IBOutlet weak var sendButton: UIButton!

   override func viewDidLoad() {
      center = UNUserNotificationCenter.current()
      center.delegate = self

      sendButton.isEnabled = false

      Task(priority: .background) {
         do {
            let authorized = try await
center.requestAuthorization(options: [.alert])
            await MainActor.run {
               self.sendButton.isEnabled = authorized
            }
```

```
        } catch {
            print("Error: \(error)")
        }
    }
  }
  @IBAction func checkAuthorization(_ sender: UIButton) {
    Task(priority: .background) {
        let authorization = await center.notificationSettings()
        let status = authorization.authorizationStatus
        if status == .authorized {
            await self.sendNotification()
        }
    }
  }
  func sendNotification() async {
    let content = UNMutableNotificationContent()
    content.title = "Reminder"
    content.body = "This is the body of the message"

    let trigger = UNTimeIntervalNotificationTrigger(timeInterval: 10,
repeats: false)

    let id = "reminder-\(UUID())"
    let request = UNNotificationRequest(identifier: id, content:
content, trigger: trigger)
    do {
        try await center.add(request)
        await MainActor.run {
            self.sendButton.isEnabled = false
        }
    } catch {
        print("Error: \(error)")
    }
  }
  func userNotificationCenter(_ center: UNUserNotificationCenter,
willPresent notification: UNNotification, withCompletionHandler
completionHandler: @escaping (UNNotificationPresentationOptions) -> Void)
{
    completionHandler([.banner])
  }
}
```

***Listing 16-16:** Showing notifications while the app is running*

Do It Yourself: Update the **ViewController** class with the code in Listing 16-16. For this example, we have removed the **provisional** parameter added to the configuration in Listing 16-14, so the notifications are not provisional anymore. Remove the application from the device and run it again. Press the button to post a notification. Wait for 10 seconds. You should see the notification on the screen while the app is running.

Basic Groups

The system automatically groups notifications together by app. For instance, if our application sends multiple notifications to the Notification Center, they will all be grouped together and only the last one will be shown to the user. This is the automatic behavior, but we can separate them in custom groups using identifiers. The **UNMutableNotificationContent** class includes the following property for this purpose.

threadIdentifier—This property sets or returns a string used to identify each group of notifications.

All the notifications with the same identifier will be grouped together. The following example separates notifications in two groups called Group One and Group Two.

```
import UIKit
import UserNotifications

class ViewController: UIViewController {
   var center: UNUserNotificationCenter!
   @IBOutlet weak var sendButton: UIButton!

   let listGroups = ["Group One", "Group Two"]
   let listMessages = ["This is message 1", "This is message 2", "This is
message 3"]

   override func viewDidLoad() {
      center = UNUserNotificationCenter.current()
      sendButton.isEnabled = false

      Task(priority: .background) {
         do {
            let authorized = try await
center.requestAuthorization(options: [.alert])
            await MainActor.run {
               self.sendButton.isEnabled = authorized
            }
         } catch {
            print("Error: \(error)")
         }
      }
   }
   @IBAction func checkAuthorization(_ sender: UIButton) {
      Task(priority: .background) {
         let authorization = await center.notificationSettings()
         if authorization.authorizationStatus == .authorized {
            await self.sendNotification()
         }
      }
   }
   func sendNotification() async {
      for group in listGroups {
         for message in listMessages {
            let content = UNMutableNotificationContent()
            content.title = "Reminder \(group)"
            content.body = message
            content.threadIdentifier = group
            let trigger = UNTimeIntervalNotificationTrigger(timeInterval:
10, repeats: false)

            let id = "reminder-\(UUID())"
            let request = UNNotificationRequest(identifier: id, content:
content, trigger: trigger)
            do {
               try await center.add(request)
            } catch {
               print("Error: \(error)")
            }
         }
      }
      await MainActor.run {
         self.sendButton.isEnabled = false
      }
   }
}
```

Listing 16-17: *Organizing notifications into groups*

For didactic purposes, we define two arrays with the name of the groups ("Group One" and "Group Two") and the messages for the notifications. In the **`sendNotification()`** method, we iterate through the arrays to create all the notifications (three per group) and tell the system to which group each notification belongs by assigning the name of the group to the **`threadIdentifier`** property. In total, we post six notifications in two groups.

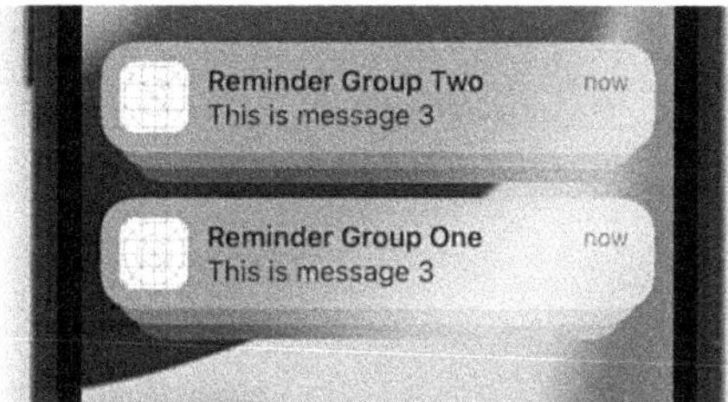

Figure 16-6: *Notifications in two groups*

Do It Yourself: Update the **`ViewController`** class with the code in Listing 16-17. Run the application. Press the button to post the notifications. Go to the Lock screen. After 10 seconds you should see all the notifications organized in two groups (Figure 16-6).

Basic Summary

Users can create notification summaries to get a single alert at a specific time in the day with all the notifications grouped together. A summary can include notifications from one or multiple apps. The tool to create a summary is available in the Notifications option of the Settings app.

Figure 16-7: *Summary option in Settings app*

To configure the summary, we must create a category and add that category to the User Notification Center. Categories are objects that define actions and behavior associated to a notification or a group of notifications. The framework offers the **`UNNotificationCategory`** class to create these objects. The following is the initializer used to configure a summary.

UNNotificationCategory(identifier: String, **actions:** [UNNotificationAction], **intentIdentifiers:** [String], **hiddenPreviewsBodyPlaceholder:** String?, **categorySummaryFormat:** String?, **options:** UNNotificationCategory-Options)—This initializer creates a category to configure a summary. The **identifier** argument is a string that identifies the category, the **actions** argument defines the actions available for the summary, the **intentIdentifiers** argument is an array of strings used to guide Siri to produce a better response, the **hiddenPreviewsBodyPlaceholder** argument is the string to show instead of the notifications when the previews are disabled, the **categorySummaryFormat** argument is the string that describes the summary, and the **options** argument is an array of properties that determine how the notifications associated to the category are going to be handled. The properties available are **`customDismissAction`** (processes the dismiss action) and **`allowInCarPlay`** (allows car play to show notifications).

The **UNUserNotificationCenter** class includes the following method to register a category in the User Notification Center.

setNotificationCategories(Set**)**—This method configures the User Notification Center to work with the types of notifications and actions we want to support. The argument is the set of categories we want to associate to the center.

When the notifications appeared in a summary, they are sorted according to their relevance. The system determines this relevance for us, but we can suggest a specific order by setting the notification's relevance ourselves. The **UNMutableNotificationContent** class includes the following property for this purpose.

relevanceScore—This property sets or returns a value of type **Double** between 0 and 1 to tell the system how to sort the app's notifications. The notification with the highest relevance gets featured in the notification summary.

The following are the modifications we need to introduce to the **sendNotification()** method from the previous example to include our notifications in a summary.

```
func sendNotification() async {
   let groupID = "Group One"
   let summaryFormat = "\(listMessages.count) messages"

   let category = UNNotificationCategory(identifier: groupID, actions:
[], intentIdentifiers: [], hiddenPreviewsBodyPlaceholder: nil,
categorySummaryFormat: summaryFormat, options: [])
   center.setNotificationCategories([category])

   for message in listMessages {
      let content = UNMutableNotificationContent()
      content.title = "Reminder"
      content.body = message
      content.threadIdentifier = groupID

      let trigger = UNTimeIntervalNotificationTrigger(timeInterval: 10,
repeats: false)

      let id = "reminder-\(UUID())"
      let request = UNNotificationRequest(identifier: id, content:
content, trigger: trigger)
      do {
         try await center.add(request)
      } catch {
         print("Error: \(error)")
      }
   }
   await MainActor.run {
      self.sendButton.isEnabled = false
   }
}
```

Listing 16-18: *Configuring a summary of notifications*

The notifications are created with the messages in the **listMessages** array introduced in the previous example. To include the notifications in the summary, we define a single group with the identifier "Group One" and create a category with a summary message that includes the number of notifications included in the summary. The rest of the process is the same as before.

If we just run the application, the notifications are displayed as before, but we can go to the Settings app and set a summary, as shown in Figure 16-7. Below is how the summary created by our app looks like when it is shown to the user.

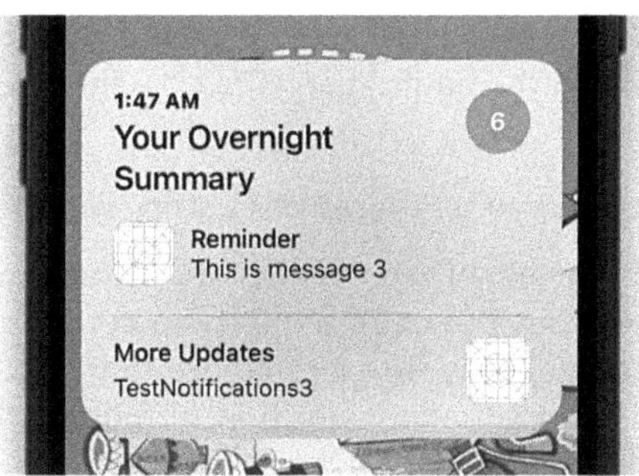

Figure 16-8: *Notifications summary in the Lock screen*

Do It Yourself: Update the **`sendNotification()`** method with the code in Listing 16-18. Press the Home button, open the Settings app, and set a summary for the application, as shown in Figure 16-7. Run the application and press the button to post the notifications. You should see a summary in the Lock screen with all the notifications at the time specified in Settings.

Basic Actions

Notifications can show custom actions in the form of buttons and input fields that the user can interact with to provide feedback without having to open our app. The actions are defined by two classes: **`UNNotificationAction`** and **`UNTextInputNotificationAction`**.

UNNotificationAction(identifier: String, **title:** String, **options:** UNNotificationActionOptions**)**—This initializer creates an action represented by a custom button. The **identifier** argument is a string that we can use to identify the action, the **title** argument is the text shown on the button, and the **options** argument is a set of properties that determine how the action should be performed. The properties available are **`authenticationRequired`** (the user is required to unlock the device), **`destructive`** (the button is highlighted), and **`foreground`** (the app is opened to perform the action).

UNTextInputNotificationAction(identifier: String, **title:** String, **options:** UNNotificationActionOptions, **textInputButtonTitle:** String, **textInput-Placeholder:** String**)**—This initializer creates an action represented by a custom button that when pressed prompts the system to display an input field. In addition to the arguments included by a normal action, these types of actions also include the **textInputButtonTitle** and **textInputPlaceholder** arguments to define the button and the placeholder for the input field.

After the actions we want to include in the notification are defined, we must create a category to group them together. The **`UNNotificationCategory`** class includes the following initializer to add actions to a notification.

UNNotificationCategory(identifier: String, **actions:** [UNNotificationAction], **intentIdentifiers:** [String], **options:** UNNotificationCategoryOptions**)**—This initializer creates a category with the actions specified by the **actions** argument. The **identifier** argument is a string that identifies the category, the **intentIdentifiers** argument is an array of strings used to guide Siri to produce a better response, and the **options** argument is an array of properties that determine how the notifications associated to the category are going to be handled. The properties available are **`customDismissAction`** (processes the dismiss action) and **`allowInCarPlay`** (allows car play to show notifications).

When an action is performed, the User Notification Center calls the **`userNotificationCenter(UNUserNotificationCenter, didReceive:, withCompletionHandler:)`**

method on its delegate. The method receives a **UNNotificationResponse** object with information about the action and the notification. The class includes the following properties to read the values.

actionIdentifier—This property sets or returns a string with the action's identifier.

notification—This property sets or returns a **UNNotification** object representing the notification. The object includes the **date** property to get the date the notification was delivered and the **request** property with a reference to the **UNNotificationRequest** object used to schedule the notification, which in turn offers the **content** property to access the values of the notification.

The following example adds an action to the notification scheduled in previous examples and implements the delegate method to process the response.

```
import UIKit
import UserNotifications

class ViewController: UIViewController, UNUserNotificationCenterDelegate{
   var center: UNUserNotificationCenter!
   @IBOutlet weak var sendButton: UIButton!

   override func viewDidLoad() {
      center = UNUserNotificationCenter.current()
      center.delegate = self

      sendButton.isEnabled = false

      Task(priority: .background) {
         do {
            let authorized = try await
center.requestAuthorization(options: [.alert])
            await MainActor.run {
               self.sendButton.isEnabled = authorized
            }
         } catch {
            print("Error: \(error)")
         }
      }
   }
   @IBAction func checkAuthorization(_ sender: UIButton) {
      Task(priority: .background) {
         let authorization = await center.notificationSettings()
         let status = authorization.authorizationStatus
         if status == .authorized {
            await self.sendNotification()
         }
      }
   }
   func sendNotification() async {
      let groupID = "listActions"
      let actionDelete = UNNotificationAction(identifier: "deleteButton",
title: "Delete", options: .destructive)
      let category = UNNotificationCategory(identifier: groupID, actions:
[actionDelete], intentIdentifiers: [], options: [])
      center.setNotificationCategories([category])

      let content = UNMutableNotificationContent()
      content.title = "Reminder"
      content.body = "This is the body of the message"
      content.categoryIdentifier = groupID
      let trigger = UNTimeIntervalNotificationTrigger(timeInterval: 10,
repeats: false)

      let id = "reminder-\(UUID())"
```

```
      let request = UNNotificationRequest(identifier: id, content:
content, trigger: trigger)
      do {
         try await center.add(request)
         await MainActor.run {
            self.sendButton.isEnabled = false
         }
      } catch {
         print("Error: \(error)")
      }
   }
   func userNotificationCenter(_ center: UNUserNotificationCenter,
didReceive response: UNNotificationResponse, withCompletionHandler
completionHandler: @escaping () -> Void) {
      let identifier = response.actionIdentifier
      if identifier == "deleteButton" {
         print("Delete Message")
      }
      completionHandler()
   }
}
```

Listing 16-19: *Adding and processing actions for notifications*

This view controller creates a destructive action with the title Delete, and includes it in a category called "listActions". Categories have to be added to the User Notification Center first with the **setNotificationCategories()** method and then assigned to the notification's **categoryIdentifier** property to configure the notification, as we did in Listing 16-18.

Actions are displayed when the user drags down the notification. In this case, the notification shows the Delete button. If the user presses this button, the User Notification Center calls the delegate method to give our application the chance to perform a task. In our example, we read the **actionIdentifier** property, compare it with the string "deleteButton" to confirm that the user pressed the Delete button, and then print a message on the console in case of success.

Figure 16-9: *Actions in a notification*

In the example of Listing 16-19, we implement a simple action that shows a button when the notification is expanded, but we can also include an action that shows an input field, so the user can provide feedback right from the screen where the notification is being displayed. The following are the changes we need to introduce to add an action of this type.

```
func sendNotification() async {
   let groupID = "listActions"
   let actionDelete = UNNotificationAction(identifier: "deleteButton",
title: "Delete", options: .destructive)
   let actionInput = UNTextInputNotificationAction(identifier:
"inputField", title: "Message", options: [])

   let category = UNNotificationCategory(identifier: groupID, actions:
[actionDelete, actionInput], intentIdentifiers: [], options: [])
   center.setNotificationCategories([category])
```

```
   let content = UNMutableNotificationContent()
   content.title = "Reminder"
   content.body = "This is the body of the message"
   content.categoryIdentifier = groupID

   let trigger = UNTimeIntervalNotificationTrigger(timeInterval: 10,
repeats: false)

   let id = "reminder-\(UUID())"
   let request = UNNotificationRequest(identifier: id, content: content,
trigger: trigger)
   do {
      try await center.add(request)
      await MainActor.run {
         self.sendButton.isEnabled = false
      }
   } catch {
      print("Error: \(error)")
   }
}
func userNotificationCenter(_ center: UNUserNotificationCenter,
didReceive response: UNNotificationResponse, withCompletionHandler
completionHandler: @escaping () -> Void) {
   let identifier = response.actionIdentifier
   if identifier == "deleteButton" {
      print("Delete Message")
   } else if identifier == "inputField" {
      print("Send: \((response as!
UNTextInputNotificationResponse).userText)")
   }
   completionHandler()
}
```

Listing 16-20: *Processing an input action*

The text inserted by the user in the text field is sent to the delegate method. The framework offers a special class to represent the response called **UNTextInputNotificationResponse**. To access the value inserted by the user, we must cast the response object to this class and then read its **userText** property, as we did in Listing 16-20. The result is shown below.

Figure 16-10: *Notification with a text field*

Do It Yourself: Update your **ViewController** class with the code in Listing 16-20 and run the application. Press the button to schedule a notification. Go to the Home screen and wait until the notification is displayed. Expand the notification to see the actions. Click the Message button, insert a value, and press the Send button. You should see the same text printed on the console.

Medium 16.3 Key/Value Observing

KVO (Key/Value Observing) is a system we can use to perform a task when the value of a property is modified. This is similar to what the **didSet()** method does for the properties of our own structures and classes (see Property Observers in Chapter 3), with the difference that some predefined classes provided by Apple come ready to work with this system and therefore we can monitor the values of their properties as we do with our own from anywhere in the code.

There are several situations in which KVO may be useful. For example, we may have a property that reflects the status of an operation. The problem is that we do not know when the status is going to change, and which are the objects that must be notified when a change occurs. Constantly checking the property from every object to see if its value has changed is not practical. KVO allows us to add observers to every object that needs to keep an eye on the property. Every time the property is modified, the system notifies these observers, so the objects can perform the task they need, such as updating the interface or initiating a new operation.

Medium KVC

For the KVO system to be able to monitor the values of a property, the object in which the property was defined must comply to the **NSKeyValueCoding** protocol. This protocol defines another system called KVC (Key/Value Coding) that allows us to access properties using their names as keys. Instead of using dot notation to access the values of a property, we call methods defined in this protocol with a string that identifies the property we want to modify. The following are the most frequently used.

setValue(Any?, **forKeyPath:** String**)**—This method assigns a value to the property specified by the **forKeyPath** argument. The first argument is the value we want to assign to the property and the **forKeyPath** argument is a string with the name of the property.

value(forKey: String**)**—This method retrieves the value of the property identified by the **forKey** argument. The argument is a string with the name of the property.

Some of the frameworks provided by Apple include classes that are ready to work with KVC, but we can define our own. An easy way to make our custom classes KVC compliant is to declare them as subclasses of the **NSObject** class. This is the class from which the rest of the Objective-C classes are created, and it already includes an implementation of the protocol. The following example illustrates how to define a subclass of **NSObject** called **MyControl**. Notice that because KVC is a system developed in Objective-C the properties must be preceded by the **@objc** prefix.

```
import Foundation

class MyControl: NSObject {
   @objc var round = false
}
```

Listing 16-21: *Defining a custom class to work with KVC*

Because the **MyControl** class is a subclass of **NSObject**, we can call the **NSKeyValue-Coding** protocol methods on instances of this class to set or retrieve the value of the **round** property. In the following example, we present a **ViewController** class that creates an instance of **MyControl** and modifies the value of the **round** property every time the user changes the value of a Stepper. The example assumes that the scene contains an interface with a Stepper and a label.

```
import UIKit

class ViewController: UIViewController {
   @IBOutlet weak var counterLabel: UILabel!
   var control: MyControl!

   override func viewDidLoad() {
      super.viewDidLoad()
      control = MyControl()
   }
   @IBAction func updateValue(_ sender: UIStepper) {
      let current = Int(sender.value)
      if current % 10 == 0 {
         control.setValue(true, forKey: "round")
      } else {
         control.setValue(false, forKey: "round")
      }
      counterLabel.text = String(current)
   }
}
```

Listing 16-22: *Modifying property values using KVC*

The **ViewController** class in Listing 16-22 creates an instance of the **MyControl** class and then implements an Action for the Stepper to change the value of the **round** property every time the value of the Stepper is modified. The Action gets the Stepper's current value and then sets the value of the **round** property to **true** or **false** depending on whether the current value is multiple of 10 or not.

Medium KVO

When properties are set using the **setValue()** method instead of the = sign, as we did in the last example, they automatically become KVO compliant and therefore they may be observed from other objects. The process requires the objects to become observers. For this purpose, Foundation includes the **NSKeyValueObserving** protocol, to which the **UIViewController** class conforms by default. The following are some of the methods defined by the protocol to add and remove observers.

addObserver(NSObject, **forKeyPath:** String, **options:** NSKeyValue-ObservingOptions, **context:** UnsafeMutablePointer?**)**—This method adds an observer to the object. The first argument is a reference to the observer (usually **self**), the **forKeyPath** argument is a string with the name or the path to the property, the **options** argument is a Set with enumeration values that determine the values sent to the observer (possible values are **new**, **old**, **initial**, and **prior**), and the **context** argument is a generic value that identifies the observer (used when a class and its subclasses observe the same property).

removeObserver(NSObject, **forKeyPath:** String, **context:** UnsafeMutable-Pointer?**)**—This method removes an observer. The arguments are the same values specified in the **addObserver()** method when the observer was added.

With KVO, an object can observe the property of another object and perform a task when the value of the property changes. For this purpose, the **NSKeyValueObserving** protocol defines the following method.

observeValue(forKeyPath: String?, **of:** Any?, **change:** [NSKeyValue-ChangeKey : Any]?, **context:** UnsafeMutableRawPointer?**)**—This method is called on the object when there is a change in the property the object is observing. The **forKeyPath** argument is a string with the name or the path to the property, the **of**

argument is a reference to the object where the change occurred, the **change** argument is a dictionary with the description of the changes, and the **context** argument is the value that identifies the observer.

To observe a value, we must add the observer with the **addObserver()** method and override the **observeValue()** method to perform a task when a change occurs, as shown next.

```
import UIKit

class ViewController: UIViewController {
   @IBOutlet weak var counterLabel: UILabel!
   var control: MyControl!

   override func viewDidLoad() {
      super.viewDidLoad()
      control = MyControl()
      control.addObserver(self, forKeyPath: "round", options: [],
context: nil)
   }
   @IBAction func updateValue(_ sender: UIStepper) {
      let current = Int(sender.value)
      if current % 10 == 0 {
         control.setValue(true, forKey: "round")
      } else {
         control.setValue(false, forKey: "round")
      }
      counterLabel.text = String(current)
   }
   override func observeValue(forKeyPath keyPath: String?, of object:
Any?, change: [NSKeyValueChangeKey : Any]?, context:
UnsafeMutableRawPointer?) {
      if keyPath == "round" {
         if control.round {
            counterLabel.textColor = UIColor.red
         } else {
            counterLabel.textColor = UIColor.black
         }
      }
   }
}
```

Listing 16-23: *Observing the value of a property*

This example updates the previous **ViewController** class to add an observer to monitor the value of the **round** property. When the user modifies the value of the Stepper, the **updateValue()** method is called and the value of the **round** property is modified with the **setValue()** method. This prompts the property to report the change. The observer added to the **ViewController** class is notified of the change and executes the **observeValue()** method. In this method, we check if the name or path of the property matches the name or path of the property we want to read and then perform the task according to its value. In this example, if the value of **round** is **true**, we change the color of the label to red, and if it is **false** we change it back to black.

Do It Yourself: Create a new project. Add a Stepper and a label to the scene. Connect the Stepper with an Action called **updateValue()** and the label with an Outlet called **counterLabel**. Create a Swift file called **MyControl** for the code in Listing 16-21. Complete the **ViewController** class with the code in Listing 16-23 and run the application. Press the Stepper to change the value. The **counterLabel** label should turn red every time the value is multiple of 10.

Setting the value of the property with the **setValue()** method prompts the property to notify the change, but this means that every time we want the changes in a property to be noticed by the observers we have to perform those changes calling the **setValue()** method. If we want every change to be reported, including those performed with traditional methods like the = sign, we need to make the property compliant to KVO by implementing some of the methods provided by the **NSKeyValueObserving** protocol. The simplest way to do this is by calling the following protocol methods from the property's **didSet()** and **willSet()** methods.

willChangeValue(forKey: String)—This method informs the class that the value of the property is about to change. The **forKey** argument is a string with the property's name or path.

didChangeValue(forKey: String)—This method informs the class that the value of the property was changed. The **forKey** argument is a string with the property's name or path.

The following example implements these two methods to make the **round** property report the changes before and after they happen.

```
import Foundation

class MyControl: NSObject {
   @objc var round = false {
      didSet {
         self.didChangeValue(forKey: "round")
      }
      willSet {
         self.willChangeValue(forKey: "round")
      }
   }
}
```

Listing 16-24: *Reporting changes*

Now, we can assign new values to the **round** property as we always do and get the property to report the changes. The following example shows the new action for the Stepper.

```
@IBAction func updateValue(_ sender: UIStepper) {
   let current = Int(sender.value)
   if current % 10 == 0 {
      control.round = true
   } else {
      control.round = false
   }
   counterLabel.text = String(current)
}
```

Listing 16-25: *Working with a KVO compliant property*

Do It Yourself: Update the **MyControl** class with the code in Listing 16-24 and the **updateValue()** method of the **ViewController** class with the code in Listing 16-25. Run the application. Again, you should see the label changing colors according to the Stepper's current value.

IMPORTANT: With Key/Value Observing you can only observe the properties of one object from another. To observe properties of the same object you can use Property Observers (see Chapter 3). Usually, you do not need this technique to observe values in your own classes, but some frameworks include classes that require the use of Key/Value Observing, as we will see later.

Chapter 17
iCloud

Basic 17.1 Data in the Cloud

These days, users own more than one device. If we create an application that works on multiple devices, we must provide a way for users to share their data, otherwise they will have to insert the same information on every device they own. But the only way to do it effectively is through a server. Data from one device is stored on a server so that it can be retrieved later from other devices. Setting up a server to run this kind of system is complicated and costly. To provide a standard solution, Apple created a free system called *iCloud*. iCloud allows applications to synchronize data across devices using Apple servers. It provides three basic services: Key-Value Storage, to store single values, Document Storage, to store files, and CloudKit Storage, to store structured data.

Basic Enabling iCloud

iCloud must be enabled for each application. The system requires entitlements to authorize our app to use the service and a container where our app's data will be stored. Fortunately, Xcode can set up everything for us by just selecting an option in the Signing & Capabilities panel, found inside the app's settings window. The panel includes a + button at the top-left corner to add a new capability to the application (Figure 17-1, number 1). The button opens a view with all the capabilities available, as shown below. The capability is added by clicking on it and pressing Return.

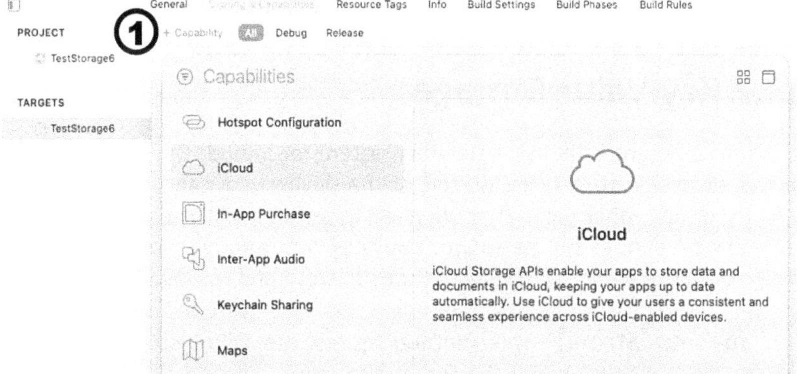

Figure 17-1: *Activating iCloud for our app*

After iCloud is added to the app, it is shown on the panel, below the signing section. From here, we can select the services we want to activate for our app and Xcode takes care of creating the entitlements. Figure 17-2, below, shows the panel with the Key-Value storage service activated.

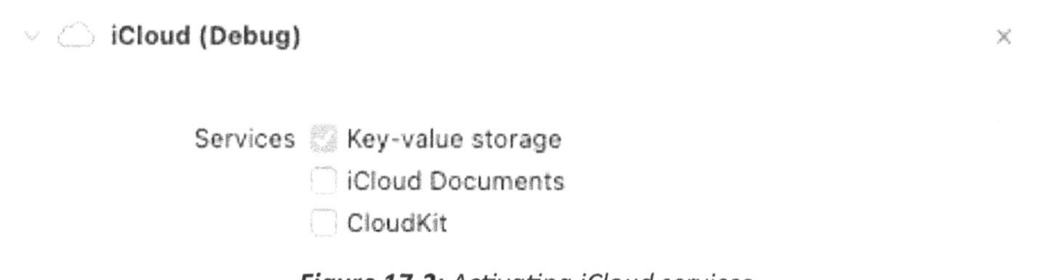

Figure 17-2: *Activating iCloud services*

Do It Yourself: Create a new project. Click on the app's settings option at the top of the Navigator Area (Figure 5-12, number 6) and open the Signing & Capabilities panel. Click on the + button at the top-left corner to add a capability (Figure 17-1, number 1). Select the iCloud option, press return, and check the option Key-value storage. This iCloud service is now available in your application.

Basic Testing Devices

The best way to test iCloud is by running the app in two different devices, but Apple has made iCloud services available in the simulator as well. Thanks to this feature, we can synchronize data between a device and the simulator to test our app.

For the devices and the simulators to be able to access iCloud services, we must register our iCloud account in the Settings app. We have to go to the Home screen, access the Settings app, tap on the option Sign in to your iPhone/iPad (Figure 17-3, center), and sign in to Apple's services with our Apple ID. The process must be repeated for every device or simulator we want to use.

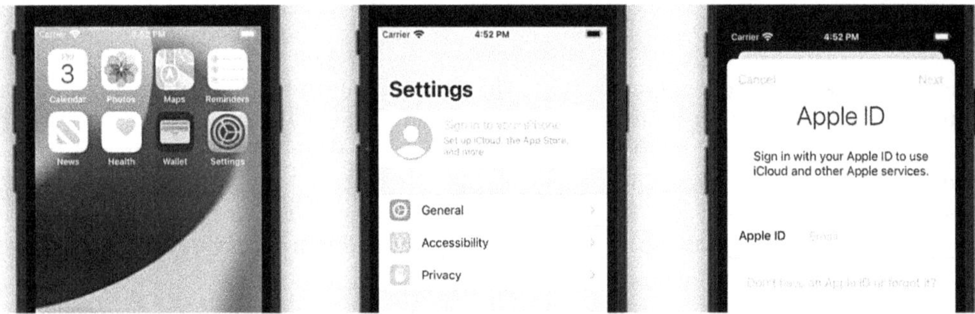

Figure 17-3: *iCloud account in the simulator*

Basic 17.2 Key-Value Storage

The Key-Value storage system is the User Defaults system for iCloud. It works the same way, but all the data is stored on iCloud servers instead of the device. We can use it to store the app's preferences, states, or any other value that we need to automatically set on each device owned by the user. Foundation defines the **`NSUbiquitousKeyValueStore`** class to provide access to this system. The class includes the following methods to store and retrieve values.

set(Value, **forKey:** String**)**—This method stores the value specified by the first argument with the key specified by the **forKey** argument. The class provides versions of this method for every data type we are allowed to store in the system, such as **`String`**, **`Bool`**, **`Data`**, **`Double`**, **`Int64`**, dictionaries, arrays, and Property List values (**`NSNumber`**, **`NSString`**, **`NSDate`**, **`NSArray`**, **`NSDictionary`**, **`NSData`**, and the equivalents in Swift).

bool(forKey: String**)**—This method retrieves a value of type **`Bool`**.

double(forKey: String**)**—This method retrieves a value of type **`Double`**.

longLong(forKey: String**)**—This method retrieves a value of type **`Int64`**.

string(forKey: String**)**—This method retrieves a value of type **`String`**.

array(forKey: String**)**—This method retrieves an array.

dictionary(forKey: String**)**—This method retrieves a dictionary.

data(forKey: String**)**—This method retrieves a value of type **`Data`**.

object(forKey: String**)**—This method retrieves an object.

To store or access a value, we must initialize an **NSUbiquitousKeyValueStore** object and then call its methods. The object takes care of establishing the connection with iCloud and downloading or uploading the values. As we already mentioned, the system is used to storing discrete values that represent the user's preferences or the app's state. For example, we may have a Stepper that lets the user set a limit on the number of items the app can manage.

Figure 17-4: *Interface to test Key-Value storage*

If the user decides to set the limit to 5 in one device, the same limit should be set when the application is executed on a different device. To achieve this, we must read the value from iCloud when the view is loaded and store it back when the user sets a new one. The following is the view controller necessary for this application.

```
import UIKit

class ViewController: UIViewController {
   @IBOutlet weak var stepper: UIStepper!
   @IBOutlet weak var counter: UILabel!
   var kvStorage: NSUbiquitousKeyValueStore!

   override func viewDidLoad() {
      super.viewDidLoad()
      kvStorage = NSUbiquitousKeyValueStore()
      let control = kvStorage.double(forKey: "control")
      stepper.value = control
      counter.text = String(control)
   }
   @IBAction func changeValue(_ sender: UIStepper) {
      let current = stepper.value
      counter.text = String(current)
      kvStorage.set(current, forKey: "control")
      kvStorage.synchronize()
   }
}
```

Listing 17-1: *Storing setting values in iCloud*

This example creates the **NSUbiquitousKeyValueStore** object as soon as the view is loaded and reads a value of type **Double** identified with the key "control". Like it happens with some of the methods included in the **UserDefaults** class, the **double()** method used in this example returns 0 if the value is not found, so the first time the application is executed, the value assigned to the label will be 0. To update the value, we have created an Action for the Stepper called **changeValue()**. In this method, we get the current value of the Stepper, assign it to the label to reflect the change on the screen, and then store the value in iCloud with the "control" key using the **set()** method. If the user opens the application in a different device, the process starts again by reading the value associated with the "control" key from iCloud, but this time instead of returning 0 it will find the last number stored by the **set()** method.

Notice that we have executed a method called **synchronize()** after storing a new value. This is a method provided by the **NSUbiquitousKeyValueStore** class to force the system to send the new value to iCloud right away. It is not always necessary, only when we want to make sure that the value is there as soon as possible.

Do It Yourself: Create a new project. Add a Stepper and a label to the scene, as illustrated in Figure 17-4. Connect the Stepper to the **ViewController** class with an Outlet called **stepper** and the label with an Outlet called **counter**. Connect the Stepper with an Action called **changeValue()** and complete the **ViewController** class with the code in Listing 17-1. Run the application. Press the Stepper's button to change the value to 5. Wait a few seconds for the information to be uploaded. Stop the application and run it again. The label should contain the value 5 this time. If you run the app on a different device or simulator, you should see the value 5 again on the screen (remember to activate the same iCloud account in any of the simulators or devices you try).

IMPORTANT: The simulator does not update the information automatically. Most of the time, you must force the update. If you modify the value on your device and do not see it changing on the simulator, open the Features menu at the top of the screen and select the option Trigger iCloud Sync. This will synchronize the application with iCloud and update the values right away.

The previous example stores in iCloud a value associated with the "control" key, and every time the app is executed the value is retrieved from iCloud servers and shown on the screen. The problem is that at this moment the application does not know when the value was modified from another device. If we launch the app on an iPhone, set the value to 5, and then launch it again on an iPad, we will see the value 5 on the iPad's screen, but modifying the value thereafter will not produce any effect on the other device. To report the changes, the **NSUbiquitousKey-ValueStore** class defines the following notification.

didChangeExternallyNotification—This notification is posted by the system when a change in the values of the Key-Value storage is detected.

In the following example, we listen to this notification to update the value every time is changed from another device.

```
import UIKit

class ViewController: UIViewController {
   @IBOutlet weak var stepper: UIStepper!
   @IBOutlet weak var counter: UILabel!
   var kvStorage: NSUbiquitousKeyValueStore!

   override func viewDidLoad() {
      super.viewDidLoad()
      kvStorage = NSUbiquitousKeyValueStore()
      let control = kvStorage.double(forKey: "control")
      stepper.value = control
      counter.text = String(control)

      Task(priority: .high) {
         await receiveNotifications()
      }
   }
   func receiveNotifications() async {
      let center = NotificationCenter.default
      let name =
NSUbiquitousKeyValueStore.didChangeExternallyNotification
      for await notification in center.notifications(named: name, object:
kvStorage) {
         if notification.name == name {
            await MainActor.run {
               let control = kvStorage.double(forKey: "control")
               stepper.value = control
```

```
                    counter.text = String(control)
                }
            }
        }
    }
    @IBAction func changeValue(_ sender: UIStepper) {
        let current = stepper.value
        counter.text = String(current)
        kvStorage.set(current, forKey: "control")
        kvStorage.synchronize()
    }
}
```

Listing 17-2: *Updating the interface when a new value is received*

The first thing we do in this view controller is to create a task in the **viewDidLoad()** method to call an asynchronous method that listens to **didChangeExternallyNotification** notifications, so every device running the application knows when the value was modified from another device.

When a notification is received, we read the new value and update the interface. Now, we can have the application running simultaneously on different devices and the user will see the value automatically changing on the screen when it is modified from another device.

Do It Yourself: Update the **ViewController** class with the code in Listing 17-2. Run the application simultaneously in two devices. Modify the value on one device and check the other to see how the label changes (it may take up to a few minutes for the data to be transferred from one device to another). If you use the simulator, remember to select the option Trigger iCloud Sync from the Features menu.

Basic 17.3 iCloud Documents

The Key-Value storage system was developed to store small values. The purpose is to allow users to set preferences or configuration parameters across devices. Although very useful, it presents some limitations, especially on the amount of data we can store (currently no more than 1 megabyte). If what we need is to store large amounts of data, we can activate the iCloud Documents option in the Capabilities panel and upload files instead.

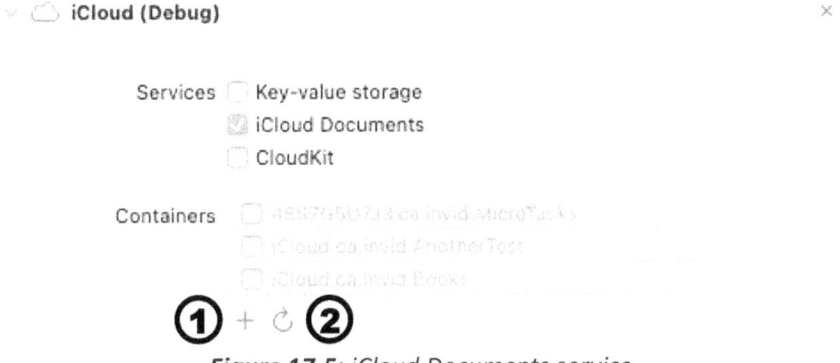

Figure 17-5: *iCloud Documents service*

The operative system uses a container to store iCloud files. This container is a folder in the app's storage space where iCloud files are created. Once a file is added, modified, or removed from this container, the system automatically reports the changes to iCloud, so the copies of the app running in other devices can modify their own container to stay synchronized. To create a container for our app, we must press the + button (Figure 17-5, number 1). This opens a window to insert the name.

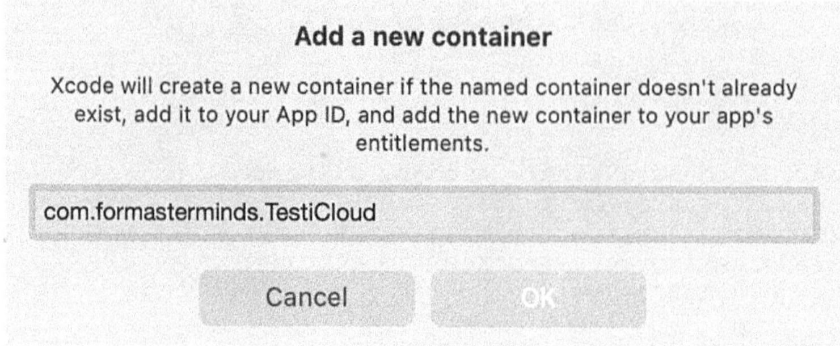

Figure 17-6: *iCloud Container*

The name must be unique, and the best way to guarantee this is to use the app's bundle identifier. In Figure 17-6, we use the bundle identifier to create the container for an app called TestiCloud. Once the container is created, we should press the Refresh button to make sure the information is uploaded to Apple servers right away (Figure 17-5, number 2). After this, the container is added and selected as the active container for the application.

An iCloud container is called *ubiquitous container* because its content is shared with other devices and therefore available everywhere. The **FileManager** class includes properties and methods to work with a ubiquitous container. The following are the most frequently used.

url(forUbiquityContainerIdentifier: String?**)**—This method returns the URL of the app's iCloud container. The **forUbiquityContainerIdentifier** argument is the name of the container we want to access. The value **nil** returns the container which name matches the Bundle identifier.

evictUbiquitousItem(at: URL**)**—This method removes the local copy of the document at the URL specified by the **at** argument.

Basic Documents

Although the files are stored in a container in the device and synchronized by the system automatically, working with iCloud presents some challenges that the **FileManager** class cannot overcome. The most important issue is coordination. Because of the unreliability of network connections, at any moment iCloud may find different versions of the same file. Modifications that were introduced to a file from one device may not have reached iCloud and therefore may later conflict with updates introduced from another device. The application must decide which version of the file to preserve or what data is more valuable when the file is edited from two different devices at the same time. These issues are not easy to solve. Considering all the challenges developers face, Apple added a class to UIKit called **UIDocument**. The class includes capabilities like progression reports, automatic thumbnail generation, undo manager, and others that simplify working with documents in iCloud.

The **UIDocument** class was not designed to be implemented directly in our code; it is like an interface between the app's data and the files we use to store it. To take advantage of this class, we must create a subclass and override its methods. Once we define the subclass, we can create the object with the following initializer.

UIDocument(fileURL: URL**)**—This initializer creates a new **UIDocument** object. The **fileURL** argument is a **URL** structure with the location of the file in the iCloud's container.

The following are the methods we need to override in the **UIDocument** subclass to provide the data for the file and to retrieve it later.

contents(forType: String**)**—This method is called when the **UIDocument** object needs to store the content of the document on file. The method must return an object with the document's data (usually a **Data** structure). The **forType** argument identifies the file's type (by default, it is determined from the file's extension).

load(fromContents: Any, **ofType:** String?**)**—This method is called when the **UIDocument** object loads the content of the document from the file. The **fromContents** argument is an object with the content of the file (usually a **Data** structure that is internally turned into an **NSData** object), and the **ofType** argument is a string that identifies the file's type (by default, it is determined from the file's extension).

Once an object is created from our **UIDocument** subclass, we can manage the file from the asynchronous methods provided by the class. The following are the most frequently used.

open()—This asynchronous method asks the **UIDocument** object to open the file and load its content.

save(to: URL, **for:** SaveOperation**)**—This asynchronous method asks the **UIDocument** object to save the content of the document on file. The **for** argument is an enumeration called **SaveOperation** that indicates the type of operation to perform. The values available are **forCreating** (to save the file for the first time) and **forOverwriting** (to overwrite the file's current version).

close()—This asynchronous method saves any pending changes and closes the document.

Basic Metadata Query

Accessing the files is also complicated in iCloud. We cannot just get a list of files with methods like **contentsOfDirectory()** from the **FileManager** class because there could be some files that have not been downloaded yet to the device. What we can do instead is to get the information pertaining to the files. This data is called *metadata*, and refers to all the information associated with a particular file, such as its name, the date it was created, etc. To get the files' metadata, Foundation defines the **NSMetadataQuery** class. This class provides the properties and methods necessary to retrieve the information and watch for updates.

predicate—This property sets or returns the predicate for the query. It is an optional of type **NSPredicate**.

sortDescriptors—This property sets or returns the sort descriptors for the query. It is an array of **NSSortDescriptor** objects.

searchScopes—This property sets or returns a value that indicates the scope of the query. It is an array with constants that represent a predefined scope. The constants available for iOS are **NSMetadataQueryUbiquitousDocumentsScope** (searches all files in the Documents directory of the iCloud's container) and **NSMetadataQuery-UbiquitousDataScope** (searches all the files that are not in the Documents directory of the iCloud's container).

results—This property returns an array with the query's results. By default, the array contains **NSMetadataItem** objects with the metadata of every file found.

resultCount—This property returns the number of results produced by the query.

result(at: Int**)**—This method returns the **NSMetadataItem** object from the query's results array at the index specified by the **at** argument.

start()—This method initiates the query.

stop()—This method stops the query.

enableUpdates()—This method enables query updates.

disableUpdates()—This method disables query updates.

The **NSMetadataQuery** class also includes some notifications to report when new data is available. The following are the most frequently used.

NSMetadataQueryDidUpdate—This notification is posted when the results of the query changed.

NSMetadataQueryDidFinishGathering—This notification is posted when the query finishes retrieving all the information.

The results of a query are returned by the **results** property in the form of an array of **NSMetadataItem** objects. This is a simple class created to contain the arguments of a file. The class provides the following method to retrieve the values.

value(forAttribute: String)—This method returns the value of the file's attribute determined by the **forAtttribute** argument. The **NSMetadataItem** class defines a list of constants to represent the attributes. The constants available are **NSMetadataItem-FSNameKey** (file's name), **NSMetadataItemDisplayNameKey** (document's name), **NSMetadataItemURLKey** (file's URL), **NSMetadataItemPathKey** (file's path), **NSMetadataItemFSSizeKey** (file's size), **NSMetadataItemFSCreationDateKey** (date), and **NSMetadataItemFSContentChangeDateKey** (date the file was last modified).

Basic Single Document

The interface for an application capable of processing documents must include a way for the user to select the document and the tools to edit its content. For the following example, we will work with only one document to keep it simple. The initial scene includes a button connected to a second scene containing a Text View to edit the document's content.

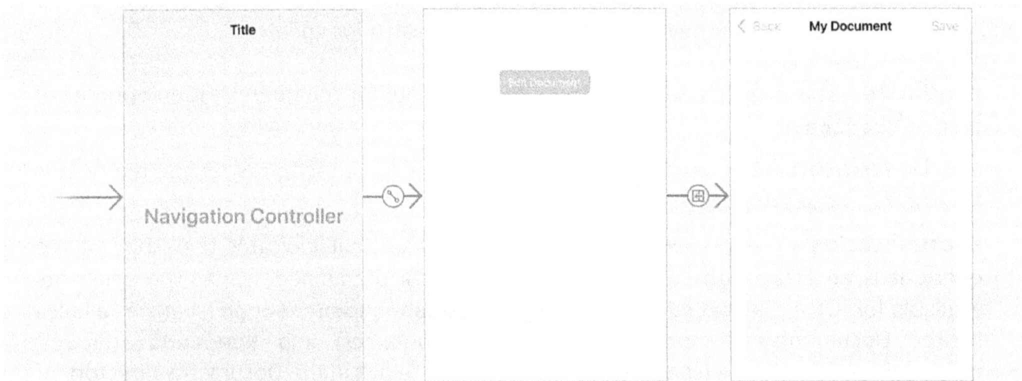

Figure 17-7: *Interface to edit a document*

Do It Yourself: Create a new project. Embed the scene in a Navigation Controller. Add a button to the scene. Add a second scene to the Storyboard. Connect the button with a Show segue to the second scene. Add a bar button with the title Save to the Navigation Bar of the second scene. Add a Text View to the second scene. Click on the app's settings option at the top of the Navigator Area and open the Signing & Capabilities panel. Click on the + button at the top-left corner to add a capability. Select the iCloud option and check the option iCloud Documents (Figure 17-5). Press the + button to add a container. Insert the app's bundle identifier for the container's name and press the OK button (you can find the bundle identifier on top of the iCloud section). If the name of the container appears in red, press the Refresh button to upload the information to Apple servers (Figure 17-5, number 2).

The first step to set up the system is to create the **UIDocument** subclass that is going to take care of our documents. As always, it is recommendable to create a separate file for the subclass. For this example, we call it **MyDocument**.

```
import UIKit

class MyDocument: UIDocument {
   var fileContent: Data?

   override func contents(forType typeName: String) throws -> Any {
      return fileContent ?? Data()
   }
   override func load(fromContents contents: Any, ofType typeName:
String?) throws {
      if let data = contents as? Data, !data.isEmpty {
         fileContent = data
      }
   }
}
```

Listing 17-3: *Creating the document*

The subclass needs at least three elements: a property to temporarily store the file's content, the **contents()** method to provide the data to store on file, and the **load()** method to get the data from the file. When the **UIDocument** object is asked to store or load the data in the file, it calls these methods and use the property as a proxy to move the data around.

The only purpose of our initial scene is to provide the button to open the editor, so all the code for our example goes in the view controller of the second scene. We called this view controller **EditionViewController**. In this class, we must get the file and create the **MyDocument** object to represent it. We begin by defining the properties and the initial statements.

```
import UIKit

class EditionViewController: UIViewController {
   @IBOutlet weak var mycontent: UITextView!
   var document: MyDocument!
   var metaData: NSMetadataQuery!

   override func viewDidLoad() {
      super.viewDidLoad()
      Task(priority: .high) {
         await receiveMetadata()
      }
      metaData = NSMetadataQuery()
      metaData.predicate = NSPredicate(format: "%K == %@",
NSMetadataItemFSNameKey, "myfile.dat")
      metaData.searchScopes = [NSMetadataQueryUbiquitousDocumentsScope]
      metaData.start()
   }
   func receiveMetadata() async {
      let center = NotificationCenter.default
      let name = NSNotification.Name.NSMetadataQueryDidFinishGathering
      for await notification in center.notifications(named: name, object:
nil) {
         await metadataReceived(notification: notification as
NSNotification)
      }
   }
}
```

Listing 17-4: *Loading the document*

Because of the logic of our application, we need a property to store the reference to the **MyDocument** object we are going to use to access the file, and a property to reference the **NSMetadataQuery** object we need to search for the file in iCloud. In Listing 17-4, we call these properties **document** and **metaData**.

The first thing we do in our view controller is to call an asynchronous method to listen to notifications, and then initialize the **NSMetadataQuery** object. This object checks whether the file exists and gets the metadata. The object's predicate is set to look for a specific file called myfile.dat, which is the only file managed by this application, and the query was configured to look into the iCloud's Documents directory with the **NSMetadataQueryUbiquitousDocumentsScope** variable because this is the recommended directory for our files. After the **NSMetadataQuery** object is set, we start the process with the **start()** method.

When the **NSMetadataQuery** object finishes gathering the data, it posts an **NSMetadataQueryDidFinishGathering** notification. In the **receiveMetadata()** method, we build a loop to get these notifications and call another asynchronous method to process the data received. The following is the implementation of this method.

```
func metadataReceived(notification: NSNotification) async {
   if metaData.resultCount > 0 {
      let file = metaData.result(at: 0) as! NSMetadataItem
      let fileURL = file.value(forAttribute: NSMetadataItemURLKey) as!
URL
      document = MyDocument(fileURL: fileURL)

      let success = await document.open()
      if success {
         if let data = self.document.fileContent {
            await MainActor.run {
               self.mycontent.text = String(data: data, encoding: .utf8)
            }
         }
      }
   } else {
      let content: String = await MainActor.run {
         let text = self.mycontent.text ?? ""
         return text
      }
      await initializeDocument(content: content)
   }
}
func initializeDocument(content: String) async {
   let manager = FileManager.default
   if let fileURL = manager.url(forUbiquityContainerIdentifier: nil) {
      let documentURL = fileURL.appendingPathComponent("Documents/
myfile.dat")

      if let data = content.data(using: .utf8) {
         document = MyDocument(fileURL: documentURL)
         document.fileContent = data
         if manager.fileExists(atPath: documentURL.path) {
            await document.save(to: documentURL, for: .forOverwriting)
         } else {
            await document.save(to: documentURL, for: .forCreating)
         }
      }
   }
}
```

Listing 17-5: *Processing query results*

The **receiveMetadata()** method of Listing 17-5 checks whether the query found a file or not by reading the **resultCount** property. If this property returns a value greater than 0, we get the first element with the **result()** method (we are only working with one file), get its URL with the **value()** method, and use it to create the **MyDocument** object. This tells the **MyDocument** object what is the file's URL, but we still need to call the **open()** method to open it. This method asks the instance of **MyDocument** to load the content of the file. The instance then executes its **load()** method and assigns the content to its **fileContent** property. The data is then converted into a string with the **String** initializer and assigned to the Text View to show it on the screen.

On the other hand, if the file does not exist, we call another asynchronous method to generate the URL and create a new file. In this case, we take advantage of a method provided by the **FileManager** class to get iCloud locations called **url(forUbiquityContainerIdentifier:)**. This method returns the URL of the location of our app's iCloud container. Because an app can have several containers, the method takes an argument to specify the container's identifier (declared as **nil** to use the container by default). The URL returned by this method is the root directory, so we append the Documents directory and the file's name to create the file. With the final URL, we create a **MyDocument** object, check if the file exists, and call the **save()** method to overwrite it or create it, respectively. Internally, the **MyDocument** instance calls its **contents()** method to get the content and create the file.

The codes added so far to the **EditionViewController** class load or create a file and show its content on the screen, but we still need to store the changes when the document is saved by the user. The following is the Action method for the Save button and some auxiliary methods to save and close the document.

```
@IBAction func saveDocument(_ sender: UIBarButtonItem) {
   Task(priority: .high) {
      await storeDocument()
      await closeDocument()
      await MainActor.run {
         closeScene()
      }
   }
}
func storeDocument() async {
   let content: String = await MainActor.run {
      let text = self.mycontent.text ?? ""
      return text
   }
   let manager = FileManager.default
   if let fileURL = manager.url(forUbiquityContainerIdentifier: nil) {
      let documentURL = fileURL.appendingPathComponent("Documents/
myfile.dat")
      if let data = content.data(using: .utf8) {
         document.fileContent = data
         await document.save(to: documentURL, for: .forOverwriting)
      }
   }
}
func closeDocument() async {
   await document.close()
}
func closeScene() {
   navigationController?.popViewController(animated: true)
}
override func viewDidDisappear(_ animated: Bool) {
   Task(priority: .high) {
      await closeDocument()
   }
}
```

Listing 17-6: *Saving the document*

The **saveDocument()** method gets the file's URL again, and then calls the **storeDocument()** method to store the document, the **closeDocument()** method to close it, and the **closeScene()** method to remove the scene. In the **storeDocument()** method, we get the text from the Text View, assign it to the **fileContent** property of the **MyDocument** object, and then call the **save()** method to save it on file. The operation assigned to the method is **forOverwriting** because at this point, we already know that there is a file available, and we just need to update its content. To make sure that the document is always closed, we call the **closeDocument()** method after the document is saved and when the scene is remove (the user pressed the Back button).

Do It Yourself: Create a new file with a subclass of **UIDocument** called **MyDocument** and complete the class with the code in Listing 17-3. Create a subclass of **UIViewController** called **EditionViewController** and assign it to the second scene. Connect the Text View with an Outlet called **mycontent**. Complete the class with the code in Listing 17-4 and the methods in Listing 17-5. Connect the Save button with an action called **saveDocument()** and complete the method and the class with the code in Listing 17-6. Run the application. Press the Edit Document button, insert some text in the Text View and press the Save button. Run the app on a different device and press the Edit Document button again. You should see the text inserted before on the screen. If you use the simulator, remember to select the Trigger iCloud Sync option from the Features menu to force the synchronization.

Basic Multiple Documents

The initial scene of our previous example offers a single button to open a document and display its content on the screen, however, most applications allow users to create and manage all the documents they need. An **NSMetadataQuery** object generates a live query. The query keeps looking for documents until we tell it to stop, and this is how we work with multiple documents in iCloud. To illustrate how the process works, we will replace the initial scene of our example with a Table View Controller, as shown next.

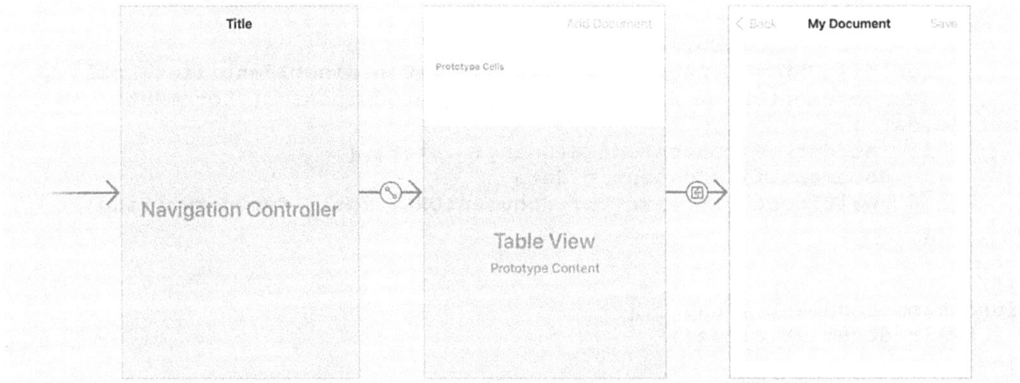

Figure 17-8: *Interface to work with multiple documents*

Do It Yourself: Delete the initial scene of the interface introduced in Figure 17-7. Add a Table View Controller in its place. Connect the Navigation Controller to the Table View Controller with a Root View Controller segue. Connect the Table View Controller to the second scene with a Show segue and give the segue the identifier "showDocument". Add a bar button to the Table View Controller with the title Add Document. Keep the design of the second scene the same as before.

The Table View Controller must create a query to get the documents available and then show their names on the table. We called this class **DocumentsViewController**. The following code defines the properties we need to manage the data and configure the query.

```
import UIKit

class DocumentsViewController: UITableViewController {
   var dataSource: UITableViewDiffableDataSource<Int, String>!
   var documentsList: [String] = []
   var metaData: NSMetadataQuery!

   override func viewDidLoad() {
      super.viewDidLoad()
      tableView.register(UITableViewCell.self, forCellReuseIdentifier:
"myCell")
      prepareDataSource()
      prepareSnapshot()
      receiveMetadata()

      metaData = NSMetadataQuery()
      metaData.searchScopes = [NSMetadataQueryUbiquitousDocumentsScope]
      metaData.start()
   }
   func receiveMetadata() {
      let center = NotificationCenter.default
      Task(priority: .high) {
         let name1 =
NSNotification.Name.NSMetadataQueryDidFinishGathering
         for await notification in center.notifications(named: name1,
object: nil) {
            updateList(notification: notification as NSNotification)
         }
      }
      Task(priority: .high) {
         let name2 = NSNotification.Name.NSMetadataQueryDidUpdate
         for await notification in center.notifications(named: name2,
object: nil) {
            updateList(notification: notification as NSNotification)
         }
      }
   }
}
```

Listing 17-7: *Initiating the query*

Because we are not only getting the list of documents available but also monitoring iCloud for changes, we check two notifications: the **NSMetadataQueryDidFinishGathering** notification to know when the process of gathering the initial data is over, and the **NSMetadataQueryDidUpdate** notification to know when updates become available. In the view controller of Listing 17-7, we call a method to perform two tasks, one for each notification. When a notification is received, we call the **updateList()** method to update the table with the current files.

```
func updateList(notification: NSNotification) {
   metaData.disableUpdates()
   for item in metaData.results as! [NSMetadataItem] {
      let name = item.value(forAttribute: NSMetadataItemFSNameKey) as!
String
      if documentsList.firstIndex(of: name) == nil {
         documentsList.append(name)
      }
   }
```

```
   documentsList.sort(by: { (value1, value2) in value1 < value2 })
   metaData.enableUpdates()

   Task(priority: .high) {
      await MainActor.run {
         prepareSnapshot()
      }
   }
}
```

Listing 17-8: *Keeping the table up to date*

Every time the query gets information, it posts notifications to let our code know what happened. To avoid conflicts with the data being processed and the new data received, we must pause the query until the process is over. This is done by the **disableUpdates()** and **enableUpdates()** methods of the **NSMetadataQuery** class. In the code of Listing 17-8, we call these methods at the beginning and the end to make sure that the **updateList()** method is not executed again until we get the new information and refresh the table.

Usually, an application like this gets the values it needs from the results returned by the query and stores them in a place the rest of the view controller can read, such as a property, a model, or a more complex storage system like Core Data. For this example, we defined a single property called **documentsList** to contain an array with the names of the documents. Because the **updateList()** method is called when the query finishes gathering the data and also when it finds changes, we need to check for duplicates before introducing a new name into this array. The code in Listing 17-8 creates a loop to go through every new value, gets the attribute for the name, and checks if it already exists in the array with the **firstIndex(of:)** method. Comparing the value returned by this method to **nil**, we make sure that there are no duplicates on the list. After the list is updated, the snapshot is recreated, and the new information is shown on the screen.

The methods to create the diffable data source and the snapshot don't require anything new, but for simplicity, we are going to use an integer to identify the sections (Integers conform to the **Hashable** protocol).

```
func prepareDataSource() {
   dataSource = UITableViewDiffableDataSource<Int, String>(tableView:
tableView) { tableView, indexPath, item in
      let cell = self.tableView.dequeueReusableCell(withIdentifier:
"myCell", for: indexPath)
      var config = cell.defaultContentConfiguration()
      config.text = item
      cell.contentConfiguration = config
      return cell
   }
}
func prepareSnapshot() {
   var snapshot = NSDiffableDataSourceSnapshot<Int, String>()
   snapshot.appendSections([0])
   snapshot.appendItems(documentsList)
   dataSource.apply(snapshot)
}
```

Listing 17-9: *Populating the table*

Every time a cell is selected, we must send the file's name to the second scene. For this purpose, we need to implement the **tableView(UITableView, didSelectRowAt:)** method to perform the segue and the **prepare()** method to send the value.

```
override func tableView(_ tableView: UITableView, didSelectRowAt
indexPath: IndexPath) {
   performSegue(withIdentifier: "showDocument", sender: self)
}
override func prepare(for segue: UIStoryboardSegue, sender: Any?) {
   if segue.identifier == "showDocument" {
      let controller = segue.destination as! EditionViewController
      if let path = tableView.indexPathForSelectedRow {
         if let item = dataSource.itemIdentifier(for: path) {
            controller.selected = item
         }
      }
   }
}
```

Listing 17-10: *Sending the name of the selected document to the second scene*

The **DocumentsViewController** class is not complete until we include the code necessary for the user to create new documents. To simplify this example, we decided to create an Alert View with a Text Field to insert the name of the new document. The following example defines the Action for the Add Document button required to create the new document and store it in iCloud.

```
@IBAction func addDocument(_ sender: UIBarButtonItem) {
   let alert = UIAlertController(title: "New File", message: nil,
preferredStyle: .alert)
   let cancel = UIAlertAction(title: "Cancel", style: .cancel, handler:
nil)
   alert.addAction(cancel)
   let action = UIAlertAction(title: "Create", style: .default, handler:
{ (action) in
      if let fields = alert.textFields, let file = fields.first?.text {
         if !file.isEmpty && self.documentsList.firstIndex(of: file) ==
nil {
            Task(priority: .high) {
               await self.createNewDocument(fileName: file)
               await MainActor.run {
                  self.prepareSnapshot()
               }
            }
         }
      }
   })
   alert.addAction(action)
   alert.addTextField(configurationHandler: { (textField) in
      textField.placeholder = "Insert name and extension"
   })
   present(alert, animated: true, completion: nil)
}
func createNewDocument(fileName: String) async {
   let manager = FileManager.default
   if let fileURL = manager.url(forUbiquityContainerIdentifier: nil) {
      let documentURL = fileURL.appendingPathComponent("Documents/\
(fileName)")
      let document = MyDocument(fileURL: documentURL)
      await document.save(to: documentURL, for: .forCreating)
   }
}
```

Listing 17-11: *Creating new documents*

The code in Listing 17-11 creates an Alert View with a Text Field and a button with the title Create. When this button is pressed, we get the text in the Text Field (the first in the array returned by the **textFields** property), confirm that the string is not empty, check if a file with that name already exists, and if not, call an asynchronous method to create the new document and save it.

Do It Yourself: Create a subclass of **UITableViewController** called **DocumentsViewController** and assign it to the Table View Controller added as the initial scene. Update the class with the code in Listing 17-7. Add the methods in Listings 17-8, 17-9, 17-10 and 17-11 to the class, and connect the Add Document button to the **addDocument()** Action.

In the **EditionViewController** class, we do not need to create a new document anymore, we just have to read the selected document, show it on the screen, and save the changes introduced by the user.

```
import UIKit

class EditionViewController: UIViewController {
   @IBOutlet weak var mycontent: UITextView!
   var document: MyDocument!
   var documentURL: URL!
   var selected: String!

   override func viewDidLoad() {
      super.viewDidLoad()
      Task(priority: .high) {
         await openDocument()
      }
   }
   func openDocument() async {
      let manager = FileManager.default
      if let fileURL = manager.url(forUbiquityContainerIdentifier: nil) {
         documentURL = fileURL.appendingPathComponent("Documents/\
(selected!)")
         document = MyDocument(fileURL: documentURL)
         let success = await document.open()
         if success {
            if let data = self.document.fileContent {
               await MainActor.run {
                  self.mycontent.text = String(data: data,
encoding: .utf8)
               }
            }
         }
      }
   }
   @IBAction func saveDocument(_ sender: UIBarButtonItem) {
      Task(priority: .high) {
         await storeDocument()
         await closeDocument()
         await MainActor.run {
            closeScene()
         }
      }
   }
   func storeDocument() async {
      let content: String = await MainActor.run {
         let text = self.mycontent.text ?? ""
         return text
      }
```

```
        if let data = content.data(using: .utf8) {
            document.fileContent = data
            await document.save(to: documentURL, for: .forOverwriting)
        }
    }
    func closeDocument() async {
        await document.close()
    }
    func closeScene() {
        navigationController?.popViewController(animated: true)
    }
    override func viewDidDisappear(_ animated: Bool) {
        super.viewDidDisappear(animated)
        Task(priority: .high) {
            await closeDocument()
        }
    }
}
```

Listing 17-12: *Reading and modifying a document*

When this scene is loaded, it opens the file with the name specified by the **selected** property, reads its content, creates the string from the data, and assigns it to the Text View to show the content on the screen. If the user taps the Save button, the process is inverted; we convert the text into data and save the file.

Do It Yourself: Update the **EditionViewController** class with the code in Listing 17-12. Run the application. Press the Add Document button. Insert the name and extension of the document you want to create, and press Create. Run the application on a different device. The document you just created should appear on the device's screen. Select the document, insert some text, and press the Save button. After a moment, the document should contain the same text on both devices.

IMPORTANT: In these examples, we have stored only a single string in the documents, but we can archive all the values we want, including custom classes, as we did in the examples in Chapter 15. When working with documents that manage content of several files, like text files and image files, instead of encoding all together in one file it is recommended to use a file wrapper. The wrapper is created with objects of the **NSFileWrapper** class. The topic goes beyond the scope of this book. For more information, visit our website and follow the links for this chapter.

Basic 17.4 CloudKit

CloudKit is a database system in iCloud. Using this system, we can store structured data online with different levels of accessibility. The system offers three types of databases to determine who has access to the information.

- **Private Database** to store data that is accessible only to the user.
- **Public Database** to store data that is accessible to every user running the app.
- **Shared Database** to store data the user wants to share with other users.

As we did with the rest of the iCloud services, the first step to use CloudKit is to activate it from the Signing & Capabilities panel.

iCloud

Services Key-value storage
iCloud Documents
CloudKit

Containers iCloud.ca.invid.AnotherTest
48S7G5U7J3.ca.invid.MicroTasks
iCloud.ca.invid.Books

Figure 17-9: CloudKit service

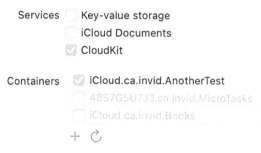

CloudKit requires a container to manage the databases. If the container is not automatically generated by Xcode when we activate the CloudKit service, we must create it ourselves, as we did before for the iCloud Documents service.

Because CloudKit uses Remote Notifications to report changes in the databases, when we activate CloudKit, Xcode automatically activates an additional service called *Push Notifications*.

Push Notifications

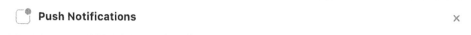

Figure 17-10: Push Notifications

Remote Notifications are like the Local Notifications introduced in Chapter 16, but instead of being posted by the app they are sent from a server to inform our app or the user that something changed or needs attention. The Remote Notifications posted by CloudKit are sent from Apple servers when something changes in the databases. Because this may happen not only when the user is working with the app but also when the app is in the background, to get these notifications, we must add the Background Mode capability and activate two services called *Background Fetch* and *Remote Notifications*.

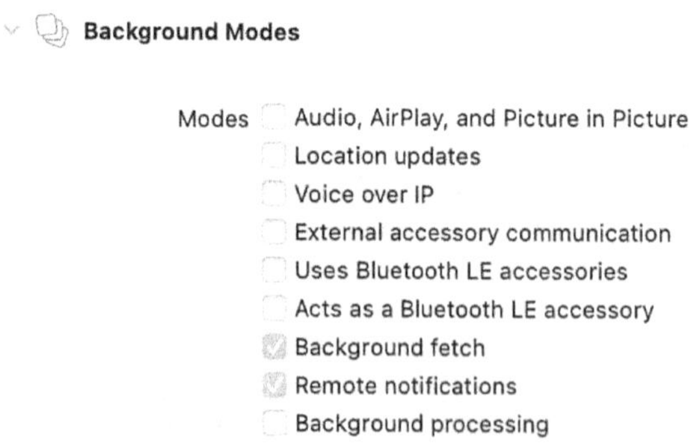

Figure 17-11: Background Mode

Do It Yourself: Create a project. Click on the settings option at the top of the Navigator Area and open the Signing & Capabilities panel. Click on the + button at the top-left corner to add a capability. Select the iCloud option and press return. Repeat the process to add the Background Modes capability. In the Background Modes section, check the options Background fetch and Remote Notifications (Figure 17-11). In the iCloud section, check the option CloudKit. Press the + button to add a container (see Figure 17-5, number 1), insert the app's bundle identifier as the container's name, and press the OK button (you can find the bundle identifier at the top of the panel). If the name of the container appears in red, press the Refresh button to upload the information to Apple servers (see Figure 17-5, number 2).

Basic Container

When CloudKit is activated from the Capabilities panel, Xcode creates entitlements to authorize the app to use the service and the container for the app's databases. The container is like a space in Apple's servers designated to our app. The CloudKit framework provides a class called **CKContainer** to access the container and the databases. Because an app may have more than one container, the class includes an initializer to get a reference to a specific container and also a type method to get a reference to the container by default.

CKContainer(identifier: String)—This initializer creates the **CKContainer** object that references the container identified with the string specified by the **identifier** argument. It is required when working with multiple containers or the container's name is different from the Bundle's identifier.

default()—This type method returns the **CKContainer** object that references the container by default (the container which name is equal to the Bundle's identifier).

Container objects provide the following properties to get access to each database.

privateCloudDatabase—This property returns a **CKDatabase** object with a reference to the user's Private database.

publicCloudDatabase—This property returns a **CKDatabase** object with a reference to the app's Public database.

sharedCloudDatabase—This property returns a **CKDatabase** object with a reference to the user's Shared database.

CloudKit databases have specific purposes and functionalities. The Private database is used when we want the user to be able to share private information among his or her own devices (only the user can access the information stored in this database), and the Public and Shared databases are used to share information between users. (The information stored in the Public database is accessible to all the users running our app and the information stored in the Shared database is accessible to the users with whom the user decides to share the data.)

The data is stored in the database as records and records are stored in zones. The Private and Public databases include a default zone, but the Private and Shared databases also work with custom zones (called Shared Zones in a Shared database), as illustrated below.

Figure 17-12: *Database configuration*

Basic Records

Once we have decided which database we are going to use, we must generate records to store the user's data. Records are objects that store information as key/value pairs. These objects are classified by types to determine the characteristics of the record. For example, if we want to store records that contain information about books, we can use the type "Books" (a type is analog to the Entities in Core Data). The framework provides the **CKRecord** class to create and manage records.

CKRecord(recordType: String, **recordID:** CKRecord.ID**)**—This initializer creates a **CKRecord** object of the type and with the identifier specified by the arguments. The **recordType** argument is the type's identifier, and the **recordID** argument is the record's identifier.

Records are identified with an object that includes a name and a reference to the zone the record belongs to (if a custom identifier is not specified, the record is stored with an identifier generated by CloudKit). To create and access the identifier and its values, the **CKRecord** class defines the **ID** class with the following initializers and properties.

CKRecord.ID(recordName: String**)**—This initializer creates a **CKRecord.ID** object to identify a record. The **recordName** argument is the name we want to give to the record.

CKRecord.ID(recordName: String, **zoneID:** CKRecordZone.ID**)**—This initializer creates a **CKRecord.ID** object to identify a record stored with the name and in the zone specified by the arguments. The **recordName** argument is the name we want to give to the record, and the **zoneID** argument is the identifier of the custom zone where we want to store the record.

recordName—This property returns a string with the name of the record.

zoneID—This property returns a **CKRecordZone.ID** object with the identifier of the zone to which the record belongs.

The **CKRecord** class offers properties to set or get the record's identifier and other attributes. The following are the most frequently used.

recordID—This property returns the **CKRecord.ID** object that identifies the record.

recordType—This property returns a string that determines the record's type.

recordChangeTag—This property returns a string with the tag assigned to the record (each record is assigned a tag by the server).

creationDate—This property returns a **Date** value with the date in which the record was created.

modificationDate—This property returns a **Date** value that indicates the last time the record was modified.

Because the values of a record are stored as key/value pairs, we can use square brackets to read and modify them (as we do with dictionaries), but the class also includes the following methods.

setObject(Value?, **forKey:** String**)**—This method sets or updates a value in the record. The fist argument is the value we want to store, and the **forKey** argument is the key we want to use to identify the value. The value must be of any of the following types: **NSString**, **NSNumber**, **NSData**, **NSDate**, **NSArray**, **CLLocation**, **CKAsset**, and **Reference**.

object(forKey: String**)**—This method returns the value associated with the key specified by the **forKey** argument. The value is returned as a generic **CKRecordValue** type that we must cast to the right data type.

Basic Zones

As illustrated in Figure 17-12, the Public database can only store records in the default zone, but the Private and Shared databases can include custom zones. In the case of the Private database, the custom zones are optional (although they are required for synchronization, as we will see later). Zones are like sections inside a database to separate records that are not related. For example, we may have an app that stores locations, like the names of cities and countries, but also allows the user to store a list of Christmas gifts. In cases like this, we can create a zone to store the records that include information about cities and countries and another zone to store the records that include information about the gifts. The CloudKit framework provides the **CKRecordZone** class to represent the zones. The class includes an initializer to create new custom zones and a type method to get a reference to the zone by default.

CKRecordZone(zoneName: String**)**—This initializer creates a **CKRecordZone** object to represent a zone with the name specified by the **zoneName** argument.

default()—This type method returns the **CKRecordZone** object that represents the zone by default in the database.

Basic Query

When we want to access data stored in CloudKit, we must download the records from the database and read their values. Records may be fetched from a database one by one using their identifiers or in a batch using a query. To define a query, the framework provides the **CKQuery** class. The class includes the following initializer and properties.

CKQuery(recordType: String, **predicate:** NSPredicate**)**—This initializer creates a **CKQuery** object to fetch multiple records from a database. The **recordType** argument specifies the type of records we want to fetch, and the **predicate** argument determines the matching criteria we want to use to select the records.

recordType—This property sets or returns a string that determines the type of records we want to fetch.

predicate—This property sets or returns an **NSPredicate** object that defines the matching criteria for the query.

sortDescriptors—This property sets or returns an array of **NSSortDescriptor** objects that determine the order of the records returned by the query.

Basic Operations

CloudKit is an online service and therefore any task may take time to process. For this reason, the CloudKit framework uses asynchronous operations to access the information on the servers. An operation must be created for every process we want to perform on a database, including storing, reading, and organizing records. These operations are like Swift asynchronous tasks but created from classes defined in the Foundation framework. The CloudKit framework includes its own subclasses of the Foundation classes to define operations. There is a base class called **CKDatabaseOperation**, and then several subclasses for every operation we need. Once an operation is defined, it must be added to the **CKDatabase** object that represents the database we want to modify. The **CKDatabase** class offers the following method for this purpose.

add(CKDatabaseOperation**)**—This method executes the operation specified by the argument. The argument is an object of a subclass of the **CKDatabaseOperation** class.

Although we can create single operations and assign them to the database, as we will see later, the **CKDatabase** class also offers convenient methods to generate and execute the most common. The following are the methods available to process records.

record(for: CKRecord.ID**)**—This asynchronous method fetches the record with the ID specified by the **for** argument. The method returns a **CKRecord** object with the record or an error if the record is not found.

save(CKRecord**)**—This asynchronous method stores a record in the database (if the record exists, it updates its values). The argument is a reference to the record we want to store.

deleteRecord(withID: CKRecord.ID**)**—This asynchronous method deletes from the database the record with the identifier specified by the **withID** argument.

The following are the methods provided by the **CKDatabase** class to process zones.

recordZone(for: CKRecordZone.ID**)**—This asynchronous method fetches the zone with the ID specified by the **for** argument. The method returns a **CKRecordZone** object representing the zone that was fetched or an error if the zone is not found.

allRecordZones()—This asynchronous method fetches all the zones available in the database. The method returns an array of **CKRecordZone** objects representing the zones that were fetched or an error if no zones are found.

save(CKRecordZone**)**—This asynchronous method creates a zone in the database. The argument is the object representing the zone we want to create.

deleteRecordZone(withID: CKRecordZone.ID**)**—This asynchronous method deletes from the database the zone with the ID specified by the **withID** argument.

To query multiple records, the **CKDatabase** class includes the following convenient method.

records(matching: CKQuery, **inZoneWith:** CKRecordZone.ID?, **desiredKeys:** [CKRecord.FieldKey]?, **resultsLimit:** Int**)**—This asynchronous method performs the query specified by the **matching** argument in the zone specified by the **inZoneWith** argument. The **desiredKeys** argument is an array of the values we want the records to include, and the **resultsLimit** argument determines the number of records we want to fetch (the value 0 returns all the records that match the query). The method returns a tuple with two values called **matchResults** and **queryCursor**. The **matchResults** value is an array of tuples with two values: the record identifier and a **Result** with the records and errors found. On the other hand, the **queryCursor** value is a cursor we can use to fetch more records that match this query.

records(continuingMatchFrom: Cursor, **desiredKeys:** Dictionary, **resultsLimit:** Int**)**—This asynchronous method creates an operation that fetches records starting from the cursor specified by the **continuingMatchFrom** argument. The cursor is an object that configures a query to retrieve the remaining results of a previous query. The **desiredKeys** argument is an array of the values we want the records to include, and the **resultsLimit** argument determines the number of records we want to fetch (the value 0 returns all the records that match the query). The method returns a tuple with two values called **matchResults** and **queryCursor**. The **matchResults** value is an array of tuples with two values: the record identifier and a **Result** enumeration value with the records and errors found. On the other hand, the **queryCursor** value is a cursor we can use to fetch more records that match this query.

Medium Batch Operations

Although the methods provided by the **CKDatabase** class are very convenient and easy to implement, they only perform one request at a time. The problem is that CloudKit servers have a limit on the number of operations we can perform per second (currently 40 requests per second per user are allowed), so if our application relies heavily on CloudKit, at one point some of the requests might be rejected. The solution is to create operations that perform multiple requests at once. The CloudKit framework defines three subclasses of the **CKDatabaseOperation** class for this purpose. The **CKModifySubscriptionsOperation** class creates an operation to add or modify subscriptions, the **CKModifyRecordZonesOperation** class is used to add or modify record zones, and the **CKModifyRecordsOperation** class is for adding and modifying records.

CKModifySubscriptionsOperation(subscriptionsToSave: [CKSubscription], **subscriptionIDsToDelete:** [CKSubscription.ID]**)**—This initializer returns an operation that adds or modifies one or more subscriptions. The **subscriptionsToSave** argument is an array with the subscriptions we want to add or modify, and the **subscriptionIDsToDelete** is an array with the identifiers of the subscriptions we want to delete from the server.

CKModifyRecordZonesOperation(recordZonesToSave: [CKRecordZone], **recordZoneIDsToDelete:** [CKRecordZone.ID]**)**—This initializer returns an operation that adds or modifies one or more record zones. The **recordZonesToSave** argument is an array with the record zones we want to add or modify, and the **recordZoneIDsToDelete** is an array with the identifiers of the record zones we want to delete from the server.

CKModifyRecordsOperation(recordsToSave: [CKRecord], **recordIDsTo-Delete:** [CKRecord.ID]**)**—This operation adds or modifies one or more records. The **recordsToSave** argument is an array with the records we want to add or modify, and the **recordIDsToDelete** argument is an array with the identifiers of the records we want to delete from the server.

The operations must be initialized and then added to the database with the **add()** method of the **CKDatabase** class. Each initializer offers the options to modify elements and remove them. If we only need to perform one task, the other can be declared as **nil**.

Basic References

Records of different types are usually related. For example, along with records of type Countries we may have records of type Cities to store information about the cities of each country. To create these relationships, records may include references. References are objects that store information about a connection between one record and another. They are created from the **Reference** class defined inside the **CKRecord** class. The following are the **Reference** initializers.

CKRecord.Reference(recordID: CKRecord.ID, **action:** CKRecord.Reference-Action**)**—This initializer creates a **Reference** object pointing to the record identified with the ID specified by the **recordID** argument. The **action** argument is an enumeration that determines what the database should do with the record when the record that is referencing is deleted. The possible values are **none** (nothing is done) and **deleteSelf** (when the record referenced by the reference is deleted, the record with the reference is deleted as well).

CKRecord.Reference(record: CKRecord, **action:** CKRecord.ReferenceAction**)** —This initializer creates a **Reference** object pointing to the record specified by the **record** argument. The **action** argument is an enumeration that determines what the database should do with the record when the record that is referencing is deleted. The possible values are **none** (nothing is done) and **deleteSelf** (when the record referenced by the reference is deleted, the record with the reference is deleted as well).

References in CloudKit are called *Back References* because they are assigned to the record that is the children of another record. Following our example, the reference should be assigned to the city and not the country, as illustrated next.

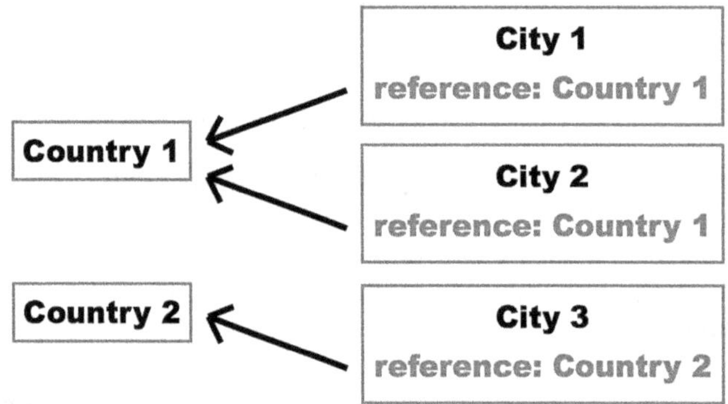

Figure 17-13: *Back references*

Basic CloudKit Dashboard

CloudKit creates a model of our app's database on its servers as records are added to the database. For example, if our app stores records of type "Books", the first time a record is created, CloudKit adds the type "Books" to the list of record types available for our app and creates fields to represent each of the record's values. This way, the system sets up the database's structure from the data we store during development, saving us the trouble of configuring the database beforehand (we do not have to create a model as we do with Core Data). But there are some configuration parameters that the system cannot determine and we need to set up ourselves. For this purpose, Apple provides the CloudKit dashboard. This is an online control panel that we can use to manage the CloudKit databases, add, update, or remove records, and configure the model.

The panel is available at **icloud.developer.apple.com/dashboard/** or by clicking on the CloudKit Dashboard button at the bottom of the iCloud section in the Signing & Capabilities panel. The dashboard's home page includes four buttons to access the tools available. We can configure the database, check how our database is performing, check user activity, and manage our account.

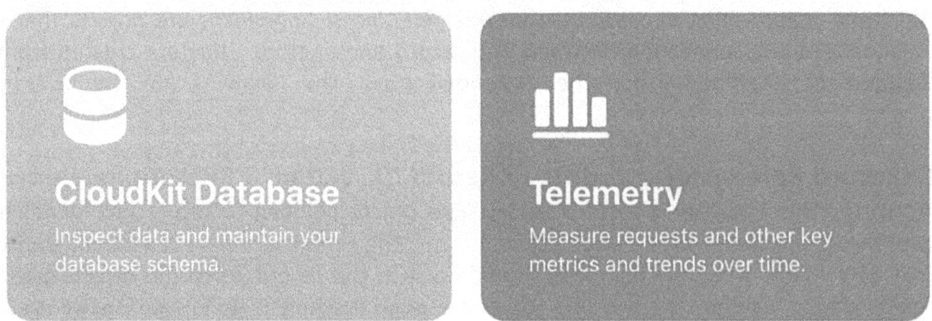

Figure 17-14: *Main menu*

If we click on the CloudKit Database button, a panel is loaded to edit the database. The panel includes an option at the top to select the container (Figure 17-15, number 1), a bar on the left to edit the data and the schema (the model), and a bar on the right to show and edit the values.

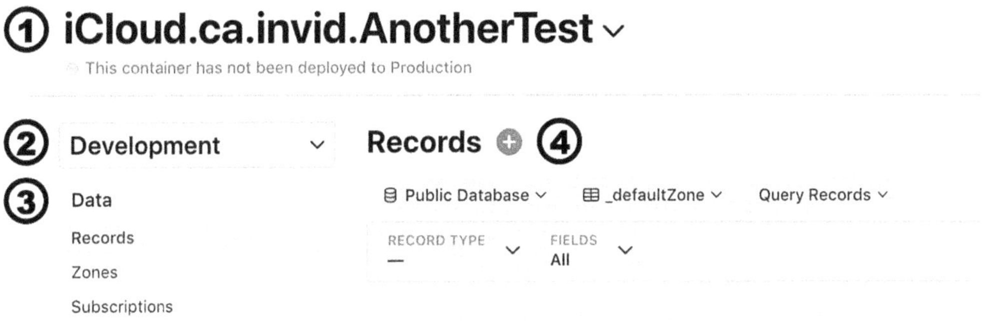

① iCloud.ca.invid.AnotherTest
This container has not been deployed to Production
② Development
③ Data
Records
Zones
Subscriptions
Records ④
Public Database
_defaultZone
Query Records
RECORD TYPE
—
FIELDS
All

Figure 17-15: *Database panel*

The bar on the left includes a button to select from two configurations: Development or Production (Figure 17-15, number 2). The Development option shows the configuration of the database we use during development. This is the database we use while we are developing our app. The Production option shows the configuration of the database that we are going to deliver with our app (the one that is going to be available to our users).

During development, we can store information in the database for testing. Below the configuration option is the Data section (Figure 17-16, number 3) where we can edit the data store by our application, including records, zones, and subscriptions. The panel also offer an option on the right to add records (Figure 17-15, number 4), and a list of values to edit.

As we already explained, the schema (the database model) is automatically created by CloudKit servers when we save records from our app during development. For instance, if our app creates a Books record, the server creates a record type called Books and adds it to the database model. In theory, this is enough to create the model, but in practice we always need to erase record types or values that we don't use anymore and add or modify others that the app may need later. For this purpose, the dashboard provides access to the schema on the left-side bar.

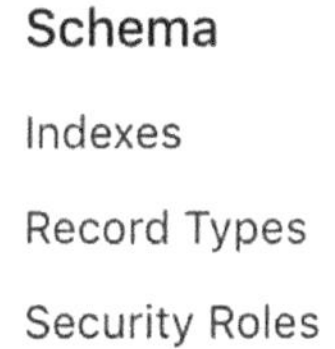

Figure 17-16: *Database schema*

From the Record Types option, we can add, modify, or delete record types (Entities) and their values (Attributes). The option to add a new record type is at the top of the panel (Figure 17-17, number 1), and the record types already created are listed below (Figure 17-17, number 2).

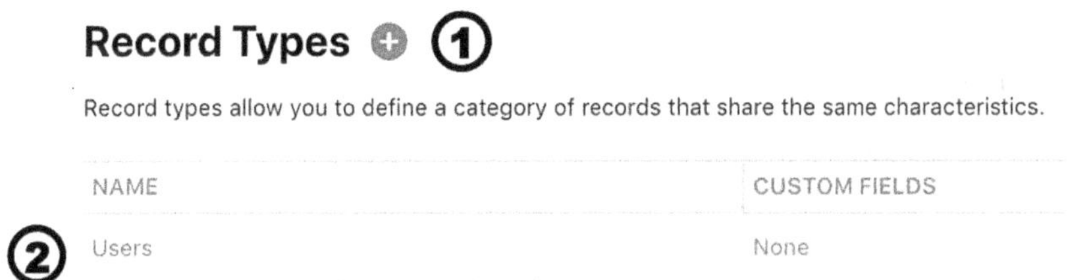

Figure 17-17: *Record types*

Basic Implementing CloudKit

To illustrate how to work with CloudKit databases, we are going to create a simple application that allows the user to save a list of locations. The interface presents two Table View Controllers inside a Navigation Controller to insert and list the names of countries and cities.

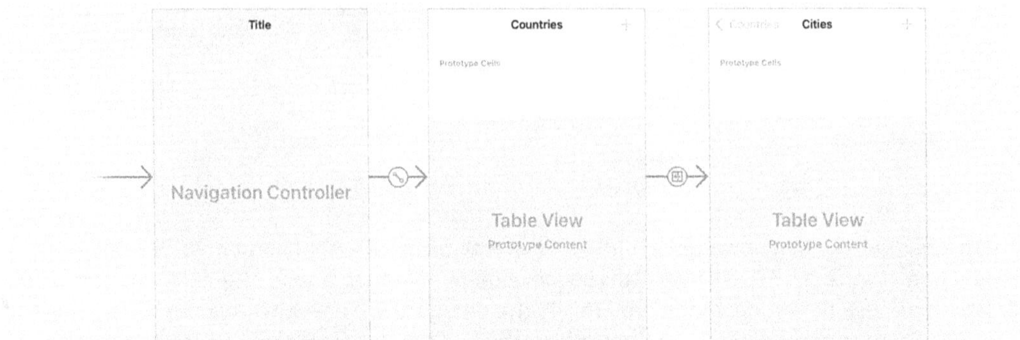

Figure 17-18: *Interface to work with CloudKit*

Do It Yourself: Create a new project. Remove the initial scene and add a Table View Controller. Embed the scene in a Navigation Controller. Assign the Navigation Controller as the initial scene from the Attributes Inspector panel. Add a second Table View Controller. Connect the first scene to the second scene with a Show segue. Give the segue the identifier "showCities". Add a bar button of type Add to both scenes. Assign the title Countries to the first scene and Cities to the second scene, as shown in Figure 17-18.

Although this time we are downloading the information from the CloudKit servers, we still need a model to temporarily store the records, manage the database, and define the diffable data sources. As always, we call it **`ApplicationData`**.

```
import UIKit
import CloudKit

enum Sections {
   case main
}
class ApplicationData {
   var database: CKDatabase!
   var selectedCountry: CKRecord.ID!

   var dataSourceCountries: UITableViewDiffableDataSource<Sections,
CKRecord.ID>!
   var listCountries: [CKRecord] = []

   var dataSourceCities: UITableViewDiffableDataSource<Sections,
CKRecord.ID>!
   var listCities: [CKRecord] = []

   init() {
      let container = CKContainer.default()
      database = container.privateCloudDatabase
   }
}
var AppData = ApplicationData()
```

Listing 17-13: *Creating the model*

Besides the properties to store the diffable data sources for the countries and cities and the arrays to store the records, we define two more properties: the **database** property to store a reference to the CloudKit's database and the **selectedCountry** property to know which country was selected by the user from the initial scene. The **database** property is initialized in the **init()** method with a reference to the Private Database (we use the private database because we only want the user to be able to share the data between his or her own devices).

In this example, we get a reference to the CloudKit container with the **default()** method, but if the name of the container is different from the app's bundle, we need to implement the **CKContainer** initializer with the right identifier, as in **let container = CKContainer (identifier: "iCloud.com.mydomain.containername")**.

Each Table View Controller defines its own diffable data source and provides the code to download the records from CloudKit servers and add more. The following is the view controller we need for the countries. We call it **CountriesViewController**.

```
import UIKit
import CloudKit

class CountriesViewController: UITableViewController {
   override func viewDidLoad() {
      super.viewDidLoad()
      tableView.register(UITableViewCell.self, forCellReuseIdentifier:
"countriesCell")

      Task(priority: .high) {
         await readCountries()
      }
      prepareDataSource()
   }
   func readCountries() async {
      let predicate = NSPredicate(format: "TRUEPREDICATE")
      let query = CKQuery(recordType: "Countries", predicate: predicate)
      do {
         let list = try await AppData.database.records(matching: query,
inZoneWith: nil, desiredKeys: nil, resultsLimit: 0)
         AppData.listCountries = []
         for (_, result) in list.matchResults {
            if let record = try? result.get() {
               AppData.listCountries.append(record)
            }
         }
         await MainActor.run {
            prepareSnapshot()
         }
      } catch {
         print("Error: \(error)")
      }
   }
   override func tableView(_ tableView: UITableView, didSelectRowAt
indexPath: IndexPath) {
      performSegue(withIdentifier: "showCities", sender: self)
   }
   override func prepare(for segue: UIStoryboardSegue, sender: Any?) {
      if segue.identifier == "showCities" {
         if let path = self.tableView.indexPathForSelectedRow {
            if let record =
AppData.dataSourceCountries.itemIdentifier(for: path) {
               AppData.selectedCountry = record
            }
         }
      }
   }
```

```
   func prepareDataSource() {
      AppData.dataSourceCountries =
UITableViewDiffableDataSource<Sections, CKRecord.ID>(tableView:
tableView) { tableView, indexPath, recordID in
         let cell = tableView.dequeueReusableCell(withIdentifier:
"countriesCell", for: indexPath)
         if let item = AppData.listCountries.first(where: { $0.recordID
== recordID }) {
            var config = cell.defaultContentConfiguration()
            config.text = item["name"] as? String
            cell.contentConfiguration = config
         }
         return cell
      }
   }
   func prepareSnapshot() {
      var snapshot = NSDiffableDataSourceSnapshot<Sections,
CKRecord.ID>()
      snapshot.appendSections([.main])
      snapshot.appendItems(AppData.listCountries.map({ $0.recordID }))
      AppData.dataSourceCountries.apply(snapshot)
   }
   @IBAction func addCountry(_ sender: UIBarButtonItem) {
      let alert = UIAlertController(title: "Insert Country", message:
nil, preferredStyle: .alert)
      let cancel = UIAlertAction(title: "Cancel", style: .cancel,
handler: nil)
      alert.addAction(cancel)
      let action = UIAlertAction(title: "Save", style: .default, handler:
{ (action) in
         if let fields = alert.textFields, let name = fields.first?.text{
            Task(priority: .high) {
               await self.insertCountry(name: name)
            }
         }
      })
      alert.addAction(action)
      alert.addTextField(configurationHandler: nil)
      present(alert, animated: true, completion: nil)
   }
   func insertCountry(name: String) async {
      let text = name.trimmingCharacters(in: .whitespaces)
      if !text.isEmpty {
         let id = CKRecord.ID(recordName: "idcountry-\(UUID())")
         let record = CKRecord(recordType: "Countries", recordID: id)
         record.setObject(text as NSString, forKey: "name")

         do {
            try await AppData.database.save(record)
            AppData.listCountries.append(record)

            await MainActor.run {
               prepareSnapshot()
            }
         } catch {
            print("Error: \(error)")
         }
      }
   }
}
```

Listing 17-14: *Reading and storing countries in the Private database*

This is a long view controller, but it is easy to understand if we read it part by part. We begin by creating a task that calls the **readCountries()** method to get the countries already stored in the CloudKit database. In this method, we define a predicate with the TRUEPREDICATE keyword and a query for records of type Countries. The type tells the server to only look for countries, and the TRUEPREDICATE keyword determines that the predicate will always return the value **true**, so we get back all the records available. If the query doesn't return any errors, we get the records from the **matchResults** value, add them to the **listCountries** array, and update the snapshot.

To let the user add a new country, we define an Action for the bar button called **addCountry()**. When the user presses the button, we create an Alert View with a Text Field inside. After the user inserts a name and presses the Save button, we call the **insertCountry()** method in the model with this value to add the record to the database. This method defines a record identifier with the string "idcountry" followed by a random value generated by the **UUID()** function (the identifiers must be unique). With this identifier, we create a **CKRecord** object of type Countries, add a property called *name* with the value received by the method, and finally save it in CloudKit servers with the **save()** method of the **CKDatabase** object. This method generates an operation that communicates with the servers asynchronously. If there is no error, we add the record to the **listCountries** property and update the snapshot (the record is added to the array and displayed on the Table View only if it is successfully added to the CloudKit database).

The rest of the code is the same used to configure Table Views before. Notice that the diffable data source and the snapshot work with the record identifiers. To read this value from the **CKRecord** objects we get from the server, we use the **recordID** property provided by the **CKRecord** class.

The **CountriesViewController** class includes the **tableView(UITableView, didSelectRowAt:)** method to perform the "showCities" segue when a country is selected by the user. We have also implemented the **prepare()** method to assign the record identifier of the selected country to the **selectedCountry** property in the model, so the view controller of the second scene can show the list of cities that belong to that country. We called this view controller **CitiesViewController**.

```
import UIKit
import CloudKit

class CitiesViewController: UITableViewController {
   override func viewDidLoad() {
      super.viewDidLoad()
      tableView.register(UITableViewCell.self, forCellReuseIdentifier:
"citiesCell")

      Task(priority: .high) {
         await readCities()
      }
      prepareDataSource()
   }
   func readCities() async {
      if AppData.selectedCountry != nil {
         let predicate = NSPredicate(format: "country = %@",
AppData.selectedCountry)
         let query = CKQuery(recordType: "Cities", predicate: predicate)
         do {
            let list = try await AppData.database.records(matching:
query, inZoneWith: nil, desiredKeys: nil, resultsLimit: 0)
            AppData.listCities = []
            for (_, result) in list.matchResults {
               if let record = try? result.get() {
                  AppData.listCities.append(record)
               }
            }
```

```
            await MainActor.run {
               prepareSnapshot()
            }
         } catch {
            print("Error: \(error)")
         }
      }
   }
   func prepareDataSource() {
      AppData.dataSourceCities = UITableViewDiffableDataSource<Sections,
CKRecord.ID>(tableView: tableView) { tableView, indexPath, recordID in
         let cell = tableView.dequeueReusableCell(withIdentifier:
"citiesCell", for: indexPath)
         if let item = AppData.listCities.first(where: { $0.recordID ==
recordID }) {
            var config = cell.defaultContentConfiguration()
            config.text = item["name"] as? String
            cell.contentConfiguration = config
         }
         return cell
      }
   }
   func prepareSnapshot() {
      var snapshot = NSDiffableDataSourceSnapshot<Sections,
CKRecord.ID>()
      snapshot.appendSections([.main])
      snapshot.appendItems(AppData.listCities.map({ $0.recordID }))
      AppData.dataSourceCities.apply(snapshot)
   }
   @IBAction func addCity(_ sender: UIBarButtonItem) {
      let alert = UIAlertController(title: "Insert City", message: nil,
preferredStyle: .alert)
      let cancel = UIAlertAction(title: "Cancel", style: .cancel,
handler: nil)
      alert.addAction(cancel)
      let action = UIAlertAction(title: "Save", style: .default, handler:
{ (action) in
         if let fields = alert.textFields, let name = fields.first?.text
{
            Task(priority: .high) {
               await self.insertCity(name: name)
            }
         }
      })
      alert.addAction(action)
      alert.addTextField(configurationHandler: nil)
      present(alert, animated: true, completion: nil)
   }
   func insertCity(name: String) async {
      let text = name.trimmingCharacters(in: .whitespaces)
      if !text.isEmpty {
         let id = CKRecord.ID(recordName: "idcity-\(UUID())")
         let record = CKRecord(recordType: "Cities", recordID: id)
         record.setObject(text as NSString, forKey: "name")
         let reference = CKRecord.Reference(recordID:
AppData.selectedCountry, action: .deleteSelf)
         record.setObject(reference, forKey: "country")

         do {
            try await AppData.database.save(record)
            AppData.listCities.append(record)

            await MainActor.run {
               prepareSnapshot()
            }
```

```
            } catch {
               print("Error: \(error)")
            }
         }
      }
   }
```

Listing 17-15: Storing cities in the Private database

This is also a long view controller, but it performs the same tasks as the view controller for the countries. The only difference is that instead of getting all the cities stored in the database, we only get the cities that belong to the country selected by the user. For this purpose, the predicate gets only the cities with a country key equal to the value of the **`selectedCountry`** property.

The value of this property is also required when the user inserts a new city. The record is created as before, but this time we create a **`Reference`** object with the country's identifier and an action of type **`deleteSelf`**, so when the record of the country is deleted, this record is deleted as well.

Do It Yourself: Create a Swift file called ApplicationData.swift for the code in Listing 17-13. Create a subclass of **`UITableViewController`** called **`CountriesViewController`**, assign it to the initial scene, and complete it with the code in Listing 17-14. Connect the bar button of this scene with the Action **`addCountry()`**. Create another subclass of **`UITableViewController`** called **`CitiesViewController`**, assign it to the second scene, and complete it with the code in Listing 17-15. Connect the bar button of this scene with the Action **`addCity()`**. Run the application and press the bar button to insert a country.

The application is ready. When the user inserts a new value, the code creates a record and uploads it to CloudKit servers, but if we stop and start the application again, the countries are not shown on the screen anymore. This is because we haven't defined the required indexes. CloudKit automatically creates indexes for every key we include in the records, except for the record's identifier. Therefore, when we query the Cities records by their country attribute to get the cities that belong to the selected country, CloudKit knows how to find and return those records, but when we try to retrieve the Countries records without a predicate, CloudKit tries to fetch them by the record identifiers and fails because there is no index associated to that attribute (called *recordName*). To create an index for this attribute, we need to go to the dashboard, click on the Indexes option in the Schema section, and click on the Countries record type to modify it.

When we click on a record, the panel shows the list of indexes available. By default, the Countries records contains three indexes for the name attribute, but no index for the record's identifier.

"Countries" Indexes

FIELD	INDEX TYPE	
name	QUERYABLE	⊖
name	SEARCHABLE	⊖
name	SORTABLE	⊖

***Figure 17-19:** Record's indexes*

To add an index, we must press the Add Basic Index button at the bottom of the list. The panel opens a form to configure a new index.

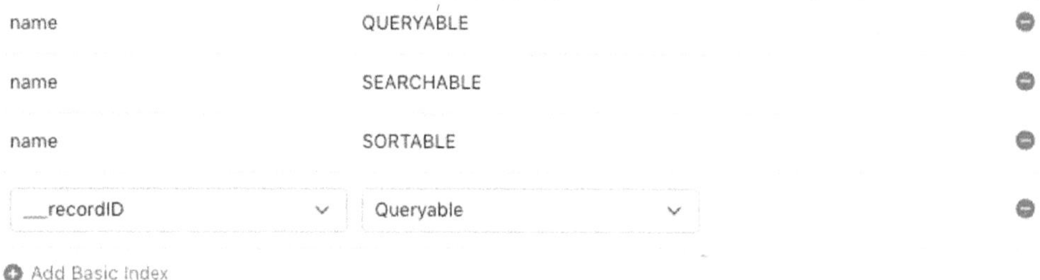

Figure 17-20: *Index configuration*

There are three types of indexes: Queryable (it can be included in a query), Searchable (it can be searched), and Sortable (it can be sorted). By default, all these indexes are associated to custom attributes but not to the record's identifier. When we query the database from the **`readCountries()`** method in the model, we do not specify any field in the predicate and therefore the system fetches the records by their identifiers, which is described in the database as recordID (recordName). For this reason, to retrieve the countries in our example, we must add a Queryable index to the recordID field of the Countries record type, as shown in figure 17-20.

Once we select the recordID field and the Queryable index, we can press the Save button to save the changes. Now, if we run the application again from Xcode, the records added to the database are shown on the table.

Basic Assets

Records may include files, and the files may contain anything from pictures to sound or even videos. To add a file to a record, we must create an asset with the **`CKAsset`** class. The class includes the following initializer.

CKAsset(fileURL: URL**)**—This initializer creates a **`CKAsset`** object with the content of the file in the location determined by the **fileURL** argument.

Assets are added to a record with a key, as any other value. For our example, we are going to store a picture in the Cities records and add a scene to show the picture when a city is selected.

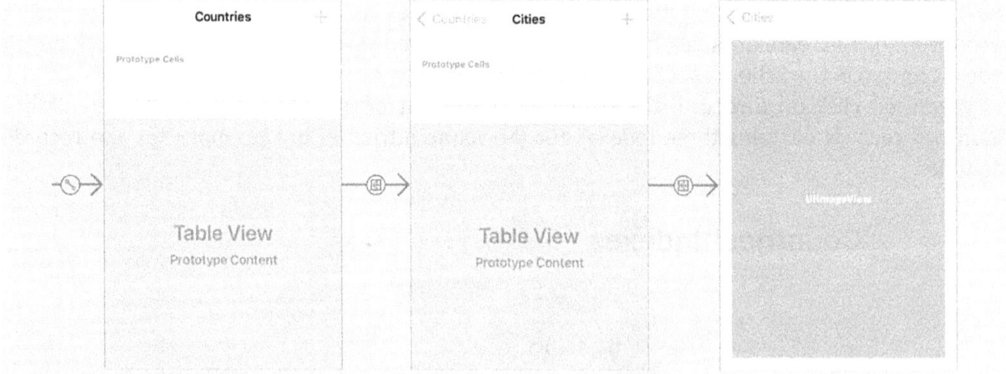

Figure 17-21: *Interface to store and show assets*

Do It Yourself: Add a new scene to the Storyboard. Connect the second scene to the new scene with a Show segue and give the segue the identifier "showPicture". Add an Image View to the new scene, as shown in Figure 17-21.

The following are the changes we have to introduce to the **`insertCity()`** method in the **`CitiesViewController`** class to get the URL of the image and assign the asset to the record.

```
func insertCity(name: String) async {
   let text = name.trimmingCharacters(in: .whitespaces)
   if !text.isEmpty {
      let id = CKRecord.ID(recordName: "idcity-\(UUID())")
      let record = CKRecord(recordType: "Cities", recordID: id)
      record.setObject(text as NSString, forKey: "name")
      let reference = CKRecord.Reference(recordID:
AppData.selectedCountry, action: .deleteSelf)
      record.setObject(reference, forKey: "country")

      let bundle = Bundle.main
      if let fileURL = bundle.url(forResource: "Toronto", withExtension:
"jpg") {
         let asset = CKAsset(fileURL: fileURL)
         record.setObject(asset, forKey: "picture")
      }
      do {
         try await AppData.database.save(record)
         AppData.listCities.append(record)
         await MainActor.run {
            prepareSnapshot()
         }
      } catch {
         print("Error: \(error)")
      }
   }
}
```

Listing 17-16: *Storing assets*

In addition to the previous information, the **insertCity()** method now gets the URL of an image included in the project called Toronto.jpg, creates a **CKAsset** object with it, and assigns the object to the record of every city with the "picture" key. Now, besides the name, a file with this image will be stored for every city inserted by the user.

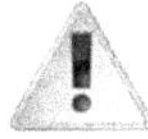

IMPORTANT: In this example, we load an image from the bundle. If you want to use an image from the Assets Catalog, you must temporarily store it in a file and then use the file's URL to create the asset. For an example, see the code in Listing 16-13. We will study how to get images from the Photo Library and take photos from the camera in Chapter 18.

To get the asset back, we have to implement the **prepare()** method in the **CitiesViewController** class to pass the record identifier of the selected city to the view controller in charge of showing the image to the user.

```
override func tableView(_ tableView: UITableView, didSelectRowAt
indexPath: IndexPath) {
   performSegue(withIdentifier: "showPicture", sender: self)
}
override func prepare(for segue: UIStoryboardSegue, sender: Any?) {
   if segue.identifier == "showPicture" {
      if let path = self.tableView.indexPathForSelectedRow {
         if let item = AppData.dataSourceCities.itemIdentifier(for:path){
            let controller = segue.destination as! PicturesViewController
            controller.selectedCity = item
         }
      }
   }
}
```

Listing 17-17: *Passing the selected city to the view controller*

Because the values stored in the **listCities** array are references to the records of every city, to show the image on the screen we just need to read the asset from the record, create an image with it, and assign it to the Image View. All this process is done by the view controller of the scene added in Figure 17-21. We call this view controller **PicturesViewController**.

```
import UIKit
import CloudKit

class PicturesViewController: UIViewController {
   @IBOutlet weak var cityPicture: UIImageView!
   var selectedCity: CKRecord.ID!

   override func viewDidLoad() {
      if let item = AppData.listCities.first(where: { $0.recordID ==
selectedCity }) {
         if let asset = item["picture"] as? CKAsset, let url =
asset.fileURL {
            self.cityPicture.image = UIImage(contentsOfFile: url.path)
         }
      }
   }
}
```

Listing 17-18: *Reading assets*

How to read the asset stored in the record depends on the type of content managed by the asset. In this example, we must use the asset's path to create a **UIImage** object and then assign this object to the **UIImageView** on the interface. As a result, every time the user selects a city, the asset is turned into an image and shown on the screen.

Do It Yourself: Update the **CitiesViewController** class with the methods in Listings 17-16 and 17-17. Download the Toronto.jpg picture from our website and add the file to your project. Create a subclass of the **UIViewController** class called **PicturesViewController** and assign it to the last scene. Complete the class with the code in Listing 17-18. Connect the Image View with the Outlet called **cityPicture**. Run the application, select a country, and add a new city. Select the city. You should see the Toronto.jpg image on the screen.

Basic Subscriptions

The previous example fetches the records available and shows them on the screen every time the scene is loaded. This means that records added to the database from another device will not be visible until the scene is loaded again. This is not the behavior expected by the users. When working with applications that store information online, users expect the information to be updated as soon as it becomes available. To provide this feature, CloudKit implements subscriptions.

Subscriptions are queries stored by our application in CloudKit servers. When a change occurs in the database, the query detects the modification and triggers the delivery of a Remote Notification from the iCloud servers to the copy of the app that registered the subscription.

Database subscriptions are created from the **CKDatabaseSubscription** class (a subclass of a more generic class called **CKSubscription**). The class includes the following initializer.

CKDatabaseSubscription(subscriptionID: String)—This initializer creates a **CKDatabaseSubscription** object that represents a subscription with the identifier specified by the **subscriptionID** argument.

Subscriptions are also added to CloudKit servers with an operation. The **CKDatabase** class offers convenient methods to create these operations.

save(CKSubscription**)**—This asynchronous method stores in the servers the subscription specified by the argument.

deleteSubscription(withID: String**)**—This asynchronous method removes from the server the subscription with the identifier specified by the **withID** argument.

After our app registers a subscription in the server, we must listen to Remote Notifications and download the changes. The first thing our application needs to do to be able to receive these notifications is to register with the iCloud servers. The **UIApplication** class offers the following method for this purpose.

registerForRemoteNotifications()—This method registers the app in the iCloud servers to receive Remote Notifications. A token is generated to identify each copy of our app, so the notifications are delivered to the right user.

To report to our application that a Remote Notification was received, the **UIApplication** object calls a method in the app's delegate. The following is the method defined by the **UIApplicationDelegate** class for this purpose.

application(UIApplication, **didReceiveRemoteNotification:** Dictionary, **fetchCompletionHandler:** Block**)**—This method is called by the application on its delegate when a Remote Notification is received. The **didReceiveRemoteNotification** argument is a dictionary with information about the notification, and the **fetchCompletionHandler** argument is a closure that we must execute after all the custom tasks are performed. The closure must be called with a value that describes the result of the operation. For this purpose, UIKit offers the **UIBackgroundFetchResult** enumeration with the values **newData** (new data was downloaded), **noData** (no data was downloaded), and **failed** (the app failed to download the data).

Setting up a subscription on CloudKit servers requires us to follow several steps. To begin with, we must call the **registerForRemoteNotifications()** method of the **UIApplication** object as soon as the application is launched to tell the system that we want to register the application to receive Remote Notifications from iCloud servers (Apple's Push Notification service). If the registration is successful, the system calls the delegate method introduced above every time a notification is received, so we need to implement that method as well, as shown next.

```
import UIKit
import CloudKit

@main
class AppDelegate: UIResponder, UIApplicationDelegate {
   func application(_ application: UIApplication,
didFinishLaunchingWithOptions launchOptions:
[UIApplication.LaunchOptionsKey: Any]?) -> Bool {
      let userSettings = UserDefaults.standard
      let values = ["subscriptionSaved": false, "zoneCreated": false]
      userSettings.register(defaults: values)

      application.registerForRemoteNotifications()
      Task(priority: .background) {
         await AppData.configureDatabase()
      }
      return true
   }
```

```
    func application(_ application: UIApplication,
didReceiveRemoteNotification userInfo: [AnyHashable : Any],
fetchCompletionHandler completionHandler: @escaping
(UIBackgroundFetchResult) -> Void) {
        let notification = CKNotification(fromRemoteNotificationDictionary:
userInfo) as? CKDatabaseNotification
        guard notification != nil else {
            completionHandler(.failed)
            return
        }
        AppData.checkUpdates(finishClosure: { (result) in
            completionHandler(result)
        })
    }
    func application(_ application: UIApplication,
configurationForConnecting connectingSceneSession: UISceneSession,
options: UIScene.ConnectionOptions) -> UISceneConfiguration {
        return UISceneConfiguration(name: "Default Configuration",
sessionRole: connectingSceneSession.role)
    }
}
```

Listing 17-19: *Processing Remote Notifications*

Subscriptions only report changes in customs zones. Therefore, if we want to receive notifications, besides creating the subscription we also must create a record zone and store all our records in it. This is the reason why, the first thing we do when the application is launched, is to store two Boolean values in the User Defaults database called "subscriptionSaved" and "zoneCreated". These values will be used later to check whether we have already created the subscription and the custom zone. After these values are set, we call the **registerForRemoteNotifications()** method on the **UIApplication** object to register the application with iCloud servers and an asynchronous method in our model called **configureDatabase()** that we are going to define later to create the subscription and the custom zone.

The **registerForRemoteNotifications()** method prepares the application to receive notifications, but the notifications are processed by the delegate method. The first thing we do in this method is to check whether the notification received is a notification sent by a CloudKit server. For this purpose, the CloudKit framework includes the **CKNotification** class with properties we can use to process the dictionary received by the method. The class includes the following initializer.

CKNotification(fromRemoteNotificationDictionary: Dictionary)—This initializer creates a **CKNotification** object from the information included in the notification (the value of the **userInfo** parameter in the delegate method).

Because CloudKit servers can send other types of notifications, we also check whether the notification received is of type **CKDatabaseNotification**. In case of success, we proceed to download the data.

Before going through the process of downloading the new information from CloudKit servers, we must consider that the system requires us to report the result of the operation. Notifications may be received when the application is closed or in the background. If this happens, the system launches our application and puts it in the background to allow it to contact the servers and process the information. But because this process consumes resources, the system needs to know when the operation is over and therefore it requires us to report it by calling the closure received by the **completionHandler** parameter with a value of the **UIBackgroundFetchResult** enumeration that determines what happened (**newData** if we downloaded new data, **noData** if there was nothing to download, and **failed** if the process failed). By calling the closure, we tell the system that the process is over, but because the operations are performed asynchronously, we can't do it until they are finished. That's the reason why, in the example of Listing 17-19, we execute a method in the model called **checkUpdates()** that takes a closure. This method downloads the new information and executes the closure when finished. This way, we can call the **completionHandler** closure after all the operations were performed.

IMPORTANT: The **UIApplicationDelegate** class also defines an asynchronous method to receive remote notifications called **application (UIApplication, didReceiveRemoteNotification: Dictionary)**. In this example, we are using concurrent operations, but if you need to perform asynchronous operations, you may implement this method instead.

The next step is to implement the methods that are going to contact the CloudKit servers and process the information. In the application's delegate, we called two methods of our **ApplicationData** class: the **configureDatabase()** method to create the subscription and the zone, and the **checkUpdates()** method to download and process the information. The following is our implementation of the **configureDatabase()** method. (This example assumes that we are working with the model introduced in Listing 17-13.)

```
func configureDatabase() async {
   let userSettings = UserDefaults.standard
   if !userSettings.bool(forKey: "subscriptionSaved") {
      let newSubscription = CKDatabaseSubscription(subscriptionID:
"updatesDatabase")
      let info = CKSubscription.NotificationInfo()
      info.shouldSendContentAvailable = true
      newSubscription.notificationInfo = info

      do {
         try await database.save(newSubscription)
         userSettings.set(true, forKey: "subscriptionSaved")
      } catch {
         print("Error: \(error)")
      }
   }
   if !userSettings.bool(forKey: "zoneCreated") {
      let newZone = CKRecordZone(zoneName: "listPlaces")
      do {
         try await database.save(newZone)
         userSettings.set(true, forKey: "zoneCreated")
      } catch {
         print("Error: \(error)")
      }
   }
}
```

Listing 17-20: *Configuring the database*

The first thing we do in the **configureDatabase()** method is to check the subscriptionSaved value in the User Defaults to know if the subscription was already created. If not, we use the **CKDatabaseSubscription** initializer to create a subscription with the name updatesDatabase and then define the **notificationInfo** property to configure the notifications that are going to be sent by the server. For this purpose, the framework defines the **CKNotificationInfo** class. This class includes multiple properties to configure Remote Notifications for CloudKit, but database subscriptions only require us to set the **shouldSendContentAvailable** property to **true**. After this, the subscription is saved on the server with the **save()** method of the **CKDatabase** object and the subscriptionSaved value is changed to **true** if the operation is successful.

The next step is to create the custom zone. Again, we check the Boolean value stored in User Defaults to know if there is a custom zone already on the server, and if not, we create one called listPlaces to store our records. If the operation is successful, we assign the value **`true`** to the zoneCreated value, so the app knows that the zone was already created.

Next, we must define the **`checkUpdates()`** method to download and process the changes in the database. But first, we need to think about how we are going to organize our code. Every process executed in CloudKit servers is performed by asynchronous operations. This means that we need to think about the order in which the operations are executed. For some, the order doesn't matter, but for others it is crucial. For instance, we cannot store records in a zone before the zone is created. As we have seen in Chapter 14, we can use Swift concurrency to control the order in which operations are performed, but CloudKit operations are already concurrent. Therefore, depending on the requirements of our application, it may be better to implement closures to execute code only after an operation is over, and this is the approach we take in this example. The procedure is as follows. Every time we call the **`checkUpdates()`** method to download the data, we send a closure to the method with the code we want to execute once the operation is over. This way, we make sure that the operations are over before doing anything else.

```
func checkUpdates(finishClosure: @escaping (UIBackgroundFetchResult) ->
Void) {
   Task(priority: .background) {
      await configureDatabase()
      downloadUpdates(finishClosure: finishClosure)
   }
}
```

Listing 17-21: *Initiating the process to get the updates from the server*

The **`checkUpdates()`** method calls the **`configureDatabase()`** method again to make sure that the database is configured properly.

To simplify the code, we moved the statements to an additional method called **`downloadUpdates()`**. So after we confirm that the zone was created, we call this method with a reference to the closure received by the **`checkUpdates()`** method. (We pass the closure from one method to another and execute it after all the operations are over, as we will see next.)

IMPORTANT: Passing closures from one method to another is a way to control the order in which the code is executed when we use concurrent operations. We chose this programming pattern for this example because it simplifies the code, but as we mentioned before, in some cases may be better to implement Swift concurrency. For more information, see Chapter 14.

Before implementing the **`downloadUpdates()`** method and process the changes in the database, we ought to study the operations provided by the CloudKit framework for this purpose. The operation to fetch the list of changes available in the database is created from a subclass of the **`CKDatabaseOperation`** class called **`CKFetchDatabaseChangesOperation`**. This class includes the following initializer.

CKFetchDatabaseChangesOperation(previousServerChangeToken: CKServerChangeToken?)—This initializer creates an operation to fetch changes from a database. The argument is a token that determines which changes were already fetched. If we specify a token, only the changes that occurred after the token was created are fetched.

The class also includes properties to define completion handlers for every step of the process.

recordZoneWithIDChangedBlock—This property sets a closure that is executed to report which zones present changes. The closure receives a value of type **`CKRecordZone.ID`** with the identifier of the zone that changed.

changeTokenUpdatedBlock—This property sets a closure that is executed to provide the last database token. The closure receives an object of type **`CKServerChangeToken`** with the current token that we can store to send to subsequent operations.

fetchDatabaseChangesResultBlock—This property sets a closure that is executed when the operation is over. The closure receives a **`Result`** enumeration to report the success or failure of the operation. The enumeration value includes a tuple and a **`CKError`** value to report errors. The tuple includes two values: a **`CKServerChangeToken`** object with the last token and a Boolean value that indicates if there are more changes available.

After the completion of this operation, we must perform another operation to download the changes. For this purpose, the framework includes the **`CKFetchRecordZoneChanges-Operation`** class with the following initializer.

CKFetchRecordZoneChangesOperation(recordZoneIDs: [CKRecordZone.ID], **configurationsByRecordZoneID:** Dictionary**)**—This initializer creates an operation to download changes from a database. The **recordZoneIDs** argument is an array with the IDs of all the zones that present changes, and the **configurationsByRecordZoneID** argument is a dictionary with configuration values for each zone. The dictionary takes **`CKRecordZone.ID`** objects as keys and options determined by an object of the **`ZoneConfiguration`** class included in the **`CKFetchRecordZoneChangesOperation`** class. The class includes three properties to define the options: **`desiredKeys`** (array of strings with the keys we want to retrieve), **`previousServerChangeToken`** (**`CKServerChangeToken`** object with the current token), and **`resultsLimit`** (integer that determines the number of records to retrieve).

The **`CKFetchRecordZoneChangesOperation`** class also includes properties to define completion handlers for every step of the process.

recordWasChangedBlock—This property sets a closure that is executed when a new or updated record is downloaded. The closure receives two values: a **`CKRecord.ID`** with the identifier of the record that changed, and a **`Result`** enumeration value to report the success or failure of the operation. The enumeration includes two values: a **`CKRecord`** object with the record that changed and a **`CKError`** value to report errors.

recordWithIDWasDeletedBlock—This property sets a closure that is executed when the operation finds a deleted record. The closure receives two values: a **`CKRecord.ID`** object with the identifier of the record that was deleted, and a string with the record's type.

recordZoneChangeTokensUpdatedBlock—This property sets a closure that is executed when the change token for the zone is updated. The closure receives three values: a **`CKRecordZone.ID`** with the identifier of the zone associated to the token, a **`CKServerChangeToken`** object with the current token, and a **`Data`** structure with the last token sent by the app to the server.

recordZoneFetchResultBlock—This property sets a closure that is executed when the operation finishes downloading the changes of a zone. The closure receives two values: a **`CKRecordZone.ID`** with the zone's identifier, and a **`Result`** enumeration value to report the success or failure of the operation. The enumeration includes two values: a tuple and a **`CKError`** value to report errors. In turn, the tuple includes three values: a **`CKServerChangeToken`** object with the current token, a **`Data`** structure with the last token sent to the server, and a Boolean value that indicates if there are more changes available.

fetchRecordZoneChangesResultBlock—This property sets a closure that is executed after the operation is over. The closure receives a **Result** enumeration value to report errors.

CloudKit servers use tokens to know which changes were already sent to every copy of the app, so the information is not downloaded twice from the same device. If a device stores or modifies a record, the server generates a new token, so next time a device accesses the servers only the changes introduced after the last token will be downloaded, as shown in Figure 17-22.

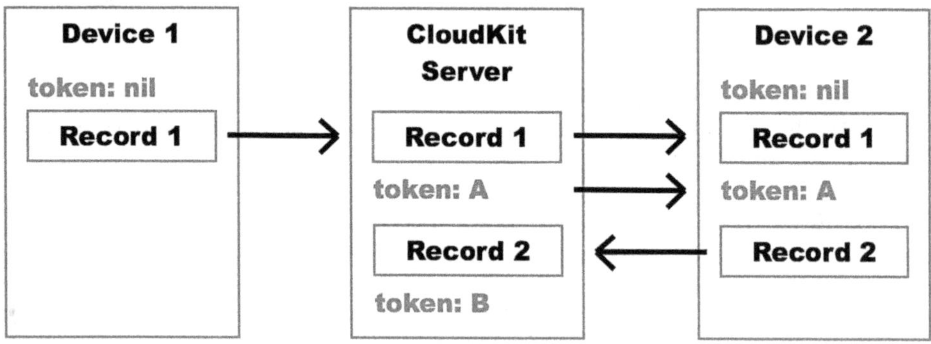

Figure 17-22: *Tokens*

In the process depicted in Figure 17-22, the app in Device 1 stores a new record in the server (Record 1). To report the changes, the server generates a new token (A). When the app in Device 2 connects to the server, the server detects that this device does not have the latest token, so it returns Record 1 and the current token (A) to update the state in this device. If later the user decides to create a new record from Device 2 (Record 2), a new token will be created (B). The next time Device 1 connects to the server, it will find that its token is different from the server's token, so it will download the modifications inserted after token A.

Tokens are great because they allow us to only get the latest changes, but this process is not automatic, we are responsible of storing the current tokens and preserve the state of our app. The server creates a token for the database and a token for each of the custom zones. For our example, we need two tokens: one to keep track of the changes in the database and another for the custom zone created by the **configureDatabase()** method. To work with these values, we are going to use two variables **changeToken** for the database token and **fetchChangeToken** for the token of our custom zone, and we are going to store them permanently in User Settings for future reference. All this process is performed by the **downloadUpdates()** method, as shown next.

```
func downloadUpdates(finishClosure: @escaping (UIBackgroundFetchResult)
-> Void) {
   var changeToken: CKServerChangeToken!
   var changeZoneToken: CKServerChangeToken!

   let userSettings = UserDefaults.standard
   if let data = userSettings.value(forKey: "changeToken") as? Data {
      if let token = try? NSKeyedUnarchiver.unarchivedObject(ofClass:
CKServerChangeToken.self, from: data) {
         changeToken = token
      }
   }
```

```
   if let data = userSettings.value(forKey: "changeZoneToken") as? Data {
      if let token = try? NSKeyedUnarchiver.unarchivedObject(ofClass:
CKServerChangeToken.self, from: data) {
         changeZoneToken = token
      }
   }
   var zonesIDs: [CKRecordZone.ID] = []
   let operation =
CKFetchDatabaseChangesOperation(previousServerChangeToken: changeToken)
   operation.recordZoneWithIDChangedBlock = { zoneID in
      zonesIDs.append(zoneID)
   }
   operation.changeTokenUpdatedBlock = { token in
      changeToken = token
   }
   operation.fetchDatabaseChangesResultBlock = { result in
      guard let values = try? result.get() else {
         finishClosure(UIBackgroundFetchResult.failed)
         return
      }
      if zonesIDs.isEmpty {
         finishClosure(UIBackgroundFetchResult.noData)
      } else {
         changeToken = values.serverChangeToken

         let configuration =
CKFetchRecordZoneChangesOperation.ZoneConfiguration()
         configuration.previousServerChangeToken = changeZoneToken
         let fetchOperation =
CKFetchRecordZoneChangesOperation(recordZoneIDs: zonesIDs,
configurationsByRecordZoneID: [zonesIDs[0]: configuration])

         fetchOperation.recordWasChangedBlock = { recordID, result in
            guard let record = try? result.get() else {
               print("Error")
               return
            }
            if record.recordType == "Countries" {
               let index = self.listCountries.firstIndex(where: { item in
                  return item.recordID == recordID
               })
               if index != nil {
                  self.listCountries[index!] = record
               } else {
                  self.listCountries.append(record)
               }
            } else if record.recordType == "Cities" {
               if let country = record["country"] as? CKRecord.Reference{
                  if country.recordID == self.selectedCountry {
                     let index = self.listCities.firstIndex(where: { item
in
                        return item.recordID == record.recordID
                     })
                     if index != nil {
                        self.listCities[index!] = record
                     } else {
                        self.listCities.append(record)
                     }
                  }
               }
            }
         }
         fetchOperation.recordWithIDWasDeletedBlock = { recordID,
recordType in
            if recordType == "Countries" {
```

```
            let index = self.listCountries.firstIndex(where: { item in
               return item.recordID == recordID
            })
            if index != nil {
               self.listCountries.remove(at: index!)
            }
         } else if recordType == "Cities" {
            let index = self.listCities.firstIndex(where: { item in
               return item.recordID == recordID
            })
            if index != nil {
               self.listCities.remove(at: index!)
            }
         }
      }
      fetchOperation.recordZoneChangeTokensUpdatedBlock = { zoneID,
token, data in
         changeZoneToken = token
      }
      fetchOperation.recordZoneFetchResultBlock = { zoneID, result in
         guard let values = try? result.get() else {
            print("Error")
            return
         }
         changeZoneToken = values.serverChangeToken
      }
      fetchOperation.fetchRecordZoneChangesResultBlock = { result in
         switch result {
            case .failure(_):
               finishClosure(UIBackgroundFetchResult.failed)
               return
            default:
               break
         }
         if changeToken != nil {
            if let data = try?
NSKeyedArchiver.archivedData(withRootObject: changeToken!,
requiringSecureCoding: false) {
               userSettings.set(data, forKey: "changeToken")
            }
         }
         if changeZoneToken != nil {
            if let data = try?
NSKeyedArchiver.archivedData(withRootObject: changeZoneToken!,
requiringSecureCoding: false) {
               userSettings.set(data, forKey: "changeZoneToken")
            }
         }
         Task(priority: .background) {
            await self.updateInterface()
         }
         finishClosure(UIBackgroundFetchResult.newData)
      }
      self.database.add(fetchOperation)
   }
}
database.add(operation)
}
func updateInterface() async {
   await MainActor.run {
      var snapshotCountries = NSDiffableDataSourceSnapshot<Sections,
CKRecord.ID>()
      snapshotCountries.appendSections([.main])
      snapshotCountries.appendItems(listCountries.map({ $0.recordID }))
      dataSourceCountries?.apply(snapshotCountries)
```

```
      var snapshotCities = NSDiffableDataSourceSnapshot<Sections,
CKRecord.ID>()
      snapshotCities.appendSections([.main])
      snapshotCities.appendItems(listCities.map({ $0.recordID }))
      dataSourceCities?.apply(snapshotCities)
   }
}
```

Listing 17-22: *Getting the updates from the server*

This is a very long method that we need to study piece by piece. As mentioned before, we start by defining the properties we are going to use to store the tokens (one for the database and another for the custom zone). Next, we check if there are tokens already stored in the User Defaults database. Because the tokens are instances of the **CKServerChangeToken** class, we can't store their values directly in User Defaults, we must first convert them into **Data** structures. This is the reason why, when we read the values, we cast them as **Data** with the **as?** operator and then unarchive them with the **unarchivedObject()** method of the **NSKeyedUnarchiver** class (see Chapter 15).

Next, we configure the operations necessary to get the updates from the server. We must perform two operations on the database, one to download the list of changes available and another to download the actual changes and show them to the user. The operations are performed and then the results are reported to the closures assigned to their properties.

The first operation we need to perform is the **CKFetchDatabaseChangesOperation** operation. The initializer requires the previous token to get only the changes that are not available on the device, so we pass the value of the **changeToken** property. Next, we define the closures for each of its properties. This operation includes three properties, one to report the zones that changed, one to report the creation of a new database token, and another to report the conclusion of the operation. The first property defined in our example is **recordZoneWithIDChangedBlock**. The closure assigned to this property is executed every time the system finds a zone whose content has changed. In this closure, we add the zone ID to an array to keep a reference of each zone that changed.

Something similar happens with the closure assigned next to the **changeToken-UpdatedBlock** property. This closure is executed every time the system decides to perform the operation again to download the changes in separate processes. To make sure that we only receive the changes that we did not process yet, we use this closure to update the **changeToken** property with the current token.

The last property we have defined for this operation is **fetchDatabaseChanges-ResultBlock**. The closure assigned to this property is executed to let the app know that the operation is over, and this is how we know that we have all the information we need to begin downloading the changes with the second operation. This closure receives a **Result** enumeration value, which includes a tuple with two values and an **Error** value to report errors. If no values are returned, we execute the **finishClosure** closure with the value **failed** and the operation is over. On the other hand, if there are values available, we check if the **zoneIDs** array contains any zone ID. If it is empty, it means that there are no changes available and therefore we execute the **finishClosure** closure with the value **noData**, but if the array is not empty, we store the last token in the **changeToken** variable and configure the **CKFetchRecordZoneChangesOperation** operation to download the changes.

The **CKFetchRecordZoneChangesOperation** operation is performed over the zones that changed, so we must initialize it with the array of zone identifiers generated by the previous operation. The initializer also requires a dictionary with the zone identifiers as keys and **ZoneConfiguration** objects that include the previous token for each zone as values. Because in this example we only work with one zone, we read the first element of the **zonesIDs** array to get the identifier of our custom zone and provide a **ZoneConfiguration** object with the current token for the zone stored in the **changeZoneToken** property.

This operation works like the previous one. The changes are fetched, and the results are reported to the closures assigned to its properties. The first property declared in Listing 17-22 is

recordWasChangedBlock. The closure assigned to this property is called every time a new or updated record is received. Here, we check if the record is of type Countries or Cities and store it in the corresponding array. When the record is of type Countries, we use the **firstIndex(where:)** method to look for duplicates. If the record already exists in the array, we update its values, otherwise, we add the record to the list. We do something similar for the Cities records, except this time we first check whether the record contains a reference to a country and only update or add the record to the array if the reference corresponds to the country currently selected by the user (the **listCities** array only contains the cities of the selected country).

The closure of the **recordWithIDWasDeletedBlock** property defined next is executed every time the app receives the ID of a deleted record (a record that was deleted from the CloudKit database). In this case, we do the same as before but instead of updating or adding the record we remove it from the list with the **remove()** method.

The closures of the next two properties, **recordZoneChangeTokensUpdatedBlock** and **recordZoneFetchResultBlock**, are executed when the process completes a cycle, either because the system decides to download the data in multiple processes, or the operation finished fetching the changes in a zone. Depending on the characteristics of our application, we may need to perform some tasks in these closures, but in our example, we just store the current token in the **changeZoneToken** property so the next time the operation is performed we only get the changes we have not downloaded yet.

Finally, the closure assigned to the **fetchRecordZoneChangesResultBlock** property is executed to report that the operation is over. The closure receives a **Result** value to report errors. If there is an error, we call the **finishClosure** closure with the value **failed** to tell the system that the operation failed, otherwise, we store the current tokens in the User Defaults database, call the **updateInterface()** method to update the interface, and finally call the **finishClosure** closure with the value **newData**, to tell the system that new data has been downloaded. Notice that to store the tokens we must turn them into **Data** structures and encode them with the **archivedData()** method of the **NSKeyedArchiver** class (see Chapter 15).

Lastly, after the definition of each operation and their properties, we call the **add()** method of the **CKDatabase** object to add them to the database.

There is one more change we must perform for the subscription to work. So far, we have stored the records in the zone by default, but as we already mentioned, subscriptions require the records to be stored in a custom zone. The following are the changes we must introduce to the **insertCountry()**method of the **CountriesViewController** class to store the records inside the listPlaces zone created before.

```
func insertCountry(name: String) async {
   await AppData.configureDatabase()

   let text = name.trimmingCharacters(in: .whitespaces)
   if !text.isEmpty {
      let zone = CKRecordZone(zoneName: "listPlaces")
      let id = CKRecord.ID(recordName: "idcountry-\(UUID())", zoneID:
zone.zoneID)
      let record = CKRecord(recordType: "Countries", recordID: id)
      record.setObject(text as NSString, forKey: "name")

      do {
         try await AppData.database.save(record)
         AppData.listCountries.append(record)

         await MainActor.run {
            prepareSnapshot()
         }
```

```
        } catch {
            print("Error: \(error)")
        }
    }
}
```

Listing 17-23: Storing the Countries records in a custom zone

All we need to do to store a record in a custom zone is to create the **CKRecordZone** object and use the zone identifier to create the **CKRecord.ID** object, as we did in this example.

The following are the same changes applied to the **insertCity()** method of the **CitiesViewController** class to store the Cities records in the custom zone.

```
func insertCity(name: String) async {
    await AppData.configureDatabase()

    let text = name.trimmingCharacters(in: .whitespaces)
    if !text.isEmpty {
        let zone = CKRecordZone(zoneName: "listPlaces")
        let id = CKRecord.ID(recordName: "idcity-\(UUID())", zoneID:
zone.zoneID)
        let record = CKRecord(recordType: "Cities", recordID: id)
        record.setObject(text as NSString, forKey: "name")
        let reference = CKRecord.Reference(recordID:
AppData.selectedCountry, action: .deleteSelf)
        record.setObject(reference, forKey: "country")

        let bundle = Bundle.main
        if let fileURL = bundle.url(forResource: "Toronto", withExtension:
"jpg") {
            let asset = CKAsset(fileURL: fileURL)
            record.setObject(asset, forKey: "picture")
        }
        do {
            try await AppData.database.save(record)
            AppData.listCities.append(record)

            await MainActor.run {
                prepareSnapshot()
            }
        } catch {
            print("Error: \(error)")
        }
    }
}
```

Listing 17-24: Storing the Cities records in a custom zone

Notice that the first thing we do in both methods is to call the **configureDatabase()** method. We call this method again, so every time a record is inserted, we check that the subscription and the zone were already added to the database.

Do It Yourself: Update the **AppDelegate** class with the code in Listing 17-19. Add the methods in Listings 17-20, 17-21, and 17-22 to the **ApplicationData** class. Update the **insertCountry()** method of the **CountriesView-Controller** class with the code in Listing 17-23 and the **insertCity()** method of the **CitiesViewController** class with the code in Listing 17-24. Run the application in two different devices and insert a new country. You should see the country appear on the screen of the second device.

IMPORTANT: Remote Notifications can only be tested on a real device (they do not work on the simulator). If you only have one device, you can test your applications by adding records from the CloudKit dashboard.

Medium Errors

Errors are an important part of CloudKit. The service is highly dependable on the network and how reliable it is. If the device is disconnected or the connection is not good enough, the operations are not performed or may be lost. CloudKit does not provide a standard solution for these situations, it just returns an error and expects our app to solve the problem. If the user creates a new record but at that moment the device is disconnected from the Internet, our app is responsible for registering the incident and trying again later.

The most common error is related to the user's iCloud account. Every user must have an iCloud account to access CloudKit servers. If an iCloud account is not set on the device or has restrictions due to Parental Control or Device Management, the app will not be able to connect to the servers. The **CKContainer** class offers the following method to check the status of the user's account.

accountStatus()—This asynchronous method attempts to access the user's iCloud account and returns a **CKAccountStatus** enumeration to report the current state. The enumeration includes the values **couldNotDetermine**, **available**, **restricted**, and **noAccount**.

If the status of the iCloud account changes while the app is running, the system posts a notification that we can use to perform updates and synchronization tasks.

CKAccountChanged—This notification is posted by the system when the status of the user's iCloud account registered on the device changes.

We should always check if the servers are available before trying to perform an operation and warn the user about it. For instance, we can modify the **insertCountry()** method in our model to check the status of the connection before introducing a new record.

```
func insertCountry(name: String) async {
   await AppData.configureDatabase()
   do {
      let container = CKContainer.default()
      let status = try await container.accountStatus()
      if status != CKAccountStatus.available {
         print("iCloud Not Available")
         return
      }
   } catch {
      print("Error: \(error)")
      return
   }
   let text = name.trimmingCharacters(in: .whitespaces)
   if !text.isEmpty {
      let zone = CKRecordZone(zoneName: "listPlaces")
      let id = CKRecord.ID(recordName: "idcountry-\(UUID())", zoneID:
zone.zoneID)
      let record = CKRecord(recordType: "Countries", recordID: id)
      record.setObject(text as NSString, forKey: "name")

      do {
         try await AppData.database.save(record)
         AppData.listCountries.append(record)
```

```
            await MainActor.run {
               prepareSnapshot()
            }
         } catch {
            print("Error: \(error)")
         }
      }
   }
```

Listing 17-25: Checking CloudKit availability

This example checks the status of the account and prints a message on the console if an error occurs or the status is other than **available**. If an error occurs, the code returns from the function without letting the user insert the new record.

Do It Yourself: Update the **insertCountry()** method in the **CountriesViewController** class with the code in Listing 17-25. Run the application in a device and activate Airplane Mode from Settings. Add a new country. You should see a **CKError** on the console that reads "Network Unavailable".

IMPORTANT: Of course, this example is just for didactic purposes. The information inserted by the user should be stored locally and then uploaded to the servers when the connection becomes available again. This requires storing the information locally, checking for errors, marking every value inserted by the user as uploaded or not, and constantly trying to upload the values again when the operation failed before, which may involve hundreds of lines of code. Fortunately, Apple offers a better solution that integrates CloudKit with Core Data and takes care of everything for us. We will learn more about it in the next section of this chapter.

In the last example, we just checked whether an error occurred or not and proceeded accordingly, but we can also identify the type of error returned by the operation. Errors are objects that conform to the **Error** protocol. Every time we want to read an error, we must cast it to the right type. In CloudKit, the errors are of type **CKError**, which is a structure initialized from an object of type **NSError** and therefore it inherits the following property to return the error code.

code—This property returns a value that identifies the error found. The property is of type **CKError.Code**; an enumeration inside the **CKError** structure with values that represent all the errors produced by CloudKit. The list of values available is extensive. The most frequently used are **partialFailure**, **networkUnavailable**, **networkFailure**, **serviceUnavailable**, **unknownItem**, **operationCancelled**, **changeToken-Expired**, **quotaExceeded**, **zoneNotFound**, and **limitExceeded**.

The following example implements the **recordZone()** method of the **CKDatabase** object to check whether a zone exists in the database. In the **catch** block, we cast the value of the **error** parameter as a **CKError** structure and then compare the value of its **code** property with the value **zoneNotFound** of the **Code** enumeration. If the values match, it means that the zone we tried to access does not exist.

```
func checkZones() async {
   let newZone = CKRecordZone(zoneName: "myNewZone")
   do {
      try await database.recordZone(for: newZone.zoneID)
   } catch {
```

```
         if let error = error as? CKError {
            if error.code == CKError.Code.zoneNotFound {
               print("Not found")
            } else {
               print("Zone Found")
            }
         }
      }
   }
```

Listing 17-26: *Checking for errors*

Do It Yourself: Add the **checkZones()** method in Listing 17-26 to the **ApplicationData** class. Call this method from an asynchronous task in the **ApplicationData** initializer. Run the application. You should see the message "Not Found" on the console (there is no zone called "myNewZone").

Medium CloudKit and Core Data

Loading the information from CloudKit every time the app is launched is not practical or even reliable. The device may get disconnected, the servers may not be always available, or the response may take too long to arrive. For these reasons, Subscriptions are usually implemented to keep data updated in a local storage. The application stores the information in a local storage, like a Core Data Persistent Store, and uses CloudKit to share that data with other devices and keep them synchronized. Using CloudKit in this manner, we can create an application that automatically uploads and downloads the data to the servers, so we always display the same information to the user no matter where the app is running.

As we already mentioned in the previous section of this chapter, synchronizing a Core Data Persistent Store with a CloudKit database requires controlling the information that is uploaded and downloaded from the servers, checking for errors, solving conflicts, and making sure that no value is duplicated or lost. Because this work is pretty much the same for all applications, Apple offers an API that performs all these standard tasks for us. All we need to do is to create the Core Data stack with the **NSPersistentCloudKitContainer** class instead of the **NSPersistentContainer** class and the Persistent Store is automatically synchronized with CloudKit servers. This class is a subclass of the **NSPersistentContainer** class and therefore it includes the same initializer.

NSPersistentCloudKitContainer(name: String**)**—This initializer creates a Persistent Store with the name specified by the **name** argument.

Besides the common properties, like the **viewContext** property that returns a reference to the context, this subclass also includes the following methods in case our application needs to retrieve records manually.

record(for: NSManagedObjectID**)**—This method returns a **CKRecord** object with the record that corresponds to the Core Data object specified by the **for** argument. The argument is the object's identifier (returned by the **objectID** property). If no record is found, the method returns **nil**.

records(for: [NSManagedObjectID]**)**—This method returns an array of **CKRecord** objects with the records that correspond to the Core Data objects specified by the **for** argument. The argument is an array of identifiers (returned by the **objectID** property).

recordID(for: NSManagedObjectID**)**—This method returns a **CKRecord.ID** value with the identifier of the record that corresponds to the Core Data object specified by the **for** argument. The argument is the object's identifier (returned by the **objectID** property).

recordIDs(for: [NSManagedObjectID])—This method returns an array of **CKRecord.ID** values with the identifiers of the records that correspond to the Core Data objects specified by the **for** argument. The argument is an array of object identifiers (returned by the **objectID** property).

The **NSPersistentCloudKitContainer** object automatically resolves conflicts for us, but we must configure the context to determine how those conflicts are going to be resolved. The **NSManagedObjectContext** class includes the following properties for this purpose.

automaticallyMergesChangesFromParent—This property sets or returns a Boolean value that determines whether the changes in the Persistent Store and the context are automatically merged.

mergePolicy—This property sets or returns an object that decides the policy that the context is going to use to merge the changes in the Persistent Store and the context. The Core Data framework defines global variables to set standard policies. The **NSErrorMergePolicy** variable returns an error if the objects are different, the **NSMergeByPropertyStoreTrumpMergePolicy** variable replaces the changes in memory by the external changes, the **NSMergeByPropertyObjectTrumpMergePolicy** replaces the external changes by the changes in memory, the **NSOverwriteMergePolicy** variable replaces the values in the Persistent Store by the current changes, and the **NSRollbackMergePolicy** uses the version of the objects in the Persistent Store.

Because of this amazing API, creating an application that stores information locally in a Persistent Store and synchronizes that data with a CloudKit database is extremely simple. All we need to do is to define the Core Data stack with the **NSPersistentCloudKitContainer** class and then create the Core Data application as we always do. For instance, we can reproduce the previous example to store countries and cities and all the objects will be uploaded to CloudKit servers and shared between devices. The following is the Core Data model we need for this application.

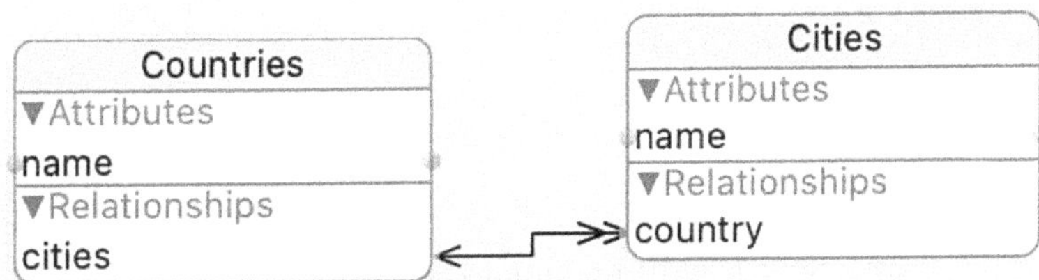

Figure 17-23: *Core Data Model*

For this example, we only need two entities, Countries and Cities, with only one attribute each of type String called *name*, and a relationship from one entity to the other (the relationship in the Countries entity must be set to To-Many because a country can have many cities).

There is one more requirement for the model to be ready to work with CloudKit. We must select the Configuration (Figure 17-24, number 1) and check the option Used with CloudKit in the Data Model Inspector panel (Figure 17-24, number 2), so all the objects stored for these entities are synchronized with CloudKit.

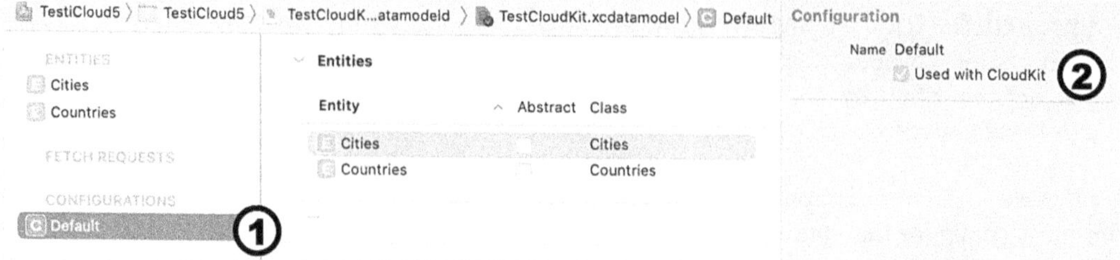

Figure 17-24: Used with CloudKit option

Do It Yourself: Create a new project. Open the Signing & Capabilities panel, add the iCloud capability, and check the CloudKit option (see Figure 17-14). Add a container with the name of the app's bundle and press the Refresh button. Add the Background Modes capability and check the options Background fetch and Remote Notifications. Create a Core Data model from the File menu. Add two entities to the model called Countries and Cities. Add an attribute of type String to both entities called name. Add a To-Many relationship to the Countries entity called cities and a To-One relationship to the Cities entity called country. Select the Inverse value in the relationship (countries for the Cities entity and cities for the Countries entity). Select the Default configuration (Figure 17-24, number 1) and check the Used with CloudKit option (Figure 17-24, number 2).

IMPORTANT: If you need to define some Entities only for local storage, you can create a custom configuration, assign those Entities to the new configuration, and deactivate the option Used with CloudKit. After this, the objects stored for those Entities will not be uploaded to CloudKit.

Once the application is configured to work with CloudKit and the Core Data model is ready, we can work on our code. First, we must initialize the Core Data stack in the **AppDelegate** class, as we did in Chapter 15.

```
import UIKit
import CoreData

@main
class AppDelegate: UIResponder, UIApplicationDelegate {
   func application(_ application: UIApplication,
didFinishLaunchingWithOptions launchOptions:
[UIApplication.LaunchOptionsKey: Any]?) -> Bool {
      return true
   }
   lazy var persistentContainer: NSPersistentCloudKitContainer = {
      let container = NSPersistentCloudKitContainer(name: "AnotherTest")
      container.loadPersistentStores(completionHandler:
{ (storeDescription, error) in
         if let error = error as NSError? {
            fatalError("Unresolved error \(error), \(error.userInfo)")
         }
      })
      container.viewContext.automaticallyMergesChangesFromParent = true
      container.viewContext.mergePolicy =
NSMergeByPropertyObjectTrumpMergePolicy
      return container
   }()
   func application(_ application: UIApplication,
configurationForConnecting connectingSceneSession: UISceneSession,
options: UIScene.ConnectionOptions) -> UISceneConfiguration {
```

```
      return UISceneConfiguration(name: "Default Configuration", 
sessionRole: connectingSceneSession.role)
   }
}
```

Listing 17-27: *Preparing Core Data to work with CloudKit*

The **persistentContainer** property is set as before, but instead of returning an **NSPersistentContainer** value it returns an **NSPersistentCloudKitContainer** value to synchronize the Persistent Store with CloudKit servers. Another difference with previous examples is that now we must tell the context that we need to merge the changes and how to do it. For this purpose, we assign the value **true** to the **automaticallyMergesChanges-FromParent** property and the value **NSMergeByPropertyObjectTrumpMergePolicy** to the **mergePolicy** property.

And that's all it takes. From now on, all the changes introduced in the Persistent Store are going to be uploaded to CloudKit and every device running the application is going to be automatically synchronized. For this example, we are going to implement the same interface as before, with two Table View Controllers to list the countries and cities, as shown below.

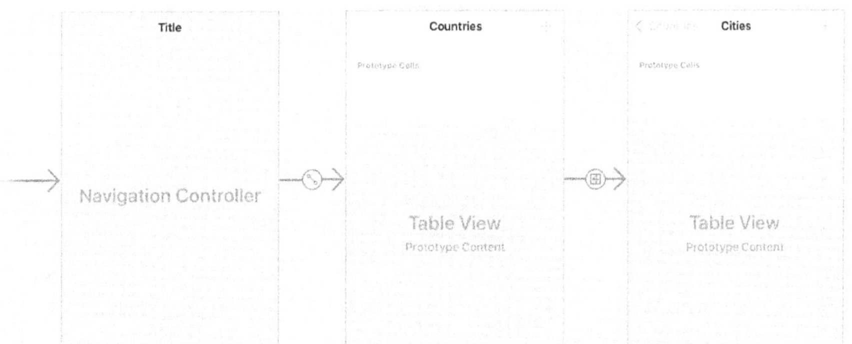

Figure 17-25: *Interface to work with Core Data and CloudKit*

In the model, we only need properties to store the diffable data sources and the Fetched Results Controllers for both Table View Controllers.

```
import UIKit
import CoreData
import CloudKit

enum Sections {
   case main
}
class ApplicationData {
   var selectedCountry: Countries!

   var dataSourceCountries: UITableViewDiffableDataSource<Sections, 
NSManagedObjectID>!
   var fetchedControllerCountries: NSFetchedResultsController<Countries>!

   var dataSourceCities: UITableViewDiffableDataSource<Sections, 
NSManagedObjectID>!
   var fetchedControllerCities: NSFetchedResultsController<Cities>!
}
var AppData = ApplicationData()
```

Listing 17-28: *Defining the model to work with CloudKit*

The Table View Controllers are the same as before. All we need to do is to define the Fetched Results Controller and add or remove objects from the Core Data Persistent Store. The system takes care of uploading the changes to CloudKit servers and updating the Persistent Store with the changes introduced from other devices. The following is the view controller to list and add countries.

```
import UIKit
import CoreData

class CountriesViewController: UITableViewController,
NSFetchedResultsControllerDelegate {
   var context: NSManagedObjectContext!

   override func viewDidLoad() {
      super.viewDidLoad()
      let app = UIApplication.shared
      let appDelegate = app.delegate as! AppDelegate
      context = appDelegate.persistentContainer.viewContext

      tableView.register(UITableViewCell.self, forCellReuseIdentifier:
"countriesCell")
      prepareDataSource()
      prepareFetchedController()
   }
   func prepareDataSource() {
      AppData.dataSourceCountries =
UITableViewDiffableDataSource<Sections, NSManagedObjectID>(tableView:
tableView) { tableView, indexPath, countryID in
         let cell = tableView.dequeueReusableCell(withIdentifier:
"countriesCell", for: indexPath)
         if let country = try? self.context.existingObject(with:
countryID) as? Countries {
            var config = cell.defaultContentConfiguration()
            config.text = country.name
            cell.contentConfiguration = config
         }
         return cell
      }
   }
   func prepareFetchedController() {
      let request: NSFetchRequest<Countries> = Countries.fetchRequest()
      let sort = NSSortDescriptor(key: "name", ascending: true, selector:
#selector(NSString.caseInsensitiveCompare(_:)))
      request.sortDescriptors = [sort]
      AppData.fetchedControllerCountries =
NSFetchedResultsController(fetchRequest: request, managedObjectContext:
context, sectionNameKeyPath: nil, cacheName: nil)
      AppData.fetchedControllerCountries.delegate = self
      try? AppData.fetchedControllerCountries.performFetch()
   }
   func controller(_ controller:
NSFetchedResultsController<NSFetchRequestResult>, didChangeContentWith
snapshot: NSDiffableDataSourceSnapshotReference) {
      let newsnapshot = snapshot as
NSDiffableDataSourceSnapshot<Sections, NSManagedObjectID>
      AppData.dataSourceCountries.apply(newsnapshot)
   }
   override func tableView(_ tableView: UITableView, didSelectRowAt
indexPath: IndexPath) {
      performSegue(withIdentifier: "showCities", sender: self)
   }
```

```
    override func prepare(for segue: UIStoryboardSegue, sender: Any?) {
        if segue.identifier == "showCities" {
            if let path = tableView.indexPathForSelectedRow {
                if let countryID =
AppData.dataSourceCountries.itemIdentifier(for: path) {
                    if let country = try? context.existingObject(with:
countryID) as? Countries {
                        AppData.selectedCountry = country
                    }
                }
            }
        }
    }
    @IBAction func addCountry(_ sender: UIBarButtonItem) {
        let alert = UIAlertController(title: "Insert Country", message:
nil, preferredStyle: .alert)
        let cancel = UIAlertAction(title: "Cancel", style: .cancel,
handler: nil)
        alert.addAction(cancel)
        let action = UIAlertAction(title: "Save", style: .default, handler:
{ (action) in
            if let fields = alert.textFields, let text = fields.first?.text{
                let name = text.trimmingCharacters(in: .whitespaces)
                if !name.isEmpty {
                    let newCountry = Countries(context: self.context)
                    newCountry.name = name
                    try? self.context.save()

                    do {
                        try AppData.fetchedControllerCountries.performFetch()
                    } catch {
                        print("Error")
                    }
                }
            }
        })
        alert.addAction(action)
        alert.addTextField(configurationHandler: nil)
        present(alert, animated: true, completion: nil)
    }
}
```

***Listing 17-29:** Listing the countries stored in the Persistent Store*

The code is the same implemented to work with Core Data before. We set up the Fetched Results Controller to get the **Countries** objects, and the diffable data source to feed the table with this data. To allow the user to add new countries, we create an Alert View with a Text Field and a Save button. When the user inserts a name and taps the Save button, the closure for the button creates a new **Countries** object and saves the context. The system updates the Persistent Store with this information, but because we use an **NSPersistentCloudKit-Container** object to manage it, the **Countries** object is automatically turned into a **CKRecord** and uploaded to CloudKit servers. When we open the application on a second device, the process is inverted; the **CKRecord** object is downloaded from CloudKit, turned into a **Countries** object, and added to the Persistent Store.

The view controller for the second scene is similar, but this time we are processing **Cities** objects instead.

```
import UIKit
import CoreData

class CitiesViewController: UITableViewController,
NSFetchedResultsControllerDelegate {
   var context: NSManagedObjectContext!

   override func viewDidLoad() {
      super.viewDidLoad()
      let app = UIApplication.shared
      let appDelegate = app.delegate as! AppDelegate
      context = appDelegate.persistentContainer.viewContext
      tableView.register(UITableViewCell.self, forCellReuseIdentifier:
"citiesCell")
      prepareDataSource()
      prepareFetchedController()
   }
   func prepareDataSource() {
      AppData.dataSourceCities = UITableViewDiffableDataSource<Sections,
NSManagedObjectID>(tableView: tableView) {tableView, indexPath, cityID in
         let cell = tableView.dequeueReusableCell(withIdentifier:
"citiesCell", for: indexPath)
         if let city = try? self.context.existingObject(with: cityID) as?
Cities {
            var config = cell.defaultContentConfiguration()
            config.text = city.name
            cell.contentConfiguration = config
         }
         return cell
      }
   }
   func prepareFetchedController() {
      let request: NSFetchRequest<Cities> = Cities.fetchRequest()
      request.predicate = NSPredicate(format: "country = %@",
AppData.selectedCountry)
      let sort = NSSortDescriptor(key: "name", ascending: true, selector:
#selector(NSString.caseInsensitiveCompare(_:)))
      request.sortDescriptors = [sort]
      AppData.fetchedControllerCities =
NSFetchedResultsController(fetchRequest: request, managedObjectContext:
context, sectionNameKeyPath: nil, cacheName: nil)
      AppData.fetchedControllerCities.delegate = self
      try? AppData.fetchedControllerCities.performFetch()
   }
   func controller(_ controller:
NSFetchedResultsController<NSFetchRequestResult>, didChangeContentWith
snapshot: NSDiffableDataSourceSnapshotReference) {
      let newsnapshot = snapshot as
NSDiffableDataSourceSnapshot<Sections, NSManagedObjectID>
      AppData.dataSourceCities.apply(newsnapshot)
   }
   @IBAction func addCity(_ sender: UIBarButtonItem) {
      let alert = UIAlertController(title: "Insert City", message: nil,
preferredStyle: .alert)
      let cancel = UIAlertAction(title: "Cancel", style: .cancel,
handler: nil)
      alert.addAction(cancel)
      let action = UIAlertAction(title: "Save", style: .default, handler:
{ (action) in
         if let fields = alert.textFields, let text = fields.first?.text{
            let name = text.trimmingCharacters(in: .whitespaces)
```

```
            if !name.isEmpty {
               let newCity = Cities(context: self.context)
               newCity.name = name
               newCity.country = AppData.selectedCountry
               try? self.context.save()

               do {
                  try AppData.fetchedControllerCities.performFetch()
               } catch {
                  print("Error")
               }
            }
         }
      })
      alert.addAction(action)
      alert.addTextField(configurationHandler: nil)
      present(alert, animated: true, completion: nil)
   }
}
```

Listing 17-30: *Listing the cities of a country*

The view controller gets the **Countries** object representing the country selected by the user from the **selectedCountry** property and creates a predicate to only retrieve the cities that belong to that country. To create the relationship, we also assign this value to the **country** property of the new **Cities** object when the user inserts a new city. The system uploads this object to CloudKit servers and creates the connection between the records for us.

Do It Yourself: Update the **AppDelegate** class with the code in Listing 17-27 (remember to replace the name in the **NSPersistentCloudKitContainer** initializer with the name of your Core Data model). Replace the initial scene with two Table View Controllers embedded in a Navigation Controller (Figure 17-25). Connect the first scene to the second scene with a Show segue and identify the segue with the name "showCities". Add bar buttons of type Add to both scenes (Figure 17-25). Create a Swift file called ApplicationData.swift for the model in Listing 17-28. Create a **UITableViewController** subclass call **CountriesViewController** for the first scene and another called **CitiesViewController** for the second scene. Connect the buttons on each scene with Actions called **addCountry()** and **addCity()** respectively. Update the view controllers with the codes in Listings 17-29 and 17-30. Run the application in two devices. Press the Add Country button and insert a new country. After a few seconds, you should see the same value appear on the second device. Repeat the process for the cities.

Because we are using a Fetched Results Controller to manage the data for the Table Views, the **Countries** and **Cities** objects added to the Persistent Store and their relationships are automatically updated and shown to the user. No matter where the new values are added from, locally or remotely, they always appear on the screen in every device that is running our application. But when we are not presenting the values with a Fetched Results Controller, we must take care of updating the interface ourselves. For this purpose, we must configure the Core Data stack to publish a notification when something changes in the Persistent Store, and perform the necessary updates every time that notification is received.

The first thing we need to control this process is a reference to the object in charge of creating and loading the Persistent Store. This is an object defined by the **NSPersistentStore-Description** class. The **NSPersistentContainer** class includes the following property to get it.

persistentStoreDescriptions—This property returns an array containing the **NSPersistentStoreDescription** objects in charge of every Persistent Store managed by the Core Data stack.

Once we get the **NSPersistentStoreDescription** object that represents the Persistent Store, we must set an option in the object to get it to post notifications every time the content of the Persistent Store changes. The class includes the following method for this purpose.

setOption(Value, **forKey:** String**)**—This method sets an option in the **NSPersistentStoreDescription** object for the key specified by the **forKey** argument and with a value determined by the first argument.

The Core Data framework defines a global variable called **NSPersistentStoreRemoteChangeNotificationPostOptionKey** with the key required to get the **NSPersistentStoreDescription** object to post notifications every time it detects changes in the Persistent Store.

The notification posted by the **NSPersistentStoreDescription** object is called **NSPersistentStoreRemoteChange**, but this notification is sent by an object that coordinates the information between the Persistent Store and the context. This object is created from the **NSPersistentStoreCoordinator** class. The **NSManagedObjectContext** class includes the following property to get a reference to this object.

persistentStoreCoordinator—This property returns a reference to the **NSPersistentStoreCoordinator** object assigned to the context.

With all these tools, we can now configure the Core Data stack to send and process notifications whenever something changes in the Persistent Store. The following is a possible implementation.

```
import UIKit
import CoreData

@main
class AppDelegate: UIResponder, UIApplicationDelegate {
   func application(_ application: UIApplication,
didFinishLaunchingWithOptions launchOptions:
[UIApplication.LaunchOptionsKey: Any]?) -> Bool {
      return true
   }
   lazy var persistentContainer: NSPersistentCloudKitContainer = {
      let container = NSPersistentCloudKitContainer(name: "AnotherTest")

      if let description = container.persistentStoreDescriptions.first {
         description.setOption(true as NSNumber, forKey:
NSPersistentStoreRemoteChangeNotificationPostOptionKey)
      }
      container.loadPersistentStores(completionHandler:
{ (storeDescription, error) in
         if let error = error as NSError? {
            fatalError("Unresolved error \(error), \(error.userInfo)")
         }
      })
      container.viewContext.automaticallyMergesChangesFromParent = true
      container.viewContext.mergePolicy =
NSMergeByPropertyObjectTrumpMergePolicy
      return container
   }()
```

```
   func application(_ application: UIApplication,
configurationForConnecting connectingSceneSession: UISceneSession,
options: UIScene.ConnectionOptions) -> UISceneConfiguration {
      return UISceneConfiguration(name: "Default Configuration",
sessionRole: connectingSceneSession.role)
   }
}
```

Listing 17-31: *Posting notifications when the Persistent Store changes*

The configuration must be set before the Persistent Store is loaded, so after the **NSPersistentCloudKitContainer** object is created, we get the **NSPersistentStore-Description** object representing the only Persistent Store in our stack (the first element of the array), and then set the **NSPersistentStoreRemoteChangeNotificationPostOptionKey** option with the value **true** to get it to send notifications. Notice that the **setOption()** method only takes objects that inherit from the **NSObject** class, so we had to convert the Boolean value into an **NSNumber** object for the option to be set.

Now, we can listen to the **NSPersistentStoreRemoteChange** notification from any of our view controllers and update the interface accordingly. To test this example, we are going to generate a task from the **CountriesViewController** class to print a message on the console when a notification is received.

```
override func viewDidLoad() {
   super.viewDidLoad()
   let app = UIApplication.shared
   let appDelegate = app.delegate as! AppDelegate
   context = appDelegate.persistentContainer.viewContext

   tableView.register(UITableViewCell.self, forCellReuseIdentifier:
"countriesCell")
   prepareDataSource()
   prepareFetchedController()

   Task(priority: .high) {
      let center = NotificationCenter.default
      for await _ in
center.notifications(named: .NSPersistentStoreRemoteChange, object: nil)
{
         print("--- Data Updated")
      }
   }
}
```

Listing 17-32: *Updating the interface when the Persistent Store changes*

This is like what we have done in previous examples. The **viewDidLoad()** method creates an asynchronous task that runs a **for in** loop to read the asynchronous sequence returned by the **notifications()** method. Every time a notification is posted by the Persistent Store, a cycle of the loop is executed. In this example, we just print a message, but receiving these notifications means that the Persistent Store was modified from the device or by data received from CloudKit servers, so we should update the interface accordingly.

Do It Yourself: Update the **AppDelegate** class with the code in Listing 17-31. Update the **viewDidLoad()** method in the **CountriesViewController** class with the method in Listing 17-32. Run the application in two devices. Press the Add Country button and insert a new country. After a few seconds, you should see the same value appear on the second device and a message on the console.

Basic Deploy to Production

In CloudKit's dashboard, at the bottom of the left panel, there is a list of options to work with the database schema (the record types, attributes, subscriptions, zones, etc.). We can export the schema, import a schema from our computer, reset the schema to start from scratch, and deploy the schema to production. This last option is the one we need to select when we want to prepare our app for distribution (to be sold in the App Store).

The Deploy Schema Changes option opens a panel where we can see the features that are going to be transferred to the Production environment. This includes record types and indexes, but it does not include records (values added for testing). If we agree, we must press the Deploy button to finish the process, and our database in CloudKit will be ready for distribution.

IMPORTANT: The Production environment is used by apps that are submitted to Apple for distribution. This step is required for your application to be published in the App Store. If you don't deploy the changes to production, the database is not going to be available to your users. To learn how to submit your app to the App Store, read Chapter 23.

Chapter 18
Media

Basic 18.1 Media

These days, personal devices are primarily used for processing pictures, videos, and sound, and Apple devices are no exception. UIKit can display an image with an **UIImageView** view, but other frameworks are required to process the image, present a video on the screen, or play sounds. In this chapter, we introduce the tools provided by Apple for this purpose.

Basic Camera

One of the most common uses of mobile devices is to take and store photos, and that is why no device is sold without a camera anymore. Because of how normal it is for an application to access the camera and manage pictures, UIKit offers a controller with built-in functionality that provides all the tools necessary for the user to take pictures and record videos. The class to create this controller is called **UIImagePickerController**. The following are some of the properties included in this class for configuration.

sourceType—This property sets or returns a value that determines the type of source we want to use to get the pictures. It is an enumeration called **SourceType** included in the **UIImagePickerController** class. At this moment, only the value **camera** is available.

mediaTypes—This property sets or returns a value that determines the type of media we want to work with. It takes an array of strings with the values that represent every media we want to use. The most common values are public.image for pictures and public.movie for videos. (These values can be represented by the constants **kUTTypeImage** and **kUTTypeMovie**.)

cameraCaptureMode—This property sets or returns a value that determines the capture mode used by the camera. It is an enumeration called **CameraCaptureMode** included in the **UIImagePickerController** class. The values available are **photo** and **video**.

cameraFlashMode—This property sets or returns a value that determines the flash mode used by the camera. It is an enumeration called **CameraFlashMode** included in the **UIImagePickerController** class. The values available are **on**, **off**, and **auto**.

allowsEditing—This property sets or returns a Boolean value that determines if the user is allowed to edit the image.

videoQuality—This property sets or returns a value that determines the quality of the recorded video. It is an enumeration called **QualityType** included in the **UIImagePickerController** class. The values available are **typeHigh**, **typeMedium**, **typeLow**, **type640x480**, **typeIFrame960x540**, and **typeIFrame1280x720**.

The **UIImagePickerController** class also offers the following type methods to detect the source available and the type of media it can manage.

isSourceTypeAvailable(SourceType**)**—This type method returns a Boolean value that indicates if the source specified by the argument is supported by the device. The argument is an enumeration called **SourceType** included in the **UIImagePickerController** class. At this moment, only the value **camera** is available.

availableMediaTypes(for: SourceType**)**—This type method returns an array with strings that represent the media types available for the source specified by the argument. The argument is an enumeration called **`SourceType`** included in the **`UIImagePickerController`** class. At this moment, only the value **`camera`** is available.

isCameraDeviceAvailable(CameraDevice**)**—This type method returns a Boolean value that indicates if the camera specified by the argument is available on the device. The argument is an enumeration called **`CameraDevice`** included in the **`UIImagePickerController`** class. The values available are **`rear`** and **`front`**.

The **`UIImagePickerController`** class creates a new scene where the user can take pictures or record videos. After the image or the video are created, the scene must be dismissed, and the media processed. The way our code gets access to the media and knows when to dismiss the scene is through a delegate that conforms to the **`UIImagePickerControllerDelegate`** protocol. The protocol includes the following methods.

imagePickerController(UIImagePickerController, **didFinishPickingMediaWithInfo:** Dictionary**)**—This method is called on the delegate when the user finishes taking the image or recording the video. The second argument contains a dictionary with the information about the media. The values in the dictionary are identified with properties of the **`InfoKey`** structure included in the **`UIImagePickerController`** class. The properties available are **`cropRect`**, **`editedImage`**, **`imageURL`**, **`livePhoto`**, **`mediaMetadata`**, **`mediaType`**, **`mediaURL`**, and **`originalImage`**.

imagePickerControllerDidCancel(UIImagePickerController**)**—This method is called on the delegate when the user cancels the process.

These are all the tools we need to take a picture or record a video and process it. But before accessing the camera, we must ask the user for authorization. The process is automatic, but it requires adding an option in the info.plist file that tells the user what the application is going to do with the camera.

We have introduced the info.plist file before. This is a file included in every Xcode template that contains configuration values for the application. The values are identified with keys and each key may contain other keys, in a hierarchical structure. When we select this file from the Navigator Area, Xcode shows an editor with the current values and a button at the top to add more.

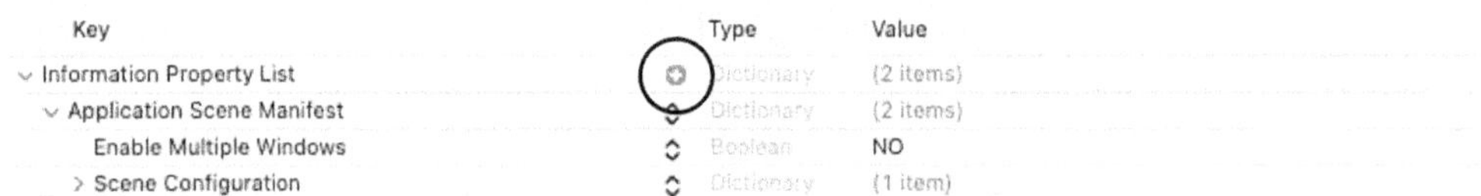

Key
Type
Value
Information Property List
Dictionary
(2 items)
Application Scene Manifest
Dictionary
(2 items)
Enable Multiple Windows
Boolean
NO
Scene Configuration
Dictionary
(1 item)

Figure 18-1: *Content of the info.plist file*

If we move the mouse over an item, the editor shows a + button to add another item to the item's hierarchy. For example, to add a new option to the main list, we click on the + button of the root item called "Information Property List" (circled in Figure 18-1). The editor now shows a list of possible options to choose from. The option to request authorization to use the camera is called "Privacy - Camera Usage Description". After the option is selected, we must insert the text we want to show to the user as the option's value, as illustrated below.

Key	Type	Value
Information Property List	Dictionary	(4 items)
Privacy - Camera Usage Description	String	We need to access the camera to take a picture

Figure 18-2: *Camera Usage Description option*

Once the configuration is ready, we can begin working on our app. Because the Image Picker Controller opens a new scene, the interface usually includes an action to open it. For this example, we have decided to keep it simple and include just an Image View to show the image taken by the user, and a button called Take Picture to open the scene generated by the controller.

Figure 18-3: *Interface to work with the camera*

The view controller that acts as the delegate of the **UIImagePickerController** controller is required to conform to two protocols: **UINavigationControllerDelegate** and **UIImagePickerControllerDelegate**. The following example includes an Action for the Take Picture button that creates, configures, and presents a **UIImagePickerController** controller to take pictures from the camera. The class also implements the method defined in the **UIImagePickerControllerDelegate** protocol to process the media.

```
import UIKit

class ViewController: UIViewController, UINavigationControllerDelegate, 
UIImagePickerControllerDelegate {
   @IBOutlet weak var pictureView: UIImageView!

   @IBAction func takePicture(_ sender: UIButton) {
      let mediaPicker = UIImagePickerController()
      mediaPicker.delegate = self
      let sourceAvailable = 
UIImagePickerController.isSourceTypeAvailable(.camera)

      if sourceAvailable {
         mediaPicker.sourceType = .camera
         mediaPicker.mediaTypes = ["public.image"]
         mediaPicker.allowsEditing = false
         mediaPicker.cameraCaptureMode = .photo
         present(mediaPicker, animated: true, completion: nil)
      } else {
         print("The media is not available")
      }
   }
   func imagePickerController(_ picker: UIImagePickerController, 
didFinishPickingMediaWithInfo info: [UIImagePickerController.InfoKey : 
Any]) {
      let picture = info[.originalImage] as! UIImage
      pictureView.image = picture
      dismiss(animated: true, completion: nil)
   }
}
```

Listing 18-1: *Taking a picture*

When the button is pressed, the **takePicture()** method creates an instance of the **UIImagePickerController** class and assigns the **ViewController** object as its delegate. Next, it checks if the camera is available and presents the controller in case of success, or shows a message on the console otherwise.

Before calling the **present()** method to show the scene on the screen, the code configures the controller. The **sourceType** property is assigned the value **camera** to tell the controller that we want to get a picture from the camera, the **mediaTypes** property is assigned the value public.image to set images as the only media we want to retrieve, the **allowEditing** property is set as **false** to not let the user edit the image, and the **cameraCaptureMode** property is assigned the value **photo** to only allow the user to take pictures. The scene created by the controller is shown below (center).

Figure 18-4: *Camera's interface*

The camera's interface includes buttons to control the camera and take the picture. After a picture is taken, a new set of buttons is shown to allow the user to select the picture or take another one. If the user decides to use the current picture, the controller calls the **imagePickerController()** method on its delegate to report the action. This method receives a value called **info** that we can read to get the media returned by the controller and process it (store it in a file, Core Data, or show it on the screen). In our example, we read the value of the **originalImage** key to get a **UIImage** object that represents the picture taken by the user and assign this object to the Image View to show it on the screen (Figure 18-4, right).

Do It Yourself: Create a new project. Add an Image View and a button to the scene (Figure 18-3). Connect the Image View to the **ViewController** class with an Outlet called **pictureView** and the button with an Action called **takePicture()**. Complete the **ViewController** class with the code in Listing 18-1. Add the "Privacy - Camera Usage Description" option to the info.plist file with the text you want to show to the user. Run the application and press the button. Take a picture and press the button to use it.

Basic Storing Pictures

In the previous example, we show the picture on the screen, but we can store it in a file or in a Core Data Persistent Store. An alternative, sometimes useful when working with the camera, is to store the picture in the device's Photo Library so that it is accessible to other applications. The UIKit framework offers two functions to store images and videos.

UIImageWriteToSavedPhotosAlbum(UIImage, Any?, Selector?, UnsafeMutableRawPointer?**)**—This function adds the image specified by the first argument to the camera roll. The second argument is a reference to the object that contains the method we want to execute when the process is over, the third argument is a selector that represents that method, and the last argument is an object with data to pass to the method.

UISaveVideoAtPathToSavedPhotosAlbum(String, Any?, Selector?, UnsafeMutableRawPointer?**)**—This function adds the video to the camera roll at the path indicated by the first argument. The second argument is a reference to the object that contains the method we want to execute when the process is over, the third argument is a selector that represents that method, and the last argument is an object with additional data for the method.

These functions store the picture or video taken by the camera in the Photo Library and then call a method to report the result of the operation. We can declare the target object and the selector as **`nil`** if we don't want to know what happened, or define a method in our view controller to handle the response. This method can have any name we want, but it is required to have a specific definition that includes three parameters. For images, the parameters are **`(image: UIImage, didFinishSavingWithError error: NSError?, contextInfo: UnsafeRawPointer)`** and for videos the parameters are **`(video: String, didFinishSavingWithError error: NSError?, contextInfo: UnsafeRawPointer)`**. In the following example, we show the picture on the screen, store it in the Photo Library, and open an Alert View to inform the user that the picture was stored on the device.

```
import UIKit

class ViewController: UIViewController, UINavigationControllerDelegate,
UIImagePickerControllerDelegate {
   @IBOutlet weak var pictureView: UIImageView!

   @IBAction func takePicture(_ sender: UIButton) {
      let mediaPicker = UIImagePickerController()
      mediaPicker.delegate = self
      let sourceAvailable =
UIImagePickerController.isSourceTypeAvailable(.camera)
      if sourceAvailable {
         mediaPicker.sourceType = .camera
         present(mediaPicker, animated: true, completion: nil)
      } else {
         print("The media is not available")
      }
   }
   func imagePickerController(_ picker: UIImagePickerController,
didFinishPickingMediaWithInfo info: [UIImagePickerController.InfoKey :
Any]) {
      let picture = info[.originalImage] as! UIImage
      pictureView.image = picture
      UIImageWriteToSavedPhotosAlbum(picture, self,
#selector(confirmImage(image:didFinishSavingWithError:contextInfo:)),
nil)
      dismiss(animated: true, completion: nil)
   }
   @objc func confirmImage(image: UIImage, didFinishSavingWithError
error: NSError?, contextInfo: UnsafeRawPointer) {
      if error == nil {
         let alert = UIAlertController(title: "Picture Saved", message:
"The picture was added to your photos", preferredStyle: .alert)
         let action = UIAlertAction(title: "OK", style: .default,
handler: nil)
         alert.addAction(action)
         present(alert, animated: true, completion: nil)
      } else {
         print("Error")
      }
   }
}
```

Listing 18-2: *Storing pictures in the Photo Library*

When we get the media from the Photo Library, the system takes care of the security aspects for us, but when we try to store new pictures or videos in the device, we must configure the app to ask the user for authorization. As always, this is done from the info.plist file. In this case, we must add the option "Privacy - Photo Library Additions Usage Description" with the message we want to show to the user when authorization is requested.

Do It Yourself: Update the **`ViewController`** class with the code in Listing 18-2. Add the option "Privacy - Photo Library Additions Usage Description" to the info.plist file to get access to the Photo Library. Run the application and take a picture. You should see an Alert View with the message "Picture Saved" and the picture should be available in your device's Photo Library.

Basic Photo Library

The same way there is a predefined view controller for the camera, there is also another for the Photo Library. This controller is created from the **`PHPickerViewController`** class, defined in the PhotosUI framework. The class includes the following initializer.

PHPickerViewController(configuration: PHPickerConfiguration**)**—This initializer creates a **`PHPickerViewController`** object with the configuration specified by the **configuration** argument.

The initializer requires a **`PHPickerConfiguration`** structure for configuration. The structure includes the following initializer.

PHPickerConfiguration(photoLibrary: PHPhotoLibrary**)**—This initializer creates a **`PHPickerConfiguration`** structure to access the Photo Library. The **`PHPhotoLibrary`** class includes a type method called **`shared()`** to return a reference to the device's Photo Library.

The **`PHPickerConfiguration`** structure also includes the following properties to specify the configuration.

filter—This property sets or returns a value that determines the type of media displayed by the controller. It is a structure of type **`PHPickerFilter`** with the properties **`images`**, **`livePhotos`**, and **`videos`**.

selectionLimit—This property sets or returns an integer value that determines the number of resources the user can select from the picker. A value of 0 allows the user to select unlimited resources.

selection—This property sets or returns a value that determines the type of selection to perform when multiple selection is allowed. It is an enumeration called **`Selection`** with the values **`ordered`** and **`default`**.

preselectedAssetIdentifiers—This property sets or returns an array with strings that identify the selected items. It is used to show the picker with preselected items.

Like the **`UIImagePickerController`** class, the **`PHPickerViewController`** class calls a method on its delegate to provide information about the media selected by the user. The class includes the **`delegate`** property to set this delegate and the framework includes the **`PHPickerViewControllerDelegate`** protocol, which defines the following method.

picker(PHPickerViewController, **didFinishPicking:** [PHPickerResult]**)**—This method is called on the delegate after the user selects an image or a video from the picker. The **didFinishPicking** argument is an array of **`PHPickerResult`** structures representing each asset selected by the user.

The resources selected by the user are returned as **PHPickerResult** structures. This is a wrapper with information about the asset and an **NSItemProvider** object with the actual resource. The **PHPickerResult** structure includes two properties to return these values.

itemProvider—This property returns the **NSItemProvider** object with the images or videos selected by the user.

assetIdentifier—This property returns a string with the name assigned to the resource.

The **NSItemProvider** class was design to transmit resources, such as data or files, between services. It is used during drag and drop or copy and paste operations, but it is also implemented by the **PHPickerViewController** class to return the images or videos selected by the user. The **NSItemProvider** class includes the following methods for this purpose.

canLoadObject(ofClass: Class**)**—This method returns a Boolean value that indicates whether the resource contained by the **NSItemProvider** object can be converted to an object of the class specified by the **ofClass** argument.

loadObject(ofClass: Class, **completionHandler:** Closure**)**—This method asynchronously loads the resource contained by the **NSItemProvider** object, cast the object to the class specified by the **ofClass** argument, and calls a closure with the result. The closure receives two values: an object that conforms to the **NSItemProviderReading** protocol with the actual data, and a second value to report errors.

The **PHPickerViewController** class generates a modal scene to allow the user to select an image or a video from the Photo Library, so we also have to present the scene with the **present()** method, as we did for the **UIImagePickerController** controller. But first, we must define a **PHPickerConfiguration** object to configure the picker, as shown in the following example.

```
import UIKit
import PhotosUI

class ViewController: UIViewController, PHPickerViewControllerDelegate {
   @IBOutlet weak var pictureView: UIImageView!

   @IBAction func takePicture(_ sender: UIButton) {
      var configuration = PHPickerConfiguration(photoLibrary: .shared())
      configuration.filter = .images
      configuration.selectionLimit = 1

      let picker = PHPickerViewController(configuration: configuration)
      picker.delegate = self
      present(picker, animated: true)
   }
   func picker(_ picker: PHPickerViewController, didFinishPicking
results: [PHPickerResult]) {
      if let itemProvider = results.first?.itemProvider {
         if itemProvider.canLoadObject(ofClass: UIImage.self) {
            itemProvider.loadObject(ofClass: UIImage.self) { item, error
in
               if let image = item as? UIImage {
                  Task(priority: .background) {
                     await MainActor.run {
                        self.pictureView.image = image
                     }
                  }
               }
            }
         }
      }
```

```
        dismiss(animated: true, completion: nil)
    }
}
```

Listing 18-3: *Selecting a picture from the Photo Library*

In this example, we import the PhotosUI framework to be able to present a **PHPickerViewController** controller and get our view controller to conform to the **PHPickerViewControllerDelegate** protocol to process the response. The code assumes that we are using the same interface introduced in Figure 18-3. When the user presses the Take Picture button, we define the **PHPickerConfiguration** class to configure the picker to show images and allow the user to select only one. Next, the **PHPickerViewController** object is created, and the picker is presented on the screen.

When the user selects a resource, the **PHPickerViewController** object calls the protocol method on its delegate. The method receives an array of **PHPickerResult** structures with all the resources selected by the user, but because our picker was configured to only allow the user to select one picture, we read the first value to get the **NSItemProvider** object that contains this asset. Next, we check that the asset can be converted into a **UIImage** object with the **canLoadObject()** method (making sure that the user selected an image), and call the **loadObject(ofClass:)** method to load the image. The result is shown below.

Figure 18-5: *Photo Library's interface (center)*

By default, the **PHPickerViewController** is presented in a full screen sheet, but we can take advantage of the bigger screens offered by iPads to show the scene with a different format, such as a popover. All we need to do is to configure the presentation style of the view controller and set the required parameters. The following example shows the scene in a popover.

```
import UIKit
import PhotosUI

class ViewController: UIViewController, PHPickerViewControllerDelegate {
   @IBOutlet weak var pictureView: UIImageView!
   @IBOutlet weak var pictureButton: UIButton!

   @IBAction func takePicture(_ sender: UIButton) {
      var configuration = PHPickerConfiguration(photoLibrary: .shared())
      configuration.filter = .images
      configuration.selectionLimit = 1

      let picker = PHPickerViewController(configuration: configuration)
      picker.delegate = self

      picker.modalPresentationStyle = .popover
      if let popover = picker.popoverPresentationController {
         popover.sourceView = pictureButton
```

```
            popover.sourceRect = pictureButton.bounds
            popover.permittedArrowDirections = [.up]
        }
        present(picker, animated: true)
    }
    func picker(_ picker: PHPickerViewController, didFinishPicking
results: [PHPickerResult]) {
        if let itemProvider = results.first?.itemProvider {
            if itemProvider.canLoadObject(ofClass: UIImage.self) {
                itemProvider.loadObject(ofClass: UIImage.self) { item, error
in
                    if let image = item as? UIImage {
                        Task(priority: .background) {
                            await MainActor.run {
                                self.pictureView.image = image
                            }
                        }
                    }
                }
            }
        }
        dismiss(animated: true, completion: nil)
    }
}
```

Listing 18-4: *Showing the picker in a popover*

In this example, we anchor the popover to the Take Picture button, so the scene is shown below the button, close to where the user's finger is. If we open the scene on a device with a small screen, the system shows it full screen, but if we do it on an iPad, the system creates a popover presentation controller and assigns it to the **popoverPresentationController** property. If this property is not **nil**, we set the values for the presentation and the scene is presented as a popover (see Action Sheets in Chapter 13, Listing 13-6).

Do It Yourself: Connect the Take Picture button to the **ViewController** class with an Outlet called **pictureButton**. Update the **ViewController** class with the code in Listing 18-4. Run the application on an iPad and press the Take Picture button. The Photo Library should open in a popover.

In these examples, we have set the **selectionLimit** property to 1, so the user could only select one picture at a time, but the **PHPickerViewController** allows multiple selection. All we need to do is to assign the value 0 to the **selectionLimit** property and the feature is enabled. But if we want to allow the user to modify the selection later, we must store the selected pictures in a model and configure the picker with these values so that the user can see which pictures were selected before and make changes. There are multiple ways to achieve this. For our example, we are going to use a simple model, like those implemented before, with a custom class to store all the information.

```
import UIKit

enum Sections {
    case main
}
class ItemsData: Identifiable {
    let id: String!
    let image: UIImage!
    let title: String!
```

```
    init(_ id: String, _ image: UIImage, _ title: String) {
        self.id = id
        self.image = image
        self.title = title
    }
}
class ApplicationData {
    var listPictures: [ItemsData] = []
    var dataSource: UITableViewDiffableDataSource<Sections, ItemsData.ID>!
}
var AppData = ApplicationData()
```

Listing 18-5: *Defining the model to keep track of the selection*

The **ItemsData** class includes three properties: the **id** property to store the picture's identifier, a **UIImage** object with the image, and a string with the name suggested by the picker for the picture. As always, we store these values in an array and define the diffable data source with the **id** property.

To display the list of pictures selected by the user, we need a small interface with a Table View Controller embedded in a Navigation Controller and a button in the Navigation Bar to open the picker.

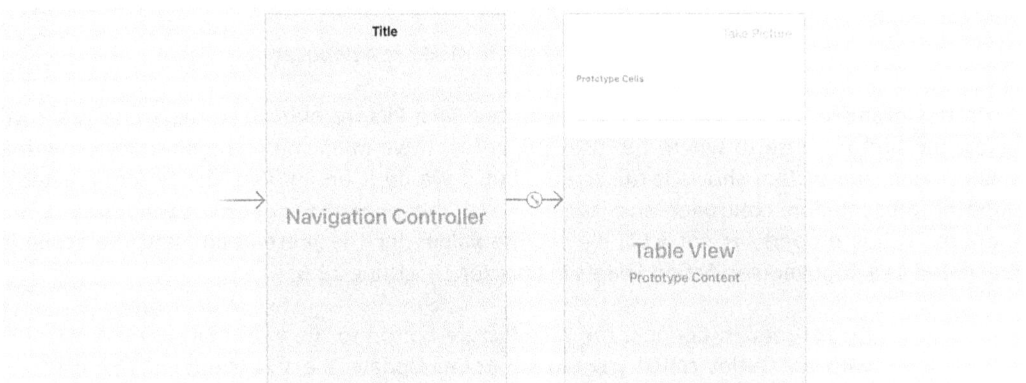

Figure 18-6: *Interface to test multiple selection*

The purpose of the application is to show the list of pictures selected by the user on the table and allow the user to open the picker and change the selection at any time. The pictures are stored in an array in the model, and each picture is identified by a unique identifier assigned by the picker. The following is a possible implementation for the view controller.

```
import UIKit
import PhotosUI

class PicturesViewController: UITableViewController,
PHPickerViewControllerDelegate {
    override func viewDidLoad() {
        super.viewDidLoad()
        tableView.register(UITableViewCell.self, forCellReuseIdentifier:
"myCell")
        prepareDataSource()
        prepareSnapshot()
    }
    func prepareDataSource() {
        AppData.dataSource = UITableViewDiffableDataSource<Sections,
ItemsData.ID>(tableView: tableView) { tableView, indexPath, itemID in
            let cell = self.tableView.dequeueReusableCell(withIdentifier:
"myCell", for: indexPath)
```

```
         if let item = AppData.listPictures.first(where: { $0.id ==
itemID }) {
            var config = cell.defaultContentConfiguration()
            config.text = item.title
            config.image = item.image
            config.imageProperties.maximumSize = CGSize(width: 100,
height: 80)
            config.imageProperties.cornerRadius = 10
            config.imageProperties.reservedLayoutSize = CGSize(width:
100, height: 80)
            cell.contentConfiguration = config
         }
         return cell
      }
   }
   func prepareSnapshot() {
      var snapshot = NSDiffableDataSourceSnapshot<Sections,
ItemsData.ID>()
      snapshot.appendSections([.main])
      snapshot.appendItems(AppData.listPictures.map({ $0.id }))
      AppData.dataSource.apply(snapshot)
   }
   @IBAction func takePicture(_ sender: UIBarButtonItem) {
      var configuration = PHPickerConfiguration(photoLibrary: .shared())
      configuration.filter = .images
      configuration.selectionLimit = 0
      configuration.preselectedAssetIdentifiers =
AppData.listPictures.map { $0.id }

      let picker = PHPickerViewController(configuration: configuration)
      picker.delegate = self
      present(picker, animated: true)
   }
   func picker(_ picker: PHPickerViewController, didFinishPicking
results: [PHPickerResult]) {
      AppData.listPictures = AppData.listPictures.filter { value in
         if results.contains(where: { $0.assetIdentifier == value.id }) {
            return true
         } else {
            return false
         }
      }
      prepareSnapshot()

      for result in results {
         if !AppData.listPictures.contains(where: { $0.id ==
result.assetIdentifier }) {
            loadItem(item: result)
         }
      }
      dismiss(animated: true, completion: nil)
   }
   func loadItem(item: PHPickerResult) {
      let provider = item.itemProvider
      let fileName = provider.suggestedName ?? "Undefined"
      let assetID = item.assetIdentifier ?? ""

      if provider.canLoadObject(ofClass: UIImage.self) {
         provider.loadObject(ofClass: UIImage.self) { item, error in
            if let image = item as? UIImage {
               if let thumbnail = self.getThumbnail(image: image) {
                  let newItem = ItemsData(assetID, thumbnail, fileName)
                  AppData.listPictures.append(newItem)
                  Task(priority: .high) {
                     await MainActor.run {
```

```
                           self.preparSnapshot()
                        }
                     }
                  }
               }
            }
         }
      }
   func getThumbnail(image: UIImage) -> UIImage? {
      let imageWidth = image.size.width
      let imageHeight = image.size.height
      let scaleFactor = (imageWidth > imageHeight) ? 100 / imageWidth : 
80 / imageHeight
      if let thumbnail = image.preparingThumbnail(of: CGSize(width: 
imageWidth * scaleFactor, height: imageHeight * scaleFactor)) {
         return thumbnail
      } else {
         return nil
      }
   }
}
```

Listing 18-6: *Displaying the pictures selected by the user*

The code begins by defining the diffable data source and the snapshot, with only a minor change from previous examples. This is because the images retrieved from the Photo Library may be of different sizes, so we set the **reservedLayoutSize** property to configure the size of the column and make sure the pictures and the text are aligned.

The picker is configured as before, but now we assign the value 0 to the **selectionLimit** property to allow multiple selection and an array of identifiers to the **preselectedAssetIdentifiers** property so that the pictures previously selected by the user are already selected in the picker.

In the delegate method, we perform two operations. First, we filter the values in the model. This is to remove from the model the pictures that were deselected by the user, so if the user selects a picture and then opens the picker again and deselects it, the picture is removed from the model and not shown on the table anymore. After the **listPictures** array is filtered, we update the snapshot and then proceed to load the new items selected by the user. To simplify the code, we moved the loading process to another method called **loadItem()**. In this method, we get the name and the identifier assigned to the picture from the **suggestedName** and **assetIdentifier** properties, then check if the image can be extracted from the asset as we did in previous examples, and finally create the new **ItemsData** object and add it to the model. Notice that so save resources, we do not store the original image in the model, we create a thumbnail with the **preparingThumbnail()** method and store this image instead (see Images in Chapter 5).

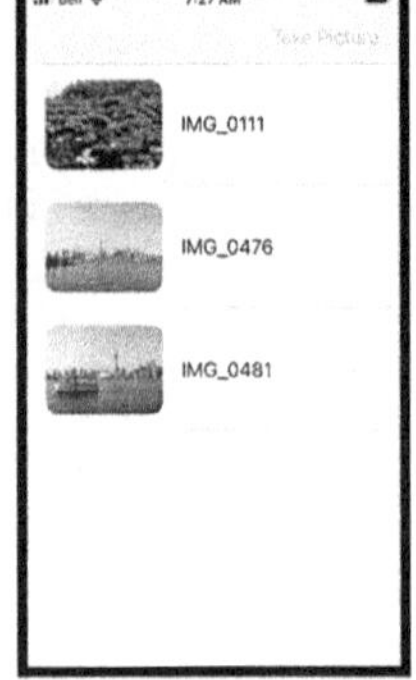

Figure 18-7: *Multiple selection*

Do It Yourself: Create a new project. Replace the scene with a Table View Controller embedded in a Navigation Controller. Add a Bar Button Item to the Navigation Bar (see Figure 18-6). Create a Swift file called ApplicationData.swift for the model in Listing 18-5. Create a subclass of **`UITableViewController`** called **`PicturesViewController`** and assign it to the Table View Controller. Connect the Bar Button Item to this class with an Action called **`takePicture()`**. Complete the class with the code in Listing 18-6. Run the application, press the button, and select a few pictures. Press the Add button. You should see the selected pictures on the table (Figure 18-7). Open the picker again and deselect some pictures. The deselected pictures should be removed from the table.

Medium Custom Camera

The **`UIImagePickerController`** controller is built from classes defined in the AV Foundation framework. This framework provides the codes necessary to process media and control input devices, like the camera and the microphone. Thus, we can use the classes in this framework directly to build our own controller and customize the process and the interface.

Creating our own controller to access the camera and retrieve information demands the manipulation and coordination of several systems. We need to configure the input from the camera and the microphone, process the data received from these inputs, show a preview to the user, and generate the output in the form of an image, live photo, video, or audio. Figure 18-8 illustrates all the elements involved.

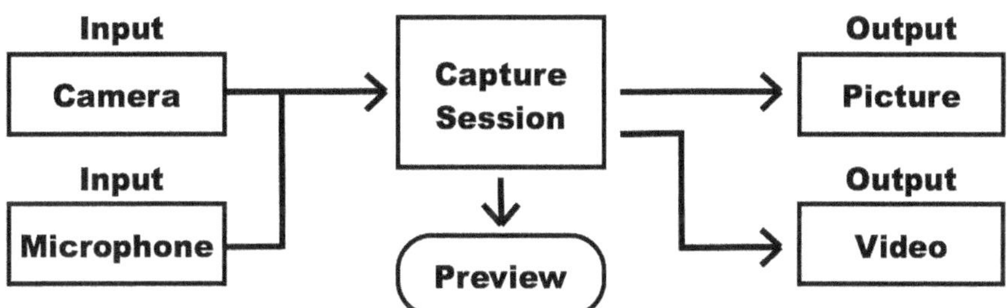

***Figure 18-8:** System to capture media*

The first thing we need to do to build this structure is to determine the input devices. The AV Foundation framework defines the **`AVCaptureDevice`** class for this purpose. An instance of this class can represent any type of input device, including cameras and microphones. The following are some of the methods included in the class to access and manage a device.

default(for: AVMediaType**)**—This type method returns an **`AVCaptureDevice`** object that represents the default capture device for the media specified by the argument. The **for** argument is a structure of type **`AVMediaType`** with properties to define the type of media. The properties available to work with the cameras and microphones are **`video`** and **`audio`**.

requestAccess(for: AVMediaType**)**—This asynchronous type method asks the user for permission to access the device. The **for** argument is a structure of type **`AVMediaType`** with properties to define the type of media. The properties available to work with the cameras and microphones are **`video`** and **`audio`**.

authorizationStatus(for: AVMediaType**)**—This type method returns a value that determines the status of the authorization to use the device. The **for** argument is a structure of type **`AVMediaType`** with properties to define the type of media. The properties available to work with the cameras and microphones are **`video`** and **`audio`**. The method returns an enumeration of type **`AVAuthorizationStatus`** with the values **`notDetermined`**, **`restricted`**, **`denied`**, and **`authorized`**.

An instance of the **AVCaptureDevice** class represents a capture device. To define this device as an input device, we must create an object that controls the ports and connections. The framework defines the **AVCaptureDeviceInput** class for this purpose. The class includes the following initializer to create the input object for the device.

AVCaptureDeviceInput(device: AVCaptureDevice**)**—This initializer creates an input for the device specified by the **device** argument.

In addition to inputs, we also need outputs to process the data captured by the device. The framework defines subclasses of a base class called **AVCaptureOutput** to describe the outputs. There are several subclasses available, such as **AVCaptureVideoDataOutput** to process the frames of a video, and **AVCaptureAudioDataOutput** to get the audio, but the most frequently used is the **AVCapturePhotoOutput** to capture a single video frame (take a picture). This class works with a delegate that conforms to the **AVCapturePhotoCaptureDelegate** protocol, which among other methods defines the following to return a still image.

photoOutput(AVCapturePhotoOutput, **didFinishProcessingPhoto:** AVCapturePhoto, **error:** Error?**)**—This method is called on the delegate after the image is captured. The **didFinishProcessingPhoto** argument is a container with information about the image, and the **error** argument is used to report errors.

To control the flow of data from input to output, the framework defines the **AVCaptureSession** class. From an instance of this class, we can control the inputs and outputs and determine when the process begins and ends by calling the following methods.

addInput(AVCaptureInput**)**—This method adds an input to the capture session. The argument represents the input device we want to add.

addOutput(AVCaptureOutput**)**—This method adds an output to the capture session. The argument represents the output we want to generate from the capture session.

startRunning()—This method starts the capture session.

stopRunning()—This method stops the capture session.

The framework also defines the **AVCaptureVideoPreviewLayer** class to show a preview to the user. This class creates a sublayer to display the video captured by the input device. The class includes the following initializer and properties to create and manage the preview layer.

AVCaptureVideoPreviewLayer(session: AVCaptureSession**)**—This initializer creates an **AVCaptureVideoPreviewLayer** object with a preview layer connected to the capture session defined by the **session** argument.

videoGravity—This property defines how the video adjust its size to the size of the preview layer. It is an enumeration of type **AVLayerVideoGravity** with the values **resizeAspect**, **resizeAspectFill**, and **resize**.

connection—This property returns an object of type **AVCaptureConnection** that defines the connection between the capture session and the preview layer.

The input, output, and preview layers are connected to the capture session by objects of the **AVCaptureConnection** class. The class manages the information of the connection, including ports and data. The following are some of the properties provided by this class.

videoOrientation—This property sets or returns the orientation of the video. It is an enumeration of type **AVCaptureVideoOrientation** with the values **portrait**, **portraitUpsideDown**, **landscapeRight**, and **landscapeLeft**.

isVideoOrientationSupported—This property returns a Boolean value that determines whether it is possible to set the video orientation or not.

Because the scene is not generated by a controller anymore, we must create our own. Figure 18-9, below, introduces the interface we have created for this example. The initial scene was embedded in a Navigation Controller and an additional scene was included to manage the camera. The initial scene includes an Image View to show the picture taken by the user, and a bar button to open the second scene. The second scene has an empty view to which we will add the preview layer, and a narrow view at the bottom added over the preview view with a button to let the user take a picture.

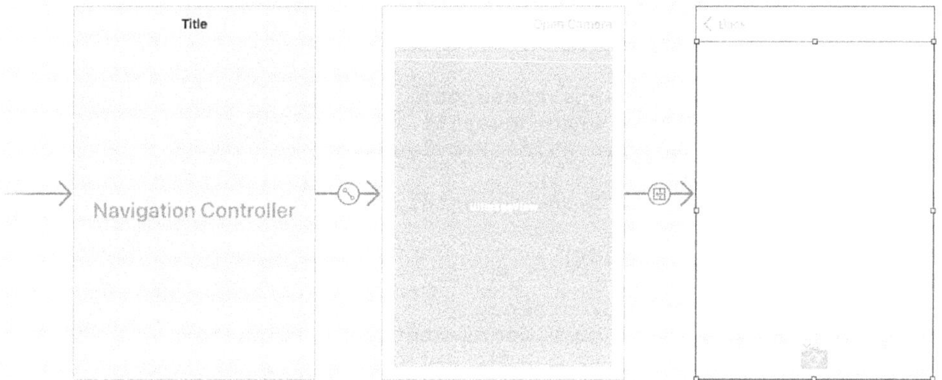

Figure 18-9: *Custom controller for the camera*

Do It Yourself: Create a new project. Embed the initial scene in a Navigation Controller. Add an Image View and a bar button to the initial scene (Figure 18-9, center). Add a new scene to the Storyboard. Connect the bar button to the second scene with a Show segue. Add an empty view to the second scene with a gray background and a Height constraint of 60 points (the option in the Library to add empty views is called *View*). Click on the background color of this view and select the option Custom to open the color picker. Set an Opacity value of 50% to make it translucent. Pin this view to the bottom of the main view and add a button at the center (Figure 18-9, right). Select an SF Symbol for the button from the Attributes Inspector panel. Add another empty view for the preview layer and pin it to the edges of the main view to adopt the size of the screen (highlighted in Figure 18-9, right). Move this view to the back from the Document Outline panel or from the Editor menu to position it behind the toolbar.

The view controller for the initial scene only needs to get the picture from the second scene and show it on the screen. For this example, we have decided to create an Action that we are going to connect to an Unwind Segue to get the image from the second scene and assign it to the Image View (the image will be stored in a property called **picture**).

```
import UIKit

class ViewController: UIViewController {
   @IBOutlet weak var pictureView: UIImageView!

   @IBAction func goBack(_ segue: UIStoryboardSegue) {
      let controller = segue.source as! CameraViewController
      pictureView.image = controller.picture
   }
}
```

Listing 18-7: *Displaying the picture on the screen*

For the second scene, we have created a subclass of **UIViewController** called **CameraViewController**. In this view controller, we must follow a series of steps to activate the camera, let the user take a picture, and process the image. But before even accessing the camera we must ask the user for permission. This is done automatically when we use a **UIImagePickerController** controller, but in a custom controller we must do it ourselves with the type methods provided by the **AVCaptureDevice** class, as shown next.

```
import UIKit
import AVFoundation

class CameraViewController: UIViewController,
AVCapturePhotoCaptureDelegate {
   @IBOutlet weak var cameraView: UIView!

   var captureSession: AVCaptureSession!
   var stillImage: AVCapturePhotoOutput!
   var previewLayer: AVCaptureVideoPreviewLayer!
   var picture: UIImage!
   var imageOrientation: UIImage.Orientation!

   override func viewDidLoad() {
      super.viewDidLoad()
      let device = UIDevice.current
      device.beginGeneratingDeviceOrientationNotifications()

      let status = AVCaptureDevice.authorizationStatus(for: .video)
      if status == .authorized {
         prepareCamera()
      } else if status == .notDetermined {
         Task(priority: .high) {
            await askAuthorization()
         }
      } else {
         notAuthorized()
      }
   }
   func askAuthorization() async {
      let granted = await AVCaptureDevice.requestAccess(for: .video)
      await MainActor.run {
         if granted {
            self.prepareCamera()
         } else {
            self.notAuthorized()
         }
      }
   }
}
```

Listing 18-8: *Asking for permission to use the camera*

The **authorizationStatus()** method returns an **AVAuthorizationStatus** value to inform the current status of the authorization. If the value is **authorized**, it means that we have been previously authorized and can use the camera, but if the value is **notDetermined**, we must call the **requestAccess()** method to ask for permission. This is an asynchronous method, so we create a task and implement it to ask for permission to use the camera. After the user responds, the method returns a value of type **Bool** to report the result.

We use two methods to respond to each situation. The **prepareCamera()** method is executed every time the code detects that we are authorized to use the camera, and the **notAuthorized()** method is executed otherwise. In the following implementation of the latter, we show and Alert View to inform the situation to the user.

```
func notAuthorized() {
   let alert = UIAlertController(title: "No Camera", message: "This app
is not authorized to use the camera. You can authorize access from the
Settings app.", preferredStyle: .alert)
   let action = UIAlertAction(title: "OK", style: .default, handler: nil)
   alert.addAction(action)
   present(alert, animated: true, completion: nil)
}
```

Listing 18-9: *Informing the user that the camera is not available*

The **prepareCamera()** method is where we begin to build the network of objects introduced in Figure 18-8. This method gets a reference to the default capture device for video and creates the inputs and outputs we need to capture a still image (to take a picture).

```
func prepareCamera() {
   captureSession = AVCaptureSession()
   if let device = AVCaptureDevice.default(for: AVMediaType.video) {
      if let input = try? AVCaptureDeviceInput(device: device) {
         captureSession.addInput(input)
         stillImage = AVCapturePhotoOutput()
         captureSession.addOutput(stillImage)
         showCamera()
      } else {
         notAuthorized()
      }
   } else {
      notAuthorized()
   }
}
```

Listing 18-10: *Initializing the camera*

We can create and add to the session all the inputs and outputs we need, in any possible order, but because the **AVCaptureDeviceInput()** initializer throws an error, we use it first. This initializer creates an object that manages the input for the capture device. If the initializer is successful, we add it to the capture session with the **addInput()** method and then create the output. For this example we have decided to use the session to capture a still image, so we use the **AVCapturePhotoOutput** class to create the output and add it to the session with the **addOutput()** method.

After adding the inputs and outputs to the capture session, the **prepareCamera()** method executes an additional method called **showCamera()** to generate the preview layer and show the video generated by the camera on the screen. In this method, we create the layer and set its size and orientation.

```
func showCamera() {
   view.setNeedsLayout()
   view.layoutIfNeeded()
   let width = cameraView.bounds.size.width
   let height = cameraView.bounds.size.height

   previewLayer = AVCaptureVideoPreviewLayer(session: captureSession)
   previewLayer.videoGravity = .resizeAspectFill
   previewLayer.frame = CGRect(x: 0, y: 0, width: width, height: height)

   let videoOrientation = getCurrentOrientation()
   let connection = previewLayer.connection
   connection?.videoOrientation = videoOrientation
```

```
   let layer = cameraView.layer
   layer.addSublayer(previewLayer)
   captureSession.startRunning()
}
```

__Listing 18-11:__ Displaying the video from the camera

The **AVCaptureVideoPreviewLayer()** initializer creates a layer that we have to adjust to the size of its view and add as a sublayer of the current view's layer. But setting the position and size of the layer does not determine how its content is going to be shown. The video coming from the camera could have a different size and orientation. How the video is going to adjust to the size of the layer is determined by the value of the layer's **videoGravity** property, but the orientation is set from the connection between the capture session and the preview layer. This is the reason why, after setting the value of the **videoGravity** property and the layer's frame, we get a reference to the connection from the layer's **connection** property. By modifying the **videoOrientation** property of the connection, we can adjust the orientation according to the device's orientation and finally add the sublayer to the view's layer with the **addSublayer()** method. When the sublayer is ready, the capture session can be initiated with the **startRunning()** method.

IMPORTANT: When a view draws its content, the graphics are stored in a layer that can be processed by the hardware and presented on the screen. The view layer is created from a class provided by the Core Animation framework called **CALayer**. In iOS, every view automatically includes a layer. To provide access to this layer, the **UIView** class includes the **layer** property (implemented in Listing 18-11). For more information, visit our website and follow the links for this chapter.

To determine the orientation, we define a method called **getCurrentOrientation()**. We need to know the device's orientation to be able to define the orientation of the preview layer and the orientation of the image taken by the camera. For these reasons, our method returns the **AVCaptureVideoOrientation** value we need to set the orientation of the preview layer and stores a **UIImage.Orientation** value in the **imageOrientation** property to set the image's orientation later.

```
func getCurrentOrientation() -> AVCaptureVideoOrientation {
   var currentOrientation: AVCaptureVideoOrientation!
   let deviceOrientation = UIDevice.current.orientation

   switch deviceOrientation {
      case .landscapeLeft:
         currentOrientation = AVCaptureVideoOrientation.landscapeRight
         imageOrientation = .up
      case .landscapeRight:
         currentOrientation = AVCaptureVideoOrientation.landscapeLeft
         imageOrientation = .down
      case .portrait:
         currentOrientation = AVCaptureVideoOrientation.portrait
         imageOrientation = .right
      case .portraitUpsideDown:
         currentOrientation =
AVCaptureVideoOrientation.portraitUpsideDown
         imageOrientation = .left
      default:
         if UIDevice.current.orientation.isLandscape {
            currentOrientation = AVCaptureVideoOrientation.landscapeRight
            imageOrientation = .up
```

```
        } else {
           currentOrientation = AVCaptureVideoOrientation.portrait
           imageOrientation = .right
        }
        break
   }
   return currentOrientation
}
```

Listing 18-12: Detecting the device's orientation

IMPORTANT: The camera always encodes the image in its native orientation, which is landscape-right. In consequence, when the device is in portrait mode, we must set the orientation of the image to right, when it is in landscape-left mode, we must set the image's orientation to up, and when it is in landscape-right mode, we must set it to down. Also, the landscape orientation of the video is the opposite of the device, therefore when the device is in the landscape-right orientation, the video orientation is landscape-left, and vice versa.

At this point, the video is playing on the screen and the system is ready to perform a capture. To allow the user to take a picture, we must connect the button added at the bottom of the view (Figure 18-9, right) to an Action in the `CameraViewController` class. The process to capture an image is initiated by the output object. The `AVCapturePhotoOutput` class we use to capture a still image offers the following method for this purpose.

capturePhoto(with: AVCapturePhotoSettings, **delegate:** AVCapturePhoto-CaptureDelegate**)**—This method initiates a photo capture with the settings specified by the **with** argument. The **delegate** argument is a reference to the object that implements the methods of the `AVCapturePhotoCaptureDelegate` protocol to receive the data generated by the output.

The type of photo captured by the output is determined by an `AVCapturePhotoSettings` object. The class includes multiple initializers. The following are the most frequently used.

AVCapturePhotoSettings()—This initializer creates an `AVCapturePhotoSettings` object with the format by default.

AVCapturePhotoSettings(format: Dictionary**)**—This initializer creates a `AVCapturePhotoSettings` object with the format specified by the **format** argument. The argument is a dictionary with keys and values to set the characteristics of the image. Some of the keys available are `kCVPixelBufferPixelFormatTypeKey` (uncompressed format), `AVVideoCodecKey` (compressed format), `AVVideoQualityKey` (compression quality).

The following are some of the properties available in this class to configure the image and the preview.

previewPhotoFormat—This property set or returns a dictionary with keys and values that determine the characteristics of the preview image. The keys available are `kCVPixelBufferPixelFormatTypeKey` (uncompressed format), `kCVPixelBuffer-WidthKey` (maximum width) and `kCVPixelBufferHeightKey` (maximum height).

flashMode—This property sets or returns the flash mode used when the image is captured. It is an enumeration of type `FlashMode` with the values **on**, **off**, and **auto**.

isHighResolutionPhotoEnabled—This property is a Boolean value that determines if the image is going to be taken in high resolution.

To capture an image, we prepare the settings with an **AVCapturePhotoSettings** object, call the **capturePhoto()** method of the **AVCapturePhotoOutput** object, and define the delegate method that is going to process the image returned. The following example implements the delegate method and an Action to initiate the process when the user presses the button.

```
@IBAction func takePicture(_ sender: UIButton) {
   let settings = AVCapturePhotoSettings()
   stillImage.capturePhoto(with: settings, delegate: self)
}
func photoOutput(_ output: AVCapturePhotoOutput, didFinishProcessingPhoto
photo: AVCapturePhoto, error: Error?) {
   let scale = UIScreen.main.scale

   if let imageData = photo.cgImageRepresentation() {
      picture = UIImage(cgImage: imageData, scale: scale, orientation:
imageOrientation)
      performSegue(withIdentifier: "goBackSegue", sender: self)
   }
}
```

***Listing 18-13:** Taking a picture*

When the user presses the button to take the picture, the **takePicture()** method calls the **capturePhoto()** method to ask the output object to capture an image. After the image is captured, this object sends the result to the delegate method. The value received by the method is an object of type **AVCapturePhoto**, which is a container with information about the image. The class includes two convenient methods to get the data representing the image.

fileDataRepresentation()—This method returns a data representation of the image that we can use to create a **UIImage** object.

cgImageRepresentation()—This method returns the image as a **CGImage** object.

In our example, we have implemented the **cgImageRepresentation()** method. This method returns a **CGImage** object that we can use to create the **UIImage** object. The **CGImage** class is defined by the Core Graphics framework to provide a low-level representation of images. The reason why we decided to create the **UIImage** object from a **CGImage** value is because the **UIImage** class includes a convenient initializer that takes this object and the image's scale and orientation and returns a **UIImage** object with that configuration (see Images in Chapter 5). In the view controller of Listing 18-13, the scale is taken from the screen scale, and the orientation is provided by the **imageOrientation** property. This sets the image scale the same as the screen and the orientation according to the orientation of the device when the picture was taken, so the image is always displayed correctly.

After the image is processed, we trigger the Unwind Segue identified with the string "goBackSegue" to take the user back to the initial scene. This is the Unwind Segue we must create for the **goBack()** Action included in the **ViewController** class of Listing 18-7.

The controller for the camera is ready, but there is one more method we need to add to the **CameraViewController** class to adapt the preview layer to the orientation of the device. As we have done before for other projects in this book, we can implement the **viewWillTransition()** method to get the new size of the main view and adjust the preview layer accordingly.

```
override func viewWillTransition(to size: CGSize, with coordinator:
UIViewControllerTransitionCoordinator) {
   super.viewWillTransition(to: size, with: coordinator)
   if previewLayer != nil {
      previewLayer.frame.size = size
```

```
        let videoOrientation = getCurrentOrientation()
        let connection = previewLayer.connection
        connection?.videoOrientation = videoOrientation
    }
}
```

Listing 18-14: *Rotating the preview layer*

Do It Yourself: Update the **`ViewController`** class with the code in Listing 18-7. Create a subclass of **`UIViewController`** called **`CameraViewController`** and assign it to the second scene. Connect the view for the preview layer with an Outlet called **`cameraView`**. Complete the class with the code in Listing 18-8. Add the methods in Listings 18-9, 18-10, 18-11, and 18-12 to this class. Connect the button in the second scene to an Action called **`takePicture()`** and complete the method with the code in Listing 18-13. Complete the **`CameraViewController`** class with the method in Listing 18-14. Create an Unwind Segue between this scene and the **`goBack()`** method of the **`ViewController`** class and give it the identifier "goBackSegue". Remember to add the option "Privacy - Camera Usage Description" to the info.plist file. Run the application and take a picture.

Basic AVKit Framework

In addition to the scene created by the **`UIImagePickerController`** class to take pictures, we can also create a scene with standard controls to play videos. The framework that provides this feature is called *AVKit*, and the class is called **`AVPlayerViewController`**. This class creates a player with the controls necessary for the user to play a video. The following are some of its properties, used to define and configure the player.

player—This property sets the player that provides the media for the controller to play. It is an object of type **`AVPlayer`**.

showsPlaybackControls—This property is a Boolean value that determines whether the player is going to show the controls or just the video.

The controller defines the player and presents the interface for the user to control the video, but the video is played by an object of the **`AVPlayer`** class. The class includes the following initializer to use with AVKit.

AVPlayer(url: URL**)**—This initializer creates an **`AVPlayer`** object to play the media stored in the URL indicated by the argument.

The **`AVPlayer`** class also includes properties and methods to control the playback.

volume—This property sets or returns a value that determines the player's volume. It is a value of type **`Float`** between 0.0 and 1.0.

isMuted—This property is a Boolean value that determines whether the player's audio is muted or not.

rate—This property sets or returns a **`Float`** value that determines the rate at which the media is being played. A value of 0.0 pauses the video and 1.0 sets the normal rate.

play()—This method begins playback.

pause()—This method pauses playback.

addPeriodicTimeObserver(forInterval: CMTime, **queue:** DispatchQueue?, **using:** Closure)—This method adds an observer that executes a closure every certain period of time. The **forInterval** argument determines the time between executions, the **queue** argument is the queue in which the closure should be executed (the main queue is recommended), and the **using** argument is the closure we want to execute. The closure receives a value of type **CMTime** with the time at which the closure was called.

The following example shows how to create, configure, and open an **AVPlayerViewController** controller.

```
import UIKit
import AVFoundation
import AVKit

class ViewController: UIViewController {
   @IBAction func playVideo(_ sender: UIButton) {
      let bundle = Bundle.main
      let videoURL = bundle.url(forResource: "trailer", withExtension:
"mp4")
      let player = AVPlayer(url: videoURL!)
      let controller = AVPlayerViewController()
      controller.player = player
      present(controller, animated: true, completion: {
         player.play()
      })
   }
}
```

Listing 18-15: *Using a standard video player*

This example assumes that we have a button in the initial scene connected to an Action in the **ViewController** class called **playVideo()**. When the button is pressed, the method creates the **AVPlayer** object from a URL, initializes the **AVPlayerViewController** controller, assigns the player object to the controller's **player** property, and presents the controller on the screen. In this example we use the completion handler of the **present()** method to play the video as soon as the view is loaded, but we can let the user decide.

Figure 18-10: *AVKit video player*
© Copyright 2008, Blender Foundation / www.bigbuckbunny.org

Do It Yourself: Create a new project. Add a button called Play Video to the initial scene. Connect the button to an Action called **playVideo()**. Complete the **ViewController** class with the code in Listing 18-15. Download the trailer.mp4 file from our website and add it to your project (remember to mark the option Add to Target). Run the application and press the button. A new scene is shown on the screen with a standard video player. Press the X button in the view to remove it.

Medium Custom Video Player

The standard video player created by the AVKit framework is designed with classes defined by the AVFoundation framework. There is a class in charge of the asset (video or audio), a class in charge of providing the media to the player, a class in charge of playing the media, and a class in charge of displaying the media on the screen. By implementing these classes, we can create our own player. Figure 18-11, below, shows the required structure.

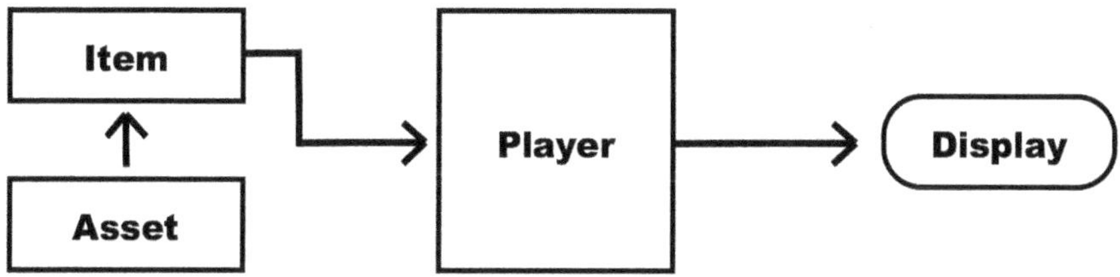

Figure 18-11: *System to play media*

Let's see the elements one by one, starting from the asset. An asset is composed of one or more tracks of media, including video, audio, subtitles, etc. The AVFoundation framework defines a class called **`AVAsset`** to load an asset. The class includes the following initializer.

AVAsset(url: URL**)**—This initializer creates an **`AVAsset`** object with the media in the location indicated by the **url** argument. The argument is a **`URL`** structure with the location of a local or remote resource.

An asset contains static information and cannot manage its status when it is being played. To control the asset, the framework defines the **`AVPlayerItem`** class. With this class, we can reference an asset and manage its timeline. The class includes multiple initializers, including the following.

AVPlayerItem(asset: AVAsset**)**—This initializer creates an **`AVPlayerItem`** object to represent the asset defined by the **asset** argument.

The **`AVPlayerItem`** class also includes properties and methods to control the asset's status. The following are the most frequently used.

status—This property returns a value that indicates the status of the player item. It is an enumeration called **`Status`** with the values **`unknown`**, **`readyToPlay`**, and **`failed`**.

duration—This property returns a value that indicates the duration of the player item. It is a structure of type **`CMTime`**.

currentTime()—This method returns a **`CMTime`** value with the item's current time.

seek(to: CMTime**)**—This asynchronous method moves the playback cursor to the time specified by the **to** argument.

The **`AVPlayerItem`** object manages the information necessary for playback but it does not play the media; this is done by an instance of the **`AVPlayer`** class. This is the same class we used with the **`AVPlayerViewController`** object to play videos. The class includes the following initializer to create a player from an **`AVPlayerItem`** object.

AVPlayer(playerItem: AVPlayerItem**)**—This initializer creates an **`AVPlayer`** object to play the media represented by the **playerItem** argument.

The last object required by the structure is the one in charge of displaying the media on the screen. This is a subclass of the **CALayer** class called **AVPlayerLayer** that provides the code necessary to draw the frames. The class includes the following initializer and property to create and configure the layer.

AVPlayerLayer(player: AVPlayer**)**—This initializer creates an **AVPlayerLayer** object associated with the player specified by the **player** argument.

videoGravity—This property defines how the video adjusts its size to the preview layer's size. It is a **AVLayerVideoGravity** structure with the type properties **resize**, **resizeAspect**, and **resizeAspectFill**.

All these classes define the system we need to play media, but we also need a way to control time. Because the precision of floating-point values is not suitable for media playback, the framework implements, among other things, the **CMTime** structure from an old framework called Core Media. The structure contains multiple values to represent time as a fraction. The most important are **value** and **timescale**, which represent the numerator and denominator, respectively. For example, if we want to create a **CMTime** structure to represent 0.5 seconds, we may declare 1 as the numerator and 2 as the denominator (1 divided by 2 is equal to 0.5). The class includes initializers and type properties to create these values. The following are the most frequently used.

CMTime(value: CMTimeValue, **timescale:** CMTimeScale**)**—This initializer creates a **CMTime** structure with the values specified by the **value** and **timescale** arguments. The arguments are integers of type **Int64** and **Int32**, respectively.

CMTime(seconds: Double, **preferredTimescale:** CMTimeScale**)**—This initializer creates a **CMTime** structure from a floating-point value that represents the seconds and a timescale. The **seconds** argument determines the seconds we want to assign to the structure, and the **preferredTimescale** argument determines the scale we want to use. A value of 1 preserves the value in seconds assigned to the first argument.

zero—This type property returns a **CMTime** structure with a value of 0.

The **CMTime** structure also includes multiple properties to set and retrieve the values. The following are the most frequently used.

seconds—This property returns the time in seconds. It is of type **Double**.

value—This property returns the value of a **CMTime** structure.

timescale—This property returns the time scale of a **CMTime** structure.

The process to create a player is straightforward. We must load the asset (**AVAsset**), create the item to manage the asset (**AVPlayerItem**), add the item to the player (**AVPlayer**), and associate the player to a layer to display the media on the screen (**AVPlayerLayer**). But playing the media requires an additional step. The media does not become immediately available and therefore, we cannot play it right away; we must wait until enough frames have been loaded for the media to be ready to play. The status is reported by the **status** property of the **AVPlayerItem** object, so we must add an observer for this property to start playing the media only after the property returns the value **readyToPlay** (see KVO in Chapter 16)

The following code shows how to build a video player. The example assumes that we have added a file called trailer.mp4 to the project and have an interface with a single scene that includes an empty view pinned to the edges.

```
import UIKit
import AVFoundation

class ViewController: UIViewController {
   @IBOutlet weak var videoView: UIView!
   var playerItem: AVPlayerItem!
   var player: AVPlayer!
   var playerLayer: AVPlayerLayer!

   override func viewDidLoad() {
      super.viewDidLoad()
      let bundle = Bundle.main
      let videoURL = bundle.url(forResource: "trailer", withExtension:
"mp4")
      let asset = AVAsset(url: videoURL!)
      playerItem = AVPlayerItem(asset: asset)
      playerItem.addObserver(self, forKeyPath: "status", options: [],
context: nil)

      player = AVPlayer(playerItem: playerItem)
      playerLayer = AVPlayerLayer(player: player)

      playerLayer.frame = view.bounds
      let layer = videoView.layer
      layer.addSublayer(playerLayer)
   }
   override func observeValue(forKeyPath keyPath: String?, of object:
Any?, change: [NSKeyValueChangeKey : Any]?, context:
UnsafeMutableRawPointer?) {
      if keyPath == "status" {
         if playerItem.status == .readyToPlay {
            playerItem.removeObserver(self, forKeyPath: "status")
            player.play()
         }
      }
   }
   override func viewWillTransition(to size: CGSize, with coordinator:
UIViewControllerTransitionCoordinator) {
      super.viewWillTransition(to: size, with: coordinator)
      playerLayer.frame.size = size
   }
}
```

Listing 18-16: *Building a video player*

In this example, we load the video from the bundle and create the player structure as soon as the scene is loaded. The player is associated with an **AVPlayerLayer** layer and the layer is added as a sublayer of the view where we want to show the video, but the video does not start until the value of the **status** property is **readyToPlay**.

The size of the layer for the player is defined according to the size of the view (**playerLayer.frame = view.bounds**). Because this value is not determined by constraints, it must be updated every time the device is rotated. This is why at the end of the view controller we added the **viewWillTransition()** method. Before rotating the interface, the system calls this method to report the size that the main view is going to adopt at the end of the rotation. By changing the layer's size to this value, we adapt the video to any orientation.

Do It Yourself: Create a project. Add an empty view to the scene. Connect the view to the **ViewController** class with an Outlet called **videoView**. Complete the class with the code in Listing 18-16. Download the file trailer.mp4 from our website and add it to your project (remember to mark the option Add to Target). Run the application. The video should start playing as soon as the application is launched.

The previous example plays the video, but it does not provide any tools for the user to control the process. The **AVPlayer** class includes methods to play, pause, and check the state of the media, but we are responsible for creating the interface. Figure 18-12, below, introduces a new interface with the view to show the video and an additional view in front of it with a button and a Progress View to allow the user to play the video and see the progression over time.

Figure 18-12: *Controls for a custom video player*

How we control the process and respond to the interface depends on the requirements of our application. For this example, we have decided to define two properties to keep track of the state of the media, **ready** and **playing**. The **ready** property will be **true** when the media is ready to play and the **playing** property will be **true** while the media is being played. The following are the definition of the properties and the initial configuration required by our application.

```
import UIKit
import AVFoundation

class ViewController: UIViewController {
   @IBOutlet weak var videoView: UIView!
   @IBOutlet weak var playButton: UIButton!
   @IBOutlet weak var progressBar: UIProgressView!
   var playerItem: AVPlayerItem!
   var player: AVPlayer!
   var playerLayer: AVPlayerLayer!
   var ready = false
   var playing = false

   override func viewDidLoad() {
      super.viewDidLoad()
      playButton.isEnabled = false
      let bundle = Bundle.main
      let videoURL = bundle.url(forResource: "trailer", withExtension:
"mp4")

      let asset = AVAsset(url: videoURL!)
      playerItem = AVPlayerItem(asset: asset)
      playerItem.addObserver(self, forKeyPath: "status", options: [],
context: nil)
      player = AVPlayer(playerItem: playerItem)
      playerLayer = AVPlayerLayer(player: player)
      playerLayer.frame = view.bounds
      let layer = videoView.layer
      layer.addSublayer(playerLayer)
   }
}
```

Listing 18-17: *Preparing the video player*

In Listing 18-17, we add a few more Outlets to the **ViewController** class to reference the elements of the interface and disable the Play button until the video is ready to play, but the code to prepare the player remains the same. The difference is in how the video is played because this time we need to wait until the user presses the Play button. This change appears in the **observeValue()** method. Instead of playing the video when the value of the **status** property changes to **readyToPlay**, we assign the value **true** to the **ready** property to let the rest of the code know that the video is ready to be played. But this is not all the method has to do. We must also register an observer to keep the progress bar updated while the video is being played.

The AV Foundation framework offers the **addPeriodicTimeObserver()** method to create an observer. The method requires a **CMTime** value to determine the frequency in which the code will be executed, a reference to the main queue (the Main Actor), and a closure with the code we want to execute every time the observer is triggered.

```
override func observeValue(forKeyPath keyPath: String?, of object: Any?,
change: [NSKeyValueChangeKey : Any]?, context: UnsafeMutableRawPointer?)
{
   if keyPath == "status" {
      if playerItem.status == .readyToPlay {
         ready = true
         playButton.isEnabled = true
         playerItem.removeObserver(self, forKeyPath: "status")

         let interval = CMTime(value: 1, timescale: 2)
         player.addPeriodicTimeObserver(forInterval: interval,
queue: .main, using: { [unowned self] time in
            let duration = self.playerItem.duration
            let position = time.seconds / duration.seconds
            self.progressBar.progress = Float(position)
         })
      }
   }
}
```

Listing 18-18: *Updating the progress bar*

In Listing 18-18, we create a **CMTime** value to represent a time of 0.5 seconds, and then use it in the call of the **addPeriodicTimeObserver()** method to register the observer. After this, the closure provided to the observer will be executed every 0.5 seconds during playback. In this closure, we get the current time and the duration of the video in seconds and calculate the right position of the progress bar by turning seconds into a value between 0.0 and 1.0 (the minimum and maximum values of a Progress View by default).

IMPORTANT: The **addPeriodicTimeObserver()** method doesn't work with Swift concurrency. Instead, it requires the thread to be defined by a **DispatchQueue** object. This is an old class defined by the Dispatch framework to create asynchronous tasks. The class includes a type property called **main** to define a task for the main queue (the Main Actor), and this is how we make sure that the closure assigned to this method runs in the main queue. Notice that this closure is required to define **self** as **unowned** to ensure that the reference does not create a strong reference cycle.

The player and the progress bar are ready, so the only thing left is to add the Action for the Play button. This is a simple method that executes the player's **play()** or **pause()** methods depending on the value of the **playing** property.

```
@IBAction func playVideo(_ sender: UIButton) {
   if ready {
      if playing {
         player.pause()
         playing = false

         var current = playButton.configuration
         current?.title = "Play"
         playButton.configuration = current
      } else {
         player.play()
         playing = true

         var current = playButton.configuration
         current?.title = "Pause"
         playButton.configuration = current
      }
   }
}
```

Listing 18-19: *Playing and pausing the video*

Figure 18-13: *Custom video player*

Do It Yourself: Add a view with a height of 45 points and pin it to the bottom and the sides of the main view to represent the control bar for the video player. Change the color of the bar to gray. Click on the color, select the Custom option to open the Color Picker, and declare an opacity of 50%. Include a button called Play and a Progress View inside (Figure 18-12). Select the Progress View and assign the value 0 to it from the Attributes Inspector panel. Connect the button, and the Progress View with Outlets called **playButton** and **progressBar**. Connect the Play button with an Action called **playVideo()**. Update the **ViewController** class with the codes in Listings 18-17, 18-18, and 18-19. Remember to add the **viewWillTransition()** method of Listing 18-16 to adapt the layer to any orientation. Run the application and press Play.

IMPORTANT: You cannot only play videos from files added to the project (local), but also from the Web (remote). All you need to do is to create a **URL** structure with the URL pointing to the file you want to play and use it as the source for the asset. There is a restriction though. You can only play remote files that are stored in secure servers (only URLs starting with https://). In Chapter 19, we will learn how to create **URL** structures to access remote documents and how to configure the application to be able to work with unsecured URLs.

The **addPeriodicTimeObserver()** method allows us to update the controls, but we can also listen to notifications to respond to changes in the state of the player. The **AVPlayerItem** class defines several notifications to report events that happened during playback. For example, we can listen to the **AVPlayerItemDidPlayToEndTime** notification to know when the video has finished.

```
func checkEnding() async {
   let center = NotificationCenter.default
   let name = NSNotification.Name.AVPlayerItemDidPlayToEndTime
   for await _ in center.notifications(named: name, object: playerItem) {
      await playerItem.seek(to: CMTime.zero)

      await MainActor.run {
         var current = self.playButton.configuration
         current?.title = "Play"
         self.playButton.configuration = current
         self.playing = false
      }
   }
}
```

Listing 18-20: *Detecting when the video finishes playing*

This method creates a **for in** loop to listen to the **AVPlayerItemDidPlayToEndTime** notification. Every time a video finishes playing, the player posts this notification. Inside the loop, we call the **seek()** method to move the player back to the beginning (time zero), and then reset the controls to allow the user to play the video again.

To start running this loop, we must call the **checkEnding()** method from an asynchronous task as soon as the scene is loaded. The following is the code we need to add to the **viewDidLoad()** method of our view controller to begin this process.

```
Task(priority: .high) {
   await checkEnding()
}
```

Listing 18-21: *Initiating the asynchronous task to listen to player notifications*

Do It Yourself: Add the method in Listing 18-20 to the **ViewController** class and the code in Listing 18-21 to the **viewDidLoad()** method. Run the application, press the Play button, and let the video play to the end. Press the Play button to play it again.

If we want to play multiple videos in sequence, we could use this notification to assign a new asset to the **AVPlayer** object, but the framework offers a subclass of the **AVPlayer** class called **AVQueuePlayer** designed specifically for this purpose. The class creates a playlist from an array of **AVPlayerItem** objects. The following are the class initializer and some of its methods.

AVQueuePlayer(items: [AVPlayerItem]**)**—This initializer creates a play list with the items specified by the **items** argument.

advanceToNextItem()—This method plays the next item on the list.

insert(AVPlayerItem, **after:** AVPlayerItem?**)**—This method inserts a new item to the list.

remove(AVPlayerItem**)**—This method removes an item from the list.

All we need to do to play a sequence of videos is to create the **AVPlayerItem** objects to load each video and create an **AVQueuePlayer** object to replace the **AVPlayer** object we have used so far. The following example introduces the necessary modifications to the **ViewController** class of Listing 18-17 to play two videos called videobeaches.mp4 and videotrees.mp4.

```
import UIKit
import AVFoundation

class ViewController: UIViewController {
   @IBOutlet weak var videoView: UIView!
   @IBOutlet weak var playButton: UIButton!
   @IBOutlet weak var progressBar: UIProgressView!

   var playerItem: AVPlayerItem!
   var player: AVQueuePlayer!
   var playerLayer: AVPlayerLayer!
   var ready = false
   var playing = false

   override func viewDidLoad() {
      super.viewDidLoad()
      playButton.isEnabled = false

      let bundle = Bundle.main
      let videoURL1 = bundle.url(forResource: "videobeaches",
withExtension: "mp4")
      let asset1 = AVAsset(url: videoURL1!)
      playerItem = AVPlayerItem(asset: asset1)
      playerItem.addObserver(self, forKeyPath: "status", options: [],
context: nil)

      let videoURL2 = bundle.url(forResource: "videotrees",
withExtension: "mp4")
      let asset2 = AVAsset(url: videoURL2!)
      let playerItem2 = AVPlayerItem(asset: asset2)

      player = AVQueuePlayer(items: [playerItem, playerItem2])

      playerLayer = AVPlayerLayer(player: player)
      playerLayer.frame = view.bounds
      let layer = videoView.layer
      layer.addSublayer(playerLayer)
   }
}
```

Listing 18-22: *Playing a list of videos*

Do It Yourself: Update the code in the **`ViewController`** class of Listing 18-17 with the code in Listing 18-22. Download the videos videobeaches.mp4 and videotrees.mp4 from our website and add them to your project. Remember to include the methods in Listings 18-18 and 18-19, and also the **`viewWillTransition()`** method of Listing 18-16. Run the application. The videos should be played one after another.

Basic 18.2 Color Picker

Along with the predefined controllers for the camera, video, and Photo Library, UIKit includes a controller to allow the user to pick a color. It is defined by the **`UIColorPickerViewController`** class. Once the object is created, we can configure the picker with the following properties.

selectedColor—This property sets or returns the selected color. It is of type **`UIColor`**.

supportsAlpha—This property sets or returns a Boolean value that determines whether the user is allowed to select the color's alpha level.

The framework also includes the **UIColorPickerViewControllerDelegate** protocol with the following methods to respond to actions performed by the user on the picker.

colorPickerViewControllerDidFinish(UIColorPickerViewController**)**—This method is called on the delegate when the user closes the picker.

colorPickerViewController(UIColorPickerViewController, **didSelect:** UIColor, **continuously:** Bool**)**—This method is called on the delegate when the user selects a color.

The following example illustrates how to set up a color picker, configure its values, and get the color selected by the user. The code assumes that we have a button on the interface connected to an Action in the **ViewController** class called **openColorPicker()**.

```
import UIKit

class ViewController: UIViewController,
UIColorPickerViewControllerDelegate {
   var picker: UIColorPickerViewController!
   var selected: UIColor!

   override func viewDidLoad() {
      super.viewDidLoad()
      picker = UIColorPickerViewController()
      picker.delegate = self
   }
   @IBAction func openColorPicker(_ sender: UIButton) {
      if let color = selected {
         picker.selectedColor = color
      }
      present(picker, animated: true, completion: nil)
   }
   func colorPickerViewController(_ viewController:
UIColorPickerViewController, didSelect color: UIColor, continuously:
Bool) {
      selected = color
      view.backgroundColor = selected
      picker.dismiss(animated: true, completion: nil)
   }
}
```

Listing 18-23: *Presenting a color picker*

The view controller in Listing 18-23 conforms to the **UIColorPickerViewController-Delegate** protocol and defines two properties: the **picker** property to store a reference to the controller, and the **selected** property to store the last color selected by the user. When the main view is loaded, we create the controller and assign the **ViewController** object as its delegate. The view controller also includes an Action connected to a button on the interface. When the button is pressed, the code in this method checks whether a color was already selected and assigns it to the picker's **selectedColor** property, so the picker always shows the last color selected by the user. Finally, the color picker controller is presented on the screen, as we did before for other controllers.

In the delegate method, we get the color selected by the user from the **selectedColor** property, assign it to the view's background, and dismiss the controller. The result is shown below.

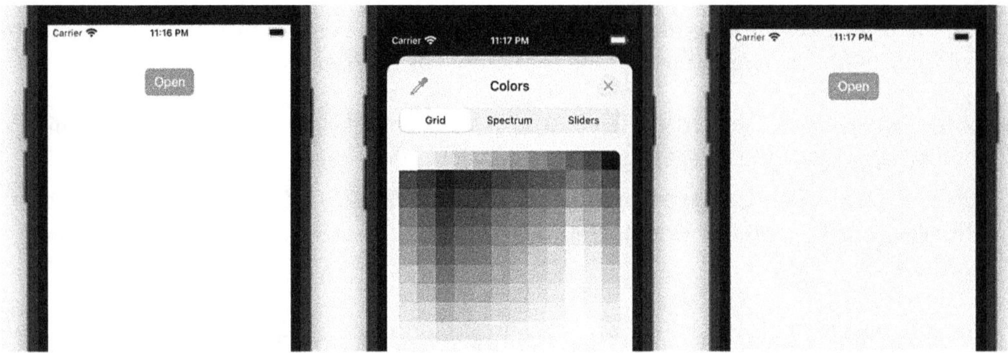

Figure 18-14: *Color picker*

Do It Yourself: Create a new project. Add a button to the scene (Figure 18-14, left). Connect the button to the **`ViewController`** class with an Action called **`openColorPicker()`**. Update the view controller with the code in Listing 18-23. Run the application, press the button, and select a color. You should see something like Figure 18-14. If you want the user to be able to change the selection before closing the picker, remove the call to the **`dismiss()`** method.

Chapter 19
Web

Basic 19.1 Links

The most important aspect of the Web is the ease with which we can access documents with a simple link. A link is a short text or an image that is associated with a URL that determines the location of a document. When the user clicks or taps the text or image representing the link, the document is opened. Links were designed for the Web, but we can add them to our applications and let the system decide where to open the document. For instance, if the link contains a web address, the system opens the browser to load the document.

Web addresses are created from **URL** structures. We have used these types of structures before to determine the location of files, but we can also use them to access remote documents. The class includes the following initializers to create a URL.

URL(string: String**)**—This initializer creates a **URL** structure with the URL specified by the **string** argument.

URL(string: String, **relativeTo:** URL?**)**—This initializer creates a **URL** structure with the URL specified by the arguments. The URL is created by adding the value of the **string** argument to the value of the **relativeTo** argument. For example, if the value of the **string** argument is "http://www.formasterminds.com" and the value of the **relativeTo** argument is "index.php", the **URL** structure will contain the URL "http://www.formasterminds.com/index.php".

URL(dataRepresentation: Data, **relativeTo:** URL?, **isAbsolute:** Bool**)**—This initializer creates a **URL** structure with the URL specified by the arguments. The URL is created by adding the value of the **dataRepresentation** argument to the value of the **relativeTo** argument. The **isAbsolute** argument is a Boolean value that determines if the URL is absolute or not (it includes all the information required to access the resource).

The **URL** structure is just a container for the location of the document we want to open, but the document is opened from the Scene (the window). The **UIScene** class offers the following method for this purpose.

open(URL, **options:** OpenExternalURLOptions?**)**—This asynchronous method opens the URL specified by the first argument. The **options** argument is an object that configures the operation (defined as **nil** to set standard options). The method returns a Boolean value that determines whether the document was opened or not.

The following example opens the website www.formasterminds.com when a button is pressed. The code creates the **URL** structure from a string, gets a reference to the Scene managing the window from the **windowScene** property provided by the **UIWindow** class, and finally calls the **open()** method on this Scene to open the URL. The system reads the URL, detects that it is a web address and opens the browser to load the website.

```
import UIKit

class ViewController: UIViewController {
   @IBAction func openWeb(_ sender: UIButton) {
      let web = "http://www.formasterminds.com"
      if let webURL = URL(string: web) {
         Task(priority: .high) {
            await openURL(url: webURL)
         }
```

```
      }
   }
   @MainActor func openURL(url: URL) async {
      let scene = view.window?.windowScene
      await scene?.open(url, options: nil)
   }
}
```

Listing 19-1: Opening a website

Do It Yourself: Create a new project. Add a button to the initial scene and connect it to the **ViewController** class with an Action called **openWeb()**. Complete the **ViewController** class with the code in Listing 19-1. Run the application and press the button. The system should open the browser and load the website.

In the last example, we have defined the URL in code, but sometimes the URL is provided by the user or taken from another document. In cases like this, the URL may contain characters that are not allowed and can cause the location to be impossible to identify. To make sure that the URL is valid, we must turn unsafe characters into percent-encoding characters. These are characters represented by the % sign followed by a hexadecimal number. Fortunately, there are methods that can correct unsafe characters in a string for us. We have studied a method like this provided by the **String** structure in Chapter 15. The **data(using: Encoding, allowLossyConversion: Bool)** method turns a string into a **Data** structure using a type of encoding that automatically corrects the characters.

```
import UIKit

class ViewController: UIViewController {
   @IBAction func openWeb(_ sender: UIButton) {
      let web = "http://www.formasterminds.com"
      if let dataURL = web.data(using: String.Encoding.utf8,
allowLossyConversion: false) {
         if let webURL = URL(dataRepresentation: dataURL, relativeTo:
nil, isAbsolute: true) {
            Task(priority: .high) {
               await openURL(url: webURL)
            }
         }
      }
   }
   @MainActor func openURL(url: URL) async {
      let scene = view.window?.windowScene
      await scene?.open(url, options: nil)
   }
}
```

Listing 19-2: Encoding URLs

The **utf8** format used in the code of Listing 19-2 works with ASCII characters and therefore it is suitable for the creation of URLs. The **data(using:)** method returns a **Data** structure containing the URL, so we create the **URL** with the initializer appropriate for this type of value. Once the **URL** structure is created, the process to open the URL is the same.

19.2 Safari View Controller

Links provide access to the Web from our app, but they open the document in an external application. Considering how important it is for applications to capture the user's attention, Apple includes a framework called SafariServices. This framework allows us to incorporate the Safari browser into our app to offer a better experience to our users. The framework includes the **SFSafariViewController** class to create a scene to display web pages and tools for navigation.

SFSafariViewController(url: URL**)**—This initializer creates a new Safari View Controller that automatically loads the website indicated by the **url** argument.

SFSafariViewController(url: URL, **configuration:** Configuration**)**—This initializer creates a new Safari View Controller with the configuration specified by the **configuration** argument that automatically loads the website indicated by the **url** argument. The **configuration** argument is a property of an object of the **Configuration** class included in the **SFSafariViewController** class. The properties available are **entersReaderIfAvailable** and **barCollapsingEnabled**.

To include a Safari View Controller in our app, we must create the controller with one of the initializers and present it with the **present()** method, as we did for previous controllers. The following example creates a Safari View Controller to load the website www.formasterminds.com. The code assumes that we have included a button in the main view connected to an Action called **openWeb()**, as we did for the previous examples.

```
import UIKit
import SafariServices

class ViewController: UIViewController {
   @IBAction func openWeb(_ sender: UIButton) {
      let url = URL(string: "http://www.formasterminds.com")
      let controller = SFSafariViewController(url: url!)
      present(controller, animated: true, completion: nil)
   }
}
```

Listing 19-3: *Loading a website with a Safari View Controller*

Do It Yourself: Update the **ViewController** class with the code in Listing 19-3. Run the application and press the button. The system opens a scene with a browser and all the tools required for navigation, including a Done button to close it.

The **SFSafariViewController** class also offers the following properties for configuration.

dismissButtonStyle—This property sets or returns a value that determines the type of button the view controller is going to show to dismiss the scene. It is an enumeration of type **DismissButtonStyle** with the values **done** (default), **close**, and **cancel**.

preferredBarTintColor—This property sets or returns a **UIColor** value that determines the color of the bars.

preferredControlTintColor—This property sets or returns a **UIColor** value that determines the color of the controls.

The following example takes advantage of these properties to get the colors of the bars to match the colors used by the www.formasterminds.com website.

```
import UIKit
import SafariServices

class ViewController: UIViewController {
   @IBAction func openWeb(_ sender: UIButton) {
      let url = URL(string: "http://www.formasterminds.com")

      let controller = SFSafariViewController(url: url!)
      controller.dismissButtonStyle = .close
      controller.preferredBarTintColor = UIColor(red: 81/255, green:
91/255, blue: 119/255, alpha: 1.0)
      controller.preferredControlTintColor = UIColor.white

      present(controller, animated: true, completion: nil)
   }
}
```

Listing 19-4: *Configuring the scene*

The code in this example also modifies the **dismissButtonStyle** property to change the type of button shown by the browser to close the scene from Done to Close.

Figure 19-1: *Custom Safari View Controller*

When the user scrolls the page, the controller collapses the bars to make more room for the content. This makes difficult for the user to dismiss the scene or use the tools. If we think that it would be better for our app to always keep the bars visible and at their original size, we can initialize the controller with a configuration object and assign the value **false** to the **barCollapsingEnabled** property.

The **Configuration** class provides a simple initializer with no parameters. Once the object is created, we can configure its properties and assign it to the Safari View Controller from the controller's initializer, as shown in the following example.

```
import UIKit
import SafariServices

class ViewController: UIViewController {
   @IBAction func openWeb(_ sender: UIButton) {
      let url = URL(string: "http://www.formasterminds.com")

      let config = SFSafariViewController.Configuration()
      config.barCollapsingEnabled = false
      let controller = SFSafariViewController(url: url!, configuration:
config)
      present(controller, animated: true, completion: nil)
   }
}
```

Listing 19-5: *Displaying the bars in their original size*

Do It Yourself: Update the **ViewController** class with the code in Listing 19-5. Run the application and scroll the page. The bars should stay at the same size and the buttons should always be visible.

The framework also defines the **SFSafariViewControllerDelegate** protocol, so we can assign a delegate to the Safari View Controller to control the process. The following are some of the methods defined by this protocol.

safariViewController(SFSafariViewController, **didCompleteInitialLoad:** Bool**)**—This method is called by the controller when the initial website finish loading.

safariViewControllerDidFinish(SFSafariViewController**)**—This method is called by the controller when the scene is dismissed (the user pressed the Done button).

The Safari View Controller includes the **delegate** property to define a delegate. The following example assigns the **ViewController** class as the delegate and implements the **safariViewControllerDidFinish()** method to deactivate the button on the interface when the user dismisses the scene (the user is only able to open the scene once).

```
import UIKit
import SafariServices

class ViewController: UIViewController, SFSafariViewControllerDelegate {
   @IBOutlet weak var openButton: UIButton!

   @IBAction func openWeb(_ sender: UIButton) {
      let url = URL(string: "http://www.formasterminds.com")
      let controller = SFSafariViewController(url: url!)
      controller.delegate = self
      present(controller, animated: true, completion: nil)
   }
   func safariViewControllerDidFinish(_ controller:
SFSafariViewController){
      openButton.isEnabled = false
   }
}
```

Listing 19-6: *Assigning a delegate to the Safari View Controller*

Do It Yourself: Update the **ViewController** class with the code in Listing 19-6. Connect the button in the scene with the **openButton** Outlet. Run the application, press the button, and press Done to close the Safari View Controller. The button should be disabled.

19.3 WebKit Framework

Including a Safari web browser in our interface is a good way to keep the users inside our app, but in some cases this option is not customizable enough. To provide more alternatives, Apple offers the WebKit framework. With this framework we can display web content within a view. The class provided for this purpose is a subclass of **UIView** called **WKWebView**.

WKWebView(frame: CGRect, **configuration:** WKWebViewConfiguration**)**—This initializer creates a **WKWebView** object with the size determined by the **frame** argument and the configuration set by the **configuration** argument.

The Library also includes an option to add a WebKit View to a scene in the Storyboard.

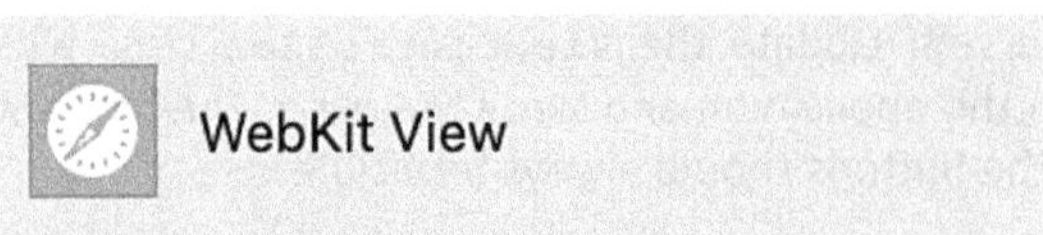

Figure 19-2: *WebKit View option in the Library*

The following are some of the properties and methods defined in the **WKWebView** class to load and manage the content.

title—This property returns a string with the title of the current page.

url—This property returns a URL structure with the URL of the current page.

customUserAgent—This property sets or returns a string with the name of the user agent (**nil** by default).

isLoading—This property returns a Boolean value that indicates if the view is in the process of loading a URL.

canGoBack—This property returns a Boolean value that indicates if the view can navigate to the previews page.

canGoForward—This property returns a Boolean value that indicates if the view can navigate to the next page.

estimatedProgress—This property returns a value of type **Double** between 0.0 and 1.0 that indicates the fraction of the content that has been already loaded.

load(URLRequest**)**—This method loads the content of a URL. The argument is the request for the URL we want to open.

goBack()—This method navigates to the previous page on the list.

goForward()—This method navigates to the next page on the list.

go(to: WKBackForwardListItem**)**—This method navigates to the page indicated by the argument. The **to** argument is an object that represents a page in the navigation list.

reload()—This method reloads the current page (it refreshes the page).

stopLoading()—This method stops the view from loading the content.

URLs are addresses that indicate the location of a file, but they also establish the kind of protocol we are going to use to set the connection. The UIKit framework offers the **URLRequest** structure to manage this information. The structure includes the following initializers.

URLRequest(url: URL, **cachePolicy:** CachePolicy, **timeoutInterval:** TimeInterval**)**—This initializer creates a **URLRequest** structure for the URL and protocol specified by the **url** argument (the information of the protocol is taken from the URL itself). The **cachePolicy** argument is an enumeration that determines how the request will work with the cache. The possible values are: **useProtocolCachePolicy** (default), **reloadIgnoringLocalCacheData**, **reloadIgnoringLocalAndRemoteCacheData**, **reloadIgnoringCacheData**, **returnCacheDataElseLoad**, **returnCacheDataDontLoad**, and **reloadRevalidatingCacheData**. The **timeoutInterval** argument is the maximum time allowed for the system to process the request (60.0 seconds by default).

A WebKit View can report the state of the content to a delegate. For this purpose, the framework defines the **WKNavigationDelegate** protocol. The following are some of its methods.

webView(WKWebView, **decidePolicyFor:** WKNavigationAction, **decisionHandler:** Block**)**—This method is called on the delegate to determine if the view should process a request. The **decidePolicyFor** argument is an object with information about the request, and the **decisionHandler** argument is a closure that we must execute to communicate our decision to the system. The closure takes a value of type **`WKNavigationActionPolicy`**, an enumeration with the properties **`cancel`** and **`allow`**.

webView(WKWebView, **didStartProvisionalNavigation:** WKNavigation!**)**—This method is called on the delegate when the view begins loading new content.

webView(WKWebView, **didFinish:** WKNavigation!**)**—This method is called on the delegate when the view finishes loading the content.

webView(WKWebView, **didFailProvisionalNavigation:** WKNavigation!, **withError:** Error**)**—This method is called on the delegate when an error occurs.

webView(WKWebView, **didReceiveServerRedirectForProvisionalNavigation:** WKNavigation!**)**—This method is called on the delegate when the server redirects the navigator to a different destination.

The process to load a website in a WebKit View is simple. We get the URL, create a request, and ask the view to load it.

```
import UIKit
import WebKit

class ViewController: UIViewController {
   @IBOutlet weak var webView: WKWebView!

   override func viewDidLoad() {
      super.viewDidLoad()

      if let webURL = URL(string: "https://www.google.com") {
         let request = URLRequest(url: webURL)
         webView.load(request)
      }
   }
}
```

Listing 19-7: *Loading a website with a WebKit View*

This example assumes that we have added a WebKit View to the interface from the Library, and it is connected to the **`ViewController`** class with an Outlet called **`webView`**. To prepare the request, we get the **`URL`** structure with the address we want to access and initialize the **`URLRequest`** structure with values by default (only the URL is required). Finally, the request is loaded with the **`load()`** method and the website is shown on the screen.

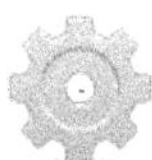

Do It Yourself: Create a project. Add a WebKit View to the scene. Connect the WebKit View to the **`ViewController`** class with an Outlet called **`webView`**. Complete the **`ViewController`** class with the code in Listing 19-7. Run the application. You should see Google's website on the screen.

With this process, we can load any website we want, including those specified or selected by the user (we just need to prepare the URL the way we did before for links in Listing 19-2). But users need more control over the content. For instance, if we use the previous example to perform a Google search, we will notice right away that there is no way to go back to the previous page or navigate back to the beginning. WebKit Views offer several methods to manipulate their content, and delegate methods to respond to changes, but we must provide the tools for navigation, as shown in the following example.

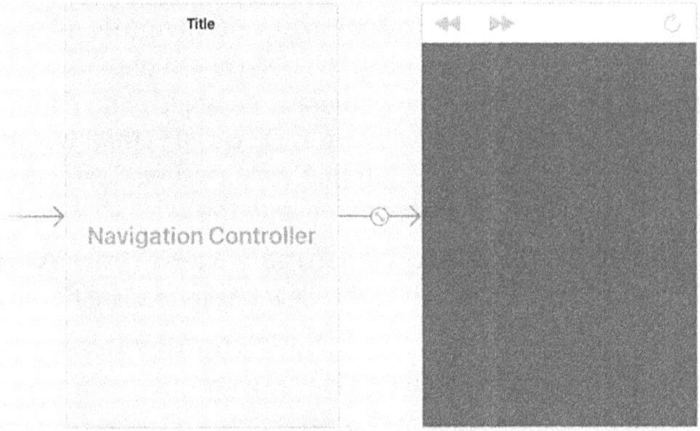

Figure 19-3: *Custom web browser for our application*

In this interface, we have embedded the scene in a Navigation Controller and added three buttons to the Navigation Bar to let the user go back, move forward, and refresh the page.

Before modifying the content of a WebKit View we need to know what we can and cannot do. For example, we can only go back if the user has already navigated forward. This is when the delegate methods become useful. Implementing the protocol methods, we can check the status of the content every time a new document is loaded, as shown next.

```
import UIKit
import WebKit

class ViewController: UIViewController, WKNavigationDelegate {
   @IBOutlet weak var backButton: UIBarButtonItem!
   @IBOutlet weak var forwardButton: UIBarButtonItem!
   @IBOutlet weak var refreshButton: UIBarButtonItem!
   @IBOutlet weak var webView: WKWebView!

   override func viewDidLoad() {
      super.viewDidLoad()
      updateButtons()

      webView.navigationDelegate = self
      if let webURL = URL(string: "https://www.google.com") {
         let request = URLRequest(url: webURL)
         webView.load(request)
      }
   }
   @IBAction func moveBack(_ sender: UIBarButtonItem) {
      webView.goBack()
   }
   @IBAction func moveForward(_ sender: UIBarButtonItem) {
      webView.goForward()
   }
   @IBAction func refresh(_ sender: UIBarButtonItem) {
      webView.reload()
   }
   func webView(_ webView: WKWebView, decidePolicyFor navigationAction:
WKNavigationAction, decisionHandler: @escaping (WKNavigationActionPolicy)
-> Void) {
      if webView.isLoading {
         updateButtons()
      }
      decisionHandler(.allow)
   }
   func updateButtons() {
      backButton.isEnabled = webView.canGoBack
```

```
        forwardButton.isEnabled = webView.canGoForward
    }
}
```

Listing 19-8: Implementing a custom web browser

The **WKWebView** class includes the **navigationDelegate** property to designate a delegate for the view. In Listing 19-8, we assign the view controller as the delegate and then implement the **webView(WKWebView, decidePolicyFor:, decisionHandler:)** method to modify the interface every time a new page is loaded. This method is called by the view to ask permission before navigating to new content and therefore is perfect to control the buttons on the interface. The method may be called multiple times per action, so we check whether the view is loading new content with the **isLoading** method, and then call our **updateButtons()** method to update the buttons. This method considers the values returned by the **canGoBack** and **canGoForward** properties to enable or disable the buttons, so the buttons to navigate back and forward are only enabled when there are documents to go to.

Do It Yourself: Create a project. Embed the initial scene in a Navigation Controller. Add a WebKit View to the scene and pin it to the sides of the main view. Connect the WebKit View with an Outlet called **webView**. Add three Bar Buttons to the Navigation Bar (you can change the appearance of the buttons from the System Item option in the Attributes Inspector panel). Connect the buttons to Outlets called **backButton**, **forwardButton**, and **refreshButton**, and to Actions called **moveBack()**, **moveForward()**, and **refresh()**. Complete the **ViewController** class with the code in Listing 19-8. Run the application and search for a word. Click on a link in the results. The buttons in the Navigation Bar should be enabled and disabled according to your location in the browsing history.

Medium App Transport Security

In the latest examples, we open secure URLs (URLs that begin with the prefix https://), because these are the URLs allowed by default. iOS implements a system called App Transport Security (ATS) to block insecure URLs, like those starting with the prefix http:// (without the s). If we need to load insecure URLs, such as http://www.formasterminds.com, we can configure our app from the info.plist file to circumvent this security measure for all the websites or specific domains. The option to configure the App Transport Security system is called "App Transport Security Settings", as shown below.

Key	Type	Value
∨ Information Property List	Dictionary	(2 items)
> App Transport Security Settings	Dictionary	(0 items)
> Application Scene Manifest	Dictionary	(2 items)

Figure 19-4: Option to configure App Transport Security

The interface includes a + button on the right side of the item to add values to that item. In this case, the button has two functions: if the arrow on the left is pointing to the item (closed), a new item is added to the main list, but if the arrow is pointing down (expanded), the new item is added to the item as a new value (we can click the arrow to close or expand the item). Values added to an item are shown below the item with a little indentation to reflect the hierarchy. The value we need to add to the App Transport Security Settings item to allow insecure URLs to be opened is called "Allow Arbitrary Loads", as shown below.

Key		Type	Value
⌄ Information Property List		Dictionary	(2 items)
⌄ App Transport Security Settings	◊	Dictionary	(1 item)
Allow Arbitrary Loads	◊	Boolean	YES
> Application Scene Manifest	◊	Dictionary	(2 items)

Figure 19-5: *App Transport Security configured to allow insecure URLs*

The Allow Arbitrary Loads key takes a Boolean value specified with the strings YES and NO (or 1 and 0, respectively). Setting this key to YES (1) allows any URL to be opened. If what we want is to allow only specific domains, we must use the Exception Domains key and add to the key additional items with the domains we want to include. These items in turn require at least three more items with the keys **`NSIncludesSubdomains`** (Boolean), **`NSTemporaryException-AllowsInsecureHTTPLoads`** (Boolean), and **`NSTemporaryExceptionMinimumTLSVersion`** (String). For example, the following configuration allows documents from the formasterminds.com domain to be opened.

Key		Type	Value
⌄ Information Property List		Dictionary	(2 items)
⌄ App Transport Security Settings	◊	Dictionary	(1 item)
⌄ Exception Domains	◊	Dictionary	(1 item)
⌄ formasterminds.com		Dictionary	(3 items)
NSTemporaryExceptionMinimumTLSVersion		String	TLSv1.1
NSTemporaryExceptionAllowsInsecureHTTPLo...		Boolean	1
NSIncludesSubdomains		Boolean	1
> Application Scene Manifest	◊	Dictionary	(2 items)

Figure 19-6: *App Transport Security configured to allow URLs from formasterminds.com*

Basic 19.4 Web Content

The Safari View Controller and the WebKit views were designed to show content to the user, but the capacity to integrate that content with our app is limited. Sometimes all we need is to extract a piece of information from a document or process the data instead of showing the entire content as it is. In cases like this, we must load the document in the background and analyze it to extract only what we need. Foundation includes a group of classes to get content referenced by a URL. The main class is called **`URLSession`**. This class creates a session that manages an HTTP connection to obtain data and download or upload files. The following are the initializers and type property provided by the class to create the session.

URLSession(configuration: URLSessionConfiguration**)**—This initializer creates a new session with the configuration set by the argument. The **configuration** argument is an object that specifies the session's behavior.

URLSession(configuration: URLSessionConfiguration, **delegate:** URLSessionDelegate?, **delegateQueue:** OperationQueue?**)**—This initializer creates a new session with the configuration set by the arguments. The **configuration** argument is an object that specifies the session's behavior, the **delegate** argument is a reference to the delegate object we want to assign to the session, and the **delegateQueue** argument is the queue in which the delegate methods are going to be executed.

shared—This type property returns a standard session with a configuration by default that is suitable to perform basic requests.

The session sets up the connection, but it does not perform any tasks. To download or upload data we must implement the following methods defined in the **`URLSession`** class.

data(from: URL, **delegate:** URLSessionTaskDelegate?**)**—This asynchronous method adds a task to the session to download the data at the URL indicated by the **from** argument. The **delegate** argument is the delegate object used by the task to report updates during the process. The method returns a tuple with two values: a **Data** structure with the data returned by the server and a **URLResponse** object with the status of the request.

download(from: URL, **delegate:** URLSessionTaskDelegate?**)**—This asynchronous method adds a task to the session to download the file at the URL indicated by the **from** argument. The **delegate** argument is the delegate object used by the task to report updates during the process. The method returns a tuple with two values: a **URL** structure that indicates the location of the downloaded file and a **URLResponse** object with the status of the request.

bytes(from: URL, **delegate:** URLSessionTaskDelegate?**)**—This asynchronous method adds a task to the session to download a sequence of bytes from the URL indicated by the **from** argument. The **delegate** argument is the delegate object used by the task to report updates during the process. The method returns a tuple with two values: a **AsyncBytes** structure with an asynchronous sequence of bytes and a **URLResponse** object with the status of the request.

The following are the methods defined by the class to upload data and files.

upload(for: URLRequest, **from:** Data, **delegate:** URLSessionTaskDelegate?**)**—This asynchronous method adds a task to the session to upload the data indicated by the **from** argument. The **delegate** argument is the delegate object used by the task to report updates during the process. The method returns a tuple with two values: a **Data** structure with the data returned by the server and a **URLResponse** object with the status of the request.

upload(for: URLRequest, **fromFile:** URL, **delegate:** URLSessionTask-Delegate?**)**—This asynchronous method adds a task to the session to upload the file in the URL indicated by the **fromFile** argument. The **delegate** argument is the delegate object used by the task to report updates during the process. The method returns a tuple with two values: a **Data** structure with the data returned by the server and a **URLResponse** object with the status of the request.

These methods are asynchronous. When they finish downloading or uploading the data, they return the result. For example, if we use the **data()** method to get data from a website, the value returned includes a value with the data and an object of type **URLResponse** with the status of the request. When we access a URL using the HTTP protocol, the response is represented by an object of type **HTTPURLResponse** (a subclass of **URLResponse**). This class includes the **statusCode** property to return a code that determines the status of the request. There are several codes available to determine things like the success of the request (200) or more drastic situations like when the website has been moved to a different address (301). If all we want is to make sure that the data was downloaded correctly, we can check if the value of the **statusCode** property is equal to 200 before processing anything. The following example shows how to perform a basic request.

```
import UIKit

class ViewController: UIViewController {
   override func viewDidLoad() {
      super.viewDidLoad()
      Task(priority: .high) {
         await loadWebsite()
      }
   }
```

```
   func loadWebsite() async {
      let session = URLSession.shared
      let webURL = URL(string: "https://www.yahoo.com")
      do {
         let (data, response) = try await session.data(from: webURL!)
         if let resp = response as? HTTPURLResponse {
            let status = resp.statusCode
            if status == 200 {
               let content = String(data: data, encoding:
String.Encoding.ascii)
               print(content!)
            } else {
               print("Error: \(status)")
            }
         }
      } catch {
         print("Error: \(error)")
      }
   }
}
```

Listing 19-9: *Loading a remote document*

To download data, all we need is a session and a URL. The **data()** method is asynchronous, so we place the code inside an asynchronous method and run a task that calls this method as soon as the scene is loaded. In this example, we load the website at www.yahoo.com and print the content on the console. Because we are just loading a single web page, the standard session returned by the **shared** property is more than enough. When the task is finished, we turn the data into a string with the **String()** initializer and then print the string on the console.

A standard session like the one we used in this example comes with a configuration by default that is suitable for most situations, but a custom session requires its own configuration. To configure a session, Foundation provides a class called **URLSessionConfiguration** with type methods and properties to set a specific configuration. The following is the type property we can use to get a configuration object with values by default.

default—This property returns a **URLSessionConfiguration** object with default settings.

Once we get a basic object, we can adapt it to the requirements of our application. The following are some of the properties offered by the **URLSessionConfiguration** class to modify the configuration.

allowsCellularAccess—This property sets or returns a Boolean value that determines if the connection should be made when the device is connected to a cellular network.

timeoutIntervalForRequest—This property sets or returns a **TimeInterval** value (a typealias of **Double**) that determines the number of seconds the session should wait for a request to be answered. The value by default is 60.

waitsForConnectivity—This property sets or returns a Boolean value that determines if the session should wait to perform the request until the device gets connected to the network. The value by default is **false**.

Working with custom sessions only requires us to change how the session is initialized, but the rest of the code remains the same.

```
import UIKit

class ViewController: UIViewController {
   override func viewDidLoad() {
      super.viewDidLoad()
      Task(priority: .high) {
         await loadWebsite()
      }
   }
   func loadWebsite() async {
      let config = URLSessionConfiguration.default
      config.waitsForConnectivity = true
      let session = URLSession(configuration: config)
      let webURL = URL(string: "https://www.yahoo.com")

      do {
         let (data, response) = try await session.data(from: webURL!)
         if let resp = response as? HTTPURLResponse {
            let status = resp.statusCode
            if status == 200 {
               let content = String(data: data, encoding:
String.Encoding.ascii)
               print(content!)
            } else {
               print("Error: \(status)")
            }
         }
      } catch {
         print("Error: \(error)")
      }
   }
}
```

Listing 19-10: *Instantiating a custom session*

Do It Yourself: Create a new project. Update the **ViewController** class with the codes in Listings 19-9 or 19-10. Run the application. You should see the HTML code of Yahoo's website printed on the console.

In the previous example, we didn't implement the **delegate** argument of the **data()** method. This argument is optional, but we can declare it if we need to respond to changes during the process. The framework defines the **URLSessionTaskDelegate** protocol to create this delegate object. The protocol defines several methods. The following are the most frequently used.

urlSession(URLSession, **task:** URLSessionTask, **didReceive:** URL-AuthenticationChallenge, **completionHandler:** Closure**)**—This method is called on the delegate when authentication is requested by the server. Our implementation must call the completion handler received by the method with two arguments that define the settings and credentials.

urlSession(URLSession, **task:** URLSessionTask, **willPerformHTTP-Redirection:** HTTPURLResponse, **newRequest:** URLRequest, **completion-Handler:** Block**)**—This method is called on the delegate when the server redirected the connection to another URL. Our implementation must call the completion handler received by the method with an argument that defines the new request (the value of the **newRequest** argument) or the value **nil** if we do not want to follow the redirection.

Some websites, like www.yahoo.com, send the user to a different address that contains a version of the website customized to the user's location and preferences. This means that the URL we provide does not represent the final destination; the server does not return any data but instead redirects the user to another document. In cases like this, we can define a custom session with a delegate and then implement the method of the **URLSessionTaskDelegate** protocol to determine what we want to do when the server is redirecting our application.

```
import UIKit

class ViewController: UIViewController, URLSessionTaskDelegate {
   override func viewDidLoad() {
      super.viewDidLoad()
      Task(priority: .high) {
         await loadWebsite()
      }
   }
   func loadWebsite() async {
      let config = URLSessionConfiguration.default
      config.waitsForConnectivity = true
      let session = URLSession(configuration: config)
      let webURL = URL(string: "https://www.yahoo.com")

      do {
         let (data, response) = try await session.data(from: webURL!,
delegate: self)
         if let resp = response as? HTTPURLResponse {
            let status = resp.statusCode
            if status == 200 {
               let content = String(data: data, encoding:
String.Encoding.ascii)
               print(content!)
            } else {
               print("Error: \(status)")
            }
         }
      } catch {
         print("Error: \(error)")
      }
   }
   func urlSession(_ session: URLSession, task: URLSessionTask,
willPerformHTTPRedirection response: HTTPURLResponse, newRequest request:
URLRequest) async -> URLRequest? {
      return request
   }
}
```

***Listing 19-11:** Following a redirection*

In this example, we define the **ViewController** class as the delegate and return the new request. Every time the server asks for a redirection, the protocol method is called and the request with the new URL is executed. The process repeats until the destination is reached and then the content of that document is printed on the console.

Basic JSON

Normal websites return documents written in HTML code. This is the basic language implemented by every website on the Internet. It is composed of predefined tags that take care of organizing the document's content. For example, the tags <title> and </title> enclose the title of the document, so we can use string methods to find the location of the last character of the <title> tag and the first character of the </title> tag and then cut the text in the middle to extract the title. The problem with this approach is that most tags in HTML have the same name, making it very difficult to identify the information we want to retrieve. Also, websites do not follow a predefined structure and their code may change without a warning. If we create an app that extracts information from the HTML code of a web page, it may not only be illegal, but it could also stop working before the app is submitted to the App Store. This is not only a problem for mobile applications but also for web applications in general. The solution was found a long time ago with the creation of formatting languages that have the sole purpose of sharing data on the Web. Some are programming languages and others are just format specifications, like JSON.

JSON (Javascript Object Notation) defines a dictionary-like notation to identify data. Every piece of data is stored with a key/value pair and related values are enclosed in braces. The advantage of this format is that the information is easy to find. Every value has a unique key.

Because of the format, JSON files can easily be converted into Swift structures that we can process as any other structure in our code. Foundation includes the **JSONDecoder** class to decode JSON data into Swift structures and the **JSONEncoder** class to encode Swift structures into JSON data. These classes include their respective methods to decode and encode the values.

decode(Type, **from:** Data**)**—This method returns a value of the data type specified by the first argument with the information contained by the **from** argument. The **from** argument is a **Data** structure that contains the JSON data we want to decode.

encode(Value**)**—This method returns a JSON representation of the data provided by the argument.

For a structure to be decodable, it must conform to the **Codable** protocol. This is a protocol that defines initializers and methods required to encode and decode the values of the properties (see Chapter 15). For example, the following is a JSON file that contains information about a book.

```
{
   "title": "The Shining",
   "author": "Stephen King"
}
```

Listing 19-12: *JSON file*

To convert this data to a value we can process in Swift, we must define a structure that conforms to the **Codable** protocol and includes all the properties required to represent the values we want to read.

```
struct Book: Codable {
   let title: String
   let author: String
}
```

Listing 19-13: *Swift structure to decode JSON data*

Because the **Book** structure conforms to the **Codable** protocol, it is ready for coding and decoding, so we can use it to read the JSON file of Listing 19-12. The following view controller demonstrates how to turn that JSON data into a **Book** structure and read its values.

```
import UIKit

class ViewController: UIViewController {
   override func viewDidLoad() {
      super.viewDidLoad()
      let bundle = Bundle.main
      let jsonURL = bundle.url(forResource: "books", withExtension:
"json")
      let jsonData = FileManager.default.contents(atPath: jsonURL!.path)
```

```
        let decoder = JSONDecoder()
        do {
           let info = try decoder.decode(Book.self, from: jsonData!)
           print("Title: \(info.title)")
           print("Author: \(info.author)")
        } catch {
           print("Error: \(error)")
        }
     }
  }
```

Listing 19-14: *Decoding JSON data*

This example assumes that we have created a file called books.json with the JSON code of Listing 19-12. Once we read the file from the bundle and get its content, we create a **JSONDecoder** object and then call the **decode()** method on it to turn the data into a **Book** structure. The values of this structure are finally printed on the console to confirm that the process was successful.

Do It Yourself: Create a new project. Create a text file called books.json with the JSON code of Listing 19-12 and add it to the project. Create a Swift file called Book.swift with the structure in Listing 19-13. Update the **ViewController** class with the code in Listing 19-14. Run the application. You should see the values in the JSON file printed on the console.

The previous example explains how to read and decode a JSON file stored in the bundle, but this information is usually downloaded from online services. The JSON documents provided by these services are dynamically generated and contain only the information requested by the application. For instance, the website www.openweathermap.org offers a service that generates JSON documents with information about the weather for specific locations (https://openweathermap.org/api).

To illustrate how to access and process the documents produced by these services, we are going to read posts from a website called JSONPlaceholder that generates phony documents. The process doesn't introduce anything new. We must load the document with a **URLSession** and then decode it with a **JSONDecoder** object, as we did before.

The document we are going to download for this example is located at https://jsonplaceholder.typicode.com/posts. The JSON code generated by this document includes multiple items, each with four values called userId, id, title, and body. The following model includes the structure we need to decode these values.

```
import UIKit

enum Sections {
   case main
}
struct Post: Codable, Identifiable {
   var id: Int
   var userId: Int
   var title: String
   var body: String
}
class ApplicationData {
   var listPosts: [Post] = []
   var dataSource: UITableViewDiffableDataSource<Sections, Post.ID>!
}
var AppData = ApplicationData()
```

Listing 19-15: *Defining a model to decode posts*

We made the **Post** structure conform to the **Identifiable** protocol to list the values on a Table View (the **Int** data type is Hashable). The following is the view controller for this table.

```
import UIKit

class PostsViewController: UITableViewController {
   override func viewDidLoad() {
      super.viewDidLoad()
      tableView.register(UITableViewCell.self, forCellReuseIdentifier:
"myCell")
      prepareDataSource()

      Task(priority: .high) {
         await loadWebsite()
      }
   }
   func loadWebsite() async {
      let session = URLSession.shared
      let webURL = URL(string: "https://jsonplaceholder.typicode.com/
posts")
      do {
         let (data, response) = try await session.data(from: webURL!)
         if let resp = response as? HTTPURLResponse {
            let status = resp.statusCode
            if status == 200 {
               let decoder = JSONDecoder()
               AppData.listPosts = (try? decoder.decode([Post].self,
from: data)) ?? []
               await MainActor.run {
                  self.prepareSnapshot()
               }
            }
         }
      } catch {
         print("Error: \(error)")
      }
   }
   func prepareDataSource() {
      AppData.dataSource = UITableViewDiffableDataSource<Sections,
Post.ID>(tableView: tableView) { tableView, indexPath, itemID in
         let cell = tableView.dequeueReusableCell(withIdentifier:
"myCell", for: indexPath)
         if let item = AppData.listPosts.first(where: { $0.id ==
itemID }) {
            var config = cell.defaultContentConfiguration()
            config.text = item.title
            config.secondaryText = item.body
            cell.contentConfiguration = config
         }
         return cell
      }
   }
   func prepareSnapshot() {
      var snapshot = NSDiffableDataSourceSnapshot<Sections, Post.ID>()
      snapshot.appendSections([.main])
      snapshot.appendItems(AppData.listPosts.map { $0.id })
      AppData.dataSource.apply(snapshot)
   }
}
```

Listing 19-16: *Decoding JSON data from the Web*

This example assumes that the initial scene in the interface has been replaced by a Table View Controller. When the scene is loaded, we create an asynchronous task to download the JSON file at the URL https://jsonplaceholder.typicode.com/posts. If the status of the response is 200, which means the data has been downloaded successfully, we decode it into an array of **`Post`** structures, assign the array to the **`listPosts`** property in the model, and update the snapshot to display the values on the screen. The result is shown below.

Figure 19-7: *List of posts downloaded from the Web*

Do It Yourself: Create a new project. Replace the initial scene with a Table View Controller. Create a subclass of **`UITableViewController`** with the name **`PostsViewController`** and assign it to the new scene. Update this class with the code in Listing 19-16. Create a Swift file called ApplicationData.swift for the model in Listing 19-15. Run the application. You should see the list of posts on the screen.

IMPORTANT: The keys used in a JSON document are selected by the developer. Every developer decides what keys to use and how to structure the information. To know the keys used to construct the hierarchy, you need to load the JSON document in your browser or find examples on the website.

Chapter 20
Map Kit

Basic 20.1 Map Kit View

Often, users need to visualize their location or the places they want to go on a map to position themselves in the world. For these kinds of applications, Apple offers the MapKit framework. The framework includes all the tools necessary to create and configure maps with which users can interact to find places and obtain information.

Maps are presented on the screen with a view created from a subclass of **`UIView`** called **`MKMapView`**. The view takes care of loading the map, managing user interaction, and displaying custom content generated by our application.

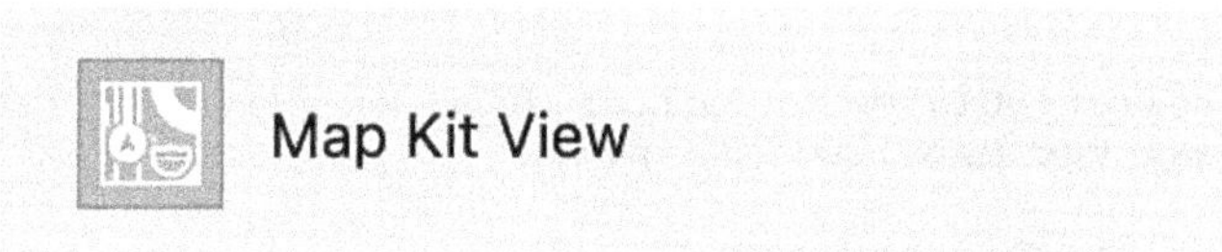

Figure 20-1: *Map Kit View option in the Library*

Like a regular view, a Map Kit View can be pinned to the sides of the main view or other elements. Figure 20-2 introduces the interface we are going to use for the following examples. The scene includes a Map Kit View and a bar button to interact with the map.

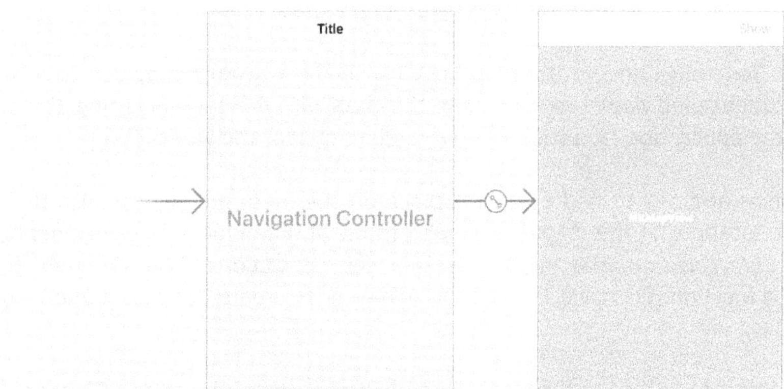

Figure 20-2: *Interface with a Map Kit View*

Do It Yourself: Create a new project. Embed the scene in a Navigation Controller. Add a Map Kit View to the scene and pin it to the Safe Area. Add a bar button called Show, as in Figure 20-2. We will use this button later to select locations. Run the application. You should see the map of the world on the screen.

Basic Configuring the Map

A Map Kit View can show the map in different styles, and let the user zoom, pan, or rotate the map to find a location. The **`MKMapView`** class includes properties to configure these features.

mapType—This property sets or returns a value that determines the style of the map. It is an enumeration of type **`MKMapType`** with the values **`standard`** (default), **`mutedStandard`**, **`satellite`**, **`hybrid`**, **`satelliteFlyover`**, and **`hybridFlyover`**.

isZoomEnabled—This property sets or returns a Boolean value that determines if the user can zoom the map (**true** by default).

isScrollEnabled—This property sets or returns a Boolean value that determines if the user can scroll the map (**true** by default).

isRotateEnabled—This property sets or returns a Boolean value that determines if the user can rotate the map (**true** by default).

isPitchEnabled—This property sets or returns a Boolean value that determines if the camera's pitch angle is considered when rendering the map (**true** by default).

To modify the map, we must import the MapKit framework and then change the values of these properties. The following example defines the style of the map and disables rotation.

```
import UIKit
import MapKit

class ViewController: UIViewController {
   @IBOutlet weak var mapView: MKMapView!

   override func viewDidLoad() {
      super.viewDidLoad()
      mapView.mapType = .satellite
      mapView.isRotateEnabled = false
   }
}
```

Listing 20-1: *Configuring the map*

Do It Yourself: Connect the Map Kit View to the **ViewController** class with an Outlet called **mapView**. Complete the class with the code in Listing 20-1 and run the application. You should see a satellite map of the world.

Users can zoom in and out to find a specific place on the map, but we can also do it from code. To determine locations in the map, the MapKit framework implements values defined in a framework called *Core Location*. The most important class is **CLLocation**, designed to store information about a location. The class includes an initializer to create the object and properties to retrieve the values.

CLLocation(latitude: CLLocationDegrees, **longitude:** CLLocationDegrees**)**—This initializer creates a **CLLocation** object with the location determined by the arguments. The **CLLocationDegrees** data type is a typealias of **Double**.

coordinate—This property returns the location's coordinates. It is a structure of type **CLLocationCoordinate2D** with the **latitude** and **longitude** properties.

horizontalAccuracy—This property returns a value that determines the accuracy of the location's latitude and longitude. It is of type **CLLocationAccuracy** (a typealias of **Double**).

verticalAccuracy—This property returns a value that determines the accuracy of the location's altitude. It is of type **CLLocationAccuracy** (a typealias of **Double**).

altitude—This property returns the altitude of the location in meters. It is of type **CLLocationDistance** (a typealias of **Double**).

The **CLLocation** class also includes a practical method to calculate the distance between two **CLLocation** objects.

distance(from: CLLocation**)**—This method returns a value that determines the distance between the location in the **CLLocation** object and the location determined by the **from** argument. The argument is a **CLLocation** object with the location we want to compare. The value returned is of type **CLLocationDistance** (a typealias of **Double**).

These values define the location, but the map is scrolled to those locations by properties and methods of the **MKMapView** class. The following are the ones available to get the values of the area currently displayed on the screen or set a new one.

region—This property returns an **MKCoordinateRegion** structure with values that determine the area currently displayed on the screen.

centerCoordinate—This property returns a **CLLocationCoordinate2D** structure with the coordinates at the center of the visible area.

setRegion(MKCoordinateRegion, **animated:** Bool**)**—This method sets the map's visible region. The first argument is a structure that contains a **CLLocation-Coordinate2D** value to determine the region's center coordinates, and a value of type **MKCoordinateSpan** to determine the region's size in degrees. The **animated** argument determines if the transition to the region will be animated.

setCenter(CLLocationCoordinate2D, **animated:** Bool**)**—This method sets the region's coordinates. The first argument specifies the latitude and longitude, and the **animated** argument determines if the transition to the location will be animated.

The **MKCoordinateRegion** structure is created from a **CLLocationCoordinate2D** structure that contains the properties **latitude** and **longitude** to return the latitude and longitude of the location, and an **MKCoordinateSpan** structure that contains the size of the region in degrees. Because the degrees of an area can be difficult to calculate, the framework defines an initializer for this structure to set the size of the region in meters.

MKCoordinateRegion(center: CLLocationCoordinate2D, **latitudinalMeters:** CLLocationDistance, **longitudinalMeters:** CLLocationDistance**)**—This initializer creates an **MKCoordinateRegion** structure with the values determined by its arguments. The first argument specifies the region's coordinates, and the second and third arguments determine the vertical and horizontal size of the region in meters.

The following example implements this structure to show an area of 1000 meters around the location of one of the Apple Stores in New York.

```
import UIKit
import MapKit

class ViewController: UIViewController {
   @IBOutlet weak var mapView: MKMapView!

   override func viewDidLoad() {
      super.viewDidLoad()
      let location = CLLocation(latitude: 40.7637825011971, longitude:
-73.9731328627541)
      let region = MKCoordinateRegion(center: location.coordinate,
latitudinalMeters: 1000, longitudinalMeters: 1000)
      mapView.setRegion(region, animated: false)
   }
}
```

Listing 20-2: *Displaying a region*

This code creates a **CLLocation** object with the coordinates of the Apple Store, defines a region around that area, and finally sets the map's visible region with the **setRegion()** method. This time, instead of the entire world, the Map Kit View shows an area of New York City.

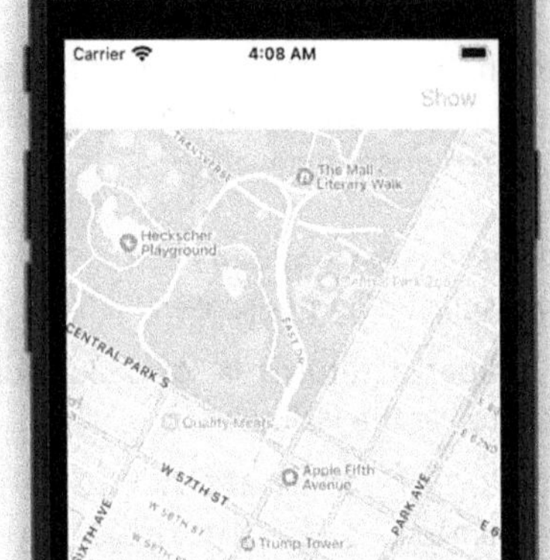

Figure 20-3: *Map showing a specific region of New York City*

Do It Yourself: Update the **ViewController** class with the code in Listing 20-2. Run the application. You should see an area of New York City with the Apple Store at the center.

Basic Annotations

The previous example sets the visible area around the Apple Store. Because this is a relevant location, the map shows an icon with the name of the store, but this is not always the case. Most locations do not show any reference at all, and the user has to guess where the exact location actually is. To add graphics to the map to mark a location, we use annotations.

Annotations provide additional information of a particular location. They are associated with a view that can display an image to represent the annotation, such as a pin, the title and subtitle of the location, and a subview, called *Callout*, to show additional information. Figure 20-4, below, illustrates how an annotation looks like on the map.

Figure 20-4: *Annotation on the map*

What the framework describes as annotations are objects that define the basic aspects of an annotation, like the coordinates in which the annotation will appear, the image that will represent the location, and the title and subtitle to show along with it. The MapKit framework includes the **MKAnnotation** protocol to create these objects. The protocol defines the following properties.

coordinate—This property sets or returns a **CLLocationCoordinate2D** structure that determines the annotation's latitude and longitude.

title—This property sets or returns a string with the annotation's title.

subtitle—This property sets or returns a string with the annotation's subtitle.

To create annotations, we must define a class that conforms to this protocol and implements at least the three properties mentioned above.

```
import MapKit

class MyAnnotation: NSObject, MKAnnotation {
   var coordinate: CLLocationCoordinate2D
   var title: String?
   var subtitle: String?

   init(coordinate: CLLocationCoordinate2D) {
      self.coordinate = coordinate
   }
}
```

Listing 20-3: *Defining an annotation*

Annotations are created from our custom class and then added to the map. The **MKMapView** class offers the following properties and methods to add, remove, and manage annotations.

annotations—This property returns an array of **MKAnnotation** objects that represent the annotations already added to the map.

addAnnotation(MKAnnotation**)**—This method adds an annotation to the map. The argument is an object of a class that conforms to the **MKAnnotation** protocol.

addAnnotations([MKAnnotation]**)**—This method adds multiple annotations to the map. The argument is an array of objects of a class that conforms to the **MKAnnotation** protocol.

removeAnnotation(MKAnnotation**)**—This method removes an annotation. The argument is a reference to the object that represents the annotation.

removeAnnotations([MKAnnotation]**)**—This method removes multiple annotations. The argument is an array of objects that represent the annotations we want to remove.

showAnnotations([MKAnnotation], **animated:** Bool**)**—This method zooms on a region that includes the annotations specified by the first argument. The **animated** argument indicates if the process will be animated.

selectAnnotation(MKAnnotation, **animated:** Bool**)**—This method selects an annotation (it shows the annotation as if the user had tapped on it). The first argument is an object that represents the annotation we want to select, and the **animated** argument indicates if the process will be animated.

deselectAnnotation(MKAnnotation?, **animated:** Bool**)**—This method deselects an annotation. The first argument is an object that represents the annotation we want to deselect, and the **animated** argument indicates if the process will be animated.

The following code expands the **viewDidLoad()** method from the previous example to create an annotation from our **MyAnnotation** class and adds it to the map.

```
import UIKit
import MapKit

class ViewController: UIViewController {
   @IBOutlet weak var mapView: MKMapView!

   override func viewDidLoad() {
      super.viewDidLoad()
```

```
        let location = CLLocation(latitude: 40.7637825011971, longitude:
-73.9731328627541)
        let region = MKCoordinateRegion(center: location.coordinate,
latitudinalMeters: 1000, longitudinalMeters: 1000)
        mapView.setRegion(region, animated: false)

        let annotation = MyAnnotation(coordinate: location.coordinate)
        annotation.title = "Apple Store"
        annotation.subtitle = "Think Different"
        mapView.addAnnotation(annotation)
    }
}
```

Listing 20-4: *Adding an annotation*

By default, the Map Kit View generates a view to show the annotation on the map. The view contains an image that represents a pin and the title below. When the annotation is selected, the view shows a larger image and the subtitle, as illustrated next.

Figure 20-5: *Annotation with a view by default*

Do It Yourself: Add to your project a Swift file called MyAnnotation.swift for the code in Listing 20-3. Update the **`ViewController`** class with the code in Listing 20-4. Run the application and tap on the pin to expand it (Figure 20-5).

IMPORTANT: The MapKit framework includes the **`MKPointAnnotation`** class to create basic annotations. If your annotations only require the values of the **`coordinate`**, **`title`**, and **`subtitle`** properties, you can create them from this class instead of defining your own (see Listing 20-12, below).

As we already mentioned, an annotation object determines where the annotation is located, but the annotation view is the element responsible for displaying the graphic that points to the coordinates of the annotation. If we do not provide a view for the annotation, the system creates one by default from a class called **`MKMarkerAnnotationView`**. The views created from this class include the balloon shown in Figure 20-5, always with the same icon and in the same color. If we want to change the configuration of the view, we must create our own objects. For this purpose, the **`MKMarkerAnnotationView`** class includes the following initializer and properties.

MKMarkerAnnotationView(annotation: MKAnnotation?, **reuseIdentifier:** String?**)**—This initializer creates an annotation view of type marker for the annotation specified by the **annotation** argument. The **annotation** argument is a reference to the annotation object we want to associate with the view, and the **reuseIdentifier** argument is a string the Map Kit View needs to be able to reuse the view to display multiple annotations.

glyphText—This property sets or returns the text displayed in the balloon.

markerTintColor—This property sets or returns a **`UIColor`** value that determines the color of the balloon.

glyphTintColor—This property sets or returns a **`UIColor`** value that determines the color of the text in the balloon.

glyphImage—This property sets or returns a **UIImage** object with the image displayed in the balloon. The image must be of a size of 20 x 20 points.

selectedGlyphImage—This property sets or returns a **UIImage** object with the image displayed in the balloon when it is selected. The image must be of a size of 40 x 40 points.

titleVisibility—This property sets or returns a value that determines whether the title will be visible or not. It is an enumeration of type **MKFeatureVisibility** with the values **adaptive**, **hidden**, and **visible**.

subtitleVisibility—This property sets or returns a value that determines whether the subtitle will be visible or not. It is an enumeration of type **MKFeatureVisibility** with the values **adaptive**, **hidden**, and **visible**.

Annotations are added to the map and then the Map Kit View checks which ones are inside the visible area and requests the views to display. When the Map Kit View needs a view, it calls a delegate method to get it. The method is defined in the **MKMapViewDelegate** protocol. To provide a custom view for each annotation, we must conform to this protocol and implement the following method.

mapView(MKMapView, **viewFor:** MKAnnotation**)**—This method is called on the delegate when the Map Kit View needs a view to show an annotation. The **viewFor** argument is a reference to the object that represents the annotation the map is going to display.

Like the cells of a Table View, annotation views are reusable. We must create the view inside the delegate method, assign an identifier to it, and then use the same view again for other annotations. The **MKMapView** class includes the following method to get a reusable view.

dequeueReusableAnnotationView(withIdentifier: String**)**—This method returns an **MKAnnotationView** object with the view identified by the **withIdentifier** argument. The argument is the same string declared when the view was created.

The **ViewController** class in the following example conforms to the **MKMapViewDelegate** protocol and implements the delegate method to create a custom view for our annotation.

```
import UIKit
import MapKit

class ViewController: UIViewController, MKMapViewDelegate {
   @IBOutlet weak var mapView: MKMapView!

   override func viewDidLoad() {
      super.viewDidLoad()
      let location = CLLocation(latitude: 40.7637825011971, longitude:
-73.9731328627541)
     let region = MKCoordinateRegion(center: location.coordinate,
latitudinalMeters: 1000, longitudinalMeters: 1000)
      mapView.setRegion(region, animated: false)

      let annotation = MyAnnotation(coordinate: location.coordinate)
      annotation.title = "Apple Store"
      annotation.subtitle = "Think Different"
      mapView.addAnnotation(annotation)

      mapView.delegate = self
   }
```

```
    func mapView(_ mapView: MKMapView, viewFor annotation: MKAnnotation)
-> MKAnnotationView? {
        if let temp = annotation as? MyAnnotation {
            var aView =
mapView.dequeueReusableAnnotationView(withIdentifier: "Pins") as?
MKMarkerAnnotationView
            if aView == nil {
                aView = MKMarkerAnnotationView(annotation: temp,
reuseIdentifier: "Pins")
                aView?.glyphText = "Place"
                aView?.markerTintColor = UIColor.blue
                aView?.titleVisibility = .hidden
                aView?.subtitleVisibility = .hidden
            } else {
                aView?.annotation = annotation
            }
            return aView
        }
        return nil
    }
}
```

Listing 20-5: *Configuring the annotation view*

The code in Listing 20-5 sets the region we want to show, adds an annotation to the map at the coordinates of the Apple Store, and designates the **ViewController** class as the Map Kit View's delegate. The protocol method is implemented next to provide a custom view for this annotation.

When the Map Kit View is showing the selected area, it detects that there is an annotation inside and calls the **mapView(MKMapView, viewFor: MKAnnotation)** method to get its view. This method checks whether the annotation is one of our custom annotations, looks for a view with the "Pins" identifier, and if there is no view, it creates a new one. Notice that the **dequeueReusableAnnotationView()** method may return a view that was previously used for another annotation, so we must assign the new annotation to it before returning the value (**aView?.annotation = annotation**).

The configuration defined for our annotation view includes a title for the balloon, a blue background, and it hides the annotation's title and subtitle. The result is shown below.

Figure 20-6: *Custom balloon*

If we want to replace the balloon altogether, instead of using an object of the **MKMarker-AnnotationView** class, we must define our own annotation view with an object of a basic class called **MKAnnotationView** (this is the superclass of the **MKMarkerAnnotationView** class). The class includes the following initializer and properties to create and configure the view.

MKAnnotationView(annotation: MKAnnotation?, **reuseIdentifier:** String?**)**—This initializer creates an annotation view for the annotation specified by the **annotation** argument. The **annotation** argument is a reference to the annotation object we want to associate with the view, and the **reuseIdentifier** argument is a string the Map Kit View needs to be able to reuse the view to display multiple annotations.

image—This property sets or returns the image for the view.

leftCalloutAccessoryView—This property sets or returns the view displayed on the left side of the callout bubble.

rightCalloutAccessoryView—This property sets or returns the view displayed on the right side of the callout bubble.

displayPriority—This property sets or returns a value that determines the annotation's priority. It is a structure of type **MKFeatureDisplayPriority** that can be initialized with a value from 0 to 1000. The structure defines three type properties to return an object with standard values: **required** (1000), **defaultHigh** (750), and **defaultLow** (250).

clusteringIdentifier—This property sets or returns a string with the name of the group to which the annotation belongs. This identifier is used to cluster annotations when they are too close to each other.

isEnabled—This property sets or returns a Boolean value that determines if the view can be selected.

The process to create a custom view is the same as before, but instead of using the **MKMarkerAnnotationView** class to create the view, we must use the **MKAnnotationView** class.

Also, these custom views present the information in a bubble on top of the icon when the annotation is selected, so we must assign the value **true** to the **canShowCallout** property if we want the user to be able to see it. The following method creates a view with a custom image and a bubble to display the title and subtitle (the iconmap.png file is available on our website).

```
func mapView(_ mapView: MKMapView, viewFor annotation: MKAnnotation) ->
MKAnnotationView? {
   if let temp = annotation as? MyAnnotation {
      var aView = mapView.dequeueReusableAnnotationView(withIdentifier:
"Pins")
      if aView == nil {
         aView = MKAnnotationView(annotation: temp, reuseIdentifier:
"Pins")
         aView?.image = UIImage(named: "iconmap")
         aView?.canShowCallout = true
      } else {
         aView?.annotation = annotation
      }
      return aView
   }
   return nil
}
```

Listing 20-6: *Defining a custom annotation*

Our image replaces the balloon, and now the information is shown in a callout bubble when the annotation is selected.

Figure 20-7: *Custom annotation view*

Do It Yourself: Download the iconmap.png image from our website and add it to the Assets Catalog. Update the **ViewController** class from the previous example with the code in Listing 20-6. Run the application and tap on the icon. You should see something like Figure 20-7.

The annotation view is responsible for the subview that presents the annotation's callout bubble. Besides the title and the subtitle provided by the annotation, this subview can also include two small views or controls on the sides. Because these views usually contain information specific for each annotation, we must define the data required to create the views in the annotation object. This may be images, text, decoration views, etc. For example, we can add a property to the **MyAnnotation** class to include a thumbnail that helps the user identify the location.

```
import MapKit

class MyAnnotation: NSObject, MKAnnotation {
   var coordinate: CLLocationCoordinate2D
   var title: String?
   var subtitle: String?
   var picture: UIImage?

   init(coordinate: CLLocationCoordinate2D) {
      self.coordinate = coordinate
   }
}
```

Listing 20-7: *Adding custom data to an annotation*

Now, besides the title and subtitle, we can also define a thumbnail for each annotation and then display that image in the callout bubble. Depending on which side we want the thumbnail to appear, we must assign it to the **leftCalloutAccessoryView** or the **rightCallout-AccessoryView** properties, as shown next.

```
import UIKit
import MapKit

class ViewController: UIViewController, MKMapViewDelegate {
   @IBOutlet weak var mapView: MKMapView!

   override func viewDidLoad() {
      super.viewDidLoad()
      let location = CLLocation(latitude: 40.7637825011971, longitude:
-73.9731328627541)
      let region = MKCoordinateRegion(center: location.coordinate,
latitudinalMeters: 1000, longitudinalMeters: 1000)
      mapView.setRegion(region, animated: false)

      let annotation = MyAnnotation(coordinate: location.coordinate)
      annotation.title = "Apple Store"
      annotation.picture = UIImage(named: "appstore")
      mapView.addAnnotation(annotation)

      mapView.delegate = self
   }
   func mapView(_ mapView: MKMapView, viewFor annotation: MKAnnotation)
-> MKAnnotationView? {
      if let temp = annotation as? MyAnnotation {
         var aView =
mapView.dequeueReusableAnnotationView(withIdentifier: "Pins")
```

```
            if aView == nil {
               aView = MKAnnotationView(annotation: temp, reuseIdentifier:
"Pins")
               aView?.image = UIImage(named: "iconmap")
               aView?.canShowCallout = true

               let leftImage = UIImageView(image: temp.picture)
               aView?.leftCalloutAccessoryView = leftImage
            } else {
               aView?.annotation = annotation
            }
            return aView
         }
         return nil
      }
   }
```

Listing 20-8: *Configuring the callout bubble*

The delegate method in Listing 20-8 adds a small image on the left side of the callout bubble. The image is called appstore.png and contains a picture of the Apple Store (the file is available on our website). The result is shown below.

Figure 20-8: *Callout bubble with a thumbnail*

Do It Yourself: Update the **MyAnnotation** class with the code in Listing 20-7 and the **ViewController** class with the code in Listing 20-8. Download the appstore.png image from our website and add it to the Assets Catalog. Run the application and tap on the pin to open the callout bubble.

Basic User Location

Displaying the user's location on a map is easy with a Map Kit View, all we need to do is to assign some values to a few properties provided by the **MKMapView** class and the Map Kit View takes care of detecting the user's current location and show it on the map. The following are some of the properties provided by the class for this purpose.

showsUserLocation—This property sets or returns a Boolean value that determines if we want the Map Kit View to detect the user's location.

isUserLocationVisible—This property returns a Boolean value that determines if the user's location is currently visible on the map.

userLocation—This property returns an object of the **MKUserLocation** class with the user's location.

To get the Map Kit View to determine the user's current location, we must assign the value **true** to the **showsUserLocation** property, but we must also ask the user for permission. There are two types of authorization. We can ask permission to get updates only while the app is active (the app is being used by the user at the time), or all the time (even when the app moves to the background). The Core Location framework defines the **CLLocationManager** class to manage locations and get authorization from the user. The following are some of the properties and methods included in this class for this purpose.

authorizationStatus—This property returns the current authorization status. The value is an enumeration of type **CLAuthorizationStatus** with the values **notDetermined**, **restricted**, **denied**, **authorizedAlways**, and **authorized-WhenInUse**.

requestWhenInUseAuthorization()—This method asks for authorization to get the location while the app is in use.

requestAlwaysAuthorization()—This method asks for authorization to get the location when the app is active or in the background.

If the app is authorized to access the user's location, the Map Kit View shows a circle to indicate the location, but the configuration of the map doesn't change. If we want the map to show the area around the location, we must set the visible region with the **setRegion()** method, as shown next.

```
import UIKit
import MapKit

class ViewController: UIViewController {
   @IBOutlet weak var mapView: MKMapView!
   var manager: CLLocationManager!

   override func viewDidLoad() {
      super.viewDidLoad()
      manager = CLLocationManager()
      manager.requestWhenInUseAuthorization()

      mapView.mapType = .standard
      mapView.isRotateEnabled = false
      mapView.showsUserLocation = true
   }
   @IBAction func showLocation(_ sender: UIBarButtonItem) {
      let location = mapView.userLocation
      let region = MKCoordinateRegion(center: location.coordinate,
latitudinalMeters: 1000, longitudinalMeters: 1000)
      mapView.setRegion(region, animated: true)
   }
}
```

Listing 20-9: *Detecting and showing the user's location*

The first thing we do in this view controller is to ask the user for permission. The instance of the **CLLocationManager** object must remain in memory, so we store it in a property called **manager**. To ask for permission, we call the **requestWhenInUseAuthorization()** method, and to get the location, we set the Map Kit View's **showsUserLocation** property to **true**.

The process is automatic, but we must define an option in the info.plist file called "Privacy - Location When In Use Usage Description" with a string that explains the user why we need to access his or her location.

The view controller also includes an Action for the Show button to zoom in on the area, so once the location is determined, the user can tap this button to get a close-up view of his or her location.

Figure 20-9: User's location on the map

Do It Yourself: Connect the Show button with an Action called **showLocation()**. Update the **ViewController** class with the code in Listing 20-9. Add the "Privacy - Location When In Use Usage Description" option to the info.plist file. Run the application on a device. You should see a window asking for authorization. Authorize the app to access your location and press the Show button to see it on the map.

The Map Kit View constantly updates the user's location. To help us keep track of these changes over time and detect errors, the **MKMapViewDelegate** protocol defines the following methods.

mapView(MKMapView, **didUpdate:** MKUserLocation**)**—This method is called on the delegate every time a new location is determined. The **didUpdate** argument is an object with the user's current location.

mapView(MKMapView, **didFailToLocateUserWithError:** Error**)**—This method is called on the delegate when the Map Kit View cannot determine the user's location.

When the Map Kit View detects a new location, it calls the **mapView(MKMapView, didUpdate:)** method to report the result. Inside this method, we can move the center of the region to the new location or perform any other task necessary.

```
func mapView(_ mapView: MKMapView, didUpdate userLocation: MKUserLocation) {
   mapView.setCenter(userLocation.coordinate, animated: true)
}
```

Listing 20-10: Keeping track of the user's location

Do It Yourself: Add the method in Listing 20-10 to the **ViewController** class. Remember to conform to the **MKMapViewDelegate** protocol and assign the view controller as the Map Kit View delegate, as we did in Listing 20-8. Run the application and take a walk. You should see the map moving to keep your location visible.

In the previous example, we requested authorization with the **requestWhenInUse-Authorization()** method. This presents an Alert View that includes two options: Allow Once and Allow While Using App. If the user allows the app only once, every time the app is opened, it will ask for permission again, which could be frustrating. To improve the user experience, Apple provides a framework called CoreLocationUI which includes a class called **CLLocationButton** to create a button that automatically authorizes the app to access the user's location once. The class defines the following properties to configure the aspect of the button.

icon—This property sets or returns a value that defines the graphic to display on the button. It is an enumeration of type **CLLocationButtonIcon** with the values **none**, **arrowFilled**, and **arrowOutline**.

label—This property sets or returns a value that determines the text to display on the button. It is an enumeration of type **CLLocationButtonLabel** with values that represent predefined titles. The values available are **none**, **currentLocation** ("Current Location"), **sendCurrentLocation** ("Send Current Location"), **sendMyCurrentLocation** ("Send My Current Location"), **shareCurrentLocation** ("Share Current Location"), and **shareMyCurrentLocation** ("Share My Current Location").

cornerRadius—This property sets or returns a **CGFloat** value that determines the radius of the button's corners.

fontSize—This property sets or returns a **CGFloat** value that determines the size of the font.

The authorization button can only be created from code, and the best way to incorporate an element to the interface from code is to add it as the content of a Stack View. The following interface includes a Stack View at the bottom with a width of 200 points and a height of 50.

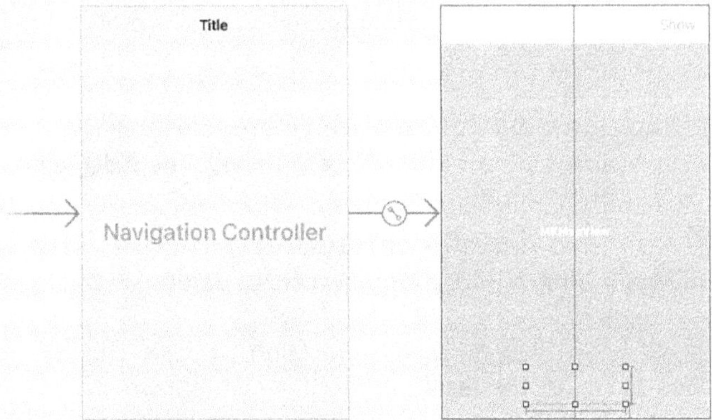

Figure 20-10: *Interface to test the authorization button*

IMPORTANT: The button must be visible and easy to read. This is the reason why the size of the Stack View is important. If Xcode considers that either the title is not readable or the icon is not visible, it will show a warning message. You should always make sure that there is enough space to display the title and icon in full.

If the user has not yet authorized the app to access his or her location, an Alert View is displayed on the screen to warn the user of what the app is about to do, but if authorization has already been granted, the location is determined immediately without prior notice. For this reason, we cannot use the location when the button is pressed, we need to wait until we are sure the location is available. And the best way to do it is by implementing the delegate method introduced before. In the following example, we show how to create a user location button and implement the delegate method to zoom in to the location when it becomes available.

```
import UIKit
import MapKit
import CoreLocationUI

class ViewController: UIViewController, MKMapViewDelegate {
   @IBOutlet weak var mapView: MKMapView!
   @IBOutlet weak var stackView: UIStackView!
```

```
    override func viewDidLoad() {
        super.viewDidLoad()
        let button = CLLocationButton()
        button.cornerRadius = 10
        button.label = .currentLocation
        stackView.addArrangedSubview(button)

        mapView.mapType = .standard
        mapView.isRotateEnabled = false
        mapView.showsUserLocation = true

        mapView.delegate = self
    }
    func mapView(_ mapView: MKMapView, didUpdate userLocation:
MKUserLocation) {
        let location = mapView.userLocation
        let region = MKCoordinateRegion(center: location.coordinate,
latitudinalMeters: 1000, longitudinalMeters: 1000)
        mapView.setRegion(region, animated: true)
    }
}
```

Listing 20-11: *Implementing the user location button*

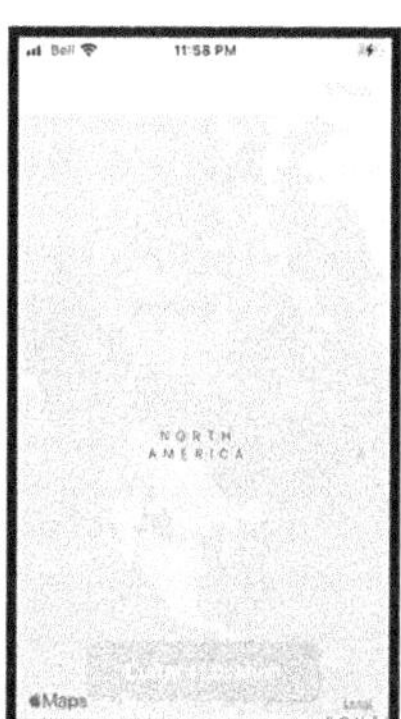

Figure 20-11: *User location button*

Do It Yourself: Add a Stack View to the scene with a Width constraint of 200 points and a Height constraint of 50. Connect this view to the **`ViewController`** class with an Outlet called **`stackView`**. Update the **`ViewController`** class with the code in Listing 20-11. Remember to disconnect the Show button in the Storyboard if you are not using it anymore. Run the application. You should see the user location button on the screen, as shown in Figure 20-11. Press the button. You should see your location on the map.

(Basic) Search

The MapKit framework incorporates a service to translate addresses into locations and find places of interest. The service is called *Local Search* and can take a freeform query string and return an array with the results. The query is created from the **`Request`** class included in the **`MKLocalSearch`** class. The following are some of the properties available for configuration.

naturalLanguageQuery—This property sets or returns a string with the term or address we want to search.

region—This property sets or returns an **`MKCoordinateRegion`** structure that determines the region in which the search is performed.

To perform a search, the **MKLocalSearch** class includes the following initializer and method.

MKLocalSearch(request: MKLocalSearchRequest**)**—This initializer creates an **MKLocalSearch** object to perform a search request.

start()—This asynchronous method performs a search and returns an **MKLocalSearch-Response** object with the results.

The search returns an **MKLocalSearchResponse** object that contains the following properties.

mapItems—This property returns an array of **MKMapItem** objects that represent the results produced by the search.

boundingRegion—This property returns an **MKCoordinateRegion** structure that determines the region occupied by the results produced by the search.

The Local Search service was designed to find all the places that match the query. The framework defines the **MKMapItem** class to represent a place. The following are some of the properties included by this class to return the data from the place.

name—This property sets or returns a string with the place's name.

phoneNumber—This property sets or returns a string with the place's phone number.

url—This property sets or returns a **URL** value with the URL of the place's website.

placemark—This property sets or returns an **MKPlacemark** object with additional information about the place.

There are different ways an app can perform a search and display the places returned. As an example, we have decided to connect the Show button to an Action that sets the region around the user's location, finds places that sell pizza, and creates the annotations to show them on the map.

```
import UIKit
import MapKit

class ViewController: UIViewController {
   @IBOutlet weak var mapView: MKMapView!
   var manager: CLLocationManager!

   override func viewDidLoad() {
      super.viewDidLoad()
      manager = CLLocationManager()
      manager.requestWhenInUseAuthorization()
      mapView.showsUserLocation = true
   }
   @IBAction func showLocation(_ sender: UIBarButtonItem) {
      let location = mapView.userLocation
      let region = MKCoordinateRegion(center: location.coordinate,
latitudinalMeters: 2000, longitudinalMeters: 2000)
      mapView.setRegion(region, animated: true)

      Task(priority: .high) {
         await setAnnotations()
      }
   }
```

```
    func setAnnotations() async {
        let request = MKLocalSearch.Request()
        request.naturalLanguageQuery = "Pizza"
        request.region = mapView.region

        let search = MKLocalSearch(request: request)
        do {
            let results = try await search.start()
            let items = results.mapItems

            await MainActor.run {
                self.mapView.removeAnnotations(self.mapView.annotations)
                for item in items {
                    if let coordinates = item.placemark.location?.coordinate {
                        let annotation = MKPointAnnotation()
                        annotation.coordinate = coordinates
                        annotation.title = item.name
                        annotation.subtitle = item.phoneNumber
                        self.mapView.addAnnotation(annotation)
                    }
                }
            }
        } catch {
            print("Error: \(error)")
        }
    }
}
```

Listing 20-12: *Searching for pizza places*

The code in Listing 20-12 defines the **`setAnnotations()`** method to search for places associated with the term "Pizza" and set the annotations for each location found. When the **`start()`** method returns the results, we remove the current annotations, get the coordinates of the location for each place, and assign the place's name and phone number to the annotation's title and subtitle.

Do It Yourself: Remove the Stack View from the interface. Connect the Show button with an Action called **`showLocations()`**. Update the **`ViewController`** class with the code in Listing 20-12. Run the application and press the Show button. You should see your location and the pizzerias in the area.

The **`setAnnotations()`** method of our example looks for places only in the current region. If the user scrolls the map to find new places, the information is not updated. To improve the application, we can take advantage of two methods defined in the **`MKMapViewDelegate`** protocol that are called when the region changes.

mapView(MKMapView, **regionWillChangeAnimated:** Bool**)**—This method is called on the delegate when the visible region is about to change.

mapView(MKMapView, **regionDidChangeAnimated:** Bool**)**—This method is called on the delegate after the visible region changed.

By implementing the **`mapView(MKMapView, regionDidChangeAnimated:)`** method, we can update the annotations every time the user scrolls the map. (Remember to conform to the **`MKMapViewDelegate`** protocol and assign the **`ViewController`** class as the Map Kit View's delegate, as we did in previous examples.)

```
func mapView(_ mapView: MKMapView, regionDidChangeAnimated animated:
Bool) {
   if mapView.userLocation.location != nil {
      Task(priority: .high) {
         await setAnnotations()
      }
   }
}
```

Listing 20-13: Updating the annotations

Medium Directions

Maps are not only used to find places but also to find routes to get from one place to another. The MapKit framework includes a set of classes to calculate a route and draw it on the map. The first class we need to implement is called **Request**, which is defined inside the **MKDirections** class. The **Request** class generates a request for a route between two locations. The following are the properties available in this class to configure the request.

source—This property sets or returns the route's starting point. It is of type **MKMapItem**.

destination—This property sets or returns the route's destination. It is of type **MKMapItem**.

requestsAlternateRoutes—This property sets or returns a Boolean value that determines whether multiple routes will be returned when available.

transportType—This property sets or returns a value that determines the type of transportation used to travel the route. It is an **MKDirectionsTransportType** structure with the properties **automobile**, **walking**, **transit**, and **any**.

departureDate—This property sets or returns a **Date** structure that determines the date of departure to help the system estimate the better route.

arrivalDate—This property sets or returns a **Date** structure that determines the date of arrival to help the system estimate the better route.

The request is sent to Apple servers for processing. The framework defines the **MKDirections** class to perform the request and process the results. The class includes the following initializer and method.

MKDirections(request: Request)—This initializer creates an **MKDirections** object with the request specified by the **request** argument.

calculate()—This asynchronous method performs the request and returns an **MKDirectionsResponse** object with the routes found.

The routes are returned as objects of the **MKRoute** class. The class includes the following properties to get the route's information.

polyline—This property sets or returns the route's geometry that we can use to draw the route on the map. It is an object of the **MKPolyline** class.

steps—This property sets or returns an array of **MKRouteStep** objects that describe every step the user needs to take to reach the destination.

advisoryNotices—This property sets or returns an array of strings with additional information that the user may need to travel the route, such as traffic jams or interruptions.

distance—This property sets or returns a **CLLocationDistance** value (a typealias of **Double**) with the route distance in meters.

expectedTravelTime—This property sets or returns a **`TimeInterval`** value with the expected travel time in seconds.

After the server returns the **`MKRoute`** object describing the route, we must present it to the user. There are different types of information we can extract from these objects, but the most interesting is the geometry provided by the **`polyline`** property, which allows us to draw the route on the map.

The Map Kit View displays the graphics in layers. There is a layer for the map, another for the labels and roads, and we can also add custom layers to display our own graphics, including the route. The value returned by the **`polyline`** property contains all the information required to create a layer that we can add to the Map Kit View to draw the route. The **`MKMapView`** class offers several methods to add and remove layers. The following are the most frequently used.

addOverlay(MKOverlay, **level:** MKOverlayLevel**)**—This method adds a layer to the Map Kit View. The first argument is an object that defines the layer, and the **level** argument is an enumeration of type **`MKOverlayLevel`** that defines the level in which the layer will be placed. The possible values are **`aboveRoads`** (places the layer above roads but below labels) and **`aboveLabels`** (places the layer above roads and labels).

removeOverlay(MKOverlay**)**—This method removes a layer from the Map Kit View.

Adding the layer to the Map Kit View is like adding an annotation. As with annotations, the Map Kit View calls a delegate method to get the information necessary to draw the layer. The following is the method defined in the **`MKMapViewDelegate`** protocol for this purpose.

mapView(MKMapView, **rendererFor:** MKOverlay**)**—This method is called on the delegate when the Map Kit View needs a renderer to draw a layer. The method must return an object of the **`MKOverlayRenderer`** class (or any of its subclasses) with the renderer we want to use to render the graphics. The **rendererFor** argument is a reference to the object that represents the layer we want to draw.

From this method, we must return a renderer configured according to how we want the layer to be drawn. The framework defines the **`MKPolylineRenderer`** class (a subclass of a subclass of the **`MKOverlayRenderer`** class) to create a renderer for a Polyline overlay.

MKPolylineRenderer(polyline: MKPolyline**)**—This initializer creates a renderer for a Polyline overlay.

The **`MKPolylineRenderer`** class inherits from its superclasses a set of properties we can use to configure the renderer. The following are the most frequently used.

fillColor—This property sets or returns a **`UIColor`** object with the color to fill the path.

strokeColor—This property sets or returns a **`UIColor`** object with the color of the stroke.

lineWidth—This property sets or returns a **`CGFloat`** value that determines the path's width.

The route's origin and destination are set with **`MKMapItem`** objects (the same type of objects we receive when we perform a search). The class includes the following initializer to create an **`MKMapItem`** object from an **`MKPlacemark`** object.

MKMapItem(placemark: MKPlacemark**)**—This initializer creates an **`MKMapItem`** object with the information provided by the argument. The **placemark** argument is an object with the information about the place (location, name, etc.).

The **MKPlacemark** class offers its own initializer to create the **MKPlacemark** object we need to initialize the **MKMapItem** object.

MKPlacemark(coordinate: CLLocationCoordinate2D**)**—This initializer creates an **MKPlacemark** object with the coordinates specified by the **coordinate** argument.

The first step to create a route is to define the **MKMapItem** objects for the starting point and destination, as we do in the following example.

```
import UIKit
import MapKit

class ViewController: UIViewController, MKMapViewDelegate {
   @IBOutlet weak var mapView: MKMapView!
   var origin: MKMapItem!
   var destination: MKMapItem!

   override func viewDidLoad() {
      super.viewDidLoad()

      let coordOrigin = CLLocationCoordinate2D(latitude:
40.7637825011971, longitude: -73.9731328627541)
      let placeOrigin = MKPlacemark(coordinate: coordOrigin)
      origin = MKMapItem(placemark: placeOrigin)

      let coordDestination = CLLocationCoordinate2D(latitude:
40.7523809365088, longitude: -73.9778321046893)
      let placeDestination = MKPlacemark(coordinate: coordDestination)
      destination = MKMapItem(placemark: placeDestination)

      let region = MKCoordinateRegion(center: coordOrigin,
latitudinalMeters: 2000, longitudinalMeters: 2000)
      mapView.setRegion(region, animated: false)
      mapView.delegate = self
   }
}
```

Listing 20-14: *Setting the route's starting point and destination*

The code in Listing 20-14 defines two properties (**origin** and **destination**) to store the information for the route's starting point and destination. When the scene is loaded, these values are initialized with the coordinates of two places in New York (the Apple Store and Grand Central Terminal) and the visible region is set around the Apple Store area. For this example, we decided to get the route when the Show button is pressed. The following are the Action for the button and the asynchronous method we need to calculate the route.

```
@IBAction func showLocation(_ sender: UIBarButtonItem) {
   let request = MKDirections.Request()
   request.source = origin
   request.destination = destination
   request.requestsAlternateRoutes = false

   Task(priority: .high) {
      await calculateRoute(request: request)
   }
}
func calculateRoute(request: MKDirections.Request) async {
   let directions = MKDirections(request: request)
   do {
      let results = try await directions.calculate()
      await MainActor.run {
         let routes = results.routes
         let route = routes.first!
```

```
            self.mapView.addOverlay(route.polyline, level: .aboveRoads)
         }
      } catch {
         print("Error: \(error)")
      }
   }
```

Listing 20-15: Calculating the route

The **showLocation()** method creates a request, assigns the location values to the **origin** and **destination** properties, and then runs an asynchronous task to perform the request. The asynchronous method creates the **MKDirections** object to process the request and then calls the **calculate()** method to get the route. This method returns the results in an **MKDirectionsResponse** object, which contains the **routes** property that returns the **MKRoute** objects with the routes. Because we set the **requestsAlternateRoutes** property to **false**, the array returned by this property only contains one route object, so we get the first element and add its Polyline overlay to the map.

The next step is to implement the **MKMapViewDelegate** protocol method to provide the renderer for the Polyline overlays.

```
func mapView(_ mapView: MKMapView, rendererFor overlay: MKOverlay) ->
MKOverlayRenderer {
   let render = MKPolylineRenderer(overlay: overlay)
   render.strokeColor = UIColor.red
   return render
}
```

Listing 20-16: Drawing the route

The protocol method in Listing 20-16 creates an **MKPolylineRenderer** object with a red stroke for the layer. This renderer draws a red line between locations, as illustrated below.

Figure 20-12: Route on the map

Do It Yourself: Update the **ViewController** class with the codes in Listings 20-14, 20-15, and 20-16. Run the application and press the Show button. You should see the route from the Apple Store to Grand Central Terminal on the map.

Because we centered the visible area at the Apple Store, the user may not be able to see the entire route unless the map is zoomed out or scrolled. There are several things we can do to improve our application, but it always depends on what we want to achieve and how the application is organized. One alternative is to define the annotations for the starting point and destination and then call the **showAnnotations()** method provided by the Map Kit View to set a visible region that includes both annotations. This way, not only will the entire route be visible, but we also make sure that the user can identify the places where the trip begins and ends.

```
func calculateRoute(request: MKDirections.Request) async {
   let directions = MKDirections(request: request)
   do {
      let results = try await directions.calculate()
      await MainActor.run {
         let routes = results.routes
         let route = routes.first!
         self.mapView.addOverlay(route.polyline, level: .aboveRoads)

         let annotation1 = MKPointAnnotation()
         annotation1.coordinate = self.origin.placemark.coordinate
         annotation1.title = "Apple Store"
         self.mapView.addAnnotation(annotation1)

         let annotation2 = MKPointAnnotation()
         annotation2.coordinate = self.destination.placemark.coordinate
         annotation2.title = "Grand Central Terminal"
         self.mapView.addAnnotation(annotation2)

         self.mapView.showAnnotations([annotation1, annotation2],
animated: true)
      }
   } catch {
      print("Error: \(error)")
   }
}
```

Listing 20-17: *Zooming out to show the route*

In the method of Listing 20-17, the annotations are added to the map when results are received from the server. Because of this, the annotations and the route are displayed at the same time and the map zooms in or out to show the entire route on the screen.

Do It Yourself: Update the **`calculateRoute()`** method with the code in Listing 20-17. Run the application and press the Show button. You should see the entire route on the screen, from the Apple Store to Grand Central Terminal.

There are two more methods defined in the **`MKMapViewDelegate`** protocol that could be useful when working with routes and destinations.

mapView(MKMapView, **didSelect:** MKAnnotationView**)**—This method is called on the delegate when an annotation view is selected.

mapView(MKMapView, **didDeselect:** MKAnnotationView**)**—This method is called on the delegate when an annotation view is deselected.

Using these methods, we can draw the route to the destination selected by the user. The following example finds coffee shops nearby the Apple Store in New York City and implements the **`mapView(MKMapView, didSelect:)`** method to get the route between the Apple Store and the selected coffee shop.

```
import UIKit
import MapKit

class ViewController: UIViewController, MKMapViewDelegate {
   @IBOutlet weak var mapView: MKMapView!
   var appleCoord: CLLocationCoordinate2D!
   var route: MKRoute?
```

```
    override func viewDidLoad() {
        super.viewDidLoad()
        appleCoord = CLLocationCoordinate2D(latitude: 40.7637825011971,
longitude: -73.9731328627541)
        let region = MKCoordinateRegion(center: appleCoord,
latitudinalMeters: 2000, longitudinalMeters: 2000)
        mapView.setRegion(region, animated: false)
        mapView.delegate = self

        Task(priority: .high) {
            let request = MKLocalSearch.Request()
            request.naturalLanguageQuery = "Coffee"
            request.region = region
            await searchCoffeePlaces(request: request)
        }
    }
    func searchCoffeePlaces(request: MKLocalSearch.Request) async {
        let search = MKLocalSearch(request: request)
        do {
            let results = try await search.start()
            await MainActor.run {
                let items = results.mapItems
                for item in items {
                    if let coordinates = item.placemark.location?.coordinate {
                        let annotation = MKPointAnnotation()
                        annotation.coordinate = coordinates
                        annotation.title = item.name
                        annotation.subtitle = item.phoneNumber
                        self.mapView.addAnnotation(annotation)
                    }
                }
            }
        } catch {
            print("Error: \(error)")
        }
    }
    func mapView(_ mapView: MKMapView, didSelect view: MKAnnotationView) {
        if let destinationCoord = view.annotation?.coordinate {
            let placeOrigin = MKPlacemark(coordinate: appleCoord)
            let origin = MKMapItem(placemark: placeOrigin)
            origin.name = "Apple Store"

            let placeDestination = MKPlacemark(coordinate: destinationCoord)
            let destination = MKMapItem(placemark: placeDestination)
            destination.name = view.annotation?.title!

            let request = MKDirections.Request()
            request.source = origin
            request.destination = destination
            request.transportType = .walking
            request.requestsAlternateRoutes = false

            Task(priority: .high) {
                await calculateRoute(request: request)
            }
        }
    }
    func calculateRoute(request: MKDirections.Request) async {
        let directions = MKDirections(request: request)
        do {
            let results = try await directions.calculate()
            await MainActor.run {
                let routes = results.routes
                if let oldRoute = self.route {
                 self.mapView.removeOverlay(oldRoute.polyline)
                    self.route = nil
```

```
            }
            self.route = routes.first!
            self.mapView.addOverlay(self.route!.polyline,
level: .aboveRoads)
         }
      } catch {
         print("Error: \(error)")
      }
   }
   func mapView(_ mapView: MKMapView, rendererFor overlay: MKOverlay) ->
MKOverlayRenderer {
      let render = MKPolylineRenderer(overlay: overlay)
      render.strokeColor = UIColor.red
      return render
   }
}
```

Listing 20-18: *Calculating routes to the destinations selected by the user*

The code in Listing 20-18 does not introduce anything new. We search for places related to the word "Coffee" around the Apple Store, create annotations for every place found, and add them to the map. When the user selects a pin, the delegate method is executed, and we use the pin's location to get the route between the Apple Store and the selected place. Because the user can select a different place after a route was added to the map, we store a reference to the route in the **route** property to be able to remove the overlay later.

Do It Yourself: Update the **ViewController** class with the code in Listing 20-18. Remember to disconnect the Show button in the Storyboard if you do not implement it anymore. Run the application and tap on a pin. You should see the route from the Apple Store to the selected place.

Route objects include additional information that may be relevant to the user, including the steps it takes to travel the route and the total distance. The next example is an Action we can connect to the Show button in our interface to display an Alert View that includes the distance and the estimated time it takes to get to the destination of the current route.

```
@IBAction func showLocation(_ sender: UIBarButtonItem) {
   if let current = route {
      let distance = current.distance
      let time = current.expectedTravelTime
      var message = "Distance: \(distance) meters \r\n"
      message += "Time: \(time) seconds"

      let alert = UIAlertController(title: "Route", message: message,
preferredStyle: .alert)
      let action = UIAlertAction(title: "OK", style: .default, handler:
nil)
      alert.addAction(action)
      present(alert, animated: true, completion: nil)
   }
}
```

Listing 20-19: *Showing additional information*

Do It Yourself: Connect the Show button with an Action called **showLocation()**. Complete the method with the code in Listing 20-19. Run the application, select a pin, wait for the route to appear, and press the Show button. You should see an Alert View with the distance and estimated time to complete the route in seconds.

Chapter 21
Drag and Drop

Basic 21.1 Drag and Drop

Drag and drop is a way to visually move data from one application to another or from two windows of the same application. It is available on devices that can share the screen with two or more windows, like iPads and Mac computers. In Mac computers, the process is simple. We open two or more windows at the same time and use the mouse to drag an element from one window to the other. On iPads, we must split the screen in two. iPads include an icon with three dots at the top that we can tap to share the screen with other applications, as shown below.

Figure 21-1: *Tool to split the screen on iPads*

When we tap on the three dots, the system shows a small window with three icons (Figure 21-1, right). The first icon assigns the whole screen to the app, the second icon splits the screen in two to show the current app on the left and an additional app on the right, and the third icon moves the app to an overlay that is displayed on top of other apps. If we tap on the second or third icons, the screen will be shared by two apps, so we can drag and drop elements between them.

Basic Drag

Drag refers to the action of dragging an element in our app to another app (or to another part of our app). For instance, we may have an application that shows pictures to the users, and we want to let them drag a picture to the Photo Library to make it available to the rest of the applications.

A drag operation is defined as an interaction between the user and the scene. The Drag and Drop framework defines the **`UIDragInteraction`** class to create it.

UIDragInteraction(delegate: UIDragInteractionDelegate**)**—This initializer creates an interaction to manage a drag operation. The **delegate** argument is a reference to the object that is going to respond to the interaction.

The interaction must be assigned to the view we want the user to be able to drag. The **`UIView`** class includes the following methods to add and remove interactions.

addInteraction(UIInteraction**)**—This method adds the interaction to the view.

removeInteraction(UIInteraction**)**—This method removes the interaction from the view.

Drag and drop is performed on elements on the screen, but the data to be transferred is determined from code. For this purpose, the Drag and Drop framework defines the **`UIDragInteractionDelegate`** protocol. When the user drags an element, the system calls methods define by this protocol to get the data and respond to changes in the state of the operation. The following are the most frequently used.

dragInteraction(UIDragInteraction, **itemsForBeginning:** UIDragSession**)**—This method is called on the delegate to get the objects to transfer to the destination app. The method must return an array of **`UIDragItem`** objects.

dragInteraction(UIDragInteraction, **previewForLifting:** UIDragItem, **session:** UIDragSession**)**—This method is called on the delegate to get the configuration of the preview (the image the user see on the screen while the element is being dragged). The method must return a **`UITargetedDragPreview`** object with the configuration.

dragInteraction(UIDragInteraction, **sessionWillBegin:** UIDragSession**)**—This method is called on the delegate when the user starts moving the element across the screen.

dragInteraction(UIDragInteraction, **session:** UIDragSession, **willEndWith:** UIDropOperation**)**—This method is called on the delegate when the user finishes dragging the element.

When a drag operation is performed, the system creates a session to manage it. Every delegate method receives a reference to this session that we can use to access the data. The session is created from a class that conforms to two protocols: **`UIDragDropSession`** and **`UIDragSession`**. These protocols define the following properties and methods to process the data.

localContext—This property returns the additional object associated to the item.

canLoadObjects(ofClass: Type**)**—This method returns a Boolean value that indicates whether the elements in the session can be converted to the data type specified by the **ofClass** argument.

hasItemsConforming(toTypeIdentifiers: [String]**)**—This method returns a Boolean value that indicates whether the session contains elements of the UTI type indicated by the **toTypeIdentifiers** argument.

When the user begins dragging an element on the screen, the interaction object calls the **`dragInteraction(UIDragInteraction, itemsForBeginning:)`** method on the delegate to get the data we want to transfer. The data can't be sent in its original format; it must be prepared for other apps to be able to read it. The Foundation framework defines the **`NSItemProvider`** class for this purpose. The class includes the following initializer to create an item provider from an object.

NSItemProvider(object: NSItemProviderWriting**)**—This initializer creates an item provider to transfer data with drag and drop and copy and paste operations. The **object** argument is an object that conforms to the **`NSItemProviderWriting`** protocol and contains the data we want to transfer.

Among others, the **`NSItemProvider`** class includes the following methods to retrieve the object.

canLoadObject(ofClass: Type**)**—This method returns a Boolean value that determines if the object in the item provider can be converted to an object of the class specified by the **ofClass** argument.

loadObject(ofClass: Type, **completionHandler:** Closure**)**—This method loads the object in the item provider, converts it to the data type specified by the **ofClass** argument, and calls the closure specified by the **completionHandler** argument when the process is over. The closure receives an array of **`NSItemProviderReading`** with the results.

Item providers require the objects that contain the data to conform to the **NSItem-ProviderWriting** protocol, which defines properties and methods to specify the data and its type. But this is usually not necessary. The most common elements users drag are images and text, and classes like **UIImage** and **NSString** already conform to this protocol.

Once we have the item provider with the object we want to transfer, we must prepare it to be used in a drag operation. The framework defines the **UIDragItem** class for this purpose.

UIDragItem(itemProvider: NSItemProvider)—This initializer creates an item to send in a drag operation. The **itemProvider** argument is the object containing the data.

itemProvider—This property returns the **NSItemProvider** object associated with the item.

localObject—This property sets or returns an additional object to associate with the item. It is useful when we need to read the content of the item from multiple methods.

Applications that allow drag and drop must include an element on the screen for the user to drag or an element for the user to drop other elements. For our example, we are going to use an Image View at the top of the screen. The following view controller implements the minimum code necessary to assign an image to the Image View and allow the user to drag it to another application.

```
import UIKit

class ViewController: UIViewController, UIDragInteractionDelegate {
   @IBOutlet weak var dragImage: UIImageView!

   override func viewDidLoad() {
      super.viewDidLoad()
      dragImage.image = UIImage(named: "husky")
      dragImage.isUserInteractionEnabled = true
      dragImage.clipsToBounds = false

      let drag = UIDragInteraction(delegate: self)
      dragImage.addInteraction(drag)
   }
   func dragInteraction(_ interaction: UIDragInteraction,
itemsForBeginning session: UIDragSession) -> [UIDragItem] {
      if let image = UIImage(named: "husky") {
         let item = NSItemProvider(object: image)
         let dragItem = UIDragItem(itemProvider: item)
         return [dragItem]
      }
      return []
   }
}
```

Listing 21-1: *Allowing the user to drag an image*

This example assumes that we have an Image View in our scene connected with an Outlet called **dragImage**. Using this Outlet, we assign the picture of a husky to the view and the value **true** to the **isUserInteractionEnabled** property to allow the user to interact with it. When the drag begins, the system shows an expanded image to indicate to the user that it is ready to initiate the operation. If the image extends outside the view's boundaries, it may be clipped. To avoid this, we assign the value **true** to the **clipsToBounds** property, so the image is always displayed in full.

Once the element to be dragged is ready, we configure the drag operation. The first step is to create the **UIDragInteraction** object and add it to the Image View. This object declares the view controller as the delegate, so we can implement the **dragInteraction(UIDrag-**

Interaction, itemsForBeginning:) method of the **UIDragInteractionDelegate** protocol to provide the data. In this method, we recreate the **UIImage** object with the picture of the husky, create the **NSItemProvider** object with this image, and include it in a **UIDragItem** object. Although this time we send only a single item, we can return multiple values and let the app on the other side decide which one to use.

The user can now drag the image of the husky to any other application. Figure 21-2, below, shows what we see when the app is opened in a split screen along with the Photo Library. If we drag the husky to the app on the right, the picture is added to the Photo Library.

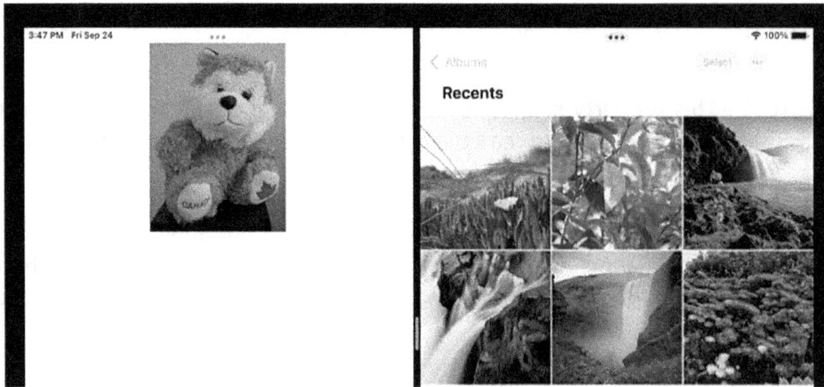

Figure 21-2: *Drag and drop operation*

Do It Yourself: Create a new project. Download the husky image from our website and add it to the Assets Catalog. Add an Image View at the top of the scene. Connect the Image View to the **ViewController** class with an Outlet called **dragImage**. Complete the view controller with the code in Listing 21-1. Run the application on an iPad. Tap the three dots at the top of the screen and select the split option in the middle (Figure 21-1). Open the Photo Library. You should see something like Figure 21-2. Drag the husky to the view on the right. The husky image should be added to the Photo Library.

The system generates a preview of the element being dragged to provide feedback to the user. Because we added the interaction to the Image View, the preview is created from this view and its content, but this is not what the user is dragging. Only the picture is going to be added to the Photo Library, not the Image View. If we want the preview to reflect this, we must customize the preview with the view we want to show instead of the view the user is dragging. For this purpose, the **UIDragInteractionDelegate** protocol includes the **dragInteraction (UIDragInteraction, previewForLifting:, session:)** method.

The preview is defined by two objects: a **UIDragPreviewTarget** object to determine for which view we are creating the preview, and a **UITargetedDragPreview** object to define the preview with the new view. The **UIDragPreviewTarget** class is a subclass of the **UIPreviewTarget** class, which includes the following initializer.

UIDragPreviewTarget(container: UIView, **center:** CGPoint**)**—This initializer creates an object that determines the view we are creating the preview for. The **container** argument is a reference to the view the user is dragging, and the **center** argument provides an anchor point for the preview.

Once we have this reference, we must define the preview with the new view. The framework defines the **UITargetedDragPreview** class for this purpose. This is a subclass of the **UITargetedPreview** class, which includes the following initializer.

UITargetedDragPreview(view: UIView, **parameters:** UIPreviewParameters, **target:** UIPreviewTarget)—This initializer creates a preview from the view specified by the **view** argument. The **parameters** argument is an object that determines the configuration of the preview. For drag operations, it is created from a subclass called **UIDragPreviewParameters**. The class includes the properties **backgroundColor** and **visiblePath** to define the background color or clip the view. The **target** argument is the **UIDragPreviewTarget** object that determines for which view we are creating the preview.

The **UITargetedDragPreview** object replaces the view dragged by the user with a new view, so we must provide this view with the content we want to display. For our example, we need to create an additional Image View to show the picture of the husky, as in the following example.

```
func dragInteraction(_ interaction: UIDragInteraction, previewForLifting
item: UIDragItem, session: UIDragSession) -> UITargetedDragPreview? {
   if let image = UIImage(named: "husky") {
      let dragView = UIImageView(frame: CGRect(x: 0, y: 0, width:
image.size.width, height: image.size.height))
      dragView.image = image

      let centerPoint = CGPoint(x: dragImage.frame.midX, y:
dragImage.frame.midY)
      let target = UIDragPreviewTarget(container: dragImage, center:
centerPoint)
      let preview = UITargetedDragPreview(view: dragView, parameters:
UIDragPreviewParameters(), target: target)
      return preview
   }
   return nil
}
```

Listing 21-2: *Defining the preview*

We not only have to provide the view but also determine the size it is going to take. In this example, we decided to give the view the size of the picture. Next, we create a **CGPoint** structure with the values in the **midX** and **midY** properties of the original view's frame and define the objects to create the preview. Notice that the **UIDragPreviewTarget** object is created with a reference of the Image View the user wants to drag and the **UITargetedDragPreview** object is created from the new Image View we just defined, so this view effectively replaces the original and now the preview only includes the picture of the husky.

Do It Yourself: Add the method in Listing 21-2 to the **ViewController** class. Run the application, split the screen, open the Photo Library, and drag the picture. You should see the picture of the husky being dragged, with no white area around it.

Basic Drop

In order for the user to be able to drop elements in our app, we must provide an element on the interface capable of receiving this data. To add this capability to a view, the framework defines the **UIDropInteraction** class, which includes the following initializer.

UIDropInteraction(delegate: UIDropInteractionDelegate)—This initializer creates an interaction to manage a drop operation. The **delegate** argument is a reference to the object that is going to respond to the interaction.

Like the drag operation, the drop operation is managed from delegate methods. The protocol is called **UIDropInteractionDelegate**. The following are the most frequently used.

dropInteraction(UIDropInteraction, **canHandle:** UIDropSession**)**—This method is called on the delegate to know if the view can receive the elements dragged by the user. The method must return a Boolean value to report the result.

dropInteraction(UIDropInteraction, **sessionDidUpdate:** UIDropSession**)**—This method is called on the delegate when the user drags an element inside the view. The method must return a **UIDropProposal** object to determine the type of operations allowed. The types of operations are defined by a **UIDropOperation** enumeration value. The values available are **cancel**, **forbidden**, **copy**, and **move**.

dropInteraction(UIDropInteraction, **performDrop:** UIDropSession**)**—This method is called on the delegate when the user performs the drop and the items are ready.

dropInteraction(UIDropInteraction, **sessionDidEnter:** UIDropSession**)**—This method is called on the delegate when the user drags the element inside the area occupied by the view.

dropInteraction(UIDropInteraction, **sessionDidExit:** UIDropSession**)**—This method is called on the delegate when the user drags the element outside the area occupied by the view.

dropInteraction(UIDropInteraction, **sessionDidEnd:** UIDropSession**)**—This method is called on the delegate when the operation is over.

The session for a drop operation is created from an object that conforms to the **UIDrop-Session** protocol. The protocol defines the following method to get the data.

loadObjects(ofClass: Type, **completion:** Closure**)**—This method gets the objects in the session that can be converted to the data type specified by the **ofClass** argument. The **completion** argument is a closure that is executed to process the result. The closure receives an array of **NSItemProviderReading** value that we must cast to the original data types.

The drop session also conforms to the **UIDragDropSession** protocol, so we can implement the **canLoadObjects(ofClass:)** method to know if the session contains a value we can process, and then call the **loadObjects(ofClass: Type, completion: Closure)** method to load the data. For instance, the following example allows the user to drag and drop an image from an external app to an Image View in the interface.

```
import UIKit

class ViewController: UIViewController, UIDropInteractionDelegate {
   @IBOutlet weak var dropImage: UIImageView!

   override func viewDidLoad() {
      super.viewDidLoad()
      dropImage.isUserInteractionEnabled = true

      let drop = UIDropInteraction(delegate: self)
      dropImage.addInteraction(drop)
   }
   func dropInteraction(_ interaction: UIDropInteraction, canHandle
session: UIDropSession) -> Bool {
      let valid = session.canLoadObjects(ofClass: UIImage.self)
      return valid
   }
```

```
    func dropInteraction(_ interaction: UIDropInteraction,
sessionDidUpdate session: UIDropSession) -> UIDropProposal {
        return UIDropProposal(operation: .copy)
    }
    func dropInteraction(_ interaction: UIDropInteraction, performDrop
session: UIDropSession) {
        session.loadObjects(ofClass: UIImage.self) { results in
            if let list = results as? [UIImage], let image = list.first {
                self.dropImage.image = image
            }
        }
    }
}
```

Listing 21-3: *Dropping images in an Image View*

As always, we first define the interaction and add it to the element on the interface that is going to respond to the operation. If the user drags an element over the view, the system calls the **dropInteraction(UIDropInteraction, sessionDidUpdate session: UIDropSession)** method to know what kind of operation is admitted by the view. In this case, all we need is to copy the image (we don't need the image to be removed at the origin), so we return a **UIDropProposal** object with the value **copy**. If the user drops the element on the view, the system first calls the **dropInteraction(UIDropInteraction, canHandle: UIDropSession)** method to know if the view can handle the values being dropped. In this method, we check if the value can be casted as a **UIImage** object with the **canLoadObjects(ofClass:)** method and return the value produced by the method (**true** if it was successful). If the value dropped by the user is valid, the system then calls the **dropInteraction(UIDropInteraction, performDrop:)** method to allow us to process the data. In this method, we get the object with the **loadObjects(ofClass:)** method, cast it to a **UIImage** object, and assign it to the Image View in the interface.

Do It Yourself: Create a new project. Add an Image View at the top of the scene. Connect the Image View to the **ViewController** class with an Outlet called **dropImage**. Complete the view controller with the code in Listing 21-3. Run the application. Split the screen and open the Photo Library (Figure 21-1 and 21-2). Drag an image from the Photo Library to your application. The image should be assigned to the Image View and show on the screen.

By implementing other delegate methods, we can have more control over the operation. For instance, we can implement the following methods to change the background color of the Image View every time the user drags an image inside or outside the view.

```
func dropInteraction(_ interaction: UIDropInteraction, sessionDidEnter
session: UIDropSession) {
   dropImage.backgroundColor = .systemTeal
}
func dropInteraction(_ interaction: UIDropInteraction, sessionDidExit
session: UIDropSession) {
   dropImage.backgroundColor = .systemBackground
}
func dropInteraction(_ interaction: UIDropInteraction, sessionDidEnd
session: UIDropSession) {
   dropImage.backgroundColor = .systemBackground
}
```

Listing 21-4: *Changing the background color*

Do It Yourself: Add the methods in Listing 21-4 to the **`ViewController`** class. Run the application, split the screen, open the Photo Library, and drag an image from the Photo Library to the application. When you enter the area of the Image View, the background color should change to Teal (green). If you drag the element outside the area of the view, the background should go back to normal.

Basic Lists

Any view can be dragged or receive a drop, but the process requires a few more steps for Table and Collection Views. These views are containers for one or more views, so the system needs to know which views are going to participate in the process and where to place the view that is being dropped. For this reason, the UIKit framework defines specific classes and protocols to control drag and drop operations performed on these elements. There are different versions for Table Views and Collection Views but they all work the same way. For instance, the framework defines the **`UICollectionViewDragDelegate`** protocol to control a drag operation for Collection Views. The following are some of the methods defined by this protocol.

collectionView(UICollectionView, **itemsForBeginning:** UIDragSession, **at:** IndexPath**)**—This method is called on the delegate to get the objects to transfer to the destination. The method must return an array of **`UIDragItem`** objects.

collectionView(UICollectionView, **dragPreviewParametersForItemAt:** IndexPath**)**—This method is called on the delegate to know which part of the cell should be shown in the preview. The method receives the cell's index path and must return a **`UIDragPreviewParameters`** object that determines the parameters of the preview. The class includes the properties **`backgroundColor`** and **`visiblePath`** to define the background color or clip the cell.

The process to drag a cell from a Collection View to another application is like the one we used before for a single Image View, but we need a Collection View Controller and a model that provides the images to display. The following is the model for this example.

```
import UIKit

enum Sections {
   case main
}
struct ItemsData: Identifiable {
   var id: UUID = UUID()
   var image: UIImage!
}
struct ApplicationData {
   var dataSource: UICollectionViewDiffableDataSource<Sections,
ItemsData.ID>!
   var items: [ItemsData] = []

   init() {
      items.append(ItemsData(image: UIImage(named: "bagels")))
      items.append(ItemsData(image: UIImage(named: "brownies")))
      items.append(ItemsData(image: UIImage(named: "butter")))
      items.append(ItemsData(image: UIImage(named: "cheese")))
      items.append(ItemsData(image: UIImage(named: "coffee")))
      items.append(ItemsData(image: UIImage(named: "cookies")))
      items.append(ItemsData(image: UIImage(named: "donuts")))
      items.append(ItemsData(image: UIImage(named: "granola")))
      items.append(ItemsData(image: UIImage(named: "juice")))
      items.append(ItemsData(image: UIImage(named: "lemonade")))
      items.append(ItemsData(image: UIImage(named: "lettuce")))
```

```
      items.append(ItemsData(image: UIImage(named: "milk")))
      items.append(ItemsData(image: UIImage(named: "oatmeal")))
      items.append(ItemsData(image: UIImage(named: "potato")))
      items.append(ItemsData(image: UIImage(named: "tomato")))
      items.append(ItemsData(image: UIImage(named: "yogurt")))
   }
}
var AppData = ApplicationData()
```

Listing 21-5: *Defining the model to test drag and drop*

We also need a cell to show the images in the Collection View. This cell is like the one we used before in the examples of Chapter 11, with the difference that now we must enable user interaction for the image and the cell's content view to allow the user to perform a drag and drop operation.

```
import UIKit

class FoodCell: UICollectionViewCell {
   let picture = UIImageView()

   override init(frame: CGRect) {
      super.init(frame: frame)
      picture.translatesAutoresizingMaskIntoConstraints = false
      picture.contentMode = .scaleAspectFit
      picture.isUserInteractionEnabled = true

      self.contentView.addSubview(picture)
      self.contentView.isUserInteractionEnabled = true

      picture.topAnchor.constraint(equalTo: self.contentView.topAnchor, 
constant: 8).isActive = true
      picture.bottomAnchor.constraint(equalTo: 
self.contentView.bottomAnchor, constant: -8).isActive = true
      picture.leadingAnchor.constraint(equalTo: 
self.contentView.leadingAnchor, constant: 8).isActive = true
      picture.trailingAnchor.constraint(equalTo: 
self.contentView.trailingAnchor, constant: -8).isActive = true
   }
   required init?(coder: NSCoder) {
       fatalError("Error")
   }
}
```

Listing 21-6: *Defining the cell to test drag and drop*

The purpose of this app is to allow the user to drag the thumbnail in a cell to another app (e.g., the Photo Library), so we must implement the two delegate methods introduced before to provide the data to be transferred and define the area of the cell used to create the preview. To designate the view controller as the delegate, we assign **`self`** to the **`dragDelegate`** property provided by the **`UICollectionView`** class, as in the following example.

```
import UIKit

class DragViewController: UICollectionViewController, 
UICollectionViewDragDelegate {
   override func viewDidLoad() {
      super.viewDidLoad()
      collectionView.dragDelegate = self
      prepareDataSource()
      prepareSnapshot()
   }
```

```
   func prepareDataSource() {
      let cellRegistration = UICollectionView.CellRegistration<FoodCell,
ItemsData.ID> { cell, indexPath, itemID in
         if let item = AppData.items.first(where: { $0.id == itemID }) {
            cell.picture.image = item.image
         }
      }
      AppData.dataSource = UICollectionViewDiffableDataSource<Sections,
ItemsData.ID>(collectionView: collectionView) { (collection, indexPath,
itemID) in
         return collection.dequeueConfiguredReusableCell(using:
cellRegistration, for: indexPath, item: itemID)
      }
   }
   func prepareSnapshot() {
      var snapshot = NSDiffableDataSourceSnapshot<Sections,
ItemsData.ID>()
      snapshot.appendSections([.main])
      snapshot.appendItems(AppData.items.map({ $0.id }))
      AppData.dataSource.apply(snapshot)
   }
   func collectionView(_ collectionView: UICollectionView,
itemsForBeginning session: UIDragSession, at indexPath: IndexPath) ->
[UIDragItem] {
      let row = indexPath.row
      if let image = AppData.items[row].image {
         let item = NSItemProvider(object: image)
         let dragItem = UIDragItem(itemProvider: item)
         return [dragItem]
      }
      return []
   }
   func collectionView(_ collectionView: UICollectionView,
dragPreviewParametersForItemAt indexPath: IndexPath) ->
UIDragPreviewParameters? {
      let cell = collectionView.cellForItem(at: indexPath) as! FoodCell
      let imageFrame = cell.picture.frame
      let preview = UIDragPreviewParameters()
      preview.visiblePath = UIBezierPath(rect: imageFrame)
      return preview
   }
}
```

Listing 21-7: *Defining a Collection View for drag and drop*

The process is the same as before, the only difference is in how we instruct the system to create the preview. What we need to do in our example is to determine the path around the area occupied by the image in the cell, so only the thumbnail is used to create the preview. The **UIDragPreviewParameters** class includes the **visiblePath** property to specify this path, which takes a value of type **UIBezierPath**. This is a class defined in the UIKit framework to create paths based on coordinate values. One of the values taken by this class is a **CGRect** structure, so we can use it to create a path from the frame of the image, as we did in this example. Once the parameters are returned, the user can drag the pictures in the Collection View to other applications.

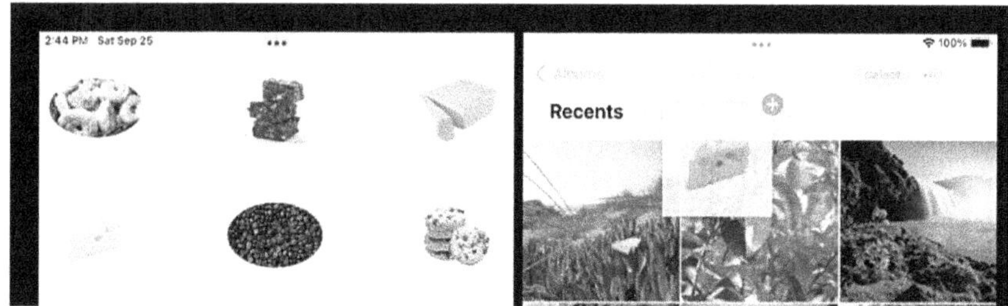

Figure 21-3: Dragging a cell from a Collection View

Do It Yourself: Create a new Project. Replace the scene with a Collection View Controller. Click on the Collection View and set the Estimate Size to None from the Size Inspector panel (see Chapter 11, Figure 11-7). Download the thumbnails from our website and add them to the Assets Catalog. Create a Swift file called ApplicationData.swift for the model in Listing 21-5. Create a subclass of **UICollectionViewCell** with the name **FoodCell**. Update this class with the code in Listing 21-6. Create a subclass of **UICollectionView-Controller** called **DragViewController** and assign it to the Collection View Controller. Update this class with the code in Listing 21-7. Run the application, split the screen, open the Photo Library, and drag one of the cells. You should see something like Figure 21-3.

Of course, we can also drop elements in the Collection View. UIKit defines the **UICollectionViewDropDelegate** protocol to control the process in a Collection View. The following are some of the methods define by the protocol.

collectionView(UICollectionView, **canHandle:** UIDropSession**)**—This method is called on the delegate to know if the Collection View can receive the elements dragged by the user. The method must return a Boolean value to report the result.

collectionView(UICollectionView, **dropSessionDidUpdate:** UIDropSession, **withDestinationIndexPath:** IndexPath?**)**—This method is called on the delegate when the user drags an element inside the Collection View. The method must return a **UICollectionViewDropProposal** object to determine the type of operations allowed. The types of operations are defined by a **UIDropOperation** enumeration value. The values available are **cancel**, **forbidden**, **copy**, and **move**.

collectionView(UICollectionView, **performDropWith:** UICollectionView-DropCoordinator**)**—This method is called on the delegate when the user performs the drop and the items are ready. The method receives an object that contains the items dragged by the user and the location in the Collection View where the items were dropped.

collectionView(UICollectionView, **dropSessionDidEnter:** UIDropSession**)**—This method is called on the delegate when the user drags the element inside the area occupied by the view.

collectionView(UICollectionView, **dropSessionDidExit:** UIDropSession**)**—This method is called on the delegate when the user drags the element outside the area occupied by the view.

When an item is dropped, the system calls the **collectionView(UICollectionView, performDropWith:)** method with a coordinator object that provides all the information required to process the item. This coordinator is created from an object that conforms to the **UICollectionViewDropCoordinator** protocol, which defines the following properties.

items—This property returns an array of objects that conform to the **UICollectionViewDropItem** protocol and contain the values of the item and its previous location (in case it was dragged from the same Collection View).

destinationIndexPath—This property returns an **IndexPath** structure with the location of the cell where the items were dropped.

The items are represented by an object that conforms to the **UICollectionViewDropItem** protocol. The protocol defines the following properties to return information about the items.

dragItem—This property returns a **UIDragItem** object with the item dropped by the user.

previewSize—This property returns a **CGSize** structure with the size of the preview.

sourceIndexPath—This property returns an **IndexPath** structure with the location of the cell that was dragged by the user.

Again, the implementation is like what we would use for a normal drop operation, but with the protocol methods defined specifically for Collection Views. The following example allows the user to drop an image in the Collection View and adds an item to the model with it.

```
import UIKit

class DropViewController: UICollectionViewController,
UICollectionViewDropDelegate {
   override func viewDidLoad() {
      super.viewDidLoad()
      collectionView.dropDelegate = self
      prepareDataSource()
      prepareSnapshot()
   }
   func prepareDataSource() {
      let cellRegistration = UICollectionView.CellRegistration<FoodCell,
ItemsData.ID> { cell, indexPath, itemID in
         if let item = AppData.items.first(where: { $0.id == itemID }) {
            cell.picture.image = item.image
         }
      }
      AppData.dataSource = UICollectionViewDiffableDataSource<Sections,
ItemsData.ID>(collectionView: collectionView) { (collection, indexPath,
itemID) in
         return collection.dequeueConfiguredReusableCell(using:
cellRegistration, for: indexPath, item: itemID)
      }
   }
   func prepareSnapshot() {
      var snapshot = NSDiffableDataSourceSnapshot<Sections,
ItemsData.ID>()
      snapshot.appendSections([.main])
      snapshot.appendItems(AppData.items.map({ $0.id }))
      AppData.dataSource.apply(snapshot)
   }
   func collectionView(_ collectionView: UICollectionView, canHandle
session: UIDropSession) -> Bool {
      let valid = session.canLoadObjects(ofClass: UIImage.self)
      return valid
   }
   func collectionView(_ collectionView: UICollectionView,
dropSessionDidUpdate session: UIDropSession, withDestinationIndexPath
destinationIndexPath: IndexPath?) -> UICollectionViewDropProposal {
      let proposal = UICollectionViewDropProposal(operation: .copy)
      return proposal
   }
```

```
    func collectionView(_ collectionView: UICollectionView,
performDropWith coordinator: UICollectionViewDropCoordinator) {
        for item in coordinator.items {
            let provider = item.dragItem.itemProvider
            provider.loadObject(ofClass: UIImage.self) { result, error in
                if error == nil {
                    if let image = result as? UIImage {
                        self.addImage(image: image)
                    }
                } else {
                    print("Error: \(error!)")
                }
            }
        }
    }
    @MainActor func addImage(image: UIImage) {
        if let thumbnail = image.preparingThumbnail(of: CGSize(width: 80,
height: 100)) {
            let newItem = ItemsData(image: thumbnail)
            AppData.items.append(newItem)
            prepareSnapshot()
        }
    }
}
```

Listing 21-8: *Dropping elements in a Collection View*

The **UICollectionView** class includes the **dropDelegate** property to declare the drop delegate. In this example, we declare the view controller as the delegate and then implement the required methods. The difference from previous examples is in how the items are processed. We read the items in the coordinator with a **for in** loop, extract the **UIDragItem** object from each item, get the item provider, and finally call the **loadObject()** method as before. Notice that the size of the image is reduced to be able to show it in a cell in the Collection View. Once we get the thumbnail, we create a new **ItemsData** structure with it, add it to the model, and update the snapshot to show it on the screen.

Do It Yourself: Create a subclass of **UICollectionViewController** called **DropViewController** and assign it to the Collection View Controller added to the interface in the previous example (instead of the **DragViewController** class assigned before). Run the application, split the screen, open the Photo Library, and drag an image from the library to the Collection View. You should see an item with that image added at the bottom.

Chapter 22
Mac Catalyst

Basic 22.1 Mac Catalyst

UIKit was developed to create applications for iPhones and iPads. Applications for Mac computers were always developed with a framework called *AppKit*. This is a completely different framework, optimized for computers and laptops, that implements its own classes and values. This means that apps developed for mobile devices don't work on Mac computers and apps for Mac computers don't work on mobile devices. Modern Macs equipped with ARM processors (e.g., M1), can run iPhone and iPad apps, but the apps run unchanged. The problem is that input and output devices on an iPhone or an iPad are different from those found on the Macs. The differences are extreme. There is no mouse on an iPhone, the computer screen is larger than the iPad screen, keyboards are different or nonexistent, and more. To offer a better user experience and take advantage of the extended capabilities of desktop and laptop computers, apps must be adapted to work on Macs. But learning how to develop an application all over again and do it for two different frameworks demand time and can be error prone. This is the reason why Apple introduced Mac Catalyst.

Mac Catalyst is a technology that allows developers to adapt iPad applications to run on Mac Computers. This means that we can develop an app that runs natively on Macs with UIKit and only a few changes.

Basic Mac Apps

The first step to turn our iPad app into a Mac app is to select the option from the app's settings. The option is in the General panel, inside the Deployment info section, as shown below.

Figure 22-1: *Mac option in the app settings*

When the Mac option is selected (Figure 22-1, number 1), Xcode opens a window to ask for confirmation and then offers an option to select the kind of adaptation we want. We can tell the system to scale the interface to look the same as the iPad or optimize it for Mac. The Optimize Interface for Mac option makes the interface look more like a native app, adding or removing spaces, styling the fonts, adapting the buttons, and more.

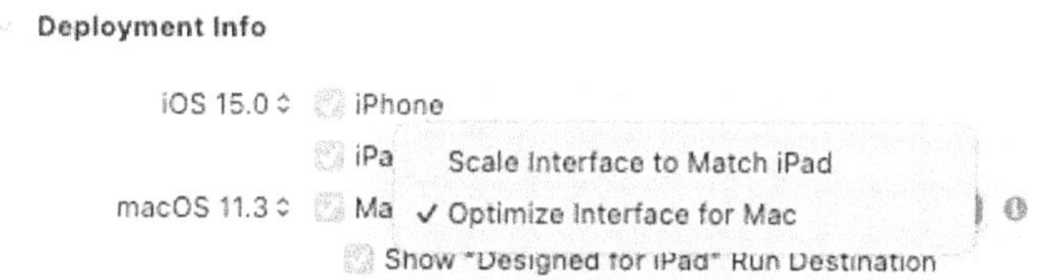

Figure 22-2: *Mac optimization*

In addition to this option, Xcode performs other changes to get the app to work on the Mac. Something we will notice right away is a new option in the Scheme called My Mac that allows us to run the application on the computer.

Figure 22-3: My Mac option

Do It Yourself: Create a new project. Click on the app's settings option in the Navigator Area (Figure 5-12, number 6), open the General panel, and click on the Mac option (Figure 22-1, number 1). Next, select the option Optimize Interface for Mac and run the application for the My Mac scheme (Figure 22-3). You should see an empty window.

Xcode also adds a bundle identifier for the Mac version of our app, and options to enable capabilities, such as access to the Camera or the Photo Library. Some of these options are automatically enabled, depending on the configuration set for the mobile version of our app, but other changes require our assistance. For example, we need to provide the icons and any images that are specific for the Mac in the Assets Catalog. The option is available in the Attributes Inspector panel. For instance, if we select the AppIcon set, and activate the Mac option from this panel (Figure 22-4, number 1), the set includes placeholders for the icons required by Macs.

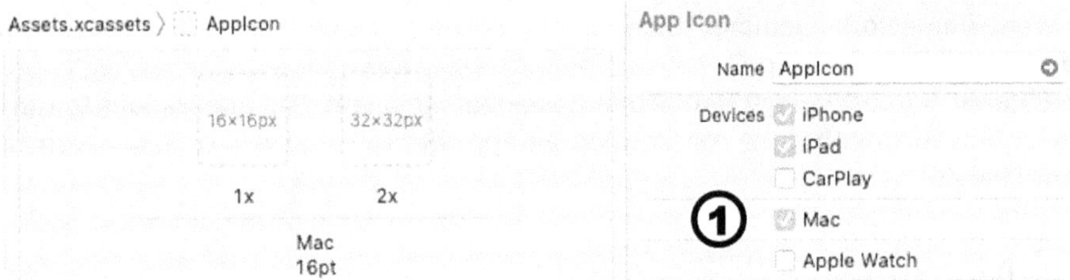

Figure 22-4: Mac icons

The Storyboard can show the scenes with a Mac layout. The option is available along with the iPad configurations, as shown below.

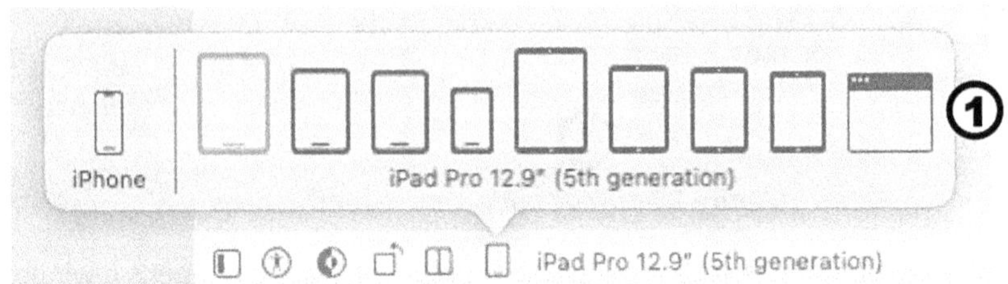

Figure 22-5: Mac configuration for the Storyboard

When we click on the Mac option (Figure 22-5, number 1), the popup window is expanded to include two more options to configure the interface to match the iPad or to be optimized for Mac. For instance, the figure below shows how a Filled button looks on an interface that matches the iPad interface (left) and when it is optimized for Mac (right).

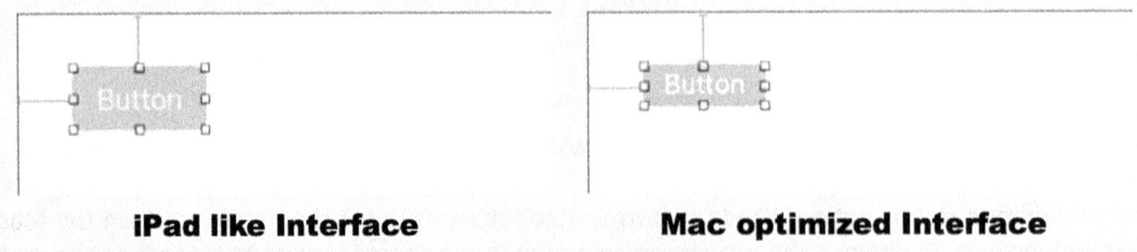

Figure 22-6: Mac interface mode

Of course, this optimization is not enough. An interface that looks good on iPads may have elements in locations that are inappropriate for Mac apps, or constraints may need adjustment for the elements to look better on the massive screens of Mac computers. To adapt the interface, we can implement the same tools provided for Size Classes (see Chapter 6). For instance, we may modify the button's top constraint in our example with a different constant for Macs. The option is called Idiom and is available when we click on the + button next to the value we want to change (Figure 22-7, number 1). In the example below, we assign a value of 50 points to the constraint when the button is shown on a Mac (Figure 22-7, number 2).

***Figure 22-7:** Values for Mac*

Basic Conditional Code

Although the system is responsible for converting UIKit code into AppKit code, more often than not we must define specific code for one platform or another. For this purpose, the Swift compiler supports conditionals. These are not normal **if else** statements, they are conditionals that are checked before the code is compiled and, therefore, we can use them to select the code we want to compile according to the target device.

Conditionals are built using the keywords **#if**, **#else**, and **#endif**. The **#if** and **#else** keywords work like the Swift conditionals **if else**, but because the code is not within a block, the **#endif** keyword is required to indicate the end.

There are several parameters we can use to set the condition, but to detect whether the application is being compiled for the Mac, we can use the **targetEnvironment()** instruction and the value **macCatalyst**, as in the following example.

```
import UIKit

class ViewController: UIViewController {
   override func viewDidLoad() {
      super.viewDidLoad()
      #if targetEnvironment(macCatalyst)
         print("Prints in Mac")
      #else
         print("Prints in iOS")
      #endif
   }
}
```

***Listing 22-1:** Detecting the platform before compiling*

This is a very simple example but illustrates how to work with these types of conditionals. If we run this project on the Mac, the message "Prints in Mac" is shown on the console, otherwise the message "Prints in iOS" is shown instead.

As we will see later, these conditionals are useful when some of the implemented classes are not supported by one system or the other, but we can also detect the system in code and implement an **if else** statement when the code in question is platform independent. As we have seen in Chapter 6, the **UITraitCollection** class includes the **userInterfaceIdiom** property for this purpose.

View controllers include the **traitCollection** property to return the **UITrait-Collection** object that defines the way the view is presented. From this property, we can check the platform and execute code accordingly.

```
import UIKit

class ViewController: UIViewController {
   override func viewDidLoad() {
      super.viewDidLoad()
      if traitCollection.userInterfaceIdiom == .mac {
         print("Prints in Mac")
      } else {
         print("Prints in iOS")
      }
   }
}
```

Listing 22-2: *Detecting the platform when the app is running*

Basic Menu

Something that iPad apps don't have is a menu bar, which is a required feature for Mac applications. To create a menu, we can add the Main Menu option to the Storyboard.

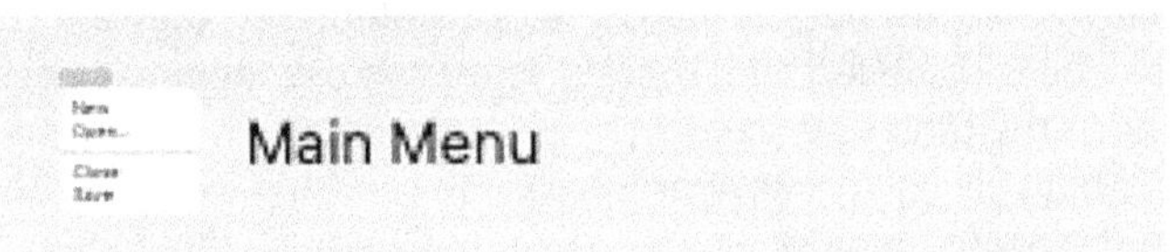

Figure 22-8: *Main Menu option in the Library*

The Main Menu option adds a menu bar to the Storyboard with system predefined options that provide basic functionality to the app.

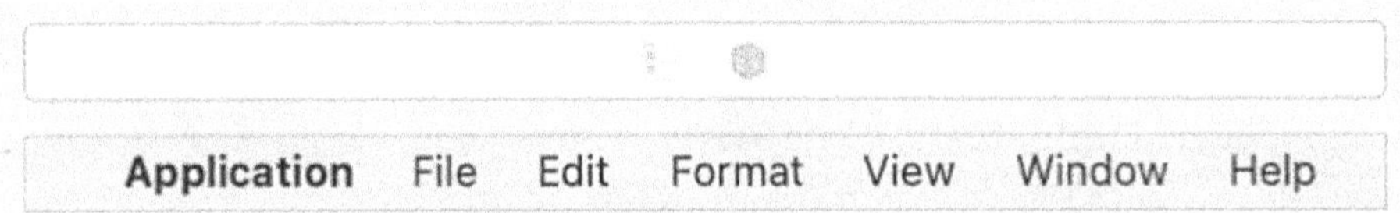

Figure 22-9: *Predefined menu*

We can double-click on a menu to see the options, select a menu or an option and press the Delete button to remove it, or edit the menus from the Document Outline panel.

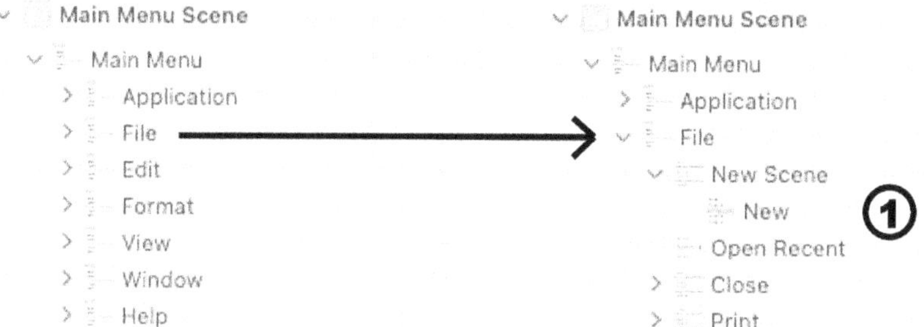

Figure 22-10: *Menu options in the Document Outline panel*

The bar is organized hierarchically. There is an element at the top representing the main menu, elements that represent each menu of the bar, such as File or Format, then elements inside that represent groups of options with similar characteristics, such as New Scene or Open Recent, and finally the elements that represent the options the user can select, such as the New option in the menu of Figure 22-10 (number 1). To delete a menu or an option, we just select it and press the Delete button, but if we want to insert a new option, we must consider whether the option is related to any of the available options, or it belongs to a separate group. For instance, if we want to insert an option that is related to the New option in the File menu, we can drag the Menu Command option from the Library to the New Scene group.

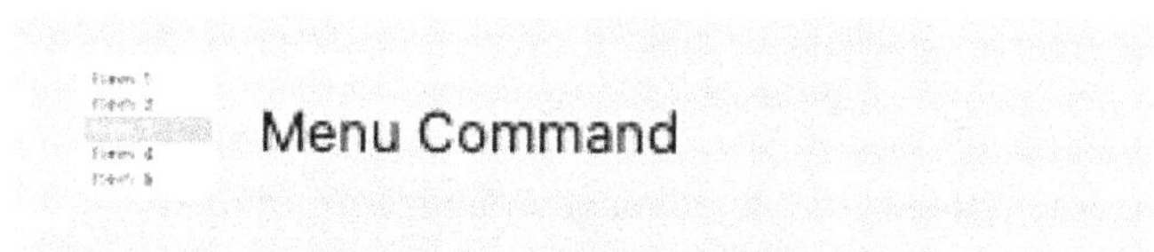

Figure 22-11: *Menu option*

The New Scene group in the File menu will now contain two options, New and Item, and the change will be reflected in the Storyboard.

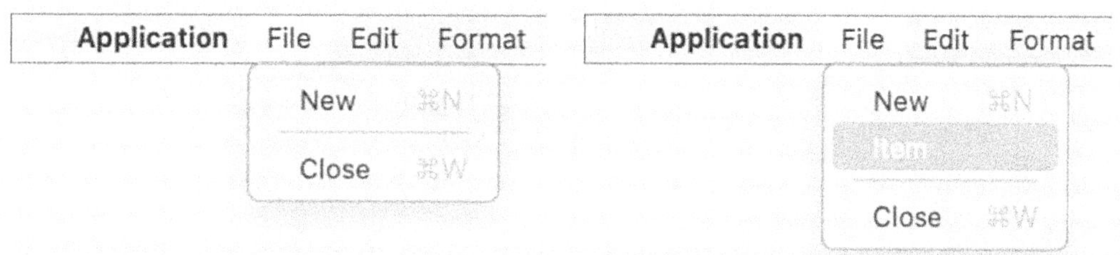

Figure 22-12: *New menu option*

In this example, we have removed a few options from the File menu and added a new one. The option is added with the title Item and no key associated to it, but we can change these values from the Storyboard or from the Attributes Inspector panel. The panel shows the values of every single attribute, including the combination of keys that perform the action. In the example below, we assign the title "Show Alert" to the option and the keys Command + S, so the user can perform the action by selecting the option from the menu or by pressing those keys.

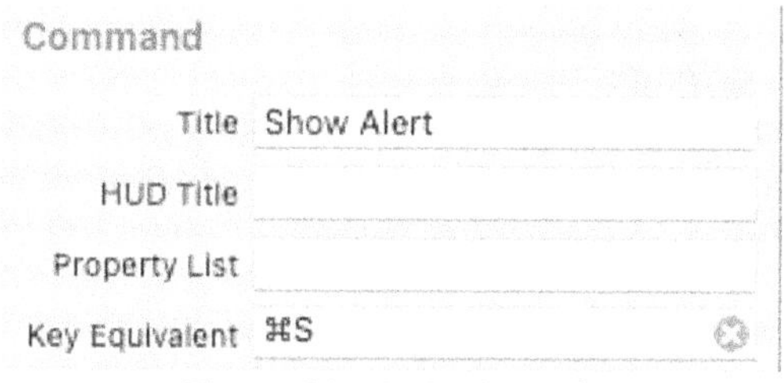

Figure 22-13: *Option title*

If our new option is not related to any of the options in the menu, we can create a new group. For this purpose, the Library includes an option called Inline Section Menu.

Figure 22-14: *Inline section option*

Dragging this option inside a menu in the Storyboard adds a group with two options. The group is called Inline Menu, and the options are called Item 1 and Item 2.

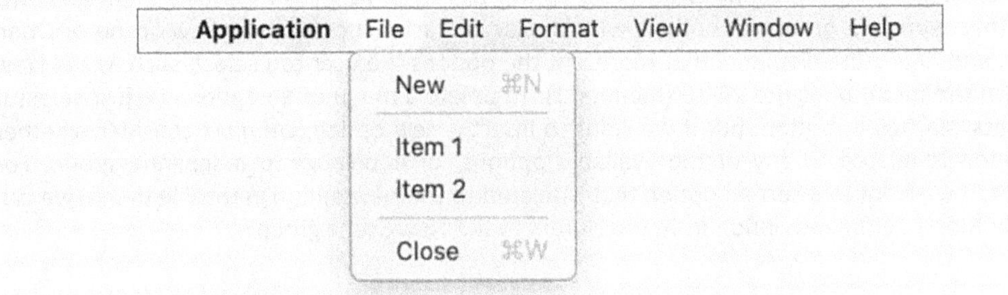

Figure 22-15: *New inline section*

There is also an option called Sub Menu to add more menus to the bar.

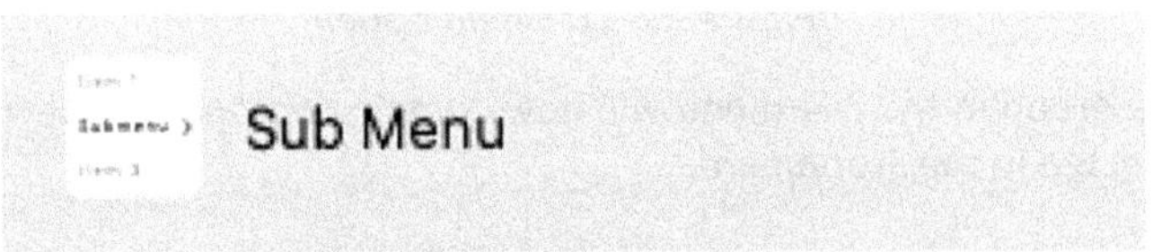

Figure 22-16: *Submenu option*

If this option is dropped on the menu bar, it adds a new menu (Figure 22-17, left), but when we drop it between the options of a menu, it adds a submenu with more options inside (Figure 22-17, right).

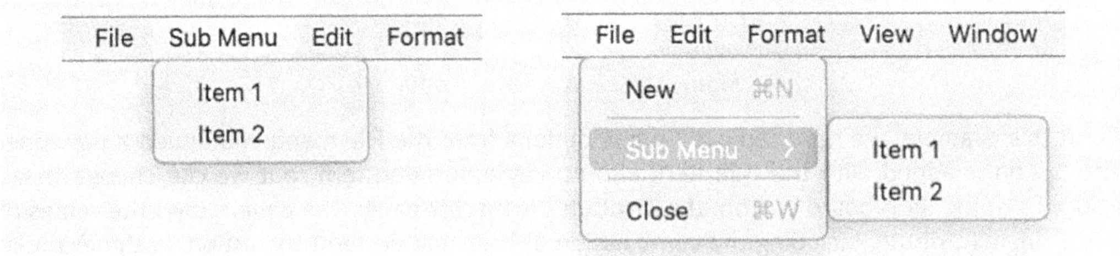

Figure 22-17: *New submenu*

After we have the option we want in the menu, we can connect it to an Action in the view controller to perform a task. This procedure is like the one we used to create Unwind Segues. We define a method with the **`@IBAction`** modifier and then select it from the Storyboard. For example, the following view controller includes an action that opens an Alert View.

```
import UIKit

class ViewController: UIViewController {
   @IBAction func showAlertView(_ sender: Any?) {
      let alert = UIAlertController(title: "Show Alert", message: "Open
from menu", preferredStyle: .alert)
      let action = UIAlertAction(title: "OK", style: .default, handler:
nil)
      alert.addAction(action)
      present(alert, animated: true, completion: nil)
   }
}
```

Listing 22-3: *Defining the action for a menu option*

With the action ready, we go to the Storyboard and Control-Drag a line from our option to the icon representing the First Responder (the view controller that is going to perform the action).

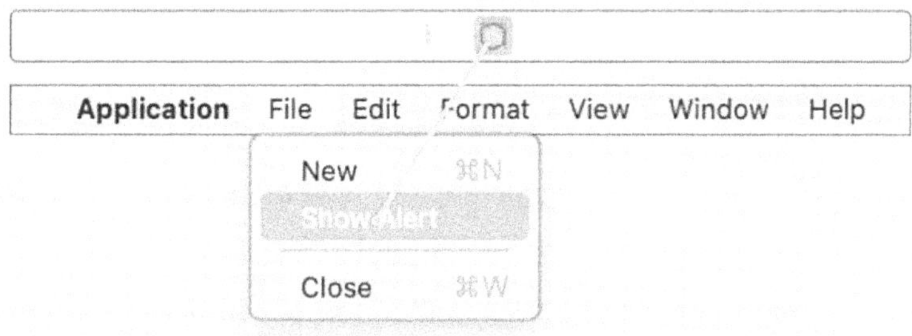

Figure 22-18: *Connecting the option to the first responder*

When the mouse is released, Xcode shows a list of all the actions in the responder chain, which includes our view controllers. The window shows all the actions predefined by the system along with the **`showAlertView()`** action we have just defined in the **`ViewController`** class.

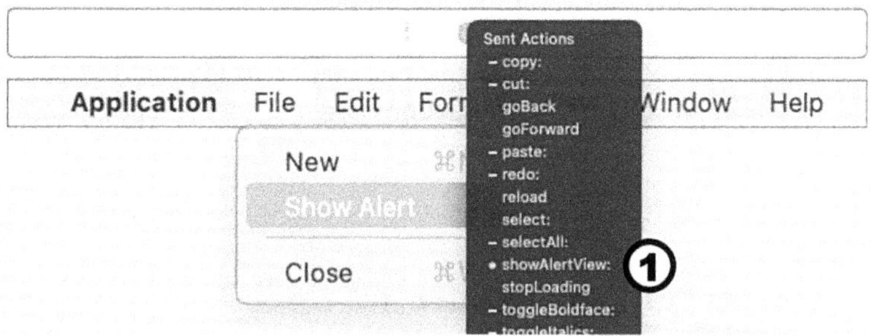

Figure 22-19: *Selecting the action for the menu option*

If we select the **`showAlertView()`** action (Figure 22-19, number 1), this method will be executed every time the user selects the Show Alert option in the menu or presses the Command + S keys.

Do It Yourself: Drag the Main Menu option from the Library to the Storyboard. Drag the Menu Command option from the Library to the Document Outline panel and put it inside the New Scene group in the File menu (or create a new group with the Inline Section Menu option). You should have a new option highlighted in blue (Figure 22-12). Select the option and change the title and the associated keys from the Attributes Inspector panel (Figure 22-13). Update the **`ViewController`** class with the code in Listing 22-3. Control-drag a line from the new option to the icon that represents the First Responder and select the Action in your view controller (Figures 22-18 and 22-19). Run the application on your Mac (My Mac scheme). Select the option from the menu or press the associated keys. You should see an Alert View popping up over the window.

Menu options sometimes change depending on the state of the app. For instance, the title of an option may change to communicate to the user that the action is now different, or the option may be disabled if it is not possible to perform the action anymore. To adapt the menu, we must reconfigure the options. Menu options are created from the **UICommand** class, which includes the following properties for configuration.

title—This property sets or returns a **String** value with the option's title.

discoverabilityTitle—This property sets or returns an optional **String** value with a message that describes the purpose of the option.

action—This property sets or returns the selector that performs the action.

attributes—This property sets or returns the option's attribute. It is a structure of type **Attributes** defined by the **UIMenuElement** class. The structure includes three type properties to configure the option: **destructive**, **disabled**, and **hidden**.

state—This property sets or returns the option's state (indicated by a checkmark on the left-hand side of the title). It is an enumeration of type **State** with the values **on**, **off**, and **mixed**.

Every time an option is about to be displayed on the screen the menu calls the following method in the view controller that performs the action to validate it.

validate(_ command: UICommand**)**—This method is called on the responder (the view controller) to validate the command. It receives a reference to the **UICommand** object that represents the option.

The **validate()** method is defined in the **UIResponder** class, which our view controllers inherit from, so we can override it to provide our own implementation. Because the method is called for every option selected by the user, the first step is to identify the option we want to modify. For this purpose, we can check the action assigned to the option with a selector, as shown next.

```
import UIKit

class ViewController: UIViewController {
   var alertDisplayed: Bool = false

   @IBAction func showAlertView(_ sender: Any?) {
      let alert = UIAlertController(title: "Show Alert", message: "Open
from menu", preferredStyle: .alert)
      let action = UIAlertAction(title: "OK", style: .default, handler:
nil)
      alert.addAction(action)
      present(alert, animated: true, completion: {
         self.alertDisplayed = true
      })
   }
   override func validate(_ command: UICommand) {
      let action = command.action
      switch action {
         case #selector(showAlertView):
```

```
            if alertDisplayed {
               command.attributes = .disabled
            }
         default:
            break
         }
      }
   }
```

Listing 22-4: Modifying a menu option

In this example, we include a Boolean property to check whether the Alert View was already opened or not. When we open the File menu, the **validate()** method is called for every option. Here, we check that the option is the one that performs the **showAlertView()** method and if the Alert View was already shown, we deactivate the option assigning the value **disabled** to the **attributes** property. Next time we open the File menu, the option is grayed out.

Do It Yourself: Update the **ViewController** class with the code in Listing 22-4. Run the application, open the File menu, and click on the Show Alert option. You should see the Alert View on the screen. Close the Alert View and open the File menu again. The Show Alert option should be disabled this time.

From the **validate()** method we can modify all the attributes of an option, but we can't remove or add options to the menu. This is a limitation we have when the menu is added to the Storyboard. If we need to modify the options available while the app is running, we must create the menu from code. The option is again provided by the **UIResponder** class, which defines the following method for this purpose.

buildMenu(with: UIMenuBuilder**)**—This method is executed by the application before the menu bar is created. The method receives a value of type **UIMenuBuilder** to provide access to the menu and options for configuration.

When the app is launched, this method is called on the **AppDelegate** class and this is our chance to customize the menu bar. The method receives a value of type **UIMenuBuilder**, which is a protocol with all the methods we need. The following are the most frequently used.

insertChild(UIMenu, **atStartOfMenu:** Identifier**)**—This method inserts an option or a group of options at the beginning of the menu indicated by the **atStartOfMenu** argument.

insertChild(UIMenu, **atEndOfMenu:** Identifier**)**—This method inserts an option or a group of options at the end of the menu indicated by the **atEndOfMenu** argument.

insertSibling(UIMenu, **beforeMenu:** Identifier**)**—This method inserts an option or a group of options before the option indicated by the **beforeMenu** argument.

insertSibling(UIMenu, **afterMenu:** Identifier**)**—This method inserts an option or a group of options after the option indicated by the **afterMenu** argument.

remove(menu: Identifier**)**—This method removes the option or group of options indicated by the **menu** argument.

There are two types of menus, the main menu at the top of the screen, and contextual menus that open when the user interacts with a view. To identify the system we are working with, the **UIMenuBuilder** protocol includes the **system** property. This property returns a **UIMenuSystem** object with information about the menu. The class includes two type properties to represent the menu system and two methods to process the menu.

main—This type property returns a reference to the main menu system (the menu bar).

context—This type property returns a reference to the context menu system.

setNeedsRebuild()—This method tells the menu system to rebuild all the menus.

setNeedsRevalidate()—This method tells the menu system that the menus need to be revalidated. It is used to update the menus when the state of the app changes.

The system creates a standard menu, as the one we added to the Storyboard before, that we can edit from code. For this purpose, the framework defines the **UIMenu** class. The class includes the following initializer.

UIMenu(title: String, **image:** UIImage?, **identifier:** Identifier?, **options:** Options, **children:** [UIMenuElement]**)**—This initializer creates a **UIMenu** object to represent a menu or an option. The **title** argument is the title of the element. The **image** argument is the image associated with the element. The **identifier** argument is the value we want to use to identify the element. The **options** argument is a structure that determines the type of element this object represents. An empty array indicates that the element is a menu (or a submenu), and the **displayInline** property indicates that the element is a menu option. Finally, the **children** argument is an array with the elements we want to add.

The options are still defined by the **UICommand** class. The class includes the following initializer to create them from code.

UICommand(title: String, **image:** UIImage?, **action:** Selector, **propertyList:** Any?, **alternates:** [UICommandAlternate], **discoverabilityTitle:** String?, **attributes:** Attributes, **state:** State**)**—This initializer creates a menu option. The **title** argument is the option's title. The **image** argument is the image associated with the option. The **action** argument is a selector with the action we want to perform when the option is selected. The **propertyList** argument is the data we want to associate with the option. The **alternates** argument is an array of alternative options. The **discoverabilityTitle** argument is a string that describes the purpose of the option. The **attributes** argument is a structure of type **Attributes** with properties to specify the style of the option (**destructive**, **disabled**, and **hidden**). And finally, the **state** argument is a **State** enumeration that specifies the option's initial state. The values available are **on**, **off**, and **mixed**.

The framework includes a subclass of **UICommand** called **UIKeyCommand** to define options that can be selected with a combination of keys.

UIKeyCommand(title: String, **image:** UIImage?, **action:** Selector, **input:** String, **modifierFlags:** UIKeyModifierFlags, **propertyList:** Any?, **alternates:** [UICommandAlternate], **discoverabilityTitle:** String?, **attributes:** Attributes, **state:** State**)**—This initializer creates an option with a shortcut key. The **title**, **image**, **action**, **propertyList**, **alternates**, **discoverabilityTitle**, **attributes**, and **state** arguments are the same defined for the **UICommand** initializer. The **input** argument is the textual representation of the key the user must press to perform the action, and the **modifierFlags** argument is a property of a structure of type **UIKeyModifierFlags** that determines the modifier key the user must press to perform the action. The properties available are **alphaShift**, **shift**, **control**, **alternate**, **command**, and **numericPad**.

The options are identified with a structure of type **Identifier** defined by the **UIMenu** class. The structure provides the following initializer to create a custom identifier.

UIMenu.Identifier(String)—This initializer creates an identifier for a menu option. The argument must be unique and therefore Apple recommends declaring it with a reverse domain, such as com.formasterminds-myapp.MyMenuBar.myOption.

The **Identifier** structure also includes type properties used to identify standard options (those included in the menu by default). The properties available are **application**, **file**, **edit**, **view**, **window**, **help**, **about**, **preferences**, **services**, **hide**, **quit**, **newScene**, **close**, **print**, **undoRedo**, **standardEdit**, **find**, **replace**, **share**, **textStyle**, **spelling**, **spellingPanel**, **spellingOptions**, **substitutions**, **substitutionsPanel**, **substitutionOptions**, **transformations**, **speech**, **lookup**, **learn**, **format**, **font**, **textSize**, **textColor**, **textStylePasteboard**, **text**, **writingDirection**, **alignment**, **toolbar**, **fullscreen**, **minimizeAndZoom**, **bringAllToFront**, and **root**.

To customize the menu bar, we must override the **buildMenu(builder: UIMenuBuilder)** method in the **AppDelegate** class. This method is called when the application is about to create the menu, so we can customize it before it is shown to the user.

The method may be called to configure the main menu or contextual menus, so we must first check that we have received a reference to the menu we want to modify and then proceed to add or remove the elements we want. The following example adds a menu called *Selection* to the main menu, next to the standard File menu.

```
import UIKit

@main
class AppDelegate: UIResponder, UIApplicationDelegate {
   func application(_ application: UIApplication,
didFinishLaunchingWithOptions launchOptions:
[UIApplication.LaunchOptionsKey: Any]?) -> Bool {
      return true
   }
   func application(_ application: UIApplication,
configurationForConnecting connectingSceneSession: UISceneSession,
options: UIScene.ConnectionOptions) -> UISceneConfiguration {
      return UISceneConfiguration(name: "Default Configuration",
sessionRole: connectingSceneSession.role)
   }
   override func buildMenu(with builder: UIMenuBuilder) {
      super.buildMenu(with: builder)

      if builder.system == .main {
         let option = UICommand(title: "Show Alert", action:
#selector(ViewController.showAlertView(_:)))
         let mymenu = UIMenu(title: "Alerts", identifier:
UIMenu.Identifier("com.formasterminds.test.alerts"), options: [],
children: [option])
         builder.insertSibling(mymenu, afterMenu: .file)
      }
   }
}
```

Listing 22-5: *Adding a menu to the menu bar*

To create a new menu, we specify the title of the **UIMenu** object, declare the **options** argument with an empty array (or ignore it), and then assign the options we want to include in the menu to the **children** argument. In this example, the menu's title is "Alerts", and an option is defined by a **UICommand** object with the title "Show Alert". The menu can be added as a new menu to the menu bar or as a submenu. This is determined by the method we use to add the menu and the identifier. In this case, we use the **insertSibling(UIMenu, afterMenu:)** method to add the menu to the main menu next to the File menu (the **file** identifier represents the File menu).

Notice that the action is defined with a selector (**#selector**) that calls the **showAlertView()** method in our view controller. This is possible because the selector looks for the method in the responder chain, which includes all the view controllers opened by the user. In this case, the selector asks the system to search for the **showAlertView()** method in the responder chain, the method is found in the **ViewController** object, and executed, showing an Alert View as before.

For the method to be found by the selector in our view controller, we need to turn the **@IBAction** into an **@objc** method, as shown next.

```
import UIKit

class ViewController: UIViewController {
   @objc func showAlertView(_ sender: Any) {
      let alert = UIAlertController(title: "Show Alert", message: "Open
from menu", preferredStyle: .alert)
      let action = UIAlertAction(title: "OK", style: .default, handler:
nil)
      alert.addAction(action)
      present(alert, animated: true, completion: nil)
   }
}
```

Listing 22-6: *Defining the action in the view controller*

The main menu now includes an additional menu called Alerts with an option called Show Alert that opens an Alert View when pressed.

Figure 22-20: *New menu added from code*

Do It Yourself: Remove the main menu added before to the Storyboard (the **buildMenu(with:)** method is not called if a menu was already defined in the Storyboard). Update the **AppDelegate** class with the code in Listing 22-5 and the **ViewController** class with the code in Listing 22-6. Run the application. You should see the Alerts menu next to the File menu, and the option should perform the same action as before.

IMPORTANT: In this example, we take advantage of the responder chain to execute a method in the view controller, but we could have defined the action inside the **AppDelegate** class and then post notifications to the view controllers or modify the model. There are different programming patterns available. For more information, visit our website and follow the links for this chapter.

Of course, we can also add the option to an existent menu or remove some of the standard menus and options included by the system, as we did before from the Storyboard. Next, we show how to add the Show Alert option to the File menu and how to remove elements.

```
import UIKit

@main
class AppDelegate: UIResponder, UIApplicationDelegate {
   func application(_ application: UIApplication,
didFinishLaunchingWithOptions launchOptions:
[UIApplication.LaunchOptionsKey: Any]?) -> Bool {
      return true
   }
   func application(_ application: UIApplication,
configurationForConnecting connectingSceneSession: UISceneSession,
options: UIScene.ConnectionOptions) -> UISceneConfiguration {
      return UISceneConfiguration(name: "Default Configuration",
sessionRole: connectingSceneSession.role)
   }
   override func buildMenu(with builder: UIMenuBuilder) {
      super.buildMenu(with: builder)

      if builder.system == .main {
         let option = UIKeyCommand(title: "Show Alert", image:
UIImage(systemName: "trash"), action:
#selector(ViewController.showAlertView(_:)), input: "S", modifierFlags:
[.command])
         let mymenu = UIMenu(title: "", identifier:
UIMenu.Identifier("com.formasterminds.test.showalert"),
options: .displayInline, children: [option])
         builder.insertSibling(mymenu, beforeMenu: .close)

         builder.remove(menu: .edit)
         builder.remove(menu: .format)
      }
   }
}
```

Listing 22-7: *Modifying the main menu*

In this example, the Show Alert option is created with the **UIKeyCommand** class, so we can assign a combination of keys to the option (Command + S). The File menu created by the system includes an option identified by the **close** value. Using this reference, we insert our option at the top of the menu and then remove the Edit and Format menus. The result is shown below.

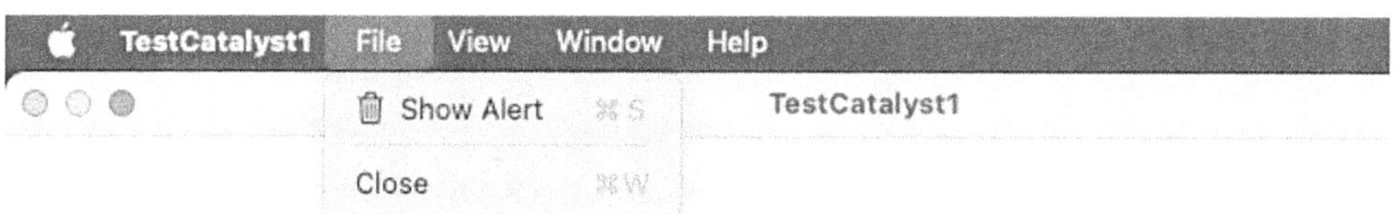

Figure 22-21: *New option in the File menu*

The option in the last example includes an image. If we need to modify this image, or any other attribute, we can implement the **validate()** method on the view controller, as we did before (see Listing 22-4), but if we want to modify the menu itself, we must ask the system to rebuild it with the **setNeedsRebuild()** method. This means storing the state of the menu in a model and rebuilding it every time the state changes. As an example, we are going to implement a simple model with just one property to determine if an option should be included or not.

```
import Foundation

struct ApplicationData {
   var includeMenu: Bool = true
}
var AppData = ApplicationData()
```

Listing 22-8: Defining a model to store the state of the menu

Now we can check the value of the **includeMenu** property in the **buildMenu(with: UIMenuBuilder)** method to include an option only when the value is **true**.

```
import UIKit

@main
class AppDelegate: UIResponder, UIApplicationDelegate {
   func application(_ application: UIApplication,
didFinishLaunchingWithOptions launchOptions:
[UIApplication.LaunchOptionsKey: Any]?) -> Bool {
      return true
   }
   func application(_ application: UIApplication,
configurationForConnecting connectingSceneSession: UISceneSession,
options: UIScene.ConnectionOptions) -> UISceneConfiguration {
      return UISceneConfiguration(name: "Default Configuration",
sessionRole: connectingSceneSession.role)
   }
   override func buildMenu(with builder: UIMenuBuilder) {
      super.buildMenu(with: builder)

      if builder.system == .main {
         if AppData.includeMenu {
            let option = UICommand(title: "Show Alert", action:
#selector(ViewController.showAlertView(_:)))
            let mymenu = UIMenu(title: "", identifier:
UIMenu.Identifier("com.formasterminds.test.showalert"),
options: .displayInline, children: [option])
            builder.insertChild(mymenu, atStartOfMenu: .file)
         }
      }
   }
}
```

Listing 22-9: Defining the menu according to the current state

In the view controller, we need to add an action to toggle the value of the **includeMenu** property when a button on the interface is pressed.

```
import UIKit

class ViewController: UIViewController {
   @IBAction func activateOption(_ sender: UIButton) {
      AppData.includeMenu.toggle()

      let main = UIMenuSystem.main
      main.setNeedsRebuild()
   }
```

```
    @objc func showAlertView(_ sender: Any) {
        let alert = UIAlertController(title: "Show Alert", message: "Open
from menu", preferredStyle: .alert)
        let action = UIAlertAction(title: "OK", style: .default, handler:
nil)
        alert.addAction(action)
        present(alert, animated: true, completion: nil)
    }
}
```

Listing 22-10: *Rebuilding the menu*

This example assumes that we have added a button to the interface and it is connected to an action called **activateOption()**. When the button is pressed, this method toggles the value of the **includeMenu** property and calls the **setNeedsRebuild()** method on the main menu. This forces the system to recreate the menu and the option is removed or added according to the property's current value.

Do It Yourself: Create a Swift file called ApplicationData.swift for the model in Listing 22-8. Update the **AppDelegate** class with the code in Listing 22-9 and the **ViewController** class with the code in Listing 22-10. Add a button to the interface and connect it to the **activateOption()** method in the view controller. Run the application. You should see the Show Alert option in the File menu. Press the button on the interface and open the File menu again. The option should be gone.

Basic Toolbar

UIKit apps include Navigation Bars to provide additional functionality, but they don't look good in Mac applications. Instead, Mac computers use a toolbar at the top of the window where we can add all the buttons we need. The toolbar is created by the **NSToolbar** class.

NSToolbar(identifier: String)—This initializer creates a toolbar. The **identifier** argument is a string we can use to identify the toolbar when there are several available.

The **NSToolbar** class includes properties to customize the bar. The following are some of the properties available for Mac applications created with Mac Catalyst.

displayMode—This property sets or returns a value that determines whether the bar is going to show icons or labels. It is a **DisplayMode** enumeration defined in the **NSToolbar** class. The values available are **iconOnly**, **labelOnly**, and **iconAndLabel**.

allowsUserCustomization—This property sets or returns a Boolean value that determines whether the user is allowed to edit the bar. If the value is **true**, a contextual menu allows the user to show the icons, the labels, or both.

The buttons on the bar are created from the **NSToolbarItem** class. The class includes the following initializer and properties to create the items.

NSToolbarItem(itemIdentifier: Identifier)—This initializer creates a new toolbar button. The **itemIdentifier** argument is a structure that contains a string to identify the item.

image—This property sets or returns the button's image.

label—This property sets or returns the button's label.

action—This property sets or returns a selector with the action to perform when the button is pressed.

The items for the toolbar are provided by a delegate object. The framework defines the **NSToolbarDelegate** protocol for this purpose. The following are some of the methods included in this protocol.

toolbarDefaultItemIdentifiers(NSToolbar**)**—This method is called on the delegate when the toolbar needs the identifiers of the items it has to show. The method must return an array of **Identifier** values with the identifiers of the items we want to include in the bar.

toolbar(NSToolbar, **itemForItemIdentifier:** Identifier, **willBeInsertedIntoToolbar:** Bool**)**—This method is called on the delegate when the toolbar needs the item with the identifier specified by the **itemForItemIdentifier** argument. The method must return an **NSToolbarItem** object with the corresponding item.

toolbarAllowedItemIdentifiers(NSToolbar**)**—This method is called on the delegate when the toolbar needs to know which items to exclude. The method must return an array of **Identifier** values with the identifiers of the items we want to exclude.

Toolbars are not available on iOS. If we try to implement any of these classes in an iOS application, we will get an error. For this reason, it is better to define the code separate from the view controller and use conditionals. This is the approach we are taking with the delegate object in the following example. We call it **MyToolbar**.

```
import UIKit

class MyToolbar: NSObject {
   #if targetEnvironment(macCatalyst)
   let firstItemID =
NSToolbarItem.Identifier("com.formasterminds.test.firstitem")
   let secondItemID =
NSToolbarItem.Identifier("com.formasterminds.test.seconditem")
   #endif
}
#if targetEnvironment(macCatalyst)
extension MyToolbar: NSToolbarDelegate {
   func toolbarDefaultItemIdentifiers(_ toolbar: NSToolbar) ->
[NSToolbarItem.Identifier] {
      let identifiers: [NSToolbarItem.Identifier] = [firstItemID,
secondItemID]
      return identifiers
   }
   func toolbar(_ toolbar: NSToolbar, itemForItemIdentifier
itemIdentifier: NSToolbarItem.Identifier, willBeInsertedIntoToolbar flag:
Bool) -> NSToolbarItem? {
      var toolbarItem: NSToolbarItem?

      if itemIdentifier == firstItemID {
         let newItem = NSToolbarItem(itemIdentifier: itemIdentifier)
         newItem.image = UIImage(systemName: "trash")
         newItem.action = #selector(ViewController.openFirstItem)
         toolbarItem = newItem
      } else if itemIdentifier == secondItemID {
         let newItem = NSToolbarItem(itemIdentifier: itemIdentifier)
         newItem.image = UIImage(systemName: "plus.app")
         newItem.action = #selector(ViewController.openSecondItem)
         toolbarItem = newItem
      }
      return toolbarItem
   }
```

```
    func toolbarAllowedItemIdentifiers(_ toolbar: NSToolbar) ->
[NSToolbarItem.Identifier] {
        let identifiers: [NSToolbarItem.Identifier] = [firstItemID,
secondItemID]
        return identifiers
    }
}
#endif
```

Listing 22-11: *Defining the toolbar's delegate*

The **Identifier** initializer requires a string to identify the item. This string could be anything, but to make sure it is unique, it is recommendable to declare it with an inverted domain. In this example, we need two, one for each item we want to include in the bar. Because they are required by different methods, we store them in two properties called **firstItemID** and **secondItemID**.

Something to consider when creating the delegate is that the **NSToolbarDelegate** protocol is not available in iOS, so we must declare the methods separated from the class, which requires creating an extension that conforms to the protocol, as we did in this example (see Extensions in Chapter 3).

The implementation of the protocol methods is simple. The **toolbarDefaultItem-Identifiers()** method must return an array with the identifiers of all the items we want to include in the bar (in our case, two), the **toolbarAllowedItemIdentifiers()** method must also return an array with the items we want to allow the toolbar to include (in this case, two), and the **toolbar(NSToolbar, itemForItemIdentifier: Identifier, willBeInserted-IntoToolbar: Bool)** method must provide the items' definitions.

The items are created from **NSToolbarItem** objects. In our example, we create two, one for each identifier. The first one includes an image of a trash can, and the second item is represented by a plus sign. The selectors behave the same way as those implemented for menu options. They search for the methods in the responder chain and execute them.

The view controller must create the **NSToolbar** object to represent the bar and assign the bar to the Scene (the window). For this purpose, the **UIWindowScene** object includes the **titlebar** property, which returns a **UITitlebar** object, which in turn includes the **toolbar** property to assign our toolbar to the Scene, as shown next.

```
import UIKit

class ViewController: UIViewController {
   var toolbarDelegate = MyToolbar()

   override func viewDidAppear(_ animated: Bool) {
      super.viewDidAppear(animated)
      #if targetEnvironment(macCatalyst)
      if let scene = view.window?.windowScene, let bar = scene.titlebar {
         let toolbar = NSToolbar(identifier: "main")
         toolbar.delegate = toolbarDelegate
         toolbar.displayMode = .iconOnly
         bar.toolbar = toolbar
      }
      #endif
   }
   @objc func openFirstItem() {
      print("First Item")
   }
   @objc func openSecondItem() {
      print("Second Item")
   }
}
```

Listing 22-12: *Creating a toolbar*

In this example, we create an instance of the **MyToolbar** class and assign the object to the delegate property of the **NSToolbar** object, so the toolbar can call the methods in this delegate object when it needs the items to show on the screen. After the delegate is defined, we configure the bar to only show icons (**iconOnly**), and then assign the bar to the Scene. The result is shown below.

***Figure 22-22:** Mac toolbar*

Do It Yourself: Create a new project. Configure the project to work on Macs from the app's settings. Create a new file with a subclass of **NSObject** called **MyToolbar** and complete the file with the code in Listing 22-11. Update the **ViewController** class with the code in Listing 22-12. Run the application on the Mac. You should see a toolbar with two buttons, as illustrated in Figure 22-22. Press the buttons. A message should be printed on the console. In this example, we just print messages on the console, but you can perform any task you want.

By default, the title on the bar is the app's name, but the **UIScene** class includes the following property to customize it.

title—This property sets or returns the toolbar's title.

subtitle—This property sets or returns the toolbar's subtitle.

The following are the changes we need to introduce to the **viewDidAppear()** method to define a custom title.

```
override func viewDidAppear(_ animated: Bool) {
   super.viewDidAppear(animated)
   #if targetEnvironment(macCatalyst)
   if let scene = view.window?.windowScene, let bar = scene.titlebar {
      let toolbar = NSToolbar(identifier: "main")
      toolbar.delegate = toolbarDelegate
      toolbar.displayMode = .iconOnly
      bar.toolbar = toolbar
      scene.title = "My App"
   }
   #endif
}
```

***Listing 22-13:** Assigning a custom title to the toolbar*

When the toolbar is displayed on the screen, the system calls a method in the view controller to make sure that the actions can be performed. The following is the method defined in the **UIResponder** class for this purpose.

canPerformAction(Selector, **withSender:** Any?**)**—This method is called in the view controller when the toolbar items are presented on the screen. The first argument is a reference to the item's action, and the **withSender** argument is a reference to the item itself.

The items are identified by the action they performed. For instance, we can disable the action that executes the **openFirstItem()** method, as shown next.

```
override func canPerformAction(_ action: Selector, withSender sender:
Any?) -> Bool {
   if action == #selector(openFirstItem) {
      return false
   }
   return true
}
```

Listing 22-14: *Disabling an item*

This method is similar to the **validate()** method we use to modify the options of a menu. We can not only implement it to disable an item but also to change it. For instance, the following method disables the first item and replaces the image of the trash can with another one to reflect a new state.

```
override func canPerformAction(_ action: Selector, withSender sender:
Any?) -> Bool {
   if action == #selector(openFirstItem) {
      if let item = sender as? NSToolbarItem {
         item.image = UIImage(systemName: "trash.slash")
      }
      return false
   }
   return true
}
```

Listing 22-15: *Modifying an item*

Do It Yourself: Add the method in Listing 22-15 to the **ViewController** class. Run the application. You should see the item with the trash can disabled and the image replaced.

Basic Gestures

Most gestures available in mobile devices are also available in Mac computer, but something users expect to be able to do on Macs that is not available in mobile devices is to perform tasks when the pointer of the mouse is moving over an element. That is called the hover gesture. UIKit includes the **UIHoverGestureRecognizer** class to detect this gesture.

UIHoverGestureRecognizer(target: Any?, **action:** Selector?**)**—This initializer creates a gesture recognizer for the hover gesture. The **target** argument is the object where the action will be executed, and the **action** argument is the method to be executed when the gesture is detected.

The hover gesture is implemented as any other (see Chapter 8). We first create an instance of the recognizer and then assign it to the view with the **addGestureRecognizer()** method.

```
import UIKit

class ViewController: UIViewController {
   override func viewDidLoad() {
      super.viewDidLoad()
      let gesture = UIHoverGestureRecognizer(target: self, action:
#selector(changeBackground))
      view.addGestureRecognizer(gesture)
   }
```

```
    @objc func changeBackground() {
        view.backgroundColor = .yellow
    }
}
```

Listing 22-16: *Adding a hover gesture recognizer*

Do It Yourself: Create a new project for the Mac. Update the **ViewController** class with the code in Listing 22-16 and run the application on the Mac. Move the mouse over the window. The view's background should change to yellow.

UIKit also includes the **UIToolTipInteraction** class to create a tooltip that shows a message if the mouse remains over a view for a few seconds. This is not required in mobile applications, but it is a useful tool for Mac applications. To create the tool, the class includes the following initializer.

UIToolTipInteraction(defaultToolTip: String)—This initializer creates a tooltip with the message specified by the **defaultToolTip** argument.

To add the tool to a view, the **UIView** class includes the following method.

addInteraction(UIInteraction**)**—This method adds an interaction to the view.

The implementation is simple. We create the tooltip with the message we want to show and add it to the view. In the following example, we add the tooltip to the main view.

```
import UIKit

class ViewController: UIViewController {
    override func viewDidLoad() {
        super.viewDidLoad()
        let tooltipInteraction = UIToolTipInteraction(defaultToolTip: "This
is the view")
        view.addInteraction(tooltipInteraction)
    }
}
```

Listing 22-17: *Adding a tooltip to a view*

Do It Yourself: Update the **ViewController** class with the code in Listing 22-17. Run the application. Move the mouse over the window and wait for a second. You should see a message popping up with the text "This is the view".

IMPORTANT: The **UIControl** class includes the **toolTip** property to define a tooltip. If your view inherits from the **UIControl** class (e.g., **UIButton**), you do not need to create a **UIToolTipInteraction** object. All you have to do is to assign the message to the **toolTip** property and the tool is created for you.

Basic Views

There are a series of small changes we may introduce to a scene to improve the interface for Mac computers. For instance, the **UISplitViewController** class includes the following properties to set up the minimum and maximum width of the primary column.

minimumPrimaryColumnWidth—This property sets or returns the minimum width of the primary column in points.

maximumPrimaryColumnWidth—This property sets or returns the maximum width of the primary column in points.

The following property is also included in the **UISplitViewController** class to apply a translucent effect to the primary column.

primaryBackgroundStyle—This property sets or returns the background style for the primary column. It is a **BackgroundStyle** enumeration value. To turn the view translucent in Mac computers, we must assign the value **sidebar**.

The **UILabel** class also includes a property useful for Mac applications.

showsExpansionTextWhenTruncated—This property sets or returns a Boolean value that determines if the system is going to expand the text when the mouse is over a label which text has been truncated (**true** if we want the system to show the full text).

Classes like **UIButton** and **UISlider** also include a property that may be helpful when the application is running on a Mac.

preferredBehavioralStyle—This property sets or returns a value that determines the style of the control. It is an enumeration of type **UIBehavioralStyle** with the values **automatic** (default), **pad**, and **mac**. If we want the control to be shown with the style used for iPads, we must assign the value **pad** to this property.

Another element that provides customization options for the Mac is the Switch. By default, the switch created by the **UISwitch** class is represented by a checkbox on Mac computers, but we can define the style with the following property.

preferredStyle—This property sets or returns a value that determines the style of the switch. It is an enumeration of type **Style** with the values **automatic**, **checkbox**, and **sliding**.

If we decide to go with a checkbox, we can also specify a label with the **title** property.

```
import UIKit

class ViewController: UIViewController {
   @IBOutlet weak var myswitch: UISwitch!

   override func viewDidLoad() {
      super.viewDidLoad()
      myswitch.preferredStyle = .checkbox
      myswitch.title = "Option"
   }
}
```

***Listing 22-18:** Configuring a switch for the Mac*

This example assumes that we have added a switch to the interface, and it is connected to the **ViewController** class with an Outlet called **myswitch**. The code makes sure that the switch is represented by a checkbox and assigns the label "Option" to it.

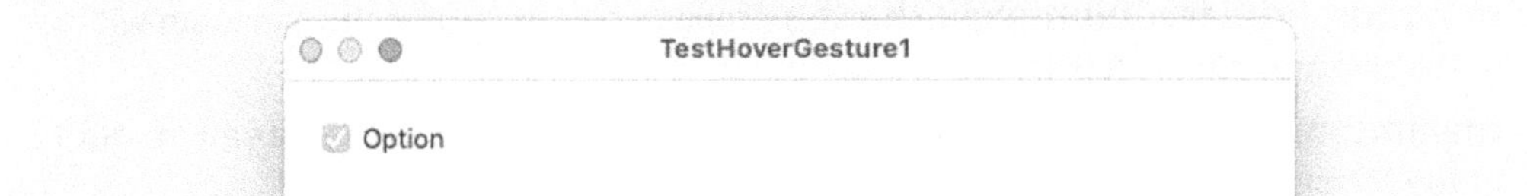

Figure 22-23: *Switch on the Mac*

Basic 22.2 Multiple Windows

iPads and Mac computers can open multiple instances of an application in separate windows (Scenes), but this feature is not enabled by default. The option to support multiple windows is available from the General panel in the project's settings, as illustrate below.

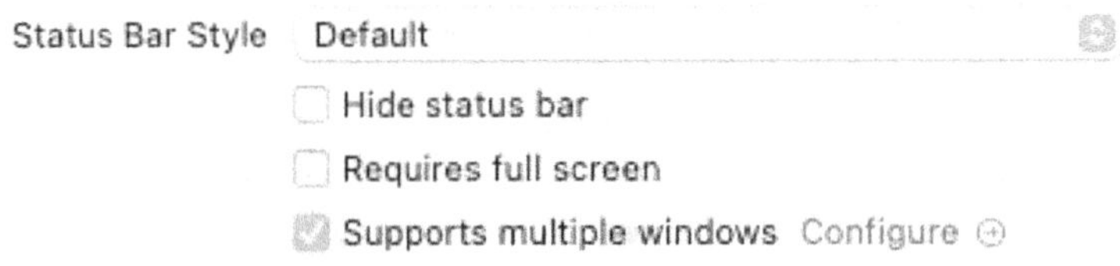

Figure 22-24: *Support Multiple Windows option*

Activating this option allows the application to work from multiple windows. iPads and Mac computers provide built-in functionality for this purpose. For instance, if we compile the app to work on the Mac, an option appears on the File menu to create a new window.

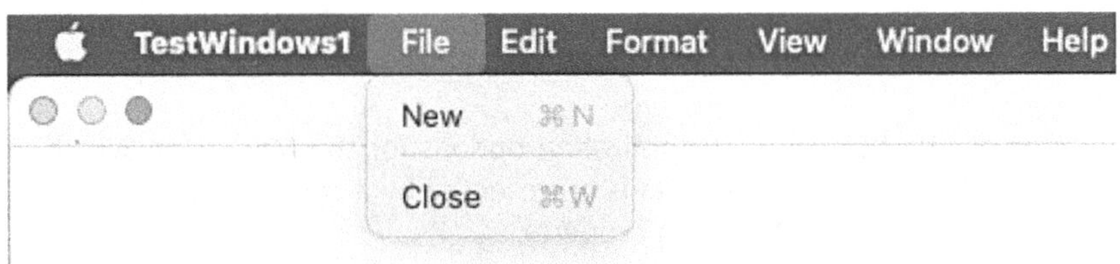

Figure 22-25: *Option to create new window*

iPads offer multiple alternatives to open the app in a new window. The easiest way is to split the screen with the bottoms at the top and open the app again (see Chapter 21, Figure 21-1). If the app allows multiple windows, two instances of the same app will share the screen.

In addition to the options provided by the system, we can open the app in a new window by creating a Scene from code. The **`UIApplication`** class offers the following methods to manage Scenes.

requestSceneSessionActivation(UISceneSession?, **userActivity:** NSUserActivity?, **options:** ActivationRequestOptions?, **errorHandler:** Closure?**)**—This method activates an existing Scene or creates a new one. The first argument is a reference to the Scene session we want to activate or the value **`nil`** if we want to create a new one. The **userActivity** argument is a reference to an object of type **`NSUserActivity`** that stores the state we want to set when the Scene is opened. The **options** argument is an object with information for the session associated with the Scene. And the **`errorHandler`** argument is the closure to be executed if an error occurs.

requestSceneSessionDestruction(UISceneSession, **options:** UISceneDestructionRequestOptions?, **errorHandler:** Closure?**)**—This method dismisses an existing Scene session. The first argument is a reference to the session we want to destroy, the **options** argument provides information on how to remove the Scene, and the **errorHandler** argument is the closure to be execute if an error occurs.

requestSceneSessionRefresh(UISceneSession**)**—This method requests the system to update the views in the Scene specified by the argument.

If all we want is to open a new window, we can just call the **requestSceneSession-Activation()** method with **nil** values, as in the following example.

```
import UIKit

class ViewController: UIViewController {
   @IBAction func openNewScene(_ sender: UIButton) {
      let app = UIApplication.shared
      app.requestSceneSessionActivation(nil, userActivity: nil, options:
nil)
   }
}
```

***Listing 22-19:** Opening a new window*

This example assumes that we have a button on the interface connected to the **ViewController** class with an action called **openNewScene()**. When the button is pressed, we get a reference to the **UIApplication** object assigned to the app and call the **requestSceneSessionActivation()** method on it to open a new window.

Do It Yourself: Create a new project. Go to the app's settings, configure the project to work on Macs, and check the Support multiple windows option to be able to open the app in multiple windows (Figure 22-24). Add a button to the interface and connect it to the **ViewController** class with an action called **openNewScene()**. Complete the class with the code in Listing 22-19 and run the application on your Mac. Click on the button to open the app in a new window.

The window opened by the example in Listing 22-19 launches an instance of the app with the configuration by default. This means that the app will display the initial screen as if it had been launched for the first time. But this is not always appropriate. Users often expect the window to be in the state it was before the app was closed. To set the initial state of the session or recover an old state, the Foundation framework defines the **NSUserActivity** class. From this class, we can create objects that contain the information required to set the state of the session or restore a previous one.

NSUserActivity(activityType: String)—This initializer creates a new **NSUserActivity** object with the name specified by the argument. The **activityType** argument is a string to identify the state.

The following are some of the properties and methods provided by the class.

title—This property sets or returns the activity's title.

userInfo—This property sets or returns a dictionary with the values required to set or restore the state represented by the object.

becomeCurrent()—This method marks the activity as the one that is currently in use.

resignCurrent()—This method deactivates the activity.

invalidate()—This method invalidates the activity.

How the state is restored depends on the characteristics of our application, but the process to store the information that represents the state is always the same. We must create an **NSUserActivity** object, store the information we are going to need to set the session in the **userInfo** property, and then use that information to configure the state of the session when a previous session or a new one is created.

To illustrate how this works, we are going to create a simple application with a Pop Up button to select a picture, an Image View to display the selected picture, and a button to open a new window.

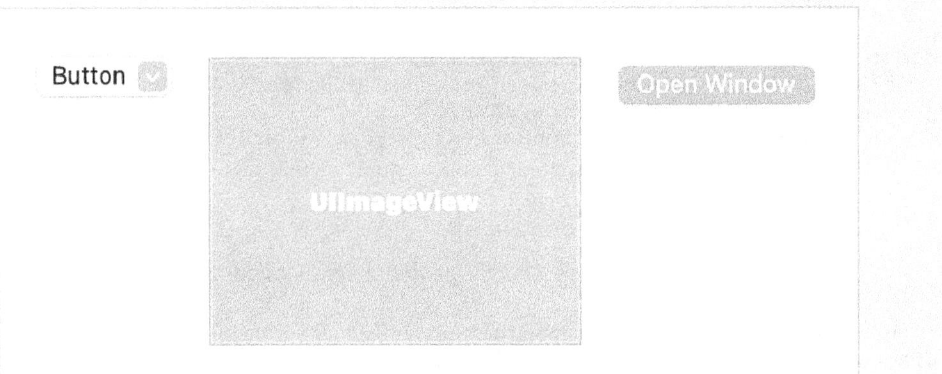

Figure 22-26: *Interface to test multiple windows on Mac*

To store the list of pictures, we need a model with at least two properties, one to store the array with the names and another to store the index of the selected picture, as shown next.

```
import Foundation

struct ApplicationData {
   var picturesList: [String]
   var selectedPicture: Int

   init() {
      picturesList = ["bagels", "brownies", "butter", "cheese", "coffee",
"cookies", "donuts", "granola", "juice", "lemonade", "lettuce", "milk",
"oatmeal", "potato", "tomato", "yogurt"]
      selectedPicture = 0
   }
}
var AppData = ApplicationData()
```

Listing 22-20: *Defining the model to test multiple windows*

In the view controller, we must feed the Pop Up button with all the values in the model and initialize the interface with the first value on the list.

```
import UIKit

class ViewController: UIViewController {
   @IBOutlet weak var myButton: UIButton!
   @IBOutlet weak var myPicture: UIImageView!

   override func viewDidLoad() {
      super.viewDidLoad()
      configureButton()
      initializePicture()
   }
   func configureButton() {
      myButton.changesSelectionAsPrimaryAction = true
      myButton.showsMenuAsPrimaryAction = true
```

```
      var listOptions: [UIAction] = []
      for (index, item) in AppData.picturesList.enumerated() {
         listOptions.append(UIAction(title: item.capitalized, identifier:
UIAction.Identifier(String(index)), handler: selectOption))
      }
      myButton.menu = UIMenu(children: listOptions)
   }
   func initializePicture() {
      let id = AppData.selectedPicture

      let action = myButton.menu?.children[id] as? UIAction
      action?.state = .on

      myPicture.image = UIImage(named: AppData.picturesList[id])
   }
   func selectOption(action: UIAction) {
      if let id = Int(action.identifier.rawValue) {
         AppData.selectedPicture = id
         myPicture.image = UIImage(named: AppData.picturesList[id])
      }
   }
   @IBAction func openNewWindow(_ sender: UIButton) {
      let activity = NSUserActivity(activityType:
"com.formasterminds.images")
      activity.userInfo?["selected"] = AppData.selectedPicture

      let app = UIApplication.shared
      app.requestSceneSessionActivation(nil, userActivity: activity,
options: nil)
   }
}
```

Listing 22-21: Storing the state in an `NSUserActivity` *object*

To configure the interface, we have defined two methods: **configureButton()** and **initializePicture()**. In the **configureButton()** method, we configure the Pop Up button with the pictures' names. First, we assign the value **true** to the **changesSelectionAsPrimaryAction** and **showsMenuAsPrimaryAction** properties to make sure that the button is rendered as a Pop Up button and the name of the selected picture is displayed on the title. And then we populate the button with the list of pictures using a **for in** loop. On the other hand, the **initializePicture()** method gets the index of the selected picture from the model and updates the Pop Up button and the Image View with it, so the selected picture is always shown on the screen.

At the end of the view controller of Listing 22-21, there is an action for the Open Window button. When the button is pressed, this method creates an **NSUserActivity** object, sets a value in the **userInfo** dictionary with the key "selected" and the index of the selected picture, and executes the **requestSceneSessionActivation()** method on the **UIApplication** object with this object to open the window.

To set the state of the Scene and get the new window to show the right image, we must read back the value stored in the **userInfo** property when the Scene is created by the **SceneDelegate** object, as shown next.

```
import UIKit

class SceneDelegate: UIResponder, UIWindowSceneDelegate {
   var window: UIWindow?

   func scene(_ scene: UIScene, willConnectTo session: UISceneSession,
options connectionOptions: UIScene.ConnectionOptions) {
      guard let _ = (scene as? UIWindowScene) else { return }
```

```
        if let activity = connectionOptions.userActivities.first(where:
{ $0.activityType == "com.formasterminds.images" }) {
            if let index = activity.userInfo?["selected"] as? Int {
                AppData.selectedPicture = index
            }
        }
    }
}
```

Listing 22-22: *Reading the state from the* `NSUserActivity` *object*

There are different ways to read the current activities set by the application. In this example, we get them from the **`userActivities`** property of the **`ConnectionOptions`** object received by the method. This property returns an array of **`NSUserActivity`** objects, so we get the first one that matches the type used by the view controller and then read the value from its **`userInfo`** property with the "selected" key. The key returns an **`Int`** value that we assign to the **`selectedPicture`** property in the model, so the currently selected picture is shown on the new window.

Do It Yourself: Remove all the elements on the interface and the code in your view controller. Add a Pop Up button, an Image View, and a button with the title Open Window to the scene, as in Figure 22-26. Connect the Pop Up button to the **`ViewController`** class with an Outlet called **`myButton`** and the Image View with an Outlet called **`myPicture`**. Connect the Open Windows button with an Action called **`openNewWindow()`**. Complete the **`ViewController`** class with the code in Listing 22-21. Create a Swift file called ApplicationData.swift for the model in Listing 22-20. Update the **`SceneDelegate`** class with the code in Listing 22-22. Download the thumbnails from our website and add them to the Assets Catalog. Run the application on the Mac or an iPad, select a picture, and click on the Open Window button. Another window should open with the same picture selected before.

IMPORTANT: In this example, we barely scratched the surface of what is possible to do when working with **`NSUserActivity`** objects and multiple windows. The topic is extensive and goes beyond the scope of this book. For more information, visit our website and follow the links for this chapter.

Chapter 23
App Store

Basic 23.1 Publishing

At the beginning of this book, we talked about Apple's strict control over the applications to which the users have access. Applications for Mac computers can be sold separately, but mobile applications can only be sold in the App Store. The process is performed from Xcode, but there are a series of requirements we need to satisfy for our app to be published and become available to the users.

- We need an Apple Developer Program membership.
- We need a Distribution Certificate.
- We need a Provisioning Profile for distribution.
- We need an App ID for each application.
- We must register the app in the App Store Connect website.
- We must create an archive with our app for each platform to send to Apple's servers.
- We must upload the archive to App Store Connect for review.

Basic Apple Developer Program

Developing and testing can be done with a free account, but publishing our app requires a membership to the Apple Developer Program. The option to enroll in this program is available on the **developer.apple.com** website. We must click on the Discover/Program options at the top of the screen, press the Enroll button, and follow the instructions to register an account for an Individual or an organization. At the time of writing, the membership costs USD 99 per year.

Basic Certificates, Provisioning Profiles, and Identifiers

Apple wants to make sure that only authorized apps are running on its devices, so it requests developers to add a cryptographic signature to each application. There are three values that are necessary to authorize the app: certificates, provisioning profiles, and identifiers. Basically, a certificate identifies the developer that publishes the application, the provisioning profile identifies the device that is allowed to run the application, and an identifier, called *App ID*, identifies the application. These values are packed along with the application's files and therefore Apple always knows who developed the app, who is authorized to run it, and in which devices.

Xcode automatically generates these values for us, so we do not have to worry about them, but Apple offers a control panel in our developer account in case we need to do it manually (the option is not available for free members). Figure 23-1 shows the menu we see after we go to developer.apple.com, click on Account, and select the option Certificates, IDs & Profiles.

Certificates, Identifiers & Profiles

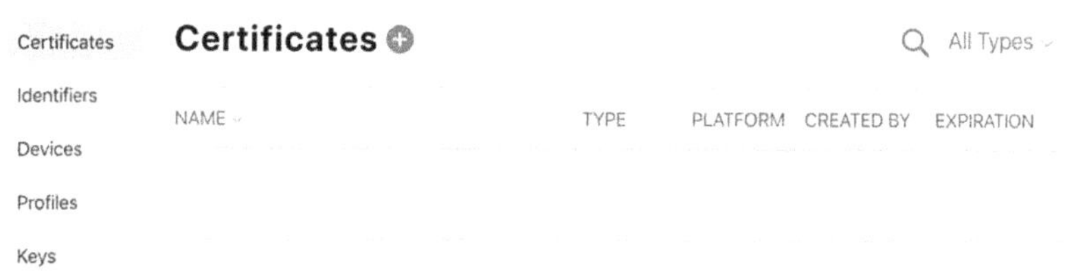

Figure 23-1: *Web page to manage certificates, provisioning profiles, and identifiers*

In this page, we can create, edit, or remove certificates, provisioning profiles and identifiers. The page contains two panels. The left panel offers a list of options to select the type of values we want to work with, and the right panel shows the list of values available and buttons to create new ones. When a value is selected, a new panel opens with tools to edit it.

Basic App Store Connect

The first step to submit our app is to create a record on Apple's servers. Apple has designated a website for this purpose, available at **appstoreconnect.apple.com**. To login, we must use the same Apple ID and password we use to access our account at developer.apple.com. Figure 23-2 illustrates the options available after logging in.

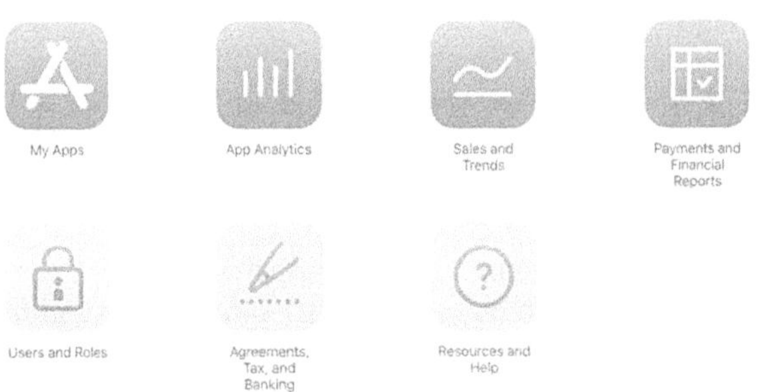

Figure 23-2: *App Store Connect menu*

From this panel, we can insert our financial information (Agreements, Tax, and Banking), publish our apps (My Apps), and see how the business is going (Sales and Trends). The first step is to create a record for the app we want to publish from the My Apps option. When we click on this icon, a new window shows the list of our apps and a + button at the top to add more.

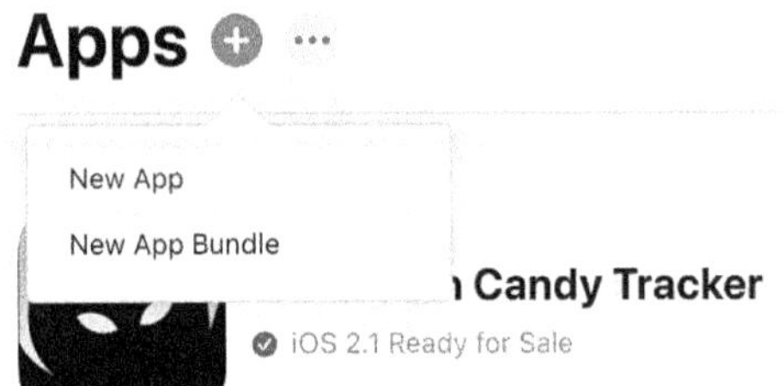

Figure 23-3: *Menu to add apps to our account*

To add a new app, we must select the New App option and insert the app's information. The first window asks for the platform we have developed the app for (in our case, iOS and macOS), the application's name, the primary language, the bundle ID, and a custom ID (SKU) that can help us identify the app later. The name and language are values we already have, and the SKU is a custom string, but the Bundle ID is a value generate by Xcode. Xcode creates a Bundle ID and submits it to Apple servers when we enable services from the capabilities panel. If our app does not use any of these services, we can register a new Bundle ID from developer.apple.com (see Figure 23-1), as explained in the form.

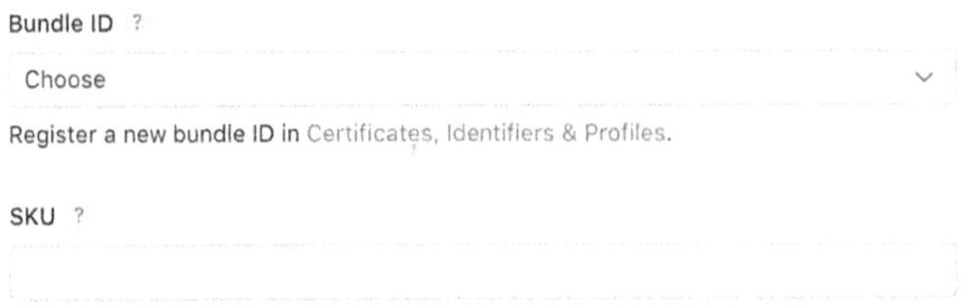

Bundle ID ?
Choose
Register a new bundle ID in Certificates, Identifiers & Profiles.
SKU ?

Figure 23-4: *Bundle ID and SKU identifier*

After these values are inserted, we can press the Create button and complete the rest of the information. This includes the app's description, screenshots, and personal information. We also must select the option Pricing and Availability on the left panel to set the price and where the application will be available. Once all the information is provided, we can finally press the Save button and go back to Xcode to upload the files.

Basic Submitting the Application

The application and its resources must be compiled for each platform in a single archive and then submitted to App Store Connect. We must create an archive for iOS devices and another for macOS. The option is available on the Xcode's Product menu, but it is only enabled when the appropriate device is selected on the Schemes. We can select a real device connected to the computer, or we can use the Any iOS Device option for iOS apps or the Any Mac option for macOS.

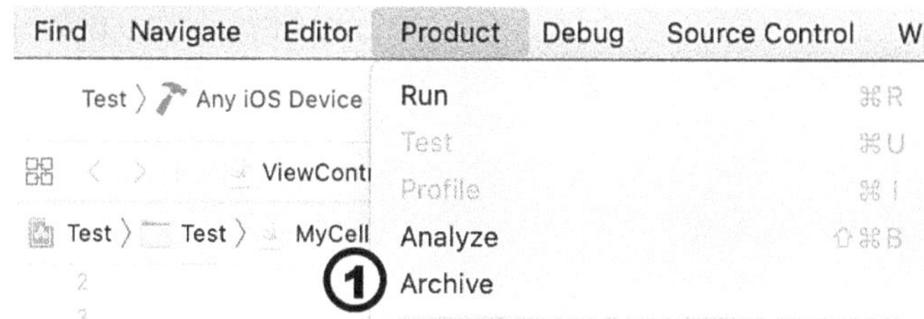

Figure 23-5: *Archive option*

After we click on this option, Xcode compiles the application and creates the archive. The next window shows the archive and offers buttons to validate and submit the app.

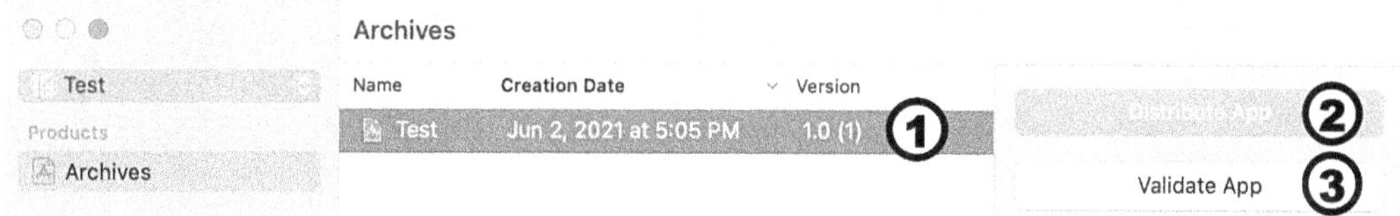

Figure 23-6: *List of archives created for our apps*

Figure 23-6 shows an archive created for an application called Test (number 1). The item representing the archive includes the date it was created, the app's version, and the number of the build (we can send multiple builds to App Store Connect and later decide which one we want to be reviewed by Apple).

IMPORTANT: The app's version and the number of the build (archive) are determined from the app's settings editor (by default, both values are set to 1.0). If we want to specify a different version, we must declare the numbers separated by one or two periods (e.g., 1.0 or 1.2.5). The values represent different revisions of our app, with the order of relevance from left to right. The actual meaning of the value is arbitrary, but we are required to change it every time an update is published to the App Store to reflect how big the update was.

Although it is not required, we should always validate the archive before submitting the app. The process allows Xcode to detect errors and suggest how to fix them. To begin the validation process, we can press the Validate App button (Figure 23-6, number 3). The first window presents options to tell Xcode how to configure the archive and what to include.

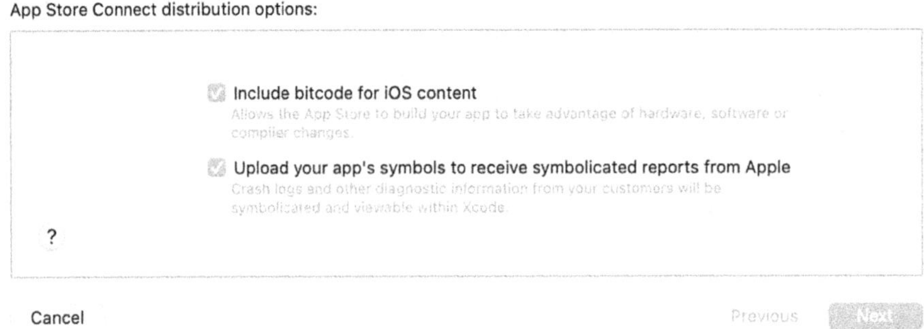

Figure 23-7: *Options to configure the archive*

All the options are recommended. The first one tells Xcode to include code that improves the app's performance, and the second uploads the necessary information for Apple to be able to report errors and perform diagnostics.

The next window allows us to select how we want to sign the app. With automatic signing, we let Xcode take care of everything for us (recommended).

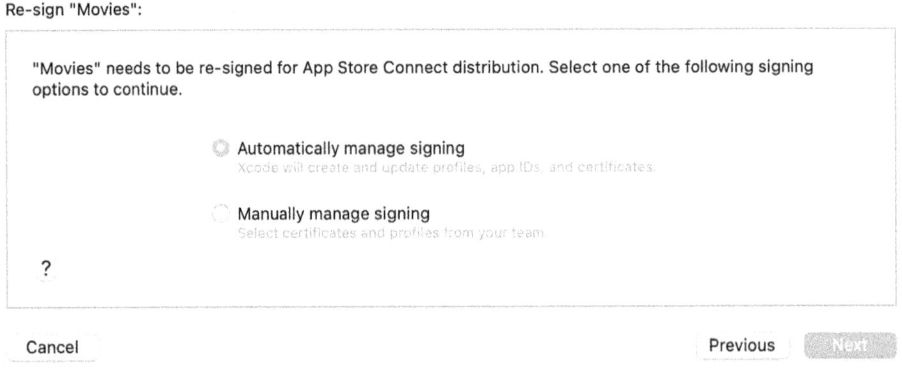

Figure 23-8: *Option to select automatic signing*

The last window displays a summary and provides a button to initiate the validation process. Once this process is over, if no errors are found, we can finally submit our app to Apple servers by pressing the Distribute App button (Figure 23-6, number 2).

As we already mentioned, we may submit multiple archives to the server (builds). For this reason, we must go back to the App Store Connect website, open the description of our application, and select the archive we just uploaded (it may take a few minutes to be available). Figure 23-9 shows the option with the archive (build) uploaded for an app in its version 3.3.

Build

BUILD	VERSION	HAS APP CLIP
1	3.3	NO

Figure 23-9: *Selecting the build to send to the App Store*

After the archive is selected, we can press the Save button to save the app's description. If all the required information was provided, we can finally press the Submit for Review button at the top of the page to submit the application. The system asks a few questions and then the application is sent for review (the message Waiting for Review is shown below the app's title).

The process takes a few days to be completed. If everything is correct, and the app is accepted, Apple sends us an email to let us know that the app has become available in the App Store.

Index

#

@

A

B

C

D

E

F

G

H

I

J

K

L

M

N

O

P

R

S

T

U

V

W

Y

Z

www.ingramcontent.com/pod-product-compliance
Lightning Source LLC
Chambersburg PA
CBHW081447050326
40690CB00015B/2706
* 9 7 8 1 7 7 7 9 7 8 2 0 4 *